Oxford Handbook of Methods in Positive Psychology

SERIES IN POSITIVE PSYCHOLOGY

SERIES EDITOR
Christopher Peterson

A Life Worth Living: Contributions to Positive Psychology
Edited by Mihaly Csikszentmihalyi and Isabella Selega Csikszentmihalyi

Oxford Handbook of Methods in Positive Psychology
Edited by Anthony D. Ong and Manfred H. M. van Dulmen

Oxford Handbook of Methods in Positive Psychology

Edited by

Anthony D. Ong
Manfred H. M. van Dulmen

OXFORD
UNIVERSITY PRESS

2007

OXFORD
UNIVERSITY PRESS

Oxford University Press, Inc., publishes works that further
Oxford University's objective of excellence
in research, scholarship, and education.

Oxford   New York
Auckland   Cape Town   Dar es Salaam   Hong Kong   Karachi
Kuala Lumpur   Madrid   Melbourne   Mexico City   Nairobi
New Delhi   Shanghai   Taipei   Toronto

With offices in
Argentina   Austria   Brazil   Chile   Czech Republic   France   Greece
Guatemala   Hungary   Italy   Japan   Poland   Portugal   Singapore
South Korea   Switzerland   Thailand   Turkey   Ukraine   Vietnam

Library of Congress Cataloging-in-Publication Data
Oxford handbook of methods in positive psychology / edited by
Anthony D. Ong and Manfred H. M. van Dulmen.
    p.   cm.—(Series in positive psychology)
   Includes bibliographical references and index.
   ISBN-13: 978-0-19-517218-8
   ISBN 0-19-517218-3
1. Positive psychology—Research—Methodology.   I. Ong, Anthony D.
II. Van Dulmen, Manfred H. M.   III. Series.
   BF204.6.O94   2006
   150'.72—dc22   2005021707

9 8 7 6 5 4 3 2 1

Printed in the United States of America
on acid-free paper

Foreword

C. R. Snyder and Shane J. Lopez

When Zach (son of CRS) was 4 years old, he was witnessing a young bird's first attempt to take off from its nest. Moving its wings furiously, however, seemed to get the neophyte flyer absolutely nowhere. To this, Zach pronounced, "Lots of flappin', but not much flyin'." In some ways, the same conservative appraisal can be made of positive psychology science and practice. For positive psychology to fulfill its magnificent potential and truly take off, it must embrace the very best in methodology, design, sampling, statistical procedures, and inference making and become more relevant to all people. Without these features, the finest in positive psychology theories and applications will be "flappin', but not much flyin'." This is why the present handbook holds such promise for the evolution of positive psychology.

In a relatively short time, there already have been a myriad of books on the theory, assessment, and applications of positive psychology, along with the appearance of texts for courses on this topic. As important as these other books in positive psychology have been, we previously have not had a foundational source that can guide future research. With the publication of the *Oxford Handbook of Methods in Positive Psychology*, however, the positive psychology initiative has a set of scientific plans and re-

sources that will help us produce the very best in psychological research and empirically supported practice.

If and when we reach the point where subsequent generations of positive psychologists are trained in and use the methods described in this volume, then positive psychology will have a chance of gaining respect in the field of psychology and the sciences more generally. In exploring the full range of humankind, with its strengths and limitations, the most accurate pictures will emerge when the best methods are invoked.

If we are to practice methodological rigor, we also will need to obtain samples that include people from all over this planet of ours. Positive psychology cannot, make that must not, be just a white American phenomenon. So too must positive psychology study persons from all ethnic and racial backgrounds, men and women, the young and old, those with disabilities and those without, and people from every social class in their societies, and so on. To act in any other way would not only be poor research, but it would create a science directed toward the few. Instead, positive psychology must be about the many. What this means for researchers is more work, and there is no way around this fact. It is more difficult to sample completely rather than to gather a sample of convenience. The 21st-century positive psychologist should be taught not to tolerate the old ways of doing business—the sufficiency of gathering a few male college students in a research project.

Our point is more than the run-of-the-mill call for diversity. Indeed, not only must we be thorough and inclusive in sampling all types of people as we develop the research base of positive psychology, but we also must learn and then apply a wide range of methodologies so as to triangulate our findings. The use of multiple methodological techniques is mandatory for a first-class science. Alas, the days of self-report questionnaires alone are over. We must look at a variety of behaviors that people exhibit, and move beyond the sole focus upon the individual. There is much to be learned from people interacting in dyads and even larger units. Likewise, our science will include the latest in technologies, and the 21st-century positive psychology research will buttress its findings with evoked potential readings, fMRI scans, and a multitude of other procedures and instruments that heretofore were thought only to be within the purview of the "hard" sciences. Likewise, some among us will become expert at measuring the role and impact of genetics. Quite simply, the only viable future for positive psychology is for it to become a hard science. Our sole motivation is not to avoid the "soft" label, but rather to conduct science in its most sophisticated manner. If respect comes to positive psychology along

the way—and it will—this will be a welcome bonus.

Last, we must be extremely open to new ideas and thinking about the many assets that humans exhibit. But along with such openness to new viewpoints about the virtues of humankind, we must remain extremely skeptical of new data and the associated inferences that are made. When any one positive psychology scientist performs methodologically flawed research, this hurts all positive psychologists. When any one positive psychology scientist makes an unwarranted inference, this undermines all of our efforts. This is why we need to embrace the many new and exciting ideas in this volume, and make sure that our students know these methods even better than we do.

Whenever we see a colleague making an inappropriate inference from his or her data in a talk, a publication, or a newspaper interview, we need to do the difficult thing and step forward to caution that colleague and the audience. Positive psychology is a collective endeavor, and when we approach our scientific foundation, methods, and principles with the utmost seriousness, our behavior will demand and beget respect. With the methods described in this handbook and the accompanying efforts of many serious scientists, positive psychology has the potential to move from "flappin' to flyin'." This volume is an important step in this direction. As such, we thank the editors Anthony Ong and Manfred van Dulmen, along with the chapter authors.

Preface

This volume is a follow-up to the *Handbook of Positive Psychology*, published by Oxford University Press in 2002. Since the publication of that first volume, scores of studies and books have proliferated on the psychology of human flourishing and on positive psychology in general. Running in parallel, however, have also been tremendous advances in the field of measurement and analysis of change. The purpose of this volume is to highlight these advances and their applications to illuminating new research initiatives in the emerging field of positive psychology. This book is therefore addressed to all those whose philosophical and intellectual leanings express themselves in a concern with the determinants and dynamics of human potentials.

At the risk of sounding defensive, we feel we should address a criticism that is often leveled at advocates of positive psychology. It has now become a common refrain that people who endorse hypotheses about human strengths and virtues do so because they want the world to be a more friendly and hospitable place. It is therefore worth underscoring here that our goal in this volume is not to paint a rosy picture of human behavior or to provide a general theory of positive psychology. It would be a great benefit of a theory if it gave one substantive insight in determining whether and how much individuals are capable of reaching their full potentials. But this benefit would not be a reason for believing that theory, and the lack of it does not provide a sound basis for rejecting one. If anything, accepting the book's claims only highlights the difficulties of settling these matters with confidence. Rather, the general goal of this volume is to provide a conception of what kinds of work need to be done and what kinds of questions need to be asked if we are to advance understanding of the nature of individual traits that promote optimal well-being, how these traits develop and change across the life span, the factors that threaten and undermine their maintenance, and the mechanisms that support and promote their growth.

Our general aim is to bring together a set of chapters, written by recognized leaders in the field, that focus on state-of-the art methods and related topics. The related topics include those that address methods for estimating variability and change at the level of the individual; those that point out methods for identifying reliability of measurements within and across individuals; and those that identify methods for separating individual differences in growth from aspects of phenomena that exhibit shorter-term variability over time.

A second goal is to bring together, in a single volume, a set of chapters that review and evaluate the utility of methods that currently are underutilized, but which are particularly appropriate to the investigation of substantive issues in positive psychology. The goal in these chapters is to describe a set of promising research initiatives, areas within positive psychology that are currently creating significant interdisciplinary breakthroughs and in which research over the next several years is likely to yield major advances.

Finally, this volume seeks to initiate a dialogue between basic and applied researchers—and ultimately with the reader—on the subject of how best to understand the nature and development of human potentials. As such, the general focus of this volume is not on persuading but on inquiring, and its aim is directed at neither advancing nor endorsing particular hypotheses but rather at opening new perspectives on thinking about the dynamics of positive human health. Ultimately, the book is an attempt to place the focus on human deficits and human strengths in a new light, a light that shows their connections to other problems and that directs our way of thinking about them along paths that have long been unexplored.

Anthony D. Ong
Manfred H. M. van Dulmen

Acknowledgments

The original impetus for this volume occurred during a meeting of the Summer Institute of Positive Psychology held in Monchanin, Delaware, on August 9–15, 2002. This volume, more than most, reflects the energies not of the editors but of the many who were involved in its creation. We are grateful to Martin Seligman, who was the first to graciously listen to our ideas about this book, and then urged us to follow through with them. We also wish to thank Catharine Carlin and her associate, Jennifer Rappaport, at Oxford University Press for their patience, tact, and invaluable assistance throughout the editorial process.

We owe a great intellectual debt to our teachers, John L. Horn and Harold D. Grotevant, quintessential developmental psychologists who—long before it was in vogue—combined psychological theory with the rigors of empirical research to ask the kind of intuitive questions of human potential that would later reveal remarkable understanding. Their commitment to clarity and depth and truth and passion have given us the standard toward which we aspire. We are also grateful to the battalion of scholars whose imaginative sweep of ideas have shaped our thinking over the years: Alan Acock, David Almeida, Jason Allaire, Paul Baltes, C. S. Bergeman, Toni Bisconti, Steve Boker, John Cacioppo, Sy-Miin Chow, Nancy Cobb, Andrew Collins, Mihaly Csikszentmihalyi, Bob Cudeck, Edward Deci, Ed Diener, Lisa Edwards, Byron Egeland, Robert Emmons, Xitao Fan, William Fleeson, Barbara Fredrickson, Shelly Gable, Paolo Ghisletta, Megan Gunnar, Scott Hofer, Alice Isen, Corey Keyes, Larry Kurdek, Randy Larsen, Shane Lopez, Scott Maxwell, Michael McCullough, Brent Miller, Dan Mroczek, John Nesselroade, Jean Phinney, Harry Reis, Richard Ryan, Carol Ryff, Martin Seligman, Alan Sroufe, C. R. Synder, Kimberly Wallace, David Walsh, Rich Weinberg, David Weiss, Elaine Wethington, and Alex Zautra.

At the institutional level, we are grateful to the University of Notre Dame and Kent State University for generously providing the intellectual climate and institutional support needed to undertake and complete this work. Finally, we wish to thank our friends and family whose encouragement made this work possible. Most of all, we thank the authors whose work is featured herein. We have learned much from them. We hope you do as well.

Contents

Contributors

Glenn G. Affleck, University of Connecticut, Farmington, Connecticut

Jasmina Burdzovic Andreas, Harvard University, Cambridge, Massachusetts

C. S. Bergeman, University of Notre Dame, Notre Dame, Indiana

Toni L. Bisconti, University of New Hampshire, Durham, New Hampshire

Steven M. Boker, University of Notre Dame, Notre Dame, Indiana

Daniel E. Bontempo, Pennsylvania State University, University Párk, Pennsylvania

Dwayne T. Brandon, Johns Hopkins University, Baltimore, Maryland

Kirk Warren Brown, Virginia Commonwealth University, Richmond, Virginia

Fred B. Bryant, Loyola University Chicago, Chicago, Illinois

John T. Cacioppo, University of Chicago, Chicago, Illinois

Mike W. L. Cheung, University of Hong Kong, Hong Kong

Sy-Miin Chow, University of Notre Dame, Notre Dame, Indiana

Mihaly Csikszentmihalyi, Claremont Graduate University, Claremont, California

Mary C. Davis, Arizona State University, Tempe Arizona

Paul G. Devereux, University of Nevada, Reno, Nevada

Lisa M. Edwards, Marquette University, Milwaukee, Wisconsin

Michael Eid, Free University of Berlin, Germany

Amir Erez, University of Florida, Gainesville, Florida

Robert Fasman, Arizona State University, Tempe, Arizona

Diane H. Felmlee, University of California, Davis, California

Emilio Ferrer, University of California, Davis, California

William Fleeson, Wake Forest University, Winston-Salem, North Carolina

Frank Fujita, Indiana University, South Bend, Indiana

Shelly L. Gable, University of California, Los Angeles, California

Paolo Ghisletta, University of Geneva, Switzerland

Judith Glück, University of Vienna, Austria

Paul W. Griffin, Pace University, Pleasantville, New York

Kevin J. Grimm, University of Virginia, Charlottesville, Virginia

Louise C. Hawkley, University of Chicago, Chicago, Illinois

Kathi L. Heffner, Ohio University, Athens, Ohio

Samuel M. Y. Ho, University of Hong Kong, Hong Kong

Scott M. Hofer, Pennsylvania State University, University Park, Pennsylvania

Karen Hooker, Oregon State University, Corvallis, Oregon

John L. Horn, University of Southern California, Los Angeles, California

Derek M. Isaacowitz, Brandeis University, Waltham, Massachusetts

Alice M. Isen, Cornell University, Ithaca, New York

Constance J. Jones, California State University, Fresno, California

Brigitte Khoury, American University of Beirut Medical Center, Lebanon

Scott P. King, Loyola University Chicago, Chicago, Illinois

Ute Kunzmann, International University Bremen, Bremen, Germany

Jennifer G. La Guardia, University of Waterloo, Ontario, Canada

Rolf Langeheine, University of Kiel, Germany

Randy J. Larsen, Washington University, St. Louis, Missouri

Shane J. Lopez, University of Kansas, Lawrence, Kansas

Richard E. Lucas, Michigan State University, East Lansing, Michigan

Gerald Matthews, University of Cincinnati, Cincinnati, Ohio

Scott E. Maxwell, University of Notre Dame, Notre Dame, Indiana

Robert R. McCrae, National Institute on Aging, Baltimore, Maryland

Michael E. McCullough, University of Miami, Coral Gables, Florida

Daniel K. Mroczek, Purdue University, West Lafayette, Indiana

Julie K. Norem, Wellesley College, Wellesley, Massachusetts

Shigehiro Oishi, University of Virginia, Charlottesville, Virginia

Anthony D. Ong, Cornell University, Ithaca, New York

Nansook Park, University of Rhode Island, Kingston, Rhode Island

Christopher Peterson, University of Michigan, Ann Arbor, Michigan

Kristopher J. Preacher, University of Kansas, Lawrence, Kansas

Nilam Ram, University of Virginia, Charlottesville, Virginia

Kevin L. Rand, Indiana University–Purdue University Indianapolis, Indianapolis, Indiana

Richard D. Roberts, ETS Center for New Constructs, Princeton, New Jersey

Richard M. Ryan, University of Rochester, Rochester, New York

Ulrich Schimmack, University of Toronto at Mississauga, Ontario, Canada

Jennifer A. Schmidt, Northern Illinois University, DeKalb, Illinois

David Schuldberg, The University of Montana, Missoula, Montana

David J. Shernoff, Northern Illinois University, DeKalb, Illinois

Kim Shifren, Towson University, Towson, Maryland

Colette M. Smart, Loyola University Chicago, Chicago, Illinois

C. R. Snyder, University of Kansas, Lawrence, Kansas

Christiane Spiel, University of Vienna, Austria

Antje Stange, Max Planck Institute for Human Development, Berlin, Germany

Howard Tennen, University of Connecticut, Farmington, Connecticut

Antonio Terracciano, National Institute on Aging, Baltimore, Maryland

Todd M. Thrash, College of William & Mary, Williamsburg, Virginia

Stacey S. Tiberio, University of Notre Dame, Notre Dame, Indiana

Penelope K. Trickett, University of Southern California, Los Angeles, California

Manfred H. M. van Dulmen, Kent State University, Kent, Ohio

K. A. Wallace, University of Montana, Missoula, Montana

David A. Walsh, University of Southern California, Los Angeles, California

Keith E. Whitfield, Duke University, Durham, North Carolina

Alex J. Zautra, Arizona State University, Tempe, Arizona

Moshe Zeidner, University of Haifa, Mt. Carmel, Israel

John M. Zelenski, Carleton University, Ottawa, Ontario, Canada

Introduction

The chapters that follow provide a selective presentation of an emerging yet diverse field of inquiry known as positive psychology. This inquiry can be located within a broad developmental framework. Central to the framework is the view that variation and change are hallmarks of human behavior. Throughout, we take the position that modeling processes of variability and change can help to reveal how long-term trajectories of gains and losses that are reasonably consistent across different individuals may differ dramatically within individuals; clarify how complex trajectories of intraindividual changes are contoured by selective individual-difference variables; separate intraindividual differences in developmental growth from aspects of temporal phenomena that exhibit shorter-term variability over time; demonstrate how dimensions of interindividual differences may be used to explain important, adaptive intraindividual processes; and elucidate, through the use of qualitative analyses, how individual development is embedded in multiple contexts (e.g., biological, familial, historical, social, and cultural).

The volume is an attempt to speak to a growing sense, among researchers, of the need to embark on inquiries that integrate person-centered and variable-centered research across disciplines (Kessel, Rosenfield, & Anderson, 2003). In contrast to other volumes that cover highly specialized topics within the respective fields of measurement and analysis of change (Collins & Horn, 1991; Collins & Sayer, 2001) and positive psychology (e.g., Aspinwall & Staudinger, 2002; Kahneman, Diener, & Schwarz, 1999; Keyes & Haidt, 2002; Snyder & Lopez, 2002), this volume seeks to bring into high relief research opportunities that are at the intersection of several active sub-disciplines of life span psychology, developmental methodology, and the psychology of positive human health and well-being. As such, the book attempts to integrate, into a single accessible volume, findings from specialized areas to form a general conceptual framework that could serve both as a scaffold for the planning and implementation of emerging ideas and as an inducement to explore new empirical methods.

The volume will be of interest to applied researchers across disciplinary boundaries within the social sciences (anthropology, philosophy, sociology) and subdisciplinary boundaries within the behavioral sciences (clinical, cognitive, developmental, personality, social, as well as gerontology and health). Our goal, however, is not to address the handful of people who already are conversant with all these areas, but to reach people who know something about only one area, or even about none of them at all. As such, the chapters are written for an audience with no formal exposure to multivariate statistics and advanced measurement issues. The presentation is conceptually rather than mathematically oriented, the use of formulas is kept to a minimum, and many examples are offered of the application of current innovative methods to a wide variety of substantive research problems.

This approach has benefited our own thinking about issues in positive psychology; we think that it will benefit our readers as well.

Organization of the Volume

The volume is organized around five unifying themes of change (Baltes & Nesselroade, 1979): reliable differences across people assessed on a single occasion (interindividual differences); reliable variability (intraindividual variability) and change (intraindividual change) within a single person assessed repeatedly; and reliable differences across people in patterns of within-person variability (interindividual differences in intraindividual variability) and change (interindividual differences in intraindividual change). Although these five conceptual themes provide the subtext for most of the chapters, readers should bear in mind that these themes are themselves related and that individual contributions to this volume commonly address more than one theme.

Within each conceptual theme, exemplary research initiatives are identified that link advances in methodology with scientific investigations of human strengths. Each methodological chapter presents the fundamental conceptual aspects of important measurement issues and methods for evaluating variability and change, acquaints the reader with the assumptions and research contexts within which the analyses are often used, and is followed by substantive chapters that review or illustrate specific applications to specialized areas within positive psychology.

Part I focuses on methods for evaluating short-term intraindividual variability (i.e., P-technique analysis) and applications to the study of well-being and psychological health across the life span. Part II presents methods for investigating change over time at the level of the individual (i.e., dynamic factor analysis) and applications to research on affective processes in both dyads and persons with Parkinson's disease. Part III concentrates on measurement issues in individual differences research (i.e., construct validation, measurement invariance, experimental manipulation, genetic covariation, qualitative assessments) and applications to studies of hope and optimism, cross-cultural assessments of well-being and personality, positive emotions, emotional intelligence, extraversion, laughter, the heritability of personality, character strengths, wisdom, and resilience. Part IV presents methods for exploring interindividual differences in intraindividual variability (i.e., spectral analysis, item-response models, dynamic systems analysis) and applications to the study of affect, forgiveness, bereavement, dyadic interactions, and stress and coping. Part V focuses on methods for examining interindividual differences in growth and change over time (i.e., latent growth analysis, hierarchical linear modeling, latent class analysis) and applications to research on body image and perceived physical competence, positive psychological interventions, defensive pessimism and self-esteem, extraversion, inspiration, motivation, intimate relationships, positive emotions, social connectedness, flow experiences, and subjective well-being.

Although the substantive chapters in this volume provide a rich offering of scholarly breadth, in the end, we concluded that they could not profitably be ordered in any single way. To assist the reader in choosing the course of substantive reading, in table 1 the chapters are presented in order by chapter, and their major content category or theme is listed. We hope this format lends a sense of coherence to the volume as a whole and stimulates readers to integrate the rich diversity of methodological perspectives and depth of theoretical information about the analysis of positive psychological phenomena.

References

Aspinwall, L. G., & Staudinger, U. M. (Eds.). (2003). *A psychology of human strengths: Fundamental questions and future directions for a positive psychology.* Washington, DC: American Psychological Association.

Baltes, P. B., & Nesselroade, J. R. (1979). History and rationale of longitudinal research. In J. R. Nesselroade & P. B. Baltes (Eds.), *Longitudinal research in the study of behavior and development* (pp. 1-39). New York: Academic Press.

Collins, L. M., & Horn, J. L. (Eds.). (1991). *Best methods for the analysis of change.* Washington, DC: American Psychological Association.

Collins, L. M., & Sayer, A. G. (Eds.). (2001). *New methods for the analysis of change.* Washington, DC: American Psychological Association.

Kahneman, D., Diener, E., & Schwarz, N. (Eds.). (1999). *Well-being: The foundations of hedonic psychology.* New York: Russell-Sage.

Kessel, F., Rosenfield, P. L., & Anderson, N. B. (Eds.). (2003). *Expanding the boundaries of health and social science: Case studies in interdisciplinary innovation*: London: Oxford University Press.

Keyes, C. L. M., & Haidt, J. (Eds.). (2003). *Flourishing: Positive psychology and the life well lived*. Washington, DC: American Psychological Association.

Snyder, C. R., & Lopez, S. L. (Eds.). (2002). *Handbook of positive psychology*. New York: Oxford University Press.

TABLE 1 Major Content Areas Addressed by Chapters

Chapter	Author(s)	Culture, Creativity	Lifespan Development	Emotion, Stress	Health, Well-Being	Positive Interventions	Self, Personality	Social Relations	Religion, Motivation
1	Jones			×			×		
2	Ong et al.				×	×			
3	Shifren & Hooker			×	×				
4	Ferrer			×				×	×
5	Bryant et al.			×	×		×		
6	Edwards et al.		×	×	×		×		
7	Schimmack	×		×	×		×		
8	Lucas	×		×			×		
9	Oishi	×		×			×		
10	Ho & Cheung	×			×	×		×	
11	Bontempo & Hofer		×		×				
12	McCrae et al.	×	×				×		
13	Matthews et al.			×		×	×	×	
14	Zelenski			×			×		×
15	Isaacowitz		×	×			×		×
16	Devereux & Heffner			×	×	×		×	
17	Isen & Erez			×					
18	Bergeman & Ong	×	×	×			×		
19	Whitfield & Brandon	×	×		×				
20	Park & Peterson	×	×			×	×		
21	Kunzmann & Stange	×	×	×		×	×		×
22	Wallace & Bergeman	×	×	×		×			×

(continued)

TABLE 1 (*Continued*)

Chapter	Author(s)	Culture, Creativity	Lifespan Development	Emotion, Stress	Health, Well-Being	Positive Interventions	Self Personality	Social Relations	Religion, Motivation
23	Larsen			×	×		×		
24	Glück & Spiel		×				×		
25	Chow et al.			×					×
26	McCullough & Boker		×	×			×	×	
27	Bisconti & Bergeman		×	×				×	
28	Felmlee				×			×	
29	Schuldberg			×	×	×	×		
30	Maxwell & Tiberio			×			×		
31	Ghisletta & Trickett		×	×	×		×		
32	Mroczek & Griffin		×	×		×	×		
33	Norem & Andreas			×			×	×	×
34	Zautra et al.			×	×		×	×	
35	Fleeson			×			×	×	×
36	Thrash			×			×		×
37	Brown & Ryan			×	×	×		×	×
38	Schmidt et al.	×	×				×		×
39	Hawkley et al.			×				×	
40	Gable & La Guardia			×				×	×
41	Eid			×	×		×		
42	Eid & Langeheine			×	×		×		

I

Intraindividual Variability

1

P-Technique Factor Analysis as a Tool for Exploring Psychological Health

Constance J. Jones

Recent collections of work (e.g., Keyes & Haidt, 2003; Snyder & Lopez, 2002) clearly illustrate the diversity of approaches that may be employed to explore positive psychology. Internet-using adults (e.g., Srivastava, John, Gosling, & Potter, 2003), psychiatric patients (e.g., Brekke & Long, 2000), and those ubiquitous college students (e.g., Butler, Hokanson, & Flynn, 1994) all have served as participants in studies of psychological health. Self-reported (e.g., Helson & Klohnen, 1998), clinician-reported (e.g., Vaillant, 1977), microanalytic (e.g., Diener, Larsen, & Emmons, 1984), and macroanalytic (e.g., Crosnoe & Elder, 2002) variables all have usefully detailed the myriad facets of psychological health. Studies also differ in terms of the number of assessments obtained per participant. While many investigations involve a single cross-sectional assessment, others involve multiple assessments, sometimes over 100 per respondent. The time span of longitudinal assessments can range enormously—for example, from 20 minutes (Fridlund, Cottam, & Fowler, 1982) to nearly 50 years (Jones & Meredith, 2000).

Of course, such diversity of approaches gives great breadth and depth to our understanding of psychological health. It is helpful, however, to occasionally partition studies by population, variable, or selected research design to more clearly understand themes as they emerge in the literature. Ong and van Dulmen designed this volume to partition studies by research design, differentiating cross-sectional from short-term and long-term longitudinal designs, and single-participant from multiple-participant designs. Naturally, distinctions become somewhat fuzzy in application, but by creating such contrasts, results from various studies of positive psychology may be more clearly illuminated.

In this chapter, the particular value of short-term longitudinal single-participant studies is detailed. Such designs focus explicitly on how particular individuals vary in their scores, collected repeatedly across a specified period of time. This form of research design is quite different from those typically used. The vast majority of research detailing positive human behavior attempts to capture individuals' unwavering characteristic "trait" qualities—who is optimistic, who is not; who has high self-esteem, who has low; who is resilient, who is not? And such approaches have taken us far in our understanding of psychological health (e.g., see chapters 5–19, this volume).

How can short-term longitudinal single-participant studies, with their collection and exploration of intraindividual variability data, advance science? An increasing number of researchers have cogently argued that expanding our exploration of human behavior to include both stable-trait and labile-state characteristics may have valuable payoffs (e.g., Lamiell, 1981; Nesselroade, 1988; Nesselroade & Boker, 1994; Watson & Clark, 1994). By focusing on individuals' variability within a particular time frame, we fully recognize and explore the dynamic qualities of real human behavior. A direct examination of variability at the level of the individual is clearly superior to inferences regarding intraindividual variability made by aggregating across data collected from individuals at a single point in time (e.g., Lamiell, 1981; Nesselroade & Ford, 1985).

Data Obtained From Short-Term Longitudinal, Single-Participant Studies

An example of a simplified short-term longitudinal single-participant study might involve asking Jack to report, daily for 100 consecutive days, his levels of elation, intellectual curiosity, and sociability (working from Fredrickson's, 2002, ideas that positive emotions are linked to expanding intellectual and social resources). Taking a univariate focus, we could examine the skew and kurtosis of Jack's distribution of elation scores, for example, across the 100-day period. This would provide information about the range and commonality of particular levels of elation reported by Jack across that time period. A simple standard deviation of Jack's response would give an index of the temporal stability of Jack's elation levels. Taking a bivariate focus, the cross-time correlation between Jack's elation and intellectual curiosity levels, for example, would indicate if, on days Jack is elated, he also tends to feel especially intellectually curious (or especially incurious). And finally, taking a multivariate focus, if all possible bivariate correlation coefficients were submitted to a factor analysis, the number and nature of the dimensions underlying variability in reported variables could be uncovered. This form of factor analysis—performed with multiple (generally more than three) variables collected repeatedly from a single individual—is termed *P-technique factor analysis*, and is discussed in more detail below. (Although of primary focus here, note that the standard deviation, correlation, and factor analysis are but a subset of statistics appropriate for the analysis of data collected from short-term longitudinal, single-subject designs; e.g., Larsen, 1987, 1989.)

The Magnitude of Intraindividual Variability: Connections to Psychological Health

Although the primary focus of this chapter is the utility of a multivariate correlational approach to intraindividual variability, first briefly consider the benefits of examining simple measures of the magnitude of intraindividual variability, here in connection to psychological health. Of the host of variables appropriate for capturing psychological health, a subset clearly shows important levels of intraindividual variability. In particular, individuals' moods, affects, or emotions, thought to be sensitively responsive to intrapsychic as well as environmental changes, nearly by definition show meaningful and reliable intraindividual variability. Other more stable characteristics may also show meaningful patterns of day-to-day variability, including self-esteem, self-description, perceptions of control, and the like.

Generally, we might first ask if magnitude of intraindividual variability is a stable attribute of individuals. Current research indicates this is, in fact, the case. Measures of intraindividual variability of affect (usually the standard deviation of scores collected across a period of many days) have been successfully used to differentiate more emotionally reactive, labile individuals from more emotionally predictable, stable individuals (e.g., Eid & Diener, 1999; Penner, Shiffman, Paty, & Fritzsche, 1994). Researchers differ with respect to their willingness to combine variables representing positive and negative affect; many argue that positive affect differs from negative affect in terms of its evolutionary role and process mechanisms (e.g., Fredrickson, 2002; Watson & Clark, 1994). However, empirical research tends to indicate that individuals' intraindividual variability in positive affect and negative affect are significantly positively correlated (e.g., Eid & Diener, 1999; Larson, Csikszentmihalyi, & Graef, 1980; Penner et al., 1994), and that a composite measure of mood variability can be successfully created and employed. Degree of intraindividual variability also appears to be a stable characteristic for measures of self-esteem (Butler et al., 1994), self-description (Charles & Pasupathi, 2003), and perceived control (Eizenman, Nesselroade, Featherman, & Rowe, 1997).

We may then proceed to ask if magnitude of intraindividual variability is related to various conceptions of psychological health. Current research indicates, most generally, that magnitude of intraindividual variability in mood tends to be negatively associated with measures of psychological health. Among adolescents (who are, as expected, generally more moody than adults (Larson et al., 1980), those who are more emotionally labile are more likely to be depressed (Larson, Raffaelli, Richards, Ham, & Jewell, 1990; Silk, Steinberg, & Morris, 2003) and show problem behaviors (Silk et al., 2003) than those who are more emotionally stable. Adult women with greater affective variability are rated as having less well-established Eriksonian identities (Tobacyk, 1981) than less affectively variable women. Greater intraindividual variability in negative affect is associated with higher neuroticism (Eid & Diener, 1999) and higher overall levels of negative affect (Watson & Clark, 1994). Those with greater intraindividual variability in self-esteem and greater intraindividual variability in self-descriptions show more negative affect overall (Butler et al., 1994; Charles & Pasupathi, 2003) than less labile individuals. A study of older individuals' variability in locus of control indicated that those who showed the most intraindividual variability in that construct were the most likely to be dead 6 years later (Eizenman et al., 1997).

Wessman and Ricks' (1966) important early study of 18 Harvard men and 25 Radcliffe women laid the groundwork for much later work regarding mood variability. Their focus on the magnitude of intraindividual variability centered on the daily report of elation, a single item from their 16-item Personal Feelings Scale. Elation scores ranged from 1 ("Utter depression and gloom. Completely down. All is black and leaden") to 10 ("Complete elation. Rapturous joy and soaring ecstacy"). Each evening for 42 consecutive evenings, students indicated how they had felt that day, on average (along with the level of their most elated and least elated moment of the day). The simple standard deviation of each individual's day-to-day report of elation served as a measure of stability (stable-variable) and was found to be uncorrelated with the overall level of elation, averaged across 42 days (unhappy-happy) for both men and women. Wessman and Ricks' case studies of a happy and stable, happy and variable, unhappy and stable, and unhappy and variable man, respectively, illustrate the power of an idiographic approach to the study of psychological health (chapter 3 gives details regarding intraindividual variability in subjective well-being).

Why Move Beyond Measures of Magnitude of Intraindividual Variability?

Clearly, magnitude of intraindividual variability holds promise for a continued general understanding of psychological health. However, indices of magnitude of intraindividual variability, whether taken from single or multiple variables, do not capture all the information present in a stream of scores obtained across time. The nature of the autocorrelations, given a single variable and the nature of simultaneous and time-lagged correlations, given multiple variables, can provide important additional information regarding the dynamic processes of human behavior. P-technique factor analysis proves to be a powerful statistical technique for capturing multivariate connections between variables, individual by individual.

What Is P-Technique Factor Analysis?

P-technique factor analysis is generally best described in contrast to the more commonly used R-technique factor analysis. Cattell (1988) labeled various forms of factor analysis depending upon the type of data submitted for analysis. Employing his three-dimensional data box, traditional R-technique factor analysis involves sampling N individuals' scores on p variables at a single point in time (see figure 1.1). R, a $p \times p$ correlation matrix (typically), is then created to indicate how variables tend to vary together at a single point in time for a group of individuals: Do individuals who score high on one variable tend to also score high or low on other collected variables? To better elucidate interdependencies in large correlation matrices, factor analysis can be used to decompose the original correlation matrix R into several new and useful matrices:

$$R_{p \times p} = A_{p \times m} L_{m \times m} A'_{m \times p} + T_{p \times p}$$

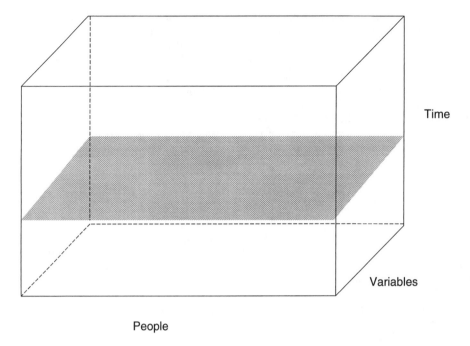

Time

Variables

People

Figure 1.1 Cattell's three-dimensional data box: R-technique factor analysis.

Employing exploratory procedures, the researcher would first determine the "correct" number of underlying dimensions, or factors, that exist in the data. The number of factors, m, indicates the relative complexity of the correlational patterns in the data; more factors indicate greater complexity. A, the factor-loading matrix, indicates how the original variables are related to the factors, and L, the factor intercorrelation matrix, indicates how the m factors are related to one another. If L contains 1s down the diagonal and 0s elsewhere (e.g., the factors are not correlated with one another), the solution is said to be orthogonal; otherwise, the solution is said to be oblique (A' is simply A transposed). T is a matrix of unique variances (see, e.g., Gorsuch, 1983). Confirmatory procedures are also possible and often prove powerful. For a reasoned discussion of the value of both exploratory and confirmatory factor analytic procedures, see Nesselroade (1994).

Traditional R-technique factor analysis has been proven enormously useful in simplifying and elucidating intractable correlation matrices, although it is not without controversy (Gould, 1996). Clearly, one weakness of R-technique factor analysis is that results may not generalize to other, unassessed, points in time. Sample size can also be a concern—data collected from at least 100 individuals give more robust results.

Procedures for P-technique factor analysis are identical to procedures for R-technique factor analysis. The difference between the two techniques lies in the "slice" of data taken from the data box (see figure 1.2). For P-technique factor analysis, p variables are assessed across t time points for a single individual. R, a $p \times p$ correlation matrix (typically), is then created to indicate how variables tend to vary together for a single individual across a number of time points: When a single individual scores high on one variable, does he or she also tend to score high or low on other collected variables?

With P-technique factor analysis, the number of factors, m, serves as a measure of the complexity of the correlational patterns of data for that particular individual. The factor loading matrix, A, indicates how particular variables are related to that individual's idiosyncratic factors, and the factor intercorrelation matrix, L, indicates how the individual's factors are related to one another; factors may be either orthogonal or oblique. Clearly, one weakness of P-technique factor analysis is that results may not generalize to other, unassessed, individuals. And, once again, sample size can be a concern—100 or more repeated assessments from focus individuals are desirable.

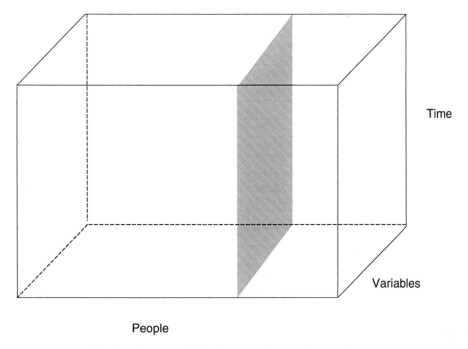

Figure 1.2 Cattell's three-dimensional data box: P-technique factor analysis.

P-Technique Factor Analysis: Connections to Psychological Health

Moving beyond the magnitude of intraindividual variability, P-technique factor analysis allows the exploration of the complexity of associations among multiple variables collected across time (the number of factors) and the nature of the dimensions underlying the associations among multiple variables collected across time (the factor loading and factor intercorrelation patterns). This information may be more generally connected to various conceptions of psychological health.

Classic P-technique factor analysis involves data collected from a single focus unit of observation (individual, dyad, etc.). Within the domain of positive psychology, Mintz and Luborsky (1970) illustrate a creative use of classic P-technique factor analysis. Verbatim transcriptions of 9 of 21 psychotherapy sessions with a college freshman experiencing "feelings of inferiority" were used to provide the raw data. A total of 60 segments (each segment consisting of three therapist and three patient statements) were scored on 18 variables, including therapist empathy, warmth, and directiveness, and patient anxiety, hopefulness, and dependency. Four orthogonal factors,

describing the underlying dimensions seen in the interrelationships among the 18 manifest variables, were extracted: Patient Health, Patient Involvement, Therapist Natural Directiveness, and Therapist Empathic Approach. Results thus indicated, for this particular individual's psychotherapy sessions, four separate and unique dimensions. By correlating factor scores with linear, quadratic, and cubic orthogonal polynomials, Mintz and Luborsky were able to illustrate transformations in the psychotherapeutic process for this young man: His distress was highest midway through therapy; his involvement initially rose, then dropped sharply.

Extensions of P-Technique Factor Analysis

Early in the use of P-technique factor analysis, criticism began mounting regarding the generalizability of results obtained from a single individual. Although P-technique factor analysis can provide fascinating insights into the complexity and process of change for a single individual, skeptics immediately point out the difficulties inherent in generalizing nomothetic law from results based on a single individual. Statisticians also warned that P-technique data violate the assumption of independent responses (e.g., Holtzman, 1963), an assumption more easily met when data are provided by different individuals. Fortunately, advances in design and statistical procedures address these concerns.

Chain P-Technique Factor Analysis

In order to address the weakness of establishing general principles based on data collected from single individuals, researchers first attempted an extension of classic P-technique factor analysis, termed chain P-technique factor analysis. Chain P-technique factor analysis differs from classic P-technique in that intraindividual variability data from multiple respondents are collected and analyzed. However, in this case, data from all respondents are chained together or merged to create a single correlation matrix. This matrix is then submitted to factor analysis, with the assumption that all individuals share the same level of multivariate complexity and the same structure of intraindividual variability. For example, Russell, Bryant, and Estrada (1996) selected, from a pool of 35 50-minute child therapy session transcripts (involving three different clinicians and three different patients), three approximately 15-minute segments deemed high-quality and three deemed low-quality, based on ratings from 33 items. Each of the six segments were subsequently rated, utterance by utterance, on an additional set of 39 items (15 were retained) said to give an overall view of psychotherapeutic interaction between clinician and client. Data from the three high-quality segments were chained together and factor analyzed, producing three orthogonal clinician-oriented factors: Responsive Informing, Initiatory Questioning, and Positive Regard. Similar factors emerged from the three low-quality sessions' data, chained together.

Unfortunately, the assumption required by chain P-technique—that all individuals (or, in this case, that all clinician-patient interactions of a particular quality) share the same number and type of dimensions—is often untenable. Thus, results from chain P-technique, although often intriguing (e.g., Friedman, 2003), may be somewhat suspect. Fortunately, an important statistical development addresses the concerns inherent in chain P-technique (Nesselroade & Molenaar, 1999). A confirmatory statistical procedure allows not only the testing of the equivalence of individual data sets before chaining, but also the

testing of the need for modeling lags in repeated measurement data sets. It is clear that confirmatory statistical modeling will play an increasingly large role in various future applications of P-technique factor analysis.

Replicated P-Technique Factor Analysis

Understanding the importance of collecting data from multiple individuals, yet unwilling to automatically generalize across individuals, other researchers have employed so-called replicated P-technique factor analysis. Replicated P-technique factor analysis involves performing a classic P-technique factor analysis for each individual in the sample, then generalizing across individuals, but only if the number and nature of obtained factors are similar. Replicated P-technique factor analysis is enormously powerful in that it builds nomothetic law created only after summarization across individuals, each understood using careful idiographic procedures, is justified (for a review, see Jones & Nesselroade, 1990).

Zevon and Tellegen's (1982) analyses of data from 23 college students classically demonstrate the power of replicated P-technique factor analysis. Each student completed a 60-item mood checklist (e.g., attentive, hostile, shy) daily for a total of 90 days. Separate P-technique factor analyses for each individual indicated 20 of 23 students produced two orthogonal factors, one representing positive affect, and the other, negative affect. One participant produced three factors: a positive affect, a negative affect, and an anger factor. The remaining two individuals, when asked to complete an adjective-sorting task using the 60 mood items, were found to be interpreting adjectives in an idiosyncratic manner; their results remained unique.

In their analyses, Zevon and Tellegen (1982) attended to both the number and nature of factors obtained. Disregarding the characteristics of the factor loading pattern and factor intercorrelation matrices extracted, some authors have utilized replicated P-technique factor analysis simply to obtain the number of factors produced by each respondent's data or the percentage of variance explained by the first factor obtained. Greater intraindividual data complexity is indicated by greater numbers of factors extracted or less variance predicted by the first factor.

Wessman and Ricks (1966), for example, found that the number of factors extracted from students' mood data predicted variability in elation: Those with more complex affective responses experienced more consistent elation levels. Similarly, Tobacyk (1981) found that those with more complex affective responses showed less affective variability overall. A study of individuals' complexity of emotional response fits nicely with newer theoretical ideas regarding the importance of this dimension of emotional experiences (e.g., Labouvie-Vief & Medler, 2002) and the idea that healthy regulation of emotion may involve coordinated, finely tuned balancing of both positive and negative affect (Carstensen, Pasupathi, Mayr, & Nesselroade, 2000; Fredrickson, 2002).

Dynamic P-Technique Factor Analysis

An additional criticism of classic P-technique factor analysis is that serial dependencies, such that systematic relationships between an individual's responses at time t and at time $t + 1$, may exist in the data. Such dependencies violate traditional factor analytic assumptions and are not eliminated or incorporated in the traditional P-technique or replicated P-technique statistical model. Fortunately, an expansion of P-technique, so-called dynamic P-technique factor analysis, has been created to address these concerns (Molenaar, 1985). Researchers using dynamic factor analysis input an enlarged correlation matrix, which includes not only simultaneous correlations but also lagged covariances and correlations. In this case, both the length of the lag and the number of factors must be selected before the factor loading and factor intercorrelation matrices are interpreted. The number of lags is generally set large initially, then reduced if results indicate this is justified. For example, using data collected daily, if a researcher believes, at maximum, scores collected 2 days ago may be related to scores collected today (lag 2), a Toeplitz-transformed matrix (see Wood & Brown, 1994) containing simultaneous (today-today), lag 1 (yesterday-today), and lag 2 (two days ago-today) correlations and covariances is created and then analyzed.

For example, Shifren, Hooker, Wood, and Nesselroade (1997) employed dynamic P-technique factor analysis, replicated across 12 individuals diagnosed with Parkinson's disease. Respondents completed an affect questionnaire daily for 70 consecutive days; 5 of the 12 showed sufficient intraindividual variability in both positive and negative affect for full analyses. A sequence of increasingly complex models were fit to each individual's data, moving from one to two factors, zero to one lag, and uncorrelated to

correlated error structures. Three respondents produced one factor, and two produced two; one respondent needed no lag, and four needed a lag of one; no respondent showed correlated error structures. Such results clearly illustrate the folly of blithely summarizing across individuals, assuming patterns of intraindividual variability are similar. Results also indicate, particularly for the study of affect, that day-to-day carryover effects are important to capture and model.

P-Technique Factor Analysis and Psychological Health: The Future

Psychology's renewed interest in a holistic view of human behavior (e.g., Magnussen, 1995)—including emphasis of individuals' uniqueness, types of individuals, multivariate assessment, and sophisticated statistical models that allow exploration of intraindividual variability and interindividual differences in intraindividual variability—bodes well for the continued use of both traditional and expanded versions of P-technique factor analysis.

With respect to an understanding of psychological health, results from P-technique factor analysis can provide important clarity regarding how labile constructs such as mood, as well as more stable constructs such as self-esteem, vary across time for single individuals—the high points and low points reached, the overall amount of intraindividual variability, the complexity of intraindividual variability, and the structure of intraindividual variability. Through the use of expansions of P-technique, including replicated P-technique, dynamic P-technique, and chain P-technique, researchers may begin to create powerful nomothetic law based on careful consideration of individuals' unique constellations of behavior; by ensuring that generalization occurs only across genuinely similar individuals, the progress of science quickens.

References

Brekke, J. S., & Long, J. D. (2000). Community-based psychosocial rehabilitation and prospective change in functional, clinical, and subjective experience variables in schizophrenia. *Schizophrenia Bulletin, 26,* 667–680.

Butler, A. C., Hokanson, J. E., & Flynn, H. A. (1994). A comparison of self-esteem lability and low trait self-esteem as vulnerability factors for depression. *Journal of Personality and Social Psychology, 66,* 166–177.

Carstensen, L. L., Pasupathi, M., Mayr, U., & Nesselroade, J. R. (2000). Emotional experience in everyday life across the adult life span. *Journal of Personality and Social Psychology, 79,* 644–655.

Cattell, R. B. (1988). The data box: Its ordering of total resources in terms of possible relational systems. In J. R. Nesselroade & R. B. Cattell (Eds.), *Handbook of multivariate experimental psychology* (pp. 69–130). New York: Plenum Press.

Charles, S. T., & Pasupathi, M. (2003). Age-related patterns of variability in self-descriptions: Implications for everyday affective experience. *Psychology and Aging, 18,* 524–536.

Crosnoe, R., & Elder, G. H. Jr. (2002). Successful adaptation in later years: A life course approach to aging. *Social Psychology Quarterly, 65,* 309–328.

Diener, E., Larsen, R. J., & Emmons, R. A. (1984). Person × situation interactions: Choice of situations and congruence response models. *Journal of Personality and Social Psychology, 47,* 580–592.

Eid, M., & Diener, E. (1999). Intraindividual variability in affect: Reliability, validity, and personality correlates. *Journal of Personality and Social Psychology, 76,* 662–676.

Eizenman, D. R., Nesselroade, J. R., Featherman, D. L., & Rowe, J. W. (1997). Intraindividual variability in perceived control in an older sample: The MacArthur Successful Aging Studies. *Psychology and Aging, 12,* 489–502.

Fredrickson, B. L. (2002). Positive emotions. In C. R. Snyder & S. J. Lopez (Eds.), *Handbook of positive psychology* (pp. 120–134). Oxford: Oxford University Press.

Fridlund, A. J., Cottam, G. L., & Fowler, S. C. (1982). In search of the general tension factor: Tensional patterning during auditory stimulation. *Psychophysiology, 19,* 136–145.

Friedman, B. H. (2003). Idiodynamics vis-à-vis psychophysiology: An idiodynamic portrayal of cardiovascular reactivity. *Journal of Applied Psychoanalytic Studies, 5,* 425–441.

Gorsuch, R. L. (1983). *Factor analysis.* Hillsdale, NJ: Erlbaum.

Gould, S. J. (1996). *The mismeasure of man.* New York: Norton.

Helson, R., & Klohnen, E. C. (1998). Affective coloring of personality from young adulthood to midlife. *Personality and Social Psychology Bulletin, 24,* 241–252.

Holtzman, W. H. (1963). Statistical models for the study of change in the single case. In C. W. Harris (Ed.), *Problems in measuring change* (pp. 199–211). Madison: University of Wisconsin Press.

Jones, C. J., & Meredith, W. (2000). Developmental paths of psychological health from early adolescence to later adulthood. *Psychology and Aging, 15,* 351–360.

Jones, C. J., & Nesselroade, J. R. (1990). Multivariate, replicated, single-subject, repeated measures designs and P-technique factor analysis: A review of intraindividual change studies. *Experimental Aging Research, 16,* 171–183.

Keyes, C. L. M., & Haidt, J. (Eds.). (2003). *Flourishing: Positive psychology and the life well lived.* Washington, DC: American Psychological Association.

Labouvie-Vief, G., & Medler, M. (2002). Affect optimization and affect complexity: Models and styles of regulation in adulthood. *Psychology and Aging, 17,* 571–588.

Lamiell, J. T. (1981). Toward an idiothetic psychology of personality. *American Psychologist, 36,* 276–289.

Larsen, R. J. (1987). The stability of mood variability: A spectral analytic approach to daily mood assessments. *Journal of Personality and Social Psychology, 52,* 1195–1204.

Larsen, R. J. (1989). A process approach to personality psychology: Utilizing time as a facet of data. In D. M. Buss & N. Cantor (Eds.), *Personality psychology: Recent trends and emerging directions* (pp. 177–193). New York: Springer-Verlag.

Larson, R., Csikszentmihalyi, M., & Graef, R. (1980). Mood variability and the psychosocial adjustment of adolescent. *Journal of Youth and Adolescence, 9,* 469–490.

Larson, R., Raffaelli, M., Richards, M. H., Ham, M., & Jewell, L. (1990). Ecology of depression in late childhood and early adolescence: A profile of daily states and activities. *Journal of Abnormal Psychology, 99,* 92–102.

Magnusson, D. (1995). Individual development: A holistic, integrated model. In P. Moen, G. H. Elder Jr., & K. Lüscher (Eds.), *Examining lives in context* (pp. 19–60). Washington, DC: American Psychological Association.

Mintz, J., & Luborsky, L. (1970). P-technique factor analysis in psychotherapy research: An illustration of a method. *Psychotherapy: Theory, Research, and Practice, 7,* 13–18.

Molenaar, P. C. M. (1985). A dynamic factor model for the analysis of multivariate time series. *Psychometrika, 50,* 181–202.

Nesselroade, J. R. (1988). Some implications of the trait-state distinction for the study of development over the lifespan: The case of personality. In P. B. Baltes, D. L. Featherman, & R. M. Lerner

(Eds.), *Life-span development and behavior* (pp. 163–189). Hillsdale, NJ: Erlbaum.

Nesselroade, J. R. (1994). Exploratory factor analysis with latent variables and the study of processes of development and change. In A. von Eye & C. C. Clogg (Eds.), *Latent variable analysis* (pp. 131–154). Thousand Oaks, CA: Sage.

Nesselroade, J. R., & Boker, S. M. (1994). Assessing constancy and change. In T. F. Heatherton & J. L. Weinberger (Eds.), *Can personality change?* (pp. 121–147). Washington, DC: American Psychological Association.

Nesselroade, J. R., & Ford, D. H. (1985). P-technique comes of age: Multivariate, replicated, single-subject designs for research on older adults. *Research on Aging, 7,* 46–80.

Nesselroade, J. R., & Molenaar, P. C. M. (1999). Pooling lagged covariance structures based on short, multivariate time series for dynamic factor analysis. In R. H. Hoyle (Ed.), *Statistical strategies for small sample research* (pp. 223–250). Thousand Oaks, CA: Sage.

Penner, L. A., Shiffman, S., Paty, J. A., & Fritzsche, B. A. (1994). Individual differences in intraperson variability in mood. *Journal of Personality and Social Psychology, 66,* 712–721.

Russell, R. L., Bryant, F. B., & Estrada, A. U. (1996). Confirmatory P-technique analyses of therapist discourse: High- versus low-quality child therapy sessions. *Journal of Consulting and Clinical Psychology, 64,* 1366–1376.

Shifren, K., Hooker, K., Wood, P., & Nesselroade, J. R. (1997). Structure and variation of mood in individuals with Parkinson's disease: A dynamic factor analysis. *Psychology and Aging, 12,* 328–339.

Silk, J. S., Steinberg, L., & Morris, A. S. (2003). Adolescents' emotion regulation in daily life: Links to depressive symptoms and problem behavior. *Child Development, 74,* 1869–1880.

Snyder, C. R., & Lopez, S. J. (Eds.). (2002). *Handbook of positive psychology.* Oxford: Oxford University Press.

Srivastava, S., John, O., Gosling, S. D., & Potter, J. (2003). Development of personality in early and middle adulthood: Set like plaster or persistent change? *Journal of Personality and Social Psychology, 84,* 1041–1053.

Tobacyk, J. (1981). Personality differentiation, effectiveness of personality integration, and mood in female college students. *Journal of Personality and Social Psychology, 41,* 348–356.

Vaillant, G. (1977). *Adaptation to life.* Boston: Little, Brown.

Watson, D., & Clark, L. A. (1994). The vicissitudes of mood: A schematic model. In P. Ekman & R. J. Davidson (Eds.), *The nature of emotion: Fundamental questions* (pp. 400–405). New York: Oxford University Press.

Wessman, A. E., & Ricks, D. F. (1966). *Mood and personality.* New York: Holt, Rinehart, and Winston.

Wood, P., & Brown, D. (1994). The study of intraindividual differences by means of dynamic factor models: Rationale, implementation, and interpretation. *Psychological Bulletin, 116,* 166–186.

Zevon, M. A., & Tellegen, A. (1982). The structure of mood change: An idiographic/nomothetic analysis. *Journal of Personality and Social Psychology, 43,* 111–122.

2

Stepping Into the Light

Modeling the Intraindividual Dimensions of Hedonic and Eudaemonic Well-Being

Anthony D. Ong, John L. Horn, and David A. Walsh

Over the past three decades, the scientific study of positive human health and well-being has been driven by two major philosophical perspectives, one emphasizing *hedonism* or happiness and the other emphasizing *eudaemonism* or self-actualization (cf. Ryan & Deci, 2000; Waterman, 1993). These perspectives have shaped two prominent theories of positive health: the theory of subjective well-being (SWB; see Diener, 1984; Diener, Suh, Lucas, & Smith, 1999, for reviews) and the theory of psychological well-being (PWB; see Ryff, 1995; Ryff & Singer, 2000, for reviews). Although both theories aim to describe how people evaluate their lives, each gives emphasis to different aspects of this evaluation. Subjective well-being defines evaluations in terms of three elements: judgments of positive and negative affect (Diener & Emmons, 1984; Watson, Clark, & Tellegen, 1988) and overall life satisfaction (Andrews & Withey, 1976). In contrast, PWB parses well-being into six elements: judgments of self-acceptance, personal growth, purpose in life, positive relations with others, environmental mastery, and autonomy (Ryff, 1989; Ryff & Keyes, 1995).

Considerable progress has been made in identifying and measuring the separate elements of SWB and PWB. Reliable trait measures of these elements have been developed—the Positive and Negative Affect Schedule (PANAS; Watson et al., 1988), the Satisfaction With Life Scale (SWLS; Diener, Emmons, Larsen, & Griffin, 1985), and the Psychological Well-Being Scales (Ryff, 1989). Different forms of evidence have been put forth to indicate the validity of these elements. Evidence of discriminant validity of SWB elements has been indicated with multitrait, multimethod analyses (Lucas, Diener, & Suh, 1996). Evidence of convergent validity of PWB elements has been indicated with common factor analyses (Ryff & Keyes, 1995). And evidence for the convergent and discriminant validity of all nine SWB and PWB elements has been indicated with confirmatory factor analyses (Keyes, Shmotkin, & Ryff, 2002). Thus, it has become clear that the phenomenon referred to as *positive health* is a mosaic of many component parts. This mosaic can be partitioned into a parsimonious set of dimensions, indicating measurements, that fairly completely account for individual differences among a large number of these components. Although this foundational evidence has provided a basis for understanding the phenomena of positive health, other basic information is needed to establish the nature of the phenomena.

In this chapter, we highlight the importance of taking a process approach to understanding positive human health (Ryff & Singer, 1998). We call attention to designs that include multiple individuals, variables, and occasions of measurement; methods of data collection that target immediate reports from individuals in their natural environments; and analytic techniques that are well suited for the study of within-person phenomena. We provide an example of how these methods can be applied to questions concerning the short-term temporal stability versus variability of SWB and PWB constructs. We conclude with a brief consideration of the gains that can be made by thinking carefully and deeply about individual lives.

Beyond Nomothetic Questions

At the outset, we underscore the importance of adopting a conception of positive health that encompasses more than traits or individual differences. We argue that the dominance of the *nomothetic approach*, in which lawful relations among variables across individuals are examined, has largely shifted investigators' attention away from temporally unfolding relations among variables measured within an individual, best captured by the *idiographic approach* (Allport, 1937). That is, while aggregate, between-person analyses have yielded converging evidence for the construct validity of well-being measures, very little attention has been given to investigating intraindividual, within-person relations among these elements.

What Is Gained From an Intraindividual Approach?

We contend that at the center of understanding individual variation and change is the in-depth study of a single individual's development followed by careful generalizations on the basis of an integration of studies of many such single cases.

Indeed, a long research tradition—beginning with Ebbinghaus (1885) and then Lewin (1935), Allport (1937), Stern (1938), Stevens (1951), Rosenzweig (1951), Cattell (1963), Horn (1972), Wohlwill (1973), Lamiell (1981), Larsen (1989), McAdams (1990), and Nesselroade (1991) among others—has shown that characteristics of the person (e.g., memory, motivation, abilities), rather than being fixed and unchanging over time, are subject to fluctuations in expression brought about by psychological and social influences. In contrast to the classical nomothetic view, an intraindividual perspective necessitates that before group variability can be understood, the intraindividual variability of a single person must be understood (cf. Kratochwill, 1978; Rogosa & Willett, 1985).

Can reliable patterns of SWB and PWB be identified within individuals studied through time? Are the patterns so identified within a single individual generalizable across individuals? Such questions necessitate repeated measurements. Whereas several studies have gone beyond a single measurement-occasion design (Kleban, Lawton, Nesselroade, & Parmelee, 1992; Larsen & Kasimatis, 1990; Wessman & Ricks, 1966; Zevon & Tellegen, 1982), broad sampling of occasions, or the study of intraindividual variability, has largely been a neglected focus in well-being research. This contrasts to other areas of research in which meaningful patterns of intraindividual variability have been demonstrated across a range of psychological phenomena, including studies of personality (Cattell & Cross, 1952), psychotherapy (Luborsky & Mintz, 1972), human abilities (Horn, 1972), locus of control (Roberts & Nesselroade, 1986), temperament (Hooker, Nesselroade, Nesselroade, & Lerner, 1987), work values (Schulenberg, Vondracek, & Nesselroade, 1988), depression (Lawton, Parmelee, Katz, & Nesselroade, 1996), Parkinson's disease (Shifren, Hooker, Wood, & Nesselroade, 1997), and emotional complexity (Carstensen, Pasupathi, Mayr, & Nesselroade, 2000). Taken as a whole, this broad collection of studies provides extensive evidence that many individual differences dimensions that are traditionally assumed to reflect stable between-person variation manifest significant occasion-to-occasion within-person variability.

Supplementing Intraindividual Inquiry With Tests of Measurement Invariance

Implicit in the comparison of groups and individuals is the assumption of equivalence of measurement. This assumption, however, is rarely tested directly in well-being research. Yet the interpretation of either between- or within-person results, based on nonequivalent measurements, is riddled with ambiguity (Horn, McArdle, & Mason, 1983; Meredith, 1964; Meredith & Horn, 2001; see also chapter 11, this volume). Measurement invariance is fundamentally important for evaluating intraindividual evidence. For in each case, before any construct validation results can be sensibly interpreted, there must be assurances that the scales measure the same attributes in the same way in different groups and circumstances. If scales do not measure (a) the same factors in the same way in different groupings of people or (b) in the same people measured in different places and times, there is no logical basis for interpreting the results of analyses of differences between means or variances or correlations or patterns of relationships (cf. Horn & McArdle, 1992; Meredith & Horn, 2001).

Do people interpret the items of SWB and PWB scales in comparable ways? A consistent finding in the literature is that women score slightly lower than men on measures of SWB (see Lucas & Gohm, 2000; for a review), but significantly higher than men on PWB measures of positive relations with others and personal growth (Ryff & Keyes, 1995; Ryff, Lee, Essex, & Schmutte, 1994). Although these observed differences may reflect valid psychological differences between men and women, it is also possible that the item content of certain SWB and PWB measures may differentially capture aspects of well-being that women are more likely to endorse, while the item content of other measures may summarize aspects of well-being that men are more likely to endorse.

Establishing the measurement invariance of well-being instruments provides evidence not only that respondents from different groups can be legitimately compared on the same instrument, but also that observed group mean differences in raw scores reflect valid and meaningful group differences at the level of the latent variables assumed to underlie those scores (Meredith & Horn, 2001). Though no such evidence has been adduced, evidence of measurement invariance across time is a necessary prerequisite for understanding all other evidence pertaining to the temporal validity of SWB and PWB measures (Horn & McArdle, 1992; Meredith & Horn, 2001).

Implementing the Intraindividual Approach

Full explication of the intraindividual agenda requires specification of appropriate research designs, description of methods of data collection, and clarification of analytic techniques. To illustrate the intraindividual approach to well-being outcomes, we summarize findings from a preliminary study designed to probe the intraindividual dimensions of SWB and PWB. We highlight the utility of (a) multivariate replicated single-subject repeated measures (MRSRM) designs, with (b) an accompanying method of data collection (experience sampling), and (c) analytic techniques (P-technique factor analysis). Arguments are presented that bear on the value of these methods as underutilized procedures that appear particularly appropriate to the investigation of short-term intraindividual variability in well-being. Throughout, we argue that the strength of the intraindividual approach is an essential shift away from cross-sectional single-variable explanations toward person-centered accounts of positive health and well-being.

MRSRM Designs

MRSRM designs are rooted in Cattell's covariation chart or data box (Cattell, 1952, 1966). MRSRM designs have been employed predominantly in studies of intraindividual variability and change (Cattell, 1952; Jones & Nesselroade, 1990; Nesselroade & Jones, 1991) and share in common (1) repeated measurements of the same person, (2) a focus on the individual person, and (3) a multivariate approach (see Jones & Nesselroade, 1990, for a review).

MRSRM designs provide a basis for disentangling ambiguities inherent in one-occasion studies. These ambiguities have been described in detail by Nesselroade (1991). When participants are measured on only one occasion, the interindividual variability in the measurements can reflect all of three sources: (1) stable differences among people (traits), (2) within-person variability (state or function fluctuations), and (3) across-time measurement error. These three possible sources of variation are inextricably confounded when data are obtained on only one occasion, and it is impossible to separate them. MRSRM designs allow for patterns of within-person variability to be separately identified and thus distinguished from patterns of between-person differences.

Experience-Sampling Procedures

Experience-sampling procedures stand in contrast to standard self-report procedures. Although a form of self-report, experience sampling does not rely on memory or a need for respondent aggregation. In addition, the experience-sampling procedures have methodological advantages that are connected to the use of MRSRM designs. First, experience-sampling procedures allow individuals to report their behavior and experiences over the range of situational circumstances experienced in everyday life. Second, they allow for statistical modeling of behavior over time. Third and most important, experience-sampling procedures can test, rather than assume, the validity of the nomothetic approach. This assumption can be tested by summarizing experience or behavior within an individual over time (and across situations), and by testing if the pattern generalizes across individuals in the sample (Larsen, 1989; West & Hepworth, 1991).

Experience-sampling procedures have been applied successfully to study an array of psychological phenomena that include the study of behaviors, such as alcohol consumption (Swendsen et al., 2000), smoking (Jamner, Shapior, & Jarvik, 1999), eating (Steiger, Gauvin, Jabalpurwala, Seguin, & Stotland, 1999), and symptom reporting (Larsen & Kasimatis, 1991); stress (Bolger & Schilling, 1991); emotional experience, such as the discreteness of emotional experience (Barrett, 1997), the trajectory of emotional experience (Marco & Suls, 1993), the variability in emotional experience (Larsen, 1987), and gender differences in emotional experience (Barrett et al., 1998); interpersonal processes, such as intimacy in dyads (Laurenceau, Barrett, & Pietromonaco, 1998), family process (Larson & Almeida, 1999), social support (Harlow & Cantor, 1995), and attachment processes (Pietromonaco & Feldman Barrett, 2000); and personality (Fleeson, Malanos, & Achille, 2002); as well as psychophysiological responding, such as ambulatory blood pressure (Holt-Lunstad, Uchino, Smith, Cerny, & Nealey-Moore, 2003). In sum, experience-sampling procedures facilitate ecologically valid research. In the broadest sense, ESM procedures are well-suited for idiographic research (Allport, 1937).

P-Technique Factor Analysis

P-technique factor analysis is a covariation technique particularly appropriate for studying intraindividual variability. In the well-being literature, the most common application focuses on the common factor model, in which correlation coefficients are computed across individuals. This application represents what Cattell (1966) labeled R-technique factor analysis. In this analysis, the data matrix has variables as columns and subjects as rows. Variables are factored and subjects are replicates of the relationships among the variables. This analysis is used to reduce the number of variables or to explore or confirm theory regarding the underlying structure of the variables. However, there are other research questions that cannot be answered using R-technique, such as questions concerning how individual lives are dynamically organized through time.

In contrast to R-technique—an analytic technique suitable for traditional cross-sectional designs—P-technique factor analysis is a covariation technique that is aimed directly at the investigation of patterns of intraindividual variability. Introduced in the 1940s (Cattell, 1947a, 1947b), P-technique is a method used to show variation in scores for the same person at different points in time. Unlike R-technique analyses, in P-technique applications, there are no individual differences because only one person is measured. Rather, the differences reflect variability in an individual's scores from one occasion to another. Obtained factors are interpreted as patterns of intraindividual variability for a particular individual over the period observations are made, and the factor pattern delineates the structure of variability over time. The difference between P-technique and traditional R-technique thus lies in the type of data analyzed, not in the actual statistical analysis (Jones & Nesselroade, 1990; see also chapter 1, this volume). Because of its emphasis on multivariate assessment repeated over many occasions of measurement, P-technique not only emphasizes explicitly the study of intraindivdual variability (Cattell, 1966; Horn, 1972), but also is well-suited for MRSRM designs (Nesselroade & Ford, 1985).

Study Description

Because little is known about the intraindividual dimensions of SWB and PWB, it is unclear whether the within-person factor structure, derived from P-technique analyses, is comparable to the between-person structure that typically emerges from R-technique analyses. Can reliable patterns of SWB and PWB variability be identified within individuals studied across time? Is the pattern of variability, identified within a single person, generalizable across individuals? We investigated these questions with a sample of young adults ($n = 9$) for whom intensive repeated measurements of well-being were available. Eight females and one male volunteered for the study. Participants were all undergraduate psychology majors who were similar in age (ranging from 19 to 21 years of age). All participants remained in the study until the end of data collection.

Measures and Procedure

We assessed momentary eudaemonic (i.e., autonomy, personal mastery, personal growth, self-acceptance, positive relations with others, purpose in life) and hedonic (i.e., life satisfaction, positive affect, negative affect) well-being with three-item scales. In accordance with previous scale adaptations for P-technique work (e.g., Lebo & Nesselroade, 1978), words and phrases were developed to comply with the frequently repeated-measures nature of the research. Participants indicated on a seven-point scale (1 = not at all; 7 = extremely) the degree to which they were currently feeling each of the nine hypothesized SWB and PWB states.

We used computerized experience-sampling procedures. These procedures involve data that is collected by handheld Palm Pilots. Each palmtop was programmed to run on custom software called the Experience Sampling Program (Feldman-Barrett & Barrett, 2001). Audible prompts signaled participants to record their experiences. Prompting lasted for 10 minutes or until the participant responded. If the participant did not respond within 10 minutes, the trial was recorded as missed. If a participant did respond, the item responses and corresponding reaction times were recorded.

During the ensuing week, participants were signaled 10 times each day. Signals were programmed to occur at random intervals within a 12-hour block. The begin and end times of each block were specified by the participant. Because participants were signaled 10 times each day, each block was split into 10 intervals of equal length. For example, if the specified period was between 10:00 A.M. and 10:00 P.M., 10 intervals of approximately 72 minutes each would be created. In this example, signaling would occur at a random time within each interval. The first trial would occur at random between 10:00 A.M. and 11:12 A.M., the next between 11:12 A.M. and 1:24 P.M., and so on. *Random* therefore means *random within each interval.* Participants were encouraged to contact the laboratory if procedural questions or problems arose and periodic e-mails were sent to participants to ensure that the highest quality data were obtained. Participants came into the laboratory once a week to transfer (or "hotsync") their data to a master computer, eliminating error-prone manual data entry. In all, participants recorded their experiences 10 times per day, across a 61-day period.

Preliminary Analyses

Missing information ranged from 2% to 10% across participants. In accordance with principles explicated in McArdle (1994), Jöreskog, Sörbom, du Toit, and du Toit (2000), Schafer (1999), and Rubin (1987), values for missing information were estimated with second-order random imputation using the multiple imputation procedures implemented in LISREL 8.50 (Jöreskog et al., 2000). Second-order imputation refers to the use of total scores to impute values for time points that are missing. Random imputation refers to a procedure for adding random elements over multiple imputations to minimize inflation in commonalities due to capitalization on sample-specific variation.

Following multiple imputations of missing information, the initial aspect of data analysis consisted of examining the distributions of all variables, separately for each participant, to evaluate response variability. The distributions for the 27 item variables in which missing information had been replaced were carefully examined to determine if the data were suitable for factoring. In item data, particularly in studies of repeated measurements, it is not uncommon to find that some respondents use only a few of the available response possibilities. Factoring such data produces factors that mainly indicate only similarities in the odd distributions of the variables. One suggestion for avoiding problems of finding (and misinterpreting) such factors is to ensure that data for factoring include only items that have no more than 80% of responses in one category and no more than 90% of responses in two categories (Jones & Nesselroade, 1990; Lebo

& Nesselroade, 1978). The item data for each participant of the present study were examined to determine if any such distributions were found. This inspection revealed that there were no instances of these conditions for any item for any participant. In no case did a participant use fewer than four of the seven scale points in endorsing an item. All items for all participants had substantial variances. Thus all items were retained for subsequent analyses.

Replicability of SWB and PWB Factor Structure Across Participants

Prior studies in which hedonic and eudaemonic well-being were assessed cross-sectionally demonstrate that SWB and PWB are related, but distinct, constructs (Keyes et al., 2002). That is, the best-fitting model is one that posits two correlated latent constructs rather than one general factor or two orthogonal factors. Thus, although correlated, each construct retains its distinctiveness as a separate component of overall well-being. We examined the replicability of the hypothesized oblique two-factor structure in idiographic data. Measurement equivalence for the covariances of the nine participants was examined by positing and comparing several factorial invariance models within the framework of multiple-group confirmatory factor analysis (Jöreskog, 1969).

Configural Invariance

A configural invariance model was fitted to establish a basis for further comparisons. In this model, the number of factors and the variables that are salient in each factor are set to be the same for each participant, but the magnitudes and the order of the magnitudes of the salient loadings are allowed to vary. Thus, for each participant considered separately, an oblique two-factor model was specified and fitted. Each of the three items hypothesized to measure a factor was estimated to have non-zero factor pattern relationships with one hypothesized factor and that factor alone. On the basis of prior research (i.e., Keyes et al., 2002), the hypothesized SWB and PWB factors were allowed to be correlated. Although precisely the same configural model was fitted for each participant, the pattern coefficients of the models for different participants were not constrained to be proportional or equal across participants. This model, thus, does not provide a statistical sampling basis

for testing hypotheses of invariance of measurement of factors (Horn et al., 1983; Thurston, 1947).

The results for these analyses are provided in table 2.1. The chi-square, goodness-of-fit index (GFI), and standardized root mean squared residual (SRMR) indices of goodness of fit are listed separately for models of the covariances of each participant. The separate chi-squares are ranked order from smallest to largest and are listed under the heading χ^2 Contributions. The sum of these chi-squares (i.e., total $\chi^2 = 5,027.23$) can be compared with the sum of the chi-squares for the null model, which required no common factors (i.e., null model $\chi^2 = 31,911.26$). The difference between these two chi-squares (i.e., $\Delta\chi^2 = 26,884.03$, with $df = 495$) indicates that the covariances clearly are not zero and that the two-factor configural-invariant model describes a substantial amount of these nonchance covariations. The SRMR indices of fit for the individual cases and the root-mean-square error of approximation (RMSEA) for fits that are pooled over all participants indicate that a two-factor model provides a good description of the covariance data for each participant. Scanning down the list of χ^2 contributions, SRMRs, and GFIs for the configural invariance model shown in table 2.1, however, one can see that for Participant 9, the fit of the model is notably poorer than the fit for the other participants

Metric Invariance

A metric invariance model was specified in the same way as the configural model: the factor intercorrelations were not required to be the same, nor were the commonalities of variables constrained to be equal. However, the factor pattern relationships between the variables and the factors were constrained to be the same for all participants. Metric invariance is necessary to support a hypothesis of measurement invariance. If a hypothesis of metric invariance can be retained, it is evidence that the same common factors, measured in the same way, are indicated in the samples over which the invariance obtains (Horn, 1991; Horn & McArdle, 1992; Meredith & Horn, 2001).

The fit of the metric invariance model is indicated by the statistics in table 2.1. To facilitate comparisons with the configural invariance model, the ordering of the participants is kept the same. Perhaps the first thing to notice from the metric

TABLE 2.1 Intraindividual Measurement Invariance Analyses of Two-Factor Oblique Model

Model	χ^2	df	χ^2/df	χ^2 Contribution	% Contribution	GFI	SRMR	RMSEA	TLI	PNFI	$\Delta\chi^2$	Δdf
Null model	31,911.26	3, 159	10.10									
Configural model	5,027.23	2, 664	1.89			0.91	0.05	0.04	0.91	0.89	26,884.03**	495
1				353.53	7.03	0.96	0.04					
6				447.51	8.90	0.95	0.04					
8				450.60	8.96	0.95	0.05					
3				465.81	9.27	0.95	0.04					
4				499.76	9.94	0.94	0.05					
5				520.02	10.34	0.94	0.05					
2				553.47	11.01	0.94	0.05					
7				589.21	11.72	0.94	0.06					
9				1,147.32	22.82	0.88	0.09					
Metric model	12,489.73	2, 880	4.34			0.89	0.08	0.07	0.88	0.76	7,462.51**	216
1				947.09	7.58	0.90	0.06					
6				953.25	7.63	0.89	0.06					
8				1,177.50	9.43	0.88	0.06					
3				1,133.93	9.08	0.88	0.09					
4				1,334.54	10.69	0.87	0.10					
5				1,368.48	10.96	0.85	0.08					
2				1,390.16	11.13	0.88	0.06					
7				1,666.31	13.34	0.81	0.07					
9				2,518.46	20.16	0.78	0.14					

Note: GFI = goodness-of-fit index; RMSEA = root-mean-square error of approximation; TLI = Tucker-Lewis index; SRMR = standardized root mean squared residual; PNFI = parsimony normed fit index; configural invariance = test of invariant number of factors; metric invariance = test of invariant factor loadings.

**$p < .01$.

invariance results shown in table 2.1 is the sum of the of χ^2 contributions of the separate participants (i.e., total $\chi^2 = 12,489.73$, with $df = 2,880$). The $\Delta\chi^2$ for comparing this model with the null model (i.e., $\Delta\chi^2 = 31,911.26 - 12,489.73 = 19,421.53$, $df = 279$) indicates again that the data of the individual participants is clearly not random and suggests that a metric invariant model might be valid for these data. However, the difference in the pooled chi-square for this model with the pooled chi-square for the configural invariant model (i.e., $\Delta\chi^2 = 12,489.73 - 5,027.23 = 7,462.50$, with $df = 216$) indicates that the measurement invariant model does not fit the data of all participants. The pooled SRMR (.08), RMSEA (.07), parsimony normed fit index (PNFI; .76), and GFI (.89) lend additional support for rejecting the hypothesis that the factor loadings are equivalent across participants. Scanning down the list of χ^2 contributions, SRMRs, and GFIs for the metric invariance model shown in table 2.1, it can be seen that, again, a disproportionate amount of the misfit of the model is in Participant 9's data. However, the magnitude of the information indicating misfit is substantial also for some of the other participants. The results thus generally indicate that despite configural similarity in the factor structures of different persons, the factors are not manifested in the same way in all participants.

Partial Metric Invariance

It is possible that measurement-invariant models are valid for subsets of participants in the present study. For purposes of constructing hypotheses to be examined in further study, it can be useful to find indications of how participants and variables might be sampled to find invariance in future studies. One possible reason why a two-factor measurement invariance model does not fit the data for all persons in the present study is that the number of common factors required to account for the within-person covariances is somewhat different for different participants. The finding that a configural model of two factors provides a reasonable description of the data for all the participants suggests that two SWB and PWB factors can be measured in all these persons. Nevertheless, the amount of variance on some of the factors could be so low for the data of some participants that it would be of little value in accounting for their covariance data. This would be indicated by a finding that fewer than two factors would adequately

account for the covariance data of some participants.

One hypothesis that seems plausible derives from consideration of the results for the participant whose data provided a poor fit in both tests of configural and measurement invariance. Review of the baseline models revealed that the model specifications for Participant 9 required eight cross-loadings, in addition to 16 error covariances, over and above the initially hypothesized model. Making these adjustments—allowing parameters representing these relationships to be estimated for Participant 9—while constraining all other parameters to be equal across participants yielded a model fit in which indices of fit (e.g., SRMR = .05, GFI = .91) suggested metric invariance. Had the model been hypothesized a priori, this would be an example of what is termed *partial measurement invariance* (Byrne, Shavelson, & Muthen, 1989).

Construct Validity in Intraindividual Research

Construct validity encompasses both the validation of a construct and the validation of a measuring instrument. In validating a construct, evidence is sought in support of the hypothesized relations among aspects of the same construct and among different constructs. These theoretical connections underlie the nomological network of hypothesized constructs (Cattell, 1964; Cronbach & Meehl, 1955). Validation of a measuring instrument, in contrast, demands empirical evidence that the traits purported to be measured are, in fact, the ones actually measured. In the case of a multidimensional phenomenon, evidence of construct validity is demonstrated if the dimensions of the phenomenon exhibit a factor structure that is consistent with the underlying theory (McArdle, 1996; McArdle & Prescott, 1992). The results of the current study thus provide partial support for the construct validity of SWB and PWB indicators both at the theoretical and measurement levels.

Although prior research has pointed to the possibility that the intraindividual dimensions of hedonic well-being are independent of, but related to, eudaemonic well-being, little empirical evidence has been provided to support this hypothesis (Keyes et al., 2002). To the best of our knowledge, our tests of within-person variation in SWB and PWB are entirely new and, as such, must be interpreted conservatively. In some ways, however, they provide the most original contribution of this research. That is, the results indicate that intraindividual variability in SWB and PWB is, in fact, structured and not simply unpredictable variability. Because occasions and variables were more extensively sampled than persons, the results are more likely generalizable within persons across a similar sampling of occasions and selection of variables. Although the research focused on short-term intraindividual variability in individuals' hedonic and eudaemonic well-being, it should be viewed as suggesting the possibility of more general intraindividual variations in well-being phenomena (Horn, 1972; Nesselroade, 1991).

Bringing Positive Human Health Into Focus

Pragmatic limitations often lead to an unavoidably incomplete selection of variables (Little, Lindenberger, & Nesselroade, 1999). This is also true of the research reported herein. We close this chapter with a brief consideration of issues that might profitably be considered in future research. First, we strongly endorse the view that the scientific study of human development requires invariance (Meredith & Horn, 2001; see also chapter 11, this volume). What does it mean to be well, and how can it be shown that the same principles that govern well-being under certain conditions also apply under different conditions? What, for example, are the factors that allow resilient individuals to have higher reserves of hedonic and eudaemonic well-being to draw upon when confronted with significant life challenges? Are resilient individuals simply more adept at cultivating an open and tolerant view of stress, what it means, how to cope if it sticks around, how to feel when it goes away, and what to feel when it returns? These questions underscore the importance of combining idiographic and nomothetic approaches (Cattell & Cross, 1952; Horn, 1972; Zevon & Tellegen, 1982; see also chapter 35, this volume) to document how the dynamic interplay between person and context contributes to the thematic structure of individual lives.

Second, we highlight the need to study positive health as a long-term process. A considerable body of research has now demonstrated that affective-cognitive structures change throughout the life span, becoming increasingly complex and differentiated (Labouvie-Vief, 2003; Labouvie-Vief & Medler, 2002). Other evidence suggests that affect complexity, particularly in later life,

represents a resilience resource that may help to account for the adaptive ways by which emotions are orchestrated in the face of stress (Ong & Bergeman, 2004a, 2004b; Ong, Bergeman, & Bisconti, 2004). How is the structural relationship between hedonic and eudaemonic well-being maintained over an extended period of time? Does this structural relationship remain consistent or is it phenomenologically distinct at different points in the life span? Does early life advantage, in the form of high hedonic and eudaemonic well-being, serve to modify the effects of later-life adversity? Does the accumulation of positive experiences in later life serve to avert or forestall trajectories of negative outcomes that otherwise would emanate from early life challenges? Including longitudinal assessments of both SWB and PWB would significantly strengthen understanding of the long-term sequelae, as well as developmental significance of hedonic and eudaemonic well-being.

Third, extant studies of well-being, from childhood through old age, have given limited attention to how hedonic and eudaemonic well-being may vary systematically across cultural contexts (see chapter 9, this volume). Although there is an extensive literature of mental health problems among members of social groups that differ in race and ethnicity (cf. Williams & Collins, 1995; Williams & Colwick, 2001), relatively little attention has been given to investigations of mechanisms that account for hedonic and eudaemonic disparities among aging racial and ethnic minority populations. At the cross-sectional level, there is considerable ethnic and racial variation in mental health outcomes. For example, despite their lower levels of physical health (Hughes & Thomas, 1998), African Americans have lower rates of psychiatric illnesses when compared with Anglo-Americans (Williams & Harris-Reid, 1999). Needed are studies that clarify how cultural resources (e.g., spirituality, positive family relations) provide protection from mental illness, as well as maintenance of wellness, in racial and ethnic minority populations (see chapter 10, this volume).

Fourth, there is a need for greater attention to the biological substrates of hedonic and eudaemonic well-being (see Ryff, Singer, & Love, 2004). How do high SWB and PWB confer biological protection against illness and disease? Like the contouring of well-being, a multidimensional approach to the study of positive biological functioning may afford greater specificity in the potential mechanisms underlying the health benefits of SWB and PWB. In a related vein, we see a need for studies that (a) link he-donic and eudaemonic processes to multiple physiological systems (e.g., cardiovascular, en-docrine, and immune functioning) and (b) track their dynamic relations through time (Uchino, Cacioppo, & Kiecolt-Glaser, 1996; see also chapter 16, this volume).

Fifth, we underscore the need for interventions that foster psychological growth and well-being in the face of adversity. Examples of such inter-ventions include attempts to develop short-term, well-being-enhancing psychotherapeutic strate-gies to prevent relapse among those suffering from major depression (Fava, 1999; Fava, Rafa-nelli, Grandi, Conti, & Belluardo, 1998). To these prior investigations, we note that the combina-tion of randomized and time series designs pres-ents a rich opportunity to examine the real-world effects of interventions based on a positive health agenda (Ryff et al., 2004). Such investigations, we believe, may have important implications for what it means to flourish in the face of difficulty (Ryff & Singer, 2002), by shedding light on the many ways in which those undergoing various life challenges are able to see beyond their pre-dicaments to define a language of wellness that reflects their own intellect and aesthetic.

Finally, like many in this volume, we see a need for greater use of methodologies that are sensitive to dynamic changes (Boker & Nessel-roade, 2002; Chow, Nesselroade, Shifren, & McArdle, 2004; Nesselroade & Ghisletta, 2003; Nesselroade, McArdle, Aggen, & Meyers, 2002). The dynamics of positive human health have generally been characterized in terms of ho-meostasis for well over a century (see Stagner, 1951). This view presumes that a healthy system will always try to maintain a normal steady state. However, recent research is beginning to challenge this view. Dynamic changes such as developmental transitions, rhythms, and even instabilities are now seen as important charac-teristics of optimal health (cf. Bonanno, 2004; Nesselroade & Featherman, 1997). Needed, therefore, are more studies that make use of innovative analytic technique (e.g., dynamic factor analysis, dynamic systems analysis) for addressing process research questions within a positive health framework.

Coda

We started this chapter by noting that under-standing human development requires the care-ful study of individuals, one at a time, from multiple perspectives. The individual person may be a highly variable unit. But the search for reliable patterns or themes around which a life is organized, we argue, is the first step to identi-fying principles of development that are appli-cable to at least some, if not all, individuals. What are the turning points in a given life that define well-being and hone resilience? What are the different meanings that are ascribed to the diversity of life pathways encountered? How do these meanings develop and how do they change over the life course? Are there common themes that shore up idiosyncratic lives? And if we study those common themes, can we learn something about how to build and improve upon our own strengths and potentials? The answers to such pressing questions oblige researchers perennially interested in the study of in-traindividual variability to step into the light.

Acknowledgments   Preparation of this chapter was supported, in part, by a traineeship from National Institute on Aging (AG00156) and a dissertation award from the Society for Multi-variate Experimental Psychology (SMEP).

References

Allport, F. H. (1937). Teleonomic description in the study of personality. *Character and Personality: A Quarterly for Psychodiagnostic and Allied Studies, 5*, 202–214.

Andrews, F. M., & Withey, S. B. (1976). *Social indicators of well-being: Americans' perception of life quality.* New York: Plenum Press.

Barrett, L. F. (1997). The relationships among mo-mentary emotion experiences, personality de-scriptions, and retrospective ratings of emotion. *Personality and Social Psychology Bulletin, 23*, 1100–1110.

Barrett, L. F., Robin, L., Pietromonaco, P. R., & Eyssell, K. M. (1998). Are women the ''more emotional'' sex? Evidence from emotional ex-periences in social context. *Cognition and Emotion, 12*(4), 555–578.

Boker, S. M., & Nesselroade, J. R. (2002). A method for modeling the intrinsic dynamics of in-traindividual variability: Recovering the pa-rameters of simulated oscillators in multi-wave panel data. *Multivariate Behavioral Research, 37*(1), 127–160.

Bolger, N., & Schilling, E. A. (1991). Personality and the problems of everyday life: The role of neuroticism in exposure and reactivity to daily stressors. *Journal of Personality, 59*(3), 355–386.

Bonanno, G. (2004). Loss, trauma, and human resilience: Have we underestimated the human capacity to thrive after extremely aversive events? *American Psychologist, 59*, 20–28.

Byrne, B. M., Shavelson, R. J., & Muthen, B. (1989). Testing for the equivalence of factor covariance and mean structures: The issue of partial measurement invariance. *Psychological Bulletin, 105*(3), 456–466.

Carstensen, L. L., Pasupathi, M., Mayr, U., & Nesselroade, J. R. (2000). Emotional experience in everyday life across the adult life span. *Journal of Personality and Social Psychology, 79*(4), 644–655.

Cattell, R. B. (1947a). Confirmation and clarification of primary personality factors. *Psychometrika, 12*, 197–220.Cattell, R. B. (1947b). A demonstration of P-technique in determining personality structure. *American Psychologist, 2*, 426.

Cattell, R. B. (1952). P-technique factorization and the determination of individual dynamic structure. *Journal of Clinical Psychology, 8*(1), 5–10.

Cattell, R. B. (1963). The structure of change by P-technique and incremental R-technique. In C. W. Harris (Ed.), *Problems in measuring change* (pp. 167–198). Madison: University of Wisconsin Press.

Cattell, R. B. (1964). Validity and reliability: A proposed more basic set of concepts. *Journal of Educational Psychology, 55*, 1–22.

Cattell, R. B. (Ed.). (1966). *Handbook of multivariate experimental psychology.* Chicago: Rand McNally.

Cattell, R. B., & Cross, K. (1952). Comparisons of the ergic and self-sentiment structures found in dynamic traits by R- and P-techniques. *Journal of Personality, 21*, 250–271.

Chow, S. M., Nesselroade, J. R., Shifren, K., & McArdle, J. J. (2004). Dynamic structure of emotions among individuals with Parkinson's disease. *Structural Equation Modeling, 11*(4), 560–582.

Cronbach, L. J., & Meehl, P. E. (1955). Construct validity in psychological tests. *Psychological Bulletin, 52*, 281–302.

Diener, E. (1984). Subjective well-being. *Psychological Bulletin, 95*, 542–575.

Diener, E., & Emmons, R. A. (1984). The independence of positive and negative affect. *Journal of Personality and Social Psychology, 47*, 1105–1117.

Diener, E., Emmons, R. A., Larsen, R. J., & Griffin, S. (1985). The Satisfaction With Life Scale. *Journal of Personality Assessment, 49*(1), 71–75.

Diener, E., Suh, E., Lucas, R., & Smith, H. (1999). Subjective well-being: Three decades of progress. *Psychological Bulletin, 125*, 276–302.

Ebbinghaus, H. (1885). *Über das Gedächtnis.* Leipzig: Duncker and Humblot.

Fava, G. A. (1999). Well-being therapy: Conceptual and technical issues. *Psychotherapy and Psychosomatics, 68*, 171–179.

Fava, G. A., Rafanelli, C., Grandi, S., Conti, S., & Belluardo, P. (1998). Prevention of recurrent depression with cognitive behavioral therapy. *Archives of General Psychiatry, 55*, 816–821.

Feldman-Barrett, L., & Barrett, D. J. (2001). Computerized experience-sampling: How technology facilitates the study of conscious experience. *Social Science Computer Review, 19*, 175–185.

Fleeson, W., Malanos, A., & Achille, N. (2002). An intra-individual process approach to the relationship between extraversion and positive affect: Is acting extraverted as "good" as being extraverted? *Journal of Personality and Social Psychology, 83*, 1409–1422.

Harlow, R. E., & Cantor, N. (1995). To whom do people turn when things go poorly: Task orientational and functional social contacts. *Journal of Personality and Social Psychology, 69*, 329–340.

Holt-Lunstad, J., Uchino, B. N., & Smith, T. W., Cerny, C. B., & Nealey-Moore, J. B. (2003). Social relationships and ambulatory blood pressure: Structural and qualitative predictors of cardiovascular function during everyday social interactions. *Health Psychology, 22*, 388–397.

Hooker, K., Nesselroade, D. W., Nesselroade, J. R., & Lerner, R. M. (1987). The structure of intraindividual temperament in the context of mother-child dyads: P-technique factor analyses of short-term change. *Developmental Psychology, 23*(3), 332–346.

Horn, J. L. (1972). State, trait, and change dimensions of intelligence. *British Journal of Educational Psychology, 42*, 159–185.

Horn, J. L. (1991). Discussions of issues in factorial invariance. In L. M. Collins & J. L. Horn (Eds.), *Best methods for the analysis of change* (pp. 114–125). Washington, DC: American Psychological Association.

Horn, J. L., & McArdle, J. J. (1992). A practical and theoretical guide to measurement invariance in aging research. *Experimental Aging Research, 18*(3), 117–144.

Horn, J. L., McArdle, J. J., & Mason, R. (1983). When is invariance not invariant: A practical scientist's look at the ethereal concept of factor invariance. *Southern Psychologist, 1*(4), 179–188.

Hughes, M., & Thomas, M. (1998). The continuing significance of race revisited: A study of race, class and quality of life in America, 1972–1996. *American Sociological Review, 63,* 785–795.

Jamner, L. D., Shapiro, D., & Jarvik, M. E. (1999). Nicotine reduces the frequency of anger reports in smokers and nonsmokers with high but not low hostility: An ambulatory study. *Experimental and Clinical Psychopharmacology, 7,* 454–463.

Jones, C. J., & Nesselroade, J. R. (1990). Multivariate, replicated, single-subject, repeated measures designs and P-technique factor analysis: A review of intraindividual change studies. *Experimental Aging Research, 16*(4), 171–183.

Jöreskog, K. G. (1969). A general approach to confirmatory maximun likelihood factor analysis. *Psychometrika, 34*(2), 183–202.

Jöreskog, K. G., & Sörbom, D. (1993). *LISREL 8 user's reference guide.* Chicago: Scientific Software.

Jöreskog, K. G., Sörbom, D., du Toit, S., & du Toit, M. (2000). *LISREL 8: New statistical features.* Chicago: Scientific Software International.

Keyes, C. L., Shmotkin, D., & Ryff, C. D. (2002). Optimizing well-being: The empirical encounter of two traditions. *Journal of Personality and Social Psychology, 82,* 1007–1022.

Kleban, M. H., Lawton, M., Nesselroade, J. R., & Parmelee, P. (1992). The structure of variation in affect among depressed and nondepressed elders. *Journals of Gerontology, 47*(3), P190–P198.

Kratochwill, T. R. (1978). *Single subject research.* New York: Academic Press.

Labouvie-Vief, G. (2003). Dynamic integration: Affect, cognition, and the self in adulthood. *Current Directions in Psychological Science, 12*(6), 201–206.

Labouvie-Vief, G., & Medler, M. (2002). Affect optimization and affect complexity: Modes and styles of regulation in adulthood. *Psychology and Aging, 17*(4), 571–587.

Lamiell, J. T. (1981). Toward an idiothetic psychology of personality. *American Psychologist, 36*(3), 276–289.

Larsen, R. J. (1987). The stability of mood variability: A spectral analytic approach to daily mood assessments. *Journal of Personality and Social Psychology, 52,* 1195–1204.

Larsen, R. J. (1989). A process approach to personality: Utilizing time as a facet of data. In D. Buss & N. Cantor (Eds.), *Personality psychology: Recent trends and emerging directions* (pp. 177–193). New York: Springer-Verlag.

Larsen, R. J., & Kasimatis, M. (1990). Individual differences in entrainment of mood to the weekly calendar. *Journal of Personality and Social Psychology, 58*(1), 164–171.

Larsen, R., & Kasimatis, M. (1991). Day-to-day physical symptoms: Individual differences in the occurrence, duration, and emotional concomitants of minor daily illnesses. *Journal of Personality, 59,* 387–424.

Larson, R., & Almeida, D. (1999). Emotional transmission in the daily lives of families: A new paradigm for studying family process. *Journal of Marriage and the Family, 61,* 5–20.

Laurenceau, J. P., Barrett, L. F., & Pietromonaco, P. R. (1998). Intimacy as an interpersonal process: The importance of self-disclosure, partner disclosure, and perceived partner responsiveness in interpersonal exchanges. *Journal of Personality and Social Psychology, 74,* 1238–1251.

Lawton, M., Parmelee, P. A., Katz, I. R., & Nesselroade, J. (1996). Affective states in normal and depressed older people. *Journals of Gerontology: Series B: Psychological Sciences and Social Sciences, 51B*(6), P309–P316.

Lebo, M. A., & Nesselroade, J. R. (1978). Intraindividual differences dimensions of mood change during pregnancy identified in five P-technique factor analyses. *Journal of Research in Personality, 12*(2), 205–224.

Lewin, K. (1935). *A dynamic theory of personality.* New York: McGraw-Hill.

Little, T. D., Lindenberger, U., & Nesselroade, J. R. (1999). On selecting indicators for multivariate measurement and modeling with latent variables: When "good" indicators are bad and "bad" indicators are good. *Psychological Methods, 4*(2), 192–211.

Luborsky, L., & Mintz, J. (1972). The contribution of P-technique to personality, psychotherapy, and psychosomatic research. In R. M. Dreger (Ed.), *Multivariate personality research: Contributions to the understanding of personality in honor of Raymond B. Cattell* (pp. 387–410). Baton Rouge, LA: Claitor's.

Lucas, R. E., Diener, E., & Suh, E. M. (1996). Discriminant validity of well-being measures. *Journal of Personality and Social Psychology, 71,* 616–628.

Lucas, R. E., & Gohm, C. (2000). Age and sex differences in subjective well-being across cultures. In E. Diener & E. M. Suh (Eds.), *Culture and subjective well-being* (pp. 291–318). Cambridge, MA: MIT Press.

Marco, C. A., & Suls, J. (1993). Daily stress and the trajectory of mood: Spillover, response assimilation, contrast, and chronic negative affectivity. *Journal of Personality and Social Psychology, 64,* 1053–1063.

McAdams, D. P. (1990). *The person: An introduction to personality psychology*: San Diego, CA: Harcourt Brace Jovanovich.

McArdle, J. J. (1994). Structural factor analysis experiments with incomplete data. *Multivariate Behavioral Research, 29*(4), 409–454.

McArdle, J. J. (1996). Current directions in structural factor analysis. *Current Directions in Psychological Science, 4*, 11–18.

McArdle, J. J., & Prescott, C. A. (1992). Age-based construct validation using structural equation modeling. *Experimental Aging Research, 18*(3–4), 87–115.

Meredith, W. (1964). Notes on factorial invariance. *Psychometrika, 29*, 177–185.

Meredith, W., & Horn, J. L. (2001). The role of factorial invariance in modeling growth and change. In L. M. Collins & A. G. Sayer (Eds.), *New methods for the analysis of change* (pp. 203–240). Washington, DC: American Psychological Association.

Nesselroade, J. R. (1991). Interindividual differences in intraindividual change. In L. M. Collins & J. L. Horn (Eds.), *Best methods for the analysis of change: Recent advances, unanswered questions, future directions* (pp. 92–105). Washington, DC: American Psychological Association.

Nesselroade, J. R., & Featherman, D. L. (1997). Establishing a reference frame against which to chart age-related changes. In M. A. Hardy (Ed.), *Studying aging and social change: Conceptual and methodological issues* (pp. 191–205). Thousand Oaks, CA: Sage.

Nesselroade, J. R., & Ford, D. H. (1985). P-technique comes of age: Multivariate, replicated, single-subject designs for research on older adults. *Research on Aging, 7*(1), 46–80.

Nesselroade, J. R., & Ghisletta, P. (2003). Structuring and measuring change over the life span. In U. Lindenberger & U. M. Staudinger (Eds.), *Understanding human development: Dialogues with lifespan psychology* (pp. 317–337). Dordrecht, Netherlands: Kluwer.

Nesselroade, J. R., & Jones, C. J. (1991). Multi-modal selection effects in the study of adult development: A perspective on multivariate, replicated, single-subject, repeated measures designs. *Experimental Aging Research, 17*, 21–27.

Nesselroade, J. R., McArdle, J. J., Aggen, S. H., & Meyers, J. M. (2002). Dynamic factor analysis models for representing process in multivariate time-series. In S. L. Hershberger & D. S. Moskowitz (Eds.), *Modeling intraindividual variability with repeated measures data: Methods and applications* (pp. 235–265). Mahwah, NJ: Erlbaum.

Ong, A. D., & Bergeman, C. S. (2004a). The complexity of emotions in later life. *Journal of Gerontology: Psychological Sciences, 59B*(3), 55–60.

Ong, A. D., & Bergeman, C. S. (2004b). Resilience and adaptation to stress in later life: Empirical perspectives and conceptual implications. *Ageing International, 29*, 219–246.

Ong, A., Bergeman, C. S., & Bisconti, T. L. (2004). The role of daily positive affect during conjugal bereavement. *Journal of Gerontology, 59B*, P158–P167.

Pietromonaco, P. R., & Feldman Barrett, L. (2000). Internal working models: What do we really know about the self in relation to others? *Review of General Psychology, 4*, 155–175.

Roberts, M. L., & Nesselroade, J. R. (1986). Intraindividual variability in perceived locus of control in adults: P-technique factor analyses of short-term change. *Journal of Research in Personality, 20*(4), 529–545.

Rogosa, D. R., & Willett, J. B. (1985). Understanding correlates of change by modeling individual differences in growth. *Psychometrika, 50*, 203–228.

Rosenzweig, S. (1951). Idiodynamics in personality theory with special reference to projective methods. *Psychological Review, 58*, 213–223.

Rubin, D. B. (1987). *Multiple imputation for nonresponse in surveys.* New York: John Wiley.

Ryan, R. M., & Deci, E. L. (2000). On happiness and human potentials: A review of research on hedonic and eudaimonic well-being. *Annual Review of Psychology, 52*, 141–166.

Ryff, C. D. (1989). Happiness is everything, or is it? Explorations on the meaning of psychological well-being. *Journal of Personality and Social Psychology, 57*, 1069–1081.

Ryff, C. D. (1995). Psychological well-being in adult life. *Current Directions in Psychology, 4*(4), 99–104.

Ryff, C. D., & Keyes, C. L. (1995). The structure of psychological well being revisited. *Journal of Personality and Social Psychology, 69*, 719–727.

Ryff, C. D., Lee, Y. H., Essex, M. J., & Schmutte, P. S. (1994). My children and me: Midlife evaluations of grown children and self. *Psychology and Aging, 9*, 195–205.

Ryff, C. D., & Singer, B. (1998). The contours of positive human health. *Psychological Inquiry, 9*(1), 1–28.

Ryff, C. D., & Singer, B. (2000). Interpersonal flourishing: A positive health agenda for the new millennium. *Personality and Social Psychology Review, 4*(1), 30–44.

Ryff, C. D., & Singer, B. (2002). Flourishing under fire: Resilience as a prototype of challenged thriving. In C. L. M. Keyes & J. Haidt (Eds.), *Flourishing: Positive psychology and the life well-lived* (pp. 15–36). Washington, DC: American Psychological Association.

Ryff, C. D., Singer, B. H., & Love, G. D. (2004). Positive health: Connecting well-being with biology. *Philosophical Transactions of the Royal Society of London, 359,* 1383–1394.

Schafer, J. L. (1999). *Multiple imputation: A primer.* Statistical Methods in Medical Research, 8, 3–15. Schulenberg, J. E., Vondracek, F. W., & Nesselroade, J. R. (1988). Patterns of short-term changes in individuals' work values: P-technique factor analyses of intraindividual variability. *Multivariate Behavioral Research, 23*(3), 377–395.

Shifren, K., Hooker, K., Wood, P., & Nesselroade, J. R. (1997). Structure and variation of mood in individuals with Parkinson's disease: A dynamic factor analysis. *Psychology and Aging, 12*(2), 328–339.

Stagner, R. (1951). Homeostasis as a unifying concept in personality theory. *Psychological Review, 58,* 5–17.

Steiger, H., Gauvin, L., Jabalpurwala, S., Seguin, J. R., & Stotland, S. (1999). Hypersensitivity to social interactions in bulimic syndromes: Relationship to binge eating. *Journal of Consulting and Clinical Psychology, 67,* 765–775.

Stern, W. (1938). *General psychology from a personalistic standpoint.* New York: Philosophical Library.

Stevens, S. S. (1951). Mathematics measurement and psychophysics. In S. S. Stevens (Ed.), *Handbook of experimental psychology* (pp. 1–49). New York:Wiley.

Swendsen, J. D., Tennen, H., Carney, M. A., Affleck, G., Willard, A., & Hromi, A. (2000). Mood and alcohol consumption: An experience sampling test of the self-medication hypothesis. *Journal of Abnormal Psychology, 109,* 198–204.

Thurston, L. L. (1947). *Multiple factor analysis: A development and expansion of vectors of the mind.* Chicago: University of Chicago Press.

Uchino, B. N., Cacioppo, J. T., & Kiecolt-Glaser, J. K. (1996). The relationship between social support and physiological processes: A review with emphasis on underlying mechanisms and implications for health. *Psychological Bulletin, 119,* 488–531.

Waterman, A. S. (1993). Two conceptions of happiness: Contrasts of personal expressiveness (eudemonia) and hedonic enjoyment. *Journal of Personality and Social Psychology, 64*(4), 678–691.

Watson, D., Clark, L. A., & Tellegen, A. (1988). Development and validation of brief measures of positive and negative affect: The PANAS scales. *Journal of Personality and Social Psychology, 54,* 1063–1070.

Wessman, A. E., & Ricks, D. F. (1966). *Mood and personality.* New York: Holt, Rinehart and Winston.

West, S. G., & Hepworth, J. T. (1991). Statistical issues in the study of temporal data: Daily experiences. *Journal of Personality, 59*(3), 609–662.

Williams, D. R., & Collins, C. (1995). U.S. socioeconomic and racial differences in health: Patterns and explanations. *Annual Review of Sociology, 21,* 349–386.

Williams, D. R., & Colwick, M. (2001). Race, ethnicity, and aging. In R. H. Binstock (Ed.), *Handbook of aging and the social sciences* (5th ed., pp. 160–178). San Diego, CA: Academic Press.

Williams, D. R., & Harris-Reid, M. (1999). Race and mental health: Emerging patterns and promising approaches. In A. Horwitz & T. L. Scheid (Eds.), *A handbook for the study of mental health* (pp. 295–314). New York: Cambridge University Press.

Wohlwill, J. F. (1973). *The study of behavioral development.* New York: Academic Press.

Zevon, M. A., & Tellegen, A. (1982). The structure of mood change: An idiographic/nomothetic analysis. *Journal of Personality and Social Psychology, 43,* 111–122.

II

Intraindividual Change

3

The Structure of Daily Positive Affect for Persons With Parkinson's Disease

A Dynamic Factor Analysis

Kim Shifren and Karen Hooker

There is an impressive literature on the positive aspects of living with chronic diseases such as diabetes mellitus, multiple sclerosis, coronary heart disease, and various forms of cancer (Benyamini, Idler, Leventhal, & Leventhal, 2000; Fournier, deRidder, & Bensing, 2003; Reich, Zautra, & Davis, 2003; Symister & Friend, 2003). Though this body of literature had been steadily growing since 1990, it increased substantially after the introduction of positive psychology (e.g., Peterson, 2000). Researchers interested in any aspect of the positive side of individuals and how they deal with illness and other negative life events have been encouraged to conduct studies that do not focus solely on the negative side of coping processes and outcomes. In fact, researchers have found that state-positive affect (i.e., short-term positive affect) is related to health while trait-positive affect is not (Casten, Lawton, Winter, Kleban, & Sando, 1997). Researchers have also discussed the adaptive functions of positive affect (PA) in the coping process, especially when dealing with chronic stressors (Folkman & Maskowitz, 2000).

Despite our knowledge of the positive aspects of living with a chronic disease, there is still much that remains unknown. This is especially true for individuals living with Parkinson's disease (PD). To date, most research on nonmedical aspects of PD remains largely focused on the negative aspects of PD, such as depression (e.g., McDonald, Richard, & DeLong, 2003). Some prior research on PD shows that individuals can have positive experiences living with PD (Brod, Mendelsohn, & Roberts, 1998; Marr, 1991), and maintain and increase levels of optimism (Shifren, 1996). While this is helpful in portraying a more balanced view of living with PD, it still does not capture the essence of daily mood, especially positive mood, experiences with PD.

In this chapter, we present the structure and lag relationship of positive mood items among individuals with PD using a technique called dynamic factor analysis (DFA; Molenaar, 1985; Molenaar, deGooijer, & Schmitz, 1992; Wood & Brown, 1994). Our chapter begins with a brief discussion of the kinds of questions that can be addressed when using the process approach to assess mood. Next, we discuss how the process approach we use helps address questions of interest for individuals with PD that can be assessed only with this approach. Third, we provide a background on the issues that have been understudied in the field of PD, and our reasons for examining positive mood in persons living with PD. In addition, we discuss the specific methodological technique we used to examine positive mood in those with PD, and we present the findings from our sample. Furthermore, we discuss the more recent techniques that have been used to examine mood, especially positive mood, in individuals with PD.

The Necessity of Using an Intraindividual Approach for Understanding Process

Traditional approaches to research on emotion, based on cross-sectional data, or data assessment at only a few points in time, provide general summaries across individuals. However, they do not address the variability that individuals experience day-to-day or within-day. Within-individual variability in emotion may be theoretically important, because if variability within an individual is large, it may provide information that is more useful for prediction than information provided by the more traditional nomethetic designs (Nesselroade & Salthouse, 2004). For example, in a study of older adults, variability in perceived control predicted mortality 5 years later, whereas mean level of control did not (Eisenman, Nesselroade, Featherman, & Rowe, 1997). Increased variability in emotions within an individual may be seen as early signs of mental illness in that individual. On the other hand, more variability in emotions could mean the individual is more flexible and able to adapt to a changing environment. These are interesting ideas to test that simply cannot be studied with traditional approaches. A strength of intraindividual research designs is that it allows for the manifestation of stability while being sensitive enough to reveal changes taking place within individuals.

To understand the true nature of individuals' emotions, we must assess emotions at multiple time points (i.e., within or across days for each individual) to determine within-individual variability in emotions. Assessments of emotions within days allows us to ask questions about the influence of one's morning emotions on one's

nighttime emotions. Perhaps in some individuals, feelings of anger and sadness in the morning can have a pervasive effect all day, keeping their spirits low. However, for other individuals, anger and sadness diminish quickly, and they maintain a happy mood the rest of the day and night. Assessments of emotions across days allows us to determine the influence of one's emotions yesterday on one's emotions today. For example, some individuals may show strong lingering effects of joy and contentment from yesterday to today, while other individuals may show no evidence of this lagged effect. Studies designed to address both within- and across-day emotions can address both within- and across-day time lag relationships in individuals' emotions.

Designs that capture the unique role of time (i.e., minutes, hours, days, weeks) along with the individual's characteristics allow us to see a very different picture of emotions. Researchers argue that the average within-individual standard deviation on a variable is comparable to a 12- to 27-year age difference with cross-sectional data, and changes of this magnitude increase with age. Consequently, there may be less precision in estimates of age effects for variables assessed in older individuals when using traditional approaches to assess these variables (Nesselroade & Salthouse, 2004).

Process Approach and Emotional Complexity

Researchers have used a design that includes the time component to capture the frequency, intensity, and complexity of emotions in a sample of European American and African American adults, 18–94 years old (Carstensen, Pasupathi, Mayr, & Nesselroade, 2000). In an experience sampling study (i.e., participants were beeped five random times a day for 1 week and were instructed to write down their emotions), Carstensen et al. (2000) found that individuals' perceptions of the intensity of their positive and negative emotions did not differ by age. They also found that positive emotions were stable, but negative emotions were unstable in older adults. Carstensen et al. (2000) argued that their results support better emotion regulation as one ages. They also found greater factorial complexity in emotions in older individuals, supporting the idea of increasing differentiation throughout development (Labouvie-Vief & Medler, 2002).

Process Approach and PD

When you want to know how individuals really feel about living with chronic diseases such as PD, your questions need to address more than general notions about mood. For example, do individuals with PD show changes in the frequency, intensity, and complexity of their moods over time? In relation to this chapter, here is another important question. Is it possible to live with PD and still have many positive emotions on a daily basis?

Here is an example of 2 days in the life of someone with PD to provide a small picture of how complex the study of mood in PD may be. On Saturday, your golf game was interrupted by a sudden bout of rigidity, keeping you frozen in place in front of your friends, leaving you embarrassed, ashamed, humiliated, and depressed. On Sunday, your granddaughter paid you a surprise visit, a surprise that you treasure dearly, despite the symptoms of your disease. You felt moments of intense happiness, but you also worried that yesterday's rigidity might reoccur in front of your granddaughter. Techniques such as DFA that include the time component in analyses allow researchers to determine if and how experiences one day impact experiences the next day. The DFA technique can address questions about the frequency, intensity, and emotional complexity of individuals with PD, questions not adequately addressed in any prior studies on PD.

Background

PD is a chronic neurological condition that is generally characterized by tremors, rigidity, slowness of movement, and loss of balance (Stern, 1990), and PD is estimated to affect about 1% of the population over age 50 and 2.5% of individuals over age 70 (Marsh, 2000). The life expectancy for individuals with PD is only slightly less than average (Stern, 1990). Individuals with PD experience symptoms that can be unpredictable, fluctuating from day to day; consequently, symptoms can profoundly affect daily functioning and social activities (cf. Dakof & Mendelsohn, 1986).

Most prior research has focused on negative aspects of PD and has provided little insight into the daily experience of living with PD. Negative aspects of living with PD was a dominant theme in the literature by 1990 (for example, see Dakof & Mendelsohn, 1989; Frazier, Cotrell, & Hooker, 2003; Mendelsohn, Dakof, & Skaff, 1995; Shifren, Hooker, Wood, & Nesselroade, 1997). For example, individuals with PD were considered depressed more often than individuals with other degenerative diseases (Mayeux, 1987). In fact, depressive symptoms are experienced by 30 to 50 percent of the PD population (Buntington & Fitzsimmons, 1991). Researchers have shown that individuals in the early stages of PD reported negative emotions, including guilt and anger (Levin & Weiner, 1987), while in the later stages of PD individuals reported other negative emotions including irritability, pessimism, and feelings of dissatisfaction, all symptoms characteristic of depressive symptomatology. Furthermore, researchers found some indirect evidence that NA was involved in the PD process itself. Brown and MacCarthy (1990) found that dysphoric and pessimistic aspects of depression were associated with an increase in the severity of disability, while Dakof and Mendelsohn (1989) found that individuals with reports of flat affect showed more physical impairment than individuals with reports of variability in affect. Currently, there is debate on the confounding relationship between psychiatric disorders and PD (Norman, Tröster, Fields, & Brooks, 2002).

By 1990, there was still little information about the daily experience of living with PD (see Raos, Huber, & Bornstein, 1992). One exception is that researchers have found that mood tends to fluctuate in relation to motor fluctuations, with decreased mood when immobile and elevated mood when mobile (Hegeman, Wallace, & Kurlan, 2001). Because PD symptoms vary from day to day, the general absence of studies examining daily aspects of PD is surprising. Furthermore, researchers have shown that chronically ill individuals have both good days and bad days (e.g., Charmaz, 1991). Research on PD indicates that those with PD present a complex picture of mood that requires more systematic and careful study.

It was clear to us that short-term variation in mood was a necessary focus for research on PD. Therefore, we designed our study to begin to fill an important gap in the literature on PD by including PA in our study of individuals' mood and by obtaining a daily assessment of mood. (This work was part of a larger set of variables assessed for the first author's dissertation; Shifren, 1994.)

Method of Study

A chronic disease such as PD permeates all aspects of the individual's daily living (Affleck, Tennen, Urrows, & Higgins, 1994; Charmaz, 1991; Livneh & Antonak, 1994); therefore, intensive observations were needed to identify the structure, variability, and correlates of mood. To date, most research on mood structure is examined by factor analytic modeling procedures (see Reich et al., 2003, for a review of the dimensions of affect and modeling techniques). One method for studying variability within individuals is known as P-technique factor analysis. Although this methodology was pioneered by Cattell (Cattell, Cattell, & Rhymer, 1947) over a half century ago, it has more recently gained stature as a well-accepted way to study change (e.g., see Jones & Nesselroade, 1990, for a review). In this approach, variables are measured over many occasions for a single individual. The variables are factor analyzed in the usual manner, and the resulting factors represent patterns of systematic change for that individual. The occasions essentially become the N for the study.

In order to address the more nomothetic question about the generalizability of factors, more than one persona can be included in the study design; each person's data representing in effect a replication of the study (e.g., Zevon & Tellegen, 1982). This design is known in the literature as a multivariate replicated single-subject repeated measures (MRSRM) design (e.g., Jones & Nesselroade, 1990; McArdle & Nesselroade, 1994; Nesselroade & Featherman, 1991). The MRSRM design allows enough occasions of measurement to establish the patterns of within-individual variability in mood and enough participants to address aspects of generalizability across individuals.

One problem with P-technique factor analysis is that it reflects only concurrent relationships among variables and ignores any lagged relationships among them (e.g., Holtzman, 1963; Molenaar, 1985). P-technique cannot capture the influence of variables that may affect mood, and mood itself, which may increase or decrease over several occasions of measurement rather than rising or falling erratically from one occasion to the next.

At the time of this study, a refinement of P-technique factor analysis, DFA (Molenaar, 1985; Molenaar et al., 1992; Wood & Brown, 1994), was available to provide one with a fit for the common factor model and take account of lagged relationships (serial dependence; Wood & Brown, 1994). When lagged relationships are present in the repeated measures, the DFA model represents it with "extra" patterns of loadings. These extra patterns of loadings do not mean more factors are needed to account for the data. Rather, the extra loading patterns show the lagged relationships between factors and variables. For example, one's observed scores today might be influenced by today's factor scores and to a lesser extent by yesterday's factor scores. Today's influence would be indicated by a lag-0 factor-loading pattern (the usual factor-loading pattern) and yesterday's influence by a lag-1 factor-loading pattern. If one fits the DFA model to data with no lagged relationship, the results simplify to simple P-technique factor solution.

In sum, DFA and, to a lesser extent, P-technique factor analysis show the complexity of day-to-day mood variation through dimensionality (number of factors) and the way mood indicators are related through time (lagged relationships). One individual's mood variability might be accurately characterized by one dimension ("feeling good" versus "feeling bad") that alternates unpredictably from day to day, a P-technique factor. However, another individual's mood variability might require multiple dimensions, feeling good about some things and feeling bad about others, that persist differentially over time (e.g., how I feel today is affected both by today's events and, to some extent, by how I felt yesterday).

Brief Description of Method

The study was completed by 12 individuals (7 females, 5 males) with a confirmed diagnosis of PD (for details on recruitment techniques, see Shifren et al., 1997). All participants were Caucasian, and their age ranged from 59 to 81 ($M = 68.75$, $SD = 7.24$) years. Socioeconomic status was based on Hollingshead's (1975) four-factor scale, with an average of 41.67 ($SD = 8.82$), indicating that individuals were technical workers, minor professionals, or owned medium-sized businesses (Hollingshead, 1975). Also, 11 individuals had been married an average of 35.33 ($SD = 15.59$) years, and one individual was a widow. Participants had been diagnosed with PD at least 2 years before this study, and they had PD an average of 6.08 ($SD = 2.64$) years. We screened for cognitive impairment with a shortened version of the Folstein Mini-Mental Status Exam (MMSE; Folstein, Folstein, & McHugh, 1975) to ensure individuals could complete the study. The participants' average score on the MMSE was 29.1 (1.2), indicating little, if any, cognitive impairment. Individuals were screened for basic activities of daily living (ADL) limitations. None of the participants needed help with basic and instrumental ADLs.

PA was measured with the Positive and Negative Affect Schedule (PANAS; Watson, Clark, & Tellegen, 1988). The published paper does include measurement of negative affect (see Shifren et al., 1997, for details). The PANAS measure contains 10 PA items, and it has been used in studies of both trait and state affect (e.g., Watson, 1988). The positive-affect items included the following terms: enthusiastic, interested, determined, excited, alert, active, strong, proud, inspired, and attentive. The PANAS has good convergent and good discriminant validity with well-known measures (Watson et al., 1988) and has demonstrated high internal consistency in previous research (Shifren & Hooker, 1995). Responses could range from 1 (not at all) to 5 (all the time). Individuals could score up to 50 points on PA. The order of the PANAS items was randomized on three different forms in the present study to control for possible order effects. Coefficient alpha ranged from .84 to .99 for PA, across all individuals for each of the 70 days.

An initial interview was conducted in the home of each participant. Participants completed the first questionnaire while the experimenter was in a room nearby. Each participant then answered a series of initial interview questions. Individuals were given a packet of materials including 70 measures with mood items for the 70-day study. Each form was identified for a given day and listed the participant's ID number. Also, 70 small envelopes were provided with instructions to complete the questionnaires every evening at precisely the same time, to place the completed questionnaire in its envelope, and to seal it.

Research on the "on/off phenomenon" in PD has shown that nighttime (end of the day or bedtime) is often the time associated with the off period (e.g., Nissenbaum, Quinn, Brown, & Toone, 1987). The on/off period of PD occurs in relation to levodopa medication after individuals have been on this medication for about 5 years, and the off period (return of PD symptoms) is often associated with parallel mood changes (Nissenbaum et al., 1987). Though research on the relation between mood and the on/off phenomenon has been inconclusive, we chose the evening to decrease the likelihood of a consistent bias toward

one set of mood characteristics over another in this sample. The evening (between 5 and 7 P.M. for this study) provided individuals with a middle-of-the-day recording time because the morning and afternoon activities would be completed, yet the dinner and bedtime activities were not.

Participants were told to place blank questionnaires in envelopes for the evenings they were not able to complete the questionnaires, and 10 medium-sized, self-addressed and stamped envelopes were provided, so that participants could send the materials back to the experimenter once a week with the measures for that week. This ensured individuals could not examine previous-week responses to the items. Individuals were called twice a week for the 10-week period to address any concerns and to enhance compliance. Each participant was paid $50.00 for completing the study.

Findings

In preliminary analyses, demographic characteristics were correlated with positive affect. Age was inversely correlated with positive affect ($r = -.57$, $p = .05$, $N = 10$). No other demographic variables were correlated significantly with positive affect. DFAs were conducted on the seven PA items that showed variability over all 12 participants (i.e., determined, interested, enthusiastic, attentive, strong, active, alert). Before proceeding with the DFA, the data were detrended and normalized to eliminate skewness (see Shifren et al., 1997, for details on detrending of data). DFA was conducted on the detrended and normalized data for each individual (see Wood & Brown, 1994, for a detailed review of the procedure and stand-alone software–based program). A one-factor P-technique model was first fitted to each individual's data to provide a reference (null model) against which the fit of subsequent models could be compared using incremental-fit statistics. The subsequently fitted DFA models represented a series of feasible values for the number of factors and the number of lags needed to represent the repeated measurements. Two additional null models used for model fit evaluation included a P-technique factor model augmented with a lagged error structure, and a one-factor one-lag model. The former model differs from a regular P-technique model by allowing for some serial dependence in the data, provided that it is due not to the common factors but rather to the unique factors.

The number of factors was assumed, a priori, to be one or two and the number of lags to be zero or one. These assumptions were based on prior research on mood structure and lag in mood (e.g., Larsen & Kasimatis, 1991; Lawton, Kleban, Dean, Rajagopal, & Parmelee, 1992; Shifren & Hooker, 1995; Watson et al., 1988). In each of the 12 participants' DFA, six models were fitted sequentially: (1) a standard P-technique model, (2)–(3) a dynamic one-factor model with loadings at lags zero and one, (4) a dynamic two-factor model with zero lag loadings, and (5)–(6) a dynamic two-factor model with loadings at lags zero and one. To determine models that best represented the data, we looked at comparative fit indices and factor-loading patterns, as well as the parsimony of the models (e.g., Molenaar, 1985; Molenaar et al., 1992; Wood & Brown, 1994).

Assessment of Model Fit

Based on prior research (cf. Wood & Brown, 1994), we chose four comparative fit indices for differentiating between models including: (1) the nonnormed fit index (NNFI; Bentler & Bonett, 1980); (2) Akaike's (1987) information criterion (AIC2); (3) the normed fit index (NFI; Bentler & Bonett, 1980); and (4) Type II Schwarz's (1978) Bayesian information criterion (SBIC2). The DFA application is such a new approach that there are very few guidelines for evaluating the fit indices. We accepted a minimum value of .30 as indicating a dynamic factor pattern in the data (see Wood & Brown, 1994). Moreover, our use of the indices was mainly to determine the cases where ordinary P-technique solutions were acceptable versus cases in which dynamic factor solutions were best.

In order to be interpreted as supporting a dynamic factor model, the corresponding four incremental fit indices had to maintain a .30 cutoff value across the three null models: (1) P-technique without correlated error, (2) P-technique with correlated error, and (3) a one-factor one-lag model (Wood and Brown, 1994). To illustrate how we evaluated the tabular information, consider Subject 1 (table 3.1). Subject 1's fit indices were .30 or higher across all three null model comparisons in table 3.1 for both the 2Factor 0Lag and 2Factor 1Lag models. We interpreted this outcome as favoring a dynamic factor model but did not choose between the 2Factor 0Lag and 2Factor 1Lag alternatives.

The fit indices for our sample provided the following factor structures: (1) nine P-technique models (Subjects 2, 3, 4, 5, 7, 8, 9, 10, and 12),

and (2) three dynamic factor models (Subjects 1, 6, and 11). As noted earlier, we did not make precise model specifications based on fit indices. Instead, we used the indices to distinguish between dynamic factor models and traditional P-technique models.

Interpretation of Factor Loadings

Basing decisions about best-fitting models on fit indices alone may not provide the most accurate representations of the factor structures. Wood and Brown (1994) discussed the subjective nature of using fit index cutoff values to decide among specific models. It is an arbitrary determination that can be influenced, in part, by the number of occasions of measurement. Therefore, factor loadings can be examined to help ascertain the model with the most plausible representation of the data. Factor loadings are regression-like weights, and they describe the relationship of the observed variables on the latent variables. We examined the factor loadings to determine if they were consistent with the decisions based on the incremental fit indices. If the pattern of the factor loadings was not consistent with the models chosen solely on fit indices, we reconsidered the model selection and tried to determine: (1) if a dynamic factor model better explained the structure of the data than a simple P-technique model, or (2) if a one-factor model sufficiently explained data that had previously been viewed as requiring a two-factor model.

For the DFA on PA, illustrative factor loadings are presented for a two-factor one-lag model (ID 1) in table 3.2. The columns of factor loadings are identified by both a factor number and a lag number (0Lag, 1Lag). 0Lag indicates that today's factor score influences today's scores on the variables. A 1Lag indicates that yesterday's factor score influences today's scores on the variables.

Summary of DFA Analyses

On the basis of fit indices and factor loadings, the following patterns for the DFA of PA were as follows: (a) 2Factor 1Lag models (Subjects 1, 6); (b) 1Factor 1Lag models (Subjects 2, 5, 7, 10, 11, 12); and (c) P-technique models (Subjects 3, 4, 8, 9). Consistent with some of the patterns found above, PA items tended to show substantial determination by yesterday's general affective dimension levels. For example, in half the sample, today's level of "alertness" was influenced by yesterday's level on the general affect dimen-

TABLE 3.1 Determining Presence of Dynamic Factor Models for Positive Affect in Parkinson's Disease Patient Using Type II Incremental Fit Values

Participant	Model	P-Technique With No Correlated Errors				P-Technique With Autocorrelated Errors				1Factor 1Lag With Autocorrelated Errors			
		NFI	NNFI	AIC2	SBIC2	NFI	NNFI	AIC2	SBIC2	NFI	NNFI	AIC2	SBIC2
1	1Factor 0Lag	.19	.08	.18	.13	.00	.00	.00	.00	.00	.00	.00	.00
	1Factor 1Lag	.10	−.10	.06	−.01	−.11	−.20	−.15	−.17	.00	.00	.00	.00
	2Factor 0Lag	.43	.37	.46	.42	.30	.31	.34	.33	.37	.43	.43	.43
	2Factor 1Lag	.57	.49	.61	.56	.47	.45	.52	.49	.52	.54	.58	.57

Note: NFI = normed fit index (also called the Bentler-Bonett normed fit index; Bentler & Bonett, 1980); NNFI = nonnormed fit index (also called the Tucker-Lewis index; Bentler & Bonett, 1980); AIC2 = Akaike's (1987) information criterion; SBIC2 = type II Schwarz's (1978) Bayesian information criterion. This table includes fit values for detrended DFA models run with the DFA macroprogram (see Shifren et al., 1997, for details). The information in this table is part of a larger table published in Shifren et al. (1997).

TABLE 3.2 Two-Factor One-Lag Model of Positive Affect Variables Represented With Factor Loadings in Parkinson's Disease Patient

Variable	1Factor 0Lag	1Factor 1Lag	2Factor 0Lag	2Factor 1Lag
Determined	−.15**	.48***	−.48***	.17**
Interested	.29***	.75***	.08	.31***
Enthusiastic	−.20***	.46***	−.56***	.06
Attentive	.25***	.81***	.09	.08
Strong	−.22***	.34***	−.83***	.38***
Active	.37***	.62***	−.00	.35***
Alert	.31***	.49***	−.57***	.30***

Note. The above data represent the factor loadings for Participant 1.
**$p = .01$, ***$p = .001$

sion. For three individuals (Subjects 7, 11, and 12), today's level of "determined" was influenced by yesterday's general factor level but not by today's. For three individuals (Subjects 5, 10, and 12), today's score on "strong" was influenced primarily by yesterday's score on the general affect factor. In contrast, for two individuals (Subjects 7 and 11), today's scores on "strong" were determined by today's factor scores rather than by yesterday's.

Our finding that positive affect structures differ across persons not only in terms of dimensionality but also in terms of lagged influences on positive affect reinforces the need to study intraindividual phenomena (e.g., mood) by intraindividual methods. We selected a sample that was homogeneous with regard to disease type, functional abilities, and cognitive impairment; however, the results showed heterogeneity for the structure and variation of mood in those with PD. Several prior studies on frail elderly have also shown heterogeneity in the structure and variation of mood (e.g., Kleban, Lawton, Nesselroade, & Parmelee, 1992; Lawton et al., 1992). The current and prior findings show why it is important not to make nomethetic generalizations concerning positive mood structure both within and across groups.

The fact that responses to mood items today are determined in part by yesterday's mood is not surprising. However, the tools to examine this aspect of mood are a recent development. DFA revealed, for example, that for some participants the kind of day one was having was influenced substantially by yesterday's mood whereas for others it was not. Earlier approaches to modeling mood such as P-technique factor analysis did not produce this kind of information about the way mood changes from day to day.

Researchers have argued that individuals who are trying to conserve their resources will show a unidimensional mood structure (e.g., Lawton et al., 1992), and conservation of resources is likely to happen in those with chronic illnesses (Kleban et al., 1992). However, our findings indicated that some individuals with PD do not display a unidimensional positive mood structure. Even those who show a unidimensional positive mood structure can show a variety of mood change patterns because of differences in the lagged relationships that influence their positive mood. Lagged relationships in individuals with PD may reflect a measure of flexibility to adapt to the varying and unpredictable course of disease (Labouvie-Vief & DeVoe, 1991).

Despite the interesting results found in this study, we caution readers about making generalizations from this study. First, the sample of individuals is small and further replications of mood structure findings in persons living with PD are desirable. Second, individuals in this sample suffered little to no cognitive or functional impairment. Better generalizations could be made in future research by broadening the basis of comparison to include those with greater levels of impairment. Third, extension of this line of research to other physically debilitating diseases such as arthritis or diabetes is needed to get a better understanding of mood structure in chronic disease groups.

Recent Work on Mood in Individuals With PD

As stated in the beginning of this chapter, research on positive mood in those with PD is still sparse. There are a few noteworthy exceptions. Schneider et al. (2003) studied high-frequency electrical stimulation of the subthalamic nucleus with 12 individuals diagnosed with PD. They found that this therapy technique was associated with more positive self-reported mood in individuals with PD. Hegeman et al. (2001) examined a sample of 16 PD patients, and they had participants complete hourly diaries for 7 days that included mood, anxiety, and motor states using visual analog scales. They found hourly fluctuations in emotional states and individual differences in patterns of emotional fluctuations.

Colleagues in the United States as well as Europe have updated the work on the original sample of 12 PD patients described in this chapter through advanced statistical techniques not available prior to 1999 (see Chow, Nesselrode, Shifren, & McArdle, 2004; Timmerman, 2001). Our discussion is based on the work done in the United States as this update was focused on positive and negative mood items (Chow et al., 2004), while the work in Europe was described in different terms (see Timmerman, 2001, for details). Using a procedure designed by Nesselroade and Molenaar (1999) for determining homogeneous subgroups of individuals based on each individual's lagged covariance matrix, Chow et al. (2004) were able to consolidate the individual differences in mood profiles from the original sample of PD patients. In addition, they determined the patterns of mood fluctuations among the subgroups using a statistical technique called direct autoregressive factor score (DAFS) model. To our knowledge, this approach is the newest one to be used with mood items in PD patients. Their findings are discussed briefly; however, details concerning exact statistical procedures can be found in Chow et al. (2004).

Chow et al. (2004) found that individuals' positive mood items had a strong autoregressive effect (i.e., much evidence of lagged relationship within and between positive mood items). However, the impact of the lagged relationship only lasted for a day. For example, yesterday's positive mood affected today's positive mood. There was no evidence of a weekly mood cycle for individuals with PD in this sample.

Finally, since the time of the work described in this chapter, researchers have refined and redefined the PA label of the PANAS to better reflect what those items capture at the individual level. Today, researchers now view PA as *positive activation* rather than *positive affect*, and PANAS descriptors are shown to load on high levels of activation (Watson, Wiese, Vaidya, & Tellegen, 1999). Thus, future work on positive mood

items in PD patients should reflect more recent theoretical ideas about the mood scales being used in research as well as including up-to-date analytic approaches to capturing factor structure and lag relationships in these individuals.

Acknowledgments   We are deeply grateful to the individuals with Parkinson's disease who dedicated much time and effort to completion of this 70-day study. This research was supported by a dissertation grant award received by Kim Shifren for her dissertation work, Graduate School, Syracuse University, Syracuse, New York. Some of the data were collected while Kim Shifren and Karen Hooker were supported by an NIMH grant no. R03-MH46637 awarded to Karen Hooker. All data analyses were performed with the valuable help of Phillip Wood, PhD, and John Nesselroade, PhD, and correspondence between authors on the data analyses were conducted while the first author was at the University of Florida.

References

Affleck, G., Tennen, H., Urrows, S., & Higgins, P. (1994). Person and contextual features of daily stress reactivity: Individual differences in relations of undesirable daily events with mood disturbance and chronic pain intensity. *Journal of Personality and Social Psychology, 66,* 329–340.

Akaike, H. (1987). Factor analysis and AIC. *Psychometrika, 52,* 333–342.

Benyamini, Y., Idler, E. L., Leventhal, H., & Leventhal, E. A. (2000). Positive affect and function as influences on self-assessments of health: Expanding our view beyond illness and disability. *Journal of Gerontology: Psychological Sciences, 55B*(2), P107–P116.

Bentler, P. M., & Bonett, D. G. (1980). Significance tests and goodness of fit in the analysis of covariance structures. *Psychological Bulletin, 88,* 588–606.

Brod, M., Mendelsohn, G. A., & Roberts, B. (1998). Patients experiences of Parkinson's disease. *Journal of Gerontology: Psychological Sciences, 53B*(4), P213–P222.

Brown, R. G., & MacCarthy, B. (1990). Psychiatric morbidity in patients with Parkinson's disease. *Psychological Medicine, 20,* 77–87.

Buntington, L. K., & Fitzsimmons, B. (1991). Depression in Parkinson's disease. *Journal of Neuroscience Nursing, 23,* 158–164.

Carstensen, L. L., Pasupathi, M., Mayr, U., & Nesselroade, J. R. (2000). Emotional experience in everyday life across the adult life span. *Journal of Personality and Social Psychology, 79*, 644–655.

Casten, R. J., Lawton, M. P., Winter, L., Kleban, M., & Sando, R. L. (1997). The relationship of health to affect assessed both state and trait form: How does age impact the relationship? *Aging and Mental Health, 1*, 230–237.

Cattell, R. B. (1952). The three basic factor-analytic research designs: Their interrelations and derivatives. *Psychological Bulletin, 49*, 499–520.

Cattell, R. B., Cattell, A. K. S., & Rhymer, R. M. (1947). P-technique demonstrated in determining psychophysical source traits in a normal individual. *Psychometrika, 12*, 267–288.

Charmaz, K. (1991). *Good days, bad days: The self in chronic illness and time.* New Brunswick, NJ: Rutgers University Press.

Chow, S. M., Nesselroade, J. R., Shifren, K., & McArdle, J. J. (2004). Dynamic coupling of positive and negative affect among individuals with Parkinson's disease. *Structural Equation Modeling, 11*, 560–582.

Dakof, G. A., & Mendelsohn, G. A. (1986). Parkinson's disease: The psychological aspects of a chronic illness. *Psychological Bulletin, 99*, 375–387.

Dakof, G. A., & Mendelsohn, G. A. (1989). Patterns of adaptation to Parkinson's disease. *Health Psychology, 8*, 355–372.

Eisenman, D. R., Nesselroade, J. R., Featherman, D. L., & Rowe, J. W. (1997). Intraindividual variability in perceived control in an older sample: The MacArthur Successful Aging Studies. *Psychology and Aging, 12*, 489–502.

Folkman, S., & Maskowitz, J. T. (2000). Positive affect and the other side of coping. *American Psychologist, 55*, 647–654.

Folstein, M. F., Folstein, S. E., & McHugh, P. R. (1975). "Mini-mental state": A practical method for grading the cognitive state of patients for the clinician. *Journal of Psychiatric Research, 12*, 189–198.

Fournier, M., deRidder, D., & Bensing, J. (2003). Is optimism sensitive to the stressors of chronic disease? The impact of type I diabetes mellitus and multiple sclerosis on optimistic beliefs. *Psychology and Health, 18*(3), 277–294.

Frazier, L. D., Cotrell, V., & Hooker, K. (2003). Possible selves and illness: A comparison of individuals with Parkinson's disease, early-stage Alzheimer's disease, and healthy older adults. *International Journal of Behavioral Development, 27*, 1–11.

Hegeman, I. R., Wallace, A. J., & Kurlan, R. (2001). Relationship between mood and motor fluctuations in Parkinson's disease. *Journal of Neuropsychiatry and Clinical Neuroscience, 13*(1), 35–41.

Hollingshead, A. B. (1975). *A four-factor index of social status.* New Haven, CT: Yale University Press.

Holtzman, W. H. (1963). Statistical models for the study of change in the single case. In C. W. Harris (Ed.), *Problems in measuring change* (pp. 190–211). Madison: University of Wisconsin Press.

Jones, C. J., & Nesselroade, J. R. (1990). Multivariate, replicated, single-subject, repeated measures designs and P-technique factor analysis: A review of intraindividual change studies. *Experimental Aging Research, 16*, 171–183.

Kleban, M. H., Lawton, M. P., Nesselroade, J. R., & Parmelee, P. (1992). The structure of variation in affect among depressed and nondepressed elders. *Journal of Gerontology: Psychological Sciences, 47*, P190–P198.

Labouvie-Vief, G., & DeVoe, M. R. (1991). Emotional regulation in adulthood and later life: A developmental view. *Annual Review of Gerontology and Geriatrics, 11*, 172–194.

Labouvie-Vief, G., & Medler, M. (2002). Affect optimization and affect complexity: Modes and styles of regulation in adulthood. *Psychology and Aging, 17*, 571–588.

Larsen, R. J., & Kasimatis, M. (1991). Day-to-day physical symptoms: Individual differences in the occurence, duration, and emotional concomitants of minor daily illnesses. *Journal of Personality, 59*, 387–423.

Lawton, M. P., Kleban, M. H., Dean, J., Rajagopal, D., & Parmelee, P. A. (1992). The factorial generality of brief positive and negative affect measures. *Journal of Gerontology: Psychological Sciences, 47*, P228–P237.

Levin, B. E., & Weiner, W. J. (1987). Psychosocial aspects. In W. C. Koller (Ed.), *Handbook of Parkinson's disease* (pp. 465–474). New York: Marcel Dekker.

Livneh, H., & Antonak, R. F. (1994). Indirect methods to measure attitudes toward persons with disabilities. *Rehabilitation Education, 8*, 103–137.

Marr, J. (1991). The experience of living with Parkinson's disease. *Journal of Neuroscience Nursing, 23*, 325–330.

Marsh, L. (2000). Neuropsychiatric aspects of Parkinson's disease. *Psychosomatics, 41*(1), 15–38.

Mayeux, R. (1987). Mental state. In W. W. Koller (Ed.), *Handbook of Parkinson's disease* (pp. 127–144). New York: Marcel Dekker.

McArdle, J. J., & Nesselroade, J. R. (1994). Using multivariate data to structure developmental change. In S. H. Cohen & H. W. Reese (Eds.), *Life-span developmental psychology: Methodological contributions* (pp. 223–267). The West Virginia University conferences on life-span developmental psychology. Hillsdale, NJ: Erlbaum.

McDonald, W. M., Richard, I. H., & DeLong, M. R. (2003). Prevalence, etiology, and treatment of depression in Parkinson's disease. *Biological Psychiatry, 54*(3), 363–375.

Mendelsohn, G. A., Dakof, G. A., & Skaff, M. (1995). Personality change in Parkinson's disease patients: Chronic disease and aging. *Journal of Personality, 63*(2), 233–258.

Molenaar, P. C. (1985). A dynamic factor model for the analysis of multivariate time series. *Psychometrika, 50,* 181–202.

Molenaar, P. C., deGooijer, J. G., & Schmitz, B. (1992). Dynamic factor analysis of nonstationary multivariate time series. *Psychometrika, 57,* 333–349.

Nesselroade, J. R., & Featherman, D. L. (1991). Intraindividual variability in older adults' depression scores: Some implications for developmental theory and longitudinal research. In D. Magnusson, L. Berman, G. Rudinger, & Y. B. Torestad (Eds.), *Problems and methods in longitudinal research: Stability and change* (pp. 47–66). London: Cambridge University Press.

Nesselroade, J. R., & Ford, D. H. (1985). P-technique comes of age: Multivariate, replicated, single-subject designs for research on older adults. *Research on Aging, 7,* 46–80.

Nesselroade, J. R., & Molenaar, P. C. M. (1999). Pooling lagged covariance structures based on short, multivariate time-series for dynamic factor analysis. In R. H. Hoyle (Ed.), *Statistical strategies for small sample research* (pp. 224–251). Newbury Park, CA: Sage.

Nesselroade, J. R., & Salthouse, T. A. (2004). Methodological and theoretical implications of intraindividual variability in perceptual-motor performance. *Journal of Gerontology: Psychological Sciences, 59B,* P49–P55.

Nissenbaum, H., Quinn, N. P., Brown, R. G., & Toone, B. K. (1987). Mood swings associated with the "on-off" phenomenon in Parkinson's disease. *Psychological Medicine, 17,* 899–904.

Norman, S., Tröster, A. I., Fields, J. A., & Brooks, R. (2002). Effects of depression and Parkinson's disease on cognitive functioning. *Journal of Neuropsychiatry and Clinical Neuroscience, 14*(1), 31–36.

Peterson, C. (2000). The future of optimism. *American Psychologist, 55,* 44–55.

Raos, M., Huber, S. J., & Bornstein, R. A. (1992). Emotional changes with multiple sclerosis and Parkinson's disease. *Journal of Consulting and Clinical Psychology, 60,* 369–378.

Reich, J. W., Zautra, A., & Davis, M. (2003). Dimensions of affect relationships: Models and their integrative implications. *Review of General Psychology, 7,* 66–83.

Schneider, F., Habel, U., Volkmann, J., Regel, S., Kornischka, J., Sturm, V., et al. (2003). Deep brain stimulation of the subthalamic nucleus enhances emotional processing in Parkinson's disease. *Archives of General Psychiatry, 60*(3), 296–302.

Schwarz, G. (1978). Estimating the dimension of a model. *Annals of Statistics, 6,* 461–464.

Shifren, K. (1994). The relationship between optimism, self-efficacy, and the behavioral symptoms of Parkinson's disease. *Dissertation Abstracts International Section B: The Sciences and Engineering, 55*(3-B), 1204.

Shifren, K. (1996). Individual differences in the perception of optimism and disease severity: A 70 day study among individuals with Parkinson's disease. *Journal of Behavioral Medicine, 19*(3), 241–271.

Shifren, K., & Hooker, K. (1995). Daily assessments of anxiety and affect: A study among spouse caregivers. *International Journal of Behavioral Development, 18*(4), 595–607.

Shifren, K., Hooker, K., Wood, P., & Nesselroade, J. R. (1997). Structure and variation of mood in individuals with Parkinson's disease: A dynamic factor analysis. *Psychology and Aging, 12*(2), 328–339.

Stern, G. (1990). *Parkinson's Disease: The Facts.* Oxford: Oxford University Press.

Symister, P., & Friend, R. (2003). The influence of social support and problematic support on optimism and depression in chronic illness: A prospective study evaluating self-esteem as a mediator. *Health Psychology, 22*(2), 123–129.

Timmerman, M. E. (2001). *Component analysis of multisubject multivariate longitudinal data.* Groningen, The Netherlands: Stichting Drukkerij C. Regenboog.

Watson, D. (1988). Intraindividual and interindividual analyses of positive and negative affect: Their relation to health complaints, perceived stress, and daily activities. *Journal of Personality and Social Psychology, 54,* 1020–1030.

Watson, D., Clark, L. A., & Tellegen, A. (1988). Development and validation of brief measures of positive and negative affect: The PANAS scales. *Journal of Personality and Social Psychology, 54,* 1063–1070.

Watson, D., Wiese, D., Vaidya, J., & Tellegen, A. (1999). The two general activation systems of affect: Structural findings, evolutionary considerations, and psychobiological evidence. *Journal of Personality and Social Psychology, 76,* 820–838.

Wood, P., & Brown, D. (1994). The study of intra-individual differences by means of dynamic factor models: Rationale, implementation, and interpretation. *Psychological Bulletin, 116,* 166–186.

Zevon, M. A., & Tellegen, A. (1982). The structure of mood change: An idiographic/nomothetic analysis. *Journal of Personality and Social Psychology, 43,* 111–122.

4

Application of Dynamic Factor Analysis to Affective Processes in Dyads

Emilio Ferrer

Individual processes, by definition, involve psychological phenomena that occur as a function of time. These processes are dynamic in nature; that is, they change over time and involve time-lagged sequences. Because of this dynamic nature, the study of such processes at the individual level necessitates an intense set of measurements that capture the fluctuations—for example, hourly, daily, weekly, or whatever time dimension underlies the process—and the time dependency of the changes. The intraindividual variability design, in which a person is measured at multiple occasions, typically on many variables, was developed precisely for this purpose. In this chapter, I focus on dynamic factor analysis (DFA), a model that uses the intraindividual variability design, and illustrate its application to the study of affective processes in dyads.

In the 1970s, Nesselroade and Baltes (1979) listed a number of objectives for longitudinal research. The first two goals were the description of intraindividual variability and possible interpersonal differences in such intraindividual variability. The next goal, much more challenging and enduring, was to identify possible causes for intraindividual variability and interpersonal differences. These goals are applicable

to the study of dyadic interactions. Here, one informative approach is to consider the two members of the dyad as the agents bringing about the variability and underlying the dyadic process. Without disregarding possible external influences, this approach focuses on the individuals themselves as endogenous forces responsible for the dynamics in the dyad (see, e.g., Felmlee & Greenberg, 1999, and chapter 28, this volume).

DFA is a method that can capture such forces. It can describe the variability of the two individuals in the dyad and identify some of the influences that both individuals exert on the dyad as a system (Ferrer & Nesselroade, 2003). More specifically, with its focus on time-lagged relations, DFA models are suitable for examining substantive questions that involve lagged effects between the two members in a dyad. These effects represent interpersonal influences (i.e., uni- or bidirectional) with a particular time structure (i.e., lag). In addition to such interpersonal influences, DFA models allow one to investigate intraindividual change processes and test hypotheses about the factor structure of the data (e.g., which variables are most influenced by which factors? Are these influences constant over time?) and its time organization (i.e., what is the optimal number of lags for capturing the relationships? How stable is the process?). For example, applying the DFA model to dyads, a particular mood (e.g., happiness) for one person at a given day—or whatever time unit is used—is the cumulative result of that same person's general affect (e.g., positive and negative) on that day, the day before, 2 days before, and so on until the effect is no longer perceptible, together with similar influences from the affect of the other person in the dyad. Equal specifications apply to the mood for the other person in the dyad.

Dynamic Factor Analysis

DFA is an extension of Cattell's original P-technique factor analysis (Cattell, Cattell, & Rhymer, 1947; Nesselroade, McArdle, Aggen, & Meyers, 2002; Wood & Brown, 1994). The development of DFA (Brillinger, 1975; McArdle, 1982; Molenaar, 1985) overcame the major limitation of Cattell's factor analytic technique; namely, its inability to represent information about the autocorrelations and cross-correlations in the data (Anderson, 1963; Cattell, 1963; Holtzman, 1963). That is, P-technique factor analysis could depict concurrent relationships but could not capture lagged relationships or any time dependency of the underlying process. In the various specifications of the DFA, on the other hand, the relations of factors and variables can be specified across time lags, thus not being constrained to a single concurrent interval. Such relations are represented in a lagged covariance matrix that includes lagged effects up to some arbitrary number of lags; ideally, until the time interval when the process under study dissipates.

One specification of the DFA model developed by Molenaar (1985; see also Geweke, 1977; Geweke & Singleton, 1981) can be written as

$$z_{(t)} = \Lambda_{(0)} \eta_{(t)} + \Lambda_{(1)} \eta_{(t-1)}$$
$$+ \cdots + \Lambda_{(s)} \eta_{(t-s)} + \varepsilon_{(t)} \qquad (1)$$

where $z_{(t)}$ is the observed p-variate time series, $\Lambda_{(s)}$, $s = 0, 1, \ldots, j$ are $p \times q$ matrices of lagged factor loadings, $\eta_{(t)}$ is the latent q-variate factor time series, and $\varepsilon_{(t)}$ is a p-variate noise time series. This model, also called the white noise factor score model (WNFS; Nesselroade et al., 2002) and shock factor analysis model (SFA; Browne & Nesselroade, 2005), includes some key features, including different factor loading

patterns for different lags, correlated factors within lags but not across lags, and possible autocorrelational structure in the unique variances of the variables (Nesselroade et al., 2002). This specification of the DFA model has been refined to include informative features, among them the identification of an optimal lag order (Molenaar & Nesselroade, 2001).

An alternative specification of the DFA model was introduced by McArdle (1982; see also Engle & Watson, 1981; Immink, 1986) and by Nesselroade et al. (2002). This specification, called the process factor analysis model (PFA; Browne & Nesselroade, 2005; Browne & Zhang, in press), can be written as

$$z_{(t)} = \Lambda[\beta_{(1)} \eta_{(t-1)} + \cdots$$
$$+ \beta_{(s)} \eta_{(t-s)}] + \Lambda \zeta_{(t)} + \varepsilon_{(t)} \qquad (2)$$

where β_s is a matrix of weights to represent lagged regression coefficients among the latent factors. Such coefficients can represent not only autoregressions but, in the case of a multiple-factor time series, cross-lagged regressions as well (see Browne & Nesselroade, 2005). This PFA specification is a particular case of a more general PFA model that includes two parts (Browne & Nesselroade, 2005; Browne & Zhang, in press). The first part is written as

$$z_{(t)} = \Lambda \eta_{(t)} + \varepsilon_{(t)} \qquad (3)$$

where, as before, $z_{(t)}$ is a matrix of observed manifest variables measured at time t, Λ is a factor matrix invariant over time, $\eta_{(t)}$ is a vector of common factors at time t, and $\varepsilon_{(t)}$ is a vector of unique factors at time t assuming $\varepsilon_{(t)} \sim (0, D_\varepsilon)$. The second part of the model can be written as

$$\eta_{(t)} = \sum_{i=1}^{p} A_i \eta(t-i) + e(t)$$
$$+ \sum_{j=1}^{q} B_j e(t-i) \qquad (4)$$

where $e_{(t)} \sim (0, \Psi)$ is a random shock vector, the A_i are autoregressive weight matrices, and the B_j are moving average weight matrices. When $q = 0$, the last term in equation (4) is omitted and this VARMA (p, q) model becomes a VAR $(p, 0)$ PFA model that is equivalent to the one expressed in equation (2). Further details and technical comparisons between the PFA and SFA models are provided elsewhere (Browne & Nesselroade, 2005; Browne & Zhang, in press; Nesselroade et al., 2002).

Examining Dynamic Processes in Dyadic Interactions

An essential feature of any dyad is the interaction that takes place between its two members. This feature is recognized by most theoretical perspectives on close relationships, which stress the interdependence between the two members of a dyad and the importance of considering such interactions to understand dyadic processes (e.g., Ainsworth, 1973; Bowlby, 1969/1982; Cowan & Cowan, 2000; Feeney, 1999; Hazan & Shaver, 1987; Kelley & Thibaut, 1978; Minuchin, 1984; Surra & Longstreth, 1990). Such an interaction can represent different kinds of processes (e.g., behavioral, psychological), but in any of these forms, the actions and emotions of one person may influence those of the other person (Rusbult & Van Lange, 1996). In spite of this theoretical recognition, however, much of the empirical research on close relationships tends to ignore the interdependence between both members of the dyad.

One example of interdependence is emotional transmission within couples in close relationships (Hatfield, Cacioppo, & Rapson, 1994; Larson & Almeida, 1999; Thomson & Bolger, 1999). *Emotional transmission* refers to the emotional influences between the two members of a dyad. Such influences take place as part of any daily interaction, especially when involved in a romantic relationship (Gottman, 1980, 1988). Emotional transmission can become even more apparent under demanding situations. For example, Thomson and Bolger showed that the negative affect (i.e., depressed mood) of individuals who were preparing to face a stressful event (i.e., the BAR Examination) influenced their partners' feelings about their relationship, with changes in the strength of such influences as the examination approached.

Another example of dyadic processes is so-called attachment-related psychodynamics, processes related to affect regulation and attachment-system activation (Mikulincer & Shaver, 2003; Mikulincer, Shaver, & Pereg, 2003; Shaver & Mikulincer, 2002). These psychodynamics describe differences in affect-regulation strategies used by individuals as a function of attachment styles. An important feature of this work is the notion of coregulation as a process that unfolds over time and involves the two members of a couple. Evidence of such coregulatory dyadic processes exists in infant-caregiver interactions (Beebe & Lachmann, 1998; Fogel, 1992;

Schore, 2000), as well as in adult interactions (Aron & Aron, 1997; Hofer, 1984; Pipp & Harmon, 1987; see Diamond & Aspinwall, 2003, for a review).

Dyadic interactions are complex dynamic processes. Understanding this complexity is only possible through questions that consider the coregulatory and evolving nature of the dyadic processes. Some possible questions along these lines include the following: (a) What are different patterns of affective processes underlying dyadic relationships? (b) How do individuals in couples rely on each other for comfort and distress reduction? (c) Are there detectable directions (i.e., from one person to the other) in such emotional influences? (d) What is the influence of significant events—both positive and negative—on the relationships, and what are the strategies that couples use to recover from such perturbations? (e) Do differences in emotional dynamics exist as a function of other psychological processes (e.g., attachment style)?

DFA models are suitable to describe such dyadic interactions and their development over time. Moreover, they can be valuable to evaluate hypotheses about affect regulation, coregulation, and emotional transmission. As described in previous sections, specifically in equation (2), when the matrix of regression lagged effects is not diagonal, the elements in the off-diagonal can represent lagged influences between the two individuals in a dyad. These effects represent interpersonal influences (i.e., uni- or bidirectional) structured as a function of time (i.e., lag). For example, Ferrer and Nesselrode (2003) used a PFA model with cross-lagged effects to examine affective processes in one dyad. They specified a PFA with multiple factors, from both individuals in one dyad, and applied it to a multivariate time series of daily affective data. A model with positive and negative affect factors was applied to daily data from both members in the dyad. This approach was useful to: (a) capture intra- and interindividual variability in affect and identify differences in such affective structure between the two members of the dyad; (b) describe these differences in terms of factorial configuration (i.e., positive and negative affect were manifested in both persons through different variables, with less complexity for the husband) and temporal organization (i.e., the lagged effects dissipated more rapidly for the wife); and (c) detect directionality in the interpersonal affective influences (e.g., the husband's negative affect had lagged effects on the wife's positive and negative affect, but the reverse effects were not perceptible). This is an example of how dynamic factor analysis can be used to examine dyadic data.

There are a fair number of studies in which dynamic factor models have been applied to various areas of research (Hooker, Nesselroade, Nesselroade, & Lerner, 1987; Hershberger, Corneal, & Molenaar, 1994; Hershberger, Molenaar, & Corneal, 1996; Mitteness & Nesselroade, 1987; Sbarra & Ferrer, in press). Applications of dynamic factor models—or any of their precursors—to dyadic data are, however, scarce. In a pioneer study, Hooker et al. (1987) used P-technique factor analysis to examine patterns of covariation in temperament between mothers and their children, with findings showing more similar change patterns within dyads than across mothers or children. Hershberger et al. (1994; see also Hershberger et al., 1996), used DFA to investigate differences in the emotional response patterns between father-daughter and stepfather-stepdaughter dyads. The lagged effects detected from the DFA models showed that involvement over time was related to affection for daughters and fathers, but to anger and anxiety for stepdaughters and stepfathers.

An interesting issue that DFA models can address is the dynamics between individuals in a dyad. With DFA, one can model the patterns of relationships between both persons and identify bidirectional or unidirectional relationships. This issue, originally examined by Mitteness and Nesselroade (1987) using P-technique, is crucial in understanding the dynamics of dyads. With the use of DFA models, it is possible to detect, for example, unbalanced relationships, in which one person has a stronger influence on the dyad than the other, and to describe the time structure of such relationships. In the following sections, I illustrate the application of DFA to address this and other questions related to dyadic interactions.

Illustrative Data

All the analyses reported here involve data from a from a husband-wife dyad in which each person completed a daily questionnaire for 6 months. Because detailed information about the participants and measures is described elsewhere (Ferrer & Nesselroade, 2003), only selected information is presented here. The questionnaire was intended to examine daily fluctuations of affect and contained, among other items, the Positive and Negative Affect Scale (PANAS; Watson, Clark, & Tellegen, 1988). The PANAS is a 20-item scale measuring positive and negative affect. Participants are asked to the mark the extent to which they experienced each of the 20 affective states on a 5-point Likert-type scale ranging from 1 (very slightly or not at all) to 5 (extremely). Table 4.1 includes means and standard deviations of all the items for each person. The PANAS scales have demonstrated good internal consistency, reliability, and convergent and discriminant validity (Hershberger et al., 1994; Shifren et al., 1997; Watson et al., 1988).

Figure 4.1 includes plots of positive and negative affect for each person. These plots indicate that: (a) positive affect has higher scores than negative affect for both persons, (b) the husband's positive affect is substantially higher than the wife's; and, most important, (c) there is large fluctuation in both persons' positive and negative affect over time. Figure 4.2 presents the plots of selected items (i.e., upset and hostile) for which differences between husband and wife are evident. Apparent in these figures is a possible synchrony between the husband's and the wife's affective states. Illustrating how to examine and quantify such synchrony is one of the goals of this chapter. The next section includes detailed steps on how to implement DFA to explore these issues.

Individual Factor Analysis

The PANAS scales are typically assumed to contain two factors. The first set of analyses examined the structure of positive and negative affect for each person. Results from separate exploratory principal-axis factor analyses revealed a model with five factors for the wife, and a model with four factors for the husband. The obliquely rotated solution for the wife suggested a structure with the following factors: Interest (i.e., *interested, alert, attentive*), Irritability (i.e., *irritable, distressed, ashamed, upset, hostile, jittery*), Nervousness (i.e., *nervous, scared*), Excitement (i.e., *excited, inspired, nonguilty, enthusiastic, proud*), and Strength (i.e., *strong, determined, active*). The solution for the husband yielded the following four-factor structure: Interest or general positive affect (i.e., *interested, excited, inspired, strong, determined, enthusiastic, active, proud*), Distress (i.e., *distressed, nervous, scared, afraid*), Hostility (i.e., *irritable, ashamed, upset, guilty, hostile*), and Alertness (i.e., *alert, attentive, jittery*).

TABLE 4.1 Means and Standard Deviations of Items

	Wife		Husband	
Variable	M	SD	M	SD
Positive affect				
interested	3.52	.65	3.81	.73
alert	3.31	.63	2.21	.79
excited	2.04	1.06	3.23	.85
inspired	1.12	.40	2.75	.82
strong	2.40	.68	2.71	.89
determined	2.24	.90	3.49	.75
attentive	3.31	.72	3.05	.86
enthusiastic	2.37	1.18	3.35	.81
active	2.48	.73	3.05	.96
proud	1.49	.98	2.62	.81
Negative affect				
irritable	1.39	.57	1.34	.73
distressed	1.59	.81	1.52	.88
ashamed	1.01	.07	1.08	.29
upset	1.33	.70	1.36	.83
nervous	1.13	.43	1.30	.67
scared	1.01	.10	1.31	.65
hostile	1.05	.25	1.25	.58
jittery	1.02	.13	1.71	.82
afraid	1.00	.00	1.37	.70
guilty	1.02	.15	1.10	.34

Creation of Block-Toeplitz Lagged Covariance Matrices

After inspecting the factorial configuration for each person, the next analyses focus on lagged structure of the data. Here the aim is to explore the dynamic nature of affective processes for each person and to test whether adding a lag component to the covariance matrices improves upon a structure without lags, as with the P-technique models. In order to perform these analyses, a block-Toeplitz lagged covariance matrix needs to be constructed for each person. In this case, block-Toeplitz matrices of four lags were computed from the original 20×182 (variables by occasions) raw data matrix and

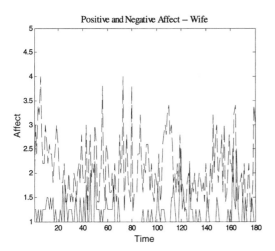
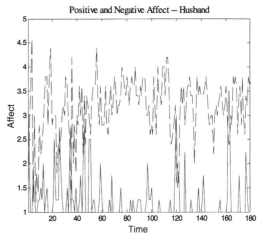

Figure 4.1 Positive and negative affect over time for each person. Dashed line represents positive affect; solid line represents negative affect.

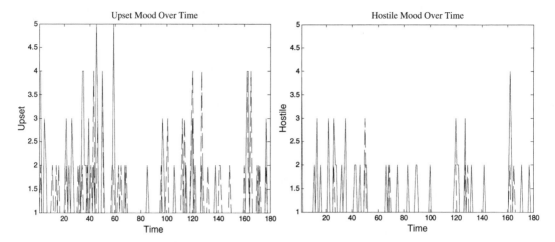

Figure 4.2 Upset and hostile mood over time for each person. Dashed line represents the variable for the wife. Solid line represents the variable for the husband.

included a number of 20×20 submatrices representing the lags 0, 1, 2, and 3.

Figure 4.3 represents a block-Toeplitz matrix of Lags 0, 1, and 2. The uppermost triangle in figure 4.3 is a symmetric covariance matrix of variables at Lag 0 (concurrent covariation). The submatrix just below contains an asymmetric covariance matrix of Lag 1. Here, the variables are lagged with themselves one time point (i.e., x_{it-1} with y_{it}, x_{it-1} with m_{it}, ... and y_{it-1} with m_{it}) to yield a 20×20 asymmetric matrix (i.e., pairing x_{it-1} with y_{it} is different than pairing y_{it-1} with x_{it}) with Lag 1 autocorrelations in the diagonal. The submatrix below is also an asymmetric covariance matrix but of Lag-2 relations. Because standard programs of covariance structures like LISREL cannot read asymmetric matrices as input, one needs to add blocks of redundant information and then free all the parameters to use up the extra degrees of freedom. The shaded areas in figure 4.3 represent such redundant blocks.

Dynamic Analyses of Individual Variability

Using the factor structure from previous analyses, WNFS or SFA dynamic factor models are now fitted to the lagged covariance matrices[1] (see figure 4.4). The results from these analyses (up to Lag 3, i.e., on 3 days) are presented in tables 4.2 and 4.3, for the wife and husband, respectively. For the wife, the variables representing positive affect are strongly influenced by

the factors[2] interest, excitement, and strength at the concurrent time (i.e., Lag 0 loadings). Such variables are also influenced, though to a lesser extent, by their factors the previous day (i.e., Lag 1 loadings), and this influence is almost dissipated when considering the factors two days ago (i.e., Lag 2 loadings; except for the variables *excited* and *strong*). For some variables, this influence is again perceptible 3 days in the past (i.e., Lag 3 loadings). Thus, the processes driving some of these positive mood variables (i.e., *excitement*) seem to endure for at least 3 days. Other variables (i.e., *alert, proud, active*) exhibit a shorter course that lasts 2 days and then dissipates. Yet others (i.e., *interested, attentive, inspired, enthusiastic, determined*) unfold in a cyclic dynamic in which they vanish after 1 or 2 days to emerge again the 3rd day.

The variables representing negative affect seem to manifest a quicker and less complex structure. Except for some variables, which do not represent affective variability of this participant at all (i.e., *jittery, nervous, scared*), the negative-affect variables are influenced by the person's affective process at the concurrent time only. The lag influence is either nonexistent (i.e., *hostile*) or very weak and expressed from the previous day (i.e., *irritable* and *upset*), or from 2 days ago (i.e., *distressed*). In one case only (i.e., *ashamed*), such an influence is again detectable from the 3rd day, after having apparently dissipated during day 2.

The results for the husband are presented in table 4.3. For this person, the positive affect

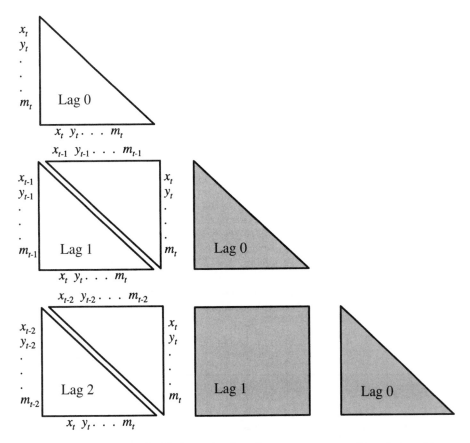

Figure 4.3 Representation of a block-Toeplitz lagged covariance matrix of Lags 0, 1, and 2.

variables are manifested in two factors: Interest (or general positive affect) and Alertness. The variables from the former factor have a strong influence from the person's positive affect at the concurrent time and this effect is also substantial from the person's affect the previous 2 days (i.e., *inspired, enthusiastic, proud*) or previous 3 days (i.e., *interested, determined*). For some variables (i.e., *strong, active*), the Lag 3 loadings have a negative sign, suggesting that low levels of positive affect 3 days ago are more likely to be followed by high strength and activity today. The variables *alert, attentive,* and *jittery* are influenced by an alertness process at the concurrent time as well as during the previous 3 days. Although such a process weakens substantially over time for the variable *attentive,* this is not the case for the variable *alert,* in which the strongest influence comes from the person's alertness at 2 to 3 days prior.

With regard to negative affect, these variables are also expressed in two factors, which correlate

moderately and positively. The variables *distressed, nervous, scared,* and *afraid* are brought about by the participant's negative affective process at the concurrent time and, even more strongly, by this process during the previous 3 days. The negative sign of the Lag 3 loadings for *distressed* and *afraid* indicate that these variables reverse after 3 days. That is, low levels of negative affect 3 days before a given occasion translate into high levels of distress and fear at the concurrent time. The rest of the negative affect variables (i.e., *irritable, ashamed, upset, guilty, hostile*) do not follow such a persistent process. On the contrary, they are strongly influenced by negative affect at the concurrent time, but this effect weakens substantially over time. Except for the variable *ashamed,* all these variables have a negative valence on their Lag 2 (or Lag 3) loadings, indicating that they follow the same reversing process explained previously. In sum, the results in this section illustrate the uniqueness of affective structures for each of the

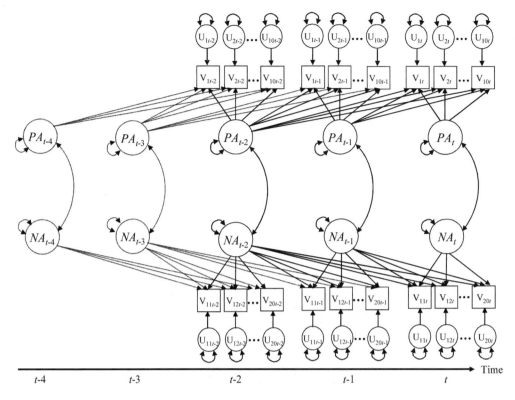

Figure 4.4 White noise factor score (WNFS) model. V = manifest variables; PA = positive affect latent factor; NA = negative affect latent factor, U = uniquenesses. The subscript t denotes the lag, where t = Lag 0, $t-1$ = Lag 1, and so on. Although not shown in this figure, autocorrelations of uniquenesses of the same variable across lags are estimated.

two persons in this study. Such singularity is manifested in both the different configurations of the affective structure and the dynamics underlying each person's affective process.

Dyadic Dynamic Analyses

This set of analyses focuses on the interrelations between the affective processes of the two persons in the dyad over time. Given the large number of items and the subsequent complexity of the block-Toeplitz lagged covariance matrix when aggregating the two participants across lags, I selected for these analyses five items denoting positive affect and five items denoting negative affect for each person.[3] To capture each person's uniqueness, the same items did not need to be selected for both individuals. Thus, a 20×182 matrix was constructed that specified four factors (i.e., positive and negative affect for each person) and covariation across three lags (i.e., 0, 1, and 2). Since

the focus of these analyses is on the factor co-variation across persons and time, a PFA $(p, 0)$ dynamic model was specified including lagged relationships among the factors through auto- and cross-lagged regressions (see figures 4.5 and 4.6). To highlight differences between husband and wife, figure 4.7 presents plots of positive and negative affect superimposed across persons. For example, the discrepancy in levels of positive affect between husband and wife is apparent in the right panel of figure 4.7, with higher values for the husband. Although it is less evident, the left panel of figure 4.7 shows negative affect for both persons and also reveals that the higher peaks correspond to the husband.

Applied to these data, such a model allows one to explore the interrelations between the participants' affective processes over time. To identify interpersonal influences in this dynamic relationship, four models positing different structural hypotheses are tested: (a) dynamic

TABLE 4.2 Parameter Estimates From WNFS Dynamic Factor Model for Wife

Estimate	Lag 0 λ_0	θ_ε	Lag 1 λ_1	Lag 2 λ_2	Lag 3 λ_3
Interest (F1)					
interested	.78	.34	.25	$-.04^{ns}$	.16
alert	.82	.31	.19	$-.06^{ns}$	$.07^{ns}$
attentive	.79	.31	.25	$.04^{ns}$	.12
Excitement (F2)					
excited	.82	.24	.22	.11	.22
inspired	.29	.86	$.01^{ns}$	$.04^{ns}$	.22
guilty	$.09^{ns}$	.95	$-.16$	$.01^{ns}$	$.13^{ns}$
enthusiastic	.87	.22	.10	$.05^{ns}$	.13
proud	.42	.75	$.08^{ns}$	$.00^{ns}$	$.11^{ns}$
Strength (F3)					
strong	.80	.32	$.11^{ns}$	.14	$-.06^{ns}$
determined	.40	.78	.13	$.09^{ns}$	.18
active	.59	.58	.26	$.06^{ns}$	$.10^{ns}$
Irritability (F4)					
irritable	.33	.87	.01	$-.11^{ns}$	$-.07^{ns}$
distressed	.72	.46	.02	.12	$-.04^{ns}$
ashamed	.35	.77	.04	$-.05^{ns}$	.33
upset	.90	.20	.02	$.10^{ns}$	$.02^{ns}$
hostile	.69	.52	$.11^{ns}$	$-.09^{ns}$	$.09^{ns}$
jittery	$-.05^{ns}$	.97	$-.17^{ns}$	$-.07^{ns}$	$.07^{ns}$
Nervousness (F5)					
nervous	$.32^{ns}$	.90	$.13^{ns}$	$-.02^{ns}$	$.00^{ns}$
scared	2.21^{ns}	-4.06^{ns}	$.09^{ns}$	$.00^{ns}$	$-.44^{ns}$
afraid	—	—	—	—	—

Shock correlations	F1	F2	F3	F4	F5
F1	1.00				
F2	.56	1.00			
F3	.46	.46	1.00		
F4	$.09^{ns}$	$.04^{ns}$	.16	1.00	
F5	$-.01^{ns}$	$-.04^{ns}$	$.03^{ns}$	$.02^{ns}$	1.00

Note: ns = parameter not accurately estimable (t value < 1.96; $p > .05$). Invariance constraints were invoked for the correlations between uniquenesses of the same variable for each lag.

influences between individuals are bidirectional (i.e., free cross-lagged regressions between the two persons); (b) dynamic influences between individuals are unidirectional (i.e., free cross-lagged regressions from Person 1 to Person 2 only); (c) dynamic influences between individuals are unidirectional (i.e., free cross-lagged regressions from Person 2 to Person 1 only); and (d) there are no dynamic influences between individuals (i.e., all cross-lagged regressions fixed to zero). Comparative fit results from these models are presented in table 4.4.

Overall, all the models yielded a good fit to these data. To evaluate the relative fit, we com-

pared their likelihood and degrees-of-freedom ratios (but see Note 1). For example, when compared with Model 1, Model 2 proves to be a significant loss in fit ($\Delta\chi^2/\Delta df = 28/8$, $p < .001$), indicating that removing the cross-lagged regressions from the husband to the wife may not be reasonable. Model 3, however, presents a negligible worsening in fit as compared with Model 1 ($\Delta\chi^2/\Delta df = 5/8$, $p > .05$), suggesting a lack of cross-lagged regressions from the wife to the husband. Model 4 tests the hypothesis of no between-person influences in these data and this idea can be accurately rejected ($\Delta\chi^2/\Delta df = 33/16$, $p < .001$). To summarize, from these analyses

TABLE 4.3 Parameter Estimates From WNFS Dynamic Factor Model for Husband

Estimate	Lag 0 λ_0	Lag 0 θ_ε	Lag 1 λ_1	Lag 2 λ_2	Lag 3 λ_3
Interest (F1)					
interested	.74	.33	.16	.26	.14
excited	.74	.39	.25	$-.01^{ns}$	.12
inspired	.57	.53	.15	.37	$.04^{ns}$
strong	.56	.52	.28	.27	$-.11$
determined	.70	.35	.24	.29	.11
enthusiastic	.82	.26	.21	.15	$.03^{ns}$
active	.56	.56	.30	.18	$-.18$
proud	.63	.54	.13	.16	$.09^{ns}$
Alertness (F4)					
alert	.25	.50	.21	.35	.47
attentive	.58	.42	.43	.10	.11
jittery	.61	.39	.26	.20	.23
Distress (F2)					
distressed	.33	.58	.43	.33	$-.15$
nervous	.15	.44	.45	.43	.41
scared	.36	.20	.49	.53	.40
afraid	.32	.12	.57	.53	$-.44$
Hostility (F3)					
irritable	.86	.10	.38	$-.22$	$.01^{ns}$
ashamed	.50	.72	.11	$-.01^{ns}$	.11
upset	.71	.39	.17	.20	$-.24$
guilty	.66	.56	.10	$-.10$	$-.01^{ns}$
hostile	.81	.31	.22	$-.10$	$-.05^{ns}$

Shock correlations	F1	F2	F3	F4
F1	1.00			
F2	.66	1.00		
F3	$-.39$	$-.41$	1.00	
F4	$-.43$	$-.50$	.53	1.00

Note: ns = parameter not accurately estimable (t value < 1.96; $p > .05$). Invariance constraints were invoked for the correlations between uniquenesses of the same variable for each lag.

it seems reasonable to conclude that unidirectional influences exist in the affective relationships between these two individuals over time. The negative affect of one person (i.e., the husband) is a process driving the dyadic system over time.

The parameter estimates from Model 3 are displayed in table 4.5. Whereas the variables comprising the positive affect factor are the same for both individuals, one variable representing negative affect is different across persons. Despite similarities in the configuration of the positive affect factor, both persons present differences in the loadings. For the wife, the variables with highest loadings on this factor are *excited* and *enthusiastic* ($\lambda_0 = .80$ and .78).

For the husband, in contrast, the variables with highest loadings are *interested* and *enthusiastic* ($\lambda_0 = .75$ and .81). With regard to negative affect, the variables with largest loadings for the wife are *upset* and *distress* ($\lambda_0 = .83$ and .65), whereas for the husband they are *hostile* and *irritable* ($\lambda_0 = .78$ and .85), although, overall, this factor seems to be more similar across persons. Further illustration of this similarity is the moderate between-persons residual correlation ($r = .56$). In contrast, the equivalent correlation for positive affect is much smaller ($r = .23$). For the husband, the residual correlation between positive and negative affect is also moderate and negative ($r = -.38$), whereas this correlation is negligible for the wife ($r = .02$, $p > .05$).

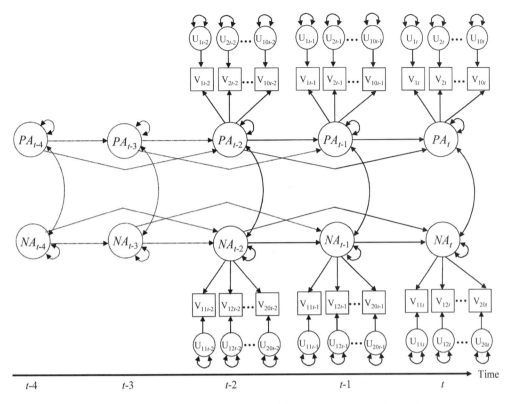

Figure 4.5 Direct autoregressive factor score (DAFS) model. V = manifest variables, PA = positive affect latent factor; NA = negative affect latent factor, U = uniquenesses. The subscript t denotes the lag, where t = Lag 0, t − 1 = Lag 1, and so on. Although not shown in this figure, autocorrelations of uniquenesses of the same variable across lags are estimated.

Note the lagged effects: auto- and cross-lagged regressions or coupling effects. For the wife, the perceptible lag effects are sparse and operate through one lag only. Positive affect is directly influenced by lag effects from positive affect (β_{t-1} = .33) and negative affect (β_{t-1} = .28), both at Lag 1. For the husband, however, there are more lag effects and they last two lags. For example, positive affect is influenced by positive and negative affect at Lag 1 (β_{t-1} = .15 and −.18, respectively) and by positive affect at Lag 2 (β_{t-2} = .27). Similarly, negative affect manifests lag effects from negative affect at both lags (β_{t-1} = .32 and β_{t-2} = −.21). The negative sign of the Lag 2 regression coefficient is in line with results of table 4.3 (i.e., negative Lag 2 loadings of the negative affect factor) and suggests a process that reverses after 2 days. Last, there are two coupling effects from the husband's negative affect to the wife that operate at Lag 1: a positive path to her negative

affect (γ_{t-1} = .40) and a negative path to her positive affect (γ_{t-1} = −.42). These coupling effects indicate that the wife's positive affect on a given day is negatively influenced by her husband's negative affect the day before. Similarly, her negative affect is positively influenced by her husband's negative affect the day before. No coupling effects are apparent from the husband's positive affect or in the opposite interpersonal direction (i.e., from the wife to the husband). Thus, the husband's negative affect here is the agent influencing the wife's subsequent emotional experience or, in other words, the leading indicator in this dynamic system of affective relationships.

Discussion

It is my goal in this chapter to present a method for modeling affective processes in dyadic in-

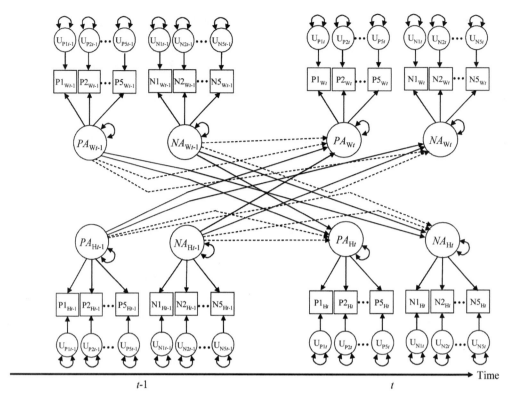

Figure 4.6 Concurrent and Lag 1 structure of the dyadic dynamic factor model. $P_1, P_2, \ldots P_5 =$ manifest positive affect variables; $N_1, N_2, \ldots N_5 =$ manifest negative affect variables; PA and $NA =$ latent positive and negative factors, U = uniquenesses. The subscripts W and H denote wife and husband, respectively. The subscript t denotes the lag, where $t =$ Lag 0, $t - 1 =$ Lag 1, and so on. For clarity purposes, only autoregressions (dashed lines) and cross-lagged regressions (or coupling, effects, solid lines) are shown. Concurrent factor-residual correlations and autocorrelations of uniquenesses are also estimated in this model.

teractions. To illustrate this possibility, I have applied dynamic factor models to time series data consisting of one couple's daily ratings of affect. These models yielded valuable information about the affective structure of each person and its daily fluctuation over time, and about the dynamics underlying the couple's affective relationship.

This chapter follows closely the analyses implemented by Ferrer and Nesselroade (2003) but with several important differences. For example, I present here results from dynamic factor models fitted to each member of the dyad separately. Furthermore, the dyadic dynamic analyses are fitted directly to items of the PANAS, as opposed to parcels created from all the items. Interestingly, the results from the dyadic dynamic analyses are equivalent in both cases.

Both approaches yielded one-lagged coupling effects from the husband's negative affect to the wife's positive and negative affect.

Although there are various techniques to analyze dyadic data, the use of dynamic factor models allows researchers to address unique questions. These models can be used with very small sample sizes, as was the case here. Moreover, in the case of multivariate data in which the factor structure of the data is pertinent to the research question, these models can describe intra- and interindividual variability that includes factor structure. Finally, the dynamic factor models allow identification of the temporal organization (i.e., lags) of dyadic interrelations and the nature of such relations (i.e., unidirectional or directional relations), with an emphasis on processes and dynamics (Browne & Nesselroade, 2005). The

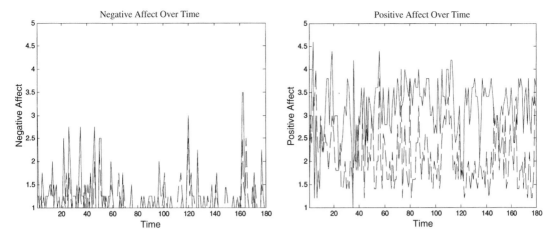

Figure 4.7 Positive and negative affect over time for each person. Dashed line represents the variable for the person. Solid line represents the variable for the husband.

model applied here is a multivariate time series with latent variables that have a lagged structure. Other techniques exist to investigate other questions related to dyadic interactions. For example, multilevel techniques can be used to distinguish among actor, partner, and interaction effects (Campbell & Kashy, 2002; Kashy & Kenny, 2000; Kenny, Mannetti, Pierro, Livi, & Kashy, 2002). Furthermore, such techniques can be combined with hierarchical dyadic models to address longitudinal data issues (Newsom, 2002; Raudenbush, Brennan, & Barnett, 1995). Even more pertinent to the study of processes in dyadic interactions is the use of nonlinear dynamics models. These models allow the specification of complex dynamics and can be fitted to longitudinal dyadic data using, for example, state space models via Kalman filtering procedures (e.g., Chow, Ferrer, & Nesselroade, in press).

The results from the analyses reported in this chapter demonstrate the utility of dynamic factor models to examine questions about dyadic interactions. These results indicate the importance of considering the two members of the dyad as agents or endogenous forces in the dynamics of the dyadic system. The application described here, however, is only one of many possibilities and can be extended to address alternative questions and to include more complex analyses. One logical extension of the current analyses is the application of the dynamic factor models to multiple dyads. A reasonable approach in that case would be to examine the affective process for each dyad separately. The covariance matrices of all dyads could then be tested for homogeneity and pooled across those groups of dyads with similar covariance structure (Nesselroade & Molenaar, 1999). Finally, the dynamic factor

TABLE 4.4 Goodness-of-Fit Indices of the PFA Dyadic Dynamic Factor Model (Two-Lag Structure)

Model	χ^2	df	RMSEA	(p-Close Fit)	CFI	IFI	$\Delta\chi^2/df$
Model $1_{\text{Couplings W} \leftrightarrow \text{H}}$	1335	952	.034	1.00	.92	.93	—
Model $2_{\text{Couplings W} \rightarrow \text{H}}$	1363	960	.034	1.00	.92	.93	$28/8^{**}$
Model $3_{\text{Couplings W} \rightarrow \text{H}}$	1340	960	.033	1.00	.93	.94	$5/8^{ns}$
Model $4_{\text{No Couplings}}$	1368	968	.033	1.00	.92	.93	$33/16^{**}$

Note: W = wife, H = husband. All models are fitted to the same covariance matrix of Lag 2 containing 60 manifest variables (10 manifest variables per person at Lags 0, 1, and 2).

$^{**}p < .01$. ns = not significant.

TABLE 4.5 Parameter Estimates From the PFA Dyadic Dynamic Factor Model (Model 3)

Estimate	Wife		Husband	
Factor loading	λ_0 $(t{-}v)$	θ_ε $(t{-}v)$	λ_0 $(t{-}v)$	θ_ε $(t{-}v)$
interested	.40 (7)	.81 (12)	.75 (18)	.32 (8)
excited	.80 (16)	.23 (4)	.69 (15)	.46 (9)
inspired	.35 (6)	.86 (13)	.56 (12)	.65 (11)
enthusiastic	.78 (16)	.26 (5)	.81 (20)	.23 (6)
proud	.43 (7)	.74 (11)	.63 (14)	.51 (9)
upset	.83 (18)	.17 (3)	.60 (12)	.59 (10)
hostile	.60 (12)	.58 (9)	.78 (19)	.31 (8)
irritable	.29 (5)	.89 (14)	.85 (22)	.17 (85)
ashamed	.33 (5)	.88 (14)	.46 (8)	.74 (12)
distressed/guilty	.65 (13)	.49 (9)	.62 (13)	.57 (11)
Autoregressions Lag 1	β_{W-1} $(t{-}v)$		β_{H-1} $(t{-}v)$	
pos aff → pos aff	.33 (4)		.15 (3)	
pos aff → neg aff	−.09 (1)		−.10 (1)	
neg aff → pos aff	.28 (2)		−.18 (2)	
neg aff → neg aff	−.15 (1)		.32 (4)	
Autoregressions Lag 1	β_{W-2} $(t{-}v)$		β_{H-2} $(t{-}v)$	
pos aff → pos aff	.13 (1)		.27 (3)	
pos aff → neg aff	−.12 (1)		−.08 (1)	
neg aff → pos aff	.01 (0)		.05 (1)	
neg aff → neg aff	.00 (0)		−.21 (3)	
Coupling effects Lag 1	γ_{W1-1} $(t{-}v)$		γ_{H1-1} $(t{-}v)$	
pos aff → pos aff	−.18 (1)		0 (=)	
pos aff → neg aff	−.08 (1)		0 (=)	
neg aff → pos aff	−.42 (3)		0 (=)	
neg aff → neg aff	.40 (3)		0 (=)	
Coupling effects Lag 2	γ_{W1-2} $(t{-}v)$		γ_{H1-2} $(t{-}v)$	
pos aff → pos aff	.02 (0)		0 (=)	
pos aff → neg aff	.06 (1)		0 (=)	
neg aff → pos aff	.05 (0)		0 (=)	
neg aff → neg aff	.07 (0)		0 (=)	
Residual correlations (ρ_0)	PA_W	NA_W	PA_H	NA_H
pos aff (wife)	—			
neg aff (wife)	.02 (0)	—		
pos aff (husband)	.23 (3)	−.06 (1)	—	
neg aff (husband)	.05 (1)	.56 (10)	−.38 (5)	—

Note: = indicates a fixed parameter; $t{-}v = T$ value. For each person, invariance constraints were invoked for the factor loadings and uniquenesses across the three lags, regressions for each lag, and correlations between uniquenesses of the same variable for each lag.

models could then be fitted to each of these groups of dyads.

Other issues that can be addressed with these models are, for example, the influence of external variables on the affective processes of the dyad. Some of these external variables could produce a shock to the dyadic system (having a baby or finding out about an affair, as examples of positive and negative shocks). Examining how the dyad recovers from such a shock would be informative about the mechanisms underlying the dyad's dynamics. Methodological extensions of the analyses presented in this chapter include, for example, models that combine dynamics with growth and decline (Ferrer & McArdle, 2003, 2004; McArdle, 2001; McArdle & Hamagami, 2001) and models for intra- and interindividual variability with nonstationary data, either from a modeling perspective (du Toit & Browne, 2001; Hershberger et al., 1996; Molenaar, De Gooijer, & Schmitz, 1992) or using nonparametric computational approaches (Hsieh, Ferrer, & Chen, 2006a, 2006b). Finally, in light of Browne's recent papers (Browne & Zhang, 2005, in press), more work is needed to investigate the likelihood function for lagged covariance matrices.

In sum, this chapter describes possibilities for using dynamic factor models to study dyadic interactions. These models place a special emphasis on processes; that is, phenomena that occur as a function of time. In the case of dyadic relations, such a function is crucial if one wants to understand interactions that unfold over time and that involve lagged sequences. It has been my intention in this chapter to demonstrate how dynamic factor models can capture such dynamic processes.

Acknowledgments   I am grateful to Michael Browne, Aki Hamagami, Jack McArdle, John Nesselroade, Liz Saft, Dave Sbarra, and Keith Widaman for their comments and suggestions offered at different stages of this work. Support in the preparation of this chapter was provided by grant BCS-05-27766 from the National Science Foundation.

Notes

1. Browne and Zhang (2005, in press) have recently pointed out that Wishart maximum likelihood estimates are not justified for lagged covariance matrices because the $z_{(t)}$ are not independently distributed. They argue that the resulting likelihood function is not adequate and, instead, they suggest ordinary least squares as a simple and robust estimation procedure. In particular, they say, "No likelihood function is available for lagged covariance matrices under an arbitrary stationary Gaussian process. Consequently maximum likelihood estimates are not available unless a different approach based on the raw data is used. A Wishart likelihood function is sometimes used for lagged covariance matrices but this is inappropriate since the underlying assumption of independent observations is violated. The usual properties of appropriate maximum likelihood estimates and associated goodness of fit test statistics are therefore not applicable" (Browne & Zhang, 2005, p. 3). For this purpose, they have developed DyFA, a freely available software program to fit dynamic factor analysis to lagged correlation matrices.

2. Nesselroade et al. (2002) use the term "factor" in this model in line with traditional factor analysis literature. Browne and Nesselroade (2005) and Browne and Zhang (in press), however, use the term "random shocks," more along the lines of time series literature.

3. Ferrer and Nesselroade (2003) used item parcels that considered all 20 items in the PANAS scale. For each person they included three parcels for positive affect and three parcels for negative affect. Results from their analyses using the item parceling approach are comparable to the ones presented in this section.

References

Ainsworth, M. D. S. (1973). The development of infant-mother attachment. In B. M. Caldwell & H. N. Ricciuti (Eds.), *Review of child development research* (Vol. 3, pp. 1–94). Chicago: University of Chicago Press.

Anderson, T. W. (1963). The use of factor analysis in the statistical analysis of multiple time series. *Psychometrika, 28*, 1–25.

Aron, A., & Aron, E. N. (1997). Self-expansion motivation and including other in the self. In S. Duck (Ed.), *Handbook of personal relationships: Theory, research, and interventions* (2nd ed., pp. 251–270). New York: Wiley.

Beebe, B., & Lachmann, F. M. (1998). Co-constructing inner and relational processes: Self- and mutual regulation in infant research and adult treatment. *Psychoanalytic Psychology, 15*, 480–516.

Bowlby, J. (1982). *Attachment and loss: Vol. 1. Attachment* (2nd ed.). New York: Basic Books. (Original work published 1969)

Brillinger, D. R. (1975). *Time series: Data analysis and theory.* New York: Holt, Rinehart and Winston.

Browne, M. W., & Nesselroade, J. R. (2005). Representing psychological processes with dynamic factor models: Some promising uses and extensions of ARMA time series models. In A. Maydeu-Olivares & J. J. McArdle (Eds.), *Advances in psychometrics: A festschrift to Roderick P. McDonald* (pp. 415–451). Mahwah, NJ: Erlbaum.

Browne, M. W., & Zhang, J. R. (2005). User's guide to DyFA: Dynamic factor analysis of lagged correlation matrices, version 2.03 [Computer software and manual]. Retrieved from http://quantrm2.psy.ohio-state.edu/browne/

Browne, M. W., & Zhang, J. R. (in press). Developments in the factor analysis of individual time series. In R. C. MacCallum & R. Cudeck (Eds.), *Factor analysis at 100: Historical developments and future directions.* Mahwah, NJ: Erlbaum.

Campbell, L., & Kashy, D. A. (2002). Estimating actor, partner, and interaction effects for dyadic data using PROC MIXED and HLM: A guided tour. *Personal Relationships, 9*, 327–342.

Cattell, R. B. (1963). The structuring of change by P-technique and incremental R-technique. In C. W. Harris (Ed.), *Problems in measuring change* (pp. 167–198). Madison: University of Wisconsin Press.

Cattell, R. B., Cattell, A. K. S., & Rhymer, R. M. (1947). P-technique demonstrated in determining psychophysical source traits in a normal individual. *Psychometrika, 12,* 267–288.

Chow, S.-M., Ferrer, E., & Nesselroade, J. R. (in press). An unscented Kalman filter approach to the estimation of nonlinear dynamical systems models. *Multivariate Behavioral Research.*

Cowan, C. P., & Cowan, P. A. (2000). *When partners become parents: The big life change for couples.* Mahwah, NJ: Erlbaum.

Diamond, L. M., & Aspinwall, L. G. (2003). Emotion regulation across the life span: An integrative perspective emphasizing self-regulation, positive affect, and dyadic processes. *Motivation and Emotion, 27,* 125–156.

du Toit, H. C., & Browne, M. W. (2001). The covariance structure of a vector ARMA time series. In R. Cudeck, S. Du Toit, & D. Sörbom (Eds.), *Structural equation modeling: Present and future* (pp. 279–314). Lincolnwood, IL: Scientific Software International.

Engle, R., & Watson, M. (1981). A one-factor multivariate time series model of metropolitan wage rates. *Journal of the American Statistical Association, 76,* 774–781.

Feeney, J. A. (1999). Adult romantic attachment and couple relationships. In J. Cassidy & P. R. Shaver (Eds.), *Handbook of attachment: Theory, research, and clinical applications* (pp. 355–377). New York: Guilford.

Felmlee, D. H., & Greenberg, D. F. (1999). A dynamic systems model of dyadic interaction. *Journal of Mathematical Sociology, 23,* 155–180.

Ferrer, E., & McArdle, J. J. (2003). Alternative structural models for multivariate longitudinal data analysis. *Structural Equation Modeling, 10,* 493–524.

Ferrer, E., & McArdle, J. J. (2004). An experimental analysis of dynamic hypotheses about cognitive abilities and achievement from childhood to early adulthood. *Developmental Psychology, 40,* 935–952.

Ferrer, E., & Nesselroade, J. R. (2003). Modeling affective processes in dyadic relations via dynamic factor analysis. *Emotion, 3,* 344–360.

Fogel, A. (1992). Movement and communication in human infancy: The social dynamics of development. *Human Movement Science, 11,* 387–423.

Geweke, J. F. (1977). The dynamic factor analysis of economic time-series models. In D. Aigner & A. Goldberger (Eds.), *Latent variables in socioeconomic models* (pp. 365–384). Amsterdam: North-Holland Publishing Company.

Geweke, J. F., & Singleton, K. J. (1981). Maximum likelihood "confirmatory" factor analysis of economic time series. *International Economic Review, 22,* 37–54.

Gottman, J. M. (1980). *Marital interaction: Experimental investigations.* New York: Academic Press.

Gottman, J. M. (1998). Psychology and the study of the marital processes. *Annual Review of Psychology, 49,* 169–197.

Hatfield, E., Caccioppo, J. T., & Rapson, R. L. (1994). *Emotional contagion: Cambridge studies in emotion and social interaction.* Cambridge, UK: Cambridge University Press.

Hazan, C., & Shaver, P. R. (1987). Romantic love conceptualized as an attachment process. *Journal of Personality and Social Psychology, 52,* 511–524.

Hershberger, S. L., Corneal, S. E., & Molenaar, P. C. M. (1994). Dynamic factor analysis: An application to emotional response patterns underling daughter/father and stepdaughter/stepfather relationships. *Structural Equation Modeling, 2,* 31–52.

Hershberger, S. L., Molenaar, P. C. M., & Corneal, S. E. (1996). A hierarchy of univariate and multivariate structural times series models. In G. A. Marcoulides & R. E. Schumacker (Eds.), *Advanced structural equation modeling: Issues and techniques* (pp. 159–194). Mahwah, NJ: Erlbaum.

Hofer, M. (1984). Relationships as regulators: A psychobiologic perspective on bereavement. *Psychosomatic Medicine, 46,* 183–197.

Holtzman, W. H. (1963). Statistical models for the study of change in the single case. In C. W. Harris (Ed.), *Problems in measuring change* (pp. 19–211). Madison: University of Wisconsin Press.

Hooker, K., Nesselroade, D. W., Nesselroade, J. R., & Lerner, R. M. (1987). The structure of intraindividual temperament in the context of mother-child dyads: P-technique factor analyses of short-term change. *Development Psychology, 23,* 332–346.

Hsieh, F., Ferrer, E., & Chen, S. (2006a). *Dyadic dynamics I: Exploring nonstationarity of intra- and inter-individual affective processes via hierarchical segmentation and stochastic small-world network (SSWN).* Manuscript submitted for publication.

Hsieh, F., Ferrer, E., & Chen, S. (2006b). *Dyadic dynamics II: Computations of algorithmic complexity of dyadic dynamics and its synthesis via hierarchical segmentation.* Manuscript submitted for publication.

Immink, K. (1986). *Parameter estimation in Markov models and dynamic factor analysis.* Doctoral dissertation, University of Utrecht, Utrecht.

Kashy, D. A., & Kenny, D. A. (2000). The analysis of data from dyads and groups. In H. T. Reiss & C. M. Judd (Eds.), *Handbook of research methods in social psychology* (pp. 451–477). New York: Cambridge University Press.

Kelley, H. H., & Thibaut, J. W. (1978). *Interpersonal relations: A theory of interdependence.* New York: Wiley.

Kenny, D. A., Mannetti, L., Pierro, A., Livi, S., & Kashy, D. A. (2002). The statistical analysis of data from small groups. *Journal of Personality and Social Psychology, 83,* 126–137.

Larson, R. W., & Almeida, D. M. (1999). Emotional transmission in the daily lives of families: A new paradigm for studying family process. *Journal of Marriage and the Family, 61,* 5–20.

McArdle, J. J. (1982). *Structural equation modeling of an individual system: Preliminary results from "A case study of alcoholism."* Unpublished manuscript, University of Denver, Psychology Department.

McArdle, J. J. (2001). A latent difference score approach to longitudinal dynamic analysis. In R. Cudeck, S. Du Toit, & D. Sörbom (Eds.), *Structural equation modeling: Present and future* (pp. 341–380). Lincolnwood, IL: Scientific Software International.

McArdle, J. J., & Hamagami, F. (2001). Linear dynamic analyses of incomplete longitudinal data. In L. Collins & A. Sayer (Eds.), *New methods for the analysis of change* (pp. 139–175). Washington, DC: American Psychological Association.

Mikulincer, M., & Shaver, P. R. (2003). The attachment behavioral system in adulthood: Activation, psychodynamics, and interpersonal processes. In M. Zanna (Ed.), *Advances in experimental social psychology* (Vol. 35). New York: Academic Press.

Mikulincer, M., Shaver, P. R., & Pereg, D. (2003). Attachment theory and affect regulation: The dynamics, development, and cognitive consequences of attachment-related strategies. *Motivation and Emotion, 27,* 77–102.

Minuchin, S. (1984). *Families and family therapy.* Cambridge, MA: Harvard University Press.

Mitteness, L. S., & Nesselroade, J. R. (1987). Attachment in adulthood: Longitudinal investigation of mother-daughter affective interdependencies by P-technique factor analysis. *Southern Psychologist, 3,* 37–44.

Molenaar, P. C. M. (1985). A dynamic factor model for the analysis of multivariate time series. *Psychometrika, 50,* 181–202.

Molenaar, P. C. M., De Gooijer, J. G., & Schmitz, B. (1992). Dynamic factor analysis of nonstationary multivariate time series. *Psychometrika, 57,* 333–349.

Molenaar, P. C. M., & Nesselroade, J. R. (2001). Rotation in the dynamic factor modeling of multivariate stationary time series. *Psychometrika, 66,* 99–107.

Nesselroade, J. R., & Baltes, P. B. (Eds.). (1979). *Longitudinal research in the study of behavior and development.* New York: Academic Press.

Nesselroade, J. R., McArdle, J. J., Aggen, S. H., & Meyers, J. M. (2002). Alternative dynamic factor models for multivariate time-series analyses. In D. M. Moscowitz & S. L. Hershberger (Eds.), *Modeling intraindividual variability with repeated measures data: Advances and techniques* (pp. 235–265). Mahwah, NJ: Erlbaum.

Nesselroade, J. R., & Molenaar, P. C. M. (1999). Pooling lagged covariance structures based on short, multivariate time-series for dynamic factor analysis. In R. H. Hoyle (Ed.), *Statistical strategies for small sample research* (pp. 224–251). Newbury Park, CA: Sage.

Newsom, J. T. (2002). A multilevel structural equation model for dyadic data. *Structural Equation Modeling, 9,* 431–447.

Pipp, S., & Harmon, R. J. (1987). Attachment as regulation: A commentary. *Child Development, 58,* 648–652.

Raudenbush, S. W., Brennan, R. T., & Barnett, R. C. (1995). A multivariate hierarchical model for studying psychological change within married couples. *Journal of Family Psychology, 9,* 161–174.

Rusbult, C. E., & Van Lange, P. A. M. (1996). Interdependence processes. In E. T. Higgins & A. W. Kruglanski (Eds.), *Social psychology: Handbook of basic principles* (pp. 564–596). New York: Guilford.

Sbarra, D. A., & Ferrer, E. (in press). The structure and process of emotional experience following non-marital relationship dissolution: Dynamic factor analyses of love, anger, and sadness. *Emotion.*

Schore, A. N. (2000). Attachment and the regulation of the right brain. *Attachment and Human Development, 2,* 23–47.

Shaver, P. R., & Mikulincer, M. (2002). Attachment-related psychodynamics. *Attachment and Human Development, 4,* 133–161.

Shifren, K., Hooker, K., Wood, P., & Nesselroade, J. R. (1997). Structure and variation of mood in individuals with Parkinson's disease: A dynamic factor analysis. *Psychology and Aging, 12,* 328–339.

Surra, C. A., & Longstreth, M. (1990). Similarity of outcomes, interdependence, and conflict in dating relationships. *Journal of Personality and Social Psychology, 59,* 1–16.

Thomson, A., & Bolger, N. (1999). Emotional transmission in couples under stress. *Journal of Marriage and the Family, 61,* 38–48.

Watson, D., Clark, L. A., & Tellegen, A. (1988). Development and validation of brief measures of positive and negative affect: The PANAS scales. *Journal of Personality and Social Psychology, 54,* 1063–1070.

Wood, P., & Brown, D. (1994). The study of intraindividual differences by means of dynamic factor models: Rationale, implementation, and interpretation. *Psychological Bulletin, 116,* 166–186.

III

Interindividual Differences:
Measurement Issues

5

Multivariate Statistical Strategies for Construct Validation in Positive Psychology

Fred B. Bryant, Scott P. King, and Colette M. Smart

After framing issues of measurement validity within the area of positive psychology, we review traditional statistical approaches and more recent multivariate strategies for assessing content, criterion, and construct validity. We then consider various multivariate statistical strategies positive psychologists can use to (a) discriminate subscales from one another within multidimensional measurement instruments and (b) relate measurement instruments to convergent and discriminant measures in construct validation. We conclude with an integrative empirical example that uses these multivariate statistical strategies to assess the construct validity of hope and optimism as distinct concepts in positive psychology.

Construct Validation in Positive Psychology

The emergence of positive psychology as a separate research domain (Seligman, 2002; Seligman & Csikszentmihalyi, 2000) has sparked renewed interest in identifying the core constructs of positive human experience. As a result, a dizzying array of new positive concepts and corresponding measurement instruments has sprung forth, encompassing a wide variety of emotions, affective processes, personality traits, and states of mind. Yet these new concepts sometimes seem similar to others already in the psychological literature.

Consider, for example, the following conceptual triads, each of which includes positive psychological constructs that would seem related to one another to some degree: (a) elation, gladness, and joy (Lindsay-Hartz, 1981); (b) awe (Keltner & Haidt, 2003), wonder (Packer, 2002), and inspiration (Thrash & Elliot, 2003); (c) mindfulness (Langer, 1989), insight (Goldstein, 1987), and self-transcendence (Kirk, Eaves, & Martin, 1999); (d) hope (Snyder, 2000), optimism (Scheier & Carver, 1985), and positive thinking (Scheier & Carver, 1993); (e) imagination (Osborn, 1957), anticipation (Bryant, 2003), and positive daydreaming (Langens & Schmalt, 2002); (f) absorption (Tellegen & Atkinson, 1974), flow (Csikszentmihalyi, 1990), and peak experience (Maslow, 1962); and (g) flourishing (Keyes &

Haidt, 2002), capitalizing (Langston, 1994), and savoring (Bryant, 1989). This list is just the tip of the ever-growing conceptual iceberg. Within each conceptual triad, should we consider these constructs to be distinct from one another or not? And how distinct are they?

Given the range of possible human experiences, the universe of constructs potentially related to positive psychology would seem endless. But is it? Where are the limits, and how can we determine them? How can researchers know whether the positive constructs they seek to measure and explore are really distinct enough from existing constructs to warrant investigation? How can researchers determine whether two instruments actually measure different concepts in positive psychology, or whether in fact both instruments tap the same thing? In general, how can positive psychologists empirically establish the limits of conceptual diversity and measurement breadth? This chapter presents a set of multivariate statistical methods that researchers in positive psychology can use to address these questions.

The Necessity of Adequate Preoperational Explication

If you want to determine whether a construct is distinct, you must first understand its meaning. Otherwise, there is no standard to use in deciding whether the conditions necessary for inferring the construct's presence exist in the first place (Bryant, 2000). Likewise, it is impossible to know whether one construct is different from another construct, unless you can clearly define both constructs. For example, is the concept of delight, as measured by one self-report instrument, conceptually distinct from glee, as measured by another instrument? Clearly, it depends on how you define these different terms.

Although this point may seem obvious, it serves to emphasize the absolute necessity of what has been termed *preoperational explication* (Cook & Campbell, 1979), or the a priori formulation of a clear and explicit definition of the underlying concept of interest. Before deciding how to measure a particular construct (i.e., at the preoperational stage), positive psychologists should carefully identify the key ingredients or necessary components that compose the construct, and should specify what distinguishes it from related but separate constructs. Otherwise, construct validation will be problematic.

Measurement Validity

At the heart of these issues lies the concept of test validity (Messick, 1980; Wainer & Braun, 1988), or what we will call *measurement validity* (Bryant, 2000)—that is, whether an instrument actually measures what it is intended to measure. Although others (e.g., Cronbach & Meehl, 1955) have termed this same notion *construct validity*, in this chapter we conceptualize measurement validity more broadly as consisting of three main components (see also McDonald, 1999): (a) *content validity*, the degree to which an instrument covers all relevant aspects of the conceptual or behavioral domain it is intended to measure; (b) *criterion validity*, the degree to which an instrument can be used to predict a relevant, external outcome (i.e., a criterion measure); and (c) *construct validity*, the degree of confidence one can have in labeling measurements in theory-relevant terms. These three broad aspects of measurement validity concern an instrument's thoroughness of measurement coverage, strength of predictive utility, and accuracy of conceptual meaning, respectively (Bryant, 2000). This tripartite conception of measurement validity is consistent with the model adopted in current testing standards and guidelines in psychology and education (American Educational Research Association, American Psychological Association, & National Council on Measurement in Education, 1985) and in personnel selection (Uniform Guidelines, 1978). For a fascinating account of the historical development of test validity, see Angoff (1988).

Assessing Content Validity

Traditionally, the content validity of an instrument has been evaluated by means of one's subjective impression in judging the degree to which the instrument's items cover the topics they are supposed to cover. This approach may involve "mild forms of quantification" (McDonald, 1999, p. 204), in which one computes the percentage of items matched to intended content domains or the percentage of intended domains not matched to items (see Hambleton, 1980). Thus, if a theorist defined the construct of "thriving" as a positive state in which individuals exhibit high self-esteem, are consistently optimistic, and find meaning in life, then an appropriate measure of thriving would need to include assessments of self-esteem, optimism, and meaning in order to have content validity. A narrower conceptual definition of "thriving" as being successful at one's career would require less breadth in content coverage.

A somewhat more rigorous approach to assessing the content validity of an instrument is to select a panel of judges based on their expertise in a given research area, and then use them to conduct an independent "confirmatory content validation" (McDonald, 1999). In this procedure, judges can be given formal conceptual definitions of the intended domains of coverage and then can be asked to sort an instrument's items into conceptual domains. To gauge content validity, researchers can then compute a variety of descriptive indices of interrater agreement (see Haynes, Richard, & Kubany, 1995). As a form of content analysis, however, such descriptive, impressionistic approaches have limited ability to test alternative hypotheses about the structure of an instrument systematically. As Nunnally (1978) noted, "inevitably content validity rests mainly on appeals to reason regarding the adequacy with which important content has been sampled" (p. 93).

Confirmatory factor analysis (CFA), in contrast, provides a more precise estimate of the degree to which necessary aspects of a construct are well represented within a particular measure (Bryant, 2000; Bryant & Yarnold, 1995). The notion of whether the conceptual components hypothesized to make up an instrument actually underlie people's responses to the instrument has been termed *factorial validity* or *structural validity* (Bryant, 2000). Structural validity can be considered a specific form of content validity. CFA is particularly well suited to evaluating the structural validity of measurement instruments.

Unidimensional Structural Validity

Researchers can use CFA in several ways to assess an instrument's structural validity. For a unidimensional instrument intended to assess a unitary construct, one can use CFA to impose a one-factor measurement model on responses to the instrument and then use the resulting goodness-of-fit statistics to gauge model adequacy. Good model fit would signify that the instrument reflects a single underlying construct as intended, and would support structural validity (Hoyle & Smith, 1994). Researchers rely on a variety of different fit statistics to judge a model's goodness of fit.

Some goodness-of-fit statistics—such as the root-mean-square error of approximation (RMSEA; Steiger, 1990), the standardized root-mean-square residual (SRMR; Jöreskog & Sörbom, 1996), and the goodness-of-fit index (GFI; Jöreskog & Sörbom, 1996)—are measures of absolute model fit. RMSEA reflects the size of the residuals that result when using the model to predict the data, adjusting for model complexity, with smaller values indicating better fit. According to Browne and Cudeck (1993), RMSEA < .05 represents close fit; RMSEA between .05 and .08 represents reasonably close fit; and RMSEA > .10 represents an unacceptable model. SRMR also reflects the size of the fitted residuals, with smaller values reflecting better model fit; Hu and Bentler (1998) recommended a cutoff value close to .08 for SRMR. Analogous to R^2 in multiple regression, GFI reflects the proportion of available variance-covariance information in the data that the given model explains, with larger GFI values representing better model fit. Bentler and Bonett (1980) recommended that measurement models have GFI values of at least .90. Other goodness-of-fit statistics—such as the nonnormed fit index (NNFI; Tucker & Lewis, 1973) and the comparative fit index (CFI; Bentler, 1990)—are measures of relative model fit. NNFI and CFI indicate how much better the given model fits the data relative to a null model, which assumes sampling error alone explains covariation among observed measures (i.e., no common variance exists among measured variables). Bentler and Bonett (1980) recommended that measurement models have relative fit indices of at least .90. One can also inspect the squared multiple correlations (R^2s) for the individual items in the one-factor CFA solution to determine the proportion of variance in each item that reflects the underlying construct. This approach provides an estimate of the reliability of each item as an indicator of the concept being measured (with lower R^2s reflecting instances of underrepresented content).

As a tool for assessing structural validity, CFA provides distinct advantages over exploratory factor analysis (EFA). CFA enables researchers to compare the goodness-of-fit of nested alternative measurement models systematically, using the likelihood ratio test (Bentler, 1995; Bollen, 1989), whereas model contrasts are more descriptive in EFA. CFA also allows researchers to examine parsimonious versions of factor models constraining items to load only on certain factors and not others, whereas EFA necessarily involves saturated models in which all items load on all factors. In addition, multigroup CFA permits researchers to test directly the degree to which structural validity generalizes across multiple samples, whereas such comparisons can be done only descriptively with EFA (Bryant & Yarnold, 1995).

Multidimensional Structural Validity

For a multidimensional instrument intended to assess multiple factors, one can use CFA to obtain likelihood-ratio tests (Bentler, 1995; Bollen, 1989) by contrasting the goodness-of-fit chi-square values (and accompanying degrees of freedom) of nested, competing measurement models representing alternative conceptualizations of the underlying construct: (a) one model representing the instrument's intended multidimensional structure (full structural validity); (b) another model representing a more parsimonious unidimensional structure in which all of the instrument's items are collapsed into a single factor (the absence of structural validity); and (c) other bidimensional or multidimensional models reflecting various combinations of two or more subscales into one (partial structural validity). The model with a significantly smaller chi-square value provides a superior goodness-of-fit. Within each intended factor, items' squared multiple correlations can again be used to identify specific aspects of the particular dimension that are inadequately sampled. One can also compare the mean, median, and standard deviation of R^2 across multiple factors, to evaluate the relative precision of content coverage across subscales. In these ways, researchers can use CFA to assess more precisely the degree to which a particular measurement instrument shows evidence of content validity.

Illustrating the use of CFA to evaluate multidimensional structural validity, Bryant (1989) investigated a four-factor model of perceived control for 15 items intended to distinguish beliefs about one's capacity to avoid negative outcomes, cope with negative outcomes, obtain positive outcomes, and savor positive outcomes. To assess the structural validity of this four-factor model, Bryant (1989) contrasted its goodness of fit in a sample of 524 undergraduates with the fit of seven simpler measurement models that embodied more parsimonious views on the structure of perceived control: (a) a one-factor model that assumed perceived control is

unidimensional; (b) a pair of two-factor models that assumed people assess personal control separately in relation to positive and negative experience, or in relation to outcomes and feelings in response to outcomes; (c) four three-factor models that represented various combinations of the four control beliefs (i.e., control over negative outcomes, negative feelings, and global positive experience; control over positive outcomes, positive feelings, and global negative experience; control over negative outcomes, positive outcomes, and global feelings; and control over negative feelings, positive feelings, and global outcomes). Supporting the multidimensionality of perceived control, each multifactor model fit the data significantly better than did the one-factor model; and supporting structural validity, the intended four-factor model provided the best fit to the data.

Assessing Criterion Validity

Typically, researchers have evaluated an instrument's criterion validity by determining the degree of statistical accuracy it provides in predicting scores on a well-accepted "gold standard" indicator of the particular concept in question (i.e., a criterion measure), or in discriminating groups of individuals known to differ on the underlying concept (i.e., criterion groups). Thus, a psychologist who developed a measure of "interest in positive psychology" might assess its criterion validity by using scores on the measure to predict the number of books or articles on positive psychology individuals have read, or to discriminate a group of positive psychologists from a group of depression researchers.

Criterion validation can take one of three different forms, depending on when the data for the criterion measure or groups were collected: *prospective* (criterion measured at a later time than the predictor), *concurrent* (criterion and predictor measured at the same time), or *retrospective* (criterion measured at an earlier time than the predictor). Compared to the other two forms of validation, prospective validation generally provides the strongest evidence concerning criterion validity, assuming the process of measuring the predictor could not reasonably be expected to influence the criterion (Anastasi, 1988). However, concurrent validation is far more common in the psychological literature, because of the reduced cost and greater convenience of gathering all data at once. Retrospective validation generally provides the weakest form of criterion validity, especially when the criterion is measured via respondent recall (due to the fact that knowledge of the present may distort recall). However, using archival records to assess the criterion retrospectively can reduce this problem (Webb, Campbell, Schwartz, Sechrest, & Grove, 1981).

Traditional Statistical Strategies

Traditionally, researchers have assessed the criterion validity of an instrument in relation to: (a) *criterion measures* by means of correlation coefficients (with a single predictor variable) or multiple regression analyses (with multiple predictor variables, or to include control variables), to examine the degree of association between scores on the instrument and scores on criterion measures; and (b) *criterion groups* by means of binary (two groups) or multinomial (three or more groups) logistic regression analysis or discriminant analysis (two or more groups), to examine the predictive utility of the instrument in differentiating the multiple groups. When using an attribute to discriminate multiple criterion groups, a more powerful statistical method is optimal data analysis (ODA; Soltysik & Yarnold, 1993; Yarnold & Soltysik, 2005), which identifies optimal cut scores for continuous predictors (or optimal decision rules for categorical predictors) and their exact probabilities, to achieve maximum classification accuracy. Advantages of ODA over traditional methods include its inherent ability to maximize classification accuracy, lack of distributional assumptions, and use of "jackknife" resampling procedures to test the expected cross-sample generalizability of results (Soltysik & Yarnold, 1993). In jackknife resampling, each observation is removed from the sample one at a time. An optimal model is obtained using the remaining subsample, and this model is used to classify the single removed observation. The classification results are stored and tabulated across all observations.

Structural Equation Modeling Approaches

Researchers can use structural equation modeling (SEM) in several ways to assess an instrument's criterion validity when the criterion is measured on a continuous, equal-interval scale. For a unidimensional instrument intended to assess a unitary construct, one can use SEM to represent the instrument and criterion measure as separate latent variables within the same measurement model, and then inspect the standardized covariance (i.e., Pearson correlation coefficient) between the two latent variables to determine the proportion of variance the instrument shares with the criterion measure. The advantage of this approach over traditional correlational analysis is that it disattenuates the correlation between scores on the instrument and scores on the criterion for the effects of unreliability (Hoyle & Smith, 1994; Judd, Jessor, & Donovan, 1986).

As an alternative, one can also use SEM to model the unitary construct underlying the instrument as an exogenous (predictor) latent variable (along with any additional predictors whose effects are to be controlled statistically) and the criterion measure as an endogenous (outcome) latent variable, and then regress the endogenous latent variable on the exogenous latent variable (and additional covariates). This latter approach provides both standardized and unstandardized regression coefficients for assessing the validity of the instrument as a predictor of the criterion measure, as well as the squared multiple correlation for structural equations (R^2), indicating the proportion of variance the exogenous latent variable explains in the endogenous latent variable. Unlike traditional multiple regression, this approach adjusts regression coefficients and squared multiple correlations for attenuation due to unreliability in the measured variables, and accommodates multiple criterion measures in a single structural model.

For a multidimensional instrument intended to assess a multifaceted construct, one can use SEM to represent the underlying construct as a set of correlated, exogenous latent variables, each representing a different dimension or factor of the instrument being validated. For a correlational analysis, the criterion measure can also be included as an additional exogenous latent variable in the same measurement model, and the factor intercorrelations can be examined to assess criterion validity. For a regression analysis, the endogenous criterion measure can be regressed as a latent variable onto these multiple exogenous predictors also modeled as latent variables, to obtain both standardized and unstandardized regression coefficients for each of the instrument's subscales, as well as an overall squared multiple correlation for the criterion variable. When the correlations among the subscales of a multidimensional instrument are moderate to high, the regression approach provides an advantage over a multiconstruct measurement model, because it assesses the unique relation between each subscale and the criterion measure holding constant at their mean the predictive effects of the other subscales (Hoyle & Smith, 1994). Alternatively, if the instrument's multiple dimensions are moderately to strongly intercorrelated, then one can use SEM to construct a hierarchical measurement model for the instrument, consisting of a single, overarching, second-order exogenous "super" factor that influences responses to each of the endogenous first-order factors; and this global second-order factor can be used to predict the endogenous criterion measure (Bentler, 1995; Byrne, 1998; Jöreskog & Sörbom, 1996).

Assessing Construct Validity

Because notions of meaning and conceptual interpretation are by definition subjective, establishing the construct validity of a measure is inherently challenging. Because construct validation (i.e., the process of assessing or demonstrating that a particular measure assesses one concept rather than another) necessarily requires comparing and contrasting measures of similar or dissimilar concepts, more techniques exist for assessing construct validity than for assessing any other form of measurement validity, and these techniques are generally more complex. The task of construct validation is further complicated by the fact that it requires researchers to identify a network of key constructs associated with the particular concept or phenomenon of interest, and to explicate the pattern of interrelationships that should exist among them. Such a broadly integrative theoretical framework is known as a *nomological net* (Cronbach & Meehl, 1955), and the issue of whether obtained data patterns match theoretical predictions is known as *nomological validity*. We distinguish among three main types of construct validity: incremental, convergent, and discriminant (see Bryant, 2000). Although each of these forms of construct validity can be examined separately, convergent and discriminant validity are more typically examined together in

the same data set; incremental validity is often considered to be a variant of both criterion and discriminant validity.

Incremental Validity

Incremental validity (Sechrest, 1963) concerns the degree to which a particular measure provides explanatory power over and above another measure in predicting a relevant criterion. This issue can be viewed as a special case of discriminant criterion validity, in which one evaluates the degree to which a particular measure provides unique information in predicting a criterion, after first considering one or more other measures. For example, if the presence of happiness is truly distinct from the absence of depression, then a measure of happiness should explain a statistically reliable amount of variance in predicting overall subjective well-being, after first controlling for the relationship between depression and overall subjective well-being. Otherwise, happiness would lack incremental validity in relation to depression as a predictor of subjective well-being.

Incremental validity is commonly evaluated by means of hierarchical stepwise multiple regression, where one tests the statistical significance of the increase in the proportion of variance explained in the dependent variable (i.e., R^2, the squared multiple correlation) when adding a particular predictor variable, over and above the other predictors already in the regression model. Alternatively, researchers can compute a squared partial correlation coefficient that reveals the strength of the bivariate relationship, after first removing from both variables the variance shared with other predictors. For example, Chang and D'Zurilla (1996) tested the incremental validity of positive problem orientation (i.e., a constructive, problem-solving cognitive set) in relation to optimism and positive affectivity in predicting adaptive problem-engagement coping. Hierarchical regression analysis revealed positive problem orientation added a significant proportion of variance in predicting problem-solving coping and cognitive restructuring above and beyond the effects of optimism and positive affectivity; and squared partial correlations indicated optimism and positive affectivity shared 27% and 30% of their variance, respectively, with positive problem-solving orientation. This incremental validity evidence supports the notion that positive problem-solving orientation does not merely reflect optimism or positive affectivity.

Convergent Validity

Convergent validity concerns the degree to which one particular measure of a construct relates to other measures of the same underlying construct. Measures that supposedly assess the same concept should relate highly to each other, if they are in fact valid measures of the same underlying construct. In the simplest bivariate case, researchers assess the convergent validity of an instrument in relation to a single measure of the same construct using a correlation coefficient or linear regression analysis. If this single measure represents the existing gold standard means of assessing the underlying concept, then this approach is really nothing more than criterion validation (DeVellis, 1991).

Although researchers use levels of statistical significance to determine whether one measure correlates (converges) with another, p values are a function of sample size, and they do not directly estimate effect size or the strength of association. A more informative index of effect size in this case is the squared correlation coefficient (r^2), which represents the proportion of variance the two measures share. According to Cohen (1988, pp. 79–80), $r = .1$ (or $r^2 = .01$) is a small effect; $r = .3$ (or $r^2 = .09$) is a medium-sized effect; and $r \geq .5$ (or $r^2 \geq .25$) is a large effect. In judging the degree of convergence between two measures, it is also useful to consider the proportion of variance that is unique to each measure ($1 - r^2$). Indeed, the ratio of common variance to unique variance can be used to interpret the degree of convergent validity. Note that $r = .71$ ($r^2 = .50$) represents a critical threshold, above which the two measures have more variance in common than each has uniquely, and $r = .82$ ($r^2 = .67$) signifies that the two measures are twice as convergent as divergent ($1 - r^2 = .33$).

However, using only a single measure to assess convergent validity has limitations. In particular, the variance two measures share can be a product not only of a common underlying construct, but also of a shared method of assessment (Campbell & Fiske, 1959). For example, one would expect a self-report measure of playfulness to correlate more strongly with other self-report measures of playfulness than with behavioral observations of playfulness. But un-

less one uses multiple methods of measurement, there is no way to disentangle trait variance from method variance. In addition, evidence concerning convergence with measures of the same construct is more interpretable when judged in relation to divergence from measures of related but conceptually distinct constructs (Campbell & Fiske, 1959; Cook & Campbell, 1979). This observation leads us logically to the second type of construct validity.

Discriminant Validity

Discriminant validity concerns the degree to which a particular measure of a given construct diverges from measures of related, but separate, constructs. Measures that supposedly assess different concepts should not relate too highly to each other, if they are in fact valid measures of different underlying constructs. Discriminant validity is sometimes referred to as divergent validity. In the simplest bivariate case, researchers use a correlation coefficient or linear regression to assess the discriminant validity of an instrument in relation to a single measure of a conceptually similar construct that should be distinct. As with convergent validity, the proportion of unique variance for the two measures ($1 - r^2$) provides an index of the degree of discriminant validity observed.

Traditional Statistical Strategies

As noted above, however, convergent and discriminant validity are more often evaluated in relation to one another, by including within the same study multiple criterion measures, some of which are hypothesized to show stronger relationships than others to the instrument being validated. Traditionally, researchers have tested these hypothesized patterns of association by "eyeballing" the resulting set of correlation coefficients, using the observed magnitudes of correlations and their associated levels of statistical significance to judge the particular instrument's construct validity. For example, a positive psychologist might test the construct validity of a new trait measure of "serenity" by seeing if its correlations with trait measures of calmness and tranquility were stronger (convergence) than its correlations with trait measures of elation and joy (discrimination). Likewise, when validating a multidimensional instrument, researchers typically develop a "nomological net" identifying key constructs associated with each subscale and formulate hypotheses about which particular subscales should relate more strongly to one or another of these key constructs. A classic traditional statistical strategy for assessing convergent and discriminant validity within the same study is Campbell and Fiske's (1959) set of evaluative criteria for interpreting patterns of association among multiple constructs measured in multiple ways in a so-called multitrait-multimethod matrix. Researchers should keep in mind that construct validation requires measures of convergent or discriminant constructs themselves to be valid indicators of these key constructs (Carmines & Zeller, 1978).

Problems With Traditional Approaches to Assessing Construct Validity

When examining patterns of correlation across multiple measures to assess convergent and discriminant validity, several cautions are noteworthy. First, as noted earlier, the correlation between two measures reflects not only the extent to which they share a common underlying construct, but also the extent to which they share a common method of assessment (Campbell & Fiske, 1959). Thus, construct validity evidence becomes suspect if the measures hypothesized to be convergent are assessed using the same method as the instrument being validated, whereas the measures hypothesized to be divergent are assessed using a different method. In this case, shared methods of assessment would be expected to boost convergent validity coefficients relative to discriminant validity coefficients, even if identical constructs were assessed in both cases.

Second, because unreliability in measurement attenuates (i.e., dilutes) the strength of observed correlations (Carmines & Zeller, 1978; McDonald, 1999), differences in the reliabilities of the measures included in construct validation can produce artifactual evidence of convergent and discriminant validity. An important tenet of classical test theory is that the maximum attainable correlation between two measures equals the square root of the product of their reliabilities (McDonald, 1999; Nunnally, 1978). Thus, if two different constructs were actually identical, but were measured using instruments with reliabilities of .8 and .7, scores on the two instruments would correlate only .75, (i.e., $\sqrt{.56}$)—spurious evidence that the two constructs share only slightly more than half of their variance ($r^2 = .56$).

Furthermore, if the measures selected to represent convergent constructs are more reliable than the measures selected to represent divergent constructs, then this fact alone would tend to produce the hypothesized pattern of correlations (Bollen, 1989). Consider a positive psychologist who assessed the construct validity of a new measure of perceived entitlement by correlating its scores with two criterion variables that had differential reliability. Imagine that the new measure of perceived entitlement had a reliability of .70, the first criterion measure of assertiveness had a reliability of .95, and the second criterion measure of extraversion had a reliability of .55. What results would emerge if the two criterion measures each in fact correlated perfectly with perceived entitlement? In this case, differential reliability in the criterion variables would produce an observed correlation of .82 between entitlement and assertiveness ($r^2 = .67$), but only .62 between entitlement and extraversion ($r^2 = .38$)—an apparent difference that provides spurious evidence of the construct validity of the entitlement measure.

In developing new instruments, positive psychologists should pay close attention to the reliabilities of the measures used in construct validation. In cases where reliability coefficients differ appreciably across measures, then they should compare results when adjusting validity correlations for attenuation due to unreliability. This correction for attenuation involves dividing the observed correlation by the square root of the product of the reliabilities of each measure to obtain a reliability-adjusted correlation (see Carmines & Zeller, 1978; McDonald, 1999). However, caution is necessary in applying this correction formula, because underestimates of reliability will overcorrect the observed correlation and make it larger than it should be (McDonald, 1999).

Reliability Assessment

As an index of internal consistency reliability for composite measures consisting of continuous-scale items, researchers most often use coefficient alpha (α; Cronbach, 1951; Guttman, 1945), which provides a lower bound on the proportion of total variance in test scores attributable to true score (i.e., the underlying concept) as opposed to measurement error when unit-weighting each item (McDonald, 1999; Nunnally, 1978). An alternative index of reliability is coefficient omega

(ω; McDonald, 1970, 1999), which estimates the ratio of true-score variance to total variance based on the observed relations between the individual items and the underlying construct (Bacon, Sauer, & Young, 1995). When composite measures are based on binary items, researchers typically use the generalization of coefficient alpha formulated by Kuder and Richardson (1937), known as K-R 20.

Yet there remains no agreement as to how low an instrument's reliability can be before it should be considered untrustworthy. Different psychometric writers have proposed different criteria in this regard. For example, Nunnally (1978) recommended .70 as a minimally acceptable value for coefficient alpha. Providing finer-grained advice, Kline (1998, p. 194) suggested that instruments with reliabilities below .50 should be avoided; reliabilities around .70 are adequate; values around .80 are very good; and values around .90 are excellent. Alternatively, DeVellis (1991, p. 85) proposed a series of ranges for judging reliability coefficients as unacceptable (<.60), undesirable (.60–.65), minimally acceptable (.65–.70), respectable (.70–.80), and very good (.80–.90), with coefficients much above .90 signifying the need to reduce the number of scale items. In general, .70 seems to be a reasonable cutoff value for minimally acceptable reliability. However, because coefficients of internal consistency increase as a function of the number of composite items, scales that consist of many items but that have only minimal reliability are in need of psychometric refinement (DeVellis, 1991; Streiner, 2003).

Besides the problem of differential reliability across measures, there are other major drawbacks to relying merely on visual inspection to establish convergent and discriminant validity. Namely, this eyeball approach: (a) is inherently subjective and allows one's expectations to shape interpretations of results via confirmatory bias; (b) is purely descriptive and provides no information about the likelihood that sampling error explains observed variation among correlations; (c) is prone to capitalize on chance by increasing the number of Type I (false positive) errors across multiple statistical tests; and (d) does not directly address the question of how closely the observed pattern of correlations matches the theoretically predicted pattern. To overcome these limitations, researchers need a more rigorous, multivariate approach for testing hypothesized differences in the size of correlations across multiple measures.

Comparing Correlated Correlation Coefficients

Along these lines, we recommend positive psychologists use a versatile, but underutilized, set of statistical methods developed by Meng, Rosenthal, and Rubin (1992) when comparing and contrasting correlations as a means of assessing construct validity. Extending earlier work by Dunn and Clark (1969) using Fisher's Z_r transformation, Meng et al.'s (1992) methods provide a powerful means of testing hypothesized patterns of convergence and divergence systematically among a set of correlated correlation coefficients. The logic of this general approach is as follows: "Just as researchers can construct contrasts to test the relative ordering of means [in ANOVA], they can equally construct contrasts to assess the relative ordering of correlation coefficients, even when those correlation coefficients are correlated with one another" (Westen & Rosenthal, 2003, p. 610).

Using Meng et al.'s (1992) approach, one first formulates a focused set of a priori hypotheses about the relative magnitude of correlations between the measure being validated and a set of competing criterion measures, and then translates these hypotheses into a set of orthogonal contrast weights that captures the expected pattern of interrelationships. One then applies these contrast weights to the Fisher r-to-z transformed values of the observed correlations in a set of hand-computed formulas (also using the median intercorrelation among the criterion measures, and the mean r^2 for the entire set of correlations), to obtain an overall Z test, which provides a one-tailed p value under the standard normal curve. A statistically significant Z value (i.e., $Z > 1.64$, $p < .05$) indicates that the observed pattern of correlations fits the hypothesized pattern. Meng et al. (1992, pp. 173–174) provide all necessary formulas, along with a worked example (see also Westen & Rosenthal, 2003, pp. 610–611). Although researchers can also use this approach simply to test whether one variable correlates more strongly with a second variable than with a third variable (Meng et al., 1992, p. 173), its greatest value is as a tool for assessing nomological validity within a larger set of variables, by testing focused, a priori hypotheses about convergent and discriminant validity.

As an illustrative example, albeit from the domain of negative psychology, Brockway, Carlson, Jones, and Bryant (2002) used Meng et al's computational methods to evaluate the convergent and discriminant validity of a new instrument containing separate subscales for assessing student cynicism toward policy, academic, social, and institutional facets of college experience. Because the Policy and Academic subscales involved specific frustrations about leadership and organizational issues, these researchers hypothesized that criterion measures of organizational cynicism and cynicism toward organizational change would each correlate more strongly with the Policy and Academic subscales than with the Social and Institutional subscales. For each criterion measure, testing this set of hypotheses involved a planned contrast of correlated correlation coefficients, applying orthogonal weights of $+1$, $+1$, -1, -1 to the correlations with the four respective cynicism subscales. Supporting the hypotheses, Policy and Academic cynicism correlated more strongly with the criterion measures of organization cynicism, $Z = 5.56$, $p < .0001$, and cynicism toward organizational change, $Z = 5.87$, $p < .0001$, than did Social and Institutional cynicism. Also confirming hypotheses, additional tests of discriminant validity revealed that Academic cynicism correlated more strongly with cumulative GPA across prior semesters, $Z = 2.41$, $p < .01$, and with subsequent GPA, $Z = 3.31$, $p < .001$, than did Policy, Social, and Institutional cynicism. In contrast to the simple visual inspection of correlations, Meng et al.'s (1992) statistical method provides a more systematic means of directly testing hypotheses about convergent and discriminant validity.

Indices of Construct Validity

Extending this approach as well as the work of Rosenthal, Rosnow, and Rubin (2000), Westen and Rosenthal (2003) have proposed two useful summary indices (i.e., correlation coefficients) for quantifying overall construct validity. These indices provide effect size estimates of the extent to which an observed pattern of correlations between the measure being validated and a set of criterion measures matches a theoretically predicted pattern of correlations. The first index of construct validity—the "alerting" correlation $(r_{\text{alerting-CV}})$—is the simple correlation between (a) the hypothesized pattern of correlations among the measure being validated and the criterion variables correlated with that measure, and (b) the observed pattern of correlations. This index reflects how well the predicted profile of

correlations accurately portrays the observed profile of correlations. The second index of construct validity—the "contrast" correlation $(r_{\text{contrast-CV}})$—combines information about (a) the median intercorrelation among the criterion variables, and (b) the absolute values of the correlations between the measure being validated and the criterion variables, to gauge the degree of correspondence between the contrast weights and individual scores. Westen and Rosenthal (2003) present formulas for computing these two indices and for determining 95% confidence intervals, as well as a worked example.

A limitation of Meng et al.'s (1992) approach is that it assumes all measures are equally reliable and ignores differences in reliability across the multiple measures being correlated. To overcome this limitation, researchers could first correct observed correlations for attenuation due to unreliability, before testing the degree to which the obtained pattern of correlations matches the hypothesized pattern. Alternatively, one can use Meng et al.'s (1992) methods to analyze factor intercorrelations from a CFA solution, to adjust for differences in measurement error.

Another potentially powerful approach to evaluating convergent and discriminant validity within the same study is the so-called multitrait-multimethod matrix (MTMMM; Campbell & Fiske, 1959), in which a researcher assesses two or more constructs (or traits) using two or more measurement techniques (or methods) and then analyzes the intercorrelations among these various measurements. A variety of different statistical approaches are currently available, many of which entail different forms of CFA. Readers interested in constructing and analyzing MTMMM data should consult Bagozzi (1993), Bryant (2003), Fiske (1982), Marsh and Grayson (1995), and Wothke (1996).

By providing an effective means of adjusting for differences in reliability across multiple measures, SEM offers a variety of other useful techniques for assessing convergent and discriminant validity within the same study. We now consider each of these approaches in turn, organizing them with respect to statistical strategies for: (a) discriminating different subscales from one another within multidimensional measurement instruments, (b) relating total scores for unidimensional instruments to convergent and divergent constructs, and (c) testing hypotheses about differential relationships between multiple constructs and multiple validational measures.

Discriminating Subscales From One Another Within a Multidimensional Instrument

The most basic form of discriminant validity for a multidimensional measurement instrument concerns the issue of whether the constituent subscales can be reliably differentiated from each other. These subscales show discriminant validity to the extent that multiple factors intercorrelate imperfectly (Judd et al., 1986). Thus, a crucial test of discriminant validity for a multidimensional instrument is the difference between the goodness-of-fit chi-square values of two competing measurement models (with accompanying difference in degrees of freedom): (a) the baseline multifactor model consisting of all of the instrument's constituent subscales, and (b) a nested comparison model consisting of a single global factor. Evidence that the multifactor model fits the data significantly better than the one-factor model supports the structural and discriminant validity of the multidimensional measurement model.

Illustrating this approach, Bryant, Yarnold, and Grimm (1996) used CFA to test the discriminant validity of a three-factor model for a subset of 27 items from the Affect Intensity Measure (AIM; Larsen, 1984) in relation to the one-factor model originally presumed to underlie this instrument. Relative to the one-factor model, the three-factor model fit the data of two large independent samples significantly better and explained more of the common variance in responses to the set of AIM items. These findings support the structural and discriminant validity of the multidimensional model of affect intensity.

Another assessment of discriminant validity within a multidimensional CFA model involves an omnibus test of the homogeneity of factor intercorrelations, or the question of whether the factors are equally related to one another. Although it is unnecessary for factors to be differentially interrelated in order for discriminant validity to exist, heterogeneity of factor intercorrelations supports the notion that the factors do not all measure the same facets of the construct. A test of the homogeneity of factor intercorrelations can be implemented by contrasting the goodness-of-fit chi-square values of two competing measurement models (with associated difference in degrees of freedom): (a) a baseline model consisting of the multidimensional model in question, and (b) a nested

version of the multidimensional model in which one imposes equality constraints (Bentler, 1995; Jöreskog & Sörbom, 1996) on the subdiagonal elements of the matrix of standardized factor variance-covariances. A significant difference between these two goodness-of-fit chi-square values signifies overall heterogeneity in factor intercorrelations, evidence supporting the discriminant validity of the instrument's subscales. Having rejected the null hypothesis of homogeneity, one can then use pairs of equality constraints to pinpoint subscales correlating more strongly, less strongly, or equivalently with one another.

Along these lines, Bryant (2003) developed a multidimensional self-report measure of beliefs about one's ability to savor positive experience, consisting of correlated subscales reflecting pleasure through anticipation, savoring the moment, and reminiscence. CFA results revealed the intended three-factor model fit the data of 415 undergraduates significantly better than a one-factor model, and tests of equality constraints indicated beliefs about one's ability to savor the moment have more to do with the perceived ability to savor through reminiscence than they do with the perceived ability to savor through anticipation. These results support the discriminant validity of the three-factor model.

Relating a Unidimensional Instrument to Convergent and Discriminant Measures

In evaluating a measurement instrument's convergent and discriminant validity in relation to external criterion measures, the simplest case involves a unidimensional instrument that provides a single, global total score, such as the Satisfaction With Life Scale (Diener, Emmons, Larsen, & Griffin, 1985) or the Rosenberg Self-Esteem Scale (Rosenberg, 1965). Evaluating construct validity becomes more complicated when the instrument being validated is multidimensional or when one wishes to distinguish multiple instruments from one another. Nevertheless, the logic and mechanics are largely the same as for a unidimensional instrument. Given a unidimensional instrument, the aim is to assess the degree to which the total score for the particular instrument converges with other measures of the same construct or diverges from measures of related, but separate, constructs. Three types of SEM analyses can be used to assess these issues statistically, depending on the nature of the relationships between the focal construct being validated and the constructs being used as convergent and discriminant criteria: (a) combining versus separating the focal construct and the criterion constructs in alternative measurement models; (b) comparing factor intercorrelations within a comprehensive measurement model; and (c) comparing regression coefficients when using the instrument to predict multiple criterion measures.

Combining Versus Separating the Focal Construct and the Criterion Constructs

One basic approach to testing the convergent or discriminant validity of a unidimensional instrument is to contrast the goodness-of-fit chi-square values of two alternative measurement models for the same set of measured variables: (a) a model that distinguishes between the instrument being validated and the criterion measures, and (b) a competing model that merges the instrument and the criterion measures into a single combined factor. To support convergent validity, the model that differentiates the instrument and the convergent criteria should fit the data no better than the model that merges the two sets of measures. To support discriminant validity, the model that differentiates the instrument and the discriminant criteria should fit the data significantly better than the model that merges the two sets of measures.

As an example, Bryant (1989) adopted this approach to evaluate the discriminant validity of self-report measures of the ability to savor positive outcomes and cope with negative outcomes, using criterion measures of subjective well-being (i.e., happiness and gratification) and subjective distress (i.e., strain and perceived vulnerability). If beliefs about savoring and coping are truly distinct from measures of well-being and distress, then a three-factor CFA model that includes separate factors for perceived control (with savoring and coping beliefs as indicators), subjective well-being, and subjective distress should fit the data significantly better than a two-factor model that includes (a) happiness, gratification, and savoring beliefs as indicators of subjective well-being, and (b) strain, perceived vulnerability, and coping beliefs as indicators of subjective distress. Supporting the discriminant validity of the measures of savoring and coping, the three-factor model fit the data significantly better than did the two-factor model.

Comparing Factor Intercorrelations

A second CFA approach to assessing the convergent and discriminant validity of a unidimensional instrument is to specify a measurement model that includes both the instrument being validated and the criterion measures, and then use equality constraints to test hypotheses about differences in the magnitude of specific factor intercorrelations. The key here is to constrain two correlations to be equal: (a) the correlation between the instrument and the convergent criteria, and (b) the correlation between the instrument and the discriminant criteria. With this approach, one once again uses the likelihood-ratio test (Bentler, 1995; Bollen, 1989) to contrast the goodness of fit of two competing measurement models, a baseline model containing no equality constraints and a nested model constraining two or more factor intercorrelations to be equal in magnitude. A statistically significant difference in the chi-square values of these two models indicates that the equality constraint(s) worsen model fit, demonstrates that the designated factor intercorrelations are in fact different, and supports convergent and discriminant validity.

To illustrate, Bryant and Baxter (1997) used this approach to assess the convergent and discriminant validity of two separate instruments designed to tap positive automatic cognition [the Automatic Thoughts Questionnaire–Positive (ATQ-P; Ingram & Wisnicki, 1988)] and negative automatic cognition (the Automatic Thoughts Questionnaire-Negative, ATQ-N; Hollon & Kendall, 1980) in relation to measures of positive and negative affect. Supporting the construct validity of both instruments, hierarchical CFA with equality constraints revealed that second-order positive automatic thought was more strongly correlated with positive affect than with negative affect, whereas second-order negative automatic thought was more strongly correlated with negative affect than with positive affect.

There is, however, an important caveat to keep in mind when using this approach to test differences in the strength of association as a form of convergent and discriminant validity. When comparing a factor intercorrelation that is expected be positive (e.g., ATQ-P score correlated with positive affect) with a factor intercorrelation that is expected to be negative (e.g., ATQ-P score correlated negative affect), it is essential to compare the absolute magnitude of these intercorrelations rather than allowing the difference in their signs to contribute to their apparent inequality. Whereas imposing a simple equality constraint confounds the magnitude and sign of the factor intercorrelations, imposing an algebraic constraint (Bentler, 1995; Jöreskog & Sörbom, 1996) overcomes this problem. Specifically, one can define the first factor intercorrelation to be equal to the second factor intercorrelation multiplied by −1, instead of simply equating the magnitude of the two factor intercorrelations. Alternatively, one can recode the one measure to be the same direction as the other, and then use an ordinary equality constraint to compare factor intercorrelations.

When more than two convergent or discriminant criterion measures are at hand, at least two options are available for testing whether the observed pattern of factor intercorrelations fits the theoretically predicted pattern. First, researchers can use Meng et al.'s (1992) procedure to apply a pattern of orthogonal weights to the factor intercorrelations, to embody the expected magnitudes of the correlations relative to one another. If the weights correspond to the observed pattern of correlations, then a statistically significant Z value emerges. With this approach, researchers can also use Westen and Rosenthal's (2003) correlational indices to quantify overall construct validity.

Alternatively, researchers can use CFA to impose algebraic constraints on multiple sets of factor intercorrelations, in order to test the validity of hypothesized differences in magnitude. For example, one can constrain the average magnitude of a group of factor intercorrelations to be equal to the average magnitude of another group of factor intercorrelations (Jöreskog & Sörbom, 1996). If the two groups of correlations are in fact different, then the model that contains the algebraic constraint should produce a significantly larger goodness-of-fit chi-square value when compared to a baseline model that contains no algebraic constraints. Note that Meng et al.'s (1992) approach yields a statistically significant result if the pattern of correlations matches the hypothesized set of orthogonal weights, and provides a one-tailed directional test of the hypothesized pattern of factor intercorrelations. The CFA approach, on the other hand, yields a statistically significant result if the correlational pattern violates the assumption of equality, and provides a two-tailed nondirectional test, unless one first confirms that the average magnitude of

the two sets of correlations are in the expected direction and then halves the p value for the likelihood-ratio test.

Comparing Regression Coefficients Using the Instrument to Predict Criterion Measures

A third strategy for assessing the construct validity of a unidimensional measurement instrument is to use SEM to represent the unidimensional instrument as an exogenous latent variable and the validational constructs as endogenous latent variables in a latent variable path model. Once again, one can use equality (or algebraic) constraints to test hypotheses about differences in the magnitude of unstandardized regression coefficients across multiple outcome measures via the likelihood-ratio test. The difference in the goodness-of-fit chi-square values (with accompanying difference in degrees of freedom) for two alternative path models—a baseline model containing no between-parameter constraints, and a nested comparison model containing one or more between-parameter constraints—provides a test of convergent and discriminant validity. As when testing criterion validity, an advantage of this regression-based path modeling approach over the correlational measurement modeling approach is that it allows one to include covariates as additional predictors in the model, or to examine changes in outcome measures over time by including baseline measures as additional predictors.

However, with this strategy, researchers must be careful not to compare apples and oranges. When comparing path coefficients in latent variable models, one must remember these values represent unstandardized regression coefficients reflecting the expected change in each dependent variable associated with a one-unit increase in the predictor variable. In many cases, these dependent variables will have been assessed using entirely different scales with different measurement units (e.g., dollars versus millimeters, hours versus IQ points, years versus ounces). Unless one converts the scales of these dependent variables into the same metric, then the regression coefficients being compared will differ even if the correlation between the predictor and each of the dependent variables is identical. Ignoring this issue can produce spurious results. Although researchers may be tempted to avoid the problem of noncomparable regression coefficients by standardizing measured variables prior to analysis (see Bryant & Yarnold, 1995; Maruyama, 1998), this approach should be avoided because it forces variables to have identical variances and produces incorrect standard errors in SEM solutions (Cudeck, 1989; Kline, 1998).

An Integrative Example

We conclude by presenting an integrative example within the area of positive psychology that illustrates the use of many of these SEM-based strategies for construct validation within the same study. This example is from research by Bryant and Cvengros (2004) addressing the question of whether hope and optimism are more accurately conceptualized as manifestations of the same global trait, or as two separate constructs. Using procedures outlined in this chapter, these researchers used SEM to evaluate: (a) the structural validity of separate instruments designed to assess hope (the Adult Hope Scale, AHS; Snyder et al., 1991) and optimism (the Life Orientation Test, LOT; Scheier & Carver, 1985); (b) the structure of hope and optimism measures and the strength of their interrelationships when analyzed together; (c) differences in the strength of the relations between hope and optimism subscales and validational criterion measures; and (d) differences in convergent and divergent patterns of association when using higher-order constructs of hope and optimism to predict key criterion variables.

The researchers began by using CFA to analyze the responses of 347 college students to each instrument separately, in order to test the structural validity of the bidimensional measurement models presumed to underlie the AHS (Agency and Pathways subscales) and the LOT (Optimism and Pessimism subscales). Supporting structural validity, for each instrument a one-factor model provided only a mediocre goodness of fit to the data, whereas the intended two-factor model fit the data well and was a statistically significant improvement in fit over the unidimensional model.

Having established structural validity, the researchers used CFA to discriminate the Hope and Optimism subscales from each other, to determine the appropriate measurement model when responses to the Hope and Optimism measures are analyzed together. In particular, they evaluated the goodness of fit of four alternative measurement models for the combined AHS (8 items) and LOT (8 items) data: (a) a one-factor model that assumes all 16 items reflect a single, global dimension termed Future Orientation; (b) a four-factor model that assumes that four correlated dimensions (Agency, Pathways, Optimism, and Pessimism) underlie responses to the 16 items; (c) a higher-order model in which a single second-order factor (Future Orientation) underlies the covariation among four first-order factors (Agency, Pathways, Optimism, and Pessimism); and (d) a higher-order model consisting of two correlated second-order factors (Hope and Optimism), the first of which underlies the covariation between the first-order factors of Agency and Pathways, and the second of which underlies the covariation between the first-order factors of Optimism and Pessimism. As hypothesized, the one-factor model fit the combined LOT and AHS data poorly, whereas the four-factor model fit the combined data well and significantly better than the one-factor model. Imposing equality constraints on the factor intercorrelations in the combined four-factor model, Bryant and Cvengros (2004) found the Optimism subscale correlated equally with both Agency and Pathways, but the Pessimism subscale correlated more strongly with Agency than with Pathways. These results support the discriminant validity of the Optimism and Hope subscales, and they suggest optimism and hope have most in common their respective components of pessimism and agency.

Having assessed the discriminant validity of the factors underlying each separate instrument, Bryant and Cvengros (2004) next evaluated the goodness of fit of the two higher-order measurement models for the hope and optimism data analyzed together—one model containing a single second-order factor (Future Orientation) influencing all four first-order factors, the other containing two correlated second-order factors (Hope influencing the two first-order AHS factors; Optimism influencing the two first-order LOT factors). Both models fit the data well. But supporting the notion that hope and optimism are distinct constructs, the model with separate second-order Optimism and Hope factors fit the combined LOT and AHS data significantly better than the model with a single second-order factor.

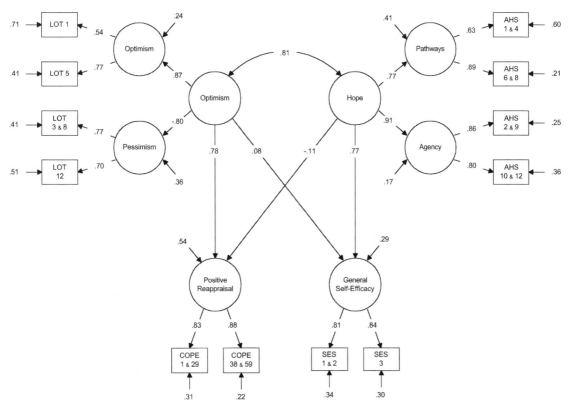

Figure 5.1 Standardized parameter estimates from structural equation modeling via LISREL 8 (Jöreskog & Sörbom, 1996) using the second-order factors of Hope and Optimism to predict the criterion measures of Positive Reappraisal Coping and General Self-Efficacy. Rectangles represent measured variables (or items), and circles represent latent variables (or factors). Arrow-headed straight lines connecting latent variables to measured variables represent standardized factor loadings (λ). The two-headed curved line connecting the second-order latent variables represents a factor correlation (ϕ). Arrow-headed straight lines connecting latent variables represent standardized regression coefficients relating second-order factors to first-order factors (γ). The small arrow-headed straight line to each measured variable indicates the proportion of measurement error. The small arrow-headed line to each first-order factor indicates the proportion of residual variance unrelated to the second-order factor. The "item parcels" that served as measured variables for the Optimism, Hope, and Positive Reappraisal latent variables were means of pairs of scores from the Life Orientation test (LOT; Scheier & Carver, 1985), Adult Hope Scale (AHS; Snyder et al., 1991), and COPE (Carver, Scheier, & Weintraub, 1989). The two "item parcels" that served as measured variables for the General Self-Efficacy latent variable were formed from three composite subscales of the Self-Efficacy Scale (SES; Sherer, Maddux, Mercandante, Prentice-Dunn, Jacobs, & Rogers, 1982). From Bryant, F. B., & Cvengros, J. A. (2004). Distinguishing hope and optimism: Two sides of a coin, or two separate coins? *Journal of Social and Clinical Psychology, 23,* 273–302. Copyright by Guilford Publications. Adapted with permission.

How strongly related are hope and optimism? The correlation (standardized ϕ) between the two second-order factors in the higher-order model was .80, $p < .00001$, indicating that hope and optimism share roughly two-thirds ($\phi^2 = 64\%$) of their variance. Thus, when controlling for measurement error, the two concepts have about twice as much in common as they have separate from each other. The Pearson correlation between unit-weighted total scores for the AHS and the LOT was .54 ($p < .00001$), representing 29% shared variance. Clearly, unreliability in the AHS and LOT attenuates the apparent strength of the relationship between hope and optimism total scores.

In the final stage of their analyses, Bryant and Cvengros (2004) used two latent-variable path models to test further the discriminant validity of the first-order hope and optimism subscales and of the second-order hope and optimism factors as predictors of criterion measures of coping and self-efficacy. The first path model contained four correlated, exogenous (predictor) latent variables (Agency, Pathways, Optimism, and Pessimism), each influencing the endogenous (outcome) latent variables of Positive Reappraisal and General Self-Efficacy. This model allowed a test of discriminant validity within each pair of factors in the bidimensional models of Hope and Optimism. The second path model contained two correlated second-order factors (Hope as defined by the two first-order AHS factors, and Optimism as defined by the two first-order LOT factors), each influencing the endogenous latent variables of Positive Reappraisal and General Self-Efficacy. This model allowed a test of the hypothesis that hope would be a stronger predictor than optimism of positive reinterpretation as a coping style, whereas optimism would be a stronger predictor than hope of general self-efficacy (see figure 5.1). To minimize the number of estimated parameters in structural models, the first-order Agency and Pathways subscales and the latent variables representing the validational criteria were each represented by a pair of "item parcels" (i.e., the mean of different subsets of items) as measured indicators. To make the unstandardized regression coefficients for hope (scores ranging from 1 to 8) and optimism (scores ranging from 0 to 4) comparable, the researchers first converted the indicators for optimism into an eight-point metric equivalent to the metric for hope, by multiplying optimism scores by 1.75 and adding 1 (so that optimism scores ranged from 1 to 8).

The first latent variable path model provided an acceptable goodness-of-fit to the combined data for the LOT, AHS, and criterion measures, $\chi^2(45, n = 347) = 95.2$, RMSEA = .058, GFI = .96, CFI = .97, NNFI = .96. All parameter estimates were statistically significant at one-tailed $p < .011$, except for the effect of second-order Hope on Positive Reappraisal (two-tailed $p > .62$) and the effect of second-order Optimism on General Self-Efficacy (two-tailed $p > .64$). Table 5.1 presents the standardized regression coefficients for Optimism, Pessimism, Pathways, and Agency as predictors of coping and self-efficacy,

for this latent-variable path model. Initial tests of homogeneity in path coefficients for each criterion measure (i.e., the absence of discriminant validity) indicated the four hope and optimism factors had different relationships with Positive Reappraisal and General Self-Efficacy. Confirming hypotheses, respective algebraic and equality constraints revealed that within the Optimism domain, the Optimism subscale was a stronger predictor of Positive Reappraisal than was the Pessimism subscale; and within the Hope domain, the Agency subscale was a stronger predictor of General Self-Efficacy than was the Pathways subscale. These findings support the discriminant validity of the bidimensional models of optimism and hope.

As tests of incremental validity, additional multiple regression analyses of mean subscale scores revealed that: (a) entering Agency and Pathways as a set of predictors after first entering Optimism and Pessimism significantly improved the variance explained in both Positive Reinterpretation, $\Delta R^2 = .04$, $F(2, 343) = 9.3$, $p < .0002$, and General Self-Efficacy, $\Delta R^2 = .18$, $F(2, 341) = 60.2$, $p < .00001$; and (b) entering Optimism and Pessimism as a set of predictors after first entering Agency and Pathways significantly improved the variance explained in both Positive Reinterpretation, $\Delta R^2 = .16$, $F(2, 343) = 43.3$, $p < .00001$, and General Self-Efficacy, $\Delta R^2 = .05$, $F(2, 341) = 18.0$, $p < .00001$. These findings support the incremental validity of the hope and optimism constructs.

The second latent-variable path model also provided an acceptable fit to the combined data. Figure 5.1 displays the standardized parameter estimates for this latent variable path model. Confirming predictions, equality constraints on path coefficients indicated second-order Optimism had a stronger influence on the use of positive reappraisal as a coping strategy than did second-order Hope, whereas second-order Hope had a stronger influence on general self-efficacy than did second-order Optimism (see figure 5.1). Indeed, controlling for the influence of the other second-order trait, Optimism was a statistically significant predictor of positive reappraisal, whereas Hope was not; and Hope was a statistically significant predictor of general self-efficacy, whereas Optimism was not. These results clearly suggest that hope and optimism are distinguishable in terms of their differential relations with the tendency to reframe stressors in a

TABLE 5.1 Standardized Regression Coefficients From Latent Variable Path Model Using Optimism and Hope Subscales to Predict Criterion Measures

| Dimensions of Optimism and Hope | Criterion Measures | | | |
| | Positive Reappraisal | | General Self-Efficacy | |
	γ	$p <$	γ	$p <$
Optimism	.57	.0004	.05	.32
Pessimism	.02	.96	−.26	.005
Pathways	.07	.26	.05	.30
Agency	.10	.18	.56	.00001
R^2	.45		.67	

Note: Tabled are completely standardized γ (gamma) coefficients from structural equation modeling conducted via LISREL 8 (Jöreskog & Sörbom, 1996). These coefficients reflect the degree of association between latent constructs adjusted for differences in measurement reliability. All p values are one-tailed, except for the p value associated with the path coefficient linking pessimism to positive reappraisal coping. Initial tests of homogeneity among path coefficients in each column (i.e., the absence of discriminant validity) revealed that the four hope and optimism factors had different relationships with Positive Reappraisal, $\Delta\chi^2(3, n = 339) = 49.9$, $p < .00001$, and with General Self-Efficacy, $\Delta\chi^2(3, n = 339) = 112.7$, $p < .00001$. From: Bryant, F. B., & Cvengros, J. A. (2004). Distinguishing hope and optimism: Two sides of a coin, or two separate coins? *Journal of Social and Clinical Psychology, 23*, 273–302. Copyright by Guilford Publications. Adapted with permission.

positive light and to expect personal mastery and success.

Conclusion

In conclusion, the statistical strategies we have presented provide a multivariate toolbox for use in validating new constructs and measurement instruments in positive psychology. Each statistical approach represents a different way of addressing the question of whether a particular instrument actually measures what it is supposed to measure. Table 5.2 summarizes these statistical approaches to measurement validation in terms of the types of validity issues involved, the specific questions addressed, the kinds of statistical analyses required, and the critical pieces of information these analyses provide.

However, we do not mean to imply that these particular methods are the only ways of using multivariate statistics to assess measurement validity. On the contrary, countless other statistical techniques can, under particular circumstances, provide valuable information about measurement validity. Multigroup structural equation modeling is a case in point. For example, given appropriate a priori hypotheses about discriminant validity, researchers can use multigroup CFA with equality (or algebraic) constraints between groups to test whether two or more latent variables are more strongly intercorrelated for one group than for another. This approach controls for differences in unreliability in the measured variables both within and between groups. In addition, researchers can use multigroup latent variable path modeling with between-group constraints to test whether one particular construct is a stronger predictor of a criterion measure in one group than in another group (Hayduk, 1987, 1996; Hoyle & Smith, 1994). Truly, the only limit to the range and versatility of multivariate statistical applications to construct validation is the creativity and imagination of the researcher.

Acknowledgments   The authors wish to thank Gerhard Mels and Steven Miller for helpful feedback on an earlier draft of this chapter. This chapter is dedicated to the memory of Merrilee Miles Bryant.

TABLE 5.2 Summary of Different Multivariate Statistical Approaches to Measurement Validation

Type of Validity	Question Addressed	Type of Statistical Analysis	Critical Results
Content/structural	Does the particular measure embody the dimension(s) it is intended to reflect?	Confirmatory factor analysis (CFA) comparing alternative measurement models for a given instrument	For unidimensional instrument: goodness-of-fit statistics for one-factor model
			For multidimensional instrument: likelihood-ratio test comparing one-factor and multifactor models
Criterion	Does the particular measure or measures predict a relevant, external outcome (or criterion)?	Correlation or multiple regression analysis using the measure(s) to predict the criterion	r, p value, and r^2 for correlation; regression coefficient, p value, and R^2 from regression model
		CFA including the measure(s) and the criterion as latent variables in a measurement model	Correlation between the measure(s) and criterion variable disattenuated for effects of unreliability
		Latent variable path model using the measure(s) to predict the criterion	Logistic or discriminant coefficient, p value, R^2, and percentage of classification accuracy
	Does the particular measure or measures discriminate groups of individuals known to differ on the underlying concept (or criterion groups)?	Binary or multinomial logistic regression, or discriminant analysis, using the measure(s) to predict criterion groups	Regression coefficient(s), p value(s), and R^2, adjusted for measurement error
		Optimal data analysis (ODA) using the measure(s) to discriminate criterion groups (Soltysik & Yarnold, 1993)	Percentage accuracy of classification, exact p value, effect strength, estimate of expected cross-sample generalizability of results
Incremental	Does the measure provide explanatory power over and above another measure or measures in predicting a relevant criterion?	Hierarchical stepwise multiple regression predicting the criterion, first entering the other measures, and then entering the given measure	Regression coefficient and p value; ΔR^2 with associated F statistic and p value
		Partial correlation coefficient relating the given measure to the criterion, first removing from each the variance shared with other measures	Partial r, p value, and partial r^2

Construct (in two forms, often assessed together):			
Convergent	How confident can we be in labeling the measure in theory-relevant terms? Is the particular measure correlated with other measures of the same underlying construct?	Z test for hypothesized pattern of differences in correlation coefficients interrelating the various measures (Meng, et al., 1992)	Z value and one-tailed p value
		Indices for quantifying overall construct validity in terms of how closely the observed pattern of correlations matches the predicted pattern of correlations (Weston & Rosenthal, 2003)	$r_{\text{alerting-CV}}$ and $r_{\text{contrast-CV}}$, confidence intervals, and p values
Discriminant	Is the particular measure uncorrelated with measures of similar but separate constructs?	CFA applied to multitrait-multimethod matrix (Campbell & Fiske, 1959)	Goodness-of-fit statistics for null, trait, method, and trait-method models, factor loadings, factor intercorrelations, standardized error terms
		Discriminating different subscales from one another within a multidimensional instrument via CFA with equality constraints	Likelihood-ratio test comparing one-factor and multifactor models or comparing factor intercorrelations
		Relating unidimensional instruments to convergent and discriminant criterion measures via CFA or latent variable path modeling with equality constraints	Likelihood-ratio test comparing measurement models combining versus separating focal construct and criterion measures, or comparing factor intercorrelations or regression coefficients
		Testing hypotheses about differential relationships between multiple constructs and multiple criterion measures via CFA or latent variable path modeling with equality constraints	Likelihood-ratio test comparing factor intercorrelations within a comprehensive measurement model, or comparing regression coefficients

References

American Educational Research Association, American Psychological Association, & National Council on Measurement in Education. (1985). *Standards for educational and psychological testing.* Washington, DC: American Psychological Association.

Anastasi, A. (1988). *Psychological testing* (6th ed.). Upper Saddle River, NJ: Prentice-Hall.

Angoff, W. H. (1988). Validity: An evolving concept. In H. Wainer & H. I. Braun (Eds.), *Test validity* (pp. 19–32). Hillsdale, NJ: Erlbaum.

Bacon, D. R., Sauer, P., & Young, M. (1995). Composite reliability in structural equations modeling. *Educational and Psychological Measurement, 55,* 394–406.

Bagozzi, R. P. (1993). Assessing construct validity in personality research: Applications to measures of self-esteem. *Journal of Research in Personality, 27,* 49–87.

Bentler, P. M. (1990). Comparative fit indexes in structural models. *Psychological Bulletin, 107,* 238–246.

Bentler, P. M. (1995). *EQS structural equations program manual.* Encino, CA: Multivariate Software.

Bentler, P. M., & Bonett, D.G. (1980). Significance tests and goodness-of-fit in the analysis of covariance structures. *Psychological Bulletin, 88,* 588–606.

Bollen, K. A. (1989). *Structural equations with latent variables.* New York: Wiley.

Brockway, J. H., Carlson, K. A., Jones, S. K., & Bryant, F. B. (2002). Development and validation of a scale for measuring cynical attitudes toward college. *Journal of Educational Psychology, 94,* 210–224.

Browne, M. W., & Cudeck, R. (1993). Alternative ways of assessing model fit. In K. A. Bollen & J. S. Long (Eds.), *Testing structural equation models* (pp. 136–162). Newbury Park, CA: Sage.

Bryant, F. B. (1989). A four-factor model of perceived control: Avoiding, coping, obtaining, and savoring. *Journal of Personality, 57,* 773–797.

Bryant, F. B. (2000). Assessing the validity of measurement. In L. G. Grimm & P. R. Yarnold (Eds.), *Reading and understanding more multivariate statistics* (pp. 99–146). Washington, DC: American Psychological Association.

Bryant, F. B. (2003). Savoring Beliefs Inventory (SBI): A scale for measuring beliefs about savouring. *Journal of Mental Health, 12,* 175–196.

Bryant, F. B., & Baxter, W. J. (1997). The structure of positive and negative automatic cognition. *Cognition and Emotion, 11,* 225–258.

Bryant, F. B., & Cvengros, J. A. (2004). Distinguishing hope and optimism: Two sides of a coin, or two separate coins? *Journal of Social and Clinical Psychology, 23,* 273–302.

Bryant, F. B., & Yarnold, P. R. (1995). Principal-components analysis and exploratory and confirmatory factor analysis. In L. G. Grimm & P. R. Yarnold (Eds.), *Reading and understanding multivariate statistics* (pp. 99–136). Washington, DC: American Psychological Association.

Bryant, F. B., Yarnold, P. R., & Grimm, L. G. (1996). Toward a measurement model of the Affect Intensity Measure: A three-factor structure. *Journal of Research in Personality, 30,* 223–247.

Byrne, B. M. (1998). *Structural equation modeling with LISREL, PRELIS, and SIMPLIS: Basic concepts, applications, and programming.* Mahwah, NJ: Erlbaum.

Campbell, D. T., & Fiske, D. W. (1959). Convergent and discriminant validity by the multitrait-multimethod matrix. *Psychological Bulletin, 56,* 81–105.

Carmines, E. G., & Zeller, R. A. (1978). *Reliability and validity assessment.* Beverly Hills, CA: Sage.

Carver, C. S., Scheier, M. F., & Weintraub, J. K. (1989). Assessing coping strategies: A theoretically based approach. *Journal of Personality and Social Psychology, 56,* 267–283.

Chang, E. C., & D'Zurilla, T. J. (1996). Relations between problem orientation and optimism, pessimism, and trait affectivity: A construct validation study. *Behavioral Research and Therapy, 34,* 185–194.

Cohen, J. (1988). *Statistical power analysis for the behavioral sciences* (2nd ed.). Hillsdale, NJ: Erlbaum.

Cook, T. D., & Campbell, D. T. (1979). *Quasi-experimentation: Design and analysis issues for field settings.* Chicago: Rand McNally.

Cronbach, L. J. (1951). Coefficient alpha and the internal structure of tests. *Psychometrika, 16,* 297–334.

Cronbach, L. J., & Meehl, P. E. (1955). Construct validity in psychological tests. *Psychological Bulletin, 52,* 281–302.

Csikszentmihalyi, M. (1990). *Flow: The psychology of optimal experience.* New York: Harper and Row.

Cudeck, R. (1989). Analysis of correlation matrices using covariance structure models. *Psychological Bulletin, 105,* 317–327.

DeVellis, R. F. (1991). *Scale development: Theory and applications.* Newbury Park, CA: Sage.

Diener, E., Emmons, R. A., Larsen, R. J., & Griffin, S. (1985). The Satisfaction With Life Scale. *Journal of Personality Assessment, 41,* 71–75.

Dunn, O. J., & Clark, V. A. (1969). Correlation coefficients measured on the same individuals. *Journal of the American Statistical Association, 64,* 366–377.

Fiske, D. W. (1982). Convergent-discriminant validation in measurements and research strategies. In D. Brinberg & L. Kidder (Eds.), *New directions for methodology of social and behavioral science: Forms of validity in research* (Vol. 12, pp. 79–92). San Francisco: Jossey-Bass.

Goldstein, J. (1987). *The experience of insight.* Boston: Shambhala.

Guttman, L. (1945). A basis for analyzing test-retest reliability. *Psychometrika, 10,* 255–282.

Hambleton, R. K. (1980). Test score validity and standard setting methods. In R. A. Berk (Ed.), *Criterion-references measurement: The state of the art* (pp. 45–123). Baltimore, MD: Johns Hopkins University Press.

Hayduk, L. A. (1987). *Structural equation modeling with LISREL: Essentials and advances.* Baltimore, MD: Johns Hopkins University Press.

Hayduk, L. A. (1996). *LISREL issues, debates, and strategies.* Baltimore, MD: Johns Hopkins University Press.

Haynes, S. N., Richard, D. C. S., & Kubany, E. S. (1995). Content validity in psychological assessment: A functional approach to concept and methods. *Psychological Assessment, 7,* 238–247.

Hollon, S. D., & Kendall, P. C. (1980). Cognitive self-statements in depression: Development of an automatic thoughts questionnaire. *Cognitive Therapy and Research, 4,* 383–395.

Hoyle, R. H., & Smith, G. T. (1994). Formulating clinical research hypotheses as structural equation models: A conceptual overview. *Journal of Consulting and Clinical Psychology, 62,* 429–440.

Hu, L.-T., & Bentler, P. M. (1998). Fit indices in covariance structure modeling: Sensitivity to underparameterized model misspecification. *Psychological Methods, 3,* 424–453.

Ingram, R. E., & Wisnicki, K. S. (1988). Assessment of positive automatic cognition. *Journal of Consulting and Clinical Psychology, 56,* 898–902.

Jöreskog, K. G., & Sörbom, D. (1996). *LISREL 8: User's reference guide.* Chicago: Scientific Software International.

Judd, C. M., Jessor, R., & Donovan, J. E. (1986). Structural equation models and personality research. *Journal of Personality, 54,* 149–198.

Keltner, D., & Haidt, J. (2003). Approaching awe, a moral, spiritual, and aesthetic emotion. *Cognition and Emotion, 17,* 297–314.

Keyes, C. L. M., & Haidt, J. (Eds.). (2002). *Flourishing: Positive psychology and the life well-lived.* Washington, DC: American Psychological Association.

Kirk, K. M., Eaves, L. J., & Martin, N. G. (1999). Self-transcendence as a measure of spirituality in a sample of older Australian twins. *Twin Research, 2,* 61–87.

Kline, R. B. (1998). *Principles and practice of structural equation modeling.* New York: Guilford.

Kuder, G. F., & Richardson, M. W. (1937). The theory of the estimation of test reliability. *Psychometrika, 2,* 151–160.

Langens, T. A., & Schmalt, H.-D. (2002). Emotional consequences of positive daydreaming: The moderating role of fear of failure. *Personality and Social Psychology Bulletin, 28,* 1725–1735.

Langer, E. (1989). *Mindfulness.* Reading, MA: Addison Wesley.

Langston, C. A. (1994). Capitalizing on and coping with daily-life events: Expressive responses to positive events. *Journal of Personality and Social Psychology, 67,* 1112–1125.

Larsen, R. J. (1984). Theory and measurement of affect intensity as an individual difference characteristic. *Dissertation Abstracts International, 85,* 2297B. (University Microfilms No. 84-22112)

Lindsay-Hartz, J. (1981). Elation, gladness, and joy. In J. de Rivera (Ed.), *Conceptual encounter: A method for the exploration of human experience* (pp. 163–224). Washington, DC: University Press of America.

Marsh, H. W., & Grayson, D. (1995). Latent variable models of multitrait-multimethod data. In R. H. Hoyle (Ed.), *Structural equation modeling: Concepts, issues, and applications* (pp. 177–198). Thousand Oaks, CA: Sage.

Maruyama, G. M. (1998). *Basics of structural equation modeling.* Thousand Oaks, CA: Sage.

Maslow, A. (1962). *Toward a psychology of being.* Princeton, NJ: Van Nostrand.

McDonald, R. P. (1970). The theoretical foundations of common factor analysis, principal factor analysis, and alpha factor analysis. *British Journal of Mathematical and Statistical Psychology, 23,* 1–21.

McDonald, R. P. (1999). *Test theory: A unified treatment.* Mahwah, NJ: Erlbaum.

Meng, X.-L., Rosenthal, R., & Rubin, D. B. (1992). Comparing correlated correlation coefficients. *Psychological Bulletin, 111,* 172–175.

Messick, S. (1980). Test validity and the ethics of measurement. *American Psychologist, 30,* 955–966.

Nunnally, J. C. (1978). *Psychometric theory.* New York: McGraw-Hill.

Osborn, A. F. (1957). *Applied imagination.* New York: Springer.

Packer, T. (2002). *The wonder of presence*. Boston: Shambhala.

Rosenberg, M. (1985). *Society and the adolescent self-image*. Princeton, NJ: Princeton University Press.

Rosenthal, R., Rosnow, R. L., & Rubin, D. B. (2000). *Contrasts and effect sizes in behavioral research: A correlational approach*. New York: Cambridge University Press.

Scheier, M. F., & Carver, C. S. (1985). Optimism, coping, and health: Assessment and implications of generalized outcome expectancies. *Health Psychology, 4*, 219–247.

Scheier, M. F., & Carver, C. S. (1993). On the power of positive thinking: Benefits of being optimistic. *Current Directions in Psychological Science, 2*, 26–30.

Sechrest, L. (1963). Incremental validity: A recommendation. *Educational and Psychological Measurement, 23*, 153–158.

Seligman, M. E. P. (2002). *Authentic happiness*. New York: Free Press.

Seligman, M. E. P., & Csikszentmihalyi, M. (2000). Positive psychology: An introduction. *American Psychologist, 55*, 5–14.

Sherer, M., Maddux, J. E., Mercandante, B., Prentice-Dunn, S., Jacobs, B., & Rogers, R. W. (1982). The self-efficacy scale: Construction and validation. *Psychological Reports, 51*, 663–671.

Snyder, C. R. (Ed.). (2000). *The handbook of hope: Theory, measures, and applications*. San Diego, CA: Academic Press.

Snyder, C. R., Harris, C., Anderson, J. R., Holleran, S. A., Irving, L. M., Sigmon, S. T., et al. (1991). The will and the ways: Development and validation of an individual-differences measure of hope. *Journal of Personality and Social Psychology, 60*, 570–585.

Soltysik, R. C., & Yarnold, P. R. (1993). *ODA 1.0: Optimal data analysis for DOS*. Chicago: Optimal Data Analysis.

Steiger, J. H. (1990). Structural model evaluation and modification: An interval estimation approach. *Multivariate Behavioral Research, 25*, 173–180.

Streiner, D. L. (2003). Starting at the beginning: An introduction to coefficient alpha and internal consistency. *Journal of Personality Assessment, 80*, 99–103.

Tellegen, A., & Atkinson, G. (1974). Openness to absorbing and self-altering experiences ("absorption"), a trait related to hypnotic susceptibility. *Journal of Abnormal Psychology, 83*, 268–277.

Thrash, T. M., & Elliot, A. J. (2003). Inspiration as a psychological construct. *Journal of Personality and Social Psychology, 84*, 871–889.

Tucker, L. R., & Lewis, C. (1973). A reliability coefficient for maximum likelihood factor analysis. *Psychomterika, 38*, 1–10.

Uniform Guidelines on Employee Selection Procedures (1978); 43 Fed. Reg. 38,290 (August 25, 1978); Equal Employment Opportunity Commission, 29 C.F.R. pt. 1607.

Wainer, H., & Braun, H. I. (Eds.). (1988). *Test validity*. Hillsdale, NJ: Erlbaum.

Webb, E. J., Campbell, D. T., Schwartz, R. D., Sechrest, L., & Grove, J. B. (1981). *Nonreactive measures in the social sciences* (2nd ed.). Boston: Houghton-Mifflin.

Westen, D., & Rosenthal, R. (2003). Quantifying construct validity: Two simple measures. *Journal of Personality and Social Psychology, 84*, 608–618.

Wothke, W. (1996). Models for multitrait-multimethod matrix analysis. In G. A. Marcoulides & R. E. Schumacker (Eds.), *Advanced structural equation modeling: Issues and applications* (pp. 7–56). Mahwah, NJ: Erlbaum.

Yarnold, P. R., & Soltysik, R. C. (2005). *Optimal data analysis: A guidebook with software for Windows*. Washington, DC: American Psychological Association.

6

Understanding Hope

A Review of Measurement and Construct Validity Research

Lisa M. Edwards, Kevin L. Rand, Shane J. Lopez, and C. R. Snyder

Hope has been discussed by philosophers, theologians, educators, and scientists, to name but a few groups of people, over the preceding two millennia. During the last 15 years, C. R. Snyder and his colleagues at the University of Kansas have developed a theory and associated measures of the hope construct that have received extensive, detailed attention both within and outside the field of psychology. In this chapter, we describe Snyder's hope model and some of the research findings that have supported the validity of this construct. Beginning with a conceptual definition of hope, we move to relevant findings about the usefulness of hope in the lives of individuals in various life arenas. We describe measures developed for assessing hope in children and adults, as well as current issues associated with the validity of hope measurement. Finally, we discuss future directions for further investigation of hope.

The Hope Model

Hope has been conceptualized as pathways and agency goal-directed thinking (Snyder, Irving, & Anderson, 1991). As such, this new approach, which has been called hope theory, contrasts with previous emotion-based or unidimensional models (Snyder, Cheavens, & Michael, 1999). More specifically, Snyder, Irving, et al. (1991, p. 287) defined hope as "a positive motivational state that is based on an interactively derived sense of successful (a) agency (goal-directed energy) and (b) pathways (planning to meet goals)." This model involves three interrelated cognitive components—goals, agency, and pathways (Snyder, Ilardi, Michael, & Cheavens, 2000). Pathways and agency thinking are additive, reciprocal, and positively related, but they are not synonymous, nor does either component alone define hope.

Snyder proposes that goals are the targets of mental action sequences (Snyder, Ilardi, et al., 2000). As the anchor of hope theory (Snyder, 1994b), goals need to be sufficiently important to occupy a person's conscious thought (Snyder, 2000). Furthermore, the goals that necessitate hope must fall somewhere in the middle of a probability of attainment continuum going from goals that are absolutely certain of being achieved to those that are untenable. To reach goals, people must perceive that they are capable of imagining one or more routes to their goals. Snyder (1994b) defined pathway thinking, also known as waypower, as the "mental capacity we can call on to find one or more effective ways to reach our goals" (p. 8). When barriers to block desired goals emerge, as they inevitably do, the mental flexibility of pathway thinking allows people to navigate around those obstacles so as to find alternate routes.

Snyder (2000) defines agency as "the motivational component to propel people along their imagined routes to goals" (p. 10). Also known as willpower, agency reflects the perceived ability to initiate and sustain movement toward a goal, along with the capacity to channel mental energy toward alternate routes if barriers are encountered. Thus, agency reflects a reservoir of determination-like thoughts such as "I know I can do this," and "I'll try," which help people to move toward their desired goals (Snyder, 1994b).

As can be seen in Snyder's (2002) goal-directed thought sequence of hope theory (figure 6.1, moving from left to right), agency and pathways thoughts are learned throughout childhood and adolescence. These learned thoughts continually influence subsequent emotions, such that successful goal pursuits of high-hope individuals cast a positive emotional set over the process in general (see Emotion Set to the right of the Pathways and Agency Thoughts). Likewise, individuals who lack hope may enter the thought sequence with negative feelings toward goal pursuits. Continuing through the goal-directed thought sequence, individuals then enter the pre-event analysis phase, during which they appraise the outcome value of a goal. Goals that are sufficiently important and that are based on a person's own standards are likely to be more appealing to the individual. Once a goal is chosen and an individual begins moving toward goal attainment, agency and pathways thoughts are activated and are utilized to again appraise the goal outcome value. As can be seen, this sequence allows for

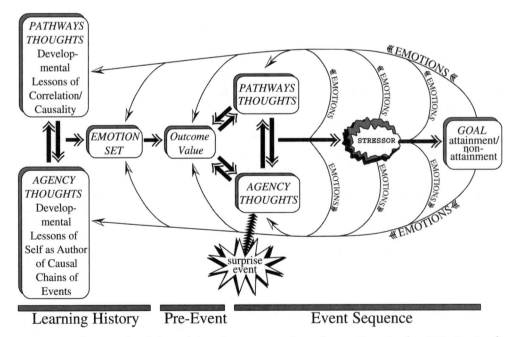

Figure 6.1. Schematic of goal-directed thought sequence in hope theory. (From Snyder, 2002. Reprinted with permission from author.)

"check-backs" such that goals can be judged and modified at different points.

It should be noted that most individuals encounter stressors in the goal pursuit (see figure 6.1), which are challenges of sufficient magnitude to potentially jeopardize the hopeful thought. As expected, low-hope individuals are more likely to be affected by stressors and "become derailed in their goal pursuits" (Snyder, 2002, p. 255). In contrast, high-hope individuals will likely view the stressor as a challenge and be able to harness agency and pathways thoughts toward overcoming this obstacle. As individuals progress toward goal attainment, the success feedback from overcoming the stressor reinforces the individuals' hopeful thinking. Thus the hope theory model involves feedback and feed-forward emotion-based mechanisms that serve to direct current and future goal attainment.

Research Findings About Hope in Children, Youth, and Adults

Researchers have investigated Snyder's model of hope and its relation to several positive correlates. Using the Children's Hope Scale (Snyder, Hoza, et al., 1997) and the Adult Hope Scale (Snyder, Harris, et al., 1991), hope has been studied in its relation to psychological adjustment, health outcomes, and athletic and academic performance (Snyder, 2002).

Psychological Adjustment

Snyder, Harris, et al. (1991) found that scores on the Hope Scale correlated positively with several measures of psychological adjustment, including optimism, control perceptions, problem-solving, positive affect, and self-esteem. With respect to relationships, high-hope adults have been shown to form strong attachments to others (Snyder, Cheavens, & Sympson, 1997) and report having had close bonds to caregivers as children (Rieger, 1993). Furthermore, increased social competence (Snyder, Hoza, et al., 1997), less loneliness (Sympson, 1999), and more perceived social support (Barnum, Snyder, Rapoff, Mani, & Thompson, 1998) all have been related to higher levels of hope.

Further support for the relationship between hope and psychological adjustment is suggested from research with children. In a study investigating children's hope, Snyder, Hoza, et al. (1997) found that hope scores were positively correlated with children's perceptions of athletic ability, physical appearance, social acceptance, and scholastic competence, thereby suggesting that hope is related to children's beliefs about their abilities to accomplish goals (Snyder, Sympson, Michael, & Cheavens, 2000). Snyder, Hoza, et al. (1997) also found that higher hope was related to lower levels of depression in children.

Physical Health

Hope also appears to be related to coping behaviors exhibited by people with health concerns and those surviving illness. In people coping with spinal cord injuries, Elliott, Witty, Herrick, and Hoffman (1991) found that higher hope was associated with lower risk for depression and a more adaptive coping style. Barnum, Snyder, Rapoff, Mani, and Thompson (1998) found that adolescent burn survivors with higher hope related to caregivers more positively and also engaged in fewer activities that undermined recovery. Among adults living with severe arthritis (Laird, 1992), blindness (Jackson, Taylor, Palmatier, Elliott, & Elliott, 1998), and fibromyalgia (Affleck & Tennen, 1996), higher hope was related to better adjustment in coping. Finally, Stanton et al. (2000) found that emotional expression and hope predicted perceived health and a sense of vigor in participants with breast cancer.

Academic and Athletic Performance

Although hope scores are not significantly correlated to intelligence, children and adults with higher hope scores have been shown to perform better on standardized achievement measures such as semester grades, graduation rates, and the Iowa Test of Basic Skills (Snyder, Harris, et al., 1991; Snyder, Hoza, et al., 1997; Snyder, Ilardi, et al., 2000). In a study of male and female college students who were followed for 6 years, it was found that Hope Scale scores significantly predicted higher grade point averages and lower dropout rates, even after controlling for college entrance examination scores (Snyder et al., 2002; Snyder, Wiklund, & Cheavens, 1999). In the arena of athletics, results from a study by Curry, Snyder, Cook, Ruby, and Rehm (1997) suggest that hope scores account for much of the variance related to female collegiates' track performance at track meets, even when ratings of natural ability, self-esteem, confidence, and locus of control were statistically controlled. Brown, Curry, Hagstrom, and Sandstedt (1999) also found that high-hope girls attending a summer sport camp were less likely than low-hope girls to consider quitting their sports, and they also set more sport-specific goals.

Measuring Hope: Traditional Methods for Supporting Scale Validity

Several scales have been developed by Snyder and colleagues to assess hope in adults and children: the Adult Dispositional Hope Scale, the Children's Hope Scale, and the State Hope Scale. One of the most important questions to be answered in the development of any psychological measure is whether it measures what it is purported to measure. In other words, is the scale valid? The historical approach for establishing the validity of a scale is first to establish its reliability, demonstrate a factor structure that is consistent with theory, and then to present a variety of correlational evidence, the sum of which is intended to establish the construct validity of the scale. In the following sections, the ways in which this approach has been used with three hope measures will be reviewed.

Adult Dispositional Hope Scale

Also known as the Goals Scale, in order to make its purpose less obvious to respondents, the Hope Scale was originally described in a 1989 article (Snyder, 1989), and later described in greater detail by Snyder, Irving, et al., in 1991. The Hope Scale is a self-report measure of 12 items. Participants taking the Hope Scale are asked to rate statements using a four-point Likert scale from 1 (definitely false) to 4 (definitely true). The highest possible score is 32, and the lowest is 8.[1] The Hope Scale contains four items that measure agency (e.g., "I energetically pursue my goals"), and four items that tap appraisals of persons' abilities to find pathways to navigate their goals under both unimpeded and impeded circumstances (e.g., "I can think of many ways to get out of a jam"). Four of the 12 items are distracters that are not scored for the total hope score but are aimed at making the scale content less obvious. Consistent with the hope theory developed by Snyder and his colleagues, the Hope Scale provides an agency subscale score, a pathways subscale score, and a total hope score. According to norms developed by Snyder, Harris, et al. (1991), average scores for college and noncollege samples of adults are approximately 24, with significantly lower Hope Scale scores for individuals who are inpatients at psychiatric hospitals or those who are seeking psychological treatment (Snyder, 1995). The Hope Scale scores of women and men were virtually the same across the samples used to develop norms.

Reliability

The overall Hope Scale has demonstrated sound internal reliability, with Cronbach alphas ranging from .74 to .88 (Cramer & Dyrkacz, 1998; Snyder, Harris, et al., 1991; Sumerlin, 1997). Both subscales have shown adequate internal reliability. Cronbach alphas have ranged from .70 to .84 for the Agency scale and from .63 to .86 for the Pathways scale (Cramer & Dyrkacz, 1998; Snyder et al., 1991; Sumerlin, 1997).

In addition, the Hope Scale has been shown to be temporally stable. In college samples, the test-retest reliability was .85 over a 3-week period (Anderson, 1988), .73 over an 8-week interval (Harney, 1989), and from .76 to .82 over a 10-week interval (Gibb, 1990; Yoshinobu, 1989).

Factor Structure

The initial factor structure of the Hope Scale was consistent with the two-factor theory of hope. Principal-components exploratory factor analysis with oblique rotation suggested two main factors that accounted for 52% to 63% of the variance across eight different samples (Snyder, Harris, et al., 1991). As expected, the agency items loaded highly on Factor 1, but not on Factor 2, whereas the pathways items loaded only on Factor 2. Although these subscales were separate, they were positively correlated ($r = .38$ to .69) across eight different samples (Cramer & Dyrkacz, 1998; Magaletta & Oliver, 1999; Snyder, Harris, et al., 1991; Sumerlin, 1997). These findings are consistent with the contention that the Hope Scale consists of two separate but related subscales for agency and pathways thought.

Validity

The convergent validity of the Hope Scale has been shown through its predicted correlations with several other scales that have been designed to measure similar concepts. For example, the Hope Scale correlated positively $(r = .60)$ with the original version of the Life Orientation Test (Scheier & Carver, 1985), a measure of trait optimism (Gibb, 1990). The Hope Scale also has correlated positively with measures of success expectations, self-esteem, self-actualization, and meaning in life (see Cheavens, Gum, & Snyder, 2000, for a review). Similarly, the Hope Scale has correlated negatively with several scales measuring concepts that are antithetical to hope. These scales include hopelessness, depression, suicidal ideations, and psychopathology (see Cheavens et al., 2000, for a review).

The discriminant validity of the Hope Scale was tested by correlating it with the Self-Consciousness Scale (Fenigstein, Scheier, & Buss, 1975). This measure was selected because there was no theoretical basis for predicting differences in self-consciousness between high- and low-hope individuals. As expected, the Hope Scale did not correlate significantly with either subscale of the Self-Consciousness Scale (Gibb, 1990).

The incremental validity of the Hope Scale was tested by examining the unique variance that it yielded when compared with other variables in predicting the same outcome variables. The goal of such tests of predictive utility was to ascertain the degree to which the Hope Scale scores augmented the predictive capabilities of other measures. For example, Sigmon and Snyder (1990) reported that the Hope Scale correlated positively with positive affect and negatively with negative affect, as measured by the Positive and Negative Affect Scale (PANAS; Watson, Clark, & Tellegen, 1988). Moreover, when both the Hope Scale and the PANAS were entered into a regression equation predicting scores on the planning subscale of the COPE (Carver, Scheier, & Weintraub, 1989), the Hope Scale accounted for significant unique variance in COPE scores beyond that accounted for by the PANAS. Similarly, when using problem-focused coping from the revised Ways of Coping Scale (Folkman & Lazarus, 1985) as the criterion variable, the Hope Scale accounted for significant unique variance beyond that accounted for by scores on the trait form of the State-Trait Anxiety Inventory (Spielberger, Gorsuch, & Luchene, 1970) and the Taylor Manifest Anxiety Scale (Taylor, 1954). In another study, Hope Scale scores accounted for unique variance in

general well-being beyond that accounted for by measures of self-efficacy and optimism (Magaletta & Oliver, 1999).

Taken together, these findings suggest that Hope Scale scores account for unique variance over other indices in predicting a variety of criterion variables. Hence, although hope is related to concepts such as positive and negative affect, optimism, and self-efficacy, it is not identical to any of them (Cheavens et al., 2000).

Children's Hope Scale

The Children's Hope Scale (CHS; Snyder, Hoza, et al., 1997) is a six-item measure designed for children ages 8 to 16. Three items on the CHS measure agency (e.g., "I think I am doing pretty well"), whereas the other three items measure pathways (e.g., "I can think of many ways to get the things in life that are most important to me"). Participants taking the CHS are asked to rate statements using a six-point Likert scale from 1 (none of the time) to 6 (all of the time). The highest possible score is 32, and the lowest is 8. Total hope scores can range from 6 to 36, while Agency and Pathways subscale scores can range from 3 to 18. According to norms developed by Snyder, Hoza, et al., the average level of hope on the CHS is 25.

Reliability

The CHS has shown acceptable internal reliabilities across six samples of children, with Cronbach alphas ranging from .72 to .86 (Snyder, Hoza, et al., 1997). Because this scale is intended to assess overall hope only, reliabilities for the individual components were not assessed. The temporal stability of the CHS has been demonstrated over a 1-month interval in two samples of children with test-retest correlations of .71 and .73.

Factor Structure

A principal-components factor analysis with varimax rotations was conducted on an earlier, 12-item version of the CHS requesting two factors. Three agency and three pathway items were discarded from the scale based on weak or equivalent loadings on one of the two factors. The resulting six-item scale was subjected to the same factor analysis. As expected, the three agency items loaded strongly on Factor 1 and not

Factor 2, and the three pathways items loaded strongly on Factor 2 and not Factor 1. These two factors accounted for 32.5% and 25.9% of the variance in the sample (Snyder, Hoza, et al., 1997). In addition, these two factors were positively correlated in two samples of children ($r = .52$ and .61). These findings are consistent with the theory that hope consists of two separate, but related types of thought (i.e., agency and pathways).

Validity

Convergent validity of the CHS was demonstrated in several ways. First, children's scores on the CHS correlated significantly and positively with knowledgeable observers' judgments of their hope levels—both at the beginning and end of a 1-month interval ($r = .37$ and .38). Second, scores on the CHS correlated positively with scores on various measures of children's self-perceived competence and control, including self-perceptions in areas of scholastics, social acceptance, athletics, physical appearance, and behavioral conduct. Also, higher scores on the CHS were related to children linking themselves to positive events and distancing themselves from negative ones. Finally, CHS scores correlated positively with an index of self-worth and negatively with scores on the Children's Depression Inventory (Kovacs, 1985; see Moon & Snyder, 2000, for a review).

Discriminant validity was demonstrated by showing that higher CHS scores were not related to greater intelligence. More specifically, CHS scores did not correlate with the Verbal score ($r = .04$), the Performance score ($r = .04$), or the Full-Scale score ($r = .03$) of the WISC-R (Wechsler, 1974) or the WISC-III (Wechsler, 1991). In contrast, CHS scores demonstrated predictive validity by correlating positively with scores on the Iowa Test of Basic Skills (Hieronymous & Hoover, 1985), which is a measure of achievement rather than intelligence.

Finally, incremental validity was tested by examining the extent to which CHS scores predicted achievement beyond other available measures. Using scores on the Iowa Test of Basic Skills as the criterion variable, CHS scores predicted significant and unique variance above and beyond that accounted for by scores on the Global Self-Worth Scale of the Self Perception Profile for Children (Harter, 1985). Hence, although hope in children is positively related to

an elevated sense of self-worth, there is more to CHS scores than mere self-worth.

Adult State Hope Scale

The State Hope Scale (SHS; Snyder et al., 1996) is a six-item self-report scale that was developed to assess goal-directed thinking in a given moment. Respondents are asked to rate items based on how they think about themselves right now using an eight-point Likert scale from 1 (definitely false) to 8 (definitely true). Three items tap agency and three items tap pathways, and total state hope scores can range from 6 to 48.

Reliability

In a study of college students, Snyder et al. (1996) had participants complete the SHS every day for 29 consecutive days. The internal reliability for the total SHS was excellent, with Cronbach alphas ranging from .82 to .95. For the Agency subscale, the Cronbach alphas ranged from .83 to .95, and for the Pathways subscale the Cronbach alphas ranged from .74 to .93 (see Feldman & Snyder, 2000, for a complete review).

Because state constructs are by nature variable, the test-retest reliability of the SHS was expected to fluctuate considerably. Consistent with this hypothesis, Snyder et al. (1996) found that the correlations between any two days ranged from .48 to .93. Hence, the SHS shows a relatively high level of lability, which is appropriate for a temporally specific measure.

Factor Analysis

Snyder et al. (1996) had 240 students complete the eight-item SHS for 29 consecutive days. These responses were submitted to a principal-components factor analysis, with oblique rotations and the request of extracting two variables. One of the agency items loaded highest on agency for only half of the 29 days and was subsequently dropped. In order to maintain an equal number of items on each subscale, one of the pathways items was dropped as well. Another factor analysis was conducted using the remaining six items. This analysis yielded clear support for the two-factor model, with the three agency items loading only on Factor 1 and the three pathways items loading only on Factor 2.

The total variance accounted for by each of these two factors in the 29 factor analyses ranged from 72% to 87%.

Validity

The convergent validity for the SHS was supported by the finding that its scores correlated positively with scores on the trait Hope Scale ($r = .78$ and $.79$). In addition, because it was hypothesized that higher levels of hope should lead to high levels of positive affect and low levels of negative affect, significant correlations were expected between the SHS and the PANAS. As expected, Snyder et al. (1996) found that scores on the SHS correlated significantly and positively with state positive affect scores and significantly and negatively with negative affect scores. Finally, because higher self-esteem is thought to be the result of successful goal pursuits, it was hypothesized that scores on the SHS would correlate positively with self-esteem. Consistent with this prediction, SHS scores correlated significantly and positively with scores on the State Self-Esteem Scale (Heatherton & Polivy, 1991).

The incremental validity of the SHS was tested by having participants list major events and thoughts that occurred on each of 27 consecutive days and rate them on a seven-point scale ($1 =$ extremely negative to $7 =$ extremely positive), in addition to providing an overall rating for each day based on this same scale. Snyder et al. (1996) examined whether the relationships between SHS scores and these ratings of positive/negative events, positive/negative thoughts, and positive/negative days were attenuated when the variance accounted for by scores on the trait Hope Scale was partialled out. Even after accounting for trait hope, scores on the SHS still were significantly correlated with ratings of daily events, ratings of daily thoughts, and overall daily ratings. This suggests that scores on the SHS account for unique variance in important outcome measures beyond that accounted for by scores on the trait Hope Scale.

The validity of the SHS also was supported by two manipulation studies. In the first study, participants were randomly assigned to one of four groups: (1) a success group, (2) a failure group, (3) a neutral group, and (4) a control group. The first three groups were given a set of 20 anagrams to solve. The success group received 20 success-inducing/easy anagrams, the failure group received 20 failure-inducing/difficult anagrams, and the neutral group received a combination of 10 success-inducing/easy anagrams and 10 failure-inducing/difficult anagrams. In addition, each of these three groups received performance feedback consistent with their group membership (i.e., success feedback, failure feedback, or neutral feedback). Participants in the control group were asked to sit quietly for 6 minutes. All participants completed the SHS, State Self-Esteem Scale, and the state PANAS before and after the anagram task or the control waiting period. As expected, analysis of covariance revealed the predicted Feedback Condition × Time of Assessment interaction, with an increase in SHS scores for the success group, no change in SHS scores for the neutral or control groups, and a significant decrease in SHS scores for the failure group.

A second study achieved similar results to the first manipulation study by placing participants in three groups: (1) instructed to imagine past successes, (2) instructed to imagine past failures, or (3) instructed to sit quietly. The results were as hypothesized: there was a significant increase in the SHS scores for participants in the successful event recall group, no change in the SHS scores for participants in the control group, and a significant decrease in the SHS scores for participants in the unsuccessful event recall group. These results remained even after controlling for the common variances related to state self-esteem and state positive and negative affect. Hence, state hope appears to fluctuate in response to feedback about performance on goal-oriented tasks (e.g., solving anagrams), or when simply thinking about past successes or failures in goal pursuits (see Feldman & Snyder, 2000, for a review).

Current Issues Associated With the Validity of Hope Measurement

Having reviewed the use of traditional approaches to validating three measures of hope, in this section we discuss the development of current issues concerning the validity of the Adult Hope Scale specifically. An initial confirmatory factor analysis (CFA), which supported previous theory and research regarding the scoring and use of the Adult Hope Scale, is described. In addition, the development and validation of a new Goal-Specific Hope Scale for adults is discussed.

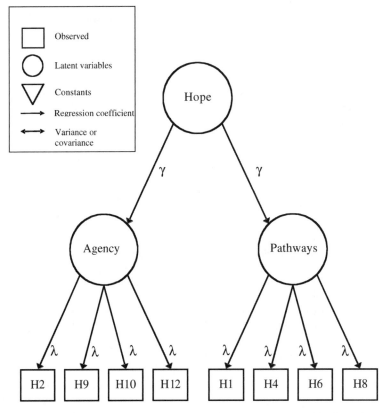

Figure 6.2 Conceptual path diagram of the higher-order factor model of Snyder's Hope Scale. λ = loading of scale item onto latent variable; γ = loading of latent variable onto a higher order latent variable.

CFA Within a Latent Variable Modeling Framework

Although the techniques described in the preceding sections have represented the standards at those times for establishing an instrument's validity, newer and better techniques have been developed. For example, exploratory principal-components factor analysis is a common method for better understanding the relationships between items on an instrument and the underlying constructs these items supposedly measure. Nevertheless, the use of CFA, comparing the statistical fit of a hypothesized model to important alternative models, is now the preferred approach for testing the underlying structure of a scale (Bollen, 1989; Jöreskog & Sörbom, 1988).

To date, the Adult Hope Scale is the only measure of hope that has been analyzed using

this approach. The initial CFA was conducted by Babyak, Snyder, and Yoshinobu (1993). One of the goals of this CFA was to evaluate the tenability the hypothesized two-factor (i.e., Agency and Pathways) model of the hope construct.[2] According to Snyder, Harris, et al. (1991), these separate-but-related factors operate interactively to provide an overall sense of hope. In factor analytic terms, this hypothesized model would consist of two first-order latent constructs (i.e., agency and pathways), which would be driven by a third, second-order construct (i.e., hope; see figure 6.2).

In addition to testing the hypothesized structure of the hope construct, CFA within a latent variable modeling framework can provide information about the scoring and implementation of the Hope Scale. There are several questions that can be addressed: Do the items on the Hope Scale separately indicate agency and pathways thinking? Should any of the items be differentially weighted in terms of their contribution to estimating the underlying constructs? Does it make sense to derive a total hope score from these two subscales and, if so, should researchers make use of the subscale scores or the total scale score in terms of assessing the sequelae of hopeful thinking?

Babyak et al. (1993) collected data on the Hope Scale from four independent samples ($N = 955$, 472, 630, and 696). All analyses of model fit were conducted on each sample separately. The first step in examining the structure of the underlying constructs as measured by the Hope Scale was to test the fit of a model in which all of the observed variables were unrelated (i.e., none of the individual scale items loaded on any factors). Although this "null" model did not fit the observed data well, it was important because it was used as the baseline for comparison of all other models. Consistent with CFA techniques, two competing models of hope (i.e., one-factor versus two-factor) were then tested across all four samples. By comparing the values of the various fit statistics, the authors determined that the two-factor model fit the observed data better than the one-factor model. In a subsequent analysis, Babyak et al. examined if a two-factor model (i.e., agency and pathways) with hope as a higher-order construct was tenable based on the observed data (see figure 6.2). This comparison showed that a model with no higher-order construct was a poorer fit of the observed data than the higher-order two-factor model.

These results support Snyder, Harris, et al.'s (1991) theory that two separate types of thought processes (i.e., agency and pathways) interact to produce hope. This finding is important because it suggests that although the Hope Scale measures both agency and pathways, the total hope score may be the more meaningful index of hopeful thinking. It is when agency and pathways work in tandem that hope is an effective predictor of measures of adjustment. In other words, the CFA conducted by Babyak et al. (1993) supports the practical use of the total hope score as a singular entity, because it demonstrates that this multidimensional construct has a single underlying latent variable (i.e., hope; see Carver, 1989). Based on this information, research using the Hope Scale would be most valid when examining the effects of the total hope score on psychological and physical well-being.

The Goal-Specific Hope Scale

A new measure of hope has been developed in the Snyder laboratory to measure hope at a more specific level. According to Snyder's (1994a) theory, hope occurs at various levels of specificity. The most commonly researched level to date has been dispositional hope. Theoretically, however, hope also exists at the domain level. Stated in other words, an individual may have varying levels of hope in different goal-pursuit arenas of her life. She may have high hope for goals in her professional life, whereas at the same time she may have slightly lower hope for goals in her social life. Although an individual's hope in each life domain is based initially on her trait hope, the domain-specific levels begin to vary as goal success or failure feedback is accrued.

Snyder and colleagues hypothesize that an individual can have a hope level for each particular goal in his or her goal-pursuit repertoire. For example, although a student may have high hope for achieving an A in her biology class, she is less hopeful about her ability to achieve an A in her history class. In an effort to measure hope at this level of specificity, Snyder and colleagues have developed the Goal-Specific Hope Scale (GSHS; Feldman, Rand, Kahle, & Snyder, 2001). The GSHS is a six-item scale designed to measure an individual's hope level for a specific goal. It includes three agency items (e.g., "I energetically pursue this goal") and three pathways items (e.g., "I can think of many ways to achieve this goal"). Two separate scores are obtained for agency and pathways. A total hope score can be calculated by adding the agency and pathways items. Keeping the specified goal in mind, the respondent indicates his or her level of agreement with each item on an eight-point Likert scale ranging from 1 "definitely false" to 8 "definitely true." Scores on the GSHS for an individual's five most important goals have been shown to moderately correlate with her or his trait hope ($r = .53$; Feldman et al., 2001). Cronbach alphas for this scale have ranged from .46 to .80, with more important goals showing greater internal consistency. Higher scores are indicative of higher hope for the specific goal.

Theoretically, hope for a specific goal initially is based on an individual's trait hope level. In other words, when a person begins a goal pursuit, his or her hope for that particular goal is interpolated from his or her overall level of hope. As the process of pursuing the goal begins, the goal-specific hope level adjusts according to feedback regarding the relative success or failure experienced pertaining to that particular goal. Conceptually, therefore, at the beginning of a goal pursuit, trait and goal-specific hope will be redundant. As the process progresses, however, trait and goal-specific hope levels will bifurcate, depending on the relative success or failure experienced in the particular goal pursuit. Trait hope levels should remain relatively stable, whereas goal-specific hope should be much more labile and responsive to success or failure feedback.

In an effort to validate the GSHS, Rand and Snyder (2004) gathered data from undergraduate students taking a personality psychology course. The data were collected over the entire semester, measuring students' trait hope and goal-specific hope at four time points corresponding to the students receiving performance feedback about course exams. Students were asked to set a goal for a final course grade, and that goal was used to gather goal-specific hope information. The aim of this study was to examine how goal-specific hope is influenced over time by trait hope and performance feedback. The findings were consistent with the hypotheses regarding goal-specific hope, and the findings will be submitted for publication soon.

Future Directions

Over the last 50 years, scholarly interest in hope has burgeoned. Social scientists, like Snyder and others, carefully have operationalized the hope construct by refining theories, conducting rigorous research, and validating brief scales. While theoretically grounded measures have brought increased clarity to our understanding of hope, enigmatic and philosophical musings on hope have led to some definitional confusion and ambiguity. Hence, we recommend that the incremental validity and value of old and new conceptualizations and measures of hope be carefully scrutinized. Specific to the measurement of hope as operationalized by Snyder, we believe that further examination of the cross-cultural applicability is warranted, as is additional validation research on domain-specific and goal-specific measures. Also, we recommend that psychometric researchers develop heteromethod measurement approaches, building on existing observation reports and narrative techniques, which combine multiple sources of hope data.

Regarding further development of domain-specific and goal-specific hope measures, preliminary scale development research must be bolstered by further psychometric study. The value of these measures will be determined by incremental validity studies that have yet to be conducted. In particular, the Domain-Specific Hope Scale is in the process of being refined, such that the revised version will include more arenas and will contain items tapping agency, pathways, and goals. Similarly, plans for revising the adult-trait Hope Scale, the SHS, and the CHS exist in order to include specific items about goals as well.

As mentioned previously, the GSHS (Feldman et al., 2001) is currently being validated. An important step in validating the GSHS as a measure of goal-specific hope is demonstrating that the underlying factor structure is consistent with hope theory (i.e., is a two-factor model consisting of agency and pathways). In addition, goal-specific hope initially should be redundant with trait hope, but subsequently respond to success or failure feedback regarding the particular goal pursuit in question. In other words, changes in goal-specific hope over time should be a function of both previous levels of goal-specific hope and previous levels of trait hope. In order to simultaneously demonstrate the factor structure of hope and its dynamic growth pattern over time, latent difference score (LDS) analysis will be utilized. The strategies to be used are based on those outlined by McArdle and Hamagami (2001), and the interested reader is referred to their work and related work for a more thorough explanation of the LDS method.

Although brief self-report measures have made the rigorous study of hope possible, multimethod assessment of hope could advance the science related to this strength. For example, we recommend that researchers refine existing observational measures (e.g., Snyder, Harris, et al., 1991; Snyder & McDermott, 1998) and combine them with self-report measures to obtain a multi-informant estimate of hope. It may even be possible to develop standardized tasks from which hope can be inferred through quantification of the goal, pathways, and agency in the behaviors. These aggregated hope scores may be less influenced by systematic bias than individual reports and they may shed more light on the domain specificity of hopeful pursuits.

Clinical use of an existing narrative measure of hope (Vance, 1996) suggests that narrative accounts of hopeful goal pursuits could provide valuable, in-depth data on how pathways and agency thinking contribute to positive life outcomes. The development of reliable and valid content analysis procedures would mine the hopefulness embedded in personal statements and essays and help researchers to retroactively link personal hope with past performance and to predict future success based on current hope.

Notes

1. Since 1993, the Hope Scale has used an eight-point Likert scale. Consequently, the highest possible score is now 64. This change was made in an effort to increase the variability of scores.

2. Recall that exploratory factor analyses supported the two-factor model across eight different samples (Snyder, Harris, et al., 1991).

References

Affleck, G., & Tennen, H. (1996). Construing benefits from adversity: Adaptational significance and dispositional underpinnings. *Journal of Personality, 64,* 899–922.

Anderson, J. R. (1988). *The role of hope in appraisal, goal-setting, expectancy, and coping.* Unpublished doctoral dissertation, Department of Psychology, University of Kansas, Lawrence.

Babyak, M. A., Snyder, C. R., & Yoshinobu, L. (1993). Psychometric properties of the Hope Scale: A confirmatory factor analysis. *Journal of Research in Personality, 27,* 154–169.

Barnum, D. D., Snyder, C. R., Rapoff, M. A., Mani, M. M., & Thompson, R. (1998). Hope and social support in the psychological adjustment of children who have survived burn injuries and matched controls. *Children's Health Care, 27,* 15–30.

Bollen, K. A. (1989). *Structural equations with latent variables.* New York: Wiley.

Brown, M., Curry, L. A., Hagstrom, H., & Sandstedt, S. (1999, August). *Female teenage athletes, sport participation, self-esteem, and hope.* Paper presented at the Association for the Advancement of Applied Sport Psychology, Banff, Alberta, Canada.

Carver, C. S. (1989). How should multifaceted personality constructs be tested? Issues illustrated by self-monitoring, attributional style, and hardiness. *Journal of Personality and Social Psychology, 56,* 577–585.

Carver, M. F., Scheier, C. S., & Weintraub, J. K. (1989). Assessing coping strategies: A theoretically based approach. *Journal of Personality and Social Psychology, 56,* 267–283.

Cheavens, J., Gum, A., & Snyder, C. R. (2000). The Trait Hope Scale. In J. Maltby, C. A. Lewis, & A. Hill (Eds.), *Handbook of psychological tests* (Vol. 1, pp. 248–258). Lampeter, UK: Edwin Mellen Press.

Cramer, K. M., & Dyrkacz, L. (1998). Differential prediction of maladjustment scores with the Snyder hope scales. *Psychological Reports, 83,* 1035–1041.

Curry, L. A., Snyder, C. R., Cook, D. L., Ruby, B. C., & Rehm, M. (1997). The role of hope in student-athlete academic and sport achievement. *Journal of Personality and Social Psychology, 73,* 1257–1267.

Elliott, T., Witty, T., Herrick, S., & Hoffman, J. (1991). Negotiating reality after physical loss: Hope, depression, and disability. *Journal of Personality and Social Psychology, 61,* 608–613.

Feldman, D. B., Rand, K. L., Kahle, K., & Snyder, C. R. (2001). *Development and validation of the Goal Specific Hope Scale.* Unpublished manuscript, University of Kansas, Lawrence.

Feldman, D. B., & Snyder, C. R. (2000). The State Hope Scale. In J. Maltby, C. A. Lewis, & A. Hill (Eds.), *Handbook of psychological tests* (Vol. 1, pp. 240–245). Lampeter, UK: Edwin Mellen Press.

Fenigstein, A., Scheier, M. F., & Buss, A. H. (1975). Public and private self-consciousness: Assessment and theory. *Journal of Consulting and Clinical Psychology, 43,* 522–527.

Folkman, S., & Lazarus, R. S. (1985). If it changes it must be a process: Study of emotion and coping during three stages of college examination. *Journal of Personality and Social Psychology, 48,* 150–170.

Gibb, J. (1990). *The Hope Scale revisited: Further validation of a measure of individual differences in the hope motive.* Unpublished master's thesis, University of Illinois at Urbana-Champaign.

Harney, P. (1989). *The Hope Scale: Exploration of construct validity and its influence on health.* Unpublished master's thesis, University of Kansas, Lawrence.

Harter, S. (1985). *Manual for the Self-Perception Profile for Children: Revision of the Perceived Competence Scale for Children.* Denver, CO: University of Denver Press.

Heatherton, T. F., & Polivy, J. (1991). Development and validation of a scale measuring state self-esteem. *Journal of Personality and Social Psychology, 60,* 895–910.

Hieronymous, A. N., & Hoover, H. D. (1985). *Iowa Test of Basic Skills.* Chicago: Riverside.

Jackson, W. T., Taylor, R. E., Palmatier, A. D., Elliott, T. R., & Elliott, J. L. (1998). Negotiating the reality of visual impairment: Hope, coping, and functional ability. *Journal of Clinical Psychology in Medical Settings, 5,* 173–185.

Jöreskog, K., & Sörbom, D. (1988). *LISREL 7: A guide to the program and applications.* Chicago: SPSS.

Kovacs, M. (1985). The natural history and course of depressive disorders in childhood. *Psychiatric Annals, 15,* 387–389.

Laird, S. (1992). *A preliminary investigation into prayer as a coping technique for adult patients with arthritis.* Unpublished doctoral dissertation, Department of Psychology, University of Kansas, Lawrence.

Magaletta, P. R., & Oliver, J. M. (1999). The hope construct, will, and ways: Their relations with self-efficacy, optimism, and general well-being. *Journal of Clinical Psychology, 55,* 539–551.

McArdle, J. J., & Hamagami, F. (2001). Latent difference score structural models for linear dynamic analyses with incomplete longitudinal data. In L. Collins & A. Sayer (Eds.), *New methods for the analysis of change: Decade of behavior* (pp. 139–175). Washington, DC: American Psychological Association.

Moon, C., & Snyder, C. R. (2000). Children's Hope Scale. In J. Maltby, C. A. Lewis, & A. Hill (Eds.), *Handbook of psychological tests* (Vol. 1, pp. 160–166). Lampeter, UK: Edwin Mellen Press.

Rand, K. L., & Snyder, C. R. (2004). *Advancing hope theory: Delineating the boundaries and improving the assessment of hope in a sample of college students.* Unpublished manuscript.

Rieger, E. (1993). *Correlates of adult hope, including high- and low-hope adults' recollection of parents.* Psychology honors thesis, Department of Psychology, University of Kansas, Lawrence.

Scheier, C. S., & Carver, M. F. (1985). Optimism, coping, and health: Assessment and implications of generalized outcome expectancies. *Health Psychology, 4,* 219–247.

Sigmon, S. T., & Snyder, C. R. (1990). *Positive and negative affect as a counter-explanation for the relationship between hope and coping strategies.* Unpublished manuscript, Department of Psychology, University of Kansas, Lawrence.

Snyder, C. R. (1989). Reality negotiation: From excuses to hope and beyond. *Journal of Social and Clinical Psychology, 8,* 130–157.

Snyder, C. R. (1994a). Hope and optimism. In V. S. Ramachandran (Ed.), *Encyclopedia of human behavior* (pp. 535–542). San Diego, CA: Academic Press.

Snyder, C. R. (1994b). *The psychology of hope: You can get there from here.* New York: Free Press.

Snyder, C. R. (1995). Conceptualizing, measuring, and nurturing hope. *Journal of Counseling and Development, 73,* 355–360.

Snyder, C. R. (2000). The past and possible futures of hope. *Journal of Social and Clinical Psychology, 19,* 11–28.

Snyder, C. R. (2002). Hope theory: Rainbows in the mind. *Psychological Inquiry, 13,* 249–275.

Snyder, C. R., Cheavens, J., & Michael, S. T. (1999). Hoping. In C. R. Snyder (Ed.), *Coping: The psychology of what works* (pp. 205–231). New York: Oxford University Press.

Snyder, C. R., Cheavens, J., & Sympson, S. C. (1997). Hope: An individual motive for social commerce. *Group Dynamics: Theory, Research, and Practice, 1,* 107–118.

Snyder, C. R., Harris, C., Anderson, J. R., Holleran, S. A., Irving, L. M., Sigmon, S. T., et al. (1991). The will and the ways: Development and validation of an individual-differences measure of hope. *Journal of Personality and Social Psychology, 60,* 570–585.

Snyder, C. R., Hoza, B., Pelham, W. E., Rapoff, M., Ware, L., Danovsky, M., Highberger, L., Rubinstein, H., & Stahl, K. J. (1997). The development and validation of the Children's Hope Scale. *Journal of Pediatric Psychology, 22,* 399–421.

Snyder, C. R., Ilardi, S. S., Michael, S. T., & Cheavens, J. (2000). Hope theory: Updating a common process for psychological change. In C. R. Snyder & R. E. Ingram (Eds.), *Handbook of psychotherapy: The process and practices of psychological change* (pp. 128–153). New York: Wiley.

Snyder, C. R., Irving, L., & Anderson, J. R. (1991). Hope and health: Measuring the will and the ways. In C. R. Snyder & D. R. Forsyth (Eds.), *Handbook of social and clinical psychology: The health perspective* (pp. 285–305). Elmsford, NY: Pergamon Press.

Snyder, C. R., & McDermott, D. (1998). *Development and validation of observational instruments for rating children's hope.* Presented at the Kansas Conference in Clinical Child Psychology, Translating Research into Practice, Lawrence.

Snyder, C. R., Shorey, H., Cheavens, J., Pulvers, K. M., Adams III, V. H., & Wiklund, C. (2002). Hope and academic success in college. *Journal of Educational Psychology, 94,* 820–826.

Snyder, C. R., Sympson, S. C., Michael, S. T., & Cheavens, J. (2000). The optimism and hope constructs: Variants on a positive expectancy theme. In E. C. Chang (Ed.), *Optimism and pessimism* (pp. 103–124). Washington, DC: American Psychological Association.

Snyder, C. R., Sympson, S. C., Ybasco, F. C., Borders, T. F., Babyak, M. A., & Higgins, R. L. (1996). Development and validation of the State Hope Scale. *Journal of Personality and Social Psychology, 70,* 321–335.

Snyder, C. R., Wiklund, C., & Cheavens, J. (1999, August). *Hope and success in college.* Paper presented at the annual conference of the American Psychological Association, Boston.

Spielberger, C. D., Gorsuch, R. L., & Luchene, R. E. (1970). *The State-Trait Anxiety Inventory.* Palo Alto, CA: Consulting Psychologists Press.

Stanton, A. L., Danoff-Burg, S., Cameron, C., Bishop, M., Collins, C. A., Kirk, S. B., et al. (2000). Emotionally expressive coping predicts psychological and physical adjustment to breast cancer. *Journal of Consulting and Clinical Psychology, 68,* 875–882.

Sumerlin, J. R. (1997). Self-actualization and hope. *Journal of Social Behavior and Personality, 12,* 1101–1110.

Sympson, S. (1999). *Validation of the Domain Specific Hope Scale.* Unpublished doctoral dissertation, Department of Psychology, University of Kansas, Lawrence.

Taylor, J. A. (1954). A personality scale of manifest anxiety. *Journal of Abnormal and Social Psychology, 48,* 285–290.

Vance, M. (1996). *Measuring hope in personal narratives: The development and validation of the Narrative Hope Scale.* Unpublished doctoral dissertation, Department of Psychology, University of Kansas, Lawrence.

Watson, D., Clark, L. A., & Tellegen, A. (1988). Development and validation of brief measures of positive and negative affect: The PANAS scales. *Journal of Personality and Social Psychology, 54,* 1063–1070.

Wechsler, D. (1974). *Wechsler Intelligence Scale for Children* (Rev. ed.). New York: Psychological Corp.

Wechsler, D. (1991). *Wechsler Intelligence Scale for Children* (3rd ed.). San Antonio: Psychological Corp./Harcourt Brace Jovanovich.

Yoshinobu, L. R. (1989). *Construct validation of the Hope Scale: Agency and pathways components.* Unpublished master's thesis, Department of Psychology, University of Kansas, Lawrence.

7

Methodological Issues in the Assessment of the Affective Component of Subjective Well-Being

Ulrich Schimmack

One important area of positive psychology examines happiness and subjective well-being (SWB; Diener, 2000). Diener (1984) noted that SWB has an affective and a cognitive component. The cognitive component of SWB is assessed with life satisfaction judgments (Diener, Emmons, Larsen, & Griffin, 1985). The affective component assesses the amount of pleasant and unpleasant experiences in people's lives (e.g., Schimmack, Diener, & Oishi, 2002).

Early on, SWB researchers noted the limitations of research programs that focused exclusively on negative states such as depression and anxiety. In an influential article, Diener (1984) proposed that SWB is more than the absence of negative affect (NA). Although low levels of NA are important for SWB, high levels of positive affect (PA) are also important. Diener's (1984) conception of SWB in terms of high PA and low NA implies that PA and NA are separable components of SWB. In other words, measures of PA show discriminant validity from measures of NA. If PA and NA were bipolar opposites, then minimization of NA would also maximize PA. In contrast, the distinction of PA

and NA as separate components of SWB implies that PA and NA have different causes and consequences. The conceptualization of PA and NA as separate dimensions of SWB created a heated debate in the affect literature (Diener, 1999). This chapter gives a brief overview of the debate with a focus on the methodological issues that have fuelled the debate.

Positive Affect and Negative Affect

In the early 1980s, several independent lines of research converged on the view that PA and NA are separable (i.e., not bipolar opposite) dimensions. Factor analyses of self-reported affects often resulted in two factors, with pleasant items loading on one factor and unpleasant items loading on the other factor. Personality researchers noted that PA and NA are related to different personality traits. Whereas extraversion is a stronger predictor of PA than NA, neuroticism is a stronger predictor of NA than PA (Costa & McCrae, 1980). These findings provided the foundation for the distinction between PA and

NA (Diener, 1984; see Diener & Lucas, 1999, for a review).

Discriminant Validity of PA and NA: A Method Artifact?

Green, Goldman, and Salovey (1993) presented the first serious challenge to the view of PA and NA as separable dimensions. They proposed that evidence of discriminant validity of PA and NA scales is a method artifact. In particular, an acquiescence bias would bias the correlation between observed ratings of PA and NA in a positive direction because respondents with an acquiescence bias agree to PA items and NA items independent of their actual level of SWB. Green et al. (1993) proposed a multiformat approach to control for the influence of response styles. Concretely, PA and NA were assessed with multiple response formats such as Likert scales and adjective checklists. The data were analyzed with structural equation models. Structural equation models essentially decomposed the variance in each item into two variance components: variance that was shared with other response formats, and variance that was unique to a particular response format. The first variance component is assumed to reflect valid variance, whereas the second component reflects both random measurement error and systematic measurement error due to response styles. The model also allowed for correlated error variances between measures that used the same response format. The magnitude of these correlations reflects the influence of systematic measurement error. Green et al.'s (1993) multiformat studies yielded format-independent correlations between PA and NA that approached −1 ($\sim$ −.90), indicating that respondents' level of PA was highly inversely related to their level of NA. This finding has been widely cited as evidence against the assumption that PA and NA are separable dimensions.

Only a few years after Green et al.'s (1993) challenge, Diener, Smith, and Fujita (1995) reexamined the relation between PA and NA by means of a multitrait multimethod analysis. PA and NA were assessed with three different methods, namely (a) retrospective self-reports, (b) daily diaries, and (c) informant reports. This approach has several advantages over the multiformat procedure used by Green et al. (1993). First, daily diary data control for memory biases in retrospective self-reports and informant reports. Thus, any variance that is shared between daily diary reports and retrospective reports is relatively free of memory biases. Second, self-reports and informant reports are made by different individuals. Thus, shared variance between these measures is free of response styles. Importantly, the use of informant report is superior to Green et al.'s multiformat procedure, which assumes that response styles are unique to a particular response format. Thus, the multiformat procedure fails to control for response styles that are common to all response formats. For example, people who respond in a social desirable manner on one format are also likely to do so on other formats. Using structural equation modeling, Diener et al. (1995) found that the method-free correlation between PA and NA was −.44. This finding contradicts Green et al.'s (1993) conclusion that PA and NA lack discriminant validity once random and systematic measurement error are controlled. Subsequently, I review attempts to reconcile the divergent results of Green et al. (1993) and Diener et al. (1995).

Cultural Variation in the Relation Between PA and NA

Bagozzi, Wong, and Yi (1999) proposed that the relation between PA and NA varies across samples. They presented empirical support for this hypothesis in a cross-cultural study. The correlations between PA and NA were less negative in East Asian cultures than in Western cultures. The authors attributed this finding to dialectic thinking in Asian philosophy. In cultures with dialectic thinking, opposite affective states are seen as compatible, which leads to weaker negative correlations between PA and NA. Schimmack, Oishi, and Diener (2002) extended Bagozzi et al.'s findings in a larger cross-cultural study of 38 nations. The data revealed that weaker negative correlations were indeed unique to East Asian cultures and not a general characteristic of non-Western cultures. However, Schimmack, Oishi, et al. (2002) also noted that even nondialectic samples had rather modest negative correlations compared to Green et al.'s (1993) findings. In addition, it has to be noted that Green et al. and Diener et al. (1995) both used North American student samples. Thus, cultural variations in the relation between PA and NA are theoretically important, but they cannot explain the inconsistent findings across North American samples. One weakness of Bagozzi et al.'s (1999) and Schimmack, Oishi, et al.'s (2002) studies was the reliance on self-reports with a single method. Thus, the finding of discriminant validity in these studies could be due to response styles.

Item Content of PA and NA Measures

Watson and Tellegen (1999) provided an alternative explanation for discrepant results regarding the discriminant validity of PA and NA (see also Tellegen, Watson, & Clark, 1999). Accordingly, evidence for discriminant validity of PA and NA depends on the item content of PA and NA scales. Green et al.'s (1993) challenge to the discriminant validity of PA and NA was limited to scales that equated PA with happiness and NA with sadness. In contrast, multimethod and multiformat studies with other PA and NA scales showed clear evidence of discriminant validity (Green et al., 1993; Lucas, Diener, & Suh, 1996). However, Watson and Tellegen's (1999) explanation overlooked that Diener et al.'s (1995) study included happiness and sadness as components of PA and NA. Furthermore, Diener et al. (1995) reported the method-free correlation between happiness and sadness. This correlation ($r = -.47$) also supported discriminant validity and contradicts Green et al.'s (1993) finding of much stronger correlations that approach -1. Furthermore, Diener et al.'s (1995) data showed that the correlation between happiness and sadness was not dramatically different from correlations between happiness and other unpleasant emotions ($r -.33$ to $-.37$). This finding is consistent with other findings that correlations between PA and NA measures do not vary dramatically with scale content (Schimmack, 2003; Schimmack, Oishi, et al., 2002; Watson, 1988; Zelenski & Larsen, 2000). Thus, item content of PA and NA scales alone is unable to reconcile the findings of Green et al. (1993) and Diener et al. (1995).

Symmetrical Versus Asymmetrical Response Formats

Schimmack, Bockenholt, and Reisenzein (2002) offered another explanation for the discrepancy between the findings of Green et al. (1993) and Diener et al. (1995). They proposed that the authors used different response formats, which produced different correlations between PA and NA. Numerous articles in the affect literature had demonstrated that the correlation between PA and NA varies with the nature of a response format (e.g., Meddis, 1972; Russell & Carroll,

1999). Meddis (1972) distinguished asymmetrical and symmetrical formats. Asymmetrical formats have a single rejection category and multiple acceptance categories (e.g., not at all, a little, a lot). Symmetrical formats have an equal number of rejection and acceptance categories (e.g., strongly disagree, disagree, neither, agree, strongly agree). Symmetrical formats imply a bipolar construct because it is meaningless to distinguish degrees of absence. For example, it does not make sense to be slightly not happy or strongly not happy. Thus, faced with a symmetrical scale, respondents assume that multiple rejection categories should be used to indicate the extent to which the opposite construct is present. For example, slightly not happy is translated into slightly sad and strongly not happy is translated into strongly sad. Three of the four response formats in Green et al.'s (1993) study were symmetrical formats that respondents were likely to interpret as bipolar scales (cf. Russell & Carroll, 1999). In contrast, Diener et al. (1995) used asymmetrical formats for the retrospective self-reports and informant reports as well as the daily diary data. Thus, the nature of the response formats provides a simple explanation for the divergent findings.

Schimmack, Bockenholt, et al. (2002) tested this explanation in a series of studies. One study demonstrated that the correlation between PA and NA could be predicted on the basis of an independent measure of respondents' interpretation of the response format. Another study demonstrated that PA and NA were only moderately negative correlated when multiple asymmetrical formats were used. Schimmack, Bockenholt, et al. (2002) also demonstrated that Green et al.'s (1993) explanation for their strong negative correlation was incorrect. The authors had attributed their finding to the ability of studies that vary response formats to control systematic measurement error. A reexamination of their own data revealed that none of their three rating scales were significantly influenced by systematic measurement error. Thus, each of their symmetric response formats alone would have produced evidence for bipolarity after controlling for random measurement error alone.

Schimmack, Bockenholt, et al.'s (2002) findings provide evidence that the nature of response formats explains the discrepant findings regarding PA and NA in the literature. This finding leads to the important question of which response formats provide valid information about the relation between PA and NA. I argue that asymmetrical formats with a single rejection category are superior to symmetrical formats. The reason is that symmetrical formats are interpreted as bipolar scales, which is inappropriate for investigations of the relation between PA and NA. If the negative pole of a PA measure is defined as high levels of NA and the negative pole of a NA measure is defined as high levels of PA, then the two measures must be inversely related. Indeed, any correlation lower than −1 must be due to measurement error, but cannot be interpreted as evidence for discriminant validity of PA and NA. Thus, an assessment of PA and NA with asymmetrical scales is required to study the relation between variation in PA and NA.

Pearson Correlation Versus Polychoric Correlations

Although response formats play an important role in determining the correlation between PA and NA, other methodological factors may also influence the relation. Some researchers have discussed the possibility that the Pearson correlation is an inappropriate statistical test (Eid, Notz, Schwenkmezger, & Steyer, 1994; Tellegen et al., 1999). The reason is that the Pearson correlation assumes that observed variables are normally distributed. If variables are not normally distributed, Pearson correlations provide attenuated estimates of the relation between two variables.

The assumption of normal distributions is typically violated for state measures of NA. Most people report not feeling any negative affect, which leads to positively skewed item distributions (e.g., Schimmack, 2003). Polychoric correlation coefficients rectify the problem of nonnormal distributions by mapping nonnormally distributed observed variables onto a normally distributed latent variable. A polychoric correlation coefficient estimates the association between two latent normally distributed variables for observed variables that do not fulfill the normal-distribution assumption of Pearson correlations.

Tellegen et al. (1999) used polychoric correlations to estimate the correlation between happiness and sadness. They also used structural equation modeling to control random measurement error. The polychoric correlation between happiness and sadness was −.77, which is a considerably more negative correlation than the Pearson correlation found by Diener et al. (1995). A model that further controlled for acquiescence biases produced an even stronger negative correlation $(r = -.91)$. This finding suggests that evidence for discriminant validity of PA and NA in Diener et al.'s (1995) study may have been due to an inappropriate use of the Pearson correlation with nonnormally distributed variables. However, other findings in the literature cast doubt on this interpretation. First, Tellegen et al. (1999) did not report the Pearson correlation for the same data set. Thus, it is unknown whether a Pearson correlation would have produced substantially different results. Eid et al. (1994) compared factor structures based on Pearson correlations and polychoric correlations and found that the "differences between both models are small" (p. 211). Watson and Tellegen (1999) reported that the Pearson correlation between single items of happiness and sadness was only slightly less negative $(r = -.48)$ than the polychoric correlation $(r = -.57)$. Furthermore, Diener et al. (1995) examined trait affect. Unlike state measures of NA, trait measures of NA tend to conform better to the assumption of normal distributions. Thus, it is likely that Diener et al. (1995) would have obtained similar findings if they had used polychoric correlations.

So far, nobody has compared Pearson and polychoric correlations with trait measures of PA and NA. For this purpose, I analyzed two new data sets. One study asked 517 students how often they experienced happiness and sadness in general. The response format was a 7-point scale ranging from 1 (almost never) to 7 (nearly always). The second study asked 819 students how often they felt happiness and sadness in the past month (30 days). The response format was an 8-point scale ranging from 0 (never, 0%) to 7 (always, 100%). Each affect was assessed with three items to control for random measurement error. The items were happy, cheerful, and joyful for PA and sad, depressed, and blue for NA. The correlation between PA and NA was tested using structural equation modeling. Each model had two factors and the three items of each construct loaded on one of the two factors. Separate models were tested with Pearson and with polychoric correlation coefficients. Models with polychoric correlation coefficients require large sample sizes and the number of participants increases exponentially with the number of response categories. To obtain robust estimates of polychoric correlations, models were tested with the original 7-point and 8-point response formats and with data that reduced the number of response categories to three by combining neighboring response categories (see Eid et al., 1994). The estimated correlations with all response categories and combined categories were virtually identical. Thus, the results with the full response format are reported. Polychoric correlation coefficients were nearly equivalent to Pearson correlations. For affect in general, the Pearson correlation was $r = -.37$ and the polychoric correlation was $r = -.38$. For affect in the past month, the Pearson correlation was $r = -.46$ and the polychoric correlation was $r = -.45$. The reason for this small effect of the statistical coefficient can be found in the distribution of the various measures. Neither the happiness scale (skewness $= -0.33$, -0.15; general and past month, respectively) nor the sadness scale (skewness $= 0.41$, 0.68) deviated dramatically from normality.

To examine the influence of the type of correlation coefficient on analyses of state NA and PA, I examined the correlation between ratings of momentary PA and NA in a large student sample ($N = 710$; see Schimmack & Reisenzein, 2002). PA was assessed with the items pleasant, good, and positive. NA was assessed with the items unpleasant, bad, and negative. Responses were made on a 4-point scale ranging from 0 (not at all) to 3 (strongly). Consistent with expectations, the NA scale was positively skewed (skewness $= 1.40$), whereas PA was approximately normally distributed (skewness $= -0.42$). The data were analyzed with the same structural equation model as the trait data. Models were tested with the full 4-point scale and a reduced 3-point scale that combined the least frequently used category with the neighbor category. This was 0 for the PA items and 3 for the NA items. Both models provided virtually identical results and the results for the 4-point scale are reported. The Pearson correlation was estimated to be $r = -.61$, whereas the polychoric correlation was estimated to be $r = -.66$. This finding shows that Pearson correlations are likely to attenuate the correlation between PA and NA in analyses of state affect due to the skewed distribution of NA items. However, the effect is modest and cannot explain the discriminant validity of PA and NA.

Aggregation Versus Retrospective Trait Measures

As noted earlier, response styles seem to have a negligible effect on the correlation between PA and NA. However, recent publications pointed out that response styles may produce systematic measurement error in studies that aggregate state measures to obtain trait measures (Schimmack, 2003; Schimmack, Bockenholt, et al., 2002; Watson & Tellegen, 2002). The reason is that aggregation increases the amount of systematic variance, which applies equally to systematic trait variance and systematic measurement error. In support of this hypothesis, Schimmack, Bockenholt, et al. (2002) demonstrated that Diener et al.'s (1995) daily diary data systematically underestimated the correlation between PA and NA in comparison to the retrospective self-reports and informant reports. Schimmack, Bockenholt, et al. estimated that aggregated response styles change correlations by about .2. A similar estimate was obtained by Schimmack (2003) using a different measure of response styles. Participants rated a set of facial expressions of emotions using the same response format. Assuming that ratings of others' emotions are independent of individuals' own levels of PA and NA, correlations between self-ratings and rating of facial expressions reflect the influence of response styles. Controlling for response styles, the correlation between aggregated momentary rating of PA and NA changed from .02 to $-.15$. Watson and Tellegen (2002) report similar discrepancies between uncorrected and corrected correlations of aggregated PA and NA measures. The influence of systematic measurement error can explain the near-zero correlations between happiness and sadness in studies that used aggregated momentary ratings (e.g., Schimmack, 2003; Zelenski & Larsen, 2000). The true correlations are likely to be negative and similar to those obtained in Diener et al.'s (1995) multimethod study. However, even these negative correlations would still support the discriminant validity of PA and NA.

Variation in PA-NA Correlations: A Mini Meta-Analysis

The review of methodological issues in the measurement of PA and NA has uncovered several factors that influence the correlation between PA and NA. For a quantitative assessment of the contribution of these factors to the variation in PA-NA correlation, I conducted a meta-analysis. The point of the meta-analysis was not to include all studies of the correlation between PA and NA. Rather, the focus was on studies that varied across the different factors that may contribute to variation in the

TABLE 7.1 Independent Variables and PA-NA Correlations in Studies Used for the Mini Meta-Analysis

Study	SM/MM	Format	State/Trait	Statistic	Aggregation	Correlation
Green et al. (1993) Study 1	1	1	1	0	0	−.85
Green et al. (1993) Study 2	1	1	1	0	0	−.91
Diener et al. (1995)	1	0	0	0	0	−.47
Barrett & Russell (1998) Study 1	1	1	1	0	0	−.93
Barrett & Russell (1998) Study 2	1	1	1	0	0	−.93
Russell & Carroll (1999) 1	0	0	1	0	0	−.46
Russell & Carroll (1999) 2	0	0	1	0	0	−.51
Russell & Carroll (1999) 3	0	0	1	0	0	−.56
Russell & Carroll (1999) 4	0	1	1	0	0	−.79
Tellegen et al. (1999)	0	0	1	1	0	−.77
Tellegen et al. (1999)	0	0	1	1	0	−.91
Watson & Tellegen (1999)	0	0	1	0	0	−.48
Watson & Tellegen (1999)	0	0	1	1	0	−.57
Zelenski & Larsen (2000) WS	0	0	1	0	0	−.30
Zelenski & Larsen (2000) AGG	0	0	0	0	0	−.13
Schimmack, Bockenholt, et al. (2002)	1	0	1	0	0	−.52
Schimmack et al. (2002) NA	0	0	0	0	0	−.34
Schimmack et al. (2002) A	0	0	0	0	1	−.13
Schimmack (2003) WS	0	0	1	0	0	−.22
Schimmack (2003) AGG	0	0	0	0	1	−.02
Schimmack (2004) General	0	0	0	0	0	−.37
Schimmack (2004) General	0	0	0	1	0	−.38
Schimmack (2004) Month	0	0	0	0	0	−.46
Schimmack (2004) Month	0	0	0	1	0	−.45
Schimmack & Reisenzein (2002)	0	0	1	0	0	−.61
Schimmack & Reisenzein (2002)	0	0	1	1	0	−.66

Note: SM/MM = single method/multimethod study, NAv not Asian dialectic, A = Asian dialectic, WS = within-subject, AGG = aggregated states.

PA-NA correlation. Table 7.1 lists all the studies that were included in the analyses. It also lists the variables that were used as predictors of variation in PA-NA correlations, namely single-method versus multimethod assessment, symmetric versus asymmetric response format, state versus trait affect, Pearson versus polychoric correlation coefficient, and one-time versus aggregate assessment. The PA-NA correlations show a large range of variability that would support models of near independence ($r = -.02$) to approximate bipolarity ($r = -.93$). Table 7.2 shows the correlation among predictors and their correlation with the PA-NA correlation coefficients. First, it is remarkable that most of the predictors are only weakly related to each other, indicating that the meta-analysis covers a range of studies with different characteristics. Second, the simple correlations indicated that response format is the strongest

TABLE 7.2 Correlations Between Method Factors and PA-NA Correlations

	Method	Format	State/Trait	Statistic	Aggregation	Correlation
Method	—					
Format	.66*	—				
State/trait	.23	.38	—			
Statistic	−.28	−.25	−.04	—		
Aggregate	−.17	−.15	−.39	−.15	—	
Correlation	−.58*	−.74*	−.63*	−.11	.52*	—

*$p < .05$.

predictor of PA-NA correlations. This finding is consistent with studies that directly examined the effect of response format on PA-NA correlation (Meddis, 1972; Russell & Carroll, 1999; Schimmack, Bockenholt, et al., 2002). A regression analysis with format and method as predictors revealed that format predicted unique variance in PA-NA correlations ($\beta = -.64$), whereas method had no significant effect ($\beta = -.16$), $t < 1$. This finding confirms Schimmack, Bockenholt, et al.'s conclusion that multimethod studies produce correlations similar to those of single-format studies if the nature of the formats is the same.

When PA-NA correlations were regressed onto format, state versus trait, type of correlation coefficient, and aggregation, all predictors contributed significantly to the prediction of PA-NA correlations. The model explained 83% of the variance in PA-NA correlations across studies.

$$PA\text{-}NA \; CORR = -.33 - .41 \; format \\ + .25 \; aggregation \\ - .15 \; state/trait \\ - .15 \; statistic$$

This formula implies that the correlation with asymmetrical formats is $-.33$, whereas the correlation with symmetrical formats is $-.74$. As noted earlier, symmetrical formats are unsuitable for the examination of the relation between PA and NA. Thus, format should be set to zero. With format set to zero, the formula is

$$PA\text{-}NA \; CORR = -.33 + .25 \; aggregation \\ - .15 \; state/trait \\ - .15 \; statistic$$

As noted earlier, aggregation attenuates the true correlation due to the influences of systematic measurement error. Thus, aggregation should be set to zero, which simplifies the formula further.

$$PA\text{-}NA \; CORR = -.33 - .15 \; state/trait \\ - .15 \; statistic$$

The final formula suggests that PA-NA correlation can range from $-.33$ to $-.63$, with stronger correlations for studies of states than traits and studies that use polychoric rather than Pearson correlations. An examination of the residuals showed no major discrepancies between actual and predicted scores. The biggest discrepancy was found for Schimmack's (2003) finding of a within-subject PA-NA correlation

of $r = -.22$, which was predicted to be $r = -.47$. As Schimmack's (2003) finding is based on single item indicators, the attenuated correlation is likely due to random measurement error.

In sum, this review has revealed several factors that contribute to the inconsistent findings of the discriminant validity of PA and NA. The strongest effect was obtained for the type of response format used. The strongest challenge to discriminant validity stems from studies with symmetrical response formats. These formats are unsuitable for the investigation of the relation between PA and NA because respondents interpret them as bipolar scales. On the other hand, studies with aggregated state measures overestimate discriminant validity due to response styles that become more notable with aggregation. The use of polychoric versus Pearson correlation has a small effect on the results that is negligible for tests of discriminant validity. Furthermore, the effect is likely to be stronger for state measures than for trait measures. State PA and NA show slightly more negative correlations than trait measures, but the difference is also quite small. To conclude, the present review reveals that Diener et al.'s (1995) multimethod study provided valid information about the discriminant validity of PA and NA, whereas Green et al.'s (1993) challenge was due to the reliance on inappropriate symmetrical formats.

The present analyses also do not confirm Tellegen et al.'s (1999) finding that state measures of PA and NA are bipolar opposites with happiness and sadness as PA and NA items. The meta-analysis predicts a polychoric correlation of $r = -.63$, which corresponds to the analysis of Schimmack and Reisenzein's (2002) data ($r = -.66$), but is considerably weaker than Tellegen et al.'s (1999) estimate ($r = -.91$). Tellegen et al.'s (1999) study is unique in several ways, but each of these methodological factors alone is unable to explain their results. First, Tellegen et al. (1999) examined state affect, whereas Diener et al. (1995) examined trait affect. However, Schimmack (2001, 2005) demonstrated that even state measures of pleasure and displeasure show discriminant validity. Second, Tellegen et al. (1999) used polychoric correlation coefficients. However, other studies with polychoric correlation coefficients still support discriminant validity, although the negative correlations are quite strong (Eid et al., 1994). Third, Tellegen et al. (1999) controlled response styles. However, Schimmack, Bockenholt, et al.

(2002) found no systematic effect of response styles on one-time assessments of PA and NA, and Watson and Tellegen (2002) also argued that response styles do not have a strong effect on single assessments of PA and NA. With correlations in the range of −.6 to −1, it becomes increasingly difficult to examine discriminant validity. As noted by Russell and Carroll (1999), evidence for discriminant validity rests on the assumption that researchers have successfully eliminated and controlled any source of measurement error. As this assumption is impossible to prove, it remains possible to defend bipolar models of state PA and NA. Fortunately, studies that go beyond psychometric analyses overcome this problem. These studies are reviewed next.

Mixed Feelings

Russell and Carroll (1999) argued that discriminant validity does not necessarily imply that PA and NA are separate affects. It is important to note, however, that their argument is limited to state measures of PA and NA with asymmetrical scales. Russell and Carroll's (1999) argument is best explained with a visual illustration. Figure 7.1 shows asymmetrical PA and NA scales that ranges from 0 (not at all) to 3 (extremely). The figure is a contingency table of the different levels of PA and NA. The hypothetical data pattern in figure 7.1 assumes that PA and NA are mutually exclusive. If somebody feels happy, he or she cannot feel sad at the same time and vice versa. Thus for any value greater than zero on PA, the value for NA must be zero, and for any value greater than zero on NA, the value for PA must be zero.

Mutually exclusive states of PA and NA do not produce a linear relationship between PA and NA. Indeed, Pearson correlations between PA and NA can range from close to zero up to −1, depending on the distribution of PA and NA (see Schimmack, 2001, for an illustration). If a study samples mostly weak affective experiences, the linear correlation is closer to zero. If a study samples mostly intense affective experiences of both valences, the linear correlation becomes increasingly negative. Russell and Carroll's (1999) model of mutually exclusive states of PA and NA is compatible with traditional notions of discriminant validity. The reason is that, in figure 7.1, it is impossible to predict PA values from NA values and vice versa. For example, when NA is 0, PA can range from 0 to 3, and when PA is 0, NA can range from 0 to 3. As a result, asymmetrical scales of PA and NA provide unique information about an individual's SWB, even when PA and NA are mutually exclusive.

However, Russell and Carroll's (1999) model suggests that it is unnecessary to measure PA and NA separately because a single bipolar measure that covers the full range of PA and NA provides the same information as separate measures of PA and NA. For the hypothetical data pattern in figure 7.1, a bipolar measure that ranges from −3 to +3 allows perfect prediction of the unipolar PA and NA scores in figure 7.1.

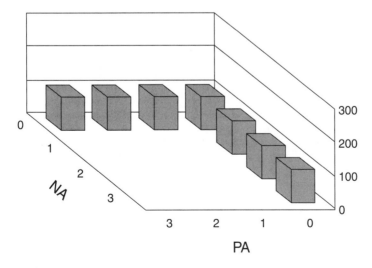

Figure 7.1 Russell and Carroll's model of mutually exclusive states of PA and NA.

For example, if the score on the bipolar measure is −2, then the NA score is 2 and the PA score is 0. If the bipolar score is +2, then PA is 2 and NA is 0. Thus, Russell and Carroll's (1999) model still poses a serious challenge to the notion of PA and NA as separate dimensions of SWB. However, the challenge assumes that state PA and NA are indeed mutually exclusive. Only a few studies have tested this hypothesis.

The first empirical test of Russell and Carroll's (1999) bipolar model was carried out by Diener and Iran-Nejad (1986; see also Beebe-Center, 1932, for a review of earlier, introspective studies of this issue). The authors asked participants to rate their affective experience on a set of affect items during everyday emotional experiences. Diener and Iran-Nejad (1986) found that high levels of PA and NA are mutually exclusive, but low levels of PA and NA are not (see figure 7.2 for an illustration). This finding undermines the assumption that state PA and NA are mutually exclusive.

Russell and Carroll (1999) argued that data patterns like Diener and Iran-Nejad's (1986) are methodological artifacts due to the selection of inappropriate items, inappropriate response formats, random measurement error, and response styles. However, several more recent studies have carefully controlled for potential method artifacts and still found evidence for mixed feelings; that is, concurrent reports of PA and NA (Hemenover & Schimmack, 2004; Hunter, Schellenberg, & Schimmack, 2006; Larsen, McGraw, & Cacioppo, 2001; Larsen, McGraw, Mellers, & Cacioppo, 2004; Schimmack, 2001, 2005; Schimmack & Colcombe, in press).

To demonstrate the validity of reports of mixed feelings, these studies used an experimental approach with a control condition. The common assumption of these studies is that reports of mixed feelings should vary across situations. Only ambivalent situations that can be appraised in a positive or negative manner should elicit mixed feelings. As a result, models with separate dimensions of PA and NA and Russell and Carroll's (1999) model make different predictions about reports of mixed feelings in different situations. Russell and Carroll's model assumes that reports of mixed feelings are due to method artifacts. Thus, the model predicts that reports of mixed feelings are the same across different situations. In contrast, models with separate dimensions of PA and NA assume that reports of mixed feelings are more frequent and more intense during ambivalent situations than during unambiguous situations.

Schimmack (2001) tested these predictions in a study of changes in affective experiences. A model with mutually exclusive states of PA and NA has to explain how affect changes when people experience one affect (e.g., PA) and are confronted with a stimulus of the opposite valence (e.g., a negative stimulus). To illustrate, imagine somebody walking along a beach in a good mood. At this moment, the individual experiences PA and NA is absent. Then the individual notices trash on the beach. How does this event influence the individual's affective experience? A model with mutually exclusive experiences of PA and NA would have to assume one of two scenarios. First, the trash fully ruins the pleasant experience of being on a sunny beach.

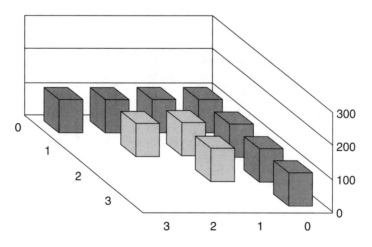

Figure 7.2 Schematic display of Diener and Iran-Nejad's (1986) findings.

Accordingly, the individual now feels NA without PA. Second, the trash merely reduces the intensity of PA, but NA remains absent. In contrast, a model with separate dimensions of PA and NA allows for the possibility that the trash induces feelings of NA without fully suppressing the initial feeling of PA, although its intensity may be reduced.

The different predictions were tested in an experiment with a mild negative mood induction. Before the mood induction, most participants reported moderate levels of PA and the absence of NA. After the mood induction, PA decreased in intensity and NA increased. Because participants started with a moderate level of PA, they still experienced PA after the mood induction. As a result, more participants experienced mixed feelings of PA and NA after the mood induction than before the mood induction. Given the significant difference in the frequency and intensity of mixed feelings between the two conditions, the results cannot be attributed to measurement artifacts. Thus, Schimmack's (2001) results are consistent with Diener and Iran-Nejad's (1986) model of separate dimensions of PA and NA and inconsistent with Russell and Carroll's (1999) model of mutually exclusive experiences of PA and NA.

Schimmack (2005) replicated and extended these findings. One extension was the manipulation of the order and the time lag between the pleasure and displeasure items. Neither of these variables had an effect on the intensity of mixed feelings after the experiment, despite a large sample size ($N = 901$). This finding suggests that reports of mixed feelings were not due to changes in affective experiences over the course of the mood assessment.

Larsen, McGraw, and Cacioppo (2001) examined experiences of happiness and sadness in ordinary situations and in ambivalent situations that could elicit happiness and sadness, such as viewing a happy and sad movie (*Life Is Beautiful*) or leaving one's dorm on graduation day. The authors found that participants reported more mixed feelings of happiness and sadness during the ambivalent situations than in normal control situations.

Schimmack and Colcombe (in press) used an old paradigm by Kellogg (1915) to examine mixed feelings. Participants were confronted with presentations of two emotional pictures. Presentations of ambivalent picture pairs elicited more intense mixed feelings than presentations of unambiguous picture pairs.

Larsen et al. (2004) found further evidence for mixed feelings with a gambling paradigm. Each gamble had two possible outcomes of the same valence (e.g., winning $5 or $12). The authors proposed that affective reactions are determined by the valence of the actual outcome (i.e., wins elicit PA, losses elicit NA) and the discrepancy with the alternative outcome (i.e., winning $5 is less desirable than winning $12). Some situations are unambiguously positive or negative (e.g., winning $12 in a gamble with $5 and $12 payoffs). Other situations are ambiguous because they are desirable in one way (winning $5), but undesirable in another way (not winning $12). Larsen et al. (2004) predicted and found that ambiguous outcomes elicited mixed feelings more frequently and intensely than unambiguous outcomes. Furthermore, the intensity of mixed feelings varied with the discrepancy between the obtained and not-obtained outcome. That is, the strongest mixed feelings were obtained for winning $5 and not winning $12, and for losing $5 and not losing $12.

A second study addressed the concern that participants experienced PA and NA in rapid alternations rather than concurrently. For this purpose, participants had to press separate keys for PA and NA as long as they experienced either affect. Rather than alternating their responses, participants pressed both keys for extended periods of time. This finding suggests that PA and NA are separate affects that can be experienced concurrently.

Whereas the previous studies focused on pleasure and displeasure and happiness and sadness, Hemenover and Schimmack (2004) examined the compatibility of two other affects, namely amusement and disgust. Participants watched a film clip with disgusting humor. Participants reported mixed feelings of disgust and amusement more frequently after than before the film clip.

Hunter et al. (2006) examined affective reactions to music. It is well known that tempo (fast vs. slow) and mode (major vs. minor) influence affective reactions to music in opposite ways. Fast music in major mode is happy, whereas slow music in minor mode is sad. Hunter et al. (2006) found that music with conflicting affective cues (e.g., fast minor or slow major) elicit more intense mixed feelings than music with consistent affective cues (e.g., fast major or slow minor).

In sum, these findings indicate that experiences of PA and NA are not mutually exclusive. As a result, it impossible to infer levels of PA and NA from a single bipolar score. For example, a score of +1 on a bipolar scale could be due to +1 PA and 0 NA, +2 PA and +1 NA, or +3 PA and + 2 NA. Thus, even studies of momentary experiences of PA and NA are more consistent with the view that PA and NA are separable dimensions of SWB (Cacioppo & Berntson, 1994; Diener & Iran-Nejad, 1986).

PA and NA Scales

The previous section did not distinguish between different measures of PA and NA because all measures of PA and NA show discriminant validity independent of item content. Furthermore, different measures of PA and NA also often show high convergent validity (Watson, 1988). Thus, it is likely that different PA or NA scales yield similar results. Nevertheless, some studies have revealed discrepant results with different measures of PA and NA. Most of these studies have focused on a comparison of the Positive and Negative Affect Schedule (PANAS; Watson, Clark, & Tellegen, 1988) with other measures of PA and NA. The PANAS scales differ from other scales in that they were developed on the basis of a psychometric model of affect that postulates two orthogonal dimensions. To obtain this objective, the scales include some items (e.g., alert, interested) that are uncommon on other measures, and they do not include items (e.g., happy, sad) that are common on other scales. These variations in item content can explain why PANAS scales sometimes produce different results than other scales.

Patrick and Lavoro (1997) examined affective reactions to pictures from the International Affective Picture System (IAPS). The IAPS contains a wide range of pictures from extremely positive to extremely negative ones. The authors hypothesized that positive pictures influence PANAS-PA, but have no effect on PANAS-NA, and negative pictures influence PANAS-NA but have no effect on PANAS-PA. Contrary to this prediction, negative pictures produced an increase in PANAS-PA. Patrick and Lavoro (1997) found that the increase in PANAS-PA in response to negative pictures was due to activation items of the PANAS-PA scale such as alert, attentive, and interested. These items reflect engagement with a stimulus but do not reveal the evaluation of a stimulus. Patrick and Lavoro's (1997) findings suggest that the PA scale of the PANAS does not provide unambiguous information about SWB because it includes activation items that reflect engagement with a stimulus independent of valence.

Another relevant finding concerns the effect of weekdays versus weekends on PA. Typically, people report more pleasant experiences on weekends than on weekdays (e.g., Stone, Hedges, Neale, & Satin, 1985). In contrast, Clark and Watson (1988) found no differences in PANAS-PA between weekdays and weekends. Egloff, Tausch, Kohlmann, and Krohne (1995) directly compared PANAS-PA and another PA scale and found significantly effects of weekend versus weekday for the ordinary PA scale, but not for PANAS-PA. Once more, this finding can be attributed to the activation component of PANAS-PA, which is likely to be higher during weekdays than weekends.

Egloff et al. (1995) also found different effects of time of day on PANAS-PA and other measures of PA. Whereas PANAS-PA increases from morning until early afternoon and then decreases in the evening, other PA scales do not show the same pattern. Again, this finding can be explained by the inclusion of activation items in the PANAS. Items such as alert reflect energetic arousal (Schimmack & Reisenzein, 2002; Thayer, 1989), and it is well known that energetic arousal has a circadian rhythm. However, pleasant affects such as happy do not show the same rhythm. Thus, scales that focus on positive valence are unlikely to show a circadian rhythm.

Schimmack (2003) compared the predictive validity of various PA items for life satisfaction judgments. Affect was assessed in an experience sampling study. The aggregated ratings of momentary happiness were a better predictor of life satisfaction than a scale that combined happiness with pride and affection. Thus, the PANAS-PA scale, which intentionally does not include happiness or related items, is likely to underestimate the contribution of affective experiences to well-being.

In sum, different PA and NA measures are likely to produce similar results because they show high convergent validity. However, different PA and NA measures are not identical and do produce different results in some situations. Thus, the best strategy might be a multidimensional assessment of PA and NA and a careful examination of specific affects (Diener et al., 1995).

Validity of Different Methods

Besides item content, researchers have to choose between methods for the assessment of PA and NA. The most common methods are self-reports, informant reports, and aggregated momentary/diary data. Each method has advantages and disadvantages. Thus, the best assessment of SWB is based on a multimethod assessment (Diener et al., 1995). However, multimethod assessments are costly and impractical in routine studies of SWB. Thus, it is important to examine the strengths and weaknesses of individual methods.

One approach examines the correlations of different methods to each other. A method with a larger amount of valid variance should be correlated more highly with other methods. Diener et al.'s (1995) multimethod study revealed that the correlation between self-reports and daily diary data of PA ($r = .68$) was higher than the correlations of these two methods with informant reports ($r = .53, .55$, respectively). For NA, correlations between self-reports and daily diary data ($r = .67$) were also higher than those with informant reports ($r = .39$, $r = .34$). This pattern of correlations suggests that retrospective self-reports and daily diary data contain equal amounts of valid variance, and more valid variance than informant reports. However, the comparison may be biased by systematic measurement variance that is common to retrospective self-reports and daily diary data. For example, socially desirable responding could inflate PA scores on both measures.

More conclusive evidence requires three truly independent methods. To my knowledge, the only study that fulfills this requirement is a multimethod study of personality traits that predict SWB, namely the depression facet of neuroticism and the positive emotion facet of extraversion (see Schimmack, Oishi, Furr, & Funder, 2004). Funder, Kolar, and Blackman (1995) reported the correlations between self-reports and three sets of informant reports, namely parents, college friends, and hometown friends, for trait measures of depression and positive emotions. For depression, the self-informant correlations ($rs = .27$ to $.43$) were stronger than the correlations among informant reports ($rs = .16$ to $.26$). For positive emotions, the self-informant correlations ($rs = .26, .34, .36$) were also stronger than the correlations among informant reports ($rs = .12$ to 33). This finding also suggests that self-reports of SWB contain more valid variance than informant reports. Funder et al. (1995) also explained why this is the case. Different informants see individuals in different contexts. Support for this hypothesis stems from much higher informant-informant correlations within each set of informants. For example, the correlations be-

tween mothers' and fathers' reports were $r = .65$ and $r = .52$ for depression and positive emotions, respectively.

Comparisons of retrospective and aggregated measures are virtually absent. Most studies have compared retrospective judgments to aggregated measures, assuming that aggregated daily ratings are more valid. However, as noted earlier, aggregated measures are biased by systematic measurement error and this bias may be more severe than the bias in retrospective ratings. Indeed, Watson and Tellegen (2002) suggested that aggregated measures that do not control for systematic measurement error are less valid than retrospective ratings. To examine this issue, I analyzed data from a daily diary study (see Schimmack, Oishi, Diener, & Suh, 2000 for details). In this study, participants rated the frequency of various emotions in the past 3 weeks. The first ratings were made before a 3-week daily diary study. Afterward, participants recorded the frequency of the same emotions each day for 3 weeks. At the end of the daily diary study, participants repeated retrospective ratings of the past 3 weeks. Importantly, these judgments covered the same 3-week period as the daily diary study. Thus, the second set of retrospective judgments is influenced by the daily recording of emotions (see Schimmack, 2002). Informant reports were used as an unbiased validation criterion. Informants completed questionnaires about life satisfaction (SWLS; Diener et al., 1985), and a short questionnaire of the Big Five. Extraversion and neuroticism were used as validation criteria because these two traits are strong predictors of SWB (Diener & Lucas, 1999).

Table 7.3 shows the results. All three measures of PA and NA predict informant reports of life satisfaction. All three measures of PA predict informant reports of extraversion, and all three measures of NA predict informant reports of neuroticism. This pattern is consistent with the theoretical model that extraversion is a disposition to experience more PA, neuroticism is a disposition to experience more NA, and life satisfaction is in part determined by the hedonic balance of PA and NA (Costa & McCrae, 1980; Diener & Lucas, 1999; Schimmack, Diener, et al., 2002). Hierarchical regression analyses revealed that retrospective postdiary ratings explained significantly more variance in neuroticism and extraversion than prediary reports. Daily diary ratings explained significantly more variance in life satisfaction and neuroticism scores than prediary ratings. Prediary self-ratings did not

TABLE 7.3 Prediction of Informant Reports of Life Satisfaction (SWLS), Extraversion, and Neuroticism

Criterion	Beta PA	Beta NA	R2
SWLS			
Self-report prediary	.19*	−.19*	.10
Self-report postdiary	.24*	−.20*	.12
Daily diary	.32*	−.34*	.15
Neuroticism			
Self-report prediary	−.08	.34*	.14
Self-report postdiary	−.18*	.35*	.19
Daily diary	−.28*	.43*	.18
Extraversion			
Self-report prediary	.23*	.01	.05
Self-report postdiary	.31*	−.07	.11
Daily diary	.19*	−.15	.04

*$p < .05$.

explain unique variance in criterion variables after controlling for postdiary ratings or daily diary data. Thus, the results suggest that daily diary data contain slightly more valid variance than retrospective ratings that are made without prior daily recording of emotions. However, even retrospective judgments prior to the daily diary study revealed predictive validity and are useful in routine studies of SWB.

Conclusion

This review examined methodological issues in the assessment of the affective component of SWB. Key conclusions were that PA and NA are separable components of SWB. The empirical relation between these dimensions depends on several methodological factors. Researchers should use asymmetric scales for the assessment of PA and NA, and they should be aware that aggregates of repeated assessments are likely to be biased by systematic measurement error. This systematic bias can be controlled in various ways (Schimmack, 2003; Watson & Tellegen, 2002). Researchers should also pay attention to the item content of PA and NA scales, as different scales sometimes produce different results. Multimethod studies are desirable, but studies with a single method are likely to produce valid results most of the time. One-time self-reports of SWB will remain the most commonly used method as they provide valid

information and are much easier to obtain than other data.

References

Bagozzi, R. P., Wong, N., & Yi, Y. (1999). The role of culture and gender in the relationship between positive and negative affect. *Cognition and Emotion, 13,* 641–672.

Barrett, L. F., & Russell, J.A. (1998). Independence and bipolarity in the structure of current affect. *Journal of Personality and Social Psychology, 74*(4), 967–984.

Beebe-Center, J. G. (1932). *Psychology of pleasantness and unpleasantness.* New York: Van Nostrand.

Cacioppo, J. T., & Berntson, G. G. (1994). Relationship between attitudes and evaluative space: A critical review, with emphasis on the separability of positive and negative substrates. *Psychological Bulletin, 115,* 401–423.

Clark, L. A., & Watson, D. (1988). Mood and the mundane: Relations between daily life events and self-reported mood. *Journal of Personality and Social Psychology, 54,* 296–308.

Costa, P. T., & McCrae, R. R. (1980). Influence of extraversion and neuroticism on subjective well-being: Happy and unhappy people. *Journal of Personality and Social Psychology, 38,* 668–678.

Diener, E. (1984). Subjective well-being. *Psychological Bulletin, 95,* 542–575.

Diener, E. (1999). Introduction to the special section on the structure of emotion. *Journal of Personality and Social Psychology, 76,* 803–804.

Diener, E. (2000). Subjective well-being: The science of happiness and a proposal for a national index. *American Psychologist, 55,* 34–43.

Diener, E., Emmons, R. A., Larsen, R. J., & Griffin, S. (1985). The Satisfaction With Life Scale. *Journal of Personality Assessment, 49,* 71–75.

Diener, E., & Iran-Nejad, A. (1986). The relationship in experience between different types of affect. *Journal of Personality and Social Psychology, 50,* 1031–1038.

Diener, E., & Lucas, R. E. (1999). Personality and subjective well-being. In D. Kahneman, E. Diener, & N. Schwarz (Eds.), *Well-being: The foundations of hedonic psychology* (pp. 213–229) New York: Russell Sage.

Diener, E., Smith, H., & Fujita, F. (1995). The personality structure of affect. *Journal of Personality and Social Psychology, 69,* 130–141.

Egloff, B., Tausch, A., Kohlmann, C., & Krohne, H. W. (1995). Relationships between time of day, day of the week, and positive mood: Exploring the role of the mood measure. *Motivation and Emotion, 19,* 99–110.

Eid, M., Notz, P., Schwenkmezger, P., & Steyer, R. (1994). Are mood dimensions monopolar? A review of empirical results and investigations with factor analyses of continuous and categorical variables as well as findings from a new study. *Zeitschrift fuer Differentielle und Diagnostische Psychologie, 15,* 211–233.

Funder, D. C., Kolar, D. C., & Blackman, M. C. (1995). Agreement among judges of personality: Interpersonal relations, similarity, and acquaintanceship. *Journal of Personality and Social Psychology, 69,* 656–672.

Green, D. P., Goldman, S. L., & Salovey, P. (1993). Measurement error masks bipolarity in affect ratings. *Journal of Personality and Social Psychology, 64,* 1029–1041.

Hemenover, S. H., & Schimmack, U. (2004). *That's disgusting! . . . , but very amusing: Mixed feelings of amusement and disgust.* Manuscript under review.

Hunter, P. G., Schellenberg, E. G., & Schimmack, U. (2006). *Mixed moods: Affective responses to music with conflicting cues.* Manuscript under review.

Kellogg, C. E. (1915). Alternation and interference of feelings. *Psychological Monographs, 18,* 1–94.

Larsen, J. T., McGraw, A. P., & Cacioppo, J. T. (2001). Can people feel happy and sad at the same time? *Journal of Personality and Social Psychology, 81,* 684–696.

Larsen, J. T., McGraw, A. P., Mellers, B. A., & Cacioppo, J. T. (2004). The agony of victory and thrill of defeat: Mixed emotional reactions to disappointing wins and relieving losses. *Psychological Science, 15,* 325–330.

Lucas, R. E., Diener, E., & Suh, E. (1996). Discriminant validity of well-being measures. *Journal of Personality and Social Psychology, 71,* 616–628.

Meddis, R. (1972). Bipolar factors in affect adjective checklists. *British Journal of Social and Clinical Psychology, 11,* 178–184.

Patrick, C. J., & Lavoro, S. A. (1997). Ratings of emotional response to pictorial stimuli: Positive and negative affect dimensions. *Motivation and Emotion, 21,* 297–322.

Russell, J. A., & Carroll, J. M. (1999). The phoenix of bipolarity: Reply to Watson and Tellegen (1999). *Psychological Bulletin, 125,* 611–617.

Schimmack, U. (2001). Pleasure, displeasure, and mixed feelings? Are semantic opposites mutually exclusive? *Cognition and Emotion, 15,* 81–97.

Schimmack, U. (2002). Frequency judgments of emotions: The cognitive basis of personality assessment. In P. Sedelmeier & T. Betsch (Eds.), *Frequency processing and cognition* (pp. 189–204). Oxford: Oxford University Press.

Schimmack, U. (2003). Affect measurement in experience sampling research. Journal of *Happiness Studies, 4,* 79–106.

Schimmack, U. (2004). Unpublished data.

Schimmack, U. (2005). Response latencies of pleasure and displeasure ratings: Further evidence for mixed feelings. *Cognition and Emotion, 19,* 671–691.

Schimmack, U., Bockenholt, U., & Reisenzein, R. (2002). Response styles in affect ratings: Making a mountain out of a molehill. *Journal of Personality Assessment, 78,* 461–483.

Schimmack, U., & Colcombe, S. (in press). *Eliciting mixed feelings with the paired-picture paradigm: A tribute to Kellogg (1915).* Cognition and Emotion.

Schimmack, U., Diener, E., & Oishi, S. (2002). Life-satisfaction is a momentary judgment and a stable personality characteristic: The use of chronically accessible and stable sources. *Journal of Personality, 70,* 345–385.

Schimmack, U., Oishi, S., & Diener, E. (2002). Cultural influences on the relation between pleasant emotions and unpleasant emotions: Asian dialectic philosophies or individualism-collectivism? *Cognition and Emotion, 16,* 705–719.

Schimmack, U, Oishi, S., Diener, E., & Suh, M. (2000). Facets of affective experiences: A new look at the relation between pleasant and unpleasant affect. *Personality and Social Psychology Bulletin, 26,* 655–668.

Schimmack, U., Oishi, S., Furr, B. M., & Funder, D. C. (2004). Personality and life satisfaction: A facet level analysis. *Personality and Social Psychology Bulletin, 30,* 1062–1075.

Schimmack, U., & Reisenzein, R. (2002). Experiencing activation: Energetic arousal and tense arousal are not mixtures of valence and activation. *Emotion, 2,* 412–417.

Stone, A. A., Hedges, S. M., Neale, J. M., & Satin, M. S. (1985). Prospective and cross-sectional mood reports offer no evidence of a ''blue Monday'' phenomenon. *Journal of Personality and Social Psychology, 49,* 129–134.

Tellegen, A., Watson, D., & Clark, L. A. (1999). On the dimensional and hierarchical structure of affect. *Psychological Science, 10,* 297–303.

Thayer, R. E. (1989). *The biopsychology of mood and arousal.* London: Oxford University Press.

Watson, D. (1988). The vicissitudes of mood measurement: Effects of varying descriptors, time frames, and response formats on measures of positive and negative affect. *Journal of Personality and Social Psychology, 55,* 128–141.

Watson, D., Clark, L. A., & Tellegen, A. (1988). Development and validation of brief measures of positive and negative affect: The PANAS scales. *Journal of Personality and Social Psychology, 54,* 1063–1070.

Watson, D., & Tellegen, A. (1999). Issues in dimensional structure of affect—Effects of descriptors, measurement error, and response formats: Comment on Russell and Carroll (1999). *Psychological Bulletin, 125,* 601–610.

Watson, D., & Tellegen, A. (2002). Aggregation, acquiescence, and the assessment of trait affectivity. *Journal of Research in Personality, 36,* 589–597.

Zelenski, J. M., & Larsen, R. J. (2000). The distribution of basic emotions in everyday life: A state and trait perspective from experience sampling data. *Journal of Research in Personality, 34,* 178–197.

8

Using Structural Equation Models to Validate Measures of Positive Emotions

Richard E. Lucas

Positive emotions play an important role in a comprehensive positive psychology. First and foremost, positive emotions serve as an indicator that one's life is on the right track. Diener and Lucas (2000) reviewed evidence that positive emotions are strongly related to individuals' overall evaluations of their lives. By measuring positive emotions and correlating this outcome with various predictor variables, researchers can identify the characteristics that are necessary for a good life. In addition, by measuring positive emotions following interventions, researchers can determine the best ways to increase well-being. Thus, positive emotional experiences serve as a useful outcome variable in investigations of the good life.

Yet emotional experiences do more than just provide a criterion variable for researchers determined to improve people's lives. Emotions are functional, and recent research shows that positive emotions can influence important outcomes. Positive emotions have been shown to affect creativity, sociability, and confidence, and they can even lead to greater income, better health, and longer lives (see Lyubomirsky, King, & Diener, 2005, for a review). Fredrickson (1998, 2001) has integrated these findings in a theory

about the nature and function of positive emotions. In her broaden-and-build theory, Fredrickson (2002) posits that positive emotions *"broaden* people's momentary thought-action repertoires and *build* their enduring personal resources" (p. 122). Thus, by fostering positive emotions, psychologists can potentially increase other positive characteristics and outcomes in individuals' lives.

Positive emotions are also stable over time (Watson & Walker, 1996), and thus they serve as an important individual difference variable in positive psychology (Watson, 2002). In fact, individual differences in positive emotionality are strongly correlated with the widely studied personality trait of extraversion (Lucas & Fujita, 2000). Based on this finding, a number of researchers have suggested that the combined extraversion/positive emotionality disposition is one of between two and five of the most basic personality dimensions that exist (Elliot & Thrash, 2002; Tellegen, 1985; Watson & Clark, 1997). Thus, investigations into the factors that lead to stable individual differences in positive emotions have implications for a variety of theories in positive psychology and personality more generally.

As is true with any psychological construct, the measurement of positive emotions can benefit from the use of advanced quantitative techniques such as structural equation modeling. Structural equation modeling "is a comprehensive statistical approach to testing hypotheses about relations among observed and latent variables" (Hoyle, 1995b, p. 1). As this broad definition suggests, the approach comprises multiple specific techniques linked by a general focus on developing testable models that describe the links among observed and latent variables. For instance, multiple measures of a construct can be assessed and modeled to eliminate measurement error or to determine whether a variety of measures cohere. In addition, specialized models can be tested to rule out artifactual explanations of research findings involving measures of positive emotions. In this chapter, I use the term *structural equation modeling* broadly, and I focus on various specific applications of this general technique.

In the following pages, I first review definitional and conceptual issues regarding positive emotions. Next, I cover some basic structural equation modeling techniques that can be used to evaluate the psychometric properties of positive emotion measures. Finally, I discuss some unique theoretical issues that can be addressed using specialized structural equation modeling techniques. Throughout the chapter, I discuss advantages and disadvantages of these techniques when compared to alternative methods of analysis.

Definitions and Conceptual Issues

Structural equation models are designed to test hypotheses about associations among variables. Thus, when using these techniques to validate measures of positive emotions, it is first necessary to have strong theories about the nature of the construct. Researchers can use these theories to develop predictions about how various measures will relate to one another. They can then use structural equation modeling techniques to test whether these predictions hold. For instance, a researcher may acquire self-report, informant-report, and physiological measures of positive emotions and may use structural equation modeling techniques to model an underlying latent trait. However, this model only makes sense if one believes that (a) emotions have characteristic physiological concomitants, (b) people

can accurately recognize and report on their own emotions, and (c) signs of these internal emotions leak out and can be recognized by others. Thus, before structural equation modeling techniques can be used, researchers must deal with issues regarding the definition of positive emotions.

Unfortunately, this is not a simple task. Even for the broader category of emotions in general, there is no single, widely agreed upon definition (Frijda, 1999; Kleinginna & Kleinginna, 1981; Larsen & Fredrickson, 1999; Ortony & Turner, 1990). Instead, existing definitions incorporate a variety of features that have been proposed by one theorist or another to be central. Frijda, for instance, listed five central components. He argued that an emotion includes: (a) a valenced appraisal of the current environment, (b) a valenced feeling state (also known as affect), (c) an action tendency, (d) a distinct pattern of physiological changes, and (e) a change in cognitive activity. Of course it is possible that no single component is a necessary feature. Fredrickson (1998), for instance, argued that positive emotions do not always have specific action tendencies.

Attempts to define emotions are further complicated by the fact that people may mean different things when they use this term. For instance, researchers have distinguished among positive emotions, positive moods, and positive affective traits (Lucas, Diener, & Larsen, 2003; Rosenberg, 1998), yet all three are often linked under a single term. When researchers use the term in a precise way, emotions are typically thought of as short-lived reactions to specific positive or negative events (Frijda, 1999). Moods are longer-lived states that do not necessarily occur in reaction to anything specific (Morris, 1999). And affective traits are the stable individual differences that result from consistent levels of positive moods or emotions. The conceptual confusion is exacerbated by the fact that emotions, moods, and affective traits are difficult to separate empirically. For instance, if we ask a person how he or she is feeling, it is difficult to determine whether that person is experiencing a mood or an emotion. Similarly, when researchers administer emotion questions multiple times over the course of an entire day, are they capturing emotions, moods, or an affective disposition? The answer to such questions may influence the models that emotion researchers construct. For instance, although emotions may be accompanied by strong action tendencies, moods may not. Thus, measures that focus on action tendencies may be expected to exhibit different relations with other components depending on whether moods or emotions are assessed. In this chapter, I use the terms *positive emotions* and *positive affect* very inclusively, though occasionally I specify which aspect of positive emotions I am describing when necessary.

Once one has an idea about the nature and definition of positive emotions, one must decide which specific emotions to assess. This decision can be guided by structural models of emotion—models that attempt to provide a comprehensive description of the associations among various emotion concepts. In general, there are two types of structural models. *Basic emotion models* posit that there is a small number of qualitatively distinct emotions and that all other emotions result from combinations of these basic components (see Ortony & Turner, 1990, for a review). For example, basic emotions may be those that have distinct action tendencies, and more complex emotional experiences may result from the simultaneous elicitation of multiple action tendencies. Unfortunately, there is much disagreement about the criteria that psychologists should use to identify the basic emotions (Ekman, 1992a, 1992b; Izard, 1992; Panksepp, 1992; Turner & Ortony, 1992. Facial expressions, action tendencies, physiological patterns, and cognitive appraisals have all been nominated as necessary criteria, though a consensus about which of these is most important has not been reached. Lucas et al. (2003) noted, however, that most basic emotion models posit the existence of only one general positive emotion (variously labeled joy, happiness, elation, or pleasure). Models that do include more specific positive emotions have included courage, hope, love, wonder, inspiration, interest, desire, and contentment.

An alternative to basic emotion models are *dimensional models* of emotional experience. Proponents of these models reject the notion that there are qualitatively distinct categories of emotions and instead focus on the similarities among different emotions. For instance, when participants report on their emotions over time, certain emotions tend to co-occur. Similarly, certain trait-level emotional experiences often cluster together. Dimensional theorists investigate the covariance among various emotion terms and hope to reduce the large set of emotions to a smaller set of more basic underlying

dimensions. Some even argue that these basic dimensions will inform theories about distinct (possibly physiological) systems that are responsible for broad categories of behaviors, cognitions, and affective experiences (e.g., Tellegen, 1985).

As with the basic emotion models, there is some disagreement about the nature and number of underlying emotion dimensions. Some researchers argue that three dimensions are needed to account for the variance in emotional experience (e.g., Schimmack & Grob, 2000). Others suggest that only two dimensions are required (e.g., Russell, 1980; Watson & Tellegen, 1985). For instance, Russell argued that most emotional experiences can be described in terms of independent pleasantness and arousal dimensions. The emotion "excited" would consist of high pleasantness and high arousal, whereas the emotion "content" would consist of high pleasantness and low arousal. Watson and Tellegen argued that these dimensions should be rotated 45 degrees to create a high-arousal positive affect dimension (renamed "positive activation"; Watson, Wiese, Vaidya, & Tellegen, 1999) and a high-arousal negative affect dimension (renamed "negative activation"). Watson, Tellegen, and their colleagues posited that this rotation is preferable because these rotated dimensions are more closely aligned with two basic personality dimensions: extraversion and neuroticism (Tellegen, 1985; Watson et al., 1999; though see Lucas & Fujita, 2000; Lucas & Baird, 2004, for contrary evidence).

Regardless of the rotation that is used, many dimensional theorists argue that emotions take the form of a circumplex. According to this view, distinct emotions can be arranged in a circle around the point formed by the intersection of the two independent dimensions (Larsen & Diener, 1992). Different emotional experiences result from different combinations of the underlying dimensions, and the similarities among various emotions can be described by their distance from one another on the circumference of the circle. Two emotions that are located 90 degrees from one another should be uncorrelated, whereas emotions that are opposite one another on the circumplex should be perfectly inversely correlated.

Each of these conceptual and definitional debates can lead to specific predictions about the way that various emotion measures relate to one another. Flexible structural equation models provide powerful ways to test various emotion models against one another and also to ensure that emotion measures are valid. For instance, if emotions truly are multicomponential, then the various components should be measurable and they should cohere over time. Similarly, the various structural models imply that various emotion terms should relate to one another in predictable ways. Thus, these models can be tested to determine whether any specific model can be rejected. In the next sections, I review the ways that structural equation modeling techniques have been applied to validating measures of positive emotions. I begin by describing basic psychometric models that are not unique to the construct of positive emotions, and then I move to more specific models that are uniquely suited to testing hypotheses about the nature of positive emotion measures.

Using Structural Equation Models to Test Psychometric Properties

In many ways, positive emotions are no different from any other construct. If the construct is valid, researchers should be able to measure it, and the measures should have desirable psychometric characteristics including reliability, convergent validity, and discriminant validity. Multiple methods of assessment should cohere, and alternative explanations regarding the nature of the construct should be able to be ruled out. As numerous general books and chapters on structural equation modeling have shown (e.g., Bollen, 1989b; Hoyle, 1995a), there are a number of basic models that can be used to investigate whether measures have desirable psychometric properties.

For instance, two of the most basic criteria that must be met to demonstrate construct validity are the criteria of convergent and discriminant validity (Campbell & Fiske, 1959). If a construct is valid, different measures of the same construct should cohere (convergent validity), and these measures should be distinguishable from measures of different constructs (discriminant validity). To assess these forms of validity, multitrait-multimethod analyses can be conducted. According to the logic of multitrait-multimethod analyses, correlations among different types of positive emotion measures should be strong enough to suggest that they each measure a single underlying trait. In addition, correlations between positive emotions and different constructs assessed using the same

method should not be so strong as to suggest that method variance overwhelms the valid trait variance in the scale.

Although multitrait-multimethod matrices provide a useful way to demonstrate convergent and discriminant validity, interpretation of these matrices is subjective and difficult. For instance, Lucas, Diener, and Suh (1996) examined the convergent and discriminant validity of five constructs—positive affect, negative affect, life satisfaction, self-esteem, and optimism—using a "vote-counting" procedure. In each of three studies, each construct was measured using either two or three methods. Multitrait-multimethod matrices were constructed, and correlations were examined to determine whether they met Campbell and Fiske's (1959) criteria. The total number of successes was compared to the total number of failures to give an overall picture of validity. Although support for the validity of the constructs was found, conclusions were somewhat subjective. How many successes are required to accept the constructs as valid? How different do correlations have to be to suggest that two constructs are truly discriminable?

Structural equation modeling analyses of multitrait-multimethod matrices can provide strong answers to questions about convergent and discriminant validity (Eid, 2000; Kenny & Kashy, 1992; Marsh & Grayson, 1995). Separate trait and method factors can be modeled, and correlations among trait factors can be examined. To demonstrate, I reanalyzed the matrices from Study 1 of Lucas et al. (1996) to assess the validity of the measures. Each of the five traits was assessed in three ways: self-report, self-report measures 1 month later, and informant reports. Following Eid's advice, I tested a model with five latent trait factors and two latent method factors (one less method factor than the total number of methods that were used). The basic outline of this model is shown in figure 8.1 (ignore the parameter labels for now). The model was identified by constraining the latent variances to be equal to 1. In all models that I present, I report the chi-square, chi-square divided by degrees of freedom, the incremental fit index (IFI; Bollen, 1989a), the Tucker-Lewis index (TLI; Tucker & Lewis, 1973), and the root mean square error of approximation (RMSEA).

The model presented in figure 8.1 fit the data well: $\chi^2 (70) = 102.89$, $p < .01$, $\chi^2/df = 1.47$, IFI = 1.00, TLI = 1.00, RMSEA = .05. Thus, the various measures of each construct cohered well enough to support a model with five distinct

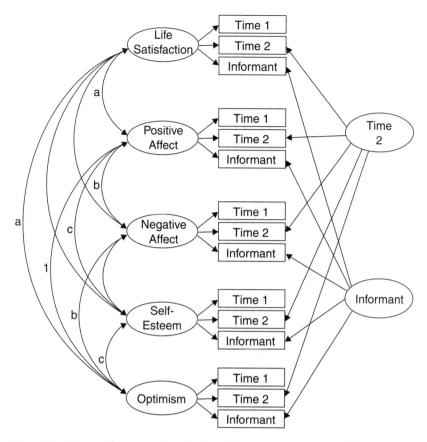

Figure 8.1 Using multitrait-multimethod models to test convergent and discriminant validity.

latent traits, a result that supports the convergent validity of these measures. However, the model also provides information about discriminant validity, and the estimated correlations among the latent traits suggest that there is reason for concern. Although the correlation between positive and negative affect was just −.16, the correlations between positive affect and life satisfaction, optimism, and self-esteem were relatively high: .63, .70, and .63, respectively. The question that emerges from this analysis is whether a correlation as high as .70 is strong enough to suggest that two constructs are really the same. Fortunately, structural equation models allow researchers to test such a hypothesis explicitly.

The parameter labels in figure 8.1 show constraints that can be made to determine whether positive affect is distinguishable from the construct of optimism. In this model (as in the unconstrained model described previously), I have identified the model by constraining the

variances of the latent trait factors to be 1. Once this is done, one can test a more restricted model by constraining the covariance between positive emotions and optimism to be 1 and by constraining the correlations between positive affect and each other construct to be the same as the correlations between optimism and these same constructs (paths that are constrained to equality have the same parameter labels in figure 8.1). An alternative way to test this model would be to delete either the positive affect or optimism latent trait and add paths from the remaining latent trait to the indicators for the variable that was removed (these two models are equivalent). After making this constraint, the model fit was satisfactory by some indexes, but significantly worse than the unconstrained model: χ^2 (74) = 200.66, $p < .01$, $\chi^2/df = 2.71$, IFI = 0.99, TLI = 0.98, RMSEA = .09. The change in χ^2 (with four degrees of freedom) was a significant 97.78. Thus, positive affect and optimism, although strongly correlated, are distinguishable.

Strong conclusions about convergent and discriminant validity of positive emotion measures simply cannot be made by examining the pattern of correlations in a multitrait-multimethod matrix. Thus, structural equation models provide a better test of these important psychometric criteria. Unfortunately, multitrait-multimethod matrix models have their own set of problems, foremost among them that they are often difficult to estimate (Kenny & Kashy, 1992; Marsh & Grayson, 1995). In fact, in attempting to test the discriminant validity of positive emotions from the Lucas et al. (1996) studies, I could not test a model with just three latent traits (positive affect, negative affect, and life satisfaction). This model resulted in a non-positive-definite matrix that prevented the model from being estimated.[1] In addition, when I tried to test a similar model using the data from Study 2 from Lucas et al., the model could not be estimated when all five traits were included. I could only run a model using four of the five traits. Thus, researchers may find that despite their best intentions, they may not be able to test convergent and discriminant validity in multitrait-multimethod matrices using structural equation modeling techniques. However, it is often possible to overcome these problems by modeling the multiple traits and multiple methods in different ways. Kenny and Kashy (1999), Eid (2000), and Marsh and Grayson (1995) are recommended as resources for those who do wish to use these models.

A second psychometric concern that researchers can investigate using structural equation models is the extent to which the measurement properties of positive emotion scales are invariant across different samples. For instance, some researchers may want to translate existing positive emotion scales into different languages. If translation is not perfect, items may mean different things in different versions of the scale. If this were the case, the items would correlate differently with one another. Thus, structural equation models that explicitly test whether items relate to one another in the same way across languages provide a test of the accuracy of the scale translation.

However, measurement invariance models are applicable in many more general situations outside of cross-cultural research. Even with perfect translations or among participants that speak the same language, indicators of an underlying latent trait may be differentially related to one another. For instance, Diener and Suh (1998) suggested that age-related changes in

positive emotions may occur differently for high-arousal emotions than for low-arousal emotions. Thus, positive emotions of varying arousal levels may relate to one another differently among samples of the young and old. Structural equation models that test for measurement invariance can be used to determine whether the same underlying latent trait is being measured in the same way across different samples (Reise, Widaman, & Pugh, 1993; Widaman & Reise, 1997).

To demonstrate this approach, I used data from the second International College Student study, which was run by Ed Diener and colleagues. In this study, over 10,000 students from 48 nations answered a variety of questions about subjective well-being and emotions. I wanted to know whether four positive emotions (pleasant, happy, cheerful, and pride) would (a) cohere well enough to support a single-factor model, (b) exhibit the same associations across two Western nations (the United States and Spain), and (c) exhibit the same associations in a non-Western nation (Korea). I first fit a single-factor model in which each of the four emotions loaded on a single latent trait and all parameters were estimated separately for each of the three nations (the model was identified by constraining the path from one indicator to the latent variable to be 1). This model fit reasonably well: χ^2 (6) = 15.098, $p < .05$, $\chi^2/df = 2.52$, IFI = 1.00, TLI = 1.00, RMSEA = .04. I next constrained the three free factor loadings and the latent variance to be equal across the U.S. and Spanish samples. This led to a nonsignificant increase in the chi-square, $\Delta\chi^2$ (4) = 6.5, ns. Finally, I constrained the three free factor loadings and the latent variance to be equal in all three samples. This, too, led to a nonsignificant increase in the chi-square, both when compared to the full unconstrained model, $\Delta\chi^2$ (8) = 13.6, ns, and when compared to the U.S./Spain constrained model, $\Delta\chi^2$ (4) = 7.1, ns. Thus, it appears that the same latent positive affect trait is being measured in these three nations.

As Tomarken and Waller (2003) have pointed out, one must be careful even when interpreting models that clearly fit well. It is possible that certain well-fitting parts of the model may compensate for particularly poor-fitting parts of the model when global fit indexes are used. For instance, there are theoretical reasons to expect that the emotion of pride may exhibit different relations with other positive emotion variables in collectivist cultures than it does in individualist cultures (Eid & Diener, 2001). However, when we constrain the loadings for all emotion terms to be equal across nations simultaneously, a large decrease in fit due to this one constraint may be hidden by the lack of change in fit when the other three parameters are constrained. Thus, it is often useful to examine specific, theoretically relevant constraints separately. In this case, it turns out that even when we constrain the loading for pride separately, the change in fit is not significant: $\Delta\chi^2 (1) = 1.4$, *ns*. Thus, it appears as though these four positive emotion variables exhibit similar single-factor structures in college students from the United States, Spain, and Korea.

Techniques for assessing measurement invariance are very flexible and can be used to test a variety of hypotheses about the performance of measures across samples or over time. For instance, although I constrained factor loadings and variances in the models tested above, one could also test whether mean levels are the same across samples (Little, 1997). And, of course, these techniques are not only restricted to analyses at the item level. Lucas, Diener, Grob, Suh, and Shao (2000) used means and covariance structural analyses to show that different types of positive emotion measures (frequency of positive affect, intensity of positive affect, and the experience of high-arousal positive affect) related to one another in similar ways in the United States, other individualistic nations, and collectivistic nations. Thus, these techniques can provide important information about the ways that scales behave across samples.

Because structural equation modeling techniques are flexible, a variety of other psychometric issues can be tested. For instance, researchers may have concerns about specific types of systematic error in their measures. It is possible that scales tap into unwanted response sets or response styles. Structural equation modeling techniques can be used to test these hypotheses. For example, Fossum and Barrett (2000) suggested that the associations between positive affect and the personality trait of extraversion could result from stable individual differences in the tendency to respond to items on the basis of evaluative content. To test this hypothesis, the authors acquired multiple measures of extraversion and multiple measures of the tendency to respond on the basis of evaluative content. They then constructed a structural equation model designed to assess whether evaluation mediated the link between personality and affect. By using multiple measures to assess evaluation, the authors were able to avoid one common criticism of tests of mediational models, namely that mediation can only be tested when the mediator is measured reliably. Fossum and Barrett found that although evaluation was related to both extraversion and positive affect, it could not completely mediate the association between the two. This suggests that the two constructs are linked by some process other than a simple tendency to respond positively to evaluative content.

Eid and Diener (2004) used structural equation models to determine whether irrelevant situational factors (namely fluctuating levels of mood) influenced judgments of supposedly stable levels of affect and subjective well-being. Schwarz and Strack (1999) argued that when making global judgments of subjective well-being, respondents often rely on their current mood rather than systematically reviewing their recent affective experiences. Thus, Schwarz and Strack argued, any situational factors that can influence current mood should also be able to influence judgments of long-term subjective well-being (a fact that would reduce the validity of these measures). Eid and Diener pointed out that if this possibility were correct, then global judgments of well-being should be relatively unstable over time (or at least as unstable as momentary mood) and should change as momentary mood changes.

To test this possibility, Eid and Diener (2004) assessed subjective well-being components (including trait levels of positive affect) three times over a 2-month period. In addition, they assessed current mood at each occasion. Finally, they tested a multistate-multitrait-multiconstruct model that allowed them to separate measurement error from occasion-specific deviations and stable individual differences in each of the measures. Specifically, their models included latent trait factors, latent occasion factors, and latent construct (trait mood versus state mood) factors. This model allowed them to determine the reliability, consistency, and occasion specificity for each of the two positive affect components they assessed (love and joy). In accordance with their hypothesis (and contrary to the previous experimental work), Eid and Diener found that for the trait positive affect scales, (a) consistency coefficients were almost as high as the reliabilities, (b) occasion-specific components were relatively small (usually accounting for just 9–17% of the variance), and (c) correlations with occasion-specific mood were often small. Thus, they concluded that trait measures of positive emotions are not strongly influenced by irrelevant situational factors, and that trait measures are valid.

Together, these examples show that structural equation models can be applied in a variety of ways to provide strong evidence about the validity of positive emotion measures. Although I covered only a few basic psychometric questions, most concerns about the quality of measures can be addressed using these flexible techniques. All one must do is to translate psychometric concerns into testable predictions regarding the precise ways that different measures relate to one another. For instance, if a researcher believes that a research finding involving positive emotions results from a systematic method variance factor, all he or she needs to do is to measure multiple constructs using that method and control for this method factor in a structural equation model. The extent to which we can reject alternative explanations provides strong support for the quality of positive emotions measures.

Using Structural Equation Models to Test Conceptual Questions

The models described in the previous section can be applied to test the psychometric properties of any measure, not just those that tap positive emotions. Yet, as noted previously, there are certain characteristics of positive emotions and positive emotion models that make them particularly well suited to be tested using structural equation modeling techniques. Specifically, most models of emotion assume that different emotion variables will relate to one another in predictable ways. Therefore, structural equation models can be adapted to test these hypotheses. In this section, I review some of the ways that these techniques have been used to test theoretical questions about positive emotions.

Number of Dimensions

One of the biggest debates within the field has centered on the extent to which any single dimensional model of emotions has more empirical support than others. As noted previously, some researchers claim that there are two independent pleasantness and arousal dimensions that underlie emotional experiences (e.g., Russell, 1980), whereas others claim that rotated

positive activation and negative activation (Watson et al., 1999) or energetic arousal and tense arousal dimensions (Thayer, 1989) are preferable. Yet a more fundamental debate concerns the extent to which two-dimensional models are truly more appropriate than models with more than two dimensions. For instance, Schimmack and Grob (2000) argued that there is a long history of support for three-dimensional models among European researchers (e.g., Matthews, Jones, & Chamberlain, 1990; Sjoberg, Svensson, & Persson, 1979; Steyer, Schwenkmezger, Notz, & Eid, 1994, cited in Schimmack & Grob). These researchers have found support for a model that includes three dimensions marked by pleasure-displeasure, awake-tired, and tension-relaxation.

It is possible, using structural equation modeling, to test the relative fit of two-dimensional models versus three-dimensional models. To do so, Schimmack and Grob (2000) assessed a variety of affect items reflecting the three dimensions found in the European models. If two-dimensional models are correct, the three-dimensional model should be able to be reduced to a more parsimonious two-factor structure. Schimmack and Grob first tested a three-factor model with freely estimated correlations among the different factors. This model fit the data well. Because the three factors correlated moderately to strongly with one another, it was conceivable that the reduced two-factor model would fit. Therefore, Schimmack and Grob went on to test whether these correlations were strong enough to suggest that a more parsimonious two-factor model could account for the data equally well.

The authors tested this possibility by constructing a variety of theoretically based two-factor models (also see Schimmack & Reisenzein, 2002). For instance, one two-factor model suggests that awake-tired and tense-relaxed are indicators of a single underlying activation factor. If this model were correct, the correlation between the latent awake-tired and tense-relaxed variables should be able to be constrained to 1. Schimmack and Grob (2000) showed that making such a constraint leads to a considerable reduction in fit. Thus, awake-tired and tense-relaxed cannot be reduced to a single dimension. Other models suggest that the experience of pleasure is simply the result of the combined activation of underlying energetic arousal and tense arousal dimensions. Schimmack and Grob tested this model by adding directional paths to the latent pleasantness trait from their latent awake-tired and tense-relaxed traits. Although this model is equivalent to their own three-factor model, they were able to investigate the amount of variance that is accounted for in the pleasantness trait. In accordance with their hypothesis that pleasantness is not simply the sum of energetic arousal and tense arousal, only 57% of the variance in pleasantness could be explained by the other two dimensions.

It is interesting to note that although two-factor solutions are often found in exploratory factor analysis of mood and emotion terms (though see Church, Katigbak, Reyes, & Jensen, 1999, for an exception), two-factor models are rarely confirmed using structural equation modeling techniques (Watson et al., 1999). Although there are some conceptual reasons why this may be the case (see Church et al., for a discussion), the models tested by Schimmack and Grob (2000) suggest that three factors provide a better description of core affective experiences than do two-factor models. In addition, Schimmack and Grob illustrated how structural equation models can be constructed to test a variety of theoretical predictions. In addition to just testing nested two- and three-factor models, these authors were able to use distinct but mathematically equivalent models to determine whether the parameters from the models match different theories' predictions. Thus, their paper makes an important point about the use of structural equation models. Researchers should not simply limit themselves to comparing the fit of various nested models. Although models must fit well to be interpretable and models must be nested for statistical tests of relative fit to be conducted, the parameters themselves can provide important information about the extent to which various models of positive emotions provide an accurate description of the data.

Bipolarity of Affect

A second debate that has been informed by research using structural equation modeling techniques is the debate regarding bipolarity of positive and negative affect. As long as research on emotions has been conducted, psychologists have debated whether positive and negative emotions reflect two poles of a single underlying dimension (see Green, Goldman, & Salovey, 1993, for a review). According to the bipolar perspective, positive emotions such as happiness are polar opposites of negative emotions such as sadness. Thus, according to this perspective,

positive and negative emotions cannot be exhibited at the same time and should show correlations that approach -1.

Although the bipolar perspective is intuitively appealing, there is somewhat greater consensus that positive and negative emotions are not in fact perfectly inversely correlated, but instead form two independent dimensions (Diener, Suh, Lucas, & Smith, 1999). Independence theorists might not suggest that individuals can experience intense happiness at the same time as intense sadness, but they do allow for some co-occurrence of positive and negative emotions and mood, and they predict that people's long-term levels of positive affect will be independent from their long-term levels of negative affect (Diener & Emmons, 1984).

Debates about bipolarity have raged for years, with most studies using simple correlational analyses to provide support for their hypotheses. However, in 1993, Green et al. argued that these studies led to flawed findings because they failed to take random error and systematic response styles into account. These authors suggested that "when one adjusts for random and systematic error in positive and negative affect, correlations between the two that at first seem close to 0 are revealed to be closer to -1.00 and support a largely bipolar structure" (p. 1029). Thus, it seemed, questions about the bipolarity of positive and negative affect could be answered once and for all using structural equation modeling techniques. Green et al. went on to conduct three studies in which participants completed a variety of emotion items using a variety of response formats (including checklists, Likert scales, and agree-disagree scales). They showed that when multiple methods were used to model latent positive and negative affect factors, the two factors correlated around $-.85$, a finding that supports the bipolarity perspective.

However, Schimmack, Bockenholt, and Reisenzein (2002) showed that support for the bipolar structure was not as strong as Green et al.'s (1993) study initially suggested. Although it was true that the correlations between the latent traits in their models did approach -1, it was not the case that the raw correlations in their studies approached 0. Instead, many of the raw correlations were around $-.60$. In addition, Schimmack et al. pointed out, a number of studies that had been conducted since the publication of Green et al.'s study used multiple methods of assessment, and these studies often (though not always) found weak to moderate correlations between latent positive and negative affect factors. Finally, Schimmack et al. pointed out that if shared method variance deflates the negative correlations among oppositely valenced affect items, then there should be strong positive covariances among the error terms for indicators that share the same method. Schimmack et al. conducted two studies to demonstrate that these method effects were very weak and could only deflate correlations to a slight extent.

So what could account for the discrepancies across studies? Schimmack et al. (2002) argued that the answer had nothing to do with measurement error, and instead was related to participants' interpretation of the response scales that various researchers had used. Specifically, the authors showed that when participants are asked to report whether they are "happy" using a scale that ranges from "strongly disagree" to "strongly agree," participants often interpret that scale as bipolar. In other words, if they were experiencing low levels of happiness (without the experience of sadness), they would use the midpoint of the scale. If, on the other hand, participants are asked to rate how happy they are using a Likert scale that ranges from "not at all" to "a great deal," they will be more likely to use "not at all" to indicate low levels of happiness. Thus, Schimmack et al. argued, discrepancies across studies had nothing to do with measurement error (random or systematic), and instead resulted from the use of different response scales. This conclusion is supported by a number of studies that have used multiple methods of assessing positive and negative affect and still found relatively low correlations among the two constructs (e.g., Diener, Smith, & Fujita, 1995; Lucas et al., 1996; Schmukle, Egloff, & Burns, 2002). However, it is clear that the size of the correlation between positive and negative affect will depend greatly on the specific affect items that are included and response scales that are used.

Structural equation modeling techniques play an important role in debates about bipolarity. As Green et al. (1993) pointed out, it is absolutely essential that multiple methods of assessment are used to measure positive emotions. However, researchers must be careful to make sure that all aspects of the model accord with the hypotheses that the models are designed to test. Green et al. argued that measures of different emotions that are assessed using the same method are infused with systematic and random error, but they did not incorporate this aspect of the hypothesis into their models. A Schimmack et al. (2002) demonstrated, there are certain questions that simply cannot be answered with the structural equation models alone, and these techniques must be used with additional correlation and experimental work to provide strong tests of the underlying theories.

Circumplex Structure

Researchers who advocate for two-factor models generally posit some variation of a circumplex structure (see Larsen & Diener, 1992; Remington, Fabrigar, & Visser, 2000; Russell, 1980; Watson et al., 1999). According to circumplex models, emotion terms should be able to be arranged in a circle around the point formed by the intersection of the two independent dimensions. Correlations among emotion terms should decrease as the angle of separation approaches 90 degrees, and then become more strongly negative as the angle of separation approaches 180 degrees. As Remington et al. (2000) pointed out in a review of this literature, most early attempts to verify the circumplex structure of emotional experiences used principal components or multidimensional scaling analyses. Analyses could be conducted and emotion terms plotted in two-dimensional space to determine whether the emotions appeared to show a circular pattern. Most of these studies supported a basic circumplex structure, but these studies were limited by their inability to provide statistical tests regarding the extent to which the data conformed to the hypothesized structure.

Recent developments in structural equation modeling have allowed researchers to use more rigorous tests to evaluate the extent to which emotions form a circumplex. As Fabrigar, Visser, and Browne (1997) have shown, specialized models can be constructed to test the hypothesis that the correlation between two emotion terms is a function of the angle of their separation. Standard structural equation modeling techniques can be used, and global fit indexes can determine whether the model fits the data.

Attempts to validate circumplex models using these techniques have had mixed success. In their review of the evidence for these models, Watson et al. (1999) suggested that in most cases, circumplex models do not fit the data well. However, Remington et al. (2000) conducted a more comprehensive review and reanalysis of more than 47 studies, and they provided a somewhat more optimistic assessment. Using the RMSEA to evaluate the fit of the models,

Remington et al. found that the median fit of all models was in the "acceptable" range (RMSEA = .073). Of the 47 data sets, 9 demonstrated a good fit (RMSEA <.05), 20 had acceptable fit (RMSEA between .05 and .08), 7 had marginal fit (RMSEA between .08 and .10) and 11 had poor fit. Furthermore, Remington et al. identified a number of factors that affected the fit of the models. For instance, model fit was better when state affect items were used than when trait items were used. Although the use of structural equation modeling techniques has not provided a complete resolution to questions about circumplex structure, it provides an important tool to evaluate the extent to which the model can be supported and it allows research to focus on the factors that might affect the nature of these associations.

Hierarchical Models

Although researches have debated the merits of basic emotion models and dimensional models of emotion, some researchers have suggested that the debate can be resolved by instead focusing on hierarchical models (Tellegen, Watson, & Clark, 1999; Watson, 2000). According to hierarchical models, it is possible to identify distinct basic emotions that can may share the same valence, but can be empirically distinguished from one another. The emotions that can be distinguished are often those suggested to be basic by theorists who work from a basic emotion perspective (Church et al., 1999). However, at a higher-order level, these distinct emotions may correlate to form global positive and negative affect factors.

A number of researchers have investigated this possibility and used structural equation modeling techniques to test for hierarchical structures. For instance, Diener et al., (1995) conducted a systematic analysis of emotion models from a variety of research traditions. Specifically, they reviewed the literature on cognitive, biological-evolutionary, and empirical approaches to emotion, and they selected a set of emotion terms that had been investigated by researchers from within these traditions. Diener et al. then acquired multiple reports (self-reports, informant reports, and experience-sampling reports) for each emotion. Then, using the type of multitrait-multimethod matrix analysis described in previous sections, they examined the hierarchical structure of the emotion terms. In accordance with their predictions, Diener et al. (1995) found that a hierarchical model fit the data well. At the

lower level of the model, two specific positive emotions, joy and love, could be distinguished from one another. These two basic emotions also formed a higher-order positive affect factor that was distinct from but moderately correlated with a negative affect factor (which, in turn, consisted of four lower-level factors: shame, fear, sadness, and anger). Trierweiler, Eid, and Lischetzke (2002) found support for a similar hierarchical structure in their examination of emotional expressivity.

Church et al. (1999) investigated a similar question in multiple samples of Filipino high school and college students. In this study, the authors developed a comprehensive list of emotion words in the Tagalog language. They then used exploratory factor analysis to identify 12 distinct clusters of positive and negative emotion words. Then, in a separate sample, they used confirmatory factor analysis to test a hierarchical structure of positive and negative affect. Because of model complexity concerns, they could not test a full, three-level hierarchical model (with items, primary emotions, and higher-level emotional dimensions as the levels). Instead, they tested three separate models to determine whether (a) the various positive emotion items had a four-factor structure, (b) the various negative emotions items had an eight-factor structure, and (c) the 12 basic emotion scales (created from the summed items) had a two-factor positive and negative affect structure. In accordance with their hypotheses, all models fit well, demonstrating that the hierarchical model of affect provided a useful description of the covariance among these emotion terms.

Hierarchical models of emotions have the potential to resolve debates between theorists from the basic emotion perspective and theorists from the dimensional perspective. Structural equation models have shown that these hierarchical models provide a good description of the relations among the various emotion terms. Yet different researchers come to different conclusions about the specific emotions that should be included in the hierarchy. In two distinct theoretical analyses, Fredrickson (1998) and Watson (2000) came up with two different lists of basic positive emotions. Fredrickson suggested that positive emotions could be separated into distinct joy, interest, contentment, and love dimensions (though she leaves open the possibility that other distinct positive emotions exist), whereas Watson suggested that the lower-order positive emotion dimensions were joviality, self-assuredness, and attention. In their empirical analyses, Diener et al. (1995) identified two positive emotions: joy and love. And in their study of Filipino emotional experiences, Church et al. (1999) identified four: happy, active, calm, and unperturbed. The differences across studies, while troubling, can be easily explained by focusing on the methods that each researcher used to select the items for their models. Some researchers started with natural language, some started with a theoretical analysis, and some used a combination of these approaches. Thus, even in studies that use structural equation models to confirm hierarchical models of emotions, the results depend on the input variables. Therefore, although structural equation modeling techniques have the potential to provide important information about the structure of emotional experiences, researchers must still arrive at some consensus about the indicators that should be included in these models before the advanced quantitative techniques can answer questions about the underlying theory.

Some Cautions About the Use of Structural Equation Modeling Techniques

In much of this chapter, I have emphasized the advantages of using structural equation modeling techniques to validate measures and models of positive emotions. This optimism regarding the value of these techniques results from the fact that they are broad, diverse, and incredibly flexible. In fact, many analytic procedures that are not typically linked under the banner of structural equation modeling can really be thought of as special cases of this more general class of techniques. Thus, it is hard to argue that there are many disadvantages of using structural equation models when investigating the validity of positive emotion measures. There are certainly cases for which this technique may be inappropriate; but when it is appropriate, structural equation modeling is often the most powerful and most flexible choice available.

Yet difficulties emerge when using these techniques. Some of these difficulties are practical in nature, others are theoretical. For instance, structural equation modeling often requires large sample sizes. In certain situations, structural equation modeling may not be needed, and it may be more efficient to use less data-intensive analytic techniques. In addition, structural equation modeling requires a fair

amount of knowledge. There are many decisions regarding model specification and modification that must be made, and researchers with little training can easily make mistakes. For certain questions, the benefit of using these techniques may not be worth the added risk of mistakes.

Even experienced researchers, however, may face difficult issues when using structural equation modeling techniques. Because structural equation modeling is, in many ways, more complicated than other readily available analytic techniques, there are still many unanswered questions about the appropriate way to conduct these analyses. For instance, questions about criteria for evaluating model fit are still being debated. Thus, researchers who use these techniques may find themselves facing questions that cannot easily be answered.

Finally, some researchers (particularly inexperienced researchers) may misinterpret the results they obtain from structural equation modeling analyses. The process of testing structural equation models is somewhat different from the processes involved in other analytic techniques, and this process (along with some unfortunate terminology) may lead to overconfidence in the results. Some researchers may believe that their analyses "confirm" that their hypothesized model is correct, when all they have really shown is that their model is not inconsistent with the data they have collected. As Tomarken and Waller (2003) have noted, there are often many alternative models that may fit just as well as a hypothesized model. Researchers need to make sure that they have enough knowledge about the technique to ensure that they can draw appropriate conclusions about the results they obtain.

Summary

Positive emotions serve three roles within the domain of positive psychology. First, they serve as useful criterion variables for researchers interested in improving the quality of people's lives. Second, positive emotions are functional and can have important implications for desirable outcomes in people's lives. Finally, positive emotions are stable over time, and investigations into the processes that are responsible for these stable individual differences may provide insight into the nature of other individual differences that allow people to maintain strengths and positive characteristics over time. Yet even though positive emotions play a prominent role within this discipline, they are also somewhat difficult to assess. One cannot directly see positive emotions, and questions about the quality of positive emotion measures will always exist. Because of these difficulties, advanced quantitative methods like structural equation modeling techniques are essential. Structural equation models have been used to establish the validity of positive emotion measures, to rule out artifactual explanations of important research findings, and to clarify the nature and structure of affective experiences. Over the past decade, these techniques have been used with increasing frequency, and a number of central questions have been answered with a greater degree of certainty than could have been attained without structural equation models. Future research will benefit from continued and expanded use of these techniques to model the multifaceted and multicomponential construct of positive emotions.

Note

1. Nonpositive definite matrices can occur for many different reasons (including missing data, collinearities, outliers and nonnormal data, and empirical underidentification). In certain cases, these problems can be remedied and models can be estimated without changing the model itself. For more information about nonpositive definite matrices and strategies for dealing with this issue, see Wothke, 1995.

References

Bollen, K. A. (1989a). A new incremental fit index for general structural equation models. *Sociological Methods & Research, 16,* 492–503.

Bollen, K. A. (1989b). *Structural equations with latent variables.* Oxford: John Wiley.

Campbell, D. T., & Fiske, D. W. (1959). Convergent and discriminant validation by the multitrait-multimethod matrix. *Psychological Bulletin, 56,* 81–105.

Church, A. T., Katigbak, M. S., Reyes, J. A. S., & Jensen, S. M. (1999). The structure of affect on a non-Western culture: Evidence for cross-cultural comparability. *Journal of Personality, 67*(3), 505–534.

Diener, E., & Emmons, R. A. (1984). The independence of positive and negative affect. *Journal of Personality and Social Psychology, 47,* 1105–1117.

Diener, E., & Lucas, R. E. (2000). Subjective emotional well-being. In M. Lewis & J. M. Haviland (Eds.), *Handbook of emotions* (2nd ed.) (pp. 325–337). New York: Guilford.

Diener, E., Smith, H., & Fujita, F. (1995). The personality structure of affect. *Journal of Personality and Social Psychology, 69*(1), 130–141.

Diener, E., & Suh, M. E. (1998). Subjective well-being and age: An international analysis. In K. W. Schaie & M. P. Lawton (Eds.), *Annual review of gerontology and geriatrics, Vol. 17: Focus on emotion and adult development* (pp. 304–324). New York: Springer.

Diener, E., Suh, E. M., Lucas, R. E., & Smith, H. L. (1999). Subjective well-being: Three decades of progress. *Psychological Bulletin, 125*(2), 276–302.

Eid, M. (2000). A multitrait-multimethod model with minimal assumptions. *Psychometrika, 65*(2), 241–261.

Eid, M., & Diener, E. (2001). Norms for experiencing emotions in different cultures: Inter- and intranational differences. *Journal of Personality and Social Psychology, 81,* 869–885.

Eid, M., & Diener, E. (2004). global judgments of subjective well-being: Situational variability and long-term stability. *Social Indicators Research, 65,* 245–277.

Ekman, P. (1992a). An argument for basic emotions. *Cognition and Emotion, 6*(3–4), 169–200.

Ekman, P. (1992b). Are there basic emotions? *Psychological Review, 99,* 550–553.

Elliot, A. J., & Thrash, T. M. (2002). Approach-avoidance motivation in personality approach and avoidance temperaments and goals. *Journal of Personality and Social Psychology, 82,* 804–818.

Fabrigar, L. R., Visser, P. S., & Browne, M. W. (1997). Conceptual and methodological issues in testing the circumplex structure of data in personality and social psychology. *Personality and Social Psychology Review, 1*(3), 184–203.

Fossum, T. A., & Barrett, L. F. (2000). Distinguishing evaluation from description in the personality-emotion relationship. *Personality and Social Psychology Bulletin, 26,* 669–678.

Fredrickson, B. L. (1998). What good are positive emotions? *Review of General Psychology, 2*(3), 300–319.

Fredrickson, B. L. (2001). The role of positive emotions in positive psychology: The broaden-and-build theory of positive emotions. *American Psychologist, 56*(3), 218–226.

Fredrickson, B. L. (2002). Positive emotions. In C. R. Snyder & S. J. Lopez (Eds.), *Handbook of positive psychology* (pp. 120–134). London: Oxford University Press.

Frijda, N. H. (1999). Emotions and hedonic experience. In D. Kahneman & E. Diener (Eds.), *Well being: The foundations of hedonic psychology* (pp. 190–210). New York: Russell Sage.

Green, D. P., Goldman, S. L., & Salovey, P. (1993). Measurement error masks bipolarity in affect ratings. *Journal of Personality and Social Psychology, 64,* 1029–1041.

Hoyle, R. H. (Ed.). (1995a). *Structural equation modeling: Concepts, issues, and applications.* Thousand Oaks, CA: Sage.

Hoyle, R. H. (1995b). The structural equation modeling approach: Basic concepts and fundamental issues. In R. H. Hoyle (Ed.), *Structural equation modeling: Concepts, issues, and applications* (pp. 1–15). Thousand Oaks, CA: Sage.

Izard, C. E. (1992). Basic emotions, relations among emotions, and emotion-cognition relations. *Psychological Review, 99,* 561–565.

Kenny, D. A., & Kashy, D. A. (1992). Analysis of the multitrait-multimethod matrix by confirmatory factor analysis. *Psychological Bulletin, 112*(1), 165–172.

Kleinginna, P. R., & Kleinginna, A. M. (1981). A categorized list of emotion definitions, with suggestions for a consensual definition. *Motivation and Emotion, 5*(4), 345–379.

Larsen, R. J., & Diener, E. (1992). Promises and problems with the circumplex model of emotion. In M. S. Clark (Ed.), *Emotion: Review of personality and social psychology, No. 13* (pp. 25–59). Thousand Oaks, CA: Sage.

Larsen, R. J., & Fredrickson, B. L. (1999). Measurement issues in emotion research. In D. Kahneman & E. Diener (Eds.), *Well being: The foundations of hedonic psychology* (pp. 40–60). New York: Russell Sage.

Little, T. D. (1997). Mean and covariance structures (MACS) analyses of cross-cultural data: Practical and theoretical issues. *Multivariate Behavioral Research, 32*(1), 53–76.

Lucas, R. E., & Baird, B. M. (2004). Extraversion and emotional reactivity. *Journal of Personality and Social Psychology, 86,* 473–485.

Lucas, R. E., Diener, E., Grob, A., Suh, E. M., & Shao, L. (2000). Cross-cultural evidence for the fundamental features of extraversion. *Journal of Personality and Social Psychology, 79*(3), 452–468.

Lucas, R. E., Diener, E., & Larsen, R. J. (2003). Measuring positive emotions. In S. J. Lopez (Ed.), *Positive psychological assessment: A handbook of models and measures* (pp. 201–218). Washington, DC: American Psychological Association.

Lucas, R. E., Diener, E., & Suh, E. (1996). Discriminant validity of well-being measures. *Journal of Personality and Social Psychology, 71*(3), 616–628.

Lucas, R. E., & Fujita, F. (2000). Factors influencing the relation between extraversion and pleasant affect. *Journal of Personality and Social Psychology, 79,* 1039–1056.

Lyubomirsky, S., King, L., & Diener, E. (2005). The benefits of frequent positive affect: Does happiness lead to success? *Psychological Bulletin, 131,* 803–855.

Marsh, H. W., & Grayson, D. (1995). Latent variable models of multitrait-multimethod data. In R. H. Hoyle (Ed.), *Structural equation modeling: Concepts, issues, and applications* (pp. 177–198). Thousand Oaks, CA: Sage.

Matthews, G., Jones, D. M., & Chamberlain, A. G. (1990). Refining the measurement of mood: The UWIST Mood Adjective Checklist. *British Journal of Psychology, 81*(1), 17–42.

Morris, W. N. (1999). The mood system. In D. Kahneman, E. Diener, & N. Schwarz (Eds.), *Well-being: The foundations of hedonic psychology* (pp. 169–189). New York: Russell Sage.

Ortony, A., & Turner, T. J. (1990). What's basic about basic emotions? *Psychological Review, 97*(3), 315–331.

Panksepp, J. (1992). A critical role for "affective neuroscience" in resolving what is basic about basic emotions. *Psychological Review, 99,* 554–560.

Reise, S. P., Widaman, K. F., & Pugh, R. H. (1993). Confirmatory factor analysis and item response theory: Two approaches for exploring measurement invariance. *Psychological Bulletin, 114*(3), 552–566.

Remington, N. A., Fabrigar, L. R., & Visser, P. S. (2000). Reexamining the circumplex model of affect. *Journal of Personality and Social Psychology, 79*(2), 286–300.

Rosenberg, E. L. (1998). Levels of analysis and the organization of affect. *Review of General Psychology, 2*(3), 247–270.

Russell, J. A. (1980). A circumplex model of affect. *Journal of Personality and Social Psychology, 39,* 1161–1178.

Schimmack, U., Bockenholt, U., & Reisenzein, R. (2002). Response styles in affect ratings: Making a mountain out of a molehill. *Journal of Personality Assessment, 78*(3), 461–483.

Schimmack, U., & Grob, A. (2000). Dimensional models of core affect: A quantitative comparison by means of structural equation modeling. *European Journal of Personality, 14*(4), 325–345.

Schimmack, U., & Reisenzein, R. (2002). Experiencing activation: Energetic arousal and tense arousal are not mixtures of valence and activation. *Emotion, 2*(4), 412–417.

Schmukle, S. C., Egloff, B., & Burns, L. R. (2002). The relationship between positive and negative affect in the Positive and Negative Affect Schedule. *Journal of Research in Personality, 36*(5), 463–475.

Schwarz, N., & Strack, F. (1999). Reports of subjective well-being: Judgmental processes and their methodological implications. In D. Kahneman & E. Diener (Eds.), *Well being: The foundations of hedonic psychology* (pp. 61–84). New York: Russell Sage.

Sjoberg, L., Svensson, E., & Persson, L. O. (1979). The measurement of mood. *Scandinavian Journal of Psychology, 20,* 1–18.

Steyer, R., Schwenkmezger, P., Notz, P., & Eid, M. (1994). Testtheoretische Analysen des Mehrdimensionalen Befindlichkeitsfragebogen (MDBF). [Theoretical analysis of a multidimensional mood questionnaire (MDBF)]. *Diagnostica, 40*(4), 320–328.

Tellegen, A. (1985). Structures of mood and personality and their relevance to assessing anxiety, with an emphasis on self-report. In A. H. Tuma & J. D. Maser (Eds.), *Anxiety and the anxiety disorders* (pp. 681–706). Hillsdale, NJ: Erlbaum.

Tellegen, A., Watson, D., & Clark, L. A. (1999). On the dimensional and hierarchical structure of affect. *Psychological Science, 10*(4), 297–303.

Thayer, R. E. (1989). *The biopsychology of mood.* New York: Oxford University Press.

Tomarken, A. J., & Waller, N. G. (2003). Potential problems with "well fitting" models. *Journal of Abnormal Psychology, 112*(4), 578–598.

Trierweiler, L. I., Eid, M., & Lischetzke, T. (2002). The structure of emotional expressivity: Each emotion counts. *Journal of Personality and Social Psychology, 82,* 1023–1040.

Tucker, L. R., & Lewis, C. (1973). A reliability coefficient for maximum likelihood factor analysis. *Psychometrika, 38,* 1–10.

Turner, T. J. & Ortony, A. (1992). Basic emotions: Can conflicting criteria converge? *Psychological Review, 99,* 566–571.

Watson, D. (2000). *Mood and temperament.* New York: Guilford.

Watson, D. (2002). Positive affectivity: The disposition to experience pleasurable emotional states. In C. R. Snyder & S. J. Lopez (Eds.), *Handbook of positive psychology* (pp. 106–119). London: Oxford University Press.

Watson, D., & Clark, L. A. (1997). Extraversion and its positive emotional core. In R. Hogan, J. A. Johnson, et al. (Eds.), *Handbook of personality psychology* (pp. 767–793). San Diego, CA: Academic Press.

Watson, D., & Tellegen, A. (1985). Toward a consensual structure of mood. *Psychological Bulletin, 98*(2), 219–235.

Watson, D., & Walker, L. M. (1996). The long-term stability and predictive validity of trait measures of affect. *Journal of Personality and Social Psychology, 70*(3), 567–577.

Watson, D., Wiese, D., Vaidya, J., & Tellegen, A. (1999). The two general activation systems of affect: Structural findings, evolutionary considerations, and psychobiological evidence. *Journal of Personality and Social Psychology, 76,* 820–838.

Widaman, K. F., & Reise, S. P. (1997). Exploring the measurement invariance of psychological instruments: Applications in the substance use domain. In K. J. Bryant & M. Windle (Eds.), *The science of prevention: Methodological advances from alcohol and substance abuse research* (pp. 281–324). Washington, DC: American Psychological Association.

Wothke, W. (1995). Nonpositive definite matrices in structural modeling. In R. H. Hoyle (Ed.), *Structural equation modeling: Concepts, issues, and applications* (pp. 256–293). Thousand Oaks, CA: Sage.

9

The Application of Structural Equation Modeling and Item Response Theory to Cross-Cultural Positive Psychology Research

Shigehiro Oishi

Many positive psychology researchers are interested in life satisfaction, positive emotions, optimism, meaning in life, relationship quality, and other human strengths. Although the mental health movement came earlier (Jahoda, 1958; Rogers, 1961), the contemporary positive psychology movement started in the late 1990s in the United States (Seligman & Csikszentmihalyi, 2000). With the globalization of psychology and society in general, the application of these key constructs to diverse populations has become a critical issue. This chapter addresses the basic measurement issues in cross-cultural research of positive psychology, using structural equation modeling (SEM) and item response theory (IRT).

The Importance of Qualitative Research

This chapter focuses on the application of SEM and IRT because the establishment of measurement equivalence is critical for cross-cultural comparisons, and measurement equivalence can be best tested across cultures using these techniques (e.g., there is no formal test for equivalence of two Cronbach's alphas, to my knowledge). Before I discuss SEM and IRT, however, the importance of qualitative research should be recognized (see Denzin & Lincoln, 2000, for general review on qualitative research). If researchers are interested in cross-cultural similarities and differences in a positive psychological construct (e.g., life satisfaction), the first recommended step is to conduct qualitative research. Researchers might interview natives of the target culture to examine whether they understand the concept that researchers are interested in and use it in a comparable fashion. If the informants have no idea about what researchers are inquiring, then researchers need to explain the phenomenon they are interested in and obtain the indigenous concept that corresponds to that phenomenon first.

If the comparable concept exists, then researchers want to find out whether the meaning of this concept is similar. The lack of a comparable concept or a drastic difference in the meaning of the concept is by itself of interest to positive psychologists. For instance, Lu and Gilmore (2004) asked participants to describe what happiness is to them personally. Whereas many Americans college students described happiness as "an intense feeling" and "excitement," many Chinese described it as "a calm, peaceful feeling" and "a sense of equilibrium." This suggests that the meaning and correlates of "happiness" might be quite different between Americans and Chinese. Similarly, Adams and Plaut (2003) asked Ghanaians and Americans what a friend meant to them. Whereas Americans described a friend in all positive terms, many Ghanaians mentioned that they should be cautious with friends. Also, whereas Americans felt "pity" toward those who have no friends, Ghanaians accused such persons because Ghanaians interpreted that persons without friends are those who are not willing to help or share their wealth. These qualitative investigations reveal important cultural differences in key positive psychological constructs.

Cultural anthropologists Usha Menon and Richard Shweder (1994) identified the indigenous concept *lajya*, in the Orissa region of India first via a field study of an iconic representation of the Great Mother Goddess of Hinduism. They discovered that the icon is a collective representation of *lajya*, or "biting a tongue." The best English translation of *lajya* is shame, though it also means shyness and embarrassment. Oriyas believe that *lajya* (shame) is a feminine virtue that is both powerful and good. Menon and Shweder went on to test cultural differences in the meaning of shame via a simple categorization task. Participants were asked to pick one emotion that is most different from the rest. The target emotions were *raga* (anger), *sukha* (happy), and *lajya* (shame). Indians in the Orissa region viewed anger as the most different from shame and happy, whereas many Americans viewed happy as most different from anger and shame. For Oriyas, shame is instrumental to maintaining harmonious relationships with others, whereas anger is detrimental to harmonious relationships. Anger is detrimental to social relationships in the United States, as well. The critical difference, however, was that the instrumental value of emotion in social relationships did not come to mind naturally among Americans, whereas that was the first dimension that came to mind among Oriyas. Instead, the pleasant versus unpleasant dimen-

sion was the first to come to mind for many Americans. This might suggest that for Oriyas a "good person" is somebody who can feel shame in an appropriate situation, whereas for Americans a "good person" is somebody who feels happy but does not feel angry much.

Likewise, cultural psychologists Hazel Markus and Shinobu Kitayama (1998) asked Japanese and American college students to describe who they are. Whereas many Americans used positive traits (e.g., responsible, persistent) to describe who they are, many Japanese used negative (e.g., undisciplined) as well as positive traits. Markus and Kitayama argued that Americans tend to have a need to view themselves in a positive light, whereas Japanese tend to have a need to view themselves in a critical light. An ideal person in the United States has many positive traits and no negative traits, whereas an ideal person in Japan has some negative as well as positive traits. Although the rest of the chapter discusses quantitative analyses of cross-cultural data based on psychological scales, qualitative analyses such as these provide invaluable insight as to what it means to "be well" and what is "positive." As discussed later, the qualitative analyses are indispensable not only at the initial stage of investigation (e.g., item selection and scale development), but also later when interpreting the quantitative analyses of cross-cultural data. In sum, qualitative analyses and anthropological knowledge are crucial for understanding what positive psychology is across cultures.

Traditional Approaches to Measurement Issues

Once the researcher is certain that the comparable concept exists in the target culture, then data can be collected. Traditionally, various reliability indices (e.g., internal consistency, test-retest) are used to examine the measurement equivalence. If a life satisfaction scale in China had an internal consistency coefficient of .80, for instance, the researcher might assume that this scale is reliable in China. Some researcher might compute the sum score of the scale, classify the participants into quartiles, and examine if each item of the scale discriminates the highest 25% from the lowest 25%. Yet another popular approach is to use exploratory factor analysis, followed by the evaluation of the similarity of factor loadings (Van de Vijver & Leung, 2001). The similarity of factor structure and loadings can be examined by formal tests such as Tucker's phi (values greater than .90 are considered comparable; see McCrae & Costa, 1997, for an example). Although these analyses are easy to conduct and provide some insight into the equivalence of the scale and items, there are some limitations as well. First, the internal consistency coefficient is a function of the number of items as well as interitem correlations (Cortina, 1993). Even if the average interitem correlation is relatively low (e.g., .20), Cronbach's alpha would be over .80 if the scale contained more than 20 items. Thus, high Cronbach's alpha itself does not guarantee either unidimensionality or equivalence. Second, even when the reliability coefficients are identical between two groups, there could be a large difference in specific item-total score correlations. For instance, the item-total score correlation might be .80, .60, and .35 for items 1, 2, and 3 in group A, whereas it might be .35, .80, and .60 in group B. The aforementioned item discrimination analysis relies on the observed score, which includes measurement errors. Thus, the sum score, upon which the classification was based, could be biased itself, which in turn could compromise the whole analysis. The use of exploratory factor analysis is still of value. Some researchers (Van de Vijver & Leung, 2001) prefer exploratory factor analysis with formal tests of factor structures to confirmatory factor analysis because confirmatory factor analysis assumes a priori factor structure, is a stricter test of measurement equivalence, and seems to result in a rejection of predicted factor structure even when the differences appear small. When the main research question is concerned with structural issues (e.g., relations between optimism and life satisfaction across cultures), confirmatory factor analysis can be easily extended to test such

structural questions. In other words, a measurement model (e.g., equivalence of optimism items and life satisfaction items across cultures) and a structural model (e.g., the relation between latent optimism and latent life satisfaction across cultures) can be simultaneously tested in the framework of structural equation modeling, whereas exploratory factor analysis cannot be easily extended to test the structural questions (after testing the measurement equivalence through exploratory factor analysis in each sample, separate analyses have to be conducted to test the structural questions).

Structural Equation Modeling

SEM is a method in which the sample covariances are compared with the covariances predicted by a theory and a conceptual model. Many of the widely used statistical techniques (e.g., regression analysis, factor analysis, ANOVA) can be conceived of as special cases of SEM (Bollen, 1989). The proposed model is tested by its closeness to the obtained covariance structure. There are two aspects of SEM. One is a measurement model, which is concerned with the relations between a latent variable and indicator variables. The other is a structural model, which is concerned with the relations among latent variables. In figure 9.1, the measurement model involves the relation between a latent variable, PA (positive affect), and four indicator variables, joy, content, affection, and pride, and the relation between a latent variable, LS (life satisfaction), and five items. The structural model is concerned with the relation between latent variables PA and LS. In this example, PA is called the exogenous (or independent) latent

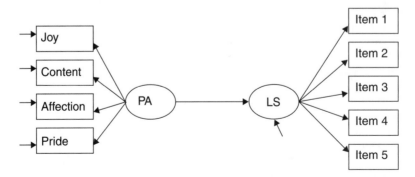

Figure 9.1 An example of measurement model and structural model. PA = positive affect; LS = life satisfaction.

variable and LS is called the endogenous (or dependent) latent variable. The measurement model is equivalent of typical confirmatory factor analysis.

Overall fit of the model is evaluated by several fit indices (see Hu & Bentler, 1998, for a more detailed discussion on fit indices; see Bollen, 1989; Hoyle, 1995, for SEM in general). If chi-squared is nonsignificant, this indicates that the obtained covariance structure is close to the predicted structure. Chi-squared is not an ideal overall fit index, however, when sample size is very large or very small and the distribution of key variables is skewed. When the sample size is very large (e.g., 1,000), chi-squared may be significant, even when the difference between the observed covariance structure and the predicted structure is negligible. In contrast, when the sample size is small, even when the discrepancy between the observed and predicted models is large, the chi-square test might be nonsignificant. Several indices are proposed to address the limitations of the chi-square test. One of the most often used indices is the goodness-of-fit index (GFI). GFI indicates the amount of observed variance and covariance information that can be accounted for by the predicted model. A related index is adjusted goodness-of-fit index (AGFI), which adjusts GFI for the degrees of freedom. The difference between GFI and AGFI is analogous to R^2 and adjusted R^2 in regression analysis. Typically, GFI and AGFI greater than .90 are considered indicators of good fit. Whereas GFI and AGFI are absolute indices, Tucker and Lewis's (1973) Tucker-Lewis index (TLI) and Bentler and Bonnett's (1980) non-normed fit index (NNFI) are incremental fit indices, which compare a common baseline model with the specified model. Bentler and Bonnett (1980) stated, "In our experience models with overall fit indices of less than 0.9 can usually be improved substantially" (p. 600), suggesting that NNFI greater than 0.90 is deemed acceptable. A problem with TLI and NNFI is that they could be outside of the 0–1 range (Muller, 1996). More recently, the normed comparative fit index (CFI) was developed to address this issue (see Widaman & Thompson, 2003, however, for a cautionary note concerning the interpretation of incremental fit indices). Root mean square error of approximation (RMSEA) is another often-used index, which assesses badness of fit of a model per degree of freedom. RMSEA is 0 if a model fits data perfectly. According to Browne and Cudeck (1992), a 0.05 value of RMSEA is

considered as good fit, 0.08 as reasonable fit, and 0.10 or greater as poor fit.

In typical research contexts, nested models are compared to determine which model fits the obtained data better. The most common way to compare nested models is to examine whether chi-square differences are significant. If the model with fewer degrees of freedom and the model with more degrees of freedom are not different in chi-square value (i.e., $\Delta\chi^2$ is nonsignificant), then the parsimonious model is more appropriate than the less parsimonious model. As with the chi-square test, however, chi-square difference is also sensitive to sample size. Namely, chi-square difference tends to be significant when the sample size is large.

Many cross-cultural psychologists have used SEM to examine psychometric properties. For instance, Vittersø, Røysamb, and Diener (2002) used SEM to examine the factor structure of the Satisfaction With Life Scale (SWLS; Diener, Emmons, Larsen, & Griffin, 1985) in 41 nations. The SWLS consists of five items (cf. the LS model in figure 9.1). These researchers examined the fit of a one-factor model in each of 41 nations, separately. In all 41 nations, CFI estimates were above .90. However, 15 nations had RMSEA values above .10 (Bahrain, Denmark, Estonia, Ghana, Guam, Hungary, Indonesia, Nigeria, Pakistan, Singapore, Slovenia, Taiwan, Tanzania, Thailand, and Zimbabwe). For example, Denmark had CFI of .939, yet had RMSEA of .157. This study illustrates divergence between different fit indices and illuminates the importance of considering multiple fit indices to reach an appropriate interpretation of the overall fit. Moreover, it is important to note that the fit indices of one sample (e.g., the United States) could not be statistically tested against those of another (e.g., Taiwan) when the one-factor structure was modeled separately. Thus, this approach does not provide a formal test of measurement equivalence across samples.

Instead of fitting the one-factor model for one sample at a time, one can simultaneously examine whether the SWLS has the same factor structure and loadings across different samples using multigroup SEM. First, the researcher should obtain fit indices of the baseline (unconstrained) model that allows for different factor loadings between samples. Second, one should obtain fit indices of the constrained model that sets all the factor loadings to be equal between groups. Measurement equivalence is established if the constrained model's fit indices are as good as the baseline model (e.g., nonsignificant change in chi-square). In my own work (Oishi, 2006), for instance, the baseline model of the data from 543 Chinese college students and 438 American college students yielded the following fit indices: χ^2 (10) = 50.292, $p < .01$, GFI = .980, CFI = .975, TLI = .95, RMSEA = .064. The fully constrained model yielded a significantly worse fit in terms of chi-square change: $\Delta\chi^2$ (4) = 22.857, $p < .01$, although other fit indices were similar to the baseline model: GFI = .969, CFI = .963, TLI = .948, RMSEA = .066. The partially constrained model in which factor loadings of items 4 and 5 ("So far I have gotten the important things I want in life" and "If I could live my life over, I would change almost nothing") were allowed to differ between the groups yielded a fit not significantly different from the baseline model: $\Delta\chi^2$ (2) = 3.807, ns, GFI = .978, CFI = .974, TLI = .957, RMSEA = .060. Using the strict rule (chi-square difference rather than overall fit), Items 1 to 3 were equivalent, whereas Items 4 and 5 revealed significant differences in factor loadings between our American and Chinese samples. Using the less strict rule (i.e., the overall fit indices such as RMSEA), the fully constrained model was acceptable.

An important next question is "Why were Items 4 and 5 different in the United States and China, while the first three items were equivalent?" To help answer this question, it is instructive to go back to the cultural psychology literature. For example, Markus and Kitayama's (1998) findings on cultural differences in self-enhancement versus self-criticism help us interpret the above finding. Assuming that Chinese share the self-critical tendency of Japanese, it is not difficult to imagine self-critical Chinese disagreeing with the statements such as "So far, I have gotten the important things I want in life" and "If I could live my life over again, I would change almost nothing," even when they are generally satisfied with the conditions of their lives. Lu and Gilmore's (2004) findings also indicate that pride and excitement might not be ideal emotions for Chinese. Item 4, which is concerned with the accomplishment of personally important goals, should be related to intense emotions such as pride and excitement. Because many Chinese do not consider pride and excitement to be ideal emotions, Items 4 and 5 do not "hang together" with other items. In short, multigroup SEM provides invaluable information about the measurement equivalence of a psychological scale. However, when measurement

discrepancy was found, cultural psychology literatures offer an insight into the reason why some items show cultural differences, while others do not.

Beyond measurement equivalence, another interesting application of SEM is testing the structural equivalence of key positive psychology constructs. We (Schimmack, Radhakrishnan, Oishi, Dzokoto, & Ahadi, 2002) used SEM to examine cultural differences in the structural relations among extraversion, neuroticism, hedonic balance (positive – negative emotions), and life satisfaction. In this study, American and German participants were grouped as individualists and Japanese, Mexicans, and Ghanaians were grouped together as collectivists (namely, five samples were reduced to two samples). First, we examined and established the measurement equivalence between Americans and Germans (as in the above example, we compared the unconstrained model with the constrained model and checked whether chi-square difference was statistically significant). Second, we examined and established the measurement equivalence between Japanese, Mexicans, and Ghanaians. Finally, the measurement equivalence between individualistic and collectivistic groups was tested and established. Then, we went on to examine whether the links between extraversion and hedonic balance and between neuroticism and hedonic balance were equivalent between these two groups. The first model assessed the fit of the unconstrained model, in which the structural relations were allowed to differ between groups. The second model assessed the fit of the constrained model, in which the structural relations were set to be equal between the two groups. The constrained model did not differ from the unconstrained model ($\Delta\chi^2$ [1] < 1.00, ns), indicating that the strength of association between neuroticism and hedonic balance and extraversion and hedonic balance was equivalent between these two groups. Next, we tested whether the link between hedonic balance and life satisfaction was the same between these two groups. The comparison of the unconstrained and constrained models revealed a significant difference in chi-square, $\Delta\chi^2$ (1) = 12.00, $p < .01$. Whereas the standardized regression coefficient was .76 between hedonic balance and life satisfaction in the individualist group, it was .48 in the collectivist group. In sum, our study demonstrated that extraversion and neuroticism were related to emotional experience in a similar way in both individualist and collectivist cultures, but the degree to which life satisfaction judgments were based on emotional experience was stronger in individualist cultures than in collectivist cultures (i.e., replicating Suh, Diener, Oishi, & Triandis, 1998).

Traditionally, researchers used two alternative approaches to test whether structural relations are different across cultures. First, a correlation coefficient between hedonic balance and life satisfaction can be computed in the individualist group and the other computed in the collectivist group separately, and then compared by a z test after converting correlation coefficients by Fisher's z transformation (see Hays, 1994, for the formula; an r-to-z transformation table is available in most statistics books). Alternatively, a regression analysis with an interaction term can be used to test whether the size of association between hedonic balance and life satisfaction is different between two cultural groups (i.e., predicting life satisfaction from hedonic balance, the group, and the interaction term; see Oishi & Diener, 2001, for an example). Although these analyses yield similar results, one major disadvantage of these traditional approaches is the effect of measurement error. Pearson correlation coefficients and observed scores used in a regression analysis are plagued with measurement error. In cross-cultural psychology, this problem can be exacerbated, as two groups might have different amounts of measurement error. Suppose the observed correlation between optimism and life satisfaction in an American sample was .50, whereas the observed correlation in a Chinese sample was .30. Further, suppose that these coefficients were significantly different from each other. Can we conclude that the strength of association between the two variables is different between the two cultures? Not for certain. If the reliabilities of the scales used in China were substantially lower than those in the United States, then the difference in the observed correlations could be due to the difference in measurement error rather than difference in the size of the "true" association. For example, if optimism and life satisfaction scales had reliability coefficients of .90 and .88 in the American sample, and .65 and .62 in the Chinese sample, the maximum correlation that these two scales can theoretically have is not 1.00, but .89 in the American sample and .63 in the Chinese sample. Correcting for measurement error, then, the disattenuated correlation coefficient would be .56 for the American sample, while it would be .48 for the Chinese sample.

Clearly, the cultural difference in observed correlation coefficients was not due to "true" differences but due to a differential amount of measurement error in the two samples. One major advantage of SEM used in Schimmack et al. (2002) is that measurement error was removed before testing the structural relations. Thus, the difference we found in the strength of association between hedonic balance and life satisfaction could not be due to the differential amount of measurement error in two groups. In short, SEM provides an opportunity to test not only measurement equivalence, but also theoretical models concerning structural relations while accounting for measurement error.

Item Response Theory

IRT is yet another sophisticated method of assessing measurement equivalence in multiple groups. IRT is different from classical test theory (CTT) in several important ways (see Embretson & Reise, 2000 ; Hambleton & Swaminathan, 1985, for details). Most psychometric information presented in psychology (e.g., Cronbach's alpha, test-retest reliability coefficient) is based on CTT. In CTT, observed-score variance is partitioned into true-score variance and error. Reliability is defined as the proportion of true variance in observed-score variance. Error variance comes from either occasions (in test-retest reliability) or item sampling (in internal consistency). One reliability coefficient for an entire scale is often computed for each sample in CTT. The most significant difference between CTT and IRT in the present context is concerned with the standard error of measurement. Whereas the standard error of measurement is assumed to apply to the whole sample in CTT, it varies depending on the latent trait score in IRT (typically, there is less reliability for those with extreme latent scores). In other words, additional sources of error can be considered in IRT, such as a person's latent score and person-by-item interaction. Cronbach's alpha, a quintessential CTT reliability index, does not provide information about person-by-item interaction, namely, whether some items measured some individuals better than others. In IRT, this interaction is considered.

Second, in IRT even if two individuals answered the same number of items "correctly" (or "yes" responses), the person who correctly answered more difficult items (or those who said "yes" to the items less frequently endorsed) would receive a higher total score than the other who correctly answered less difficult items in IRT. In CTT, these two individuals would have the same observed score.

There are several IRT models. The simplest model is the one-parameter logistic model (1 PL model), or Rasch model. The formula is the following:

$$Ln \ (Pix/[1 - Pix]) = \theta x - \beta i$$

In this model, the natural logarithm of the odds ratio of "passing" the item is modeled as the difference between person X's latent score, θx, and Item I's difficulty βi. If person X's latent score was 1 (i.e., 1 *SD* above the mean) and Item I's difficulty was .5 (i.e., a person with .5 *SD* above the mean would have a 50% probability of passing this item), then the natural logarithm of the odds ratio of person X's passing this item is .5. The second version of the Rasch model is the following:

$$Pix = \exp(\theta x - \beta i)/[1 + \exp(\theta x - \beta i)]$$

where *Pix* indicates the probability of person X passing Item I. In the present example, if you insert $\theta x = 1.00$ and $\beta i = .50$ to the formula, you would know that person X has a 62.24% probability of passing Item I.

For positive psychology research, the two-parameter logistic model (2PL model) is perhaps most relevant. In the two-parameter logistic model, an item discrimination parameter is included in addition to an item difficulty parameter. An item discrimination parameter (α parameter) indicates how well this item captures the latent trait that it is supposed to measure. This is conceptually equivalent to item–total score correlation in CTT and item–factor correlation in factor analysis. The 2PL model can be expressed as follows:

$$Pix = \exp[\alpha(\theta x - \beta i)]/[1 + \exp(\alpha(\theta x - \beta i))]$$

As you can see, the only difference between the 1PL and 2PL models is a multiplier, α (the item discrimination parameter). Namely, the difference between the latent trait score and item difficulty has a greater impact on the probability in the items that discriminate participants better than other items that do not discriminate participants as well in the 2PL model. For example, suppose Item 1 had an item discrimination of

$\alpha = 1$, whereas Item 2 had an item discrimination of $\alpha = 2$. Further suppose that both items had an item difficulty of $\beta = .50$. The person with a latent trait score of 1.00 has a 62.24% probability of passing Item 1, whereas the same person has a 73.11% probability of passing Item 2. In other words, even when θx and βi are the same, *Pix* can be different, depending on the item discrimination parameter. Most important, when estimating a latent trait score, the 2PL model takes into account item discrimination as well as item difficulty, and therefore, the better items (those with higher item discrimination) have greater weight in estimating the latent trait score than do other items (this is an advantage of the 2PL model over the 1PL and CTT).

So far, all the examples assumed that items were dichotomous (i.e., pass or fail; yes or no). In many scales used in positive psychology research, however, items are multiple ordered-response categories (e.g., strongly disagree, disagree, neither agree nor disagree, agree, strongly agree). Samejima (1969) developed a graded-response model of IRT that is appropriate for polytomous items. Whereas there was one item difficulty parameter in the dichotomous model, there are $k - 1$ item difficulty parameters in the polymotous model, where k is the number of response categories (e.g., there are two b parameters for a 3-point scale). In the case of the 3-point scale, the b1 parameter indicates the level of latent score that has the equal probability of endorsing 1 and 2, whereas the b2 parameter indicates the level of latent score in which the probability of endorsing 2 and 3 is equal. If b1 is $-.25$ and b2 is .75, then people whose latent trait score is below $-.25$ are most likely to endorse response category 1, whereas people whose latent score is between $-.25$ and .75 have the greatest probability of endorsing response category 2, and those higher than .75 are most likely to endorse response category 3.

I conducted DIF (differential item functioning) analysis on the Positive Affect (PA) subscale of PANAS (Watson, Clark, & Tellegen, 1988) among American and Chinese college student respondents, using the Multilog 7.03 program. Participants rated the frequency with which they felt 10 positive emotions (i.e., interested, excited, strong, enthusiastic, proud, active, attentive, alert, inspired, determined) during the past month on a 5-point scale (1 = very slightly or not at all; 2 = a little, 3 = moderately, 4 = quite a bit, 5 = extremely). Figure 9.2 indicates the item characteristic curves (ICC) of *determined* for

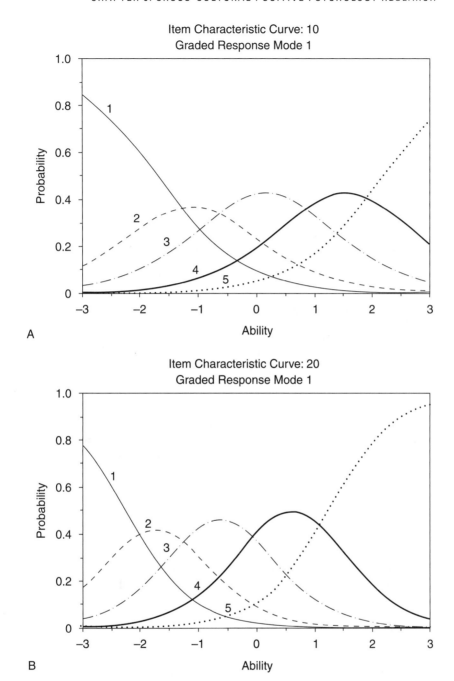

Figure 9.2 Item characteristic curve of *determined* for Chinese and American samples. (A) Chinese; (B) American.

Chinese and American respondents. The *x* axis indicates respondents' latent PA score (in *z* scores: for instance, −1 means −1 *SD* below mean) and the *y* axis indicates the probability of endorsing a particular response category. First, the ICC of Chinese responses to *determined* indicates that Chinese with 3 *SD* below the mean latent PA had over 80% probability of endorsing response category 1 (very slightly or not at all), whereas Chinese with 1 *SD* below the mean had the greatest likelihood of endorsing response category 2 (a little). Chinese with the average PA were most likely to endorse response category 3 (moderately), whereas Chinese with 1 SD above the mean were most likely to endorse response category 4 (quite a bit) and Chinese with more than 2 SD above the mean were likely to endorse response category 5 (extremely). All in all, the ICC indicates that this was a "good" item, as the most likely response increases as latent PA score increases. The ICC of *determined* for American respondents also shows a similar pattern. The most likely response increases from 1 to 5, as latent PA score increases from -3 to $+3$. Comparing Chinese and American ICCs for *determined*, it is clear that the item difficulty parameters are different between the two groups. For instance, whereas the highest response category, 5, was most likely to be endorsed by respondents with latent PA score of greater than 2 SD among Chinese, it was most likely to be endorsed by responses with latent PA score of greater than 1 SD among Americans. Similarly, response category 3 was the most likely response for Chinese with the average latent PA, whereas response category 4 was the most likely response for Americans with the average latent PA.

Reise, Widaman, and Pugh (1993) proposed a formal test of cultural differences in item response patterns. These researchers compared the negative twice the log likelihood in the baseline model, in which all the parameters were allowed to differ between two groups, and the negative twice the log likelihood in the constrained model, in which item parameters of one item were constrained to be the same between the two groups. The difference in the negative twice the log likelihood, or the G^2 index, can be evaluated against the chi-square distribution. If G^2 index is significant, then the item under scrutiny is deemed a DIF item. If G^2 index is not significant, then the item under scrutiny is deemed equivalent between groups. The G^2 value for the model that constrained the item parameters for *determined* was 17.4 (5), $p < .01$. Thus, although the ICCs appear comparable between the two samples, *determined* was a DIF item according to the G^2 test.

Next, figure 9.3 illustrates the ICC of *proud* for Chinese and American college students. It is clear from the ICC that *proud* was a "bad" item for Chinese because the most likely response was 1 (very slightly or not at all) for more than half of the participants (participants with latent PA score of less than .50 SD), and response category 5 was not the most likely response even among Chinese with 2 SD above the mean. Furthermore, there was no clear shift in the most likely response category as latent PA score increased. In contrast, American ICC for *proud* showed a clear shift in the most likely response as latent PA score increased. The cultural difference in the ICCs of *proud* is also consistent with Lu and Gilmore's (2004) qualitative analysis of happiness. Thus, *proud* was clearly a "good" item for Americans and a "bad" item for Chinese. Not surprisingly, the G^2 value was greatest when the item parameters for *proud* were constrained, 142.4, $p < .0001$. Among the 10 items, the most comparable positive emotion item was *strong*. Figure 9.4 shows the ICCs of *strong* for Chinese and American respondents. The G^2 value was 17.4. With $df = 5$, the G^2 value should be less than 11.07 to be comparable. Thus, according to the G^2 test, even *strong*, which appears comparable in the ICCs, was deemed a DIF item. As discussed later, the G^2 test might be too stringent when the sample size is quite large (here combined sample size is over 1,000).

Beyond the examination of item bias, DIF analysis illuminates theoretical issues. For instance, the ICCs of *proud* indicate that Chinese who frequently feel other positive emotions (e.g., excited, enthusiastic, interested, determined) do not feel proud, whereas Americans who experience a lot of other positive emotions feel proud quite often, as well. Consistent with the self-enhancement versus self-criticism literature (e.g., Heine, Lehman, Markus, & Kitayama, 1999; Markus & Kitayama, 1991), pride is a signature positive emotion among typically self-enhancing Americans, whereas it might not be a positive emotion among typically self-critical Chinese. The DIF on pride is also consistent with Lu and Gilmore's (2004) qualitative analysis of happiness in the United States and China. Thus, the above example illustrates that IRT analyses can reveal what positive emotions are in different cultures.

Similarly, I used the Multilog 7.03 program to examine the measurement equivalence of the SWLS between Chinese and American college students (Oishi, 2006). When assessed by SEM, only Items 4 and 5 showed cultural differences. When assessed by IRT, however, Items 1, 3, 4, and 5 were deemed DIF items. Interestingly, Reise et al. (1993) also found similar discrepancies between the SEM and IRT analyses. When assessed by SEM, only *distress* showed

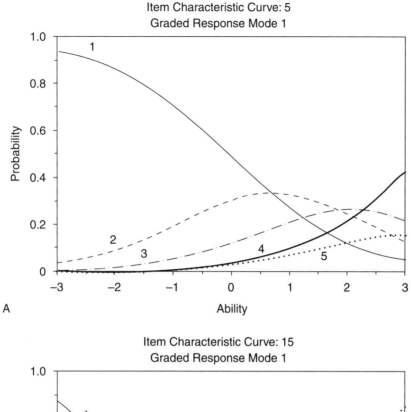

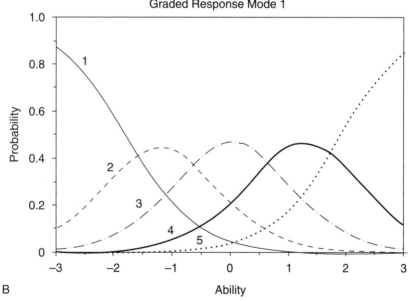

Figure 9.3 Item characteristic curve for *proud* for Chinese and American samples. (A) Chinese; (B) American.

cultural differences. When assessed by IRT, *worried* and *jittery* as well as *distress* showed cultural differences. A major difference between SEM and IRT is that SEM estimates only the item discrimination (factor loadings are con-ceptually equivalent to item discrimination in dichotomous items), whereas IRT estimates both item discrimination and item difficulty. In ty-pical SEM, summary statistics, such as correla-tion or covariance matrix, are used for analysis.

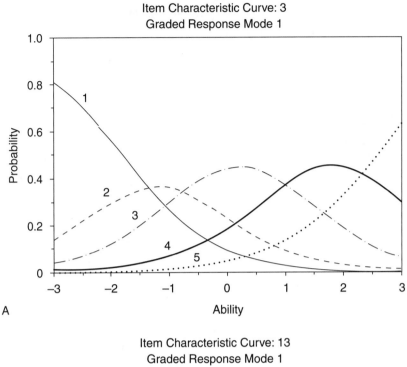

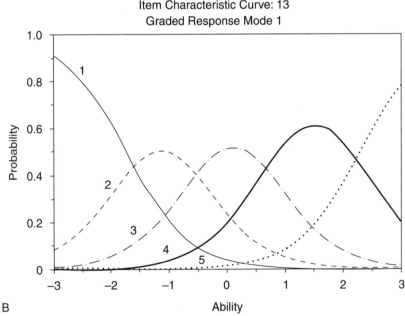

Figure 9.4 Item characteristic curve of *strong* for Chinese and American samples.
(A) Chinese; (B) American.

In such analyses, information about item difficulty, or item means, is not utilized. In other words, multigroup SEM does not test whether two groups differed on item difficulty. Although full-information item factor analysis (Bock, Gibbons, & Muraki, 1988) utilizes both covariance and item means (or item difficulty parameters in binary data), virtually all multigroup SEMs are based on the covariance or correlation matrix and provide information on the equivalence of item discrimination only. In contrast, IRT examines the equivalence of item difficulty as well as item discrimination. Thus, IRT presents a more stringent test of measurement equivalence than SEM.

Before closing, some limitations of SEM and IRT should be noted. First, both SEM and IRT require a large sample size. IRT, in particular, requires a large sample size (often 500 or more). Thus, the application of IRT is limited to data sets with large numbers of respondents. Second, software programs for IRT analysis (e.g., Multilog) are not as user-friendly as the software programs for traditional statistical analyses. The Multilog 7.03 program, however, is much more user-friendly than the older versions. I expect that future IRT programs will continue to be much more user-friendly. Third, as noted by Reise et al. (1993), fit indices are not as well-developed for IRT analyses as for SEM analyses. As in chi-square difference, G^2 seems to be sensitive to sample size. Therefore, mechanical reliance on the G^2 index should be avoided. There are fewer limitations in SEM than IRT in terms of sample size requirements and fit indices. When the sample size is small, SEM can be used for observable variables, instead of latent variables. IRT also cannot test psychological processes such as mediation and moderation. In this respect, SEM is a flexible method that allows for testing cultural variation in psychological processes (e.g., Schimmack et al., 2002) as well as measurement equivalence across cultures. As greater understanding of positive psychological variables rests on delineations of mediators and moderators, SEM will be a handy tool.

Conclusion

The present chapter has delineated the limitations of the traditional approaches to measurement equivalence across cultures. IRT presents the most stringent test available to date for measurement equivalence between two groups. SEM provides flexible ways of testing structural relations and processes, while accounting for a differential amount of measurement error across cultures. I believe that the scientific potentials of cross-cultural positive psychology will be best fulfilled with the establishment of measurement equivalence by IRT and the exploration of mediational processes by SEM. Equally important, the interpretation of culture differences in measurement and structural models

requires intimate knowledge of the target cultures. To this end, qualitative research on cultures complements qualitative research using IRT and SEM.

References

Adams, G., & Plaut, V. C. (2003). The cultural grounding of personal relationships: Friendship in North American and West African worlds. *Personal Relationships, 10,* 333–347.

Bentler, P. M., & Bonnett, D. G. (1980). Significance tests and goodness-of-fit in the analysis of covariance structures. *Psychological Bulletin, 88,* 588–600.

Bock, R. D., Gibbons, R., & Muraki, E. J. (1988). Full information item factor analysis. *Applied Psychological Measurement, 12,* 261–280.

Bollen, K. A. (1989). *Structural equations with latent variables.* New York: Wiley.

Browne, M. W., & Cudeck, R. (1992). Alternative ways of assessing model fit. *Sociological Methods and Research, 21,* 230–258.

Cortina, J. M. (1993). What is coefficient alpha? An examination of theory and applications. *Journal of Applied Psychology, 78,* 98–104.

Denzin, N. K., & Lincoln, Y. S. (2000). *Handbook of qualitative research.* London: Sage.

Diener, E., Emmons, R. A., Larsen, R. J., & Griffin, S. (1985). The Satisfaction With Life Scale. *Journal of Personality Assessment, 49,* 71–75.

Embretson, S. E., & Reise, S. P. (2000). *Item response theory for psychologists.* Mahwah, NJ: Erlbaum.

Hambleton, R. K., & Swaminathan, H. (1985). *Item response theory: Principles and applications.* Boston: Kluwer-Nijhoff.

Hays, W. L. (1994). *Statistics* (5th ed). Orlando, FL: Harcourt Brace.

Heine, S. J., Lehman, D. R., Markus, H. R., & Kitayama, S. (1999). Is there a universal need for positive self-regard? *Psychological Review, 106,* 766–794.

Hoyle, R. H. (1995). *Structural equation modeling: Concepts, issues, and applications.* Thousand Oaks, CA: Sage.

Hu, L., & Bentler, P. M. (1998). Fit indices in covariance structure modeling: Sensitivity to underparameterized model misspecification. *Psychological Method, 3,* 424–453.

Jahoda, M. (1958). *Current concepts of positive mental health.* New York: Basic Books.

Lu, L., & Gilmour, R. (2004). Culture and conceptions of happiness: Individual oriented and social oriented subjective well-being. *Journal of Happiness Studies, 5,* 269–291.

Markus, H. R., & Kitayama, S. (1991). Culture and the self: Implications for cognition, emotion, and motivation. *Psychological Review, 98,* 224–253.

Markus, H. R., & Kitayama, S. (1998). The cultural psychology of personality. *Journal of Cross-Cultural Psychology, 29,* 63–87.

McCrae, R. R., & Costa, P. T. (1997). Personality trait structure as a human universal. *American Psychologist, 52,* 509–516.

Menon, U., & Shweder, R. A. (1994). Kali's tongue: Cultural psychology and the power of shame in Orissa, India. In S. Kitayama & H. R. Markus (Eds.), *Emotion and culture* (pp. 241–284). Washington, DC: American Psychological Association.

Muller, R. O. (1996). *Basic principles of structural equation modeling: An introduction to LISREL and EQS.* New York: Springer.

Oishi, S. (2006). The concept of life satisfaction across cultures: An IRT analysis. *Journal of Research in Personality, 40,* 411–423.

Oishi, S., & Diener, E. (2001). Goals, culture, and subjective well-being. *Personality and Social Psychology Bulletin, 27,* 1674–1682.

Reise, S. P., Widaman, K. F., & Pugh, R. H. (1993). Confirmatory factory analysis and item response theory: Two approaches for exploring measurement invariance. *Psychological Bulletin, 114,* 552–566.

Rogers, C. R. (1961). *On becoming a person: A therapist's view of psychotherapy.* Boston: Houghton Mifflin.

Samejima, F. (1969). Estimation of latent ability using a response pattern of graded scores. *Psychometric Monograph, 17.*

Schimmack, U., Radhakrishnan, P., Oishi, S., Dzokoto, V., & Ahadi, S. (2002). Culture, personality, and subjective well-being: Integrating process models of life satisfaction. *Journal of Personality and Social Psychology, 82,* 582–593.

Seligman, M. E. P., & Csikszentmihalyi, M. (2000). Positive psychology: An introduction. *American Psychologist, 55,* 5–14.

Suh, E., Diener, E., Oishi, S., & Triandis, H. C. (1998). The shifting basis of life satisfaction judgments across cultures: Emotions versus norms. *Journal of Personality and Social Psychology, 74,* 482–493.

Tucker, L. R., & Lewis, C. (1973). A reliability coefficient for maximum likelihood factor analysis. *Psychometrika, 38,* 1–10.

Van de Vijver, F. J. R., & Leung, K. (2001). Personality in cultural context: Methodological issues. *Journal of Personality, 69,* 1007–1031.

Vitterso, J., Roysamb, E., & Diener, E. (2002). The concept of life satisfaction across cultures: Exploring its diverse meaning and relation to economic wealth. In E. Gullone & R. Cummins (Eds.), *The niversality of subjective wellbeing indicators* (pp. 81–103). Dordrecht: Kluwer.

Watson, D., Clark, L. A., & Tellegen, A. (1988). Development and validation of a brief measure of positive and negative affect: The PANAS scales. *Journal of Personality and Social Psychology, 54,* 1063–1070.

Widaman, K. F., & Thompson, J. S. (2003). On specifying the null model for incremental fit indices in structural equation modeling. *Psychological Methods, 8,* 16–37.

10

Using the Combined Etic-Emic Approach to Develop a Measurement of Interpersonal Subjective Well-Being in Chinese Populations

Samuel M. Y. Ho and Mike W. L. Cheung

Positive psychology originated in the West and is gaining a lot of interest among psychologists in different parts of the world. As positive psychology moves East, a major challenge for many positive psychology researchers in Asia is how to define and measure positive psychological constructs (e.g., subjective well-being, flow, gratitude, etc.) properly. The easiest approach is to translate the Western instruments and use them directly in non-Western populations. However, many researchers have raised issues on the comparability of the instruments across cultures (e.g., Cheung, Leung, & Ben-Porath, 2003). The key issues are the equivalence of translations, cultural relevance, measurement equivalence of the constructs, and the validity of the adapted instruments (Lonner & Berry, 1986).

In terms of statistical techniques in testing the applicability of instruments in another culture, structural equation modeling (SEM; Bollen, 1989) has been found useful for many researchers (e.g., Caprara, Barbaranelli, Bermudez, Maslach, & Ruch, 2000; Cheung, Leung, & Au, in press; van de Vijver & Leung, 1997). SEM is a flexible modeling technique that can be considered as a unified technique for many existing multivariate techniques, such as regression analysis, path analysis, factor analysis, ANOVA to MANCOVA, canonical correlation analysis, and growth curve modeling. It is easy to observe that applications using SEM as analysis techniques have increased dramatically in these few decades (MacCallum & Austin, 2000). Confirmatory factor analysis (CFA), a special case of SEM without imposing any structural relationship among the latent variables, is usually used to study the factor structures of the instruments. Other statistical techniques are also useful in testing the validity of the proposed instruments in another culture, for instance, item response theory, multidimensional scaling, and exploratory factor analysis (see van de Vijver & Leung, 1997). In this chapter, we focus on CFA only because many research hypotheses related to the measurement properties can be formulated and tested under the framework of CFA.

There are two main objectives in this chapter. First, we introduce the general approaches and procedures on developing instruments in cross-cultural studies. We show how CFA can be used as the multivariate technique for these procedures. Second, we use our studies on subjective well-being (SWB) in Chinese populations to demonstrate how we apply CFA in positive psychology measurement studies. Apart from showing that interpersonal relationships are essential to the SWB of Chinese, we also illustrate how the procedures introduced can be applied in research settings.

Approaches to Developing Instruments in Non-Western Cultures

Hofstede (1980) classified many Western countries (or cultures) as individualistic whereas many Eastern countries were classified as collectivistic. In individualistic cultures, people tend to define themselves primarily as separate individuals, whereas people in collectivistic cultures tend to define themselves by tight social networks such as in-groups versus out-groups. Since many of the existing psychological instruments in positive psychology were developed in Western cultures, researchers face the question of how to measure similar constructs in non-Western cultures.

Generally speaking, there are three approaches to developing psychological instruments in non-Western cultures. They are etic, emic, and combined emic-etic approaches. The terms *etics* and *emics* were coined by Pike (1954) by dropping the first syllable *phon* from the terms *phonetics* and *phonemics* in linguistics. Etics refers to studying a phenomenon with a culture-free approach or outsider perspective, whereas emics refers to studying a phenomenon with a culture-specific approach or insider perspective. After his introduction, the terminology of etics and emics was widely accepted in many disciplines such as anthropology (Headland, 1990) and cross-cultural psychology (Berry, Poortinga, Segall, & Dasen, 1992) in explaining methodologies related to cultures. As both etic and emic approaches have their own advantages and limitations, some researchers suggested combining these two approaches, which is sometimes termed a combined etic-emic approach (e.g., Hui & Triandis, 1985). The combined etic-emic approach tries to keep the advantages of both etics and emics. There are many theoretical differences among these approaches, especially on the assumption of the universality and generalizability of theory.

Etic Approach

An etic approach was widely used in scale development in the past. Western instruments such as the Minnesota Multiphasic Personality Inventory (MMPI; Hathaway & McKinley, 1967) and the Beck Depression Inventory (BDI; Beck & Steen, 1987) have been translated and administered in many non-Western cultures. The basic assumption is that theories developed in the West are universal. Thus, researchers can simply translate and apply the instruments developed in the West to a non-Western culture directly without considering culture as an issue. This approach has been called *imposed etic* (Berry, 1969) because the applicability of the theory is imposed, rather than tested, from one culture to another. A slightly modified approach is to take the universality of theory as an empirical issue. Instead of assuming that Western instruments are applicable to non-Western cultures, researchers can adapt the Western instruments and test their validities. This slightly modified etic approach is often used in clinical health psychology research.

For example, in two independent studies, we have administered the Chinese translated versions of the Mini-Mental Adjustment to Cancer Scale (Mini-MAC; Watson et al., 1994) and Posttraumatic Growth Inventory (PTGI; Tedeschi & Calhoun, 1996) to Chinese cancer patients in Hong Kong. Using both exploratory and confirmatory factor analysis techniques, we have found out that the factor structures of both scales need modifications to suit our Chinese cancer patients (Ho, Chan, & Ho, 2004; Ho, Wong, Chan, Watson, & Tsui, 2003). One example in positive psychology measurement is the Chinese Revised Life Orientation Test (CLOT-R; Lai, Cheung, Lee, & Yu, 1998). Lai et al. (1998) administered the CLOT-R to samples in Hong Kong ($n = 404$) and Beijing ($n = 328$) independently. Both exploratory and confirmatory factor analyses showed that the positive and negative items of the CLOT-R should be independently scored into two factors of optimism and pessimism, especially among the Beijing sample.

CFA can be applied in a number of ways to validate the instruments based on the etic approach. The first method is to apply a single-group CFA analysis of the proposed instrument in a local population. If the proposed model fits the non-Western population reasonably, we have evidence supporting the applicability of the proposed model. If the proposed model is rejected, researchers know that there is something wrong with the instrument applied to the non-Western population.

Single-group CFA analysis seems reasonably good enough for researchers studying the universality of the instruments when the interests are to test whether the patterns of factor structure are the same in different cultures. However, single-group CFA analysis does not tell us whether the loadings are the same in Western and non-Western populations. Multiple-group CFA analysis can be used to study the equivalence (or invariance) of the measurements in two or more cultures. If the instrument is found equivalent in two samples, we have evidence supporting that the instruments are measuring the same constructs to the same extent (e.g., Byrne, 2003; Little, 1997; van de Vijver & Leung, 1997).

There are several levels (or forms) of equivalence, and all of them can be tested empirically within the multiple-group CFA approach (Cheung & Rensvold, 2002; Vandenberg & Lance, 2000). The first (least restrictive) form is the configural equivalence in which the patterns of the factor loadings are the same in different cultures. In other words, the items are loaded on the same set of latent factors in different cultures. The second (more restrictive) form is the metric equivalence, meaning that the factor loadings are the same in different cultures. If the null hypothesis of metric equivalence is not rejected, it suggests that the instruments are measuring the same constructs to the same extent in different cultures. If the instruments are not equivalent in two different groups, even simple mean differences are not meaningful because the scores obtained are not comparable in different cultures (Vandenberg & Lance, 2000). Thus, metric equivalence is a prerequisite for comparing group mean differences across cultures.

There are other more restrictive forms of equivalence, such as residual equivalence (items having equal reliabilities across cultures) and structural equivalence (constructs having equal correlations across cultures). Since the above models are nested with each other—for instance, metric equivalence is nested within configural equivalence—a chi-square difference test can be used to test the significance of the applied restrictions. Cheung and Rensvold (2002) argued that the chi-square difference test depends too much on the sample size. The null hypothesis of equivalence is surely rejected in large samples. They suggested that a value change of the comparative fit index (CFI; Benter, 1990) smaller than 0.01 in model comparison indicates that the null hypothesis of equivalence should not be rejected. Interested readers can refer to Vandenberg and Lance (2000) for a review.

Since the same theory or instrument is used in different cultures, comparisons of the findings across cultures are feasible. Evidence for the theories accumulated from the West can be used to support the conceptual and psychometric properties of the instruments. Moreover, whether the theory is universal can be tested empirically by using CFA as outlined above. The main criticism is that the meaning of constructs in some cultures may be distorted or different even if the same instrument is used. Moreover, important emic (local) concepts are usually ignored under the etic approach (Berry et al., 1992). Even if the Western theory is applicable, the theory and its measurements are not maximized for ecological validity in the local populations because relevant key concepts and measurements are ignored.

Emic Approach

Although the etic approach has been dominated in adapting instruments to non-Western populations, there have been many attempts to develop emic or indigenous theories and instruments. The emic approach suggests that behaviors are culture-specific. Thus, researchers need to develop theories and instruments sensitive to local contexts in order to increase ecological validity. Cheung et al. (2003) provided a review of indigenous psychological assessment in Asia.

Perhaps the most well-known example among cross-cultural psychologists is the indigenous concept of filial piety in the Confucian ethic, for instance, in Chinese societies (Ho, 1996). It was found that filial piety is related to many behaviors among Chinese, for instance, counseling (Kwan, 2000), family cohesion (Cheung, Lee, & Chan, 1994), and parenting practices (Pearson & Rao, 2003). These findings suggest that locally developed instruments are required to predict behaviors in their local contexts. As another example of the emic approach in measurement, we have created an item pool of grief reactions based on psychotherapy records of bereaved adults in Hong Kong and developed a Grief Reaction Assessment Form (GRAF) as an indigenous measurement of grief reaction among the Chinese (Ho, Chow, Chan, & Tsui, 2002).

The applications of CFA in testing instruments developed locally are similar to those in the etic approach. Single-group analyses are usually used because researchers developing local instruments seldom care about whether their instruments are applicable to the West or not.

Since the instruments are developed and validated locally, the ecological validity of the instruments is generally maximized. This is the main reason why researchers are increasingly interested in the applications of indigenous assessments related to Asian values in the United States, because of the large population of Asian immigrants (Kim, Atkinson, & Yang, 1999). Indigenous theories can also shed light on general theory development in psychology by providing new insights into old problems from a different perspective (e.g., Kim, 2000). The disadvantage is the noncomparability of the results in different cultures, because the theories and instruments are tailor-made for particular cultures. Even if researchers are interested in exporting their theories and instruments to other cultures, locally developed instruments are usually difficult to translate accurately to other cultures.

Emic-Etic Approach

Etic and emic approaches can be considered as two extremes with their own advantages and limitations. An approach somewhat between them is the combined emic-etic approach (e.g., Hui & Triandis, 1985). The idea is that researchers can identify etic constructs that appear to be universal first. The construct can be measured locally or other emic constructs can be added. Then the combined instrument can be tested by itself or with other etic instruments to demonstrate the uniqueness of the emic items. CFA can be used in the joint factor analysis to test the uniqueness of the emic items.

One recent example from our research is the development of a Death Metaphor Scale (DMS; Cheung & Ho, 2004) to measure personal perception of death among the Chinese. We administered the 18-item Revised Death Fantasy Scale (RDFS; McLennan & Stewart, 1997) (etic) together with 12 self-developed items (emic) to 100 college students in Hong Kong. Exploratory factor analysis revealed, as with the RDFS, a two-factor model with positive and negative death metaphor subscales. The final 18-item DMS consists of 4 newly created items from us and another 14 items from the RDFS.

The advantage of the combined emic-etic approach is that the etic constructs are comparable to other well-established instruments in the West while the emic constructs can maximize ecological validity. Using the DMS again as an example, we have found that both the Positive Metaphor and Negative Metaphor scores of the DMS have comparable Cronbach's reliability alphas to those of the corresponding subscales of the RDFS. On the other hand, the DMS scores correlated with Templer's Death Anxiety Scale (DAS; Templer, 1970) in the expected direction but not the scores of the RDFS (Cheung & Ho, 2004). Thus, this emic trait can maximize the ecological validity of the instrument locally.

Another advantage of the emic-etic approach is what van de Vijver and Leung (1997) called the convergence approach in cross-cultural research. They suggested that findings on the combined etic-emic approach can also be tested in other cultures to develop universal theory. For instance, it has been generally believed that interpersonal relatedness is only relevant to the Chinese and some other Asian cultures like the Japanese. However, the findings of Cheung et al. (2003) suggested that this construct may also be relevant to other cultures. Thus, this construct can be exported to other cultures for testing.

The major limitation of this approach is that it demands time and resources because instrument developers have to consider both etic and emic theories. This means that researchers have to understand both theories and instruments developed in the West and constructs derived locally.

Application: Interpersonal Model of SWB in Chinese Populations

In this section, we are going to use the combined emic-etic approach to investigate SWB in Chinese populations. The original theory and measurements developed by Diener are considered etic since these items are generally valid across cultures, whereas the newly added items are based on the emic approach to Chinese culture.

In recent years, there has been a significant increase in research on SWB. Data are now available that enable a better understanding of satisfaction with life (or happiness), and the factors affecting it, across nations (Diener, 2000; Diener & Diener, 1995, 1996; Diener, Diener, & Diener, 1995; Diener, Gohm, Suh, & Oishi, 2000; Diener & Oishi, 2000; Diener & Suh, 1999; Diener, Suh, Smith, & Shao, 1995; Lyubomirsky, 2001; Lyubomirsky & Lepper, 1999; Seligman, 2002; Suh, 2000a; Suh, Diener, Oishi, & Triandis, 1998). SWB represents a person's own evaluation of his or her happiness in terms of both life satisfaction (cognitive evaluations) and affect (Diener, 1984; Ratzlaff, Matsumoto, Kouznetsova, Raroque, & Ray, 2000). We now know that: (1) people in most nations are generally happy except for those in very poor societies (Diener, 2000; Diener & Diener, 1996); (2) SWB increases with wealth, perhaps up to a point where further increases in wealth seem to have little effect on SWB (Diener, 2000; Diener & Diener, 1995; Diener & Oishi, 2000); and (3) individualism is positively correlated with SWB across nations (Diener & Diener, 1995; Diener, Diener et al., 1995).

Diener (2000) noted that the Chinese thought less frequently about happiness (mean score = 4.43 on a 7-point scale, ranked lowest among 17 nations), and consider happiness to be less important (mean score = 5.91 on a 7-point scale; the third lowest among 17 nations) than people of other nations. Their SWB level, however, was not particularly low (average score = 7.29 on a 10-point scale, ranked 18 among 29 nations), despite the fact that their purchasing power parity (PPP) was among the lowest of all nations included in the study.

However, the present concept and assessment of SWB focuses mainly on self-appraisal of one's own condition and may not be totally relevant to addressing the interpersonal dimension of happiness in collective culture. It is evident that the Chinese are relationally oriented (Ho, 1995, 1997, 1998). The SWB of Chinese people has been found to be more dependent on harmonious relationships and interdependent goal attainments than has been found in other cultural groups (Kwan, Bond, & Singelis, 1997; Oishi & Diener, 2001; Suh, 2000b). Furthermore, the Chinese are more dependent on social norms (others' approval of life satisfaction) to evaluate SWB than their Western counterparts (Suh et al., 1998). Finally, because of their relational orientation, the self-identity of the Chinese is more variable (depending on the social context) than consistent (Yeh & Hwang, 2000). It is logical to predict that situation-appropriate self-flexibility affects Chinese people's SWB more than situation-independent self-consistency. Although systematic studies in this area have not, apparently, been carried out among the Chinese, there is evidence to support this hypothesis in a series of studies conducted among Korean and American participants (Suh, 2000a).

Our studies on clinical health psychology also support the proposition that the Chinese tend to be very concerned about the well-being of their significant others. In a study of decisional considerations relating to hereditary colon cancer screening, Ho, Ho, Chan, Kwan, and Tsui (2003) asked 62 patients to evaluate the pros and cons of knowing the genetic testing results, as well as sharing the results with relatives. Their results show that the highest scored items in each category ("I want to learn whether my children are at risk"; "I am concerned about my family's reactions"; "Because my relatives could do something to reduce their risk of cancer"; "My relatives would be worried about getting colon cancer") are concerned with the well-being of significant others. In another study to establish a grief assessment inventory for the Chinese, Ho et al. (2002) found that a culturally specific item—"I do not want to abandon him/her (the deceased)"[1]—obtained the highest ranked score among bereaved adults in Hong Kong. The word *abandon* in Chinese carries the connotation that the one being abandoned is suffering as a result. These results can be interpreted as representing the Chinese belief that the deceased has continuous linkage with the family (Chan & Mak, 2000; Moser, 1975) on the one hand, and their concern about the well-being of the loved one after his or her death on the other hand. More recently, there is evidence showing that Chinese cancer survivors reported positive changes in two distinct dimensions: the interpersonal dimension and the intrapersonal dimension (Ho et al., 2004).

Based on the above findings, we have hypothesized an interpersonal dimension of SWB that appears to be neglected in the existing literature. This new dimension of SWB may explain some of the salient cross-cultural findings (e.g., the results of Diener, 2000) on SWB as well as having potential significant contribution to cross-cultural comparison and positive intervention. A more detailed explanation of this interpersonal dimension of SWB is provided below.

A New Dimension of Subjective Well-Being

Chinese people tend to use metaphorical expressions and rhetorical figures to communicate ideas (Williams, 1920). The Chinese language is rich in metaphor, and many Chinese characters (word symbols) originated from collective mental representations of phenomena. To understand what happiness means in Chinese, we first discuss a symbol of happiness from the *I Ching* (*The Book of Changes*)—an ancient book that is still very popular in Chinese-speaking societies. The symbol for happiness and satisfaction (*Dui*; Rutt, 1996) from the *I Ching* is shown in figure 10.1.

The symbol is formed by two identical overlapping symbols, each representing either a smiling face or a lake. The key words for this hexagram are: express yourself, join with others, persuade, inspire and enjoy (Karcher, 1995). The two smiling faces symbolize two people talking to each other.[2] Thus, communicating with others and forming harmonious relationships cultivate happiness. This is consistent with the interdependent nature of the Chinese, mentioned above (Markus & Kitayama, 1991; Singelis, 1994; Singelis, Bond, Sharkey, & Lai, 1999; Yeh & Hwang, 2000). However, there is another dimension of happiness depicted in the symbol, which is that happiness can also be gained through the encouragement of others (Wing, 1987). Happiness can be obtained either by cheering people up and freeing them from constraint, or through expressing oneself openly and interacting with others (Karcher, 1995). This "you are happy and therefore I am happy" dimension of happiness does not appear to be emphasized in the existing literature relating to SWB, but may be relevant to the Chinese and even to people of other cultures. This dimension

of happiness is referred to in this chapter as *interpersonal SWB*.

Confirmatory Factor Analytic Studies of Interpersonal SWB

We have conducted three studies to investigate interpersonal SWB among the Chinese. Only the factor analysis results are presented here because of their relevance to the topic of this chapter.

Study 1: Beijing Sample

This study expanded the Chinese version of the original Satisfaction With Life Scale (SWLS; Diener, Emmons, Larson, & Griffin, 1985; Shek, 1995) by adding onto it another five items (e.g., "In most ways my *family members'* life is close to my ideal"; "The conditions of my *family members'* lives are excellent"; "My *family members* are satisfied with their lives"; "So far I believe my *family members* have gotten the important things they want in life"; "If my *family members* could live their lives over, I believe they would change almost nothing")[3] to measure interpersonal SWB. We then administered this expanded version of the SWLS online to 296 (167 men; 129 women) second-year bachelor degree students at Tsinghua University in Beijing, China. All participants were native Chinese, born and raised in China. Mean age of

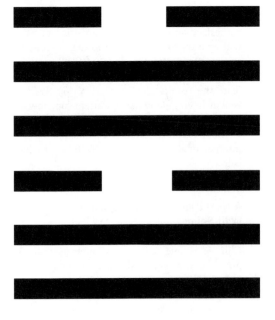

Figure 10.1 Hexagram 58 of *I Ching*: *Dui* (Satisfaction). This hexagram is formed by two identical overlapping symbols, with each symbol representing either a smiling face or a lake.

the participants was 18.41 years (range = 17–21 years, $SD = .85$). There was no sex difference in terms of age; $t(290) = .16$, $p = .87$. Exploratory factor analysis with varimax rotation revealed three factors. The first factor consisted of six items. Three are intrapersonal items (swb_a4, swb_a7, swb_a8) from the original C-SWLS and the other three are interpersonal items (swb_a6, swb_a9, swb_a10) created for this study. This factor accounted for 37.06% of the total variance and had a Cronbach's alpha value of .85. Factor II consisted of two interpersonal items and had a modest internal reliability alpha of .53. Finally, Factor III had two items from the original C-SWLS. This factor, however, had a low alpha value of .13 (table 10.1).

In summary, both Factor II and Factor III had modest to low internal reliabilities and each accounted for a relatively small percentage of the total variance. Since Factor I contained both the relational and self-oriented items, we decided to exclude items in Factors II and III in Study 2. Consequently, the 6 items from Factor I were

selected for a subsequent study. This 6-item scale to measure both the intrapersonal and interpersonal dimensions of SWB is called the Expanded Satisfaction With Life Scale (E-SWLS).

Study 2: Beijing Sample

Study 1 provided preliminary support to our proposition that there exists an interpersonal dimension of SWB and this dimension could be measured by the 6-item E-SWLS. In Study 2 ($n = 485$), we aimed to examine the factorial validity of the 6-item E-SWLS by CFA. We had hypothesized, a priori, two models to be examined in this study. The first is a first-order single-factor model with the interpersonal and intrapersonal items loaded onto a single factor. The second model is a first-order two-factor model with interpersonal SWB and intrapersonal SWB as separated but related identities. We changed the method of data collection from online survey to face-to-face group survey in

TABLE 10.1 Exploratory Factor Analysis Results (Beijing Sample, $n = 296$)

	Factor		
	I	II	III
Factor I (37.06% of variance; $\alpha = .85$)			
(swb_a9) So far I believe my family members have gotten the important things they want in life.	.803		−.174
(swb_a8) The conditions of my life are excellent.*	.793		
(swb_a7) I am satisfied with life.*	.790		
(swb_a6) In most ways my family members' lives are close to my ideal.	.777		
(swb_a10) The conditions of my family members' lives are excellent.	.767	.225	−.227
(swb_a4) So far I have gotten the important things I want in life.*	.589	−.120	.354
Factor II (14.77% of variance; $\alpha = .53$)			
(swb_a2) If my *family members* could live their lives over, I believe, they would change almost nothing.		.798	
(swb_a3) *My family members* are satisfied with their lives.		.796	
Factor III (10.33% of variance, $\alpha = .13$)			
(swb_a1) In most ways my life is close to my ideal.	−.179	.271	.753
(swb_a5) If I could live my life over, I would change almost nothing.	.367	−.124	.573

Note: Items with an asterisk are original items of the SWLS (Diener, 1985). There are two pairs of parallel items in Factor I: swb_a4_swb_a9 and swb_a8–swb_a10. The wordings of items in a pair are almost identical except that the first item in a pair focuses on self whereas the second item focuses on family members. We had decided to assign correlated error terms to items in each pair in the confirmatory factor analyses of subsequent studies.

order to ensure that all participants completed the questionnaire under similar conditions.

In Beijing, China, 485 students completed the E-SWLS together with other psychometric inventories. There were 262 (54.0%) first-year students from Tsinghua University and 223 (46.0%) senior high school students. The university sample included 189 men (72.1%) and 73 women (27.9%). The high school sample had 124 men (55.6%) and 99 women (44.4%). There were more men in the university sample than the high school sample, $\chi^2(1) = 14.39$, $p < .0001$. The mean age of the university sample was 18.42 years ($SD = .85$; men $= 18.48 \pm .81$ and women $= 18.30 \pm .92$) and that of the high school sample was 15.41 years ($SD = .55$; men $= 15.49 \pm .52$ and women $= 15.32 \pm .57$). The university sample had higher mean age than the high school sample, $t(478) = 45.40$, $p < .001$.

We conducted two CFAs by using AMOS (Analysis of Moment Structures) Version 4 (Arbuckle, 1999a, 1999b). Maximum-likelihood estimation method was used to test the covariance matrix to determine how well the model fit the data. Apart from a standard chi-square test, several other fit indices are also reported, including the goodness-of-fit index (GFI; Jöreskog & Sörbom, 1993), the adjusted goodness-of-fit index (AGFI; Jöreskog & Sörbom, 1993), CFI, the Tucker-Lewis index (TLI; Benter & Bonett, 1980; Bollen, 1989; Marsh, Balla, & McDonald, 1988), and the root mean square error of approximation (RMSEA; Browne & Cudeck, 1993). Akaike's information criteria (AIC; Akaike, 1987) and the consistent version of the AIC (CAIC; Bozdogan, 1987) were used to compare the two models, with smaller values representing a better fit of the hypothesized model (Byrne, 2001; Hu & Bentler, 1995).

The path diagrams and the fit indices of both models under investigation are shown in figures 10.2 and 10.3. We had made an a priori decision to include two correlated errors in the path diagrams before the CFA. The first correlated error was between swb_a4 "So far I have gotten the important things I want in life" and swb_a9 "So far I believe my family members have gotten the important things they want in life." The second correlated error was between swb_a8 "The conditions of my life are excellent" and swb_a10 "The conditions of my family members' lives are excellent." The specifications of these error terms were justified by the semantic similarity of the respective items. The reliability coefficients according to this Beijing sample were:

intrapersonal SWB, $\alpha = .42$; interpersonal SWB, $\alpha = .64$; total SWB, $\alpha = .67$.

The single-factor model moderately fit this sample of data according to the fit indices. However, the two-factor model achieved an excellent fit. The AIC and CAIC indices showed that the two-factor model achieved a better fit than the single-factor model in this population.

Study 3: Hong Kong Sample

Study 2 used a sample in Beijing that represented a traditional Chinese (collective) culture. It would be interesting to examine which one of the two models can better fit a sample in Hong Kong where East meets West. In Study 3, we asked 1,635 hospital staff to complete the E-SWLS, together with other psychological inventories to test which of the two models in Study 2 could better fit the Hong Kong sample. Note that we used an etic approach in Study 3—we used the models established among Beijing samples and imposed them on a Hong Kong sample to compare their goodness-of-fit indices.

There were 1,188 women (72.7%) in this sample. The occupations of the participants were: nurse (40.1%), support staff (40.3%), health care professional (other than doctor or nurse; 11.6%), medical doctor (4.6%), and management/administrator (3.4%). A majority (69.9%) of the participants were between 35 and 44 years old. Another 26.8% of them were above 45 years. CFA results of the two models are shown in table 10.2. The same correlated errors were specified in the path diagrams as in Study 2. The two-factor model again achieved a significantly better fit in our Hong Kong sample. The reliability coefficients of this Hong Kong sample were: intrapersonal SWB, $\alpha = .86$; interpersonal SWB, $\alpha = .86$; total SWB, $\alpha = .90$.

To further test whether the two-factor CFA model was equivalent in the Beijing and Hong Kong samples, we conducted a multiple-group analysis by imposing various degrees of restriction (Byrne, 2003; Little, 1997). Apart from relying on the formal chi-square test statistics, which are very sensitive to sample size, we also used the goodness-of-fit indices, especially the CFI, suggested by Cheung and Rensvold (2002). The results suggest that the factor loadings (Model 2) and the factor correlations (Model 3) are invariant in the Beijing and Hong Kong samples. In other words, the two-factor CFA model was measuring the same construct to the same extent in the two samples (Model 2).

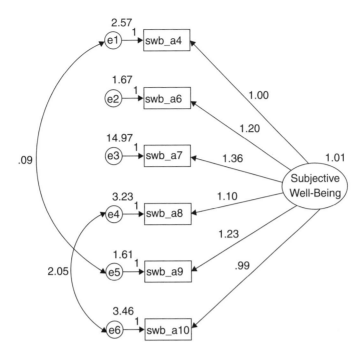

χ	df	p	GFI	AGFI	CFI	TLI	RMSEA	AIC	CAIC
26.30	7	≤.000	.982	.947	.974	.943	.075	54.30	126.879

Figure 10.2 First-order single-factor model of the Extended Satisfaction With Life Scale (Beijing sample, $n = 485$).

Moreover, the factor correlation between interpersonal and intrapersonal SWB was .80, which was equal in these two samples (Model 3). Furthermore, the hypothesis of equal reliability was not supported (Model 4). This is consistent with our previously reported alpha coefficients showing that the reliabilities of interpersonal and intrapersonal SWS were higher in the Hong Kong sample than in the Beijing sample.

The issue of reliability in different samples is worthy to be addressed here because it demonstrates the superiority of CFA over conventional approaches in estimating the correlations among constructs. As shown in Studies 2 and 3, the scales have higher reliabilities in Hong Kong samples than in Beijing samples. Conventionally, we estimated the correlation between interpersonal and intrapersonal SWB by creating the composite scores on their corresponding items. The calculated correlations in Beijing and Hong Kong samples were .54 and .72, respec-

tively. By using Fisher's z transformation, the z statistic on the equivalence of the population correlations was 34.44, which is statistically significant. Researchers may (wrongly) conclude that the strength of relationship between interpersonal and intrapersonal SWB is different in these two samples. By using multiple-group CFA, the estimated correlations in the Beijing and Hong Kong samples were .84 and .79, respectively. Two important points are noted. First, the estimated correlations are usually higher than those based on composite scores, especially in the Beijing sample, because CFA can account for the measurement unreliability (e.g., Fan, 2003). Second, Model 3 in table 10.3 suggests that the strength of relationship between interpersonal and intrapersonal SWB is the same ($r = .80$) in the Beijing and Hong Kong samples. To sum up, the two-factor SWB model measured the same construct in Beijing and Hong Kong samples. Moreover, their strength of

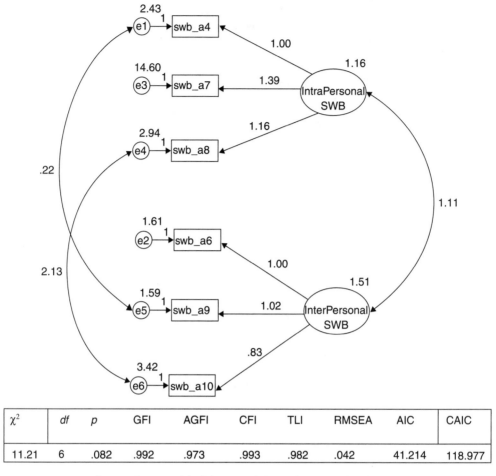

χ^2	df	p	GFI	AGFI	CFI	TLI	RMSEA	AIC	CAIC
11.21	6	.082	.992	.973	.993	.982	.042	41.214	118.977

Figure 10.3 First-order two-factor model of the Extended Satisfaction With Life Scale (Beijing sample, $n = 485$).

relationship was also the same in these two samples. We can conclude that the E-SWLS scale measures the same constructs to the same extent among people in Beijing and Hong Kong. Comparison of the scores (e.g., mean differences) obtained by the E-SWLS between Beijing and Hong Kong samples is therefore justified.

Summary and Conclusion

Human beings are capable of deriving true happiness from the happiness of significant others, and this dimension of happiness should be relevant to the overall SWB of a person. The present concept and assessment of SWB focuses mainly

TABLE 10.2 Confirmatory Factor Analysis Results of the Extended Satisfaction With Life Scale (Hong Kong Sample, $n = 1635$)

Model	χ^2	df	p	GFI	AGFI	CFI	TLI	RMSEA	AIC	CAIC
First-order single-factor	745.793	7	<.000	.857	.570	.883	.750	.254	773.793	863.384
First-order two-factor	102.512	6	<.000	.980	.929	.985	.962	.099	132.512	228.503

TABLE 10.3 Multigroup Analysis Results Comparing the Beijing and Hong Kong Samples

Model	χ^2	df	p for χ^2	$\Delta\chi^2$	Δdf	p for $\Delta\chi^2$	CFI	TLI	RMSEA
Baseline	113.72	12	<.001				0.990	0.975	0.089
Equal factor loadings	123.42	16	<.001	9.70	4	.046	0.989	0.980	0.079
Equal factor loadings and factor variances and covariances	125.89	19	<.001	2.47	3	.481	0.990	0.983	0.072
Equal factor loadings, factor variances and covariances, and error variances and covariances	3,191.35	27	<.001	3,065.46	8	<.001	0.690	0.656	0.354

Note: All models are compared with the previous model.

on self-appraisal of one's well-being and may not explain the total SWB experience of people in collective cultures, like the Chinese. According to our hypothesis, Chinese may think about the happiness of significant others and incorporate this appraisal into their own happiness. This chapter describes our attempt to investigate this interpersonal dimension of SWB among Chinese people. We have used the combined etic-emic approach to guide our investigation by adopting the original SWLS (Diener et al., 1985) and adding to it another five interpersonal items created by ourselves. We have selected six from this initial item pool, based on the exploratory factor analysis result among a group of participants in Beijing in Study 1, for further examination. We refer to this 6-item scale as the Expanded Satisfaction With Life Scale (E-SWLS). Three items are etic components from the orginal SWLS and measure intrapersonal SWB. Another three items are emic components that measure interpersonal SWB. We then conducted two studies, one in Beijing and another in Hong Kong, to compare two models of SWB among the Chinese. One is a single-factor model with both interpersonal and intrapersonal components integrated together. This integrated model is consistent with the argument that the self versus other self-construal is more enmeshed among people in collective cultures (Markus & Kitayama, 1991; Singelis et al., 1999). Another is a two-factor model with two separated but related SWB dimensions: the interpersonal and the intrapersonal. The mind-body relationship could be used as an analogy to help us understand these two models. In some cultures, the body and the mind are considered separate entities. The body refers to our physical being and the mind refers to our mental being. In other cultures (e.g., Chinese), the body and the mind are regarded as an integrated whole. Similarly, we propose that in some cultures interpersonal and intrapersonal SWB would be more separated, and in other cultures the two constructs would be more integrated.

Our results showed that the two-factor model can fit both the Beijing and the Hong Kong data significantly better than the singlefactor integrated model. Hence, similar to optimism (Lai & Yue, 2000), SWB among the Chinese can be conceptualized as having two separated but related components: the interpersonal and the intrapersonal. For future studies, we are planning to study whether these two dimensions of SWB will vary among people in different cultures as well as different age groups. Besides, from an intervention point of view, we would like to see whether change in the SWB of significant others would have a consequently important impact on the SWB of self.

Our examples of SWB demonstrate the advantages of using the combined etic-emic approach in cross-cultural positive psychology measurement. First, the etic (intrapersonal) items were found to be applicable to the samples in Beijing and Hong Kong while the emic (interpersonal) items were found to be distinctive from the etic items. These suggest that the interpersonal dimension of SWB may be an important but neglected dimension in Chinese populations. Moreover, the multigroup CFA analysis results show that the E-SWLS is measuring interpersonal SWB and intrapersonal SWB to the same extent in both cities. This will facilitate comparison of results across cultures. Following the convergence approach suggested by van de Vijver and Leung (1997), we suggest that the intrapersonal and interpersonal dimensions of SWB measured by the E-SWLS may also be applicable to non-Chinese. We hope that these findings can shed light on the theory and measurement development of SWB.

Acknowledgments The authors would like to thank Professor Fumin Fan of Tsinghua University for collecting data for us in Beijing, China. We would also like to express our sincere gratitude to Mrs. Rosalie S. Y. Kwong and her staff at Corporate Clinical Psychology Services, Oasis Center for Personal Growth and Crisis Intervention, Hospital Authority, for their support in the Hong Kong study.

Notes

1. The original item was set in Chinese and there is no direct translation of this culture-specific item. The present translation only carries the essential meaning of the original item.
2. The two lakes represent openness (lake) upon openness (lake), which form the condition for an exchange of ideas (Wing, 1987).
3. We used *family members* in our scale since most Chinese will consider their family members as their most significant others. Future users may change *family members* to other significant persons (e.g., partners, children) according to their needs.

References

Akaike, H. (1987). Factor analysis and AIC. *Psychometrika, 52,* 317–332.
Arbuckle, J. L. (1999a). *AMOS 4.0 (Version 4.0)*. Chicago: Smallwaters.
Arbuckle, J. L. (1999b). *AMOS 4.0 user's guide.* Chicago: Smallwaters.
Beck, A., & Steen, R. A. (1987). *Beck Depression Inventory manual.* San Antonio, TX: Psychological Corporation.
Benter, P. M. (1990). Comparative fit indices in structural models. *Psychological Bulletin, 107,* 238–246.
Benter, P. M., & Bonett, D. G. (1980). Significance tests and goodness of fit in the analysis of covariance structures. *Psychological Bulletin, 88,* 588–606.
Berry, J. W. (1969). On cross-cultural comparability. *International Journal of Psychology, 4,* 119–128.
Berry, J. W., Poortinga, Y. H., Segall, M. H., & Dasen, P. R. (1992). *Cross-cultural psychology: Research and applications.* New York: Cambridge University Press.

Bollen, K. A. (1989). *Structural equations with latent variables.* New York: Wiley.
Bozdogan, H. (1987). Model selection and Akaike's information criteria (AIC): The general theory and its analytical extensions. *Psychometrika, 50,* 345–370.
Browne, M. W., & Cudeck, R. (1993). Alternative ways of assessing model fit. In K. A. Bollen & J. S. Long (Eds.), *Testing structural equation models* (pp. 136–162). Newbury Park, CA: Sage.
Byrne, B. M. (2001). *Structural equation modeling with AMOS: Basic concepts, applications, and programming.* Mahwah, NJ: Erlbaum.
Byrne, B. M. (2003). The issue of measurement invariance revisited. *Journal of Cross-Cultural Psychology, 34,* 155–175.
Caprara, G. V., Barbaranelli, C., Bermudez, J., Maslach, C., & Ruch, W. (2000). Multivariate methods for the comparison of factor structures in cross-cultural reserach: An illustration with the Big Five Questionnaire. *Journal of Cross-Cultural Psychology, 31,* 437–464.
Chan, C. L.-w., & Mak, J. M.-h. (2000). Benefits and drawbacks of Chinese rituals surrounding care for the dying. In R. Fielding & C. L.-w. Chan (Eds.), *Psychosocial oncology and palliative care in Hong Kong: The first decade* (pp. 255–270). Hong Kong: Hong Kong University Press.
Cheung, C., Lee, J., & Chan, C. (1994). Explicating filial piety in relation to family cohesion. *Journal of Social Behavioral and Personality, 9,* 565–580.
Cheung, F. M., Leung, F. T., & Ben-Porath, Y. S. (2003). Psychological assessment in Asia: Introduction to the special section. *Psychological Assessment, 15,* 243–247.
Cheung, G. W., & Rensvold, R. B. (2002). Evaluating goodness-of-fit indexes for testing measurement invariance. *Structural Equation Modeling, 9,* 233–255.
Cheung, M. W. L., Leung, K., & Au, K. (in press). Evaluating multilevel models in cross-cultural research: An illustration with Social Axioms. *Journal of Cross-Cultural Psychology.*
Cheung, W.-s., & Ho, S. M. Y. (2004). The use of death metaphors to understand personal meaning of death among Hong Kong Chinese undergraduates. *Death Studies, 28,* 47–62.
Diener, E. (1984). Subjective well-being. *Psychological Bulletin, 95,* 542–575.
Diener, E. (2000). Subjective well-being. *American Psychologist, 55*(1), 34–43.
Diener, E., & Diener, C. (1996). Most people are happy. *Psychological Science, 7*(3), 181–185.
Diener, E., Diener, C., & Diener, M. (1995). Factors predicting the subjective well-being of nations. *Journal of Personality and Social Psychology, 69*(5), 851–864.

Diener, E., & Diener, M. (1995). Cross-cultural correlates of life satisfaction and self-esteem. *Journal of Personality and Social Psychology, 68*(4), 653–663.

Diener, E., Emmons, R. A., Larson, R. J., & Griffin, S. (1985). The Satisfaction With Life Scale. *Journal of Personality Assessment, 49,* 71–75.

Diener, E., Gohm, C. L., Suh, E., & Oishi, S. (2000). Similarity of the relations between marital status and subjective well-being across cultures. *Journal of Cross-Cultural Psychology, 31*(4), 419–436.

Diener, E., & Oishi, S. (2000). Money and happiness: Income and subjective well-being across nations. In E. Diener & E. Suh (Eds.), *Culture and subjective well-being* (pp. 185–218). Cambridge, MA: MIT Press.

Diener, E., & Suh, E. M. (1999). National differences in subjective well-being. In D. Kahneman, E. Diener, & N. Schwartz (Eds.), *Well-being: The foundations of hedonic psychology* (pp. 434–450). New York: Russell Sage.

Diener, E., Suh, E. M., Smith, H., & Shao, L. (1995). National differences in reported subjective well-being: Why do they occur? *Social Indicators Research, 34*(1), 7–32.

Fan, X. (2003). Two approaches for correcting correlation attenuation caused by measurement error: Implications for research practice. *Educational and Psychological Measurement, 63,* 915–930.

Hathaway, S. R., & McKinley, J. C. (1967). *Minnesota Multiphasic Personality Inventory Manual, Revised.* New York: Psychological Corporation.

Headland, T. N. (1990). A dialogue between Kenneth Pike and Marvin Harris on emics and etics. In T. N. Headland, K. L. Pike, & M. Harris (Eds.), *Emics and etics: The insider/outsider debate* (pp. 13–27). Newbury Park, CA: Sage.

Ho, D. Y. F. (1995). Selfhood and identity in Confucianism, Taosim, Buddhism, and Hinduism: Contrasts with the West. *Journal for the Theory of Social Behavior, 25*(2), 115–139.

Ho, D. Y. F. (1996). Filial piety and its psychological consequences. In M. H. Bond (Ed.), *The handbook of Chinese psychology* (pp. 155–165). Hong Kong: Oxford University Press.

Ho, D. Y. F. (1997). *Relational counseling: An Asian perspective on therapeutic intervention.* Paper presented at the the 55th Annual Convention of the International Council of Psychologists, Graz, Austria.

Ho, D. Y. F. (1998). Indigenous psychologies: Asian perspectives. *Journal of Cross-Cultural Psychology, 29*(1), 88–103.

Ho, S. M. Y., Chan, C. L. W., & Ho, R. T. H. (2004). Post-traumatic growth in Chinese cancer survivors. *Psycho-Oncology, 13*(6), 377–389.

Ho, S. M. Y., Chow, A. Y. M., Chan, C. L.-w., & Tsui, Y. K. Y. (2002). The assessment of grief among Hong Kong Chinese: A preliminary report. *Death Studies, 26,* 91–98.

Ho, S. M. Y., Ho, J. W. C., Chan, C. L. W., Kwan, K., & Tsui, Y. K. Y. (2003). Decisional consideration of hereditary colon cancer genetic test results among Hong Kong Chinese adults. *Cancer Epidemiology, Biomarkers and Prevention, 12*(5), 426–432.

Ho, S. M. Y., Wong, K. F., Chan, C. L.-w., Watson, M., & Tsui, Y. K. Y. (2003). Psychometric properties of the Chinese version of the Mini Mental Adjustment to Cancer (Mini-MAC) Scale. *Psycho-Oncology, 12*(6), 547–556.

Hofstede, G. (1980). *Culture's consequences: International differences in work-related values.* Beverly Hills, CA: Sage.

Hu, L. T., & Bentler, P. M. (1995). Evaluating model fit. In R. H. Hoyle (Ed.), *Structural equation modeling: Concepts, issues, and applications* (pp. 76–99). Thousand Oaks, CA: Sage.

Hui, C. H., & Triandis, H. C. (1985). Measurement in cross-cultural psychology: A review and comparison of strategies. *Journal of Cross-Cultural Psychology, 16,* 131–152.

Jöreskog, K. G., & Sörbom, D. (1993). *LISREL VIII: A guide to the program and applications.* Nororesville, IN: Scientific Software.

Karcher, S. (1995). *The elements of the I Ching.* Shaftesbury, Dorset: Element.

Kim, B. S. K., Atkinson, D. R., & Yang, P. H. (1999). The Asian Values Scale: Development, factor analysis, validation, and reliability. *Journal of Counseling Psychology, 46,* 342–352.

Kim, U. (2000). Indigenous, cultural, and cross-cultural psychology: A theoretical, conceptual, and epistemological analysis. *Asian Journal of Social Psychology, 3,* 265–287.

Kwan, K. L. K. (2000). Counseling Chinese peoples: Perspectives of filial piety. *Asian Journal of Counseling, 7,* 23–41.

Kwan, V. S. Y., Bond, M. H., & Singelis, T. M. (1997). Pancultural explanations for life satisfaction: Adding relational harmony to self-esteem. *Journal of Personality and Social Psychology, 73,* 1038–1051.

Lai, J. C. L., Cheung, H., Lee, W. M., & Yu, H. (1998). The utility of the revised Life Orientation Test to measure optimism among Hong Kong Chinese. *International Journal of Psychology, 33,* 45–56.

Lai, J. C. L., & Yue, X. (2000). Measuring optimism in Hong Kong and mainland Chinese with the revised Life Orientation Test. *Personality and Individual Differences, 28*(4), 781–796.

Little, T. D. (1997). Mean and covariance structures (MACS) analyses of cross-cultural data: Practical and theoretical issues. *Multivariate Behavioral Research, 323,* 53–76.

Lonner, W. J., & Berry, J. W. (1986). *Field methods in cross-cultural research.* Beverly Hills, CA: Sage.

Lyubomirsky, S. (2001). Why are some people happier than others? The role of cognitive and motivational processes in well-being. *American Psychologist, 56,* 239–249.

Lyubomirsky, S., & Lepper, H. S. (1999). A measure of subjective happiness: Preliminary reliability and construct validation. *Social Indicators Research, 46,* 137–155.

MacCallum, R. C., & Austin, J. T. (2000). Applications of structural equation modeling in psychological research. *Annual Review of Psychology, 51,* 201–226.

Markus, H. R., & Kitayama, S. (1991). Culture and the self: Implications for cognition, emotion, and motivation. *Psychological Review, 98,* 224–253.

Marsh, H. W., Balla, J. R., & McDonald, P. P. (1988). Goodness-of-fit indices in confirmatory factor analysis: The effect of sample size. *Psychological Bulletin, 103,* 391–410.

McLennan, J., & Stewart, C. A. (1997). Using metaphors to assess anticipatory perceptions of personal death. *Journal of Psychology Interdisciplinary and Applied, 131*(3), 333–343.

Moser, M. J. (1975). Death in Chinese: A two-dimensional analysis. *Journal of Thanatology, 3,* 169–185.

Oishi, S., & Diener, E. (2001). Goals, culture, and subjective well-being. *Personality and Social Psychology Bulletin, 27,* 1674–1682.

Pearson, E., & Rao, N. (2003). Socialization goals, parenting practices, and peer competence in Chinese and English preschoolers. *Early Child Development and Care, 173,* 131–146.

Pike, K. L. (1954). *Language in relation to a unified theory of the structure of human behavior.* Glendale, CA: Summer Institute of Linguistics.

Ratzlaff, C., Matsumoto, D., Kouznetsova, N., Raroque, J., & Ray, R. (2000). Individual psychological culture and subjective well-being. In E. Diener & E. Suh (Eds.), *Culture and subjective well-being* (pp. 37–59). Cambridge, MA: MIT Press.

Rutt, R. (1996). *The book of changes (Zhouyi).* London: Curzon Press.

Seligman, M. E. P. (2002). *Authentic happiness.* New York: Free Press.

Shek, D. T. (1995). Gender differences in marital adjustment and marital satisfaction in Chinese married adults. *Sex Roles, 32,* 699–715.

Singelis, T. M. (1994). The measurement of independent and interdependent self-construals. *Personality and Social Psychology Bulletin, 20*(5), 580–591.

Singelis, T. M., Bond, M. H., Sharkey, W. F., & Lai, C. S. Y. (1999). Unpackaging culture's influence on self-esteem and embarrassability: The role of self-construals. *Journal of Cross-Cultural Psychology, 30*(3), 315–341.

Suh, E. M. (2000a). Culture, identity consistency, and subjective well-being. *Dissertation Abstracts International: Section B. The Sciences and Engineering, 60*(9-B), 4950.

Suh, E. M. (2000b). Self, the hyphen between culture and subjective well-being. In E. Diener & E. Suh (Eds.), *Culture and subjective well-being* (pp. 63–86). Cambridge, MA: MIT Press.

Suh, E., Diener, E., Oishi, S., & Triandis, H. C. (1998). The shifting basis of life satisfaction judgments across cultures: Emotions versus norms. *Journal of Personality and Social Psychology, 74*(2), 482–493.

Tedeschi, R. G., & Calhoun, L. G. (1996). The Posttraumatic Growth Inventory: Measuring the positive legacy of trauma. *Journal of Traumatic Stress, 9*(3), 455–471.

Templer, T. D. (1970). The construction and validation of the Death Anxiety Scale. *Journal of General Psychology, 82,* 165–177.

Vandenberg, R. J., & Lance, C. E. (2000). A review and synthesis of the measurement invariance literature: Suggestions, practices, and recommendations for organizational research. *Organizational Research Methods, 3,* 4–69.

van de Vijver, F., & Leung, K. (1997). *Method and data analysis for cross-cultural research.* Thousand Oaks, CA: Sage.

Watson, M., Law, M., dos Santos, M., Greer, S., Baruch, J., & Bliss, J. (1994). The Mini-MAC: Further development of the Mental Adjustment to Cancer Scale. *Journal of Psychosocial Oncology, 12*(3), 33–46.

Williams, C. A. S. (1920). *A manual of Chinese metaphor: Being a selection of typical Chinese metaphors, with explanatory notes and indices.* Shanghai: Statistical Department of the Inspectorate General.

Wing, R. L. (1987). *The illustrated I Ching.* Wellingborough, Northamptonshire: Aquarium Press.

Yeh, C. J., & Hwang, M. Y. (2000). Interdependence in ethnic identity and self: Implications for theory and practice. *Journal of Counseling and Development, 78*(4), 420–429.

11

Assessing Factorial Invariance in Cross-Sectional and Longitudinal Studies

Daniel E. Bontempo and Scott M. Hofer

The issue of factorial invariance (FI), or more specifically the subset of FI tests that pertain to measurement equivalence, is in essence an issue of construct validity. At the conceptual level, a measure is valid when it accurately operationalizes the construct it purports to measure. The operationalization calibrates manifest indicators to theoretical constructs, which are latent in the sense that they are not directly observed. When a construct is used across multiple groups of individuals or on multiple occasions for the same individuals, the construct's measurement is invariant (and scores may be quantitatively compared) only when the construct's operationalization functions equivalently for each group or occasion. This is defined as *measurement invariance*, and multigroup requirements can be mathematically formulated (Meredith, 1993). In practice, invariance of measurements obtained in different groups is often assumed without formal test. This occurs when scale items are summed (i.e., unit-weighted) or latent factor scores (a loading-weighted sum of scale items) are calculated across groups or occasions without first establishing that the score's meaning is invariant for each group or across occasions. For a construct operationalized as the

common factor of a set of manifest indicators, measurement invariance can be demonstrated by testing a sequence of invariance hypotheses focusing on the loadings, intercepts, specific factors, and some structural elements of the common-factor measurement model. These hypotheses provide evidence for the validity of subsequent score comparisons across groups or occasions.

Factor analytic models attempt to model the observed covariances among the manifest indicators by decomposing each item's variance into a linear composite of a single common factor accounting for the common variance or covariance of the indicators and a specific factor containing systematic variance and error unique to each indicator. A linear model (i.e., intercept and slope) relates each manifest indicator to each latent factor. Figure 11.1 illustrates the parameters of the common-factor measurement model. The latent common factor is represented by the large ellipse, the manifest indicators by the four rectangles, and the linear relationships by regression-like loadings (l_i) and intercepts (i_i). The specific factors (or uniquenesses) are shown by the circles on the left. The magnitudes of the loadings are used to interpret the meaning of the

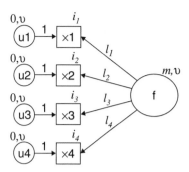

Figure 11.1 Common-factor measurement model showing factor means, factor variances, indicator intercepts, and indicator loadings.

construct because the loading is an indication of the strength of the association between the indicator and the construct. The interpretation of a loading is the amount of change observed in the indicator for a one-unit change in the common factor. The intercepts represent how much of each indicator exists when the latent common factor is zero. The model fit, or how successfully the model accounts for the observed covariances, is given by a chi-square fit statistic. Several additional nonstatistical relative fit indices are also commonly used (Bentler, 1990; Cheung & Rensvold, 2002; Hu & Bentler, 1999).

Factorial invariance is subordinate to measurement invariance. Measurement equivalence or invariance requires that functional relationships between theoretical constructs and their observed measures function equivalently across groups or occasions. The methodology to demonstrate such equivalence must be worked out for distinct measurement models (e.g., classical test theory, item response theory, factor analytic). Each measurement model attempts to represent the functional relationships between constructs and observed measures using a parsimonious and useful set of parameters (e.g., loadings, intercepts, factor variances, factor means). The factor analytic model uses a linear calibration (i.e., intercept and slope) to relate observed measures to latent constructs. Thus, factorial invariance refers to definitions and methodology to demonstrate measurement equivalence within the factor analytic model. Measurement equivalence or invariance, as the more general and abstract concept, can be thought of as unrestricted while demonstration of FI must approximate measurement invariance under additional assumptions and limitations of the factor analytic

model (for a more formal treatment of assumptions, see Meredith, 1993, p. 532). At a minimum, the construct must be factorial (i.e., the items have substantial covariance, and a common factor can account for the observed item covariances) in each group in addition to exhibiting across-group equivalence of key parameters. Also, estimation of factor-analytic models requires specific parameter constraints to achieve mathematical identification and comparable multigroup scaling (Reise, Widaman, & Pugh, 1993). (We discuss model identification in the procedural section.)

The importance of FI tests may vary with type of study, but the most important distinction is between scale development efforts and structural equation models utilizing latent factors. A review of the FI literature (Vandenberg & Lance, 2000) found that researchers across a broad spectrum of social science disciplines such as individual differences, education, aging, cross-cultural psychology, developmental psychology, criminology, and the organizational sciences have utilized FI tests to further investigations of test bias, the assessment of longitudinal change, cross-cultural comparisons, and psychometric scale development. In factor analytic structural equation models (FASEM), FI tests are of interest because the observation that measurement operations differ across groups or occasions may generate new theory, yield new knowledge, or lead to improvement of measures. However, biased latent factor scores may not occur if the differential measurement properties are modeled so that the latent factors in each group or occasion constitute the best available measure of the constructs of interest. However, in scale development efforts, subsequent manifest scoring is anticipated, where any across-group differences in measurement will create bias. In other words, manifest scores may reflect group differences that are due to measurement and not true differences on the underlying construct.

As noted above, FI procedures apply a sequence of tests to detect if the parameters of the common-factor measurement model are equivalent in each group. These tests are nested because the same parameters are used in each model, and each successive model imposes additional parameter constraints. As seen in figure 11.1, we can test for equivalent loadings, intercepts, and specific-factor variances. While we can also evaluate the equivalence of the common-factor mean and variance, these equivalences are not an aspect of FI. FASEM permits simultaneous estimation of model parameters in two or more groups and consequently permits testing of across-group parameter equivalence (Jöreskog, 1971; Sörbom, 1974). Tests involve the statistical comparison of model fit for a full model with the parameters freely estimated in each group, and a nested (reduced) model where parameters are constrained to be equivalent across groups. A sequence of tests begins with no equivalency constraints, and in a series of subsequent tests respectively applies constraints to the loadings, intercepts, and unique variances.

For a more concrete illustration of the importance of FI analyses, we offer a hypothetical example using the Satisfaction With Life Scale (SWLS; Diener, Emmons, Larsen, & Griffin, 1985; Pavot & Diener, 1993). The SWLS is a short, five-item instrument designed to measure global cognitive judgments of one's life. Pavot and Diener noted that this scale has shown good psychometric properties across numerous independent samples (e.g., unidimensionality, high and uniform factor loadings, temporal stability, language translation). There has also been some examination of the measurement invariance of the SWLS (Atienza, Balaguer, & Garcia Merita, 2003; Pons, Atienza, Balaguer, & Garcia Merita, 2000; Shevlin, Brunsden, & Miles, 1998). These five items query ideal life conditions or satisfaction with circumstances. Each item uses a 7-point response option ranging from *strongly disagree* to *strongly agree*. The actual items and standardized loadings averaged across several studies reviewed by Pavot and Denier (1993) are shown in table 11.1.

If the magnitude of the SWLS item loadings had a substantially different profile in another group (e.g., .11, .71, .72, .91, .62), the latent SWLS construct would be subject to a qualitatively different interpretation, and unambiguous quantitative group comparisons could not be made. In table 11.1, interpretation of the SWLS construct is dominated by an actual-ideal comparison of life circumstances (item 1, 0.84), but other items have similarly large loadings. In the hypothetical alternate profile given above, the interpretation would be dominated by the fourth item (0.91, having gotten important things), with other items having relatively lower importance (and the first item would effectively no longer load on the latent construct). By contrast, consider a second hypothetical alternate profile where only the order of the first two items (i.e., close to ideal, and conditions of life) was reversed across two groups. In this case, it would be very difficult to argue that the SWLS construct had qualitatively different interpretations in each group. Unfortunately, there is currently no well-articulated system for describing degrees of noninvariance, or providing confidence intervals for the bias that might result from minor or moderate departures from absolute invariance; we will return to this point.

Factorial invariance, like the larger enterprise of measurement, has been fairly well developed by decades of work, but it is also an ongoing enterprise with some unresolved issues and the frequent requirement for researchers to make judgments about its application. For single-construct models with a unidimensional common factor like the SWLS example above, procedures are fairly clear. For more complex models with multiple common factors, multidimensional constructs, or indicators at different levels of aggregation, there are more unresolved questions and consequently greater demands on judgment. More important, invariance requirements in the context of scale development differ from the invariance needs of a single study using FASEM and ad hoc measures of more holistic constructs. More precisely, each study's ability to tolerate some degree of misfit differs. Scale development efforts, where subsequent manifest use is anticipated, have the strictest invariance requirements. FASEM models may be unconcerned with some FI tests if they do not relate to the parameters of interest. Full discussion of topics such as indicator aggregation, construct breadth, and construct dimensionality are beyond the scope of this chapter, but we touch on some of these topics in our discussion. A good synthesis of these topics into a single conceptual framework is provided by Bagozzi and Edwards (1998).

In this chapter, we provide an overview of established methods utilizing FASEM to evaluate

TABLE 11.1 SWLS Items and Average Standardized Loadings

Loadings	Item Text
0.84	In most ways my life is close to my ideal.
0.81	The conditions of my life are excellent.
0.81	I am satisfied with my life.
0.74	So far I have gotten the important things I want in life.
0.71	If I could live my life over, I would change almost nothing.

FI in cross-sectional and longitudinal studies. The methodology discussed here is based on the theoretical work of Meredith (Meredith, 1993; Meredith & Horn, 2001) and FASEM estimation procedures described by Jöreskog (1971) and Sörbom (1974). In addition, Vandenberg and Lance's (2000) review of the invariance literature has been indispensable for identifying discrepant practices and nomenclature in the applied literature, as well as highlighting aspects of invariance analyses where further work is needed.

Our intention is to provide a straightforward conceptual and procedural introduction for substantive researchers who have some understanding of FASEM but are less familiar with the measurement equivalency literature. We have three main goals:

- Provide a clear conceptual understanding of the meaning, importance, and limitations of FI procedures.
- Deliver a clear procedural guide that details the sequence of FI tests and the parameter constraints employed for each successive test.
- Assist researchers in the application of FI procedures by providing sufficient introduction to circumstances where theory or the investigator's judgment may need to supersede an inflexible application of the full sequence of FI tests.

Achieving these goals will require some discussion of the factor analytic measurement model and the key parameters that are involved in FI tests. Also, while an unequivocal procedural cookbook will be of interest to many readers, it would be problematic not to address some of the discrepant recommendations and vocabulary in the invariance literature (Vandenberg & Lance, 2000) because failure to do so would hamper readers who want to pursue the FI literature in greater depth. It is also our intent to highlight the important role that the researcher plays in scrutinizing, judging, and interpreting results throughout FI procedures. Based on these goals, the remainder of this chapter is organized into three broad sections. We begin by clarifying some important factor analytic concepts and terminology, noting problematic inconsistencies in the FI literature, and adopting a clearly defined terminology. Next we discuss each of the nested FI tests in detail. Conceptual issues as well as more detailed instructions to implement each test are discussed. Finally, we address a

selection of special topics, recent developments, and unresolved issues pertaining to the evaluation of FI.

Distinctions, Definitions, and Conventions

The purpose of this section is to provide important distinctions and background information to facilitate a more detailed discussion of nested FI tests. It is important note that FI procedures are not suited to all constructs. Next, we discuss which parameters in FASEM must be invariant for measurement equivalency and distinguish other parameters for which invariance constitutes a substantive hypothesis. Finally, we address some of the disorganization Vandenberg and Lance (2000) noted in the invariance literature, and adopt a clear terminology for the remainder of the discussion.

The Common-Factor Measurement Model

At the outset, it is important to make a point about latent constructs, causality, and the common-factor measurement model, because FI tests apply only to the common-factor measurement model. Many constructs of interest in positive psychology (e.g., optimism, motivation, intelligence, subjective well-being, hope, self-esteem, perseverance) are operationalized as common-factor constructs, but not all constructs use this model. In the common-factor model, the latent construct is conceptualized as causing the observed item responses, and thus the arrows point toward the indicators (see figure 11.1). In this sense, the items reflect the latent construct; and as purported parallel reflectors of the common latent factor, they would have a large degree of covariation. It is this covariation that makes possible exploratory factor analysis (EFA) and confirmatory factor analysis (CFA). In these analyses, the known mean, variance, and covariance of the indicators is modeled in terms of the model parameters (i.e., the variance of latent common and specific factors, the loading of the items onto the factors, and the item intercepts). Like residuals in regression analyses, the means of the latent specific factors are fixed at zero. The common factor is called a *reflective construct*, and the indicators are designated *effect indicators*. Indicators (scale items) are viewed as a sample taken from a population of parallel reflectors, and the justification for using a small sample of all potential reflectors lies in their conceptualization as parallel (i.e., interchangeable).

In contrast, a latent construct could be conceptualized as emerging from the aggregation of a number of formative indicators. For example, the construct of *life stress overload* might be operationalized as acknowledging a sufficiently large number of common life stressors such as the death of a pet or the serious illness of a family member. In this case, the indicators are conceptualized as causing the latent construct and are not required to have any particular covariation with other items. In other words, you have life stress overload due in part to the death of your pet as opposed to your pet dying because you have life stress overload. Your family member falling ill does not increase the expectation that your pet will die. This type of latent construct is called an *emergent construct*, and the indicators are designated as formative indicators. (For further discussion of reflective and formative measurement models, see Bollen & Lennox's, 1991, discussion of reflective, formative, and mixed constructs. Also see Edwards & Bagozzi's, 2000, discussion of latent constructs and causality. See Diamantopoulos & Winklhofer, 2001, for further discussion of formative measurement operationalization.) The evaluation of FI does not apply to formative measures. The important implication of this short discussion of measurement models is that a determination that a measure utilizes the common-factor measurement model must be made prerequisite to considerations of FI. The consequence of incorrect conclusions that may be drawn under the false assumption of a common-factor measurement model are further elaborated by MacCallum and Browne (1993).

It is also important to understand that a measurement model almost certainly departs from reality, which has important implications for the discussion of FI. George Box (1976) pointed out that all models are wrong, but some models are useful. To begin with, models make assumptions (e.g., the indicators are parallel reflections, or the specific-factor variances are uncorrelated) and estimates of model parameters may be biased when assumptions are violated. We return to this point later when we talk about a baseline model for nested FI tests. Second, a model is an attempt at a parsimonious representation of reality, or at least reality as represented by empirical data. Meredith (1993) notes that these concepts "are idealizations... their

validity and existence in the real world of psychological measurement and research can never be finally established in practice" (p. 540). Nothing about the common-factor measurement model presumes the common factors to be real entities. This link is made when the researcher adopts a realist philosophy (Borsboom, Mellenbergh, & van Heerden, 2003). While the theoretical role of the common factor is to be an underlying truth that is free of measurement error, and an entity that is there to be reflected by the indicators, its estimate is only a mathematical partitioning of the indicator variance. EFA procedures operate by extracting common factors until all that remains is a set of uncorrelated specific factors. CFA procedures partition out the indicators' common variance, attribute the remaining variance to specific factors and, given this partitioning, permit an implied covariance matrix to be statistically compared with the actual sample covariance matrix. In short, the common-factor estimates depend on the particular indicators. With the inclusion of an additional indicator, or by using one less indicator, or by substituting a parallel indicator, the common-variance estimate (in any given sample) changes. The assumption we must make is that the change is small and yields no practical difference in the qualitative interpretation of the construct. We will return to these ideas when we consider the baseline model and a construct's centroid.

Local Independence

A central factor-analytic assumption of uncorrelated specific factors is actually problematic in the context of factorial invariance. This condition of uncorrelated specific factors is called *local independence*. Local in the sense that conditioned on the common factor(s), which is purported to explain all of the covariance among any set of indicators, the specific factors should retain no covariance. Therefore, local independence is inextricably bound with the estimation of the common factor. We have already noted that a model is never expected to perfectly match reality, but the problem in a multigroup context is that what is factorial (i.e., meets the local independence assumption) in the full population may have correlated specific factors in selected (e.g., gender, age, culture) subgroups (Meredith, 1993; Meredith & Horn, 2001). Correlated specific factors can also result when several indicators share method variance, or pertain to a subdimension of a common factor that is not quite unidimensional. On the one hand, we want the construct to be factorial in each group (including meeting local independence assumptions) and to have equivalent parameters across groups. On the other hand, it can be demonstrated using selection theory (Meredith, 1964, 1993) that local independence in each group is unlikely.

In practice, this dilemma is resolved by permitting some correlations among selected specific factors. This is especially true for the longitudinal case, where it is important to allow the specific factor for each indicator to correlate across occasions. In this sense, each indicator shares method variance with its replicate at each occasion. To avoid capitalizing on chance, it is desirable that these correlations be specified a priori. In any event, it is incumbent on the researcher to discuss and justify any nonstandard specifications included in the model.

Identification and Scaling

The issue of identification of CFA models is another area where assumptions of the factor-analytic model create difficulties for FI procedures. A CFA model is said to be *identified* when two conditions are met: (1) the model is mathematically identified, and (2) the scale of the factors has been established. *Mathematical identification* means that there must not be more unknown parameters to be estimated than the number of known moments (i.e., means, variances, covariances) in the observed data. This generally necessitates three or more indicators for each common factor, although some multiple-construct FASEM models containing related factors with only two indicators might be successfully estimated. *Scaling* requires that the latent factor be given a metric. In CFA models, the relationship between loadings and latent factor variance is indeterminate, because the loadings are in part dependent on the units of the factor. (Recall that the interpretation of the loading is the amount of change in the observed indicator for a one-unit change in the latent factor.) Yet as an unobserved abstraction, the latent factor has no absolute units, and a convenient scaling must be imposed. In practice, either the factor variance or one of the loadings is fixed to unity. When an arbitrary indicator's loading (reference item) is fixed to 1, the factor's variance is in the same scale as that indicator, and the other estimated loadings are relative to

the fixed loading. Alternatively, when the factor's variance is fixed to 1, the loading is semi-standardized in that it expresses the change in the observed indicator for a one-standard-deviation change in the latent factor. Choosing different options for scaling will result in numerically different unstandardized parameter estimates (but identical standardized estimates). Choosing which CFA parameter to constrain for identification purposes may yield more or less conveniently interpretable scaling.

In multigroup FASEM, scaling and FI have a crucial intersection. It has been asserted that only invariant factors (i.e., they are calibrated to their manifest indicators in an equivalent manner) can be unambiguously compared across groups, but now it can be seen that the problem is due to scaling. Unless there are invariant latent factors, scaling differences will prevent direct comparison. This introduces a couple of issues. First, although it is desirable to test all parameters for invariance, identification requires fixing some parameters. Second, the choice of which parameter to fix (use as the reference item) can yield different estimates. This is called the *standardization problem* (Reise et al., 1993; Rensvold & Cheung, 2001; Vandenberg & Lance, 2000). We will return to this problem when we discuss item-level FI tests.

What Must Be Versus What Can Be Invariant

There is some confusion in the literature about the number, naming, and sequence of invariance tests required (Vandenberg & Lance, 2000). Different terms are used for the same concept, distinct concepts are referred to with the same term, important FI tests are sometimes skipped without comment, and frequently tests that extend beyond measurement equivalency are presented as if they are required. The issue can be phrased thus: What about the factor needs to be the same in each group in order to make valid comparisons? Figure 11.1 also illustrates what needs to be invariant across groups to establish measurement equivalency. The common factor is interpreted by the loadings of its indicators, and equivalent loadings are clearly needed; but four distinct aspects of measurement equivalence can be articulated.[1]

- Configural: The same indicators are suitable (have nonzero loadings) in each group.
- Metric: The loading profile must define the same common factor in each group.

TABLE 11.2 Synthesis of Meredith's (1993) Comparability Prerequisites with Vandenberg and Lance's (2000) Recommended Test Names

Intended Purpose	Meredith's Prerequisites	Vandenberg & Lance's Test Names	Implementation
Qualitative comparability		Configural Invariance	Comparable factor composition (pattern of loadings), same simple structure specified in each group
Quantitative comparability of common-factor variances	Weak factorial invariance	Metric invariance	Add equality/proportionality constraints on common-factor loadings
Quantitative comparability of common-factor means, variances, and covariances	Strong factorial invariance	Metric and scalar invariance	Add equality constraints on intercepts (scalar invariance)
Unambiguous quantitative comparability of manifest composite scores	Strict factorial invariance	Metric, scalar, and uniqueness invariance	Add equality constraints on uniquenesses (i.e., specific-factor variances)
Generalizability, cross-construct validity	Structural invariance	Invariant factor variances	Constrain common-factor variances to be equal
		Invariant factor covariances	Constrain common-factor covariances to be equal
		Equal factor means	Constrain common-factor means to be equal

- Scalar: The manifest item intercepts need to be the same across groups.
- Strict: The specific factors for each indicator should exert a comparable influence across groups.

Meredith (1993) introduced the terms *metric* and *scalar* for the respective invariance hypotheses related to loadings and intercepts, and uses the term *strong factorial invariance* when configural, metric, and scalar invariance hypotheses are all retained. He does not name the invariance hypothesis related to specific factors, but uses the term *strict factorial invariance* when invariant specific factors and the hypotheses for strong factorial invariance all hold. (Specific factors are also commonly referred to as the item's *uniqueness*.) A logic of lexical ordering (i.e., weak, strong, strict) has led to the use of the term *weak factorial invariance* when only configural and metric aspects of invariance are obtained (Hofer, 1994; Hofer, Horn, & Eber, 1997; Reise et al., 1993), although this term was not used by Meredith. The term *structural invariance* (SI) has been used to refer to any additional invariance hypotheses because these tests pertain to the common factors and their interrelationships, but not to the measurement model of each common

factor. Some confusion in the literature may have resulted from the existence of two different naming schemes. *Weak, strong, strict,* and *structural* refer to cumulative degrees of invariance. *Configural, metric, scalar, uniquenesses, factor variances, factor covariance,* and *factor means* each name a separate invariance hypotheses.

Table 11.2 provides a synthesis of Meredith's (1993) terminology and Vandenberg and Lance's (2000) recommended names for each FI hypothesis. The leftmost column indicates what type of comparisons could be made as each successive hypothesis is retained. The rightmost column specifies the constraints required to frame each invariance hypothesis. The first three invariance hypotheses are *configural, metric,* and *scalar.* Together these constitute *strong FI.* The fourth test is for invariant uniquenesses, and together with configural, metric, and scalar hypotheses constitutes *strict FI.* The last three tests extend beyond measurement equivalency and pertain to SI of model parameters outside of the measurement models.

When models are extended beyond the single measurement model shown in figure 11.1 to include multiple common factors, their respective measurement models, and the structural relations among common factors (see figure 11.2),

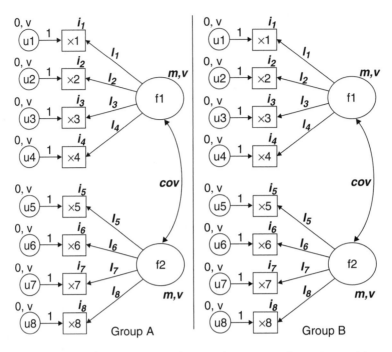

Figure 11.2 Two-factor, two-group factor analytic structural equation model with intragroup factor covariance.

the distinction of what can be invariant versus what must be invariant is very important. Misconceptions arise because FASEM permits factor-related invariance tests that extend beyond measurement equivalency concerns. Jöreskog (1971) stated that "any parameter in the factor analysis models (factor loadings, factor variances, factor covariances, and unique variances) for the different groups may be assigned an arbitrary value or constrained to be equal to some other parameter.... Various hypotheses can be tested by computing several solutions under different specifications. The method is capable of dealing with any degree of invariance" (p. 409). However, invariance tests of factor variances, factor means, covariances, or structural relations pertain to substantive hypotheses and do not speak to measurement equivalence. Unfortunately, references to factorial invariance in the literature often fail to make this distinction. There are situations where SI tests are of substantive interest, and equality constraints might be used to test these substantive hypotheses. However, factor means, factor variances, and factor covariances are not expected to be invariant across groups under most selection conditions (Meredith & Horn, 2001), and failure to obtain levels of SI should not be seen as prob-

lematic. SI hypotheses may provide further evidence of construct validity (i.e., convergent), but not in the sense of measurement equivalence. The rationale for testing aspects of SI should always be articulated.

A final distinction between what must be and what can be invariant involves the purpose of the study. As noted above, in FASEM recommendations can differ based on the investigator's ultimate goals. Vandenberg and Lance (2000) observed that various authorities deferred to the needs of the study to determine which tests were necessary. They asserted, "Like all statistical analyses, the aims and goals of the study should determine which specific ME/I tests are undertaken and the ordering in which they are undertaken" (p. 18). (Note ME/I is their term for factorial invariance.) In the course of scale development, the tests of scalar invariance and invariant uniquenesses are essential because summing the scale to create a manifest indicator introduces some systematic bias whenever strict FI has not been demonstrated. Meredith (1993) distinguished the scientific use (i.e., FASEM) of tests from the practical (i.e., manifest score) use of tests. Classical test theory (Lord & Novick, 1968) views items as composed of true score and error components. Under aggregation, the error components cancel each other and the composite is expected to be more reliable and valid than any single item. Unlike error, differences in intercepts and specific factors are systematic and thus will aggregate. A composite may then be less reliable or valid than any single item. Meredith introduced the concept of the practical test user versus the scientific use of tests to underscore this point: "For the practical user of tests and other measures, strict factorial invariance is essential" (p. 542). It is very important that scale developers, who should anticipate the manifest use of their scale, keep this point in mind when they encounter claims that a particular FI tests (e.g., scalar invariance or invariant uniquenesses) are of lesser importance.

Adopting a Uniform Terminology

Many of the discrepancies in the FI literature highlighted by Vandenberg and Lance (2000) stem from terminology. First, the term *factorial invariance* is often used to loosely refer to both the measurement as well as other structural equivalencies that can be tested in a FASEM framework. Also, in longitudinal research, the terms *stationarity* and *stability* have been used to respectively refer to FI and SI. In other instances, the terms *congeneric, tau equivalent,* and *parallel forms* are sometimes used in FI discussions that draw on Classical test theory (Lord & Novick, 1968; Traub, 1994); but there is only a limited alignment with the rest of the FI literature. Congeneric is synonymous with configural invariance, and parallel forms is substantially the same as strict FI. However, tau equivalence requires equal within-group loadings for a construct and does not have a counterpart in the FI literature (for illustration, see Pitts, West, & Tein, 1996).

In the interests of a clear and precise terminology, we use the term *factorial invariance* (FI) to denote both a desirable measurement property and a set of FASEM procedures; also we adopt Vandenberg and Lance's (2000) names for the specific invariance hypotheses (see table 11.2).[2] We also distinguish FI as hypotheses concerning the measurement model (i.e., configural, metric, scalar, and invariant specific factors) from SI as hypotheses about additional FASEM parameters that are not part of the measurement model (e.g., factor variances, factor covariances).

Factorial Invariance Procedures

The goal of this section is to deliver clear procedural information as well as further conceptual understanding of each FI or SI test. We begin with consideration of the data to be analyzed and comments on the sequence of FI tests. Next we discuss each FI/SI test in detail.

Analysis of FI must be based on raw data or a covariance matrix augmented with means. Comparison of mean structure across groups should be the most anticipated use of developed scales. Analyses based on correlations (where differences in group level and variability have been removed), as is typical (but not necessary) in independent rotation factor analysis (e.g., varimax, promax) and Procrustean rotation, will not establish a basis for unambiguous interpretation of factors in different groups.

A sequence of FI models from fewest across-group constraints to most constrained (i.e., fully invariant) is recommended. Initial work on simultaneous CFA (Jöreskog, 1971; Sörbom, 1974) did outline a procedure that began with the fully invariant model and then proceeded to models which increasingly relaxed constraints if the fit of the fully invariant model was poor. However, Bentler (2000) discussed this issue and noted that comparing increasingly constrained models to an unconstrained baseline has the desirable property that each test is independent. When comparisons are instead made to the fully constrained model, then each test is not independent. But in practice, software can generally estimate fully constrained models with less problems than fully unconstrained models because the latter have many more parameters. Ultimately some judgment will be required on the part of the investigator if there are problems estimating the fully unconstrained baseline model we recommend.

Also, an initial omnibus test of equivalent sample covariance matrices across groups is not recommended. Vandenberg and Lance (2000) advocate this initial omnibus test, and stipulate no further invariance tests if this model fits well. However, excellent fit in one part of the model may mask departures from invariance in other parts of the model when an omnibus test is utilized. Since FI hypotheses pertain to the factor-analytic measurement parameters, a test of all parameters is less precise.

Configural Invariance

In configural invariance, freely estimated (unconstrained) parameters require that the same indicators load on the common factor in each group.[3] The pairing of indicators and common factors reflects theory and a priori assumptions of the investigator. Good model fit provides evidence that a common factor with the same indicators (i.e., congeneric) exists in each group. However, this model does not allow unambiguous quantitative comparisons to be made. The importance of the configural model is its role as a baseline (full model) for subsequent restricted (reduced) model comparisons.

We recommend one particular method of identifying the configural model, although there are several options. To identify the model, the factor means and variances must be given a scale in each group. To identify the common factor,[4] the mean and variance of the factor could be fixed, or the intercept and loading of one of the indicators (denoted as the reference item) could be fixed, permitting the factor mean and variance to be estimated. A hybrid option involves fixing the factor mean and variance in one group (the reference group), and then propagating the scale to other groups by placing across-groups equality constraints on the loading (and intercept) of a reference item.[5] Each alternative involves the same degrees of freedom and will yield the same model fit. Only the scaling of the unstandardized parameter estimates will differ. For interpretability considerations, the hybrid option is used by Reise and colleagues (Reise et al., 1993; Widaman & Reise, 1997), and is also recommended here.

Choosing which indicator to use as the reference item can be done on a theoretical or statistical basis. The model fit is not affected by this choice. Theoretically, it might be convenient to choose an indicator that has the highest face validity with respect to the proposed latent construct. On a more statistical basis, an indicator that had the largest loading in prior EFA studies could be chosen. If EFA has previously been conducted within each group, an indicator having a relatively large loading and consistent loading across groups would be desirable because these circumstances suggest that this indicator has an invariant relation with the common factor.

To summarize the recommendation for constraints on the configural model:

1. The same model (i.e., the same indicators) is specified in each group.
2. The variance of the common factor is fixed to one in the reference group.
3. The mean of the common factor is fixed to zero in the reference group.

4. The intercept and loading of a suitable indicator is constrained to be equivalent across groups.
5. All other nonfixed parameters are freely estimated.

The configural model scales the mean and variance of each group's common factor relative to the common factor in the reference group, but interpretation of any differences is still ambiguous because the ratio of these differences may change if a different reference item was used. For example, if the common factor variance in the second group is twice the variance in the first group when the first indicator is used for identification, it may not be twice as large in the scaling that results if the second indicator is used instead (for further discussion, see Widaman & Reise, 1997). The ratio of factor differences is preserved only when both the intercept and loading of the reference item are held invariant.

At this point, it is useful to consider different meanings for configural invariance and baseline models. The two terms are generally used synonymously, and they are synonymous in FASEM models with a single unidimensional construct. The importance of baseline is that it is the model with freely estimated parameters against which subsequent nested models with constrained parameters will be compared. For simple models, the implication of configural (when a good fit is indicated) is only that the construct (and the given indicators) is factorial in each group. In the cases of multidimensional constructs or FASEM with multiple common factors, some thought should be given to univariate versus multivariate FI testing. In these more encompassing models, baseline retains the same meaning, but configural has much greater importance. Not only is the suitability of the indicators for each common factor tested but, in addition, simple structure is tested. The additional meaning is that the indicators for each common factor have no cross-loadings on the other common factors.

Issues of simple structure can be problematic because factors are sensitive to their context. Each common factor varies (hopefully slightly) over alternate sets of indicators, but also each indicator's cross-loadings (and consequently the definition of each common factor) vary with the nature of the other common factors in the model. Vandenberg (2002) discusses an example where a two-construct model of self-esteem and job satisfaction might exhibit simple structure, but a two-construct model with self-esteem and self-efficacy would not exhibit simple structure. In the latter case, configural invariance might not be obtained if the associations denoted by the cross-loadings could not be absorbed by the association among the common factors. In this example, we can see that the invariance required by simple structure really pertains to the zero loadings (omitted paths) in the model. This is more demanding than the case with a single unidimensional common factor for which cross-loadings are meaningless.

Is it better to test the measurement for each common factor in isolation, or to study measurement properties in the multivariate (i.e. multiple common factors) context in which subsequent analyses will be conducted? It depends on several considerations. If multivariate tests are conducted and the FI hypothesis is rejected, univariate FI tests will ultimately be required to find whether all or only some constructs lack invariance. Also, multivariate tests could be misleading. Since fit applies to the whole model, it is possible that several perfectly invariant factors could mask problematic noninvariance in another factor. One option is to demonstrate invariance for each common factor in isolation, and then estimate a multivariate model where measurement parameters are fixed to the previously determined values. There is some question as to the proper degrees of freedom when parameters are fixed in this way. An exhaustive investigation might compare univariate and multivariate analyses to explore any differences in the results obtained. In addition, multitrait multimethod models have been developed to properly deal with method variance, and cross-loadings are an integral part of these models. Finally, longitudinal models might want to investigate the lagged effect of specific indicators, and this too requires cross-loadings.

Meredith (1993) also discussed simple structure as problematic in the context of FI tests. Simple structure is actually an answer to the undesirable tendency of factors to shift definitions in response to their context. This definition is conceptualized as the construct's centroid in a conceptual domain (Little, Cunningham, Shahar, & Widaman, 2002). To increase the comparability of factors across studies, a narrower construct (shifted in the conceptual domain) defined only by the salient loadings (e.g., above .4) is chosen over the slightly broader construct defined by all loadings. The implicit assumption is that the salient loadings capture the construct's centroid, and that the small cross-loadings can be

ignored in a manner similar to random error. Although for multidimensional constructs where it is most reasonable to expect some cross-loadings because all indicators pertain to the same higher-order factor, the influence of non-salient loadings should not be treated like error. Meredith initially stated, "Simply identified invariant models should be fit first and simple structure specifications introduced subsequently" (p. 542). Later Meredith and Horn (2001) reiterated the same assertion: "Let invariance take precedence over meta-theory, such as that of simple structure" (p. 236). They discussed this topic and recommended that investigators conduct FI tests with saturated factor patterns and subsequently impose simple structure (p. 209), but this recommendation has been all but ignored. Also, many applications benefit from simple structure. Scale development begs for simple structure. Studies using existing measures in complex structural models are also facilitated by simple structure. Perhaps only when an investigator is examining relationships among a number of factors that are defined by indicators available in a given data set (e.g., the investigator selects four survey items to indicate job commitment) does Meredith's saturated-model advice become more applicable.

Once again, we see that there is no single correct answer and that decisions must consider the purpose of the study and the need for fine-grained versus more holistic constructs. The degree of imprecision (and associated costs) that can be tolerated must also be taken into account.

Metric Invariance (Weak Factorial Invariance)

This level of invariance involves additionally constraining the loadings to be equivalent in each group while permitting the factor variances and covariances to vary across groups. That the factor loadings are found to be invariant is not to say that they are identical, since the factor variances and covariances are free to vary across groups. Rather, we say that the factor loadings in one group are proportionally equivalent to corresponding loadings in other groups. In other words, loadings standardized to the common-factor variance would each differ from the corresponding loading in another group by the same proportion—the ratio of the variance in each group. It is essential that the common-factor variances are freely estimated in all but the first group. This condition is what creates a test of proportionality when equality constraints are imposed on the loadings. As a more parsimonious model, the fit will be poorer than the fit of the configural model. The question, though, is "Is the fit significantly worse?" If not, metric invariance has been demonstrated.

To summarize the required constraints:

1. Constrain the loading for each indicator to be equivalent across groups.
2. If an alternative baseline identification was used, free the estimates of the common-factor mean and variance in all but the first group.

Metric invariance permits interpretation of differences in common-factor variances. Because the slope aspect of the linear indicator-factor calibrations now function the same way in each group, each common-factor variance has the same metric (units). At this point, standardized relationships (beta weights, correlations) between the common factor and other constructs could be interpreted. Unstandardized regression weights or covariances are still problematic because the magnitudes of these values depend on the common-factor mean, which is still subject to scaling bias until intercepts are held invariant (Widaman & Reise, 1997).

Scalar Invariance (Strong Factorial— Metric and Scalar)

Meredith's strong FI requires both metric and scalar invariance, and consequently the indicator's intercepts are now constrained to be equivalent across groups. This requires the model to account for all mean differences in the indicators solely through the common-factor mean. The intercept anchors the linear indicator-factor calibration, because the intercept value denotes how much of the indicator there is when the common factor is zero. Recall that this is directly analogous to the intercept in ordinary least squares regression, and the common factor is the predictor. (In fact, since the common factor mean in the first group is fixed to zero, this effectively centers the common factor, and thus for the first group each intercept is the observed indicator's mean.) With the additional constraints on the intercepts, the common factor in each group is on the same scale. The question is, "Does this model fit well enough?" Once again, as a more parsimonious model, the fit will be worse. If the fit does not significantly deteriorate, this is evidence that all group differences in observed indicator means can be explained by group differences in the common-factor mean.

To summarize the required constraints:

1. Constrain the loading for each indicator to be equivalent across groups.
2. If not done previously, the common-factor means must be estimated in all but the first group, where the parameter is fixed to zero.

Invariant intercepts are one of the more inconsistent and misunderstood areas in the FI literature. Meredith (1993; Meredith & Horn, 2001) was very clear about the need to place across-group equality constraints on the intercepts (i.e., test for scalar invariance), thereby forcing the common-factor mean to convey as much of group mean differences as possible. Likewise, Widaman and Reise (1997) reiterated, "Strong factorial invariance constraints must be imposed to represent and test group mean differences on the latent variables in any meaningful fashion" (p. 294). Inconsistent recommendations about the need to test for scalar invariance may to some extent be explained by observing that many older studies did not model the mean structure and would not have mentioned this step. Also, intercepts have often been treated like error and presumed to have random fluctuations from sample to sample (Vandenberg & Lance, 2000), but systematic across-group intercept differences are easily imagined (e.g., a more lenient group that does not score zero when the true level of the construct really is zero).

Unfortunately, the discussion of intercepts provided by Vandenberg and Lance (2000) creates some confusion. They note that item "intercept differences may not reflect biases (undesirable) but response threshold differences that might be predicted based on known group differences (desirable), for example, between inexperienced versus highly experienced employees" (p. 38), and argue that there may sometimes be good reasons not to require invariant intercepts. This is true in special cases, but Meredith's (1993) practical and scientific test users must be recalled. The scientific user working in a FASEM framework may be interested in any across-groups intercept differences, but for the practical user (i.e., a scale developer), intercept differences are always undesirable. Also, it must also be understood that theoretical prediction of across-group intercept differences does not change the fact that across-group comparisons of common-factor means requires invariant intercepts. The scientific study of across-group intercept differences is a valid enterprise, but these studies must admit the potential of scaling issues making comparisons of factor means ambiguous. For the practical test user, and for those scientific test users interested in comparing factor means and covariances, strong FI is required. Meredith and Horn (2001, p. 218) provided an applied example where strong FI is not supported, and they discussed a strategy that may be followed if the scalar invariance model cannot be retained.

Invariant Uniquenesses (Strict Factorial Invariance—Metric, Scalar, and Uniquenesses)

This test requires the additional constraint of invariant specific-factor variances as well as the constraints for metric and scalar invariance. This model tests the across-group equivalency of specific-factor influences on the manifest items, and thus may not be necessary when working with common factors in FASEM contexts. On the other hand, if the scale is being validated for subsequent use as a manifest composite, then this test is very important because, unlike random error, specific-factor biases do aggregate. This point is at the heart of Meredith's (1993) distinction between practical and scientific use of measures. Less than fully invariant models may serve the scientist by aligning with a substantial theoretical framework, or by generating new knowledge about the constructs involved. For the practical (i.e., manifest) use of measures, strict factorial invariance should be demonstrated to ensure that individuals are treated with fairness and equity.

The constraint for this test is straightforward:

Constrain the variance of each specific factor to be equivalent across groups.

There are many reasons to expect that the hypothesis of strict FI will be rejected. Meredith's (1964, 1993) selection theory suggests that specific-factor variances (and covariances) will generally vary across groups. Also, developmental constructs frequently show age-related increases in mean and variance. It is reasonable to expect this to be reflected in both common and specific factors. Yet constraining specific-factor variances to be equal across groups and the

manner in which specific factors are identified (i.e., single loading fixed to 1) does not permit these differences.

Although not necessary for subsequent FASEM analyses, there are a number of reasons to conduct this test anyway. Specific factors are not error, and so it can be informative to scrutinize them. If they are large relative to common factors, the issue of swollen specifics or poor study design should be considered. If the reliability of observed indicators is of interest, this test as well as a test for invariant common-factor variances will be needed. Finally, the test is easy to conduct with software available today. If strict invariance is not demonstrated, the investigator can then alert Meredith's practical users that the measure is unsuitable as a manifest indicator.

The issue of swollen specific factors and the opposite condition of inappropriately swollen common factors occurs when insufficient or inappropriate indicators are used. This goes back to the point that a factor (whether common or specific) is defined in terms of the company it keeps. Meredith and Horn (2001) offer the example of indicators for a spatial visualization factor that are also associated with the related concept of spatial orientation. Used with other visualization indicators that do not have a spatial orientation component, the specific factors for the contaminated items would be swollen by the variance associated with spatial orientation. If only similarly contaminated indicators are used, the specific factors will be much smaller, but the common factor will contain the variance associated with both spatial visualization and spatial orientation. In the first case, knowledge about the true structure of spatial abilities may be lost. In the latter case, the interpretation of the common factor may be broader than the study design intended. These issues are related to more general discussion of study design and measurement, and go beyond the scope of FI. The reason for this short tangent is to underscore the point that specific factors are important and tests of specific-factor invariance or other scrutiny should not be lightly dismissed—especially given the small effort required to conduct and report this test.

Structural Invariance

The following three invariance hypotheses involve the equivalence of common-factor means, variances, and covariances in structural models. The associated invariance hypotheses do not pertain to measurement equivalence, although they may have measurement implications (e.g., longitudinal stability). A brief comment on each is provided.

Invariant Common-Factor Variances

There are two situations in which this hypothesis may have measurement implications: reliability and subsequent regressions. As noted earlier, strict FI does not permit statements about the reliability of the observed measure in each group. Vandenberg and Lance (2000) assert that reliabilities may be inferred from specific factors only when the common-factor variances are equivalent. Subsequent regressions of the common factor on other constructs may be biased if due to restriction of range if there are large discrepancies across groups. Since our recommended model identification has fixed the factor variance in the first group, this SI test can be implemented by fixing the variance in other groups to the same value (e.g., 1).

Invariant Common-Factor Covariances

Situations in which this hypothesis has measurement implications include longitudinal stability and the structure of second-order common-factors. In longitudinal models, high covariances among the common factors for each occasion indicate stability in individual differences (i.e., the rank order remains largely the same). For further discussion and several examples, see Pitts et al. (1996). Also, across-group equivalences of covariances among first-order common factors speaks to the invariance of any

second-order factors. The utility of examining common-factor covariances versus a model in which the first-order factors are used as indicators of (i.e., have loadings on) a second-order factor is not clear.

Invariant Common-Factor Means

This hypothesis is usually substantive and corresponds to a *t* test or ANOVA comparison of means. When there are more than two groups, the test is an omnibus test, and follow-up models that release the equality constraint for common-factor means across specific groups would be needed. The advantage over traditional ANOVA is that the common factors are presumed to be free of measurement error. Since our recommended model identification has fixed the factor mean in the first group, this SI test can be implemented by fixing the means in other groups to the same value (e.g., 0), resulting in a combined test of across-group equivalence of both item intercepts and common-factor means.

Multigroup Versus Multioccasion

Several important differences exist when testing for invariance across occasions as opposed to invariance across groups. Figure 11.3 shows a three-occasion model for a single construct with four indicators. At each occasion, the same indicators are used. Unlike the cross-sectional model in figure 11.1, which is replicated in each group, this is a single group model containing all three occasions. A second difference is that the specific factor for each indicator is permitted to

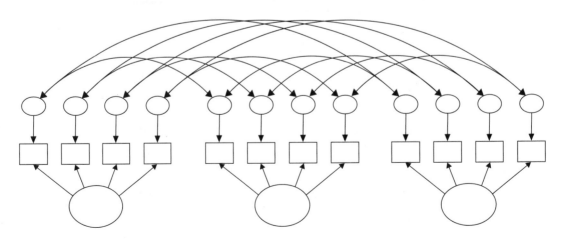

Figure 11.3 Multioccasion model.

covary with the specific factors for the same indicator at each subsequent occasion. This presumes method variance specific to each indicator.

When multioccasion models are used in a context where considerable age-based change is expected, bias may result unless age heterogeneity is small compared to the amount of change expected. This issue relates to selection theory (Meredith, 1964) and has been briefly discussed (Meredith & Horn, 2001, see pp. 225–226), but a full and clear treatment is still needed. To illustrate, consider a sample of individuals between 20 and 25 years of age at the first occasion, and successive occasions 8 years apart. The expectation is that the construct of interest will develop over the 16-year period studied. However, this same developmental gradient would be apparent across the 5-year age span in the sample. This will violate local independence by inducing positive lagged correlations among different indicators that the common factors or their covariation are unable to absorb. This can never be fully avoided, and study design must mitigate this problem by keeping age bands narrow with respect to the amount of developmental change anticipated over the course of the study.

Special Topics

Special topics that deserve further discussion are partial measurement invariance (PMI), aggregated indicators, relative fit indices, substantive hypotheses that a priori specify conditions where measurement invariance is not expected, and polytomous indicators. Each of these topics has received some treatment in the literature. PMI (Byrne, Shavelson, & Muthen, 1989) and relative fit indices (Bentler, 1990) may have received the most attention. Rensvold and Chueng's (2001) factor ratio test which identified invariant item subsets is a less known alternative to PMI. Each approach may offer some basis to proceed if necessary levels of invariance are not obtained. Aggregation has received limited theoretical attention (Bagozzi & Edwards, 1998; Little et al., 2002), but is a common practice. Finally, it is generally understood that we can learn something fundamental about our measurement and conceptualization of constructs when invariance does not obtain; this is the consolation prize when invariance is seen as prerequisite. However, there are interesting substantive hypotheses, especially in developmental

or intervention studies, that can be supported by demonstrating that invariance does not obtain. While more questions than answers are provided in this section, these topics lead to increased understanding of FI meanings and limitations, as well as the importance of the investigator's use of theory and judgment.

Partial Measurement Invariance

PMI (Byrne et al., 1989) is the idea that some invariance (some parameters fixed and others free across groups) is better than abandoning analyses when confronted with lack of invariance. Vandenberg and Lance (2000) reviewed 14 studies whose primary focus was the use of CFA methodology to test aspects of FI and found that tests of PMI were the most frequently discussed additional tests, and that some investigators tested PMI in conjunction with each test of measurement and structural invariance. Several issues are worth reviewing. First, recommendations about acceptable amounts (how many parameters) and locations (e.g., loadings, intercepts, specific factors) of PMI vary from as few as two (Byrne et al., 1989) to a preponderance of the most salient loadings (Reise et al., 1993). Second, Byrne and colleagues introduced the concept in the context of metric invariance. The argument was that if two or more loadings were invariant, then the metric of the common factor was equivalent across groups, and factor comparisons could still be made. Intercepts were not discussed. Yet it might be expected that common factor means would exhibit the most bias under PMI, and the rationale for PMI of intercepts is much less clear. Third, while invariant specific-factor variances are not needed for FASEM analyses, the PMI of specific factors would not eliminate bias for Meredith's practical test user. PMI may only be defensible for work in FASEM frameworks, but see work (Millsap & Kwok, 2004), which develops a framework for evaluating PMI bias for manifest composite scores.

Intuitively, some invariance should yield less bias than no invariance, but this has not been proven; more important, the improvement is not quantified. Vandenberg (2002) found no algebraic or simulation evidence supporting PMI, stating, "Regardless of what form the research stream takes, it will be necessary to show how the means are adjusted for in the presence of partial metric invariance (or, for that matter, partial invariance of any of the other tests subsequent to the metric invariance test)" (p. 152).

This issue is an instance of the larger question, how much bias does lack of invariance introduce? Rejection of an invariance hypothesis means that the discrepancy introduced by invariance constraints is significant. It does not indicate how much bias is involved. This would be a function of the sample size, the complexity of the model, and the narrow versus holistic nature of the construct. Consider OLS regression, where highly significant effects might be found but the magnitude of these effects has little practical consequence. What is needed is knowledge of the threshold where lack of invariance presents significant practical bias for a particular study. What we have, though, is a statistical test of when factor-analytic parameters are significantly different. Because there are presently no definitive answers, sound theoretical frameworks, understanding the meanings and limitations of invariance tests, and good judgment on the part of the investigator are all crucial. For more detailed discussion, see Vandenberg's (2002) discussion of sensitivity and susceptibility in FI testing.

Millsap and Kwok (2004) have suggested a framework for making judgments about sensitivity under conditions of PMI. They compare respondents whose factor score is above the 75th percentile to those respondents whose manifest composite score is above the 75th percentile. This creates a four-cell typology of true positives (factor above, composite above), false positives (factor below, composite above), true negatives (factor below, composite below), and false negatives (factor above, composite below). Bias due to PMI is quantified as across-group shifts in sensitivity and specificity, and thus the practical consequences of PMI can be considered.

Locating Misfit Within Invariance Models

Closely related to PMI is the question of which parameters need to be unconstrained in order to obtain a well-fitting PMI model. Inspection of the unconstrained and constrained models is a possible starting place, but standardization and proportionality may make important inequalities difficult to see. The most desirable starting place would be theoretical expectations for particular loadings or intercepts to be problematic, but in practice locating sources of noninvariance is often more exploratory. Most SEM software implements modification indices (Bentler, 1980; Chou & Bentler, 1990) that identify the most

poorly fitting parameters. The values of such modification indices denote the estimated drop in the chi-square value (misfit) of the model that would occur if the restricted parameter in question were freely estimated. It is very important to understand that this kind of respecification may overfit the model to the data and consequently suffer a lack of generalizability (Tomarken & Waller, 2003).

Locating Invariant Item Subsets With the Factor-Ratio Test

Procedures developed by Rensvold and Cheung (2001) address known item-level standardization problems and offer an alternative to PMI by identifying item subsets that demonstrate invariance. Rensvold and Cheung's factor-ratio test (FRT) is a systematic process of testing metric invariance for individual indicators and combining the results to identify multiple overlapping item subsets that display invariance. The FRT avoids identification-related bias inherent in PMI solutions and other less systematic approaches to item-level FI testing. In short, the FI test of any one indicator occurs in the context of another indicator (or indicators in the case of the fully constrained baseline) used for identification. In other words, more than the desired constraint is actually being tested. This is called the *standardization problem*. Cheung and Rensvold (1999) provided an algebraic demonstration of the potential bias that may result. It must be noted that item subsets may assess a narrower construct, and in some circumstances this may be unacceptable. In other circumstances, the narrower but invariant measure may be preferred. If the purpose is scale development and a measure with optimal psychometric properties is the desired outcome, dropping problematic items seems logical—especially if a sufficient number of indicators were being retained. In longitudinal models with manifest indicators (e.g., growth modeling of several related constructs), a narrower but invariant measure might also be preferred. However, if the investigator's requirements are limited to FASEM analyses, a PMI approach might be more promising—especially if most of the indicators were invariant.

The FRT procedure addresses the standardization issue by multiply testing each indicator in the identification context of each of the other indicators. In this way, noninvariant pairs are identified. Invariant subsets are then formed by taking each combination of indicators that does not include more than one member of a bad pair. The researcher is now able to select among subsets based on size or theoretical concerns (e.g., preferring the second largest subset because it contains the indicator with the highest loading). It also becomes possible to attend to indicators appearing in all or most sets versus indicators found in fewer sets. This procedure has been described in detail (Cheung & Rensvold, 1999; Rensvold & Cheung, 2001). Rensvold and Cheung also describe algorithms that find all invariant subsets given a list of bad pairs, and provide an applied example. The FRT procedure should also benefit from further study and development. As described, the procedure focuses on metric invariance. It seems plausible that this could be extended to determinations based on both metric and scalar invariance, but this has not been explicitly examined.

Relative Fit Indices in FI/SI Tests

Work to develop criteria for the use of relative fit indices in FI tests (Cheung & Rensvold, 2002) is related to issues of sensitivity. The chi-square and chi-square difference statistics used to assess model fit and model differences are sensitive to sample size and the number of degrees of freedom. To address this issue, relative goodness-of-fit indices (GFI), which locate the model relative to the worst- or best-fitting models possible, were developed (Bentler, 1990; Hu & Bentler, 1999). Unlike chi-square, no p-value is involved; rather, guidelines are offered for cutoff values that denote good and excellent fit. Many of these indices are routinely produced by today's SEM software packages. Investigators are advised to obtain convergence of both chi-square and several GFIs, and in cases of very large samples are instructed to attend to GFI information when chi-square statistics may be too sensitive. Until recently, however, there were no GFI difference guidelines. Cheung and Rensvold (2002) used simulation studies to evaluate various GFI indicators and to determine thresholds for GFI difference, and this work shows promise.

Aggregation

Aggregation refers to using indicators that are a composite (generally an average) of multiple items. This is more common for ability-related constructs like intelligence, where multiple trials might be averaged, or composite scores on several batteries used as individual indicators. For constructs that entail values, attitudes, judgments, or dispositions, item-level indicators are generally used (e.g., self-esteem). Disaggregated models generally yield narrower, more circumscribed constructs, but the SWLS used as an example at the beginning of this chapter is a holistic construct with item-level indicators. Pro-aggregation arguments draw on conceptions of error in classical test theory, focus on the poorer distributional properties of items, or cite the benefits of models with fewer parameters to estimate. The cons of aggregation include objection to any manipulation between empirical observation and analysis, loss of opportunity to observe the relationships among variables (i.e., cross-loading, correlated specifics), or potential misspecification of constructs—especially their dimensionality. The use of aggregation has been controversial for decades (Little et al., 2002). What does each parcel mean—how is it interpreted? In a sense, parceling is invariance by fiat.

Does aggregation affect invariance testing? Rather than assert a yes/no or good/bad answer, once again the purpose of the study and the judgment of the investigator come into play. Parceling has the least risk of introducing bias when the construct is unidimensional and the domain is narrow. If there are indicator cross-loads, parceling may provide the appearance of configural invariance but build undesirable variance into the common factor. Little et al. (2002) offered the example of an item with salient loadings on both depression and anxiety. If aggregated with other items and used to indicate depression, some of the anxiety variance enters the common factor. If the goal of the study is to understand the psychometric properties of the measure, fully disaggregated models will be needed. On the other hand, Bagozzi and Edwards (1998) noted that the fully disaggregated model will be the most difficult to fit and the least likely to demonstrate invariance. Decisions determined by the investigator's desired level of generality in the construct are special cases of the larger issues of sensitivity and susceptibility (Millsap & Kwok, 2004; Vandenberg, 2002), which may in turn be subsumed under the very broad issue of construct validity (Kane, 2001). Concern focuses on tolerance for a shift in meaning of the common factor. As with PMI, aggregation forces attention to the issue of how much shift in meaning any particular study can tolerate.

One related idea is *implicit aggregation.* When responding to items that reflect values, attitudes, or judgments, subjects implicitly aggregate across occasions and circumstances. This is analogous to aggregating across recollections of state to provide an estimate of trait. Items could be designed to elicit a greater or lesser degree of implicit aggregation. Consider Diener's (Pavot, Diener, Colvin, & Sandvik, 1991) conceptualization of the process by which his SWLS items assess global life satisfaction:

> Life satisfaction refers to a judgmental process, in which individuals assess the quality of their lives on the basis of their own unique set of criteria...a conscious cognitive judgment of one's life in which the criteria for judgment are up to the person.... Individuals are also likely to have unique criteria for a good life as well, which in some cases might outweigh the common benchmarks in importance. Furthermore, individuals may have very different standards for success in each of these areas of their lives. Thus, it is necessary to assess an individual's global judgment of his or her life rather than only his or her satisfaction with specific domains. (p. 164)

Pavot and Diener reported that the SWLS scale appears highly unidimensional with the common factor accounting for around 66% of the observed variance.

It is unclear how concerns about parceling and dimensionality play out when the aggregation is implicit. Since the SWLS anticipates respondents' use of individual and unique criteria, one could argue that there should be more stringent requirements for invariance at the item level because the implicit aggregation over unique and individual criteria has buffered the structural and metric invariance that occurs at the lower level of individual criteria. Alternatively, given the holistic emphasis of the SWLS and the idea that individualized weighting of SWLS items might exist, one could still argue for less stringent invariance requirements. Again, the informed judgment of the researcher, the population being studied, and the purpose for which the measurement is being made should all be involved in considerations of factorial invariance.

A Priori Lack of Invariance

Traditional uses of FI seek to establish a basis for concluding that differences on latent variables

are true changes on the construct of interest by demonstrating lack of any measurement bias. For multioccasion invariance, the true change is interpreted as development, and evidence of measurement bias precludes unambiguous statements about development because the apparent change may be due in whole or part to changes in measurement properties. This is the threat to internal validity called *instrumentation.* In fact, the often-invoked image of the rubber yardstick is a particularly apt analogy for the stretching, shrinking, or shifting of units that a lack of metric or scalar invariance implies. In this sense, FI analyses are seen as prerequisite to the substantive questions of interest.

Alternatively, it is also important to consider studies where lack of invariance may be desired in order to further substantive hypotheses. While evidence of differential measurement presents an opportunity to learn something about the construct of interest, this opportunity is often viewed as a consolation prize. The planned analyses cannot be conducted because measures lack invariance, but something can be learned anyway. On the other hand, there are often theoretical reasons to expect changes in the factor structure (i.e., number of common factors, factor intercorrelations) in a developmental framework. For example, theories of cognitive ability have often postulated an early-life differentiation and a late-life dedifferentiation of intelligence. In early life one general factor differentiates into multiple distinct factors, and in late life multiple cognitive factors return to a single factor or, in a weaker scenario, intelligence becomes more unified as the intercorrelations (Abad, Colom, Juan Espinosa, & Garcia, 2003; Anstey, Hofer, & Luszcz, 2003; Schmidt & Botwinick, 1989) of cognitive factors increase. In another example, it would not be too difficult to imagine how the structure of self-perception might be perturbed by puberty. The implicit aggregation of actual-ideal comparisons in physical (attractiveness, athleticism) and social (acceptance, dating) domains should reflect physical, social, cognitive, and identity-related changes that accompany puberty. In this case, a hypothesis about the development of self-perception might be advanced by the lack of invariance. Theory based on a priori predictions is required.

To further explore this idea, consider the SWLS items in table 11.1. The fifth item, "If I could live my life over...," has the lowest loading. It is also reported to have the lowest item-total correlation across several studies (Pavot & Diener, 1993). Pavot and Diener speculated that this may be because this item refers to the past while the others invoke the present. A substantive hypothesis might be that this item and one or more of the others would load on a second factor in elder samples. Perhaps drawing on Erikson's idea of integrity versus despair, older adults might exhibit a second factor related to paths not taken. FI tests could be used to evaluate this hypothesis.

Alpha, Beta, Gamma Change Typology

In the case of cognitively mediated constructs, three change outcomes are possible. The alpha, beta, gamma (ABG) change typology (Golembiewski, 1989; Riordan, 2001) distinguishes true development on the construct from two types of differential measurement. Alpha change is true change on the construct. Beta change is differential calibration of the measure to the construct. This constitutes an instrumentation threat to validity. Gamma change involves a reconceptualization of the construct as in the hypothetical SWLS example above. Gamma change entails a validity threat from maturation or history. Invariance hypotheses based on the ABG change framework may be especially valuable to positive psychology researchers because many constructs in positive psychology are cognitively mediated and because interventions are of interest. Supporting a priori predictions of beta or gamma change as a result of development or intervention would provide strong empirical validation for theoretical frameworks.

Further work is needed to synthesize ABG and FI literatures. Procedures have been described to explore ABG change in a covariance modeling framework (Millsap & Hartog, 1988; Schmitt, 1982) at both individual and group levels (Schmitt, Pulakos, & Lieblein, 1984). Metric and scalar invariance as well as differences in common-factor variance are linked to beta change. Unlike multigroup studies where factor variances are expected to vary across groups, in multi-occasion studies (especially closely spaced occasions), a change in common-factor variance at least raises the possibility that measurement recalibration has occurred. Gamma change is linked to configural noninvariance and noninvariant common-factor covariances. Millsap and Hartog (1988) described a two-group (experimental, control) two-occasion (pre-, posttest) model where invariance hypotheses concern the regression coefficient of the posttest on the pretest to provide additional information about beta change. Unfortunately, some recommended ABG procedures run counter to recommended FI procedures. For example, earlier work ignored the intercepts (Schaubroeck & Green, 1989), although later applied work did include intercepts (Vandenberg & Self, 1993). Also, procedures described by Millsap and Hartog test for invariant covariances before imposing restrictions for metric and scalar invariance. These discrepancies beg further synthesis.

Polytomous Indicators

The increasing capability of standard SEM packages to handle polytomous indicators facilitates appropriate FASEM and FI analyses for many measures that do not have continuous indicators. Polytomous indicators are important because many test and survey items use ordinal response options with five or fewer choices. Under assumptions of continuous and normally distributed indicators, polytomous indicators have poor distributional properties that may introduce serious misspecification problems or may bias fit statistics. The distributions for these indicators, even when symmetrical, can only offer a poor approximation of a normal distribution, and in practice are often very asymmetric (e.g., zero inflated). Modeling polychoric (ordinal-ordinal) and polyserial (ordinal-continuous) correlations (an option available in multiple packages, e.g., LISREL, EQS, MPlus) permits unbiased parameter estimates. It should be noted that ordinal indicators with as few as four levels and reasonable symmetry (i.e., a hump in the middle) can be successfully modeled as continuous and normally distributed indicators. However, the fully disaggregated models that are necessary for detailed study of measurement relations have not been possible for many measures of interest in positive psychology because they use yes/no responses or elicit highly skewed response distributions.

Specification, identification, and interpretation of polytomous models does require more FASEM proficiency. Modeling polychoric correlations utilizes additional latent continuous variables underlying the manifest polytomous indicators, and additional parameter constraints are required to identify these models because there are more unknowns. In addition to the mean and variance of these latent response variables, $m-1$ threshold parameters (where m is the number of response options) are are needed for each item to actually connect the observed items to the measurement model. Since these threshold parameters are what actually connect the observed data to the measurement model, testing the hypothesis of threshold invariance is important.

The LISREL and MPlus approaches to polychoric models differ. Detailed discussion of these procedures, or comparisons of their implementation across software packages, is largely missing from the literature. LISREL utilizes a preprocessor (PRELIS) to compute the polychoric correlation matrix subsequently submitted to LISREL. A four-part series discussing ordinal data, including a multigroup example and some references to invariance, is provided on the LISREL home page (http://www.ssicentral.com/lisrel/mainlis.htm). Likewise, the producer of MPlus provides a Web note (Muthén & Asparouhov, 2002) discussing multigroup models with polytomous indicators, including some discussion of factorial invariance procedures. The Web note also offers a brief comparison of the LISREL and MPlus implementations. It is asserted in the Web note that MPlus is more flexible than LISREL in regard to item thresholds because the polychoric correlations and threshold parameter estimates are computed at the same time, while LISREL requires the PRELIS preprocessor (p. 15). Millsap and Yun-Tien (2004) also offer a limited comparison of the LISREL and MPlus implementations. The baseline model recommended by Millsap and Yun-Tien achieves identification by placing across-group equilivancy constraints on the first level of each item's threshold parameters. This approach is less attractive for dichotomous items where there is only one threshold because the result is no test of threshold invariance. In this case, an alternative baseline using across-group constraints on the residual variance of the latent response variables may be useful (Bontempo, 2006).

Summary

Factorial invariance and the larger enterprise of measurement are foundational aspects of good science. This is especially true in the social sciences generally, and particularly in fields such as positive psychology where important objects of study are latent constructs whose nature and validity are simultaneously derived from consideration of a set of interrelationships with other latent and observed constructs. Factorial

invariance is also essential for developmental studies that implicitly require the comparability of constructs over time (e.g., growth modeling). Many of the conflicting proscriptions in the FI literature can be reconciled in historical context (i.e., mean structure introduced more recently) or by considering the investigator's purpose in terms of the level of holism desired in the construct (e.g., issues of aggregation or PMI) or a particular study's ability to tolerate some ambiguity concerning the construct's centroid (manifest versus FASEM uses and Meredith's practical user of tests). FI procedures are well established and increasingly facilitated by powerful SEM software packages, and we have described the model parameterization and constraints recommended to test factorial invariance. However, the investigator's perspicuity and judgment regarding both FI and larger measurement issues can not be automated or reduced to the inflexible application of hard rules.

One of the most desirable developments would be theory and methodology to set boundaries on the biases associated with noninvariance. Analogous to moving from p-values to confidence intervals in the more general statistical literature, new methods might replace scenarios that reject invariance hypotheses at a particular probability level, with confidence intervals for the evaluation of substantive effects that become increasingly wide under increasing conditions of noninvariance. This would subsume issues of configural invariance, PMI, aggregation, narrow versus holistic constructs, and sensitivity or susceptibility. More recent work (Millsap & Kwok, 2004) constitutes an important advance in this direction.

Further treatment of the ABG change typology (Golembiewski, 1989; Riordan, 2001) should be very useful to positive psychologists. Further integration of ABG and its associated methodologies (Millsap & Hartog, 1988; Schmitt, 1982; Schmitt et al., 1984; Vandenberg & Self, 1993) with established FI procedures should be of particular benefit to positive psychology because of its potential in developmental and intervention research. Substantive hypotheses about the effects of development or intervention could be tested with a priori hypotheses of noninvariance at specific locations within the FASEM framework.

Factorial invariance, like measurement, is an ongoing enterprise, and we have endeavored to provide a conceptual map of current limitations and unresolved issues that should allow readers to be informed consumers of subsequent developments in the FI literature. At the same time, FI procedures are currently at a high level of development and should be routinely applied today, without waiting for future developments.

Notes

1. Also, see the clear and accessible development using matrix equations with attention to the presence or absence of group subscripts (indicating constraints) provided by Widaman and Reise (1997).

2. Vandenberg and Lance (2000) preferred the term *measurement equivalence/invariance* (ME/I) over FI, but this is rejected because there is an established FI literature, and the term ME/I confounds FI and SI tests.

3. For univariate measurement models, no invariance requirements are actually tested by the configural model; but for models with multiple common factors, the configural model requires invariance of the zero (unspecified) cross-loadings. In the latter case, this is also a test of simple structure.

4. Identification of specific factors is accomplished by fixing the mean to zero and the single loading to one.

5. It is important to note that in this case the reference item is not fixed, but only constrained.

References

Abad, F. J., Colom, R., Juan Espinosa, M., & Garcia, L. F. (2003). Intelligence differentiation in adult samples. *Intelligence, 31*(2), 157–166.

Anstey, K. J., Hofer, S. M., & Luszcz, M. A. (2003). Cross-sectional and longitudinal patterns of de-differentiation in late-life cognitive and sensory function: The effects of age, ability, attrition, and occasion of measurement. *Journal of Experimental Psychology: General, 132*(3), 470–487.

Atienza, F. L., Balaguer, I., & Garcia Merita, M. (2003). Satisfaction With Life Scale: Analysis of factorial invariance across sexes. *Personality and Individual Differences, 35*, 1255–1260.

Bagozzi, R. P., & Edwards, J. R. (1998). A general approach for representing constructs in organizational research. *Organizational Research Methods, 1*(1), 45–87.

Bentler, P. M. (1980). Multivariate analysis with latent variables: Causal modeling. *Annual Review of Psychology, 31*, 419–456.

Bentler, P. M. (1990). Comparative fix indexes in structural models. *Psychological Bulletin, 107*(2), 238–246.

Bentler, P. M. (2000). Rites, wrongs, and gold in model testing. *Structural Equation Modeling, 7*(1), 82–91.

Bollen, K., & Lennox, R. (1991). Conventional wisdom on measurement: A structural equation perspective. *Psychological Bulletin, 110*(2), 305–314.

Bontempo, D. E. (2006). *Applied olytomous actor odels: Specification, nvariance esting, and easurement ssues.* Unpublished doctoral dissertation, The Pennsylvania State University.

Borsboom, D., Mellenbergh, G. J., & van Heerden, J. (2003). The theoretical status of latent variables. *Psychological Review, 110*(2), 203–219.

Box, G. (1976). Science and statistics. *Journal of the American Statistical Association, 71*, 791–799.

Byrne, B. M., Shavelson, R. J., & Muthen, B. (1989). Testing for the equivalence of factor covariance and mean structures: The issue of partial measurement invariance. *Psychological Bulletin, 105*(3), 456–466.

Cheung, G. W., & Rensvold, R. B. (1999). Testing factorial invariance across groups: A reconceptualization and proposed new method. *Journal of Management, 25*(1), 1–27.

Cheung, G. W., & Rensvold, R. B. (2002). Evaluating goodness-of-fit indexes for testing measurement invariance. *Structural Equation Modeling, 9*(2), 233–255.

Chou, C. P., & Bentler, P. M. (1990). Model modification in covariance structure modeling: A comparison among likelihood ratio, Lagrange multiplier, and Wald tests. *Multivariate Behavioral Research, 25*(1), 115–136.

Diamantopoulos, A., & Winklhofer, H. M. (2001). Index construction with formative indicators: An alternative to scale development. *Journal of Marketing Research, 38*(2), 269–277.

Diener, E., Emmons, R. A., Larsen, R. J., & Griffin, S. (1985). The Satisfaction With Life Scale. *Journal of Personality Assessment, 49*(1), 71–75.

Edwards, J. R., & Bagozzi, R. P. (2000). On the nature and direction of relationships between constructs and measures. *Psychological Methods, 5*(2), 155–174.

Golembiewski, R. T. (1989). The alpha, beta, gamma change typology: Perspectives on acceptance as well as resistance. *Group and Organization Studies, 14*(2), 150–154.

Hofer, S. M. (1994). *On the structure of personality and the relationship of personality to fluid and crystallized intelligence in adulthood.* Unpublished PhD dissertation, University of Southern California. Copies available exclusively from Micrographics Department, Doheny Library, USC, Los Angeles, CA.

Hofer, S. M., Horn, J. L., & Eber, H. W. (1997). A robust five-factor structure of the 16PF: Evidence from independent rotation and confirmatory factorial invariance procedures. *Personality and Individual Differences, 23,* 247–269.

Hu, L. T., & Bentler, P. M. (1999). Cutoff criteria for fit indexes in covariance structure analysis: Conventional criteria versus new alternatives. *Structural Equation Modeling, 6*(1), 1–55.

Jöreskog, K. G. (1971). Simultaneous factor analysis in several populations. *Psychometrika, 36*(4), 409–426.

Kane, M. T. (2001). Current concerns in validity theory. *Journal of Educational Measurement, 38*(4), 319–342.

Little, T. D., Cunningham, W. A., Shahar, G., & Widaman, K. F. (2002). To parcel or not to parcel: Exploring the question, weighing the merits. *Structural Equation Modeling, 9*(2), 151–173.

Lord, F. M., & Novick, M. R. (1968). *Statistical theories of mental test scores.* Reading, MA: Addison-Wesley.

MacCallum, R. C., & Browne, M. W. (1993). The use of causal indicators in covariance structure models: Some practical issues. *Psychological Bulletin, 114*(3), 533–541.

Meredith, W. (1964). Notes on factorial invariance. *Psychometrika, 29,* 177–185.

Meredith, W. (1993). Measurement invariance, factor analysis and factorial invariance. *Psychometrika, 58*(4), 525–543.

Meredith, W., & Horn, J. L. (2001). The role of factorial invariance in modeling growth and change. In L. M. Collins (Ed.), *New methods for the analysis of change* (pp. 203–240). Washington, DC: American Psychological Association.

Millsap, R. E., & Hartog, S. B. (1988). Alpha, beta, and gamma change in evaluation research: A structural equation approach. *Journal of Applied Psychology, 73*(3), 574–584.

Millsap, R. E., & Kwok, O. M. (2004). Evaluating the impact of partial factorial invariance on selection in two populations. *Psychological Methods, 9*(1), 93–115.

Millsap, R. E., & Yun-Tien, J. (2004). Assessing factorial invariance in ordered-categorical measures. *Multivariate Behavioral Research, 39*(3), 479–515.

Muthén, B., & Asparouhov, T. (2002, December 9). Latent variable analysis with categorical outcomes: Multiple-group and growth modeling in Mplus. Mplus Web Notes: No. 4 Version 5. Retrieved January 20, 2004, from http://www.statmodel.com/mplus/examples/webnotes/CatMGLong.pdf.

Pavot, W. G., & Diener, E. (1993). Review of the Satisfaction With Life Scale. *Psychological Assessment, 5*(2), 164–172.

Pavot, W. G., Diener, E., Colvin, C. R., & Sandvik, E. (1991). Further validation of the Satisfaction With Life Scale: Evidence for the cross-method convergence of well-being measures. *Journal of Personality Assessment, 57*(1), 149–161.

Pitts, S. C., West, S. G., & Tein, J. Y. (1996). Longitudinal measurement models in evaluation research: Examining stability and change. *Evaluation and Program Planning, 19*(4), 333–350.

Pons, D., Atienza, F. L., Balaguer, I., & Garcia Merita, M. L. (2000). Satisfaction With Life Scale: Analysis of factorial invariance for adolescents and elderly persons. *Perceptual and Motor Skills, 91*(1), 62–68.

Reise, S. P., Widaman, K. F., & Pugh, R. H. (1993). Confirmatory factor analysis and item response theory: Two approaches for exploring measurement invariance. *Psychological Bulletin, 114*(3), 552–566.

Rensvold, R. B., & Cheung, G. W. (2001). Testing for metric invariance using structural equation models. In C. A. Schriesheim & L. L. Neider (Eds.), *Equivalence in measurement* (Vol. 1, pp. 21–50). Greenwich, CT: Information Age.

Riordan, C. M. (2001). Alpha, beta, and gamma change. In C. A. Schriesheim & L. L. Neider (Eds.), *Equivalence in measurement* (Vol. 1, pp. 51–98). Greenwich, CT: Information Age.

Schaubroeck, J., & Green, S. G. (1989). Confirmatory factor analytic procedures for assessing change during organizational entry. *Journal of Applied Psychology, 74*(6), 892–900.

Schmidt, D. F., & Botwinick, J. (1989). A factorial analysis of the age dedifferentiation hypothesis. In V. L. Bengtson (Ed.), *The course of later life: Research and reflections* (pp. 87–92). New York: Springer.

Schmitt, N. W. (1982). The use of analysis of covariance structures to assess beta and gamma change. *Multivariate Behavioral Research, 17*(3), 343–358.

Schmitt, N. W., Pulakos, E. D., & Lieblein, A. (1984). Comparison of three techniques to assess group-level beta and gamma change. *Applied Psychological Measurement, 8*(3), 249–260.

Shevlin, M., Brunsden, V., & Miles, J. N. V. (1998). Satisfaction With Life Scale: Analysis of factorial invariance, mean structures and reliability. *Personality and Individual Differences, 25*(5), 911–916.

Sörbom, D. (1974). A general method for studying differences in factor means and factor structures between groups. *British Journal of Mathematical and Statistical Psychology, 28,* 229–239.

Tomarken, A. J., & Waller, N. G. (2003). Potential problems with "well fitting" models. *Journal of Abnormal Psychology, 112*(4), 578–598.

Traub, R. E. (1994). *Reliability for the social sciences: Theory and applications.* Thousand Oaks, CA: Sage.

Vandenberg, R. J. (2002). Toward a further understanding of an improvement in measurement invariance methods and procedures. *Organizational Research Methods, 5*(2), 139–158.

Vandenberg, R. J., & Lance, C. E. (2000). A review and synthesis of the measurement invariance literature: Suggestions, practices, and recommendations for organizational research. *Organizational Research Methods, 3*(1), 4–69.

Vandenberg, R. J., & Self, R. M. (1993). Assessing newcomers' changing commitments to the organization during the first 6 months of work. *Journal of Applied Psychology, 78*(4), 557–568.

Widaman, K. F., & Reise, S. P. (1997). Exploring the measurement invariance of psychological instruments: Applications in the substance use domain. In K. J. Bryant & M. Windle (Eds.), *The science of prevention: Methodological advances from alcohol and substance abuse research* (pp. 281–324). Washington, DC: American Psychological Association.

12

Dolce Far Niente

The Positive Psychology of Personality Stability and Invariance

Robert R. McCrae, Antonio Terracciano, and Brigitte Khoury

When Costa and McCrae first published their findings on the stability of personality in adulthood (Costa & McCrae, 1978, 1980b; Costa, McCrae, & Arenberg, 1980) the results were met not only with skepticism, but also with hostility and scorn. Developmentalist Orville Brim, in an interview in *Psychology Today* (Rubin, 1981), was quoted as saying "When you focus on stability . . . you're looking at the dregs—the people who have gotten stuck. You want to look at how a person grows and changes, not at how a person stays the same" (p. 24). Costa and McCrae were once half-jokingly introduced at a symposium as "the Antichrists of adult development."

Years later, when McCrae and Costa (1997b) showed constancy of personality trait factor structures across cultures, a similar reaction was evident in some quarters. As Bond (2000) wrote, "among many cross-cultural psychologists there is concern about importing tests developed out of a Western cultural logic . . . into alien cultural systems. Berry (1969) labeled this an *imposed etic* strategy—it was *imposed* presumably because the test measuring the construct was

pressed on the host culture, distorting and dominating its own voice; it was *etic* because it innocently presumed that the construct being measured was coherent and functioned similarly in all cultures" (p. 64).

Thus, findings of stability and invariance are often unpalatable to psychologists, and perhaps especially to advocates of positive psychology. This movement has its historical roots in humanistic psychology (Maddi & Costa, 1972), as seen, for example, in Maslow's (1954) studies of exceptional individuals like Abraham Lincoln and Eleanor Roosevelt. Maslow's motivational psychology postulates that, under favorable conditions, people will focus their attention on more and more lofty goals. Rogers also believed that growth and change are the norm and that stability is the result of defensive processes that can and ought to be transcended (Rogers & Dymond, 1954).

The objection to invariance in personality factor structure has a somewhat different basis: psychologists' appreciation of cultural diversity and their reluctance even to appear to assert the superiority of Western models to those of other cultures. Bond (2000) noted "an obvious liberal political concern" (p. 64) in the arguments about an imposed etic, and Gergen (2001) stated flatly that "universalizing tendencies approximate neocolonialism" (p. 809). Multiculturalism is, of course, distinct from positive psychology, but both share attitudes that favor change and variety over stability and invariance.

In this chapter, we briefly review the evidence for the temporal stability of personality traits in adulthood and the invariance of factor structure across cultures. We focus on research designs and statistical methods for assessing stability and invariance. Finally, we hope to argue that stability and invariance are neither negative nor oppressive and should be valued for their positive contributions to human life.

Personality Stability

The assertion that personality is generally stable in adulthood perplexes some people because they adopt a different definition of personality than most of the researchers in this field. If one defines personality in terms of the self or the self-concept, then change is likely the norm: People think of themselves first as children, then as adults and perhaps parents, and later as grandparents. Similarly, if one adopts a behaviorist perspective and conceives of personality as the sum of learned responses, change is more or less inevitable, because learning is a lifelong process. But researchers concerned with stability and change in personality are typically interested in *traits*, the (relatively) enduring dispositions that influence styles of action and experience. Although they are sometimes called *needs* (Jackson, 1984), *folk concepts* (Gough, 1987), or *types* (Myers, 1962), the scales of most personality inventories usually measure traits and are in general related to one (or more) of five trait dimensions commonly called neuroticism (N), extraversion (E), openness to experience (O), agreeableness (A), and conscientiousness (C; McCrae, 1989). For example, O is related to the need for change (Costa & McCrae, 1988), the folk concept of flexibility (McCrae, Costa, & Piedmont, 1993), and the intuitive type (McCrae & Costa, 1989), as well as such traits as curiosity, aesthetic sensitivity, and tolerance for ambiguity (McCrae & Costa, 1997a).

From this perspective, questions about stability and change in personality boil down to what happens to the level of personality traits over time and as a result of life experience. There are several different senses in which personality traits might be called stable, and they are addressed by different design and analytic strategies.

Most important are the stability of mean levels and the stability of individual differences. The stability of mean levels implies that the average levels of traits remain constant at different times or ages; the stability of individual differences implies that people retain their standing on a trait dimension relative to others. It is essential to note that these two forms of stability are conceptually and statistically independent. It is possible for mean levels to remain constant although individuals fluctuate wildly—think of the collective mood of spectators at a sporting event, where first one team and then the other scores. Similarly, it is possible to maintain relative ranking despite marked changes in mean levels. High school seniors have much greater cognitive ability than first graders, but the smartest seniors are likely to have been the smartest first graders.

There are at least two other ways in which stability or change might be manifested. Traits might change relative to each other. One could, for example, change from being more agreeable than extraverted to being more extraverted than agreeable. This is known as *ipsative change*, and it is most commonly examined with instruments that use a forced-choice distribution, such as the California Q-Set (Block, 1961; Costa, McCrae, & Siegler, 1999). It is also possible that the variance in traits might change with time, even though the mean levels and rank order are stable. However, there is little evidence that this happens in the case of personality traits (McCrae, 1993).

The Stability of Mean Levels

Aging is a natural process that we can observe, but not manipulate, and people are born at one particular point in time and live during a particular segment of history. These facts complicate the search for stability and change in mean levels.

Other things being equal, if a trait increases as people age, older people would show higher levels than younger people. This is the basis of cross-sectional research designs, which compare individuals of different ages on a single occasion. The trouble is that other things are not equal; in particular, people who are different ages at a given time must have been born at different times, and birth cohort may account for observed differences. For example, 85% of Americans in their 20s are high school graduates, whereas only 70% of the over-65 population are (see U.S. Census Bureau, n.d.) But this cross-sectional comparison surely does not mean that people lose years of education as they age. This is a birth cohort effect, and birth cohort effects are an invariable confound in interpreting cross-sectional studies.

The way to circumvent them is by measuring people born at the same time when they are different ages. This can be done in two ways. The first is the conventional longitudinal study, in which people are assessed two or more times over a reasonably long interval. At first glance, this seems to be a foolproof design, because subjects are used as their own control. If scores on a trait go up across administrations, it must mean the trait has increased. Unfortunately, this would be true only if scales were pure and absolute measures of the traits they assess, and they are not. Two sources of error are commonly noted, *practice effects* and *time-of-measurement effects*. Practice effects occur when people respond differently the second or subsequent time because they have been exposed to the test the first time. For example, scores on vocabulary tests may improve with time if the same items are asked, because some respondents may have made a deliberate effort to learn the words they did not know. Practice effects are a serious problem for cognitive tests, but less serious for personality scales, where items have no single correct answer.

Methodologists have devised some ways around this problem. The first is the parallel form, in which different (and hence unpracticed) items are used to assess the same trait on the second occasion. The second is the cross-sequential design (Schaie, 1965), in which different people are measured on different occasions. A sample of people born in the same year could be randomly assigned to be tested now or 10 years from now. Differences between the groups might be due to aging, but could not be due to practice, because everyone was tested only once.

Both longitudinal and cross-sequential designs, however, are subject to time-of-measurement effects. Such effects are often seen in attitude surveys. For example, in the United States, tolerance for gay men and lesbians has increased markedly over the past 30 years, and would

presumably show up on both longitudinal and cross-sequential studies of attitudes—but this change has nothing to do with aging.[1] Again, time of measurement may affect response style: More individuals might acknowledge on a survey now that they were gay than would have done so 30 years ago, although the real number may not have changed.

For all these reasons, inferring stability or change in mean levels is difficult; ultimately, scientific judgment is required to weigh evidence from all sources and come to reasonable conclusions (Costa & McCrae, 1982). If the same effect is seen in longitudinal, cross-sequential, and cross-sectional studies, then it is most probably a true aging effect; if it is seen in only one of these, artifacts are likely.

Consider age changes in the mean levels of traits between college age and middle adulthood. Separate norms are provided for the Revised NEO Personality Inventory (NEO-PI-R; Costa & McCrae, 1989, 1992a), because six separate college samples and a military recruit sample showed consistently different scores from adults: College-age respondents were higher in N, E, and O, and lower in A and C. These findings are also consistent with longitudinal studies conducted in this portion of the life span (Jessor, 1983; McGue, Bacon, & Lykken, 1993), except that studies conducted within the 4 years of college suggest that O increases rather than declines (Gray, Haig, Vaidya, & Watson, 2001; Robins, Fraley, Roberts, & Trzesniewski, 2001). It appears that levels of O peak sometime in the early 20s.

These conclusions are also supported by another line of evidence: cross-cultural studies. If differences between American students and adults were due to birth cohort effects instead of aging, it would mean that traits are shaped by some feature of the environment that has changed during the lifetime of today's adults. Most or all Americans share these historical changes. But life has changed in very different ways for people who grew up in the People's Republic of China or Zimbabwe or Croatia, so one would expect different patterns of cohort effects in these places. In fact, however, age differences resemble the American pattern in all those cultures (McCrae et al., 1999; Piedmont, Bain, McCrae, & Costa, 2002; Yang, McCrae, & Costa, 1998). Such findings make it more plausible that age differences in personality trait levels reflect true maturational changes.

Note that all the designs so far considered allow statistical tests of difference or change, not tests of stability. The claim that a personality trait level is stable is necessarily the assertion of a null finding, which is always problematic. The initial claims for personality stability in adulthood were based not on the complete absence of significant age differences or changes, but on the failure to find consistent changes across different instruments and designs (Costa & McCrae, 1980b; McCrae & Costa, 1984). For example, in adults over age 30 there are small but significant positive correlations of C with age (Costa & McCrae, 1992a). But a 6-year longitudinal study of 40-year-olds showed a small but significant decline in C (Costa, Herbst, McCrae, & Siegler, 2000). The most parsimonious interpretation of this pair of findings is that C is stable in adulthood.

Null findings are compromised by small sample sizes; it is almost certain that significant effects can be found if sufficiently large samples are studied. For example, Srivastava, John, Gosling, and Potter (2003) found the 60-year-olds were only one-quarter standard deviation lower in N than 21-year-olds, but that difference was highly significant in their sample of 132,515. Despite the awesome size of this study, interpretation is difficult. Not only was this a cross-sectional study, it was also an Internet study whose representativeness is easily questioned.

Considering all available data, at present it seems likely that there are continued changes in N, E, and O after age 30, but that they are small in magnitude. It is unclear whether A and C show maturational changes in this time period (but see Terracciano, McCrae, Brant, & Costa, 2005). What we can conclude with reasonable certainty is that, if A and C change, the magnitude of the change is quite modest. If either showed marked increases with age, it would have been apparent by now. McCrae and Costa (2003) estimated that changes in the five factors are around one-third standard deviation between age 30 and age 70. Mean personality trait levels are not absolutely fixed, but they are predominantly stable.

The Stability of Individual Differences

It is somewhat easier to discuss rank order stability, because only longitudinal studies are relevant, and the correlation across occasions is easily interpreted. Costa and McCrae (1997) reviewed available studies and found median retest correlations ranging from .34 to .77, with an overall median of .56. A later meta-analysis (Roberts & DelVecchio, 2000) estimated stabil-

ity coefficients of .64 at age 30 and .74 after age 50, and argued from this that personality has not fully stabilized until age 50. Meta-analyses, however, combine different instruments, intervals, and samples. More direct tests of the hypothesis that stability is higher at age 50 than at age 30 come from studies in which the same instruments were administered to different age groups at the same times. In such comparisons (McCrae & Costa, 2003; Terracciano, Costa, & McCrae, in press), adults in their 30s and 40s show equivalent levels of stability to those found in older adults, values close to Roberts and DelVecchio's .74.

Stability coefficients near .74 suggest that half of the variance in personality is stable, whereas half changes. That interpretation, however, rests on the assumption that the scales used are perfectly reliable, and of course they are not. Disattenuated correlations are a better basis for estimating the true stability of personality. Observed stability coefficients could be corrected using short-term retest reliabilities (but not internal consistency reliabilities, which assess something quite different). McCrae, Yik, Trapnell, Bond, and Paulhus (1998) reported 2-year retest correlations of .83 to .91; disattentuation using those values would suggest that the true stability coefficient is near .85, accounting for nearly three quarters of the variance.

This argument, however, leaves out of account the time interval over which stability is assessed, and there is evidence that the magnitude of stability coefficients declines over longer intervals. Using Guilford-Zimmerman Temperament Survey (GZTS; Guilford, Zimmerman, & Guilford, 1976) data spanning 24 years and estimation techniques provided by Heise (1969), Costa and McCrae (1992b) reported estimated true score stabilities of from .70 to .87, and they projected that about 60% of the variance in personality traits would be stable across the half-century from age 30 to age 80. Later estimates (Terracciano et al., in press) raised that figure to 80%.

The remaining 20% is currently unexplained. Many psychologists believe that traits are reshaped by life experience, but demonstrations of such effects are scattered. Roberts, Caspi, and Moffit (2003) examined personality at age 18 and again at age 26, and assessed the work environment at age 26. Personality changes over that interval were associated with work variables, although the causal ordering was ambiguous: It is possible that change occurred between ages 18 and 21, and subsequent work variables were the result rather than the cause of personality change. Small personality changes that might be attributable to the environment have been reported in older adults (Costa et al., 2000; Helson & Picano, 1990). It remains to be seen whether such changes are replicable, or whether they are flukes or artifacts. Although of great theoretical interest, such findings do not challenge the basic assertion that individual differences in personality traits are highly stable after age 30.

The analytic methods we have described are those that have traditionally been used in studies of adult personality development. More sophisticated approaches have been advocated (see chapter 11, this volume), and are beginning to be used (e.g., Terracciano et al., 2005). Small, Hertzog, Hultsch, and Dixon (2003) reported longitudinal confirmatory factor analyses of NEO Personality Inventory (Costa & McCrae, 1985) data in a sample of 223 adults initially aged 55–85 and followed for 6 years. Their results confirmed the conclusions of more conventional analyses: "There is evidence for stability in both the factor structure . . . [and] individual differences in personality over the 6-year interval. This suggests that not only is the between-person level of stability relatively stable over time, but the nature of the interrelationships among the subscales and factors also remains invariant longitudinally" (p. P172).

The Positive Value of Personality Trait Stability

Findings of personality trait stability are unpopular not only with adult developmentalists but also with laypersons (Hale, 1981). Transcendentalist Ralph Waldo Emerson was one of the first to notice that people "are all creatures of given temperament, which will appear in a given character, whose boundaries they will never pass" (Emerson, 1844/1990), and he was bitterly disappointed by that fact. "I had thought that the value of life lay in its inscrutable possibilities," he wrote, and complained that "temperament puts all divinity to rout" (quoted in McCrae & Costa, 1994).

For those who are high in N and low in E, and thus temperamentally unhappy (Costa & McCrae, 1980a), stability is not a pleasant prospect, and they may wish to concentrate on evidence that effective psychotherapy can modify personality traits somewhat (Santor, Bagby, & Joffe, 1997). Fortunately, most people consider themselves happy (Robinson, Solberg, Vargas, &

Tamir, 2003), and for them findings of stability ought to be reassuring. In particular, studies of aging populations dispel the myth that old age is invariably accompanied by depression and social withdrawal (McCrae & Costa, 2003). Open individuals need not fear that they will become rigid with age, and conservatives can rest assured that they will remain true to their principles.

Stability of personality does not mean stagnation in life. Jean-Jacques Rousseau led a kaleidoscopic life, turning from music to social philosophy to literature to botany, yet he remained high in O throughout (McCrae, 1996). People who are closed to experience may lead less eventful lives, but that is just as they prefer. Again, an enduringly high level of E can lead to an ever-expanding circle of friends.

A life filled with "inscrutable possibilities" might be exciting, but it could also be frustrating and hazardous. Imagine spending years in medical school only to find you had lost all interest in medicine. Imagine marrying a kind and loving spouse who suddenly turned abusive. We can construct for ourselves a satisfying life only if we and those around us are somewhat predictable over long periods of time, and personality stability is one of the major sources of predictable behavior. Social psychologists (Nussbaum, Trope, & Liberman, 2003) have shown that people do make long-term predictions on the basis of their traits; perhaps cognitive mechanisms have evolved to capitalize on the stability of dispositions.

Finally, it should be noted that we are not in bondage to our traits, because we *are* our traits. Most people include them in their spontaneous self-concept (McCrae & Costa, 1988), and we feel most authentic when we are acting in ways that are consistent with our enduring dispositions (Sheldon, Ryan, Rawsthorne, & Ilardi, 1997). Erikson (1950) considered the goal of psychosocial development to be ego integrity, a state in which one accepts "one's one and only life cycle as something that had to be" (p. 268). Most adults come to accept their one and only personality, and positive psychologists would be wise to accept the stability of personality.

The Invariance of Personality Trait Structure

One of the concerns of positive psychology is an understanding of group differences, because that understanding may lead to improvements in human life. For example, we might contrast the personality traits of great artists with those of less gifted individuals to see what conditions might foster creativity in all of us (e.g., MacKinnon, 1962). Again, we might compare experienced meditators with nonmeditators to test the hypothesis that meditation enhances self-esteem (Shapiro, Schwartz, & Santerre, 2002).

Such comparisons are all based on the assumption that the constructs being measured are invariant across groups[2]—that self-esteem in meditators is qualitatively identical to self-esteem in others. That assumption is rarely questioned, except in the context of cross-cultural research. Differences in language highlight difference in constructs; it is often questioned whether a particular idea can even be expressed in another language. Anthropologists and cross-cultural researchers are acutely aware that culture profoundly shapes perceptions and evaluations of the world, and that different cultures may give rise to different psychologies, with entirely different constructs (Gergen, Gulerce, Lock, & Misra, 1996). As Lopez and colleagues (2002) note, this problem has not yet been adequately addressed in positive psychology: "Surprisingly, few attempts have been made to directly evaluate the cross-cultural equivalence of constructs such as hope and optimism" (p. 703).

Evaluating equivalence, like any other assessment of construct validity, is an intricate and problematic task. Normally we expect equivalent scales to have similar correlates, but the correlates of a construct may differ across cultures. Life satisfaction is strongly related to feelings of positive and negative affect in individualistic, Western nations, but less so in collectivistic cultures (Suh, Diener, Oishi, & Triandis, 1998). Under these conditions, is life satisfaction the same construct in East and West?

Such complexities aside, the basic process of establishing construct equivalence is through an examination of convergent and discriminant validities, and when multi-item scales or multiscale inventories are involved, factor analysis is a useful tool. Factors are defined by clusters of variables that covary independently of the other variables in the analysis; that is, they show convergent relations to some variables and discriminant relations to others. In American studies, assertiveness, sociability, and positive affect all covary to define an Extraversion factor. Replicating that factor in other cultures provides prima facie evidence that the defining scales all retain construct validity.

There are at least two methods of assessing factor invariance. The more familiar employs structural equation modeling (Byrne, 2001): Confirmatory factor analysis (CFA) is conducted in two or more samples simultaneously, under the constraint that the factor loadings must be equal. If an unconstrained model fits better, the hypothesis of invariance is rejected. (For a more detailed discussion of these techniques, see chapter 11, this volume.) The primary advantage of this approach is that it provides a statistical test of invariance; indices of fit also quantify the similarity of the two factor matrices.

Although mathematically elegant, there are problems with CFA when applied to real data. Most crucially, CFA often rejects models that appear to be empirically robust and accepts models that are not replicable (McCrae, Zonderman, Costa, Bond, & Paunonen, 1996). As ten Berge (2000) noted, "applied psychologists, facing 'improved' psychometric methods, are well advised to demand empirical evidence for the alleged superiority of the innovations" (p. 139). Although CFA is no longer an innovation, it is not clear that such evidence has ever been provided. CFA appears to be overly sensitive to departures from a multivariate normal distribution and, as typically used, is not appropriate for instruments that lack clear simple structure (Church & Burke, 1994).

McCrae and colleagues suggested an alternative, based on Tucker's (1951) congruence coefficient, φ. This is a simple measure of the proportionality of factor loadings across two factors; high values suggest that the factor is replicated, and if all the factors are replicated, the structure itself can be considered invariant. Use of this approach, however, raises several issues.

First, there is no widely accepted test for the statistical significance of φ (but see Chan, Ho, Leung, Chan, & Yung, 1999), which is essentially an effect size. Rules of thumb are needed to decide if congruence is sufficiently large to warrant the judgment of replication. The most common rule is .90, but Haven and ten Berge (1977) offered evidence that expert human judges consider factors to be replicated when congruences are as low as .85.

Second, φ considers only the similarity of factor loadings across variables. A fuller evaluation also looks at the similarity of each variable's loadings across factors. A factor defined by five of six intended variables might have an acceptable φ, but the cross-cultural researcher needs to know that one of the scales is of questionable validity in translation. McCrae and colleagues (1996) recommended calculating variable congruence coefficients and a total congruence coefficient in addition to factor congruence coefficients.

Third, exploratory factor analysis is usually followed by factor rotation (typically varimax). If the variables under study are in fact simply structured, it is appropriate to compare varimax-rotated factors. But in the study of personality traits, joint loadings on two or more factors is common, and interpersonal traits (E and A facets) tend to form a circumplex (Wiggins, 1979). In these circumstances, minor variations in scale intercorrelations can lead to dramatic differences in the position of the varimax axes, and thus to misleadingly low congruences. McCrae and colleagues (1996) therefore suggested that the evaluation of congruences be preceded by an orthogonal Procrustes rotation to best match the target. Like conventional CFA, this method defines a target, finds the solution that best approximates it, and then evaluates the fit, and one simulation study reported that "factor analysis with Procrustes rotation was more accurate than confirmatory factor analysis in fitting the specified model to the sample data" (Williams, 1995, p. 4629).

Despite the unfortunate name of this procedure, Procrustes rotation does not force the data to fit a mold; it merely selects the best fit from among the infinite number of possible and mathematically equivalent rotations. McCrae and colleagues (1996) used Monte Carlo methods to show that large congruence coefficients will almost never occur by chance following Procrustes rotation.

An Empirical Example

The first application of this procedure was in analyses of data from Hong Kong and Japan. In both cases, translations of the NEO-PI-R (Costa & McCrae, 1992a) were used. The NEO-PI-R consists of 30 facet scales, 6 for each of the five factors. The instrument has been used in some 1,500 studies and is known to have a highly replicable structure in American samples of men and women. A sample of 1,000 adults was selected to provide norms for the instrument, and the factor structure of the 30 facet scales in that sample is used as the target for Procrustes rotations. The Hong Kong data clearly replicated the American normative structure even before

Procrustes rotation, with factor congruence coefficients ranging from .92 to .97. In the Japanese varimax solution, however, the familiar E and A factors were replaced by intermediate factors interpreted as Dominance and Love. After a rotation of about 35°, E and A factors appeared, and all five factor congruence coefficients exceeded .92.

Similar results have been found in a broad array of cultures, from India (Lodhi, Deo, & Belhekar, 2002) to Iceland (Costa, McCrae, & Jónsson, 2002). Most of these studies, however, have employed self-reports of personality traits, and none has been conducted in an Arabic culture. In this chapter, we examine the factor structure of observer ratings of personality in Lebanon. Although there is an authorized Arabic translation of the NEO-PI-R (personal communication, A. J. Hanna, January 10, 1999), the participants in this research were students at the American University of Beirut, and they completed the English version. Students were asked to think of a native Lebanese citizen they knew well and provide personality ratings; the raters were randomly assigned to rate an adult (over age 40) or college age (18–21) male or female.

Lebanon is a small country (4,036 square miles) located in the Middle East and considered part of the Arab world. It is bounded on the north and east by Syria, on the west by the Mediterranean Sea, and on the south by Israel. The population was estimated in 2003 to be approximately 3.7 million. Although Arabic is the official language, French is the second most commonly used language, and English is also widely spoken. Unlike most Arab countries, Lebanon is characterized by religious and cultural diversity. The population consists of 70% Moslems and 30% Christians (Darwiche, 2001).

Between 1975 and 1991, a civil war tore the country apart. Since 1991, however, the country has witnessed government reform and a rebirth in its infrastructure, economy, and tourism industry. Despite being part of the Arab world, Lebanon has always had a mixture of Arabic and Mediterranean European influences. This is seen in freedom of the press, the numerous Western schools and universities, an openness to different cultures, and the ability of many people to speak two or more foreign languages.

The American University of Beirut (AUB) is a private, independent, nonsectarian institution of higher learning chartered by the state of New York. AUB offers programs leading to both the bachelor's and master's degrees. It is coeducational, with English as the language of instruction, and is one of the most prestigious universities in the Arab world.

The participants in our study were male and female undergraduate students in AUB enrolled in an Introduction to Psychology course. They came from various departments and faculties and were all sufficiently proficient in the English language to have the questionnaires administered to them in English during their class time.

Results are presented in table 12.1. The 30 NEO-PI-R facet scales are grouped according to the factor on which they are intended to load. The first five data columns present factor loadings from a varimax rotation, and it is already clear that the Lebanese structure closely resembles the American. All but three facets have loadings above .40 on their intended factor; in all but four cases, this is their largest loading. Tucker's congruence coefficient values range from .87 to .94,

TABLE 12.1 Factor Loadings and Congruence Coefficients for Lebanese Students' Ratings of College-Age and Adult Targets

NEO-PI-R Facet Scale	Varimax Factor					Procrustes Factor[a]					
	N	E	O	A	C	N	E	O	A	C	VC[b]
N1: Anxiety	**.77**	.03	−.07	−.15	.12	**.76**	.03	−.12	−.03	.20	.92**
N2: Angry Hostility	**.42**	−.02	−.03	−**.67**	.07	**.50**	.02	−.06	−**.60**	.14	.93*
N3: Depression	**.66**	−.05	.25	−.01	−.26	**.69**	−.02	.19	.07	−.21	.96**
N4: Self-Consciousness	**.60**	−.12	−.26	.01	−.13	**.58**	−.16	−.29	.08	−.06	.94**
N5: Impulsiveness	.35	.24	.19	−.38	−.30	**.43**	.28	.11	−.32	−.27	.97**
N6: Vulnerability	**.62**	.01	−.02	−.15	−**.56**	**.68**	−.00	−.10	−.08	−**.49**	.97**
E1: Warmth	−.06	**.73**	.21	**.43**	.06	−.12	**.73**	.12	**.46**	.01	.98**
E2: Gregariousness	−.08	**.77**	.08	.01	−.20	−.07	**.77**	−.04	.04	−.23	.95**
E3: Assertiveness	−.34	.33	−.06	−**.45**	**.49**	−.32	.36	−.06	−**.46**	**.47**	.89*
E4: Activity	.12	.38	.28	−.32	.37	.14	**.44**	.23	−.26	.37	.98**
E5: Excitement Seeking	−.16	**.42**	**.49**	−.06	−.37	−.09	**.48**	**.41**	−.07	−**.42**	.70
E6: Positive Emotions	.05	**.58**	**.48**	.25	−.02	.04	**.63**	.39	.29	−.07	.90*
O1: Fantasy	.14	.13	**.65**	.01	−.35	.21	.21	**.59**	.03	−.38	.97*
O2: Aesthetics	.13	.02	**.78**	.09	.18	.15	.13	**.77**	.11	.14	.99**
O3: Feelings	.27	.36	**.52**	−.02	.23	.28	**.44**	**.46**	.05	.22	.98**
O4: Actions	−.17	.17	**.57**	−.11	−.18	−.10	.25	**.54**	−.13	−.23	.91*
O5: Ideas	−.16	−.02	**.53**	.11	**.50**	−.18	.06	**.57**	.10	**.45**	.86*
O6: Values	−.27	.06	**.56**	.20	.06	−.26	.13	**.57**	.16	−.01	.88*
A1: Trust	−.18	.37	.12	**.61**	−.02	−.26	.35	.09	**.60**	−.08	.96**
A2: Straightforwardness	.00	.07	−.05	**.69**	.35	−.13	.03	−.03	**.70**	.32	.95**
A3: Altruism	−.04	**.45**	.09	**.61**	**.45**	−.17	**.43**	.06	**.64**	**.40**	.97**
A4: Compliance	−.02	.03	−.05	**.81**	−.02	−.13	−.03	−.04	**.80**	−.06	.99**
A5: Modesty	−.06	−.13	.21	**.76**	.16	−.16	−.14	.25	**.74**	.11	.68
A6: Tender-Mindedness	.12	.28	.08	**.61**	.28	.01	.26	.06	**.65**	.25	.94**
C1: Competence	−.19	.08	.11	.07	**.80**	−.26	.11	.16	.07	**.77**	.97**
C2: Order	.09	−.16	−.03	.09	**.72**	.01	−.15	.03	.12	**.72**	.90**
C3: Dutifulness	.02	.04	−.03	.27	**.82**	−.09	.04	.02	.30	**.80**	.98**
C4: Achievement Striving	−.09	.01	−.01	−.15	**.83**	−.14	.04	.04	−.13	**.82**	.96**
C5: Self-Discipline	−.10	−.04	.01	.16	**.88**	−.20	−.02	.08	.17	**.86**	.94**
C6: Deliberation	−.15	−.10	−.12	.28	**.76**	−.26	−.11	−.04	.27	**.74**	.96**
Factor Congruence[c]	.94	.93	.87	.94	.94	.96**	.95**	.87**	.95**	.93**	.93**

Note: These are principal components, N = 200 raters of college-age and adult targets. Loadings greater than |.40| are given in boldface.
[a]Targeted to American normative factor structure.
[b]Variable congruence coefficients; total congruence coefficient in the last row.
[c]Congruence with American normative factor structure.
*Congruence higher than that of 95% of rotations from random data.
**Congruence higher than that of 99% of rotations from random data.

suggesting that all replicate their American counterparts (Haven & ten Berge, 1977).

The next five columns show the result of Procrustes rotation, maximizing alignment with the American normative structure. It shows a modest improvement in fit, particularly for the N and E factors. All but one of the facets now loads over .40 on the intended factor, and in all but two cases, this is their largest loading. The total congruence coefficient is .93, suggesting very substantial agreement.

The last column presents variable congruence coefficients, which are instructive in two regards. First, the two variables that show a higher loading on what was intended to be a secondary factor, N2: Angry Hostility and E3: Assertiveness, both have significant variable congruence coefficients. In each case, the pattern of loadings across factors resembles the American structure overall; the only difference is a slight shift in emphasis. For example, in the United States, Angry Hostility is chiefly high N and secondarily low A; in Lebanon the pattern is reversed. Second, two of the facets, E5: Excitement Seeking and A5: Modesty, have nonsignificant variable congruences. In the case of E5, the loadings on O and C are unexpectedly large; in the case of A5, the sign is reversed for several small secondary loadings. One would not conclude from this single, small-scale study that Excitement Seeking and Modesty are qualitatively different in Lebanon than in the United States, but if replicated in future studies in Lebanon or other Arabic countries, such findings would merit reinterpretation of these scales and their culturally conditioned meanings.

Evaluating Invariance

Procrustes rotation is a method designed to evaluate the invariance of factor structures. It does not force structures to be the same; in fact, its most impressive use is in studies that demonstrate that some factor structures cannot be replicated, even after Procrustes rotation (Gosling & John, 1998). But Procrustes rotation is arguably not the optimal way to identify variations in structure if they are there. Just as the etic approach begins with a predefined set of variables that may not be the most relevant in another culture, so Procrustes rotation begins with a predefined number of factors that also may not be optimal. If the imported variables are meaningless, or if the target factor structure is clearly not replicable in a new culture, congruence coefficients will show it. At that point, it would be time to reevaluate the translation, or the conditions of administration, or perhaps the whole imposed etic enterprise.

But so far, cross-cultural studies have provided overwhelming evidence that the structure of personality traits—the five-factor model (FFM)—is a human universal (McCrae & Allik, 2002). There may well be additional emic factors, unique to particular cultures (Cheung & Leung, 1998), but all human groups seem to be differentiated along the lines of the five basic factors.

This may be unappealing to extreme multiculturalists (Gergen et al., 1996) and cultural psychologists (Shweder & Sullivan, 1990) who celebrate the absolute uniqueness of each different culture. But it should be welcome news to positive psychologists. Most of the constructs with which they are concerned—hope, creativity, humor, joy, spirituality, self-efficacy, wisdom, gratitude, forgiveness—are conceptually and empirically tied to personality traits in the FFM (e.g., McCrae, 1987; McCullough, Bellah, Kilpatrick, & Johnson, 2001; Watson, 2002). The implication of cultural invariance in the FFM is that many of these positive psychology constructs are also likely to have a universal core, and what we learn about creativity or optimism in American research may well be applicable around the world—and vice versa. If the basic constructs of psychology were created or reshuffled arbitrarily by each culture—if personality structure were not invariant—psychology as a science and as a helping profession would necessarily become purely ethnocentric, with each culture's psychologists tending only to their own people. Instead, a single positive psychology is in a position to help all humankind.

There are also implications for disseminating these findings to psychology students and the general public. Universalism, defined as "understanding, appreciation, tolerance, and protection for the welfare of all people and for nature" (Schwartz, 1994, p. 89) is one of 10 pancultural values identified by Schwartz, and it is surely promoted by the cross-cultural invariance of personality structure. A careful consideration of that finding conveys two basic ideas: First, people everywhere show a range of individual differences, because without variation there could be no covariation along the lines of the familiar FFM. Learning about the FFM develops an appreciation for human individuality, and works in particular against ethnic stereotypes. Second, the ways in which people differ are everywhere the same: Every culture has introverts and extraverts, liberals and conservatives, achievers and slackers. In this important respect, all peoples are alike. Surely at this point in the history of the world it is worthwhile to contemplate table 12.1 and recall that Americans and Arabs share a common humanity.

Change is good and variety is good, but sometimes it is sweet to do nothing.

Notes

1. Time-sequential designs, comparing individuals tested at the same age but at different times, can be used to assess time-of-measurement effects.
2. In addition, such comparisons assume scalar equivalence (van de Vijver & Leung, 1997), that is, a common origin and equivalent unit of measurement. Readers will note that the same requirements are implicit in the longitudinal studies of mean level change previously discussed.

References

Berry, J. W. (1969). On cross-cultural comparability. *International Journal of Psychology, 4*, 119–128.

Block, J. (1961). *The Q-sort method in personality assessment and psychiatric research.* Springfield, IL: Charles C Thomas.

Bond, M. H. (2000). Localizing the imperial outreach: The Big Five and more in Chinese culture. *American Behavioral Scientist, 44*, 63–72.

Byrne, B. M. (2001). *Structural equation modeling with AMOS: Basic concepts, applications, and programming.* Mahwah, NJ: Erlbaum.

Chan, W., Ho, R. M., Leung, K., Chan, D. S. K., & Yung, Y. F. (1999). An alternative method for evaluating congruence coefficients with Procrustes rotation: A bootstrap procedure. *Psychological Methods, 4*, 378–402.

Cheung, F. M., & Leung, K. (1998). Indigenous personality measures: Chinese examples. *Journal of Cross-Cultural Psychology, 29*, 233–248.

Church, A. T., & Burke, P. J. (1994). Exploratory and confirmatory tests of the Big Five and Tellegen's three- and four-dimensional models. *Journal of Personality and Social Psychology, 66*, 93–114.

Costa, P. T., Jr., Herbst, J. H., McCrae, R. R., & Siegler, I. C. (2000). Personality at midlife: Stability, intrinsic maturation, and response to life events. *Assessment, 7*, 365–378.

Costa, P. T., Jr., & McCrae, R. R. (1978). Objective personality assessment. In M. Storandt, I. C. Siegler, & M. F. Elias (Eds.), *The clinical psychology of aging* (pp. 119–143). New York: Plenum.

Costa, P. T., Jr., & McCrae, R. R. (1980a). Influence of extraversion and neuroticism on subjective well-being: Happy and unhappy people. *Journal of Personality and Social Psychology, 38*, 668–678.

Costa, P. T., Jr., & McCrae, R. R. (1980b). Still stable after all these years: Personality as a key to some issues in adulthood and old age. In P. B. Baltes & O. G. Brim, Jr. (Eds.), *Life span development and behavior* (Vol. 3, pp. 65–102). New York: Academic Press.

Costa, P. T., Jr., & McCrae, R. R. (1982). An approach to the attribution of age, period, and cohort effects. *Psychological Bulletin, 92*, 238–250.

Costa, P. T., Jr., & McCrae, R. R. (1985). *The NEO Personality Inventory manual.* Odessa, FL: Psychological Assessment Resources.

Costa, P. T., Jr., & McCrae, R. R. (1988). From catalog to classification: Murray's needs and the five-factor model. *Journal of Personality and Social Psychology, 55*, 258–265.

Costa, P. T., Jr., & McCrae, R. R. (1989). *The NEO-PI/NEO-FFI manual supplement.* Odessa, FL: Psychological Assessment Resources.

Costa, P. T., Jr., & McCrae, R. R. (1992a). *Revised NEO Personality Inventory (NEO-PI-R) and NEO Five-Factor Inventory (NEO-FFI) professional manual.* Odessa, FL: Psychological Assessment Resources.

Costa, P. T., Jr., & McCrae, R. R. (1992b). Trait psychology comes of age. In T. B. Sonderegger (Ed.), *Nebraska Symposium on Motivation: Psychology and aging* (pp. 169–204). Lincoln: University of Nebraska Press.

Costa, P. T., Jr., & McCrae, R. R. (1997). Longitudinal stability of adult personality. In R. Hogan, J. A. Johnson, & S. R. Briggs (Eds.), *Handbook of personality psychology* (pp. 269–290). New York: Academic Press.

Costa, P. T., Jr., McCrae, R. R., & Arenberg, D. (1980). Enduring dispositions in adult males. *Journal of Personality and Social Psychology, 38*, 793–800.

Costa, P. T., Jr., McCrae, R. R., & Jónsson, F. H. (2002). Validity and utility of the Revised NEO Personality Inventory: Examples from Europe. In B. De Raad & M. Perugini (Eds.), *Big five assessment* (pp. 61–77). Göttingen, Germany: Hogrefe and Huber.

Costa, P. T., Jr., McCrae, R. R., & Siegler, I. C. (1999). Continuity and change over the adult life cycle: Personality and personality disorders. In C. R. Cloninger (Ed.), *Personality and psychopathology* (pp. 129–154). Washington, DC: American Psychiatric Press.

Darwiche, F. (2001). Lebanon. In M. Ember & C. R. Ember (Eds.), *Countries and their cultures* (Vol. 3, pp. 1266–1273). New York: Macmillian Reference USA.

Emerson, R. W. (1990). Experience. In *Essays: First and second series.* New York: Vintage. (Original work published in 1844)

Erikson, E. H. (1950). *Childhood and society.* New York: Norton.

Gergen, K. J. (2001). Psychological science in a postmodern context. *American Psychologist, 56,* 803–813.

Gergen, K. J., Gulerce, A., Lock, A., & Misra, G. (1996). Psychological science in cultural context. *American Psychologist, 51,* 496–503.

Gosling, S. D., & John, O. P. (1998, May). *Personality dimensions in dogs, cats, and hyenas.* Paper presented at the Annual Meeting of the American Psychological Society, Washington, DC.

Gough, H. G. (1987). *California Psychological Inventory administrator's guide.* Palo Alto, CA: Consulting Psychologists Press.

Gray, E. K., Haig, J., Vaidya, J., & Watson, D. (2001, February). *Personality stability in young adulthood.* Paper presented at the second annual meeting of the Society for Personality and Social Psychology, San Antonio, TX.

Guilford, J. S., Zimmerman, W. S., & Guilford, J. P. (1976). *The Guilford-Zimmerman Temperament Survey handbook: Twenty-five years of research and application.* San Diego, CA: EdITS.

Hale, E. (1981, June 8). Your personality—you're stuck with it. *Idaho Statesman.*

Haven, S., & ten Berge, J. M. F. (1977). *Tucker's coefficient of congruence as a measure of factorial invariance: An empirical study* (Heymans Bulletin 290 EX). University of Groningen, The Netherlands.

Heise, D. R. (1969). Separating reliability and stability in test-retest correlation. *American Sociological Review, 34,* 93–101.

Helson, R., & Picano, J. (1990). Is the traditional role bad for women? *Journal of Personality and Social Psychology, 59,* 311–320.

Jackson, D. N. (1984). *Personality Research Form manual* (3rd ed.). Port Huron, MI: Research Psychologists Press.

Jessor, R. (1983). The stability of change: Psychosocial development from adolescence to young adulthood. In D. Magnusson & V. L. Allen (Eds.), *Human development: An interactional perspective* (pp. 321–341). New York: Academic Press.

Lodhi, P. H., Deo, S., & Belhekar, V. M. (2002). The five-factor model of personality: Measurement and correlates in the Indian context. In R. R. McCrae & J. Allik (Eds.), *The five-factor*

model of personality across cultures (pp. 227–248). New York: Kluwer Academic/Plenum.

Lopez, S. J., Prosser, E. C., Edwards, L. M., Magyar-Moe, J. L., Neufeld, J. E., & Rasmussen, H. N. (2002). Putting positive psychology in a multicultural context. In C. R. Snyder & S. J. Lopez (Eds.), *Handbook of positive psychology* (pp. 700–714). New York: Oxford University Press.

MacKinnon, D. W. (1962). The nature and nurture of creative talent. *American Psychologist, 17,* 484–495.

Maddi, S. R., & Costa, P. T., Jr. (1972). *Humanism in personology: Allport, Maslow and Murray.* Chicago: Aldine.

Maslow, A. H. (1954). *Motivation and personality.* New York: Harper and Row.

McCrae, R. R. (1987). Creativity, divergent thinking, and openness to experience. *Journal of Personality and Social Psychology, 52,* 1258–1265.

McCrae, R. R. (1989). Why I advocate the five-factor model: Joint analyses of the NEO-PI and other instruments. In D. M. Buss & N. Cantor (Eds.), *Personality psychology: Recent trends and emerging directions* (pp. 237–245). New York: Springer-Verlag.

McCrae, R. R. (1993). Curiouser and curiouser! Modifications to a paradoxical theory of personality coherence. *Psychological Inquiry, 4,* 300–303.

McCrae, R. R. (1996). Social consequences of experiential openness. *Psychological Bulletin, 120,* 323–337.

McCrae, R. R., & Allik, J. (Eds.). (2002). *The five-factor model of personality across cultures.* New York: Kluwer Academic/Plenum.

McCrae, R. R., & Costa, P. T., Jr. (1984). *Emerging lives, enduring dispositions: Personality in adulthood.* Boston: Little, Brown.

McCrae, R. R., & Costa, P. T., Jr. (1988). Age, personality, and the spontaneous self-concept. *Journal of Gerontology: Social Sciences, 43,* S177–S185.

McCrae, R. R., & Costa, P. T., Jr. (1989). Reinterpreting the Myers-Briggs Type Indicator from the perspective of the five-factor model of personality. *Journal of Personality, 57,* 17–40.

McCrae, R. R., & Costa, P. T., Jr. (1994). The stability of personality: Observations and evaluations. *Current Directions in Psychological Science, 3,* 173–175.

McCrae, R. R., & Costa, P. T., Jr. (1997a). Conceptions and correlates of openness to experience. In R. Hogan, J. A. Johnson, & S. R. Briggs (Eds.), *Handbook of personality psychology* (pp. 269–290). Orlando, FL: Academic Press.

McCrae, R. R., & Costa, P. T., Jr. (1997b). Personality trait structure as a human universal. *American Psychologist, 52,* 509–516.

McCrae, R. R., & Costa, P. T., Jr. (2003). *Personality in adulthood: A five-factor theory perspective* (2nd ed.). New York: Guilford.

McCrae, R. R., Costa, P. T., Jr., de Lima, M. P., Simões, A., Ostendorf, F., et al. (1999). Age differences in personality across the adult life span: Parallels in five cultures. *Developmental Psychology, 35,* 466–477.

McCrae, R. R., Costa, P. T., Jr., & Piedmont, R. L. (1993). Folk concepts, natural language, and psychological constructs: The California Psychological Inventory and the five-factor model. *Journal of Personality, 61,* 1–26.

McCrae, R. R., Yik, M. S. M., Trapnell, P. D., Bond, M. H., & Paulhus, D. L. (1998). Interpreting personality profiles across cultures: Bilingual, acculturation, and peer rating studies of Chinese undergraduates. *Journal of Personality and Social Psychology, 74,* 1041–1055.

McCrae, R. R., Zonderman, A. B., Costa, P. T., Jr., Bond, M. H., & Paunonen, S. V. (1996). Evaluating replicability of factors in the Revised NEO Personality Inventory: Confirmatory factor analysis versus Procrustes rotation. *Journal of Personality and Social Psychology, 70,* 552–566.

McCullough, M. E., Bellah, C. G., Kilpatrick, S. D., & Johnson, J. L. (2001). Vengefulness: Relationships with forgiveness, rumination, well-being, and the Big Five. *Personality and Social Psychology Bulletin, 27,* 601–610.

McGue, M., Bacon, S., & Lykken, D. T. (1993). Personality stability and change in early adulthood: A behavioral genetic analysis. *Developmental Psychology, 29,* 96–109.

Myers, I. B. (1962). *Manual: The Myers-Briggs Type Indicator.* Palo Alto, CA: Consulting Psychologists Press.

Nussbaum, S., Trope, Y., & Liberman, N. (2003). Creeping dispositionism: The temporal dynamics of behavior prediction. *Journal of Personality and Social Psychology, 84,* 485–497.

Piedmont, R. L., Bain, E., McCrae, R. R., & Costa, P. T., Jr. (2002). The applicability of the five-factor model in a Sub-Saharan culture: The NEO-PI-R in Shona. In R. R. McCrae & J. Allik (Eds.), *The five-factor model of personality across cultures* (pp. 155–173). New York: Kluwer Academic/ Plenum.

Roberts, B., Caspi, A., & Moffitt, T. E. (2003). Work experiences and personality development in young adulthood. *Journal of Personality and Social Psychology, 84,* 582–593.

Roberts, B. W., & DelVecchio, W. F. (2000). The rank-order consistency of personality traits from childhood to old age: A quantitative review of longitudinal studies. *Psychological Bulletin, 126,* 3–25.

Robins, R. W., Fraley, R. C., Roberts, B. W., & Trzesniewski, K. H. (2001). A longitudinal study of personality change in young adulthood. *Journal of Personality, 69,* 617–640.

Robinson, M. D., Solberg, E. C., Vargas, P. T., & Tamir, M. (2003). Trait as default: Extraversion, subjective well-being, and the distinction between neutral and positive events. *Journal of Personality and Social Psychology, 85,* 517–527.

Rogers, C. R., & Dymond, R. F. (Eds.). (1954). *Psychotherapy and personality change.* Chicago: University of Chicago Press.

Rubin, Z. (1981). Does personality really change after 20? *Psychology Today, 15,* 18–27.

Santor, D. A., Bagby, R. M., & Joffe, R. T. (1997). Evaluating stability and change in personality and depression. *Journal of Personality and Social Psychology, 73,* 1354–1362.

Schaie, K. W. (1965). A general model for the study of developmental problems *Psychological Bulletin, 64,* 92–107.

Schwartz, S. H. (1994). Beyond individualism/ collectivism: New cultural dimensions of values. In U. Kim, H. C. Triandis, C. Kagitcibasi, S.-C. Choi, & G. Yoon (Eds.), *Individualism and collectivism: Theory, method, and applications* (pp. 85–119). Thousand Oaks, CA: Sage.

Shapiro, S. L., Schwartz, G. E. R., & Santerre, C. (2002). Meditation and positive psychology. In C. R. Snyder & S. J. Lopez (Eds.), *Handbook of positive psychology* (pp. 632–645). New York: Oxford University Press.

Sheldon, K. M., Ryan, R. M., Rawsthorne, L. J., & Ilardi, B. (1997). Trait self and true self: Cross-role variation in the Big Five personality traits and its relations with psychological authenticity and subjective well-being. *Journal of Personality and Social Psychology, 73,* 1380–1393.

Shweder, R. A., & Sullivan, M. A. (1990). The semiotic subject of cultural psychology. In L. A. Pervin (Ed.), *Handbook of personality: Theory and research* (pp. 399–416). New York: Guilford.

Small, B. J., Hertzog, C., Hultsch, D. F., & Dixon, R. L. (2003). Stability and change in adult personality over 6 years: Findings from the Victoria Longitudinal Study. *Journal of Gerontology: Psychological Sciences, 58B,* P166–P176.

Srivastava, S., John, O. P., Gosling, S. D., & Potter, J. (2003). Development of personality in early and middle age: Set like plaster or persistent change? *Journal of Personality and Social Psychology, 84,* 1041–1053.

Suh, E., Diener, E., Oishi, S., & Triandis, H. C. (1998). The shifting basis of life satisfaction judgments across cultures: Emotions versus norms. *Journal of Personality and Social Psychology, 74,* 482–493.

ten Berge, J. M. F. (2000). Linking reliability and factor analysis: Recent developments in some classic psychometric problems. In S. Hampson (Ed.), *Advances in personality psychology* (Vol. 1, pp. 138–156). Philadelphia: Taylor and Francis.

Terracciano, A., Costa, P. T., Jr., & McCrae, R. R. (in press). Personality plasticity after age 30. *Personality and Social Psychology Bulletin.*

Terracciano, A., McCrae, R. R., Brant, L. J., & Costa, P. T., Jr. (2005). Hierarchical linear modeling analyses of NEO-PI-R scales in the Baltimore Longitudinal Study of Aging. *Psychology and Aging, 20,* 493–506.

Tucker, L. R. (1951). *A method for synthesis of factor analysis studies* (Personnel Research Section Report No. 984). Washington, DC: Department of the Army.

U. S. Census Bureau. (n.d.). *Educational attainment of the population 15 years and over, by age, sex, race, and Hispanic origin: March 2002.* Retrieved April 27, 2006, from http://www.census.gov/population/socdemo/education/ppl-169/tab01.pdf

van de Vijver, F. J. R., & Leung, K. (1997). Methods and data analysis of comparative research. In J. W. Berry, Y. H. Poortinga, & J. Pandey (Eds.), *Handbook of cross-cultural psychology: Vol. 1. Theory and method* (pp. 257–300). Boston: Allyn and Bacon.

Watson, D. (2002). Positive affectivity: The disposition to experience pleasurable emotional states. In C. R. Snyder & S. J. Lopez (Eds.), *Handbook of positive psychology* (pp. 106–119). New York: Oxford University Press.

Wiggins, J. S. (1979). A psychological taxonomy of trait-descriptive terms: The interpersonal domain. *Journal of Personality and Social Psychology, 37,* 395–412.

Williams, H. C. (1995). Confirmatory factor analysis and common factor analysis in conjunction with Procrustes target rotation method: A comparison. *Dissertation Abstracts International, 55*(10), 4629B.

Yang, J., McCrae, R. R., & Costa, P. T., Jr. (1998). Adult age differences in personality traits in the United States and the People's Republic of China. *Journal of Gerontology: Psychological Sciences, 53B,* P375–P383.

13

Measuring Emotional Intelligence

Promises, Pitfalls, Solutions?

*Gerald Matthews, Moshe Zeidner, and
Richard D. Roberts*

From the beginnings of scientific study, intelligence researchers have been concerned with mental abilities that go beyond the narrowly cognitive (Bowman, Markham, & Roberts, 2002). At least part of this attraction appears driven by a positive, egalitarian message; that there is more to destiny than academic-cognitive intelligence (Kyllonen, Roberts, & Stankov, 2006). Thus, pioneers of the field, including Thorndike, Guilford, and Wechsler, addressed constructs such as social intelligence, with rather limited success (see Matthews, Zeidner, & Roberts, 2002). The latest construct of this kind is *emotional intelligence* (EI), which may be loosely defined as a set of interrelated abilities for identifying, understanding, and managing emotions. The concept of EI has had a far-reaching popular impact, to the extent that it has spawned several mainstream best-sellers, and been named, by the American Dialect Society, among the most useful new words or phrases of the late twentieth century.

Popular accounts of EI may be justifiably criticized for hyperbole and the advancing of claims unsupported by adequate empirical evidence. However, recent interest also owes much to more sober attempts to develop and validate tests of EI (and measures of other affective processes), which, potentially, may be as important for psychological assessment as tests of IQ (i.e., cognitive-academic intelligence). In occupational psychology, EI assessment may improve personnel selection, while training aimed at raising EI may increase productivity and employee well-being. Similarly, educational psychologists have increasingly focused on interventions that increase children's emotional competence as a means of tackling substance abuse, delinquency, and psychological maladjustment (Greenberg et al., 2003). Thus, in many ways, across a variety of subdisciplines and applications, EI may be heralded as among the most promising of the new constructs emerging in psychological science that are directed toward improving the human condition. Indeed, Salovey, Mayer, and Caruso (2002) suggested that EI belongs in positive psychology because, by contrast with traditional conceptions of IQ, the term suggests hope that people may be able to develop the emotional competencies required for success in relationships and in the workplace. The construct is also in tune with a popular zeitgeist that emphasizes personal growth and the enjoyment of high self-esteem (Matthews & Zeidner, 2003).

Recent work has resulted in EI tests that meet conventional standards for reliability and possess at least some criterion and construct validity. At the same time, as we have alluded to elsewhere, several difficulties have become apparent with theoretical and empirical approaches to understanding the concept (Matthews et al., 2002). The field is too new for any definitive judgment, but skeptical arguments include the following. Definitions of EI are often vague and incompatible with one another. The predictive validity of tests may be a consequence of confounding this construct with established ability and personality factors. Theoretical accounts of EI are often naive, and perhaps little more than laundry lists of desirable qualities. Finally, although there are successful programs for training interpersonal skills in real life, it is questionable whether the success of such programs owes much to the EI construct.

In this chapter, extending upon and updating our previous research, we aim to provide a balanced account of the accomplishments and difficulties of existing research on EI. Our thesis is that current research in fact uses the term *emotional intelligence* to refer to multiple constructs, which should be differentiated. Many of these constructs may not be true "intelligences," and we question whether they should be linked to an overarching, general EI factor. Equally problematic, some of these constructs may already be subsumed by existing theories of individual differences. Is it worthwhile developing new models for these old wines in new bottles? At the same time, individual differences in affective processes had received short shrift until recently; EI has focused scientific research on this doubtless important topic (Matthews et al., 2002). Thus, throughout this chapter we cover the promises offered by EI, and suggest domains of this emerging subdiscipline where there might be a need for more balanced discourse. Similarly, we alert the reader to certain pitfalls that may impede proper scientific progress, if due caution is not exercised. We also offer some suggestions for a more unified, scientific framework.

Assessment Issues

Thus far, by basing research on a variety of tests for the construct, EI research has followed the conventional path often traced for differential psychology. Mayer, Caruso, and Salovey (2000) introduced a distinction between ability models and mixed models of EI. Ability models define EI as a set of competencies, which may be assessed using objective tests with right or wrong answers. Mayer and his colleagues (e.g., Mayer, Salovey, Caruso, & Sitarenios, 2003) developed two influential tests of this kind, the Multifactor Emotional Intelligence Scale (MEIS) and its successor the Mayer-Salovey-Caruso Emotional Intelligence Test (MSCEIT). Both tests are based on a four-branch conceptualization of EI, which incorporates emotion perception, emotional facilitation of thought, emotional understanding, and emotion management. The MSCEIT has two subtests for each branch. Other objectively scored ability tests, such as tests for emotion perception (Davies, Stankov, & Roberts, 1998), are of much narrower scope and do not provide an overall EI score. Even so, we have suggested that they may provide theoretically enriched understanding of individual differences in emotional processes, if multiple indices are used in combination with advanced statistical techniques covered throughout this volume (MacCann, Matthews, Zeidner, & Roberts, 2003).

By contrast to a model that considers information processes and performance components pivotal, mixed models define EI as a broader collection of traits, which include abilities, personality, and motivational qualities that facilitate effective real-life adaptation and coping (e.g., Bar-On, 2000; Goleman, 1998). EI as a mixed model construct is assessed by self-report, using questionnaires that resemble, at least superficially, standard personality inventories. Questionnaires of this kind are now numerous and growing rapidly. In table 13.1, we summarize characteristics of four of the best known of these self-report measures (as well as, for comparison purposes, including a capsule description of the MSCEIT). All of these measures (including the MSCEIT) may be scored for overall EI, as well as for various subdimensions (i.e., facets) of EI.

Naturally, tests for EI should meet standard criteria relating to content validity, reliability, criterion/predictive validity, and construct validity (e.g., Anastasi & Urbina, 1997). Issues of consequential, operational, and other forms of

TABLE 13.1 Sampling Domain and Scoring Methodology of Select Self-Report and Ability Measures of Emotional Intelligence

Test	Sampling Domain	Tests	Scoring
Self-report Scales			
EQ-i (Emotional Quotient Inventory, Bar-On, 1997)	Intrapersonal, interpersonal, adaptation, stress management, general mood	15 scales (132 items)	5-point scale; self-report
ECI (Emotional Competence Inventory 360, Boyatzis et al., 2000)	Self-awareness, self-management, social awareness, social skills	19 scales (63 items)	7-point scale; self, manager, direct and peer reports
SSRI (Schutte Self-Report Index, Schutte et al., 1998)	Four-branch hierarchical model	1 test (33 items)	5-point scale; self-report
TEIque (Trait Emotional Intelligence Questionnaire, Petrides & Furnham, 2003)	Comprehensive domain sampling (mainly four-branch and EQ-i)	15 scales (144 items)	5-point scale; self-report
Ability Scale			
Mayer-Salovey-Caruso Emotional Intelligence Test Battery, Mayer, Salovey, & Caruso, 2002	Four-branch hierarchical model	8 (2 per branch)	Rating scales and multiple choice, scored for consensus (general and expert)

validity (e.g., face) should also be acceptable (see American Educational Research Association, American Psychological Association, & National Council on Measurement in Education, 1999). Beyond these properties, still further item statistics related to validity issues (e.g., factorial invariance, generalizability, fairness), although equally of interest in their own right, should be well documented. In fact, researchers have failed to capitalize fully on multivariate methods in test development. Most questionnaire studies report exploratory, but not confirmatory, factor analyses, without establishing the stability of factor solutions across different populations. Indeed, the published factor solutions of some well-known instruments may not be replicable (e.g., Petrides & Furnham, 2000). Confirmatory analyses have provided support for the Mayer-Salovey-Caruso four-branch model (Mayer, Salovey, & Caruso, 2002; Roberts, Zeidner, & Matthews, 2001). Current research has also failed to develop and test comprehensive multistratum models of the kind familiar from ability research (Carroll, 1993). Given the possible placement of EI at the crossroads of ability and personality, it is imperative that such models locate latent EI factors in relation to constructs such as general intelligence and the "Big Five" personality factors. Another neglected multivariate method is the multitrait-multimethod approach (Campbell & Fiske, 1959). The evidence for EI would be more convincing if multiple primary abilities were triangulated within a structural model using independent data sources, say, self-report, peer-report, and objective testing. A final limitation of current research—understandable in view of the novelty of the field—is the lack of prospective studies. Such studies may be especially important for demonstrating that EI (and its component facets) operate as causal agents, affording prediction of future emotional functioning. In the next section, we evaluate briefly the specific psychometric strengths and weaknesses of questionnaire and ability tests.

Content Validity

This criterion deals with conceptualization issues and the decision of which qualities should be accepted or excluded as components of EI. However, examination of the literature suggests there is no clear, consensual definition of EI and that the multitude of qualities covered by the concept appears, at times, overwhelming (Roberts, 2003).

Indeed, popular accounts of EI (e.g., Goleman, 1998) tend to define the construct by exclusion—EI represents all those positive qualities that are not IQ, including qualities such as hope, optimism, and moral character that bear little relation to ability. Much current research—especially "mixed model" research—proceeds from little more than a listing of desirable personal qualities that are linked in some way to emotion (e.g., Bar-On, 1997, 2000). Current conceptualizations leave open various issues that make it difficult to decide on the appropriate content for tests of EI. First, it is unclear the extent to which tests of EI measure (1) a basic aptitude for emotion processing (akin to fluid intelligence), (2) learned skills for handling specific contingencies (akin to crystallized intelligence), or (3) even actual outcomes of emotional encounters (akin to academic achievement). Second, current tests for EI rely on explicit verbal response, but competence may reside in implicit skills inaccessible to consciousness, such as abilities in decoding nonverbal cues or in expressing emotion. That is, current assessments emphasize declarative knowledge of emotion, but, in real-life encounters, procedural knowledge may also be critical. Third, there is uncertainty over whether EI relates to a special class of cognitions and metacognitions, supporting the regulation of emotion, or, alternatively, to some separate noncognitive emotion system (e.g., Izard, 2001).

Such differing conceptualizations have led to considerable confusion and a lack of convergence on the appropriate content for assessment devices. In defense of EI, one should bear in mind that, after over a century of research, controversy remains over the precise meaning of intelligence. However, there appears to be less implicit agreement among researchers on the content domains of EI than was the case for intelligence tests, even during the early days of testing (see Roberts, Markham, Matthews, & Zeidner, 2005). In part, at least, the full promise of EI measures (and ensuing research) depends on resolving issues surrounding content validity, an important undertaking that needs to be addressed for the field to progress.

Reliability

The development of reliable scales has been one of the successes of the field, especially with respect to coefficients of internal consistency in self-report EI measures (Matthews et al., 2002). The performance-based measures are somewhat more problematic, with reliabilities as low as .50

for certain branches (e.g., emotion management), though likely this could be improved with more rigorous item development. Moreover, MacCann, Roberts, Matthews, and Zeidner (2004) have demonstrated that reliabilities may be improved somewhat by applying the method of reciprocal averages to consensually derived scores. However, somewhat vexing for the emotion perception branch, in particular, is the issue of experimental dependence, and possibly inflated internal consistency reliability estimates that may occur (since a person's face, for example, cannot be both happy and sad; MacCann et al., 2003). Acceptable levels of test-retest reliability over periods of several months have nonetheless been reported for some questionnaire measures (Bar-On, 1997, 2000), and in this respect the MSCEIT also fares reasonably well (see Brackett & Mayer, 2003).

Criterion and Predictive Validity

Studies are equivocal in establishing the predictive validity of questionnaire measures of EI (MacCann et al., 2003), largely because of methodological deficiencies that we discuss shortly. On the positive side, Bachman, Stein, Campbell, and Sitarenios (2000) reported that more successful account officers have higher Emotional Quotient Inventory (EQ-i) scores than less successful account officers. Similarly, Slaski and Cartwright (2002) found a small relation between EQ-i scores and managerial performance ($r = 0.22$), while the ECI was found to predict university grades, albeit rather weakly (i.e., $R^2 = 0.07$ to 0.15; Rozell, Pettijohn, & Parker, 2002). However, none of these studies controlled personality or intelligence, which some would consider pivotal in the context of establishing the incremental predictive validity of EI (see e.g., Matthews et al., 2002). A study in which this was attempted found that the Schutte Self-Report Index (SSRI) predicted some well-being indices with the Big Five personality factors controlled, although the additional variance explained was small (i.e., less than 5%; see Saklofske, Austin, & Minski, 2003). A possible confound apparent in these studies too is the self-report nature of both the EI measure and the criteria, rendering positive findings less convincing than would otherwise be the case (i.e., shared "method" variance may be responsible for the relations between test and criterion variables). Furthermore, there is a risk of criterion contamination in that tests like the EQ-i include

general mood scales as part of EI, although improved mood might be better seen as an outcome of high EI.

Note that these problems seem less critical when considering the predictive validity of the performance-based scales. Thus, meaningful associations have been found between MEIS scores and self-reported empathy ($r = 0.33$ and 0.43); parental warmth ($r = 0.23$ and 0.15); life satisfaction ($r = 0.11$ and 0.28; Mayer et al., 2000; Ciarrochi, Chan, & Caputi, 2000, respectively, in each instance); and (lack of) tobacco and alcohol usage (Trinidad & Johnson, 2002). Evidence supporting the predictive validity of the newer MSCEIT is also beginning to emerge. For example, Lopes, Salovey, and Strauss (2003) showed that the MSCEIT Managing Emotions subtest correlated significantly ($0.22 < r < 0.36$) with various indices of social adjustment in a student sample. These relatively small correlations reduced (though remained significant), when Big Five personality factors were controlled. Brackett and Mayer (2003) found that both questionnaire measures and the MSCEIT were weakly predictive of criteria for deviance and academic achievement, with the Big Five and Verbal Scholastic Aptitude Test controlled.

A recent meta-analysis (van Rooy & Viswesvaran, 2004) analyzed 59 samples ($N = 9,522$) to examine relations between EI and occupational performance, although it should be noted that the analysis relied quite heavily on unpublished reports not subject to peer review evaluation. Van Rooy and Viswesvaran found an overall correlation of 0.20, corrected to a ρ of 0.23. Similar coefficients were obtained for the MEIS and several questionnaire scales. In this context, validity is similar to that of Big Five personality dimensions, but considerably less than the validities of 0.5 or so typically obtained with general intelligence measures (Schmidt & Hunter, 1998). The meta-analysis also showed that EI had some modest incremental validity over personality in predicting performance, but it did not evidence incremental validity over general mental ability.

Construct Validity

Construct validation is the process of testing whether or not a test actually measures some theoretical construct or trait (Anastasi & Urbina, 1997). The demonstration of construct validity rests on a systematic program of research that builds up a nomological network of relationships between the test and other criteria that fit prediction from theory. As mentioned earlier, theoretical accounts of EI are sparse and make few detailed predictions about how test scores might relate to relevant cognitive and neural processes. Thus, we focus here on one of the most important forms of construct validation for a new construct: its convergent and discriminant validity (Campbell & Fiske, 1959). A test should correlate highly with other variables that the theory specifies should relate to the underlying construct (convergent validity). Conversely, the test should not correlate highly with variables that are believed to index unrelated constructs (divergent validity).

The simplest test of convergent validity is whether alternate measures of the construct are strongly positively intercorrelated. However, the limited data available suggest that ability-based and questionnaire-based assessments of EI are measuring essentially different constructs. For example, Brackett and Mayer (2003) report a 0.21 correlation between their MSCEIT and Bar-On's (2000) EQ-i. Similarly, Zeidner, Shani, Matthews, and Roberts (2005) obtained a small but significant correlation of 0.25 between the SSRI and the MSCEIT. This study also showed that a sample of academically gifted children obtained higher EI scores than controls on the MSCEIT, but a lower mean score on the SSRI; clearly a problematic finding in the context of establishing convergent validity. Brackett and Mayer (2003) showed that small positive correlations between the MSCEIT and questionnaire measures drop to zero when confounding with the Big Five traits is controlled. Questionnaire measures of EI may themselves be heterogeneous. Brackett and Mayer (2003) found that the subscales of the EQ-i and SSRI loaded on separate, though correlated, factors. The EQ-i factor had a large negative loading for neuroticism, whereas the SSRI factor had high loadings for psychological well-being (PWB). Perhaps there is a "positive self-report EI" related to PWB constructs such as personal growth and positive relations, and a "negative self-report EI" related to stress resistance and freedom from anxiety and depression.

Another test of convergent validity is whether EI measures correlate with standard general intelligence or g. If it is assumed that all mental abilities form a positive manifold (Bowman et al., 2002)—that is, they tend to intercorrelate positively—then tests for EI should be at least modestly positively correlated with g. Table 13.2

summarizes some illustrative data, across a range of measures of intelligence, academic achievement, and EI tests and their subscales. The MEIS and MSCEIT pass this test of convergent validity, although they appear to relate to measures of acculturated knowledge (i.e., Gc) rather than fluid intelligence (i.e., Gf, which is closer to the general intelligence construct; see Roberts et al., 2005). However, questionnaire measures are consistently unrelated to general intelligence, indeed sometimes being even negative in sign. Van Rooy and Viswesvaran's (2004) meta-analysis reported corrected correlations of 0.33 for the MEIS and cognitive ability (9 studies: $N = 2,196$), and 0.09 for other measures and cognitive ability (10 studies: $N = 1,962$), without differentiating Gf from Gc.

Divergent validity requires that the test is psychometrically distinct from tests for other constructs. In this case, the requirement is that tests for EI are distinct from ability and personality scales. The MEIS and MSCEIT meet this criterion. Their correlations with various measures of intelligence, although consistent and seemingly replicable, are typically less than 0.4. Several studies (e.g., Lopes et al., 2003; Roberts, Zeidner, & Matthews, 2001) have correlated one or other of these tests with the Big Five personality traits. EI typically correlates with high agreeableness, low neuroticism, and high conscientiousness, but correlation magnitudes are usually less than 0.3.

By contrast, questionnaire scales for the EI are highly correlated with established traits. McCrae (2000) identified considerable overlap in content between these scales and measures of the Big Five traits. Table 13.3 summarizes some illustrative studies (and for the sake of completeness, we also include some findings with the MSCEIT in this table). The EQ-i is strongly correlated with low scores on traits representing negative affectivity, including neuroticism and trait anxiety (Bar-On, 1997, 2000; Brackett & Mayer, 2003; Dawda & Hart, 2000; Newsome, Day, & Catano, 2000). Correlation magnitudes typically range from 0.6 to 0.8. The EQ-i is also substantially correlated with high extraversion, high conscientiousness, and agreeableness. Thus, the EQ-i appears, in general, to be largely a proxy for these traits from the five-factor model (FFM).

The SSRI appears to be better distinguished from the Big Five than the EQ-i, but there is still demonstrably substantial overlap. Saklofske et al. (2003) found that the strongest correlate of

TABLE 13.2 Representative Correlations With Intelligence and Scholastic Achievement for EI Measures (and Subscales)

	Vocabulary	Verbal SAT	Math SAT	GPA
Ability Measures of EI				
MSCEIT total (Brackett & Mayer, 2003)	—	.32	—	—
MSCEIT total (Lopes, Salovey, & Strauss, 2003)	.17	−.04	−.03	—
MSCEIT Branch 1	.06	−.10	−.09	−.04
MSCEIT Branch 2	−.03	−.22	−.06	−.01
MSCEIT Branch 3	.39	.36	.19	.23
MSCEIT Branch 4	.05	−.10	−.13	.10
Self-Report Measures of EI				
EQ-i (Brackett & Mayer, 2003)	—	−.03	—	—
SSRI (Brackett & Mayer, 2003)	—	.05	—	—
SSRI (Zeidner et al., 2005)	−.02	—	—	—

	Matching	Analogies	Sequences	Construction
Self-Report Measures of EI				
EQ-i Total (Derkson et al., 2002)	.06	.05	.08	.09
Intrapersonal	.02	.03	.07	.08
Interpersonal	.01	−.06	−.04	−.03
Adaptability	.06	.08	.09	.10
Stress management	.11	.11	.11	.11
General mood	.07	.07	.10	.11

TABLE 13.3 Representative Correlations With Personality for EI Measures (and Subscales)

	O	C	E	A	N
Ability Measures of EI					
MSCEIT total (Lopes et al., 2003)	−.22	.23	.03	.32	−.12
MSCEIT Branch 1	−.13	.11	−.04	.19	−.07
MSCEIT Branch 2	−.28	.12	−.10	.24	−.03
MSCEIT Branch 3	−.01	.22	.10	.15	−.09
MSCEIT Branch 4	−.22	.24	.06	.33	−.15
MSCEIT total (Brackett & Mayer, 2003)	.25	.03	.11	.28	−.08
Self-Report Measures of EI					
EQ-i total (Dawda & Hart, 2000)	−.12	.51	.52	.43	−.62
EQ-i total (Dawda & Hart, 2000)	.17	.33	.56	.43	−.72
ECI Self-Awareness (Sala, 2002)	.28	.30	.47	.00	−.07
ECI Social Awareness (Sala, 2002)	.23	.21	.24	.03	−.10
ECI Self-Management (Sala, 2002)	.20	.33	.24	−.02	−.20
ECI Social Skills (Sala, 2002)	.22	.39	.49	.08	−.11
SSRI (Saklofske et al., 2003)	.27	.38	.51	.18	−.37
TEIque (Petrides & Furnham, 2003)	.47	.22	.69	.02	−.73
TEIque (Petrides & Furnham, 2003)	.44	.34	.68	−.04	−.70

Note: O = Openness to Experience; C = Conscientiousness; E = Extraversion; A = Agreeableness; N = Neuroticism.

EI as assessed by the SSRI was high extraversion ($r = 0.51$), although EI also correlated between 0.3 and 0.4 with high conscientiousness and low neuroticism. The FFM does not provide an exhaustive account of personality. Although the issue has been neglected in existing research, questionnaire-based assessments of more narrowly defined "midlevel" traits such as empathy, self-esteem, hardiness, and (low) impulsivity may also contribute to variance in EI shared with established traits. This possibility leaves self-reported EI open to a potentially damning problem: If these constructs are taken into account, the utility of the new construct of EI is uncertain; what can EI explain that comprehensive assessment of personality constructs cannot?

Other Psychometric Properties

The extent to which other psychometric properties of these measures have been established is surprisingly scant. For example, it has yet to be determined whether the factor structure of the MSCEIT is the same for disparate ethnic groups, across gender, or as a function of age. No information is given either concerning the relation between the earlier version of the ability test (i.e., MEIS) and its revision (i.e., the MSCEIT). These shortcomings are noticeable in the context of other standardized, psychological tests that are operational, where such issues are contemporaneously given detailed treatment in test manuals and other forms of supporting documentation. Similarly, differential item function analysis, polytomous item response theory (IRT) models, and testing concepts using structural equation modeling offer promise if applied with due caution to (and sometimes in combination with) the assessment of EI (see e.g., Thissen & Wainer, 2001). These methodologies certainly present themselves as directions for future research to resolve a number of validity issues, some of which we are currently pursuing with colleagues in various research centers around the world.

The Outlook for Ability Tests

The preceding exposition suggests that ability tests such as the MSCEIT merit further investigation. At least so far as total EI score is concerned, they meet conventional criteria for reliability and convergent-divergent validity. There are encouraging signs of criterion validity

and even incremental validity (Lopes et al., 2003). Our reservations about the MSCEIT relate primarily to content validity. It appears to measure some interesting dispositional qualities, but are those qualities truly a form of intelligence?

One reason for questioning the status of the MEIS and MSCEIT concerns scoring. Fundamental to measuring intelligence is the notion of veridical scoring (Guttman & Levy, 1991); there should be a clearly justified correct answer for each item. The scoring problem has dogged precursors of today's EI tests, such as scales for social intelligence: How can we say with certainty what is the best way to resolve problematic social encounters? Mayer et al. (e.g., 2000) have adopted two principal scoring methods. *Expert scoring* relies on a panel of psychologists with expertise in emotion to decide the correct answers. The problems here are that experts are fallible, that academic psychologists may possess declarative but not procedural knowledge of emotion, and that some items may simply not have a correct answer, in that the best response may depend on circumstance and contextual factors. *Consensus scoring* allocates credit to test takers to the extent that their responses match those of a large normative sample, on the grounds that the "best" ways of interpreting and managing emotion are socially defined. The obvious problem is that the consensus viewpoint may not in fact be correct; beliefs about emotion may be affected by culturally defined stereotypes, for example.

In defense of the tests, Mayer et al. (2002) showed a high degree of convergence between expert and consensus scoring of the MSCEIT, correcting a lower degree of convergence demonstrated for the MEIS (Roberts et al., 2001). However, doubts remain over whether the experts may just be reproducing shared cultural beliefs. Furthermore, although Mayer et al. (2002) favored consensus scoring, the method introduces measurement problems. By definition, the consensus response to a difficult item is incorrect. Thus, the method obviates the possibility of including difficult items that might separate emotional geniuses from the merely emotionally competent (Zeidner, Matthews, & Roberts, 2001). It also appears that consensually scored tests result in very high levels of kurtosis and negative skew, and thus statistical analysis assuming multivariate normality cannot be validly applied to them (MacCann et al., 2003). In fact, MacCann et al. (2004) showed that scores can be normal only if scale reliability is low; that is, it appears unlikely that consensus-scored tests can be both reliable and normally distributed.[1] Further research might focus on improving the validity of expert judgments, which appear less susceptible to these statistical difficulties, or other scoring metrics (deviation from expert scores, for example).

Thus, future research should explore whether the MSCEIT predicts genuine differences in emotional competence. One technique that has been highly successful in validating orthodox intelligence tests is to show that the tests predict performance on simple information-processing tasks requiring no specialized knowledge (e.g., Kyllonen & Roberts, 2003). Mayer et al.'s four-branch conceptualization of EI seems to require that the MSCEIT should predict, for example, chronometric measures of recognition, recoding, and response selection taken from tasks with emotional stimuli. Thus far, there is little relevant evidence to test this proposition, although a recent, as yet unpublished, study by the current authors sheds some light on this issue. Reid et al. (2006) had participants complete the MSCEIT as well as standard experimental measures of emotion perception in voices (i.e., Recognition of Affect in a Foreign Language, RAFL) and faces (i.e., Japanese and Caucasian Brief Affect Recognition Test, JACBART), and the Emotional Stroop. It was hypothesized that these measures, which are based on some combination of speed and accuracy of response and otherwise conceptually similar to the MSCEIT, would share moderate-to-large correlation with the consensually scored subscales. Instead, correlations were low and even sometimes opposite in sign to that predicted by theory.

Alternative interpretations of performance on the MEIS and MSCEIT are also possible if one considers the way in which the test is scored. For example, Zeidner et al. (2001) suggested that rather than representing a basic aptitude for handling emotion, performance-based EI actually assesses acquired, culturally shaped social-emotional knowledge, such as "feeling rules" and "display rules" that indicate the appropriate meanings to be assigned to social encounters and acceptable forms of expressing emotion. Thus construed, one possibility is that EI represents the extent of learning and knowledge of this kind; Ackerman (1996) has identified what might be an analogous broad factor of declarative knowledge (*Gk*) of academic learning, which is distinct from fluid and crystallized intelligence.

Another interpretation is that the "ability" tests measure the congruence of the person with the surrounding culture. Someone who follows cultural norms in interpreting and managing emotion is likely to be better adapted simply through being in tune with other people. Thus, the MSCEIT may assess a genuinely adaptive quality, but one that relates to goodness of fit with the social environment rather than to an ability per se.

The Outlook for Questionnaire Measures

We are more pessimistic concerning the outlook for questionnaire scales that rely on self-reports of competence. Although these scales are typically reliable and valid, they fail tests of convergent and divergent validity, deriving much of their criterion validity from overlap with existing personality constructs. Developers of these tests must also confront the fundamental difficulty that they appear to be overly dependent on self-insight. Indeed, there is a paradox here that the tests rely on the emotionally illiterate person possessing insight into his or her lack of emotional competence, although poor self-understanding is seen as one of the hallmarks of low EI. The problem is demonstrated empirically by Dunning, Johnson, Ehrlinger, and Kruger's (2003) findings showing that poor performers are often "blissfully unaware of their incompetence" (p. 83). In addition, self-reports of intelligence correlate only at about 0.3 with objective intelligence (Paulhus, Lysy, & Yik, 1998), and studies show that self-reports of some aspects of emotional functioning are unrelated to objective measures. For example, a meta-analysis (Davis & Kraus, 1997) established that self-reports of empathy are unrelated to objective measures of person perception.

Nevertheless, further development of questionnaires may add usefully to the range of individual difference constructs—although not necessarily to ability constructs. Although the total EI score on existing questionnaires tends to overlap considerably with the Big Five, some of the variance in subscales appears more distinct from personality (e.g., Petrides & Furnham, 2001). Saklofske et al. (2003) showed that factors derived from the SSRI that related to emotion appraisal and emotion utilization showed no correlations greater than 0.3 with any Big Five factor; by contrast, optimism and social skills factors were substantially confounded with personality.

Fractionating "Emotional Intelligence"

Thus far, we have found two reasons for supposing that tests for EI may refer to multiple constructs that are only weakly related to one another. First, objective and questionnaire-based tests for EI fail the Campbell and Fiske (1959) convergent validity test. For example, the SSRI (Schutte et al., 1998), although based on the Mayer-Salovey-Caruso conceptual model, correlates at less than 0.3 with these authors' own test (e.g., Zeidner et al., 2005). The correlation of the MSCEIT with the self-report instrument is actually less than its correlations with general intelligence and some personality constructs. Second, our examination of content validity suggests that that there are important domains of emotional competence, including information processing and proceduralized skills, which may not be well covered by existing instruments.

Thus, current research may mistakenly label multifarious constructs as emotional intelligence while neglecting other relevant constructs. Some of these constructs may be true abilities, in that they confer an unequivocal adaptive advantage, whereas others relate more to personality and styles of behavior conferring both adaptive benefits and costs (Matthews & Zeidner, 2000). Thus, advances in assessment of these different constructs require a clearer initial conceptualization of the domain. In table 13.4 we briefly list four discrete sets of constructs that appear to differ psychometrically, as well as the key processes to which they relate and their adaptive significance. This table also draws parallels with similar constructs from the literature on intelligence, as well as providing some comments on developmental influences that likely operate in each instance. In the passages that follow, we discuss these four classes of construct in more depth.

Temperament

Dimensions of childhood temperament (e.g., negative affectivity, extraversion/surgency, and effortful control; Rothbart & Jones, 1998) map onto adult personality dimensions (e.g., neuroticism, extraversion, and conscientiousness), overlapping substantially with self-report scales for EI. Complexes of various biological and cognitive processes support such dimensions, the adaptive consequences of which are intricate and multifaceted (Matthews et al., 2002). For example, distress-prone children have difficulties in interacting with the caregiver, but vulnerability to distress may also attract the caregiver's attention and promote risk avoidance. Similarly, neuroticism (or negative affectivity) in adults confers a mixture of costs and benefits (Matthews et al., 2002). Temperamental factors are critical for emotional functioning, but they are not in themselves abilities.

Information Processing

Factors that define aptitudes for processing emotional stimuli may contribute to emotional competence. For example, there appears to be a factor for accurate emotion perception defined by objective tests, including the JACBART, RAFL, and Emotional Stroop (Reid et al., 2006). Other factors might relate to individual differences in memory, reasoning, and response generation. There is little evidence on whether distinct factors for processing emotive stimuli exist, but, if so, they would constitute true abilities. A general factor for such abilities might correspond to fluid intelligence in the abilities domain. However, the adaptive value of such factors remains to be explored; it is unclear that, for example, rapid processing of positive stimuli and slow processing of negative stimuli is necessarily beneficial.

Emotional Self-Confidence

A novel aspect of EI research is the assessment of beliefs that one can manage emotion and interpersonal encounters: that is, self-reported confidence in regulating one's own emotional states and in dealing with emotive situations. Emotional self-confidence may be at the core of second-generation questionnaires such as that of Petrides and Furnham (2003), which separate such qualities from traditional personality measures. Thus, the construct is akin to self-rated intelligence. At the process level, we might compare it to allied self-knowledge such as self-esteem and self-efficacy. As such, self-confidence is likely to be more dependent on learning within specific contexts than is temperament (see Bandura, 1999). Like self-esteem, high emotional self-confidence may be predominantly adaptive, but with a "dark side" (Baumeister, Smart, & Boden, 1996), which may take the form of narcissism, denial of problems, and excessive self-enhancement.

TABLE 13.4 Multiple Types of Construct That May Contribute to Emotional Competence

Construct	Possible Current Measure	Equivalent in IQ Research	Key Processes	Adaptive Significance	Developmental Influences
Temperament	Scales for Big Five EQ-i (Bar-On, 1997)	None	Neural and cognitive processes controlling arousal, attention, and reinforcement sensitivity	Mixed: most temperamental factors confer a mixture of costs and benefits	Genetics and early learning
Information processing	JACBART, Emotional Stroop, RAFL	Choice RT, inspection time, working memory	Specific processing modules	Uncertain: Is speed of processing necessarily adaptive?	Genetics and early learning
Emotional self-confidence	SSRI subcomponents Petrides-Furnham	Self-assessed intelligence	Self-concept and self-regulation	Predominantly but not exclusively positive: presumed similar to self-esteem	Learning and socialization: e.g., mastery experiences, modeling, direct reinforcement (in emotive contexts)
Emotional knowledge and skills	MSCEIT	Gc and/or Gk	Multiple acquired procedural and declarative skills	Adaptive within context for learning: may be irrelevant or counterproductive in other contexts	Learning, socialization, and training of specific skills and knowlege

Emotional Knowledge

Emotional competence may also relate to acquired, contextualized skills for handling specific encounters or problems, such as calming a friend who is upset. As with cognitive skills, such emotional skills may be numerous and highly specialized for specific problems. Similarly, depending on level of practice and the stimulus-response mapping (varied or consistent), skills vary on an explicit-implicit continuum. Implicit skills perhaps resemble crystallized intelligence, whereas explicit skills might correspond to Ackerman's (1996) *Gk*, that is, declarative knowledge of emotional matters. It is likely that the understanding and management of emotions branches of the MSCEIT assess explicit skills, while implicit skills are poorly assessed by existing EI tests. Generally, increased knowledge is adaptive, but it may transfer poorly across different situations or contexts.

Conclusions and Future Directions

In the case of intelligence, the top-down approach of seeking a single general factor was ultimately successful, certainly in the context of modern multistratum models of human cognitive abilities (Carroll, 1993). However, the analysis herein suggests that emotional competence may be a more elusive and multifaceted construct than cognitive competence and, consequently, attempts to identify a general factor directly may not succeed. Instead, researchers should focus on developing measures with acceptable content validity for each of the various domains identified herein. Such efforts may support a bottom-up approach of testing the multistratum models that may (or may not) include a general factor of EI. However, at this early stage of research, it is unknown whether we require a pyramid of emotional constructs with EI at the top, twin peaks for IQ and EI, or some more complex structure with no general factor for emotion. It may also be simplistic to locate EI at the center of positive psychology. Some of the various EI constructs we have discriminated relate more to negative qualities such as the absence of stress, anxiety, and depression than they do to positive well-being. Indeed, in the wider context of how people deal with emotional life challenges, it may be somewhat artificial to separate positive and negative experiences (Lazarus 2003; Matthews & Zeidner, 2003).

One of the most promising avenues for test development may come from experimental paradigms derived from the literature on emotions, in line with Cronbach's (1957) call to integrate experimental and individual differences. Aside from sampling emotion recognition in voices and faces and the Emotional Stroop, future experimental paradigms might include variations on the Wisconsin card-sorting task utilizing emotional stimuli (Heaton, 1981), variations on perceptual speed tasks utilizing emotional stimuli (e.g., finding and circling sad faces among an array of sad, scared, and angry faces), or variations on implicit memory and retrieval tasks utilizing emotional stimuli. In concert with item development specialists, studies employing versions of these paradigms inside multivariate designs will likely prove profitable to EI research in the immediate future (Kyllonen & Roberts, 2003). Indeed, at this writing, multivariate studies along these lines were being either conducted or planned at each of the authors' host institutions.

Development of stronger psychometric models must proceed in parallel with theory development. As with personality constructs, a richer understanding of emotional competence resides in processes subsumed by qualitatively different levels of description (i.e., neural functioning, information processing, and high-level cognition, especially that related to ascertaining the personal meaning of social encounters). Thus, further progress requires the integration of various subfields of emotion. The different types of construct identified here may be linked developmentally. Zeidner, Matthews, Roberts, and McCann (2003) reviewed evidence suggesting that temperament shapes emotional skill acquisition, which in turn may influence self-aware understanding of emotion. Again, insights from multiple branches of psychology are required, encompassing the influence of child-caregiver interaction on neural development, emotional socialization and learning processes, and self-directed development as the child becomes increasingly autonomous.

Advances in both assessment and theory are needed to reap whatever practical benefits may accrue from a better understanding of individual differences in competence. Currently, gusto for promoting emotional competence in real-world settings exceeds the contribution to psychological science made by EI. In occupational psychology, inflated claims that the predictive validity of "EQ" exceeds that of IQ remain unsubstantiated by data. Indeed, although EI may predict well-being at work (Slaski & Cartwright, 2002), there is little evidence that current tests predict any objective index of work performance with ability and personality controlled (Zeidner, Matthews, & Roberts, 2004).

In the educational context, Zins, Weissberg, Wang, and Walberg (2004) define social-emotional learning (SEL) as teaching children to be self-aware, socially cognizant, able to make responsible decisions, and competent in self-management and relationship-management skills. These authors describe instructional techniques that promote SEL. They also emphasize that person-centered approaches are insufficient; the learning environment must also be supportive of SEL. Programs instantiating these principles have a good record of success: Greenberg et al. (2003) reviewed meta-analyses suggesting beneficial outcomes on mental health, antisocial behaviors, and academic performance and learning.

Given such successes, one is tempted to ask what recent conceptions of EI can add to existing work. In fact, it seems that educational programs are prone to capitalize on enthusiasm for EI, although the interventions are directed toward specific skills, for example, for conflict-resolution or impulse control, rather than some general competence (see Zeidner, Roberts, Matthews, 2002, for a review). Research has not addressed the key issue of whether it is more cost effective to train for some general competence, or to focus on specific skills.

Supposing general competencies exist, the practical techniques of choice depend critically on which conception of competence is adopted. The different conceptions identified here can loosely be divided into those primarily dependent on gene-environment interaction in early childhood (temperament, information processing) and those that, although potentially influenced by such constitutional factors, are most directly influenced by learning and socialization (emotional self-confidence, specific skills, and knowledge). In principle, temperament and basic information-processing competences might be altered in infancy and early childhood. However, without an adaptive analysis, there is little basis for choosing to do so. We might be able to train faster recognition of emotion in faces, for example, but would this ability really help the child, or society at large? Similarly, we might wonder if it is desirable for children to be raised to be insensitive to distress. Work on older children and adults may be better directed toward investigating aptitude æ treatment interactions (Snow, 1978) that allow people to make best use of their emotional dispositions and aptitudes.

By contrast, emotional self-confidence, declarative knowledge, and procedural skills may be trained at any stage of life, given the active cooperation of the learner. Again, an adaptive analysis is needed to tell us whether social resources should be allocated to such an enterprise. We might train emotional self-confidence by assisting the person through learning experiences that build a sense of mastery. Generally, this seems like a worthy goal, but is there a danger of also building narcissism, inflated self-worth, and indifference to personal flaws and limitations? Training procedural and declarative emotional knowledge appears to be safe, but, as with any skill, the person also requires insight into its range of applicability.

To conclude, the hyperbolic claims made in the early days of emotional intelligence study are verifiably false. The first wave of EI research has had some success at a "proof-of-concept" level, in showing that there exist interesting personal qualities that may add to our existing understanding of ability and personality, in both theory and practice. At the same time, we have noted various difficulties in validating the various assessment instruments that have been developed. For further progress, the next wave of research requires a multifactorial conception of emotional competence, without assuming the existence of a broad EI or EQ factor analogous to general cognitive intelligence. Discriminating factors related to temperament, information processing, emotional self-confidence, and emotional knowledge provides a coherent rationale for mapping the factor space of individual differences in emotional functioning. It is also essential to focus more on the person-situation transaction and contextual moderators of individual difference factors. Such research may lead us to more effective practical interventions, but only time and further research will tell us whether training EI offers any advantage over training specific skills.

Notes

The ideas expressed in this chapter are those of the authors and not necessarily those of the Educational Testing Service.

1. Whether or not this assertion is correct, under all circumstances, should perhaps be tested using simulations. Suffice to say the logic has been articulated by MacCann et al. (2004) thus: "The most basic property of consensus scoring (that the majority are correct, and therefore receive the most credit) is set on a 'collision course' with a basic fact about test reliability (that in internally consistent tests, high-ability people correctly answering one item are also likely to correctly answer other items), ensuring that test scores cannot be both normally distributed and reliable" (p. 659).

References

Ackerman, P. L. (1996). A theory of adult intellectual development: Process, personality, interests, and knowledge. *Intelligence, 22,* 227–257.

American Educational Research Association, American Psychological Association, & National Council on Measurement in Education. (1999). *Standards for educational and psychological testing.* Washington, DC: American Psychological Association.

Anastasi, A., & Urbina, S. (1997). *Psychological testing* (7th ed.). Princeton, NJ: Prentice Hall.

Bachman, J., Stein, S., Campbell, K., & Sitarenios, G. (2000). Emotional intelligence in the collection of debt. *International Journal of Selection and Assessment, 8,* 176–182.

Bandura, A. (1999). Self-efficacy: Toward a unifying theory of behavioral change. In R. F. Baumeister (Ed.), *The self in social psychology* (pp. 285–298). Philadelphia: Psychology Press.

Bar-On, R. (1997). *Bar-on Emotional Quotient Inventory (EQ-i): Technical manual.* Toronto: Multi-Health Systems.

Bar-On, R. (2000). Emotional and social intelligence: Insights from the Emotional Quotient Inventory. In R. Bar-On & J. D. A. Parker (Eds.), *The handbook of emotional intelligence* (pp. 363–388). San Francisco: Jossey-Bass.

Baumeister, R. F., Smart, L., & Boden, J. M. (1996). Relation of threatened egotism to violence and aggression: The dark side of high self-esteem. *Psychological Review, 103,* 5–33.

Bowman, D., Markham, P. M., & Roberts, R. D. (2002). Expanding the frontier of human cognitive abilities: So much more than (plain) *g! Learning and Individual Differences, 13,* 127–158.

Boyatzis, R. E., Goleman, D., & Rhee, K. (2000). Clustering competence in emotional intelligence: Insights from the Emotional Competence Inventory. In R. Bar-On & J. D. A. Parker (Eds.), *Handbook of emotional intelligence* (pp. 343–362). San Francisco: Jossey-Bass.

Brackett, M. A., & Mayer, J. D. (2003). Convergent, discriminant, and incremental validity of competing measures of emotional intelligence. *Personality and Social Psychology Bulletin, 29,* 1147–1158.

Campbell, D. T., & Fiske, D. (1959). Convergent and discriminant validation by the multitrait-multimethod matrix. *Psychological Bulletin, 56,* 81–104.

Carroll, J. B. (1993). *Human cognitive abilities: A survey of factor-analytic studies.* New York: Cambridge University Press.

Ciarrochi, J., Chan, A., & Caputi, P. (2000). A critical evaluation of the emotional intelligence construct. *Personality and Individual Differences, 28,* 539–561.

Cronbach, L. J. (1957). The two disciplines of scientific psychology. *American Psychologist, 12,* 671–684.

Davies, M., Stankov, L., & Roberts, R. D. (1998). Emotional intelligence: In search of an elusive construct. *Journal of Personality and Social Psychology, 75,* 989–1015.

Davis, M. H., & Kraus, L. A. (1997). Personality and empathic accuracy. In W. Ickes, W. John, et al. (Eds.), *Empathic accuracy* (pp.144–168). New York: Guilford.

Dawda, D., & Hart, S. D. (2000). Assessing emotional intelligence: Reliability and validity of the Bar-On Emotional Quotient Inventory (EQ-i) in university students. *Personality and Individual Differences, 28,* 797–812.

Derksen, J., Kramer, I., & Katzko, M. (2002). Does a self-report measure for emotional intelligence assess something different than general intelligence? *Personality and Individual Differences, 32,* 37–48.

Dunning, D., Johnson, K., Ehrlinger, J., & Kruger, J. (2003). Why people fail to recognize their own incompetence. *Current Directions in Psychological Science, 12,* 83–87.

Goleman, D. P. (1998). *Working with emotional intelligence.* New York: Bantam Books.

Greenberg, M. T., Weissberg, R. P., O'Brien, M.U., Zins, J. E., Fredericks, L., Resnik, H., et al. (2003). Enhancing school-based prevention and youth development through coordinated social, emotional, and academic learning. *American Psychologist, 58,* 466–474.

Guttman, L., & Levy, S. (1991). Two structural laws for intelligence tests. *Intelligence, 15,* 79–103.

Heaton, R. K. (1981) *Wisconsin Card Sorting Test manual.* Odessa, FL: Psychological Assessment Resources.

Izard, C. E. (2001). Emotional intelligence or adaptive emotions. *Emotion, 1,* 249–257.

Kyllonen, P. C., & Roberts, R. D. (2003). Cognitive processes assessment. In R. Fernandez-Ballesteros (Ed.), *Encyclopedia of psychological assessment* (Vol. 1). London: Sage.

Kyllonen, P. C., Roberts, R. D., & Stankov, L. (Eds.). (2006). *Extending intelligence: Enhancement and new constructs*. Mahwah, NJ: Erlbaum.

Lazarus, R. S. (2003). Does the positive psychology movement have legs? *Psychological Inquiry, 14,* 93–109.

Lopes, P. N., Salovey, P., & Strauss, R. (2003). Emotional intelligence, personality, and the perceived quality of social relationships. *Personality and Individual Differences, 35,* 641–658.

MacCann, C., Matthews, G., Zeidner, M., & Roberts, R. D. (2003). Psychological assessment of emotional intelligence: A review of self-report and performance-based testing. *International Journal of Organizational Assessment, 11,* 247–274.

MacCann, C., Roberts, R. D., Matthews, G., & Zeidner, M. (2004). Consensus scoring and empirical option weighting of performance-based Emotional Intelligence (EI) tests. *Personality and Individual Differences, 36,* 645–662.

Matthews, G., & Zeidner, M. (2000). Emotional intelligence, adaptation to stressful encounters and health outcomes. In R. Bar-On & J. D. A. Parker (Eds.), *Handbook of emotional intelligence* (pp. 459–489). San Francisco: Jossey-Bass.

Matthews, G., & Zeidner, M. (2003). Negative appraisals of positive psychology: A mixed-valence endorsement of Lazarus. *Psychological Inquiry, 14,* 137–143.

Matthews, G., Zeidner, M., & Roberts, R. D. (2002). *Emotional intelligence: Science and myth.* Cambridge, MA: MIT Press.

Mayer, J. D., Caruso, D. R., & Salovey, P. (2000). Selecting a measure of emotional intelligence: The case for ability scales. In R. Bar-On & J. D. A. Parker (Eds.), *Handbook of emotional intelligence* (pp. 320–342). San Francisco: Jossey-Bass.

Mayer, J. D., Salovey, P., & Caruso, D. R. (2002). *Mayer-Salovey-Caruso Emotional Intelligence Test (MSCEIT) user's manual.* Toronto: Multi-Health Systems.

Mayer, J. D., Salovey, P., Caruso, D. R., & Sitarenios, G. (2003). Modeling and measuring emotional intelligence with the MSCEIT V2.0. *Emotion, 3,* 97–105.

McCrae, R. R. (2000). Emotional intelligence from the perspective of the five-factor model of personality. In R. Bar-On & J. D. A. Parker (Eds.), *Handbook of emotional intelligence* (pp. 263–276). San Francisco: Jossey-Bass.

Newsome, S., Day, A. L., & Catano, V. M. (2000). Assessing the predictive validity of emotional intelligence. *Personality and Individual Differences, 29,* 1005–1016.

Paulhus, D. L., Lysy, D. C., & Yik, M. S. M. (1998). Self-report measures of intelligence: Are they useful proxies as IQ tests? *Journal of Personality, 66,* 525–554.

Petrides, K. V., & Furnham, A. (2000). On the dimensional structure of emotional intelligence. *Personality and Individual Differences, 29,* 313–320.

Petrides, K. V., & Furnham, A. (2001). Trait emotional intelligence: Psychometric investigation with reference to established trait taxonomies. *European Journal of Personality, 15,* 425–448.

Petrides, K. V., & Furnham, A. (2003). Trait emotional intelligence: Behavioral validation in two studies of emotion recognition and reactivity to mood induction. *European Journal of Personality, 17,* 39–57.

Reid, J., O'Brien, K., Roberts, R. D., MacCann, C., Rouse, J. R., Matthews, G., et al. (2006). *Out with the old and in with the new? Emotional intelligence may meet traditional standards required of "intelligence"!* Manuscript in preparation.

Roberts, R. D. (2003). Emotional intelligence: Pop psychology or new construct? *Contemporary Psychology: APA Review of Books, 48,* 853–855.

Roberts, R. D., Markham, P. M., Zeidner, M., & Matthews, G. (2005). Assessing intelligence: Past, present, and future. In O. Wilhelm & R. Engle (Eds.), *Understanding and measuring intelligence,* pp. 333–360. Thousand Oaks, CA: Sage.

Roberts, R. D., Zeidner, M., & Matthews, G. (2001). Does emotional intelligence meet traditional standards for an intelligence? Some new data and conclusions. *Emotion, 1,* 196–231.

Rothbart, M. K., & Jones, L. B. (1998). Temperament, self-regulation, and education. *School Psychology Review, 27,* 479–491.

Rozell, E. J., Pettijohn, C. E., & Parker, R. S. (2002). An empirical evaluation of emotional intelligence: The impact on management development. *Journal of Management Development, 21,* 272–289.

Saklofske, D. H., Austin, E. J., & Minski, P. S. (2003). Factor structure and validity of a trait emotional intelligence measure. *Personality and Individual Differences, 34,* 707–721.

Sala, F. (2002). *Emotional Competence Inventory: Technical manual.* Hay Group, McClelland Center for Research and Innovation. Retrieved March 31, 2003, from http://www.eiconsortium.org/research/ECI_Tech_Manual.pdf

Salovey, P., Mayer, J. D., & Caruso, D. (2002). The positive psychology of emotional intelligence. In

C. R. Snyder & S. J. Lopez (Eds.), *Handbook of positive psychology* (pp. 159–171). London: Oxford University Press.

Schmidt, F. L., & Hunter, J. E. (1998). The validity and utility of selection methods in personnel psychology: Practical and theoretical implications of 85 years of research findings. *Psychological Bulletin, 124,* 262–274.

Schutte, N. S., Malouff, J. M., Hall, L. E., Haggerty, D. J., Cooper, J. T., Golden, C. J., et al. (1998). Development and validation of a measure of emotional intelligence. *Personality and Individual Differences, 25,* 167–177.

Slaski, M., & Cartwright, S. (2002). Health, performance and emotional intelligence: An exploratory study of retail managers. *Stress and Health, 18,* 63–68.

Snow, R. E. (1978). Theory and method for research on aptitude processes. *Intelligence, 2,* 225–278.

Thissen, D., & Wainer, H. (Eds.). (2001). *Test scoring.* Mahwah, NJ: Erlbaum.

Trinidad, D. R., & Johnson, C. A. (2002). The association between emotional intelligence and early adolescent tobacco and alcohol use. *Personality and Individual Differences, 32,* 95–105.

van Rooy, D. L., & Viswesvaran, C. (2004). Emotional intelligence: A meta-analytic investigation of predictive validity and nomological net. *Journal of Vocational Behavior, 65,* 71–95.

Zeidner, M., Matthews, G., & Roberts, R. D. (2001) Slow down, you move too fast: Emotional intelligence remains an "elusive" intelligence. *Emotion, 1,* 265–275.

Zeidner, M., Matthews, G., Roberts, R. D., & MacCann, C. (2003). Development of emotional intelligence: Towards a multi-level investment model. *Human Development, 46,* 69–96.

Zeidner, M., Matthews, G., & Roberts, R. D. (2004). Emotional intelligence in the workplace: A critical review. *Applied Psychology: An International Review, 53,* 371–399.

Zeidner, M., Roberts, R. D., & Matthews, G. (2002). Can emotional intelligence be schooled? A critical review. *Educational Psychologist, 37,* 215–231.

Zeidner, M., Shani, I., Matthews, G., & Roberts, R. D. (2005). Emotional intelligence in gifted versus non-gifted students: Outcomes depend on the measure. *Intelligence, 33,* 369–391.

Zins, J. E., Weissberg, R. P., Wang, M. C., & Walberg, H. J. (Eds.). (2004). *Building school success through social and emotional learning: Implications for practice and research.* New York: Teachers College Press.

14

Experimental Approaches to Individual Differences and Change

Exploring the Causes and Consequences of Extraversion

John M. Zelenski

Positive psychologists, like most other people, wish to better understand happiness. While our environments and efforts surely play roles, it is also clear that some people are dispositionally more (or less) prone to happiness. For example, the personality traits of extraversion and neuroticism are among the best predictors of happiness (negatively in the case of neuroticism; Diener & Seligman, 2002; Diener, Suh, Lucas, & Smith, 1999). Nonetheless, naming these traits does not tell us what causes individual differences in happiness. The question remains: What are the processes that underlie the traits of extraversion and neuroticism, or individual differences in happiness? That is, what, specifically, are the stable aspects of personality (e.g., genes, beliefs, etc.) that contribute to behavior and experience across situations, and how do they manifest themselves, in conjunction with changing situations, over time? For example, do extraverts put themselves into more positive environments, or do they respond more positively than introverts while sharing roughly equivalent

environments? In either case, how, at the level of psychological processes, is this accomplished (e.g., differences in attentional biases or emotional responsiveness)?

Understanding the causal processes underlying individual differences provides an attractive goal for research, but also raises significant challenges. Most obviously, individual differences (like extraversion or happiness) are not easily manipulated and, as every psychologist learned in his or her first methods course, manipulation is the key to establishing causality in psychology. These truisms likely contribute to personality research's reliance on purely correlational methods (Mallon, Kingsley, Affleck, & Tennen, 1998), and psychology's reluctance to ascribe causal status to personality effects. Although I do not suggest that researchers should manipulate stable individual differences or personality, I argue that experimental methods (i.e., where the researcher manipulates key situational variables) provide a valuable tool in individual differences research. Moreover, using personality variables to predict short-term change across carefully manipulated, theoretically relevant situations can yield persuasive insights into causal personality processes. That is, even quasi-experimental research (where the individual difference is merely measured) avoids the major causal ambiguities of purely correlational research, and allows defensible arguments about causal processes. Although most of the theories and research I discuss focus on extraversion (i.e., the relationship between extraversion and positive emotions and the causes of extraversion more broadly), the general principles can be fruitfully applied to many individual differences important to positive psychology.

Conceptual Issues

A classic definition of an individual difference variable would note that it is something internal to people, is generally stable over time, is consistent across situations, and allows us to make distinctions among individuals (i.e., describes a dimension along which people differ, or a between-subjects variable). For example, people with high subjective well-being consistently evaluate their lives more positively than people with low subjective well-being. However, as the content of this book clearly demonstrates, individual difference variables are not necessarily unchanging over time and can also include proclivities to predictable variation. In other words, absolute stability and consistency are not necessary criteria. For example, when considering the individual difference variable of affect intensity (Larsen & Diener, 1987), the "stable" aspect describes a tendency to greater change (i.e., the tendency to experience exaggerated changes in emotional state). Nonetheless, individual difference variables are stable and consistent in that the theoretical constructs are traitlike, rather than statelike (i.e., the tendency toward a type of variation is stable). In other words, variation in behavior and experience is partly the result of stable individual differences in what people bring to different situations. Whether this stable component originates from genes or experience (or some combination of both), it is almost certainly instantiated in the brain, and is theoretically separable from situational demands.

Even when variability or change is not a salient feature of individual difference variables (e.g., classic traits), the nomological networks surrounding these variables specify circumstances associated with changes in behavior. For example, we expect extraverts to be more jovial than introverts at parties, but we also expect to see a much smaller difference in joviality during final exams. The idea of nomological networks was introduced by Cronbach and Meehl (1955) as an aid to understanding and establishing construct validity for psychological tests. A test has good construct validity if a body of empirical evidence suggests that the test measures what it purports to measure. Nomological networks define the parameters of this evidence. That is, a test's designer must specify the relationships among conceptual variables (e.g., extraversion, joviality, and social situations) and their associated observable variables (i.e., the specific measurement instruments or situations), and these relationships form the nomological network. A test's construct validity is established when data are consistent with this nomological network.

Psychologists often develop tests for individual difference variables that are very difficult, if not impossible, to manipulate, such as personality characteristics. Because of this, the research traditions surrounding these variables tend to utilize correlational (i.e., nonexperimental) methods that examine statistical associations among variables, but do not include manipulations. (Consider that personality psychology's primary, or at least most publicized, contribution is the purely structural five-factor model.) This split between methodological approaches (correlational vs. experimental) was lamented long ago by Cronbach (1957), and he argued for the importance of combining experimental methods with correlational methods (see also Eysenck, 1995). More specifically, combining stable individual measures with situational manipulations is important in establishing a construct's nomological network, that is, establishing a test's validity. For example, one might test the nomological network alluded to above by measuring extraversion and joviality while manipulating the immediate environment to resemble partylike or examlike situations. In other words, a full nomological network requires propositions about the relationships among individual differences, characteristics, and situational effects (including the ways persons and situations interact). Said another way, testing the if-then relationships among variables (i.e., short-term change) provides especially compelling demonstrations of construct validity (cf. Mischel & Shoda, 1998). Experimental methods that manipulate relevant situational features provide a unique tool for establishing the construct validity of individual differences measures.

It might seem odd to include a discussion of construct validity here as this chapter is not particularly concerned with test development. However, while few would doubt the need to establish a measure's construct validity, the majority (but certainly not entirely) of current personality research correlates one-time, self-report questionnaires with each another (Mallon et al., 1998). Revisiting the idea of construct validity highlights the need for theories of causal personality processes (i.e., the nomological network), and, more important, tests of these processes. Taking a broad view, virtually all psychological research could be described as exploring nomological networks. That is, it explores the relationships among theoretical constructs (e.g., stereotypes and moods) by observing the relationships among indicators of those constructs (e.g., response times to categorize words and a particular mood manipulation). Just as experimental methods are used to test the nomological networks (i.e., causal theories) in cognitive and social psychology, personality and positive psychologists can use experimental methods to illuminate the processes underlying individual differences. That is, research that tests nomological networks also tests the causal theories contained in those networks, regardless of whether or not each node in the network can be manipulated. Experimental methods provide a particularly useful tool for exploring the causal links in these networks.

Past reliance on correlational methods may help explain empirically minded psychologists' ambivalence about ascribing causal status to personality variables. We have all repeated many times the warning contained in most undergraduate psychology textbooks, "correlation does not imply causation." Since we cannot manipulate personality, it follows that the results of individual differences research cannot imply causation. While this is necessarily true of most personality studies, personality's contributions to behavior must, in some way, reflect causal processes, even if we are unable to manipulate personality in the laboratory. Experimental methods may bring us closer to defensible causal theories of personality. That is, it is possible to manipulate key situational variables predicted to interact with individual difference variables. To the extent that these predictions reflect theories about the causes of

personality variables, such quasi-experimental methods approximate tests of causality. For example, Revelle and colleagues have tested the idea that the dimension of extraversion results from individual differences in arousal by giving caffeine to their subjects (Revelle, Amaral, & Turriff, 1976; Revelle, Humphreys, Simon, & Gilliland, 1980). Because caffeine clearly interacts with the proposed causal mechanism underlying extraversion (differences in arousal), causal interpretations of the results seem reasonable.

Although the inability to manipulate personality necessitates caveats surrounding these causal interpretations, a closer examination of the methodological strengths and limitations in experimental personality research may help mitigate the degree to which such caveats substantially alter conclusions. Purely correlational approaches typically suffer from ambiguity about the direction of any potential causal relationships. For example, knowing that extraversion and subjective well-being correlate does not tell us whether the trait of extraversion causes people to be happier or whether people who are happy tend to act more extraverted. In much experimental research, this "directionality problem" ceases to be a problem at all. For example, consider studies where individual difference variables are used to predict short-term change in response to a manipulation (a within-subject manipulation) or differences between two groups (between-subjects manipulation) exposed to different manipulations (e.g., extraversion predicting joviality in a "party" condition compared to an "exam" condition). Assuming a reasonably valid individual difference assessment, it seems silly to suggest that temporary experience or behavior could cause the stable individual difference characteristic in this situation (i.e., increased joviality in the lab could not cause the stable trait of extraversion). Instead, the experience or behavior is clearly the result of some interaction between the specific (manipulated) situation and the (assessed) stable characteristics of research participants, and therefore the direction of personality's effect is clear.[1] Administering the individual differences assessment prior to the manipulation adds further certainty to this claim, as manipulations cannot influence measurements that preceded them. In short, experimental personality research typically resolves the directionality problem by drawing on the common understanding of the state versus trait distinction. An instance of behavior or experience does not cause the stable aspects of individual differences.

Unfortunately, the classic "third-variable problem" in individual differences research is not as easily dismissed. That is, researchers can never be sure that associations between behavior and the individual difference variable they measured are not due to a highly correlated individual difference variable that they did not measure. Although this ambiguity seems intractable, it is not especially unique to individual differences research. The third-variable problem mirrors ambiguities in purely experimental research, research where few would argue with the legitimacy of causal assertions. That is, even purely experimental studies face the issue of internal validity (see Brewer, 2000; Smith, 2000). Because psychologists are typically interested in intangible theoretical constructs (e.g., stress, motivation, processing fluency, etc.), manipulations and stimulus materials are not isomorphic with these constructs, and thus it is possible that some closely related construct was actually manipulated. That is, practical limitations often prevent psychologists from cleanly manipulating a single construct of interest, raising the possibility that a third variable actually caused any observed changes in behavior. Clever designs, random assignment to conditions, and conceptual replications (i.e., using different manipulations of the same underlying construct) make third-variable explanations increasingly implausible in purely experimental research, and thus causal explanations are readily accepted.

Many of the tools used to exclude third-variable explanations in purely experimental research can similarly be applied to individual differences research. For example, using alternative individual difference assessment techniques (e.g., multiple self-report instruments, peer reports, physiological indicators, behavioral observations, performance-based tests, projective techniques, etc.) is roughly akin to conceptual replications in purely experimental research. That is, replicating an individual differences effect with a new measure helps rule out some alternative third-variable explanations. Alternatively, researchers can attempt to assess potential third variables (i.e., the highly correlated individual differences) and comparatively test their predictive ability. Additionally, some third variables may be less like problems and more like opportunities to discover shared underlying processes. Of course none of these options presents a perfect solution to potential

third-variable problems in individual differences research. Both purely experimental and experimental personality research depends on the accumulation of results from different studies using different measures and manipulations to make causal explanations increasingly convincing. Even though a single experimental personality study cannot isolate a particular individual difference with complete confidence, it can explicate process explanations linking situational variation in experience with stable individual differences.

In sum, the challenges faced by experimental individual differences research mirror those faced by purely experimental work, and thus the causal inferences it generates can be regarded with similar veracity. The following section provides an example of this kind of research, that is, testing a temperamental explanation of extraversion's link with positive emotions.

Linking Extraversion With Positive Emotions

Extraversion is somewhat atypical compared to other broad traits (e.g., those in the five-factor model of personality; see John & Srivastava, 1999) in that it already has a long tradition of causal theories and experimental research. A review of this literature goes far beyond the scope of this chapter, and such reviews already exist (e.g., Matthews & Gilliland, 1999). Among the most consistent findings is that extraversion predicts subjective well-being (happiness) and positive emotional experience. Nonetheless, knowing that this correlation exists tells us little about the processes that produce it.

McCrae and Costa (1991) outlined two broad approaches that describe causal links between personality and emotion. In the *temperamental view*, people who possess a given trait are more likely to experience certain kinds of emotions because of internal factors. That is, the person's temperament has a direct influence on the way experience leads to emotions. For example, according to the temperamental view, extraverts might experience more positive emotions because they are more likely to attend to positive information in the environment, more likely to interpret ambiguous information as positive, or simply are more reactive to positive sensations or experience. Although the temperamental view encompasses many potential processes (e.g., attention, interpretation, reactivity), they all directly influence the personality-emotion link. Potential mediators in these processes are all internal, whether emotional (reactivity) or cognitive (interpretation or attention). The temperamental aspects of people's emotional experience depend less on the situations they are in and more on what they bring to each situation. In this view, personality, and the processes it includes, moderates the influence of situations or events on experience (Judge & Larsen, 2001).

In contrast, the *instrumental view* suggests that personality's influence on emotions is indirect. For example, extraverts may spend more time in social situations, and these situations might be more likely to cause positive emotions as compared to nonsocial situations. In other words, being in social situations makes everyone happy; extraverts simply do it more (see Fleeson, Malanos, & Achille, 2002, for a similar argument). Another instrumental explanation might suggest that because the trait of extraversion is valued by most societies, people scoring high on extraversion receive more positive interpersonal feedback or opportunities for success. Although many instrumental explanations are possible, they all emphasize causal processes with indirect links between personality and emotion. In the instrumental view, the way people self-select situations or the way situations (including other people) react to different personality characteristics is more important than other internal (temperamental) sources of variation. In all instrumental explanations, the causal path between personality and emotion involves an external mediator.

Although the examples above have focused on extraversion, the distinction between temperamental and instrumental views can be extended to many individual differences. McCrae and Costa (1991) addressed the relationships between happiness and extraversion, neuroticism, conscientiousness, and agreeableness, suggesting that extraversion's and neuroticism's influences were temperamental and conscientiousness's and agreeableness's influences were instrumental. However, because their data were correlational, McCrae and Costa's intriguing suggestions remained speculative until experimental work provided empirical support. Nonetheless, distinguishing between temperamental and instrumental views begins to suggest different kinds of personality processes, a useful step in planning experimental personality research.

A specific temperamental process linking extraversion and positive emotions is suggested by Gray's (1981, 1994; Pickering, Corr, & Gray, 1999) reinforcement sensitivity theory of personality. Based primarily on animal research, Gray posited a behavioral activation system (BAS) in the brain that is sensitive to reward cues in the environment and responds by instigating approach behavior and positive affect. A functionally independent system, the behavioral inhibition system (BIS), responds to punishment cues in the environment by inhibiting ongoing behavior and generating negative affect. Said another way, the BAS mediates appetitive motivation, and the BIS mediates aversive motivation. Gray links these brain systems to personality by suggesting that individual differences in the strengths of the BAS and BIS account for the personality variables of extraversion and neuroticism. Gray has suggested that the traits of extraversion and neuroticism do not correspond directly to BAS and BIS (i.e., they are slight rotations in the same two-dimensional conceptual space). Nonetheless, extraversion is clearly more strongly linked with the BAS and neuroticism is clearly more strongly linked with the BIS (Pickering et al., 1999).

In essence, Gray provides a causal theory of extraversion. Specifically, extraverts behave in extraverted ways because they are more sensitive to reward cues (often available in social situations), and their reward sensitivity results from physiological differences in BAS functioning. To the extent that differences in BAS functioning underlie extraversion, Gray's theory also helps explain why extraverts report higher levels of happiness (i.e., due to their more frequent and intense reward experiences). To test Gray's theory and the temperamental explanation linking personality and happiness more generally, we conducted a study that utilized both correlational and experimental methods (further details can be found in Zelenski & Larsen, 1999). It examined the correlations among measures of extraversion, BAS, and positive emotional experience, and then used these personality measures to predict reactions to a laboratory mood manipulation. A final phase of the study linked this laboratory manipulation with real-world emotional experience using the experience sampling method (ESM; see Scollon, Kim-Prieto, & Diener, 2003).

Participants completed several personality questionnaires designed to measure constructs similar to extraversion, neuroticism, BAS, and BIS. Additional impulsivity scales were also included because Gray has used this term to describe the trait that might result from individual differences in BAS functioning (i.e., impulsivity rather than extraversion per se). Specific scales were the Eysenck Personality Questionnaire (EPQ; see Eysenck, Eysenck, & Barrett, 1985), the Temperament and Character Inventory (TCI; see Cloninger, Svrakic, & Przybeck, 1993), the Generalized Reward and Punishment Expectancy Scales (GRAPES; Ball & Zuckerman, 1990), BIS/BAS Scales (Carver & White, 1994), and the I7 Impulsivity Questionnaire (Eysenck, Pearson, Easting, & Allsopp, 1985).

As an initial (correlational) test of Gray's theory, we submitted all the above scales to a principle axis factor analysis with a varimax rotation. If, at the theoretical level, BAS and BIS underlie the traits of extraversion and neuroticism, we should observe a high degree of covariation among independent measures of these constructs (the scales). In other words, BAS-related scales (e.g., reward expectancy, reward responsiveness) should correlate highly with the extraversion scale, and BIS-related scales should correlate highly with the neuroticism scale. The factor analysis suggested that this was indeed the case. Three factors emerged and accounted for 49% of the variance. These factors clearly represented reward sensitivity (high loadings for extraversion and BAS scales), punishment sensitivity (high loadings for neuroticism and BIS scales), and impulsivity (high loadings for psychoticism and impulsivity measures). The emergence of this third factor suggests that impulsivity is a poor name for BAS functioning. This conclusion was further supported when the factors were correlated with the trait version of the Positive and Negative Affect Schedule (PANAS; see Watson, Clark, & Tellegen, 1988). Reward sensitivity was highly correlated with trait-positive affect ($r = .69$), but not negative affect ($r = -.20$), and punishment sensitivity was correlated with trait-negative affect ($r = .46$), but not trait-positive affect ($r = -.14$). Impulsivity was not significantly correlated with either affect scale. In sum, the pattern of correlations (including the factor analysis) was very consistent with the idea that a strong BAS underlies the trait of extraversion and a strong BIS underlies the trait of neuroticism. Similar findings have been reported by others (Elliot & Thrash, 2002; Gable, Reis, & Elliot, 2003; Zuckerman, Joireman, Kraft, & Kuhlman, 1999).

Given these findings, we can suggest that the reason extraverts report higher subjective well-being is that they are more responsive to reward cues in the environment (i.e., because extraversion correlated with BAS scales). Still, with only this correlational data, this suggestion remains weak. Other more elaborate correlational techniques and more comprehensive sampling can add strength to this suggestion. For example, Lucas, Diener, Grob, Suh, and Shao (2000) used structural equation modeling with data collected from 39 different cultures, and found that reward sensitivity (as opposed to other facets such as sociability) formed the core of extraversion across different cultures. Such data clearly strengthen the suggestion that something like a strong BAS underlies the trait of extraversion. However, experimental methods add another unique tool for testing this proposition and testing the temperamental view more generally.

According to the temperamental view, extraversion will have a direct influence on emotional experience. In other words, there is something stable within the person (e.g., a strong BAS) that causes different people to react to the same situation with more or less intense emotions. In another phase of the study introduced above, we tested the temperamental view of extraversion and neuroticism by controlling the situation through experimental mood manipulations (see also Larsen & Ketelaar, 1989, 1991; Rusting & Larsen, 1997). Participants sat in a comfortable chair as positive, negative, and neutral pictures were projected on a screen in front of them. Every participant saw all picture types (i.e., the manipulation was within-subject), but the pictures were blocked into groups of like-valenced images. After viewing each block of images, participants rated how much they were feeling *happy, disgusted, anxious, euphoric, aroused,* and *gloomy* at that moment using a 0–6 scale.

Unsurprisingly, the mood manipulations had significant effects on participants' self-reported emotions. That is, participants reported more intense positive emotions after viewing positive images ($M = 2.86$) as compared to the negative ($M = .38$) or neutral ($M = 2.68$) images. Similarly, participants reported more negative emotions after viewing the negative images ($M = 2.78$) as compared to the positive ($M = .27$) or neutral ($M = .25$) images. Although these findings are important in confirming the efficacy of the mood induction procedure, the more interesting results examine how personality predicts emotional experience across the different mood conditions. Table 14.1 shows the correlations between personality factor scores (impulsivity is omitted, but was unrelated to emotional experience) and self-reported emotions (happy and euphoric are combined as positive affect, and disgusted, anxious, and gloomy are combined as negative affect).

The temperamental view (and Gray's theory) predicts that the reward sensitivity factor will predict positive emotional experience following the positive mood induction, and this prediction is supported ($r = .30$). In other words, even though most participants reported more positive emotions following positive images, this effect was especially large for people scoring high on the extraversion and BAS measures. That is, they received a bigger boost from, or were more reactive to, the attempt to improve their mood. Similarly, the punishment sensitivity factor was expected to predict the magnitude of negative mood induction effect. This prediction was also supported ($r = .48$). Table 14.1 shows that people scoring high on neuroticism and BIS also reported significantly more negative affect following the neutral images. However, even after statistically controlling for this effect, the punishment sensitivity factor predicted greater reactivity following the negative images. That is, even though most participants found the negative images aversive, people scoring high on neuroticism and BIS found them especially disturbing.

TABLE 14.1 Self-Reported Emotional Experience and Personality by Mood Induction Condition

	Reward Sensitivity (Extraversion, BAS)	Punishment Sensitivity (Neuroticism, BIS)
Neutral Induction		
Positive affect	.13	.21
Negative affect	.05	.23*
Positive Induction		
Positive affect	.30**	.08
Negative affect	−.15	.20
Negative Induction		
Positive affect	.06	−.05
Negative affect	.13	.48**

*$p < .05$, **$p < .01$.

These results provide especially strong support for the temperamental explanation linking extraversion and neuroticism to emotional experience (and happiness more generally). The laboratory mood induction procedure ensured that the external situation was identical for all participants. Nonetheless, there was wide variation in how people responded to the mood inductions, and this variation was predicted by the personality measures. Because the situation was equal for everyone (externally), internal (temperamental) factors must account for the observed differences in emotional experience. In other words, personality had a direct effect, and thus the temperamental explanation is supported. Of course, this support for the temperamental view in no way argues against instrumental explanations. It is possible that extraverts also self-select environments more conducive to positive experiences (e.g., Fleeson et al. 2002).

Although we did not test this selection hypothesis directly, a final phase of the study investigated whether individual differences in emotional reactivity could account for happiness in day-to-day life. In other words, it investigated the external validity, or generalizability, of the laboratory findings. The fact that the same personality scales predicted both reactions to the lab mood inductions and questionnaire measures of average emotional experience (the PANAS) certainly suggests that the lab findings will generalize to the real world. On the other hand, Fowles (1987) has suggested that people's self-regulation could lead to divergences between sensitivity to intense emotions and the actual experience of intense emotions over time. Said another way, instrumental influences may contradict temperamental influences. For example, a person who reacts strongly to punishing environments may use this self-knowledge to avoid potentially threatening environments, and thus substantially reduce the experience of negative emotions. It follows that people's responses following a mood manipulation may not predict (or not predict in the same direction) their experience outside the lab. Fowles's suggestion highlights the fact that lab studies' generalizability should not be assumed.

To address the issue of generalizability (external validity), we compared participants' emotional experience in the lab with their day-to-day emotional experience in an experience-sampling phase. Participants were asked to rate their current emotional state three times a day for a month. These ratings were combined to create actual averages (as opposed to the mental averages assessed with one-time self-reports) of self-reported positive and negative emotional experience over the month. We correlated these 1-month averages with the ratings of positive (or negative) affect following the positive (or negative) laboratory mood inductions. Emotional reactivity assessed in the lab significantly correlated with emotions experienced in daily life both for positive ($r = .38$) and negative ($r = .29$) emotions. Therefore, it seems that people who respond with especially intense positive or negative emotions in the lab similarly experience more intense positive or negative emotions in day-to-day life. (The personality measures similarly predicted emotional experience in daily life.) In other words, the lab manipulation results generalize to the real world. Even if people self-regulate in ways that counteract their temperamental influences, these data suggest that such attempts are not entirely successful.

In sum, this study suggests that individual differences in reward and punishment sensitivity (BAS and BIS strength) could cause extraversion and neuroticism and, ultimately, more or less happiness. From a methodological point of view, this study indicates how experimental manipulations can probe psychological processes (e.g., temperamental versus instrumental explanations) in ways that purely correlational methods cannot. Nonetheless, it also demonstrates that combining multiple methods (factor analysis, lab manipulations, experience sampling) provides especially rich data and persuasive causal stories.

A number of other studies have shown extraversion and neuroticism predicting emotional reactivity (Gomez, Cooper, & Gomez, 2000; Gross, Sutton, & Ketelaar, 1998; Hemenover, 2003; Larsen & Ketelaar, 1989, 1991; Rusting & Larsen, 1997; but cf. Lucas & Baird, 2004), and Canli et al. (2001) found that extraversion correlates highly with the degree of amygdala activation (functional magnetic resonance imaging signal) while viewing happy faces. In addition, extraversion and neuroticism predict positive and negative cognitive biases respectively (similar to mood-congruent biases; see Rusting, 1998), further suggesting the importance of positive and negative emotionality to these traits. Other theorists have posited systems or mechanisms similar to Gray's BAS and BIS (e.g., Cloninger et al., 1993; Depue & Collins, 1999)

and these theories come together to suggest a growing consensus that views extraversion and neuroticism as individual differences in approach and avoidance motivation (Carver, Sutton, & Scheier, 2000). Despite the attractiveness of this recent theoretical integration, and a growing collection of supportive data, this relatively new consensus on extraversion largely ignores an older causal theory and the data that support it.

A Closer Look at the Causes of Extraversion

Before Gray had developed the constructs of BAS and BIS, Eysenck (1967, 1990) suggested that extraverts were underaroused compared to introverts. Assuming that there exists an optimal, moderate level of arousal, Eysenck argued that extraverts behave in more social, active, and so on (i.e., extraverted) ways to compensate for chronically low levels of arousal. In other words, extraverts seek out external stimulation to achieve optimal levels of arousal, whereas introverts require very little external stimulation, and risk becoming overaroused under stimulating conditions. Although Eysenck's theory originally identified chronically low levels of arousal as extraversion's cause, subsequent work has refined this idea such that comparatively low arousability in the presence of stimulation (rather than low tonic level) better characterizes extraversion (Stelmack, 1990).

It is worth noting that Eysenck's theory does not provide as direct an explanation for the relationship between extraversion and happiness as Gray's theory, but it is consistent with some of the instrumental examples noted above. For example, in an attempt to raise their general arousal level, extraverts may seek out social situations, and these situations may create more opportunities to experience positive emotions or develop positive relationships that lead to higher levels of overall happiness. Still, Eysenck's theory does not seem capable of explaining the emotional reactivity findings described above. In fact, Eysenck's theory might make the opposite prediction: that extraverts would be expected to respond to the emotional stimulation with a diminished response, that is, be less reactive. Nonetheless, a long tradition of research, much of it employing experimental methods, supports Eysenck's general assertion (Matthews & Gilliland, 1999).

Taken together, Eysenck's and Gray's models of personality provide two different causal process (i.e., low arousal and sensitivity to reward cues) that could underlie the trait of extraversion. By conducting lab studies, we were able to manipulate relevant features of the environment (stimulation and presence of reward cues) and, thus, simultaneously test these two potential causes (see Zelenski & Larsen, 2006 for more details). Participants ($n = 99$) in the study completed a task where clearly positive, negative, and neutral words appeared on a computer screen, and they pressed buttons on a keyboard as quickly as possible to categorize the words as positive, negative, or neutral. The main dependent measure in this task was the response latency, that is, how long it took participants to press a key. Gray's theory predicts that people scoring higher on extraversion (strong BAS) should respond more quickly to positive words (Rusting & Larsen, 1998).[2] That is, their greater reward sensitivity manifests itself in terms of preferential processing of positive information. The valence of the stimuli (words) provides a within-subject manipulation that should interact with the system Gray proposes as extraversion's cause. In other words, speed of processing should change depending on the content of the stimuli, and extraversion should predict this change.

A second within-subject manipulation was designed to tap individual differences in arousability, the central feature of Eysenck's account of extraversion. To this end, each participant actually completed the categorization task twice, once while mentally rehearsing a nine-digit number and once under normal conditions (i.e., no number). Adding this cognitive load (rehearsing the number) significantly increases the task's difficulty, adding external stimulation to the situation (Humphreys & Revelle, 1984). In Eysenck's view, extraverts are less arousable than introverts, so they are expected to perform better (compared to introverts) under conditions of higher stimulation (i.e., the cognitive load). To further clarify the task details, different sets of words were used in each task to reduce practice effects. In addition, the order of these word sets, as well as which set included the cognitive load instructions, was counterbalanced (i.e., some participants received the load instructions first, others second).[3]

Results of this study indicated that the cognitive load manipulation (mentally rehearsing the number) made the task more difficult and presumably more stimulating. That is, overall response times were significantly slower under conditions of cognitive load as compared to conditions of no load (965 msec vs. 885 msec). This finding provides support for the efficacy of the manipulation, but the more interesting findings involve differences in performance related to extraversion. Eysenck's theory predicts that people scoring high on extraversion should perform relatively better (compared to those scoring lower) under conditions of cognitive load. This prediction was supported, with extraversion predicting faster average response times under conditions of load, even when statistically controlling for average response times under conditions of no load ($\beta = -.24$). We replicated this finding in a second study using a nearly identical procedure but different word lists ($\beta = -.19$). Moreover, in both studies, extraversion predicted faster response times under conditions of load regardless of word type (positive, negative, or neutral) and after controlling for self-reported mood state (cf. Gray, 2001). These results provide support for Eysenck's causal theory of extraversion. Introverts' comparatively poor performance under conditions of cognitive load (high stimulation) can be attributed to their overarousal.

Gray's theory also received support from the results of these studies. According to Gray, the valence of the stimuli (as opposed to stimulation from the task) should be important to individual differences in task performance. Consistent with this prediction, the composite extraversion/BAS measure (see the factor analysis above) predicted faster response times to categorize words as positive, and this effect held after controlling for average response times to categorize words as neutral ($\beta = -.16$). However, a second study using a different word list did not find the same significant relationship ($\beta = -.07$, ns). One major difference between the two studies was that one used emotion words (e.g., *happy* and *sad*) where the other used merely valenced words (e.g., *money* and *death*). Extraversion predicted faster responses to the positive emotion words. Of course, other minor variations between the two studies may account for the discrepancy in findings, so the emotion-valence explanation must remain speculative pending further research.

In sum, the response time studies provided support for Eysenck's arousal theory and mixed support for Gray's reward sensitivity theory. However, it is also worth noting that although no data presented here directly contradict either theory, the results highlight problems with both. Specifically, Eysenck's theory fails to predict both the emotional reactivity findings of the mood manipulation study and extraverts' tendency to categorize positive (emotion) words more quickly. Conversely, Gray's theory has a difficult time explaining why extraversion predicted faster responses under conditions of cognitive load, regardless of word valence. In other words, because the two theories posit different mechanisms with different inputs and outputs, supportive evidence for either reveals a shortcoming of the other. Said yet another way, competitive theory testing between Eysenck's and Gray's accounts is difficult because single manipulations do not seem to yield divergent predictions. Nonetheless, experimental methods do allow a more fine-grained analysis of personality processes proposed by Eysenck and Gray. Given that experimental evidence supporting both processes (low arousability and high reward sensitivity) has already accumulated, it seems reasonable to tentatively conclude that both contribute to the trait of extraversion. Broad traits such as extraversion almost certainly encompass multiple underlying processes.

Taking a broader methodological view, these cognitive load studies provide an example of how bringing individual differences research into the lab permits novel assessment techniques. In the study described here, we used the computer tasks to probe the processes underlying extraversion. That is, we used a standard questionnaire assessment of personality and used these questionnaire scores to predict changes in performance (response times) as stimuli and task demands were manipulated. To the extent that theories about the causes of individual difference variables involve differences in cognition (e.g., expertise with different categories of information or associations between categories of information), computer tasks provide relatively easy and powerful tests of those causal theories.[4]

Open Questions and Future Directions

Although I have focused on extraversion, combining experimental methods with individual differences research more generally promises to increase our understanding of causal personality processes. For example, experimental methods are well suited to testing temperamental (as compared to instrumental) explanations linking personality and emotion. Other broad traits, such as agreeableness and conscientiousness, consistently predict happiness. McCrae and Costa (1991) speculated that instrumental explanations account for these relationships (see also Larsen, 2000), but naturalistic (experience sampling) data suggest that emotional reactivity (a temperamental effect) may also contribute (Suls, Martin, & David, 1998). A study using experimental methods, similar to the study described above, would help resolve this issue. In addition, the temperamental-instrumental distinction, and experimental methods' ability to speak to this issue, can apply far beyond the Big Five traits and emotions. For example, do emotionally intelligent people achieve success because they avoid problematic situations (instrumental explanation) or because they respond to those situations differently (temperamental explanation), or both?

This general approach can be adapted to virtually any individual difference variable, and will aid in moving these constructs from actuarial predictors to components of dynamic processes that unfold over time and across situations. Beyond the general temperamental-instrumental distinction, experimental methods provide a useful tool for testing theories that posit more specific causal processes. For example, temperamental contributions could include individual differences in attention, interpretation, emotional reactivity, and so on that explain differences in responses. Instrumental contributions also separate into more specific processes such as situational selection, evocation of others' behavior, and other forms of situational management that create objectively different environments. Because laboratory-based experimental methods allow detailed observation and superior control over theoretically relevant features of situations, the combination of experimental manipulations with individual difference measures will be especially useful in parsing these narrower processes.

Returning to the example of extraversion reveals this potential, as well as some challenges endemic to ambitious goals like developing a process understanding of individual differences. For example, although many laboratory studies now suggest that extraversion predicts increased positive emotional reactivity (to positive mood inductions), other data question the robustness or generalizability of these results. Lucas and Baird (2004) suggested that this effect is limited to high-arousal positive emotions. In addition, although we (Zelenski & Larsen, 1999) have found extraversion/BAS predicting more posi-tive reactions to good events in the real world, other experience-sampling studies have failed to find this effect (Gable, Reis, & Elliot, 2000) or have even found the reverse (Fleeson et al., 2002, Study 1). To clarify, the link between extraver-sion and positive emotions is robust across studies; the more specific finding of extraverts' increased reactivity to positive events or situa-tions is less consistent.

Although there are a variety of methodolog-ical differences across these studies, one of the most obvious results from the trade-off between naturalistic settings (with ESM), where situa-tional equivalence across research participants cannot be assumed, and manipulations (in the lab), which often gain situational equivalence by sacrificing realism. It may be that in the real world, introverts and extraverts define, and thus self-report, events and situations differ-ently from one another, or even that they differ in their ability to accurately report on features of social situations (Lieberman & Rosenthal, 2001). In other words, experience-sampling partici-pants' categorizations of situations and events may be colored by their interpretations or the intensity of their emotional experience, all of which result, in part, from individual differences in extraversion. On the other hand, it may be that extraverts' greater reactivity found with laboratory mood inductions does not always extend to their day-to-day experiences. Future studies that combine both laboratory manipu-lations and experience sampling components may help resolve these questions.

The link between extraversion and positive emotional experience may also be clarified by developing a more nuanced understanding of the narrower processes that underlie the broad trait of extraversion. In determining these compo-nents, Eysenck's low arousability and Gray's reward sensitivity provide good starting points. However, these constructs remain broad or iso-lated from all their concomitant parts in the nomological network. For example, reward sen-sitivity may include positive biases in cognitive processes such as attention, perception, judg-ment, interpretation, and memory (e.g., Reed & Derryberry, 1994; Rusting, 1999; Rusting & Larsen, 1998; Zelenski & Larsen, 2002). These stable individual differences in cognitive pro-cesses (part of, or related to, reward sensitivity) may lead people to differentially notice potential rewards or interpret ambiguous situations as rewarding. Such differences might explain why

different people select different situations (cf. instrumental explanations), or how they re-spond to situations whether or not they were intentionally selected (cf. temperamental expla-nations). In addition, the extent to which these narrower processes are engaged (and thus indi-vidual differences are apparent) likely depends on objective contextual factors (Avila, 2001). In other words, the process components of extra-version are not always switched on or respon-sible for behavior and experience in every given moment. Experimental methods' ability to iso-late these processes and manipulate contexts will yield important clues in understanding how stable aspects of individual differences unfold over time and across situations to produce a wide range of behavior and experience.

In addition, understanding extraversion (or other individual differences) as narrower pro-cesses may help provide an understanding of personality at additional levels of analysis. For example, molecular genetics has linked specific genes with personality traits (e.g., Lesch et al., 1996; Retz, Rösler, Supprian, Retz-Junginger, & Thome, 2003). However, individual genes ac-count for only a small proportion of variance in these traits—much smaller than the proportion of variance behavior geneticists suggest is due to heritability. Thus, it is likely that many different genes (influencing many processes) will be linked with single traits. Similarly, neuroima-ging studies are showing traits correlating with activation in various regions of the brain (e.g., Canli et al., 2001; Gray & Braver, 2002). That is, a broad trait will not be localized in a single re-gion of the brain. As the biological correlates of personality accumulate, it will become increas-ingly important to understand the many narrow processes that together make up broad traits like extraversion. That is, by linking an aspect of biology with a specific process (as opposed to a broad trait), we improve the utility of knowing the brain-behavior link. Again, experimental methods are well suited to isolating these nar-rower processes.

Even though they comprise a small proportion of individual differences research, experimental approaches have a long history in the field (Cronbach, 1957; Eysenck, 1990; Murray, 1938). As personality and positive psychology progress and interact with other disciplines, experimental approaches promise to further our understand-ing of causal processes underlying individ-ual differences. Ultimately these techniques, in combination with complimentary methods (such as those described in this book), will help us understand how stable constructs like extraversion contribute to constantly varying behavior and experience.

Notes

1. When thinking about the causes of behavior or experience in this situation, it is tempting to compare the relative contributions of individual differences and situational manipulations (e.g., how much happiness is due to the manipulation, and how much is due to extraversion?). However, such comparisons are of limited usefulness. First, behavior and experience require both the person and the situation, and ascribing more or less cause to one seems to negate the vital importance of the other. In addition, laboratory situations typically lack external validity (i.e., they are contrived) or, at best, can only simulate a small proportion of relevant situations in the real world. Therefore the effect sizes derived from this limited population of situations are best interpreted with caution.

2. It also seems reasonable to predict that people scoring high on neuroticism would respond more quickly to negatively valenced words (Rusting & Larsen, 1998). On the other hand, negative information often slows active responses (Cothran, Larsen, Zelenski, Prizmic, & Chien, 2006). Even if people scoring high on neuroticism are processing negative information preferentially, it is not clear that this would manifest itself as quicker responses (the BIS's function is to inhibit behavior, e.g., the button press). In any case, the data suggest that neuroticism does not correlate significantly with response times in this type of task (Rusting & Larsen, 1998, Zelenski & Larsen, 2004).

3. This type of counterbalancing is essential in experimental research where the central hypotheses directly involve the main effects of manipulations (e.g., if we were most interested in the effects of cognitive load rather than extraversion). Although counterbalancing is somewhat desirable in experimental personality research (e.g., for greater generalizability), it is less essential. As long as all participants are treated equally, practice effects or other forms of nonequivalence between experimental conditions will not alter associations with individual differences variables. That is, even when nonequivalences (like order effects) are clearly confounded with main effects, the personality effects remain valid. Therefore, rigid adherence to counterbalancing need not stifle the design creativity of experimental personality research.

4. Taking a slightly different approach, some individual difference characteristics are now operationalized as performance on computer tasks (as opposed to a more standard questionnaire assessments). That is, differences in response times across within-subject manipulations comprise the personality assessment. For example, Robinson, Solberg, Vargas, and Tamir (2003) have conceptualized habitual use of the neutral-positive dimension in categorization as a relatively stable individual difference construct (cf. Kelly, 1963) and used it in conjunction with extraversion to predict happiness. Similarly, the Implicit Association Test (Greenwald, McGhee, & Schwartz, 1998) has been adapted as an assessment tool for a great variety of individual differences. See Fazio (1990) for general, practical advice on using response time data.

References

Avila, C. (2001). Distinguishing BIS-mediated and BAS-mediated disinhibition mechanisms: A comparison of disinhibition models of Gray (1981, 1987) and of Patterson and Newman (1993). *Journal of Personality and Social Psychology, 80*(2), 311–324.

Ball, S. A., & Zuckerman, M. (1990). Sensation seeking, Eysenck's personality dimensions and reinforcement sensitivity in concept formation. *Personality and Individual Differences, 11*, 343–353.

Brewer, M. B. (2000). Research design and issues of validity. In H. T. Reis & C. M. Judd (Eds.), *Handbook of research methods in social and personality psychology* (pp. 3–16). New York: Cambridge University Press.

Canli, T., Zhao, Z., Desmond, J. E., Kang, E., Gross, J., & Gabrieli, J. D. E. (2001). An fMRI study of personality influences on brain reactivity to emotional stimuli. *Behavioral Neuroscience, 115*(1), 33–42.

Carver, C. S., Sutton, S. K., & Scheier, M. F. (2000). Action, emotion, and personality: Emerging conceptual integration. *Personality and Social Psychology Bulletin, 26*, 741–751.

Carver, C. S., & White, T. L. (1994). Behavioral inhibition, behavioral activation and affective responses to impending reward and punishment: The BIS/BAS scales. *Journal of Personality and Social Psychology, 67*, 319–333.

Cloninger, R. C., Svrakic, D. M., & Przybeck, T. R. (1993). A psychobiological model of temperament and character. *Archives of General Psychiatry, 50*, 975–990.

Cothran, D. L., Larsen, R. J., Zelenski, J. M., Prizmic, Z., & Chien, B. (2006). *Do emotion words interfere with processing emotion faces?*

Stroop-like interference versus automatic vigilance for negative information. Manuscript under review.

Cronbach, L. J. (1957). Two disciplines of scientific psychology, *American Psychologist, 12,* 671–684.

Cronbach, L. J., & Meehl, P. E. (1955). Construct validity in psychological tests. *Psychological Bulletin, 52,* 281–302.

Depue, R. A., & Collins, P. F. (1999). Neurobiology of the structure of personality: Dopamine, facilitation of incentive motivation, and extraversion. *Behavioral and Brain Sciences, 22*(3), 491–569.

Diener, E., & Seligman, M. E. P. (2002). Very happy people. *Psychological Science, 13*(1), 81–84.

Diener, E., Suh, E. M., Lucas, R. E., & Smith, H. L. (1999). Subjective well-being: Three decades of progress. *Psychological Bulletin, 125*(2), 276–302.

Elliot, A. J., & Thrash, T. M. (2002). Approach-avoidance motivation in personality: Approach and avoidance in temperaments and goals. *Journal of Personality and Social Psychology, 82*(5), 804–818.

Eysenck, H. J. (1967). *The biological basis of personality.* Springfield, IL: Charles C. Thomas.

Eysenck, H. J. (1990). Biological dimensions of personality. In L. A. Pervin (Ed.), *Handbook of personality: Theory and research* (pp. 244–276). New York: Guilford.

Eysenck, H. J. (1995). Can we study intelligence using the experimental method? *Intelligence, 20,* 217–228.

Eysenck, S. B. G., Eysenck, H. J., & Barrett, P. (1985). A revised version of the Psychoticism scale. *Personality and Individual Differences, 6,* 21–29.

Eysenck, S. B. G., Pearson, P. R., Easting, G., & Allsopp, J. F. (1985). Age norms for impulsiveness, venturesomeness and empathy in adults. *Personality and Individual Differences, 6,* 613–619.

Fazio, R. H. (1990). A practical guide to the use of response latency in social psychological research. In C. Hendrick & M. S. Clark (Eds.), *Research methods in personality and social psychology* (pp. 74–97). Newbury Park, CA: Sage.

Fleeson, W., Malanos, A. B., & Achille, N. M. (2002). An intraindividual process approach to the relationship between extraversion and positive affect: Is acting extraverted as good as being extraverted? *Journal of Personality and Social Psychology, 83*(6), 1409–1422.

Fowles, D. C. (1987). Application of a behavioral theory of motivation to the concepts of anxiety and impulsivity. *Journal of Research in Personality, 21,* 417–435.

Gable, S. L., Reis, H. T., & Elliot, A. J. (2000). Behavioral activation and inhibition in everyday life. *Journal of Personality and Social Psychology, 78*(6), 1135–1149.

Gable, S. L., Reis, H. T., & Elliot, A. J. (2003). Evidence for bivariate systems: An empirical test of appetition and aversion across domains. *Journal of Research in Personality, 37,* 349–372.

Gomez, R., Cooper, A., & Gomez, A. (2000). Susceptibility to positive and negative mood states: A test of Eysenck's, Gray's, and Newman's theories. *Personality and Individual Differences, 29,* 351–365.

Gray, J. A. (1981). A critique of Eysenck's theory of personality. In H. J. Eysenck (Ed.), *A model for personality* (pp. 246–276). New York: Springer-Verlag.

Gray, J. A. (1994). Personality dimensions and emotion systems. In P. Ekman & R. Davidson (Eds.), *The nature of emotion: Fundamental questions* (pp. 329–331). New York: Oxford University Press.

Gray, J. R. (2001). Emotional modulation of cognitive control: Approach-withdrawal states double-dissociate spatial from verbal two-back task performance. *Journal of Experimental Psychology: General, 130,* 436–452.

Gray, J. R., & Braver, T. S. (2002). Personality predicts working memory related activation in caudal anterior cingulate cortex. *Cognitive, Affective, and Behavioral Neuroscience, 2,* 64–75.

Greenwald, A. G., McGhee, D. E., & Schwartz, J. L. K. (1998). Measuring individual differences in implicit cognition: The implicit association test. *Journal of Personality and Social Psychology, 74,* 1464–1480.

Gross, J. J., Sutton, S. K., & Ketelaar, T. (1998). Relations between affect and personality: Support for the affect-level and affective-reactivity views. *Personality and Social Psychology Bulletin, 24*(3), 279–288.

Hemenover, S. H. (2003). Individual differences in rate of affect change: Studies in affect chronometry. *Journal of Personality and Social Psychology, 85*(1), 121–131.

Humphreys, M. S., & Revelle, W. (1984). Personality, motivation, and performance: A theory of the relationship between individual differences and information processing. *Psychological Review, 91,* 153–184.

John, O. P., & Srivastava, S. (1999). The Big Five trait taxonomy: History, measurement, and theoretical perspectives. In L. A. Pervin & O. P. John (Eds.), *Handbook of personality: Theory and research* (2nd ed., pp. 102–138). New York: Guilford.

Judge, T. A., & Larsen, R. J. (2001). Dispositional affect and job satisfaction: A review and theoretical extension. *Organizational Behavior and Human Decision Processes, 86*(1), 67–98.

Kelly, G. A. (1963). *A theory of personality.* New York: Norton.

Larsen, R. J. (2000). Toward a science of mood regulation. *Psychological Inquiry, 11*(3), 129–141.

Larsen, R. J., & Diener, E. (1987). Affect intensity as an individual difference characteristic: A review. *Journal of Research in Personality, 21,* 1–39.

Larsen, R. J., & Ketelaar, T. (1989). Extraversion, neuroticism and susceptibility to positive and negative mood induction procedures. *Personality and Individual Differences, 10,* 1221–1228.

Larsen, R. J., & Ketelaar, T. (1991). Personality and susceptibility to positive and negative emotional states. *Journal of Personality and Social Psychology, 61,* 132–140.

Lesch, K. P., Bengel, D., Heils, A., Sabol, S. Z., Greenberg, B. D., Petri, S., et al. (1996). Association of anxiety-related traits with a polymorphism in the serotonin transporter gene regulatory region. *Science, 274,* 1527–1531.

Lieberman, M. D., & Rosenthal, R. (2001). Why introverts can't always tell who likes them: Multitasking and nonverbal decoding. *Journal of Personality and Social Psychology, 80*(2), 294–310.

Lucas, R. E., & Baird, B. M. (2004). Extraversion and emotional reactivity. *Journal of Personality and Social Psychology, 86*(3), 473–485.

Lucas, R. E., Diener, E., Grob, A., Suh, E. M., & Shao, L. (2000). Cross-cultural evidence for the fundamental features of extraversion. *Journal of Personality and Social Psychology, 79*(3), 452–468.

Mallon, S. D., Kingsley, D., Affleck, G., & Tennen, H. (1998). Methodological trends in *Journal of Personality*: 1970–1995. *Journal of Personality, 66*(5), 671–685.

Matthews, G., & Gilliland, K. (1999). The personality theories of H. J. Eysenck and J. A. Gray: A comparative review. *Personality and Individual Differences, 26,* 583–626.

McCrae, R. R., & Costa, P. T. (1991). Adding liebe und arbeit: The full five-factor model and well-being. *Personality and Social Psychology Bulletin, 17,* 227–232.

Mischel, W., & Shoda, Y. (1998). Reconciling processing dynamics and personality dispositions. *Annual Review of Psychology, 49,* 229–258.

Murray, H. A. (1938). *Explorations in personality.* New York: Oxford University Press.

Pickering, A. D., Corr, P. J., & Gray, J. A. (1999). Interactions and reinforcement sensitivity theory: A theoretical analysis of Rusting and Larsen (1997). *Personality and Individual Differences, 26,* 356–365.

Reed, M. J., & Derryberry, D. (1994). Temperament and attention to positive and negative trait information. *Personality and Individual Differences, 18*(1), 135–147.

Retz, W., Rösler, M., Supprian, T., Retz-Junginger, P., & Thome, J. (2003). Dopamine D3 receptor gene polymorphism and violent behavior: Relation to impulsiveness and ADHD-related psychopathology. *Journal of Neural Transmission, 110,* 561–572.

Revelle, W., Amaral, P., & Turriff, S. (1976). Introversion/extroversion, time stress, and caffeine: Effect on verbal performance. *Science, 192,* 149–150.

Revelle, W., Humphreys, M. S., Simon, L., & Gilliland, K. (1980). The interactive effect of personality, time of day and caffeine: A test of the arousal model. *Journal of Experimental Psychology: General, 109,* 1–31.

Robinson, M. D., Solberg, E. C., Vargas, P. T., & Tamir, M. (2003). Trait as default: Extraversion, subjective well-being, and the distinction between neutral and positive events. *Journal of Personality and Social Psychology, 85*(3), 517–527.

Rusting, C. L. (1998). Personality, mood, and cognitive processing of emotional information: Three conceptual frameworks. *Psychological Bulletin, 124*(2), 165–196.

Rusting, C. L. (1999). Interactive effects of personality and mood on emotion-congruent memory and judgment. *Journal of Personality and Social Psychology, 77*(5), 1073–1086.

Rusting, C. L., & Larsen, R. J. (1997). Extraversion, neuroticism, and susceptibility to positive and negative affect: A test of two theoretical models. *Personality and Individual Differences, 22,* 607–612.

Rusting, C. L., & Larsen, R. J. (1998). Personality and cognitive processing of affective information. *Personality and Social Psychology Bulletin, 24*(2), 200–213.

Scollon, C. N., Kim-Prieto, C., & Diener, E. (2003). Experience sampling: Promises and pitfalls, strengths and weaknesses. *Journal of Happiness Studies, 4,* 5–34.

Smith, E. R. (2000). Research design. In H. T. Reis & C. M. Judd (Eds.), *Handbook of research methods in social and personality psychology* (pp. 17–39). New York: Cambridge University Press.

Stelmack, R. M. (1990). Biological basis of extraversion: Psychophysiological evidence. *Journal of Personality, 58,* 293–311.

Suls, J., Martin, R. & David, J. P. (1998). Person-environment fit and its limits: Agreeableness, neuroticism, and emotional reactivity to interpersonal conflict. *Personality and Social Psychology Bulletin, 24*(1), 88–98.

Watson, D., Clark, L. A., & Tellegen, A. (1988). Development and validation of brief measures of positive and negative affect: The PANAS scales. *Journal of Personality and Social Psychology, 54,* 1063–1070.

Zelenski, J. M., & Larsen, R. J. (1999). Susceptibility to affect: A comparison of three personality taxonomies. *Journal of Personality, 67*(5), 761–791.

Zelenski, J. M., & Larsen, R. J. (2002). Predicting the future: How affect-related personality traits influence likelihood judgments of future events. *Personality and Social Psychology Bulletin, 28*(7), 1000–1010.

Zelenski, J. M., & Larsen, R. J. (2006). *What causes extraversion? A test of Eysenck's and Gray's theories of personality.* Manuscript under review.

Zuckerman, M., Joireman, J., Kraft, M., & Kuhlman, D. M. (1999). Where do motivational and emotional traits fit within three factor models of personality? *Personality and Individual Differences, 26,* 487–504.

15

Understanding Individual and Age Differences in Well-Being

An Experimental Attention-Based Approach

Derek M. Isaacowitz

The idea that there may be important links between thinking and feeling is not a new one. In clinical psychology, Beck's influential theory of depression asserted that dysfunctional cognitions represent not just a symptom of depression, but rather a cardinal cause of the disorder itself. In the social cognitive study of emotion, links to cognition have been at the core of several controversial assertions. For example, the long-standing debate between Zajonc (1980, 1984) and Lazarus (1982) centered on whether cognition does or does not necessarily precede emotion. Additionally, Bower's (1981) network theory made important assertions concerning the contextual links between emotional experience and memory.

Only more recently, however, have researchers interested in the links between emotion and cognition turned from focusing either on the necessity of cognition for emotion or on the effects of emotion on memory to ask more refined questions about where and how emotion might affect cognition. In particular, rather than view-

ing information processing as a black box and using only memory measures to determine simply whether cognition had been impacted somehow by emotion, researchers have attempted to decompose information processing into more specific parts to better understand where the "action" may be linking emotion with processing of stimuli from the environment. This broader consideration led quickly to a focus on preattentional and attentional mechanisms that might permit emotion to bias information processing from the very beginning; in other words, the earliest ways in which emotion might influence cognition.

In this chapter, I review several methodologies that have been used to investigate the relationship between emotion and attentional processes. In line with the spirit of this section of the book, I attempt to focus on stable interindividual differences in emotionality as they relate to attention, but I also note important work linking state emotion with attention. After presenting particular research problems concerning age and individual differences that may be particularly suited to attentional methods, I then present several specific techniques that have been widely used for these types of inquiries: Emotional Stroop and dot-probe. I then turn my focus to very recent work using eye tracking. While the majority of the work I describe centers on negative emotional states such as depression and anxiety, more links to positive emotions and well-being will be made in describing my own most recent work.

Individual and Age Differences in Emotion and Affective Experience

It is not surprising that individuals vary in the quality of their affective states, with some individuals chronically happier than others (Diener, Suh, Lucas, & Smith, 1999). In the search to understand the psychological processes underlying these individual differences, psychologists have primarily focused on volitional mechanisms like coping (e.g., Lazarus & Folkman, 1984). More recently, however, some researchers have noted that individual differences may be expressed very early on in information processing. For example, anxiety researchers have noted that anxious individuals show an attentional preference for threatening material in the environment (e.g., Mogg & Marden, 1990); neurotics may have trouble disengaging from negative information (Derryberry & Reed, 1994); and optimists may have an attentional bias for positive stimuli (Segerstom, 2001). Thus individual difference variables that likely relate to outcomes like well-being may show their effects very early in information processing that biases that processing toward some stimuli and away from others. Investigating these biases is important to further understanding how these individual difference variables actually lead some individuals to have better and some to have worse well-being (see Isaacowitz, 2005b; Isaacowitz & Seligman, 2002).

Recent theory and research in the field of socioemotional aging has suggested similar links between attentional bias and well-being. Socioemotional selectivity theory, for example, is a motivational account of how perceived endings (such as advancing age) lead individuals to focus more on emotional content in their socioemotional lives (Carstensen, Isaacowitz, & Charles, 1999). The role of focus on or salience of emotion

in the theoretical formulation of the theory has led to investigations of age differences in processing of emotional information. While the bulk of that work has centered on the centrality of emotion in the memory of older individuals (e.g., Charles, Mather, & Carstensen, 2003; Kennedy, Mather, & Carstensen, 2004), some studies have focused instead on attention (Mather & Carstensen, 2003). Just as individual difference researchers have started to link attentional preferences and well-being, so too have socioemotional selectivity researchers started to think of attentional bias as a mechanism possibly underlying age differences in emotion regulation. As with the individual difference work, studying attention can help illuminate how exactly emotion might be increasingly well regulated as individuals get older.

As attention has become more a popular research focus for those interested in individual and age differences relevant to emotion and well-being, two primary methodologies have been employed: the Emotional Stroop and the dot-probe or probe-response task.

Methodologies for Studying Individual and Age Differences in Attentional Preference

Emotional Stroop

Perhaps the most popular methodology for studying links between emotion and attention arose from classic early work in the study of visual attention showing that individuals are slowed in their responses to a color-naming task when the word whose color is to be named is the name of another color (e.g., the word *green* written in red; participants will be slower to say that the word is written in red in this case compared to a word not written in a competing color). This Stroop effect is classically interpreted as reflecting attentional interference, as the word the color is written in grabs attention and makes the target information processing (naming the actual color in which the word is written) take longer.

While the classic Stroop task has long been used in cognitive psychology to try to unravel how attention works, experimental psychopathology researchers devised a creative use for the Stroop task. Instead of using the names of different colors to interfere with the color-naming task, these researchers proposed using emotion- ally valenced words. The reasoning was that individuals who have disorders of mood and af- fect, such as anxiety and depression, might be particularly disrupted in color naming when the content of the words was relevant to their par- ticularly disordered mood. The earliest work us- ing the Emotional Stroop was done linking anxiety with attentional and preattentive biases, based on the observation that anxious individuals seem particularly tuned in to potentially threat- ening information from the environment (e.g., Buckley, Blanchard, & Hickling, 2002; see also Williams, Watts, MacLeod, & Mathews, 1997).

More recently, the Emotional Stroop has been used not simply to investigate the role of atten- tion in pathological states like anxiety and mood disorders, but also to unravel individual differ- ences within the more normal range of affective experience. Segerstrom (2001) tested whether optimism could be linked to attentional biases using a version of the Stroop task in which the words were either positive, negative, or neutral in content. Optimists showed an attentional bias such that their responses on the color-naming task were more disrupted for positive words, whereas the color-naming latencies of pessimists were more disrupted for negative words.

While the Emotional Stroop has been quite a popular method for bringing attention to the study of emotion, several important limitations have been enumerated, suggesting that its util- ity for specifically testing for attentional biases may be limited. Most fundamentally, there is a response component inherent to the task that makes it unclear whether group differences re- sult from actual attentional interference or in- stead from differences in the responding (saying the color name) that is necessary in the task (Mogg, Millar, & Bradley, 2000).

Dot-Probe

The other traditionally popular methodology for investigating links between attention and emo- tion has also arisen primarily from experimental psychopathologists studying anxiety. The basic design is as follows: The participant views two images on a screen (either left/right or top/ bottom); after a time interval, the two images disappear and a dot appears on the screen in place of one of the images. The participant is in- structed to press the appropriate button (i.e., the button for "left" if the dot replaces the image on the left side of the screen) as quickly as possible;

the dependent variable is the response latency. In the emotional version of the dot-probe, one of the two images is emotional in nature and the other is not. Importantly, evidence of attentional preference or bias on the dot-probe is opposite in direction to the Emotional Stroop. Whereas at- tention is believed biased on the Emotional Stroop when response latencies are slower to an emo- tional than nonemotional word, on the dot- probe, response latencies should be faster when the dot appears replacing an emotion word if attention is grabbed by the emotional content (Posner, Snyder, & Davidson, 1980).

Early work using dot-probe tasks to investigate attentional mechanisms in anxiety disorders found that, indeed, anxious individuals responded faster to dots following anxiety-relevant words than they did to neutral words, whereas non- anxious individuals showed no such difference (Macleod, Mathews, & Tata, 1986).

In contrast to the research on anxiety, atten- tional studies of depression have yielded more mixed results. For example, Bradley, Mogg, and Lee (1997) found evidence for an attentional bias in depressives using a dot-probe, but another study with the Emotional Stroop failed to find evidence for a bias (Hill & Knowles, 1991).

Finally, the dot-probe has recently been used to investigate age differences in attention to emotional stimuli. According to socioemotional selectivity theory (Carstensen et al., 1999), emo- tions and emotion regulation become more sa- lient to individuals as they face contexts in which they view their futures as being limited or con- strained. Advancing age is one such life context; and indeed, older individuals appear to make social choices more based on emotion regulation goals than do young adults (Fredrickson & Carstensen, 1990). Starting from that first find- ing, Carstensen and colleagues have attempted to show more generally that the information processing of older individuals is more oriented toward emotional stimuli than the information processing of younger individuals (which may be more oriented toward factual content of stimuli). For example, older individuals appear to remember more emotional content of a text than younger adults (Carstensen & Turk-Charles, 1994).

A study using images varying in emotional valence found that, in general, younger and older adults both attended more to negative emotional images, but that age differences emerged when a memory task was added to the attention ones. Even though they had viewed negative images along with the young adults, the older participants remembered the negative emotional images less (Charles et al., 2003).

Mather and Carstensen (2003) used a dot-probe paradigm to provide additional support for the theory. In this study, pairs of faces, one emotional (positive or negative) and one neutral, served as preprobe stimuli. Older individuals were faster to respond to neutral as opposed to negative faces, whereas younger participants showed no such bias. In other words, older participants appeared to show an attentional bias away from negative information.

While studies using dot-probe methodology have made substantial contributions to the understanding of individual and age differences in processing of emotional information, these studies share the same limitations as the Emotional Stroop with regard to making conclusions about specific biases or preferences in attention. In particular, it is impossible using the dot-probe to discern whether differences in response latencies between groups result from differences in attending or responding. In other words, the faster response group may be faster in orienting toward the dot when it replaces a relevant stimulus (attentional explanation), or they may be faster in executing their response (i.e., pressing the appropriate button; a response explanation). Given that hypervigilance can be exhibited both perceptually (scanning the environment) or behaviorally (jumping at any noise), this is a nontrivial problem left open by the dot-probe technique. Moreover, this paradigm may allow for multiple attentional shifts that are difficult to interpret (Mogg et al., 2000).

Eye Tracking: A More Precise Measure of Attentional Preference and Bias

Given the limitations of the Emotional Stroop and dot-probe tasks for excluding response bias explanations for observed group differences, psychologists interested in the role of attention in emotion have turned to newer technologies that allow for the recording of attentional processes online, free from response elements. Eye tracking has been a particularly relevant technological innovation for this purpose, as newer systems allow for relatively nonobtrusive recording of eye movements in nearly real time. Eye-tracking systems used in emotion research are either head-mounted or remote; remote systems sometimes also feature magnetic head tracking in order to minimize the effects of head movement

on recording. Below, more information is provided on the particular system we use; of course, other systems may vary in their specifications.

As with Emotional Stroop and dot-probe, researchers in experimental psychopathology were the first to utilize eye-tracking technology to study the emotional bases of interindividual differences relevant to emotion and affect. Before them, it was primarily researchers interested in directly studying eye movements to understand how vision works (e.g., Rayner, 1998) or how reading relates to the psychology of language (e.g., Arnold, Eisenband, Brown-Schmidt, & Trueswell, 2000).

In the context of anxiety, researchers particularly interested in the nature of attentional bias for ambiguous negative stimuli have started to use eye tracking to delineate whether attentional bias operates in these more subtle situations for anxious individuals. Rather than showing clearly threatening words (as has been done in the other methods), Calvo and Avero (2002) used a more complex design in which threatening or non-threatening event sentences were followed by consistent or inconsistent target words. Anxious individuals showed an attention bias not in attention to the threatening sentences but instead in terms of showing faster reading of the inconsistent target. This led the authors to conclude that attentional biases in anxiety occur not in initial processing but temporally later.

To discern exactly how and why anxious individuals react so strongly to stimuli others fail to perceive as at all threatening requires a subtle set of stimuli such as those in the Calvo and Avero (2002) study. However, extending the study of attention and emotion out of particular flavors of psychopathology to a more general understanding of individual differences requires attempting to trace attentional biases in situations more naturalistic than reading text that is ambiguously or inconsistently threatening. Therefore, we have established a program of research utilizing pictorial rather than textual stimuli. The reasoning behind this is as follows: Interindividual differences in psychological constructs such as anxiety or optimism produce large behavioral differences and therefore should function in a wide range of contexts. Thus, our goal has been to utilize stimuli that might capture a relatively broad range of ways individual differences might emerge in the attention-emotion relation and to minimize the context specificity or ambiguity of the stimuli. So, for instance, in the one eye-tracker study we have done so far focused on anxiety, we took a broader view than that of Calvo and Avero. Rather than focusing simply on ambiguously threatening text, we instead used pictoral images varying in valence.

In that study (Block & Isaacowitz, 2003), we used as our stimuli a set of faces posed in emotional and nonemotional configurations. We reasoned that, unlike ambiguous words, emotional faces are almost universally recognizable and tend not to be ambiguous in valence or interpretation (Ekman, 1993). Nonetheless, individuals may still differ in their patterns of attention to these valenced faces, whether or not they are able to self-report on this in a veridical fashion. Whereas anxiety researchers using attentional measures such as eye tracking have attempted to narrow down to the most particular instances of attentional biases shown by anxious individuals, we wanted instead to broaden the search for attentional biases to better understand the most general ways in which biases may facilitate anxiety in nearly real-world settings. Therefore, we accepted the conclusion of previous studies that anxious individuals show an attentional bias for threatening stimuli and instead focused our attention on whether these biases could be extended to all negative stimuli (the negativity hypothesis; Bradley, Mogg, & Millar, 2000) or beyond that to all emotional stimuli (the emotionality hypothesis; Mogg & Marden, 1990) such that anxious individuals would be biased in their attention to many stimuli as they go about their lives, not just a small subset. To do this, we presented a sample of college students with pairs of faces from the MacBrain dataset of emotional faces (for more information, see www.macbrain.org/faces/#faces), created by having acting students pose prototypic faces for different emotions (for this study, we used only happy, sad, and neutral faces). Participants were presented with pairs featuring the same individual in a nonemotional and emotional (happy or sad) pose. Faces were counterbalanced so they varied in terms of screen position. Each pair was presented on the screen for 5 seconds, with 5 seconds of gray screen between pairs. Individuals high in trait anxiety looked more at sad faces than their nonanxious peers; however, this result was especially pronounced when the sad face was on the left and the last 3 seconds were evaluated (based on the initial left-right scan taking 2 seconds). Thus, this study provided support for the negativity but not the emotionality

hypothesis. Anxious individuals may show an attentional bias not just to threatening stimuli but instead to all negative emotional stimuli; this finding is consistent with the large differences in thoughts and behaviors that distinguish anxious and nonanxious individuals.

Eye Tracking Apparatus and Setup

Our particular methodology for eye tracking is as follows (though readers should note that this a schematic generalization for ease of presentation): First, we test all participants' vision (acuity and contrast sensitivity) to ensure that their vision is adequate for eye tracking. Following this comes any battery of pencil-and-paper personality or cognitive testing appropriate for the particular study. To begin eye tracking, we sit participants between 20 and 30 inches in front of a computer screen. Our remote tracking device is right under the computer monitor, and behind the participant is a magnet on a tall stand. A small magnetic transmitter on a headband is then placed directly over the participant's left eye; the information transmitted to the magnet concerns the position of the head in space (using coordinates from a magnetic calibration performed at installation) and is used by the analytic program to correct for head movements in recording. First, the experimenter "catches" the participants' pupil with the illumination emanating from the remote unit under the monitor, and then proceeds to run through a 9- or 17-point calibration procedure. Once calibration is complete, determined by demonstrating that where a subject looks when asked to look somewhere specifically is also found by the equipment to be gaze toward that position, the actual tracking is ready to begin. Generally, we attempt to follow the eye tracking with a recognition memory task (for example, participants might be presented with pairs of images, only one of which they had seen previously, and are asked to identify which of the two they had seen). The purpose of this is to try to contextualize any findings of attentional bias within information processing more generally. Also toward that end, we have been increasing the number of other cognitive tests to include assessment of general memory and attentional functioning, not tied to the particular study stimuli. These tests are particularly important for work on age differences in attention to socioemotional stimuli, as age effects in perceptual and cognitive processes need to be ruled out as alternative explanations before age differences in specific attentional biases can be asserted.

Our particular system records gaze position 60 times per second. It defines a fixation as 100 msec or more within about 1 degree visual angle; other recordings are considered to reflect saccades rather than fixations and are not retained for further analysis. For each study, we designate one or more areas of the image as areas of interest (AOIs). Eyenal, the data reduction program associated with the ASL eye-tracking machines (Applied Science Laboratories, Bedford, MA), will then calculate total fixation time within those AOIs. It measures these AOI fixation times in two ways: First, it produces the raw duration of total fixation within that AOI for that participant; second, it produces a percentage reflecting how much of the total fixation time the participant spent fixating on that particular AOI. Generally, we prefer the percentage over the raw duration data, for two reasons. The first has to do with interindividual variability in gaze; some individuals will saccade frequently and fixate rarely, whereas others will make many fixations. Raw duration times may be misleading in the context of these differences. Even more important, though, is the second reason, having to do with minimizing the impact of machine error on the results. If the tracker loses a participant's gaze for some period of time during a particular image presentation (but not for the entire period, in which case it would be considered missing data and would not be retained for further analysis), raw duration would again be misleading, whereas a percentage of fixation time would correct for the lost data and only provide information on how much of the time the participant was actually being successfully recorded and was fixating somewhere in which their gaze was directed specifically at that AOI.

More on Individual Differences: Optimism

Our lab's first project using eye tracking to study attention to emotional information centered on an individual difference variable, optimism, that I had studied previously (e.g., Isaacowitz & Seligman, 2002) using self-report methodology. I wondered about what active ingredient was linking optimism to well-being and noticed some discrepancy in the existing literature. On the one hand, Aspinwall and colleagues argued, based on

several studies, that optimistic individuals attended more to negative information, but only when that information was relevant to them (Aspinwall, Richter, & Hoffman, 2001). In contrast, but more in line with common language notions that optimists wear rose-colored glasses was the finding of a study by Segerstrom (2001) described above, in which optimists showed more attentional disruption to positive words and pessimists showed more disruption to negative words. I wondered whether methodological limitations could account for the discrepant findings: Aspinwall and Brunhart (1996) had used time spent before clicking to a new Web page as a raw index of attention, whereas Segerstrom used the Emotional Stroop. In the lab, we thought eye tracking might be a good way to gain a more direct understanding of the links between optimism and attention to negative information.

Therefore, we conducted a study in which participants completed a series of self-report measures and then had their eyes tracked as they viewed a series of stimuli: melanoma/skin cancer images, matched schematic line drawings (to control for contour), and faces rated as neutral by a group of coders (Isaacowitz, 2005c). Images were presented one at a time in the middle of the screen for 15 seconds, with 5 seconds of gray screen between the target images. Participants were asked to look at the images ''naturally, as if at home watching television.'' One self-report measure included in the battery was the Life Orientation Test (LOT; Scheier & Carver, 1985), a widely used test of dispositional optimism and pessimism. Following other studies, we computed a composite optimism score (dispositional optimism—dispositional pessimism) for all participants. Optimists displayed a specific attentional bias such that they looked less at the skin cancer images than did more pessimistic individuals. This also held true in a more conservative test using residual scores controlling for attentional patterns to matched schematic line drawings. No differences in attention were found to neutral faces. Finally, I statistically controlled for the other self-reported constructs, including depressive symptoms, positive and negative affect, and neuroticism. The relationship between optimism and attention to the skin cancer remained after these controls.

Several important weaknesses existed in this first study that prevented us from concluding more definitively that optimists show an attentional bias away from negative information. First, we had not measured anxiety, and this was a problem because of the data linking anxiety with attentional bias (e.g., Calvo & Avero, 2002). Second, it could be argued that our stimuli were not particularly relevant to individuals, an important critique given Aspinwall and Brunhart's (1996) finding that optimists attend more to negative information, but only when that information is relevant to them. So we conducted a second study to address some of these concerns (Study 2, Isaacowitz, 2005c). The stimuli for eye tracking were the same, but we added a self-report measure of anxiety to the group of self-report questionnaires and randomly assigned participants to get either the same instructions as in the first study (baseline condition), or a set of instructions designed to increase the relevance of the skin cancer images: "These images may be useful to you in the future in helping you identify problems on the skin in yourselves and others. So try to look at the images as you would approach any information that may prove useful to you in the future" (relevance condition). Finally, we added a recognition memory task, in which participants had to decide from a series of faces and cancer images whether or not they had seen them in the eye-tracking presentation.

Results of this study basically replicated the first study (Isaacowitz, 2005c). No differences in fixation patterns were found based on condition, so data were collapsed across condition and only differences between optimists and pessimists were evaluated. Again, optimists showed a particular attentional bias away from skin cancer images. Anxiety did not relate to attentional patterns in this study. Additionally, no memory biases were found.

Age Differences

We next wondered about age differences in attention to these negative emotional stimuli (Isaacowitz, 2005a). This issue is particularly interesting given both data and theory on emotion and aging. From an empirical perspective, numerous studies have found evidence of better affect in older individuals (e.g., Carstensen, Pasupathi, Mayr, & Nesselroade, 2000; Charles, Reynolds, & Gatz, 2001), though these gains appear not to be maintained in very old age (Isaacowitz & Smith, 2003). Socioemotional selectivity theory has been proposed as a motiva-

tional account of these findings. The original formulation of socioemotional selectivity theory (e.g., Carstensen et al., 1999) asserted that emotions in general should be more salient to older individuals, and that age-related increases in affect are therefore due to older individuals being more oriented toward emotional goals in their everyday lives. However, more recent research (e.g., Charles et al., 2003; Mather & Carstensen, 2003) has suggested not that older individuals are focused on emotion generally, but instead that they show information processing that favors positive stimuli and disregards negative stimuli. We planned to conduct the first optimism study with a sample of community-dwelling older individuals, to determine first how trackable older individuals would be, and then, if tracking was successful, to test for age differences in attentional patterns to the negative emotional stimuli. This was basically a replication of the first optimism study, as all older participants were instructed to view the stimuli naturally, as if they were at home watching television.

It was indeed a challenge to track our older participants, due to well-documented changes in vision that take place with age, including droopy eyelids and yellowing lenses (Sekuler & Sekuler, 2000). Ultimately, we were able to track 21 of 31 of our older participants, for a hit rate of 68%. This compares to a success rate of 89% in our optimism studies with young adults.

We used data from the first two optimism studies in young adults for age-comparative purposes. Only young adult participants who had received the same instructions as the older adults were included for comparative purposes; in other words, all young adults from Study 1 (in which all participants were asked to view the stimuli naturally, as if at home watching television), and all young adults from the baseline condition of Study 2 were included. Those Study 2 participants who had received the relevance manipulation were not included in these age-comparative analyses. The two samples were demographically fairly similar; however, attesting to the high educational achievement of our older participants, they actually reported more years of education (by over 4 years) than did our college-student young adult sample; this is the opposite of what often happens in cross-sectional age-comparative work. Thus, results need to be interpreted in light of this demographic difference, though controlling for years of education did not change the overall results.

Interestingly, when evaluating overall fixation patterns by age, no differences emerged for any type of stimuli. Differences did emerge, however, when considering the relationship between optimism and attention; a significant Age × Optimism interaction emerged in the prediction of fixation to the cancer images. Whereas in young adults the more optimistic individuals looked less at the cancer images than the pessimists, the opposite was true in older participants. For them, optimism was positively correlated with attention to the cancer images. These findings, with older optimists and younger pessimists looking more at the cancer than their age peers, held even after conducting several analyses to account for perceptual changes that might happen with age, both using an individual difference approach (controlling statistically for contrast sensitivity) and a psychophysical approach (testing high- and low-contrast stimuli separately).

Why should it be the case, however, that the relationship between optimism and attentional bias or preference to negative emotional stimuli should vary so dramatically between younger and older adults? While I have considered this question in more detail elsewhere (Isaacowitz, 2005a), I believe there are two primary candidates for underlying psychological mechanisms that may be important in motivating this age difference. The first is familiar from the optimism study in young adults—namely, stimulus relevance (I avoid using *salience* here because of the tradition in vision research to use salience to refer to stimulus properties, such as contour and color, rather than psychological properties having to do with an individual's motivation toward or away from the stimulus). In this account, the skin cancer images are simply more relevant to older than younger individuals. If one assumes that the relevance manipulation in the second skin cancer study with young adults was actually too weak to have any behavioral impact, this account would fit with Aspinwall et al.'s (2001) assertion that optimists attend more to negative stimuli but only when it is significantly relevant.

What I believe is a more parsimonious account, however, concerns not differential relevance of the stimuli but instead differential experience with the stimuli. Elsewhere (Isaacowitz, 2005a), I proposed three mechanisms by which experience might affect attention to emotional stimuli: habituation, expertise, and mere exposure. I believe that expertise may be

the most persuasive general mechanism: It may be that pessimists become experts at negative stimuli and thus become more efficient processors of such information, whereas it remains novel for more optimistic individuals. Obviously, this is a rather speculative account of our own findings, but general support for an expertise-related explanation comes from a number of sources.

For example, a particularly interesting study in this regard is one by Polk and Farah (1995), in which mail sorters completed a task that required them to pick a letter out of an array of other letters or digits. Workers who sort Canadian mail, in which letters and numbers are combined in zip codes (e.g., Vancouver, BC V5W 3M6), were compared with those who sort only American mail, in which zip codes are solely numeric (e.g., Waltham, MA 02454). Canadian sorters were faster at the letter-digit task, suggesting that the experience of sorting mail had changed their attentional mechanisms to similar types of tasks. This is consistent with research comparing novice and expert drivers (Crundell, Underwood, & Chapman, 1999), suggesting that the attentional processes of these groups work differently from each other. For example, experienced pilots appear to have a wider functional field of view than novices (Williams, 1995); experience changes how the attentional system functions, making it structurally different and more efficient in its operation. We are currently pursuing additional studies to further specify the nature of age-related changes in attention to emotional stimuli (e.g., Isaacowitz, Wadlinger, Goren, & Wilson, 2006).

Positive Affect and the Broaden-and-Build Model of Positive Emotions

In our studies of optimism described above, we did not find any unique effect of positive affect, based on self-report scores on the PANAS (Watson, Clark, & Tellegen, 1988). In other words, when positive affect was entered into a regression model predicting attentional bias, no significant effects were found. Rather than resulting directly from positive affect, attention seemed to be more a function of optimism, a cognitive-affective construct (Chang & Sanna, 2001). Nonetheless, there are theoretical reasons to believe that positive affect or positive emotion should relate some aspects of attention to emotional information. This is due in particular to

Fredrickson's (1998) enumeration of a broaden-and-build account of the function of positive emotions. According to the theory, whereas negative emotions function to protect an organism in dangerous situations, thereby resulting in focus of attention and action on the problem at hand, positive emotions may function in an opposite manner. First, they may occur not during acute situations, but rather during times of relative calm and need fulfillment. Second, because there is no pressing situation or problem that demands focused attention, they may instead show patterns of more diffuse attention to a wider range of information and possibilities. According to Fredrickson, this openness allows individuals to develop relationships and skills that might help them out in the future. So, for example, an individual might use a context of relative security to seek out new potential social partners, and one of these may turn out to be a long-term romantic partner. Had the individual not used that period of calm to consider new and different possibilities, that new romantic relationship may never have developed.

The attentional implications of the broaden-and-build model are quite clear: Positive emotional states should lead to wider attention. Some evidence for this assertion has been found: For example, individuals in a positive mood state were more likely than those in a sad mood state to classify images based on global properties in one study (Gasper & Clore, 2002). Heather Wadlinger and I (Wadlinger & Isaacowitz, in press) thought that this would be a perfect sort of problem to investigate using eye tracking. What we could investigate using this technology was whether induced positive affective states do lead somehow to more peripheral attentional processing, as compared with individuals in normal affective states.

To conduct this study, we used one of Alice Isen's well-established techniques for short-term positive mood induction (e.g., Carnevale & Isen, 1986; Estrada, Isen, & Young, 1997). After completing self-report measures, participants were brought to the eye-tracker room, and those in the positive mood induction condition were offered a small bag of candy in gratitude for their help with the study. They were of course asked not to eat the candy until after the experiment was over so that sugar intake would not affect the findings; participants in the control group were given a bag of candy after the study was complete. A quick manipulation check, involving

asking participants to rate how they felt on a 1–10 scale right before having their eyes tracked, suggested that that the mood induction group did indeed feel happier than their peers in the control group.

Stimuli for this study were taken from Peter Lang's International Affective Picture System (IAPS; Center for the Study of Emotion and Attention, 1999), a series of images varying in valence and arousal level. Because our interest was specifically in central versus peripheral attention, we constructed each stimulus in the eye tracker presentation to include three images from the IAPS that were matched in content and valence (and, in a second study, arousal level). The three images were then presented in an array such that one was in the center of the computer monitor, whereas the other two were in the periphery of the screen. We used five different central-peripheral presentations: horizontal, vertical, right and left diagonal, and a spatial orientation featuring a random set. Results did not vary by array, so data was collapsed across them.

The gist of the findings was that positive moods do seem to broaden attention, but only sometimes. Including stimuli of varying emotional valence and arousal level helped illuminate when positive moods do and do not broaden attention. Specifically, those individuals induced into positive affective states showed more attention to the periphery when stimuli were of high positive valence and of medium or low positive arousal. Thus, positive emotions may indeed impact attention, but only for attention to some types of stimuli. This may also help explain our failure to find unique effects of positive affect on attention in the skin cancer studies, as only neutral and negative emotional images were used in those studies.

Lingering Issues Regarding Attentional Biases

While I now believe quite strongly that using eye tracking to study attentional preferences and biases will help illuminate important issues regarding individual and age differences in socioemotional functioning, several issues linger. For example, an assertion of attentional bias requires some comparison group, such that one group shows a bias in some processing as compared to another group. But establishing baselines for comparison is no easy task. For example, should a baseline be chance, when other evidence points to differential overall visual processing by valence (e.g., Charles et al., 2003; Luo, 2003)? Several studies have found overall patterns of higher attention to negative than other stimuli, regardless of age or individual differences. Is this a bias, or is this the appropriate baseline to compare other groups to in order to determine their biases? Some theoretical and computational work will be needed to unravel this issue.

Second is the thorny issue of timing. While previous methodologies such as the Emotional Stroop and dot-probe have been critiqued for leaving ambiguous when a bias happens, an emerging area of interest and concern is when in visual attention some individuals show biases or preferences for some information. In our study of anxiety, we found biases relatively late in presentation of a stimulus (Block & Isaacowitz, 2003), whereas other researchers have found "preattentive" effects on very first fixations (Mogg et al., 2000).

Before the days of using eye tracking to study emotion, Derryberry (e.g., Derryberry & Reed, 1994) made the provocative assertion that the attentional issue in neuroticism has to do with disengagement, not engagement, from negative stimuli. Some researchers have started to look in more detail at the time course of anxiety's effects on attention (Fox, Russo, & Dutton, 2002; Rohner, 2002). It is challenging to use eye tracking to test different propositions about the time course of the attention-emotion relationship. One technique we have started using in our research is presenting our stimuli at varying time intervals (from very quick to much slower) to test whether biases reveal themselves at some durations but not at others. However, more sophisticated techniques will need to be developed to better pursue this issue in the future, with or without eye tracking.

Contextualizing Eye Tracking in Information Processing

Visual attention to emotional stimuli is a very specific kind of information processing, and an important future direction will be to better delineate how this specific type of cognition fits into processing of information more generally. One study has done this by combining eye tracking with the results of a dot-probe task in the context of smoking (Mogg, Bradley, Field, & de Houwer, 2003). The results provided converging evidence from both dot-probe and eye

tracking for an attentional preference for smoking-relevant stimuli among smokers.

But even this step toward putting eye tracking in its place with other measures does not go beyond simply measuring attention in different ways. And yet, going beyond attention to other measures of information processing will be critical to truly understand the role of attentional biases in the production and reinforcement of behavior. So, for example, we have included recognition memory tasks in several of our eye-tracker studies, and some Emotional Stroop and dot-probe studies have also included memory measures. In our own work, we have found that depressed individuals remember fewer positive faces than their nondepressed peers, but this memory effect is not rooted in any bias or preference distinguishing the groups in terms of attention (Luo, 2003). While consistent with some theory in experimental psychopathology, this does present the intriguing problem of where the bias happens. In other words, what happens between attention and memory that may account for these findings?

As we attempt to tackle both individual and age differences in our work, we have realized that it is important not only to contextualize findings using other measures relevant to the stimuli (such as memory for the faces presented) but also to evaluate general perceptual and cognitive functioning in order to make the case that any observed biases do not simply reflect differences in general vision or cognition. Of course, differential results by stimulus type suggest this (such as findings biases in the same study for some images but not others), but unless the stimulus types are perfectly matched psychophysically (a tall order), then this possibility will always exist. And in particular, when differences are observed between age groups, the immediate temptation is to conclude that they result from some more basic cognitive aging process rather than specific biases or preferences. Therefore, we now include a full battery of general cognitive tests in each of our studies: including tests of processing speed (Digit Symbol), short-term memory (Forward and Backward Digit Span), and crystallized intelligence (Vocabulary).

Future Directions

The current goal of work in my lab is to document the ways in which attentional mechanisms underlie individual and age differences in well-being and emotion regulation. Therefore, our current studies are primarily descriptive in nature: We hypothesize where theoretically we would expect to see differences in attention between groups, and then design studies to test whether or not those attentional differences actually exist. When they do, we conclude that attentional mechanisms relate to the group differences, and perhaps they serve to reinforce the group differences in output. So, for example, in our work on anxiety (Block & Isaacowitz, 2003), we found that anxious individuals fixate longer on negative faces than their nonanxious peers, particularly when on the left side of the screen and particularly after a first scan has been made of the scene. We therefore assert that this attentional bias on the part of anxious individuals may serve to reinforce their anxiety, as it in effect tunes them in more to negative aspects of their environment.

Once these differences in attention have been documented, a remaining open question involves where the different attentional patterns come from. In other words, how does it happen that anxious individuals have different attentional patterns than their nonanxious peers in the first place? Future research will need to devise ways of determining the origins of these attentional biases and preferences. Possible approaches range from computational modeling to lab-based training studies.

A final area involves linking attentional preferences and biases to later behavior. Ingenious lab-based manipulations may be able to follow processing from trackable attention to measurable behavior. While much of this remains a promissory note for the future, the gist of my argument is that eye tracking may be an invaluable resource for linking levels of analysis in pursuit of an understanding of age and individual differences in well-being. While other researchers will continue their critical work examining neural or behavioral aspects of well-being, using creative technology to understand the cognitive mechanisms linking the neural activity to the behavior will facilitate a more complete picture of the psychology of happiness.

References

Arnold, J. E., Eisenband, J., Brown-Schmidt, S., & Trueswell, J. C. (2000). The rapid use of gender information: Evidence of the time course of pronoun resolution from eyetracking. *Cognition, 76,* B13–B26.

Aspinwall, L. G., & Brunhart, S. M. (1996). Distinguishing optimism from denial: Optimistic beliefs predict attention to health threats. *Personality and Social Psychology Bulletin, 22,* 993–1003.

Aspinwall, L. G., Richter, L., & Hoffman, R. R. (2001). Understanding how optimism "works": An examination of optimists' adaptive moderation of belief and behavior. In E. C. Chang (Ed.), *Optimism and pessimism: Theory, research, and practice* (pp. 217–238). Washington, DC: American Psychological Association.

Block, D. M., & Isaacowitz, D. M. (2003). *Anxiety and preferential attention to visual stimuli in young adults.* Unpublished manuscript, Brandeis University, Waltham, MA.

Bower, G. H. (1981). Mood and memory. *American Psychologist, 36,* 129–148.

Bradley, B. P., Mogg, K., & Lee, S. C. (1997). Attentional biases for negative information in induced and naturally occuring dysphoria. *Behaviour Research and Therapy, 35,* 911–927.

Bradley, B. P., Mogg, K., & Millar, N. H. (2000). Covert and overt orienting of attention to emotional faces in anxiety. *Cognition and Emotion, 14,* 789–808.

Buckley, T. C., Blanchard, E. B., & Hickling, E. J. (2002). Automatic and strategic processing of threat stimuli: A comparison between PTSD, panic disorder, and nonanxiety controls. *Cognitive Therapy and Research, 26,* 97–115.

Calvo, M. G., & Avero, P. (2002). Eye movement assessment of emotional processing in anxiety. *Emotion, 2,* 105–117.

Carnevale, P. J., & Isen, A. M. (1986). The influence of positive affect and visual access on the discovery of integrative solutions in bilateral negotiation. *Organizational Behavior and Human Decision Processes, 37,* 1–13.

Carstensen, L. L., Isaacowitz, D. M., & Charles, S. T. (1999). Taking time seriously: A theory of socioemotional selectivity. *American Psychologist, 54,* 155–181.

Carstensen, L. L., Pasupathi, M., Mayr, U., & Nesselroade, J. (2000). Emotion experience in everyday life across the adult life span. *Journal of Personality and Social Psychology, 79,* 644–655.

Carstensen, L. L., & Turk-Charles, S. (1994). The salience of emotion across the adult life course. *Psychology and Aging, 9,* 259–264.

Center for the Study of Emotion and Attention. (1999). *International affective picture system: Digitized photographs.* Gainsville, FL: Center for Research in Psychophysiology, University of Florida.

Chang, E. C., & Sanna, L. J. (2001). Optimism, pessimism, and positive and negative affectivity in middle-aged adults: A test of a cognitive-affective model of psychological adjustment. *Psychology and Aging, 16,* 524–531.

Charles, S. T., Mather, M., & Carstensen, L. L. (2003). Aging and emotional memory: The forgettable nature of negative images for older adults. *Journal of Experimental Psychology: General, 132,* 310–324.

Charles, S. T., Reynolds, C. A., & Gatz, M. (2001). Age-related differences and change in positive and negative affect over 23 years. *Journal of Personality and Social Psychology, 80,* 136–151.

Crundell, D., Underwood, G., & Chapman, P. (1999). Driving experience and the functional field of view. *Perception, 28,* 1075–1087.

Derryberry, D., & Reed, M. A. (1994). Temperament and attention: Orienting toward and away from positive and negative signals. *Journal of Personality and Social Psychology, 66,* 1128–1139.

Diener, E., Suh, E. M., Lucas, R. E., & Smith, H. L. (1999). Subjective well-being: Three decades of progress. *Psychological Bulletin, 125,* 276–302.

Ekman, P. (1993). Facial expression and emotion. *American Psychologist, 48,* 384–392.

Estrada, C. A., Isen, A. M., & Young, M. J. (1997). Positive affect facilitates integration of information and decreases anchoring in reasoning among physicians. *Organizational Behavior and Human Decision Processes, 72,* 117–135.

Fox, E., Russo, R., & Dutton, K. (2002). Attentional bias for threat: Evidence for delayed disengagement from emotional faces. *Cognition and Emotion, 16,* 355–379.

Fredrickson, B. L. (1998). What good are positive emotions? *Review of General Psychology, 2,* 300–319.

Fredrickson, B. L., & Carstensen, L. L. (1990). Choosing social partners: How old age and anticipated endings make people more selective. *Psychology and Aging, 5,* 335–347.

Gasper, K., & Clore, G. L. (2002). Attending to the big picture: Mood and global versus local processing of visual information. *Psychological Science, 13,* 34–40.

Hill, A. B., & Knowles, T. H. (1991). Depression and the "emotional" Stroop effect. *Personality and Individual Differences, 12,* 481–485.

Isaacowitz, D. M. (2005a). An attentional perspective on successful socioemotional aging: Theory and preliminary evidence. *Research on Human Development, 2,* 115–132.

Isaacowitz, D. M. (2005b). Correlates of well-being in adulthood and old age: A tale of two optimisms. *Journal of Research in Personality, 39,* 224–244.

Isaacowitz, D. M. (2005c). The gaze of the optimist. *Personality and Social Psychology Bulletin, 31,* 407–415.

Isaacowitz, D. M., & Seligman, M. E. P. (2002). Cognitive style predictors of affect change in older adults. *International Journal of Aging and Human Development, 54,* 233–253.

Isaacowitz, D. M., & Smith, J. (2003). Positive and negative affect in very old age. *Journal of Gerontology: Psychological Sciences, 58B,* P143–P152.

Isaacowitz, D. M., Wadlinger, H. A., Goren, D., & Wilson H. R. (2006). Selective preference in visual fixation away from negative images in old age? An eye tracking study. *Psychology and Aging, 21,* 40–48.

Kennedy, Q., Mather, M., & Carstensen, L. L. (2004) The role of motivation in the age-related positive bias in autobiographical memory. *Psychological Science, 15,* 208–214.

Lazarus, R. S. (1982). Thoughts on the relations between emotion and cognition. *American Psychologist, 37,* 1019–1024.

Lazarus, R., & Folkman, S. (1984). *Stress, appraisal, and coping.* New York: Springer.

Luo, J. (2003). *Visual attention and memory bias in depression.* Unpublished manuscript, Brandeis University, Waltham, MA.

MacLeod, C., Mathews, A., & Tata, P. (1986). Attentional bias in emotional disorders. *Journal of Abnormal Psychology, 95,* 15–20.

Mather, M., & Carstensen, L. L. (2003). Aging and attentional biases for emotional faces. *Psychological Science, 14,* 409–415.

Mogg, K., Bradley, B. P., Field, M., & de Houwer, J. (2003). Eye movements to smoking-related pictures in smokers: Relationship between attentional biases and implicit and explicit measures of stimulus valence. *Addiction, 98,* 825–836.

Mogg, K., & Marden, B. (1990). Selective processing of emotional information in anxious subjects. *British Journal of Clinical Psychology, 27,* 227–229.

Mogg, K., Millar, N., & Bradley, B. P. (2000). Biases in eye movements to threatening facial expressions in generalized anxiety disorder and depressive disorder. *Journal of Abnormal Psychology, 109,* 695–704.

Polk, T. A., & Farah, M. J. (1995). Late experience alters vision. *Nature, 376,* 648–649.

Posner, M. I., Snyder, C. R., & Davidson, B. J. (1980). Attention and the detection of signals. *Journal of Experimental Psychology: General, 109,* 160–174.

Rayner, K. (1998). Eye movements in reading and information processing: Twenty years of research. *Psychological Bulletin, 124,* 372–422.

Rohner, J.-C. (2002). The time-course of visual threat processing: High trait anxious individuals eventually avert their gaze from angry faces. *Cognition and Emotion, 16,* 837–844.

Scheier, M. F., & Carver, C. S. (1985). Optimism, coping, and health: Assessment and implications of generalized outcome expectancies. *Health Psychology, 4,* 219–47.

Segerstrom, S. C. (2001). Optimism and attentional bias for negative and positive information. *Personality and Social Psychology Bulletin, 2,* 1334–1343.

Sekuler, R., & Sekuler, A. B. (2000). Visual perception and cognition. In J. G. Evans, T. F. Williams, B. L. Beattle, J.-P. Michelm, & G. K. Wilcock (Eds.), *Oxford textbook of geriatric medicine* (2nd ed., pp. 874–880). Oxford: Oxford University Press.

Wadlinger, H., & Isaacowitz, D. M. (in press). Positive affect broadens visual attention to positive stimuli. *Motivation and Emotion.*

Watson, D., Clark, L. A., & Tellegen, A. (1988). Development and validation of brief measures of positive and negative affect: The PANAS scales. *Journal of Personality and Social Psychology, 54,* 1063–1070.

Williams, J. M. G., Watts, F. N., MacLeod, C., & Mathews, A. (1997). *Cognitive psychology and emotional disorders* (2nd ed.). New York: Wiley.

Williams, L. J. (1995). Peripheral target recognition and visual field narrowing in aviators and nonaviators. *International Journal of Aviation Psychology, 5,* 215–232.

Zajonc, R. B. (1980). Feeling and thinking: Preferences need no inferences. *American Psychologist, 35,* 151–175.

Zajonc, R. B. (1984). On the primacy of affect. *American Psychologist, 39,* 117–123.

16

Psychophysiological Approaches to the Study of Laughter

Toward an Integration With Positive Psychology

Paul G. Devereux and Kathi L. Heffner

The study of laughter occupies a rather modest place in scientific inquiry. Overshadowed by the study of humor, laughter has been relegated to a subtopic occasionally examined within the study of emotion (Ruch, 1993), facial displays (van Hooff, 1972), communication (Grammer, 1990), and, of particular relevance to this chapter, well-being (Fry, 1994). Discussions of laughter and health have mostly occurred in the context of therapeutic approaches to healing and wellness without strong scientific support. The scientific neglect of laughter is not unlike the relative neglect of positive emotion in general, and therefore it is commendable that this volume seeks to incorporate the work on laughter into positive psychology.

The neglect of laughter is unfortunate because the topic of laughter has much to offer the study of positive psychology. From its benefits to the physiological system and potentially to individual health, to its indication of positive interaction and positive intraindividual emotional states, the study of laughter can inform the interpersonal, individual, and biological levels of psychological inquiry. Laughter is implicated in a wide variety of positive psychology topics (e.g., reducing perceptions of pain, reconstructing narrative, coping, resilience, creating and strengthening bonds, and mind-body linkages).[1] Given its ubiquitous occurrence in social interaction, the study of laughter should occupy a central place in social psychology as well as positive psychology.

In this chapter, we present an overview of research on laughter as it relates to positive psychology. Our focus is on psychophysiological methods as a technique in the study of laughter to inform positive psychology. In particular, we argue that this approach lends itself to addressing questions about the temporal patterning of laughter, including the identification of any potential salubrious outcomes. Utilizing a social psychophysiological perspective should be fruitful if, as we argue, it is in the social and physiological domains where laughter's benefits to health and well-being are most likely located.

We suggest that: (1) studies examining the behavior of laughing have been limited, especially studies exploring interpersonal contexts associated with laughter; (2) as a field, social psychophysiology has not readily addressed the topic of laughter with the result that many studies of laughter's physiology are atheoretical; and (3) conversely, theoretical approaches on relevant positive psychology issues like emotion and coping have not typically included laughter. Incorporating psychophysiological perspectives can help inform theory by establishing how positive psychological constructs "get under our skin" and ultimately impact health (Anderson & Armstead, 1995).

Relevance of Psychophysiological Methods to Laughter and Positive Psychology

Laughter may be less likely to be a topic of study in any one particular domain (e.g., communication studies) because of its multifaceted properties. Laughter has facial, postural, and acoustic, as well as physiological properties. In the present context, however, we suggest that laughter is a behavioral channel through which many of the positive emotions can affect physiology. It is a rapid and direct way that the social world "enters the body." Just as ignoring the mind has hindered advances in medical studies (Spiegel, 1999), it makes little sense for psychology to ignore the body. Psychological events do not operate outside of an embodied biological system. Physiology can inform affect (James, 1884) and affect informs physiology (Lazarus, 1991). Studying physiology is not a call for reductionism; rather, we argue that researchers should incorporate physiology to inform the topic of positive psychology. Therefore, explanation of phenomena must remain at the psychological level. Our approach in this chapter is in the spirit of multimethod triangulation, wherein psychophysiological measures complement self-report and behavioral data (for a discussion, see Blascovich, 2000).[2]

Over the last 20 years, the field of psychophysiology has made advances in methodology and conceptual clarity. For example, there has been movement away from measuring undifferentiated arousal to using more differentiated concepts of arousing states (see Cacioppo, Berntson, & Crites, 1996). As in all methodologies, researchers must be judicious in incorporating psychophysiology and avoid crudely applying it. An understanding of laughter and positive psychology will not advance simply by measuring physiological responses atheoretically. For example, an increase in heart rate or any other single physiological response typically fails to unambiguously index specific behaviors. Heart rate increases due to events as varied as exercise, awaiting a romantic partner, and public speaking (Blascovich, 2000, p. 119). Therefore, there is no one-to-one correspondence from physiology to behavior or from behavior to physiology (Blascovich, 2000; Cacioppo et al., 1996).

Similarly, the probability of laughter uniquely indexing one physiological state is also unlikely. There are too many varieties to laughter and too many contexts in which it occurs, especially in humans. The relationships between laughing, physiology, and positive psychology will be more reliably uncovered by studying laughter in appropriate contexts. In this chapter, we argue that the appropriate contexts for laughter would necessarily be interactional settings.

Collecting data using psychophysiological measures means that researchers do not need to rely solely on self-report. Interrupting participants' line of activity to complete questionnaires is detrimental to the environment necessary for the occurrence of laughter. In this sense, psychophysiological measures are less intrusive than self-report and they also have a much sharper temporal resolution (see Tomarken, 1995). Incorporating psychophysiological measures also allows for measuring activity that might be missed by observers or coders. For example, facial muscle activity corresponding with sad and happy memories that was not readily apparent to observers has been discriminated using psychophysiological indices (Tassinary & Cacioppo, 1992).

There has not been extensive work in positive psychology using psychophysiological methods, but some researchers have examined immune, neuroendocrine, and cardiovascular antecedents, concomitants, and sequelae of emotion, often with the goal of distinguishing between positive and negative emotion (e.g., Fredrickson, Mancuso, Branigan, & Tugade, 2000). As one example, the facial feedback hypothesis posits that emotional experiences are influenced by facial displays, and distinct muscle activity underpinning these displays indeed correlates with negative and positive affect (Ekman & Davidson, 1993; Zajonc, Murphy, & Inglehart, 1989). More research has examined physiological variables within the study of laughter compared to other issues like its acoustic properties, but the evidence is not conclusive.

In the following section, we discuss the definition and function of laughter. We then turn to laughter's associations with physiological variables. Following that, methodological considerations, theoretical contributions, and future directions in the psychophysiological study of laughter are addressed.

What Is Laughter?

A paradox exists in that everyone knows what laughter is but scientifically its measurement has been scattered, in part a reflection of laughter's complexity. A conceptually distinct definition and validated measures of laughter are still needed. Its ease of recognition may be laughter's undoing. Because of its conspicuousness, careful operationalizations may not seem as necessary.

Laughter, according to *Webster's* (1998) dictionary, is a "movement (usually involuntary) of the muscles of the face, particularly of the lips, with a peculiar expression of the eyes, indicating merriment, satisfaction, or derision, and usually attended by a sonorous and interrupted expulsion of air from the lungs." Laughter is most typically not involuntary (Provine, 1993). It can indicate much more than merriment, satisfaction, or derision and can occur without any accompanying emotion. Laughter typically comprises a distinctive respiratory-vocal-behavioral pattern and involves facial, laryngeal, and thoracic muscles, as well as the abdomen and extremities, like the limbs (Bachorowski, Smoski, & Owren, 2001; Kuhn, 1994; Ruch & Ekman, 2001). Although laughter typically includes these features, as will be discussed, there are many varieties of laughter and no characteristic of these varieties seems to be necessary or sufficient. With relevance to positive psychology, laughter can be a marker of positive affect (a dependent variable) or a means of promoting a positive end state, emotionally or otherwise, and therefore, a mediator or independent variable. Laughter can also be conceptualized as a moderator (e.g., in coping with stress or conflict). Without an accepted scientific definition, though, it is difficult enough

to study laughter, let alone attempt to identify corresponding physiological or psychological events.

Despite the popular view that laughter is the best medicine, relatively few studies can back up this assertion. In a review of the literature, Martin (2001) concluded that there is little evidence for the positive effects of laughter on health. One study that did find effects of a humor intervention did not explicitly measure laughter. Tan, Tan, Berk, Lukman, and Lukman (1997) compared cardiac rehabilitation patients who viewed humor against a control group who received the standard care conditions. The authors found that patients of both genders in the humor group had better cardiovascular health outcomes after 1 year, including fewer episodes of arrhythmias, lower blood pressure, lower urinary and plasma catecholamines, a lower requirement for beta-blockers and nitroglycerine, and a lower incidence of recurrent myocardial infarction.

As with studies of physical health, laughter-related research examining mental health and well-being has placed more emphasis on humor. In these studies, researchers have focused on the positive emotional states accompanying laughter and humor (Argyle, 1997), with the majority of research demonstrating a link between humor and reduced depression (Danzer, Dale, & Klions, 1990). Laughter in this context has been used primarily as a way to produce positive emotion, rather than as an end in itself.

Laughter Unto Itself

Researchers purporting to study laughter's effects most often attempt to induce humor by having subjects watch amusing video clips. In reports of these studies, the impact of both humor and laughter on the dependent variables of interest tend to be discussed interchangeably, often without actually measuring laughter (for a review, see Martin, 2001). Although the two are often conflated, there are only moderate correlations between humor and laughter (Provine, 1997). McGhee (1977) noted that correlations between rated funniness and the amount of smiling or laughter are low, seldom exceeding .40. As one example of this discordance, laughter occurs in jeering situations where humor is absent. Laughter is also used as a conversational signal to others, as politeness in indicating attention (O'Donnell-Trujillo & Adams, 1983) or as a signal indicating sexual interest (Grammer, 1990). Studying laughter separately from humor allows for the focus to be on the behavior of laughing and in this way, its physiological aspects can command a stronger emphasis than has occurred when laughter has been coupled with humor. For information on coping with humor or other studies using humor, see Martin (2001).

These important distinctions between laughter and humor notwithstanding, laughter is most usually indicative of positive emotion, and therefore has direct relevance for positive psychology. For clarification among laughter types, some researchers use the term *mirthful laughter* (Berk, Felten, Tan, & Bittman, 2001) to denote laughter that is associated with amusement or positive affect. To separate out their impacts on positive affect or other positive psychology constructs, laughter should be studied independently from humor, or at the very least, measured independently from humor.

Laughter is also distinct from the smile, although like humor, the two co-occur. Evolutionarily, laughing and smiling have different origins (van Hooff, 1972) and occur in different contexts (Sroufe & Waters, 1976). Much of the psychophysiological work on positive affect has looked at the smile (e.g., Larsen, Norris, & Cacioppo, 2003), particularly using electromyographic (EMG) assessment of the zygomaticus major, the muscle that pulls the cheeks from the mouth. Relative to laughter, the smile is easier to produce (the movement of one bilateral muscle, zygomaticus major), and it does not have the other components typical of laughter (e.g., respiration, torso movement, vocalization). The addition of these other factors in laughter probably help explain why the comparatively straightforward smile has received more attention. Ruch (1993) points out that relative to smiling, the exact number of additional muscles involved in laughing is not yet known.

Types of Laughter

Just as all laughter is not associated with humor, not are all laughs are alike. There are meaningful differences between shared laughter among friends and an indignant HA! Milford (1981) examined the acoustical properties of laughter from four different stimulus conditions: tension-release, humor, tickle, and social (occurring during a conversation). She found significant acoustic and temporal differences among all laughter types: The mean duration in response to tickling was 2.62 seconds, to humor 2.08 seconds, to tension release 1.3 seconds, and the shortest duration was social laughter, .88 seconds. In a similar study on the acoustic properties of laughter conducted with mother-infant dyads, Nwokah, Davies, Islam, Hsu, and Fogel (1993) also found what they called comment laughter (which occurred in conversational contexts) to be shortest in duration compared to other laughter types. Given that the duration of laughter so typical in day-to-day interactions is quite short, it is likely that examining the frequency of laughter across time is where investigators need to direct their efforts to elucidate laughter's health effects. Typically, the duration of all types of laughter seldom lasts beyond 7 seconds (Ruch, 1990, as cited in Ruch, 1993).

Despite these differences, few researchers have examined whether laughter types are physiologically unique. Fry and Savin (1988) found no differences in blood pressure between simulated laughter and felt mirth. In another study, viewing more amusing films produced an increase in cortisol (Hubert, Moller, & de Jong-Meyer, 1993), whereas laughter has been typically associated with cortisol decreases (Berk et al., 1989). There is also evidence that the type of laughter has differential outcomes on positive emotion. For example, voiced but not unvoiced laughter elicits positive affect (Bachorowski & Owren, 2001). The authors argue that the acoustical properties of laughter may be associated with inducing and maintaining arousal in listeners. To the extent that there are meaningful differences among laughter types, psychophysiological studies can and should be designed to distinguish among them.

Although it is believed that laughter is acoustically distinct at the individual level (e.g., Janice's identifiable laugh on the television show *Friends*), evidence points to the context as an important influence on distinctive laughter (Vettin & Todt, 2004). Milford's (1981) acoustical analysis of laughter samples indicated that the laughter of one individual tends to be similar to the laughter of another individual when it is produced under similar conditions. Milford also demonstrated that context as a cue source is an important consideration. When judges listened to tapes to try to classify laughter types, they were not able to make discriminations among the laughter samples when they were presented out of their communicative context. Researchers then must consider both the context of occurrence and the type of laughter.

Interpersonal Psychophysiology and the Study of Laughter

According to Provine (2000), laughter evolved not for its health benefits but because of its impact on others, and therefore positive benefits should most reliably occur within interpersonal contexts. Evolutionary accounts of laughter exist because of the generally accepted view that laughter is a homologue of the primate relaxed open-mouth display, known less formally as the play face (Darwin, 1872; Redican, 1982; van Hooff, 1972). The play face is characterized by a rather widely opened mouth, with lips that remain covering all or the greater part of the teeth (van Hooff). Theories of play that suggest it promotes the acquisition of cooperation in young animals (e.g., Fagen, 1987) also associate the context of laughter with interpersonal bonding. Because facial displays and the vigilance toward them coevolved (see Fridlund, 1994), it makes sense that researchers employ an interpersonal psychophysiology perspective to study them.

Ontogenetic explanations also describe laughter as occurring in situations of infant exploration and bonding: "when laughter occurs the baby maintains an orientation towards the agent, reaches for the object, and seeks to reproduce the situation" (Sroufe & Wunsch, 1972, p. 1340). The context for infant laughter is social, and, in particular, laughter occurs during interactional episodes in which the infant is actively engaged. For younger infants (4 months of age), physically vigorous, intrusive stimulation (i.e., tickling) is the most potent elicitation of laughter (Sroufe & Waters, 1976). As the infants grow, incongruous events (e.g., mother walking like a penguin) and finally "interesting social events," especially when the infant is the agent (rather than a passive recipient), most reliably elicit laughter (Bainum, Lounsbury, & Pollio, 1984; Sroufe & Waters). Washburn (1929) observed that strangers can seldom evoke a laugh by tickling a child. In a study using humorous video clips, children laughed in the presence of friends but not strangers (Foot, Chapman, & Smith, 1977).

Ethological research overwhelmingly supports the idea that laughter is a social event. Provine has reported that laughing was more than 30 times as likely to be performed by subjects in social than in solitary settings (Provine & Fischer, 1989). In Provine's studies, subjects when alone were more likely to speak to themselves than they were to laugh. Provine and Fischer argue that laughter is virtually nonexistent outside of social or media contexts. Laughter therefore should be studied in interpersonal contexts; however, many studies relevant to positive psychology are of people in isolation. Most typically, the studies consist of subjects being shown humorous videotapes. We argue that the study of laughter and its positive impacts should be examined using an interpersonal psychophysiology approach wherein psychophysiological recording includes two or more people engaged in social interaction (see Wagner & Calam, 1988). This perspective is congruent with Ryff and Singer's (2000) call for the physiological study of interpersonal flourishing as a means of understanding positive human health. Laughter is the ultimate accompaniment of positive interaction and part and parcel of "having quality ties to others" (Ryff & Singer, p. 31). For a more complete discussion on studying interpersonal relationships and positive psychology, see chapter 40, this volume.

Whether physiological differences exist between isolated and social or shared laughter has not been explored. Perhaps shared laughter is healthier physiologically or otherwise, compared with nonshared laughter. For example, social bonds may help "retune" physiological systems, resulting in better physiological functioning and healthier reactions to stress (see Diamond, 2001). The regular presence of shared laughter within relationships may help this retuning process. In addition, laughter promotes behavioral synchrony, which is associated with emotional contagion, and this allows for a setting wherein more positive, engaged interaction can occur (Devereux & Ginsburg, 2001b). The judicious use of humor by interactants may be undertaken to facilitate this physiological coordination and positive interactional end state.

Fry (1994) has discussed the physiological impact of laughter in producing a positive social effect: "After laughter's relaxation phase, an elevated level of mental and emotional interactiveness develops between people who have been laughing together, reflecting the infectiousness of this exhilaration" (p. 115). This elevated interactiveness may occur as a consequence of the physiological matching of persons performing similar motor actions (in this case laughter) or as a consequence of interactants having similar emotional stances when laughing together (Owren & Bachorowski, 2003; Smoski & Bachorowski, 2003). Compared to shared laughter, even less work has examined what happens physiologically to someone hearing laughter. For example, although some work has looked at responses to laughter in mother-infant dyads (see Fogel et al., 1997, for a review), it is not yet clear how laughter physiologically impacts the mother or infant.

The Physiological Study of Laughter

In psychophysiological studies of laughter, researchers have sought to identify distinctive physiological characteristics of laughter (Provine & Yong, 1991; Ruch & Ekman, 2001). With regard to the former, laughter, according to some views, is proposed to release "excess arousal" and this reduction of arousal following laughter (the relaxation phase) is seen as pleasurable and beneficial for the individual (Fry, 1994). In these approaches, laughter functions in modulating arousal (undifferentiated) in the confrontation of provocative stimuli (Porteous, 1988), often conceptualized as a response to a joke-telling sequence. The excess arousal ideas are advanced because of laughter's unique respiratory pattern. When one is laughing, there is a predominance of expiration over inspiration and the inspiration-expiration ratio during laughter is lower than in any other emotional state studied (Ruch, 1993).

More common than basic psychophysiological research on laughing have been studies of hypothesized beneficial effects of vigorous laughter, including reduced muscle tension, increased oxygenation of blood, exercising of the heart, and endorphin production (Fry, 1994; Martin 2001), but empirical support for these ideas is not strong.

Laughter does, however, have specific and potentially health-relevant physiological effects on the central nervous, muscular, respiratory, endocrine, immune, and cardiovascular systems (Fry, 1986, 1992). In light of the distinction we emphasize between humor and laughter, we do not presume the necessity of humor for these effects, only the behavior of laughing, but we encourage direct empirical testing of this assumption. Because there have been few psychophysiological studies directly assessing the act of laughter independent of humor, we present some findings with regard to humor and physiological correlates that provide a foundation from which the psychophysiological study of laughter and well-being can develop.

Cardiovascular System

Emotions are generally thought to most strongly impact the cardiovascular system given its relationship to action tendencies (Obrist, 1981; see Fredrickson & Levenson, 1998). Laughter also probably most strongly affects the cardiovascular system, including increases in heart rate, blood pressure, and owing to the expiration force produced in laughing, increases in blood oxygen. Laughter's respiratory pattern has potential health benefits, as laughing sometimes even exceeds the level of maximal voluntary exhalation (Bright, Hixon, & Hoit, 1986; Lloyd, 1938). Fry (1994) suggested:

> Increased pulmonary ventilation causes a blowing off of the excess carbon dioxide and water vapor which builds up in residual air. Air with greater oxygen concentration and less moisture content is exchanged for the "stale" air; more oxygen is available for red blood cell uptake; there is less excess moisture to encourage pulmonary bacterial growth (less chance of bronchial infection and/or pneumonia). (p. 116)

One widely held belief is that laughter is salutary because it is similar to exercise, hence the term *inner jogging* (Szabo, 2003). There are a handful of studies comparing similarities in psychological outcomes for exercise and laughter, which again is typically not directly measured. There are only a few studies directly comparing the physiology of laughter and exercise. In fact, in a study comparing laughter's caloric costs relative to aerobic exercise, the caloric cost of the laughter period was the same as a prelaughter baseline measurement (1.35 kcal/min) and the authors concluded that laughter is not exercise (Boone, Hansen, & Erlandson, 2000).

Immune and Endocrine Systems

Psychophysiological studies of laughter have not readily incorporated theory, and this is especially the case with studies that have addressed laughter's relationship to the immune system. The absence of theory means that the literature contains assorted results that do not easily cohere. A meta-analysis is warranted. If the topic of laughter is more readily incorporated into the positive psychology theoretical paradigm, an organizing framework would help the results in this area cohere. Thus far, there has been a kind of "let's measure everything and see what comes out" approach. Given the dearth of research at this point, though, exploratory studies remain important. However, these types of studies leave one open to criticisms of inflated Type I error rates (see Martin, 2001). In their place, theoretically driven studies with focused comparisons are better in terms of what can be uncovered and then explained. Theory linking the biological and psychological is improving (see for example, McEwen, 1998) but is in its infancy.

Immune variables that have been measured are: natural killer cell activity; plasma immunoglobulins; functional phenotypic markers for leukocytes including activated T cells, B cells, natural killer cells, T cells with helper and suppressor markers, cytokines, interferon-gamma, and total leukocytes with subpopulations of lymphocytes, granulocytes, and monocytes (see Berk, 2001). The primary way that laughter is believed to provide immunity benefits is by increasing transport of blood substances to body cells (Fry & Savin, 1988), thus improving immune system efficiency. Martin (2001) reported evidence from laughter studies showing increases in serum immunoglobulin A, which protects against upper respiratory infections. Other studies have found some evidence that laughter helps antibodies destroy defective or infected cells and increases the number and activity of natural killer cells and T cells (Berk, Tan, & Fry, 1993).

Laughter also influences endocrine system responding. Changes in circulating catecholamine and cortisol levels have been noted (Hubert & de Jong-Meyer, 1991; Hubert et al., 1993). In a study at Loma Linda University School of Medicine (Berk et al., 1989), blood samples were drawn before, during, and after subjects were shown a humorous video. The mirthful experience appeared to reduce dopac, a dopamine marker, serum cortisol, epinephrine, and growth hormone, indicating a reduction in stress-associated physiological activity.

The results described here are from exposure to humorous videos, and researchers have not always independently measured laughter. One study that did measure both laughter and humor found that the humorous stimulus resulted in improved immunity as measured by serum immunoglobulin A, regardless of the overt laughter expressed, as rated by observers (Labott, Ahleman, Wolever, & Martin, 1990). Given the small sample size of 16 subjects and the lack of differences in self-ratings of laughter between the expression and inhibition conditions in this study, more work is needed. However, if exposure to humor has one impact and laughing another, this finding will help further separate humor and laughter. Studies directly comparing humor and laughter are necessary.

Brain Activity

Although functional magnetic resonance imaging and electroencephalographic studies are increasing, brain pathology continues to dominate the area, especially in studies of laughter. Specific to emotion, asymmetry in the brain's anterior cortical regions is related to emotional states, and individuals with greater baseline left frontal brain activity report more positive affect than individuals with greater baseline right frontal brain activity (Tomarken, Davidson, Wheeler, & Doss, 1992). In contrast, responses to humor appear to engage the whole cerebral cortex (Derks, Bogart, & Gillikin, 1991, as cited in Berk, 2001). In designing these studies, researchers need to utilize a methodology that is able to discriminate whether the brain activity is due to humor, feelings of amusement, or laughter.

Studies that stimulate the brain produce laughter in people who then have reported that everything seemed funny (Arroyo et al., 1993). It is not clear whether the stimulation caused the feelings of mirth, whether observing themselves laughing caused the mirth, or even whether subjects attributed the laughter to their circumstances to simply provide an explanation for laughing (Fried, Wilson, MacDonald, & Behnke, 1998). However, other studies show that laughter can be generated without accompanying feelings of mirth, particularly during seizures (Georgakoulias, Vize, Jenkins, & Singounas, 1998) or when simulated (Fry & Savin, 1988). These neurological analyses distinguish pathological laughter and nonpathological laughter, cataloguing pathological laughter under the region associated with epilepsy, strokes, and circumspect brain lesions (Wild, Rodden, Grodd, & Ruch, 2003). Researchers have not yet examined health outcomes or differences in positive psychology constructs between felt and produced, mirthless laughter.

Methodological Considerations

General Issues

Depending on the particular research question or interest in laughter, it may be necessary to collaborate with other disciplines, given laughter's diverse properties. For example, researchers in audiology, communication, or comparative psychology could be consulted to help with understanding the relevant aspects of laughter.

Psychophysiological studies of emotion must independently assess the presence of emotion, and so too must the presence of laughter be measured. Simply having subjects watch humorous films is not sufficient to the study of laughter (to humor perhaps, but not laughter). Laughter must be assessed independently from humor. Just as the failure to independently verify emotion arousal was a problem in early emotion studies and was the reason why a consistent autonomic nervous system pattern could not be demonstrated (Levenson, 1988), the lack of measurement inhibits the understanding of laughter. We detail the measurement of laughter below following our discussion of physiological measurement.

If using humor to produce laughter, individual differences in humor appreciation need to be considered. Wide situational and individual differences exist in what is perceived as funny, and therefore stimuli often will not be equivalent across people and even for the same person over time. In these cases, matching ratings of amusement or stimuli funniness and manipulation checks are needed. Ratings of funniness and feelings of amusement do not measure the same thing, however, and therefore both measures should be included (Cupchik & Leventhal, 1974). Even though laughter is often conceptualized as an independent variable, few studies have matched laughter across groups. It is also best to measure frequency and intensity of laughter (e.g., using spectrograms, observer ratings, or even self-reports) to control for differences.

Unlike the difficulty timing physiological patterns that co-occur with emotions like sadness, it is relatively easy to match physiological variables with laughter's onset and offset due to laughter's conspicuousness. Studies are still needed to determine how consistently laughter is associated with emotional states and even which particular emotions correspond with laughter (Bonanno & Keltner, 2004). Observational, descriptive studies like that of Provine

and Fischer (1989) would be helpful in this regard.

Measuring Physiology

When designing studies to identify physiological correlates and consequences of laughter, basic principles of psychophysiology must be considered. These include attention to the time-dependent nature of physiological responses, the relationship of prestimulus physiological levels to the magnitude of stimulation responses, habituation and sensitization in repeated-measures designs, and individual variation in physiological responses. When developing analytical strategies, one must contend with the loss of data that accompanies technical physiological assessment, individual outliers, and the statistical dependency of sequentially sampled physiological data. A discussion of each of these principles and hurdles is beyond the scope of this chapter; however, the interested reader is encouraged to refer to McHugo and Lanzetta (1983) and Jennings and Stine (2000) for more details. We limit our discussion here to methodological considerations specific to laughter and physiology.

The psychophysiological study of laughter necessarily requires attention to motoric activation; laughter is an activity rather than some experiential state that may or may not be accompanied by overt bodily movement. Such attention is required for any research question with regard to laughter, even when the outcome of interest is not muscle activity. For instance, if one is interested in cardiovascular activity following episodes of laughter, it will be important to have some assessment of movement during the laughter episode; the degree of overall body movement during laughter can impact cardiovascular responses following laughter. This motoric activity can be directly assessed using EMG or may be obtained using observational methods (e.g., videotaping).

When the interest is in psychophysiological correlates of laughter itself, the physiological indices used will most often capture changes associated with general body movement (such as postural changes) in addition to the movement associated with laughing (facial displays and upper body movement). The former constitutes noise in the data; however, allowing for such natural movement will be a better strategy than artificially constraining it. The noise can be filtered out during collection or removed during analysis without compromising the realism of the laughter episode. Therefore, issues of signal detection and noise are important concerns (see Gratton, 2000, for a discussion of how to address these technical issues).

A more comprehensive approach to the collection of physiological data may prove more useful than capturing a single measure, as in data triangulation. For example, multiple measures of physiological systems, like the sympathetic nervous system, provide a better representation of bodily response than only measuring heart rate. In exploratory work, one could potentially include measures of brain activity, immune system parameters, and cardiovascular indices because all of these systems have been implicated in laughter. Given the lack of knowledge to date, these studies are needed. In a related vein, great variety exists with regard to laughter, and just as undifferentiated concepts of arousal no longer prove very useful, it is best to decide a priori what specific aspects of laughter are most relevant for your study. For example, if the acoustic properties or facial activity associated with laughter are the focus of the investigation, the design should follow.

The research environment is another important issue when studying laughter. Within the laboratory, the most typical methodology is to have subjects watch amusing films, but one could also record a conversation, instruct people to laugh, or direct subjects to imagine an amusing episode in their life. Relative to interpersonal psychophysiology, the relevance of relationship type and context are also important methodological considerations. It has been demonstrated that the amount and duration of laughter are different between strangers and friends (Devereux & Ginsburg, 2001a). Studies comparing laughter within different settings are also needed: Does the humorous video elicit comparable amounts and types of laughter in the lab, at home, or in other, more naturalistic environments? Given laughter's sensitivity to context, laboratory studies may be too contrived when trying to understand how laughter impacts health outcomes. Researchers typically try to produce a relaxed, playful context to promote laughter; however, that is difficult to do if one is videotaping, recording, and hooking up subjects to physiological equipment. In studies of infants, it is hard to produce laughter in the lab, especially after attaching physiological leads for EMG and other recordings (Sroufe & Waters, 1976). Experience-sampling methods wherein subjects are recorded throughout the day better

capture real-world occurrences of laughter and are potentially more relevant for the study of positive psychology.

On a final note, expectancy effects are important to consider when assessing positive psychology constructs related to benefits of laughter (Mahony, Burroughs, & Lippman, 2002), especially in light of folk wisdom promoting the idea that laughter helps with healing. An advantage to physiological assessment is reduced reliance on self-report, which in turn minimizes the likelihood of expectancy effects.

Measuring Laughter

Scales

To our knowledge, no scales currently exist that directly measure laughter. There are a few scales that attempt to measure the likelihood of using humor (Situational Humor Response Questionnaire, Martin & Lefcourt, 1984; Sense of Humor Questionnaire, Ziv, 1979). Owing to their differences, researchers should not use scales conceptualizing laughter and humor as a unipolar construct with *not humorous* and *laughing uncontrollably* as anchors. Laughter does not directly correspond to mirth or felt amusement and, therefore, researchers interested in correlating laughter with emotion states must measure emotion and, depending on the research questions, control for its presence. Using a scale may be less helpful than observing or recording laughter.

Observing Laughter

Videotaping respondents produces a permanent record and allows for a microanalysis of laughter, including frame-by-frame detail. Reliability of coders is a concern, and the reliability and validity issues discussed by Bakeman and Gottman (1997) are relevant to observational studies of laughter. Because postural changes and limb movements are associated with laughing, the placement of video cameras should be considered carefully. In addition, laughter's vocalizations are hard to record, especially at a distance (Preuschoft, 1992).

In studies in which laughter has been directly measured, detail on the methodology is often lacking. A well-defined and validated code is needed for observations of laughter just as in any observational research. One previous operationalization of laughter used for coding was the presence of "inarticulate vocal sounds of a reiterated ha-ha form" (Chapman & Wright, 1976, p. 204). This definition leaves out non-reiterated sounds and laughter without sound. Another operationalization of laughter, defined it "in terms of the onset and termination of a nonverbal vocal behavior" (Mowrer, LaPointe, & Case, 1987, p. 194). However, laughter can also occur without accompanying vocal sounds, with simply the presence of the play face, increased expirations, and trunk movements.

Acoustic Measurement

Because coding of laughter can be so tedious, researchers may want to capture laughter directly with auditory recorders. Acoustical properties of laugh episodes, including measures of frequency, rhythmicity, and amplitude, are not fully understood, and more studies like that of Nwokah et al. (1993) are needed. It is known that modifications in the vibratory pattern codetermine how laughter sounds and may be a key factor in distinguishing types of laughter (Ruch & Ekman, 2001). When laughter's acoustic properties are well identified, relationships with positive psychology can better be uncovered. Questions such as whether rhythmic laughs are physiologically healthier would be worth exploring.

Measuring Respiration

Polygraph measures of respiration have been used to quantify laughter in previous work (Fry, 1977; Svebak, 1975). Although the presence of respiration is not sufficient to capture laughter, it is a useful methodology as respiration is an essential component of laughter and unique respiratory properties of laughter exist. Because respiration alters heart rate, heart rate should be assessed independently of laughter. When measuring respiration, particular attention should be paid to the various types of laughter, as respiratory demands will be different, for example, between social laughter, comment laughter, and vigorous laughter in response to humor.

Laughter in Context: Temporal Issues

Examining what behaviors, interactions, or emotions follow laughter can help answer questions about temporal issues. For instance, what does laughter prepare us to do? Physiologically, are we better prepared for any line of action after laughing? Are we better prepared uniquely via laughter? Increases in heart rate and blood pressure typically serve to prepare one for a line of action, yet there is disagreement on whether the physiological changes associated with laughter actually do that. According to Ruch (1993), the physiological changes in laughter do not prepare us for fight-or-flight reactions, and the general lowering of muscle tonus is associated with a reduced readiness to respond attentively or with planned behavior to environmental changes. However, laughter is often observed during episodes of rough-and-tumble play in nonhuman primates, during which activity is abundant, and the play face facilitates the respiratory demands of this activity (Loizos, 1967). In order to determine what precedes, accompanies, and follows laughter physiologically, onset and offset information need to be collected.

The temporal examination of laughter should extend beyond its offset. Researchers have demonstrated that there are physiologically meaningful occurrences following laughter, especially related to relaxation (Fry, 1994). Research on the duration of elevated immune parameters shows impacts up to 12 hours following a period of laughter (Berk et al., 2001). There has not been much support for longer-term effects of laughter or of the benefits of having a sense of humor across the life span (see Martin, 2002). More longitudinal studies of laughter are required to discern the impact of laughter episodes across time. Laughter's physical benefits may arise from an accumulation of positive physiological experiences (e.g., physiological "retunement"; Diamond, 2001) that co-occur with laughter, or from laughter's ability to enhance coping with repetitive life hassles that are suggested over time to have potentially pernicious effects on bodily health processes if taken too seriously (Cacioppo et al., 1998).

Examining cyclicity patterns between people is important to determine who starts laughter, who reciprocates, and who ends a laughter episode. Spectral analysis of laughter's waveforms can be used here, as is often done with heart rate patterns of respiration (Porges & Bohrer, 1990). Milford (1981) used a real-time spectral analyzer to determine the spectral content, duration, and relative intensity of laughter in a variety of contexts. Due to the temporal data frequently collected in psychophysiology, time series analysis is also a common analytic strategy.

Considering Control Groups in Laughter Research

Identifying the equivalence of a "nonemotion" control group is not easily done. For example, in a study by the authors (Heffner, Devereux, & Ginsburg, 2005) in which subjects were instructed to write about mundane topics without referring to emotion, participants complained about the difficulty of describing events without using emotion terms. Pleasant versus unpleasant or positive versus negative emotion conditions are easier to devise and contrast with each other as compared with using a nonemotion group.

Fredrickson et al. (2000) discussed problems with "no-film" controls, arguing that cardiovascular "activity is sensitive to perceptual and attentional processes, as well as to emotional processes. As such, comparing responses to film viewing to 'doing nothing' confounds emotional content with differences in basic cognitive demands" (p. 244). Fredrickson et al. use a neutral film in their studies. These are important issues given that much of the cited work consists of control conditions with people sitting in a room together while other conditions watched humorous video.

Participants in different conditions should be matched along behavioral dimensions that necessarily have physiological concomitants, for example, by ensuring equivalent movement across participants. It is easy for a participant to comply with a request to remain stationary when watching a video, but much more difficult during studies of interactional episodes of laughter. Other studies might use comparison groups who engage in similar voiced activity like yells or forced expirations. Using subjects as their own controls can help minimize comparison issues and can be especially useful given individual differences in humor appreciation.

Theoretical Implications of the Psychophysiological Study of Laughter

To more readily advance scientific understanding, psychophysiological measures need to be embedded into broader biological and behavioral systems (Tomarken, 1995). For example, McEwen (1998) created an index which he termed *allostatic load* that connects different physiological systems to explain stress-induced wear and tear on the body. The concept of allostatic load "thus provides a unifying scheme for investigating the effects of stress on disparate physiological systems" (Kubzansky, Kawachi, & Sparrow, 1999, p. 336). Similarly, a theoretical paradigm that incorporates laughter into positive psychology would be especially welcome. Ruch's (1993) discussion of exhilaration is an example of work integrating laughter into larger theoretical constructs. Short of developing new theoretical ideas, examining predictions of laughter drawn from the metatheory of evolution and positive psychological theories could potentially be informative.

There has been research examining laughter and amusement as converses to negative emotional states and pain. McDougall (1922) called laughter the antidote of sympathetic pain. However, pain tolerance studies have not measured laughter directly, so its role therein is actually unclear (Martin, 2002). Work in the 1970s used an incompatible states approach to study humor and aggression. This research most reliably demonstrated that feelings of amusement and anger do not mutually co-occur, but distraction or attentional shift hypotheses were also proposed as explanations (Baron, 1983; McDonald & Wooten, 1988). More recently, work in positive psychology has begun to look at how positive affect like amusement might offset or undo negative affect.

Although the charges are no longer as bold as the idea that laughter is incompatible with negative states, Davidson (2000) concluded that data indicate that a function of positive affect is to inhibit concurrent negative affect. Fredrickson (2002) argued that "positive and negative emotions (or key components of them) . . . cannot fully and simultaneously coexist" (p. 127). Fredrickson's work on the undoing hypothesis provides evidence that positive emotion does not simply replace but rather undoes negative emotion, as evidenced by quicker physiological recovery following emotion episodes when positive emotion follows negative emotion (Fredrickson et al., 2000). The undoing hypothesis is especially relevant to the current discussion in light of the psychophysiological approach underpinning its formulation.

The role of laughter in undoing negative emotion should be explored. For example, differences in sympathetic and parasympathetic nervous system reactivity are not typically associated with positive emotions (Levenson, Ekman, & Friesen, 1990); however, physiological changes are associated with laughter, including increases in blood pressure and heart rate (Fry & Savin, 1988). Further, research shows that laughter returns some physiological indices to lower-than-baseline levels (Berk et al., 1989; see White & Winzelberg, 1992), suggesting that laughter could have a potentially unique role in emotional "undoing." Although laughter may not speed recovery to baseline, which is typically how undoing is operationalized, the potential for laughter to do more than undo remains intriguing, if lower-than-baseline levels are indeed consistently observed in response to laughter.

Laughter, in addition to its potential role in undoing prior emotion, can also be examined relative to other positive and negative emotions. Laughter is associated with reduced anger in samples of bereaved individuals and greater improvement in long-term functioning (Keltner & Bonanno, 1997). It is unclear whether this dissociation from distress is physiological in nature, whether cognitive processes like reinterpretation are at work, or whether this association is a result of both physiological and cognitive processes (Abel & Hester, 2002, p. 241).

It would also be fruitful for investigators to begin incorporating laughter into known physiological lines of theoretically grounded research as they relate to positive psychology. For example, social psychophysiological studies of stress have identified physiological patterns indicative of threat versus challenge states (see Blascovich & Tomaka, 1996). What might laughter offer the threat versus challenge paradigm? Is laughter associated with a challenge pattern? Can laughter annul a physiological response of threat, as suggested by the undoing hypothesis? If so, how long would that take? Do all varieties of laughter produce consistent effects? What situation could be created that both engenders laughter and a threat or challenge response?

Future Directions

Physiological studies of laughter are in their infancy. Provine and Yong (1991) have argued that more is known about bird songs than human laughter. Progress in the understanding of laughter is being made in certain areas, especially with regard to brain activity in pathological laughter, but work is needed in all areas, especially in the domain of positive psychology. Laughter continues to be overshadowed by the study of humor and is not identified centrally with any one discipline or topic of study. In this

chapter, we have argued for the relevance of laughter to positive psychology, especially when approached using psychophysiological methods. We have also presented research questions to hopefully inspire others with interest in positive psychology to pursue laughter.

Much like the research distinguishing types of smiles (e.g., Duchenne smiles), there is still a great need for descriptive work categorizing laughter. What are the characteristics of laughter, neurologically and otherwise? Under what conditions does it occur? More work is needed to determine what types of laughter are associated with which positive emotions. When is laughter linked with negative emotion, for example, anger (see Bonanno & Keltner, 2004)? Or does laughter occur only with the undoing of negative emotion?

Which properties of laughter are more closely associated with healing and positive psychology? Do positive benefits exist for all shared laughter between conspecifics or only between individuals in close relationships? For instance, the neuropeptide oxytocin is involved in the development of pair bonds and attachment (see Insel, 2000). Given laughter's relationship to bonding, perhaps laughter stimulates release of oxytocin. We await the emergence of careful, descriptive work linking physiological systems with types, kinds, and contexts of laughter, as has been done with mother-infant smile interchanges (see Bolzani, Messinger, Yale, & Dondi, 2002). Due to limited and conflicting results for laughter and well-being in general (and in particular, effects on the immune system), more replication is needed.

Identification of individual differences in laughter is also desirable, and psychophysiology methods have great potential to advance this goal. Individual differences in physiological responses exist (Duffy, 1957), and questions specific to laughter are worth exploring. Does laughter have salutary benefits equally for everyone? Similarly, very little work has examined gender differences in laughter. In their study, Lefcourt, Davidson, Prkachin, and Mills (1997) reported opposite relationships between sense of humor and systolic blood pressure for women and men. Svebak (1975) identified gender differences in laughter's respiratory patterns, with reduced abdominal muscle tonus predicting laughter in women but not men.

Intervention studies are needed to determine the extent to which laughter has positive health effects and in what areas. Is a dose-response understanding of laughter feasible? Intervention studies could examine relevant populations, such as the depressed, the elderly (see Berk, 2001), or persons susceptible to strong stress reactions. Other potential targets for interventions include people who do not have easily accessible options for exercise, such as people with quadriplegia and those who are bedridden. African Americans and men with hostility are two groups worthy of study as they are at greater risk for cardiovascular disease and exhibit greater cardiovascular reactivity to negative emotions. The excess carbon dioxide released following laughter could also have implications for people with chronic obstructive pulmonary disease. Laughter interventions have great potential to be helpful with any of these populations. Randomized controlled trials would be most useful in identifying impact.

Conclusion

The occurrence of laughter is overwhelmingly social. Therefore, to fully understand laughter's relationships to positive psychology, researchers should most typically study laughter in social settings. We have argued in this chapter that a psychophysiological approach to the study of laughter can offer much to positive psychology due to laughter's biological properties. In addition, the high daily occurrence of laughter and its significance in social relationships make it an important topic for positive psychology in general. Many of the contexts of occurrence for laughter are associated with constructs in positive psychology, including positive intra- and interindividual emotional states, coping with loss or conflict, and overcoming negative emotions. A better understanding of the origins, contexts, and functions of laughter is a necessary first step to discerning its benefits for positive psychological theorizing. Appreciating laughter in its own right, independently from its humor and smiling counterparts, will better elucidate its role in the biological, psychological, and social systems within which it is embedded. These objectives will, in turn, determine whether the much-valued hearty laugh is, indeed, the best medicine.

Acknowledgments Preparation of this chapter was supported by grant #R03AG19908-01 from the National Institute on Aging.

Notes

1. Much of the work on laughter has examined its relationship to pathology, which is beyond the scope of this chapter, but see Wild, Rodden, Grodd, and Ruch (2003).

2. For a detailed discussion of the correspondence between psychological and physiological phenomena, see Blascovich (2000) and Cacioppo, Berntson, and Crites (1996).

References

Abel, M. H., & Hester, R. (2002). The therapeutic effects of smiling. In M. H. Abel (Ed.), *An empirical reflection on the smile* (pp. 217–253). Lewiston, NY: Edwin Mellen.

Anderson, N. B., & Armstead, C. A. (1995). Toward understanding the association of SES and health: A new challenge for the biopsychosocial approach. *Psychosomatic Medicine, 57*(3), 213–225.

Argyle, M. (1997). Is happiness a cause of health? *Psychology and Health, 12*(6), 769–781.

Arroyo, S., Lesser, R. P., Gordon, B., Uematsu, S., Hart, J., Schwerdt, P., et al. (1993). Mirth, laughter and gelastic seizures. *Brain, 116,* 757–780.

Bachorowski, J. A., & Owren, M. J. (2001). Not all laughs are alike: Voiced but not unvoiced laughter readily elicits positive affect. *Psychological Science, 12*(3), 252–257.

Bachorowski, J. A., Smoski, M. J., & Owren, M. J. (2001). The acoustic features of human laughter. *Journal of the Acoustical Society of America, 110,* 1581–1597.

Bainum, C. K., Lounsbury, K. R., & Pollio, H. R. (1984). The development of laughing and smiling in nursery school children. *Child Development, 55,* 1946–1957.

Bakeman, R., & Gottman, J. (1997). *Observing interaction* (2nd ed.). New York: Cambridge.

Baron, R. A. (1983). The control of human aggression: A strategy based on incompatible responses. In R. G. Geen & E. I. Donnerstein (Eds.), *Aggression: Theoretical and empirical reviews: Vol 2. Issues in Research* (pp. 173–190). New York: Academic Press.

Berk, L. S., Felten, D. L., Tan, S. A., & Bittman, B. B. (2001). Modulation of neuroimmune parameters during the eustress of humor-associated mirthful laughter. *Alternative Therapies in Health and Medicine, 7*(2), 62–72.

Berk, L. S., Tan, S. A., & Fry, W. F. (1993). Eustress of humor associated laughter modulates specific immune system components [Abstract]. *Annals of Behavioral Medicine, 15,* S111.

Berk, L. S., Tan, S. A., Fry, W. F., Napier, B. J., Lee, J. W., Hubbard, R. W., et al. (1989). Neuroendocrine and stress hormone changes during mirthful laughter. *American Journal of the Medical Sciences, 298,* 390–396.

Berk, R. A. (2001). The active ingredients in humor: Psychophysiological benefits and risks for older adults. *Educational Gerontology, 27*(3/4), 323–339.

Blascovich, J. (2000). Using physiological indexes of psychological processes in social psychological research. In H. T. Reis & C. M. Judd (Eds.), *Handbook of research methods in social and personality psychology* (pp. 117–137). New York: Cambridge University Press.

Blascovich, J., & Tomaka, J. (1996). The biopsychosocial model of arousal regulation. In M. Zanna (Ed.), *Advances in experimental social psychology* (Vol. 28, pp. 1–51). New York: Academic Press.

Bolzani, L. H., Messinger, D. S., Yale, M., & Dondi, M. (2002). Smiling in infancy. In M. H. Abel (Ed.), *An empirical reflection on the smile* (pp. 111–135). Lewiston, NY: Edwin Mellen.

Bonanno, G. A., & Keltner, D. (2004). The coherence of emotion systems: Comparing "on-line" measures of appraisal and facial expressions, and self-report. *Cognition and Emotion, 18*(3), 431–444.

Boone, T., Hansen, S., & Erlandson, A. (2000). Cardiovascular responses to laughter: A pilot project. *Applied Nursing Research, 13*(4), 204–208.

Bright, K. E., Hixon, T. J., & Hoit, J. D. (1986). Respiration as a laughing matter. In D. L. F. Nilsen & A. P. Nilsen (Eds.), *Whimsy IV* (pp. 147–148). Tempe: Arizona State University, Department of English.

Cacioppo, J. T., Berntson, G. G., & Crites, S. L., Jr. (1996). Social neuroscience: Principles of psychophysiological arousal and response. In E. T. Higgins & A. W. Kruglanski (Eds.), *Social psychology: Handbook of basic principles* (pp. 72–84). New York: Guilford.

Cacioppo, J. T., Berntson, G. G., Malarkey, W. B., Kiecolt-Glaser, J. K., Sheridan, J. F., Poehlmann, K. M., et al. (1998). Autonomic, neuroendocrine, and immune responses to psychological stress: The reactivity hypothesis. *Annals of the New York Academy of Sciences, 840,* 664–673.

Chapman, A. J., & Wright, D. S. (1976). Social enhancement of laughter: An experimental analysis of some companion variables. *Journal of Experimental Child Psychology, 21,* 201–218.

Cupchik, G. C., & Leventhal, H. (1974). Consistency between expressive behavior and the evaluation of humorous stimuli: The role of sex and self-observation. *Journal of Personality and Social Psychology, 30,* 429–442.

Danzer, A., Dale, J., & Klions, H. L. (1990). Effects of exposure to humorous stimuli on induced depression. *Psychological Reports, 66,* 1027–1036.

Darwin, C. R. (1872). *Expression of the emotions in man and animals.* New York: D. Appleton.

Davidson, R. J. (2000). The functional neuroanatomy of affective style. In R. D. Lane & L. Nadel (Eds.), *Cognitive neuroscience of emotion* (pp. 371–388). New York: Oxford University Press.

Devereux, P. G., & Ginsburg, G. P. (2001a). Sociality effects on the production of laughter. *Journal of General Psychology, 128*(2), 227–240.

Devereux, P. G., & Ginsburg, G. P. (2001b, May). *Laughter and the development of interpersonal synchrony.* Paper presented at the annual meeting of the Western Psychological Association, Maui, HI.

Diamond, L. M. (2001). Contributions of psychophysiology to research on adult attachment: Review and recommendations. *Personality and Social Psychology Review, 5*(4), 276–295.

Duffy, E. (1957). The psychological significance of the concept of "arousal" or "activation." *Psychological Review, 64*(5), 265–275.

Ekman, P., & Davidson, R. J. (1993). Voluntary smiling changes regional brain activity. *Psychological Science, 4,* 342–345.

Fagen, R. (1987). Play, games and innovations: Sociobiological findings and unanswered questions. In C. Crawford, M. Smith, & D. Krebs (Eds.), *Sociobiology and psychology: Ideas, issues and applications* (pp. 253–268). Hillsdale, NJ: Erlbaum.

Fogel, A., Dickson, K. L., Hsu, H., Messenger, D., Nelson-Goens, G. C., & Nwokah, E. (1997). Communication of smiling and laughter in mother-infant play: Research on emotion from a dynamic systems perspective. In K. C. Barrett (Ed.), *The communication of emotion: Current research from diverse perspectives. New directions for child development,* no. 77 (pp. 5–24). San Francisco: Jossey-Bass.

Foot, H. C., Chapman, A. C., & Smith, J. R. (1977). Friendship and social responsiveness in boys and girls. *Journal of Personality and Social Psychology, 35*(6), 401–411.

Fredrickson, B. L. (2002). Positive emotions. In C. R. Snyder & S. J. Lopez (Eds.), *Handbook of positive psychology* (pp. 120–134). New York: Oxford University Press.

Fredrickson, B. L., & Levenson, R. W. (1998). Positive emotions speed recovery from the cardiovascular sequelae of negative emotions. *Cognition and Emotion, 12*(2), 191–220.

Fredrickson, B. L., Mancuso, R. A., Branigan, C., & Tugade, M. M. (2000). The undoing effect of positive emotions. *Motivation and Emotion, 24*(4), 237–258.

Fridlund, A. J. (1994). *Human facial expression: An evolutionary view.* San Diego, CA: Academic Press.

Fried, I., Wilson, C. L., MacDonald, K. A., & Behnke, E. J. (1998). Electric current stimulates laughter. *Nature, 391,* 650.

Fry, W. F. (1977). The respiratory components of mirthful laughter. *Journal of Biological Psychology, 19,* 39–50.

Fry, W. F. (1986). Humor, physiology, and the aging process. In L. Nahemow, K. A. McCluskey-Fawcett, & P. E. McGhee (Eds.), *Humor and aging* (pp. 81–98). Orlando, FL: Academic Press.

Fry, W. F. (1992). The physiological effects of humor, mirth, and laughter. *Journal of the American Medical Association, 267,* 1857–1858.

Fry, W. F. (1994). The biology of humor. *Humor, 7*(2), 111–126.

Fry, W. F., & Savin, W. M. (1988). Mirthful laughter and blood pressure. *Humor, 1*(1), 49–62.

Georgakoulias, N., Vize, C., Jenkins, A., & Singounas, E. (1998). Hypothalamic hamartomas causing gelastic epilepsy: Two cases and a review of the literature. *Seizure, 7,* 167–171.

Grammer, K. (1990). Strangers meet: Laughter and nonverbal signs of interest in opposite-sex encounters. *Journal of Nonverbal Behavior, 14*(4), 209–236.

Gratton, G. (2000). Biosignal processing. In J. T. Cacioppo, L. G. Tassinary, & G. G. Berntson (Eds.), *Handbook of psychophysiology* (2nd ed., pp. 900–923). New York: Cambridge University Press.

Heffner, K. L., Devereux, P. G., & Ginsburg, G. P. (2005, September). *Does hypertension influence older adults' cardiovascular reactivity during emotional arousal?* Poster session presented at the International Conference for the Society of Psychophysiological Research, Lisbon, Portugal.

Hubert, W., & de Jong-Meyer, R. (1991). Autonomic, neuroendocrine, and subjective responses to emotion-inducing film stimuli. *International Journal of Psychophysiology, 11,* 131–140.

Hubert, W., Moller, M., & de Jong-Meyer, R. (1993). Film-induced amusement changes in saliva cortisol levels. *Psychoneuroendocrinology, 18,* 265–272.

Insel, T. R. (2000). Toward a neurobiology of attachment. *Review of General Psychology, 4,* 176–185.

James, W. (1884). What is an emotion? *Mind, 9,* 188–205.

Jennings, J. R., & Stine, L. A. (2000). Salient method, design, and analysis concerns. In J. T. Cacioppo, L. G. Tassinary, & G. G. Berntson (Eds.), *Handbook of psychophysiology* (2nd ed., pp. 870–899). New York: Cambridge University Press.

Keltner, D., & Bonanno, G. A. (1997). A study of laughter and dissociation: Distinct correlates of laughter and smiling during bereavement. *Journal of Personality and Social Psychology, 73,* 687–702.

Kubzansky, L. D., Kawachi, I., & Sparrow, D. (1999). Socioeconomic status, hostility, and risk factor clustering in the normative aging study: Any help from the concept of allostatic load? *Annals of Behavioral Medicine, 21*(4), 330–338.

Kuhn, C. C. (1994). The stages of laughter. *Journal of Nursing Jocularity, 4*(2), 34–35.

Labott, S. M., Ahleman, S., Wolever, M. E., & Martin, R. B. (1990). The physiological and psychological effects of the expression and inhibition of emotion. *Behavioral Medicine, 16*(4), 182–189.

Larsen, J. T., Norris, C. J., & Cacioppo, J. T. (2003). Effects of positive and negative affect on electromyographic activity over *zygomaticus major* and *corrugator supercilii. Psychophysiology, 40,* 776–785.

Lazarus, R. S. (1991). *Emotion and adaptation.* New York: Oxford University Press.

Lefcourt, H. M., Davidson, K., Prkachin, K. M., & Mills, D. E. (1997). Humor as a stress moderator in the prediction of blood pressure obtained during five stressful tasks. *Journal of Research in Personality, 31,* 532–542.

Levenson, R. W. (1988). Emotion and the autonomic nervous system: A prospectus for research on autonomic specificity. In H. L. Wagner (Ed.), *Social psychophysiology and emotion: Theory and clinical applications* (pp. 17–42). Chichester, England: Wiley.

Levenson, R. W., Ekman, P., & Friesen, W. V. (1990). Voluntary facial action generates emotion-specific autonomic nervous system activity. *Psychophysiology, 27,* 363–384.

Lloyd, E. L. (1938). The respiratory mechanism in laughter. *Journal of General Psychology, 19,* 179–189.

Loizos, C. (1967). Play behavior in higher primates. In D. Morris (Ed.), *Primate ethology* (pp. 176–218). London: Weidenfeld and Nicolson.

Mahony, D. L., Burroughs, W. J., & Lippman, L. G. (2002). Perceived attributes of health-promoting laughter: A cross-generational comparison. *Journal of Psychology, 136*(2), 171–181.

Martin, R. A. (2001). Humor, laughter, and physical health: Methodological issues and research findings. *Psychological Bulletin, 127*(4), 504–519.

Martin, R. A. (2002). Is laughter the best medicine? Humor, laughter, and physical health. *Current Directions in Psychological Science, 11*(6), 216–220.

Martin, R. A., & Lefcourt, H. M. (1984). Situational Humor Response Questionnaire: Quantitative measure of sense of humor. *Journal of Personality and Social Psychology, 47*, 145–155.

McDonald, P. J., & Wooten, S. A. (1988). The influence of incompatible responses on the reduction of aggression: An alternative explanation. *Journal of Social Psychology, 128*(3), 401–406.

McDougall, W. (1922). A new theory of laughter. *Psyche, 2*, 292–303.

McEwen, B. S. (1998). Protective and damaging effects of stress mediators. *New England Journal of Medicine, 338*(3), 171–179.

McGhee, P. E. (1977). Children's humour: A review of current research trends. In A. J. Chapman & H. C. Foot (Eds.), *It's a funny thing, humour* (pp. 199–209). Oxford: Pergamon.

McHugo, G. J., & Lanzetta, J. T. (1983). Methodological decisions in social psychophysiology. In J. T. Cacioppo & R. E. Petty (Eds.), *Social psychophysiology: A sourcebook* (pp. 630–665). New York: Guilford.

Milford, P. A. (1981). Perception of laughter and its acoustical properties. *Dissertation Abstracts International, 41A*, 3779A.

Mowrer, D. E., LaPointe, L. L., & Case, J. (1987). Analysis of five acoustic correlates of laughter. *Journal of Nonverbal Behavior, 11*(3), 191–199.

Nwokah, E. E., Davies, P., Islam, A., Hsu, H., & Fogel, A. (1993). Vocal affect in three-year-olds: A quantitative acoustic analysis of child laughter. *Journal of the Acoustical Society of America, 94*(6), 3076–3090.

Obrist, P. A. (1981). *Cardiovascular psychophysiology: A perspective.* New York: Plenum.

O'Donnell-Trujillo, N., & Adams, K. (1983). Heheh in conversation: Some coordinating accomplishments of laughter. *Western Journal of Speech Communication, 47*, 175–191.

Owren, M. J., & Bachorowski, J. A. (2003). Reconsidering the evolution of nonlinguistic communication: The case of laughter. *Journal of Nonverbal Behavior, 27*(3), 183–200.

Porges, S. W., & Bohrer, R. E. (1990). The analysis of periodic processes in psychophysiological research. In J. T. Cacioppo & L. Tassinary (Eds.), *Principles of psychophysiology: Physical, social, and inferential elements* (pp. 708–753). Cambridge: Cambridge University Press.

Porteous, J. (1988). Humor as a process of defense: The evolution of laughing. *Humor, 1*(1), 63–80.

Preuschoft, S. (1992). "Laughter" and "smile" in barbary macaques. *Ethology, 91*, 220–236.

Provine, R. R. (1993). Laughter punctuates speech: Linguistic, social and gender contexts of laughter. *Ethology, 95*, 291–298.

Provine, R. R. (1997). Yawns, laughs, smiles, and talking: Naturalistic and laboratory studies of facial action and social communication. In J. A. Russell & J. M. Fernandez-Dols (Eds.), *The psychology of facial expression* (pp. 158–175). London: Cambridge University Press.

Provine, R. (2000). *Laughter: A scientific investigation.* New York: Viking Press.

Provine, R. R., & Fischer, K. R. (1989). Laughing, smiling, and talking: Relation to sleeping and social context in humans. *Ethology, 83*, 295–305.

Provine, R. R., & Yong, Y. L. (1991). Laughter: A stereotyped human vocalization. *Ethology, 89*, 115–124.

Redican, W. K. (1982). An evolutionary perspective on human facial displays. In P. Ekman (Ed.), *Emotion in the human face* (2nd ed., pp. 212–280). New York: Cambridge Press.

Ruch, W. (1993). Exhilaration and humor. In M. Lewis & J. M. Haviland (Eds.), *The handbook of emotions* (pp. 605–616). New York: Guilford.

Ruch, W., & Ekman, P. (2001). The expressive pattern of laughter. In A. Kaszniak (Ed.), *Emotion, qualia, and consciousness* (pp. 426–443). Tokyo: World Scientific.

Ryff, C. D., & Singer, B. (2000). Interpersonal flourishing: A positive health agenda for the new millennium. *Personality and Social Psychology Review, 4*(1), 30–44.

Smoski, M. J., & Bachorowski, J. A. (2003). Antiphonal laughter between friends and strangers. *Cognition and Emotion, 17*(2), 327–340.

Spiegel, D. (1999). Healing words: Emotional expression and disease outcome. *Journal of the American Medical Association, 281*(14), 1328.

Sroufe, L. A., & Waters, E. (1976). The ontogenesis of smiling and laughter: A perspective on the organization of development in infancy. *Psychological Review, 83*(3), 173–189.

Sroufe, L. A., & Wunsch, J. P. (1972). The development of laughter in the first year of life. *Child Development, 43*, 1326–1344.

Svebak, S. (1975). Respiratory patterns as predictors of laughter. *Psychophysiology, 12*(1), 62–65.

Szabo, A. (2003). The acute effects of humor and exercise on mood and anxiety. *Journal of Leisure Research, 35*(2), 152–162.

Tan, S. A., Tan, L. G., Berk, L. S., Lukman, S. T., & Lukman, L. F. (1997). Mirthful laughter: An effective adjunct in cardiac rehabilitation [Abstract]. *Canadian Journal of Cardiology, 13* (suppl B), 190.

Tassinary, L. G., & Cacioppo, J. T. (1992). Unobservable facial actions and emotion. *Psychological Science, 3*(1), 28–33.

Tomarken, A. J. (1995). A psychometric perspective on psychophysiological measures. *Psychological Assessment, 7*(3), 387–395.

Tomarken, A. J., Davidson, R. J., Wheeler, R. W., & Doss, R. (1992). Individual differences in anterior brain asymmetry and fundamental dimensions of emotion. *Journal of Personality and Social Psychology, 62,* 676–687.

van Hooff, J.A.R.A.M. (1972). A comparative approach to the phylogeny of laughter and smiling. In R. A. Hinde (Ed.), *Nonverbal communication* (pp. 209–241). Cambridge: Cambridge University Press.

Vettin, J., & Todt, D. (2004). Laughter in conversation: Features of occurrence and acoustic structure. *Journal of Nonverbal Behavior, 28*(2), 93–115.

Wagner, H. L., & Calam, R. M. (1988). Interpersonal psychophysiology and the study of the family. In H. L. Wagner (Ed.), *Social psychophysiology and emotion: Theory and clinical applications* (pp. 211–229). West Sussex, England: Wiley.

Washburn, R. W. (1929). A study of the smiling and laughing of infants in the first year of life. *Genetic Psychology Monographs, 6,* 397–537.

Webster's Revised Unabridged Dictionary. (1998). Retrieved April 6, 2004, from http://dictionary .reference.com/search?q=LAUGHTER

White, S., & Winzelberg, A. (1992). Laughter and stress. *Humor, 5*(4), 343–355.

Wild, B., Rodden, F. A., Grodd, W., & Ruch, W. (2003). Neural correlates of laughter and humour. *Brain, 126,* 2121–2138.

Zajonc, R. B., Murphy, S. T., & Inglehart, M. (1989). Feeling and facial efference: Implications of the vascular theory of emotion. *Psychological Review, 96,* 395–416.

Ziv, A. (1979). Sociometry of humor: Objectifying the subjective. *Perceptual and Motor Skills, 49,* 97–98.

17

Some Measurement Issues
in the Study of Affect

Alice M. Isen and Amir Erez

This volume addresses methods in the field of positive psychology. Within that topic, this chapter focuses on methodological issues associated with induced positive affect. In this context, we focus especially on the assessment of induced affect and its impact on other processes and behavior. In the course of this, we discuss several problems that are associated with the traditional self-report measures of affect, describe some conceptual alternatives to self-report measures, and consider some empirical alternative indicators of positive affect. We also consider some theoretical implications of the use of different methods of assessing affect. And we pay some attention to the requirements and limitations, from a measurement perspective, inherent in some of the methods of inducing positive affect that are used in the literature.

Although positive psychology consists of more than the study of emotions, it is very clear that investigating emotions or feelings is one of the major building blocks of this emerging field of study. Research on the influence of feelings (affect) on human functioning has tended to use a mix of methods—behavioral, cognitive, physiological, neuropsychological, as well as self-

report—to induce or assess the presence or impact of affect. Nonetheless, it seems that there is a growing tendency to rely, at least to some degree, on self-report measures of feeling states. In one respect, it seems to make a lot of sense to ask people directly about their emotions, because who should know better than they how they feel? However, this method of investigation has some serious limitations.

One of the problems with people's reporting their emotions is that in order to do so they need to introspect, and introspection has long been known to be a problematic method of investigation in psychology (see, e.g., Isen & Hastorf, 1982, for consideration of this issue in historical perspective). For instance, in a well-known experiment by Nisbett and Wilson (1977), the researchers asked participants to choose among five identical pairs of stockings and then asked them to explain the choice. Most participants chose the rightmost pair and therefore their decision was based only on the relative spatial position of the stockings. However, participants strongly denied that this was the reason for the decision, instead pointing to insignificant differences in color and texture of the stockings as the causes for the choice. Based on these findings, Nisbett and Wilson concluded that introspection is of little value, because people are generally unaware of response factors, or processes, affecting their behaviors. George Mandler, too, long interested in the study of consciousness as well as cognition and emotion, made that same point with regard to cognitive processes—that although people can be aware of the content of their thoughts, they are not aware of the processes involved in thinking (e.g., Mandler, 1982).

Another class of examples that pertain to the sometimes poor correspondence between what people show or report they know or think, and what they actually know, falls under the heading of the "learning–performance distinction" identified in social and developmental psychology. In many studies, it was noticed that contextual factors such as incentives, rules (sometimes subtle or implied rules), other stimulus materials present concurrently, and other factors that influence how the person thinks about the situation and conceptualizes what it is appropriate to say or do in the situation, can influence what and how much people appear to have learned in a given task situation (e.g., Bandura, 1971). For example, in a classic series of studies on learning by imitation, Bandura and associates found that people did learn and remember the behavior of the model, but did not always display all that they had learned, even when asked to do so. Under one set of conditions, when merely asked to show what they remembered, people appeared not to have learned material that indeed they had learned; but under other conditions, they displayed more of what they had learned and remembered (see Bandura, 1971, for fuller discussion of these points).

But if people cannot or will not explain their observable choices, or report what they have learned or know, can or will they accurately report their still more ambiguous and fleeting thoughts or feelings? In general, then, when conclusions are drawn on the basis of people's reports of their introspections about their feelings, not enough consideration is given to the difficulty of interpreting such statements. In addition, based on what we know from years of research in social psychology and cognitive psychology, it seems that not enough emphasis is being given to situational factors that influence feelings and, especially, report of feelings, when self-reports of feeling states are taken as measures.

In this chapter, we do not take the extreme position that self-reports or introspections about feelings and emotions are worthless, as some have said. However, we do hold that, by themselves, they are not enough to allow conclusions about emotion; and we strongly suggest that if the field of positive psychology is to make advances in scientific discovery, more rigorous methods need to be applied to supplement, and in some instances supplant, self-reports. We offer two such methods that have been successfully applied to establish research findings in other fields such as measurement and cognitive psychology.

The first method we suggest for improving research in positive psychology is to use conceptual validation, in which the convergence of different methods of research operations is used to validate findings (see Cronbach, 1960; Cronbach & Meehl, 1955, for discussion). One example is simply to use more than one way of inducing or measuring affect (or any concept), to make sure that it is the concept or feeling that is being studied, and not just one measure or one approach to measuring it, which could be flawed or not fully representative of the concept. Another example is to come at the problem in a completely different way, such as through a mix of cognitive evidence, physiological measures, or by studying a different population that is expected to perform differently, based on theoretical expectations.

For example, theories in cognitive psychology mainly rely on findings based on people's responses on tasks designed to represent particular cognitive processes. However, other methods such as information gathered about cognitive impairment in brain-damaged patients, as well as studies on brain functioning utilizing brain scans, may also be used to validate these theories. Of course, one must use caution when inferring normal processes from the responses of brain-damaged individuals, but with converging operations and multiple checks, this arena can be a source of important data. Thus, by using different lines of research and methods that provide findings that may sometimes converge or at other times diverge, fields such as cognitive psychology have refined and developed more comprehensive theories. In this chapter, we suggest that positive psychology research should benefit in the same way by using multiple methods to validate findings. We demonstrate how research using such converging operations and discriminant validation could be applied to positive psychology, by using examples from the research program on induced positive affect developed by Isen and her colleagues.

Second, we suggest the use of implicit measures to supplement or replace self-reports of affect. Here again, research in other areas of psychology has shown that unitary reliance on self-reports and introspection may be problematic. Another example from cognitive psychology illustrates this point: It has been found that complex material can be learned and remembered and yet the person may not verbalize that learning, even when asked about it. For example, Tulving, Schacter, and Stark (1982) asked participants to learn a list of rare words such as *toboggan* and, after a delay of an hour or a week, gave them a word fragment completion test (e.g., a request to fill in the blanks for the word _O_O_GA_). Participants exhibited much better performance in completing the word fragments for words they had seen earlier than for words they had not seen previously, even though they did not report having seen them previously. This and other studies have shown that "individuals can exhibit excellent memory performance even when they show no relevant introspective evidence" of the learning (Eysenck & Keane, 2003, p. 4).

Thus, methods of assessing implicit memory and learning (or implicit measures) have been very successful in revealing important facts about thinking processes in individuals. It has also been shown that contextual factors or other factors that govern people's responses can influence how much of what is known or felt is demonstrated under those particular circumstances. Thus, in this chapter we also suggest the use and development, in assessing and measuring affect, of implicit methods that may help to lessen the impact of response factors that influence responding and can interfere with accurate (or full) understanding of what people are feeling. We demonstrate how this may be done, by using some examples from current research on positive affect.

We organize this chapter by first briefly reviewing some of the problems associated with the assessment of affect using self-report measures. We then suggest and discuss the alternative methods of conceptual validation and implicit measures, and finally we conclude by indicating some of the theoretical implications and potential benefits for positive psychology research that can result from using these suggested methods.

Assessment of Affect by Means of Self-Report

The most obvious, and seemingly simple, seemingly direct, approach to affect measurement is thought to be to ask people how they feel. A closely related method involves providing people with rating scales (of the target affect of interest, and sometimes of alternative feelings, as well) and asking them to indicate on these 5-point or 7-point or 9-point (or however many points the researcher prefers or thinks optimal in the situation) scales "how much" of a given affect they are feeling, or "to what degree" they are feeling that affect, at the moment. Some of these scales have the Likert format (with "opposite" emotions at the poles, e.g., *very sad* to *very happy*, ranging from -2 to $+2$, or -3 to $+3$, and so on, with 0 as the neutral point), whereas some use the approach of assessing one feeling state at a time, with ratings ranging from 0–4 or 1–7, or 0–10, or 1–100, for example, where the lower pole represents *not at all* and the higher pole represents something like *very much* or *extremely*. Sometimes, points along the continuum are labeled with descriptive words, such as "a little bit" or "somewhat," and so on.

There are some seeming advantages to using these types of affect measures. First, they can be easily used in a variety of situations, such as in field studies, experiments, quasi-experiments, and longitudinal designs including affect-sampling studies, some utilizing handheld recording or signaling devices for time sampling. They take a very short time to answer, and they are easy to administer and analyze. They are also "face valid," in that the items appear to reflect the affect construct as defined conceptually (although in many instances they are not actually valid indicators of a person's feelings). While face validity is not considered evidence of validity from a measurement point of view, participants may regard it as important, and some researchers are taking that into consideration.

At the same time, self-report measures of affect also have some major shortcomings. In the next few sections, we discuss two of these major problems—problems with validity and problems caused by the fact that they interrupt the experimental session and direct the person's focus to themselves—that may limit the usefulness of these types of affect measures. We then describe some alternative methods for the assessment of affect.

Problems With the Validity of Self-Report Measures of Affect

Over the past 100 years of research in personality assessment, educational assessment, and testing and measurement more generally, researchers have come to understand that people's responses to straightforward questions or assessment devices aimed at measuring internal states are not direct measures of the underlying states. Instead, they are merely responses and, like all responses, are subject to many factors including some errors and biases that influence responses of many kinds (see, e.g., Cronbach, 1960; Mischel, 1968). In other words, researchers became aware of the problems of reliability and validity of the assessment devices they wanted to use, even for something like assessment of feelings. Generally, challenges to validity can be divided into two kinds: First, there are challenges that stem from unsystematic (random) error, which is represented by the concept of reliability; and second, there are systematic errors, which constitute threats to validity beyond that which occurs from low reliability.

Random Errors in Self-Reports

Some affect studies utilize measures of affect that are unreliable; as such, they cannot be valid (that is, cannot measure what they are designed to measure), because reliability sets the upper limit of validity (e.g., see Cronbach, 1960). For example, it is now well understood that a one-item scale is unreliable. Yet many researchers still use one-item scales, in particular as manipulation checks in their studies. That is, following an affect induction, many researchers then ask participants to indicate whether, or to what degree, they are feeling the state that the researcher attempted to induce. Based on such one-item manipulation checks, the researchers then try to draw conclusions about whether or not the manipulation worked. However, if the measure used as a manipulation check is in itself not a reliable and valid measure of affect, it cannot answer the question of whether the manipulation has worked. As a result, researchers may throw away useful data based on the erroneous conclusion that their manipulation did not work.

Reliability of measures may be increased by adding consistent items to a scale, and therefore affect researchers sometimes now consider including several separate items intended to assess the same target affective state (such as "how good do you feel," "how happy do you feel," "how pleased," or "good-bad," "happy-sad," "pleasant-unpleasant"), rather than just one question. Thus, the problem of reliability of the measures used in affect research may be remedied to some extent. However, in addition, as the field of measurement matured, researchers began to focus not only on the reliability of the measurement but also on other threats to validity and the need to establish the validity of any measurement or assessment device.

Validity Threats in Self-Report

Validity, as noted earlier, is the extent to which a measure actually measures what it was designed to measure; and self-report affect measures are especially vulnerable to threats to validity. This is because many factors that threaten validity can have influence when a measure involves self-report. One such factor is *response bias*, a matter related to the way a person uses the scale. For example, a person may have a tendency simply to endorse or say yes (or no) to all questions, or to use a particular position on the scale, and this, then, would work against the response's being an accurate reflection of the person's feeling or opinion on the topic or whatever is being assessed. Self-reports in general are vulnerable to factors such as response bias, in part because they involve responses on scales. This problem may be especially pronounced when affect is being assessed, because it may be that some feeling states, under some circumstances, may themselves be confounded with some response biases (e.g., extreme responding), and thus one may not know whether to regard the response as a bias or as something meaningful (though not related to the particular question asked), or as a true answer to the particular question.

Here again, the problems stemming from response bias may sometimes be ameliorated by using accepted methods of scale construction such as reverse coding, wherein scale items are included that reverse the direction of the content (i.e., if for some items the low end of the scale is labeled *not at all*, for other items the low end of the scale is tagged *a lot*, and the high end represents *not at all*). One problem with this procedure is that sometimes participants inadvertently, and without the researcher's awareness, keep using the poles of the scale that were indicated on the first item and do not carefully read the scale labels of each item individually. This, then, invalidates some or all of their responses, and the researcher does not discover the problem until after the data have been collected, if ever. Thus, some researchers forgo this safeguard, of reverse coding some of the items, and try other methods to avoid the potential for response bias.

Perhaps the best technique that researchers sometimes use, in order to be sure that any response does not represent only response bias is to include more than one affect scale in the assessment device, with some of those affects being distinct from the target one; and what they hope to find in the assessment is evidence that the affective state of interest was influenced in the expected way, while at the same time the alternative affective states were not similarly influenced. Assessing more than the one target affect state would be in keeping with the goal of trying to establish construct validity (Cronbach & Meehl, 1955) of the measurement, which we describe further in a later section. Thus, one sometimes sees a battery of four or five different affects assessed, each with two or three questions, even when the major focus is on one particular feeling state, in order to allow for this so-called discriminant validation.

Another major complication for self-report measurement of affect is that researchers who employ self-report measures of affect fundamentally disagree about the structure of affect. The disagreement about the structure of affect is reflected in two opposing viewpoints that permeate the literatures, not only of affect research but also of several applied fields (e.g., management, consumer behavior). The debate between these two opposing views has a long history (see, e.g., discussion in chapter 7, this volume; Weiss & Cropanzano, 1996, for review) and periodically each one of these models gains popularity, as more and more empirical evidence is presented to support it (Russell, 1978, 1979, 1980; Russell & Carroll, 1999a, 1999b; Watson & Clark, 1991; Watson & Tellegen, 1985, 1999). One point of view (e.g., Watson & Tellegen, 1985, 1999) claims that affect consists of two independent dimensions: positive affect (PA, called positive affectivity in this system) and negative affect (NA, negative affectivity). According to this view, low PA is a lack of PA and is not equivalent to high NA, nor is the lack of NA (i.e., low NA) equivalent to high PA. The two dimensions are considered to be completely independent and orthogonal (see Watson & Clark,

1991). The opposing view (e.g., Russell, 1978, 1979, 1980; Russell & Carroll, 1999a, 1999b) also claims that affect consists of two main independent dimensions. However, in this view, the two dimensions are *valence* and *arousal*, not positive and negative affect. Rather than perceiving PA and NA as independent, those two components of affect are viewed as the opposite ends of a valence continuum, or a bipolar dimension representing valence of affect, while the other dimension represents arousal, low versus high. Moreover, according to this point of view it makes no sense to talk about positive and negative affect as two independent dimensions, because that conceptualization allows for the conclusion (thought to be erroneous by this view) that one can experience positive and negative affect at the same time.

The lack of agreement among researchers about the structure of affect makes it problematic to determine if a given measure of affect has construct validity. For example, if one decides to measure positive affect with a scale that captures only PA (such as the PA subscale of the PANAS scale; Watson, Clark, & Tellegen, 1988) and in fact the bipolar model is correct, then the measure of affect would be both deficient (because it measures only part of the dimension) and contaminated (with indicators of arousal). Similarly, a measure that utilizes the bipolar model could produce assessments that are deficient (because it omits the arousal component of affect) and contaminated (with the negative affect dimension), if indeed the PANAS approach is correct. Until this debate is resolved, any use of self-report measures is further complicated and vulnerable to threats from such measurement validity issues, beyond the other points already considered.[1]

As has been described thus far, self-report of feelings, happy or sad, may not be a valid indicator of experienced affect, because it is a verbal response and is subject to all of the kinds of factors that influence responses (both verbal and other). In addition, however, in the case of reporting feelings, there may be pressures that make it even more likely that what people say when asked, especially during an experimental session, may not be a good indication of what they are feeling. First, they may not want to tell others what they are feeling. Second, they may not realize, themselves, exactly what they are feeling. Especially in the case of positive affect, induced by the very mild affect inductions used in much of the research on the topic, people may not know, or may not want to admit, that such a small thing made them feel happy. Research has shown that when things are going well, people may not search for causes or connections (e.g., Weiner, 1985), and thus they may not seek to discover, or realize, what they are feeling or what caused the feeling. Thus, this problem for self-report of affect is especially pronounced for positive affect, and particularly for mild positive affect.

In the case of using the self-report of affect as a "manipulation check," to make sure that the intended feeling state was in fact induced, there is also the problem of the potential for experimenter demand. That is, if the research participant gets the sense that the researcher is trying to induce a given feeling state and is then asked what he or she is feeling, the person may affirm that he or she is in that state, just to be cooperative or to appear to have the "correct" feelings or reactions in the situation.

Interference With the Ecological Validity of the Study

Thus far, we have considered several ways in which use of self-report of affect may not be appropriate because it may not be valid as an indicator of experienced feelings. In addition, however, the use of self-report of feelings may actually undermine the ecological validity of the entire study. (Self-reports may interfere with the ecological validity of field studies, quasi experiments, and longitudinal studies, as well as of experiments; however, because of space limitations, here we discuss only problems that self-reports may cause in experiments.) Consider, first, that the affect inductions that have usually been used are mild; that they are accomplished by means of everyday events, such as receiving a small free sample, finding change in the coin return of a public telephone, being informed of success on a puzzle or other inconsequential task, seeing 5 minutes of a nonsexual, nonaggressive comedy film, and the like; and that they are intended to be subtle and not call attention to the feelings that are being induced (or the fact that feelings are being studied). The affect inductions have been designed to represent everyday, relatively common, good feelings, the kinds of things that may happen frequently and that do not interrupt ongoing activity but rather allow the person to continue with what he or she is doing. For example, in some instances the studies obtain the responses of

people in shopping malls or other public places where they naturally go about their lives (and even in laboratories, people's natural, nonreactive responses are sought). The studies attempt to induce affect without distracting people or focusing their attention on their feelings. Sometimes the participants in the study do not even know that they are participating in a study (e.g., Isen & Levin, 1972, Study 2; Isen, Clark, & Schwartz, 1976), and in most of the studies they usually do not know that the focus of the experiment is on their feelings. These two points should be emphasized: The affect inductions are intended to induce a feeling state that people may experience frequently, not rare strong emotion; and they are designed to occur in a way that seems natural to the participant, and does not capture attention or interrupt the ongoing task, so that the person keeps on engaging in the task (and the researcher can assess the impact of the feelings on the ongoing task performance).

Against this background, then, we can see another reason that self-report measures of induced affect may pose problems in studies where the affect induction is subtle and meant to be unobtrusive or ecologically valid: Not only are they open to biases, experimental influences, and response effects, as discussed so far, but in addition, by asking directly about the person's feelings, such self-report measures of affect may undermine the very subtlety and unobtrusiveness that the researchers sought in designing the study. Thus, in such situations self-report measures can also undermine the ecological validity of the study. That is, the studies are usually designed to represent affect naturally, without distracting people or focusing their attention on the fact that the researchers are interested in their affective reactions to the events. By doing this, the researchers hope to create situations that represent the real-world situations in which affect may occur and have influence in daily life. This effort would be undermined, however, by direct questions about participants' feelings, with no other apparent reason for asking about feelings.

Finally, the use of self-report measures of feelings is problematic in studies that are focused on examining affect's influence on other tasks or processes, because direct questions about the affect that the participant is feeling may interrupt the task performance that is the dependent measure of interest, and thus may interfere with performance. Another way in which such questions may interrupt and interfere with the task itself is that the unexpected, unexplained question about affective state may make participants self-conscious or suspicious about the experimenter's intent, or both, and cause a complete change of focus.

It should be noted, however, that many of these problems may be ameliorated if the design of the study includes affect induction by means of some stimulus such as a film, slides, musical selection, or so forth, on which the questions about feelings can be centered. For example, when films are used (but presented as materials being pretested for a different study), the film can be followed by questions (several affect scales) about how the film made the person feel, and in such a case the affect question only serves to follow through on the cover story and will not make the participant suspicious or reveal that the purpose of the film was to induce affect for the actual study that is about to take place. In the same way, the participant is not likely to be focused on his or her feelings during the next activity, the main dependent measure of the actual study.

In contrast, some other means of affect induction may exacerbate the problems associated with self-report measures of affect. Sometimes researchers induce affect by asking participants to imagine being in an affective state of a given type, such as negative affect, positive affect, anger, fear, happiness, or whatever, or to recall occasions in the past on which they experienced an affective state of a given type. In such a context, self-report measures of affect are even more problematic than they are in studies using less reactive affect inductions. That is, these kinds of affect inductions involve people's full awareness of the experimenter's intent to alter their feeling states, as well as their full cooperation and effort to induce the state requested by the researcher. For this reason, such studies necessarily involve assessing affect only when participants know that their feelings are the topic of study and when they are focusing on their feelings. Further, although self-report measures of affect in this context are not subject to the concern that they will alert the participant to the fact that his or her feelings are the subject of study (because the affect induction has already done that), they still do suffer from most of the other drawbacks associated with self-reports of people's feeling states already mentioned.

Beyond that, however, such a method of affect induction raises several additional concerns that are especially problematic if self-reports of feeling states are used as affect measures. First, this type of affect induction renders self-reports of affective state even more vulnerable to experimenter demand or other experimenter effects or experimental artifacts, and thus use of a self-report measure of induced affect as a manipulation check or dependent measure would be especially questionable with this type of affect induction. This is because not only does the participant know what affective state the researcher wanted to induce, but he or she is also responsible for inducing the state successfully. Consequently, when the participant is asked about his or her state, there is great pressure to affirm that the requested one has been induced and is now being felt. Other problems associated with this method of affect induction are discussed in a later section.

Thus, in sum, even though some people still consider self-report as the sine qua non of the presence of a feeling state, the foregoing discussions have illustrated that simply asking people how they feel, as a way of assessing affect—either for a manipulation check or as part of a dependent measure—is not as simple as it seems, and certainly is not a direct assessment of feelings at all. Self-report of affect is a response or a set of responses, and it is subject to all of the concerns that surround obtaining participants' responses—factors such as not only response bias but also experimenter demand and experimenter bias, social-desirability and self-presentational concerns, and so forth, all of which have been found to play a role in participants' responses during an experimental session (see Rosenthal & Rosnow, 1969, for discussion). Thus, we next present some alternatives to self-report as ways to assess affect.

Alternatives to Self-Report

In this section, we suggest two alternatives to self-report in the study of affect. We first suggest that researchers should apply the process of conceptual validation of induced affect in their studies—that is, use converging operations and discriminant validation of the concept (or affective state) being studied. Although this applies to all forms of studies, including field studies and quasi experiments as well as experiments (see Schwab, 1999, for discussion), here we focus on the validation of affect manipulations in experiments utilizing induced affect.[2] Taking steps to validate the induced affect manipulation itself will increase confidence that it is affect that is induced and not anything else, which should render the use of self-reports of affect unnecessary in those studies. Second, we suggest the use of some implicit measures of affect (which actually can also be seen as part of the conceptual validation of the affect induction), which do not call subjects' attention to their emotions. In the discussion of implicit measures, we also indicate how these measures might be used in field studies as well as in experiments.

Conceptual Validation of Affect

As described above, self-reports of affect, as either manipulation checks or as dependent measures, are potentially problematic in experiments in several ways, including their unproven validity and their potential incompatibility with the experimental setting. An alternative approach, based on a conceptual validation method that was worked out by the field and applied widely in work ranging from personality assessment to test construction to experimentation, involves the concept of construct validity (see, e.g., Cronbach & Meehl, 1955). Put simply, methods based on this approach involve establishing a conceptual basis for the validity of the intended measure. In the next section, we present only a brief overview of some of the basic principles of conceptual validation, but one that we hope can be useful in validation of intervening variables such as affect, in experiments.

The process of conceptual validation of a procedure requires several steps. First, the manipulations should fit with theory, or at least be logically consistent with it, but they should not be put in place in a way that biases the outcome in favor of the theory or the hypotheses (Schwab, 1999). Second, researchers need to specify what has been called the *nomological network* (Cronbach & Meehl, 1955), wherein the relationship of the construct under investigation with other similar constructs is investigated. One component of the nomological network is the test of convergent validity. Convergent validity concerns the extent to which alternative operations of the construct are correlated or have the same or similar impact on theoretically relevant variables (Schwab, 1999). In the case of induced affect, convergent validity can be established by the convergence of various ways of inducing that same affect (i.e., converging operations). That is, if a new affect induction

method or operation is valid, it should display similar effects on a given dependent variable to those observed with other ways of representing that affective state.

Converging Operations

This method—conceptual validation, including conceptual validation of affect—utilizes triangulation on the construct or concept of the intended affective state. Triangulation involves using several different methods to represent the concept or feeling state and seeing that they all produce the same or compatible effects. This is what one would expect if that feeling, and not just something associated with one particular operationalization or way of representing that feeling state, is having influence. One example of the use of this method involves presenting evidence from *converging operations*, or different forms of affect induction that all converge on, or triangulate on, the constructs under study.

For example, in a series of experiments by Isen and her students, intended to study the influence of positive affect on helping behavior, affect was induced first by means of success on a task, and it was found that those who had succeeded donated more to a charity collection can (Isen, 1970, Study 1) and were also more helpful to a person who dropped books and papers that she was carrying (Studies 2 and 3). Following this, however, positive affect was induced by means of receipt of a cookie while studying in a library (Isen & Levin, 1972, Study 1) and by finding money in the coin return of a telephone booth in a shopping mall (Isen & Levin, 1972, Study 2). Helping was measured by rate of volunteering to serve as a helpful (as contrasted with a distracting) coexperimenter in an experiment (Study 1), and by willingness to help a person pick up papers she had dropped as she passed by the telephone in the mall (Study 2). In subsequent experiments, positive affect was induced by receipt of a small gift or free sample (three stationery note cards, tied with a small piece of ribbon) from a person posing as a representative of the stationery company, and the helping measure was the person's willingness to make a call for someone who telephoned him or her with a request (Isen et al., 1976).

The purpose of using those diverse affect inductions, such as success, good fortune, receiving an unexpected small gift, seeing 5 minutes of a comedy film, and others, was to establish that it was the positive affect generated by the inductions, and not something else about a particular method of positive-affect induction, that caused the observed effect. This inference is possible because the various inductions used are very different and do not share a same alternative interpretation, so that when they are observed to have the same impact on the dependent variable of interest (for example, helping), their impact is most parsimoniously interpreted as resulting from the one quality or factor that they share, induction of happy feelings.

After the affect manipulation was established in this series of studies, in subsequent experiments, similar affect-induction methods were used to extend the affect findings into the cognitive domain, showing that positive affect, induced in some of these same ways (e.g., free sample, success on a task, etc.) and in additional ways (e.g., humor), influenced memory, judgment, risk preference, cognitive organization, and problem-solving, in several different contexts (e.g., Isen, Daubman, & Gorgoglione, 1987; Isen, Daubman, & Nowicki, 1987; Isen & Geva, 1987; Isen, Johnson, Mertz, & Robinson, 1985; Isen & Patrick, 1983; Isen & Shalker, 1982; Isen, Shalker, Clark, & Karp, 1978). Thus, over a series of experiments, the construct of positive affect was established, empirically, by the conceptual method of converging operations. The nature of positive affect and the range of its effects were, similarly, explored and clarified by converging and discriminant operations on the dependent measure of helping (and, later, cognitive processes), because different measures of helping were used, and then different measures of cognitive organization were used. Thus, by this iterative process, using converging operations on both the independent (positive affect) and the dependent variables (i.e., helping, problem solving, decision making), researchers can establish the construct validity of affect without relying on self-report measures.

Discriminant Validation

Another component of the nomological network is discriminant validity. As Campbell (1960) noted, discriminant validity is "the requirement that a test not correlate too highly with measures from which it is supposed to differ" (p. 548). In the case of induced affect, discriminant validity means that the operation is not confounded with other constructs such as arousal or cognitive load, and that it should not influence tasks that are not expected to be influenced by the particular intended affective state.

This, then, means that not everything should have the same impact as positive affect, and not everything should be influenced in the same way by positive affect. Thus, the use of discriminant validation involves helping to confirm that positive affect has been induced by seeing that things not expected to be influenced by it indeed are not influenced by the induction. Since absence of an effect is most often difficult to interpret, this technique involves including dependent measures or conditions that are *not* expected to be influenced by the affective state, along with some that *are* expected to be influenced, or influential, with the expectation that a statistical interaction between that variable and positive affect will occur. That is, the expectation is that there will be an interaction between the affect variable and the two kinds of conditions or circumstances or dependent measures (one of which is predicted to be influenced and one of which is not expected to be influenced).

For example, in the article by Isen and Levin (1972) described above, there was not only a dependent measure designed to represent helping, but the experiment (Study 1) also included a measure designed to represent willingness to distract, rather than to help, people who were trying to study. The purpose of including the willingness-to-distract measure was to see whether positive affect promotes helping specifically, and to rule out alternative interpretations of the participant's behavior. That is, without the additional conditions that tested affect's influence on willingness to distract, it might have been argued that induced positive affect led people to be not so much helpful, but rather, energized and willing to do anything just to be active, or to be more compliant and willing to do whatever was requested or suggested. The results obtained, a crossover interaction wherein people in positive affect were more willing than controls to help but less willing to distract, show that positive affect, in fact, does not promote all behavior equally—it does not simply energize people and prompt them to do anything, just in order to be active, and it does not lead to compliance or willingness to agree to all behaviors or requests—but rather it promotes helping specifically. If the studies had not provided opportunities for not only helping but also other behaviors to be observed, it would not have been possible to have drawn these conclusions.

To recapitulate, then, an example of a study lacking in discriminant validity would be one in which the affect induction influenced all measures included in the study (say, both willingness to help and willingness to distract, in the example used above), even those not expected to be influenced by affect, or one in which only one dependent measure was included in the series of studies,[3] so that the researchers would not have any way of knowing the limits of the effect. In these examples, the lack of discriminant validity would be in the dependent measure.

An example of affect *inductions* that may not provide for discriminant validity may be those that ask participants to imagine themselves in a given affective state or to remember a time when they felt happy, angry, afraid, or whatever. (This type of induction was considered briefly earlier in this chapter, in the context of the problems they exacerbate when self-reports of affect are employed as measures; now we consider them in the context of the fact that they undermine discriminant validity.) In this case, the experimenter has given up control of the details of the affect induction, and the lack of discriminant validity comes from the fact that the affect induction may be confounded with other factors, such as cognitive load, intensity of affect, complexity of the memory chosen, mixed emotions (which the researcher cannot foresee or detect) about the situation recalled, and so on. That is, by giving up control and asking participants to create or choose almost everything about the affective state and the cognitive content that will be studied, if an effect is obtained, the researcher loses the ability to know for sure that the kind of affective state he or she envisioned when requesting that it be induced—and only that affect—influenced the dependent measure being investigated, and produced the effect. For example, if participants choose affective experiences that differ in complexity at the same time that they differ in valence, then any difference observed on a dependent measure such as problem solving could be coming from the extra complexity or cognitive load in the affective example chosen or retrieved by the participant, rather than exclusively from the affect itself that was intended by the researcher. And, if this is more likely with one type of affect than another, or with affect than with a control condition, then the manipulation would be confounded and therefore unable to reveal anything about the effect of the affect itself.

This kind of confounding is also a reason that, more generally, even with other types of affect induction, one cannot compare two affective states—say, positive and negative affect or happiness and sadness or happiness and anger—directly in an experiment. This is because one cannot be sure that comparable degrees of positive and negative affect are being induced, that the positive and negative memories chosen are equally effective in inducing any feelings, that positive and negative affect are being induced to the same intensity level, or that the positive and negative memories selected by the participants are equally cognitively demanding (see Isen, 1984, p. 210 ff. for discussion). It is easy to see that comparing very intense negative affect with mild positive affect, for example, or vice versa, would not seem a fair test of the relative effects of the two types of states. It is also easy to see that this problem would be exacerbated by use of an "imagine" or "recall-a-time-when" technique for inducing affect, because a participant might recall an extremely negative and complex event such as a funeral in the negative condition, but a more common, moderate, simple event such as a picnic in the positive condition.

Related to the issue of discriminant validity is the fact that we do not know whether strong affect would have the same or a similar effect as those that have been observed with mild, common feelings. This is a topic that has not been extensively investigated as yet, but that seems appropriate for study. However, there is some reason to believe that the effects of intense affect could be quite different—different in kind, rather than just in magnitude—from the effects of mild, pleasant affect. This is because important keys to positive affect's facilitating influence on thinking and social interaction may lie in what the mild feelings lead the person to think about, and in the fact that such affect can occur without interrupting the other ongoing activity in which the person is engaged. Intense affect, or focused emotion, in contrast, may be distracting or demanding of attention, changing both the thoughts that are brought to mind or easily accessible, and the likelihood of the person's continuing to focus on the other task. Thus, the impact on cognition that intense affect may have could be quite different from the impact that mild positive affect has—both because of the thoughts that are cued by the intense affect and because of the interruption of the ongoing task that becomes likely. This, however, remains to be investigated.

Compatibility With Theory and Existing Data

Along with converging operations and discriminant validity, another way of establishing the construct validity of an affect induction is to investigate whether the results obtained with this operation are compatible with theoretical expectations. That is, as information about the influence of an affective state, say positive affect, is gathered, over many studies and as represented in the literature, the field comes to understand and expect certain effects of that state. Thus, if a new affect induction or measurement tool produces radically different relationships with established dependent variables, it may be considered suspicious as a method of inducing the known affective state, at least until these results are widely replicated. In contrast, if the results obtained with this new method fit well with the established streams of research, that would help to validate the new operation.

For example, it has been well established, by many programs of research, that positive affect promotes creative problem solving and innovation (e.g., Estrada, Isen, & Young, 1994; Greene & Noice, 1988; Isen, Daubman, & Nowicki, 1987; Staw & Barsade, 1993, just to name a few). Thus, whatever else one is studying, one should also expect to find more unusual, though appropriate, responding and more evidence of innovative thinking and a problem-solving approach among people in whom positive affect has been induced (and a reduction in the dominance of the most typical response, even though it should not become completely unavailable).

At the same time, deriving predictions from previous findings need not—in fact, should not—be limited to deducing only simple, incremental steps that consider only one aspect of a phenomenon at a time. Consider, for example, that not only has positive affect been shown to lead to more innovative thinking and problem solving, but it has also been found to give rise to risk aversion in dangerous or high-risk situations (e.g., Isen & Patrick, 1983; Isen & Geva, 1987; Isen, Nygren, & Ashby, 1988; Nygren, Isen, Taylor, & Dulin, 1996), and from those findings one expects that people in positive affect will behave self-protectively in situations of real danger. These two facts about the effects of positive affect, just like examples of the process under discussion, can be considered at the same time and thus may lead to unique or unexpected predictions that help to confirm that the affective state has indeed been induced, at the same time that they advance the field's understanding of positive affect, as they suggest new expectations about positive affect.

This kind of process of building on previous findings, employing converging representations of the affective state, and ensuring discriminant validation of the state by inclusion of tasks or operations that are not expected to produce similar effects, lies at the heart of conceptual validation of positive affect—and indeed of all otherwise unobservable intervening variables. Thus, over programs of research, or several studies cumulatively, the fact that positive affect is the cause of the observed effects can be established conceptually and empirically.

In the preceding section, we have attempted to present a brief summary of the topic of conceptual validation of unseen intervening variables such as affect, and we have laid out some procedures that can be used to help establish that affect has been induced as intended in studies. Our consideration of this topic serves to highlight the importance, and the difficulty, of establishing the validity of any measurement attempted—even seemingly simple ones such as assessment of feelings. Because of space limitations, we cannot undertake a full discussion of the concept and implementation of construct validity in this chapter. However, the interested reader is referred to work by Cronbach and his colleagues (e.g., Cronbach, 1960; Cronbach & Meehl, 1955), by Campbell, Fiske, and their colleagues (e.g., Campbell & Fiske, 1959; Cook & Campbell, 1979), and by Garner and colleagues (e.g., Garner, Hake, & Eriksen, 1956), and others, for more discussion of this important idea and related issues such as those discussed above.

Implicit Measures of Affect

Another alternative to self-report measures of affect are what might be called *implicit measures* of affect. These would include measures or responses by the participant that do not involve any direct expression of affect, or any answer to a direct question about current feeling state, but that can be taken to indicate the presence of positive affect, because they assess something that has previously been shown to be promoted by positive affect (see Isen, 1984, for discussion). These have been used at various times in the literature, sometimes under other names, such as *unobtrusive measures* (e.g., Webb, Campbell, Schwartz, & Sechrest, 1966), but they are enjoying a resurgence in popularity now, because of the current interest in implicit memory in the cognitive psychology literature (e.g., Schachter, 1989).

An example of a study that used an implicit measure of this kind is one by Estrada et al. (1994), which attempted to induce positive affect in physicians who were about to undertake a diagnostic problem but first asked the physicians to solve seven items of moderate difficulty taken from the Remote Associates Test (RAT), a task previously used to measure creativity (Mednick, Mednick, & Mednick, 1964) and previously shown to be influenced by positive affect (Isen, Daubman, & Nowicki, 1987). In that way, while the authors were actually interested in investigating the impact of positive affect on medical diagnostic problem solving, they were able to confirm, first, that affect had been induced by their affect induction, because the doctors randomly assigned to the positive-affect condition did, in fact, perform better on the RAT items.

Thus, the inclusion of the implicit affect manipulation check served two purposes: First, it helped to establish that (as expected) affect could be induced among physicians and would have an impact on their task performance, as had been observed previously with college students. This is a fact that has surprised many nonphysicians (but not many physicians). Second, the inclusion of the nonobvious manipulation check would have been invaluable if the effect on the diagnostic process had not been observed, because it would have enabled the researchers to know that any failure to find differences on the diagnostic problem was not attributable to failure of the affect induction. As it turned out, there was a facilitative effect of the induced positive affect on the diagnostic process, and so that function of the manipulation check was not needed; however, it was important to be able to assess the presence of an effect without asking the physicians for a self-report of their feeling state.

In another article, researchers used five implicit measures, across two studies, to show that positive affect was induced by sampling a refreshing drink, and in one study also compared those implicit measures with two explicit ratings of the beverage (Isen, Labroo, & Durlach, 2004). The implicit measures used, besides performance on the RAT, which has been described above, were based on previous findings that positive affect, induced in several different ways, compared with control, gives rise to a broader range of first associates to neutral stimuli, resulting in nontypical first associates to neutral stimuli (Isen et al., 1985) and also increases accessibility of positive material in memory, resulting in a more positive cognitive context (e.g., Isen & Shalker, 1982; Isen et al., 1978). The other implicit measures used, then, were prevalence of nontypical first associates, and of positive first associates, to neutral words, and prevalence of nontypical, and of positive, word-fragment-completion words. The explicit ratings were not direct questions about affect or feelings, but they did ask explicitly about the refreshingness and pleasantness of the beverage. The results indicated that the implicit measures and explicit ratings of the beverage corresponded, and they also suggested some ways in which the implicit ratings can be used more flexibly than explicit questions about target stimuli.

The content of word-fragment completions has also been used in studies in cognitive psychology and clinical psychology, to infer relevant feelings or thoughts, and may be able to be adapted to serve as implicit measures of affect. For instance, Eysenck, McLeod, and Mathews (1987) asked participants to write down auditorily presented words that were homophones having both a threat-related and a neutral interpretation (i.e., die, dye; pain, pane) and used this method as a measure of cognitive interpretive bias caused by anxiety. Similarly, researchers may be able to use other homophones to measure other emotions and mood states implicitly.

Thus, such implicit measures of affect may be used to provide assurance that the affective state has been induced, and they eliminate the need to rely on verbal self-reports—which we have argued are of unknown validity. At the same time, we make note of the need to establish any measure of affect, following many of the principles outlined here, before such a measure can be comfortably used as an implicit measure of affect. That is, any implicit measure of affect must be used with multiple affect inductions, multiple other dependent measures that triangulate on the affective concept intended and discriminate it from other responses or feeling states, must be logically and empirically compatible with theory and the body of accumulated data on the topic, and so on, before it can be used as an implicit indicator of the intended affect state. One cannot, for example, just come up with a hunch that some outcome will indicate the presence of the desired state and, after one study demonstrating that it does have a relationship with some affective state (say, induced in one way, in one situation, with one dependent measure, and so on), use that outcome as evidence itself that a class of affective states (for example, positive affect or negative affect or anxiety) has been induced. That is, the researcher must establish the whole nomological net, or at least provide substantial evidence for the nomological net, before it would be possible to use a given response as an implicit measure of a feeling state.

Theoretical Implications

We started this chapter by arguing that these methods of conceptual validation and implicit measures have been successfully used in fields of study such as cognitive psychology, and we demonstrated how they have also been used to validate findings in positive affect research. However, we believe that these methods could also be applied to other emotion-related research.

For example, although, as we demonstrated in this chapter, conceptual validation has been used with positive affect research, this method has not been extensively applied to the investigation of induced negative affect. This may be part of the reason that the effect of negative affect on a variety of dependent variables appears to be less consistent than results obtained from induced positive affect. Conceptually validating methods of inducing negative affect may be quite complex, because negative affect may be heterogeneous in nature (see e.g., Isen, 1990, for discussion). For example, inducing sadness may be very different from inducing anxiety; the experience of these two states seems very different; and the consequences of inducing these two states may differ considerably. Therefore, several dependent variables may be required in order to validate methods of inducing negative affect, and these may differ for anxiety, sadness, anger, hostility, or other negative affect states that are being induced. Thus, an extensive program of research employing converging operations and ensuring discriminant validation, using different method of inducing negative affect, may greatly benefit this line of research.

The use of implicit measures of affect in other areas of positive psychology may also be helpful for advancing theory in positive psychology. For example, in this volume Ulrich Schimmack describes the continuing debate about the structure of affect (chapter 7). He also describes some of the method artifacts created by self-report that make for difficulty in interpreting the nature of the relationship between positive affect and negative affect. We suggest that the use of implicit measures of affect could be a useful tool in alleviating this kind of problem, because such measures may be less open to some of the biases that he identifies, such as acquiescence bias and cross-cultural differences, described in chapter 7. That is, because the tendency of some participants to respond indiscriminately positively to items should not influence implicit measures of affect such as the RAT, this kind of implicit measure may get around that kind of bias. Similarly, there may be implicit measures that would not be influenced by the dialectic thinking attributed to Asian culture. These would have to be determined based on a full understanding of the processes and effects involved with such proposed dialectic thinking, of course. Thus, if one reason that researchers find contradictory results regarding the relationship between positive affect and negative affect lies in artifacts related to self-reports, then the use of implicit measures of affect may help in solving this ongoing debate.

Besides the issue of that continuing debate, another arena that could benefit from use of implicit affect measures is research on subjective well-being (SWB). Some of the problems of self-report measures that we have mentioned, such as factors related to demand or self-presentation, and unwanted induced affect caused by the use of the self-report affect measures themselves, may also affect the SWB line of research. Thus, it may be useful to validate, using implicit measures, some of the findings that are reported in SWB research. For example, instead of using self-report measures in the daily diary data-gathering method described by Schimmack, researchers may be able to use different implicit measures on various days along with or instead of the self-report measures.

Of course, a lot of scientific effort will need to be devoted to developing these measures if they are to be used in positive psychology research. However, researchers in the field may be able to borrow some implicit measures that have already been developed in other fields of research. For example, as noted in this chapter, work on positive affect has already begun to develop such measures and methods, and as noted earlier in describing the study by Eysenck et al. (1987), from cognitive psychology, the homophone/word-fragment method may be borrowed, although it will need to be adapted to fit affect research. Other methods used by cognitive psychologists may also be adapted to be used as measures of affect. For another example, ratings of neutral products may be adopted from marketing research, and tendencies to engage in extra-role behaviors (as rated by self or supervisors) may be adopted from organizational behavior research, as implicit measures of affect. Obviously, all of these methods will need to be validated themselves before they can be used in this way as implicit measures of affect, because their interpretation cannot simply be assumed. However, the conceptual validation method described in this chapter, using converging operations and discriminant validation, could be used to identify useful implicit measures and strengthen their acceptability.

Summary

In this chapter, we have tried to address some of the methodological concerns surrounding the study of affect. We have presented arguments against the simplistic use of self-report measures of affect in research settings, pointing out problems with the validity and interpretation of self-report responses, and noted the need to validate such responses. We have urged that self-reports be used only where they do not compromise the experimental situation, and only in conjunction with other indicators of affect, triangulating on the concept of the affective state intended by any affect induction. We also noted the special problems that attend to use of techniques such as the "imagine" or "remember-a-time-when" technique of affect induction. Even though these kinds of affect-induction methods, and self-report measures used as checks on the effectiveness of the intended affect induction, or as the dependent measure, seem convenient, we have suggested alternative methods of measurement, based on a conceptual validation of affect and implicit measures; and we have urged integration of such principles into studies of affect.

What became clear to us while writing this chapter is that, although a lot of headway has been made in positive psychology research in the last 30 years, a lot more needs to be done. We also believe that a lot of progress in this field of study will be achieved if researchers integrate what has been learned in related fields over the years and stay careful to maintain only scientifically rigorous and valid methods of investigation. Clearly, many studies use rigorous methods; however, as the field is progressing and growing, we also sense that some researchers may be tempted to use convenient methods that, unfortunately, carry some of the risks to validity and correct interpretation that we have identified here. We hope, instead, that positive psychology will continue to integrate the rich and well-researched concepts and methods developed over the years in the fields of measurement theory and testing into its own work, as it develops its own strengths and, in turn, helps to advance those same and other areas of thought and research.

Notes

1. This debate about the structure (and nature) of affect may be relevant to the findings that thus far in the empirical literature on the influence of induced affect, positive and negative affect have not been found to have parallel or opposite effects. For example, in the literature on helping, it has been found that positive affect generally facilitates helping; however, the opposite has not always been found for negative affect (sadness), where instead sometimes sadness leads to less helping, sometimes to more helping, and sometimes its effects are no different from those of a control group (see, e.g., Isen, 1984, 1990, for discussions). Similarly, in the cognitive literature, although positive affect has been found to cue positive material in memory (e.g., Isen et al., 1978; Teasdale & Fogarty, 1979), a parallel effect for sadness has not generally been observed—that is, sadness has not been found to cue negative material in memory or has been found to do so in an attenuated fashion (e.g., Isen, 1985; Isen et al., 1978; Snyder & White, 1982; Teasdale, Taylor, & Fogarty, 1980), except under special, focusing, circumstances such as use of hypnosis as the affect-induction technique (e.g., Bower, 1981).

2. Appropriate conceptual validation should be applied to all measures of affect used in all forms of studies, including field studies and quasi experiments, as well as experiments (see Schwab, 1999, for discussion). However, the details of how to apply conceptual validation in field studies may differ from those that are applicable in experiments; and a full treatment of all of the various considerations in all different settings of research is beyond the scope of this chapter.

3. Sometimes one cannot include multiple measures in a single study, but in that case one can include more than one study on the topic.

References

Bandura, A. (1971). *Social learning theory.* New York: General Learning Press.

Bower, G. H. (1981). Mood and memory. *American Psychologist, 36,* 129–148.

Campbell, D. T. (1960). Recommendation for APA test standards regarding constructs, trait, or discriminant validity. *American Psychologist, 15,* 546–553.

Campbell, D. T., & Fiske, D. W. (1959). Convergent and discriminant validation by the multi-trait, multi-method matrix. *Psychological Bulletin, 56,* 81–105.

Cook, T. D., & Campbell, D. T. (1979). *Quasi-experimentation.* Boston: Houghton Mifflin.

Cronbach, L. J. (1960). *Essentials of psychological testing* (2nd ed.). New York: Harper.

Cronbach, L. J., & Meehl, P. E. (1955). Construct validity in psychological tests. *Psychological Bulletin, 52,* 281–302.

Estrada, C. A., Isen, A. M., & Young, M. J. (1994). Positive affect influences creative problem solving and reported source of practice satisfaction in physicians. *Motivation and Emotion, 18,* 285–299.

Eysenck, M. W., & Keane, M. K. (2003). *Cognitive psychology* (4th ed.). East Sussex, England: Psychological Press.

Eysenck, M. W., MacLeod, C., & Mathews, A. (1987). Cognitive functioning and anxiety. *Psychological Research, 49,* 189–195.

Garner, W. R., Hake, H. W., & Eriksen, C. W. (1956). Operationism and the concept of perception. *Psychological Review, 63,* 149–159.

Greene, T. R., & Noice, H. (1988). Influence of positive affect upon creative thinking and problem solving in children. *Psychological Reports, 63,* 895–898.

Isen, A. M. (1970). Success, failure attention and reactions to others: The warm glow of success. *Journal of Personality and Social Psychology, 17,* 107–112.

Isen, A. M. (1984). Toward understanding the role of affect in cognition. In R. Wyer & T. Srull (Eds.), *Handbook of social cognition* (pp. 179–236). Hillsdale, NJ: Erlbaum.

Isen, A. M. (1985). The asymmetry of happiness and sadness in effects on memory in normal college students. *Journal of Experimental Psychology: General, 114,* 388–391.

Isen, A. M. (1990). The influence of positive and negative affect on cognitive organization: Implications for development. In N. Stein, B. Leventhal, & T. Trabasso (Eds.), *Psychological and biological processes in the development of emotion* (pp. 75–94). Hillsdale, NJ: Erlbaum.

Isen, A. M., Clark, M. S., & Schwartz, M. F. (1976). Duration of the effect of good mood on helping: "Footprints on the sands of time." *Journal of Personality and Social Psychology, 34,* 385–393.

Isen, A. M., Daubman, K. A., & Gorgoglione, J. M. (1987). The influence of positive affect on cognitive organization: Implications for education. In R. Snow & M. Farr (Eds.), *Aptitude, learning, and instruction: Affective and conative factors* (pp. 143–164). Hillsdale, NJ: Erlbaum.

Isen, A. M., Daubman, K. A., & Nowicki, G. P. (1987). Positive affect facilitates creative problem solving. *Journal of Personality and Social Psychology, 52,* 1122–1131.

Isen, A. M., & Geva, N. (1987). The influence of positive affect on acceptable level of risk: The person with a large canoe has a large worry. *Organizational Behavior and Human Decision Processes, 39,* 145–154.

Isen, A. M., & Hastorf, A. H. (1982). Some perspectives on cognitive social psychology. In A. H. Hastorf & A. M. Isen (Eds.), *Cognitive social psychology* (pp. 1–31). New York: Elsevier.

Isen, A. M., Johnson, M. M. S., Mertz, E., & Robinson, F. G. (1985). The influence of positive affect on the unusualness of word association. *Journal of Personality and Social Psychology, 48,* 1413–1426.

Isen, A. M., Labroo, A. A., & Durlach, P. (2004). An influence of product and brand name on positive affect: Implicit and explicit measures. *Motivation and Emotion, 28,* 43–63.

Isen, A. M., & Levin, P. F. (1972). The effect of feeling good on helping: Cookies and kindness. *Journal of Personality and Social Psychology, 21,* 384–388.

Isen, A. M., Nygren, T. E., & Ashby, F. G. (1988). The influence of positive affect on the perceived utility of gains and losses. *Journal of Personality and Social Psychology, 55,* 710–717.

Isen, A. M., & Patrick, R. E. (1987). The effect of positive feelings on risk taking: When the chips are down. *Organizational Behavior and Human Performance, 31,* 194–202.

Isen, A. M., & Shalker, T. E. (1982). Do you "accentuate the positive, eliminate the negative" when you are in a good mood? *Social Psychology Quarterly, 45,* 58–63.

Isen, A. M., Shalker, T. E., Clark, M., & Karp, L. (1978). Affect, accessibility of material in memory and behavior: A cognitive loop? *Journal of Personality and social Psychology, 36,* 1–12.

Mandler, G. (1982). The structure of value: Accounting for taste. In M. S. Clark & S. T. Fiske (Eds.), *Affect and cognition: 17th Annual*

Carnegie Symposium on Cognition. Hillsdale, NJ: Erlbaum.

Mednick, M. T., Mednick, S. A., & Mednick, E. V. (1964). Incubation of creative performance and specific associative priming. *Journal of Abnormal and Social Psychology, 69,* 84–88.

Mischel, W. (1968). *Personality and assessment.* New York: Wiley.

Nisbett, J. M., & Wilson, T. D. (1977). Telling more than we can know: Verbal reports on mental processes. *Psychological Review, 84,* 231–259.

Nygren, T. E., Isen, A. M., Taylor, P. J., & Dulin, J. (1996). The influence of positive affect on the decision rule in risk situations: Focus on outcome (and especially avoidance of loss) rather than probability. *Organizational Behavior and Human Decision Processes, 66*(1), 59–72.

Rosenthal, R., & Rosnow, R. L. (Eds.). (1969). *Artifact in behavioral research.* New York: Academic Press.

Russell, J. A. (1978). Evidence of convergent validity on the dimensions of affect. *Journal of Personality and Social Psychology, 36,* 1152–1168.

Russell, J. A. (1979). Affective space is bipolar. *Journal of Personality and Social Psychology, 37,* 345–356.

Russell, J. A. (1980). A circumplex model of affect. *Journal of Personality and Social Psychology, 39,* 1161–1178.

Russell, J. A., & Carroll, J. M. (1999a). On the bipolarity of positive and negative affect. *Psychological Bulletin, 125,* 3–30.

Russell, J. A., & Carroll, J. M. (1999b). The phoenix of bipolarity: Reply to Watson and Tellegen. *Psychological Bulletin, 125,* 611–617.

Schachter, D. L. (1989). Implicit memory: History and current status. *Journal of Experimental Psychology: Learning, Memory, and Cognition, 13,* 501–518.

Schwab, D. P. (1999). *Research methods for organizational studies.* Mahwah, NJ: Erlbaum.

Staw, B. M., & Barsade, S. G. (1993). Affect and managerial performance: A test of the sadder-but-wiser vs. happier-and-smarter hypotheses. *Administrative Science Quarterly, 38,* 304–331.

Snyder, M., & White, E. (1982). Moods and memories: Elation, depression, and remembering the events of one's life. *Journal of Personality, 50,* 149–167.

Teasdale, J. D., & Fogarty, S. J. (1979). Differential effects of induced mood on retrieval of pleasant and unpleasant events from episodic memory. *Journal of Abnormal Psychology, 88,* 248–257.

Teasdale, J. D., Taylor, R., & Fogarty, S. J. (1980). Effects of induced elation-depression on the accessibility of memories of happy and unhappy experiences. *Behavior Research and Therapy, 18,* 339–346.

Tulving, E., Schacter, D. L., & Stark, H. A. (1982). Priming effects in word-fragment completion are independent of recognition memory. *Journal of Experimental Psychology: Learning, Memory, and Cognition, 17,* 595–617.

Watson, D., & Clark, L. A. (1991). Self- versus peer ratings of specific emotional traits: Evidence of convergent and discriminant validity. *Journal of Personality and Social Psychology, 60,* 927–940.

Watson, D., Clark, L. A., & Tellegen, A. (1988). Development and validation of brief measures of positive and negative affect: The PANAS scales. *Journal of Personality and Social Psychology, 54,* 1063–1070.

Watson, D., & Tellegen, A. (1985). Toward a consensual structure of mood. *Psychological Bulletin, 98,* 219–235.

Watson, D., & Tellegen, A. (1999). Issues in dimensional structure of affect—Effects of descriptors, measurement error, and response formats: Comment on Russell and Carroll (1999). *Psychological Bulletin, 125,* 601–610.

Webb, E. J., Campbell, D. T., Schwartz, R. D., & Sechrest, L. (1966). *Unobtrusive measures: Normative research in the social sciences.* Oxford: Rand McNally.

Weiner, B. (1985). "Spontaneous" causal thinking. *Psychological Bulletin, 97,* 74–84.

Weiss, H., & Cropanzano, R. (1996). Affective events theory: A theoretical discussion of the structure, causes and consequences of affective experiences at work. In L. L. Cummings & B. M. Staw (Eds.), *Research in organizational behavior* (Vol. 18, pp. 1–74). Greenwich, CT: JAI.

18

Natural Experiments

What Behavioral Genetic Approaches Can Tell Us About Human Potential

C. S. Bergeman and Anthony D. Ong

Variation is a hallmark of human development. Implied in every question about an individual's development, thus, is another question: How did the person get this way? And, relatedly, What kind of person will he or she become? Such questions are neither invented by nor restricted to academic psychologists. Reflections on religion, physics, education, and philosophy all lead to the issue of biological propensity and individual agency, and one has only to read Dostoyevsky to get a sense of the exigency with which these issues may be felt. Indeed, questions concerning the influence of nature versus nurture speak to the very core of what it means to be human. Does genetic inheritance restrict our range of purposeful behavior? At the same time, individual variation in genetic makeup also begs a question about identity, one that all identical twins probably struggle with to some extent: If you cannot hear the beat of your own heart, who are you?

Comprehensive understanding of the complexities of human development, thus, requires methodologies that permit the assembly of an ever-expansive puzzle, the pieces of which come from different domains of inquiry. Behavior genetics is a theory and a set of methodologies that can help to bridge the arc between the language of genes and the influence of the environment (cf. Bergeman, 1997; Plomin, DeFries, & McClearn, 1990). In this chapter, we identify and describe research designs (family, twin, and adoption) and analytical techniques (univariate, multivariate, and longitudinal model-fitting analyses; DeFries-Fulker analysis) commonly used in behavioral genetic research. We discuss and summarize the strengths and limitations of these approaches. In the final section, we provide a sketch of the important ways in which a behavioral genetic perspective can both inform and enhance research in positive psychology.

Understanding Genes and Environment

Because of the multidimensional nature of human behavior, it is unlikely that a single direct gene contributes to the range of individual differences in personalities, abilities, and temperaments. Thus, it is important to keep in mind that there are no genes for happiness or resilience; rather, biological channels are indirect, and genetic influences are in reality just influences, propensities that nudge development in one direction instead of another. That is, genes work like blueprints, directing the assembly and regulation of proteins (Plomin, DeFries, McClearn, & McGuffin, 2000). Each gene codes for a specific sequence of amino acids, and these proteins then interact with other physiological and environmental factors. The behavior genetic approach thus takes into consideration the influence of many genes as well as environmental factors to explain normal variation in complex behavioral traits.

As a descriptive statistic, *heritability* is defined as the proportion of phenotypic variance in a population that is due to genetic variance (Falconer & McKay, 1996; Lush, 1940), which in turn can be partitioned into two types—additive and nonadditive. According to quantitative genetic theory (Falconer & McKay, 1996), *additive genetic variance* is the extent to which there is a linear relation among the alleles (alternate forms of a gene) contributing to a particular trait (i.e., the more alleles for a particular trait that a person has, the more of that characteristic the individual will have as well), whereas *nonadditive genetic variance* represents genetic influences due to *dominance* (interactions between alleles at a single locus), as well as the variance due to the higher-order interactions (interactions between alleles at different loci), called *epistasis*. Phenotypic differences among individuals can also be due to environmental differences and, interestingly, behavioral genetic research provides some of the most conclusive evidence for the salience of environmental influences on development. The environmental component of variance can be separated into those factors that contribute to phenotypic similarity among family members, referred to by different researchers as *shared, common,* or *between-family variance,* and those environmental influences that make family members different from one another, termed *nonshared, specific,* or *within-family variance* (see Carey, 2003).

What is perhaps even more relevant to the understanding of how attributes related to human potential are developed and maintained is the interface between genes and environment. Genetic and environmental influences have been suggested to intersect in two major ways—via interactions and correlations. *Genotype-environment* (GE) *interactions* reflect the fact that because of their genetic propensities, some individuals are more responsive to specific aspects of the environment (Bergeman & Plomin, 1989). That is, the impact of the environment is contingent on a person's genetic predispositions, and some individuals are more likely than others to be selectively steered toward environments that they find most compatible. Related to this is the *diathesis-stress model* (Monroe & Simons, 1991), in which a specific genetic propensity (the diathesis) produces a vulnerability to stressful environmental influences, which results in a negative outcome. Although the focus of the diathesis-stress model has been applied mainly to studies of psychopathology, it is surely applicable to research in resilience and other aspects of positive psychology.

Genotype-environment correlation literally refers to a correlation between genetic deviations and environmental differences as they affect a trait (Plomin, DeFries, & Loehlin, 1977). Three types of GE correlations have been posited—passive, reactive, and active. Passive GE correlation suggests that because they share both genes and family environment with their parents, children can passively inherit environments that are correlated with their genetic tendencies. Reactive, or evocative, GE correlations relate to experiences of the child that derive from the reactions of other people to their genetic propensities; in other words, people react differently to individuals of different genotypes. Finally, active GE correlation is sometimes called niche-picking and describes the situation in which children actively seek or even create environments that are correlated to their genetic makeup. This last type of genetic predisposition may play a crucial role in the way the genotype plays out in development (Scarr & McCartney, 1983). Although GE correlations are often conceptualized in a positive way (i.e., the environment supports, or even accentuates, the genetic propensity), it can also work in the other direction as well. That is, environments can be provided or created that counteract one's hereditary predisposition.

The focus of behavioral genetic research, therefore, is the relative contribution of genetic and environmental influences on individual differences in behavior, and their confluence. Three types of research paradigms are typically used—family, twin, and adoption designs—and are described below.

Research Designs

Family Studies

Family studies include information from a variety of kinship relations, including parents and offspring, siblings, half-siblings, grandparents, aunts, uncles, and cousins (see Morton, 1974; Morton & MacLean, 1974; Neale & Cardon, 1992). Quantitative genetic theory specifies the relative amount of resemblance expected for different types of family relationships (see Falconer, 1980, for a complete discussion). For example, first-degree relatives, such as full siblings or parents and their offspring, are more similar genetically than are second-degree relatives, such as half-siblings. If heredity is important for a particular behavior, pairs of individuals who are more similar genetically should be more phenotypically (showing outward manifestation of the characteristic of interest) similar as well. If heredity is not important, then the differences in genetic similarity should not affect the resemblance of these pairs of individuals. From an environmental perspective, the same premise applies: To the extent that shared environment is important, in-

dividuals who live together should be more similar than those who do not. These suppositions are the foundation of behavioral genetic theory.

The conceptual design depicted in figure 18.1 is an illustration of familial data that could be used in model-fitting analyses (Boomsma, Martin, & Neale, 1989). The design in the diagram incorporates three generations of family members. The first generation (G1), in this example, includes a husband and wife and their siblings. In the second generation (G2), two children of the proband and spouse are included, and the third generation (G3) includes the grandchildren of the original husband and wife, two per child. The design allows for comparisons of sibling relationships across three generations, parent-offspring relations across two generations, aunt-uncle/niece-nephew relations across two generations, grandparent-grandchild relations from G1 to G3, and cousin relationships in G3. In addition, the effects of *assortative mating* (the tendency for like to marry like) can also be assessed. To the extent that there is assortative mating for the characteristic of interest, estimates of heritability will be overestimated (see Buss, 1984, 1985; Plomin, DeFries, et al.,

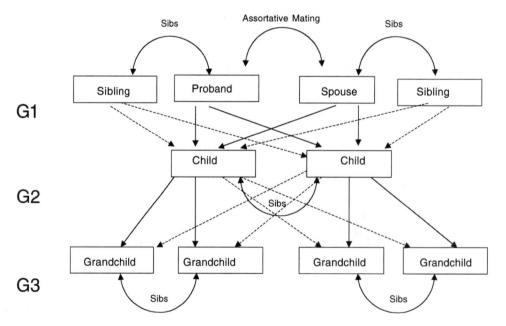

Figure 18.1 Schematic of family design including sibling relationships at all three generations (G), parent-offspring relationships at two generations, aunt-uncle/niece-nephew relations at two generations, grandparent-grandchild relations at one generation (not shown), and cousin relations at one generation (not shown).

1990, for a thorough discussion of these issues). Model-fitting techniques are especially useful when combination designs that yield different familial correlations are employed (Jinks & Fulker, 1970).

Unfortunately, the family design itself cannot unambiguously disentangle the contribution of heredity and shared environment on family influence (Plomin, DeFries, et al., 1990). This is not only because members of a family share both, but also because environmental similarity goes along with genetic relatedness. That is, the closer the genetic resemblance, the greater the likelihood that these individuals also share similar environments (i.e., full sibs share more environmental influences than do cousins). Thus, the contribution of shared genes and shared environment contributing to family resemblance for characteristics of interest is referred to as *familiality*. Although family studies cannot definitively estimate genetic and environmental sources of familial resemblance, they are valuable for several reasons (Bergeman, 1997; Plomin, DeFries, et al., 1990). First, family studies suggest upper-limit estimates of the influences of additive genetic effects (genetic effects that "breed true" among siblings or parent-offspring relations), which can be no greater than twice the phenotypic correlation between first-degree relatives (and might be substantially less if shared environment is important). Second, family studies provide important comparison data for the results of twin and adoption studies. Because the purpose of behavioral genetic research is to provide information that is broadly generalizable, and because twins or adoptees may have characteristics that make them different from the general population, data that provide a comparison to twin and adoption research paradigms is essential to the external validity of behavioral genetic research. An important contribution of the family design, then, is to identify characteristics that "run in families"—whether for genetic or environmental reasons—that may warrant further exploration and to provide an upper-limit estimate of genetic and shared family environmental influence.

Twin Design

One of the most common behavioral genetic designs is the use of identical and fraternal twins, referred to as the *twin method* (Segal, 1999). There is a plethora of twin studies, including multiple Scandinavian twin registries (e.g., Danish, Finnish, Swedish) as well as other international twin studies (e.g., Australian, Russian); registries developed from military databases (e.g., Vietnam Era Twin Registry), and those developed at universities (e.g., Virginia, Minnesota, Louisville). Twin registries have also been developed for specific age groups (e.g., the Octo-Twin Registry was developed to study characteristics of interest in twins over the age of 80) or subcultures (e.g., Black Elderly Twin Study).

Monozygotic (MZ) twins are genetically identical and share 100% of all hereditary influences, whereas dizygotic (DZ) or fraternal twins share 50% (on average) of the genetic influences that operate additively and 25% of nonadditive influences. Fraternal twins are no more similar genetically than any other pair of full siblings. There are several advantages to using twins. First, twins are plentiful, accounting for approximately 1 in 85 live births (Plomin et al., 2000). Second, twins are the same age at the same time and they share the same family environment to a greater extent than do siblings. This *equal environment assumption* allows for the relative impact of genes and environment to be distinguished.

Figure 18.2 represents a simple path diagram for the analysis of data from twins (see Boomsma et al., 1989). Phenotype Twin 1 represents the score of one member of the twin pair on the characteristic of interest, and Phenotype Twin 2 refers to the score of the other twin. G and Es refer to genotypic and shared environmental variables, respectively. The model assumes that r_g (the genetic correlation) is 1.0 for identical (MZ) twins and 0.5 for fraternal (DZ) twins if the genetic influences operate in an additive manner, and 1.0 for MZ and 0.25 for DZ twins if the genetic influences operate in a nonadditive way (i.e., via dominance or epistasis); r_e (the environmental correlation) is specified as 1.0 if the twins are reared together (T), and 0.0 if the twins are reared apart (A). It is important to remember that this does not mean that the actual correlation for a particular trait is 1.0 for either genetic or environmental reasons; it reflects the fact that identical twins (MZ) reared together (T) share all of the hereditary influences on the trait of interest as well as 100% of the environmental effects that occur as a result of living together. Because the parameter labeled En represents nonshared environmental influences that do not contribute to twin

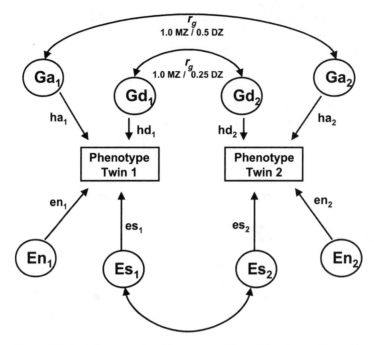

Figure 18.2 Path diagram of model to assess additive (a) and nonadditive (d) genetic (g) and shared (s) and nonshared (n) environmental (e) influences on a phenotype of interest.

similarity (including error of measurement), the latent parameters are not connected by paths. Although it is possible to use patterns of correlations among individuals who differ in genetic relatedness and environmental overlap to estimate genetic and environmental influences on behaviors, the testing of explicit models has become the standard in the field (see Boomsma et al., 1989; Neale & Cardon, 1992).

One potential problem that must be addressed when using twin designs is to ensure an accurate zygosity diagnosis. Historically, investigators have used a questionnaire method to assess zygosity, which is based on questions regarding highly heritable traits, such as eye color, hair color, and hair texture, that are influenced by a network of many genes. In fact, one question, "When you were children, did [parents, siblings, other family members, friends, strangers] have difficulty telling you apart?" works pretty well. To be mistaken for another person requires that many heritable characteristics are identical. Interestingly, just asking twins whether they are identical versus fraternal is not a very accurate method, as about 40% of twins misclassify themselves (Scarr & Carter-Saltzman, 1979). Now it is possible to perform highly accurate blood analyses to determine whether twins are iden-

tical or fraternal. That is, if any of the genetic markers are different, the twins are considered dizygotic. Additionally, molecular genetic techniques can be used to look at DNA "fingerprints." Assessments that compare the use of questionnaires with blood markers suggest that the paper-and-pencil methods correlate greater than .90 with blood marker analysis (Chen et al., 1999). Inaccurate zygosity determination will result in lowered estimates of heritability. Because estimates of heritability using the twin design are based on the difference in resemblance between the two types of twins, misclassifying MZ and DZ twins will result in an inflated DZ correlation (because it contains MZ pairs), and the MZ correlation will be lessened based on the number of DZ pairs that are included. The elevated DZ correlation and lowered MZ correlation will result in less difference, and a lower estimate of heritability.

The second potential problem when using twins is the violation of the equal environments assumption. That is, if identical twins are treated more similarly for nongenetic reasons than are fraternal twins, and if that treatment is related to the behavior of interest, then the increased resemblance of identical twins could be due to environment, not heredity. Similarly, it is possible for twins or siblings to either emulate or differentiate themselves from their co-twin or other family member, resulting in what has been termed *imitation* and *contrast effects*, respectively (Carey, 1986). Parents evaluating their children may also contrast them, even though there is little difference between them for the trait of interest (Eaves, 1976; Neale & Stevenson, 1989). Violations of this assumption necessarily affect estimates of genetic and environmental parameters. Research to test the reasonableness of the equal environment assumption has indicated that although identical twins are treated more similarly than fraternal twins, it is only in situations in which the parent is responding to some aspect of the child's behavior (Bouchard & Propping, 1993). That is, the parents themselves do not initiate those activities, but rather respond to the more similar behavior of the monozygotic twins (Kendler et al., 1993; Lytton, 1977). In fact, research has indicated that twins are treated according to their actual zygosity and not their perceived zygosity when zygosity is misclassified (Scarr & Carter-Saltzman, 1979).

A related issue is the extent to which twins are representative of the general population. There is no doubt that young twins are different from other single-born children. For example, they are typically premature (Phillips, 1993) and have a greater incidence of obstetric complications (MacGillivray, Campbell, & Thompson, 1988); their parents are more fully absorbed in basic caretaking; and they are often delayed in language development (Rutter & Redshaw, 1991). Thus, at least some caution is warranted when generalizing the results from twin studies to the broader population, especially when the focus is on infancy or early childhood.

Finally, the twin method (like all behavioral genetic designs) is dependent on the use of large samples because the focus is on the difference between two correlations, and the differences between correlations have large errors of estimation (Martin, Eaves, Kearsey, & Davies, 1978). Studies based on small samples result in limited power and can result in an underestimation of the salient contributions of genes and shared environment.

Adoption Design

The adoption design severs the relationship between shared environment and shared heredity. Genetically related individuals adopted apart (and reared in uncorrelated environments) will resemble each other only for genetic reasons. Genetically unrelated individuals adopted together into the same family will only resemble each other for reasons of shared environment. The best example is identical twins reared apart. Resemblance between these pairs (expressed as a correlation) can be attributed to heredity, because unlike identical twins reared together, resemblance is not due to shared environment. An obvious limitation of studies of identical twins reared apart is that they are rare, but there are several major behavioral genetic studies that contain reared-apart twins (e.g., Minnesota Study of Twins Reared Apart; Swedish Adoption/Twin Study of Aging).

It is more common to use comparisons of first-degree relatives (biological parents and adopted-away offspring) in adoption studies (examples include the Colorado Adoption Project and the Texas Adoption Project). Figure 18.3 depicts the full adoption design in which there is information from the biological parent (typically the mother), the adoptive parent (again, typically the mother as she provides the best comparison with the biological mother), and the adopted child. In assessments of first-degree relatives, who on average share 50% of their genetic resemblance, the correlation only estimates one half of the genetic influences for any given behavior of interest; therefore, the correlation for first-degree relatives must be doubled to estimate heritability. The other part of the adoption design investigates the resemblance for a particular trait among genetically unrelated individuals living in the same adoptive family, which makes it possible to look at parent-offspring resemblance or sibling resemblance that may contribute to shared rearing environment. This similarity, described as a correlation, is a direct estimate of the importance of being reared in the same family to the characteristics of interest.

A potential problem in adoption research is *selective placement*, which is the placement of adopted-apart relatives into environments that are correlated for characteristics that affect the trait under study (Plomin, DeFries, et al., 1990). For example, a biological mother giving her child up for adoption might have a very positive, optimistic attitude and might want to make sure that the adoptive parents have the same outlook on life. The adoption agency might specifically try to match the adopted child to parents with this trait, creating a placement situation that is

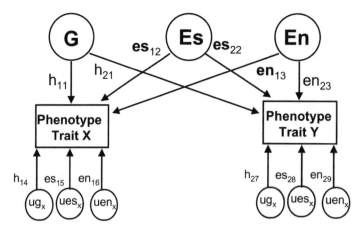

Figure 18.3. Path diagram of adoption design.

not entirely random for the characteristic of interest (see Carey, 2003, for additional discussion of this issue). To the extent that there is genetic influence on the trait being studied, selective placement increases the resemblance between adoptive parents and their adopted child and, to the extent that shared environmental influences are important, it will also increase the resemblance between birth parents and their adopted-away children. This confound results in an overestimation of both shared genes and shared environment, because when assessing the biological relationship, the correlation will indirectly contain the environmental influence of the adoptive parents. Similarly, the assessment of shared environment contains additional variance indirectly assessed from the relationship with the biological parent, which should be attributed to heredity. It is possible, however, to explicitly test whether there is a correlation in the trait of interest between the biological and adoptive parents and, if so, to model that relationship in the analyses.

Using a Genetically Informative Design to Understand the Importance of the Environment

In addition to model-fitting analyses, data from behavioral genetic designs can be interpreted using a regression technique termed DeFries-Fulker (DF) analysis (DeFries & Fulker, 1985). There are several advantages of using DF analysis (Rodgers & McGue, 1994). First, the approach is conceptually straightforward and can

be used to estimate heritability and common environmental influences on population parameters in either selected or unselected samples with multiple kinship levels (e.g., proband, siblings, children, grandchildren, twins). Second, the approach is very flexible, permitting the evaluation of variables that may interact with the traits of interest, such as gender or age. Finally, DF analysis can offer the advantage of controlling for genetic influences so that measured indicators of shared and nonshared environment can be studied without the usual genetic-environmental confounds that have plagued the literature.

The "augmented model" fits the following regression equation to the data:

$$K_1 = b_0 + b_1 K_2 + b_2 R + b_3 (K_2 \times R) + e \quad (1)$$

in which K_1 and K_2 are scores on a given trait from a kinship pair, R is the coefficient of genetic relatedness (i.e., 1.0 for MZ twins, .50 for DZ twins, siblings, or parent-offspring, and .25 for grandparent/grandchild and aunt/uncle/niece/nephew), the bs are estimated least-squares regression weights, and e is the residual of the model. The interaction term $(K_2 \times R)$ is the product of the co-twin/family member's score and the coefficient of relatedness. When the beta value associated with this interaction term is significant, kin resemblance is conditioned on the degree of genetic relatedness, hence the trait is heritable. The b_1 coefficient represents twin/kin resemblance independent of genetic resemblance, and thus estimates shared environmental variation. Specifically, b_1 and b_3 are the estimates of shared environment (e_s^2) and heredity (h^2), respectively; and apply to any level of genetic relatedness. It should be noted that this particular approach assumes an additive genetic model (see Waller, 1994, for the nonadditive model), assortative mating, and equal environmental influences across kinship categories.

One problem with this procedure is that individuals may be a part of more than one kinship pair (e.g., an individual may be both a parent and a sibling, or a co-twin and a child). In this case, a correlated error structure can result and thereby violate the assumption of independence. Rodgers and McGue (1994) suggested that one possible solution involves coding the data within the context of a design that actually estimates the variance-covariance structure across members of a family (e.g., treating the different family members as repeated treatments in a repeated-measures design and using multivariate analysis). Alternatively, maximum-likelihood methods may be used that explicitly model correlated errors.

The DF regression analyses can also be used to assess the influence of nonshared environment. Specifically, the environmental influences that contribute to differences between twins or other family members can be assessed by adding specific environmental measures to these analyses (Rodgers, Rowe, & Li, 1994). The residuals depicted by e in Equation 1 contain a combination of measurement error and the influences on the trait that are systematic, but do not operate to make twin/kin pairs similar to one another. These latter influences are what are referred to in the behavioral genetic literature as nonshared or unique environmental influences.

To assess nonshared environmental influences, variables that may act to make individuals different from one another must be identified. Although one would want to assess theoretically relevant attributes, possible examples include differences in aspects of social support or intrafamilial relationships, differential parental treatment, or the experience of specific life events. When a score defining the differences in environmental influence for two members of a twin/kinship pair is included in the analysis, differences due to a systematic relationship to the residual of the DF model can be estimated. If the addition of a variable of this type increases the R^2 of the model, there is evidence that the variable (and possibly other variables correlated with it) is an explicit source of nonshared in-

fluence. Furthermore, if this difference score interacts with the genetic coefficient reflecting the level of relatedness of the pairs (R), the type of nonshared environment is suggested to have a genetic component. The genetic component acting to make related individuals different from one another is a source of nonshared *genetic* influence (Rodgers et al., 1994). Thus, an additional source of variance that this formulation can account for is the genetic influences that contribute to differences between family members. The equations to specify nonshared genetic and environmental influence are as follows:

$$K_1 = b_0 + b_1 K_2 + b_2 R + b_3 (K_2 \times R) \\ + b_4 ENVDIFF + e \tag{2}$$

$$K_1 = b_0 + b_1 K_2 + b_2 R + b_3 (K_2 \times R) \\ + b_4 ENVDIFF + b_5 (ENVDIFF \times R) + e \tag{3}$$

in which the Ks are the scores for Kin 1 and Kin 2 on the trait of interest (as before) and R is the coefficient of genetic relatedness. *ENVDIFF* is a difference score, from the two kin on a specifically measured environmental source (e.g., life events, social support, or family environment) that might account for differences between them on the trait. The bs are least squares regression coefficients, and the e is the error term or residual. Within these models, the *ENVDIFF* variable provides tests for a nonshared environmental influence, whereas the interaction term of this difference score with R provides a test for nonshared genetic influence, given that the nonshared environmental influence has been detected. The significance of the parameters is determined by comparison of R^2 change when the nonshared environmental or genetic (interaction term) parameters are added to the model. An advantage of this approach is that the model strategy can be applied to more than one measure of nonshared environment.

Multivariate and Longitudinal Analyses

Multivariate model-fitting techniques allow the family, twin, or adoption design to be used to assess genetic and environmental factors mediating the covariation among measures (see Boomsma et al., 1989; Neale & Cardon, 1992, for details). Information about genetic and environmental mediation is especially useful for investigating the causes of phenotypic correlations

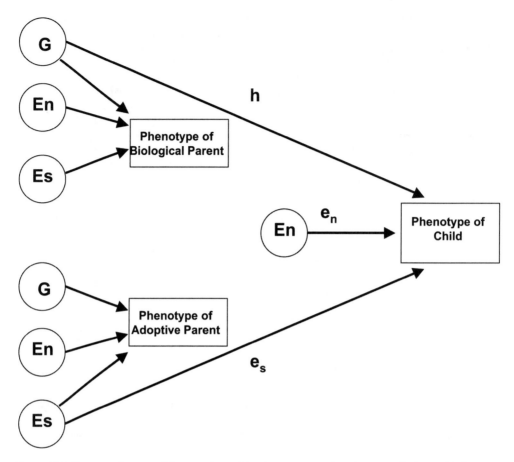

Figure 18.4 Common-factor model to test the multivariate genetic and environmental relationship between two traits of interest. Model assesses both common (G, Es, and En) and unique (Ug, Ues, Uen) components of covariance.

between behaviors of interest. Figure 18.3 represents a path model for a twin design that describes common factors for genetic (G) and environmental (Es or En) sources of variance and covariance for two different phenotypes (labeled X and Y). The model also specifies unique sources of genetic (ug) and environmental (ues and uen) influence for these two traits. For example, research has indicated that there is a phenotypic relationship between aspects of social support (e.g., Trait X) and positive affect and life satisfaction (e.g., Trait Y) in older samples (Bergeman, Plomin, Pedersen, & McClearn, 1991; Kessler et al., 1992). The assumption is that being more socially connected promotes positive psychological and subjective well-being. The direct conclusion from this work is that interventions directed at changing social relations can result in a positive outcome. What if the relation between these attributes is more complex? What if heredity plays a role in the extent to which individuals create and maintain social support networks? What if environmental experiences (e.g., loss of a spouse, move to a new residence, health problems) affect both social relationships and well-being outcomes? The multivariate studies cited above (Bergeman et al., 1991; Kendler et al., 1992) support this more complex interpretation, because the genetic and nonshared environmental factors that contribute to the perceived adequacy of the support network (for example) also contribute to the assessment of life satisfaction. Thus, behavioral genetic designs can assess the extent to which the phenotypic relationship between two attributes of interest is mediated genetically, environmentally, or both. As a result, it is an important mechanism to inform both intervention and prevention strategies.

Developmental behavioral genetics merges developmental questions with behavioral theories and methodologies. One of the most basic developmental questions is whether the contributions of genetic and environmental factors differ with age (Plomin, 1986). That is, are the genetic and environmental influences on positive affect in adolescence the same factors that impact individual differences in etiology in adulthood? Conversely, are the physiological and social changes associated with puberty due to inherently different genes and environmental factors than those experienced in later adulthood? The answers to these questions are most often assessed cross-sectionally by comparing subjects of different ages within studies or by comparing results across studies that focus on different age groups. Unfortunately, these approaches do not consider the extent to which the contributions of genes and environment change with development. Thus, cross-sectional research can provide information about age differences, but not about age changes, in genetic and environmental influences. As a result, the comparison of individuals in different age groups may reflect cohort differences rather than the developmental processes that occur as individuals age. For example, characteristics associated with specific cohorts (e.g., wars, political events) or factors related to historical change (e.g., increase in divorce rate, changes in affluence, medical advances) can contribute to different estimates of genetic and environmental influence on behavior. This occurs because heritability is a population-specific parameter, and quantitative genetic parameter estimates change when genetic and environmental sources of variation change (see Bergeman, 1997).

One common misconception is that if a particular behavior of interest is heritable, it is stable, but traits that exhibit longitudinal stability are not necessarily influenced by genetic factors, and traits that show strong heritability are not necessarily stable (Bergeman & Plomin, 1996). That is, the influence of a given set of genes may show continuous effects during development, or new genes may come into play at certain developmental stages (Hahn, Hewitt, Henderson, & Benno, 1990). Similarly, the influence of the environment may be uniform over time, or the quality of environmental effects may fluctuate across the life span.

Analyses to explicitly test changes in genetic and environmental influences over time have been developed (see Neale, Boker, Bergeman, & Maes, 2006). Figure 18.5 is one such model that represents a phenotype of interest at three different points in time (see Bergeman, Neiderhiser, Pedersen, & Plomin, 2001). G1, G2, and G3 represent the latent genetic effects on the trait of interest, whereas E1, E2, and E3 similarly represent the environmental influences at each measurement occasion. The age-to-age genetic correlations (r_g) indicate the extent to which genetic effects at one measurement occasion or age are correlated with genetic effects at another, with a genetic correlation of 1.0 indicating perfect overlap and 0.0 indicating that a completely different gene or set of genes affect the trait at the two points in time (see Carey, 1988, for making inferences based on genetic correlations). Longitudinal designs can be used to explicitly assess the extent to which the genetic and environmental factors salient at one age are related to the genetic and environmental factors at another. Loosely interpreted, the genetic correlation indicates the extent to which there is overlap in the genetic effects operating at two or more ages, regardless of the relative contribution to the phenotypic variance. Thus, the genetic correlation can be substantial even though the heritability is low and vice versa. Environmental correlations can be conceptualized in a similar way.

Traditionally, the variance due to age is statistically controlled for in behavioral genetic analyses or removed by selecting participants from narrow age bands because age effects cannot be assigned to either a genetic or an environmental component of variance (see McGue & Bouchard, 1984, for details). Thus, caution should be exercised when generalizing the results beyond the age or cohort of the samples used, because without a longitudinal design, there is no way to disentangle effects due to age (age change) versus experience (age differences). Additionally, even if estimates of heritability do not change with age, levels of heritability can be the same at two ages for different genetic reasons. That is, the genes that affect the trait at one age could be different from the genes that affect the trait at another age, but the overall magnitude of genetic effects (heritability) could be the same at the two ages. Longitudinal behavioral genetic designs can explicitly differentiate these effects. Thus, longitudinal designs are crucial in

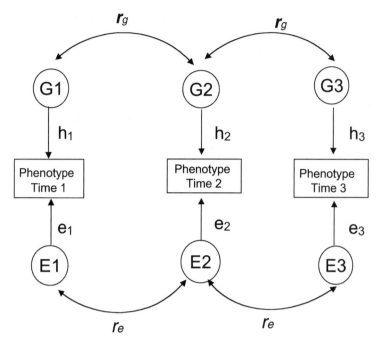

Figure 18.5. Path model depicting continuity and change over time in genetic and environmental influences on a phenotype of interest.

the study of stability or change in genetic and environmental effects.

Implications for Theory and Research in Positive Psychology

In this chapter, we have argued that the influence of nature and nurture often operate in tandem to shape our perceptions of the past and understanding of what lies in the future. Indeed, a mass of evidence now attests to the basic notion that our perceptions of the world around us are influenced by an internalized representation for living that we have developed over time. Thus, in a subtle fashion, one that is often not within reach of conscious awareness, the way in which the narrative of our life unfolds is shaped by both our personal blueprint and the carousel of important life events we carry inside our heads.

Research in behavioral genetics suggests that there are no complex traits that are entirely heritable, and that aspects of personality, cognitive functioning, and attitudes that are the focus of research in positive psychology show heritabilites between 30% and 50% (Berge-

man, 1997; McGue & Bouchard, 1998; Plomin, Owen, & McGuffin, 1994). What we often lose sight of is that behavioral genetic methodologies also provide the most compelling support for the importance of the environment. Interestingly, this approach has shown that although the environment is extremely important to the development of these characteristics, it does not work in the way that we initially thought. That is, we often assume that the important developmental dynamics in the family work to make family members similar to one another, but research has indicated that it works to make them different (Plomin & Daniels, 1987). In fact, children growing up in the same family lead surprisingly different lives (Dunn & Plomin, 1990).

Family similarity is typically due to shared genes, and the environmental factors at play work on an individual-by-individual basis, rather than a family-by-family basis (Plomin et al., 2000). Future work on understanding the role of the environment from a positive psychology perspective will need to focus on the specific aspects of the environment that might be particularly relevant to the development of traits such as openness, resilience, and positive affect. To better understand this process, studies must be designed to assess environmental influences separately for individual members of a family. For example, parents typically report that they treat their children very similarly, but siblings perceive the treatment from their parents very differently (Plomin & Daniels, 1987). Thus, if you ask parents about their parenting behaviors, you may get a very different picture of what is happening in the family than if you ask the individual children.

The Sibling Inventory of Differential Experience (Daniels & Plomin, 1985) is an example of a measure that was designed to explicitly assess the ways in which siblings perceive parental control and warmth, sibling interactions (e.g., antagonism, jealousy, caretaking, closeness), and peer relationships (e.g., college orientation, delinquency, popularity). Once differences in sibling experiences are identified, then the next step is to see whether these differential experiences relate to differences in the outcomes of interest, and ultimately the direction of those effects. That is, the siblings could elicit differences in environmental experiences rather than be affected by them. One project designed specifically to test these important environmental influences is the Nonshared Environment and Adolescent Development (NEAD) Project (see Reiss, Neiderhiser, Hetherington, & Plomin, 2000). The DF analysis is an ideal analytical technique to test nonshared environmental influences on behavioral outcomes.

Another counterintuitive result of behavioral genetic research is the notion that just labeling a variable as a measure of the environment (e.g., life events, social support) does not make it one. In fact, research has indicated that if you treat these "environmental" measures as phenotypes, they too show a genetic component (Plomin, 1994; Plomin & Bergeman, 1991). For example, scores of studies have shown that many measures of the "environment" are influenced by genetic characteristics, including social support (Bergeman et al., 1990; Kessler et al., 1992), family environment (Plomin, McClearn, Pedersen, Nesselroade, & Bergeman, 1989; Plomin et al., 1988), parenting behavior (Rowe, 1981), life events (Plomin et al., 1990), and socioeconomic status (Lichtenstein, Hershberger, & Pedersen, 1995; Lichtenstein, Pedersen, & McClearn, 1992). Thus, when examining ways in which differences in environmental variables relate to positive outcomes, it is important to consider the extent to which genetic or environmental factors mediate this relationship.

Research on resilience has suggested that some individuals thrive in the face of stressful life events whereas others do not (cf. Curtis & Cicchetti, 2003; Rutter, 2003). The assumption is that if researchers can identify the factors associated with personality or life circumstances that contribute to these protective mechanisms, then prevention and intervention strategies can be developed to enhance resilience. Behavioral genetic methodologies can be used to evaluate questions of this type. For example, research indicates that a substantial portion (estimates have suggested as much as 43%) of differences in individuals' experience and perception of life events is due to genetic differences between them (Plomin, DeFries, et al., 1990). This may not be as paradoxical as it sounds. Many life events reflect the behavior of individuals and, as such, treating these environmental measures as phenotypes may indirectly tap into genetic influences on personality attributes like sensation seeking or risk taking, cognitive ability, health, or interpersonal relationships. The result is that many of the genetic factors that influence resilience also influence the perception and experience of stressful life events, and these environment → development relationships are mediated genetically. Although this approach increases the complexities of understanding the development and maintenance of characteristics associated with positive psychology, it also informs the fact that individuals respond differently to intervention and prevention strategies, and we are unlikely to find a magic solution to produce positive outcomes in all people all the time.

Also important will be understanding the complex biological and environmental pathways that link up the influences of nature and nurture. For example, studies suggest that people with certain genetic propensities are more likely to experience related environments, and these genotype-environment correlations can work in passive, active, and reactive ways (Plomin et al., 1977). In fact, there is much interest in the ways in which people create their own environments and the extent to which genetic propensities are at play in this process (Scarr & McCartney, 1983). Specifically, it has been hypothesized that it is one's genetic propensities that drive one's environmental experiences (G → E). For example, parents can pass on attributes of an optimistic personality genetically and also provide an environment high in positive expectation. Additionally, friends and family may be more likely to provide social support to individuals who they view as being predispositionally resilient. Individuals with a penchant toward positive affect may surround themselves with family members and friends who also have a positive outlook on life. Behavioral genetic methodologies, such as the combined family-adoption design, that permit assessments of the importance of GE correlations will make important contributions to our understanding of the ways in which genes and environment interrelate.

Genes and environments also interact in a more traditional analysis-of-variance way (Bergeman & Plomin, 1996). That is, after assessing for the main effects of genes and environment, a G × E interaction can also be tested. Significant G × E interactions suggest that the effects of the environment differentially impact individuals with certain genetic predispositions. The concept of GE interaction represents an important perspective for understanding environmental influences on individual development. Rearing environments might differentially affect the expression of genetic propensities; similarly, the effects of the environment on development might depend on an individual's genotype (see Bergeman & Plomin, 1989). Rather than searching for environmental influences that equally affect all individuals on average, GE interaction focuses on environmental influences that may powerfully affect only a small group of individuals with certain genetic proclivities.

Although this has not been explicitly tested, openness to experience is a good example—that is, genetic predispositions for openness may be expressed differently in restrictive versus permissive environments. In other words, the opportunity for children to develop an interest in novel ideas, artistic sensitivity, depth of feeling, behavioral flexibility, intellectual curiosity, and unconventional attitudes might be constrained by a conservative family environment, in which parental attitudes and behaviors favor authoritarianism, whereas a more responsive family environment characterized by permissive or authoritative parental behaviors might enhance the characteristics of behavioral flexibility, nontraditional attitudes, and preferences for complexity, which are all motivational aspects of openness. Thus, interventions aimed at producing optimal outcomes may work well for some individuals but not for others. These examples of the interface between genes and environment may well be an important component in the development of resilience and essential to

understanding many attributes of positive psychology. The adoption design is an ideal mechanism for estimating GE interactions, because the sources of genetic and environmental variance can be separated.

Research in the fields of behavioral genetics and positive psychology also needs to focus on how genes have an effect on the behaviors of interest and how these genetic influences unfold with development. Thus, an additional area of future research is to assess how the relative importance of genes and environments change with development. Two general hypotheses have been posited to describe the potential change in the relative influences of genetic and environmental factors across the life span. First, developmental behavioral geneticists have suggested that when heritability changes with development, it increases (Plomin, 1986; Plomin & Thompson, 1988). According to this view, it is expected that an attribute like openness to experience would be more heritable in adulthood than in childhood. Indeed, Scarr and McCartney (1983) proposed that as individuals become older, they gain increasing control over their environment and become more active in selecting environments that support or even promote their genetic tendencies. Under this scenario, individuals who have a genetic predisposition toward openness to experience may be more likely to marry someone with a similar outlook on life, select an occupation or engage in hobbies that facilitate intellectual growth, or associate with friends, family, and coworkers who take advantage of novel experiences and exchange ideas. Although this view intertwines genetic and environmental influences, Scarr and McCartney argue that it is the genetic propensity that produces the environmental experience.

Proponents of an alternative hypothesis about the relative influences of nature and nurture across the life span suggest that as individuals have a greater number of life experiences, the impact of the environment will play an increasingly important role in determining the course of human development (Baltes, Reese, & Lipsitt, 1980; McCartney, Harris, & Bernieri, 1990). As a result, it is speculated that heritability will decrease with age, and environmental influences, especially of the nonshared type, will become more salient. According to this view, as an individual experiences a greater diversity of environmental opportunities, his or her openness to new experience will increasingly be shaped by the past. Thus, someone who is open to experience may become more narrow and rigid over time in a monotonous job, with a couch potato spouse, and a lack of intellectual stimulation. At this point, empirical support for either of these hypotheses is lacking because the majority of the research in this area is based on cross-sectional analyses, and these cause-effect relationships are difficult to unravel, even with sophisticated longitudinal designs. It is important to remember, however, that in all behavioral genetic research, heritability and environmentality are considered static estimates because they are based on findings from a certain population at a given point in time; different estimates of heritability (and environmentality) can be obtained from samples of participants who have vastly different experiences due to their cohort, socioeconomic status, culture, or other factors that contribute to differential experience.

Behavioral genetic research over the past three decades has focused on genetic and environmental components of variance for individual differences in a wide array of behavioral characteristics. It is important to keep in mind that just because something is genetic does not mean that it is immutable and cannot be changed. In fact, the research in this area suggests that the development of complex traits is due not only to the impact of genes and environment working in tandem, but to the dynamic interrelation between them as well. Thus, as we age, the delicate dance of individuation becomes more complex and our repertoire of choreography expands: We incorporate steps of autonomy, learn to tolerate dips of disappointment, and practice acceptance of change. Although behavior genetic methodologies represent a useful tool for exploring questions about human potential and positive psychology in general, it will be the interface of multiple approaches, each using a different lens to view positive psychological phenomena, that will lead to greater understanding of the complexities and intricacies of human potential.

References

Baltes, P. B., Reese, H. W., & Lipsitt, L. P. (1980). Life-span developmental psychology. *Annual Review of Psychology, 31,* 65–110.

Bergeman, C. S. (1997). *Aging: Genetic and environmental influences*: Thousand Oaks, CA: Sage.

Bergeman, C. S., Neiderhiser, J. M., Pedersen, N. L., & Plomin, R. (2001). Genetic and environmental influences on social support in later life: A longitudinal analysis. *International Journal of Aging and Human Development, 53,* 107–135.

Bergeman, C. S., & Plomin, R. (1989). Genotype-environment interaction. In J. S. Bruner & M. H. Bornstein (Eds.), *Interaction in human development* (pp. 157–171). Hillsdale, NJ: Erlbaum.

Bergeman, C. S., & Plomin, R. (1996). Behavioral genetics. In J. E. Birren (Ed.), *Encyclopedia of gerontology* (Vol. 1, pp. 163–172). Orlando, FL: Academic Press.

Bergeman, C. S., Plomin, R., Pedersen, N. L., & McClearn, G. E. (1991). Genetic mediation of the relationship between social support and psychological well-being. *Psychology and Aging, 6,* 640–646.

Bergeman, C. S., Plomin, R., Pedersen, N. L., McClearn, G. E., et al. (1990). Genetic and environmental influences on social support: The Swedish Adoption/Twin Study of Aging. *Journals of Gerontology, 45,* P101–P106.

Boomsma, D. I., Martin, N. G., & Neale, M. C. (1989). Genetic analysis of twin and family data: Structural modeling using LISREL. *Behavior Genetics, 19,* 5–7.

Bouchard, T. J., Jr., & Propping, P. (Eds.). (1993). *Twins as a tool of behavioral genetics.* Oxford: John Wiley.

Buss, D. M. (1984). Marital assortment for personality dispositions: Assessment with three different data sources. *Behavior Genetics, 14,* 111–123.

Buss, D. M. (1985). Human mate selection. *American Scientist, 73,* 47–51.

Carey, G. (1986). Sibling imitation and contrast effects. *Behavior Genetics, 16,* 319–341.

Carey, G. (1988). Inferences about genetic correlations. *Behavior Genetics, 18,* 329–338.

Carey, G. (2003). *Human genetics for the social sciences.* London: Sage.

Chen, W. J., Chang, H. W., Lin, C. C., Chang, C., Chiu, Y. N., & Soong, W. T. (1999). Diagnosis of zygosity by questionnaire and polymarker polymerase chain reaction in young twins. *Behavior Genetics, 29,* 115–123.

Curtis, W., & Cicchetti, D. (2003). Moving research on resilience into the 21st century: Theoretical and methodological considerations in examining the biological contributors to resilience. *Development and Psychopathology, 15,* 773–810.

Daniels, D., & Plomin, R. (1985). Differential experience of siblings in the same family. *Developmental Psychology, 21*(5), 747–760.

DeFries, J. C., & Fulker, D. W. (1985). Multiple regression analysis of twin data. *Behavior Genetics, 15,* 467–473.

Dunn, J., & Plomin, R. (1990). *Separate lives: Why siblings are so different*: New York: Basic Books.

Eaves, L. J. (1976). A model for sibling effects in man. *Heredity, 36,* 205–241.

Falconer, D. S. (1980). *Introduction to quantitative genetics* (2nd ed.). New York: Wiley.

Falconer, D. S., & McKay, T. F. (1996). *Introduction to quantitative genetics* (4th ed.). Harlow, UK: Longman.

Hahn, M. E., Hewitt, J. K., Henderson, N. D., & Benno, R. H. (1990). *Developmental behavioral genetics: Neural, biometrical and evolutionary approaches.* New York: Oxford University Press.

Jinks, J. L., & Fulker, D. W. (1970). Comparison of the biometrical genetical, MAVA, and classical approaches to the analysis of human behavior. *Psychological Bulletin, 75,* 311–349.

Kendler, K. S., Neale, M. C., Kessler, R. C., Heath, A. C., et al. (1992). Familial influences on the clinical characteristics of major depression: A twin study. *Acta Psychiatrica Scandinavica, 86,* 371–378.

Kendler, K. S., Neale, M. C., Kessler, R. C., Heath, A. C., et al. (1993). A test of the equal-environment assumption in twin studies of psychiatric illness. *Behavior Genetics, 23,* 21–27.

Kessler, R. C., Kendler, K. S., Heath, A. C., Neale, M. C., et al. (1992). Social support, depressed mood, and adjustment to stress: A genetic epidemiologic investigation. *Journal of Personality and Social Psychology, 62,* 257–272.

Lichtenstein, P., Hershberger, S. L., & Pedersen, N. L. (1995). Dimensions of occupations: Genetic and environmental influences. *Journal of Biosocial Science, 27,* 193–206.

Lichtenstein, P., Pedersen, N. L., & McClearn, G. E. (1992). The origins of individual differences in occupational status and educational level: A study of twins reared apart and together. *Acta Sociologica, 35,* 13–31.

Lush, J. L. (1940). Intra-sire correlations or regressions of offspring on dam as a method of estimating heritability of characteristics. *Proceedings of the American Society for Animal Production, 33,* 293–301.

Lytton, H. (1977). Do parents create, or respond to, differences in twins? *Developmental Psychology, 13,* 456–459.

MacGillivray, I., Campbell, D. M., & Thompson, B. (Eds.). (1988). *Twinning and twins.* Chichester, UK: Wiley.

Martin, N. G., Eaves, L. J., Kearsey, M. J., & Davies, P. (1978). The power of the classical twin study. *Heredity, 40,* 97–116.

McCartney, K., Harris, M. J., & Bernieri, F. (1990). Growing up and growing apart: A developmental meta-analysis of twin studies. *Psychological Bulletin, 107*(2), 226–237.

McGue, M., & Bouchard, T. J. (1984). Adjustment of twin data for the effects of age and sex. *Behavior Genetics, 14,* 325–343.

McGue, M., & Bouchard, T. J., Jr. (1998). Genetic and environmental influences on human behavioral differences. *Annual Review of Neuroscience, 21,* 1–24.

Monroe, S. M., & Simons, A. D. (1991). Diathesis-stress theories in the context of life stress research: Implications for the depressive disorders. *Psychological Bulletin, 110,* 406–425.

Morton, N. E. (1974). Analysis of family resemblance: I. Introduction. *American Journal of Human Genetics, 26,* 318–330.

Morton, N. E., & MacLean, C. J. (1974). Analysis of family resemblance: III. Complex segregation of quantitative traits. *American Journal of Human Genetics, 26,* 489–503.

Neale, M. C., Boker, S. M., Bergeman, C. S., & Maes, H. H. (2006). The utility of genetically informative data in the study of development. In C. S. Bergeman and S. M. Boker (Ed.), *Quantitative methodology in aging research* (pp. 219–327). Mahwah, NJ: Erlbaum.

Neale, M. C., & Cardon, L. R. (1992). *Methodology for genetic studies of twins and families*: New York: Kluwer Academic/Plenum.

Neale, M. C., & Stevenson, J. (1989). "Rater bias in the EASI temperament scales: A twin study": Erratum. *Journal of Personality and Social Psychology, 56,* 845.

Phillips, D. J. (1993). Twin studies in medical research: Can they tell us whether diseases are genetically determined? *Lancet, 341,* 1008–1009.

Plomin, R. (1986). *Development, genetics, and psychology*: Hillsdale, NJ: Erlbaum.

Plomin, R. (1994). *Genetics and experience: The interplay between nature and nurture.* Newbury Park, CA: Sage.

Plomin, R., & Bergeman, C. S. (1991). The nature of nurture: Genetic influence on "environmental" measures. *Behavioral and Brain Sciences, 14,* 373–427.

Plomin, R., & Daniels, D. (1987). Why are children in the same family so different from one another? *Behavioral and Brain Sciences, 10,* 1–16.

Plomin, R., DeFries, J. C., & Loehlin, J. C. (1977). Genotype-environment interaction and correlation in the analysis of human behavior. *Psychological Bulletin, 84,* 309–322.

Plomin, R., DeFries, J. C., & McClearn, G. E. (1990). *Behavioral genetics: A primer* (2nd ed.). New York: W. H. Freeman.

Plomin, R., DeFries, J. C., McClearn, G. E., & McGuffin, P. (Eds.). (2000). *Behavioral genetics.* New York: Worth.

Plomin, R., Lichtenstein, P., Pedersen, N. L., McClearn, G. E., et al. (1990). Genetic influence on life events during the last half of the life span. *Psychology and Aging, 5,* 25–30.

Plomin, R., McClearn, G. E., Pedersen, N. L., Nesselroade, J. R., et al. (1988). Genetic influence on childhood family environment perceived retrospectively from the last half of the life span. *Developmental Psychology, 24,* 738–745.

Plomin, R., McClearn, G. E., Pedersen, N. L., Nesselroade, J. R., & Bergeman, C. S. (1989). Genetic influence on adults' ratings of their current family environment. *Journal of Marriage and the Family, 51,* 791–803.

Plomin, R., Owen, M. J., & McGuffin, P. (1994). The genetic basis of complex human behaviors. *Science, 264,* 1733–1739.

Plomin, R., & Thompson, L. (1988). Life-span developmental behavioral genetics. In D. L. Featherman & P. B. Baltes (Eds.), *Life span development and behavior* (Vol. 8, pp. 1–31). Hillsdale, NJ: Erlbaum.

Reiss, D., Neiderhiser, J. M., Hetherington, E. M., & Plomin, R. (2000). *The relationship code: Deciphering genetic and social influences on adolescent development.* Cambridge, MA: Harvard University Press.

Rodgers, J. L., & McGue, M. (1994). A simple algebraic demonstration of the validity of DeFries-Fulker analysis in unselected samples with multiple kinship levels. *Behavior Genetics, 24,* 259–262.

Rodgers, J. L., Rowe, D. C., & Li, C. (1994). Beyond nature versus nurture: DF analysis of nonshared influences on problem behaviors. *Developmental Psychology, 30,* 374–384.

Rowe, D. C. (1981). Environmental and genetic influences on dimensions of perceived parenting: A twin study. *Developmental Psychology, 17,* 203–208.

Rutter, M. (2003). Genetic influences on risk and protection: Implications for understanding resilience. In S. S. Luthar (Ed.), *Resilience and vulnerability: Adaptation in the context of childhood adversities* (pp. 489–509). New York: Cambridge University Press.

Rutter, M., & Redshaw, J. (1991). Growing up as a twin: Twin singleton differences in psychological development. *Journal of Child Psychology and Psychiatry and Allied Disciplines, 32,* 885–895.

Scarr, S., & Carter-Saltzman, L. (1979). Twin method: Defense of a critical assumption. *Behavior Genetics, 9,* 527–542.

Scarr, S., & McCartney, K. (1983). How people make their own environments: A theory of genotype left-arrow environment effects. *Child Development, 54,* 424–435.

Segal, N. L. (1999). *Entwined lives: Twins and what they tell us about human behavior:* New York: Dutton.

Waller, N. G. (1994). A DeFries and Fulker model for genetic nonadditivity. *Behavior Genetics, 24,* 149–153.

19

Cultural Aspects of Quantitative Genetic Investigations

Keith E. Whitfield and Dwayne T. Brandon

The fields of quantitative genetics, adult development, and aging as well as cultural psychology often draw from perspectives in positive psychology to explain phenomena within their disciplines. The discussion in this chapter is on using positive psychology perspectives to further elucidate the complicated relationships found in the integration of adult development and aging research with cultural psychology, using a quantitative genetic approach to examine individual differences.

Social scientists have long been engaged in an epic search for the sources of individual variation in the development and aging of humans. Research has led to various methodologies in an effort to account for the differences found between people. One of those methodologies is quantitative genetics, which, in part, grew out of opposition to the "environmentalist" view that only factors from the environment are involved in interindividual variability (Plomin, Defries, McClearn, & Rutter, 1997). However, the absence of environmental causal factors in molecular genetic models and theories swings the pendulum of reductionism too far in the opposite direction.

One criticism that could be levied against some of the past literature in the field of quantitative genetics is that there appears to be an emphasis on findings concerning genetic influences over findings of environmental influences. A review of quantitative genetic studies reveals that no phenotype has been found to arise solely from heritable influences. Environmental influences always play a role in accounting for interindividual variability, whether they are shared among family members or unique to individuals.

The National Human Genome Research Institute of the National Institutes of Health announced in June 2000 that they had developed a working draft of the human genome. This historic event places science on the doorstep of limitless possibilities including new insights about diseases and how to treat them. Knowing the sequence of the genome, however, is only the beginning. Equally important will be our knowledge of how the environment influences health, disease, and complex behaviors associated with aging. One must keep in mind that quantitative genetic techniques assess the collective contribution of genes and environment, not nature versus nurture.

Previous research on the significant impact that sociodemographic factors play in contributing to disease processes and complex behaviors is perhaps our best indicator that science must avoid the reductionistic view (Whitfield, Weidner, Clark, & Anderson, 2002), a view that assumes knowing and manipulating the genome will cure all our ills. Rather, we must understand how genetic and environmental influences work in concert to account for behavioral and health variables. Much of what produces differences in health and disease among ethnic minorities are behaviors that are interwoven in the fabric of being called culture. Herein lies one of the new fields of focus for those who study cultural psychology. To integrate these perspectives, those who use quantitative genetic methods will need to understand the underlying effect genes have on health, behavior, and aging within complex environments or cultures. We may find that the polymorphisms that occur in genotypes are destructive or protective factors related to disease and health that are created, modified, or triggered by cultural and contextual factors. The challenge, in order for research on these perspectives to move forward, is that interdisciplinary teams of scientists will need to work together to best answer these questions (Shields et al., 2005).

The purpose of this chapter is to present one view of how to approach the complex interplay of genetics and sociocultural environmental factors with adult development and aging. Understanding aging involves appreciating not only the current conditions being experienced but recognizing starting points and the paths taken in reaching later life. Across individuals, this constellation of events is varied and complex. The quantitative genetic approach to understanding interindividual differences has important implications for assessing sociocultural influences across the life course (Whitfield & Brandon, 2000; Whitfield & McClearn, 2005).

Sociocultural influences are represented in the environmental components of quantitative genetic methods. However, such influences are embedded in history and may differentially impact the aging process. For instance, because African Americans have historically experienced a lifetime of racism and discrimination, interindividual variability among the aged in this group involves influences from the environment that range from segregated housing to threats of violence to expectations of poor performance on intelligence tests, which must be accounted for and appreciated in quantitative genetic studies. These kinds of sociocultural influences contrib-ute to the possibility of differential heritabilities between African Americans and the majority culture if one attempts to make comparisons (discussed later in greater detail).

Cultural differences among nations may also have an impact on quantitative genetic studies. An example of the importance of culture (world cultures) in quantitative genetic studies of smoking has been reported by Heath and Madden (1995). In an analysis of the available twin data on risk of being a current smoker, they found differences in genetic and environmental estimates between studies using similar assessment protocols but samples from different countries: Finland, Sweden, and America.

One hypothesis posed about the outcome of quantitative genetic studies on older populations is that, as individuals age, nonshared environmental influences increase and have a significant impact on individual variability. This idea is derived from a hypothesis from life span developmental theory, which suggests that as people age they accumulate experiences that shape the phenotype of interest. There is evidence to the contrary from quantitative genetic research that greater nonshared environmental variation with increased age is not the case for phenotypes such as general cognitive abilities (see Pedersen, Plomin, Nesselroade, & McClearn, 1992). However, population estimates of the sources of individual variability derived from the majority culture may not be applicable to ethnic minority groups. If modeled appropriately, phenotypes such as cognitive abilities may show significant environmental influence in ethnic minority samples or comparisons of cross-national samples. For example, because African Americans have experienced the pervasive environmental force of discriminatory practices in schooling and employment opportunities throughout their life course, estimates of environmental influences on cognitive functioning may be greater compared to Caucasians. Conceptually, one would predict that discriminatory practices impacted African American families as well as individuals, so both shared as well as nonshared environmental estimates would be affected.

It can be argued that quantitative genetic approaches to individual differences have not been fully appreciated or used to the extent that these rich sources of data provide information about aging. For example, many of these designs utilize identical and fraternal twin pairs as subjects, and usually only intact pairs are included in the analyses. One of the primary potential selection biases in research of older twins is the issue of mortality (Simmons et al., 1997). Given the decreased probability that two individuals will live into late life due to increasing risk for mortality from disease or accidents, these twin pairs could be considered what some have called successful agers (Rowe & Kahn, 1985). As cited in Simmons et al. (1997), twin samples may be biased toward healthier individuals because of higher refusal rates when one or both are ailing and the removal of the more frail, due to the mortality of one twin. The well-documented differences in mortality across ethnic groups may be important in the extension of quantitative genetic studies of aging among ethnic minority groups. African Americans, for example, experience significantly higher mortality than Caucasians, with the age- and gender-adjusted death rate from all causes being 60% higher in African Americans than in Caucasians, a trend that persists until age 85 (U.S. Department of Health and Human Services, 1995). This differential produces a life expectancy gap between African Americans and Caucasians of 8.2 years for men and 5.9 years for women. These findings suggest the probability of recruiting intact African American twin pairs in late life may be less than that for Caucasians. Then, do population mortality rates create differences between intact twin pairs and members of nonintact pairs in psychological, social, or health dimensions of adulthood and later life for African Americans? Using quantitative genetic methods (i.e., twin studies) to address this question can provide valuable insight about successful aging for African Americans.

One of the most recent twin studies of aging is the Carolina African American Twin Study of Aging (CAATSA; Whitfield, Brandon, Wiggins, Vogler, & McClearn, 2003). The CAATSA project attempts to in part address issues of health disparities using a quantitative genetic perspective. This is a somewhat unusual perspective because many scientists believe that the study of health disparities should focus on social factors (Whitfield, 2005). Some have suggested that the outcome of genetic explanations will lead to incorrect assumptions about the origin of disparities as well as racist conclusions about health and health behaviors. Our perspective is that much of science is fraught with those same problems without the complicated history of behavioral genetics. We use a positive psychology perspective to suggest in much of our findings that genes are part of the biological milieu

that works in concert with environmental and social factors to account for the disparities that are observed between majority and minority groups. Our study is one of the very few in-person studies of African American twins.

CAATSA was designed to examine the proportion of genetic and environmental influences on health in a sample of older adult African American twins between 25 and 89 years of age. Preliminary analysis of data from the CAATSA suggests that the disparities in blood pressure experienced by African Americans do influence the mortality of older twins. Whitfield et al., (2003) found that after controlling demographic variables, only blood pressures differed between members of intact twin pairs and surviving members of nonintact twin pairs. It appears that using only pairs in research on older African American twins may represent a bias in estimating origins of individual variability in some examinations of health.

In the following sections, we review the results from cross-cultural research that has focused on three broad domains: health, personality, and cognition. We examine several instances of differential outcomes of cross-cultural comparisons in an attempt to provide insight on how culture impacts environmental influences.

Health

One of the most common health disparities experienced by African Americans as a group is hypertension. African Americans have one of the highest rates of hypertension in the world (Joint National Committee on Prevention, Detection, Evaluation and Treatment of High Blood Pressure VI, 1997) and are estimated to have a prevalence nearly two times that of Caucasians (Anderson, McNeilly, & Meyers,1991; Centers for Disease Control and Prevention, 2005). This disease affects approximately 65% of African American elders between the ages of 65 and 74 and is predictive of functional decline (Wagner, Grothaus, Hect, & LaCroix, 1991). Earlier studies have focused on understanding sources of variance in systolic blood pressure (SBP) and diastolic blood pressure (DBP), which are recognized as risk factors for cardiovascular disease (Alderman, 1999; Lee, Rosner, & Weiss, 1999; Palatini & Julius, 1997).

Several theories have been proposed to account for the disparity in rates of hypertension.

Some theories have suggested that genetic factors related to sodium retention are dominant in determining blood pressure among African Americans (Harshfield & Grim, 1997; Wilson & Grim, 1991). In contrast, other theories posit that environmental factors such as racism (Anderson, McNeilly, & Myers, 1993; Clark, Anderson, Clark, & Williams, 1999) or socioeconomic stress (Pickering, 1999) are dominant in determining blood pressure among African Americans. However, few studies have employed the twin or family design to address the relative contribution of genetic and environmental factors in determining blood pressure among African Americans.

Previous twin and family studies have estimated the heritability of blood pressure among Caucasian populations to range from .44 to .64 for SBP, and .34 to .73 for DBP (Ditto, 1993; Fagard et al., 1995; Harrap, 1994; Hong, de Faire, Heller, McClearn, & Pedersen, 1994). In a review by Harrap (1994), previous studies show that genetic factors account for 30% to 60% of the variance in blood pressure. Using preliminary data from the CAATSA, we found a large proportion of the individual variability in blood pressure for African American adults arises from genetic sources. Heritabilities for this sample of African American twins ranged from .44 to .52 for DBP and SBP respectively, after controlling for the effects of antihypertensive medication. These heritability estimates are similar to previous studies that have used the classic twin design.

Previous research has shown that forced expiratory volume (FEV) is a useful predictor of remaining life in older adults (e.g., Burrows, 1990; Tager, Segal, Speizer, & Weiss, 1988). Epidemiological studies have investigated the decline of FEV as an indicator of chronic airway obstructive disease (e.g., Burrows, Bloom, Traver, & Cline, 1987), the presence and course of asthma (Enright, Lebowitz, & Cockroft, 1994), and as a measure of the effects of air pollution (Dockery et al., 1985).

Although there is considerable interindividual variability in level and rate of change in FEV, very few studies have assessed the sources of this variability. In an analysis of the influence of genetic and environmental factors on FEV in Swedish twins, McClearn, Svartengren, Pedersen, Heller, and Plomin (1994) found substantial influence of genetic factors on FEV in middle and late adulthood. They found that 57% of the individual variation (in the young-old group) was due to genetic factors, and the remainder of the variance was due to nonshared environmental factors.

In a study of Russian adult twins, Whitfield, Grant, Ravich-Scherbo, Marutina, and Ibatoulina (1999) attempted to replicate results from the McClearn et al. (1994) study of Swedish twins. After the affects of age, gender, height, and smoking were partialled out of FEV, quantitative genetic analyses were conducted. Shared environmental effects were significant, accounting for 47% of the variance in FEV, while genetic effects accounted for only 28% of the variance.

The proportion of variance on FEV that was attributable to genetic factors was greater (57%) for the Swedish than for the Russian sample (28%). In addition, shared environmental influences were not important in the Swedish sample but accounted for nearly half of the variance in the Russian sample. We assume that there are not substantial genetic differences at the population level between Swedish and Russian twins, so the difference in these results is likely due to environmental influences. While there could be allelic differences between the populations, due to the complexity of this phenotype, there are likely multiple genes involved and the probability of allelic differences across multiple sites that affect this phenotype in a significant manner is assumed to be low.

Hypotheses about how the contextual and situational factors influence the genetic and environmental estimates between these two samples could take at least two forms: (1) Recent sociopolitical changes have made Russian dizygotic twins more alike than Swedish dizygotic twins, or (2) long-standing cultural influences make Russian dizygotic twins more alike than Swedish dizygotic twins.

Using preliminary data from the CAATSA, we calculated another group's genetic and environmental estimates for FEV and found that 30% was attributable to genetic influences, 10% to shared environmental influences, and 60% to nonshared environmental forces. What do these differences in estimates mean? The estimates for any phenotype are constrained by the larger cultural influences that exist for the sample under study but suggest that there are critical cultural factors that contribute to individual variability in FEV. In addition, comparisons of within-group age variability and differences in raw variances between groups might be dimensions of future studies of these populations.

Personality

Quantitative genetic studies have consistently shown that personality is genetically influenced. Studies conducted in Sweden, Australia, Britain, Finland, and the United States report fairly robust heritabilities (40%–50%) for personality traits such as neuroticism and extroversion (Saudino et al., 1999). In most of these studies, unique but not shared environmental influences also significantly contribute to variance in personality. A study of personality in Russian adult twins adds to this body of literature. The authors examined Russian twins because of the unique, homogenizing culture Communism attempted to create in Russia (Saudino et al., 1999). Such circumstances may have resulted in a reduced contribution from unique environmental influences or an increased contribution from shared environmental components of variance.

Using model fitting, Saudino et al. (1999) found significant heritabilities for neuroticism (49%), extraversion (59%), monotony avoidance (53%), and impulsivity (49%). These results are consistent with data from previous twin studies of personality, which suggest similar genetic influence on personality traits across different cultures.

Cognition

As cited earlier, evidence indicates that general cognitive abilities do not show a significant increase in nonshared environmental influences as people age. However, this does not mean that cultural factors do not have an impact on cognitive abilities as people grow older. The results of previous research suggested that heritability for some cognitive tasks, specifically memory performance, may decrease with age (Finkel, Pedersen, McGue, & McClearn, 1995). If so, differences in the environmental components across studies may arise from cultural differences that exist in different countries and populations.

In the literature, there are two examples of cross-cultural comparisons of cognitive abilities that are useful for our purposes here. While their primary intent was not to examine the impact of culture on genetic and environmental estimates of cognitive ability, comparisons of the data from Sweden and the United States provide an opportunity to examine the possible cultural differences in the sources of individual vari-

ability in cognitive functioning. In the first example, Finkel, Pedersen, McGue, and McClearn (1995) examined the varying degrees to which genetics and environment influence cognitive abilities across the life span. They compared data obtained from two twin studies, the Minnesota Twin Study of Adult Development and Aging (MTSADA) and the Swedish Adoption/Twin Study of Aging (SATSA). Finkel et al. investigated the heritability of IQ. They found that heritability estimates for IQ were 81% for the MTSADA sample (the best-fitting model included the entire sample as one group, 27–88 years of age) in contrast to estimates from SATSA, which were 80% for the young and middle cohort (27–49 and 50–64 years of age) and 54% for the older cohort (64–88 years of age). The authors explained these estimates as population-specific phenomena. They also suggested that the decrease with age in heritability for the Swedish sample could actually be created by an increase in environmental variance. Conversely, there appears to be stability in environmental variance for the sample from the United States.

Similar results were found in an examination of genetic and environmental influences on memory. While there were no age differences in heritability estimates of the memory factor, Finkel, Pedersen, and McGue (1995) found that average heritabilities for memory and the measures used to construct the memory factor were less for SATSA (.49 and .37) than for MTSADA (.60 and .56).

So there do appear to be some differences in estimates of individual differences in cognitive functioning across cultural groups. These findings reflect differences in education and other factors that influence the course of cognitive function as we age. These compelling findings require further elaboration and specific tests of differences in variance estimates. The identification of differences also requires attention and appropriate interpretations for similarities and differences once identified from closer systematic scrutiny.

Differential Heritabilities

A potentially troubling result that may be produced by a quantitative genetic study that compares ethnic or cultural groups is finding a lower heritability for a desirable phenotype or higher heritability for undesirable characteristics in comparison to the majority group counterparts. The danger here is the possible interpretation that the majority population may posses a "superior set of genes" because they show a higher heritability on a positive or desirable phenotype. This kind of interpretation is erroneous given the assumptions of quantitative genetic methodology.

There are (at least) three plausible interpretations that could account for differences in the proportions of environmental and genetic influences between ethnic and cultural groups. For demonstrative purposes, we have provided a hypothetical example of results from twin data on life satisfaction in older African Americans and Caucasians in table 19.1. In this example, we find that there is greater similarity between fraternal or dizygotic twins in the sample of African American twins than in the Caucasian sample. Furthermore, there is a greater difference between the similarities in identical twins as compared to dizygotic twins in the Caucasian sample relative to the African American sample. One hypothesis for these differences in proportions of genetic and environmental influences between the two groups is that genes play a greater role in influencing individual differences in the Caucasian group than in the African American group. A second interpretation is that environmental factors are such powerful influences in the African American group that much of the differences between individuals in this group are accounted for by factors that are shared within families and extrafamilial factors. A third possible interpretation of this example is that, in this case, genes are important in the

African American group, but the genetic expression of this particular phenotype does not account for as much individual variation as environmental influences.

We consider the third explanation to be the most plausible in most cases. The expression of any phenotype is the result of genetic and environmental factors working in concert. Variations in the genetic makeup of different ethnic minority groups are considered by some to be so small that, genetically, the two groups are very similar (see Bamshad, 2005). The influences driving the expressed phenotype are found in differing proportions because the environment, which acts in concert with, and in addition to, an individual's genetic constitution, is different across groups. Thus, the sociocultural influences that affect environments produce different proportions of genetic and environmental influences. These three interpretations need to be tested empirically. For example, one could use these interpretations to try to explain the ethnic group differences in risk for Alzheimer's disease by the *ApoE4* genotype. The literature suggests that African Americans and other groups with *ApoE4* alleles are not at the same risk for Alzheimer's as Caucasians with the same genotype (e.g., Tang et al., 1998). It is not clear if this demonstrates the complexity of the genetic influences that underlie Alzheimer's such as epistasis or gene-environment interactions or how environments work to protect African Americans.

If comparisons are made between the estimates of individual variation from African Americans and other ethnic groups using a

TABLE 19.1 An Example of Twin Study Results for Life Satisfaction

Twin Type	African Americans	Caucasians
	Intrapair Correlations	
Monozygotic twin correlation	.60	.60
Dizygotic twin correlation	.55	.35
Proportions of Variance (%)		
Genetic heritability	.10	.50
Environment		
Shared	.50	.10
Nonshared	.40	.40

Note: These proportions can be calculated using the correlations provided and the following formulas: Heritability $= Mz - (Dz * 2)$; Shared environment $= (2 * Dz) - Mz$; Nonshared environment $= 1 - (\text{heritability} + \text{shared environment})$.

quantitative genetic approach, it is also possible that the resulting genetic and environmental components of variance will be identical in proportion. However, different mechanisms may be driving this similarity. These methods are limited in that they provide descriptions of the proportions of influences but do not identify the specific factors within each of the components of variance.

Thus, a limitation of these types of analyses is that the proportion of genetic and environmental sources is identified but the specific environmental factors impacting each are not assessed. The environment has, of course, an important impact on any behavior a social scientist selects to study. It is suggested here that a combination of traditional social scientific inquiry and a quantitative genetic approach would allow one to model specific environmental influences (e.g., education, income, occupation, family attitudes and values, racism, etc.) in light of their overall contribution to interindividual variation. This could be accomplished through experimental manipulation using a co-twin control method or assessing an environmental factor and incorporating it into the decomposition of environmental proportion of variance.

Modeling Cultural or Ethnic Influences

Structural equation modeling (SEM), or biometrical modeling, is used to fit observed data to models of genetic and environmental effects and is the preferred method for data analysis among most quantitative geneticists. These SEM techniques use variance and covariances to provide parameter estimates of the relative contribution of genetic and environmental influences (for review, see Neale & Cardon, 1992).

There are SEM models that account for the contribution of age to estimates of variance (Neale & Cardon, 1992), but models have not been suggested that incorporate cultural influences. The closest approximation has been the work of Eaves and others, who have developed models of cultural transmission. These models use data from parents and offspring to account for the nongenetic transfer of information from parent to offspring (Eaves, 1976; Eaves, Fulker, & Heath, 1989). This approach proposes that cultural inheritance may act on genetic and environmental differences between individuals (Eaves, 1976). While there are numerous ways one could consider extending models of genetic

and environmental influence to ascertain cultural factors, we offer four obvious explanatory approaches for consideration:

1. Culture is encompassed in the shared environmental component of the traditional ACE (where A = additive genetic influences, C = common or shared environmental influences, and E = unique environmental influences) model.
2. Cultural influences are distributed in the shared and nonshared environmental components of the ACE model.
3. Cultural influences represent an additional component that is not modeled in the traditional ACE model represented in figure 19.1.
4. Testing constraints of a multigroup model that tests equality or invariance across groups of identical and fraternal twins from at least two cultural groups (see figure 19.2).

The cultural relevance model presented in the third scenario assumes that there is intrapair variance that is not constrained by an expectation of similarity as in the case of the shared environmental component. Furthermore, this variance is not specific to the individuals, as is the case of the nonshared environmental component, but impacts both twins. This component would represent the cultural norms and structural constraints that can interact to systematically alter the meaning of different factors in behavioral processes. For example, Dressler (1985) studied how active coping styles moderated the effects of stressors differently for males and females. For females, active coping buffered the effects of stressors, but active coping exacerbated the effects of stressors for males. These results are consistent with the social and cultural

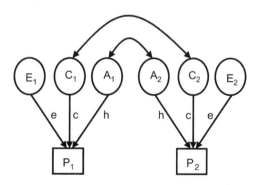

Figure 19.1 ACE model.

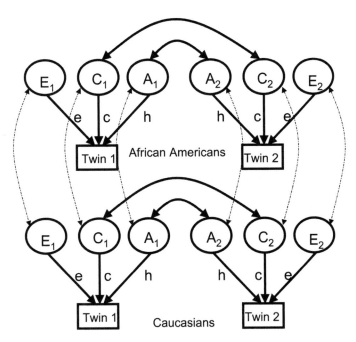

Figure 19.2 Constraint model.

context of the community and with cultural norms governing gender roles within the community. The cultural norms would not necessarily impact twins to the same degree such that these effects could be considered shared environmental effects (the assumption in the twin model is a correlation of 1.00 for shared environmental influences). In the model proposed, those influences could be estimated rather than being considered error and embodied in the nonshared environmental component.

The fourth model would be similar to performing a test of homogeneity of variance. In performing such a comparison, it might be useful to first perform a test of homogeneity of variance between the groups at the phenotypic level and then conduct the model fitting to examine potential invariance across the components.

Several levels of invariance could be tested: configural, metric, strong factorial, and strict factorial (Meredith, 1993). Obtaining configural invariance, the same pattern of factor loadings but not strictly equivalent factor loadings across groups, provides evidence that qualitative similarity exists across the groups being compared. If the factor loadings in one group are proportionally equivalent to corresponding loadings in the other group, metric invariance is attained and factors can be unambiguously compared

across groups. Strong and strict factorial invariance are conditions where the mean intercepts and unique variances are found to be equivalent across the groups, respectively. Strict factorial invariance is necessary for comparisons of factor level means.

Conclusion

In this chapter, we have presented three central issues relevant in examining sociocultural influences in quantitative genetic studies: (1) avoiding genetic determinism, (2) differential heritabilities, and (3) modeling cultural influences. Collaborations among quantitative geneticists, behavioral and social scientists, and biomedical researchers can provide further elaboration on the impact of sociocultural influences on genetic and environmental estimates. With the significant advances to date, and those to come gathered from sequencing the human genome, a better understanding and identification of genes that influence individual differences in the context of environment should be possible. The parallel integration of environmental sources of variance should provide an ever-clearer picture of how genes and environment coalesce to create individual variability as we age to result in resilience.

With the substantial diversification of the United States on the horizon, how cultural factors are involved in genetic and environmental interplays will represent an interesting, important, and vital challenge to interdisciplinary scientists. Departure from past racist views of genes and environment among people of different races is needed for advancement and enlightenment. While there is much current discussion about the place of race as a category in research on genetics (for a review, see Shields et al., 2005), how the social influence of factors that are derived from people's perceptions and assumptions of differences between people will continue to exist in our society and create inequities for issues related to the quality of life such as health. If we can continue to develop and test cultural models of genetic and environmental influences, there is significant and exciting promise for understanding not just individuals within particular groups but factors that vary across society that impact health and mental health.

References

Alderman, M. H. (1999). A new model of risk: Implications of increasing pulse pressure and systolic blood pressure on cardiovascular disease. *Journal of Hypertension, 17* (Suppl. 5), S25–S28.

Anderson, N. B., McNeilly, M. D., & Meyers, H. (1991). Autonomic reactivity and hypertension in blacks: A review and proposed model. *Ethnicity and Disease, 1*, 154–170.

Anderson, N. B., McNeilly, M. D., & Myers, H. (1993). A biopsychosocial model of race differences in vascular reactivity. In J. Bloscovich & E. S. Katkin (Eds.), *Cardiovascular reactivity to psychological stress and disease* (pp. 83–108). Washington, DC: American Psychological Association.

Bamshad, M. (2005). Genetic influences on health: Does race matter? *JAMA, 294*(8), 937–946.

Burrows, B. (1990). Airways obstructive diseases: Pathogenic mechanisms and natural histories of the disorders. *Obstructive Lung Disease, 74*, 547–559.

Burrows, B., Bloom, J. W., Traver, G. A., & Cline, M. G. (1987). The course and prognosis of different forms of chronic airways obstruction in a sample from the general population. *New England Journal of Medicine, 317*, 1309–1314.

Centers for Disease Control and Prevention. (2005). Racial/ethnic disparities in prevalence, treatment and control of hypertension: United States 1999–2002. *MMWR Morbidity and Mortality Weekly Report, 54*, 7–9.

Clark, R., Anderson, N. B., Clark, V. R., & Williams (1999). Racism as a stressor for African Americans: A biopsychosocial model. *American Psychologist, 54*, 805–816.

Ditto, B. (1993). Familial influences on heart rate, blood pressure, and self-report anxiety responses to stress: Results from 100 twin pairs. *Psychophysiology, 30*, 635–645.

Dockery, D. W., Ware, J. H., Ferris, B. G., Jr, Glicksberg, D. S., Fay, M. E., Spiro, A., 3rd, et al. (1985). Distribution of forced expiratory volume in one second and forced vital capacity in healthy, white, adult never-smokers in six U.S. cities. *American Review of Respiratory Disease, 131*(4), 511–520.

Dressler, W. W. (1985). The social and cultural context of coping: Action, gender and symptoms in a southern black community. *Social Science Medicine, 21*(5), 499–506.

Eaves, L. (1976). The effect of cultural transmission on continuous variation. *Heredity, 37*(1), 41–57.

Eaves, L. J., Fulker, D. W., & Heath, A. C. (1989). The effects of social homogamy and cultural inheritance on the covariances of twins and their parents: A LISREL model. *Behavior Genetics, 19*(1), 113–122.

Enright, P. L., Lebowitz, M. D., & Cockroft, D. W. (1994). Physiologic measures: Pulmonary function tests. Asthma outcome. *American Journal of Respiratory and Critical Care Medicine, 149*(2, Pt. 2), 9–18.

Fagard, R., Brguljan, J., Staessen, J., Thijs, L., Derom, C., Thomis, M., et al. (1995). Heritability of conventional and ambulatory blood pressures: A study in twins. *Hypertension, 26*, 919–924.

Finkel, D., Pedersen, N. L., & McGue, M. (1995). Genetic influences on memory performance in adulthood: Comparison of Minnesota and Swedish twin data. *Psychology and Aging, 10*(3), 437–446.

Finkel, D., Pedersen, N. L., McGue, M., & McClearn, G. E. (1995). Heritability of cognitive abilities in adult twins: Comparison of Minnesota and Swedish data. *Behavior Genetics, 25*(5), 421–431.

Harrap, S. B. (1994). Hypertension: Genes versus environment. *Lancet, 344*, 169–171.

Harshfield, G. A., & Grim, C. E. (1997). Stress hypertension: The "wrong" genes in the "wrong" environment. *Acta Physiatrica Scandinavica, 161*(Suppl. 640), 129–132.

Heath, A. C., & Madden, P.A. F. (1995). Genetic influences on smoking behavior. In J. R. Turner,

J. K. Hewitt, & L. R. Cardon (Eds.). *Behavior genetic approaches in behavioral medicine* (pp. 98–115). New York: Plenum Press.

Hong, Y., de Faire, U., Heller, D. A., McClearn, G. E., & Pedersen, N. (1994). Genetic and environmental influences on blood pressure in elderly twins. *Hypertension, 24,* 663–670.

Joint National Committee on Prevention, Detection, Evaluation and Treatment of High Blood Pressure (1997). The sixth report of the joint national committee on prevention, detection evaluation and treatment of high blood pressure. *Archives of Internal Medicine, 157,* 2413–2444.

Lee, M. T., Rosner, B. A., & Weiss, S. T. (1999). Relationship of blood pressure to cardiovascular death: The effects of pulse pressure in the elderly. *Annals of Epidemiology, 9,* 101–107.

McClearn, G. E., Svartengren, M., Pedersen, N. L., Heller, D. A., & Plomin, R. (1994). Genetic and environmental influences on pulmonary function in aging Swedish twins. *Journal of Gerontology, 49,* M264–268.

Meredith, L. (1993). Measurement, factor analysis, and factorial invariance. *Psychometrika, 58,* 525–543.

Neale, M. C., & Cardon, L. R. (1992). *Methodology for genetic studies of twins and families.* Dordrecht, Netherlands: Kluwer.

Palatini, P., & Julius, S. (1997). Heart rate and the cardiovascular risk. *Journal of Hypertension. 15,* 3–17.

Pedersen, N. L., Plomin, R., Nesselroade, J. R., & McClearn, G. E. (1992). A quantitative genetic analysis of cognitive abilities during the second half of the life span. *Psychological Science, 3,* 346–353.

Pickering, T. (1999). Cardiovascular pathways: Socioeconomic status and stress effects on hypertension and cardiovascular function. *Socioeconomic Status and Health in Industrialized Nations, 896,* 262–277.

Plomin, R., DeFries, J. C., McClearn, G. E., & Rutter, M. (1997). *Behavior genetics.* New York: W. H. Freeman.

Rowe, J. W., & Kahn, R. L. (1997). Successful aging. *Gerontologist, 37*(4), 433–440.

Saudino, K. J., Gagne, J. R., Grant, J., Ibatoulina, A., Marytuina, T., Ravich-Scherbo, I., et al. (1999). Genetic and environmental influences on personality in adult Russian twins. *International Journal of Behavioral Development, 23*(2), 375–389.

Shields, A. E., Fortun, M., Hammonds, E. M., King, P. A., Lerman, C., Rapp, R., et al. (2005). The use of race variables in genetic studies of complex traits and the goal of reducing health disparities: A transdisciplinary perspective. *American Psychologist, 60*(1), 77–103.

Simmons, S., Ljunquist, B., Johansson, B., Plomin, R., Zarit, S., & McClearn, G. (1997). Selection bias in samples of older twins? A comparison between octogenarian twins and singletons in Sweden. *Journal of Aging and Health, 9*(4), 553–567.

Tager, I. B., Segal, M. R., Speizer, F. E., & Weiss, S. T. (1988). The natural history of forced expiratory volumes: Effect of cigarette smoking and respiratory symptoms. *American Review of Respiratory Disease, 138,* 837–849.

Tang, M. X., Stern, Y., Marder, K., Bell, K., Gurland, B., Lantigua, R., et al. (1998). The APOE-epsilon4 allele and the risk of Alzheimer disease among African Americans, whites, and Hispanics. *Journal of the American Medical Association, 279,* 751–755.

U.S. Department of Health and Human Services. (1995). *Vital and health services: Trends in the health of older Americans: United States, 1994.* (Series 3: Analytic and Epidemiological Studies, No. 30.) DHHS Publication No. PHS 95-1414. Hyattsville, MD: Author.

Wagner, E. H., Grothaus, M. S., Hect, J. A., & LaCroix, A. Z. (1991). Factors associated with participation in a senior health promotion program. *Gerontologist, 31,* 598–602.

Whitfield, K. E. (2005). Studying biobehavioral aspects of health among older adult minorities. *Journal of Urban Health, 82*(2 Suppl 3), 103–110.

Whitfield, K. E., & Brandon, D. (2000). Individual differences, ethnicity, and aging: What can gerogenetic studies contribute? *African American Research Perspectives, 6*(2), 115–122.

Whitfield, K. E., Brandon, D. T., Wiggins, S. A., Vogler, G., & McClearn, G. (2003). Does intact pair status matter in the study of African American twins?: The Carolina African American Twin Study of Aging. *Experimental Aging Research, 29*(4), 1–17.

Whitfield, K. E., Grant, J. D., Ravich-Scherbo, I., Marutina, T., & Ibatoulina, A. (1999). Genetic and environmental influences on forced expiratory volume in midlife: A cross-cultural replication. *Experimental Aging Research, 25*(3), 255–266.

Whitfield, K. E., & McClearn, G. (2005). Genes, environment, race, and health. *American Psychologist, 60*(1), 104–114.

Whitfield, K. E., Weidner, G., Clark, R., & Anderson, N. B. (2002). Sociodemographic diversity and behavioral medicine. *Journal of Consulting and Clinical Psychology, 70*(3), 463–481.

Wilson, T. W., & Grim, C. E. (1991). Biohistory of slavery and blood pressure differences in blacks today: A hypothesis. *Hypertension, 17*(Suppl. I), I122–I128.

20

Methodological Issues in Positive Psychology and the Assessment of Character Strengths

Nansook Park and Christopher Peterson

Positive psychology has three pillars: positive experiences and emotions; positive traits like talents, passions, and strengths of character; and positive institutions that enable the psychological good life (Seligman & Csikszentmihalyi, 2000). For the past several years, our work has addressed the second of these pillars and specifically such character strengths as curiosity, perseverance, kindness, teamwork, and hope. The intent has been to create a consensual classification of widely valued positive traits (Peterson & Seligman, 2004) and ways of measuring these as individual differences (Peterson, Park, & Seligman, 2005). This project, the Values in Action (VIA) Classification, has been the most ambitious undertaking to date deliberately guided by the perspective of positive psychology. Its goals—a conceptual framework and an associated assessment strategy—represent necessary steps for an empirical science of positive psychology that goes beyond armchair speculations or scattered investigations.

The present contribution discusses research methods that can be used to validate this classification. In some cases, we have already

deployed these methods to good effect, and in other cases, we sketch a future research agenda. Although we have elsewhere argued that positive psychology is above all psychology, a social science with tried-and-true methods (Peterson & Park, 2003), we also address what is special when these methods are applied to the topic of optimal functioning. Accordingly, we start with an overview of positive psychology vis-à-vis research methods.

Methodological Issues in Positive Psychology

Positive psychology is an umbrella term for theories and research about what makes life most worth living. By this view, positive psychology has a history that long predates its birth. Indeed, one of the original purposes of psychology was to make the lives of ordinary people more fulfilling (Seligman, 2002), and studies of values, giftedness, health, and well-being have a sustained lineage within psychology (e.g., Jahoda, 1958; Kluckhohn, 1951; Maslow, 1954,

1962; Rogers, 1942; Terman, 1925). Contemporary volumes that gather together good examples of positive psychology work have no difficulty filling their pages, and the studies included use the full range of research methods familiar to psychologists: case histories, surveys, interviews, observations, laboratory experiments, and the like.

At the same time, positive psychology represents a sea change within the field because it is based on a different metapsychology than business-as-usual psychology. As Seligman (2002) argued, psychology in the United States since World War II has focused on understanding human problems, identifying the conditions that produce them, and devising interventions that prevent or undo their damage. The yield of these efforts has been considerable, but a perspective on the human condition as flawed and fragile has crept into psychology as a result. People are seen as victims of bad genetics or cruel environments, in denial or in recovery, and little else.

Positive psychology challenges this view. Without disagreeing that problems exist, positive psychologists additionally propose that goodness, strength, and accomplishment are as genuine as evil, weakness, and failure. What is good about people is not secondary, derivative, illusory, epiphenomenal, parasitic upon the negative, or otherwise suspect. If this proposal is taken seriously, important research implications follow.

Measures and Theories

Psychologists need to use measures that break through the zero point of pathology indices (Peterson, 2000). Mental health is not simply the absence of mental illness. Consider the Beck Depression Inventory (BDI), a widely used self-report questionnaire that assesses the extent and severity of common depressive symptoms (Beck, Ward, Mendelson, Mock, & Erbaugh, 1961). The best that one can score on the BDI is zero, but not all zero scores are interchangeable. There is a world of difference between someone who is not sad, not sluggish, and not suicidal, and someone else who bounds out of bed in the morning with good cheer and enthusiasm for what the day holds.

Also, we cannot create theories about the good life by standing theories of dysfunction on their head. The factors that enable optimal functioning are not necessarily the opposites of those that lead to poor functioning. For example, religious involvement distinguishes between

happy and unhappy people (e.g., Myers, 1993) but not between happy and extremely happy people; in this case, it is close interpersonal relationships that prove crucial (Diener & Seligman, 2002). For another example, a family with high expressed emotion is deleterious when family members have severe psychological disorders (Leff & Vaughn, 1985), but the absence of affective communication hardly makes a good family an excellent one (cf. Reis & Gable, 2003).

Settings and Samples

If one's interest is in optimal functioning, one must identify people in settings and circumstances that allow them to do their best. We call these the natural homes for positive psychology research, and they include settings in which virtuosity is recognized, celebrated, and encouraged (Peterson & Seligman, 2003b). Among the obvious examples that satisfy this rule are the workplace, sports, the performing arts, the military, and school. Studies in such settings are often segregated as applied psychology, but in the present context, this is a curious label if it means that basic psychology can stay away from these settings. We find the applied-basic partition profoundly false. Positive psychology must seek its subject matter where it is most likely to be found. These places may not always include the typical source of research participants: psychology subject pools and psychiatric clinics.

Along these lines, positive psychologists cannot rely simply on convenience samples of callow youth or troubled souls. Without putting too fine a point on it, studies of college students are somewhat suspect if our interest is with general psychology but downright bizarre if our concern is with positive psychology. For example, creativity seems better studied with accomplished artists and scientists, who meet the 10-year rule of sustained training and practice in their fields of endeavor (Hayes, 1989), than with college students generating remote associates. Courage seems better studied by interviewing bomb defusers or those who sheltered Jews in Nazi Europe (Oliner & Oliner, 1988; Rachman, 1990) than with a convenience sample of adolescents responding to hypothetical scenarios.

Longitudinal and Multivariate Designs

The good life unfolds over time, and positive psychologists must therefore undertake longitudinal studies. We do not deny that laboratory experiments can provide important insights into the topics of concern to positive psychology (cf. Fredrickson, 2001), but they provide snapshots that must eventually be placed in longer perspective. Consider these studies often cited as excellent examples of what attention to the positive can reveal:

- The forecasting of U.S. presidential elections from the positive traits of candidates (Zullow, Oettingen, Peterson, & Seligman, 1988)
- The increased life expectancy of Academy Award winners relative to runners-up (Redelmeier & Singh, 2001)
- The increased life expectancy of those who hold a positive view of aging (Levy, Slade, Kunkel, & Kasl, 2002)
- The prediction of marital satisfaction from smiles in college yearbooks (Harker & Keltner, 2001)
- The prediction of successful aging from the use of mature coping strategies by young adults (Vaillant, 2000)
- The foretelling of longevity from expressions of happiness in essays by young adults (Danner, Snowdon, & Friesen, 2001)
- The civic engagement decades later of youthful activists from the 1960s (Franz & McClelland, 1994)

All of these studies are ambitiously longitudinal. Here we approve of studies that start with young people and follow them over time to reveal the processes that produce flourishing.

In addition, routes to the good life are multiple. Positive psychology research must spread a broad net to ensure that no positive phenomenon is left behind. We disagree with Tolstoy's (1877/2000, p. 3) adage that "Happy families are all alike, [but] every unhappy family is unhappy in its own way." Happiness is just as complex as unhappiness—perhaps more so. Multivariate studies are therefore demanded, and one-size-fits-all bivariate theories have no lasting place in positive psychology. As positive psychology develops, research attention needs to go beyond surface description to address the mechanisms and processes that underlie positive phenomena.

The Sociocultural Context

The good life is one that has significance to the person who leads it. Positive psychologists must tackle meaning head-on in their research, which means it cannot be modeled on natural science approaches that study phenomena solely from the outside. Positive psychologists must take seriously stories, narratives, and accounts, the typical starting points for qualitative research. Case histories of exceptional individuals should be encouraged. Historical archives and cultural products should be consulted. The sociocultural context should always be kept in mind.

Positive psychologists must address explicitly the objection that their subject matter is a narrowly Western undertaking reflecting societal preoccupations with individualism and hedonism. In principle arguments for and against cultural relativism can be mounted, but we believe that data bear on the debate and further that no simple answer will emerge (Murdock, 1949). In some cases, what is meant by the good life will prove to be thoroughly situated in time and place, but in other cases, generalization will be possible. Consider investigations like those by Bok (1995) or Schwartz (1994) into the universality of values. Depending on the level of abstraction, given values can be described either as culture-bound or as universal.

The methodological "so what" is that the ubiquity of positive psychology constructs is partly an empirical issue and that positive psychologists should use the research strategies of cross-cultural psychology to map out their boundaries. Samples of research participants from different cultures should be studied, the equivalence of measures should be demonstrated, and constructs of concern should not just be exported (from Western cultures to elsewhere) but also imported (from elsewhere to Western cultures). Our own research on character strengths has emphasized cross-cultural commonalities, but the investigation of what is culturally unique is just as important.

Social Desirability and 360-Degree Methodology

Positive psychology must worry about the potential pitfall represented by social desirability (Crowne & Marlowe, 1964). Business-as-usual psychologists are well aware that people may minimize their problems and shortcomings when asked to report on them. Positive psychologists need to be similarly cautious when asking people to report on what is best about themselves. Indeed, issues of social desirability may play themselves out in particularly complex ways as researchers study optimal functioning.

Accordingly, the strategy of measuring social desirability with the Marlowe-Crowne Scale or the MMPI Lie Scale and then partialling these scores from analyses involving substantive constructs may not suffice. Consider that some people will exaggerate what is good about themselves—a tendency captured by social desirability scales—but that other people will do just the opposite and modestly understate their strengths and virtues—a tendency that confounds the confound, as it were. How do we know who is doing what? Furthermore, given the critical role in the good life of someone maintaining harmonious relationships with other people, the ability to present oneself well to others may not be nuisance but essence. By this point of view, positive states and traits are not contaminated by a response set of social desirability; they are socially desirable, especially when reported with fidelity.

There is no simple solution to these dilemmas except to urge positive psychologists to obtain information from multiple sources. Self-report is a good place to start, but researchers must additionally turn to knowledgeable informants as well as more objective indices of thriving. There is a temptation to treat multiple sources of information as idiosyncratically fallible but substantively interchangeable (Campbell & Fiske, 1959). Certainly, different research strategies provide checks on one another, and we would not expect different sources of information to be routinely orthogonal in what they convey. But it is also important to appreciate that each source of information can provide a unique vantage on a topic. We therefore like the metaphor of 360-degree methodology, meaning that different sources of information are not automatically combined into a single composite but rather are used to create a picture with breadth and depth (Hedge, Borman, & Birkeland, 2001). For example, in our studies of character strengths, we have found that observers (friends, parents, teachers) usually agree with research participants about the presence or absence of traits like kindness and humor that are displayed interpersonally—that is, publicly—but not necessarily about more private strengths like spirituality.

Tonic Versus Phasic Measures

Finally, because of its concern with optimal functioning, positive psychology cannot always study typical behavior. Also of interest are the high points of a person's life, the psychological equivalents of the personal bests tracked by athletes at all levels of ability. Muscle physiology distinguishes between *tonic activity* (the baseline electrical activity when muscles are idle) and *phasic activity* (the burst of electrical activity that occurs when muscles are challenged and contract). Most of psychology is about tonic activity—typical thoughts, feelings, and actions. Cognitive complexity, intelligence, and hope, for example, are all measured in the absence of any real-world challenge, with the hope that these summary measures will predict what a person actually does when challenged.

Tonic measures are at best moderate predictors of phasic action, and the $r = .30$ upper limit (the so-called personality coefficient) is familiar to all psychologists who study individual differences. For many purposes, moderate correlations are useful. But for a positive psychologist, they may miss what is most exceptional about people.

The imperfect prediction of optimal action from tonic characteristics has been called the *Harry Truman effect* (Peterson & Seligman, 2001). After a largely undistinguished life, Truman, to almost everyone's surprise, rose to the occasion upon the death of FDR to became one of the great presidents of the United States. What allowed him to do so?

We have our own answers to this question, but psychology has provided few of them. Besides work on resilience (Luthar, Cicchetti, & Becker, 2000; Masten, 2001), psychology has few accounts of rising to the occasion, even though evolution has no doubt shaped people to respond well when needed. We may all possess strengths that we do not display until we are truly challenged. Crises may not forge character, but they reveal it, and positive psychology is necessarily a phasic psychology.

The methodological implications are several. We must beware of relying only on summary measures; positive psychology research is not just census taking. We must be interested not only in variation across people but also within people. Almost no one wins multiple Congressional Medals of Honor. Civil rights pioneer Rosa Parks did not stay seated in the front of every Alabama bus she took during the 1960s. Traits remain an important subject matter for positive psychology, but researchers must consider that traits vary along the tonic-phasic continuum. The investigation of the more phasic traits require different research strategies than the investigation of the more tonic traits.

Applying Positive Psychology Methods to the Classification and Assessment of Character

In light of general issues about positive psychology methods, let us turn to an illustrative program of research—character strengths and virtues. As noted, we have made a serious effort to define and measure good character, one of positive psychology's central concerns.

In keeping with the guidelines set forth, we have approached character in its own right as an important instance of optimal functioning. We did not measure character by ascertaining the relative absence of its antonyms, and given the focus of extant psychological theories on disease and distress, we did not wed our work to an a priori theory.

We have been careful to describe our project as a classification as opposed to a taxonomy. By definition, a classification parses some part of the universe by demarcating its domain and by specifying mutually exclusive and exhaustive subcategories within that domain. Both sorts of parsing rules need to be explicit and demonstrably reliable. A classification is not to be confused with a taxonomy, which is based on a deep theory that explains the domain of concern (Bailey, 1994). If the theory that girds a taxonomy is wrong, contradictory, or inarticulate, the activity that is organized and guided becomes self-defeating. The details of our thinking about character are spelled out elsewhere (Peterson

et al., 2005; Peterson & Seligman, 2004). Here are our conclusions:

- A character strength is "a disposition to act, desire, and feel that involves the exercise of judgment and leads to a recognizable human excellence or instance of human flourishing" (Yearley, 1990, p. 13).
- Good character is composed of a family of positive traits.
- Virtuous activity involves choosing virtue for itself and in light of a justifiable life plan, which means that people can reflect on their own strengths of character and talk about them to others.
- Character strengths can be distinguished from related individual differences like talents and abilities by criteria like those summarized in table 20.1

The application of these criteria led us to identify 24 different strengths of character organized in terms of six core virtues that emerged from our surveys of influential religious and philosophical traditions (Dahlsgaard, Peterson, & Seligman, 2003). In some cases, the classification of a given strength under a core virtue can be debated. But we have not directly measured the more abstract virtues. We have measured only the more specific strengths, although we are in the process of empirically testing the hierarchical classification in table 20.2 with appropriate multivariate techniques.

What distinguishes the VIA Classification from many previous attempts to articulate good character is its simultaneous concern with assessment. Our measurement work has been

TABLE 20.1 Criteria for a Character Strength

1. Ubiquity—is widely recognized across cultures
2. Fulfilling—contributes to individual fulfillment, satisfaction, and happiness broadly construed
3. Morally valued—is valued in its own right and not for tangible outcomes it may produce
4. Does not diminish others—elevates others who witness it, producing admiration, not jealousy
5. Nonfelicitous opposite—has obvious antonyms that are negative
6. Traitlike—is an individual difference with demonstrable generality and stability
7. Measurable—has been successfully measured by researchers as an individual difference
8. Distinctiveness—is not redundant (conceptually or empirically) with other character strengths
9. Paragons—is strikingly embodied in some individuals
10. Prodigies—is precociously shown by some children or youth
11. Selective absence—is missing altogether in some individuals
12. Institutions—is the deliberate target of societal practices and rituals that try to cultivate it

TABLE 20.2 Values in Action Classification of Character Strengths

---

1. Wisdom and knowledge—cognitive strengths that entail the acquisition and use of knowledge
   - Creativity: thinking of novel and productive ways to do things
   - Curiosity: taking an interest in all of ongoing experience
   - Love of learning: mastering new skills, topics, and bodies of knowledge
   - Open-mindedness: thinking things through and examining them from all sides
   - Perspective: being able to provide wise counsel to others
2. Courage—emotional strengths that involve the exercise of will to accomplish goals in the face of opposition, external or internal
   - Authenticity: speaking the truth and presenting oneself in a genuine way
   - Bravery: not shrinking from threat, challenge, difficulty, or pain
   - Persistence: finishing what one starts
   - Zest: approaching life with excitement and energy
3. Humanity—interpersonal strengths that involve "tending and befriending" others
   - Kindness: doing favors and good deeds for others
   - Love: valuing close relations with others
   - Social intelligence: being aware of the motives and feelings of self and others
4. Justice—civic strengths that underlie healthy community life
   - Fairness: treating all people the same according to notions of fairness and justice
   - Leadership: organizing group activities and seeing that they happen
   - Teamwork: working well as member of a group or team
5. Temperance—strengths that protect against excess
   - Forgiveness: forgiving those who have done wrong
   - Modesty: letting one's accomplishments speak for themselves
   - Prudence: being careful about one's choices; not saying or doing things that might later be regretted
   - Self-regulation: Regulating what one feels and does
6. Transcendence—strengths that forge connections to the larger universe and provide meaning
   - Appreciation of beauty and excellence: noticing and appreciating beauty, excellence, and/or skilled performance in all domains of life
   - Gratitude: being aware of and thankful for the good things that happen
   - Hope: expecting the best and working to achieve it
   - Humor: liking to laugh and tease; bringing smiles to other people
   - Spirituality: having coherent beliefs about the higher purpose and meaning of life

---

deliberately broad. To date, we have devised and evaluated several different methods: (a) focus groups to flesh out the everyday meanings of character strengths among different groups (e.g., Steen, Kachorek, & Peterson, 2003); (b) self-report questionnaires suitable for adults and young people (e.g., Park & Peterson, 2005); (c) structured interviews to identify what we call signature strengths; (d) informant reports of how target individuals rise to the occasion (or not) with appropriate strengths of character (e.g., courage in the face of fear, open-mindedness when confronting difficult decisions, hope when encountering setbacks, and so on); and (e) case studies of nominated paragons of specific strengths (e.g., Peterson & Kellerman, 2002).

Among additional methods we are in the process of developing are: (f) a content analysis procedure for assessing character strengths from unstructured descriptions of self and others (Park, 2003); and (g) strategies for scoring positive traits from archived material like obituaries (Neuman, Barker, & Lee, 2003). These methods, once perfected, will greatly extend the reach of future studies to allow the investigation of good character among the quick, the dead, the famous, and the otherwise unavailable. Furthermore, they will allow longitudinal studies to be mounted retrospectively, so long as suitable verbal material for content analyses has been left behind, a strategy described as the time machine method (Peterson & Seligman, 1984).

Space does not permit a detailed description of what we have learned about the reliability and validity of these different methods for assessing strengths of character. Suffice it to say that we have successfully established the internal consistency of our questionnaire scales and their test-retest stability over several months. We have investigated the validity of our methods for assessing positive traits with the known-groups procedure and more generally by mapping out their nomological nets (e.g., Dahlsgaard, Davis, Peterson, & Seligman, 2002; Park & Peterson, 2005; Park, Peterson, & Seligman, 2004; Peterson & Seligman, 2003a; Shimai, Otake, Park, Peterson, & Seligman, 2003). We also note our ongoing attempts to devise interventions to change character strengths (Seligman et al., 2003), which embody Kurt Lewin's adage that one good way to understand a phenomenon is to try and change it. To the degree that our interventions successfully target specific character strengths as we measure them, we will have compelling evidence that they indeed are discrete individual differences captured by our assessment strategies. Although we anticipate that these different methods will converge in the strengths they identify within given individuals, we repeat our earlier point that each method will also provide unique information about good character. Indeed, the relevant data at hand already suggest convergence but not redundancy.

To develop and validate measures, we did not rely on college student samples. Although we of course believe that young adults have strengths of character, we were persuaded by previous thinkers from Aristotle to Erik Erikson that good character is most apt to be found among those who are mature, who have done more than rehearse work and love.

To reach a wide range of adults, we placed our tentative questionnaires online (e.g., at www.authentichappiness.org). Critical to the appeal of this method, we believe, is that upon completion of the measures, respondents are given instant feedback about their top five strengths. In addition to expediting our research, this strategy has taught us something about character: Being able to put a name to what one does well is intriguing and even empowering.

If it is meaningful to generalize across our 400,000-plus respondents, the typical person we have studied is an adult aged 35 to 40 who has completed several years of college, has held various jobs, and is married or living as. Females are overrepresented, by a two- or three-to-one margin. About 75% of the respondents are from the United States; the remainder are mostly from English-speaking nations (Australia, Canada, and the United Kingdom), but also represented are research participants from the rest of the world. Among U.S. respondents, the ethnic makeup of our samples approximates that of the nation as a whole, with a tilt toward European Americans.

We acknowledge that our research subjects are hardly a representative sample of the U.S. or world population, but we would like to stress the diversity of our respondents across virtually all demographic contrasts (other than computer literacy). Recently, researchers have shown that Internet studies typically enroll more diverse samples than conventional studies using psychology subject pool samples at colleges or universities and that they are as valid as traditional research methods (Gosling, Vazire, Srivastava, & John, 2004; Kraut et al., 2004). In any event, our concern has been with what is common across respondents from different groups and not what is unique, and we believe that the commonalities we have discovered are both striking and real.

Our Internet surveys have paid the dividend of a diverse sample, but we have additionally sought to establish the cross-cultural generality (or not) of our constructs by deliberately surveying people from different nations and cultures about their recognition and valuing of different strengths of character, using focus groups for nonliterate samples and written surveys for literate samples (Biswas-Diener & Diener, 2003; Peterson, Boniwell, Park, & Seligman, 2003). And our colleagues around the world have begun serious translations of our inventories into Chinese, French, German, Hindi, Italian, Japanese, Portuguese, Spanish, and Urdu.

These projects are in progress, although preliminary data are consistent with the premise of universality. Regardless, our classification contains two dozen different character strengths. Given the range of classified traits, we will likely be able to offer nuanced conclusions about their differential universality. Indeed, even within a given nation or culture, there is good reason for researchers to assess a number of different strengths. We believe that good character comprises a family of positive traits and that no one person will show all or even most of them (Walker & Pitts, 1998). We caution researchers not to zoom in prematurely on a given strength of character if it means moving the others far off focus.

Our measures of the VIA strengths allow a systematic study of character in multidimensional terms. Most existing research on good character has focused on one component of character at a time, leaving unanswered questions about the underlying structure of character within an individual. Some individuals may be wise and authentic but are neither courageous nor kind, or vice versa (Park, 2004). Furthermore, measuring a full range of positive traits may even reduce concerns about socially desirable responding by allowing most research participants to say something good about themselves. Although we are open to the possibility that some people may lack all of the strengths in our classification, the data show that virtually everyone has some notable strengths of character. We have taken to calling these *signature strengths*, and they are akin to what Allport (1961) identified decades ago as personal traits.

Signature strengths are positive traits that a person owns, celebrates, and frequently exercises. In interviews with adults, we find that everyone can readily identify a handful of strengths as very much their own, typically between three and seven (just as Allport proposed). Our hypothesis is that the exercise of signature strengths is fulfilling. Other than some preliminary studies using our structured interview, we have yet to undertake a systematic investigation of signature strengths. Here would be a good use of the multiple-case research strategy and its ability to unearth the deep meaning of conduct to individuals (Rosenwald, 1988).

Another way we have sidestepped concerns with social desirability is with ipsative scoring of our surveys. For each respondent, we rank his or her character strength scores from 1 (top) to 24 (bottom). Because someone who is high on one strength must be lower on other strengths, ipsative scoring builds dependencies into the data. However, ipsative scoring also reduces concerns about response biases, including social desirability and undue modesty. Each of the 24 strengths is ranked first for some respondents and last for others. External correlates of ipsatively scored strengths, such as subjective well-being, are much the same as the correlates of the strength scores per se, implying that our surveys tap something more than artifact.

As an initial step toward studying people at their best, we did three parallel studies of adults with respect to good character and its correlates at work, love, and play (Peterson & Seligman, 2004). Rather than asking our respondents about current jobs, current relationships, and current recreational activities (the typical research strategy when these topics are of concern), we asked them to think of their most fulfilling job, their truest love and their best friend, and their most engaging hobby, whenever these were present in their lives. (We also gave respondents the option of saying "does not apply," which some small number of them, invariably young adults, exercised.) Interestingly, respondents did not always describe their current jobs, relationships, or leisure pasttimes. The clichéd standards by which people seem to judge and even to choose among options in these domains—like salary, status, or geographical location for jobs; good looks or financial security for relationships; and unalloyed sensory pleasure for leisure activities—did not characterize what our respondents reported as the best they ever had. Instead, what people most valued was a job, a relationship, and a hobby congruent with their own particular strengths of character. Without the perspective of positive psychology to guide the design of these studies, we would not have learned these important facts about the good life.

Another way to study people at their best is to focus on consensual paragons of particular strengths. Here we have only scratched the surface, undertaking case studies of award-winning firefighters and paramedics to learn more about bravery (Peterson & Kellerman, 2002). Our primary findings suggest two necessary conditions for courageous action: (a) having overlearned the required tasks; and (b) having strong social support for doing what needs to be done regardless of fear. We plan further case studies with respect to other entries in the classification.

Future Research Directions

We have described our research efforts to date that use various quantitative and qualitative methods. However, there are additional matters to be addressed in order to advance our understanding of character strengths. First, we have not yet undertaken ambitious longitudinal studies of character strengths. We know something about their cross-sectional correlates and short-term consequences but little about the origins of positive traits, their long-term consequences, and what might be the routes between. Future studies of the natural history of good character might profitably be patterned on the Terman (1925) study of adolescent geniuses or the Grant Study of the best and brightest of Harvard University undergraduates (Vaillant, 1977) by employing large samples, longitudinal designs, and multiwave assessments but not by starting with the most fortunate or the most privileged in our society. Longitudinal studies of individuals in difficult circumstances—so-called at-risk samples—would be especially interesting if the focus were on how they rise to the occasion and flourish despite adversity.

Second, we have not yet taken seriously our own distinction between tonic and phasic strengths. Our questionnaires conceptualize and measure positive traits as if they are all displayed in stable and general ways, and we do not know if people who are habitually kind also show prodigious acts of kindness—for example, donating an organ to a stranger—or if those who typically stand up for what is right also rise mightily to the occasion as whistle-blowers at work, despite great cost to their careers and lives. Maybe yes, but maybe no if the Harry Truman effect holds. We need to answer such questions.

Third, what we wish to touch upon here is the evaluation of our classification as a whole. To evaluate the VIA Classification qua classification, it must be demonstrated that: (a) included entries meet the criteria we have set forth (exhaustiveness); (b) included entries are mutually exclusive (distinctiveness); and (c) we can add new entries and—conversely—drop old entries. We have called the VIA Classification an aspirational one, meaning that it tries to approach these ideals but does not pretend to have achieved them fully (Peterson & Seligman, 2004). The adjective *aspirational* provides wiggle room, but there are limitations to the squirming allowed. The facts of the matter bear on the classification, tentative though it may be.

How well do the entries meet the criteria that we have set forth? As table 20.3 shows, our classification seems to fare well in capturing what is meant by good character by most of our criteria. Most of the table's entries are widely recognized as morally valued individual differences that are able to be measured and are associated with various indices of fulfillment and satisfaction. For most of the strengths, we can point to nonfelicitous antonyms, to societal institutions and rituals that attempt to cultivate them, to consensual paragons who embody the strengths, and to individuals who strikingly lack them. Except for those strengths that require a certain level of cognitive development or psychosocial maturation for their meaningful display, we can also identify prodigies.

The final issue concerning the VIA Classification is the posited distinctiveness of the included strengths and their relationship to other personality constructs. For example, whether measures of the VIA strengths are distinct from Big Five

indices is not fully established. Our preliminary factor analyses identify a somewhat different structure than the Big Five, although interestingly, usually one with five factors (Park & Peterson, 2004).

In a recent study, we correlated the VIA character strengths with life satisfaction while simultaneously partialling measures of all Big Five traits; the VIA measures robustly explained life satisfaction beyond the contribution of the Big Five. Perhaps we should not be surprised that the VIA Classification is organized differently than are personality traits per se, because the starting point of the Big Five and most other lexical approaches to personality—the 18,000-plus trait terms identified decades ago by Allport and Odbert (1936)—deliberately excluded moral traits (Cawley, Martin, & Johnson, 2000).

In any event, the distinctiveness of two traits—including character strengths—is a matter of degree, best judged on conceptual and empirical grounds. So love of learning is arguably a special case of curiosity, and persistence may be a special case of self-regulation. However, correlations between these pairs of strengths suggest that they are related but still not identical (e.g., in an Internet sample of adults, $r = .65$ in the former case and $r = .47$ in the latter case).

The VIA Classification is an ongoing project, and we are open to the possibilities of dropping current entries and introducing new ones if necessary. How will this be done? Apply the criteria in table 20.1, devise a measure or use one that is already established, and show its (relative) independence from existing entries. For instance, tolerance is an additional strength that many people have suggested that we include. We are not yet persuaded. On the one hand, tolerance seems to blend the included strengths of open-mindedness and fairness. On the other hand, tolerance has connotations that preclude the moral celebration that marks the other strengths in the classification. We may tolerate bad smells or shrill sounds, but we certainly do not value them, morally or otherwise. And more to the point, to say that we tolerate people who differ from us or those who are constant sources of disappointment and annoyance does not mean that we seek them out or feel fulfilled in their presence.

Further work, both conceptual and empirical, needs to be done to understand the structure and nature of character strengths and virtues. Recent developments in measurement and statistical

TABLE 20.3 Values in Action Entries and the Criteria for a Character Strength

	1. ubiquity	2. fulfilling	3. morally valued	4. does not diminish others	5. nonfelicitous opposite	6. traitlike	7. measurable	8. distinctiveness	9. paragons	10. prodigies	11. selective absence	12. institutions
	1	2	3	4	5	6	7	8	9	10	11	12
Creativity	++	+	++	++	++	+	++	++	++	++	++	++
Curiosity	++	++	++	++	++	++	++	++	++	++	++	++
Love of learning	+	+	++	++	++	++	+	?	++	++	?	++
Open-mindedness	++	+	++	++	++	+	++	++	++	−	++	++
Perspective	++	++	++	++	++	++	++	++	++	−	++	++
Authenticity	++	++	++	++	++	+	+	+	++	++	++	++
Bravery	++	++	++	++	++	?	?	+	++	++	++	+
Persistence	++	++	+	++	++	++	+	?	++	++	++	++
Zest	++	++	++	++	++	++	++	?	++	++	++	++
Kindness	++	++	−	++	++	++	++	+	++	++	++	++
Love	++	++	++	++	++	++	++	++	++	++	++	++
Social intelligence	++	++	++	++	++	++	++	+	++	++	++	−

(continued)

TABLE 20.3 (*Continued*)

	1. ubiquity	2. fulfilling	3. morally valued	4. does not diminish others	5. nonfelicitous opposite	6. traitlike	7. measurable	8. distinctiveness	9. paragons	10. prodigies	11. selective absence	12. institutions
	1	**2**	**3**	**4**	**5**	**6**	**7**	**8**	**9**	**10**	**11**	**12**
Fairness	++	++	++	++	++	+	++	++	++	–	++	++
Leadership	++	++	++	++	++	++	++	?	++	++	++	++
Teamwork	++	++	++	++	++	+	++	?	++	++	++	++
Forgiveness	++	++	++	++	++	++	++	++	++	–	++	++
Modesty	++	+	++	++	++	+	+	++	++	–	++	++
Prudence	++	++	++	+	++	++	+	?	++	+	++	++
Self-regulation	++	++	++	++	++	++	++	++	++	++	++	++
Appreciation of beauty	++	+	+	++	++	++	+	?	++	++	++	++
Gratitude	++	++	++	++	++	++	++	++	++	+	++	++
Hope	++	++	++	++	++	++	++	+	++	++	++	++
Humor	++	++	+	++	++	++	++	++	++	++	++	++
Spirituality	++	++	++	++	++	++	++	++	++	++	++	++

++ = satisfies criterion; + = somewhat satisfies criterion; – = does not satisfy criterion; ? = unknown.

techniques can greatly advance our studies of good character. Following are a few examples.

Testing a series of hierarchically related models using structural equation modeling would help us to establish a conceptually driven but empirically validated classification of character strengths. That is, evaluating the structural relations among second-order factors of the 24 character strengths vis-à-vis the six core virtues would clarify the overall structure of the VIA classification and its associated measures.

The generality of character strengths across ethnicity, culture, age, and gender has been one of our chief interests. Lack of equivalence in the validity of the measures may lead to inappropriate interpretations of research findings based on simple comparisons of mean scores or correlates. In order to undertake valid comparisons across groups, measurement equivalence across the groups must be established with multiple group confirmatory factor analysis (Meredith, 1993).

Understanding the development of good character is also one of our ultimate goals, and as noted, longitudinal investigations are needed. Because of the multidimensional complexity of character, this is a quite challenging goal given the limitations of conventional statistical techniques. However, with new developments in latent growth modeling, these limitations can be surmounted (Curran & Muthén, 1999) to shed light on the normative development of character strengths as well as the predictors and correlates of individual differences in growth patterns and growth rates of the individual components of good character. We expect that this method will identify those who own particular strengths and how their development is different from or the same as others'. The long-term benefit will be information that can inform deliberate intervention programs.

Last, but importantly, we are very interested in studying various profiles of character strengths. Using cluster analysis, we would like to identify various profiles of character strengths and establish the psychosocial and behavioral characteristics of individuals who have particular profiles. Are there modal types of people defined by the strengths they do or do not possess? We have speculated about the possible roles played by configurations of strengths but have not yet investigated them (cf. Peterson & Seligman, 2004). For example, the strength of humor may not be especially valued or valuable in its own right but might take on considerable significance

when coupled with other strengths of character like leadership or love.

Conclusion

The new field of positive psychology requires equally new perspectives on theories and methods. As much as traditional approaches can contribute to the goals of positive psychology, there are additional issues to be considered when the subject matter of research entails thriving. In the present contribution, we have discussed these issues and how they bear on the assessment of character strengths. Good character matters, to positive psychology and to the larger society (Hunter, 2000). The VIA project is the first major project explicitly inspired by positive psychology. Our studies have demonstrated that strengths of character can be specified and measured as a multidimensional construct. Challenging but exciting tasks are ahead of us. With the help of state-of-art quantitative as well as qualitative methods, we will eventually know more about strengths of character and how to cultivate them.

References

Allport, G. W. (1961). *Pattern and growth in personality.* New York: Holt, Rinehart, and Winston.

Allport, G. W., & Odbert, H. S. (1936). Trait-names: A psycho-lexical study. *Psychological Monographs, 47*(Whole No. 211), 1–171.

Bailey, K. D. (1994). *Typologies and taxonomies: An introduction to classification techniques.* Thousand Oaks, CA: Sage.

Beck, A. T., Ward, C. H., Mendelson, M. N., Mock, J., & Erbaugh, J. (1961). An inventory for measuring depression. *Archives of General Psychiatry, 4,* 561–571.

Biswas-Diener, R., & Diener, E. (2003). *From the equator to the north pole: A study of character strengths.* Unpublished manuscript, Portland, OR.

Bok, S. (1995). *Common values.* Columbia, MO: University of Missouri Press.

Campbell, D. T., & Fiske, D. W. (1959). Convergent and discriminant validation by the multitrait-multimethod matrix. *Psychological Bulletin, 56,* 81–105.

Cawley, M. J., Martin, J. E., & Johnson, J. A. (2000). A virtues approach to personality. *Personality and Individual Differences, 28,* 997–1013.

Crowne, D. P., & Marlowe, D. (1964). *The approval motive: Studies in evaluative dependence*. New York: Wiley.

Curran, P. J., & Muthén, B. O. (1999). The application of latent curve analysis to testing developmental theories in intervention research. *American Journal of Community Psychology, 2*, 567–595.

Dahlsgaard, K., Davis, D., Peterson, C., & Seligman, M. E. P. (2002, October 4). *Is virtue more than its own reward?* Poster presented at the first Positive Psychology International Summit, Washington, DC.

Dahlsgaard, K., Peterson, C., & Seligman, M. E. P. (2005). Shared virtue: The convergence of valued human strengths across culture and history. *Review of General Psychology, 9*, 209–213.

Danner, D. D., Snowdon, D. A., & Friesen, W. V. (2001). Positive emotions in early life and longevity: Findings from the nun study. *Journal of Personality and Social Psychology, 80*, 804–813.

Diener, E., & Seligman, M. E. P. (2002). Very happy people. *Psychological Science, 13*, 80–83.

Franz, C. E., & McClelland, D. C. (1994). Lives of women and men active in the social protests of the 1960s: A longitudinal study. *Journal of Personality and Social Psychology, 66*, 196–205.

Fredrickson, B. L. (2001). The role of positive emotions in positive psychology: The broaden-and-build theory of positive emotions. *American Psychologist, 56*, 218–226.

Gosling, S. D., Vazire, S., Srivastava, S., & John, O. P. (2004). Should we trust Web-based studies? A comparative analysis of six preconceptions about Internet questionnaires. *American Psychologist, 59*, 93–104.

Harker, L. A., & Keltner, D. (2001). Expressions of positive emotion in women's college yearbook pictures and their relationship to personality and life outcomes across adulthood. *Journal of Personality and Social Psychology, 80*, 112–124.

Hayes, J. R. (1989). *The complete problem solver* (2nd ed.). Hillsdale, NJ: Erlbaum.

Hedge, J. W., Borman, W. C., & Birkeland, S. A. (2001). History and development of multisource feedback as a methodology. In D. W. Bracken, C. W. Timmreck, & A. H. Church (Eds.), *The handbook of multisource feedback* (pp. 15–32). San Francisco: Jossey-Bass.

Hunter, J. D. (2000). *The death of character: Moral education in an age without good or evil*. New York: Basic Books.

Jahoda, M. (1958). *Current concepts of positive mental health*. New York: Basic Books.

Kluckhohn, C. K. M. (1951). Values and value orientations in the theory of action. In T. Parsons & E. Shils (Eds.), *Toward a general theory of action* (pp. 388–433). Cambridge, MA: Harvard University Press.

Kraut, R., Olson, J., Banaji, M., Bruckman, A., Cohen, J., & Couper, M. (2004). Psychological research online: Report of board of scientific affairs' advisory group on the conduct of research on the Internet. *American Psychologist, 59*, 105–117.

Leff, J., & Vaughn, C. (1985). *Expressed emotion in families: Its significance for mental illness*. New York: Guilford.

Levy, B. R., Slade, M. D., Kunkel, S. R., & Kasl, S. V. (2002). Longevity increased by positive self-perceptions of aging. *Journal of Personality and Social Psychology, 83*, 261–270.

Luthar, S. S., Cicchetti, D., & Becker, B. (2000). The construct of resilience: A critical evaluation and guidelines for future work. *Child Development, 71*, 543–562.

Maslow, A. H. (1954). *Motivation and personality*. New York: Harper and Row.

Maslow, A. H. (1962). *Toward a psychology of being*. Princeton, NJ: Van Nostrand.

Masten, A. S. (2001). Ordinary magic: Resilience processes in development. *American Psychologist, 56*, 227–238.

Meredith, W. (1993). Measurement invariance, factor analysis and factorial invariance. *Psychometrika, 58*, 525–543.

Murdock, G. P. (1949). *Social structure*. New York: Macmillan.

Myers, D. G. (1993). *The pursuit of happiness*. New York: Avon Books.

Neuman, E., Barker, B., & Lee, F. (2003). *Character strengths in obituaries*. Unpublished data, University of Michigan.

Oliner, S., & Oliner, P. (1988). *The altruistic personality*. New York: Free Press.

Park, N. (2003). *Parental descriptions of young children's character*. Unpublished data, University of Rhode Island.

Park, N. (2004). Character strengths and positive youth development. *Annals of the American Academy of Political and Social Science, 591*, 40–54.

Park, N., & Peterson, C. (2004). *Character strengths and the Big Five*. Manuscript in preparation, University of Rhode Island.

Park, N., & Peterson, C. (2005). The Values in Action Inventory of Character Strengths for Youth. In K. A. Moore & L. H. Lippman (Eds.), *What do children need to flourish? Conceptualizing and measuring indicators of positive development* (pp. 13–23). New York: Springer.

Park, N., Peterson, C., & Seligman, M. E. P. (2004). Strengths of character and well-being.

Journal of Social and Clinical Psychology, 23, 603–619.

Peterson, C. (2000). The future of optimism. *American Psychologist, 55,* 44–55.

Peterson, C., Boniwell, I., Park, N., & Seligman, M. E. P. (2003). *Cross-national survey of character strengths.* Unpublished data, University of Michigan .

Peterson, C., & Kellerman, R. (2002). *Interviews with courageous firefighters and paramedics.* Unpublished data, University of Michigan.

Peterson, C., & Park, N. (2003). Positive psychology as the evenhanded positive psychologist views it. *Psychological Inquiry, 14,* 141–146.

Peterson, C., Park, N., & Seligman, M. E. P. (2005). Assessment of character strengths. In G. P. Koocher, J. C. Norcross, & S. S. Hill, III (Eds.), *Psychologists' desk reference* (2nd ed.), (pp. 93–98). New York: Oxford University Press.

Peterson, C., & Seligman, M. E. P. (1984). Causal explanations as a risk factor for depression: Theory and evidence. *Psychological Review, 91,* 347–374.

Peterson, C., & Seligman, M. E. P. (2001). How can we allow character to matter? University of Michigan Business School Leading in Trying Times Webpage. Retrieved December 7, 2003, from http://www.bus.umich.edu/leading/index.html

Peterson, C., & Seligman, M. E. P. (2003a). Character strengths before and after 9/11. *Psychological Science, 14,* 381–384.

Peterson, C., & Seligman, M. E. P. (2003b). Positive organizational studies: Thirteen lessons from positive psychology. In K. S. Cameron, J. E. Dutton, & R. E. Quinn (Eds.), *Positive organizational scholarship: Foundations of a new discipline* (pp. 14–27). San Francisco: Berrett-Koehler.

Peterson, C., & Seligman, M. E. P. (2004). *Character strengths and virtues: A handbook and classification.* New York: Oxford University Press.

Rachman, S. J. (1990). *Fear and courage* (2nd ed.). New York: W. H. Freeman.

Redelmeier, D. A., & Singh, S. M. (2001). Survival in Academy Award–winning actors and actresses. *Annals of Internal Medicine, 134,* 955–962.

Reis, H. T., & Gable, S. L. (2003). Toward a positive psychology of relationships. In C. L. M. Keyes & J. Haidt (Eds.), *Positive psychology and the life well-lived* (pp. 129–159). Washington, DC: American Psychological Association.

Rogers, C. R. (1942). *Counseling and psychotherapy: Newer concepts in practice.* Boston: Houghton Mifflin.

Rosenwald, G. C. (1988). A theory of multiple-case research. *Journal of Personality, 56,* 239–264.

Schwartz, S. H. (1994). Are there universal aspects in the structure and content of human values? *Journal of Social Issues, 50*(4), 19–45.

Seligman, M. E. P. (2002). *Authentic happiness.* New York: Free Press.

Seligman, M. E. P., & Csikszentmihalyi, M. (2000). Positive psychology: An introduction. *American Psychologist, 55,* 5–14.

Seligman, M. E. P., Reivich, K., Gillham, J., Peterson, C., Duckworth, A., Steen, T., et al. (2003). *Lessons for the pleasant life, the good life, and the meaningful life.* Unpublished manuscript, University of Pennsylvania.

Shimai, S., Otake, K., Park, N., Peterson, C., & Seligman, M. E. P. (2003). *Convergence of character strengths in American and Japanese young adults.* Unpublished manuscript, Kobe College, Japan.

Steen, T. A., Kachorek, L. V., & Peterson, C. (2003). Character strengths among youth. *Journal of Youth and Adolescence, 32,* 5–16.

Terman, L. M. (1925). *Genetic studies of genius: Vol. 1. Mental and physical traits of a thousand gifted children.* Stanford, CA: Stanford University Press.

Tolstoy, L. (2000). *Anna Karenina.* New York: Modern Library. (Original work published 1877)

Vaillant, G. E. (1977). *Adaptation to life.* Boston: Little, Brown.

Vaillant, G. E. (2000). *Aging well.* Boston: Little, Brown.

Walker, L. J., & Pitts, R. C. (1998). Naturalistic conceptions of moral maturity. *Developmental Psychology, 34,* 403–419.

Yearley, L. H. (1990). *Mencius and Aquinas: Theories of virtue and conceptions of courage.* Albany: State University of New York Press.

Zullow, H., Oettingen, G., Peterson, C., & Seligman, M. E. P. (1988). Explanatory style and pessimism in the historical record: CAVing LBJ, presidential candidates, and East versus West Berlin. *American Psychologist, 43,* 673–682.

21

Wisdom as a Classical Human Strength

Psychological Conceptualizations and Empirical Inquiry

Ute Kunzmann and Antje Stange

Positive psychologists value the investigation of positive traits and subjective experiences, including happiness, self-efficacy, and optimism (e.g., Aspinwall & Staudinger, 2003; Seligman & Csikszentmihalyi, 2000). The field of positive psychology would be incomplete, however, if it failed to incorporate human strengths such as empathy, altruism, or morality—even if these characteristics do not necessarily guarantee a constant experiencing of positive feelings, but rather require the ability to tolerate and make use of mixed and negative experiences, at least occasionally.

In this chapter, we consider a human strength that has been prized since antiquity in philosophical and religious writings, namely, wisdom (e.g., Assmann, 1994; Hall, 1922; Kekes, 1996). At the core of this concept is the notion of a perfect, perhaps utopian, integration of knowledge and character, mind and virtue (e.g., Baltes & Kunzmann, 2003; Baltes & Staudinger, 2000). Although the psychology of wisdom is a relatively new field, several promising psychological models of wisdom have been developed during the last two decades (for reviews, see Baltes & Staudinger, 2000; Kramer, 2000; Kunzmann &

Baltes, 2005; Sternberg, 1998). In these models, wisdom is thought to be different from other human strengths in that it facilitates an integrative and holistic approach toward life's challenges and problems—an approach that embraces past, present, and future dimensions of phenomena, values different points of views, considers contextual variations, and acknowledges the uncertainties inherent in any sense-making of the past, present, and future.

A second important feature of wisdom is that it is inherently an intra- and interpersonal concept. In this sense, wisdom has been said to refer to time-tested knowledge that guides our behavior in ways that optimize productivity on the level of individuals, groups, and even society (e.g., Baltes & Staudinger, 2000; Kramer, 2000; Sternberg, 1998).

Finally, although wisdom has been linked to a good life at all times, its acquisition during ontogenesis may be incompatible with a hedonic life orientation and a predominantly pleasurable, sheltered, and passive life (e.g., Baltes, Glück, & Kunzmann, 2002; Kunzmann & Baltes, 2003a). Given their interest in maximizing a common good, for example, wiser people are likely to partake in behaviors that contribute, rather than consume, resources (Kramer, 2000; Kunzmann & Baltes, 2003a; Sternberg, 1998). Moreover, an interest in understanding the complexity of life, including the blending of developmental gains and losses, most likely is associated with emotional complexity (e.g., Labouvie-Vief, 1990) and with what has been called "constructivistic" melancholy (Baltes, 1997a).

While there appears to be considerable agreement on several important ideas about the definition, development, and functions of wisdom, all existing psychological wisdom models encompass their unique features. The purpose of this chapter is to discuss the different ways in which wisdom has been theoretically defined and empirically operationalized in psychological research. As a first step, we introduce elements of wisdom that were revealed in an analysis of cultural-historical work on wisdom (Baltes, 2004; Baltes & Staudinger, 2000) and in past work on laypeople's theories about wisdom and wise persons (e.g., Clayton & Birren, 1980; Holliday & Chandler, 1986; Sternberg, 1985). Thereafter, we review three psychological lines of research that have conceptualizatized wisdom as an aspect of mature personality development (e.g., Erikson, 1959; Wink & Helson, 1997), as postformal and dialectical thinking (e.g., Kramer, 1990, 2000; Labouvie-Vief, 1990), and as an expanded form of pragmatic intelligence (e.g., Baltes & Smith, 1990; Baltes & Staudinger, 2000; Sternberg, 1998). We compare these three approaches to define and assess wisdom and discuss implications of conceptualizing wisdom in each of the three ways. In our concluding remarks, we discuss several avenues for future work and especially consider multivariate methods suited to address timely topics in the field of wisdom research.

Cultural-Historical Work and Implicit Theories

Given that wisdom is an enormously rich and broad concept with a variety of meanings, developing a comprehensive psychological definition and operationalization of wisdom is challenging. A first starting point toward a psychological definition of wisdom is considering relevant cultural-historical work. According to Baltes (1993, 2004), seven general characteristics of wisdom have been mentioned repeatedly in cultural-historical conceptualizations of wisdom (see also Assmann, 1994; Clayton & Birren, 1980).

Specifically, wisdom is thought to (1) address difficult problems regarding the meaning and conduct and life; (2) represent truly outstanding knowledge, judgment, and advice; (3) be a perfect integration of knowledge and character, mind and virtue; (4) coordinate and promote individual and societal growth; (5) involve balance and modulation; (6) include an awareness of the limits of knowledge and uncertainties of the world; and (7) be difficult to achieve but easy to recognize. Together, the seven properties constitute a general conceptualization of wisdom representing agreed-upon properties of this concept. This working model can help evaluate psychological definitions of wisdom, especially in terms of their comprehensiveness.

A second starting point for the development of psychological wisdom models is evidence from implicit theories on wisdom. This line of research has investigated the beliefs and mental representations laypeople have about wisdom and wise persons (Clayton & Birren, 1980; Holliday & Chandler, 1986; Sternberg, 1985). To investigate this question empirically, laypeople have been instructed to rate a large set of attributes (e.g., smart, cheerful, helpful, loving, foolish, relaxed) according to the degree to which each is typical of wisdom or wise persons. To establish conceptual differentiation, participants also rate how typical the same attributes are for other concepts such as creativity or intelligence.

The main findings of this line of research can be summarized as follows. First, laypeople can clearly distinguish wisdom from other human capacities such as intelligence or creativity. Second, in laypeople's conceptions, wisdom represents human excellence. Third, lay conceptions emphasize the multidimensional nature of wisdom. Given that the existing studies differ in the attributes rated by the participants as being more or less typical of wisdom, it is not surprising that the nature and number of the extracted dimensions differ somewhat across studies. However, implicit theories of wisdom consistently entail a coalition of cognitive (e.g., outstanding knowledge about the world), social (e.g., empathic concern, the ability to give good advice), emotional (e.g., affect sensitivity and regulation), and motivational (e.g., personal growth) capacities.

There is much overlap between implicit theories of wisdom and conceptualizations of wisdom in cultural-historical and philosophical work; however, these two approaches to defining the nature of wisdom have different strengths. Philosophical and cultural-historical work offers an abstract, comprehensive, and systematic description of the wisdom concept. Implicit theories on wisdom are less comprehensive and more specific in terms of the elements that might be subsumed under this concept. This is understandable given that laypeople typically have not articulated an abstract framework of wisdom as a theoretical construct; rather, their representations are likely to be linked to specific exemplars and experiences. When considered together, philosophical and implicit approaches to wisdom provide an excellent background for explicit psychological work on wisdom and a comparison of different conceptual models and empirical paradigms.

Psychological Definitions of Wisdom: Three Approaches

In our view, there should be sufficient agreement between psychological wisdom models and conceptualizations of wisdom held by laypeople and philosophers. However, psychological researchers are interested in formulating a definition of wisdom that can be used for empirical assessment and, in addition, permits the empirical investigation of the factors associated with the acquisition and expression of wisdom (e.g., Baltes & Staudinger, 2000; Helson & Srivastava, 2002; Sternberg, 1998). Developing definitions of wisdom that allow the operationalization and measurement of wisdom-related performance may have led to relatively narrow conceptualizations of this concept, each emphasizing different aspects of wisdom. In the following sections, we discuss three major approaches to the definition and assessment of wisdom in psychological research.

Wisdom as Mature Personality Development

In this tradition, wisdom has been conceptualized as a mature part of the individual's personality that develops relatively late during adulthood. Erikson's (1959) work is an example of this tradition. For Erikson, personality development requires the attainment and successful resolution of a sequence of psychosocial crises, each emerging at a particular stage in the life cycle. Wisdom is thought to result from resolving the final crisis occurring in old age when a person faces his or her own death and dying. Erikson proposed that dealing with death and dying can result in either despair or integrity (i.e., wisdom). Resolution with integrity means that a person can accept that life comes to a conclusion. This insight allows one to have a detached concern with life and to evaluate problems from a holistic and abstract perspective. According to more recent conceptualizations of the wise personality (e.g., Wink & Helson, 1997), another late stage of personality development is also relevant to wisdom, namely, the seventh stage dealing with generativity versus self-absorption and stagnation. The feeling that one is responsible for passing one's knowledge and experience on to future generations is generally considered a central aspect of wisdom.

In the meantime, several self-report questionnaires have been developed that assess the two Erikson-based final stages of personality development: integrity and generativity (e.g., McAdams & de St. Aubin, 1992; Ryff & Heincke, 1983). For example, Ryff and Heincke defined integrity as adapting to the triumphs and disappointments of being and viewing one's past life as inevitable, appropriate, and meaningful and generativity as having a concern for guiding the next generation and a responsibility for those younger in age. The authors developed 16 traitlike self-descriptive items to assess each dimension (e.g., "I feel generally contented with what I have accomplished in my life" was one item for integrity).

Cronbach's alphas for both scales were satisfactory (integrity: $\alpha = .80$; generativity: $\alpha = .79$). As predicted by the authors, older adults scored higher on generativity and integrity than middle-aged and younger adults. There is also work that established the validity of the two scales. Orwoll and Perlmutter (1990) reported a study in which they compared older adults nominated as wise and older adults nominated as creative. Wise nominees were found to score significantly higher on both generativity and integrity than creative nominees or older adults from the general population who participated in Ryff and Heincke's (1983) study.

Helson and her colleagues have taken another personality-based approach to wisdom (e.g., Helson & Srivastava, 2002; Wink & Helson, 1997). Based on Achenbaum and Orwoll's ideas (Achenbaum & Orwoll, 1991; Orwoll & Achenbaum, 1993), the authors distinguished two components of wisdom, practical and transcendent wisdom. Practical and transcendent wisdom both reflect interpersonal development (empathy, understanding, maturity in relationships). In addition, practical but not transcendent wisdom reflects intrapersonal development (mature affective responses, self-knowledge, integrity), whereas transcendent but not practical wisdom reflects interest and skill in the transpersonal domain (self-transcendence, recognition of the limits of knowledge, philosophical/spiritual commitments).

To assess practical wisdom, the authors created an 18-item scale consisting of adjectives from the Adjective Check List (ACL; Gough & Heilbrun, 1983). The adjectives were chosen by judges to be indicative (i.e., clear thinking, fair-minded, insightful, intelligent, interest wide, mature, realistic, reasonable, reflective, thoughtful, tolerant, understanding, wise) and contraindicative (i.e., immature, intolerant, reckless, shallow) of a wise person. Given that the ACL has a dichotomous yes-no response format, an individual's wisdom score consists of the number of indicative adjectives checked as being self-descriptive minus the number of nonindicative adjectives checked. This scale has been employed as a self-report and an observer-report measure (Helson & Srivastava, 2002; Wink & Helson, 1997) in two long-term longitudinal studies of about $N = $ 100 women and their partners. At the first wave of data collection in 1958, the women studied at Mills College, a private women's college in Oakland. In this sample, the practical wisdom scale's reliability was satisfactory (range $\alpha = .74$ to $\alpha = .81$).

Transcendent wisdom was assessed with an open-ended question, namely, "Would you give an example of wisdom you have acquired and how you came by it?" Four judges rated self-descriptive statements in response to this question on a five-point scale. A statement received a high score if it was abstract, insightful, and reflected philosophical or spiritual depth, an integration of thought and affect, as well as an awareness of the complexity and limits of knowledge. Cronbach's alpha coefficients were reported as a measure of the mean interrater agreement among four raters. All alpha coefficients were greater than .80.

As the authors expected, practical and transcendent wisdom were positively related, but the correlation between these two measures was relatively low, ranging from $r = .16$ to $r = .26$ in different groups of the sample. This low correlation suggests that practical and transcendent wisdom are not two poles of the same underlying wisdom dimension; rather, they seem to constitute two highly distinct dimensions that should be assessed separately. Studying practical and transcendent wisdom individually also allows more differentiated questions about precursors, correlates, and consequences of wisdom. In fact, initial research suggests that practical and transcendent wisdom do have different correlates and relate to different classes of variables (Wink & Helson, 1997). Specifically, practical but not transcendent wisdom showed a positive correlation with dominance (confidence, prosocial initiative, goal directedness), generativity, and empathy as measured by the CPI. Transcendent but not practical wisdom was positively associated with cognitive complexity (openness, flexibility) and intuition sensation as measured by the Myers-Briggs Type Indicators Inventory (Myers & McCaully, 1985). Other variables were positively correlated with both dimensions of wisdom, namely, Loevinger's (1976) measure of ego development as well as with psychological mindedness, insight, and autonomy as measured by the California Personality Inventory (CPI; Gough, 1987). Neither practical nor transcendent wisdom was related to work status or life satisfaction. Consistent with implicit wisdom theories (e.g., Holliday & Chandler, 1986), Wink and Helson (1997) found that practical wisdom increased from early to middle adulthood and that professional specialization (psychotherapy) contributed to these age-related gains.

A third approach to defining wisdom in the tradition of personality research is Ardelt's (2003) work. Based on Clayton and Birren's (1980) studies on implicit theories about wise persons, Ardelt has defined wisdom as an integration of reflective, cognitive, and affective elements. Ardelt views the reflective dimension as a prerequisite for the acquisition of the cognitive and emotional elements. Reflection primarily refers to a person's willingness and ability to overcome subjectivity and projections by looking at phenomena and events from different perspectives. The cognitive element is defined as a person's ability to understand life, that is, to comprehend the significance and deeper meaning of phenomena. The affective dimension of wisdom is reflected in the presence of positive emotions toward others (e.g., sympathy, compassion) and the absence of indifferent or negative emotions.

Ardelt (2003) developed a self-report questionnaire to assess the dimensions of her wisdom model in a sample of older adults. She selected 14 items to represent the cognitive dimension of wisdom (e.g., "I often do not understand people's behavior"; reversed), 13 items to indicate the affective dimension (e.g., "I am easily irritated by people who argue with me"; reversed), and 12 items to assess the reflective dimensions (e.g., "I always try to look at all sides of a problem"). The internal consistencies of the three scales were satisfactory and ranged between $\alpha = .71$ and $\alpha = .85$ in a sample of $N = 180$ older adults. As to be expected, the three wisdom scales were positively interrelated (correlations ranged from $r = .30$ to $r = .50$). These small to moderate correlations again corroborate the notion that wisdom is a multidimensional concept and that the specific components of this concept should be studied individually.

In her initial study, however, Ardelt (2003) provided evidence for the predictive validity of her participants' overall wisdom score. Individual differences in wisdom were positively correlated with individual differences in several indicators of adjustment (sense of mastery, general subjective well-being, purpose in life, self-rated health) and negatively related to individual differences in indicators of maladjustment (depressive symptoms, fear of death). Wisdom was positively related to higher education, but was unrelated to marital status, gender, and ethnicity. In contrast to previous work in this tradition (e.g., Ryff & Heincke, 1983; Wink & Helson, 1997), wisdom and age were negatively interrelated ($r = -.29$). As to convergent validity, Ardelt reported that people who had been nominated as being wise independently of her wisdom definition had a significantly higher wisdom score than participants who were not nominated ($M_{nominees} = 3.71$; $M_{controls} = 3.57$; scale 1–5).

Summary

Research using the existing self-report measures of wisdom has made valuable contributions to our understanding of the wise personality. As reviewed previously, the existing measures possess acceptable reliabilities and generally show meaningful and theory-consistent associations with other variables. In our view, however, additional efforts are needed in refining the conceptualization of wisdom as part of the mature personality.

Specifically, all of the studies cited above used at least somewhat selected samples, which potentially limits the generalizability of the findings reported. Some studies failed to provide a convincing theoretical rationale for the selection of wisdom components and, maybe even more problematic, those components selected were often measured with a small and unrepresentative sample of specific items. As a result, existing personality-based conceptualizations of wisdom differ in the number and nature of the specific components subsumed under the concept of wisdom. Furthermore, given the lack of a generally accepted theoretical model of the development and functions of the wise personality, it often remains unclear whether a personality trait (e.g., affect sensitivity) represents an antecedent, constituent, or consequence of wisdom.

These problems notwithstanding, the personality-based concepts of wisdom discussed above are promising in that they all address two important facets of wisdom that have been repeatedly mentioned in laypeople's implicit theories about wise persons (e.g., Clayton & Birren, 1980; Holliday & Chandler, 1986). These two characteristics are self-development (e.g., integrity, self-knowledge) and self-transcendence (e.g., generativity, empathy). Clarifying the nature of these two self-related wisdom facets based on rigorous and systematic questionnaire development and multitrait-multimethod factor analytic work is an important direction for future research.

Future work in the area of test development and refining should also more explicitly address processes of social desirability and impression management and, more generally, the conditions under which adults of different ages are able and willing to provide valid information about their competencies. For example, under certain conditions, some people might not want to communicate that they do not possess highly valued and generally desirable traits and competencies, whereas more modest persons might consider it inappropriate to communicate that they are good advisors, highly reflective, or emotionally competent. Reinforcing our concern is Meacham's (1990) conclusion that "the essence of wisdom is to hold the attitude that knowledge is fallible and to strive for a balance between knowing and doubting" (p. 181). Applying this notion to knowledge about the self suggests that a person who reports the belief that she is wise or possesses wisdom-related traits and attitudes is likely to be not wise. In order to create unambiguous results, it is important to address these and other possible problems. Artifacts related to social desirability, communication norms, scale use, and memory biases have been studied by several researchers (e.g., Schwarz, 1999). Dealing with these problems more explicitly would surely advance the development of self-report wisdom questionnaires.

Taken together, although self-report may be the most direct and convenient method of assessing wisdom, future work in this field might benefit from combining self-report questionnaires with more objective, behavior-based methods. These methods have been developed in the two traditions of wisdom research reviewed and discussed below.

Wisdom as Postformal Stage of Cognitive Development

Theorists of cognitive development in the Piagetian tradition, or influenced by it, treat wisdom as a late stage of cognitive development characterized by the emergence of relativistic and dialectical thought (e.g., Riegel, 1973). Dialectical thinking derives from the insight that knowledge about the self, others, and the world evolves in an everlasting process of theses, antitheses, and syntheses. From this perspective, wisdom has been described as the integration of different modes of knowing (Labouvie-Vief, 1990), of opposing points of view (Kitchener & Brenner, 1990), and of different intrapsychic systems such as cognition, emotion, and motivation (Birren & Fisher, 1990; Kramer, 2000).

Kramer's approach to wisdom is one example of this tradition. She suggests that wisdom requires three elements typical of mature thought, namely, an awareness of the relativistic nature of knowledge, the acceptance of contradiction, and an integration of contradiction through dialectical thinking (Kramer, 1983, 1990, 2000). To assess this type of mature thought, Kramer and Woodruff (1986) presented participants with two dilemmas, each of which represented a conflict between two opposing elements. For example, a career dilemma centered on a woman's decision of whether to enter the workforce for the first time and discussed several pros and cons for her decision. Participants were asked to discuss possible resolutions, and the answer protocols were scored according to four categories, including awareness of the relativistic nature of knowledge, acceptance of contradictions, and integration of contradiction into the dialectic whole. Kramer and Woodruff (1986) reported that interrater agreements for these categories were satisfactory (total agreement percentage was above 85%). Consistent with their prediction,

older people scored higher on these categories than young and middle-aged adults.

The dialectical relativistic approach to cognition is also represented in work by Labouvie-Vief (e.g., Labouvie-Vief, 1990, 1998). In her cognitive adult development theory, Labouvie-Vief has suggested that mature cognition requires overcoming static, dualistic, either-or thinking in which reality is predicated into such categories as self versus other, right versus wrong, or reason versus emotion. In her view, mature cognition involves an integration of these oppositions through dynamic and contextual thinking. Labouvie-Vief (1990) proposed that two modes of knowing and their dynamic interplay are especially critical to defining wisdom. One mode, logos, reflects objective, analytical, and rational thought. The other mode, mythos, represents more concrete, contextually embedded thought that entails the subjective significance of phenomena. According to Labouvie-Vief, wisdom is the smooth and balanced dialogue between these alternative modes of knowing.

Labouvie-Vief's approach has resulted in an array of studies concerned with different facets of adult cognition, including subjective representations of the self (Labouvie-Vief, Chiodo, Goguen, Diehl, & Orwoll, 1995) and knowledge about emotion regulation (Labouvie-Vief, DeVoe, & Bulka, 1989). In these studies, participants are asked to respond to open-ended questions regarding their self-concept or emotional life and the answers are subsequently coded in terms of ascending levels of mature thought (Labouvie-Vief, 1998).

Summary

Work that conceptualizes wisdom as a postformal stage of cognitive development has described one important facet of wisdom, namely, the ability to process information about the self and the world in relativistic and integrative ways. This capacity has been repeatedly mentioned in laypeople's conceptions of wisdom and constitutes a central element of wisdom according to cultural-historical work (e.g., Baltes, 2004; Clayton & Birren, 1980).

Consistent with a competence-based conceptualization of wisdom, relativistic and dialectical thinking have been assessed by performance-based paradigms. That is, participants have been instructed to think about and reflect on life-like dilemmas of fictitious persons or aspects of their own life, including problems that they themselves have encountered in the past. These performance-based measures may allow more objective assessments of wisdom than standardized personality measures.

A potential limitation of past work in this tradition is, however, that it has not explicitly specified the contents to which reflective and dialectical processes refer and the bodies of knowledge that distinguish wisdom from other cognitive abilities. Put differently, proponents of wisdom conceptualizations in the tradition of Piaget have emphasized cognitive processes and ways of mature thinking rather than cognitive structures and knowledge contents. One direction of future work in this area is to develop a more systematic theory about the content domains to which relativistic and dialectical thinking as parts of wisdom refer. This work will help distinguish wisdom-related cognitive processes from processes that reflect mature thinking but not necessarily wisdom.

Furthermore, given that cognitive maturity is only one side of wisdom, it appears important to extend existing conceptualizations of wisdom in this tradition toward a more integrative view that also includes personality dispositions as part of wisdom. In this vein, Kramer (1990) proposed a two-component model of wisdom that encompasses a cognitive component (i.e., relativistic and dialectical thinking) and a personality component (i.e., ego development, integration of conscious and unconscious processes, affect regulation). Future research is needed that specifies the multiple ways in which the different subcomponents of these two broad factors might interact in wisdom. This work should be based on a creative combination of personality measures and relevant cognitive tests.

Wisdom as an Expanded Form of Pragmatic Intelligence

In this tradition, wisdom has been conceptualized in the context of psychometric models of intelligence (e.g., Baltes & Smith, 1990; Baltes & Staudinger, 2000; Sternberg, 1998). Robert Sternberg's wisdom model represents one example. Proceeding from his triarchic theory of intelligence, Sternberg (1998) considered tacit knowledge, a component of practical intelligence, as a core feature of wisdom. According to Sternberg (1998), tacit knowledge is action oriented, helps individuals to achieve goals they, personally value, and can be acquired only through learning from one's own experiences,

not vicariously through reading books or through others' instructions. Sternberg (1998) states that wisdom is not tacit knowledge per se; rather, wisdom is involved when people apply their tacit knowledge in order to maximize a balance of various self-interests (intrapersonal) with other people's interests (interpersonal) and aspects of the context in which they live (extrapersonal). Therefore, what sets wisdom apart from practical intelligence is its orientation toward the maximization of a common good, rather than individual well-being. Sternberg and his colleagues are currently developing open-ended tasks and coding schemes to operationalize their theoretical definition of wisdom. The tasks are complex conflict-resolution problems involving the formation of judgments, given multiple competing interests and no clear resolution of how these interests could be reconciled. Wisdom, assessed by these tasks, refers to a person's ability to identify whose interests are at stake and what the contextual factors are under which one is operating (Sternberg, 1998). It will be interesting to see how this newly developed measure relates to personality-based wisdom questionnaires and other performance-based wisdom tests.

The Berlin Wisdom Model

The Berlin wisdom model, which has been proposed by Paul Baltes and his colleagues, is another example of work that conceptualized wisdom as a highly valued form of pragmatic intelligence. This model has been developed during the last two decades and has resulted in the most systematic research program on wisdom to date (e.g., Baltes & Smith, 1990; Baltes & Staudinger, 2000; Dittmann-Kohli & Baltes, 1990; Dixon & Baltes, 1986).

Historical Background The Berlin wisdom model is embedded in a theoretical framework that highlights two distinct but interacting categories of intellectual functioning: the mechanics and the pragmatics of intelligence (Baltes, Staudinger, & Lindenberger, 1999). This framework draws on earlier theories of intelligence such as the theory of fluid and crystallized intelligence by Cattell and Horn (e.g., Cattell, 1971; Horn & Hofer, 1992). The cognitive mechanics, on the one hand, refer to the neurophysiological architecture of the brain as it has evolved during biological evolution. Speed, accuracy, and the coordination of basic information processing operations are examples of the cognitive mechanics.

Given their biological basis, the cognitive mechanics are assumed to decline relatively early in the life span. In contrast, the cognitive pragmatics are indicated by culturally transmitted bodies of knowledge. Typical examples are reading and writing skills, educational qualifications, or skills related to practical problems of everyday life. Because of the importance of experience in acquiring knowledge-based skills, the cognitive pragmatics are thought to show stability or even selected growth into old age.

According to Baltes and colleagues, wisdom represents one prototypical example of the cognitive pragmatics. The bodies of knowledge that are typical of wisdom, however, go beyond those subsumed under other more limited forms of pragmatic intelligence. In fact, the definition of wisdom as expert knowledge about fundamental life problems is meant to expand the traditional dual-process model of intellectual functioning and its close link to the psychometric method. Studying wisdom as a component of the cognitive pragmatics requires a return to the original conceptualization of intelligence as general adaptation to the changing biological and environmental conditions inevitably taking place throughout the life span (e.g., Baltes, 1997b; Dittmann-Kohli & Baltes, 1990; Kunzmann & Baltes, 2003b).

Theoretical Definition   In the Berlin paradigm, wisdom has been defined as a highly valued and outstanding expertise in dealing with fundamental problems related to the meaning and conduct of life (e.g., Baltes & Smith, 1990; Baltes & Staudinger, 1993, 2000). These problems are typically complex and ill-defined, and have multiple, yet unknown, solutions. Deciding on a particular career path, accepting the death of a loved one, dealing with personal mortality, or solving long-lasting conflicts among family members exemplify the type of problem that calls for wisdom-related expertise. In contrast, dealing with more circumscribed everyday problems requires other abilities. To solve a math problem, for example, wisdom is not particularly helpful.

Proceeding from his cultural-historical analysis of wisdom (Baltes, 2004) as well as his propositions about life span developmental theory (Baltes, 1997b), together with his colleagues, Baltes developed five criteria to describe wisdom-related products (e.g., Baltes & Smith, 1990; Baltes & Staudinger, 2000; Dittmann-Kohli & Baltes, 1990). Two criteria are considered basic in the sense that they are characteristic of all

types of expertise. These are rich factual knowledge about human nature and the life course and rich procedural knowledge about ways of dealing with fundamental life problems. The three metacriteria are thought to be unique to wisdom. These are *life span contextualism*, that is, an awareness and understanding of the many contexts of life, how they relate to each other and change over the life span; *value relativism and tolerance*, that is, an acknowledgment of individual, social, and cultural differences in values and life priorities; and *knowledge about handling uncertainty*, including the limits of one's own knowledge.

Empirical Assessment   Wisdom-related knowledge has been assessed by instructing adults of different ages to think aloud about fundamental, hypothetical but real-life problems (for detailed information about the method of thinking aloud, see Ericsson & Simon, 1984). One problem has been: "A 15-year-old girl wants to get married right away. What could one consider and do?" Participants are informed that (a) they should talk about what they think without pausing, (b) there is no right or wrong solution to the problem, (c) they can talk about specific and general aspects of the problem, and (d) they themselves should decide when they would like to finish. Participants then think aloud about a given problem without further intervention. An excerpt of a participants' response to the 15-year-old girl problem might be: "Well, on the surface, this seems like an easy problem. On average, marriage for 15-year-old girls is not a good thing. On the other hand, thinking about getting married is not the same as actually doing it. I guess many girls think about it without getting married in the end. There are situations where the average case doesn't fit. Perhaps special life circumstances are involved. The girl may have a terminal illness. Perhaps she lives in another culture . . ."

Trained raters evaluate responses such as this one by using the five criteria that were specified as defining wisdom-related knowledge. In doing so, they read the individual answer protocols and assign each protocol a score between 1 (*no correspondence*) and 7 (*high degree of correspondence*), representing the degree to which the protocol matched the ideal definition of one wisdom criterion. As Staudinger and Leipold (2003) have reported, the interrater reliabilities for the five criteria across more than 3,000 response protocols are acceptable (from $r = .73$ to $r = .93$).

Empirical Research Research in the Berlin Wisdom Project has been based on a theoretical model of the development, structure, and functions of wisdom (see figure 21.1). This model suggests a number of conditions under which wisdom is likely to develop and be maintained. As is typical for the development of any expertise, the model assumes that wisdom is acquired through an extended and intensive process of learning and practice. This process clearly requires a high degree of motivation to strive for excellence as well as supportive environmental conditions

Given that wisdom is different from other more circumscribed abilities in that it involves an integration of intellect and character, its development and refinement require a coalition of facilitative factors, namely, facilitative contexts, as determined, for example, by a person's gender, social network, or culture; expertise-specific factors such as certain life experiences, professional practice, or receiving and providing mentorship; and person-related factors such as certain intellectual capacities, personality traits, or emotional dispositions. As illustrated in figure 21.1, these three types of factors are thought to influence the development of wisdom-related knowledge because they determine the ways in which people experience the world and plan, manage, or make sense out of their lives (i.e., these factors determine the context of developmental regulation). Furthermore, all relations among the three components of the model—facilitative factors, context of developmental regulation, and wisdom-related knowledge—are meant to be bidirectional and accumulative over the life course.

Past findings were largely supportive of this theoretical model; they can be summarized as follows. First, and consistent with the idea that wisdom is an ideal, high levels of wisdom-related knowledge are rare. On a seven-point scale, with 7 representing the highest level of wisdom-related knowledge, only few study participants have received scores above 5.

Second, public figures that were nominated as being wise by a panel of journalists, independently of the Berlin definition, were among the top performers in the Berlin wisdom tasks and outperformed same-aged adults that were not nominated (Baltes, Staudinger, Maerker, & Smith, 1995). The same was true for clinical psychologists who outperformed same-aged adults with professions that do not explicitly promote the development of expertise in dealing

with fundamental life problems (Smith, Staudinger, & Baltes, 1994).

Third, the period of late adolescence and young adulthood appears to be the primary age window in which developmental gains in wisdom-related knowledge occur. In studies with adult samples, the relationship between chronological age and wisdom-related knowledge was nonsignificant (Pasupathi, Staudinger, & Baltes, 2001; Staudinger, 1999a).

Fourth, during adulthood, factors other than age predict wisdom-related knowledge. Several studies have suggested that general life experiences, professional training and practice, and certain motivational preferences such as an interest in understanding others are important contributors to wisdom-related knowledge (e.g., Staudinger, Lopez, & Baltes, 1997). The same studies have revealed that neither academic intelligence nor basic personality traits play a major role in predicting wisdom-related knowledge.

Fifth, wisdom-related knowledge plays a significant role in adults' value orientations and behavioral preferences when having conflicts with others. As reported in Kunzmann and Baltes (2003a), people with higher levels of wisdom-related knowledge report less preference for values revolving around a pleasurable and comfortable life. Instead, they report preferring self-oriented values such as personal growth and insight as well as a preference for other-oriented values related to environmental protection, societal engagement, and the well-being of friends. People with high levels of wisdom knowledge also indicate less preference for conflict management strategies that reflect either a one-sided concern with one's own interests (i.e., dominance), a one-sided concern with others' interests (i.e., submission), or no concern at all (i.e., avoidance). Rather, they prefer a cooperative approach reflecting a joint concern for their own and the opponent's interests. This evidence is consistent with the notion that wisdom is knowledge about ways of maximizing a balance between one's own and others' interests (see also Sternberg, 1998).

Sixth, the expression of wisdom-related performance can be enhanced by social and cognitive interventions. Boehmig-Krumhaar, Staudinger, and Baltes (2002) demonstrated that a memory strategy, namely, a version of the method of loci, in which participants were instructed to travel on a cloud around the world, can be used to focus people's attention on cultural relativism and

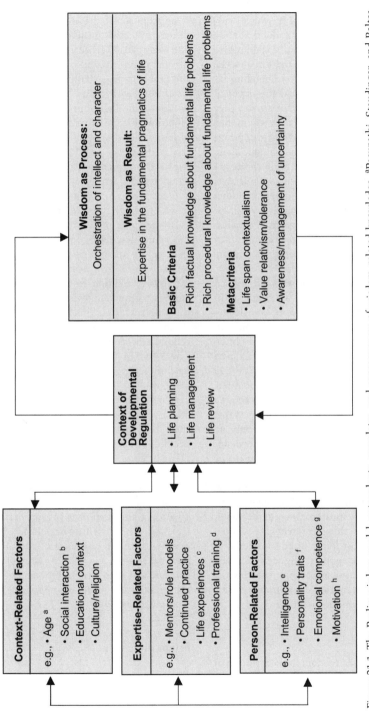

Figure 21.1 The Berlin wisdom model: antecedents, correlates, and consequences of wisdom-related knowledge. [a]Pasupathi, Staudinger, and Baltes (2000); Smith and Baltes (1990); Staudinger (1999a). [b]Staudinger and Baltes (1996). [c]Baltes, Staudinger, Maerker, and Smith (1995). [d]Smith and Baltes (1994); Staudinger and Baltes (1992). [e,f]Staudinger, Lopez, and Baltes (1996). [g,h]Kunzmann and Baltes (2003a).

tolerance. As predicted, following this intervention, participants expressed higher levels of wisdom-related knowledge, especially value relativism and tolerance. Staudinger and Baltes (1996) conducted an experiment in which study participants were asked to think aloud about a wisdom problem under several experimental conditions involving imagined and actual social interactions. Specifically, before responding individually, some participants had the opportunity to discuss the problem with a person they brought into the laboratory and with whom they usually discuss difficult life problems; others were asked to engage in an inner dialogue about the problem with a person of their choice, or simply to think about the problem on their own. Actual social dialogue and the inner-voice dialogue increased performance levels by almost one standard deviation. One important implication of these two studies is that many adults may have the capacity to perform better on wisdom tasks than they actually often do.

Seventh, in the tradition of work on implicit wisdom theories, Stange (2005) has begun to investigate the relative importance of knowledge-based and personality-based characteristics for the perception of a person as being wise. In an experimental person perception study, her participants had to evaluate an advisor's level of wisdom after they observed this advisor interacting with a young woman who talked about a serious problem. The initial findings suggest that participants' evaluations depended not only on the advisor's level of wisdom-related knowledge as expressed in his or her verbal advice to the young woman, but also on the advisor's age and nonverbal listening behavior. In fact, advisors who met all three wisdom criteria (high wisdom-related knowledge, empathic listening behavior, and older age) and thus represented a wisdom prototype were most likely to be considered as wise. This evidence supports the idea that wisdom is a multidimensional concept requiring the simultaneous consideration of experience-based, behavioral, and cognitive qualities.

Summary

Conceptualizations of wisdom in the tradition of psychometric intelligence have considered wisdom as a competence rather than a personality trait. While these models are embedded in work on intelligence, they make explicit the ways in which wisdom differs from other more limited cognitive abilities. For example, Sternberg (1998)

has emphasized that wisdom differs from practical intelligence in that it is used to maximize the attainment of a common good rather than individual interests. According to Baltes, wisdom is an example of the cognitive pragmatics but differs from other forms of pragmatic knowledge and cognitive expertise in that it refers to fundamental, that is, complex, difficult, and uncertain life problems (e.g., Baltes & Staudinger, 2000). Consistent with their theoretical definition of wisdom, the Baltes group has developed an empirical paradigm that allows the assessment of wisdom-related knowledge through a standardized performance-based procedure. As discussed above, this procedure exhibits satisfactory psychometric characteristics.

One direction for future empirical research based on the Berlin wisdom paradigm is to investigate variations of the standard assessment procedure described above. For example, tasks that require knowledge and expertise about the self and one's own development would be an interesting addition to the standard tasks focusing on general knowledge about fundamental life problems (e.g., Staudinger, 1999b).

Another potential variation concerns the procedural aspects of the Berlin wisdom interview. The standard procedure refers to an individual test setting, and interviewers do not intervene when participants think aloud about a problem at hand. One direction for future research is to use social interaction paradigms rather than individual settings when assessing people's wisdom-related knowledge. As we reviewed above, there is initial evidence that social-cognitive interventions can considerably improve a person's individual wisdom-related performance score (e.g., Staudinger & Baltes, 1996). Another option is to consider interview techniques in which interviewers pose follow-up questions to the participant. Although these methods run the risk of being less objective and standardized than the Berlin standard method, they may yield a more comprehensive picture of a person's wisdom.

Future Directions

The psychology of wisdom is a relatively young field of study, and the majority of past psychological work has been theoretical rather than empirical (e.g., Sternberg, 1990). Attention to wisdom has grown recently, however, increasing the interest in assessment methods and empirical investigations of the antecedents, correlates, and consequences of wisdom. There are at least three directions for future empirical research.

The Structure of Wisdom

Although wisdom researchers have produced many interesting substantive findings, basic research on the adequacy of the existing conceptualizations and assessment tools of wisdom is needed. One important avenue for future research is to investigate the relationships among the existing wisdom measures introduced in the literature and discussed above. It will be especially interesting to see the relations between personality-related and knowledge-based facets of this concept. Proceeding from implicit theories of wisdom and relevant cultural-historical work, we would predict a relatively low but significantly positive relationship between these two broad facets of wisdom (e.g., Baltes, 2004; Holliday & Chandler, 1986).

More generally speaking, questions about the structure of wisdom can be broken down into at least three more specific questions: (a) What is the nature of the wisdom dimensions? How can the dimensions be defined on the measurement level? (b) What is the number of wisdom dimensions? Should we conceptualize wisdom as a two-dimensional concept, as implied by the general theoretical definition of wisdom as integration of mind and virtue? (c) What are the relations among the wisdom dimensions? Is the wisdom structure hierarchical? Are all dimensions positively correlated?

Structural equation modeling (SEM) would be ideally suited to answer these and related questions (e.g., Byrne, 1998; Hoyle, 1995; Kaplan, 2000). Based on wisdom theory, past relevant empirical work, or both, this method allows testing for the hypothesized theoretical structure of the wisdom concept or the factorial structure of a particular wisdom measure. Going one step further, SEM provides tests for measurement and structural invariance across multiple groups (e.g., gender, age, or socioeconomic status) as well as over time. Two examples: It could well be that the structure of wisdom differs across cultural contexts in that certain aspects of wisdom are culture specific (e.g., they play a major role in defining wisdom in some cultures but not in others). It is also possible that the structure of wisdom becomes more differentiated with age due to the accumulation of life experience.

Although SEM effectively addresses these and related substantive issues involving the structure of wisdom, this method has rarely been used in contemporary wisdom research (for an exception, see Ardelt, 2003). Utilizing SEM would help integrate the existing wisdom models and assessment tools toward more comprehensive theoretical conceptualizations and measurement devices. Employing SEM would also advance our knowledge about the generality of contemporary wisdom models, both across subgroups of people and over time.

Convergent and Divergent Validity

A second and related avenue for future wisdom research is to continue studying the relationships between wisdom and psychological characteristics, including other human strengths (e.g., Aspinwall & Staudinger, 2003). In our view, this line of research should be based on a theoretical model of wisdom from which one can derive a priori predictions about the factors and processes that are relevant to, irrelevant to, or incompatible with the development of wisdom during ontogenesis or its expression in a given situation. We discussed such a theoretical model when reviewing work conducted in the Berlin Wisdom Project (see figure 21.1).

Again, structural equation modeling is an elegant method to test for hypotheses bearing on predictive and construct validity. Especially valuable are models that are tested in the context of multitrait-multimethod (MTMM) designs by which multiple traits are measured by multiple methods (e.g., Kenny & Kashy, 1992; Marsh & Grayson, 1995). Following the seminal work by Campbell and Fiske (1959), MTMM designs typically address the following issues: (a) convergent validity, that is, the extent to which different assessment methods concur in their measurement of different concepts; (b) discriminant validity, that is, the extent to which independent assessment methods diverge in their measurement of different traits; and (c) method effects, that is, the bias that results from using the same method in the assessment of different traits (Byrne, 1998).

Analyses of Individual Differences and Intraindividual Change

Although life span psychologists and researchers interested in aging were among the first to study wisdom from a psychological point of view (e.g.,

Baltes, Dittmann-Kohli, & Dixon, 1984; Baltes & Smith, 1990; Clayton & Birren, 1980), data used to evaluate theoretical hypotheses about age-related changes in wisdom typically refer to variability between individuals rather than within individuals over time. Put differently, the majority of past empirical work has been based on cross-sectional designs rather than on longitudinal analyses (for a notable exception, see Wink & Helson, 1997). The benefits and costs of these two data-analytic schemes are fairly well understood (e.g., Baltes, Reese, & Nesselroade, 1988). For example, cross-sectional age differences are confounded with stable differences among birth cohorts. Evaluating how and why people acquire wisdom as they grow older clearly requires longitudinal designs. It is only on the basis of longitudinal data that we can describe and explain intraindividual changes in wisdom as well as interindividual differences in the onset, amount, and direction of changes (e.g., Collins & Horn, 1991; Hertzog & Nesselroade, 2003).

Investigating short-term variability in wisdom is another avenue for future research. As reviewed above, laboratory work has suggested that wisdom-related performance can be optimized by relatively simple intervention strategies (e.g., by providing the opportunity to exchange ideas about a life problem with another person). Experience-sampling methods would provide a better understanding of the conditions that facilitate or hinder the expression of wisdom in everyday situations. It would also be interesting to know whether people who differ in their typical level of wisdom differ in the degree to which they show short-term situation-to-situation variability in their behaviors and emotions. Given that wisdom is said to involve balance and moderation, it is reasonable to assume that wiser people will exhibit a more balanced emotional life and behave more consistently when interacting with others than people with lower wisdom scores do. A number of statistical methods such as P-technique factor analyses have been developed and extended during the last two decades that help address these and related questions (e.g., Nesselroade, 1990, 2001).

We hope that we were able to convince the reader that wisdom is a concept that deserves a central place in contemporary psychological research and especially in the field of positive psychology. In our view, it is worth the effort to face the theoretical and empirical challenges involved in developing a psychology of wisdom. Certainly,

there are a number of human capacities that people can bring to bear when dealing with life's challenges and problems, including practical, emotional, or interpersonal abilities (e.g., Gardner, 1999; Salovey, Mayer, & Caruso, 2002; Sternberg, 1999). For example, creativity can help a person in dealing with a problem that requires a particular invention or social intelligence can help in a conflict with others, but how can a person coordinate his or her behavior to find solutions that are acceptable from a broader viewpoint extending over time and space? It is here that wisdom-related knowledge comes into play. Because of its holistic and integrative nature, wisdom can be seen as the most general framework that directs and optimizes individual development. For example, the presence of wisdom-related knowledge can issue warnings when we apply our emotional intelligence to harm others rather than to support them, when we do not use our intellectual capacities to develop ourselves, or when we focus too much on the present and do not consider past and future conditions. These and similar considerations should be addressed more systematically in future research on both theoretical and empirical levels.

Summary and Conclusion

In this chapter, we reviewed three ways of conceptualizing and assessing wisdom. The first related wisdom to the individual's personality; the second conceptualized wisdom as relativistic and dialectical thinking; and the third defined wisdom as a highly valued form of pragmatic intelligence. In our assessment, these wisdom models are generally in agreement with implicit theories about wise persons as well as with cultural-historical work on wisdom. Although of different origins, they share at least three ideas about the nature of wisdom: Namely, wisdom is integrative and holistic, it represents outstanding performance, and it has many desirable consequences on the levels of individuals and groups. Despite these areas of common ground, it is important to be aware of the differences among the three approaches. The magnitude and nature of these differences imply that contemporary psychological wisdom models and their operationalizations cannot be used interchangeably. The decision to use one or the other should be made in reference to specific research interests.

If one is interested in wisdom as a personality characteristic, it may be most fruitful to employ a self-report questionnaire developed to measure wisdom-related personality traits (e.g., Ardelt, 2003; Helson & Srivastava, 2002). Given the problems with standardized self-report measures, however, it seems advantageous to also base one's research on more objective and performance-based ways of assessing wisdom. Wink and Helson (1997) provided first evidence for the usefulness of employing open-ended measures that require participants to describe self-relevant traits and attitudes, which can then be rated according to several wisdom scales. Similar measures have been developed in the tradition of research on postformal cognitive adult development (e.g., Kramer & Woodruff, 1986). Tasks that have been used in the context of the Berlin wisdom model differ from those tasks in that they do not exclusively refer to the self but explicitly assess a person's general knowledge about fundamental problems regarding the meaning and conduct of life (Baltes & Staudinger, 2000). The five criteria that were developed to evaluate a person's response to those complex problems may allow the most comprehensive assessment of a person's wisdom to date.

References

Achenbaum, W. A., & Orwoll, L. (1991). Becoming wise: A psycho-gerontological interpretation of the Book of Job. *International Journal of Aging and Human Development, 32,* 21–39.

Ardelt, M. (2003). Empirical assessment of a three-dimensional wisdom scale. *Research on Aging, 25,* 275–324.

Aspinwall, L. G., & Staudinger, U. M. (Eds.). (2003). *A psychology of human strengths: Fundamental questions and future directions for a positive psychology.* Washington, DC: American Psychological Association.

Assmann, A. (1994). Wholesome knowledge: Concepts of wisdom in a historical and cross-cultural perspective. In D. L. Featherman, R. M. Lerner, & M. Perlmutter (Eds.), *Life-span development and behavior* (Vol. 12, pp. 187–224). Hillsdale, NJ: Erlbaum.

Baltes, P. B. (1993). The aging mind: Potential and limits. *Gerontologist, 33,* 580–594.

Baltes, P. B. (1997a). Wolfgang Edelstein: Über ein Wissenschaftlerleben in konstruktivistischer Melancholie [Wolfgang Edelstein: A scientific life in constructivistic melancholy]. *Reden zur Emeritierung von Wolfgang Edelstein.* Berlin, Germany: Max Planck Institute for Human Development.

Baltes, P. B. (1997b). On the incomplete architecture of human ontogeny: Selection, optimization, and compensation as foundation of developmental theory. *American Psychologist, 52,* 366–380.

Baltes, P. B. (2004). *Wisdom as orchestration of mind and virtue.* Manuscript in preparation. http://www.mpib-berlin.mpg.de/dok/full/baltes/orchestr/index.htm

Baltes, P. B., Dittmann-Kohli, F., & Dixon, R. A. (1984). New perspectives on the development of intelligence in adulthood: Toward a dual-process conception and a model of selective optimization with compensation. In P. B. Baltes & O. G. Brim Jr. (Eds.), *Life-span development and behavior* (Vol. 6, pp. 33–76). New York: Academic Press.

Baltes, P. B., Glück, J., & Kunzmann, U. (2002). Wisdom: Its structure and function in successful lifespan development. In C. R. Snyder & S. J. Lopez (Eds.), *Handbook of positive psychology* (pp. 327–350). New York: Oxford University Press.

Baltes, P. B., & Kunzmann, U. (2003). Wisdom: The peak of human excellence in the orchestration of mind and virtue. *Psychologist, 16,* 131–133.

Baltes, P. B., Reese, H. W., & Nesselroade, J. R. (1988). *Life-span developmental psychology: Introduction to research methods.* Hillsdale, NJ: Erlbaum.

Baltes, P. B., & Smith, J. (1990). The psychology of wisdom and its ontogenesis. In R. J. Sternberg (Ed.), *Wisdom: Its nature, origins, and development* (pp. 87–120). New York: Cambridge University Press.

Baltes, P. B., & Staudinger, U. M. (1993). The search for a psychology of wisdom. *Current Directions in Psychological Science, 2,* 75–80.

Baltes, P. B., & Staudinger, U. M. (2000). Wisdom: A metaheuristic (pragmatic) to orchestrate mind and virtue toward excellence. *American Psychologist, 55,* 122–136.

Baltes, P. B, Staudinger, U. M., & Lindenberger, U. (1999). Lifespan psychology: Theory and application to intellectual functioning. *Annual Review of Psychology, 50,* 471–507.

Baltes, P. B., Staudinger, U. M., Maerker, A., & Smith, J. (1995). People nominated as wise: A comparative study of wisdom-related knowledge. *Psychology and Aging, 10,* 155–166.

Birren, J. E., & Fisher, L. M. (1990). The elements of wisdom: Overview and integration. In R. J. Sternberg (Ed.), *Wisdom: Its nature, origins, and development* (pp. 317–323). New York: Cambridge University Press.

Boehmig-Krumhaar, S. A., Staudinger, U. M., & Baltes, P. B. (2002). Mehr Toleranz tut Not: läßt sich wert-relativierendes Wissen und Urteilen mit Hilfe einer wissensaktivierenden Gedächtnisstrategie verbessern? *Zeitschrift für Entwicklungspsychologie und Pädagogische Psychologie, 34,* 30–43.

Byrne, B. M. (1998). *Structural equation modeling with LISREL, PRELIS, and SIMPLIS: Basic concepts, applications, and programming.* Mahwah, NJ: Erlbaum.

Campbell, D. T., & Fiske, D. W. (1959). Convergent and discriminant validation by the multitrait-multimethod matrix. *Psychological Bulletin, 56,* 81–105.

Cattell, R. (1971). *Abilities: Their structure, growth, and action.* New York: Houghton-Mifflin.

Clayton, V. P., & Birren, J. E. (1980). The development of wisdom across the life span: A reexamination of an ancient topic. In P. B. Baltes & O. G. Brim, Jr. (Eds.), *Life-span development and behavior* (Vol. 3, pp. 103–135). New York: Academic Press.

Collins, L. M., & Horn, J. L. (1991). *Best methods for the analysis of change.* Washington, DC: American Psychological Association.

Dittmann-Kohli, F., & Baltes, P. B. (1990). Toward a neofunctionalist conception of adult intellectual development: Wisdom as a prototypical case of intellectual growth. In: *Higher stages of human development* (pp. 54–78). New York: Oxford University Press.

Dixon, R. A., & Baltes, P. B. (1986). Toward life-span research on the functions and pragmatics of intelligence. In R. J. Sternberg & R. K. Wagner (Eds.), *Practical intelligence: Nature and origins of competence in the everyday world* (pp. 203–235). Cambridge, UK: Cambridge University Press.

Ericsson, K. A., & Simon, H. A. (1984). *Protocol analysis: Verbal reports as data.* Cambridge, MA: MIT Press.

Erikson, E. H. (1959). *Identity and the life cycle.* New York: International University Press.

Gardner, H. (1999). *Intelligence reframed: Multiple intelligences for the 21st century.* New York: Basic Books.

Gough, H. G. (1987). *California Psychological Inventory administrator's guide.* Palo Alto, CA: Consulting Psychologists Press.

Gough, H. G., & Heilbrun, A. B. (1983). *The Adjective Check List manual.* Palo Alto, CA: Consulting Psychologists Press.

Hall, G. S. (1922). *Senescence: The last half of life.* New York: Appleton.

Helson, R., & Srivastava, S. (2002). Creative and wise people: Similarities, differences, and how they develop. *Personality and Social Psychology Bulletin, 28,* 1430–1440.

Hertzog, C., & Nesselroade, J. R. (2003). Assessing psychological change in adulthood: An overview of methodological issues. *Psychology and Aging, 18,* 639–657.

Holliday, S. G., & Chandler, M. J. (1986). Wisdom: Explorations in adult competence. In J. A. Meacham (Ed.), *Contributions to human development* (Vol. 17, pp. 1–96). Basel, Switzerland: Karger.

Horn, J. L., & Hofer, S. M. (1992). Major abilities and development in the adult period. In R. J. Sternberg & C. A. Berg (Eds.), *Intellectual development* (pp. 44–49). Cambridge, UK: Cambridge University Press.

Hoyle, R. H. (Ed.). (1995). *Structural equation modeling: Concepts, issues, and applications.* Thousand Oaks, CA: Sage.

Kaplan, D. (2000). *Structural equation modeling: Foundations and extensions.* Thousand Oaks, CA: Sage.

Kekes, J. (1996). *Moral wisdom and good lives.* Ithaca, NY: Cornell University Press.

Kenny, D. A., & Kashy, D. A. (1992). Analysis of multitrait-multimethod matrix by confirmatory factor analysis. *Psychological Bulletin, 112,* 165–172.

Kitchener, K. S., & Brenner, H. G. (1990). Wisdom and reflective judgment: Knowing in the face of uncertainty. In R. J. Sternberg (Ed.), *Wisdom: Its nature, origins, and development* (pp. 212–229). New York: Cambridge University Press.

Kramer, D. A. (1983). Post-formal operations? A need for further conceptualization. *Human Development, 26,* 91–105.

Kramer, D. A. (1990). Conceptualizing wisdom: the primacy of affect-cognition relations. In R. J. Sternberg (Ed.), *Wisdom: Its nature, origins, and development* (pp. 279–313). New York: Cambridge University Press.

Kramer, D. A. (2000). Wisdom as a classical source of human strength: Conceptualizing and empirical inquiry. *Journal of Social and Clinical Psychology, 19,* 83–101.

Kramer, D. A., & Woodruff, D. S. (1986). Relativistic and dialectical thought in three adult age groups. *Human Development, 29,* 280–290.

Kunzmann, U., & Baltes, P. B. (2003a). Wisdom-related knowledge: Affective, motivational, and interpersonal correlates. *Personality and Social Psychology Bulletin, 29,* 1104–1119.

Kunzmann, U., & Baltes, P. B. (2003b). Beyond the traditional scope of intelligence: Wisdom in action. In R. J. Sternberg, J. Lautry, & T. I. Lubart (Eds.), *Models of intelligence for the next millennium* (pp. 329–343). Washington, DC: American Psychological Association.

Kunzmann, U., & Baltes, P. B. (2005). The psychology of wisdom: Theoretical and empirical challenges. In R. J. Sternberg & J. Jordan (Eds.), *A handbook of wisdom: Psychological perspectives* (pp. 110–135). New York, NY: Cambridge University Press.

Labouvie-Vief, G. (1990). Wisdom as integrated thought: Historical and developmental perspectives. In R. J. Sternberg (Ed.), *Wisdom: Its nature, origins, and development* (pp. 52–83). Cambridge, MA: Cambridge University Press.

Labouvie-Vief, G. (1998). Cognitive-emotional integration in adulthood. *Annual Review of Gerontology and Geriatrics, 17,* 206–237.

Labouvie-Vief, G., Chiodo, L. M., Goguen, L. A., Diehl, M., & Orwoll, L. (1995). Representations of self across the life span. *Psychology and Aging, 10,* 404–415.

Labouvie-Vief, G., DeVoe, M., & Bulka, D. (1989). Speaking about feelings: Conceptions of emotion across the life span. *Psychology and Aging, 4,* 425–437.

Loevinger, J. (1976). *Ego development: Conception and theory.* San Francisco, CA: Jossey-Bass.

Marsh, H. W., & Grayson, D. (1995). Latent variable models of multi-trait-multimethod data. In R. H. Hoyle (Ed.), *Structural equation modeling: Concepts, issues, and applications* (pp. 177–198). Thousand Oaks, CA: Sage.

McAdams, D. P., & de St. Aubin, E. (1992). A theory of generativity and its assessment through self-report, behavioral acts, and narrative themes in autobiography. *Journal of Personality and Social Psychology, 62,* 1003–1015.

Meacham, J. A. (1990). The loss of wisdom. In R. J. Sternberg (Ed.), *Wisdom: Its nature, origins, and development* (pp. 181–211). Cambridge, MA: Cambridge University Press.

Myers, I. B., & McCaully, M. H. (1985). *Myers-Briggs Type Indicator manual.* Palo Alto, CA: Consulting Psychologists Press.

Nesselroade, J. R. (1990). Adult personality development: Issues in assessing constancy and change. In A. I. Rabin & R. A. Zucker (Eds.), *Studying persons and lives* (pp. 41–85). New York: Springer.

Nesselroade, J. R. (2001). Intraindividual variability in development within and between individuals. *European Psychologist, 6,* 187–193.

Orwoll, L., & Achenbaum, W. L. (1993). Gender and the development of wisdom. *Human Development, 36,* 274–296.

Orwoll, L., & Perlmutter, M. (1990). The study of wise persons: Integrating a personality perspective. In R. J. Sternberg (Ed.), *Wisdom: Its nature, origins, and development* (pp. 160–177). Cambridge, MA: Cambridge University Press.F

Pasupathi, M., Staudinger, U. M., & Baltes, P. B. (2001). Seeds of wisdom: Adolescents' knowledge and judgment about difficult life problems. *Developmental Psychology, 37,* 351–361.

Riegel, K. F. (1973). Dialectic operations: The final period of cognitive development. *Human Development, 16,* 346–370.

Ryff, C. D., & Heincke, S. G. (1983). Subjective organization of personality in adulthood and aging. *Journal of Personality and Social Psychology, 44,* 807–816.

Salovey, P., Mayer, J. D., & Caruso, D. (2002). The positive psychology of emotional intelligence. In C. R. Snyder & S. J. Lopez (Eds.), *Handbook of positive psychology* (pp. 159–171). New York: Oxford University Press.

Schwarz, N. (1999). Self-reports: How the questions shape the answers. *American Psychologist, 54,* 93–105.

Seligman, M. E. P., & Csikszentmihalyi, M. (2000). Positive psychology: An introduction. *American Psychologist, 55,* 5–14.

Smith, J., & Baltes, P. B. (1990). Wisdom-related knowledge: Age/cohort differences in response to life-planning problems. *Developmental Psychology, 26,* 494–505.

Smith, J., Staudinger, U. M., & Baltes, P. B. (1994). Occupational settings facilitating wisdom-related knowledge: The sample case of clinical psychologists. *Journal of Consulting and Clinical Psychology, 62,* 989–999.

Stange, A. (2005). *The social dimension of wisdom: Conditions for perceiving advice-giving persons as wise.* Unpublished doctoral dissertation, Free University of Berlin, Berlin.

Staudinger, U. M. (1999a). Older and wiser? Integrating results on the relationship between age and wisdom-related performance. *International Journal of Behavioral Development, 23,* 641–664.

Staudinger, U. M. (1999b). Social cognition and a psychological approach to an art of life. In T. M. Hess & F. Blanchard-Fields (Eds.), *Social cognition and aging* (pp. 343–375). San Diego, CA: Academic Press.

Staudinger, U. M., & Baltes, P. B. (1996). Interactive minds: A facilitative setting for wisdom-related performance? *Journal of Personality and Social Psychology, 71,* 746–762.

Staudinger, U. M., & Leipold, B. (2003). The assessment of wisdom-related performance. In S. J. Lopez & C. R. Snyder (Eds.), *Positive psychological assessment: A handbook of models and measures* (pp. 171–184). Washington, DC: American Psychological Association.

Staudinger, U. M., Lopez, D. F., & Baltes, P. B. (1997). The psychometric location of wisdom-related performance: Intelligence, personality, and more? *Personality and Social Psychology Bulletin, 23*, 1200–1214.

Sternberg, R. J. (1985). Implicit theories of intelligence, creativity, and wisdom. *Journal of Personality and Social Psychology, 49*, 607–627.

Sternberg, R. J. (Ed.). (1990). *Wisdom: Its nature, origins, and development.* New York: Cambridge University Press.

Sternberg, R. J. (1998). A balance theory of wisdom. *Review of General Psychology, 2*, 347–365.

Sternberg, R. J. (1999). The theory of successful intelligence. *Review of General Psychology, 3*, 292–316.

Wink, P., & Helson, R. (1997). Practical and transcendent wisdom: Their nature and some longitudinal findings. *Journal of Adult Development, 4*, 1–15.

22

Hardiness as a Dispositional Resource

Methods of Conceptualizing the Construct

K. A Wallace and C. S. Bergeman

Broadly defined, positive psychology encompasses the scientific examination of human strengths and virtues (Sheldon & King, 2001) at either a subjective, individual, or institutional level (Seligman & Csikszentmihalyi, 2000). Particularly relevant to the present chapter, the individual level concerns positive individual traits (i.e., positive personality traits), including, for example, forgiveness, spirituality, wisdom, and hardiness. In conjunction with researchers' growing interest in the area of positive psychology and human strengths (Aspinwall & Staudinger, 2003a), there has been an increase in substantive work on various positive personality traits such as these (e.g., Baltes, Glueck, Kunzmann, 2002; Lightsey, 1996; McCullough, Pargament, & Thoresen, 2001; Pargament & Mahoney, 2002). Despite recent growth in the field of positive psychology (e.g., Keyes & Haidt, 2003), however, considerable research is needed concerning the conceptualization and measurement of positive psychological traits.

Clearly the constructs of interest in positive psychology (i.e., strengths and virtues) are complex and multidimensional. Also complex are the interconnections that exist between strengths, resources, and healthy processes. According to Lopez and Snyder (2003), strengths are an integral part of healthy psychological growth, and thus healthy processes and life fulfillments may not develop or be attained without human strengths. Our ability to elucidate the nature of the interconnections between strengths, resources, and healthy processes depends, in part, on our ability to conceptualize, operationalize, and measure the psychological variables of interest. As a result of the importance of advancing our understanding of positive psychological constructs at this level, the purpose of the present chapter is to explore several methods for conceptualizing one such complex positive individual trait, the dispositional resilience resource referred to as hardiness.

More specifically, this chapter examines three alternative conceptualizations of hardiness, including the latent variable, synergistic, and person-focused approaches. These strategies provide a rich and complex picture of the nature of the construct as a result of integrating both a variable and person perspective. According to Magnusson (1999), the focus of a variable approach is on the variable, specifically the relationships among variables and outcomes, whereas the focus of a person approach is more holistic, with emphasis being placed on the person in context, as a wholly integrated totality. Directly relevant to the present chapter are two frequently used statistical techniques that underlie the variable approach, including regression analysis (i.e., for the synergistic conceptualization of hardiness) and structural equation modeling (i.e., for the latent variable conceptualization of hardiness). With regard to the person approach found in the present chapter, a cluster analytic strategy is employed. Ultimately, these approaches complement one another and both are necessary to fully understand not only the possible operating factors but also the functioning of the individual in context (Magnusson, 1996).

The application of the combined person- and variable-focused approaches provides an important way of thinking about hardiness as a multidimensional construct and thus helps to address current gaps in the hardiness literature. In particular, the majority of research in the hardiness literature is dominated by a variable approach, with most researchers looking at the nature of the relation between hardiness and various other constructs, as well as group mean differences in specified outcomes as a function of hardiness. Within the hardiness literature, consideration of the person in context has been minimal; the patterning of operating factors is not well understood; and certainly there has been little integration of a variable and person approach. Not only does this integrative approach emphasize the importance of a multidimensional conceptualization of hardiness, but it helps to illuminate important future research questions and advance our theoretical understanding of this positive personality trait. For example, the coupling of a person approach with a variable approach emphasizes the need to examine not only the interrelations among hardiness and other variables of interest, but also the patternings inherent within an individual's hierarchical system, how such patternings may change over time, and ultimately the underlying mechanisms involved (e.g., Magnusson, 1999). Although the examination of each of these issues is beyond the scope of the present chapter, the combined person- and variable-focused perspectives emphasize the multidimensional nature of the construct and provide a new way of thinking about the dispositional resilience resource of hardiness.

Resilience and the Hardiness Construct

Resilience is a term that has typically been used in developmental psychopathology in research on children and adolescents who are able to overcome serious psychological and environmental challenges (e.g., Farber & Egeland, 1987; Werner & Smith, 1992). The term has been defined in a number of different ways; for example, Rutter (1987) defined resilience as the positive end of the distribution of developmental outcomes among individuals at high risk. Resilience has also been viewed in terms of three different phenomena, including the attainment of a good outcome in spite of serious threat to adaptation or development (Masten, 2001), sustained competence under stress, or recovery from trauma (Masten, Best, & Garmezy, 1990). Seminal work in this field was conducted by Rutter (e.g., Rutter, 1987), who examined the children of parents diagnosed as mentally ill; Garmezy (e.g., Garmezy, Masten, & Tellegen, 1984), who investigated children from low socioeconomic backgrounds and negative family environments; and Werner (e.g., Werner, 1995; Werner & Smith, 1977), who studied a group of children, a number of whom were deemed at risk, over many years. In addition to its contribution to a focus on positive functioning, the literature on resilience has made several significant contributions, one of which is identifying a broad range of background conditions, personal characteristics, social relations, and community resources essential to our understanding of positive adaptation (Windle, 1999).

Resilience is conceptualized as a function of an individual's available protective factors. Although there is some inconsistency in the literature with regard to the use of this term (e.g., Luthar, 1993; Luthar & Cushing, 1999), protective factors have been defined in terms of direct effects, that is, in terms of biological and psychosocial factors that contribute to positive developmental outcomes (Werner, 1990). A more specific definition of the term refers to protective factors as those effects involving interactions (Garmezy et al., 1984). Here, the impact of stress (or other identified risk factor) on the outcome of interest is different depending on the level (or presence/absence) of a protective attribute. Regardless of the specific conceptualization concerning how they operate, protective factors have typically been discussed in the developmental psychopathology literature in terms of three broad categories, including dispositional attributes (e.g., hardiness), family cohesion and warmth, and the availability of external resources and supports (Garmezy, 1985). For the purposes of the present chapter, the dispositional resilience resource of hardiness will be used to illustrate several methods of conceptualizing a complex personality trait. In addition, this discussion may also begin to address current gaps in the hardiness literature (e.g., Funk, 1992; Funk & Houston, 1987; Ouellette, 1993).

Hardiness research emerged from an existential theory of personality (Kobasa & Maddi, 1977), which suggests that a person's general orientation toward life influences how stressful a given life event is perceived to be, how one deals with that stress, and consequently, the event's impact on the organism (Kobasa, 1982). As a constellation of personality traits that is hypothesized to foster stress resistance (Kobasa, 1979), hardiness comprises three components: commitment, control, and challenge. *Committed* individuals believe in the truth, importance, and value of themselves and their activities (Kobasa, 1982; Kobasa, Maddi, & Kahn, 1982) and they develop a relationship with the self and with the environment that involves both activeness and approach instead of passivity and avoidance (Kobasa et al., 1982). Individuals who display the second dimension, *control*, believe that they are efficacious in bringing about outcomes of interest, which allows them to perceive stressful life events as consequences of their own actions (Kobasa, 1982). Individuals who display the third dimension, *challenge*, believe that change is a normal part of life and necessary for growth (Kobasa et al., 1982). As such, these individuals are typically open to new experiences, cognitively flexible, and tolerant of ambiguity (Kobasa, 1982; Kobasa et al., 1982).

Despite a plethora of research on the linkages between hardiness and positive physical and psychological outcomes, including work on cognitive hardiness and coping style (Beasley, Thompson, & Davidson, 2003); hardy coping, social interaction, and self-care skills (Maddi, 2002); the moderating effects of hardiness following the experience of trauma (Waysman, Schwarzwald, & Solomon, 2001); the importance of individual and family hardiness for caregivers (Clark, 2002); the relations between hardiness, coping, stress, and illness (Soderstrom, Dolbier, Leiferman, & Steinhardt, 2000); the patterns of socioemotional functioning associated with physical hardiness (Magai, Consedine, King, & Gillespie, 2003); and hardiness as an expression of mental health (Maddi et al., 2002), the con-

ceptualization of the hardiness construct is still being questioned. That is, there is debate over whether hardiness should be conceptualized as three distinct components or as a single, unitary construct. Although both approaches have been taken, several investigators advocate the use of separate subscales because of differential predictive power across measures. In particular, some researchers argue that the three subscales are not equally effective in predicting health (Hull, Van Treuren, & Virnelli, 1987). Similarly, although commitment and challenge correlate with social support, control does not (Ganellen & Blaney, 1984). As a result, it has been suggested that hardiness is not a unitary concept and therefore its component parts should not be combined to form a composite (Hull et al., 1987). It appears, however, that the use of the composite is often the method of choice for researchers. The present chapter explores three alternative conceptualizations of this positive personality trait, including latent variable, synergistic, and person-focused approaches. A short discussion of the utility of each of these approaches, an empirical example of each, and an integrative discussion of the contributions of the approaches are presented. First, however, a brief look at the study that generated the data used in the empirical illustrations is provided.

Notre Dame Study of Optimal Aging

Data for the empirical examples included in this chapter were drawn from the Notre Dame Study of Optimal Aging, which examined the multidimensional nature of adaptation in later life. Of the various constructs assessed in this study, hardiness, depression, and life satisfaction are relevant to the analyses examined here. These attributes were assessed as part of a battery of measures collected in a mail-out survey. Participants were recruited through random calls made to every tenth household in the local phone book and from a listing of elderly individuals obtained from the local Area Agency on Aging. Individuals were residing in the northern Indiana area and ranged in age from 61 to 93 ($N = 243$, $\bar{X} = 76.62$, $SD = 6.91$). Although the sample was representative of the demographics of both an older sample and of individuals residing in the surrounding geographical area (*Indiana Fact Book*, 1992), there was a slight underrepresentation of minorities. In particular, 23% of the sample was male, 77% was female;

95.6% of the sample was White, 4% was African American, and .4% was other. In addition, 28.6% of the sample was married, 54.3% widowed, 11.0% divorced, 5.3% single, and .8% separated. Finally, 62.9% of the participants had a yearly income that was less than $15,000, 14.7% had an income that was between $15,000 and $25,000, and 22.4% had an income that was $25,000 or more.

The hardiness measure used was a modified version of the Dispositional Resilience Scale (DRS; Bartone, Ursano, Wright, & Ingraham, 1989). This measure is composed of 45 items, with 15 commitment, 15 challenge, and 15 control items. A 4-point Likert scale, ranging from 1 (*not at all true*) to 4 (*completely true*) was used to rate agreement with control, challenge, and commitment statements; a high score indicates a lack of hardiness. Items were reversed as necessary and several items were changed in order to make them more applicable to an older population (e.g., items pertaining to work were changed to include hobbies or other leisure activities). Reliability for the present study was consistent with previous research, with Cronbach's alpha equal to .72, .68, .59, and .87 for the commitment, control, and challenge subscales, and for the overall hardiness measure, respectively.

The Center for Epidemiologic Studies–Depression Scale (CES-D) was used to measure depression and emotional distress (Radloff, 1977). This scale consists of 20 items; each item presents a depressive symptom for which participants rate frequency of occurrence during the past week. Responses are made on a 4-point Likert scale and range from *rarely or none of the time* to *all or most of the time*. High scores on the scale indicate an increased amount of distress (i.e., high negative affect, low positive affect). Factor analysis indicated that two factors accounted for 46% of the variance. The two factors that emerged included negative and positive affect, which accounted for 34% and 12% of the variance, respectively. Cronbach's alpha was .90 for the full scale and .92 and .71 for negative and positive affect, respectively. These results, which suggest the presence of both a positive and a negative factor, are consistent with research that examines the two-factor affect structure (Lawton, Kleban, & Dean, 1993), and its salience in the aging process (Lawton, Kleban, Rajagopal, & Parmelee, 1992). Life satisfaction, in turn, was assessed with the Life Satisfaction Index—Form Z (Wood, Wylie, & Sheafor, 1969), which is a modified version of the Life Satisfaction Index—A (Neugarten, Havighurst, & Tobin, 1961). This scale consists of 13 items and has frequently been used with older adults. Respondents used a 5-point Likert scale that ranged from *strongly agree* to *strongly disagree*. The measure was scored in the same direction as the CES-D, with higher scores reflecting lower life satisfaction. Factor analysis revealed a principal component that accounted for 33% of the variance, and Cronbach's alpha was .84. See table 22.1 for descriptive statistics for the depression and life satisfaction measures.

Latent Variable Conceptualization of Hardiness

As mentioned previously, hardiness has typically been viewed from a composite perspective, in which the subscales are standardized and summed. Simply summing dimensions to create and test a composite construct, however, may not be the best approach because of possible explanatory confounds and the subsequent inability to assess the association between the composite measure and its component parts (Carver, 1989). Without testing the component parts, one cannot be certain how the composite measure is related to the outcome of interest. According to the latent variable perspective, in contrast, the three components of hardiness, commitment, challenge, and control, are imperfect representations from which the underlying construct emerges (Carver, 1989). With this conceptualization, the relative importance of each subcomponent of hardiness as it relates to the outcome variable of interest can be examined.

TABLE 22.1 Means and Standard Deviations by Gender and Correlations With Age for Positive Affect, Negative Affect, and Life Satisfaction

Measure	Males		Females		
	$\overline{X}$	SD	$\overline{X}$	SD	r_{age}[a]
CES-D					
Posaff	8.15	3.59	8.03	3.16	.09
Negaff	22.42	7.46	24.58	8.80	.06
LSI-Z	27.15	5.04	29.72[b]	5.30	−.04

Note: CES-D = Center for Epidemiologic Studies–Depression Scale; Posaff = positive affect; Negaff = Negative affect; LSI-Z = Life Satisfaction Index–Form Z.
[a]Sample sizes range from 155–221. [b]$t(216) = -3.11, p < .01$.

As an illustration of this method of conceptualizing the hardiness construct, model-fitting analyses were conducted to examine the structural relation between hardiness and well-being, as well as the relative contribution of each component of hardiness to the overall fit of the model. Table 22.2 includes the correlations for life satisfaction, positive affect, negative affect, commitment, control, and challenge.[1] As depicted in figure 22.1, the three subscales, commitment, control, and challenge, loaded onto the latent variable of hardiness, which was then used to predict the latent variable of well-being, which included measures of life satisfaction, positive affect, and negative affect. LISREL 8 (Jöreskog & Sörbom, 1993) was used to estimate the maximum likelihood estimates, standard errors, and goodness-of-fit indices. The full model yielded an acceptable fit, $\chi^2_{(8)} = 4.41$, $p = .82$.[2] The parameter estimates for the variables loading onto hardiness and for the variables loading onto well-being (i.e., the estimates of λ_X and of λ_Y), as well as the gamma estimate, were significant (see table 22.3), indicating that

TABLE 22.2 Intercorrelations Between Life Satisfaction, Positive Affect, Negative Affect, Commitment, Control, and Challenge

	1	2	3	4	5	6
1. Life satisfaction	—					
2. Positive affect	.28*	—				
3. Negative affect	.63**	.23*	—			
4. Commitment	.57**	.29*	.45**	—		
5. Control	.63**	.23*	.48**	.63**	—	
6. Challenge	.54**	.16	.46**	.49**	.63**	—

Note: $N = 129$.
*$p < .01$; **$p < .001$.

parameter estimates for these paths were significantly different from zero. In particular, the unstandardized loadings onto the hardiness construct were .73, .85, and .72 for commitment, control, and challenge, respectively. The unstandardized loadings onto well-being were 1.26, .45, and 1.00 (this path was set equal to 1 in order

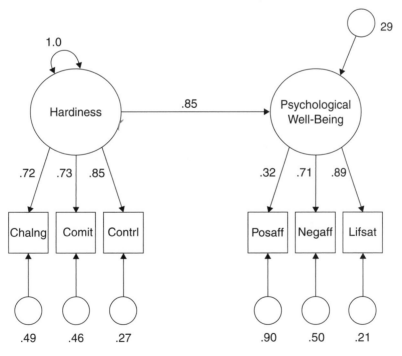

Figure 22.1 Proposed theoretical model illustrating the relationship between the latent variable of hardiness, which comprises challenge (Chalng), commitment (Comit), and control (Contrl), and well-being, which comprises positive affect (Posaff), negative affect (Negaff), and life satisfaction (Lifsat). Note that the parameter estimates are standardized; unstandardized estimates can be found in table 22.3. The chi-square for this model was, $\chi^2_{(8)} = 4.41$, $p = .82$.

TABLE 22.3 Factor Loadings and Uniqueness for Structural Model of the Effect of the Hardiness Subscales on Well-Being

Measure	Unstandardized Factor Loading	SE	Uniqueness
Commitment	.73	.08	.46
Control	.85	.08	.27
Challenge	.72	.08	.49
Life satisfaction	1.26	.16	.21
Positive affect	.45	.13	.90
Negative affect	1.00	—	.50

Note: Dash indicates the standard error was not estimated because the path was set equal to 1.00; standardized estimates are included in figure 22.1.

to estimate the model), for life satisfaction, positive affect, and negative affect, respectively. The parameter estimate for the path between hardiness and well-being was .85.

Because of the sensitivity of the chi-square statistic to sample size, additional indices were included (see Loehlin, 1992, for a discussion of these indices). The GFI, which assesses the overall degree of fit (and is not adjusted for degrees of freedom), and which should be .9 or higher, was acceptable (.99). The adjusted goodness-of-fit index (AGFI), which takes into account the degrees of freedom, and which should be .8 or higher, was acceptable (.97). The root mean square residual (RMR), which represents an average of the absolute discrepancies between the expected and the observed matrices, and which should be .05 or less, was acceptable (.02). Finally, the normed fit index (NFI), which assesses the relative comparison of the proposed to the null model, and which should be .9 or higher, was also acceptable (.99).

In addition to the test of the full model, the fit of a series of nested models was examined (see table 22.4 for goodness-of-fit indices for the

nested models). In particular, the extent to which each component of hardiness contributed to the overall fit of the model was of interest. Thus, three additional models were tested: Model 2, in which the lambda loading of commitment was set equal to 0; Model 3, in which the lambda loading of control was set equal to 0; and finally, Model 4, in which the lambda loading of challenge was set equal to 0. This procedure, which fixes the contribution of a particular part of the model (e.g., commitment, control, or challenge) to 0, assesses the change in the overall fit of the model, and thus the relative importance of each component of hardiness to the fit of the model. In comparison to the full model, Model 2 provided a significantly worse fit, $\Delta\chi^2_{(1)} = 76.51$, $p < .001$, to the data. Similarly, both Model 3, $\Delta\chi^2_{(1)} = 107.24$, $p < .001$, and Model 4, $\Delta\chi^2_{(1)} = 71.51$, $p < .001$, provided a significantly worse fit than the full model. As suggested by the model comparison results, the reduced models all provided a significantly worse fit to the data; thus the full model was the best-fitting and most parsimonious model. More specifically, the model comparison indicated that the paths from hardiness to commitment, control and challenge were all necessary in order to provide a good fit to the data.

A Synergistic Conceptualization of Hardiness

The second conceptualization of hardiness is as a synergistic construct (Carver, 1989; Funk, 1992). According to this perspective, the whole is considered to be greater than, and therefore different from, the sum of its parts. This conceptualization of the positive personality trait of hardiness allows the researcher to look beyond main effect questions to examine whether results are due primarily to one component of the construct, to additive effects of two or more of the components, to some interaction between the

TABLE 22.4 Model Comparisons for Structural Model

Model	χ^2	df	p	$\Delta\chi^2$	GFI	AGFI	RMR	NFI
Full model	4.41	8	.82	—	.99	.97	.02	.99
Model 2	80.92	9	.00	76.51	.86	.68	.24	.73
Model 3	111.65	9	.00	107.24	.84	.62	.27	.62
Model 4	75.92	9	.00	71.51	.87	.69	.23	.74

Note: GFI = goodness-of-fit index; AGFI = adjusted goodness-of-fit index; RMR = root mean square residual; NFI = normed fit index; full model = all paths estimated; Model 2 = path to commitment set equal to zero; Model 3 = path to control set equal to zero; Model 4 = path to challenge set equal to zero.

components, or to a combination of these factors (Carver, 1989). In particular, the inclusion of terms that represent the interactions between the various subcomponents of hardiness allows the researcher to look, for example, at whether the impact of one component depends on levels of another, or whether the combined impact of two components depends on levels of the third.

As an illustration of this type of approach, a series of hierarchical multiple-regression analyses was run in order to determine how well positive affect, negative affect, and life satisfaction were predicted by commitment, challenge, and control (and gender, for life satisfaction),[3] the two-way interactions between the subscales, and the three-way interaction between them (i.e., the synergistic conceptualization of hardiness). Bonferroni adjustments were made to control familywise alpha at .05; thus tests of life satisfaction, negative affect, and positive affect were compared to a critical alpha of .02. Correlational analyses revealed that the overall hardiness measure was significantly correlated with life satisfaction ($r = .22$, $p < .01$) and with negative affect ($r = .32$, $p < .001$).

The overall model with positive affect as the dependent variable was significant, $F(7, 168) = 2.61$, $p < .02$, with 10% of the variance accounted for by challenge, commitment, control, the two-way interactions between them, and the three-way interaction (see table 22.5). In particular, the three main effects were entered into the equation first; both challenge, $F(1, 168) = 7.47$, $p < .02$, which accounted for 4% of the variance, and commitment, $F(1, 168) = 7.17$, $p < .02$, which accounted for 4% of the variance, significantly predicted positive affect. For both challenge and commitment, the results were not in the expected direction, with an increased amount of challenge and commitment predicting less positive affect. Entering the two-way interactions into the equation revealed that none of them were significant predictors of positive affect. Similarly, the three-way interaction was not a significant predictor of positive affect.

The overall model assessing predictions of negative affect was significant, $F(7, 133) = 11.06$, $p < .001$, and it accounted for 37% of the variance. All three main effects were significant predictors of negative affect, $F(1, 133) = 42.85$, $p < .001$, $F(1, 133) = 19.27$, $p < .001$, $F(1, 133) = 6.45$, $p < .02$, for challenge, commitment, and control, respectively. In particular, 20% of the variance was accounted for by challenge, 9% by commitment, and 3% by control. For all three

significant main effects, the results were in the expected direction, with increased amounts of challenge, commitment, and control predicting less negative affect. As a result of the Bonferroni adjustment, none of the two-way interactions were significant. There was, however, a marginally significant interaction between control and commitment, $F(1, 133) = 4.48$, $p < .05$, which accounted for 2% of the variance. Although the three-way interaction was not significant, it suggests a trend in the data, $F(1, 133) = 3.46$, $p = .07$, and accounts for approximately 2% of the variance.

Finally, 50% of the variance in the life satisfaction model was accounted for by gender, challenge, commitment, control, the two-way interactions, and the three-way interaction,

TABLE 22.5 Summary of Hierarchical Regression Analysis for Variables Predicting Positive Affect, Negative Affect, and Life Satisfaction

Source	R^2	df	F	p	B	SE B
Positive affect	**.10**					
Chalng	.04	1	7.47	.01	−.55	1.45
Commit	.04	1	7.17	.01	−.46	1.68
Cntrl	.00	1	.54	.47	.29	1.65
Com × Con	.00	1	.10	.75	−.00	.06
Cha × Con	.00	1	.20	.65	.00	.05
Cha × Com	.02	1	2.80	.10	.02	.05
CCC	.00	1	.01	.93	−.00	.00
Negative affect	**.37**					
Chalng	.20	1	42.85	.00	6.03	3.27
Commit	.09	1	19.27	.00	5.13	3.71
Cntrl	.03	1	6.45	.01	6.75	3.79
Com × Con	.02	1	4.48	.04	−.20	.13
Cha × Con	.00	1	.18	.67	−.23	.12
Cha × Com	.00	1	.71	.40	−.18	.12
CCC	.02	1	3.46	.07	.00	.00
Life satisfaction	**.50**					
Gender	.06	1	22.19	.00	2.36	.65
Chalng	.22	1	82.43	.00	2.43	1.66
Commit	.16	1	58.82	.00	2.98	1.93
Cntrl	.03	1	11.59	.00	4.85	1.95
Com × Con	.01	1	5.14	.02	−.13	.07
Cha × Con	.00	1	.25	.62	−.11	.06
Cha × Com	.01	1	4.13	.04	−.06	.06
CCC	.01	1	2.33	.13	.00	.00

Note: Chalng = challenge; Commit = commitment; Cntrl = control; Com × Con = commitment × control interaction; Cha × Con = challenge × control interaction; Cha × Com = challenge × commitment interaction; CCC = challenge × commitment × control interaction; F values, parameter estimates, and standard errors were calculated using Type I sums of squares.

$F(8, 186) = 23.36$, $p < .001$. In this model, the main effect for gender, $F(1, 186) = 22.19$, $p < .001$, which accounted for 6% of the variance, the main effect for challenge, $F(1, 186) = 82.43$, $p < .001$, which accounted for 22% of the variance, the main effect for commitment, $F(1, 186) = 58.82$, $p < .001$, which accounted for 16% of the variance, and the main effect of control, $F(1, 186) = 11.59$, $p < .001$, which accounted for 3% of the variance, were significant. For the significant main effects of challenge, commitment, and control, the results were in the expected direction, with increased amounts of challenge, commitment, and control predicting an increased satisfaction with life. Due to the Bonferroni adjustment, none of the two-way interactions were significant predictors of life satisfaction. The two-way interaction between control and commitment, $F(1, 186) = 5.14$, $p = .02$, and between commitment and challenge, $F(1, 186) = 4.13$, $p = .04$, however, were marginally significant, with each accounting for approximately 1% of the variance. Finally, the three-way interaction between commitment, control, and challenge was not significant.

A Person-Focused Approach to the Conceptualization of Hardiness

In contrast to the latent and synergistic conceptualizations, a person-focused approach considers the criteria that help differentiate among profiles of individuals. As such, this approach moves beyond main-effect or interaction models and helps to elucidate underlying patterns in lived experiences (Masten, 2001). An important method for the person-focused approach is cluster analysis, which allows the researcher to examine a "natural" structure among the observations based on a multivariate profile (Hair, Anderson, Tatham, & Black, 1995). As an illustration of this alternative method of investigating the relationship between the hardiness construct and well-being, a cluster analysis was conducted in order to identify individuals with a similar pattern of scores across the commitment, control, and challenge components (e.g., individuals high on all three components versus those who are high on commitment and control, but not challenge). Thus, participants were clustered according to their scores on commitment, control, and challenge.

For the purposes of the present analysis, variables were standardized prior to clustering.[4] The procedure FASTCLUS (SAS Institute, 1988),

which uses the nearest centroid sorting method (Anderberg, 1973), was used. In the present study, 20 clusters were specified for the initial analysis. The number of clusters was gradually reduced, until the most acceptable cluster solution, which included 9 clusters, was reached. An examination of the standard error within clusters and the R^2 was used to identify the most acceptable solution; these values were compared for each successive clustering procedure, and an acceptable solution was found when there was a large difference in the values between clustering procedures (Aldenderfer & Blashfield, 1984; Hair et al., 1995). A difference in these values between cluster solutions suggests that two relatively dissimilar clusters have been joined; thus the number of clusters specified before the difference is the most appropriate solution (Aldenderfer & Blashfield, 1984). In the current study, a difference of this type occurred between the eighth and the ninth cluster solution. Thus the nine-cluster solution was retained (overall Within STD $= .46$; $R^2 = .79$). In addition, two participants were deleted from the analysis, having been identified as outliers during the clustering process, and 14 observations were excluded from the analysis due to missing data.

An examination of the cluster means for the nine clusters retained in the final cluster solution revealed specific patterns of scores for each cluster. In particular, Cluster 1 contained individuals approximately two standard deviations above the mean for commitment, control, and challenge, indicating that these individuals were low on all three components of hardiness (see table 22.6 for cluster descriptions). In contrast, individuals in Cluster 5 and in Cluster 8 were approximately one standard deviation or more below the mean on all three subscales. Thus, these individuals were high on all three components of hardiness. Other patterns that emerged within clusters included average scores across all three subscales (Cluster 3), average scores on two subscales, and either high or low scores on the third (e.g., Cluster 4 and Cluster 2), low scores on two subscales, and average scores on the third (e.g., Cluster 6 and Cluster 7), very low scores across all three subscales (Cluster 1), and, finally, low scores on challenge, high scores on commitment, and average scores on control (Cluster 9).

Using these cluster memberships, a 2×9 between-subjects analysis of variance (ANOVA) was used to examine the relationship between cluster membership and life satisfaction. For this

TABLE 22.6 Cluster Descriptors

Cluster #	Challenge	Commitment	Control
1	Very low	Very low	Very low
2	High	Average	Average
3	Average	Average	Average
4	Average	Average	Low
5	Very high	High	Very high
6	Average	Low	Low
7	Low	Low	Average
8	High	High	High
9	Low	High	Average

Note: Descriptors represent the cluster mean for a given scale, and categorize clusters according to whether individuals are high, low, or average on hardiness.

model (overall $R^2 = .38$), there was a significant main effect of gender, $F(1, 192) = 16.36$, $p < .001$, suggesting that on average, women were less satisfied with life than men. In addition, there was also a significant main effect of cluster membership, $F(8, 192) = 12.50$, $p < .001$. See table 22.7 for the means and standard deviations by cluster for the dependent variables. Follow-up analyses of the significant cluster membership effect revealed that individuals in Cluster 1 (i.e., participants low on commitment, challenge, and control) were significantly less satisfied with life than individuals in Clusters 2, 3, 4, 5, 8, and 9 (in general, individuals in these clusters were average or high on most of the hardiness subscales). In addition, individuals in Cluster 5 (i.e., those who were high on all three subscales) were significantly more satisfied with life than those in Clusters 2, 3, 4, 6, and 7. There was no significant difference in life satisfaction between in-

dividuals in Cluster 5 and Cluster 8, and between individuals in Cluster 3 and Cluster 4. There was no significant interaction between cluster membership and gender.

A one-way ANOVA was used to test the relationship between cluster membership and positive affect (overall $R^2 = .09$). This test revealed a significant effect of cluster membership, $F(8, 179) = 2.11$, $p < .05$. Follow-up analyses using Tukey's HSD revealed that there were no significant differences between cluster membership. Finally, a one-way ANOVA was used to examine the relationship between negative affect and cluster membership (overall $R^2 = .34$). This model was significant, $F(8, 139) = 8.79$, $p < .001$. Follow-up tests using Tukey's HSD revealed a pattern of findings similar to that obtained with life satisfaction. Specifically, individuals in Cluster 1 displayed significantly more negative affect than individuals in Clusters 2, 3, 4, 5, 7, 8, and 9. In addition, members of Cluster 5 reported significantly less negative affect than members of Clusters 6 and 7; individuals in Cluster 8 reported significantly less negative affect than individuals in Clusters 6 and 7. There was no significant difference in negative affect between members of Cluster 8 and Cluster 5, and between members of Cluster 3 and Cluster 4.

Methods of Conceptualization: An Integration

As a result of a recent surge of interest in human adaptation and flourishing (e.g., Aspinwall & Staudinger, 2003b; Keyes & Haidt, 2003) and the

TABLE 22.7 Cluster Means and Standard Deviations for Life Satisfaction, Positive Affect, and Negative Affect

Cluster #	Life Satisfaction		Positive Affect		Negative Affect	
	$\bar{X}$	SD	$\bar{X}$	SD	$\bar{X}$	SD
1	35.73	5.43	10.40	3.71	40.60	9.21
2	29.21	4.34	7.35	3.16	23.83	9.66
3	29.70	4.91	7.91	3.30	23.32	6.28
4	30.59	4.16	8.72	2.99	24.48	5.80
5	22.65	4.31	7.50	3.01	18.00	2.51
6	32.07	4.36	9.27	3.49	30.25	8.39
7	32.26	5.00	9.21	2.86	29.00	9.80
8	25.49	3.53	6.55	3.10	19.22	2.81
9	28.09	4.34	8.03	3.33	23.28	8.78

Note: A high score indicates a decreased amount of positive affect, an increased amount of negative affect, and a decreased satisfaction with life.

field of positive psychology (e.g., Snyder & Lopez, 2002), there has been an increased focus on positive personality traits such as forgiveness, hardiness, love, and wisdom. Given the complexity of these constructs, research that considers various approaches to their conceptualization is needed. The present chapter serves as a preliminary examination of one such positive personality trait, the dispositional resilience resource of hardiness. Overall, the model-fitting analysis demonstrated the importance of all three components of the construct to the fit of the model. More specifically, the model-fitting analysis was used to assess the relative contribution of commitment, control, and challenge to the hardiness construct, controlling for the presence of error. The finding that the full model is the best-fitting model is not surprising, although the testing of the relative contribution of each component, and the results suggesting that each one is necessary to the overall fit of the model, provides some evidence for the latent trait conceptualization of the hardiness construct, as well as evidence for the importance of the three distinct components. This particular conceptualization is consistent with the definition of hardiness as a constellation of personality characteristics (Kobasa, 1979). Moreover, it is compelling because it allows one to view hardiness as a multifaceted dimension that is representative of a global personality trait.

In addition to the information that the model provided regarding the conceptualization of hardiness, the finding of a significant relationship between hardiness and well-being, once error had been attenuated, provided some evidence for the predictive utility of the construct. That is, the good fit of the model suggests that it is not just error variance that is driving the relationship between hardiness and well-being. Information of this type may be particularly important given the consistently low internal consistency reliabilities of the subscales (e.g., Funk, 1992). Of course, the model tested in the present analysis is a preliminary model. Future research could examine more complex models, including assessments of the relative contribution of method variances, and addressing more explicitly issues of discriminant validity.

Of particular interest is a comparison of the results of the model-fitting analysis with the correlations calculated between the overall hardiness measure and the outcome measures (table 22.2). That is, there is an apparent discrepancy between the findings in these two analyses; in

the model-fitting analysis, the hardiness construct was related to well-being, whereas in the correlational analysis, the hardiness construct did not consistently relate to the components of well-being. One possible explanation for this apparent discrepancy may be related to error of measurement. As demonstrated in the model, there may be a relatively strong relationship between hardiness and well-being, which is less evident in the correlations between the overall hardiness measure and life satisfaction, positive affect, and negative affect as a result of measurement error. Once error has been attenuated (i.e., as in the model-fitting analysis), the underlying relationship is more evident. The findings provide some evidence for the importance of a latent trait conceptualization of hardiness in which the dimension of interest can be examined without error.

The hierarchical regression analyses were useful in assessing the extent to which positive affect, negative affect, and life satisfaction were predicted by commitment, challenge, control, the two-way interactions between them, and the three-way interaction between them. Whereas the main effects of challenge and commitment were significant in all three models, and the main effect of control was significant in predicting both life satisfaction and negative affect, control did not significantly predict positive affect. Moreover, although a significant amount of variance was accounted for in each model, the least amount of variance was accounted for in positive affect. One possible explanation for these findings may be related to the fact that the positive affect subscale comprised only four items. Thus, there may have been less reliable variance in positive affect to be explained.

Additional comparisons across models revealed that none of the two-way interactions were significant. Several of these interactions, however, were marginally significant. In particular, the interaction between control and commitment approached significance for both life satisfaction and negative affect, but not for positive affect. Finally, although none of the three-way interactions were significant, the three-way effect predicting negative affect approached significance. One possible explanation for the lack of significant interactions in the present study may be related to the issue of power, particularly given the Bonferroni adjustments that were made in order to control familywise alpha. The trend in the data, which suggested that the three-way interaction approached significance in the model predicting negative affect, provided additional evidence in support of this contention. Future studies could examine this issue, using larger, more variable samples, and thus more powerful designs. Regardless, the use of the interactive term provides one way to conceptualize the synergistic (i.e., "the whole is greater than the sum of its parts") view of the dispositional resilience resource of hardiness.

The person-centered approach, in turn, provides important information on the criteria that help differentiate profiles of individuals and the underlying patterns of lived experiences (Masten, 2001). As previously discussed, the cluster analysis was used in this chapter as an alternative method of classifying individuals on the different hardiness dimensions. This analysis provided support for the usefulness of grouping individuals according to their scores on the hardiness subscales. In general, individuals identified as low on commitment, control, and challenge were significantly less satisfied with life and significantly more depressed than those identified as average or high on the three hardiness subscales, whereas individuals classified as high hardy on all three dimensions showed the opposite pattern. One interesting trend that emerged in this analysis suggested that, with average levels of commitment and challenge, an average amount of control does not result in a better outcome (e.g., less negative affect, more satisfaction with life) than low control. Although future research is needed to clarify and replicate this finding, it could have important implications for the implementation of effective interventions, such that assessments and evaluations of all three components would be necessary.

Although the person-centered information gained from the cluster analysis is important, one possible weakness of this analysis is its subjectivity (Aldenderfer & Blashfield, 1984). That is, cluster analysis by definition is a data-driven process. Consequently, it is difficult to determine the extent to which the cluster solution obtained in the present analysis is generalizable to other samples. Additional validation of the solution, in addition to the external validation included in the current analysis, is needed. The need for validation, however, does not negate the descriptive importance of the present analysis, particularly given the significant differences found between clusters on the dependent variables. In addition, it is clear that the clustering of profiles of similar individuals on the hardiness subdimensions provides information

that is not readily accessible in either the latent-trait or synergistic approaches.

Despite the need for future research that examines the positive personality trait of dispositional hardiness, the present chapter provides important preliminary information concerning different methods for its conceptualization. Generally speaking, the latent-trait approach allows the researcher to examine relationships between the underlying hardiness construct and various positive outcomes while attenuating for error. The synergistic conceptualization, in turn, allows the researcher to consider the interactive effects of the component parts of the hardiness construct in predicting positive psychological and physical outcomes. Finally, the person-focused approach is useful when one is interested in examining the criteria used in grouping profiles of individuals or the underlying patterns of lived experience (Masten, 2001).

Considered together, the integration of a variable and person approach illustrates the multidimensionality of the construct of interest. For example, whereas the variable approaches (i.e., the latent trait and synergistic analyses) provided evidence for the predictive utility of hardiness and its component parts, the person approach (i.e., the cluster analysis) revealed interesting patterns among the subcomponents. One such pattern revealed by this typological approach, which was not evident in the variable-focused analyses, concerned the role of the control component of hardiness in the context of individuals reporting average levels of both commitment and challenge. In particular, control was an important predictor in the latent-variable model and the regression models; however, there were no differences in negative affect or life satisfaction for individuals reporting low versus average control. As suggested here, differences and similarities between different profiles may be lost (averaged over) when only a variable perspective is taken. As such, consideration of the patterns among subcomponents provides additional information about the potential functioning of the individual in context (e.g., Magnusson, 1996). Overall, it is clear that the creation of a simple hardiness composite, which is a common method in the hardiness literature, is not the best approach (e.g., Carver, 1989). Rather, this chapter presents several alternative methods, which, when combined, are useful for enhancing our understanding of dispositional resilience, the patterns among hardiness subcomponents within respondents, and the ability of hardiness and its components to predict optimal outcomes in a sample of older adults.

Although this chapter has applied these conceptualizations within the framework of the hardiness literature, these methods may be applicable more broadly. That is, the integration of a person- and variable-focused approach may be helpful in the conceptualization of other positive personality traits as well. For example, Asendorpf (2000) illustrates how a person approach may be used to complement a variable approach in the study of personality and social relationships. More generally, the combination of person- and variable-focused approaches is necessary to advance theoretical understanding in the field of positive psychology. In particular, the scientific study of human strengths, virtues, and quality of life would be incomplete without consideration of the totality of the functioning individual. Typologies, clusters, or profiles of characteristics that come together at the individual level, for example, may then be used to predict positive psychological and health outcomes. Consideration of the continuity and stability of said profiles, as well as the dynamic, changing nature of their relationships with optimal outcomes over time, are areas in which the assimilation of knowledge from both person and the variable approaches could inform the advancement of more fully integrated models of positive psychological development.

Acknowledgments This research was supported in part by a grant from the National Institute for Mental Health (1 R03 M#53895-01). In addition, the authors would like to Sara Leitsch, Erin Kelly, Tara Sillars, and Laura Sullivan for their help and support in the completion of this project.

Notes

1. The sample used in the model-fitting analysis comprised 129 participants. A listwise deletion was used; thus individuals with data missing on any of the variables were excluded from the analysis. In order to assess the extent to which the individuals excluded from the analysis differed from those included, a series of chi-square tests was conducted. Overall, individuals excluded from the analysis were not significantly different from those included on race, gender, marital status, education, or income. A *t* test, however, revealed that those ex-

cluded from the analysis were significantly older than those included, $t(241) = -4.74$, $p < .001$.

2. An examination of the assumption of normality for the variables used in the present model (i.e., moderate contamination as indicated by estimates of skewness; Micceri, 1989) revealed moderate departures from normality for both positive and negative affect. Inverse transformations were done on these variables, an adjusted correlation matrix was computed, and the full model was rerun. Neither the fit of the model nor the significance tests for the parameters were seriously perturbed by the transformations; thus the model estimated using the variables' original metric was retained.

3. Descriptive analyses revealed a significant effect of gender on life satisfaction, with women exhibiting significantly less satisfaction with life than men. Thus, gender was controlled for in this and subsequent analyses predicting life satisfaction.

4. Typically, variables are standardized in a cluster analysis in order to reduce the effects of differences in scaling or differences in variances between the variables being used to form the clusters. Thus, because several researchers have indicated that standardization has only minor effects on the final cluster solution (e.g., Aldenderfer & Blashfield, 1984; Milligan, 1980), variables were standardized in the present analysis to a mean of zero and a standard deviation of one.

References

Aldenderfer, M. S., & Blashfield, R. K. (1984). *Cluster analysis.* Newbury Park, CA: Sage.

Allred, K. D., & Smith, T. W. (1989). The hardy personality: Cognitive and physiological responses to evaluative threat. *Journal of Personality and Social Psychology, 56,* 257–266.

Anderberg, M. R. (1973). *Cluster analysis for applications.* New York: Academic Press.

Asendorpf, J. B. (2000). A person-centered approach to personality and social relationships: Findings from the Berlin Relationship Study. In L. R. Bergman, R. B. Cairns, L. Nilsson, & L. Nystedt (Eds.), *Developmental science and the holistic approach* (pp. 281–298). Mahwah, NJ: Erbaum.

Aspinwall, L. G., & Staudinger, U. M. (2003a). A psychology of human strengths: Some central issues in an emerging field. In L. G. Aspinwall & U. M. Staudinger (Eds.), *A psychology of human strengths: Fundamental questions and future directions for a positive psychology* (pp. 9–22). Washington, DC: American Psychological Association.

Aspinwall, L. G., & Staudinger, U. M. (2003b). *A psychology of human strengths: Fundamental questions and future directions for a positive psychology.* Washington, DC: American Psychological Association.

Baltes, P. B., Glueck, J., & Kunzmann, U. (2002). Wisdom: Its structure and function in regulating successful life span development. In C. R. Snyder & S. J. Lopez (Eds.), *Handbook of positive psychology* (pp. 327–347). London: Oxford University Press.

Bartone, R. T., Ursano, R. J., Wright, K. M., & Ingraham, L. H. (1989). The impact of a military air disaster on the health of assistance workers: A prospective study. *The Journal of Nervous and Mental Disease, 177,* 317–328.

Beasley, M., Thompson, T., & Davidson, J. (2003). Resilience in response to life stress: The effects of coping style and cognitive hardiness. *Personality and Individual Differences, 34,* 77–95.

Carver, C. S. (1989). How should multifaceted personality constructs be tested? Issues illustrated by self-monitoring, attributional style, and hardiness. *Journal of Personality and Social Psychology, 56,* 577–585.

Clark, P. C. (2002). Effects of individual and family hardiness on caregiver depression and fatigue. *Research in Nursing and Health, 25,* 37–48.

Farber, E. A., & Egeland, B. (1987). Invulnerability among abused and neglected children. In E. J. Anthony & B. J. Cohler (Eds.), *The invulnerable child* (pp. 253–288). New York: Guilford.

Funk, S. C. (1992). Hardiness: A review of theory and research. *Health Psychology, 11,* 335–345.

Funk, S. C., & Houston, B. K. (1987). A critical analysis of the hardiness scale's validity and utility. *Journal of Personality and Social Psychology, 53,* 572–578.

Ganellen, R. J., & Blaney, P. H. (1984). Hardiness and social support as moderators of the effects of life stress. *Journal of Personality and Social Psychology, 47,* 156–163.

Garmezy, N. (1985). Stress resistant children: The search for protective factors. In J. E. Stevensen (Ed.), *Recent research in developmental psychopathology* (pp. 213–233). Oxford: Pergamon.

Garmezy, N., Masten, A. S., & Tellegen, A. (1984). The study of stress and competence in children: A building block for developmental psychopathology. *Child Development, 55,* 97–111.

Hair, J. F., Anderson, R. E., Tatham, R. L., & Black, W. C. (1995). *Multivariate data analysis* (4th ed.). Englewood Cliffs, NJ: Prentice Hall.

Hull, J. G., Van Treuren, R. R., & Virnelli, S. (1987). Hardiness and health: A critique and alternative approach. *Journal of Personality and Social Psychology, 53,* 518–530.

Indiana Fact Book (1992). Indianapolis: State of Indiana.

Jöreskog, K. G., & Sörbom, D. (1993). *LISREL 8 user's reference guide.* Chicago: Scientific Software International.

Keyes, C. L. M., & Haidt, J. (2003). *Flourishing: Positive psychology and the life well lived.* Washington, DC: American Psychological Association.

Kobasa, S. C. (1979). Stressful life events, personality, and health: An inquiry into hardiness. *Journal of Personality and Social Psychology, 37,* 1–11.

Kobasa, S. C. (1982). The personality: Toward a social psychology of stress and health. In G. S. Sanders & J. Suls (Eds.), *Social psychology of health and illness* (pp. 3–32). Mahwah, NJ: Erlbaum.

Kobasa, S. C., & Maddi, S. R. (1977). Existential personality theory. In R. Corsini (Ed.), *Current personality theories* (pp. 243–276). Itasca, IL: Peacock.

Kobasa, S. C., Maddi, S. R., & Kahn, S. (1982). Hardiness and health: A prospective study. *Journal of Personality and Social Psychology, 42,* 168–177.

Lawton, M. P., Kleban, M. H., & Dean, J. (1993). Affect and age: Cross-sectional comparisons of structure and prevalence. *Psychology and Aging, 8,* 165–175.

Lawton, M. P., Kleban, M. H., Rajagopal, D., & Parmelee, P. A. (1992). The factorial generality of brief positive affect and negative affect measures. *Journal of Gerontology: Psychological Sciences, 47,* P228–P237.

Lightsey, O. R. (1996). What leads to wellness? The role of psychological resources in well-being. *Counseling Psychologist, 24,* 589–759.

Loehlin, J. C. (1992). *Latent variable models: An introduction to factor, path, and structural analysis* (2nd ed.). Mahwah, NJ: Erlbaum.

Lopez, S. J., & Snyder, C. R. (2003). The future of positive psychological assessment: Making a difference. In S. J. Lopez & C. R. Snyder (Eds.), *Positive psychological assessment: A handbook of models and measures* (pp. 461–468). Washington, DC: American Psychological Association.

Luthar, S. S. (1993). Annotation: Methodological and conceptual issues in research on childhood resilience. *Journal of Child Psychiatry and Psychology, 34,* 441–453.

Luthar, S. S., & Cushing, G. (1999). Measurement issues in the empirical study of resilience. In M. D. Glantz & J. L. Johnson (Eds.), *Resilience and development: Positive life adaptations* (pp. 129–160). New York: Kluwer Academic/Plenum.

Maddi, S. R. (2002). The story of hardiness: Twenty years of theorizing, research, and practice. *Consulting Psychology Journal: Practice and Research, 54,* 173–185.

Maddi, S. R., Khoshaba, D. M., Persico, M., Lu, J., Harvey, R., & Bleecker, F. (2002). The personality construct of hardiness: Relationships with comprehensive tests of personality and psychopathology. *Journal of Research in Personality, 36,* 72–85.

Magai, C., Consedine, N. S., King, A. R., & Gillespie, M. (2003). Physical hardiness and styles of socioemotional functioning in later life. *Journal of Gerontology: Psychological Sciences, 58B,* P269–P279.

Magnusson, D. (1996). Interactionism and the person approach in developmental psychology. *European Child and Adolescent Psychiatry, 5,* 18–22.

Magnusson, D. (1999). Holistic interactionism: A perspective for research on personality development. In L. A. Pervin & O. P. John (Eds.), *Handbook of personality: Theory and research* (2nd ed., pp. 219–247). New York: Guilford.

Masten, A. M. (2001). Ordinary magic: Resilience processes in development. *American Psychologist, 56,* 227–238.

Masten, A. S., Best, K. M., & Garmezy, N. (1990). Resilience and development: Contributions from the study of children who overcome adversity. *Development and psychopathology, 2,* 425–444.

McCullough, M. E., Pargament, K. I., & Thoresen, C. E. (2001). *Forgiveness: Theory, research, and practice.* New York: Guilford.

Micceri, T. (1989). The unicorn, the normal curve, and other improbable creatures. *Psychological Bulletin, 105,* 156–166.

Milligan, G. W. (1980). An examination of the effect of six types of error perturbation of fifteen clustering algorithms. *Psychometricka, 45,* 325–342.

Neugarten, B. L., Havighurst, R. J., & Tobin, S. S. (1961). The measurement of life satisfaction. *Journal of Gerontology, 16,* 134–143.

Ouellette, S. C. (1993). Inquiries into hardiness. In L. Goldberger & S. Breznitz (Eds.), *Handbook of stress: Theoretical and clinical aspects* (2nd ed., pp. 77–100). New York: Free Press.

Pargament, K. I., & Mahoney, A. (2002). Spirituality: Discovering and conserving the sacred. In C. R. Snyder & S. J. Lopez (Eds.), *Handbook of positive psychology* (pp. 646–659). London: Oxford University Press.

Radloff, L. S. (1977). A self-report depression scale for research in the general population. *Applied Psychological Measurement, 1,* 385–401.

Rutter, M. (1987). Psychosocial resilience and protective mechanisms. *American Journal of Orthopsychiatry, 57,* 316–331.

SAS Institute. (1988). *SAS/STAT user's guide* (release 6.03 ed.). Cary, NC: Author.

Seligman, M. E. P., & Csikszentmihalyi, M. (2000). Positive psychology: An introduction. *American Psychologist, 55,* 5–14.

Sheldon, K. M., & King, L. (2001). Why positive psychology is necessary. *American Psychologist, 56,* 216–217.

Snyder, C. R., & Lopez, S. L. (2002). *Handbook of positive psychology.* New York: Oxford University Press.

Soderstrom, M., Dolbier, C., Leiferman, J., & Steinhardt, M. (2000). The relationship of hardiness, coping strategies, and perceived stress to symptoms of illness. *Journal of Behavioral Medicine, 23,* 311–328.

Waysman, M., Schwarzwald, J., & Solomon, Z. (2001). Hardiness: An examination of its relationship with positive and negative long-term changes following trauma. *Journal of Traumatic Stress, 14,* 531–548.

Werner, E. E. (1990). Protective factors and individual resilience. In S. J. Meisels & J. P. Shonkoff (Eds.), *Handbook of early childhood intervention* (pp. 97–116). New York: Cambridge University Press.

Werner, E. E. (1995). Resilience in development. *Current Directions in Psychological Science, 4,* 81–85.

Werner, E. E., & Smith, R. S. (1977). *Kauai's children come of age.* Honolulu: University of Hawaii Press.

Werner, E. E., & Smith, R. S. (1992). *Overcoming the odds: High risk children from birth to adulthood.* Ithaca, NY: Cornell University Press.

Windle, M. (1999). Critical conceptual and measurement issues in the study of resilience. In M. D. Glantz & J. L. Johnson (Eds.), *Resilience and development: Positive life adaptations* (pp. 161–176). New York: Kluwer Academic/Plenum.

Wood, V., Wylie, M. L., & Sheafor, B. (1969). An analysis of a short self-report measure of life satisfaction: Correlation with rater judgments. *Journal of Gerontology, 24*(4), 465–469.

IV

Interindividual Differences in Intraindividual Variability

23

Within-Person Covariation Analysis

Applications to the Study of Affect

Randy J. Larsen

The tongue-twisting title of this section of the book—Interindividual Differences in Intraindividual Variability—hints at the combined sources of variability that are disentangled in this particular approach. The approach I have employed to disentangling such variation consists of two steps. First, within-person covariation is assessed for each subject in the sample. This step is similar to calculating a score for each subject, but in this case the "score" is the degree of some form of covariation present in each person's data stream. In the second step, between-person analyses are conducted on the covariation scores to see if meaningful individual differences can be found. These two steps can be done simultaneously with hierarchical linear models (e.g., Raudenbush & Bryk, 2002), or they can be done in two actual steps.

A quick example will bring this approach to life. I was interested in emotional reactivity to life events (Larsen & Cowan, 1988). Within persons, one would expect that, when good events happen people should be happy and when bad events happen people should be sad or distressed. In other words, the hedonic balance of one's emotional state over time should track fairly well onto the valence of the events that are happening in

one's life. This would suggest a positive correlation should be found between affect and life events calculated within persons. To examine this, we (Larsen & Cowan, 1988) had 62 subjects keep daily records of their emotions as well as provide descriptions of their best and worst events each day for 56 consecutive days. This resulted in 2,907 bad event descriptions and 3,064 good event descriptions. The events were rated by a team of raters for how objectively good or bad each event would be for the average college students (since our subjects were from this population). For our purposes, we were primarily interested in the link between bad events and negative affect, and so focus on these two variables.

From such a data set, we can then undertake an interindividual differences analysis of intraindividual variability. In the first step we correlated, for each person, his or her self-reported negative affect with the rated severity of the worst event across the 56 days of observation. These should be positive correlations, indicating that each person's day-to-day level of negative affect is covarying with the magnitude of the unpleasant events in his or her life. Across the 62 subjects, we did find that all the correlations were positive. In other words, no subject reported feeling good when bad events occurred and bad when good events occurred. However, there were subjects who had fairly low correlations between their negative affect and the bad events in their lives. The correlations ranged from essentially 0 up to .92. The person with the .92 correlation had a negative affect system that was very tightly synchronized to the events in her life. The person with the .02 correlation was essentially having negative emotions that were not at all connected to the events in his life. This within-person covariation can be thought of as the degree of linkage a person has between his or her affect and the ongoing events in his or her life.

In the second step, we tried to predict the magnitude of the linkage between affect and life events using a collection of personality variables. We found that depression scores correlated negatively with this linkage, indicating that depressed persons have negative emotional states that are unpredictable from the events in their lives. Of course, this is an obvious aspect of depressed persons, that they feel bad for no good objective reason. However, this example illustrates the notion of quantifying a process for each person, in this case, the linkage between his or her feelings and the events in his or her life, and then trying to understand individual differences in that process. Analysis of within-person covariation is part of a general analytic strategy I have called process analysis (Larsen, 1989). I turn to a description of that general model, with some emphasis on co-variation analysis. I then give three examples of within-person covariation analysis.

A Process Approach to Studying Persons

Assume that people try to regulate their ongoing moods in ways that maintain positive feelings and remediate negative feelings. The process might be much like emotional homeostasis, where the goal is to maintain some desired affective set point. Of course, life intrudes randomly, providing shocks to this homeostatic process. Feelings of stress may act much like negative feedback that calls for corrective or regulative action (Larsen, 2000). In order to observe such self-regulation, the researcher would need to study at least one person fairly intensively over time, paying careful attention to affective changes, to events from the environment, and to behavioral or cognitive strategies that the person uses to regulate feelings (Larsen & Prizmic, 2004). By observing one person for a period of time, we might be able to model his or her self-regulation system, perhaps using concepts and even the mathematics from cybernetic control theory (Hyland, 1987) or nonlinear dynamics (Pool, 1989). Observing only day-by-day fluctuation, with no model of the underlying process, we might conclude that changes in feeling states are chaotic. However, by using a model that incorporates a set point, negative feedback, and self-correcting strategies, we might see a pattern of self-regulation that appears purposeful, intelligent, and predictable.

If we observe several people in this same manner over time, we might begin to notice important individual differences in patterns of self-regulation. For example, some people might consistently exhibit one pattern of regulation (say, motivated by negative affect, or fear avoidant), while others exhibit another consistent pattern of regulation (say, motivated by positive affect or the desire to approach). An important individual difference is the temporal pattern of affect and events that might be observed, in this case whether the person is pushed by fear or pulled by desire. This example highlights how we may, on a case-by-case basis, search for order or patterning in the ongoing lives of our subjects. And these patterns may turn out to reveal important differences between the individuals we are studying. For example, who are the people who are pushed through life by fear, and how are they different from those who are pulled through life by desire? How did they get this way? What forces maintain this pattern of behavior?

The process approach (Larsen, 1989) is well-suited for addressing such questions because it begins with the individual level of analysis and then goes to the group level to search for meaningful differences between individuals. The process approach thus consists of two steps: first, each case is analyzed separately over the temporal dimension to assess some form of temporal pattern; second, an estimate of the degree to which each subject exhibits the temporal pattern is used as an individual-difference variable for comparison across subjects. This approach has much in common with the idiographic-nomothetic paradigm proposed by Epstein (1983). I prefer the term *process*, however, because there are several ways to conduct an idiographic analysis that do not take into account the temporal dimension of life events emphasized by the idiodynamic perspective (e.g., Runyon, 1983). The process approach might instead be called the idiodynamic-differential approach because it demands that the first step at the individual level of analysis be performed across time to identify temporal patterns for each subject. This approach is exactly what is done in hierarchical linear modeling (HLM; Raudenbush & Bryk, 2002). However, HLM is limited to the interindividual analysis of aspects of linear correlation, including slope and intercept, whereas the researcher may be interested in nonlinear correlational patterns (e.g., rhythmic oscillations; Boker & Nesselroade, 2002), or in other aspects of intraindividual change, such as multivariate patterns, within-subject skew, or phase relations between oscillating processes.

This process approach can serve as a heuristic for researchers who are interested in a wide variety of intraindividual patterns. Any researcher considering the temporal aspects of some substantive topic could use this approach to think through various analytic possibilities. Any phenomenon that fluctuates over time (e.g., mood, self-esteem) or that exhibits development, adaptation, adjustment, regulation, rhythm, learning, reversal, or any form of temporal covariation with one or more other variables would be appropriate topics for the process approach. The crucial point is that the researcher must be willing to observe subjects extensively over time and think a bit differently about the nature of the data so gathered.

Adding the Temporal Dimension to Our Conception of Data

Conducting observations intensively over time demands that we think differently about the

resulting data set. A typical study or experiment generates a two-dimensional data set, with persons as rows and variables as columns. In the process approach, assessment over time is extensive enough that a third dimension—time— must be added to the data set. Such a data set is schematized in figure 23.1, which represents the covariation chart or "data box" first proposed by Cattell (and which he revised several times during his career; e.g., Cattell, 1973, 1988). Cattell used the data box to demonstrate the combination of different dimensions over which one may perform correlational analyses. By including a temporal dimension, the researcher may model such concepts such as change, lability, growth, and lead-lag relations within each subject's data.

The data box provides a conceptual starting point for clarifying and organizing the within-subject (or intraindividual) phase of the process approach. The data box provides a scheme for thinking about various within-subject temporally derived parameters. Now that both time and persons are in the same data set, we can turn to the question of how to go about modeling within-person process variables at the level of the individual. In terms of the data box, we peel off one subject at a time, treating each subject as an individual time series (Gottman, 1981).

In figure 23.1, Panel A, a single variable is extracted for each subject, essentially considering each subject as a distinct univariate time series. Here the idiodynamic pattern may refer to the distributional properties of a variable over time for each subject. For example, the idiodynamic concern might be with the variability of some state over time, as in recent research on self-esteem,

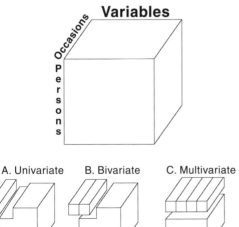

Figure 23.1 The data-box concept (from Cattell, 1966, 1973) illustrating the dimensions of variation. Panels illustrate how facets of the data box are segmented for intraindividual analyses.

which is emphasizing that some people are more variable or reactive in terms of blows to self-esteem than others (e.g., Kernis, Cornell, Sun, & Berry, 1993). In addition, a variable might be of interest to the degree that it might be rhythmic or its variability can be characterized as periodic. I mention below how spectral analysis can assist in the identification of rhythmic variability, even in the midst of apparent randomness in the temporal data. In figure 23.1, Panel B, the concern is with bivariate relationships between two variables over time for each person. The idiodynamic focus may be on the co-occurrence of those variables (first-order, within-subject correlation), the lead-lag relations between those variables (bivariate auto-regression), or the rhythmic coherence between variables (cross-spectral analysis). For example, consider the relation between work and positive emotions; for some subjects, this relationship over time might be positive (being productive is associated with being happy), whereas for others this relationship may be negative (they are unhappy when working). In figure 23.1, Panel C, multiple variables are considered simultaneously, in a multivariate time series for each subject. Here the pattern of temporal covariation among a collection of variables assessed over time is the idiodynamic focus for each subject.

For the past few years, I have been employing just such a process approach to studying personality (cf. Larsen, 1990, 1992, 1993). This approach pursues within-subject analyses of dynamic temporal patterns (idiodynamic analyses), followed by between-subject (demographic) comparisons of those temporal patterns. This approach to personality research represents not only a strategy for combined person and time sampling, but also presents a unique way of thinking about questions important to personality psychology (Larsen, 1987, 1989). In the remainder of this chapter I describe the details of this approach to personality research, which I call the process approach, and illustrate it with several examples.

Examples of Within-Person Covariation Analysis

The within-person phase of this approach can involve any of a wide variety of parameters. What is necessary is that the researcher have a clear conceptualization of what psychological process he or she wants to represent. This will then guide the researcher in formulating which within-subject quantitative parameter will serve

as an indicator. For example, we might want to know a person's average tendency on some variable, say their average affective state (Zelenski & Larsen, 2000). In this case, the mean affect score calculated over time would be a good indicator. The process so represented could be conceived as the person's set point, their steady state, or their expected value on affect. Alternatively, the researcher might be interested in variability as the within-person process, and so each person's standard deviation might be calculated and used as indicators of within-person variability.

In this chapter, I am focusing on the special case of within-person covariation. Covariation can be thought of as having three distinct varieties, corresponding to the three subpanels of figure 23.1. The obvious variety is bivariate co-variation, where two variables are examined over time for the degree of temporal overlap they exhibit. The second obvious type of covariation is the multivariate case, where multivariate statistics, such as factor analysis, can be applied to within-person data. The third variety of co-variation is autocorrelation, where a variable can be lagged in time and correlated with itself. Autocorrelation involves correlating a variable at time t with itself at time ($t + 1$, $t + 2$, $t + k$, etc.). Lagged autocorrelation can be used to indicate system memory or the duration of some phenomenon (e.g., Larsen, in press). As a special case, lagged autocorrelations can be used to detect rhythmicity in the time course of a variable. An autocorrelation series that is not monotonic suggests the presence of possible rhythms. Lagging can also be done with bivariate within-subject correlations as well, where the value of one variable is used to predict future values on another variable. In the examples below, I give demonstrations of within-person bivariate correlation, within-person autocorrelation, within-person spectral analysis, and within-person factor analysis. Each of these within-person analyses yields a covariation parameter that represents very different psychological processes in each example.

The use of a specific covariation parameter should be guided by one's scientific goals. That is, the ability to calculate a parameter is not a good rationale to proceed with a particular analysis. Rather, one should first have in mind the psychological process one wants to represent, then, from this, deduce which within-subject parameter will best accomplish that representation. In the examples below, I try to describe how the concern should first be with what one wants to represent using within-person covariation parameters.

Intraindividual Bivariate Correlation: The Emotional Impact of Minor Illnesses

The first two examples described in this chapter are drawn from Larsen and Kasimatis (1991). In this study, we started out with a main concern about the personality-health relationship. Most researchers in this area are concerned with whether or not personality predicts the occurrence of illnesses. But there are many other aspects of the personality-health link that can be investigated, especially when conceptualized in a process framework. For example, in addition to the occurrence of illnesses, another parameter of illness concerns the emotional concomitants of becoming ill. Many researchers consider emotions and moods to function something like a signal system (Larsen & Prizmic, 2004), revealing to the person his or her state of affairs. These signals may be important in self-regulation behaviors necessary to cope with illness. For example, if an individual does not feel ill during a cold, then he or she may not engage in the self-regulatory behaviors necessary to recover efficiently from the cold. If one is stoically unresponsive to illness symptoms, then one is disconnected from a source of information useful in guiding self-regulatory behaviors.

The intraindividual parameter examined in this study thus concerns the linkage between changes in a person's health status and his or her daily moods. In our study, we operationalized this intraindividual parameter as the within-subject correlation between daily mood ratings and daily symptom ratings computed across occasions for each subject. We then examined whether some people show a diminished or enhanced emotional consequence of becoming ill.

To assess the intraindividual linkage between daily mood and daily symptoms, we regressed daily mood on symptom scores over the occasions of observation for each subject. In the intraindividual regression model between mood and symptoms, we controlled for the previous three mood scores. This has the effect of removing any autocorrelation in mood that might contribute to the mood-symptom correlation, as in the following equation:

$$\text{Mood}_t = a + \beta_1 \text{Mood}_{t-3} + \beta_2 \text{Mood}_{t-2} + \beta_3 \text{Mood}_{t-1} + \beta_4 \text{Symptom}_t$$

The parameter used as the intraindividual indicator of the linkage between mood and symptoms is the β_4 parameter in the above equation. If a subject has a large β_4 parameter, it means that his or her negative emotions covary strongly with the presence of symptoms, even after controlling for autocorrelation in the mood measure. Subjects with a large β_4 parameter display affective changes that co-occur with changes in health status.

The within-subject regression coefficients—the temporal parameter indexing linkage—ranged from essentially zero to strongly positive in this sample. The larger this linkage, the more likely it is that negative moods co-occurred with symptoms for that person. In terms of the linkage between mood and symptoms, a very consistent pattern emerged among persons with Type A personality. The interindividual analyses indicated that subjects high on the Type A dimension reported higher linkages between negative moods and symptoms than subjects low on this personality measure. That is, Type A individuals tend to have negative moods when they are ill much more than persons low on Type A. Episodes of illness are more likely to be accompanied by bouts of negative affect (feeling blue, unhappy, frustrated, worried, anxious, and angry) for high Type A individuals but less so for persons low on this personality variable.

This example highlights how intraindividual variability can be assessed in terms of covariation between important variables, and that the degree of covariation may show important differences between people. In the next example, I show how intraindividual variability can be assessed in a manner that allows the researcher to estimate the relative duration of events, in this case the duration of common illnesses.

Intraindividual Lagged Autocorrelation: Predicting Future States From Past States

The dominant question in the personality-health literature is whether personality factors predict who gets sick. Results have been mixed (Depue & Monroe, 1986; Friedman & Booth-Kewley, 1987). However, one might turn the question around and ask whether personality predicts who gets better. That is, when it comes to common daily illnesses (e.g., stomachaches, headaches, respiratory infections) everyone gets ill from time to time. The personality effects may occur in who gets better faster. Said differently, personality may predict the within-subject duration of common illnesses more than the frequency or occurrence of those illnesses. Attempting to understand the course of illness demands that we study persons over time and include the intraindividual dimension in data on illness.

In the present example, we (Larsen & Kasimatis, 1991) examined the duration of common illnesses over a 2-month period in the lives of our subjects. We made the case that occurrence and duration of illnesses should be distinct processes. What causes a person to, say, catch a cold (a virus) is quite different from what causes the person to recover (rest, plenty of fluids). As such, different personality factors may be involved in the onset and recovery rate or duration of common illnesses.

For duration scores, we wanted to quantify the probabilistic degree to which symptoms persisted over contiguous observation periods for each subject. To do this, we calculated, for each person, the degree to which current symptoms

predicted symptoms on future occasions, across increasing time lags. The autocorrelation of a variable with itself, at increasing time lags, can be displayed as a correlogram. In figure 23.2 are two idealized correlograms created to illustrate differences in duration. In Panel A is a correlogram of a process that has longer duration than that displayed in Panel B. In Panel A, the autocorrelation remains significant out to Lag 8, whereas in Panel B the autocorrelation is significant out to only Lag 3. Autocorrelation is computed by correlating a variable with itself in the future. As an example, respiratory infection at Time T was correlated with respiratory infection at Times $T+1$, $T+2$, $T+3$...If symptom occurrence tends to be followed in time by further symptoms, then significant lagged autocorrelations will be found. Autocorrelations were computed separately for each subject for each of four symptom factors to model individual differences in the duration of those symp-

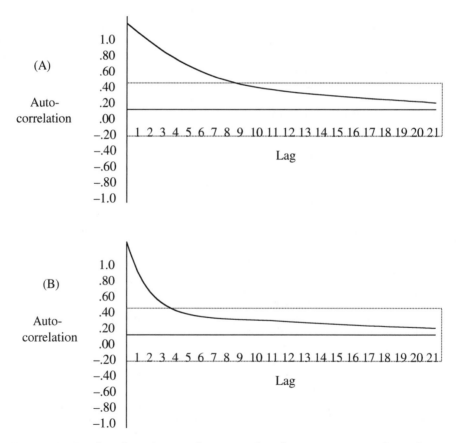

Figure 23.2 Hypothetical correlograms illustrating a long duration symptom with significant autocorrelation out to Lag 8 (A) and a shorter duration symptom with significant autocorrelation out to Lag 3 (B). Adapted from Larsen (in press).

toms over time. For each subject and symptom factor, we determined the maximum lag at which the autocorrelation remained significantly different from zero. The symptom duration variable thus represents the largest number of lags at which the autocorrelation remains significant for each symptom factor for each subject. A larger number means a longer duration of symptom.

In terms of duration, the upper respiratory factor had the longest average duration, with the average autocorrelation staying significant out to over five lags forward in time. Since three lags covered a full day in the data set, this implies that, on average, if we know a person has respiratory symptoms on one occasion, we are able to significantly predict the occurrence of symptoms almost 48 hours later. This finding does not mean that respiratory infections last only two days. Rather, the meaning of this lagged autocorrelation is that respiratory symptoms persist in a probabilistic way that allows significant predictability almost 2 days into the future, on average. By contrast, the shortest duration was found for the gastrointestional symptoms. The finding of a significant autocorrelation of only 1.6 lags into the future (on average) suggests that such symptoms do not last long (about 6 to 9 hours in this college student sample).

Symptoms of distress (urge to cry, trouble concentrating, fatigue) had a very short duration, with significant autocorrelation slightly less than two lags into the future. The symptoms reported on in this factor probably have to do with intense but temporary negative affect associated with acute stress, which is common enough among college students to produce a distinct symptom factor.

In terms of an interindividual analysis of duration, a pattern emerged such that, with the exception of respiratory symptoms, the duration of all other symptoms correlated significantly (and negatively) with anger control. That is, individuals who are less likely to act aggressively when frustrated report illness symptoms that tend to be of shorter duration compared to the more aggressive subjects.

In this example, the intraindividual parameter was the autocorrelation function for specific symptoms. It turns out that the autocorrelation function for most symptoms was negatively related to hostility, with hostile persons reporting longer-duration illnesses compared to the less hostile subjects. In our next example, we examine rhythmic variation as the intraindividual pattern of interest.

Lagged Covariation: Detecting Hidden Cycles

Lagged autocorrelation can also be used to examine data for rhythmic variability, which can be defined as directional variability that repeats itself over a specific time period. If a researcher produces a correlogram for a particular subject (as in figure 23.2), and that correlogram exhibits the normal motonic decline, then there are no hidden cycles or rhythms in that subject's data. However, if the correlogram exhibits a spike at a certain lag, with the autocorrelation function displaying a bump at a particular lag, then this is evidence of a cycle in the data set, with a period approximating the lag at which the autocorrelation spikes. In this way, autocorrelation plots are useful for detecting hidden cycles (Gottman, 1981).

The source of the following example is Larsen and Kasimatis (1990). Here we were interested in weekly rhythms in mood. We had subjects keep daily mood records for 84 consecutive days (3 months). We calculated average mood for each day of the study, and submitted this time series to spectral analysis to see if there was a weekly rhythm. There was a clear spike in the spectral density function indicating a rhythm of 7 days. In fact, a perfect sine wave with a period of 7 days correlated, locked in phase with the days of the week, correlated .63 with the raw data, which implies that approximately 40% of the variability in the aggregated daily mood scores is accounted for by a 7-day cycle.

We also had theoretical reasons for predicting that some persons would show more entrainment to this 7-day cycle than other persons. Consequently, we fit each subject's data to the 7-day sine wave and assessed the degree of fit. Here the intraindividual parameter of interest is the degree to which each subject is predictable from a 7-day sine wave. Across subjects, it turned out that introverted subjects were significantly more cyclically predictable than extraverts. Said differently, extraverts conformed less to the 7-day cycle than introverts. This finding is consistent with the notion that extraverts tend to avoid routine, and introverts tend to seek routine. Introverts seek to keep stimulation to a minimum, and one way to do this is to have a great deal of routine in their lives. Extraverts, on the other hand, enjoy stimulation and obtain it, in part, by being more unpredictable, such as not waiting for the weekend to have a party or go out to socialize.

In this third example, the intraindividual parameter of interest was the degree of predictability in each subject's moods in terms of a weekly cycle. Spectral analysis, which is based on autocorrelation functions, was used to identify the 7-day cycle. The fit of this cycle was assessed for each person, and the interindividual analyses showed that there were meaningful individual differences in that within-subject parameter. In the final example, a multivariate time series approach is taken to intraindividual variability.

Multivariate Covariation Within Persons: The Complexity of Individual Emotional Lives

In this final example of intraindividual variability, I focus on a structural analysis of each subject's temporal data using factor analysis, also called P-technique factor analysis since it is applied to single persons (Cattell, 1973). In this example, drawn from Larsen and Cutler (1996), we had subjects complete a mood report three times a day (morning, afternoon, and evening) for 2 consecutive months. This gave us, on average, 180 observation occasions for each subject. The report form completed on these occasions contained 21 emotion adjectives (e.g., happy, depressed, irritable, peppy, bored, joyful, etc.).

Many researchers employing this experience sampling technique use it to obtain average levels of affect for each person. Such estimates are reliable indicators of the person's expected level of affect, but they ignore variability and other intraindividual processes. More important, treating the data in this fashion assumes that each person has the same structure of emotion and differs from others only in the amount of the emotion experienced over time.

We wondered, however, whether subjects might actually differ from each other in the intraindividual structure of their emotional lives. If so, then we would find different factor structures between subjects when we compared factor analysis results from subject to subject.

One structural way that persons might differ from each other is in the number of factors needed to account for a fixed portion of variation in each subject's intraindividual data. This possibility was mentioned decades ago in the pioneering work of Wessman and Ricks (1966). They discussed the possibility that people may differ from each other in the complexity of emotional lives, with some subjects possibly needing many factors to account for common

variance and others needing only a few factors. However, Wessman and Ricks (1966) devoted only two pages of their book to the topic of emotional complexity and focused mainly on individual differences in mean level of emotion and emotional variability.

Zevon and Tellegen (1982) undertook an extensive factor analytic study of individual differences in intraindividual variability in affect. However, these authors assumed no difference in emotion structure and so extracted only two factors for each subject. While the first two factors show similar loadings for each subject, it nevertheless represents underextraction for some subjects. That is, the degree to which the two-factor solution accounted for variation most likely differed greatly across subjects (Zevon and Tellegen, 1982; did not report fit statistics).

In our data set, we factored the 21 mood adjectives across the 180 occasions for each subject, and we extracted as many factors as was necessary to account for half of the common variability in each subject's data. For some subjects this required only two factors, but for others it required as many as five factors. The subjects with the larger numbers of factors simply had more independent units of covariation in their data; that is, they showed a more complex covariance pattern than the subjects with fewer factors.

In a between-subjects analysis, we identified some interesting correlates of emotional complexity, and these correlates differed between the genders. Emotional complexity in males tended to correlate with indicators of maladjustment, including lower levels of happiness, more emotional variability, and psychosomatic complaints. None of these correlations were observed for women. In fact, for women, emotional complexity was positively associated with happiness. In the report (Larsen & Cutler, 1996), we went into some detail on why this might be the case. For the present purposes, however, the point of this example is to illustrate an application of a multivariate analysis of intraindividual variability. Here the parameter of interest was the factorial complexity of each subject's daily mood ratings.

Conclusion

In this chapter, I have presented a framework for thinking about intraindividual variability, which I have previously termed a *process approach* to research. I then went on to provide four examples of the use of this approach to analyze intraindividual variability in a number of different ways. In this context, the specific content and findings I presented are not as important as the examples each provides of the different ways that a researcher can conceptualize intraindividual variability.

My intention here is to inspire enthusiasm for the unique questions that can be addressed when one thinks a bit differently about data and about variability over time (West & Hepworth, 1991). When time is included in data capture, by intensively sampling experience or behavior over many occasions, then time becomes an inherent structural component of the data. As such, intraindividual variability can be analyzed in unique ways that reveal specific processes (Larsen, 1990). In particular, processes that involve patterns of intraindividual change, such as cycles or rhythms, or that involve duration or rate of change, or that involve covariation of change, either at the same time (co-occurrence) or across time (lagged covariation) are all ideal questions for study with these methods.

The type of intraindividual analyses that are possible can result in a large number of models open to investigation. A final thought thus concerns the importance of having the substantive research question dictate the analytic strategy, rather than the other way around. In contemplating whether to gather and analyze intraindividual data, one simply has to keep the research question in clear focus as a guiding principle throughout the design and analysis of the project. If researchers were to proceed on a purely inductive path, going out and gathering data without being guided by a specific question, they would be quickly overwhelmed by analytic possibilities inherent in intraindividual data. In the present examples, the research questions came first, and guided us in determining the best strategy to pursue in the modeling of intraindividual variability. Researchers need to keep a focus on the intraindividual parameters that might best serve as indicators to characterize the processes in which they are interested.

There are many questions in positive psychology that could be approached through an analysis of intraindividual variability. With a few moments of thought, several questions come to mind. For example, are happy people less reactive to negative life events, more reactive to positive life events, or both? Are happy persons faster to recover from unpleasant circumstances? Would they show shorter durations in returning to their emotional set points following a distressing event? What is the relative impact of having a skewed distribution of positive events in one's life, that is, having a few really positive events versus having many somewhat positive events? Are their interventions strategies (e.g., thankfulness training) that would lead to changes in day-to-day positive affect? The answers to these and many other questions could be obtained through the study of intraindividual variability similar to the examples provided in this chapter.

Acknowledgments   Preparation of this manuscript was supported by grant RO1-MH63732 from the National Institute of Mental Health.

References

Boker, S. M., & Nesselroade, J. R. (2002). A method for modeling the intrinsic dynamics of intraindividual variability: Recovering the parameters of simulated oscillators in multi-wave data. *Multivariate Behavioral Research, 37*, 127–160.

Cattell, R. B. (1973). *Personality and mood by questionnaire*. San Francisco: Jossey-Bass.

Cattell, R. B. (1988). The data box: Its ordering of total resources in terms of possible relational systems. In J. R. Nesselroade & R. B. Cattell (Eds.), *Handbook of multivariate experimental psychology* (2nd ed.) (pp. 69–130). New York: Plenum Press.

Epstein, S. (1983). The stability of behavior: I. On predicting most of the people much of the time. *Journal of Personality and Social Psychology, 37*, 1097–1126.

Depue, R. A. & Monroe, S. M. (1986). Conceptualization and measurement of human disorder in life stress research: The problem of chronic disturbance. *Psychological Bulletin, 99*, 36–51.

Friedman, H. S., & Booth-Kewley, S. (1987). The "disease-prone personality": A meta-analytic view of the construct. *American Psychologist, 42*, 539–555.

Gottman, J. M. (1981). *Time-series analysis: A comprehensive introduction for social scientists*. New York: Cambridge University Press.

Hyland, M. E. (1987). Control theory interpretation of psychological mechanisms of depression: Comparison of integration of several theories. *Psychological Bulletin, 102*, 109–121.

Kernis, M. H., Cornell, D. P., Sun, C, & Berry, A. (1993). There's more to self-esteem than whether it is high or low: The importance of stability of self-esteem. *Journal of Personality and Social Psychology, 65,* 1190–1204.

Larsen, R. J. (1987). The stability of mood variability: A spectral analytic approach to daily mood assessments. *Journal of Personality and Social Psychology, 52,* 1195–1204.

Larsen, R. J. (1989). A process approach to personality: Utilizing time as a facet of data. In D. Buss & N. Cantor (Eds.), *Personality psychology: Recent trends and emerging directions* (pp. 177–193). New York: Springer-Verlag.

Larsen, R. J. (1990). Spectral analysis of psychological data. In A. Von Eye (Ed.), *Statistical methods in longitudinal research: Volume II. Time series and categorical longitudinal data* (pp. 319–349). Boston: Academic Press.

Larsen, R. J. (1992). Neuroticism and selective encoding and recall of symptoms: Evidence from a combined concurrent-retrospective study. *Journal of Personality and Social Psychology, 62,* 480–488.

Larsen, R. J. (1993). Strategies and tactics for person-situation interaction. In J. Hettema & I. Deary (Eds.), *Foundations of personality* (pp. 165–173). Dordrecht, The Netherlands: Kluwer.

Larsen, R. J. (2000). Toward a science of mood regulation. *Psychological Inquiry, 11,* 129–141.

Larsen, R. J. (in press). Personality, emotion, and daily health. In A. Stone & S. Shiffman (Eds.), *The science of real-time data capture: Self-reports in health research.* New York: Oxford University Press.

Larsen, R. J., & Cowan, G. S. (1988). Internal focus of attention and depression: A study of daily experience. *Motivation and Emotion, 12,* 237–249.

Larsen, R. J., & Cutler, S. (1996). The complexity of individual emotional lives: A within-subject analysis of affect structure. *Journal of Social and Clinical Psychology, 15,* 206–230.

Larsen, R. J., & Kasimatis, M. (1990). Individual differences in entrainment of mood to the weekly calendar. *Journal of Personality and Social Psychology, 58,* 164–171.

Larsen, R. J., & Kasimatis, M. (1991). Day-to-day physical symptoms: Individual differences in the occurrence, duration, and emotional concomitants of minor daily illnesses. *Journal of Personality, 59,* 387–423.

Larsen, R. J., & Prizmic, Z. (2004). Affect regulation. In R. Baumeister & K. Vohs (Eds.), *Handbook of self-regulation research* (pp. 40–60). New York: Guilford.

Pool, R. (1989). Is it chaos, or is it just noise? *Science, 243,* 25–28.

Raudenbush, S. W., & Bryk, A. S. (2002). *Hierarchical linear models: Applications and data analysis methods* (2nd ed.). Thousand Oaks, CA: Sage.

Runyon, W. M. (1983). Idiographic goals and methods in the study of lives. *Journal of Personality, 51,* 413–437.

Wessman, A. E., & Ricks, D. F. (1966). *Mood and personality.* New York: Holt, Rinehart and Winston.

West, S., & Hepworth, J. (1991). Statistical issues in the study of temporal data: Daily experiences. *Journal of Personality, 59,* 609–662.

Zelenski, J. M., & Larsen, R. J. (2000). The distribution of emotions in everyday life: A state and trait perspective from experience sampling data. *Journal of Research in Personality, 34,* 178–197.

Zevon, M. A., & Tellegen, A. (1982). The structure of mood change: An idiographic/nomothetic analysis. *Journal of Personality and Social Psychology, 43,* 111–122.

24

Using Item Response Models to Analyze Change

Advantages and Limitations

Judith Glück and Christiane Spiel

In this chapter, we present models that measure change in people's responses to individual test or questionnaire items, as opposed to change in scores computed across a number of items. In our view, these models are well-suited for many concepts of positive psychology, because they offer a highly differentiated perspective on change. Consider, for example, changes in personality in old age. Such changes, which occur relatively late in old age and are not very large in size, have to date been described in terms of scores on personality tests such as the NEO (Costa & McCrae, 1985). For example, Smith and Baltes (1999) found in a cross-sectional analysis that from age 85 on, neuroticism is positively correlated with age, while extraversion and openness are negatively correlated with age.

Looking at such personality changes on an item level, as we suggest, would ask a different question: Do changes occur in all or in only some of the items, and are these changes all in the same direction? For example, it is quite possible that different aspects of extraversion change in different ways in old age, so that some items show changes in one direction, and others show change in the other direction, together resulting in small or no changes on the score level. In spite of these small changes, however, the meaning of the sum score would change. If at Time 1 a high score is largely the result of highly positive responses to Items 1 and 2, but at Time 2, responses to Items 1 and 2 have decreased and responses to Items 3 and 4 have increased, the substantive meaning of the sum score across the four items has changed. Item response models allow for analyzing such qualitative changes. Thus, instead of simply describing change as a quantitative increase or decrease in scores, they look at changes in the quality of constructs.

In the following, we first describe the data example—changes in personality in old age, as found in the Berlin Aging Study—that will illustrate our methods. Then, we introduce the basics of the Rasch model and show how it can be used to look at age differences in cross-sectional data. After that, we present the linear logistic model with relaxed assumptions (LLRA), a special model for analyzing change, and apply it to our longitudinal data. In the last section, we discuss both the substantive implications of the results and the applicability (and limitations of applicability) of our models in different research contexts. To conclude, we give an overview of other Rasch models for change.

Data Example

Participants

The data we analyze here were collected in the Berlin Aging Study (BASE; Baltes & Mayer, 1999). In this large-scale study, an age- and gender-stratified sample of citizens of Berlin, aged 70 to 100 years, was interviewed and tested using a variety of psychological, sociological, psychiatric, and medical measures. Follow-up data were collected at 2-year intervals. At the first time point (t1), the sample consisted of 516 individuals. Here, we analyze changes between t1 and the third time point, 4 years later, when 206 of the original 516 participants were still willing and able to participate. Due to missing data, our sample consists of 203 individuals; of these, 99 (48.8%) were male and 104 were female. For the

sake of simplicity, we denote the third BASE assessment, which is the second time point in our analysis, as t2 in the following.

One of the strengths of the models we advocate here is that they allow for comparisons of change across subgroups of individuals. For the present purpose, we were especially interested in age differences in change. As has been shown, personality traits are stable across most of the life span and show only small changes late in life (e.g., Smith & Baltes, 1999). Therefore, we divided our sample into a younger and an older age group, using the t1 age median (78.6 years) as the splitting criterion. The younger age group consisted of 102 individuals, with age means of 74.3 years ($SD = 2.5$ years) at t1 and 78.1 years ($SD = 2.6$) at t2. The older age group consisted of 101 individuals, with age means at t1 and t2 of 85.2 ($SD = 5.4$) and 89.0 years ($SD = 5.5$).

Materials

In the BASE study, a German-language short version of the scales Neuroticism, Extraversion, and Openness to Experience of the NEO-FFI (Costa & McCrae, 1985) was used (see table 24.1). The questionnaire consisted of five items

TABLE 24.1 NEO Items as Used in the Berlin Aging Study

Item Nr.	Item Text
Neuroticism	
1	When I'm under a great deal of stress, sometimes I feel like I'm going to pieces.
2	I often feel fearful or anxious.*
3	I often feel tense and jittery.
4	I often feel helpless and want someone else to solve my problems.
5	Sometimes I feel completely worthless.
Extraversion	
1	I like to have a lot of people around me.
2	I really enjoy talking to people.
3	I like to be where the action is.
4	I often get angry at the way people treat me.
5	I am a cheerful, high-spirited person.
6	I am a very active person.
Openness	
1	I like to daydream.*
2	Once I find the right way to do something, I stick to it. (recoded)
3	Poetry affects me.*
4	I like to try something new.
5	I have a very active imagination.
6	I have a lot of intellectual curiosity.

*Items differ from the original English-language NEO because negations were avoided.

measuring neuroticism, six items measuring extraversion, and six items measuring openness to experience. The items are listed in table 24.1. Responses were given on 5-point scales with the end points *does not apply to me at all* (1) and *applies very well to me* (5). For the sake of simplicity of presentation, we dichotomized the item responses, coding 1 and 2 as 0 and 3, 4, and 5 as 1 (for models for ordered response formats, see the last section of this chapter).

Changes on the Score Level

In order to compare our qualitative-change approach to the classical approach, we first analyzed whether our two age groups showed any changes over the 4-year period in their sum scores in the three scales. Figure 24.1 shows the two age groups' means in neuroticism, extraversion, and openness at the two time points.

Analyses of variance showed no significant effects of time, nor interactions of time and age group, for any scale. Significant age group differences were found for neuroticism, $F(1, 201) = 4.461$, $p = .036$, and extraversion, $F(1, 201) = 6.181$, $p = .014$. Thus, there were some cross-sectional age differences on the score level, but there was not much longitudinal change in either age group during the 4-year period under

study. Smith and Baltes (1999) analyzed cross-sectional age differences in the same data using 5-year age brackets and using scores based on the original 5-point response formats. They found negative age differences in openness and extraversion, but not in neuroticism.

The fact that age differences were found in cross-sectional but not longitudinal analyses may suggest that the age group differences are due to cohort effects only (although it is not easy to find a good theoretical explanation for such cohort effects). Another explanation would be that there are some changes, but they are too slow, or too small, to be visible in a 4-year interval. Also, changes may have occurred in some of the items but may have gotten lost in the computation of sum scores. Therefore, we analyzed longitudinal changes on the item level in spite of stability on the score level.

In the following, we first introduce the conceptual background of the Rasch model, and then use standard Rasch model tests to perform a cross-sectional comparison between the t1 data of the two age groups. In this way, we analyze whether there were qualitative differences between the younger and the older age group when they entered the study. Then we explain the rationale of the LLRA and use it to analyze changes that occurred in the two age groups between t1 and t2.

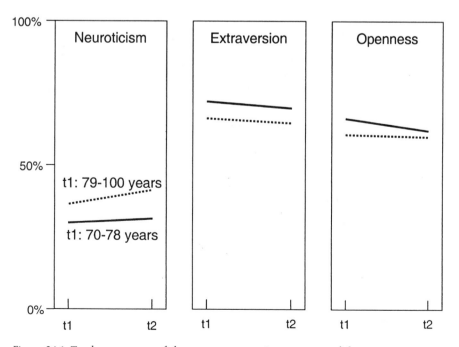

Figure 24.1 Total score means of the two age groups (in percentage of the maximum

For all analyses, we used the software LPCM-Win (Fischer & Ponocny-Seliger, 1998), which is available at SciencePlus in Groningen (http://www.scienceplus.nl). For the Rasch model, many other programs are available, and some of them can also be outsmarted to estimate LLRA parameters; however, LPCM-Win is the only one that includes the LLRA as a standard application.

The Rasch Model

In almost all psychological tests or questionnaires, item responses are coded as numbers, and scores across items are computed by adding up those numbers. However, such a score computation makes conceptual sense only if the items meet certain requirements. The original Rasch model (Rasch, 1960/1980) was a mathematical formulation of the requirements that dichotomous test items need to fulfill if their responses are to be added up to such a sum score. It is intuitively convincing that for a sum score to make substantive sense, the items that are added up should all be measuring the same construct, or, in the language of item response theory, the same latent dimension. The Rasch model shows that there should be one, and only one, latent dimension of ability (or, more generally, a latent trait) on which every individual and every item can be unequivocally positioned.

As the Rasch model was originally developed for ability tests, the Rasch terminology refers to individuals' "ability" and item "difficulty," which does not fit for questionnaires assessing personality, attitudes, and the like. However, the idea can easily be translated into the language of

such questionnaires. An individual's ability is simply that person's level of the latent trait in question (e.g., the person's degree of extraversion), and an item's difficulty is the level on the latent trait where this item discriminates best. A very "difficult" extraversion item is one to which only very extraverted participants will agree (e.g., "I like to give talks in front of a large audience"), while a very easy item is one to which almost everyone, except for very introverted individuals, will agree (e.g., "I like to go out with friends"). An individual's "ability," or position on the latent dimension, determines her probability to agree to each item of the test, given the item's position on the latent dimension. Instead of ability and difficulty parameters, we will simply speak of trait parameters and item parameters.

The model equation of the Rasch model gives an individual's probability to agree to a given item as a logistic function of the individual's trait parameter and the item parameter:

$$p(+\,|\,\theta_v, \sigma_i) = \frac{e^{\theta_v - \sigma_i}}{1 + e^{\theta_v - \sigma_i}} \qquad (1)$$

where $p(+\,|\,\theta_v, \sigma_i)$ is the probability that individual v agrees to item i, given the individual's trait parameter θ_v and the item parameter σ_i. Figure 24.2 illustrates the idea. Each item is represented by a curve that shows the probability that individuals at different points on the latent dimension will agree to this item. The item parameter is located at the point where the agreement probability is exactly 50%. Participant 1 with trait parameter θ_1 has a low probability to agree to Item 1 and an even lower probability to agree to Item 2. Participant 2, whose trait parameter θ_2 is

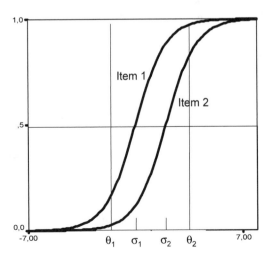

Figure 24.2 Item characteristic curves in the Rasch model.

higher than the two item parameters, has a high probability of agreeing to Item 2 and an almost perfect chance to agree to Item 1.

Thus, the agreement probability is a function of the distance between the individual's and the item's position on the latent dimension. An individual with low extraversion will have a lower probability of agreeing to all items than an individual with high extraversion. An item with a low difficulty parameter will be agreed to by more individuals than a difficult item. The crucial aspect for the present discussion is that the ordering of items on the latent dimension is independent of the subgroup of individuals analyzed. That is, it is clearly possible that a more extraverted group of people (say, windsurfing instructors) can have a higher probability of agreeing to all items of the scale than a more introverted group (say, mathematicians). However, the order of and differences between the items' positions on the latent dimension should be constant across these two groups. That is, both groups should have higher agreement rates for Item 1 than for Item 2 in the example in figure 24.2. If this is the case, an individual's probability of agreeing to an item depends on no other factor except the person's and the item's position on the latent dimension.

If these assumptions hold, the sum score of an individual's item responses is a sufficient statistic for estimating the individual's level on the latent dimension; that is, it makes mathematical sense to look only at the number of items agreed to and not at which items the individual has agreed to. In most empirical cases, however, these assumptions are not fulfilled; that is, the items cannot be ordered on a latent dimension so that the order is the same for all subgroups of individuals that may be tested. Consider our first example. If certain aspects of extraversion become more frequent in older age, whereas others become less frequent, the positions of the items on the latent dimension are not the same for younger and older individuals. That is, some items that many young people agree to may be much more difficult for older people to agree to, and the other way around. In such cases, the sum score has a different meaning across the two age groups—or in other words, computing a sum score is not sufficient for interpreting a person's item responses. For example, a younger and an older individual may have the exact same sum score in extraversion, but the quality of their extraversion, which manifests in the patterns of their item responses, may be different.

The Rasch model was developed in order to identify such cases. Georg Rasch proved mathematically that the computation of a sum score is only justified when the Rasch model holds for a test or questionnaire. (Almost all of our current tests and questionnaires do not fulfill this strict condition, however; we will come back to this point later.) How do we test whether the Rasch model holds for a test or questionnaire? There are many ways (for an overview, see Glas & Verhelst, 1995); one method, however, follows directly from the requirement that the ordering of the item difficulty parameters and the differences between them must be the same in all possible subgroups of individuals. This assumption is tested by Andersen's (1973) conditional likelihood ratio test (CLRT). For this test, the sample is divided into two predefined subgroups, for example, younger and older participants. Andersen's CLRT checks whether the Rasch model fits the data significantly better if the item difficulty parameters are estimated for the two subgroups separately than if they are estimated for the total sample. If this is the case, the item parameters in the respective subgroups are different, and the Rasch model does not hold for the item set. If there is no significant difference in fit, the test items seem to measure the same latent dimension. Technically, the test is similar to invariance tests for covariance structures, as used, for example, in structural equation modeling. The difference is, however, that we test for differences in item difficulty parameters, and not for differences in covariances.

It is important to note that just because there is no difference in item parameters between, for example, older and younger participants, the test does not necessarily fulfill the assumptions of the Rasch model. There might be differences between male and female participants or between some other subgroups more difficult to identify. Mixed Rasch models (see the last section of this chapter) offer an exploratory way to look for groups of individuals that differ in item parameters.

The Rasch model has seldom been used in the development of questionnaires. In fact, even the number of ability tests that fulfill its assumptions is quite small. The reason is that the Rasch model's criteria are very strict. For the order of item difficulties to be the same across all possible subgroups of people, an item set needs to be extremely homogeneous in content; questionnaires that fulfill this requirement could only measure very narrow traits. At the same time, a certain heterogeneity in item difficulties is important for the Rasch model to hold; thus, a Rasch-homogeneous questionnaire would need to consist of a very similar question asked in different ways so that the agreement rate varies considerably. This is sometimes achievable in ability tests, but hardly ever in personality or attitude tests. One of the remarkable advantages of the LLRA, the model for analyzing change described above, is that it does not require unidimensionality of the items involved. Before we discuss that model, however, we want to argue that the Rasch model is still a very useful instrument both in constructing scales and in understanding what exactly they measure. By identifying differences in item difficulty patterns between subgroups of individuals, researchers can learn a lot about what their scales measure. Even a researcher who does not insist on using only items that fulfill the strict criteria of the Rasch model can get to understand the construct in a new way by looking at item-response patterns. In the following, we demonstrate what this means using the NEO data.

Application of the Rasch Model to the Data Example

We used Andersen's CLRT to compare the t1 item difficulties in the younger and older age group. For neuroticism, there was no significant difference in item difficulty parameters, χ^2 (4, $N = 203$) = 4.712, $p = .318$. Thus, although the analyses on the score level reported above had shown that the older age group was higher in neuroticism than the younger age group, this was a quantitative age difference that did not involve any qualitative differences. For extraversion, we had to exclude Item 5 ("I am a cheerful, high-spirited person") from the analyses because all individuals in the younger age group agreed to this item. There was no significant difference in the parameters of the remaining five items, χ^2 (4, $N = 203$) = 5.149, $p = .272$. Thus, as with neuroticism, differences between the age groups are quantitative but not qualitative. For openness to experience, however, we found a significant difference between the two age groups, χ^2 (5, $N = 203$) = 12.783, $p = .026$. The age groups differed significantly in the parameter of Item 1 ("I like to daydream") only. We found that this was the only item to which the older group had a higher agreement rate (43%) than the younger group (39%), while all other items had lower agreement rates in the older group. Thus, although the difference is small in absolute numbers, daydreaming is a more typical

aspect of openness in the older group than in the younger group.

In the next step, we studied longitudinal changes in the item parameters of the three NEO scales. The Rasch analysis had shown only one significant age difference; however, the literature on personality and aging shows that changes occur, if at all, only in very old age (e.g., Smith & Baltes, 1999). Therefore, we expected to see some changes in the older age group over the 4-year period.

The Linear Logistic Model With Relaxed Assumptions

A number of models have been derived from the original Rasch model (see Fischer & Molenaar, 1995); however, we believe that the LLRA (Fischer, 1983, 1995a; Fischer & Formann, 1982; for applications see Glück & Indurkhya, 2001; Glück & Spiel, 1997; Spiel & Glück, 1998) is among the most ingenious inventions for two reasons. The first is that, as we will show, the LLRA allows researchers to formulate and test hypotheses about differences in change across items and across groups of people in a straightforward and technically elegant manner. The second reason is that it circumvents the most crucial practical problem in applying the Rasch model. As was just discussed, most data—especially where questionnaires, as opposed to ability tests, are concerned—do not fulfill the strict assumptions of the Rasch model. This may have led many researchers to abandon the use of the Rasch model in favor of less restrictive models.

The LLRA does not require homogeneity of the items involved. It allows for testing hypotheses about the homogeneity of *change* across items without any restrictions on item dimensionality. How is this possible? The basic idea of the LLRA is to model each item as a test of its own. The item responses at t1 are modeled as the responses to Item 1 of the test, responses at t2 are modeled as responses to Item 2, and so on. Thus, the LLRA acts as if there were as many different tests in the data as there were items, and as if each test had as many items as there were time points. To analyze change, item parameters are estimated by setting the parameter for Item 1, that is, the first time point, to zero. The parameters for the other time points are then estimated relative to t1. That is, if a positive change has occurred in the frequency of agreement to an item between t1 and t2, the parameter for Item 2 of the respective test will be positive, and if the change has been negative, the parameter will be negative. Obviously, the model can easily be extended to more than two time points, resulting in more than two items in each test.

As each item is viewed as a test of its own, the most general LLRA model has as many tests as there are items. This model is only the first step, however. Next, more restrictive models can be tested—for example, a model specifying that the differences between Item 2 and Item 1 are equal across all tests, that is, that changes between t1 and t2 are the same across all items. The model equation of the most general LLRA we use here gives the probability for participant v to agree to item i at time point t1 as

$$p(x_{vit1} = 1) = \frac{\exp(\theta_{vi})}{1 + \exp(\theta_{vi})}, \qquad (2a)$$

and the probability for participant v to agree to item i at time point t2 as

$$p(x_{vit2} = 1) = \frac{\exp(\theta_{vi} + \delta_{gi})}{1 + \exp(\theta_{vi} + \delta_{gi})}. \qquad (2b)$$

Thus, an individual's agreement probability at t1 is only dependent on θ_{vi}, that is, on that person's level of the trait that item i measures. Her agreement probability at t2 is dependent on θ_{vi} plus a change parameter δ_{gi}, which is specific to the item and to the subgroup g the person belongs to. More restrictive models assume, for example, that a smaller set of change parameters δ_g, which are group-specific but constant across all items, or change parameters δ_i, which are item-specific but the same for all groups, describe the data as well as the general model does. Using likelihood ratio tests, we compare the fit of such restrictive models against the first, most general model. The aim of these tests is to find the most parsimonious model for the data, that is, the model that requires the smallest number of parameters to describe the data well. We demonstrate the procedure in the following.

Application of the LLRA to the Data Example

Although there were no significant longitudinal changes on the score level, we wanted to test whether the older group showed changes in some of the items of the three scales, which might not have been strong enough to affect the sum scores. Therefore, we analyzed differences in the changes the younger and older age group

showed in the three NEO scales. For each scale, we first estimated the most general model, which assumed one item parameter (representing change from t1 to t2) for each item in each age group. Thus, for a six-item scale, the first model estimated 12 parameters. This model served as a base model for each scale, against which we then tested more restrictive models—for example, models assuming no change at all, no difference in change between the two groups, or no difference in change across the six items. A model is assumed to fit the data if it does not fit significantly worse than the base model.

The base model allows for all possible differences that our theory expects: differences in change between items, differences in change between age groups, and interactions, that is, differences between the age groups in the differences between items. The base model is often referred to as the quasi-saturated model, in analogy to the saturated models that are used as base models in other methods, for example, in loglinear modeling. The difference is that a truly saturated model has perfect fit because it has enough parameters to describe all changes in the data, whereas our base model assumes that changes are homogeneous within the two age groups we analyze.

In the following, we describe the model-testing process for each scale of the NEO. In the case of neuroticism, the process was brief. We first tested a model assuming no change at all. As this model did not fit the data significantly worse than the base model, χ^2 (10, $N = 203$) = 13.612, $p = .191$, there were no significant changes in either age group for any item. Thus, there was no need to test any more complex models; for neuroticism, the LLRA results confirmed the results of the analyses of variance. The same was true for openness; the no-change model fit the data acceptably, χ^2 (12, $N = 203$) = 19.605, $p = .074$. Again, the results of the LLRA are consistent with those on the score level.

For extraversion, results told a more complex story. We had to remove Items 2 and 5 because they showed changes only in one direction in the younger group (this requirement of the LLRA is discussed below). For the remaining four items, the no-change model fit the data significantly worse than the base model, χ^2 (8, $N = 203$) = 24.575, $p = .002$. Thus, in the extraversion scale, some changes did occur. The next model we tested assumed equal changes across the four items within each age group. This model did not fit the data either, χ^2 (6, $N = 203$) = 23.605,

$p < .001$. Thus, there were differences in change between the items.

In order to find a model that describes these differences well, we developed hypotheses based on theories of life-span developmental psychology, in particular, on Laura Carstensen's socioemotional selectivity theory (overview in Carstensen, Isaacowitz, & Charles, 1999). Carstensen assumes that when the end of life comes closer, older people prefer social situations that give them positive emotions (such as being with close friends or family) to situations that may be more negative but offer potential gains for the future (such as meeting new people). Second, we used findings on the development of emotionality in old age. The fact that Items 2 and 5, which refer to being cheerful and enjoying talking to people, had almost 100% agreement rates at t1 in the younger group (and therefore had to be left out of the analysis) is consistent with this theory. Items 1, 3, and 6 (see table 24.1) refer to a view of oneself as an active, outgoing person who likes to be in the center of what goes on; for these items, the theory would predict a decrease. For Item 4, we expected a different pattern. Although findings on emotionality in old age show that the duration and intensity, but not the frequency of negative emotions, decrease with old age (Carstensen, Pasupathi, Mayr, & Nesselroade, 2000), the higher dependency of very old people on the help of others suggests that they may quite often be treated in a way that gives them reason to be angry. Therefore, we did not specify a directed hypothesis for this item, but expected that it might show a different type of change than the others did.

Thus, in our next model we assumed, for each age group, one change parameter that generalizes over Items 1, 3, and 6, and a different change parameter for Item 4. This model fit the data better than the previous ones, χ^2 (4, $N = 203$) = 11.044, $p = .026$, but not really well. As we had expected changes to occur only in the older group, we next set all change parameters in the younger age group to zero. We did that in order to have fewer parameter to be estimated, which might improve model fit if the parameters were really close to zero. For the older group, we kept the two different parameters just described. This model fit the data well, χ^2 (6, $N = 203$) = 6.116, $p = .410$. Thus, in our older group, there are some qualitative changes within the extraversion scale that lead to a change in the rank order of item difficulties. Both change parameters were significantly different from zero. The change

parameter for Items 1, 2, and 4 was $-.52$ ($SE = .24$, $p = .031$), and the change parameter for Item 3 was .98 ($SE = .39$, $p = .012$). Thus, the older participants' agreement to "I like to have a lot of people around me," "I like to be where the action is," and "I am a very active person" decreased significantly, whereas their agreement to "I often get angry at the way people treat me" increased by an even higher amount.

Figure 24.3 shows the actual frequencies of agreement to each of the four items at both time points in the two age groups. The dotted lines refer to cross-sectional changes, that is, differences between the younger age group at t1 and the older age group at t2. As the figure shows, the frequencies are not perfectly described by the parameters estimated in the LLRA. There is essentially no change for "I like to be where the action is," which had a low agreement frequency to begin with. However, statistically the stability in this item does not differ from the decreases in Items 1 and 4.

Substantive Discussion of the Results

As we have shown, Rasch models allow for distinguishing quantitative and qualitative change. We first used standard Rasch model tests to analyze differences between the younger and older age group at t1. Analyses on the score level had shown that the older group was significantly lower in extraversion and higher in neuroticism than the younger group; analyses on the Rasch model showed that these differences were quantitative in nature. That is, the age group differences in agreement frequencies were about equal across all items. There was a qualitative age group difference for openness to experience, however. While trying out new things and being intellectually curious, imaginative, and affected by poetry tended to be somewhat more frequent in the younger age group, daydreaming was a more typical aspect of openness in the older group. This result fits with Carstensen's socioemotional selectivity theory as most of the aspects that are more frequent in the younger group are somewhat future- and learning-oriented aspects of openness, while daydreaming is a present-oriented aspect.

We then used the LLRA to investigate longitudinal changes in the two age groups. On the score level, we had found no such changes in either age group. The same was true on the item level for neuroticism and openness; however, for extraversion we found some qualitative changes in the

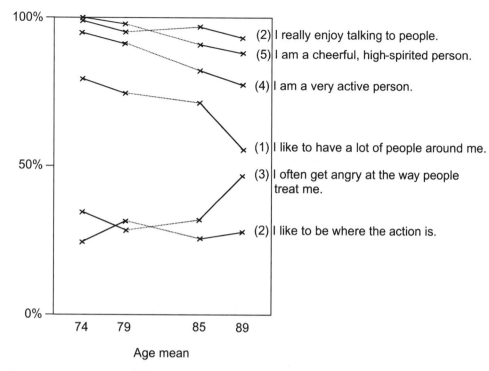

Figure 24.3 Item means of the two age groups in the extraversion scale.

older age group. Figure 24.3 shows how the substantive meaning of the extraversion scale changes in very old age. At an age of 74 years, a medium to high score in extraversion is likely to reflect, among other aspects, agreement to the item "I like to have a lot of people around me." At an age of 89 years, a medium to high score less often results from agreeing to this item, and more often results from agreeing to "I often get angry at the way people treat me." This may reflect a change in the way people treat older people, or perhaps an increasing dependency on others that leads to negative feelings when needs are not optimally fulfilled. In any case, the statement that there are no changes in extraversion even in very old age is correct on the score level, but masks relevant qualitative changes that occur within the construct.

Methodological Discussion

We hope to have demonstrated that item response models are a good means to analyze qualitative changes within constructs. Thinking about positive psychology, the idea of qualitative change may be a good way to overcome the overgeneralization that changes are always positive or negative (as far as old age is concerned, mostly negative).

A New Way of Using the Rasch Model

Using the Rasch model as a means of analyzing qualitative differences between groups is a rather new approach; most researchers have used the model only to evaluate (and, if necessary, eliminate) test items. If the computation of a sum score is valid only when the Rasch model holds for a data set, then the sum score is invalid as soon as group differences in item difficulty patterns are found. And, as discussed above, such group differences are found very frequently, especially when questionnaires are concerned and when different subgroups (e.g., male and female participants, participants with high or low scores, etc.) are considered. Thus, strictly speaking, standard scores on most of our questionnaires are not really sufficient to describe a person's trait level. This message has been largely ignored, and where it was heard, it has led most researchers to eliminate those items that cause the subgroup differences. This procedure may lead to relatively narrow constructs, possibly losing interesting information. In our data example, we would have had to eliminate daydreaming as an aspect of openness because this aspect is relatively more frequent in older than in younger participants. We believe in an alternative way to proceed: If the data do not follow the Rasch model and the total score therefore is not a sufficient descriptor, all we have to do is take the pattern of items a person has agreed to into account in interpreting this individual's responses to the test. This does not mean we have to develop a new interpretation for every response pattern we encounter in testing practice. For example, in addition to looking at the raw score, we could compare a participant's response pattern to the typical patterns of certain subgroups, for example, based on age, and gain more information on that person's qualitative expression of the trait in question. For example, some younger people may show response patterns more similar to those of the older group than to those of their own group, which would tell an interesting story.

We have used the same line of thinking to classify people into Piagetian stages of development based on their performance in a syllogism test (Spiel, Glück, & Gössler, 2001). In that case, different item solution patterns showed that people had mastered different aspects of the task. Mixed Rasch models identified three classes of participants who differed systematically in the types of items they could solve. Thus, we can infer a person's level of deductive reasoning performance from what items that person has solved, rather than from the total score.

Limitations of the Rasch Model

Researchers who use the Rasch model to study age differences in the way we have proposed here need to be aware that the model will not react to differences that are purely quantitative in nature. In our example, older and younger participants differed in their total scores in two of the three scales we studied, but the Rasch model did not find any parameter differences in these scales. This implies that older participants had higher agreement probabilities for all neuroticism items and lower agreement probabilities for all extraversion items, but there were no differences in the ordering of the items on the latent dimension. The reason the Rasch model cannot show quantitative differences is that in order to estimate its parameters, some kind of normalization is required. Either one parameter is set to zero, or the mean across all parameters

is set to zero. Therefore, if the agreement rates for all items are higher in one group than in the other, this will not affect the normalized item parameters—only differences between items will. Thus, to get the full picture, researchers need to additionally look at changes in the total score by use of standard methods such as analysis of variance.

Another general issue with the Rasch model is that it cannot estimate parameters for items that all participants, or no participant at all, agreed to. Such items will be assigned infinitely high or low parameters. It makes substantive sense that such items are not informative, and questionnaires are usually constructed so as to avoid such cases. Therefore, the problem will not occur very frequently. It did occur in our case with one item in the extraversion scale that was agreed to by all participants in the younger group, and this item could not be included in the analyses, which may be due to the dichotomization of the original response format (see below).

Using the LLRA for Analyzing Change

The LLRA is a very elegant means of directly looking at longitudinal changes in item agreement frequencies. As it specifies each item as a test of its own, item homogeneity considerations are not relevant here. In contrast to the Rasch model, the LLRA can also account for purely quantitative change. If, for example, all t2 item parameters are equal and positive, agreement to all items has increased in the exact same way; that is, there is quantitative but no qualitative change.

A disadvantage is that the LLRA does not offer any direct information on item agreement patterns within a scale. Two items may show the same amount of change, however, one item may have a very high agreement rate from the beginning and increase it even more, while the other may have a low agreement rate at t1 and become a relevant aspect of the trait only at later time points. Therefore, in order to completely understand changes within a scale, it is important to look at agreement means in addition to looking at change parameters.

Limitations of the LLRA

There are a number of limitations to using the LLRA for measuring change in practice, and they may more often become real problems than with the Rasch model. One limitation is that if in any subgroup × item combination there are no changes at all or changes in only one direction, LLRA parameters for that combination become inestimable. Such cases are rather frequent, and there is not much else to do than to remove the respective items from the analysis. In the data example above, we had to eliminate Items 2 and 5 from the extraversion scale. As figure 24.2 shows, both had extremely high agreement rates at all time points and therefore were not very informative anyway. However, there may be cases where the requirement of change in both direction poses a severe problem. If, for example, a training program works so well that all participants change in the hoped-for direction, this success leads to inapplicability of the change model. There exist some hybrid forms of the LLRA, where different items are modeled as the same item at different time points, which at least allows for analyzing differences between groups of persons (an application is given in Glück & Spiel, 1997); however, they require that the items used may fulfill the requirements of the Rasch model.

One major limitation of the LLRA at its current stage of development is that it does not allow for including missing values. Only complete data can be analyzed, unless the sample is so large that subgroups of participants with different patterns of missing values can be formed.

Incorporating Theory: Testing Predictions About Change

In looking at qualitative change, researchers may have very different starting points in terms of theoretical considerations. In some cases, clear expectations about itemwise changes may be available, whereas in other cases the analysis may be completely exploratory. Both approaches are possible with the models we have introduced here, although in our analyses we have used the more historically typical approach in each case. That is, with the Rasch model we did not make any predictions about which items should show age differences in certain directions. With the LLRA, we did incorporate such predictions in our models.

It is possible to include theoretical expectations into the Rasch model by applying the linear logistic test model (see e.g., Fischer, 1995b). This model allows for testing hypotheses about equality and inequality of item parameters across subgroups of participants and subsets of items (see e.g., Glück & Spiel, 1997). With respect to the LLRA, a researcher with a purely exploratory interest could simply look at the size and significance of the change parameters for each item in each subgroup as estimated in the base model. Especially with larger numbers of items or subgroups, however, the picture may become very complex. Then researchers may have the idea to develop more restrictive models by just grouping items according to their change parameters. Such procedures, if they are not based on an a priori theory of what the items measure, may get very close to capitalizing on chance, especially with smaller samples. Therefore, we believe that the main strength of the LLRA is in the possibility of developing parsimonious models based on theory. Ideally, if a study is designed for using the LLRA from the beginning, researchers can select items in the first place that represent different aspects of the construct in question and then use the LLRA to test hypotheses about change in these aspects.

Other Relevant Item Response Models

Models for Graded Response Categories

In our data example, we dichotomized participants' responses to the NEO items, which were originally given on a 5-point scale. We did so to simplify our presentation; however, there are a number of models for graded response formats. For example, the rating scale model (Andrich, 1978) and the partial credit model (Masters, 1982) are generalizations of the Rasch model for more than two response categories. Like the Rasch model, these two models assume that people and items can be unequivocally positioned on a latent dimension; however, they assume that there is not just one item parameter, but a parameter for each response category. The rating scale model assumes that the distances between response categories on the latent dimension are the same for all items. Therefore, it estimates only one parameter per item plus parameters for the category distances. The partial credit model does not make this assumption and estimates one parameter for each category of each item (minus some normalizations). Fischer and Parzer (1991) have developed an LLRA-type model from the rating scale model, and Fischer and Ponocny (1994) have done the same for the partial credit model.

While these models may seem optimally suited for analyzing interindividual differences and change in item response patterns, some technical problems may occur. A typical problem in our experience is that individual differences in response style can confound changes in the construct in question. When we use mixed Rasch models to identify subgroups of participants with different item parameters in data with graded response categories, a very typical finding is one group that mostly uses the most extreme categories (in our case, 1 and 5), and one group that prefers the less extreme categories (in our case, 2 and 4). Rost (1999) found two such classes when he reanalyzed the norming sample of the German NEO-FFI using mixed Rasch models. While these two response styles may tell an interesting psychological story by themselves (and may show changes in old age), they tend to mask real differences in people's agreement to each item. Therefore, although it has been shown that this can cause technical difficulties (Andrich, 1995; Jansen & Roskam, 1986) we prefer to use dichotomized items for studying qualitative change. Of course, an additional analysis of response behavior using the original number of categories is recommendable.

An Exploratory Approach

We have already briefly mentioned a different, more exploratory approach to measure change as it manifests in item difficulties. Mixed Rasch models (Rost, 1996; Rost & von Davier, 1995) allow for identifying subgroups of individuals that differ in the pattern of item difficulties. More precisely, these models assume that there are a number of subgroups of participants and that the Rasch model holds within each group, but not across groups. Each group has its own item parameters. For example, an analysis of the extraversion data with mixed Rasch models might identify two classes of participants that differ only in their agreement rate for Item 4 ("I often get angry at the way people treat me"), with Class 1 having low agreement rates and Class 2 having intermediate agreement rates to that item. Cross-sectional differences in the size of the two classes could easily be analyzed; presumably, more people in the older age group than in the younger age group would be in Class 2. An application of this type of cross-sectional analysis is given in Spiel et al. (2001). Such models also allow for looking at longitudinal change. In the example, change would probably manifest in a number of participants who were in Class 1 at t1 moving into Class 2 at t2, but few or no people moving in the opposite direction.

Applications and more extensive discussions of the mixed Rasch model approach for analyzing change can be found in Glück and Spiel (1997), and Glück, Machat, Jirasko, and Rollett (2002).

One Last Warning: Sample Size

One limitation that is common to all models we have discussed here is that they require relatively large samples. This is because as they focus on single items (or response categories) rather than on scores, they have to estimate a lot more parameters, and as they gain much of the information they use from patterns rather than sums, lots of different patterns need to be present in the data. Thus, sample size in general and the ratio of number of participants to number of items should be as large as possible. Rost (1996) showed that exact parameter estimations are possible only if the sample size is a multiple of the number of possible response patterns (for 10 dichotomous items, there are $10^2 = 1,024$ possible patterns); however, for the purpose of group comparisons, samples do not have to be that large. Ponocny (personal communication, May 2004) suggested a minimum sample size of 400 for Rasch model analyses; there exist, however, nonparametric model tests that are applicable for smaller samples (Ponocny, 2001). The sample-size problem is somewhat less severe for the LLRA than for the Rasch model because the data structure of the LLRA produces few response patterns and lots of virtual persons (each person is included once per item). However, small sample sizes may still be a problem, especially with exploratory approaches where lots of parameters are estimated.

To conclude, we hope to have demonstrated that the use of item response models for analyzing change offers more than just another way of estimating change scores. It opens up new perspectives both on qualitative changes within traits that have formerly been viewed as stable and on more differentiated types of change than general increases or decreases.

References

Andersen, E. B. (1973). A goodness of fit test for the Rasch model. *Psychometrika, 38,* 123–140.

Andrich, D. (1978). A rating formulation for ordered response categories. *Psychometrika, 43,* 357–374.

Andrich, D. (1995). Models for measurement, precision and the non-dichotomization of graded responses. *Psychometrika, 60,* 7–26.

Baltes, P. B., & Mayer, K. U. (Eds.). (1999). *The Berlin Aging Study: Aging from 70 to 100.* New York: Cambridge University Press.

Carstensen, L. L., Isaacowitz, D. M., & Charles, S. T. (1999). Taking time seriously: A theory of socioemotional selectivity. *American Psychologist, 54,* 165–181.

Carstensen, L. L., Pasupathi, M., Mayr, U., & Nesselroade, J. R. (2000). Emotional experience in everyday life across the adult life span. *Journal of Personality and Social Psychology, 79,* 644–655.

Costa, P. T., & McCrae, R. R. (1985). *The NEO Personality Inventory.* Odessa, FL: Psychological Assessment Resources.

Fischer, G. H. (1983). Logistic latent trait models with linear constraints. *Psychometrika, 48,* 3–26.

Fischer, G. H. (1995a). Linear logistic models for change. In G. H. Fischer & I. Molenaar (Eds.), *Rasch models: Foundations, recent developments, and applications* (pp. 157–180). New York: Springer.

Fischer, G. H. (1995b). The linear logistic test model. In G. H. Fischer & I. Molenaar (Eds.), *Rasch models: Foundations, recent developments, and applications* (pp. 131–155). New York: Springer.

Fischer, G. H., & Formann, A. K. (1982). Some applications of logistic latent trait models with linear constraints on the parameters. *Applied Psychological Measurement, 4,* 397–416.

Fischer, G. H., & Molenaar, I. (Eds.). (1995). *Rasch models: Foundations, recent developments, and applications.* New York: Springer.

Fischer, G. H., & Parzer, P. (1991). An extension of the rating scale model with an application to the measurement of treatment effects. *Psychometrika, 56,* 637–651.

Fischer, G. H., & Ponocny, I. (1994). An extension of the partial credit model with an application to the measurement of change. *Psychometrika, 59,* 177–192.

Fischer, G. H., & Ponocny-Seliger, E. (1998). *Structural Rasch modeling: Handbook of the usage of LPCM-Win 1.0.* Vienna: Department of Psychology, University of Vienna.

Glas, C. A. W., & Verhelst, N. D. (1995). Testing the Rasch model. In G. H. Fischer & I. Molenaar (Eds.), *Rasch models: Foundations, recent developments, and applications* (pp. 69–95). New York: Springer.

Glück, J., & Indurkhya, A. (2001). Assessing changes in the longitudinal salience of items in constructs. *Journal of Adolescent Research, 16,* 169–187.

Glück, J., & Spiel, C. (1997). Item response models for repeated measures designs: Application and limitations of four different approaches. *Methods of Psychological Research–Online, 2.* Retrieved from http://www.mpr-online.de

Glück, J., Machat, R., Jirasko, M., & Rollett, B. (2002). Training-related changes in solution strategy in a spatial test: An application of item response models. *Learning and Individual Differences, 13,* 1–22.

Jansen, P. G. W., & Roskam, E. E. (1986). Latent trait models and dichotomization of graded responses. *Psychometrika, 51,* 69–91.

Masters, G. N. (1982). A Rasch model for partial credit scoring. *Psychometrika, 47,* 149–174.

Ponocny, I. (2001). Nonparametric goodness-of-fit tests for the Rasch model. *Psychometrika, 66,* 437–459.

Rasch, G. (1980). *Probabilistic models for some intelligence and attainment tests* (expanded ed.). Chicago: University of Chicago Press. (Original work published 1960)

Rost, J. (1996). *Lehrbuch Testtheorie Testkonstruktion* [Textbook test theory—test construction]. Bern: Huber.

Rost, J. (1999). Sind die Big-Five Rasch-skalierbar? Eine Reanalyse der NEO-FFi-Normierungsdaten. [Are the Big Five Rasch scalable? A reanalysis of the NEO-FFI norm data.] *Diagnostica, 45,* 119–127.

Rost, J., & von Davier, M. (1995). Mixture distribution Rasch models. In G. H. Fischer & I. Molenaar (Eds.), *Rasch models: Foundations, recent developments, and applications* (pp. 257–268). New York: Springer.

Smith, J., & Baltes, P. B. (1999). Trends and profiles of psychological functioning in very old age. In P. B. Baltes & K. U. Mayer (Eds.), *The Berlin Aging Study: Aging from 70 to 100* (pp. 197–226). New York: Cambridge University Press.

Spiel, C., & Glück, J. (1998). Application of various item-response models for assessing change in dichotomous item score matrices. *International Journal of Behavioral Development, 22,* 517–536.

Spiel, C., Glück, J., & Gössler, H. (2001). Stability and change of unidimensionality: The sample case of deductive reasoning. *Journal of Adolescent Research, 16,* 150–168.

25

Exploring Cyclic Change in Emotion Using Item Response Models and Frequency Domain Analysis

Sy-Miin Chow, Kevin J. Grimm, Frank Fujita, and Nilam Ram

Effective mood regulation presupposes that affect and mood are dynamic and capable of change. Researchers have begun to conceptualize affect as dynamic processes (e.g., Carver & Scheier, 1990; Larsen, 2000). However, most of the analytic tools used in affect research are predominantly static. In other words, they do not account for any interdependencies in emotions that may exist over time. Very often, single-occasion factor analytic or correlational techniques are used to capture the relationships among different emotions at one point in time (e.g., Feldman Barrett, 1998; Tellegen, Watson, & Clark, 1999; Watson & Tellegen, 1985). Furthermore, even when such techniques are extended to examine how emotions unfold over time (e.g., Diener, Fujita, & Smith, 1995; Eid & Diener, 1999), they are limited in that they usually only capture linear change. Evidence is building that emotions exhibit nonlinear rather than linear patterns of change over time (e.g., diurnal and weekly cycles; Chow, Ram, Boker, Fujita, & Clore, 2005; Murray, Allen, Trinder, & Burgess, 2002; Larsen & Kasimatis, 1990; Rusting & Larsen, 1998). Taken together, these short-comings suggest that researchers should expand the study of emotion to incorporate tools for capturing nonlinear (e.g., cyclic) change.

Psychometric Properties of Affect Measures

The structure of affect has been a controversial subject over the last few decades. Recently, there has been a surge of interest in using item response models to examine the psychometric properties of affect items and their associated response formats (Baker, Rounds, & Zevon, 2000; Segura & González-Romá, 2003; Watson & Tellegen, 1999). In particular, characteristics and item locations of pleasant and unpleasant affect (denoted below as PA and UA) items were used to clarify the unipolar versus bipolar nature of these two constructs. Even though a general consensus has begun to emerge regarding the structure of affect (Tellegen, Watson, & Clark, 1999), the dimensionality of affect may still vary across individuals and contexts.

Our focus in this chapter is not to examine directly the dimensionality of PA and UA, but rather to use an item response model to evaluate the psychometric properties of affect measures, and to subsequently model the dynamics of day-to-day variability in emotion using these "reformed" measures. In presenting this item response model, that is, the rating scale model (RSM) proposed by Andrich (1978a, 1978b), we hope to illustrate some potential inadequacies of the affect scales used in this study, and highlight how item response approaches might add to existing factor analytic approaches. After obtaining emotion estimates from the RSM, we then model the cyclic change in these estimates by using frequency domain techniques. In the following sections, we first present an overview of item response models and frequency domain analysis, then provide an empirical example of their use.

Overview of Item Response Models as a Tool for Assessing Affect Measures

The measurement of ephemeral states, like momentary emotional experience, is often a challenge. However, multivariate measurement can help researchers obtain true score estimates of these ephemeral or latent constructs. We can obtain a more accurate representation of the construct of interest by taking a number of simultaneous measurements or by asking individuals to respond to a number of items. In this vein, a number of multi-item scales have been developed to tap into individuals' emotional state (e.g., PANAS; Watson & Tellegen, 1988). Either by summing over items to create a composite score or by conducting a factor analysis to obtain latent factor scores, we can obtain more accurate measurement of the construct than we could from a single measure or item. However, both methods make rather strong assumptions about the interval nature of the measurement scale and the relationship between items and the latent construct they purport to measure (Lord, 1980; Hambleton, Swaminathan & Rogers, 1991; Reise, Widaman & Pugh, 1993). Each of these strengths of the item response approach is discussed briefly in turn.

Rescaling Ordinal Data Into Interval-Level Data

Most affect measures utilize some variations of one or multiple Likert scales. By doing so, distances between categories on a Likert scale are assumed to be constant, and the resultant (supposedly ordinal) data are analyzed and treated as though they were interval-level data. Item response models, such as the Rasch model, can be used to obtain estimates of individuals' true scores without making such strong assumptions about interval-level measurement. Rather than simply assuming interval-level measurement, all measurement scales are transformed into a logit scale and, as a result, ordinal-level data are rescaled into interval-level measurement. Because all item and person estimates are placed on a common logit scale, item and person characteristics can be interpreted more meaningfully than when a simple composite score is used (Embretson & Reise, 2000).[1]

Nonlinearity Between Factors and Manifest Items

Much as factor analytic models are used to represent the relationship between manifest measures and latent factors, item response models are used to capture the relationship between a manifest item response and a latent variable (representing, e.g., an individual's trait, state, or ability level). However, in the former, the relationship between manifest measures and latent variables is confined to be linear in nature, whereas the latter uses a nonlinear monotonic function to map out the person-item relationship (Lord, 1980; Reise et al., 1993). This relationship is depicted in figure 25.1, in which the relationship between person estimates (i.e., person-latent PA and UA levels), derived from an item response model, and usual composite score (derived from summing across a set of PA items) is clearly a nonlinear one. We note, however, that item response models can be reparameterized and perfectly reproduced as a nonlinear factor analysis model (McDonald, 1982), and a rapprochement between the two approaches is thus possible.

Recently, a few researchers have used item response models to equate measures in longitudinal research (thus finding a common scale for multiple occasions of measurement) and subsequently model the patterns of change in the obtained estimates (e.g., Bond & Fox, 2001; Lee, 2003; McArdle, Grimm, Hamagami, Bowles, & Meredith, 2006; Ram et al., 2006). When item response models are used in conjunction with analytic procedures that explicitly model the

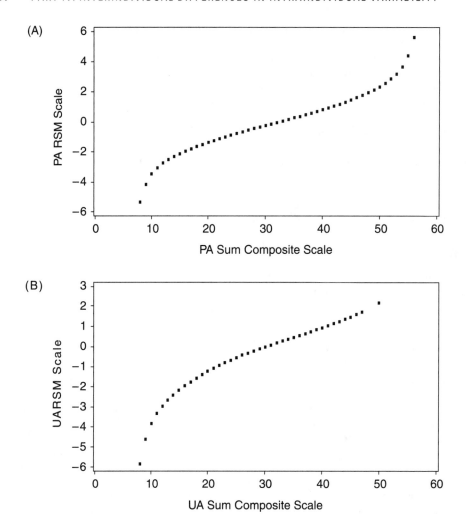

Figure 25.1 Mapping between sum composite scales and the interval-level scales derived from the rating scale model (RSM)—an item response model used in this study to yield estimates for individual PA and UA levels. PA = pleasant affect; UA = unpleasant affect.

within-person patterns of change (e.g., latent growth curve analysis, mixed-effects models, spectral analysis) or continuity between measurement occasions, researchers are able to capitalize on the powerful measurement characteristics provided by the item response model and information about change as captured by the longitudinal models. In the following section, we present an overview of a particular item response model, the RSM, and indicate how it may be applied to data in order to evaluate the measurement properties of a scale or test, determine whether the items in a scale measure the same construct, and obtain true scores that have desirable measurement properties.

The Rating Scale Model

The RSM (Andrich, 1978a, 1978b) is one of a number of models that explicitly model polytomous categorical responses (for an overview, see Embretson & Reise, 2000) within an item response framework. When fitting the RSM to item-level data, the distances between successive response categories are derived from the data rather than assumed to be equal. For instance, the distance between categories 1 and 2 may not be the same as the distance between categories 3 and 4 on a scale. Consider a five-point scale on which an individual is asked to indicate their level of pleasant affect with 1 (*not at all*), 2 (*a little*), 3 (*somewhat*), 4 (*a lot*), and 5 (*quite a lot*).

An individual who begins the day with a very low level of pleasant affect would likely indicate a very low level of PA (e.g., a response of 1). As the individual's level of pleasant affect increases past some threshold value, he or she will likely endorse the next highest category. The RSM does not assume that these thresholds (steps) are equally spaced. In other words, a relatively small increase in pleasant affect may underlie a move from *not at all* to *a little* (i.e., from 1 to 2), but a much larger increase may be needed to move someone from *somewhat* to *a lot* (i.e., from 3 to 4). In this way, the RSM can be used to incorporate nonlinearity in response categories (e.g., unequal distances between categories) into estimates of an individual's true scores.

The RSM for items with k categories and m steps between categories (where $m = k - 1$) is written as

$$P(x_{is} = j|\theta_s, \lambda_i, \delta_j) = \frac{\exp\left\{\sum_{j=0}^{x}\left[\theta_s - (\lambda_i + \delta_j)\right]\right\}}{\sum_{x=0}^{m} \exp\left\{\sum_{j=0}^{x}\left[\theta_s - (\lambda_i + \delta_j)\right]\right\}}$$

(1)

where $P(x_{is} = j|\theta_s, \lambda_i, \delta_j)$ is the probability for response x of an individual s on item i to reach up to step j ($j = 1, \ldots, m$), conditional on the individual's level of the construct (θ_s), the difficulty of item i (λ_i), and threshold of step j (δ_j; also known as the category intersection parameter. Thus, the difficulty of step j on item i, denoted below as B_{ij}, is a function of both the item difficulty level and the difficulty of step j (λ_i and δ_j, respectively), written as

$$B_{ij} = \lambda_i + \delta_j$$

(2)

Note that only one set of thresholds (δ_j) is estimated for all items in the test. In other words, it is assumed that the specific patterns of separation between categories are identical across all items, but distances between successive categories are allowed to vary within items. Thus, this model is appropriate only in cases where all items have an identical format. Items themselves, however, can vary in their difficulty levels (λ_i), meaning that different items may tap into different levels of PA. An easy item (low λ_i) may differentiate among low levels of the construct, while a difficult item (high λ_i) may differentiate among high levels of the construct.

In sum, the RSM, as one type of item response model, provides a tool for estimating a set of true

scores along a scale that has highly desirable interval level measurement properties.

Using Frequency Domain Analysis to Capture Cyclic Change

Since many psychological processes (e.g., mood regulation) unfold over time, static linear representations provide limited and at times misleading information about them. More complete understandings might be garnered by incorporating time into our representations. In fact, much has been learned about emotion from examination in the time domain (e.g., Shifren, Hooker, Wood, & Nesselroade, 1997; chapter 23, this volume). However, theories of change and the techniques used to examine them are usually grounded on linear theories of change. Including nonlinearity into our representations and theories of dynamic process may help us understand psychological processes more fully.

One way of modeling nonlinear change is to theorize and examine how individuals' behavior may be cyclic in nature. Frequency domain techniques provide us with the tools to explore and test theories about how processes unfold over time in the context of this particular type of nonlinear change (i.e., cyclic change). This class of analytic techniques is especially conducive to affect-related research because human emotions and physiological rhythms are known to display some cyclic regularity. Changes in emotions attributable to the "Blue Monday" phenomenon, circadian rhythms, women's menstrual cycles, and seasonal changes in mood are all instances of cycles that evolve according to different time scales (see findings by, e.g., Larsen & Kasimatis, 1990; Murray et al., 2002; Reid, Towell, & Golding, 2000; Rusting & Larsen, 1998).

As a whole, frequency domain analysis techniques range from the more confirmatory harmonic analysis to the more exploratory spectral analysis. In harmonic analysis, a prespecified frequency (e.g., the frequency associated with a weekly cycle) and its associated harmonic components (i.e., integer multiples of the pre-specified frequency) are directly fitted to the data in much the same way as a linear function is fitted to the data in a regression analysis. By assessing how well the model fits the data (e.g., by means of an R^2 statistic), we can assess how well an individual's data are characterized by, or how entrained an individual is to, the hypothesized cyclic process. Spectral analysis, in contrast, is used to fit a collection of frequencies to each individual's data and, in an exploratory way, identify the frequencies that are most prominent in the data. Stated briefly, frequency domain analysis provides a valuable addition to one's repertoire of research tools because parameters estimates yielded from both approaches, as we will elaborate in more detail, map well onto theoretical notions of affect.

In sum, frequency domain analysis techniques may be tools that can help us better understand the nonlinear dynamics of emotional experience. In our forthcoming example, both harmonic and spectral analyses will be used to illustrate how one might proceed in examining such notions. Particularly, we examine weekly cycles in emotion from an idiographic perspective (Allport, 1937) and explicate, where appropriate, the pros and cons of taking an idiographic versus a nomothetic approach to analyzing cyclic change.

The Basis of Frequency Domain Analysis: The Sinusoidal Model

Frequency domain analysis (including Fourier analysis or spectral analysis) is often considered as a subclass of time-series analysis (Box & Jenkins, 1976). It serves to extract regularity in single-subject multioccasion data in the form of cycles or oscillations. In this approach, an individual's time-series data are represented as a set of sinusoidal waves of different frequencies. Each sinusoid takes the form of

$$Y(t) = \mu + R\cos(\omega t + \phi) + \varepsilon(t), \qquad (3)$$

where $Y(t)$ is a time series measured from time $t = 0$ to T, R is the amplitude of oscillation, $\omega = 2\pi/\tau$ is a particular frequency of oscillation in radians, and τ the period of oscillation (in units of t), μ is the mean of the oscillation (governing vertical shift, or one's baseline affect level), ϕ is the phase (horizontal) shift of the oscillation, or time elapsed between Time 0 and the first peak of the wave, and $\varepsilon(t)$ is a time series of residuals representing portions of the data that are not accounted for by the particular sinusoidal function.

An example of a sinusoidal wave is illustrated in figure 25.2. This plot was generated using Equation 3 with $\mu = 0$, $R = 1.0$, $\phi = 3.1415$, an oscillation period, τ, of 7 (making $\omega = 2\pi/7 = .90$) and no residual ε. Interpreting the model as an illustration of daily fluctuations in an individual's emotion, μ of 0 represents the individual's average affect level over the course of 28 days. The phase, ϕ, reflects the distance (or time elapsed) between Time 0 and the first peak of the cycle (in this case, ϕ is set to $\pi = 3.1415$ radians or equivalently, 3.5 days). The amplitude parameter, R, governs the magnitude of

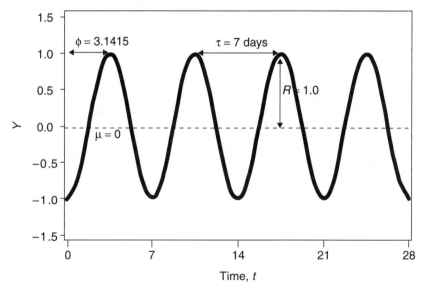

Figure 25.2 A sinusoidal wave generated using Equation 3, with a mean of $\mu = 0$, amplitude (R) of 1, period (τ; time elapsed between two successive peaks) of 7, and phase (ϕ time elapsed between Time 0 and the first peak) of π.

deviation from the average affect level, and the oscillation period, τ, represents the amount of time for the individual's emotion to complete one full cycle (in this case, $2\pi = 7$ days). In substantive research, individual differences in amplitude may indicate individual differences in affect intensity (see Larsen & Diener, 1987).

By adding together a collection of all possible sinusoidal waves with different frequencies, we can reproduce any set of time-series data; that is, $\varepsilon(t)$ becomes 0 when all the waves are summed. The main objective in conducting such an analysis is to determine if the time series contains predictable cycles. For instance, if, in decomposing an individual's data into a collection of sinusoidal waves, we find that a particular frequency (e.g., 28 days) accounts for much of the variance, we might infer the presence of a particular biological or psychological process that regularly unfolds along this time frame (e.g., a menstrual cycle). In the next section, we describe harmonic analysis and spectral analysis in further detail and summarize how they are conducted.

Harmonic Analysis

In harmonic analysis, the sinusoidal model depicted in Equation 3 with a predetermined oscillation period, τ, and its associated harmonic components (i.e., $\tau/2$, $\tau/3$, and so on; Brockwell & Davis, 2002) are fitted to a univariate time series. However, because of the model's inherent nonlinearity, fitting this model is difficult. The model can, though, be rewritten as a linear regression. We consider, in the present context, the case of only one cyclic component. In this case, Equation 3 can be re-expressed as (see Koopmans, 1995; Warner, 1998, for details):

$$Y(t) = \mu + A \cos(\omega t) + B \sin(\omega t) + \varepsilon(t) \quad (4)$$

where $\omega = 2\pi/\tau$. Here the amplitude of the wave, R (from Equation 3), is a function of the coefficients A and B, and expressed as

$$R = \sqrt{A^2 + B^2} \quad (5)$$

Likewise, the phase shift, ϕ, is function of A and B, such that

$$\phi = \tan^{-1}\left(\frac{-B}{A}\right). \quad (6)$$

Once rewritten in regression form as in Equation 4, the model can be fitted to data using or-

dinary least squares (OLS) estimation procedures. First, an a priori value for τ is chosen, since we are examining a weekly cycle, $\tau = 7$. Two dummy variables, D1 and D2, are then created: $D1 = \cos[(2\pi/\tau)^*t]$ and $D2 = \sin[(2\pi/\tau)^*t]$, where $t =$ occasion number. The dependent variable, Y, is then regressed on D1 and D2 to obtain estimates of A, B, and the variance of ε. Amplitude, R, and phase shift, ϕ, are then calculated using Equations 2 and 3 above. As with conventional regression analysis, the R^2 statistic represents the amount of variance explained by fitting a cycle of a particular frequency to the data and can be used as a measure of model fit.

Spectral Analysis

As noted earlier, spectral analysis is a more general exploratory approach to finding the dominant frequency (or frequencies) in a time series (see also Chatfield, 1996; Gottman, 1979; Warner, 1998). In essence, during a spectral analysis, a total of $T/2$ (T representing the total number of measurement occasions) orthogonal sinusoidal functions of different frequencies are fitted to the data. The particular frequencies used are a function of the number of occasions in the data, that is, the Fourier frequencies $1/T, 2/T, 3/T, \ldots$, ½. Thus, the time series is decomposed into a collection of sinusoidal functions that together account for the total variance in the series. The spectral density or percentage of variance accounted for by each individual frequency provides an indication of the dominance of that particular cycle in the data. The particular functions (frequencies) that account for significantly greater proportions of variance than would be expected under random noise conditions may characterize the processes that underlie the data. For example, if a time series shows particularly high spectral density/weight for a 7-day frequency compared to other frequencies, this can be taken as evidence that a weekly cycle underlies the data (e.g., Chow et al., 2005; Larsen & Kasimatis, 1990).

In practice, spectral analysis is usually conducted using fast Fourier transform algorithms rather than by conducting multiple OLS regression procedures as in harmonic analysis. Additionally, the spectral densities of neighboring frequencies are often weighted to smooth neighboring density estimates. More specifically, rather than assigning a weight or density to each particular frequency, weights are assigned to subsets of neighboring frequencies. This reduces the possibility of overextracting cycles within close bandwidths and estimation biases due to random fluctuations in the data. In most statistical packages, including SAS, SPSS, S-plus, R, and so on, these procedures have been automated and are relatively easy to execute. We focus here on the analysis of univariate time series. However, bivariate extensions of the techniques (e.g., cross-spectral analysis) are also viable and useful. Readers are referred to other work wherein such extensions are discussed in detail (e.g., Brockwell & Davis, 2002; Koopmans, 1995).

An Idiographic Modeling Perspective

As presented, both harmonic and spectral analyses fit the sinusoidal model (in a more restrictive form in the former and along a more exploratory line in the latter) to a univariate, multioccasion time series for a single individual. The extension to multivariate or multiperson data requires additional steps. In our analysis, we incorporate multivariate data into the time series by using a multivariate measurement model (i.e., the RSM; Andrich, 1978a, 1978b) to obtain true scores. The sinusoidal model is then fitted to the univariate time series of true scores. Extending the analysis to multiple persons requires first fitting each individual's data separately and then summarizing the individual differences in parameter estimates. We do not advocate aggregating data across individuals before conducting the analyses. Such a procedure would assume that all individuals exhibit nonlinear dynamics in exactly the same way (i.e., at the exact same frequencies and amplitudes) and at exactly the same time (i.e., the individual trajectories are not out of phase with respect to each other, or in other words, all individuals' trajectories peak on the same moment).

Given the complexity of human behavior, such strong assumptions seem unwarranted. Instead, we suggest first analyzing the dynamics of change at the individual level and then assessing the homogeneity or heterogeneity across individuals. For instance, Larsen and Kasimatis (1990; see also Larsen, 1987) compared group differences in spectral densities of average hedonic level as a function of extraversion and other predictor variables. The key here is that individual estimates have to be derived before any aggregation or group-level comparisons can be made. Thus, even though the sinusoidal model depicted in Equation 4 can be fitted as a multilevel model, the amplitude estimate (R)

obtained based on the average A parameter and average B parameter in the sample may not correspond to the average amplitude, R, of all the individual trajectories because of the nonlinear transformation involved in Equation 3. This critical point was addressed explicitly by Estes (1956): the average of a set of individual curves may be quite distinct from the curve of the average (i.e., the aggregated data). Therefore, researchers should exercise caution when deciding between an idiographic and a nomothetic approach to analyzing change and must be willing to bear the fundamental assumptions (and consequences) of each.

Combining Item Response Models and Frequency Domain Analysis

As psychologists, we face the difficulties of modeling latent processes using available measures that may or may not map well onto the underlying psychological constructs. We see great promise in combining techniques that originated from rather different traditions (e.g., Rasch and time series), with the hope that such collaborations can help answer research questions in more effective and meaningful ways.

Substantively, in trying to understand how processes unfold within the context of cyclic change, we advocate combining methods using a two-step procedure. We suggest first using multivariate item response models (e.g., RSM) to obtain estimates of each individual's emotional states, and then proceeding to examine the dynamics in the individuals' states using other procedures that explicitly model the between-occasion dependencies (e.g., frequency domain analysis). This approach is, of course, just one way of incorporating multivariate longitudinal measurement into the analysis of nonlinear within-person processes. Alternatively, the dynamic and measurement models can be fitted simultaneously using, for instance, nonlinear mixed effects and Markov chain Monte Carlo procedures (e.g., Ram et al., 2006). The two-step approach illustrated herein simply provides a more convenient and practical way of fitting the RSM and the sinusoidal model in a two-step sequence to effectively capitalize on the strengths of each. Now, using an empirical example, we demonstrate how item response models and frequency domain analysis can be combined to examine the dynamics of individuals' pleasant and unpleasant emotions.

An Empirical Example

To illustrate the data analytic techniques described above, we examined if and how emotions conform to a weekly cycle. The main question we investigated was, "Are individuals' emotions characterized by a weekly cycle?" We used longitudinal data from 176 college students (98 males, 81 females, average age = 20.24, $SD = 1.81$) who completed daily self-reports of their emotional experiences for 52 consecutive days (Diener et al., 1995). Participants were asked to rate how often they felt each of 40 emotions on a 7-point Likert-type scale (1 = *none* to 7 = *always*). With our main interest being in a 7-day cycle, only the first 49 measurement occasions were retained to yield data in multiples of this specific oscillation period. We focused our analysis on eight items considered to be markers of PA (love, affection, caring, fondness, joy, happiness, contentment, and satisfaction) and eight items measuring UA (depression, unhappiness, shame, nervousness, loneliness, sadness, anxiety, and irritation). Further details regarding the larger study and other analyses of these particular data can be found elsewhere (see Chow et al., 2005; Diener et al., 1995; Eid & Diener, 1999; Ram et al., 2006).

As explicated above, our data analysis proceeded in two phases. In the first phase, we fitted the data to the RSM to obtain true score estimates of individuals' PA and UA. In the second phase of data analysis, the detrended estimates of PA and UA derived from the RSM were used as the input time-series data for running spectral and harmonic analyses.[2] All analyses were conducted using either Winsteps (Linacre, 2002) or S-plus. Other statistical analysis packages, however, contain routines for conducting the same analyses (e.g., Parscale, PROC SPECTRA in SAS). To our knowledge, the statistical algorithms implemented in all existing spectral analysis packages currently do not handle missing data directly. Thus all spectral analysis results reported here are based on 150 participants with complete data (i.e., with all data over 49 days). For all other analyses (i.e., RSM fitting and harmonic analysis), all of the available data were utilized.

Phase 1: Fitting the RSM to Individual Data

To obtain individual RSM estimates across multiple measurements, participants were included in the data matrix multiple times (i.e., relational, person-period, or long-form data). The RSM was then fitted to all participants' PA responses across all measurement occasions simultaneously. The same procedure was repeated by using the UA responses. Item and person estimates were thus derived based on information from all occasions and persons. In other words, the measurement characteristics of the scale held across both persons and time. These estimates were then modeled over time to examine both within-person change and between-person differences.[3]

Overall, the PA data fit the RSM well (average item mean squared [MS] infit = 0.99, average MS outfit = 0.99, root mean square error [RMSE] = 0.01). The infit and outfit statistics ranged from 0.69 to 1.31, and from 0.69 to 1.26, respectively, which are within the range of acceptable fit (Wright, Linacre, Gustafson, & Martin-Löf, 1994).[4] Furthermore, all of the PA items had high correlations with the PA total score (>.70). An examination of how well the items targeted the persons (i.e., person-item map, figure 25.3A) indicated some incongruence between the relatively small range of item difficulties ($-0.60 - 0.58$) and the relatively large range of PA estimates ($-4.14 - 4.41$). Therefore, this set of items did not include words that specifically tapped into very high or very low levels of PA, and this group of individuals were not well measured at these extremes. However, given the high reliability of the person estimates (0.91), the factor scores derived from the RSM are considered to be accurate measures of individuals' true PA scores.

The category thresholds (i.e., distances between responses 1, 2, 3, . . . , 7) for the PA items were not evenly spaced (as would have been assumed in a sum composite score or standard factor analysis model). Considerable redundancy was observed among the middle categories (i.e., response categories 3, 4, and 5), indicating, for example, that a move from Category 3 to 4 only reflects a very small, practically indiscernible change in PA level (see figure 25.4A). This nonlinearity in the distances between response categories is shown in figure 25.1A, wherein the RSM PA estimates are plotted against the PA sum composite score.

The UA items also fit the RSM well (average MS infit = 1.05, average MS outfit = 0.98, RMSE = 0.02). Item infit and outfit statistics ranged from 0.74 to 1.34 and from 0.72 to 1.15, indicating an acceptable fit. The point-biserial correlations were all greater than 0.50. The person reliability is still relatively high (0.79),

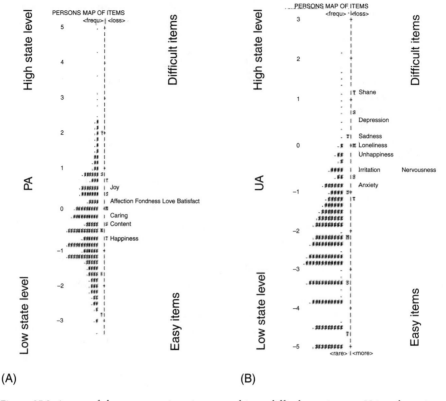

Figure 25.3 A map of the person-trait estimates and item difficulty estimates. Using the rating scale model, the person and item estimates were placed on a common scale.

but the items were not well targeted for the sample because most of the UA items were too difficult to endorse (see figure 25.3B). Again, category thresholds were not equally spaced, with relatively small differentiation at the high end of the scale (i.e., thresholds between 5, 6, and 7 were very close together; see panel B of figure 25.4). As mentioned previously, the nonlinearity in the response pattern is quite evident in figure 25.1B presented earlier.

Summary of Results From the RSM Analysis

The separation between response categories within each of PA and UA became less well defined over certain ranges of affect levels: The UA items were only able to capture very low levels of UA, whereas the middle categories for the PA scales were practically redundant. Even though the RSM cannot overcome the targeting problem in this data set (this is a problem inherent in the items and response scales), it helped place the

PA and UA responses onto a scale with measurement properties we desired. The true score estimates (θ_s) of PA and UA for each individual at each occasion were extracted from the RSM (see figures 25.5 and 25.6) and used for subsequent spectral and harmonic analyses.

Phase 2: Frequency-Domain Analyses

Using the state estimates of PA and UA derived from the RSM, we began examining the data for evidence of weekly mood cycles. We began with a spectral analysis of each individual's detrended PA and UA time series. Then, harmonic analysis was used to fit individualized 7-day cycles to PA and UA. We summarize the findings by presenting information about the distribution of a selected set of parameters.

Spectral Analysis

First, spectral analysis was used to determine the extent to which individuals' emotions might be

(A)

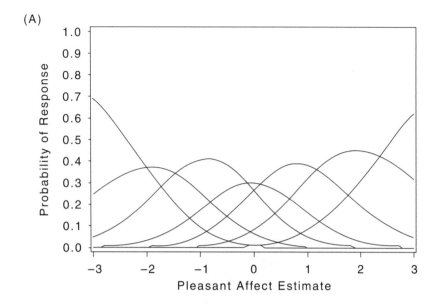

(B)

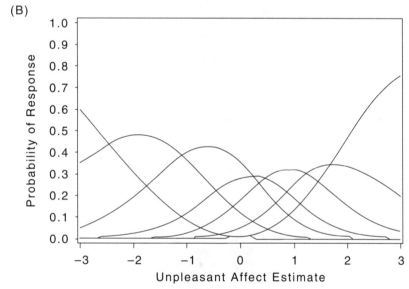

Figure 25.4 Category response curves showing the category thresholds that apply to (A) all the pleasant affect items and (B) all the unpleasant affect items. Unlike the original 7-point Likert scale, the step difficulties are freed within items, but all items are constrained to have the same step difficulties; that is, the shape of the curves is the same for all items, but the difficulty level of each item essentially shifts the whole set of curves horizontally along the x-axis (the person-measure axis).

characterized by a weekly cycle. For each individual, we obtained an estimate of which period accounted for the most variance in his or her PA and UA time series. As shown in table 25.1, the dominant cycle in individuals' PA ranged in period from 2 to 24 days (median = 8.8 days), meaning that different individuals were characterized by different lengths of cycles or patterns. Similarly, the dominant cycle for individuals' UA ranged in period from 2 to 24 days (median = 12.0 days). Thus, there appear to be substantial individual differences in how these individuals' PA and UA changed over time. That is, weekly cycles do not define how individuals' emotions progress

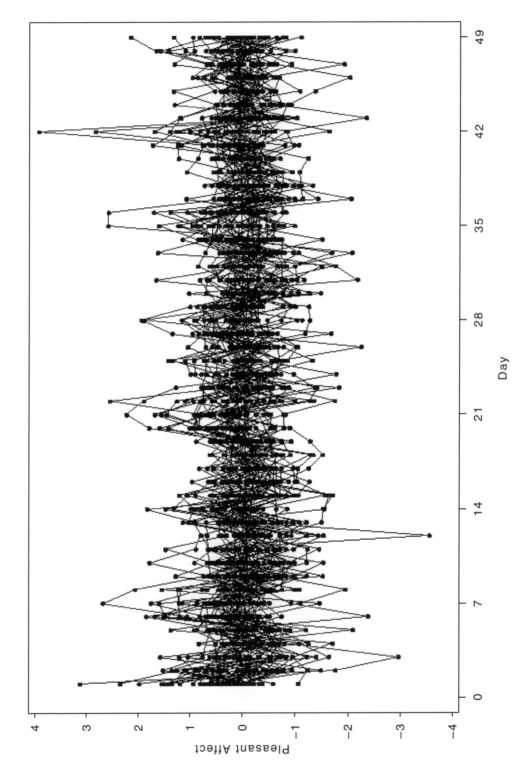

Figure 25.5 Pleasant affect estimates obtained from the RSM model—detrended to remove individual linear trends. Each individual's day-to-day level of pleasant affect is represented by a single line.

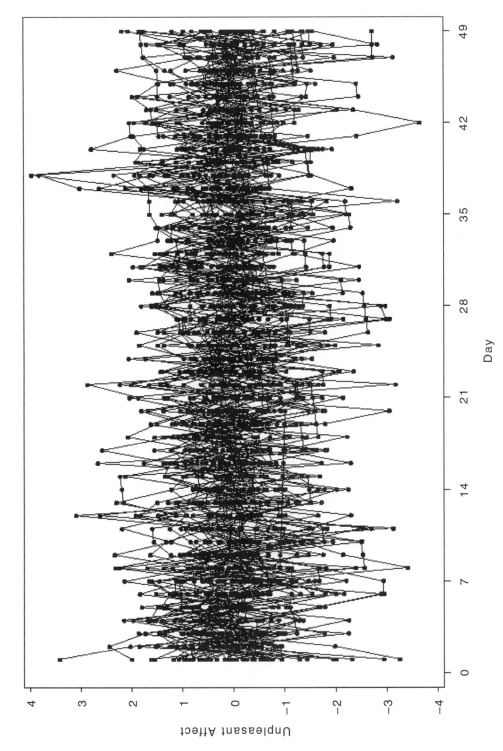

Figure 25.6 Unpleasant affect estimates obtained from the rating scale model—detrended to remove individual linear trends. Each individual's day-to-day level of unpleasant affect is represented by a single line.

TABLE 25.1 Summary of Results From Spectral and Harmonic Analyses

	Median	Mean	SD	Min	Max	N
Spectral Analysis Results						
PA dominant period (in days)	8.8	12.7	7.8	2.0	24.0	150
UA dominant period (in days)	12.0	12.5	7.9	2.0	24.0	150
PA 7-day spectral density	0.06	0.07	0.05	0.00	0.33	150
UA 7-day spectral density	0.05	0.06	0.03	0.01	0.17	150
7-Day Harmonic Analysis Results						
PA 7-day cycle, R^2	0.07	0.10	0.11	0.00	0.71	176
UA 7-day cycle, R^2	0.05	0.07	0.07	0.00	0.32	176
PA amplitude, R	0.21	0.26	0.22	0.00	1.58	176
UA amplitude, R	0.25	0.28	0.19	0.01	1.06	176
PA phase, ϕ, in days (corresponding day of peak)	0.14 (Sat)	0.15 (Sat)	1.69	−3.31 (Wed)	3.43 (Wed)	176
UA phase, ϕ in days (corresponding day of peak)	0.04 (Sat)	0.05 (Sat)	1.84	−3.36 (Wed)	3.46 (Wed)	176

Note: PA = pleasant affect; UA = unpleasant affect.

from day to day or week to week. Instead, a wide variety of characterizations are possible. That said, being particularly interested in how individuals' emotions might reflect a weekly cycle, in subsequent analyses we still concentrated on results that pertain to a 7-day period.

An individual's spectral density estimate for a particular frequency (i.e., 7-day period) can be thought of as an index of the amount of variance in the individual time series accounted for by that particular cycle (i.e., weekly cycle). The spectral density estimates for a 7-day period (see table 25.1) indicated significant individual differences in the degree to which an individual's emotions are characterized by (or entrained to, cf. Larsen & Kasimatis, 1990) weekly cycles (mean spectral density PA = 0.07, SD = 0.05; mean spectral density UA = 0.06, SD = 0.03). Note that individuals' 7-day spectral densities covered a range of values. In other words, some individuals' data can be explained well by a weekly cycle and others' not so much.

Restricted Harmonic Analysis with a Seven-Day Frequency

Finally, we fitted 7-day cycles, that is, Equation 4, to each individual's data separately. Using detrended data, wherein μ_i was zero and by fixing $\tau = 7$, we estimated the coefficients A and B using OLS regression. Individual amplitude, R, and phase, ϕ, for PA and UA were calculated as per Equations 2 and 4. The predicted weekly cycles derived from the model are shown in figures 25.7

and 25.8. As can be seen in the plots and as we noted in the spectral analysis results, there were substantial interindividual differences in how well a weekly cycle fitted individuals' time series. Here, individual R^2 statistics, indicating the percentage of variance accounted for by a weekly cycle, ranged from 0.00 to 0.71 for PA and from 0.00 to 0.32 for UA (see table 25.1). The distributions of R^2 (across individuals) for both PA and UA were relatively normally distributed with means of 0.10 (SD = 0.11) for PA and 0.07 (SD = 0.07) for UA. Furthermore, we found interindividual differences in the amplitudes (R) of PA (mean = 0.26, SD = 0.22) and UA (mean = 0.28, SD = 0.19). The range or dispersion of amplitudes indicates that some individuals showed large weekly fluctuations in their emotions, while others did not. The individual estimates of phase (ϕ), an indicator of which day of the week an individual's emotion was likely to peak, also showed interindividual differences. For PA, ϕ estimates ranged, in terms of days, from −3.5 days (Wednesday) to +3.5 days (Wednesdays). That is, depending on the individual, PA might systematically peak on any one of the 7 days of the week. The mean ϕ for PA was 0.05, indicating prototypical peaks in PA on Saturdays. For UA, ϕ estimates also showed substantial between-person differences (−3.5 to +3.5 days from Saturday). Unlike those for PA, however, the ϕ estimates for UA were not normally distributed. Instead, they conformed roughly to a trimodal distribution, with modes corresponding to weekly peaks in UA occurring for some individuals on Thursday mornings (−1.5

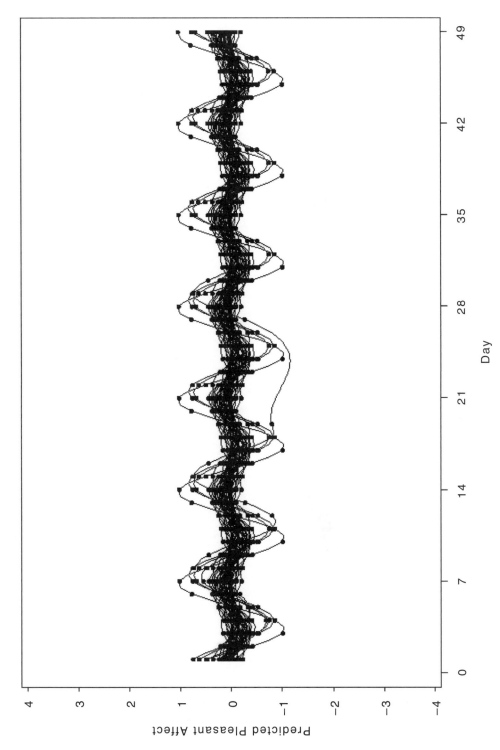

Figure 25.7 Predicted 7-day sinusoidal cycles in pleasant affect as obtained from the harmonic analysis. Each individual's predicted pattern of weekly cyclicity in pleasant affect is represented by a single line.

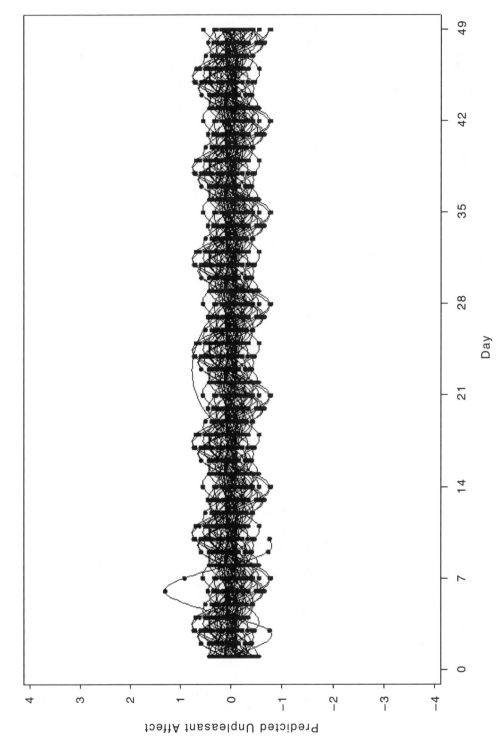

Figure 25.8 Predicted 7-day sinusoidal cycles in unpleasant affect as obtained from the harmonic analysis. Each individual's predicted pattern of weekly cyclicity in unpleasant affect is represented by a single line.

days), some on Saturday (0.0 days), and some on Monday morning (+1.5 days). As with the relatively low R^2, such results illustrate that UA exhibits less systematic patterns in its day-to-day progression.

Overall, the spectral and harmonic analysis results indicate that there are substantial individual differences in both the extent to which individuals' emotions follow a weekly cycle and in how such cycles are exhibited. Some individuals do not show evidence of a weekly cycle while some do. Some individuals show large, predictable weekly swings in their emotions and others do not. Furthermore, individual weekly cycles differ with regard to which days they peak, often without a clear indication as to when this happens for the "prototypical" person.

Brief Discussion of Empirical Findings

The purpose of this analysis was to examine if and how individuals' emotions may be characterized by a weekly cycle. Using daily reports of emotion experiences, we obtained estimates of individuals' day-to-day pleasant and unpleasant emotional states and attempted to extract patterns of weekly cyclicity from them. Generally, we found that true score estimates of PA and UA could be obtained using these particular 16 items, and that there are substantial individual differences in both the extent to which individuals' emotions follow a weekly cycle and in how such cycles are exhibited.

It is encouraging that our 8-item scales had the highly desirable measurement properties required by the RSM (i.e., overall fit to the RSM was good). This meant that true score estimates derived from the measurement model were highly interpretable and meaningful. However, the response thresholds indicated that a 7-point scale was unnecessary. The same information could have been obtained with a more parsimonious 5-point scale. This finding has relevance to the construction of scales for use in forthcoming studies of intraindividual variability in emotion and subjective well-being.

The spectral and harmonic analysis findings highlight the high degree of individual heterogeneity in how emotional experiences progress over time. There is, at least with respect to the days of the week, great diversity in the predictability of mood fluctuations. For example, the substantial interindividual differences noted in the UA peaks (i.e., phase, φ) highlight that model-derived prototypical or average cycles may in fact characterize no one. Furthermore,

the bimodal distributions found in this data mean that the cyclic wave fit to aggregated data would not correspond with an averaging of the individual curves (see similar discussion by Estes, 1956). In other words, even taking a nonlinear mixed-modeling, individual growth curve approach might lead one toward a biased set of conclusions. It is therefore paramount that while still exploring how nonlinear processes might be structured that we take caution in how we aggregate and generalize across individuals.

Conclusion

We illustrated how models from different traditions might be synthesized to provide richer descriptions of human behavior. The RSM was used to examine the patterns that existed among items and to provide an objective scale of measurement. Spectral and harmonic analyses were then used to examine the cyclic change in individuals' daily pleasant and unpleasant affect. Together, these methods allowed us to learn more about emotion cyclicity within a stronger measurement framework. Furthermore, we hope to have illustrated how multiple techniques might be combined so as to capitalize on the strengths of each. More of such combinations should be explored and utilized.

In conclusion, psychology appears to be developing an enriched notion of research design and measurement. Active theorizing and study of more dynamic notions of human behavior has led us to conclude that the traditional static or linear models are limited in what they can tell us about the complexities of human behavior. To obtain a more complete understanding, we must begin including alternative forms of inquiry that might have originated from different traditions into our research designs and methods. As we have illustrated here, some of this complexity can be modeled and studied readily using widely available methods.

Acknowledgments   The authors gratefully acknowledge the support provided by grants T32 AG20500-01 and 5 R01 AG18330 from the National Institute on Aging in the preparation of this chapter. Special thanks to John R. Nesselroade, Ryan Bowles, Tim Salthouse, and other members of the Institute for Developmental and Health Research Methodology at the University of Virginia for helpful comments on earlier versions of this work.

Notes

1. However, it is useful to note that comparison of person estimates across different groups is only possible if measurement invariance can be established (i.e., all item parameters are constrained to be the same across groups; for details, see Reise et al., 1993; Thissen, Steinberg, & Gerrard, 1986).

2. When fitting sinusoidal models, there should not be any increasing or decreasing trends existent in the data. For this reason, individual trends were removed by regressing each individual's affect series on time. Each resulting time series of residuals is then the detrended time series (i.e., with its intercept and linear slope removed).

3. In empirical applications, the basic assumptions underlying item response modeling—unidimensionality and local independence—should be checked before one proceeds to model fitting. Unidimensionality implies that a single construct underlies the set of items tested, whereas local independence means that test items are pairwise uncorrelated if person trait (or in this context, state) level is held constant statistically (Reise et al., 1993). The assumption of unidimensionality was not tested explicitly in the current example. This is because the dimensionality of PA and UA is itself a topic of debate and this issue has already been tested using this data set elsewhere (e.g., Diener et al., 1995). The local independence assumption, in contrast, was clearly violated in this analysis due to the within-person dependencies in item responses across measurement occasions. However, this is what we seek to capture later using harmonic and spectral analyses anyway, and is therefore less relevant in this particular setting. Bond and Fox (2001), for instance, have used within-person, across-occasion estimates obtained from item response models in the context of longitudinal models, and found this approach to be useful and to yield "actual individual trends rather than mere statistical artifacts" (p. 135). Of course, other kinds of dependencies (e.g., within-occasion dependencies) are still possible and could potentially lead to violation of the local independence assumption.

4. In the context of Rasch models, it is customary to assess model fit by examining the residuals of item and person fit. A general guide (although this may vary from application to application) for ranges of acceptable item mean-square values is discussed in Wright et al. (1994).

References

Allport, G. W. (1937). *Personality: A psychological interpretation*. New York: Holt, Rinehart, and Winston.

Andrich, D. (1978a). A binomial latent trait model for the study of Likert-style attitude questionnaires. *British Journal of Mathematical and Statistical Psychology, 31*, 84–98.

Andrich, D. (1978b). A rating formulation for ordered response categories. *Psychometrika, 43* (4), 561–573.

Baker, J. G., Rounds, J. B., & Zevon, M. A. (2000). A comparison of graded response and Rasch partial credit models with subjective well-being. *Journal of Educational and Behavioral Statistics, 25*(3), 253–270.

Bond, T. G., & Fox, C. (2001). *Applying the Rasch model: Fundamental measurement in the human sciences*. Mahwah, NJ: Erlbaum.

Box, G. E. P., & Jenkins, G. M. (1976). *Time series analysis: Forecasting and control.* (rev. ed.). San Francisco: Holden-Day.

Brockwell, P. J., & Davis, R. A. (2002). *Introduction to time series and forecasting* (2nd ed.). New York: Springer-Verlag.

Carver, C. S., & Scheier, M. F. (1990). Origins and functions of positive and negative affect: A control-process view. *Psychological Review, 97*(1), 19–35.

Chatfield, C. (1996). *The analysis of time series: An introduction* (5th ed.). London: Chapman and Hall.

Chow, S.-M., Ram, N., Boker, S. M., Fujita, F., & Clore, G. (2005). Emotion as a thermostat: Representing emotion regulation using a damped oscillator model. *Emotion, 5*(2), 208–225.

Diener, E., Fujita, F., & Smith, H. (1995). The personality structure of affect. *Journal of Personality and Social Psychology, 69*(1), 130–141.

Eid, M., & Diener, E. (1999). Intraindividual variability in affect: Reliability, validity and personality correlates. *Journal of Personality and Social Psychology, 76*, 662–676.

Embretson, S. E., & Reise, S. (2000). *Item response theory for psychologists*. Mahwah, NJ: Erlbaum.

Estes, W. (1956). The problem of inference from curves based on group data. *Psychological Bulletin, 53*(2), 134–140.

Feldman Barrett, L. (1998). Discrete emotions or dimensions? The role of valence focus and arousal focus. *Cognition and Emotion, 12*, 579–599.

Gottman, J. (1979). Detecting cyclicity in social interaction. *Psychological Bulletin, 86*(2), 338–348.

Hambleton, R. K., Swaminathan, H., & Rogers, H. J. (1991). *Fundamentals of item response theory*. Newbury Park, CA: Sage.

Koopmans, L. H. (1995). *The spectral analysis of time series (probability and mathematical statistics)*. San Diego, CA: Academic Press.

Larsen, R. J. (1987). The stability of mood variability: A spectral analytic approach to daily mood assessments. *Journal of Personality and Social Psychology, 52,* 1195–1204.

Larsen, R. J. (2000). Toward a science of mood regulation. *Psychological Inquiry, 11*(3), 129–141.

Larsen, R. J., & Diener, E. (1987). Affect intensity as an individual difference characteristic: A review. *Journal of Research in Personality, 52,* 1195–1204.

Larsen, R. J., & Kasimatis, M. (1990). Individual differences in entrainment of mood to the weekly calendar. *Journal of Personality and Social Psychology, 58*(1), 164–171.

Lee, O. K. (2003). Rasch simultaneous vertical equating for measuring reading growth. *Journal of Applied Measurement, 4*(1), 10–23.

Linacre, J. M. (2002). *A user's guide to WINSTEPS MINISTEPS Rasch-model computer programs.* Chicago, IL: Author.

Lord, F. M. (1980). *Applications of item response theory to practical testing problems.* Hillsdale, NJ: Erlbaum.

McArdle, J. J., Grimm, K. J., Hamagami, F., Bowles, R. P., & Meredith, W. (2006). *Modeling non-repeated measures using longitudinal structural equations.* Manuscript under review.

McDonald, R. P. (1982). Linear versus non-linear models in item response theory. *Applied Psychological Measurement, 6,* 379–396.

Murray, G., Allen, N. B., Trinder, J., & Burgess, H. (2002). Is weakened circadian rhymicity a characteristic of neuroticism? *Journal of Affective Disorders, 72*(3), 281–289.

Ram, N., Chow, S.-M., Bowles, R. P., Wang, L., Grimm, K., Fujita, F., & Nesselroade, J. R. (2006). Examining interindividual differences in cyclicity of pleasant and unpleasant affect using spectral analysis and item response modeling. *Application Reviews and Case Studies, 70,* 773–790.

Reid, S., Towell, A. D., & Golding, J. F. (2000). Seasonality, social zeitgebers and mood variability in entrainment of mood: Implications for seasonal affective disorder. *Journal of Affective Disorders, 59*(1), 47–54.

Reise, S. P., Widaman, K. F., & Pugh, P. H. (1993). Confirmatory factor analysis and item response theory: Two approaches for exploring measurement invariance. *Psychological Bulletin, 114,* 552–566.

Rusting, C. L., & Larsen, R. J. (1998). Diurnal patterns of unpleasant mood: Associations with neuroticism, depression, and anxiety. *Journal of Personality, 66*(1), 85–103.

Segura, L. S., & González-Romá, V. (2003). How do respondents construe ambiguous response formats of affect items. *Journal of Personality and Social Psychology, 85*(5), 956–968.

Shifren, K., Hooker, K. A., Wood, P. K., & Nesselroade, J. R. (1997). The structure and variation in mood in individuals with Parkinson's disease: A dynamic factor analysis. *Psychology and Aging, 12,* 328–229.

Tellegen, A., Watson, D., & Clark, L. A. (1999). On the dimensional and hierarchical structure of affect. *Psychological Science, 10*(4), 297–303.

Thissen, D., Steinberg, L., & Gerrand, M. (1986). Beyond group-mean differences: The concept of item bias. *Psychological Bulletin, 99*(1), 118–128.

Warner, R. M. (1998). *Spectral analysis of time-series data.* New York: Guilford.

Watson, D., Lee, A. C., & Tellegen, A. (1988). Development and validation of brief measures of positive and negative affect: The PANAS scale. *Journal of Personality and Social Psychology, 54,* 1063–1070.

Watson, D., & Tellegen, A. (1985). Toward a consensual structure of mood. *Psychological Bulletin, 98,* 219–235.

Watson, D., & Tellegen, A. (1999). Issues in the dimensional structure of affect—effects of descriptors, measurement error and response formats: Comment on Russell and Carroll (1999). *Psychological Bulletin, 125,* 601–610.

Wright, B. D., Linacre, J. M., Gustafson, P., & Martin-Löf, J.-E. (1994). Reasonable mean-square fit values. *Rasch Measurement Transactions, 8*(3), 370.

26

Dynamical Modeling for Studying Self-Regulatory Processes

An Example From the Study of Religious Development Over the Life Span

Michael E. McCullough and Steven M. Boker

The development of religious faith and practice over the life course has been a topic of interest to psychological theorists for over a century (Fowler, 1981; Hall, 1904). In recent years, social scientists have applied quantitative methods from modern developmental science to questions regarding the development of religious feeling, belief, and behavior over the adult life course (Argue, Johnson, & White, 1999; McCullough, Enders, Brion, & Jain, 2005; Sasaki & Suzuki, 1987). Many of the models that have been proposed by theorists such as Hall and Fowler, and the empirical tests of developmental hypotheses, have relied upon the assumption that a person's religiousness may change (or not) as a function of how old he or she is. In other words, these models and tests have assumed that it is something about getting older per se that controls religious development.

Other scientists have given a role to the effects of life events on religious development (Bahr, 1970; Ingersoll-Dayton, Krause, & Morgan, 2002;

Kelley-Moore & Ferraro, 2001; Sherkat, 1998; Stolzenberg, Blair-Loy, & Waite, 1995), providing an understanding of how the vicissitudes of life can influence people's religious beliefs and behaviors. Such research has explored, for instance, how normative events in the life cycle—going to college, getting married, having children, getting divorced, the empty nest, the death of a spouse, and the development of physical disability—can produce growth and decline in religiousness.

Together, the age-dependent perspective and the life-events perspective on religious development have shed important light on the development of religiousness over the life course. However, another developmental perspective has been ignored: A perspective based on the notion that individuals actively govern their religious belief and behavior according to an internal guidance system. This internal guidance system might be thought of as a coordinated set of psychophysiological processes comprising reference values, perceptions of one's social world, programs for behavioral action, and feedback loops that seeks to produce in individuals a degree of religiousness that enables them to flourish in their social environments, modify environments that are not working for them, and feel comfortable with what they believe and how they interact with the world.

This third perspective is not mutually exclusive of the age-dependent and life-events models of religious development, but it is distinct from them. This chapter is the first of which we are aware to extend theory and research on religious development by proposing and testing the idea that religiousness does not simply change as a function of age, or as a function of life circumstances, but rather as the result of self-regulation.

The proposition that humans are self-regulating creatures that use information about how they are changing to exert change upon their own physiological, psychological, and behavioral states must surely be one of the most foundational assumptions of any positive psychology of human behavior. However, this assumption is hardly unique to positive psychology. In one respect, the assumption that human beings are self-regulatory is utterly uncontroversial, for every organism must regulate its behavior to ensure survival. At the levels of cells, tissue, and organs, many human physiological functions are governed by homeostatic mechanisms. Blood pressure, heart rate, hunger, water balance, temperature, and respiration are all self-regulated as well, as are the body's responses to psychological and physical stress (Selye, 1956).

Many contemporary theorists in personality, social, developmental, and clinical psychology assume that psychological and behavioral processes are governed by self-regulatory processes as well. In their book *On the Self-Regulation of Behavior*, Carver and Scheier (1998) proposed "that human behavior is a continual process of moving toward, and away from, various kinds of mental goal representations, and that this movement occurs by a process of feedback control. This view treats behavior as the consequence of an internal guidance system inherent in the way living beings are organized... we refer to the guidance process as a system of *self-regulation*" (p. 2). Some of these self-regulatory processes can be conceptualized as preferred set points (e.g., weight, happiness), with individuals' biobehavioral systems attempting to keep the values of a system within a small zone of deviation from the set points. For example, it is often assumed that the biological system that controls body mass and the affective system that controls mood both regulate people toward certain ideal weights or ideal balances of positive and negative affect. In addition, the pursuit of goals, which is often a conscious process involving volitional effort, can also be viewed through the lens of self-regulation—the process by which individuals actively work to change their behavior to make it conform to their standards (Carver & Scheier, 1998; Higgins, Grant, & Shah, 1999).

Although theorists and researchers in positive psychology have also recognized that self-regulation is an important aspect of many forms of strength, resilience, and adaptation, few researchers in psychology and the behavioral sciences, and perhaps none in the domain of positive psychology, have taken advantage of the considerable advances in multivariate statistics that allow for tests of self-regulatory processes (Boker & Nesselroade, 2002; McArdle & Hamagami, 2003; Oud & Jansen, 2000). Such tools have been used to shed light on the millisecond-to-millisecond regulation of posture in infants (Boker, 2001), the day-to-day regulation of psychological well-being among recent widows (Bisconti, 2001), and the year-to-year regulation of tobacco and alcohol use among adolescents (Boker & Graham, 1998). The goal here is to introduce some of these tools to researchers interested in positive psychology and to illustrate their utility for testing hypotheses regarding the extent to which a given psychological process is governed by a self-regulatory mechanism. Many constructs that are of interest to the emerging positive psychology field are based on the notion that human behavior either is guided by self-regulatory processes (Masten & Reed, 2002) or can be conceptualized themselves as self-regulatory processes (McCullough & Witvliet, 2002), so understanding how multivariate methods can be used to study those self-regulatory processes could be a boon to scientific progress in positive psychology.

In the pages that follow, we (a) introduce some basic concepts regarding self-regulation and the differential equations that can be used to test self-regulation processes with longitudinal data; (b) introduce some theoretical background that sets the stage for considering how religious or spiritual development may be governed by self-regulation; (c) report the results of a study in which we explored self-regulatory dynamics in religious development; (d) discuss what these analyses might suggest about religious development and future work on this particular topic; and (e) offer some general recommendations to researchers who want to use these techniques in their own work.

Modeling Longitudinal Data From a Self-Regulatory Perspective

Suppose we are interested in a psychological construct that is hypothesized to regulate itself. In other words, suppose that the construct may undergo changes such that future values of the construct's indicator variables are dependent on the current value of those same variables. For instance, when the construct was far from a preferred equilibrium value or set point, change might occur such that the construct would tend to return toward the equilibrium value. Or perhaps there might be a preference for slow change rather than rapid change. Then changes that occurred too rapidly might be reduced or damped. In this case, the change itself would be changed by the self-regulation.

It is self-evident that in the preceding paragraph we relied heavily on the word *change*. Additionally, one should note that when speaking of self-regulatory processes, one is naturally led to propose models in which quantifiable measures of change are the outcome or predictor variables. For that reason, it is important to be specific about what sort of change we mean and exactly how to quantify it. To observe change, some interval of time must elapse. Thus, observed change is always relative to some interval of time. But, if we make the assumption that the construct of interest changes continuously over time, we can calculate a convenient abstract concept: instantaneous change, a derivative of the construct with respect to time.

Consider the trajectory of continuous change of a construct X over some interval of time from $t = 0$ to $t = 10$ plotted as a gray curve in figure 26.1. From $t = 0$ to $t = 2$, the construct is increasing and becoming farther from its equilibrium, followed by a period of decline in the interval from $t = 2$ to $t = 7.5$, and then finally a period of increase again. There are several observations that can be made about this trajectory. It is apparent that the construct does not stray far from its equilibrium since the slope of the curve is changing from positive to negative to positive again in a regular way. That is, when the trajectory strays too far from equilibrium, the slope changes sign and the trajectory heads back toward equilibrium.

The arrows in figure 26.1 plot the slope of the trajectory at each of seven points ($a, b, c, \ldots, g$). Another way to think about these arrows is that they plot the predicted change in the construct X at a time t if we thought there was only linear change in X. The more these linear predictions diverge from the trajectory, the more curvature in the trajectory. For instance, at points b and f there is a great deal of mismatch between the trajectory and the linear prediction. But at point d the linear prediction is quite good. For this reason, in dynamical systems we do not speak of figure 26.1 as being a nonlinear system even though the trajectory is different than a line. Recall that sometimes the trajectory curves and sometimes it does not—sometimes a line is a good approximation and sometimes it is not. In dynamical systems we ask, "Can the change, both slope and curvature, be accounted for by a system of linear equations?" If so, we call it a linear system, and if not we call it nonlinear.

Note that in figure 26.1, the farther a point is from equilibrium, the greater the mismatch between the arrow and the trajectory. In fact, in this example there is a linear relationship between the

Figure 26.1 A construct X fluctuates around its equilibrium (0 on the ordinate axis) for the time interval $t = 0$ to $t = 10$. Arrows indicate slope at each point, that is, the first derivative of the curve at that point. Change in the slope, that is, the second derivative of the curve, is indicated by the deviation between the arrowhead and the trajectory.

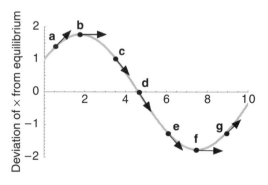

deviation from equilibrium of a chosen point on the trajectory and the second derivative of the trajectory, that is, the curvature, at that chosen point.

Now consider the five trajectories plotted in figure 26.2. Each of these trajectories has the same linear relationship between its displacement and its second derivative. But each curve has a different starting value at time $t = 0$. In psychological terms, we would say that there were no individual differences in the parameters of the self-regulation, but there were individual differences in initial conditions, that is, the values of the variables at time $t = 0$. In this case, the differences were in the initial displacement from equilibrium, but there were no individual differences in slope at time $t = 0$.

Of course, in real data, trajectories will never be so smooth and similar to one another. We must find ways to statistically aggregate data in such a way that intraindividual change and interindividual similarities are not obscured by the aggregation. If we were to simply average all of the slopes in figure 26.2, we would find that there was a modest negative slope. In fact, one can simply draw a line from the mean value of the displacement at $t = 0$ to the mean value of the displacement at $t = 10$ and this line would have exactly the mean of all of the slopes of all of the trajectories over the entire interval. Such a procedure tells us no more than would a pretest/posttest design—in either case we would learn nothing about the highly patterned intraindividual variability in these data.

In these data, such a mean slope is extremely misleading. If we chose to end our experiment at $t = 8$, the mean slope would be more negative. But if we chose to end our experiment at $t = 6$, the mean slope would be very close to zero. Finally, suppose we ended our experiment at $t = 3$. Now the line connecting the mean displacement

at $t = 0$ and the mean displacement at $t = 3$ is strongly positive. Which mean slope are we to believe? Since each individual's curve changes sign from positive to negative to positive again, the aggregation method must not aggregate over too much time or this patterned intraindividual variability will be obscured.

Suppose instead we were to aggregate a mean slope within a small interval of time and within a small set of values of displacement. For instance, in figure 26.3 a grid is superimposed and the mean slope is taken within each box of the grid for all trajectories crossing that box in the grid. The plot of the dark line segments in figure 26.3 is called an empirical slope field (Boker & McArdle, 2005). In this plot, the changes in sign of the slope become apparent. Recall that there were no individual differences in slope in the initial conditions at time $t = 0$. Note that the line segments in a column are similar to one another. Similarity in rows or in columns are a clue that helps in guiding model building in dynamical systems. We wish to build a model in which we can test for reliable relationships between derivatives of a system. Aggregating and plotting derivatives (in this case the first derivative) against a variable or variables can help reveal which of these relationships might be strong.

To create an empirical slope field, one does not need to make an assumption about where the equilibrium might be. In other words, the zero on the ordinate axis in figure 26.3 could change and the slope field would not change. This means that we can sometimes use a slope field to help determine a likely value for the equilibrium.

A word of caution is in order here: Sometimes aggregating over displacement and time is not an effective method for determining a likely equilibrium value. Suppose there were individual differences in equilibrium value; that is to say, every individual might have a separate set point

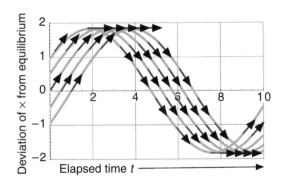

Figure 26.2 Five trajectories with the same relationship between displacement and curvature, but with different starting values.

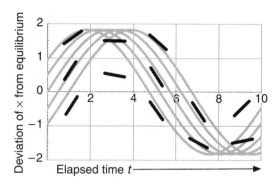

Figure 26.3 An empirical slope field. Average slope of all trajectories within each box is plotted as a single line segment centered in that box. When no trajectories cross a box, no line segment is plotted.

on the construct X. In this case, aggregating over individuals can obscure patterned intraindividual variability (i.e., the dynamics of self-regulation) that would be observed if the true individual equilibria were known. Random coefficients models provide one method for testing for individual differences in equilibria (Boker & Bisconti, 2006).

We will next consider a simple linear differential equations model that could account for self-regulating fluctuations about an equilibrium value—a second-order linear differential equation in which the curvature is a linear combination of the slope and displacement. This is often called a damped linear oscillator model because it approximates the motion of a pendulum with friction. Suppose we have measured a construct X at N occasions separated by an interval s. Then the damped linear oscillator model for the time series data $X = \{x_1, x_2, x_3, \ldots, x_N\}$ can be written

$$\ddot{x}_t = \eta x_t + \zeta \dot{x}_t + e_t \qquad (1)$$

where $\ddot{x}_t$ and $\dot{x}_t$ are the second and first derivatives of x with respect to time, η is a coefficient related to the frequency of the oscillation, ζ is a coefficient related to how quickly the oscillations

are damped to equilibrium, and e_t is a residual term.

Each of the 15 gray trajectories in figure 26.4 is the result of applying Equation 1 with the coefficients $\eta = -0.2$ and $\zeta = -0.3$ and the error term equal to zero: a completely deterministic system with no individual differences in coefficients. If there are no individual differences in coefficients, then why do the trajectories look so different from each other? These trajectories differ only in their initial conditions. There are five different values of initial displacement $\{-1, -0.4, 0.4, 0.8, 1.2\}$ and three different values of initial slope $\{0, 3, 5\}$.

One way to analyze these data would be to fit latent growth curves to the trajectories. In such a case, we would reject the hypothesis that the coefficients of these trajectories are equal. Latent growth curve analysis is widely used and is appropriate for many problems. However, growth curve analysis has drawbacks when used to specify models for self-regulation. First, as seen in this example, growth curves can confound individual differences in initial conditions with individual differences in coefficients. The way these 15 simulated individuals self-regulate is identical; only their initial conditions differ.

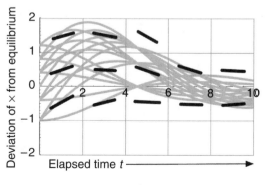

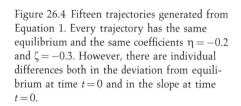

Figure 26.4 Fifteen trajectories generated from Equation 1. Every trajectory has the same equilibrium and the same coefficients $\eta = -0.2$ and $\zeta = -0.3$. However, there are individual differences both in the deviation from equilibrium at time $t = 0$ and in the slope at time $t = 0$.

Second, the parameters obtained from a growth curve analysis relate to either an aggregate trajectory or how each individual's trajectory conforms to the particular hypothesized model. These results say nothing about what might have happened if the individual had started at another initial condition.

In contrast, fitting a differential equation model to longitudinal data specifically distinguishes between model coefficients and initial conditions in such a way that a family of trajectories is implied. Each possible initial condition has associated with it a trajectory. In this way we can explore questions such as, "How similar would two individuals' trajectories be if they self-regulated differently (had different coefficients) but the same initial conditions?" Or the opposite question could be asked: "How similar would two individuals' trajectories be if they self-regulated in the same way, but had different initial conditions?"

Superimposed on figure 26.4 is an empirical slope field. Note that by simply focusing on the line segments of the slope field, we can estimate the equilibrium for this equation to be somewhere near zero. Note that except for the first interval, from $t = 0$ to $t = 2$, the slopes above zero are negative and the slopes below zero are positive. This method is used to provide a preliminary estimate of an equilibrium value for the example data analyzed later in this chapter.

Given data from trajectories such as those plotted in figure 26.4, we can fit Equation 1 if we can estimate the derivatives of the construct from the observed time series. In the example, we will use local linear approximation (Boker & Nesselroade, 2002) to estimate these derivatives and fit multilevel models in order to account for potential individual differences in self-regulation (Boker & Ghisletta, 2001).

Religious Development as a Self-Regulatory Process

At this point, we illustrate some of the concepts introduced above by analyzing some data drawn from the real world. One psychological domain in which we can ask questions about self-regulation that should be of interest to positive psychology is in the area of religious and spiritual development (Mattis, 2004; Pargament & Mahoney, 2002; Tsang & McCullough, 2003). Although researchers have found evidence that religious and spiritual changes over

the life course arise from aging per se (Argue et al., 1999; Sasaki & Suzuki, 1987) and the influence of external life events (Bahr, 1970; Ingersoll-Dayton et al., 2002; Kelley-Moore & Ferraro, 2001; Sherkat, 1998; Stolzenberg et al., 1995), spiritual or religious change over the life course probably does not result solely from age-related development and external forces acting upon individuals. To some extent, spiritual and religious changes may also be caused by self-regulation processes that are intrinsic to individual functioning. Just as heart rate has an intrinsic variability independently of any forces acting upon the organism, spirituality and religiousness may vary as a function of an intrinsic self-regulation process. As we mentioned previously, self-regulation is a process by which an organism uses information about the way its behavior is changing to modify future behavior (Boker, 2001). Insofar as the human tendency toward religiousness is ordered in such a way that the current state of an individual's religious system (i.e., the person's religiousness at time t) predicts the future behavior of the system (i.e., the same person's religiousness at time $t + 1$), this system is said to possess intrinsic dynamics (Boker & Graham, 1998), and we can posit a self-regulatory mechanism that works to achieve stability or equilibrium (Boker, 2001).

Because religiousness is at least partially based upon genetic effects (for review see D'Onofrio, Eaves, Murrelle, Maes, & Spilka, 1999) and strong effects for socialization processes (e.g., Flor & Knapp, 2001) that may set people's preferences for certain optimal degrees of religiousness, it is reasonable to expect that adults' religiousness is subject to self-regulatory processes that effectively pull their levels of religiousness toward points of equilibrium. As a result, even though aging and the vicissitudes of life (e.g., bereavement, health problems, marriage, child rearing, etc.), might create fluctuation in people's spirituality or religiousness over time, an intrinsic self-regulatory process may also be active in directing the extent to which people define their lives in terms of religion and engage in religious activities.

Intrinsic dynamics are often modeled in terms of differential equations in which accelerations in a dependent variable (i.e., the extent to which changes in religiousness at any given point in time are speeding up or slowing down, operationalized as the second derivatives of the individual's observed scores) are regressed simultaneously upon the measured value of the variable (e.g., actual scores of an individual's religiousness at a given point in time) and the rate of change in those measured values (i.e., the first derivatives of the individuals' observed scores). One dynamical model that may be of particular value for shedding light on self-regulatory processes underlying religious and spiritual change is a damped linear oscillator with a single point attractor (in which scores oscillate around one or more point attractors, with variation around the point attractors gradually becoming smaller and smaller, like a pendulum with friction).

A second dynamical model that has a substantive psychological interpretation is a damped linear oscillator model with two point attractors rather than one. In positing such a model, one proposes that religious development involves oscillation caused by two points of stability or equilibrium that exert simultaneous influences on people's religiousness over time.

In the context of religious and spiritual development, these two dynamical models have substantive psychological interpretations (for a fuller treatment, see Boker & Graham, 1998). A damped linear oscillator model with a single point attractor corresponds to a self-regulatory system in which an individual's level of religiousness oscillates between values that are higher than optimal and values that are lower than optimal, eventually converging closer and closer to a point of equilibrium. We might imagine an individual who begins adulthood with a higher-than-optimal level of religiousness (with optimal defined as the value that maximizes person-environment fit in the broadest sense), but finds the social consequences of this high level of religiousness to be unpleasant (i.e., it alienates friends and family members). As a result, a self-regulatory process pulls the individual's religiousness toward equilibrium but overshoots this optimum. At this lower-than-optimal level of religiousness, the individual experiences problems adapting to his or her social environment that are experienced as unpleasant and which being more religious is perceived to remedy. In response, the individual's self-regulatory process then attracts him or her to an increased level of religiousness, thereby overshooting the optimum but not to the same degree as before. This process of oscillation around an optimum, with better and better approximation of the optimum in each cycle, is posited to continue until a point of equilibrium is reached.

A second-order model with two attractors implies that individuals' religious trajectories are produced by oscillation around two rather than one point attractors. This might occur in a system in which it is possible to develop a high degree of person-environment fit by settling upon either of two values of religiousness. In a highly religious society such as the United States, in which one can easily find social structures and social relations that reinforce both very high and very low levels of religiousness, it is perhaps more plausible to conceive of religiousness as a two-attractor system, with people eventually settling upon very high or very low levels of religiousness over time.

A damped linear oscillator model with a single point of attraction can be specified in terms of the causal effects of a religious variable's measured values and first derivative (i.e., rate of change) on its second derivative (i.e., rate of acceleration). Referring back to Equation 1, we can write:

$$\ddot{x}_t = \eta x_t + \zeta \dot{x}_t + e_t \qquad (1)$$

where $\ddot{x}_t$ acceleration in the rate at which religiousness is changing at time t; $\zeta =$ the coefficient of damping (i.e., the speed with which individuals reduce their periodic oscillation around their equilibrium point); $\dot{x}_t =$ the rate at which religiousness is changing; $\eta =$ the square of the frequency of oscillation; $x_t =$ religiousness at time t; and $e_t =$ error in measuring the second derivative of religiousness at time t.

The only difference between a one-attractor model and a two-attractor model is the inclusion of a cubic term as a predictor of the second derivatives:

$$\ddot{x} = \eta x_t + \zeta \dot{x}_t + \xi x_t^3 + e_t \qquad (2)$$

Including the x^3 term allows religiousness to be attracted toward two equilibria instead of one.

It is possible to test the viability of these two models using the repeated measures of religious saliency that we have developed for participants in the Terman Life Cycle Study of Children With High Ability (Terman & Oden, 1947).

Participants

Over the last few years, the first author and colleagues have been using data from the Terman Life Cycle Study of Children With High Ability to shed light on questions related to the development of religiousness over the life course (McCullough et al., 2005; McCullough, Tsang, & Brion, 2003). In this previous work, we have used longitudinal research designs that are based on the assumption that an individual's religiousness at a given point in time is dependent on his or her age rather than upon a dynamical notion of how people may self-regulate religiousness to maximize person-environment fit.

The Terman study comprises data from 1,528 bright and gifted boys and girls (all of the students had intelligence quotients exceeding 135) from the state of California. The average birth year for children in the original sample was 1910. Since the study was initiated, participants have been recontacted for more than a dozen follow-up surveys.

For the present study, we used 957 (approx. 56% male, 44% female; ages in 1940 ranged from 24 to 40 yrs) of the 1,528 original participants. As of 1940, these mostly white, middle-class adults were highly educated (approximately 99% had high school diplomas; 89% had at least some college experience, 70% had at least a bachelor's degree; 45% had at least a master's degree, and 8% had a doctorate or more). Most (approximately 65%) were married (approximately 31% were single and 3% were divorced).

Measures of Religiousness

Although Terman and successive directors of the Terman longitudinal study collected a great deal of data on participants' religious lives, including dozens of items in checklist or Likert-type format, none of these items was repeated in exactly the same way across surveys. Such frustrations are not uncommon in longitudinal work (Elder, Pavalko, & Clipp, 1993), but social scientists have found a productive way to cope with them.

As in other recent work on religious development (Wink & Dillon, 2001, 2002) we used a recasting method (Elder et al., 1993) to develop a five-point rating scale for measuring the saliency or importance of religion to participants (which we called religious saliency). This measure is conceptually similar to other measures of religious saliency that have been used in previous longitudinal research on religious development among adults (e.g., Argue et al., 1999; Wink & Dillon, 2001). To use these rating scales, trained raters read all information that participants provided regarding their religious-

ness for surveys that Terman and associates conducted in 1940, 1950, 1960, 1977, 1986, and 1991. After reading the religious information on a given participant for a given year, raters then provided a single numeric rating of their perceptions of the participant's religious saliency at that point in the participant's life. Scores on this scale ranged from $-1 = partici$-pant is actively antireligious, noted by lack of personal religious interest/inclination, total lack of life satisfaction gained from religion, and some degree of hostility/suspicion toward religion or religious beliefs, to $4 = religion$ has very high importance in participant's life, as noted by very high interest in religion, very high religious inclination, or very high degree of life satisfaction gained from religion. Interrater reliability was very good (McCullough et al., 2005).

Results

Does a Visual Display of the Data Suggest That Dynamical Processes May Be at Work?

A good way to begin a project designed to examine self-regulatory processes is to acquire an inductive sense of how change actually occurs in the data. Visual displays of data are important for this purpose. Figure 26.5 is an empirical slope field of our religious saliency data (Boker & McArdle, 2005). Based on an aggregation of data from the entire sample, this figure portrays the expected slopes (that is, the rates of change) in religious saliency for combinations of age and the measured values of the variable. That is, this plot depicts the direction in which, and the rate at which, scores on the variable are likely to change after a small amount of time has elapsed. In a sense, they depict the flow of scores with the passage of time.

The empirical slope field in figure 26.5 shows that for most people, religious saliency has a fairly steep positive slope from about age 20 to about age 50, with the slopes appearing slightly steeper for individuals who score in the range $-1 < x < 0$ on religious saliency around age 20. As time passes, however, the slopes become increasingly flat for people at low levels of religious saliency (i.e., people with religious saliency scores around $x = 1$), and increasingly negative for individuals with moderate levels

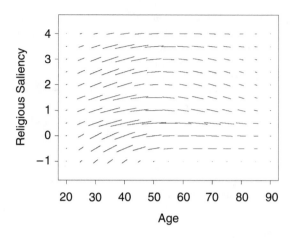

Figure 26.5 Empirical slope field for religious saliency.

of religious saliency (i.e., people scoring in the range $1 < x < 3$). This suggests that religious saliency may possess a single attractor somewhere in the lower range of the scale (i.e., people scoring in the range $-.5 < x < 1$). There is one region of the slope field plot for which low levels of religious saliency do not appear to operate as a strong attractor: the upper right corner. This region describes individuals who possess very high religious saliency scores into their mid-50s and beyond. For individuals in this region, changes in religious saliency with small changes in time are essentially zero, suggesting that religious saliency has stopped changing and is maintaining a consistently high level through the remainder of the life course. This raises the possibility that there may actually be two attractors in this system: an attractor for religious saliency scores in the range $(.5 < x < 1)$ and a second attractor around $x = 4.0$.

Testing Second-Order Differential Equations

With a feel for the data that led us to suspect that the interindividual variations in religious saliency might be created by a self-regulatory system in which people's scores were oscillating (with damping) toward one or possibly two attractors, we proceeded to test some formal differential equations. Our first model was a second-order differential equation in the form of Equation 1.

Calculating First and Second Derivatives With Local Linear Approximation

To generate the necessary first and second derivatives, we used local linear approximation

(LLA; Boker & Nesselroade, 2002), which involves estimating the first derivatives (i.e., slopes or rates of linear change) and second derivatives (e.g., rates of acceleration or curvature) for an observed value of interest based on the observed data preceding and following the observed value of interest. Therefore, estimating these derivatives requires at least three occasions of measurement per individual. Since we measured religious saliency on up to six occasions per individual, we could estimate up to four of the necessary triads (i.e., an observed value and its corresponding first and second derivatives) if we based our estimates on data drawn $\tau = 1$ time step (or measurement occasion) before and after the value for which we wish to approximate the first derivative and second derivative.

However, it is often advantageous to also develop measures of the first and second derivatives using a $\tau > 1$ (i.e., with data more than one time step or occasion of measurement before and after the measured value of interest). Using a value of $\tau > 1$ tends to help reduce the influence of measurement error by low-pass filtering the data while estimating the derivatives. Measurement error will show up as if it were an oscillation with a period of two occasions of measurement. Using observations $\{x1, x3, x5\}$ to calculate one set of derivatives and $\{x2, x4, x6\}$ to calculate a second set of derivatives means that the measurement error will tend to cancel itself out in the long run.

In such cases, to estimate the first and second derivatives for any measured value, we will look not one occasion to the left and right of the index value, but two or more occasions to the left and the right of the value of interest. So, for the analyses that we conducted, we estimated first and second derivatives using values of $\tau = 1$ (these models are referred to below as Models 1a, 2a, 3a, and 4a) and compared those results to the results that emerged from using values of $\tau = 2$ (these models are referred to below as Models 1b, 2b, 3b, and 4b).

We actually calculated four sets of models. The first and second models were second-order models that posited the existence of one point attractor. These two models differed only in the fact that in Model 1, we posited that the parameter estimates of η and ζ were the same for all individuals; that is, that there existed an underlying dynamical system that generalized to all subjects (Boker & Nesselroade, 2002). In contrast, in Model 2 we posited that these parameters varied across persons.

Models 3 and 4 were two-attractor models that posited two point attractors rather than a single one. Model 3 posited that the parameter estimates of η and ζ were the same for everyone, whereas they were permitted to differ across individuals in Model 4.

Models 1a and 1b: A Second-Order Model With One Attractor and Fixed Effects

In testing our first model—a second-order differential equation with one attractor—we assumed that every individual had the same parameters for η (the frequency parameter) and ζ (the damping parameter). Simultaneously regressing $\ddot{x}_t$ upon its corresponding values for x

and $\dot{x}_t$ as in Equation 1 yields the parameters that appear in the Model 1a and 1b columns of table 26.1. The fact that the coefficient for ζ is negative for Model 1a indicates that some damping appears to be occurring in this self-regulatory system: As time passes, the amount of oscillation around the mean becomes smaller—much like a pendulum with friction. In other words, religious saliency looks like a resilient system that manifests less and less fluctuation as time passes. Had the coefficient for ζ been positive, this would have suggested that religiousness is an excitable system in which fluctuation actually becomes greater and greater with the passage of time. The value of η was negative near zero, indicating that the system does not oscillate rapidly—in line with our expectations given the slow change observed in the empirical slope field in figure 26.5.

However, Model 1a appears inadequate, accounting for only 14% of the variance in the second derivative. This is in line with what one would expect when a slow-frequency system is evaluated with a value of $\tau = 1$ (Boker & Nesselroade, 2002). There is a built-in dependence between the value of x and $\ddot{x}_t$ that results from the LLA method of calculating derivatives. This dependence results in an expected $R^2 = 0.65$ when a second-order linear differential equation model (as we use here) is applied to normally distributed random numbers (Boker & Nesselroade, 2002). In essence, this surprising result is due to the fact that normally distributed numbers will appear to oscillate with a period

TABLE 26.1 Parameter Estimates for Differential Equation Models of Religious Saliency

	Model							
	1a One Attractor, Fixed Effects ($\tau = 1$)	1b One Attractor, Fixed Effects ($\tau = 2$)	2a One Attractor, Random Effects ($\tau = 1$)	2b One Attractor, Random Effects ($\tau = 2$)	3a Two Attractor, Fixed Effects ($\tau = 1$)	3b Two Attractor, Fixed Effects ($\tau = 2$)	4a Two Attractor, Random Effects ($\tau = 1$)	4b Two Attractor, Random Effects ($\tau = 2$)
ζ	−0.655	0.029	−0.614	−0.063	−0.654	−0.039	−0.620	−0.021
η	−0.214	−0.113	−0.206	−0.117	−0.071	−0.109	−0.060	−0.103
ξ	—	—	—	—	−0.012	−0.001	−0.013	−0.001
R^2	0.14	0.34	0.30	0.72	0.15	0.61	0.31	0.72
$\eta\tau^2$	−0.21	−0.45	−0.21	−0.47	−0.07	−0.44	−0.06	−0.41
Number of observations	2,417	869	2,417	869	2,417	869	2,417	869
Number of individuals	957	571	957	571	957	571	957	571

equal to twice the value of t used to estimate the model. However, the dependence between t and frequency results in an expected value of $\eta\tau^2 = -2.0$. We can use this fact to calculate values of $\eta\tau^2$ for Models 1a and 1b of -0.21 and -0.45, respectively. These values are far from -2.0 and indicate that the estimated period of oscillation is much slower than the expected value for normally distributed random numbers. Nevertheless, even Model 1b, which evaluated the one-attractor fixed effects model with $\tau = 2$, was not very good, accounting for only 34% of the variance in the second derivative.

Models 2a and 2b: A Second-Order Model With a Single Attractor and Random Effects

Next we evaluated a second-order differential equation with one attractor, as in Models 1a and 1b, but we also allowed the η (frequency) and ζ (damping) parameters to vary across persons. In other words, in these models we evaluated the possibility that the differences in the trajectories observed for each individual were produced not only by individual differences in initial conditions (initial displacement from equilibrium and initial rate of change), but also individual differences in frequency and damping.

Using $\tau = 1$ (Model 2a), we saw a small increase in the variance accounted for, $R^2 = .30$, but a much more impressive increase in model fit occurred when we conducted the same model using $\tau = 2$ (Model 2b). In this version of the one-attractor model with random effects, the model accounted for 72% of the variation in the second derivative of religious saliency. This sizeable increase in R^2 not only suggests that the second-order model with one attractor and random effects may provide an acceptable fit to the data, but it also suggests that using $\tau = 2$ for calculating the first and second derivatives introduces less bias to the estimates than does calculating them with $\tau = 1$ (Boker & Nesselroade, 2002). Since the value for $\eta\tau^2$ was well below 2, we need not be concerned that the fluctuations were solely the product of noise.

The length of time, λ, that elapses during one full cycle of religious saliency (also called the period) can be calculated from the estimated η parameter

$$\lambda = 2\pi\sqrt{1/-\eta,} \tag{3}$$

where 2π converts from units of radians into units of time. Using the average values $\eta = -.206$ and $-.117$ estimated from Models 2a and 2b, and recalling that time was expressed in decades, we estimate that the average period for a full cycle of religious saliency is between 140 and 180 years.

Models 3a and 3b: A Second-Order Model With Two Attractors and Fixed Effects

Because our visual inspection of the slope field plot for religious saliency hinted that a second attractor might be present, we ran a third model that permitted individuals' scores to be attracted to either of two attractors. This was accomplished by adding a coefficient to the models representing x^3. The results of these models appear as Model 3a and Model 3b in table 26.1. Using R^2 as a measure of goodness of fit, these models did not fit appreciably better than did the one-attractor models with random effects (Models 2a and 2b).

Model 4: A Second-Order Model With Two Attractors and Random Effects

In this version of the two-attractor model model, we allowed the ζ and x^3 parameters (representing the relative strength of the two attractors) to vary between persons. The coefficients for η were not random because their high correlation with x^3 ($r = -.92$). The coefficients for these models appear as Model 4a and Model 4b in table 26.1. Using R^2 as a measure of goodness of fit, these models did not fit better than did the one-attractor models with random effects (Models 2a and 2b).

Discussion

In writing this chapter, we wished to introduce readers to multivariate methods for studying self-regulation using differential equation models. We used a real data set that allowed us to examine the self-regulation of religiousness across the adult life course. As chapters on religion and spirituality in some of positive psychology's seminal volumes (Mattis, 2004; Pargament & Mahoney, 2002; Tsang & McCullough, 2003) testify, religion and spirituality are constructs with considerable relevance to the burgeoning field of positive psychology.

Using recently developed methods for studying self-regulatory systems with multiwave panel data (Boker & Ghisletta, 2001; Boker & Nesselroade, 2002), we tested several models that allowed us to examine the possibility that the importance an individual ascribes to religion is to some extent governed by the functioning of an internal guidance system that seeks to move people toward an equilibrium value. The results of the best-fitting of these models—a single-attractor model with random effects for the damping and frequency parameters—suggest that it is indeed plausible to posit that religiousness is, to some degree, self-regulatory in nature. Over the course of adulthood, individuals appear to be adjusting their levels of religiousness toward equilibrium values. As people approach their points of equilibrium, the oscillation in their religious trajectories becomes less pronounced. According to our analyses, an optimal level of religiousness, that is, one that provided equilibrium, was somewhere around a value of 1 on a scale ranging from 0 to 4. A value of 1 represents a fairly low level of religiousness, which is not terribly surprising given the fact that the individuals in this sample were considerably less religious, on average, than were the general population at large (McCullough et al., 2003). However, the indication of individual differences in coefficients for damping and frequency suggest that this single equilibrium value may be a misleading portrayal of particular individuals' equilibrium values (Boker & Nesselroade, 2002).

We were somewhat surprised to find that a two-attractor model did not perform any better than the one-attractor model, as our visual inspection of the slope field plot suggested the possibility of a second point attractor around religiousness values of 4. However, the analyses did not give any reason to favor the less parsimonious two-attractor model over the one-attractor model. Studies with greater numbers of observations per individual would have helped us to gain greater statistical power and, thus, perhaps a greater chance of detecting a second attractor if one truly existed.

As mentioned above, the fact that a model incorporating random effects provided a better fit to the data than did a model with fixed effects means that individuals differed in their damping rates and frequencies of oscillation. Individual differences in damping reflect differences in the extent to which individuals' religious systems can impose friction upon the intrinsic oscillation

that the system is also producing, thereby reducing the amount of swing above and below the equilibrium point with each oscillation. Individual differences in frequency represent individual differences in the intrinsic cycling rate of individuals' religious self-regulatory systems; that is, the number of oscillations completed in a given amount of time. Finally, individual differences in initial conditions represent individual differences between persons such that some people began an observation period with higher levels of religiousness (i.e., high levels of initial displacement from their equilibrium values) than did other people, or more positive slopes (i.e., steep upward initial trajectories) than did other people. In the self-regulation framework we have described herein, it is these individual parametric differences, along with individual differences in initial conditions, that explain the variety of longitudinal trajectories that are seen among the individuals in the Terman study.

Possible Next Steps

Having found individual differences in frequency and damping, as well as individual differences in initial conditions, it might be worthwhile to attempt to account for these individual differences. What factors might cause some individuals to experience more or less damping, or faster or slower frequencies of oscillation, than do others? Can these individual differences be attributed to individual differences in personality? Perhaps individuals with greater emotional stability experience less dramatic fluctuation around their equilibria than do others. Alternatively, perhaps people who marry spouses with levels of religiousness that are similar to their own experience greater damping—that is, greater efficiency in reducing the amount of swing around equilibrium values. To explain individual differences in initial conditions, we might look to background factors such as the degree to which individuals' parents themselves were religiously devout, which might have produced individual differences in initial conditions. Or perhaps we could look to their religious histories in adolescence to find evidence that they had undergone conversion experiences that produced positive religious slopes in early adulthood.

Differential equation modeling of self-regulatory processes is appealing in part because of the elegant way in which it produces estimates of psychologically meaningful processes. Positing that people have different damping and frequency parameters rests on the strong assumption that damping mechanisms and intrinsic frequencies actually exist somewhere under the human skin. In comparison, consider the latent growth parameters that might be used to depict the same longitudinal data in a multilevel growth curve model (Raudenbush & Bryk, 2002). Hypothesizing that interindividual differences in religious development are produced by interindividual differences in initial status values, rates of linear change, or degrees of curvature over a bounded interval, as one might in a growth curve model, does not yield parameters that have intrinsic psychological meaning: One is still left asking what mechanisms produced the interindividual differences in initial status, or linear change, or curvature. This is not to say that growth curve models are not important tools or that differential equation models are a cure-all for modeling longitudinal data. Each type of model has its place and they address rather different questions. Nevertheless, differential equation models have considerable potential to shed light on how people change.

Limitations of the Data Set and Design Recommendations for Researchers

In some respects, the Terman data set was less than ideal for testing hypotheses about self-regulation. With a maximum of six observations per person (data on people's religiousness were available from 1940, 1950, 1960, 1977, 1986, and 1991), it was possible to build a maximum of four observations per person for which a displacement, first derivative, and second derivative could be calculated (since each observation's first and second derivatives could only be calculated if values existed before and after the observation in question). Using $\tau = 2$—the degree of spacing between observations that provided us with the best fit to the data—a maximum of two observations per person were available for which the necessary triads could be established for estimating differential equations. This cut our number of observations by two thirds and the number of participants by 40%. By increasing the number of observations per person, statistical power for conducting these models would have increased, as would the analytic options and the range of dynamical questions we could have asked.

Second, because we were restricted to single-item measures of religiousness, it was impossible to control the effects of measurement error,

which might have been considerable. With two or more indicators of the construct at each time point, we could have reduced measurement error by working with aggregates of observed variables. As a result, our models would have demonstrated greater power to account for individual variation in the $\ddot{x}_t$ values.

Third, we could have developed a better understanding of religious development from these data if we were working in reference to a known perturbation in people's religious self-regulatory systems. The "pendulum with friction" is a common conceit used to frame inquiries into the self-regulatory dynamics of systems. It is easier to understand the behavior of a pendulum if we know when—and from what height—the pendulum was released. That is, it is useful to know when the perturbation occurred and how large it was.

Extending the pendulum conceit to the domain of religious change, it might be easier to understand the self-regulatory mechanisms underlying religious development if one worked with data collected before and after a known disruption to individuals' religious lives. For instance, one might study a group of individuals who had recently experienced a religious conversion as the result of attending a religious event. Alternatively, one might study religious or spiritual responses to tragedy. Recent evidence suggests that adults in the United States became, on average, slightly more spiritually inclined in the months following the terrorist attacks of September 11, 2001 (Peterson & Seligman, 2003), and there is good experimental evidence that exposing people to tragedies in the laboratory increases a questing, open-ended approach to religion (Burris, Jackson, Tarpley, & Smith, 1996; Krauss & Flaherty, 2001). The death of a spouse also appears to create temporary perturbations in widows' and widowers' religious functioning (Brown, Nesse, House, & Utz, 2004). Presumably, insofar as self-regulation actually occurs in the religious domain, these perturbations from equilibrium triggered the operation of that self-regulatory system. Laboratory methods such as those developed by Burris et al. (1996) might be used to introduce systematic religious perturbations, and differential equation models might then be used to estimate mechanisms by which people modulate the effect of the perturbations, thereby allowing researchers to explicitly test self-regulatory hypotheses about religious change.

Summary

Self-regulation is a useful concept for a comprehensive positive psychology. Goals, forgiveness, resilience, posttraumatic growth, and hardiness are but a few of the concepts central to positive psychology that lend themselves to a self-regulatory conceptualization. We hope that the present chapter has provided a brief introduction to the promise that these models might hold for theoretical work and new empirical studies in this young and promising field.

Acknowledgments   For this research we used the Terman Life Cycle Study of Children With High Ability 1922–1986 data set (made accessible 1990, machine-readable data files and microfiche data). These data were collected by L. Terman, R. Sears, L. Cronbach, and P. Sears and are available through the archive of the Henry A. Murray Research Center of the Radcliffe Institute for Advanced Study at Harvard University, 10 Garden Street, Cambridge, Massachusetts (producer and distributor).

This research was generously supported by grants from the John Templeton Foundation, the Metanexus Institute, NIA Grant No. 1R29 AG14983, and funds given by the John D. and Catherine T. MacArthur Foundation to the Henry A. Murray Research Center of the Radcliffe Institute for Advanced Study at Harvard University. We are grateful to the helpful staff of the Murray Research Center, Al Hastorf, Eleanor Walker, and Andrea Jain for their assistance.

References

Argue, A., Johnson, D. R., & White, L. K. (1999). Age and religiosity: Evidence from a three-wave panel analysis. *Journal for the Scientific Study of Religion, 38,* 423–435.

Bahr, H. M. (1970). Aging and religious disaffiliation. *Social Forces, 49,* 59–71.

Bisconti, T. L. (2001). *Widowhood in later life: A dynamical systems approach to emotion regulation.* Unpublished doctoral dissertation, University of Notre Dame.

Boker, S. M. (2001). Differential structural equation modeling of intraindividual variability. In L. M. Collins & A. G. Sayer (Eds.), *New methods for the analysis of change* (pp. 5–27).

Washington, DC: American Psychological Association.

Boker, S. M., & Bisconti, T. L. (2006). Dynamical systems modeling in aging research. In C. S. Bergeman & S. M. Boker (Eds.), *Quantitative methodology in aging research* (pp. 185–229). Mahwah, NJ: Erlbaum.

Boker, S. M., & Ghisletta, P. (2001). Random coefficients models for control parameters in dynamical systems. *Multilevel Modelling Newsletter, 13*(1), 10–17.

Boker, S. M., & Graham, J. (1998). A dynamical systems analysis of substance abuse. *Multivariate Behavioral Research, 33,* 479–507.

Boker, S. M., & McArdle, J. J. (2005). Vector field plots. In P. Armitage & T. Colton (Eds.), *Encyclopedia of Biostatistics: Vol. 8* (2nd ed., pp. 5700–5704). Chichester, UK: Wiley.

Boker, S. M., & Nesselroade, J. R. (2002). A method for modeling the intrinsic dynamics of intraindividual variability: Recovering the parameters of simulated oscillators in multi-wave panel data. *Multivariate Behavioral Research, 37,* 127–160.

Brown, S. L., Nesse, R. M., House, J., & Utz, R. L. (2004). Religion and emotional compensation: Results from a prospective study of widowhood. *Personality and Social Psychology Bulletin, 30,* 1165–1174.

Burris, C. T., Jackson, L. M., Tarpley, W. R., & Smith, G. J. (1996). Religion as quest: The self-directed pursuit of meaning. *Personality and Social Psychology Bulletin, 22,* 1068–1076.

Carver, C. S., & Scheier, M. F. (1998). *On the self-regulation of behavior.* Cambridge, UK: Cambridge University Press.

D'Onofrio, B. M., Eaves, L. J., Murrelle, L., Maes, H. H., & Spilka, B. (1999). Understanding biological and social influences on religious affiliation, attitudes, and behaviors: A behavior genetic perspective. *Journal of Personality, 67,* 953–984.

Elder, G. H., Jr., Pavalko, E. K., & Clipp, E. C. (1993). *Working with archival data: Studying lives.* Newbury Park, CA: Sage.

Flor, D. L., & Knapp, N. F. (2001). Transmission and transaction: Predicting adolescents' internalization of parental religious values. *Journal of Family Psychology, 15,* 627–645.

Fowler, J. (1981). *Stages of faith: The psychology of human development and the quest for meaning.* New York: Harper and Row.

Hall, G. S. (1904). *Adolescence, its psychology and its relations to physiology, anthropology, sociology, sex, crime, religion and education* (Vol. 1). New York: D. Appleton.

Higgins, E. T., Grant, H., & Shah, J. (1999). Self-regulation and quality of life: Emotional and non-emotional life experiences. In D. Kahneman, E. Diener, & N. Schwartz (Eds.), *Well-being: The foundations of hedonic psychology* (pp. 244–266). New York: Russell Sage.

Ingersoll-Dayton, B., Krause, N., & Morgan, D. (2002). Religious trajectories and transitions over the life course. *International Journal of Aging and Human Development, 55,* 51–70.

Kelley-Moore, J. A., & Ferraro, K. F. (2001). Functional limitations and religious service attendance in later life: Barrier and/or benefit mechanism? *Journal of Gerontology: Social Sciences, 56B,* S365–S373.

Krauss, S. W., & Flaherty, R. W. (2001). The effects of tragedies and contradictions on religion as a quest. *Journal for the Scientific Study of Religion, 40,* 113–122.

Masten, A. S., & Reed, M. J. (2002). Resilience in development. In S. J. Lopez (Ed.), *Handbook of positive psychology* (pp. 74–88). New York: Oxford University Press.

Mattis, J. (2004). Spirituality. In C. Peterson & M. E. P. Seligman (Eds.), *Character strengths and virtues: A handbook and classification* (pp. 599–622). New York: Oxford University Press/American Psychological Association.

McArdle, J. J., & Hamagami, F. (2003). Structural equation models for evaluating dynamic concepts within longitudinal twin analyses. *Behavior Genetics, 33,* 137–159.

McCullough, M. E., Enders, C. K., Brion, S. L., & Jain, A. R. (2005). The varieties of religious development in adulthood: A longitudinal investigation of religion and rational choice. *Journal of Personality and Social Psychology, 89,* 78–89.

McCullough, M. E., Tsang, J., & Brion, S. (2003). Personality traits in adolescence as predictors of religiousness on early adulthood: Findings from the Terman Longitudinal Study. *Personality and Social Psychology Bulletin, 29,* 980–991.

McCullough, M. E., & Witvliet, C. v. O. (2002). The psychology of forgiveness. In S. J. Lopez (Ed.), *Handbook of positive psychology* (pp. 446–458). New York: Oxford University Press.

Oud, J. H. L., & Jansen, R. A. R. G. (2000). Continuous time state space modeling of panel data by means of SEM. *Psychometrica, 65,* 199–215.

Pargament, K. I., & Mahoney, A. (2002). Spirituality: Discovering and conserving the sacred. In C. R. Snyder & S. J. Lopez (Eds.), *Handbook of positive psychology* (pp. 646–659). New York: Oxford University Press.

Peterson, C., & Seligman, M. E. P. (2003). Character strengths before and after September 11. *Psychological Science, 14,* 381–384.

Raudenbush, S. W., & Bryk, A. S. (2002). *Hierarchical linear models: Applications and data analysis methods* (2nd ed.). Thousand Oaks, CA: Sage.

Sasaki, M., & Suzuki, T. (1987). Changes in religious commitment in the United States, Holland and Japan. *American Journal of Sociology, 92,* 1055–1076.

Selye, H. (1956). *The stress of life.* New York: McGraw-Hill.

Sherkat, D. E. (1998). Counterculture or continuity: Competing influences on baby boomers' religious orientations and participation. *Social Forces, 76,* 1087–1115.

Stolzenberg, R. M., Blair-Loy, M., & Waite, L. J. (1995). Religious participation in early adulthood: Age and family life cycle effects on church membership. *American Sociological Review, 60,* 84–103.

Terman, L. M., & Oden, M. H. (1947). *Genetic studies of genius IV: The gifted child grows up.* Stanford, CA: Stanford University Press.

Tsang, J., & McCullough, M. E. (2003). Measuring religious constructs: A hierarchical approach to construct organization and scale selection. In C. R. Snyder (Ed.), *Handbook of positive psychological assessment* (pp. 345–360). Washington, DC: American Psychological Association.

Wink, P., & Dillon, M. (2001). Religious involvement and health outcomes in late adulthood. In T. G. Plante & A. C. Sherman (Eds.), *Faith and health* (pp. 75–106). New York: Guilford.

Wink, P., & Dillon, M. (2002). Spiritual development across the adult life course: Findings from a longitudinal study. *Journal of Adult Development, 9,* 79–94.

27

Understanding the Adjustment to Widowhood

Using Dynamical Systems to Assess and Predict Trajectories of Well-Being

Toni L. Bisconti and C. S. Bergeman

The last decade has seen an explosion of research from a new area in psychology. This area, positive psychology, emphasizes the positive aspects of well-being and functioning rather than pathology (Aspinwall & Staudinger, 2003; Seligman & Czikszentmihalyi, 2000; Thompson, 2002). In fact, human beings appear to have an extraordinary capacity to maintain emotional, psychological, and physical health despite facing a myriad of stressors (Luthar, 1991; Ryff & Singer, 2002). *Resiliency*, or the ability to maintain or regain healthy levels of functioning under difficult or stressful circumstances (Bonanno, 2004; Masten & Reed, 2002), was first introduced in the field of child psychopathology (Masten, 1999; Masten & Garmezy, 1985); the term, however, has now been used across all disciplines in psychology to describe individuals who show adaptation and growth rather than decline or pathology under challenging conditions. In understanding adjustment to widowhood, bereavement researchers have begun to apply the concept to the characteristics of individuals who successfully negotiate the process of adjusting to conjugal loss. In fact, Bonanno (2004) held that "resilience in the face of loss . . . is more common than is often believed, and that there are multiple and sometimes unexpected pathways to resilience" (p. 20). The focus of this chapter is to describe a methodology that allows for the description of trajectories of adjustment to the loss of a spouse and the identification of protective factors that may contribute to resiliency in the face of stressful life events.

The last several decades have seen an abundance of research in the area of conjugal loss (Wortman & Silver, 2001); however, it has been noted that the initial grief process has received relatively little attention (Bonanno & Kaltman, 2001). One way to examine this process is to use a methodology that allows researchers to examine fluctuations in emotional states that are commonly experienced after a significant life stressor. One such approach is dynamical systems analyses. One limitation of most, if not all, current studies of bereavement is that the process of within-person fluctuation is lost in the assessment of long-term change. For example, in a robust examination of the correlates of resiliency in widows, Bonanno, Wortman, and Nesse (2004) tried to identify the protective factors that differentiate five different types of postloss well-being trajectories, including common grief, chronic grief, chronic depression, depression followed by improvement, and resilience. Results suggested the disruption surrounding an unexpected loss is characteristic of chronic grief, whereas the more enduring emotional difficulties that are often exacerbated by the loss is more indicative of chronic depression. One of the authors' own criticisms is that the first assessment postloss was conducted 6 months after the death had occurred. They further pointed out, "earlier and more frequent assessments would have provided more reliable data about the early bereavement experiences" (Bonanno et al., 2004, p. 269). In order to truly examine the intraindividual variability in the initial experience of grief, two prerequisites must be met. First and foremost, data must be collected in the initial weeks postloss. Second, researchers must use an analytical technique sensitive to within-person oscillation.

Several questions can be uniquely examined using a dynamical systems approach. Broadly, dynamical systems analyses involve the conceptualization of change in a way that allows for the modeling of the deterministic relationships between the value of a variable and how rapidly that value changes (Boker & Bisconti, 2006). The study of aging in general, and bereavement in particular, is ready for the application of dynamical systems analysis because most topics of interest inherently involve the study of change. In fact, the ways in which we adapt and regulate our behavior in response to the changing nature of life's experiences (e.g., retirement, conjugal loss) actually defines the aging process. Using bereavement as an example, researchers have highlighted the need for conceptualizing trajectories of change and individual differences in the change process. For example, Bonnano (2004) suggested that adult resilience to loss needs to be differentiated from recovery. More specifically, he defined recovery as a trajectory in which normal functioning temporarily gives way to threshold or subthreshold psychopathology, whereas resilience reflects the ability to maintain a stable equilibrium. Dynamical systems

analyses allow researchers to explicitly delineate these trajectories and to identify factors that contribute to variability in them. Additionally, researchers will be able to examine how initial variability in emotional well-being relates to longer-term adjustment outcomes, such as depression. The study of bereavement is ripe for this new and innovative way of assessing an individual's adaptation to loss.

In the current chapter, we show how using a daily assessment design with dynamical systems analysis allows us to describe the regulation of emotional well-being following the loss of a spouse and to identify psychosocial attributes that promote stress resistance and resiliency in later life. This discussion is based on the notion that individuals who overcome the risks and challenges associated with aging, and with conjugal loss in particular, may have important resources of resilience that promote more optimal outcomes in later life. More generally, these resilience factors may influence the way in which one perceives life events (e.g., as stressful or nonstressful) or they may facilitate the coping process used to expedite recovery after the experience of an adverse event (Bergeman & Wallace, 1999). In either case, the concept of resiliency is important to understanding the antecedents and sequelae that influence the course of adaptation in human behavior.

One of the most stressful normative events experienced in later life is the loss of the spouse (Holmes & Rahe, 1967). Although many researchers have studied bereavement to advance our understanding of the short- and long-term impact of conjugal loss on physical health and psychological well-being (Wortman & Silver, 2001), much less is known about the process by which widow(er)s adjust to the death of a spouse (Blazer, 1990; Lund, Caserta, & Dimond, 1993; Morycz, 1992). Historically, researchers have examined bereavement outcomes using cross-sectional designs to compare the differences in health and well-being between widow(er)s and their married counterparts. More recently, longitudinal studies have been conducted. These studies typically begin in the first few months after the death and follow the widow(er) for a year or two postloss. Because coping with the death of a spouse is a persistent and contextual experience, research that assesses longitudinal change in adjustment is an important step for the field, but it may only elucidate part of the picture. In the current chapter, we use an additional lens to capture the components important to understanding the bereavement process, using a design and analytical technique that focuses on the assessment and prediction of intraindividual variability (in addition to change) in emotional well-being regulation following the loss of a spouse.

Understanding Emotional Reactions to Conjugal Loss

Many researchers now concur that emotions are multifaceted response tendencies that unfold over short periods of time (Fredrickson, 2002). Because many different emotional and psychological states are experienced during the grief process (Blazer, 1990), the ability to manage one's emotions has been viewed as an especially important component of well-being (Staudinger, Marsiske, & Baltes, 1993). As a result of the marked fluctuations in mood associated with loss, widowhood has been described as inducing states of emotional imbalance (Thomas, DiGiulio, & Sheehan, 1988). These *emotion dynamics* are related to the various elements of the regulatory process. That is, emotions are known to unfold over time involving alterations that have specific component parts (Thompson, 1990), including "latency, rise time, magnitude, duration, and offset of emotional responses in one or more domains" (Gross, 1999, p. 564). One approach to defining successful adjustment to an event, such as conjugal loss, is to identify an individual's ability to keep his or her distress levels within emotional bounds (Kessler, Price, & Wortman, 1985; Stroebe, Hansson, Stroebe, & Schut, 2001), often referred to as *emotion regulation*. For example, in one previous study, widows who were described as less emotionally stable and more apprehensive and anxious indicated "high distress" 2 years postloss (Vachon et al., 1982).

One recent conceptualization of bereavement that lends itself perfectly to dynamical systems is the *dual process model of coping*, which includes the stressors related to loss, the cognitive strategies that assist in adjustment to the event, and the "dynamic process of oscillation" (Stroebe & Schut, 1999, p. 212). More specifically, the dual process is described as a loss- and restoration-oriented coping. *Loss orientation* refers to concentrating on, dealing with, or processing some aspect of the loss itself. It has been suggested that loss orientation is the dominant process early on in bereavement. *Restoration orientation* focuses on what situations need to be dealt with and how

one goes about dealing with them. According to Stroebe and Schut (1999), the dynamic process of oscillation refers to the alternation between loss- and restoration-oriented coping. More specifically, at various points in the bereavement process, the widow will confront her loss (i.e., loss orientation) whereas at other times she will actively avoid thinking about it by doing new things or distracting herself from the grief (i.e., restoration orientation). This cognitive process is a regulatory mechanism, which is specified as dynamic, and oscillation is hypothesized as being necessary for successful adjustment to take place. Finally, across time, loss orientation is replaced more fully with restoration, leading to habituation to the loss (Stroebe & Schut, 1999). This model has received a considerable amount of attention in the bereavement literature; however, it has not been empirically tested due to the limitations associated with using traditional methodologies.

Although researchers have explicitly claimed that fluctuations in emotional expression are a part of successfully coping with the loss of a spouse, this idea has been very difficult to test given the cross-sectional and longitudinal methodologies typically employed in bereavement research. That is, examining specific psychological well-being outcomes as predicted concurrently or even longitudinally does not allow researchers to fully understand the fluctuations in emotional responses following the death of a spouse. Furthermore, the problem is confounded by the lack of consensus regarding how one might define emotion regulation. For example, some researchers believe that emotion regulation pertains only to the inhibition of emotional reactions, whereas others believe any definition of emotion regulation should include the maintenance as well as the enhancement of one's emotional behavior (Thompson, 1994). In the present examination, emotion regulation refers to a reduced fluctuation in daily oscillations of emotional well-being between 1 month and 4 months after the loss of a spouse.

The Assessment of Change

Delineating the adjustment to widowhood requires that researchers understand the different types of change that could be assessed and to identify a methodology and analytic technique that best captures the process of interest. For example, one could study interindividual differences, intraindividual change, or intraindividual variability. According to Baltes, Reese, and Nesselroade (1988), *interindividual differences* refer to differences between individuals on a given behavior or characteristic at one point in time and are assessed using a cross-sectional design (e.g., assessments of well-being between widows 1 year after the death of a spouse and their married counterparts); whereas *intraindividual change* refers to within-person differences in the same behavior across time and are measured using a longitudinal design (e.g., assessments of well-being in the same group of individuals 1 month and 1 year after the death of a spouse). Both of these conceptualizations of change are characterized as relatively slow changes that occur as a result of precursors, consequences, and correlates of the phenomenon of interest (Baltes, 1987). A third type of change, *intraindividual variability*, refers to relatively short-term changes that occur rapidly (Nesselroade, 1990a) and are frequently viewed as random noise, not part of the process of interest. Nesselroade (1990b) claimed that this variability, however, is not noise, but rather is indicative of changes in attributes, such as states (as opposed to traits) in the organism. The regulation of emotional well-being after a significant life event is by nature a measure of intraindividual variability, in that individuals experience marked fluctuations in state that are temporary (Fredrickson, 2002). The question then is, how do we measure this variability and analyze its importance in understanding the bereavement process? Understanding the expression of emotions after a significant life event demands that one uses a methodology that allows for the possibility of oscillation across time as well as considers time, or order, to be critical. One such approach is dynamical systems.

Assessments of Intraindividual Variability: Dynamical Systems

That all systems change and evolve in time is a primary supposition of dynamical systems analysis, and knowledge of the current state of a system can be used to predict the future state of that system (Nowak & Lowenstein, 1994). Dynamic systems are made up of dynamic variables, which are numerical representations that characterize the relevant properties of the state of the system; Nowak and Lowenstein have described two types. *Order parameters* are macroscopic global parameters internal to the system and represent intraindividual variability, whereas *control parameters* represent conditions or influences external to the system itself, but that determine the character of the observed dynamics. More specifically, control parameters represent the interindividual differences in intraindividual variability. A dynamical system could be understood geometrically, with a set of numbers $x_1(t)$, $x_2(t)$, ..., $x_n(t)$ considered to be coordinates of a point in an n-dimensional space, called a phase space (Smith & Thelen, 1993). One point in this space is the actual state of the system and described by the dynamical variables. This motion draws a curve, or a sequence of points, in the phase space that is often referred to as a trajectory. In other words, a trajectory is a set of points visited by the system during its time evolution (Nowak & Lowenstein, 1994). A phase space portrays all the potential states of a system and the transitions between them (Smith & Thelen, 1993); however, a system's trajectory typically settles into an *attractor state*, or a subset of the phase space (Nowak & Lowenstein, 1994). Although many attractor states are possible, the one relevant to the present study is a *point attractor*, in which all trajectories in the phase space tend to a single point.

A dynamical system modeling perspective was used to examine rapid fluctuations in emotional well-being in recent widows. Specifically, a model was tested that reflects a pendulum with friction that was hypothesized to best reflect the intraindividual dysregulation that may result from conjugal loss. This model is referred to as a *damped linear oscillator* (see figure 27.1). The equation for the damped linear oscillator can be expressed as a linear regression formula in which the acceleration of the pendulum is the outcome variable and the position and velocity of the pendulum are the predictor variables (Bisconti, Bergeman, & Boker, 2004; Boker, 2001). More specific to a developmental perspective, *velocity* refers to the linear change in the system (e.g., change in well-being), and *acceleration* pertains to the curvature (e.g., the speed with which the well-being change occurs). Differential equation models express effects within a system in terms of their derivatives (i.e., the instantaneous rates of change of the variables) as well as in terms of the values of the variables themselves (Boker & Graham, 1999). For example, a differential equation model of emotion regulation after conjugal loss might relate daily affect to its slope, or first derivative (i.e., how rapidly the widow's emotional well-being was changing). A more complete model might include effects related to its

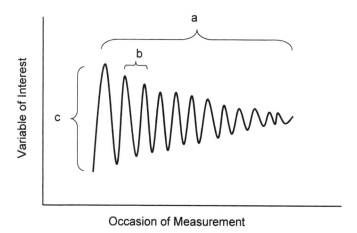

Figure 27.1 A linear oscillator model with parameters (a) damping, (b) 1/frequency, and (c) amplitude.

curvature, or second derivative (i.e., how rapidly emotional well-being was accelerating and decelerating in its change). These three parameters, initial position (emotional well-being), velocity (change), and acceleration (speed of change) are related as a dynamical system in which the relationships between them define a central tendency of a family of trajectories that any one individual might have (Boker, 2001). In order to calculate derivatives using local linear approximation, τ (time parameter) must be specified. According to previous stimulations, the most appropriate τ is the one at which the R^2 for a linear oscillator model first reaches asymptote (Boker & Nesselroade, 2002). According to Boker and Nesselroade, calculating τ based on this method introduces the least amount of bias into estimates of the frequency and damping parameters.

Intraindividual Variability in Emotional Well-Being of Recent Widows

Participants and Materials

The first phase of the study included 28 Caucasian widows from the northern Indiana and southwest Michigan area.[1] The participants ranged in age from 61 to 82 ($M = 72.21$; $SD = 5.44$); all women graduated from high school and 16 of them received some post–high school education or training. Income levels were difficult to assess at the beginning of the study because of the financial fluctuations that are common immediately following conjugal loss. At the conclusion of the daily assessment phase of the study (i.e., approximately 4 months postloss), however, five subjects reported having a yearly income between $7,500 and $15,000, 13 subjects reported an annual income between $15,000 and $25,000, three subjects reported an annual income between $25,000 and $40,000, and seven of the subjects reported making over $40,000 per year. Also, 21 of the women were in their first marriage and 7 were in their second. Widows were married between 14 and 61 years ($M = 46.25$; $SD = 12.66$). Finally, 18 of the women characterized the death as "expected" and 10 characterized it as "unexpected."

The Mental Health Inventory (MHI; Veit & Ware, 1983), which is a 36-item assessment of well-being consisting of five subscales, including anxiety, depression, emotional ties, general positive affect, and behavioral control, was initially described to participants at an interview, which took place between 18 and 42 days postloss ($M = 27.93$, $SD = 6.60$). Widows were asked to complete the MHI every day for 98 days (the surveys were mailed to participants in 14-day increments). The total score was used in the present analyses and a higher score indicates a greater amount of psychological well-being (e.g., lower depression and anxiety, higher positive affect, emotional ties, and a sense of behavioral control).

Linear Trend and Initial Variability

In order to examine the linear trend of the system, which is the traditional measure of the intraindividual change typically assessed in longitudinal bereavement studies, the following regression equation was estimated:

$$X_t = I_i + S_i t + e_t \qquad (1)$$

in which X_t represents the value of daily emotional well-being at t (days since death of spouse), I_i represents the intercept for each individual, S_i represents the slope of the overall trend (for the ith widow), t represents time (day), and e_t represents the error of measurement on the daily assessment of emotional well-being. Consistent with previous research, and as hypothesized, the overall trend is significantly positive ($t = 2.94$, $p < .01$), indicating that the intraindividual change in emotional well-being reflects positive outcomes. Specifically, the widows' levels of emotional well-being (based on the total MHI score) showed significant improvement across the 3-month duration of the study.

A second linear model was used to measure the predictability of the initial variability on the overall MHI score, by calculating the standard deviation for the first 20 scores per person. That is,

$$X_i = b_0 + b_1 \sigma_i + e_t \qquad (2)$$

in which σ_i represents the initial standard deviation of the intraindividual variability (for the ith widow) and e_t represents the error of measurement on the daily assessment of emotional well-being. It was found that the initial variability in emotion regulation does not show a relationship with mean level of well-being ($t = -1.61$, ns). That is, a person's initial oscillations of emotional well-being do not relate to their overall well-being average.

Intraindividual Variability

The next step in understanding intraindividual variability in emotions following conjugal loss was to predict the residual of each person's daily assessment score (e_i). As is indicated by Equations 1 and 2, traditional linear modeling techniques use the variability in each individual's score as an error term, which is conceptualized as noise. The purpose of the present study was to assess whether ignoring intraindividual variability results in an incomplete understanding of the bereavement process. Thus, differential equation models were fit to the data to test a linear oscillator model. In order to do this, general

linear mixed-effects modeling techniques were employed to estimate the relationship between the total score on the MHI and its derivatives. In the current study, this process involved three steps based on Boker (2001):

1. The residuals from the overall linear trend for each individual are used as intraindividual variability scores.
2. Local linear approximations to the first and second derivatives (i.e., change in emotional well-being and speed of change, respectively) of emotional well-being are calculated for each appropriate occasion of measurement.
3. The relationship between emotional well-being and its derivatives is estimated within subjects.

In order to fit a differential equation model to the data, the data were put in the form of approximations to the instantaneous first and second derivatives of emotional well-being at each occasion. For example, three consecutive measurements of MHI scores (i.e., A_1, A_2, and A_3) were used to approximate the first derivative of A (i.e., slope, or how rapidly the widow's emotional well-being changed) at the second occasion of measurement. The slope of these three consecutive scores was calculated by the average of the two slopes between A_1 and A_2 and between A_2 and A_3 (Equation 3), setting the necessary criteria for calculating derivatives at three consecutive data points.

$$\frac{dA_{1+\tau}}{dt} = \frac{(A_{1+2\tau} - A_1)}{2\tau \Delta t} \qquad (3)$$

in which $\tau = 1$ because A_1, A_2, and A_3 are successive occasions of measurement and Δt is the interval of time between measurements.

Similarly, the local linear approximation for the second derivative of A (i.e., curvature, or the acceleration or deceleration with which a widow's emotional well-being changes) at the second occasion of measurement can be calculated from the same triplet of scores A_1, A_2, and A_3 as the change in the slopes shown in Equation 4,

$$\frac{d^2 A_{1+\tau}}{dt^2} = \frac{(A_{1+2\tau} - 2A_{1+\tau} + A_1)}{\tau^2 \Delta t^2} \qquad (4)$$

A multilevel differential equation model for a damped linear oscillator of the MHI (refer again to figure 27.1) was fit to the sample of widows (see Boker & Ghisletta, 2001, for implementation details of this type of model). This model allows each widow to have a unique frequency (i.e., rate of ups and downs in emotions) and damping (i.e., regulation of emotional well-being) parameter as shown in Equations 5, 6, and 7. An assumption is made that these widows' parameters are a sample from a normal distribution of frequency and damping parameters in the population.

$$\frac{d^2 R_{ti}}{dt^2} = \zeta_i \frac{dR_{ti}}{dt} + \eta_i R_{ti} + e_{ti} \qquad (5)$$

$$\zeta_i = c_1 + u_{1i} \qquad (6)$$

$$\eta_i = c_2 + u_{2i} \qquad (7)$$

in which R_{ti} is the residual MHI score for widow i at time t, ζ_i and η_i are the damping and frequency parameters, respectively, for widow i, c_1 and c_2 are the overall mean damping and frequency parameters, and u_{1i} and u_{2i} are the damping and frequency components unique to widow i. This model was fit using the linear mixed effects function in Splus (Insightful Corporation, 2001; Pinheiro & Bates, 2000).

As previously mentioned, in order to calculate derivatives using local linear approximation, τ (the time parameter) must be specified. According to previous stimulations, the most appropriate τ is the one at which the R^2 for a linear oscillator model first reaches asymptote (Boker & Nesselroade, 2002). According to Boker and Nesselroade, calculating τ based on this method introduces the least amount of bias into estimates of the frequency and damping parameters. Additionally, in order to determine whether or not the specified model fit the data, one must calculate the overall R^2, η (frequency parameter), and ζ (damping parameter) at a particular τ (time parameter). For the model to be acceptable, the R^2 (indicating how well the first and second derivatives predict the score) must reach a level, and subsequently asymptote, at a minimum of .76 (Boker & Nesselroade, 2002), which was also the R^2 in our study, suggesting that the residual intraindividual variability in emotional well-being can be predicted by a damped oscillatory model. Furthermore, a damped linear oscillator requires that the damping parameter, ζ, is negative. Our damping parameter was $-.015$, $p < .001$, suggesting that our system significantly decays across the 98-day period. Finally, the frequency parameter, η, can be interpreted based on its

magnitude, with larger values (e.g., $-.40$) indicating more rapid oscillations and smaller values (e.g., $-.05$) indicating much slower oscillations. Our value was $-.02$, $p < .001$, suggesting a slow but significant oscillation.

Interindividual Differences Based on Social Support in Intraindividual Variability in Emotional Well-Being of Recent Widows

After identifying the order parameters (i.e., frequency and decay rate) of the system that best represent changes in daily well-being following conjugal loss, the next step was to examine factors, or control parameters, that influence the system. In other words, we wanted to identify the characteristics of individuals (e.g., aspects of personality) or their environment (e.g., familial or community support factors) that might represent important resilience mechanisms and explain individual differences in the emotion trajectories of recent widows. Researchers have long been interested in understanding how socially induced stress affects psychological health and well-being. In almost all of the stress-outcome literature, three groups of mediators have been examined, including social support, psychosocial resources (e.g., personal control), and coping efforts (Avison & Cairney, 2003). In the current program of research, these mediators were all conceptualized as part of the social support process, which is known to reduce psychological distress during times of stress and may be especially helpful in vulnerable populations, such as the elderly and the recently widowed (Taylor & Aspinwall, 1996). Furthermore, researchers have hypothesized that if a stressor is social in nature, it is likely that the mobilization of social resources will be particularly important to the adaptation process (Hansson & Carpenter, 1994). Bonanno (2004) suggested that there are multiple pathways to resilience; however, there has been a paucity of research on the attributes that distinguish resilient from nonresilient individuals in the face of conjugal loss. Research, however, has suggested two broad sources of protective mechanisms: *environmental factors*, which include features such as social network size from family and friends, and *individual factors*, which for the current investigation include the perceived control over the network's utilization and the actual mobilization of the support system in the face of a stressor (either with emotion-focused or problem-focused social coping). Although all of these factors have been linked to better psychological adjustment in recent widows, little empirical work has addressed the confluence of these components of the support process; therefore, a brief overview of the literature relating to the individual characteristics will be presented.

When social support is operationalized to reflect social integration (that is, the number of individuals one identifies as friends), researchers have reported the importance of the direct effects of social support on better psychological well-being outcomes (Taylor & Aspinwall, 1996). For example, in a study of 162 widows who were interviewed postloss, the most important variable associated with high distress at one month was the woman's perception that she was not seeing old friends as often as she did prior to her husband's death (Vachon et al., 1982). The quantity of support was also linked to greater life satisfaction in a sample of 77 widow(er)s who were bereaved for an average of 18 months (deKeijser & Schut, 1990). Although linkages between family and friend support have been established, less is known about whether there are differential effects of friend versus family support on the adjustment of recent widows. For example, research has indicated that widows' networks tend to contain more family than nonfamily members (Morgan, Neal, & Carder, 1997). What is especially important to this process is that nonfamily relationships are viewed as more flexible and more likely to be associated with positive relationships than negative ones, whereas family relations were described as commitments involving both problematic obligations and an inability to avoid undesirable behavior (Morgan, 1989).

Control specifically related to social interactions may be another important resilience mechanism related to the support process. That is, the characteristic vulnerabilities of support networks in old age suggest that it may be important for individuals to feel as if they have some degree of control over their social support network (Hansson & Remondet, 1988). This notion of social control measures the belief that if needed, an individual can call upon and receive support from his or her social network. One possible way that this type of control may underlie the process in the support-outcome relationship is that an individual's perceptions of control may be associated with increased social interaction (not necessarily an increase in the number of support providers), therefore leading to more positive perceptions of the environment. This in turn may determine whether coping behavior will occur (i.e., mobilization of the support network), and whether or not these coping behaviors will prevail in the face of stressful life events such as the death of a spouse.

Control specifically related to eliciting social support has not been examined in a widowed population; however, more general studies of control demonstrate its positive effect on psychological health. For example, in one study, an orientation toward internal locus of control at the first time point predicted lowered depression scores at subsequent time points (Stroebe & Stroebe, 1993); similar results were found in a matched sample of married individuals. One limitation to the previous research in this area is that a domain-specific control construct was not measured (i.e., social control); thus it is not known whether a sense of control over one's social network garners a similar protective effect.

The final component of the social support process is the actual mobilization of the support network, often referred to as *social coping*. Two types of coping have been identified: *problem-focused*, defined as responses aimed at eliminating or modifying the conditions that give rise to the problem, and *emotion-focused*, referring to responses geared toward the management of the emotional consequences of the stressor and the maintenance of one's emotional equilibrium (for a more complete discussion, see Lazarus & Folkman, 1984). Although most people appear to use both emotional- and problem-focused strategies, contextual differences have been found in their use (deKeijser & Schut, 1990), and each type may have an important, but separate, effect on the utilization of one's social network. For example, emotion-focused coping has been suggested to be more useful for interpersonal and relatively uncontrollable stressors (Lazarus, 1993). Seeking social support as a coping mechanism has been directly studied as a possible resilience resource in the face of stress; in this case, on the manifestation of emotions (Folkman & Lazarus, 1988). Data were based on a 1-hour interview of older adults (collected once a month for 6 months), in which subjects were asked to report the most stressful life event they had experienced during the month preceding the interview. Additionally, they were asked to fill out a coping questionnaire and to report the extent to which they experienced each of a number of emotions at the event's most stressful moment as well as at the resolution of the event. Hierarchical regression analyses of residual scores were used to analyze the data and seeking social support as a coping strategy was found to be predictive of confidence as well as happiness. A problem with the aforementioned study, and a possible explanation for the small relations (i.e., beta weights), is that it is largely based on retrospective reports. One way to answer the question of the utility of mobilizing social networks in times of stress is to assess seeking social support during a stressful life event. That is, it is important to avoid the assumption that stressful life events will mobilize support and to begin to specifically examine the perceptions of the actual mobilization in the face of a stressor (Morgan et al., 1997).

Participants and Materials

In the second phase of the analyses, the same sample of 28 Caucasian widows were used (see Bisconti, Bergeman, & Boker, in press; Bisconti et al., 2004). In addition to the daily assessment of emotional well-being (i.e., MHI), the participants completed a packet of questionnaires after the initial interview, which included measures of friend and family quantity of support, perceived social control, and emotion-focused and problem-focused social coping. More specifically, the Interview Schedule for Social Interaction (ISSI; Henderson, Duncan-Jones, Byrne, & Scott, 1980) was used to assess quantity of support from both family and friends. A subscale of the Desire for Control measure (Reid & Ziegler, 1981) was used to assess perceptions of social control. Finally, two subscales of the COPE (seeking emotional support and seeking instrumental support; Carver, Scheier, & Weintraub, 1989) were used to assess the use of emotion-focused and problem-focused social coping.

Interindividual Differences in Intraindividual Change and Intraindividual Variability

In order to estimate the predictors of amplitude (σ_i), trend (S_i), damping (ζ_i), and frequency (η_i), four second-level models were calculated, which included all of the hypothesized control parameters (see Equations 8, 9, 10, and 11, respectively, for σ_i, $S_i \zeta_i$, and η_i). These analyses allow the relative weights of each of the predictors to be estimated. The projected Level 2 models are:

$$\sigma_i = a + \beta_1(\text{fri}) + \beta_2(\text{fam}) + \beta_3(\text{con}) + \beta_4(\text{emot}) + \beta_5(\text{prob}) + e_t \quad (8)$$

$$S_i = b + \beta_1(\text{fri}) + \beta_2(\text{fam}) + \beta_3(\text{con}) + \beta_4(\text{emot}) + \beta_5(\text{prob}) + e_t \quad (9)$$

$$\zeta_i = c + \beta_1(\text{fri}) + \beta_2(\text{fam}) + \beta_3(\text{con}) + \beta_4(\text{emot}) + \beta_5(\text{prob}) + e_t \quad (10)$$

$$\eta_i = d + \beta_1(\text{fri}) + \beta_2(\text{fam}) + \beta_3(\text{con}) + \beta_4(\text{emot}) + \beta_5(\text{prob}) + e_t \quad (11)$$

in which fri = quantity of support from friends; fam = quantity of support from family; con = perceived social control; emot = emotion-focused social coping; and prob = problem-focused social coping.

The regression equations using the various protective mechanisms predicting initial variability and frequency indicated that none of the independent variables significantly predicted these aspects of the recovery trajectory. Emotion-focused coping, however, related to a quicker damping rate ($t = -1.78$, $p = .07$), whereas problem-focused coping significantly predicted a slower damping rate ($t = 3.45$, $p < .001$). In other words, individuals who mobilized their networks for emotion-focused needs were able to more quickly regulate their emotions than those who mobilized their network for problem-focused, or instrumental, needs. Similarly, the pattern of predictability in slope shows emotion-focused coping was significantly related to a steeper slope ($t = 3.66$, $p < .01$), whereas problem-focused coping related to a shallower slope ($t = -1.91$, $p = .07$). That is, individuals who used more emotion-focused coping strategies had greater overall improvement in psychological well-being than those who primarily used problem-focused coping strategies. Surprisingly, a shallower slope was also predicted by social control ($t = -2.83$, $p = .01$), indicating that the greater amount of perceived control an individual has, the less overall positive change she will experience across time. Overall, 47% of the variance was explained using the social support constructs as predictors in this model ($F = 3.22$, $p = .03$).

General Discussion and Directions for Future Research

The first objective of the studies presented in this chapter was to assess the initial process of recovery in recent widows. Specifically, the focus was on how individuals regulate emotional well-being in the second through fourth months following conjugal loss. Although emotional lability is commonly experienced after the loss of a spouse, researchers have found that most widows do eventually adjust (Blazer, 1990; Morycz, 1992). The focus of previous research has been on the outcomes, however, and not on the process by which individuals adapt. A dynamical systems approach was used to identify the intraindividual variability in emotion regulation following the loss of a spouse. This type of methodology allowed the parameters (i.e., the variability in mood, the frequency of mood shifts, and the rate at which the mood shifts decay) of the system to be estimated. The second objective was to identify interindividual differences in intraindividual change and intraindividual variability. More specifically, the dispositional and environmental factors that constitute the social support process were found to influence the overall trend of the system (i.e., intraindividual change) as well as the parameters of the emotion regulation trajectories, including frequency and damping (i.e., intraindividual variability). Because of the protective role that social support plays in the stress and coping relationship, it has been suggested that understanding the components that comprise the social support process should heighten researchers' understanding of what contributes to the regulation of well-being during difficult times (Filipp & Klauer, 1991), thus helping to elucidate resiliency in later life.

Our results are consistent with Bonanno's (2004) characterization that individuals who are resilient may display some temporary oscillations in their normal functioning but will resume a stable trajectory across time. We further our understanding of the emotional adaptation to loss as a dynamic process that varies across time, individuals, and situations. Building on prior investigations of later-life resilience (e.g., Ryff, Singer, Love, & Essex, 1998; Staudinger, Marsiske, & Baltes, 1995) and more recent characterizations of the multiple adjustment trajectories to loss (Bonanno, 2004), we distinguish between resilience as the recovery from adversity and resilience as the maintenance or growth of developmental capacities in the face stressful life events. It is the latter definition that allows for the understanding of the positive outcomes that could arise from some of life's greatest challenges. Additionally, we were able

to identify factors that distinguished different trajectories of emotion regulation, in terms of both how quickly widows experienced more positive emotions and the rate at which the emotional fluctuations following the loss of a spouse damped. More specifically, individuals who used emotion-focused social coping strategies appeared more resilient based on the slope and dampening parameters of the model, whereas those who relied on problem-focused strategies were more likely to maintain chronic disruptions in functioning.

The Role of Positive Affect

One area of research that we are currently investigating is the role that positive emotions play in the bereavement process. It has been shown that positive emotions are related to fewer mental health problems in individuals who have experienced loss (Wortman & Silver, 2001); little is known, however, about the complexity of the emotions experienced in recent widows (Ong, Bergeman, & Bisconti, 2004). Using multilevel modeling, an investigation of this issue (Ong, Bergeman, Bisconti, & Wallace, in press) utilizing the daily assessment technique described previously has yielded four major conclusions. First, when individuals are under stress, there is evidence of the "undoing" benefits of positive affect on negative affect. Second, individuals who are higher in dispositional resilience (i.e., hardiness) express more positive affect. Third, individuals who report lower resilience have a difficulty regulating their negative affect and show increased vacillation to stressful events. Finally, when present, individuals who are lower in resilience benefit even more from positive affect, particularly in the context of conjugal loss. Adding dynamical systems analyses to this growing body of work will allow investigators to determine such additional questions as whether or not the trajectory of positive affect following conjugal loss yields the same frequency and damping parameters as those found for negative affect

Similarly, understanding the role of positive affect may assist in directly testing the dual process model of coping (Stroebe & Schut, 1999). One of the basic tenets of this theory is the idea that emotions are transient. More specifically, in the early days postloss, negative affect predominates; however, as the recovery process unfolds, positive affect plays an increasingly prominent role. The gradual increase in positive affect may be another indicator of resilient individuals. A major advantage of dynamical systems analysis is that we can explicitly test this hypothesis by examining the oscillating models of both negative and positive affect across a 3-month period. More specifically, we might hypothesize negative affect to damp and positive affect to amplify across the duration of the sampling period. Additionally, we could simultaneously examine the slopes of the levels of positive versus negative affect across time, explicitly examining Stroebe and Schut's ideas of the increasing importance of positive affect as a replacement for negative affect in the adjustment to widowhood.

Long-Term Adjustment

One extension of the traditional approaches in the assessment of intraindividual change is to predict the long-term change patterns from the components of the oscillating system (i.e., initial variability, frequency, and damping). Traditionally, we use stable traits as predictors of long-term functioning; however, we could also use statelike variability to predict long-term adaptation. One potential hypothesis is that individuals who reach equilibrium more quickly will also exhibit better overall adjustment. With the design of the present study and the use of dynamical systems analyses, hypotheses such as this will be examined, allowing researchers an even more extensive understanding of the process and predictors behind the adjustment to widowhood.

For many different kinds of psychological attributes, including measures of affect, there exist coherent and systematic patterns of fluctuation (intraindividual variability) that are defined over relatively short intervals of time (Nesselroade, 1990b). The adjustment to widowhood is a complex phenomenon that requires a methodology that allows for the possibility of oscillation across time, as well as assessing intraindividual variability and intraindividual change on multiple individuals simultaneously. Because we need to assess whether one's trajectory is changing across time, more traditional techniques of growth curve analysis are inadequate. Dynamical systems is one approach that utilizes longitudinal designs that capture intraindividual variability. From a dynamical systems perspective, the death of a spouse is an event that perturbs an individual's emotional regulatory system from its normal equilibrium state. Although an ultimate reestablishment often occurs, the process is highly variable. Understanding the variability within individuals who experience conjugal loss as well as the predictors of that variability allows researchers and helping professionals to better understand the lack of uniformity in coping with such a loss. Taking a dynamical systems approach to capturing the individual differences in recent widows is a necessary step in further identifying the etiology of adjustment to conjugal loss.

Note

1. For a more thorough description of the methodology, please see Bisconti et al. (2004). Please note that although the data used in this chapter come from a sample that is larger than previously described, the methodology is identical.

References

Aspinwall. L. G., & Staudinger, U. M. (2003). A psychology of human strengths: Some critical issues of an emerging field. In L. G. Aspinwall & U. M. Staudinger (Eds.), *A psychology of human strengths: Fundamental questions and future directions for a positive psychology* (pp. 9–22). Washington, DC: American Psychological Association.

Avison, W. R., & Cairney, J. (2003). Social structure, stress, and personal control. In K. W. Schaie (Series Ed.) & S. H. Zarit, L. I. Pearlin, & K. W. Schaie (Vol. Eds.), *Societal impact on aging series: Personal control in social and life course contexts* (pp. 127–164). New York: Springer.

Baltes, P. B. (1987). Theoretical propositions of life-span developmental psychology: On the dynamics between growth and decline. *Developmental Psychology, 23*, 611–626.

Baltes, P. B., Reese, H. W., & Nesselroade, J. R. (1988). *Introduction to research methods: Life-span developmental psychology*. Hillsdale, NJ: Erlbaum.

Bergeman, C. S., & Wallace, K. A. (1999). Resiliency and aging. In T. Whitman, T. Merluzzi, & R. White (Eds.), *Psychology and medicine* (pp. 207–225). Hillsdale, NJ: Erlbaum.

Bisconti, T. L., Bergeman, C. S., & Boker, S. M. (in press). Social support as a predictor of variability: An examination of recent widows' adjustment trajectories. *Psychology and Aging*.

Bisconti, T. L., Bergeman, C. S., & Boker, S. (2004). Emotion regulation in recently bereaved widows: A dynamical systems approach. *Journal of Gerontology, 59B*, P168–P176.

Blazer, D. (1990). *Emotional problems in later life: Intervention strategies for professional caregivers* (pp. 17–30). New York: Springer.

Boker, S. M. (2001). Differential structural modeling of intraindividual variability. In L. Collins & A. Sayer (Eds.), *New methods for the analysis of change* (pp. 3–28). Washington, DC: American Psychological Association.

Boker, S. M., & Bisconti, T. L. (2004). Dynamical systems modeling of data from aging research. In C. S. Bergeman & S. M. Boker (Eds.), *Quantitative methodology in aging research.* Hillsdale, NJ: Erlbaum.

Boker, S. M., & Ghisletta, P. (2001). Random coefficients models for control parameters in dynamical systems. *Multivariate Behavioral Research, 37*(3), 405–422.

Boker, S. M., & Graham, J. (1999). A dynamical systems analysis of adolescent substance use. *Multivariate Behavioral Research, 33*(4), 479–507.

Boker, S. M., & Nesselroade, J. R. (2002). A method for modeling the intrinsic dynamics of intraindividual variability: Recovering the parameters of simulated oscillators in multi-wave panel data. *Multivariate Behavioral Research, 37*(1), 127–160.

Bonanno, G. A. (2004). Loss, trauma, and human resilience: Have we underestimated the human capacity to thrive after extremely aversive events? *American Psychologist, 59*(1), 20–28.

Bonanno, G. A., & Kaltman, S. (2001). The varieties of grief experience. *Clinical Psychology Review, 21*(5), 705–734.

Bonanno, G. A., Wortman, C. B., & Nesse, R. M. (2004). Prospective patterns of resilience and maladjustment during widowhood. *Psychology and Aging, 19*(2), 260–271.

Carver, C. S., Scheier, M. F., & Weintraub, J. K. (1989). Assessing coping strategies: A theoretically based approach. *Journal of Personality and Social Psychology, 56*(2), 267–283.

deKeijser, J., & Schut, H. (1990). Perceived support and coping with loss. In K. C. P. M. Knipscheer & T. C. Antonucci (Eds). *Social network research: Substantive issues and methodological questions* (pp. 67–82). Amsterdam: Swets and Zeitlinger.

Filipp, S.-H., & Klauer, T. (1991). Subjective well-being in the face of critical life events: The case of successful copers. In F. Strack, M. Argyle, & N. Schwarz (Eds.), *Subjective well-being: An interdisciplinary perspective* (pp. 213–234). Oxford: Pergamon Press.

Folkman, S., & Lazarus, R. S. (1988). Coping as a mediator of emotion. *Journal of Personality and Social Psychology, 54,* 466–477.

Fredrickson, B. L. (2002). Positive emotions. In C. R. Snyder & S. J. Lopez (Eds.), *Handbook of positive psychology* (pp. 120–134). New York: Oxford University Press.

Gross, J. J. (1999). Emotion regulation: Past, present, and future. *Cognition and Emotion, 13*(5), 551–573.

Hansson, R. O., & Carpenter, B. N. (1994). *Relationships in old age: Coping with the challenge of transition.* New York: Guilford.

Hansson, R. O., & Remondet, J. H. (1988). Old age and widowhood: Issues of personal control and independence. *Journal of Social Issues, 44,* 159–174.

Henderson, S., Duncan-Jones, P., Byrne, D. G., & Scott, R. (1980). Measuring social relationships: The interview schedule for social interaction. *Psychological Medicine, 10,* 723–734.

Holmes, T., & Rahe, R. (1967). The social readjustment rating scale. *Journal of Psychosomatic Research, 11,* 213–218.

Insightful Corporation. (2001). *S-plus version 6.* Seattle, WA: Author.

Kessler, R. C., Price, R. H., & Wortman, C. B. (1985). Social factors in psychopathology: Stress, social support, and coping processes. *Annual Review of Psychology, 36,* 531–572.

Lazarus, R. S. (1993). Coping theory and research: Past, present, and future. *Psychosomatic Medicine, 55,* 234–247.

Lazarun, R. S., & Folkman, S. (1984). *Stress appraisal and coping.* New York: Springer.

Lund, D. A., Caserta, M. S., & Dimond, M. R. (1993). The course of spousal bereavement. In M. S. Stroebe, W. Stroebe, & R. O. Hannson (Eds.), *Handbook of bereavement: Theory, research, and intervention* (pp. 240–254). Cambridge: Cambridge University Press.

Luthar, S. S. (1991). Vulnerability and resilience: A study of high-risk adolescents. *Child Development, 62,* 600–616.

Masten, A. S. (1999). Resilience comes of age: Reflections on the past and outlook for the next generation of research. In M. D. Glantz, J. Johnson, & L. Huffman (Eds.), *Resilience and development: Positive life adaptations* (pp. 282–296). New York: Plenum.

Masten, A. S., & Garmezy, N. (1985). Risk, vulnerability, and protective factors in developmental psychopathology. In B. B. Lahey, & A. E. Kazdin (Eds.), *Advances in clinical child psychology* (Vol. 8, pp. 1–51). New York: Plenum.

Masten, A. S., & Reed, M. J. (2002). In C. R. Snyder & S. J. Lopez (Eds.), *Handbook of positive psychology* (pp. 74–88). New York: Oxford University Press.

Morgan, D. L. (1989). Adjusting to widowhood: Do social networks really make it easier? *Gerontologist, 29,* 101–107.

Morgan, D. L., Neal, M. B., & Carder, P. C. (1997). Both what and when: The effects of positive and negative aspects of relationships on depression during the first 3 years of widowhood. *Journal of Clinical Geropsychology, 3*(1), 73–91.

Morycz, R. K. (1992). Widowhood and bereavement in late life. In V. B. Van Hasselt & M. Hersen (Eds.), *Handbook of social development: A lifespan perspective* (pp. 545–582). New York: Plenum.

Nesselroade, J. R. (1988). Some implications of the trait-state distinction for the study of development over the life-span: The case of personality. In P. B. Baltes, D. L. Featherman, & R. M. Lerner (Eds.), *Life-span development and behavior* (Vol. 8, pp. 163–189). Hillsdale, NJ: Erlbaum.

Nesselroade, J. R. (1990a). Individual differences in intraindividual change. In L. M. Collins & J. L. Horn (Eds.), *Best methods for the analysis of change: Recent advances, unanswered questions, future directions* (pp. 92–105). Washington, DC: American Psychological Association.

Nesselroade, J. R. (1990b). The warp and the woof of the developmental fabric. In R. Downs, L. Liben, & D. S. Palermo (Eds.), *Visions of development, the environment, and aesthetics: The legacy of Joachim F. Wohlwill* (pp. 213–240). Hillsdale, NJ: Erlbaum.

Nowak, A., & Lowenstein, M. (1994). Dynamical systems: A tool for social psychology? In R. R. Vallacher & A. Nowak (Eds.), *Dynamical systems in social psychology* (pp. 17–53). San Diego: Academic Press.

Ong, A., Bergeman, C. S., & Bisconti, T. L. (2004). The role of daily positive affect during conjugal bereavement. *Journal of Gerontology, 59B,* P158–P167.

Ong, A. D., Bergeman, C. S., Bisconti, T. L., & Wallace, K. A. (in press). The contours of resilience and the complexity of emotions in later life. *Journal of Personality and Social Psychology.*

Pinheiro, J. C., & Bates, D. M. (2000). *Mixed-effects models in S and S-Plus.* New York: Springer.

Reid, D. W., & Ziegler, M. (1981). The desired control measure and adjustment among the elderly. In H. M. Lefcourt (Ed.), *Research with the locus of control construct: Vol. 1. Assessment methods* (pp. 127–159). New York: Academic Press.

Ryff, C. D., & Singer, B. (2002). Flourishing under fire: Resilience as a prototype of challenged thriving. In C. L. M. Keyes & J. Haidt (Eds.), *Flourishing: Positive psychology and the life well-lived* (pp. 15–36). Washington, DC: American Psychological Association.

Ryff, C. D., Singer, B., Love, G. D., & Essex, M. J. (1998). Resilience in adulthood and later life: Defining features and dynamic processes. In J. Lomranz (Ed.), *Handbook of aging and mental health* (pp. 69–96). New York: Springer-Verlag.

Seligman, M. E. P., & Csikszentmihalyi, M. (2000). Positive psychology: An introduction. *American Psychologist, 55,* 5–14.

Smith, L. B., & Thelen, E. (1993). Can dynamic systems theory be usefully applied in areas other than motor development? In L. B. Smith & E. Thelen (Eds.), *A dynamic systems approach to development* (pp. 151–170). Cambridge, MA: MIT Press.

Staudinger, U. M., Marsiske, M., & Baltes, P. B. (1993). Resilience and levels of reserve capacity in later adulthood: Perspectives from life-span theory. *Development and Psychopathology, 5,* 541–566.

Staudinger, U. M., Marsiske, M., & Baltes, P. B. (1995). Resilience and reserve capacity in later adulthood: Potentials and limits of development across the life span. In D. Cicchetti & D. J. Cohen (Eds.), *Developmental psychopathology: Vol. 2. Risk, disorder, and adaptation* (pp. 801–847). New York: Wiley.

Stroebe, M. S., Hansson, R. O., Stroebe, W., & Schut, H. (Eds.). (2001). *Handbook of bereavement research: Consequences, coping, and care.* Washington, DC: American Psychological Association.

Stroebe, M. S., & Schut, H. (1999). The dual process model of coping with bereavement: Rationale and description. *Death Studies, 23,* 197–224.

Stroebe, W., & Stroebe, M. S. (1993). Determinants of adjustment to bereavement in younger widows and widowers. In M. S. Stroebe, W. Stroebe, & R. O. Hansson (Eds.), *Handbook of bereavement* (pp. 208–226). Cambridge: Cambridge University Press.

Taylor, S. E., & Aspinwall, L. G. (1996). Mediating and moderating processes in psychosocial stress: Appraisal, coping, resistance, and vulnerability. In H. Kaplan (Ed.), *Psychosocial stress: Perspectives on structure, theory, life-course, and methods* (pp. 71–110). San Diego: Academic Press.

Thomas, L. E., DiGiulio, R. C., & Sheehan, N. W. (1988). Identity loss and psychological crisis in widowhood: A re-evaluation. *International Journal of Aging and Human Development, 26*(3), 225–239.

Thompson, R. A. (1990). Emotion and self-regulation. In R. A. Thompson (Ed.), *Socioemotional development: Nebraska symposium on motivation* (Vol. 36, pp. 367–467). Lincoln: University of Nebraska Press.

Thompson, R. A. (1994). Emotion regulation: A theme in search of definition. *Monographs of the Society for Research in Child Development, 59* (2–3, Serial No. 240).

Thompson, S. C. (2002). The role of personal control in adaptive functioning. In C. R. Snyder & S. J. Lopez (Eds.), *Handbook of positive psychology* (pp. 202–213). New York: Oxford University Press.

Vachon, M. L. S., Rogers, J., Lyall, W. A. L., Lancee, W. J., Sheldon, A. R., & Freeman, S. J. J. (1982). Predictors and correlates of adaptation to conjugal bereavement. *American Journal of Psychiatry, 139,* 998–1002.

Veit, C. T., & Ware, Jr., J. E. (1983). The structure of psychological distress and well-being in general populations. *Journal of Consulting and Clinical Psychology, 51,* 730–742.

Wortman, C. B., & Silver, R. C. (2001). The myths of coping with loss revisited. In M. S. Stroebe, R. O. Hansson, W. Stroebe, & H. Schut (Eds.), *Handbook of bereavement research: Consequences, coping, and care* (pp. 405–429). Washington, DC: American Psychological Association.

28

Application of Dynamic Systems Analysis to Dyadic Interactions

Diane H. Felmlee

Research on close dyads assumes that individuals who comprise couples influence each other's behavior over time. A good deal of theoretical work on intimate relationships, for example, focuses on the ways in which romantic partners affect each other and their relationship. Yet interaction between members of a dyad seldom is modeled formally as an endogenous system in which each actor is allowed to directly affect change in the behavior of the other, and as a consequence we know little about the manner in which each member of a pair influences the other. A good deal of theoretical and empirical work also documents that dyadic social processes fluctuate, and that interaction among pairs of social actors is fluid. Nevertheless, there are relatively few systematic studies that investigate the types of changes that might occur over time in interdependent, dyadic social systems.

Work that ignores the dynamic nature of interaction among pairs does not acknowledge that the behavior of couples may be changing dramatically over time, and studies that rely on information gained from a one-time snapshot cannot examine a dyad's developmental trajectory. Furthermore, research that fails to apply a systems perspective toward human behavior, when that behavior is inherently dyadic, runs the danger of being misleading at a basic, conceptual level and is apt to be inaccurate empirically. Moreover, a wide range of behavior may be interdependent rather than individually shaped, especially given that the vast majority of adults are married or cohabiting and likely to be influenced by an intimate partner on a multitude of dimensions.

The purpose of this chapter, then, is to explore theoretically the notion of dyadic interaction as a dynamic, coupled system. To do this, I investigate the ramifications of several basic assumptions regarding such behavior: (1) that when two actors interact, they directly influence change in each other's behavior; (2) interaction is a dynamic process that evolves over time; (3) external, individual factors also may affect an actor's behavior; and (4) change in behavior is continuous. Here I formalize these assumptions and investigate their implications for dyadic interaction. Questions that I address include the following. What types of basic dyadic systems are there, and what are the long-term outcomes for such systems? Which paired systems are most likely to reach equilibrium over time and become stable? Which are likely to explode or decay over time?

I model interaction between two actors as a dyadic, dynamic system, using a basic system of linear differential equations developed by Felmlee and Greenberg (1999). I then explore a series of variations of this model and assess the implications of those variations for dyadic interaction over time. I begin this task by describing four basic models, each of which embodies unique assumptions regarding dyadic behavior. Next, I explore a series of four additional models that represent distinct combinations of these basic dyadic actor models. For each model, I provide an illustration of a fictional couple's behavior that could fit the observed trajectories over time. Finally, I discuss the theoretical implications of these models for dyadic interaction.

Theoretically, the models I present could apply to various types of actors, including individuals or small groups. Here I focus my illustrations on the two-person dyadic system, because it represents a reasonable starting point and because of the paucity of work on this topic. In addition, I refer to the intimate couple as an example of a dyadic system, because I assume that the behavior of each member of a couple is particularly susceptible to influence on the part of the other. To illustrate the models, I discuss the example of two actors' propensity to engage in the beneficial practice of regular physical exercise.

Background

Theoretical work on couples and close pairs relies on the basic assumption that dyadic social actors influence each other's behavior and attitudes. Interdependence theory from social psychology, for example, emphasizes that close relationships are characterized by two chains of causally interconnected events, one for each dyadic actor (Kelley & Thibaut, 1978). Family systems theorists also stress the interdependence of members of a married or cohabiting couple (e.g., Minuchin, 1984). On a broader level, social psychologists traditionally attempt to understand the ways in which individuals' thoughts, feelings, and actions are socially influenced (Allport, 1968), and empirical research repeatedly provides support for the social nature of individual behavior. We know then that social processes in general influence individual behavior. Very little empirical work, however, treats social influence as a system in which individuals

simultaneously influence change in each other's behavior. Most studies of couples treat the two partners as independent units, for example, and typically examine information from only one partner (Karney & Bradbury, 1995).

A good deal of research and theory also testifies to the dynamic nature of dyadic behavior. Developmental (e.g., Surra, 1990) and dialectical theories (e.g., Baxter & Montgomery, 1996), for instance, stress that the behavior of intimate dyads evolves over time. Longitudinal studies of couples document fluctuations in partners in a wide array of attitudes and behaviors, including conflicts (Huston & Chorost, 1994) and the balance of power (Sprecher & Felmlee, 1997). Yet the dynamic nature of dyadic interaction is seldom explicitly modeled in research. A major purpose of this chapter is to use a system of two differential equations to model dyadic interaction over time.

Applied Dynamic Modeling

Differential equation models have been applied to social behavior in several contexts (Tuma & Hannon, 1984), including the study of interaction in a group (Simon, 1957), arms races (Rapaport, 1960), and network effects on social influence (Friedkin, 1998). There are only a handful of cases, however, in which scholars have used differential equations to examine the interactive behavior of a two-actor system. Some of these exceptions include the examination of turn-taking in conversations (Buder, 1991) and the dynamic study of love between historical figures (Rinaldi, 1998). In addition, Baron, Amazeen, and Beek (1994) applied nonlinear dynamics to the development of various types of social relationships, such as minority-majority groups, ingroups and out-groups, and marriages. More recently, Gottman, Murray, Swanson, Tyson, and Swanson (2002) used dynamic models to examine emotional interaction between spouses. In one of their most noteworthy results, Gottman et al. found that couples often have multiple emotional set points, rather than only one, as suggested by earlier approaches.

Yet there is room for a great deal more applied modeling work regarding dyadic interaction over time; the surface barely has been scratched regarding the variety of applicable dynamic models for two-actor systems. There also is a need for an explication of the basic social psychological assumptions made regarding dyadic interaction and the implications of these assumptions for paired behavior over time. Such assumptions are often implicit, rather than explicit in empirical work, and making them explicit helps to reveal their ramifications. Here I formalize basic social scientific assumptions regarding dyadic interaction and examine their long-run implications for a pair of actors.

There are several advantages of the dynamic differential equation modeling approach that is used in this chapter. First, on a theoretical level, differential equations are especially useful when representing a conceptual model for a process that changes continuously, or smoothly, over time. In such models, the construct of interest, the dependent variable, is the rate of change in a phenomenon. Thus, differential equation models allow one to develop explicit theories of the mechanisms that are predicted to influence the process of change in a variable. The resulting theories are often conceptually and intuitively appealing as explanations of continuous time behavioral processes.

Alternative approaches to the study of change, such as more statistically based techniques, typically model the outcomes that result from underlying processes of change, rather than capturing the rate of change itself. Growth curves, for example, are used to investigate longitudinal trajectories of a process, and panel analyses are useful when examining change at discrete stages, whereas sequential analysis is applicable when studying series of observed events. However, dynamic equation approaches also have the advantage that their models of change can be relatively conceptually concise and yet at the same time account for quite intricate time paths. For example, a simple set of differential equations can predict complex cyclical oscillating patterns of development that are apt to have applications to dyadic interaction. These nonlinear trajectories are modeled relatively easily within a differential equation framework, and the set of equations represents a theoretical explanation of these patterns of development. More traditional, statistical techniques also could be used to represent such complicated, undulating time paths, but in practice this is rarely, if ever, done. More generally, these more traditional, statistical techniques are better geared toward describing temporal change than they are to explaining it.

Another benefit of a dynamic modeling approach is that the notion of a system equilibrium is central to differential equations. An equilibrium, or steady state, is a set point to which a self-regulating system will return if it is pushed by external forces. Many social systems, such as couples, are likely to develop self-regulating patterns of development over time. With dynamic systems, it is possible to directly investigate equilibria, as well as the speed with which a possible equilibrium will be reached. On the other hand, variability due to self-regulation in a dynamic process can be erroneously classified as measurement error if more standard, linear models for change are used (e.g., repeated measures ANOVA, random coefficient models; Boker & Nesselroade, 2002). Furthermore, an advantage of differential equation models over techniques such as a mixed-effects growth model is that these dynamic models do not require simplifying assumptions regarding the equivalence of initial conditions and independence from environmental short-term changes; these assumptions can lead to incorrect conclusions regarding complex over-time processes (Boker & Bisconti, 2006).

A final benefit of using differential equations to model change is that it is relatively straightforward to apply a mathematical systems approach in which the behavior of two actors is considered. In such system models, the behavior of each actor can influence directly the rate of change in the behavior of the other, an assumption that is potentially crucial for modeling dyadic interaction, but one that is typically not incorporated into other more statistical approaches, such as multilevel models. Systems of differential equations, similar to single equations, also often have the advantage of theoretical conciseness and intuitive attractiveness. Dynamic systems models have the potential benefit, too, of being able to capture relatively easily intricate nonlinear developments, as well as systems in which the behavior of two actors adopt distinctly divergent paths over time.

Basic Dynamic Models

The mathematical models presented here represent ideal types of interaction in dyads. They are not intended to be realistic models of human dyadic behavior, but instead represent simplified theoretical heuristics. These models demonstrate the implications over time of making certain basic assumptions about dyadic behavior. They address the following question: What can the symbolic language of differential calculus, and its rigorous system of logic, tell us about dyadic behavior if we formalize various assumptions?

The models that I present have implications for behavioral change that is continuous. There are many applications of such types of actor behavior, including, for example, change in a pair's attitudes, or other social psychological constructs, such as commitment, love, and relationship satisfaction. Other examples include the level of a particular actor behavior, such as the level of conflict, or the frequency of engaging in activities, such as the frequency of church attendance. Alternative modeling approaches have been used for endogenous systems of dyadic behavior that alters in discrete stages, such as getting married (e.g., hazard models; Tuma & Hannan, 1984) and decision making (e.g., game theory; Becker, 1981).

I present a series of models that represent change in two actors' behavior, x and y. In these models, the symbols on the left side of the equation represent the instantaneous rate of change in x or y, dx/dt or dy/dt. The right side of the equation includes either an individual component (in which an individual is influenced by his or her own behavior), a system component (in which one actor influences the other actor), or both individual and system components.

Note that time, t, is undefined in the model. It could represent years, months, days, or other intervals of time, depending on the type of behavior and the particular actors. Feelings of commitment and love, for example, might change relatively slowly, at least in well-established couples, and in that case t might represent months or years. The frequency of nonverbal cues exchanged between a pair, on the other hand, could shift by the minute.

The models that I develop are variations of the following general model (Felmlee & Greenberg, 1999):

$$dx/dt = a_1(x^* - x) + b_1(y - x)$$
$$dy/dt = a_2(y^* - y) + b_2(x - y)$$

where x and y refer to the behavior of two actors. For a detailed discussion of the analytic equilibrium solution for this model and its derivation, see Felmlee and Greenberg (1999).

Here I begin with basic models, models that separate the above general system into its component parts, and I describe possible social applications of even these very simple models. Next I systematically examine more complex

dynamic systems that represent combinations of these basic models.

The illustration of the models that I use is the amount of physical exercise undertaken by two members of a romantic couple. Physical exercise is an example of a constructive behavior that enhances the physical and mental well-being of individuals. Exercise also is intriguing because it can be either individually or dyadically determined, that is, it may or may not have a dyadic system component.

Model 1: Two Independents; Individual Model

The first model is one in which there is no system. It is a baseline model against which I intend to compare other models that incorporate a systemic component. Here I assume that the external, personal goals of two actors, x and y, influence their behavior; neither actor directly affects the behavior of the other. The model can be written as follows:

$$dx/dt = a_1(x^* - x)$$
$$dy/dt = a_2(y^* - y) \tag{1}$$

Next I present solutions for this model in which I arbitrarily set the personal standard of x at the value of 10 (i.e., $x^* = 10$) and that of y at 5 (i.e., $y^* = 5$). I vary the initial conditions in three situations. In one case, both x and y start at a point below their respective personal goals. In the second, both start at a point above their respective goals. Finally, actor x starts at a point above his or her goal, whereas actor y's starting point is lower than that of his or her goal.

This model approaches an equilibrium over time in which each actor's behavioral level approaches his or her own individual standard, regardless of the initial conditions. As can be seen in figure 28.1, the value of x approaches 10 and that of y approaches 5.

As an illustration of this model, we take the case of the amount of exercise in which a romantic pair engages over a period of 10 days. One partner (x), Rachel, has as a goal to exercise daily (10 times in a 10-day period). The other partner (y), Raymond, intends to exercise every other day (5 times in a 10-day period). Regardless of whether the individual enters the system, at a point below, at, or above a personal goal, the long-range predictions suggest that the frequency of exercise for both Rachel and Raymond will approach that of their own personal goal. Eventually, Rachel will

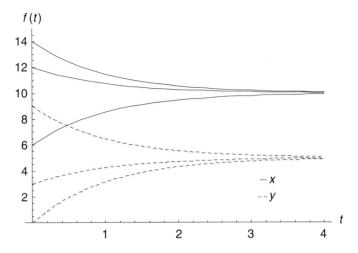

Figure 28.1 Both actors are independent.

exercise approximately daily and Raymond will exercise about every other day. Neither actor is influenced by the exercise frequencies of the other. Rachel and Raymond represent a highly independent couple, at least with respect to the practice of regular exercise.

Model 2: Two Dependents; System Model

The next model formalizes the assumption that a pair forms an endogenous system. Here the assumption is that each actor's behavior is completely dependent on that of the other; that is, the rate of change in the behavior of each actor is influenced only by the other actor's level of behavior, and by his or her own behavior, but not at all by external, individual factors.

$$dx/dt = b_1(y - x)$$
$$dy/dt = b_2(x - y)$$
(2)

As can be seen in figure 28.2, this specification suggests that both actors will converge to a level of behavior that is an average of the two initial levels of behavior, assuming that $b_1 = b_2$. Eventually, their behavior levels will be approximately the same. Furthermore, regardless of the values of b_1 and b_2, if $x = y = c$, the solution will stay at that point.

In an illustration of this model, let us assume that actor x, Laverne, and actor y, Bud, are in a

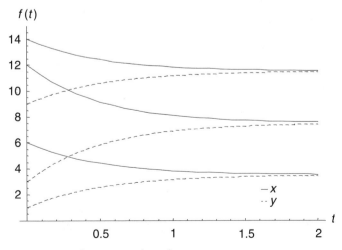

Figure 28.2 Both actors are dependent.

romantic relationship. Neither person has a clear personal or external goal for regular exercise. Instead, each partner's exercise frequency is affected by the exercise behavior of the other. Depending upon the initial starting point, each person's exercise frequency converges to that of the other. It may be, for example, that Laverne and Bud decide to exercise together, and that their exercise patterns converge because of this decision. Note that it is also possible that one partner, say Bud, could be more influenced than the other by his partner's behavior (i.e., $b_2 > b_1$). In this situation, the exercise frequency of the pair would still converge over time, but it would converge more closely to Laverne's starting point.

Model 3: Two Reactionaries; Negative Individual Components

A third basic model is one that consists solely of individual components, as in Model 1, but the coefficients in the model (a_1 and b_1) are now negative, rather than positive.

$$dx/dt = -a_1(x^* - x)$$
$$dy/dt = -a_2(y^* - y)$$
(3)

This set of equations implies that the rate of change in an actor's behavior decreases as the actor's behavioral level becomes more distant from that of an individual, external standard. If he or she has an initial starting point that is lower than an external standard, then his or her behavioral change level gets slower with time. If the actor has an initial starting point that is greater than the external standard, how-

ever, then his or her behavior will change more quickly over time. This system does not stabilize, as shown in figure 28.3.

For example, let's assume that there is a couple, Horace and Hortensia, and that neither one of them wants to act like their same-gender parent. Horace's father worked out every day, and Horace is determined not to replicate his father's regular daily exercise behavior. Hortensia's mother, on the other hand, also engaged in regular exercise, but did so every other day, and Hortensia does not want to mimic her behavior. The model suggests that if the only influence on each person's exercise behavior is the wish to differentiate his or her behavior from an external standard (e.g., the behavior of a parent), then it is quite likely that Horace and Hortensia eventually will not exercise at all on a daily basis. If they start exercising at a level below that of their respective parent, then they will continue to decrease their exercise level until they stop exercising. The model also implies, however, that if they start to exercise more frequently than their parent, that they will increase their exercise frequency until they exercise constantly, in order to differentiate their behavior from that of their parent. This second implication seems to be less realistic, although there may be cases in which an individual attempts to avoid a particular type of behavior and, in so doing, exhibits an exaggerated form of the behavior.

Model 4: Two Contrarians; Negative System Components

Another basic model is one that consists solely of system components, as in Model 2, but here the

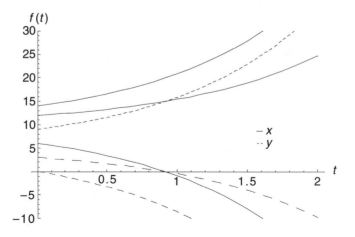

Figure 28.3 Both individual reactionaries.

coefficients for the system components (b_1 and b_2) are negative, rather than positive in sign.

$$dx/dt = -b_1(y - x)$$
$$dy/dt = -b_2(x - y) \qquad (4)$$

In this situation, the rate of change in each actor's behavior decreases, rather than increases, as the difference between the two parties' behavioral levels becomes larger. Instead of each actor trying to shorten the distance between his own and his partner's level of behavior, each one acts to increase the distance between the two.

Here, as is shown in figure 28.4, the two actors become more and more different in their behavioral levels over time ($b_1 = b_2 = -1$). The model explodes, with one member expressing higher and higher levels of the behavior, and the other actor exhibiting lower and lower levels.

An illustration of this is a couple, Mary Ellen and Betty Sue. Mary Ellen and Betty Sue influence each other's exercise patterns, but in ways that cause each other's exercise frequencies to develop in opposing directions. When one increases her rate of exercise, the other will decrease hers. Perhaps, for example, Mary Ellen is concerned about Betty Sue's health problems, and she is determined to set a good example. The less Betty Sue exercises, the more Mary Ellen steps up her workout regimen in hopes that Betty Sue will follow in her footsteps. Betty Sue, on the other hand, becomes more and more intimidated by Mary Ellen's demanding exercise program and decreases her rate of exercise as Mary Ellen's increases. In the long run, such a system results in a situation in which Mary El-

len becomes an exercise nut and works out as much as possible, whereas Betty Sue turns into a complete couch potato. Alternatively, one might infer that the situation is apt to become so unstable that the relationship between Mary Ellen and Betty Sue dissolves.

Combinations of Models 1 Through 4

More complex models can be formed by combining the basic models presented in Models 1 through 4. Next I explore four such combinations, which produce distinct trajectories over time and represent particularly interesting dynamic, dyadic interaction patterns.

Model 5: Two Cooperatives; Positive Individual and Positive System Components

Model 5 includes both individual and system components (a combination of Models 1 and 2), and the coefficients in the model are positive (see Felmlee & Greenberg, 1999). Here actors are influenced by their own individual factors as well as by the other actor's behavioral level.

$$dx/dt = a_1(x^* - x) + b_1(y - x)$$
$$dy/dt = a_2(y^* - y) + b_2(x - y) \qquad (5)$$

This system converges to a stable equilibrium over time. The steady state approached by the two actors is located between those of the two previous models, Models 1 and 2. This equilibrium represents a compromise and is located between the two actors' individual goals (see figure 28.5).

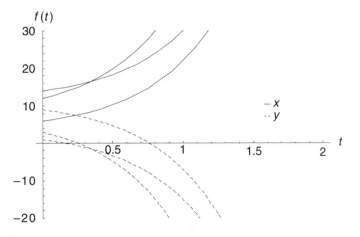

Figure 28.4 Both system contrarians.

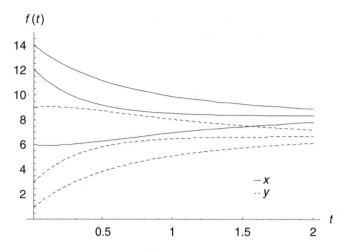

Figure 28.5 Both cooperative: positive individual and system components.

Note that several stable outcomes are possible within this basic cooperative model. For example, influence could be unequal between the partners, with one relatively dependent actor (e.g., $b_1 \neq b_2$). In this case, the equilibrium is closer to that of the more independent partner's goal.

An example of such a system is a couple, Juan and Juanita. Juan prefers daily exercise, whereas Juanita believes that every other day would suffice. In addition, Juanita, in particular, enjoys jogging with Juan, because she finds it a good time to talk with him, and therefore she exercises more often than she would otherwise. When Juanita is too busy to jog, Juan sometimes skips his morning jog as well. Eventually, Juan ends up exercising somewhat less frequently than he would if he was single, and Juanita exercises more frequently. Their eventual long-term exercise regimen represents a compromise between their two individual goals, although it is closer to Juan's individual preferences than it is to those of Juanita.

Model 6: Both Uncooperative; Positive Individual and Negative System Components

In the next variation, the model also consists of individual and system components, and the coefficients for the individual components are positive, whereas those for the system components of the model have negative coefficients.

$$dx/dt = a_1(x^* - x) - b_1(y - x)$$
$$dy/dt = a_2(y^* - y) - b_2(x - y)$$
(6)

Here the long-term behavior of the system depends on the value of the coefficients in the model. If $a_1 = a_2 = 1$, and $b_1 = b_1 = -1$, then the system explodes, with one partner's behavioral level skyrocketing and the other's plummeting over time (see figure 28.6a). When $a_1, a_1 > 2$, however, a different equilibrium situation is obtained (see figure 28.6b). In this case, an actor's goals influence his or her own behavior more than twice as much as does the behavior of the other actor. Here a steady state is approached in which one partner's behavior levels off at a very high level, whereas the other's behavior falls below zero.

As an illustration of this system, suppose that Jenny and Jessie both have strongly held, unique goals with regard to physical exercise ($a_1 = a_2 = 2.1$). Yet they are at odds with each other and tend to react negatively to each other's actions. When Jessie begins to exercise more frequently, Jenny slows down her exercise regime. Over time, the model suggests that Jenny and Jessie's exercise patterns will diverge (see figure 28.6b). In particular, Jenny will stop exercising altogether, while Jessie will level off at a relatively high frequency of exercise.

Model 7: One Cooperative; One Reactionary Cooperative

Next, I model a situation in which one actor is cooperative (see Model 5) and the other has a reactionary individual component and a

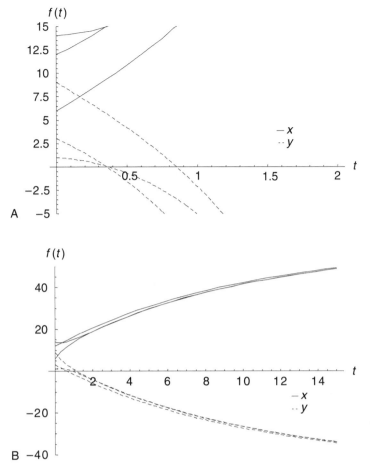

Figure 28.6 Both uncooperative: positive individual and negative system components; (A) $a_1 = a_2 = 1$; (B) $a_1 = a_2 = 2.1$.

cooperative system component. The pair of equations is as follows:

$$dx/dt = a_1(x^* - x) + b_1(y - x)$$
$$dy/dt = -a_2(y^* - y) + b_2(x - y) \tag{7}$$

The long-term behavior of this pair of actors depends upon the value of the coefficients in the model. For example, when a_2 and b_2 are both equal, this means that actor y is influenced equally by his or her own reactionary tendencies with regard to an external standard and by his or her tendency to cooperate with actor x. In this situation, the model does not reach a stable equilibrium. The actors' behaviors explode and become larger and larger in value. In the case in which b_2 greatly exceeds a_2, however, the model

does reach an equilibrium, as can be seen in figure 28.7. Here actor y's cooperative tendencies influence her or his behavior more than do her or his reactionary impulses. The equilibrium is one in which each actor's behavioral level is higher than each of his or her individual goals. Actor y ends up exhibiting much more of the behavior, however, than does actor x.

In this case, suppose we have a pair, Harry and Harriet. Harry's ideal is to exercise daily. Harriet, on the other hand, prefers not to exercise every other day. In her last relationship, she and her partner exercised together every other day, and the relationship ended badly. Harriet does not want to repeat that experience. Each person, and in particular Harry, also influences the exercise pattern of the other. In this situation, Harriet speeds up her exercise frequency over

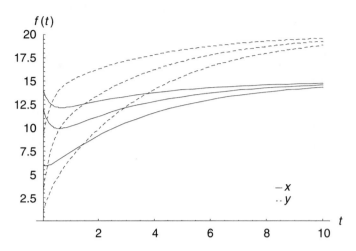

Figure 28.7 One cooperative (x); one reactionary strong cooperative (y); $b_2 = 3$.

time, in part because she is trying to close the distance between her exercise behavior and that of Harry, who begins exercising at a higher rate than does Harriet. Harriet also tries to avoid an every-other-day exercise routine, and in so doing continues to increase her rate of exercise. Harry slows down at first, because of his tendency to decrease the distance between his behavior and that of his partner. He then speeds up as Harriet continues to increase exercising. Both Harry and especially Harriet end up exercising at a relatively high level. Note that the reactionary tendencies of Harriet affect the outcomes for both actors.

Model 8: One Uncooperative; One Dependent

Next I model a situation in which an uncooperative actor is paired with a dependent. This model is of the following form:

$$dx/dt = a_1(x^* - x) - b_1(y - x)$$
$$dy/dt = b_2(x - y)$$

$$(8)$$

In this case, the outcome differs in interesting ways, depending on the value of the b_1 coefficient. When b_1 is equal to 1, for instance, the dyadic system experiences oscillations initially, but then reaches an equilibrium, that is, the system develops a dampened, oscillatory pattern (see figure 28.8a). When the coefficient b_1 is greater than 1, however, the system either os-

cillates perpetually (see figure 28.8b, $b_1 = 2$) or it exhibits exploding oscillations, that is, oscillations that get bigger and bigger over time (when $b_1 > 2$).

In an illustration of this model, a couple, Fred and Ethel, just got married. Fred prefers to be a daily exerciser, whereas Ethel likes to work out every other day. Fred, however, reacts strongly to his wife's behavior and attempts to differentiate his own exercise routine from hers. He does not intend to let his behavior be governed by his wife's. Ethel, on the other hand, wants to match her physical activity to that of her husband as closely as possible. In this situation, when Ethel begins to exercise more frequently, Fred slows down the rate at which he exercises. Then Ethel cuts back as well, in which case Fred speeds up his exercise routine, and so on. In certain specifications of the model, this oscillatory pattern could continue indefinitely.

Another illustration of this model could be the case of relationship involvement for two individuals with disparate relationship attachment styles, Eva and Everett (e.g., Bowlby, 1969; Shaver, Hazan, & Bradshaw, 1988). Suppose, for example, that Eva has a secure attachment style and therefore attempts to match her behavior to that of her romantic partner. Everett, on the other hand, has an avoidant relationship style and tends to react in the opposite way. So if Eva attempts to see Everett more frequently, Everett withdraws. When Everett withdraws, however, Eva stops calling him as often. When Eva pulls back from the relationship, Everett steps up the

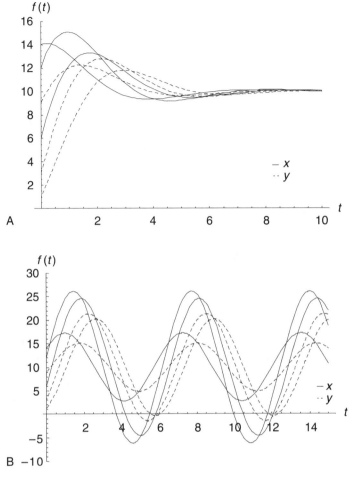

Figure 28.8 One uncooperative (x) and one dependent (y); (A) $b_1 = 1$; (B) $b_1 = 2$.

pace and contacts Eva more frequently. But when Eva reacts to his behavior by coming to see him more often, Everett again withdraws. Assuming that nothing else changes, this on-again–off-again relationship pattern could become routine for a couple, according to the theoretical model.

Implications

What can we learn from these sets of equations? First, if a pair of actors is engaged in a dyadic system in which one or both members' behavior directly influences the other, then the long-term behavior of this pair develops in a unique manner over time. The pattern of development in such a systems model departs, often dramati-

cally, from that of an independent model in which neither actor influences the behavior of the other (i.e., there is no endogenous system component to the model). Ignoring the endogenous system created by a pair of interdependent actors can be misleading, in particular when considering the long-term behavior of the pair.

For example, take the case of the contrarian couple, Mary Ellen and Betty Sue. An examination of the exercise routines of these women would lead to the conclusion that Mary Ellen is an exercise nut and that Betty Sue is a couch potato, and perhaps the inference that these behaviors reflect their personal preferences. But in fact, neither would exhibit such behavior if she were not in a relationship with the other. Furthermore, attempts to predict the exercise patterns of either individual with an equation that includes only individual variables would be very inaccurate. Only a model that included the exercise behavior of the other partner would be accurate.

Second, the models make explicit the argument that there are two ways in which one actor could be affected by the other, that is, positively or negatively. In one situation there are pressures toward conformity, and an actor attempts to more closely reflect the behavior of the other. The second situation represents pressures toward differentiation, in which a dyad member attempts to differentiate his or her behavior from that of the other member. These model components are reminiscent of Homan's (1950) argument that members of groups face two pressures, those toward uniformity, or interdependence, and those toward anomie, or independence. Here the models point out that these contradictory pressures appear in the smallest of group systems, the dyad.

Another implication of these models is that even in this relatively simple set of differential equations, there are a multitude of ways in which actors can pair up and interact with each other over time. Pairs can be cooperative, uncooperative, reactionary, or independent. One member of the pair can be cooperative, whereas the other may be uncooperative. The outcome for the pair depends on the particular combination of behavior for each member. In addition, note that the extent to which one partner is influenced by the other is a continuum. Couples could range from partners who are completely independent of each other to those in which each person's behavior is totally dependent on that of the other. The extent to which each person is influenced by the other affects the long-term behavior of the dyadic system.

Finally, we see that some dyads reach a stable equilibrium whereas others do not. In particular, if both actors are independent of each other, dependent on each other, or cooperative, then a stable, steady state is approached over time. Stability is not obtained, on the other hand, when both actors are independent reactionaries or system contrarians. In several other combinations of actors, the outcome depends on the values of the parameters, that is, the relative strength of the individual and the system model components. For example, when both partners are uncooperative, stability is possible in cases in which actors are a good deal more influenced by their respective positive individual factors than by the behavior of

their partner. In another instance, when a dependent is paired with a relatively highly uncooperative partner $(b_1 = 2)$, then a stable, repetitive, cyclical interaction pattern develops; in other specifications of the model, the system converges to a point equilibrium or produces exploding oscillations. Negative, reactionary, or contrary behavior on the part of at least one actor is necessary, but not sufficient, for instability to occur in these systems.

There are a number of directions for future work on dynamic, dyadic interaction. First, empirical data sets, consisting of repeated measurements for each partner of a couple, are necessary to test the assumptions and predictions of the model. There are several techniques that could be used to estimate the differential equation models. One approach is to integrate the differential equations over a time period corresponding to data collection and then estimate the coefficients of the integrated equations using an approach such as weighted generalized least squares (e.g., Kessler & Greenberg, 1981; Tuma & Hannan, 1984). Other procedures include the use of local linear approximations of the first and second derivatives of data (Boker & Nesselroade, 2002) and the use of latent differential equation modeling (Boker & Bisconti, in press; Ferrer & McArdle, 2003). These techniques provide possible empirical methods for capturing the dynamic theoretical processes identified by differential equation models.

On a theoretical level, the models proposed here incorporate a number of simplifying assumptions, such as the assumption that interdependent behavior is limited to pairs of actors. Individual or dyadic behavior could be part of a larger system, such as one that includes family and social network members, and the exploration of such a multiactor system is an avenue for future research. Additional work also is needed to explore more complex dynamic, dyadic models that incorporate interactions and nonlinearities that may be useful for analyzing particular types of coupled behavior (e.g., Gottman et al., 2002).

Note that the simplifying assumptions made in a good deal of other work on couples are demanding as well. Empirical studies that rely on data from only one member of the pair to analyze relationship processes, for example, implicitly assume that relationships have reached an equilibrium in which one partner is not directly influencing the other. The research presented here suggests that this is likely to be a misleading assumption, particularly at stages in a relationship where change is occurring. What may be more surprising is that these models also suggest that there are limitations to psychological and social psychological research on behavior that is typically viewed as individual. For instance, research on intraindividual topics, such as the self, cognitive styles, or attitudes, is making the implicit assumption that the particular behavior examined is not part of a dynamic, coupled system. Yet if an individual is a member of an interdependent dyad, then that person's sense of self, cognitive pattern, and personal attitudes may be directly influenced by his or her partner's respective sense of self, cognitive pattern, or attitudes. The simplifying assumptions of typical empirical work are not as obvious as those made here, however, because they are not formalized.

In conclusion, a simple two-actor system produces a multitude of intriguing outcomes over time, if we formalize several very basic assumptions, such as the assumptions that the members form an endogenous system and that this system changes over time in a smooth, continuous manner. Two partners can converge in their behavior, they can diverge completely, or their actions can oscillate repeatedly. Not surprisingly, cooperation on the part of each individual leads to stability over time. Nevertheless, in some cases, couples that are not cooperative can approach an equilibrium as well. The implications of these models point to the importance of taking into account dynamic systems of coupled behavior in studies of dyads as well as individuals.

Acknowledgments   Appreciation is expressed to David Greenberg, Scott Gartner, Larry Cohen, Emilio Ferrer, and the University of Iowa Sociology Theory Workshop for their comments on an earlier version of this chapter.

References

Allport, G. W. (1968). The historical background of modern social psychology. In G. Lindzey & E. Aronson (Eds.), *The handbook of social psychology* (Vol. 1, 2nd ed., pp. 1–80). Cambridge, MA: Addison-Wesley.

Baron, R. M., Amazeen, P. G., & Beck, P. J. (1994). "Local and global dynamics of social relations." In R. R. Vallacher & A. Nowak (Eds.), *Dynamical systems in social psychology* (pp. 11–138). San Diego, CA: Academic.

Baxter, L. A., & Montgomery, B. J. (1996). *Relating: Dialogues and dialectics.* New York: Guilford.

Becker, G. S. (1981). *A treatise on the family.* Cambridge, MA: Harvard University Press.

Boker, S. B., & Bisconti, T. L. (2006). Dynamical systems modeling in aging research. In C. S. Bergeman & S. M. Boker (Eds.), *Quantitative methodology in aging research* (pp. 185–229). Mahwah, NJ: Erlbaum.

Boker, S. B., & Nesselroade, J. R. (2002). A method for modeling the intrinsic dynamics of intraindividual variability: Recovering the parameters of simulated oscillators in multi-wave panel data. *Multivariate Behavioral Research, 37,* 127–160.

Bowlby, J. (1969). *Attachment and loss: Vol. 1.* New York: Basic Books.

Buder, E. H. (1991). A nonlinear dynamic model of social interaction. *Communication Research, 18,* 174–198.

Felmlee, D. H., & Greenberg, D. H. (1999). A dynamic systems model of dyadic interaction. *Journal of Mathematical Sociology, 23,* 155–180.

Ferrer, E., & McArdle, J. J. (2003). Alternative structural models for multivariate longitudinal data analysis. *Structural Equation Modeling, 10,* 493–524.

Friedkin, N. E. (1998). *A structural theory of social influence.* New York: Cambridge.

Gottman, J. M., Murray, J. D., Swanson, C. C., Tyson, R., & Swanson, K. R. (2002). *The mathematics of marriage.* Cambridge, MA: MIT Press.

Homans, G. C. (1950). *The human group.* New York: Harcourt, Brace and World.

Huston, T. L., & Chorost, A. F. (1994). Behavioral buffers on the effects of negativity on marital satisfaction: A longitudinal study. *Journal of Personal Relationships, 1,* 223–238.

Karney, B. R., & Bradbury, T. N. (1995). The longitudinal course of marital quality and stability: A review of theory, method, and research. *Psychological Bulletin, 1,* 3–34.

Kelley, H. H., & Thibaut, J. W. (1978). *Interpersonal relations: A theory of interdependence.* New York: Wiley.

Kessler, R. C., & Greenberg, D. F. (1981). *Linear panel analysis: Models of quantitative change.* New York: Academic Press.

Minuchin, S. (1984). *Families and family therapy.* Cambridge, MA: Harvard University Press.

Rapaport, A. (1960). *Fights, games and debates.* Ann Arbor: University of Michigan Press.

Rinaldi, S. (1998). Love dynamics: The case of linear couples. *Applied Mathematics and Computation, 95,* 181–192.

Shaver, P. R., Hazan, C., & Bradshaw, D. (1988). Love as attachment: The integration of three behavioral systems. In R. J. Sternberg &

M. L. Barnes (Eds.), *The psychology of love* (pp. 68–99). New Haven, CT: Yale University Press.

Simon, H. (1957). *Models of man.* New York: Wiley.

Sprecher, S., & Felmlee, D. (1997). The balance of power in romantic heterosexual couples over time from "his" and "her" perspectives. *Sex Roles, 37,* 361–380.

Surra, C. A. (1990). Research and theory on mate selection and premarital relationships in the 1980's. *Journal of Marriage and the Family, 52,* 844–865.

Tuma, N. B., & Hannan, M. T. (1984). *Social dynamics: Models and methods.* Orlando, FL: Academic Press.

29

Nonlinear Dynamics of Positive Psychology

Parameters, Models, and Searching for a Systems Summum Bonum

David Schuldberg

This chapter discusses new measurement and modeling techniques for positive psychology, methods grounded in the theory of nonlinear dynamical systems (NDS). The chapter's primary focus is on ways to evaluate interindividual differences in variables that assess the complexity of each person's fluctuating behavior.[1] It also discusses individual differences in descriptors summarizing the pattern or shape of a participant's variations. Whether assessing the quantity—or the quality and style—of a person's changes, the intent is to find indices of intraindividual change that can be related to interindividual differences in positive characteristics. The emphasis here is on methods based on NDS, in contrast to more traditional time-series techniques.

The chapter combines both within-subject and between-subjects analyses.[2] This two-level approach to data is relatively new; in some cases applications specific to positive psychology have yet to develop. Nevertheless, NDS and related methods have a great deal to contribute to theory and empirical work on human strengths, and the chapter describes some exemplary studies.

The chapter begins with an overview of NDS methods in psychology and nearby fields, potential applications to questions in positive psychology, and the relevance of NDS for data analysis. It discusses model-free approaches to analyses, methods that are either purely numerical or that describe patterning in data; it then reviews model fitting and testing. The chapter describes how health and positive characteristics have historically been defined as systems properties or processes. These approaches and positive psychology share interest in describing criteria for a potential supreme good in systems, a systemic summum bonum.

The chapter highlights applications of NDS to modeling and measurement of variation for studying individual differences in stress and coping. These processes are especially relevant for positive psychology and important to physical and mental health and illness. They represent dynamic phenomena, with dramatic personal variation over time, as well as marked individual stylistic differences. Coping styles have a long history of capturing both putatively pathological (when called defense mechanisms) and positive, healthy response (as resources, or components of resiliency).

Where NDS Methods Are Most Often Used

Systematic analyses of individual differences (differences between participants, interindividual differences) in the nonlinear dynamics of behavior are relatively rare; these methods are still sparsely applied in psychology. NDS techniques themselves—with an almost exclusive within-subject focus—are used most prominently in developmental (Smith & Thelen, 1993) and social psychology (Vallacher, 1994; Vallacher & Nowak, 1994; Vallacher, Nowak, Froehlich, & Rockloff, 2002), with additional applications in areas such as learning, cognition, and clinical psychology (see Abraham, Abraham, & Shaw, 1990; Masterpasqua & Perna, 1997). NDS methods are applied more widely in physiology and medicine, where notions of complexity in biological systems (West, 1990) and "complex diseases" are popular (Rees, 2002).

Of particular relevance to positive psychology, there is a fascinating and contentious literature in physiology and now psychopathology regarding whether certain NDS properties, notably chaos, are indicative of health or illness. Even here, systematic approaches to finely graduated or continuous interindividual differences have been relatively neglected, with more emphasis on characterizing health and pathology categorically, or in detecting different regimes of variability in the same person (e.g., the same person is observed when healthy and sick). Much can be gained from exploring differences in complex positive psychological processes and complex health.

The Importance of NDS to Positive Psychology

NDS theory includes three basic components. It is concerned first with *systems*, aggregations of linked interacting components. Second, system behavior is considered as *dynamic* and changing with time, observed longitudinally across multiple occasions. Third, components of the systems must include *nonlinear* causal relationships between independent and dependent variables; simply put, this means that the relationships governing these connections cannot be modeled as straight-line graphs on ordinary graph paper. This last emphasis distinguishes the NDS approach from earlier systems theories (e.g., von Bertalanffy, 1968).

Nonlinearities can occur in curvilinear dose-response relationships (where more of a good thing is not proportionately better), in stepwise or lagged responses, as nonlinear coupling of subsystems, or in the multiplicative interactions of causal variables that influence a downstream variable over time (Carver & Scheier, 2000; Schuldberg, 2006). These types of nonlinearity are all internal to a system, rather than referring to whether its global external behavior appears linear or nonlinear. It is specifically this within-system nonlinearity that technically defines NDS.[3]

In the classical theories of general systems (von Bertalanffy, 1968), living systems (Miller, 1978), and cybernetics (Weiner, 1961), systems were prized for properties of interconnectedness, feedback, regulation, reciprocal causation, holism, and equifinality; the last term overlaps with what is now called emergence and points to the appearance of new behavior, structure, or organization.

Connections between system function and health or sickness also have a long history. Sontag (1977) notes the metaphorical parallels between physical disease and the condition of a larger "body politic." Importantly, in the late 1920s Harvard physiologist Walter Cannon introduced *homeostasis* to describe normal physiological function; this represents an early and sophisticated idea of system health, what this chapter calls a systems summum bonum. Unfortunately, homeostasis has been applied indiscriminately to physiology, family and group functioning, and positive psychology; while colorful alternatives have been proposed, the concept is in need of further revision. Thus, health is commonly described as dynamic self-regulation; while positive psychology does include regulated and bounded behavior, the NDS approach suggests that well-being is not the same as equilibrium. As Cannon himself noted, even homeostasis is not completely stable, and it dissipates energy. NDS theory also represents a change in perspective in emphasizing trajectories, attractors, chaos, bifurcations (where system regimes shift), and the emergence of new forms.

Several events have led to the rise of NDS. Interest in nonlinearity was spurred—after early and visionary contributions, for example, by Poincaré—by fairly recent improvements in data-processing hardware and computational techniques. Because NDS generally cannot be described analytically (their behavior completely specified by simple equations), they often must be investigated by iterative numerical methods. Once very cumbersome, these techniques are now widely accessible.

In psychology and medicine, there is growing interest in characterizing individuals' longitudinal behavior; the next step is to go beyond single-case descriptive work to derive general findings about how changeable individuals differ. As noted, this can mean distinguishing individuals with a particular disease from those who are well, for example in so-called dynamic diseases (Belair, Glass, an der Heiden, & Milton, 1995). This chapter argues for an extension to using complexity information in conjunction with other continuous, rather than categorical, individual difference variables.

These new developments have important implications for theory and research in positive psychology:

1. Pictures of the positive should be dynamic ones, rather than still portraits. This means moving from studying components of some (probably illusory) static state or condition of being well, healthy, or virtuous. The positive is a trajectory, journey, or story. Examples are broadening and building, and "upward and outward spirals" of positive emotions (Fredrickson & Joiner, 2002; Fredrickson & Losada, 2005; Seligman, 2002), and the process of leaving boredom or anxiety and finding the flow state (see Csikszentmihalyi & Larson, 1984, pp. 264–270). Positive paths emerge from underlying dynamic processes that form the good lives we want to describe, understand, and attain. Proposing and validating these processes are tasks of modeling and model fitting, discussed near the end of the chapter. Understanding positive dynamics also allows design of interventions that emphasize shaping attractors, rely on heuristics, and honor human contradiction and disorder.

2. Positive psychology must recognize well-known nonlinearities in the effects of putative goods or virtues (Chang & Sanna, 2003). The curvilinear character of these relationships is inescapable, yet too often ignored. Discussions of the positive can fall prey to the linear virtue problem, assuming that more is better, and that good behaviors and characteristics function independently of time and context, and without interacting with other virtues and goals. In contrast, we must develop principles of nonlinear salutogenesis.

3. The positive is multivariate, as evidenced by the many domains tapped by quality of life measures (Frisch, 1998). These all represent goals that can be pursued relatively independently, suggesting that well-being emerges from modular subsystems.

4. The positive is multifactorial. There are many salutogenic agents: Virtues, personal attributes, behaviors, relationships, and environments. These function over time, as main effects and in interactions.

5. Finally, different means-end modules are not only relatively independent but also interacting and (perhaps loosely) coupled. These couplings can also contain nonlinearities.

These five items constitute a bottom-up or micro case for an NDS role in positive psychology, an argument on the basis of small mechanisms rather than the larger-scale behavior of healthy systems. Elsewhere I have called such mechanisms "somewhat-complicated systems" (Schuldberg, 2002, 2006). Not too complicated to understand and model, they can still do justice to the complexities of positive function.

There are also top-down or macro arguments for applying NDS to positive psychology. These note large-scale properties of well-being; positive psychology must acknowledge and account for the macroscopic stigmata or flags (Keating & Miller, 2000) that point to the involvement of nonlinear processes in health. As Mandell and Salk (1984) wrote, "Discontinuities, the reordering of latent patterns, the sudden emergence of new forms, and the occurrence of global disorder among healthy and well-functioning individuals are examples of phenomena well known to psychosocial clinicians" (p. 304).

Macro and micro features of NDS important for positive psychology include the fact that well-being can be bafflingly complicated, elusive, difficult to maintain, and sometimes intractable. A well-lived life includes inconsistency as well as consistency, and internal and external conflict from competing agendas, goals, strategies, and desires. We communicate mixed messages because we normally want more than one thing. There are also positive effects of mixed emotions (Larsen, Hemenover, Norris, & Cacioppo, 2002). Positive psychology may well consist of the dynamic juggling of competing interests, opponent processes, or dialectics (Linehan, 1993).

Health can also be unpredictable and surprising, with sometimes sudden, discontinuous, perverse, or unexpected change. These phenomena are referred to as tipping, nemesis effects, and blowback. Catastrophic change can occur for both good and ill, and small interventions can have large positive effects. In addition, health is startlingly robust and adaptable, deeply rich, and sometimes beautiful; it is irregular and fluctuating, and it dissipates energy. Positive psychology needs to attend to the different types (and degrees) of variability in normal functioning.

There is contemporary interest in the fact that NDS contain the possibility of technically defined chaotic behavior, with a possible overlap between chaos and health. There is also attention to systems far from equilibrium or on the edge of chaos. Cardiologist Ary Goldberger, a pioneer in applying chaos theory and related empirical techniques to medicine, has contended that "healthy systems don't want homeostasis, they want chaos" (quoted in Pool, 1989; see Goldberger & Rigney, 1991). He argues that healthy behavior is irregular, not strictly rhythmic.

The relationship between chaos and health is being debated (Glass & Mackey, 1988, pp. 179–180; Huikuri et al., 1999). We cannot make the blanket statement that chaos is the summum bonum of health; it has also been demonstrated in pathological conditions, including epilepsy, bipolar disorder, perhaps schizophrenia, and even heart disease (Weiss, Garfinkel, Spano, & Ditto, 1994). Whether or not chaos defines health, NDS have properties that make them realistic as well as frustrating, and very applicable to positive psychology. They are hard to predict and control, capable of novel creative behavior, and can demonstrate adaptability, flexibility, and resistance to entrainment by the environment (West, 1997).

This discussion has sketched both bottom-up and top-down cases for an NDS role in positive psychology. These arguments from each end must be brought together by characterizing, quantifying, and comparing behaviors of specific models in relation to the everyday or laboratory behavior of flesh-and-blood participants. Embracing NDS does not mean that all the things we already know about positive psychology and physical health are wrong. New models can be built from variables we know well, incorporate components of existing (but, at this point, generally static) causal models, and explain well-observed phenomena. The "behavioral" (Staddon, 2001) language of psychology is uniquely useful for constructing very illuminating models. A worthwhile strategy is to assemble small, relatively self-contained modular subunits that can interact and be aggregated with others to build more complicated models with bigger behaviors. In the life sciences, this has been called "reverse engineering biological complexity" (Csete & Doyle, 2002); its proponents have advocated "toy models" with self-regulative feedback loops as suitable building blocks for complicated systems.

NDS and Data Analysis

There are several approaches to assessing across-person differences in within-person variability that rely on NDS theory and related methods. This discussion is organized around two ways to conceptualize individual variability: first, via a parameter (e.g., through deriving variability metrics or complexity indices); second, as a shape or pattern, using a "trajectory vocabulary." The emphasis here is on stable features of within-person variability. However, not all authors assume that this variability is stable underneath. Gottman, Murray, Swanson, Tyson, and Swanson (2002) looked at patterns of change in couples, and other authors are interested in within-subjects differences in variability across situations, over time, or through the course of an experimental task (Vallacher et al., 2002; chapter 28, this volume).

How is this approach specifically related to research in positive psychology, as opposed to the study of deficits, or work that ignores distinctions between what is healthy and unhealthy? Wellness and illness emerge from the same systems and inhabit the same bodies. They seem to be located on continua; but, even if positive and negative differ discontinuously, they must be understood together. Still, it is easy to lose sight of what is specifically beneficial, even without pathologizing. It will be productive to focus increasing attention on what is positive in systems (Seligman & Csikszentmihalyi, 2000), especially on how positive psychology can incorporate variability. But some of the empirical methods discussed here still await application and a conceptual shift toward positive psychology.

The chapter now turns to specific ways to quantify and describe fluctuation at the level of the individual. Techniques of NDS-informed data analysis are aimed at computing individuals' levels on variability measures, and they require the researcher either to estimate parameters or to derive patterns for each of the participants, who are then compared. The assessment and classification of individuals can be done without proposing, specifying, or fitting an underlying model, but modeling helps. Without it, the work can be very much atheoretical, with a dynamic "dustbowl" quality to its empiricism. (Because the approach is dynamic, we can call this "dust devil" empiricism.) Models can simplify data analysis and add power, leading to less fishing.

Two Model-Free Ways to Characterize Dynamic Data

As noted, there are two basic ways to approach individual differences in intraindividual variability without specifying a candidate system in advance; they emphasize either parameters or patterns in variability.

The key component in one approach is the extraction of parameter values for each individual case by summarizing its time-series data. These values make up the observations for a variable to be used in between-subjects comparisons, with differing levels related to differing levels on other types of measures (e.g., correlated with self-report). While a good deal of work has been done on the derivation of dynamic indices to characterize individual cases (e.g., Abarbanel, 1996; Heath, 2000; Kantz & Schreiber, 1999; Sprott, 2003; Sprott & Rowlands, 1995), less is known about how to employ them in this large-n, between-subjects work.

There are also traditional, moment-based approaches to characterizing variation in a person's data. For example, one can compute each participant's across-time variance or standard deviation, as well as range and indices of velocity, acceleration, and still periods (Vallacher & Nowak, 1994; Vallacher et al., 2002). SPSS's

AGGREGATE procedure is very useful for computing individuals' variability indices. These summary indices of across-time variability can then be used in between-subjects analyses. While high between-individual variance often characterizes deviant groups, Larson, Csikszentmihalyi, and Graef (1980) noted that, in adolescents, within-subject variability on experience sampling ratings of affect was not related to pathology and correlated with some positive indices.

In contrast, an NDS approach derives different sorts of indices, generally ones summarizing the amount of complexity or degree of deterministic chaos[4] manifested in the fluctuations of each participant's data set. Complexity refers to the degree to which this variability represents deterministic chaos, as opposed to periodic regularity on the one hand (low complexity), or random noise on the other (very high values of fractal dimension and related measures). At a descriptive level, these provide a basis for discussing how a given phenomenon (e.g., affect variability) may be characterized as periodic, as representing deterministic chaos, or as stochastic (random). The values derived for each case refer to the degree of chaos (or, alternatively, the degree of noisiness or disorder) in an individual's data set, and can be used in interindividual analyses.

However, looking at large differences between high- and low-chaos participants presents problems; because high-dimensional chaos is indistinguishable from noise, a time series characterized as more chaotic on the basis of these statistics is also closer to stochastic, nondeterministic noise, that is to say, not characterized by deterministic chaos at all.[5] The phrases *more chaotic* and *degree of chaos* lose meaning at high values of a complexity statistic. And while different phenomena are defined by low, moderate, and high dimensional chaos (or by stochastic noise), there are also questions whether relatively small differences in these variables are meaningful.

A number of complexity statistics are available, including the fractal dimension, correlation dimension, and the largest nonnegative Lyapunov exponent; the last assesses the extent to which an attractor is "strange" or chaotic. There are also related measures of degree of apparent randomness versus determinism in a data set, including information statistics, entropy (a measure of disorder), and the BDS (Brock-Dechert-Sheinkman) statistic.

A colleague and I have taken this approach and compared indices derived from momentary fluctuations in self-reported affect to other, more traditional static and large-scale emotion measures (Schuldberg & Gottlieb, 2002). No specific dynamic model was specified in advance of data analysis, although I have suggested a toy model elsewhere (Schuldberg, 2002). Nevertheless, parameters from observed time series do provide information about the types of systems that might underlie a person's data, about the number of variables or the order of the equations required to produce the observed behavior (Sprott, 2003; West, 1990).

Methodological Difficulties Involving Complexity Indices

An additional practical question concerns the observed or theoretical distributional properties of derived dynamic parameters: What are appropriate interindividual comparisons to make, and what are the correct (e.g., parametric or nonparametric) inferential statistics to use? Another technical problems is related to the degree-of-chaos problem and connected to common misconceptions about what chaos is. There is a tendency to view chaos woodenly as either vice or virtue, a sign of either health or illness. Some now laud moderation in degree of chaos; following Aristotle, the idea of a happy medium tends to replace maximization approaches. Thus, simply testing (e.g., with correlation) for a presumed linear relationship between magnitude of a complexity statistic and self-reported affect (Schuldberg & Gottlieb, 2002) could be misleading.

Other practical difficulties concern the techniques currently available for computing complexity indices. While powerful and relatively easy-to-use software can handle these intraindividual analyses (e.g., Sprott & Rowlands, 1995; see also Kantz & Schreiber, 1999), there are limitations to how much the investigator can employ a "meat-grinder approach" (Bird, 2003) to analyses. This refers to using a single analytic technique or to relying on a program's default initial parameter settings and possibly employing batch files to automate analyses, processing data in the same way for each participant, without personalized attention.

In contrast, time series data sets often require a good deal of individual work, eyeballing, and careful selection of setup parameters for each person. One size does not fit all. Choosing the

initial values for parameters that guide the analysis (e.g., the embedding dimension) impacts the results. In addition, computation involves methods of estimation and approximation that are still somewhat unsettled. Different software may produce different values for a statistic in the same data set.

Data and Design Considerations

Of course, the data extraction methods described here require a set of observations taken over time for each of the individuals being studied. There is a good deal of disagreement about how long a time series is required to characterize either internal parameters of a model or to derive overall complexity indices. In a Monte Carlo study, Boker and Nesselrade (2002), starting out with a well-defined model common to a sample of artificial participants, estimated important model constants accurately from only three data points; they noted that when there are individual differences in these values, more points will be needed. In the case when the form of the underlying model is also unknown and not assumed, much larger data sets are generally required from each individual.

Rules of thumb about the number of points needed to make meaningful judgments about whether a time series is chaotic and to derive dynamic patterns range from under 100 to several thousand. Generally, about 1,000 points per participant will provide sufficient data for deriving an individual's complexity indices (Bird, 2003).[6] Yet, this number often cannot be met by data from repeated self-report, coding of interaction behavior, diaries, or even Ecological Momentary Assessment methods. Considerably smaller numbers of points may need to be used. Then, for the between-subjects analyses, usual considerations of power apply. Thus, two sample size issues are involved in this work: observations per participant, and number of participants.

Techniques for estimating complexity parameters also tend to assume equally spaced time-sampling intervals. This does not lend itself easily to handling missing data or usual techniques for imputation of points, although the Gottman group (Gottman et al., 2002) described reduction methods that should be able to finesse the absence of some data; they sometimes average data points over blocks. (See also Kreindler & Lumsden, 2006.) A related issue concerns potential problems from oversampling, gathering too many data points, which can introduce spurious correlations among nearby observations (Bird, 2003; Sprott, 2003).

The researcher also sometimes finds that a participant has some uncomputable complexity variables. This raises questions of interpretation: Are these data actually noisy? Was there a problem with data acquisition procedures or instrumentation? Do the data include trends or regular fluctuations that need to be removed? Is the researcher missing something regarding setting up the initial data analysis parameters for this participant?

Other methodological issues concern the meaning of behavior samples themselves and are not specific to NDS techniques; it is assumed that the investigator can legitimately treat a snippet of behavior as a sample, making inferences about larger-scale phenomena. This asserts the representativeness of limited observations and the stability and validity of the derived variables. These are often untested assumptions, although complexity indices can be computed over subsets of a time series and the values compared (Sprott, 2003).

Generally, algorithms for computing complexity indices require stationary data, with trends and regular oscillations removed. It is easy to remove a linear trend with a linear regression analysis of each participant's data, computing residuals; this provides a value for each data point with a linear component taken out. However, it is less easy to remove nonlinear trends and some oscillations. Techniques are available for evaluating the stationarity of each individual's time series (Kantz & Schreiber, 1999; Sprott, 2003; Sprott & Rowlands, 1995).

Despite the methodological difficulties and unresolved technical and theoretical issues associated with these methods, they have a tremendous amount to offer positive psychology and the social sciences in general. And we are witnessing a rapid evolution in available practical techniques.

Examples of This Type of NDS-Informed Research

I have mentioned my own work as one example of a model-free approach to assessing individual differences in intraindividual parameters derived from time series. Several other projects exemplify related strategies. Boker and Nesselroade (2002) discussed estimating different individuals' models on the basis of time-series data, emphasizing the case when the general underlying structure is known. They have done work based on a damped linear feedback model of self-regulation, an important type of system for positive psychology, related to a simple "homeostat" (see also chapter 26, this volume)

The Gottman group (Gottman et al., 2002) stands out for deriving meaningful parameters based on sequences of couples' interaction and for describing patterns for different types of dyads. The derived variables characterize couple types; they can be used in statistical analyses along with different sorts of measures and provide meaningful information for larger-scale interindividual (or, more precisely, interdyad) predications, for example, characterizing risk for divorce.

Individual Differences in Patterning

A second approach to assessing individual differences in time-series data refers to the patterning of trajectories, the paths defined by each subject's data set, and looking at different trajectories between persons. Many psychological terms relevant to positive psychology—and to mental and physical health—have essentially dynamic referents and point to paths through the "life space." These include recovery from serious illness, "Aha!" experiences in psychotherapy, creative insight, and drying out from a binge.

Finding ways to describe and classify trajectories addresses important conceptual questions about the dynamic, systems-level, or process foundations of our vocabularies of well-being. One strength of these methods is that they may produce a leap forward in understanding and quantifying the essentially dynamic meanings of basic concepts in positive psychology, for example, virtues. They may also provide empirical grounding for literary and narrative accounts of health, illness, and care (Frank, 1995; Hunter, 1991).

A first step in evaluating patterning is generally visual inspection of a pictorial representation of each participant's data to discern shape, style, or pattern. This is sometimes done with averaged group data, but summaries can obscure the phenomena of interest both visually and empirically (Heath, 2000, p. 18). These graphs are generally either simple plots of one or more variables against time, phase-space graphs (where points are plotted against a derivative or a time-lagged observation), or bivariate plots. On the basis of inspection, a number of authors claim to find chaos or attractors in their data. (An attractor is a region in phase space where the trajectory of a system tends to go and tends to linger or remain.)

This visual approach has a number of problems (Guastello, 1995, p. 93). There are not agreed-upon criteria for qualitative judgments that a picture represents a given pattern; there is not yet a good vocabulary for naming configurations, a lexicon of style. This also echoes Sprott's (2003) concern about overstating findings of chaos on the basis of quantitative indices; he warns against "joining the legions of others who have published false claims of chaos" (p. 235).

Nevertheless, visual inspection of data is important and can be very informative. It reminds the researcher to pay attention to the person when studying intraindividual variability, even when the ultimate goal is interindividual comparison. Looking at graphs can be a tonic to the practice, mentioned earlier, of conducting uniform and possibly automated derivations of parameters.

There are also more rigorous and quantitative ways to derive pattern, with several exemplary cases where researchers have extracted configurations relevant to mental health. The work on interaction patterns that predict divorce mentioned above (Gottman et al., 2002) is an excellent example. These authors built on an array of earlier findings (e.g., ratios of observed positive and negative verbalizations while couples discuss a conflict) to construct NDS models. These were then tested with data, and relevant new descriptive and empirical parameters derived for both stable and unstable couples. This combines both parameter-based methods with elements of a trajectory-based pictorial approach. The authors then developed marriage experiments, where they designed and prescribed focused marital interventions whose impact was tested for therapeutic efficacy. Gottman et al. (2002, p. 71) also provided a useful schematic for constructing, testing, and utilizing NDS models in psychological science.

Another exemplary illustration comes from the work of Metzger and her colleagues (Metzger, 2003; Morrel, Metzger, Murphy, & O'Farrell, 2006). These researchers used several different forms of multivariate and multiprocess time-series modeling (Metzger, 1995). The multiprocess approach derives specific modes of intradyad communication and assumes couples can engage in more than one mode. While the models in this research were linear ones, the overall approach to pattern derivation is relevant. The Metzger (2003) work is important for its use of multivariate time series and noteworthy in employing Bayesian techniques for model building and iterative model testing, a statistical process for settling on a best model or models in a particular case. The predominance of different interaction patterns was then assessed for each couple and used as an interindividual variable (in this case, again, "intercouple" is more accurate) in subsequent between-groups analyses. Variables referring to these interaction modes discriminated domestic-violence from nonviolent couples, and relapsing from nonrelapsing substance-abusing and domestic-violence couples. Thus, group difference predictions were made on the basis of interaction characteristics from within-couple data, and the between-group differences were cross-validated in a new subsample.

Lewis, Lamey, and Douglas (1999; see Granic & Hollenstein, 2003; Granic & Patterson, 2006) have developed a hybrid approach that they call state space grid analysis, where dyadic or two-variable behavior sequences are plotted in a state space divided into tiles. Variables can be computed for a particular pattern on a grid and then used in statistical analyses of individual differences. This combines graphical representation of dynamic patterns with quantitative methods.

Model Construction and Model Testing

While they are not required for deriving time-series variables for individual differences research, it is worthwhile to comment briefly on how the researcher can go about constructing dynamic models to match empirical data; this is an area where there is a good deal of room for fruitful research. First, it is possible to derive models from theory. One can also propose a model from intuition or knowledge grounded in existing data, by induction. What this often means today—where data with time as a variable are still relatively rare, or include only two or three longitudinal data points rather than an extended series of observations—is that researchers will construct a candidate NDS model using an existing static model that was built with cross-sectional data.

One common family of these static models includes the path, causal, or structural models constructed and tested with path analytic, regression, or structural equation techniques. Although diagrams of these models generally do contain what Arlo Guthrie referred to (in *Alice's Restaurant*) as "circles and arrows and a paragraph on the back of each one," and thus they can look like block diagrams of dynamic systems, they generally depict a frozen-in-time view of causes and correlations, or use variables in a few temporal panels. Several techniques are available for moving from a path to a systems model, and these are important for the "not everything you know is wrong" theme of this chapter: Current knowledge, often based on excellent data, is commonly presented in static causal models; we can now construct dynamic pictures based on them. An exciting question concerns how the new candidates for simple systems models will behave when time, change, and nonlinearity are taken into account.

Levine (1992) used the concept of pulse processes to show how coefficients in a path diagram can be transformed into weights in a systems model. Boker and Nesselroade (2002) demonstrated the correspondence of a very important dynamical system to an interesting variation on a classical path model. It will be interesting to extend this work to include nonlinear feedback, although this may complicate model testing. Fredrickson and Losada (2005) have proposed a dynamic model of flourishing similar to the Lorenz equations. Molenaar and Raymakers (1998) took up the problem of fitting nonlinear models. Guastello's (1995) extensive work on testing catastrophe and other NDS models is relevant here.

A related topic concerns model testing, the application of statistical fit indices to evaluate the accuracy of a particular NDS model for one or more empirical time series. There are a number of techniques for evaluating the significance and appropriateness of the value of a complexity parameter derived from a participant's empirical time series. For example, a computed value can be compared to values from various surrogate, artificial, or shuffled data sets (Heath, 2000; Kantz & Schreiber, 1999; Sprott, 2003; Sprott & Rowlands, 1995; Theiler, Eubank, Longtin, Galdrikian, & Farmer, 1992), complete with null hypothesis significance tests. In general, such techniques are now used to compare one real participant's data with artificial data sets, but they could also be adapted to group comparisons.

Somewhat less is known about fitting an entire systems model, not just testing the value of a single index related to the order of a system. Levine, Van Sell, and Rubin (1992) described one approach to model fitting. Molenaar and Raymakers (1998) provided an iterative approach to both model development and fitting. Boker (2002) also addressed goodness of fit. And van Geert (e.g., 1998), applying several dynamic growth models to language development, grappled with fitting and parameter estimation and touched on problems of individual differences.

Once a model has been fitted, it is then worthwhile to make predictions to future behavior, other individuals, or another sample. Finally, it is important to mention again the work of Guastello (1995), who has extensively studied NDS and catastrophe models. He has been a pioneer in evaluating discontinuities in empirical data, and in developing data analytic strategies for testing these models against actual data sets using regression techniques. Catastrophe models are very useful for understanding the important discontinuous phenomena involved in health and positive psychology.

From Individual to Dyadic Perspectives and Beyond

If I had been asked in graduate school what I believed was missing in understanding mental health (and in psychology in general), I would have said that we needed to take general systems theory more seriously. What I would have meant by invoking systems was that behavior should be considered in nonindividualistic terms, that the field should move beyond the "skin-encapsulated ego" to include dyads, larger groups, and potentially the whole universe.

I have changed my mind and now believe that an individual focus is quite defensible, at least in preliminary work, and that current developments in modeling really need to emphasize internal nonlinearity, rather than moving immediately beyond the lone actor. Systems contain many internal interactions. Some interesting models are closed, except for the influence of the hand fixing initial conditions; they are not externally forced or driven and can virtually ignore the environment (or the "will," for that matter), emphasizing the multiplicity of orienting and regulative processes potentially operating within one individual. An actor's performance may be solo, but one is hardly alone within oneself. (In this sense, one is never acting alone.) Note, however, that Gottman et al.'s (2002) and Metzger's (2003) studies have a dyadic focus. Some researchers studying stress and arousal regulation (Smith & Stevens, 1997) also consider both self and other (see also Granic & Hollenstein, 2003; chapter 28, this volume).

System Positives: Looking for Mr. Good-System

Returning to the relationships between NDS approaches and positive psychology, how are nonlinear dynamics relevant to specifying and understanding well-being, health, virtue, and the positive? Can characterizing intraindividual variability, via parameters or trajectories, and examining individual differences in this variability contribute to our understanding of human strengths?

Comprehensive reviews of healthy processes noted in the literature, and of the search for what has constituted a good system through the ages, are beyond this chapter. However, among the candidates for the essence of healthy system processes are maximization (now out of favor), optimization (perhaps to follow maximization), equilibrium, balance, homeostasis, consistency, coherence, regulation, and many more.

We can distinguish a (micro) parameter-setting or model-type summum bonum from a (macro) complexity-index or behavior-pattern summum bonum. Micro-systems attributes are structures, constants, settings, or initial conditions of systems that can create or produce healthy behaviors and lead to good-enough lives. Such a micro systems virtue can also be a good-enough heuristic for getting things right. Examples of these properties include redundancy, diversity, taking advantage of multiple salutogenic factors, predictive efficiency (using simple heuristics), selective compensatory strategies (or satisficing), use of thick descriptive systems and local knowledge, distributed processing, incorporating extended time frames for intervention, and probably not simplicity or parsimony (Schuldberg, 2002). Macro descriptions refer to beneficial patterns or statistical indices summarizing over a system's behavior; a macro summum bonum describes a good system as a whole. Examples include robustness, flexibility, adaptability, creativity and inventiveness, and possibly beauty.

Candidates for systemic virtues can be found in unlikely places, very far from the literatures in medicine, mental health, and ethics. For example, references to system goods occur in economics (and agricultural economics) and political science. These systems virtues are primarily micro characteristics that suggest ways that a government or economy can be healthy. For example, drawing on Schumacher's (1999) *Small Is Beautiful*, Fawcett, Mathews, and Fletcher (1980) proposed criteria for appropriate behavioral technology, which must be inexpensive, decentralized, small-scale, flexible, and adaptable. Wendell Berry (1981), describing problem solving in agriculture, emphasized appropriate scale, balance, diversity, and quality (pp. 121–123). Finally, in *Seeing Like a State*, Scott (1998) argued for the importance of "practical knowledge, informal processes, and improvisation in the face of unpredictability," and "emphasizing process, complexity, and open-endedness" (p. 6). These can provide guidelines for solving social problems while avoiding the excesses—and perhaps catastrophic systems failures—of bureaucratic, top-down solutions.

Not all health is the same; there is likely to be more than one positive psychology, with diverse "positive psyches." The recommendation here is not to describe one universal systems summum bonum, one form of the Good Life or good form of life, but to discern diverse dynamic patterns in health, to assess individual differences in beneficial dynamics, and to model the systems that live well.

Conclusion: Future Directions for NDS Approaches

I am hopeful that new developments will include the following:

1. More widespread application of NDS-based methods in positive psychology, with an emphasis on describing process virtues and virtuous processes, the "how" of living well.
2. An increase in the software available and improvement of computer applications for intraindividual data acquisition, reduction, and analysis.
3. Greater agreement on how many data points are needed for different sorts of within-subject computations.
4. Standardization of techniques and procedures for trend removal, smoothing, filtering, noise reduction, and other data preprocessing.

5. Consensus on how to compute indices, with the dissemination of appropriate cookbooks and robust, elegant, unapologetically meat-grinder recipes.

6. More attention to methods for multivariate time series (Kantz & Schreiber, 1999; Metzger, 2003; Sprott, 2003).

7. Advances in NDS model construction and fitting techniques and specification of appropriate test statistics for evaluating the correspondence of time series and model.

8. Better integration of qualitative, descriptive look and feel, even narrative accounts of trajectories, with quantitative methods. Although published pictures of phase-space diagrams and putative attractors are widespread, it is not always clear what the pictures mean and whether claims based on them are justified (Guastello, 1995). Our eyes need training in a new type of visual interpretation of data; we need connections between quantitative and eyeballing approaches.

Increasing application of techniques based on NDS theory to specifically positive psychology topics will lead to better understanding of what health and well-being really are. This will provide a way to leave behind limitations of static, linear virtues and develop a more informed, richer, dynamic account of flourishing and good-enough living.

Stress and Coping Research

As mentioned at the beginning of this chapter, stress processes represent a productive area for joining NDS methods and positive psychology. Stress and coping have diverse theories grounded in process; they are conceptually related to health, illness, and disorder, and they span normality and pathology. We have rich data, both intra- and interindividual, and some promising dynamic models are already available (Guastello, 1995; Neufeld, 1999; Smith & Stevens, 1997), along with well-specified and well-studied cross-sectional ones (Lin & Ensel, 1990).

Stress and coping also include clearcut nonlinearities: Some involve dose-response relationships linking stress and coping processes with outcomes, for example, curvilinear functions relating arousal and performance. Others concern statistical interactions among causal variables, such as buffering effects (Cohen & Wills, 1965; Schuldberg, 2006) of stress and social support on mental health. These features readily lend themselves to NDS models. Stress research is also tied to the resourcefulness, resiliency, and coping literatures, which supply models and data on positive processes (e.g., Masten et al., 1988). While several interesting dynamic models have been suggested and simulated, more work needs to be done fitting them to observations.

This field is poised to uncover new and informative models of positive functioning, to learn how to derive them and test them against data. Once dynamic systems are proposed, we need to know how to adjust them empirically and evaluate their correspondence to real behavior. NDS models are potentially deep and theoretically relevant, and they can illuminate underlying phenomena at work in positive psychology. An individual differences approach means that we can look at variability among as well as within persons, dealing with people's diversity on two levels: I am diverse with respect to myself (both contemporaneously noncoherent and very inconsistent across time), and I sometimes differ from my neighbor.

Acknowledging both types of difference—within oneself and from others—will contribute to the ecological validity of research in positive psychology. It allows us to honor and understand the complexity of the times when we are good, and the diversity of what is good for us.

Notes

1. Degree of complexity is used here to refer to the extent of deterministic chaos in a time series. There is disagreement, however, about whether these two concepts should be used interchangeably (Kantz & Schreiber, 1999; Sprott, 2003).

2. This chapter uses the term *subject* when referring to within-subject and between-subjects methods, but uses *participants* elsewhere.

3. Indeed, a nonlinear system can have more or less grossly linear macroscopic behavior, as well as behavior that is locally linear (Mandell & Salk, 1984).

4. See note 1.

5. Note that in contrast to the prevalent view that much of the variability in data is error or noise, a complexity-based approach entertains the possibility that variation is deterministic, nonrandom, and a valuable component of measurements.

6. Assuming a correlation dimension of approximately 3.

References

Abarbanel, H. D. I. (1996). *Analysis of observed chaotic data*. New York: Springer.

Abraham, F. D., Abraham, R. H., & Shaw, C. D. (1990). *A visual introduction to dynamical systems theory for psychology*. Santa Cruz, CA: Aerial Press.

Belair, J., Glass, L., an der Heiden, U., & Milton, J. (Eds.). (1995). *Dynamical disease: Mathematical analysis of human illness*. Woodbury, NY: American Institute of Physics.

Berry, W. (1981). *The gift of good land: Further essays, cultural and agricultural*. San Francisco: North Point Press.

Bird, D. (2003, August 8). *Drawing conclusions from time series*. Workshop at the 13th Annual International Convention of the Society for Chaos Theory in Psychology and the Life Sciences, Boston, MA.

Boker, S. M. (2002). Consequences of continuity: The hunt for intrinsic properties within parameters of dynamics in psychological processes. *Multivariate Behavioral Research, 37*, 405–422.

Boker, S. M., & Nesselroade, J. R. (2002). A method for modeling the intrinsic dynamics of intraindividual viability: Recovering the parameters of simulated oscillators in multi-wave panel data. *Multivariate Behavioral Research, 37*, 127–160.

Carver, C. S., & Scheier, M. F. (2000). On the structure of behavioral self-regulation. In M. Boekaerts, P. R. Pintrich, & M. Zeidner (Eds.), *Handbook of self-regulation* (pp. 41–84). San Diego, CA: Academic Press.

Chang, E. C., & Sanna, L. J. (Eds.). (2003). *Virtue, vice, and personality: The complexity of behavior*. Washington, DC: American Psychological Association.

Cohen, S., & Wills, T. A. (1965). Stress, social support, and the buffering hypothesis. *Psychological Bulletin, 98*, 310–357.

Csete, M. E., & Doyle, J. C. (2002). Reverse engineering of biological complexity. *Science, 295*, 1664–1669.

Csikszentmihalyi, M., & Larson, R. (1984). *Being adolescent: Conflict and growth in the teenage years*. New York: Basic Books.

Fawcett, S. B., Mathews, M., & Fletcher, R. K. (1980). Some promising dimensions for behavioral community psychology. *Journal of Applied Behavior Analysis, 13*, 505–518.

Frank, A. W. (1995). *The wounded storyteller: Body, illness, and ethics*. Chicago: University of Chicago Press.

Fredrickson, B. L., & Joiner, T. (2002). Positive emotions trigger upward spirals toward emotional well-being. *Psychological Science, 12*, 172–175.

Fredrickson, B. L., & Losada, M. (2005). Positive emotions and the complex dynamics of human flourishing. *American Psychologist, 60*, 678–686.

Frisch, M. B. (1998). Quality of life therapy and assessment in health care. *Clinical Psychology: Science and Practice, 5*(1), 19–40.

Goldberger, A. L., & Rigney, D. R. (1991). Nonlinear dynamics at the bedside. In L. Glass, P. Hunter, & A. McCulloch (Eds.), *Theory of heart: Biomechanics, biophysics, and nonlinear dynamics of cardiac function* (pp. 583–605). New York: Springer-Verlag.

Gottman, J. M., Murray, J. D., Swanson, C. C., Tyson, R., & Swanson, K. R. (2002). *The mathematics of marriage: Dynamic nonlinear models*. Cambridge, MA: MIT Press.

Granic, I., & Hollenstein, T. (2003). Dynamic systems methods for models of developmental psychopathology. *Development and Psychopathology, 15*, 641–669.

Granic, I., & Patterson, G. R. (2006). Toward a comprehensive model of antisocial development: A dynamic systems approach. *Psychological Review, 113*, 101–131.

Guastello, S. J. (1995). *Chaos, catastrophe, and human affairs: Applications of nonlinear dynamics to work, organizations, and social evolution*. Mahwah, NJ: Erlbaum.

Heath, R. A. (2000). *Nonlinear dynamics: Techniques and applications in psychology*. Mahwah, NJ: Erlbaum.

Huikuri, H. V., Mäkikallio, T., Airaksinen, K. E. J., Mitrani, R., Castellanos, A., & Myerburg, R. J. (1999). Measurement of heart rate variability: Clinical tool or a research toy? *Journal of the American College of Cardiology, 34*, 1878–1883.

Hunter, K. M. (1991). *Doctors' stories: The narrative structure of medical knowledge*. Princeton, NJ: Princeton University Press.

Kantz, H., & Schreiber, T. (1999). *Nonlinear time series analysis*. New York: Cambridge University Press.

Keating, D. P., & Miller, F. K. (2000). The dynamics of emotional development: Models, metaphors, and methods. In M. D. Lewis & I. Granic (Eds.), *Emotion, development, and self-organization* (pp. 373–392). New York: Cambridge University Press.

Kreindler, D. M., & Lumsden, C. J. (2006). The effects of the irregular sample and missing data in time series analysis. *Nonlinear Dynamics, Psychology, and Life Sciences, 10*, 187–214.

Larsen, J. T., Hemenover, S. H., Norris, C. J., & Cacioppo, J. T. (2002). Turning adversity to advantage: On the virtues of the coactivation of positive and negative emotions. In L. G. Aspinwall & U. M. Staudinger (Eds.), *A psychology of human strengths: Fundamental questions and future directions for a positive psychology* (pp. 211–225). Washington, DC: American Psychological Association.

Larson, R., Csikszentmihalyi, M., & Graef, R. (1980). Mood variability and the psychosocial adjustment of adolescents. *Journal of Youth and Adolescence, 9*, 469–490.

Levine, R. L. (1992). An introduction to qualitative dynamics. In R. L. Levine & H. E. Fitzgerald (Eds.), *Analysis of dynamic psychological systems: Volume 1. Basic approaches to general systems, dynamic systems, and cybernetics* (pp. 267–330). New York: Plenum.

Levine, R. L., Van Sell, M., & Rubin, B. (1992). System dynamics and the analysis of feedback processes in social and behavioral systems. In R. L. Levine & H. E. Fitzgerald (Eds.), *Analysis of dynamic psychological systems: Volume 1. Basic approaches to general systems, dynamic systems, and cybernetics* (pp. 145–266). New York: Plenum.

Lewis, M. D., Lamey, A. V., & Douglas, L. (1999). A new dynamic systems method for the analysis of early socioemotional development. *Developmental Science, 2*, 457–475.

Lin, N., & Ensel, W. M. (1989). Life stress and health: Stressors and resources. *American Sociological Review, 54*, 382–399.

Linehan, M. M. (1993). *Cognitive-behavioral treatment of borderline personality disorder.* New York: Guilford.

Mandell, A. J., & Salk, J. (1984). Developmental fusion of intuition and reason: A metabiological ontogeny. In D. Offer & M. Sabshin (Eds.), *Normality and the life cycle: A critical integration* (pp. 302–314). New York: Basic Books.

Masten, A. S., Garmezy, N., Tellegen, A., Pellegrini, D. S., Larkin, K., & Larsen, A. (1988). Competence and stress in school children: The moderating effects of individual and family qualities. *Journal of Child Psychology and Psychiatry, 29*, 745–764.

Masterpasqua, F., & Perna, P. A. (1997). *The psychological meaning of chaos: Translating theory into practice.* Washington, DC: American Psychological Association.

Metzger, M. A. (1995). Multiprocess models of cognitive and behavioral dynamics. In R. Post &

T. van Gelder (Eds.), *Mind as motion: Dynamics, behavior, and cognition* (pp. 491–526). Cambridge, MA: MIT Press.

Metzger, M. A. (2003, August 8). *Drawing conclusions from time series.* Workshop at the 13th Annual International Convention of the Society for Chaos Theory in Psychology and the Life Sciences, Boston, MA.

Miller, J. G. (1978). *Living systems.* New York: McGraw-Hill.

Molenaar, P. C. M., & Raymakers, M. E. J. (1998). Fitting nonlinear dynamical models directly to observed time series. In K. M. Newell & P. C. M. Molenaar (Eds.), *Applications of nonlinear dynamics to developmental process modeling* (pp. 269–297). Mahwah, NJ: Erlbaum.

Morrel, T. M., Metzger, M. A., Murphy, C. M., & O'Farrell, T. J. (2006). *Multivariate time-series analysis of marital interactions: Illustrations from marital violence in alcoholics.* Manuscript in preparation.

Neufeld, R. W. J. (1999). Dynamic differentials of stress and coping. *Psychological Review, 106*, 385–397.

Pool, R. (1989). Is it healthy to be chaotic? *Science, 243*, 604–607.

Rees, J. (2002, April 26). Complex disease and the new clinical sciences. *Science, 296*, 698–701.

Schuldberg, D. (2002). Theoretical contributions of complex systems to positive psychology and health: A somewhat-complicated affair. *Nonlinear Dynamics, Psychology and Life Sciences, 6*, 335–350.

Schuldberg, D. (2006). Complicato, ma non troppo: A small nonlinear model and the good life. In A. Delle Fave (Ed.), *Dimensions of well-being: Research and intervention* (pp. 552–566). Milano: Franco Angeli.

Schuldberg, D., & Gottlieb, J. (2002). Dynamics and correlates of microscopic changes in affect. *Nonlinear Dynamics, Psychology and Life Sciences, 6*, 231–257.

Schumacher, E. F. (1999). *Small is beautiful: Economics as if people matter* (25 years later with commentary). Point Roberts, WA: Martley & Marks.

Scott, J. C. (1998). *Seeing like a state: How certain schemes to improve the human condition have failed.* New Haven, CT: Yale University Press.

Seligman, M. E. P. (2002). *Authentic happiness: Using the new positive psychology to realize your potential for lasting fulfillment.* New York: Free Press.

Seligman, M. E. P., & Csikszentmihalyi, M. (2000). Positive psychology: An introduction. *American Psychologist, 55*, 5–14.

Smith, T. S., & Stevens, G. T. (1997). Biological foundations of social interaction: Computational explorations of nonlinear dynamics in arousal modulation. In R. A. Eve, S. Horsfall, & M. E. Lee (Eds.), *Chaos, complexity, and sociology: Myths, models, and theories* (pp. 197–214). Thousand Oaks, CA: Sage.

Smith, L. B., & Thelen, E. (1993). *A dynamic systems approach to development: Applications.* Cambridge, MA: MIT Press.

Sontag, S. (1977). *Illness as metaphor.* New York: Vintage.

Sprott, J. C. (2003). *Chaos and time series analysis.* New York: Oxford University Press.

Sprott, J. C., & Rowlands, G. (1995). *Chaos data analyzer: The professional version.* New York: Physics Academic Software, American Institute of Physics.

Staddon, J. E. R. (2001). *Adaptive dynamics: The theoretical analysis of behavior.* Cambridge, MA: MIT Press.

Theiler, J., Eubank, S., Longtin, A., Galdrikian, B., & Farmer, J. D. (1992). Testing for nonlinearity in time series: The method of surrogate data. *Physica D, 58,* 77–94.

Vallacher, R. R. (Ed.). (1994). *Dynamical systems in social psychology.* San Diego, CA: Academic Press.

Vallacher, R. R., & Nowak, A. (1994). The stream of social judgment. In R. R. Vallacher (Ed.), *Dynamical systems in social psychology* (pp. 251–277). San Diego, CA: Academic Press.

Vallacher, R. R., Nowak, A., Froehlich, M., & Rockloff, M. (2002). The dynamics of self-evaluation. *Personality and Social Psychology Review, 6,* 370–379.

van Geert, P. L. (1998). Dynamic modeling of cognitive and language development: From growth processes to sudden jumps and multimodality. In K. M. Newell & P. C. M. Molenaar (Eds.), *Applications of nonlinear dynamics to developmental process modeling* (pp. 129–160). Mahwah, NJ: Erlbaum.

von Bertalanffy, L. (1968). *General systems theory: Foundations, development, applications* (rev. ed.). New York: George Braziller.

Weiner, N. (1961). *Cybernetics: Or, control and communication in the animal and the machine* (2nd ed.). New York: MIT Press and Wiley.

Weiss, J. N., Garfinkel, A., Spano, M. L., & Ditto, W. L. (1994). Chaos and chaos control in biology. *Journal of Clinical Investigation, 93,* 1355–1360.

West, B. J. (1990). *Fractal physiology and chaos in medicine.* Singapore: World Scientific.

West, B. J. (1997). Chaos and related things: A tutorial. *Journal of Mind and Behavior, 18*(2–3), 103–126.

V

Interindividual Differences in Intraindividual Change

30

Multilevel Models of Change

Fundamental Concepts and Relationships to Mixed Models and Latent Growth-Curve Models

Scott E. Maxwell and Stacey S. Tiberio

In their classic article, Cronbach and Furby (1970) recommended that psychologists interested in studying change "frame their questions other ways" (p. 80). Fortunately, in the intervening years methodologists have taken up the challenge to develop better methods of understanding change. In the last two decades, new methods have appeared that offer not just new ways of analyzing data but, more important, fundamentally different conceptualizations of change itself.

The purpose of this chapter is to provide a broad overview and brief introduction to one of these ways of conceptualizing change: multilevel models. In particular, this chapter consists of several major sections: (1) a description of the types of data structures for which multilevel models are appropriate; (2) a review of standard analysis of variance (ANOVA) methods for analyzing data, to establish a context for understanding the newer methods; (3) an introduction to multilevel models for simple data structures; (4) a brief overview of the relationship between multilevel models and mixed models; and (5) a conceptual demonstration

of the comparability of multilevel models and latent growth-curve models.

It is useful to establish some terminology and notation at the beginning. Multilevel models are often also referred to as *hierarchical linear models*. In many situations, multilevel models can also be conceptualized as mixed models. Because of its popularity in psychology, we often use the abbreviation HLM to refer to the class of multilevel models. Similarly, we use the abbreviation LGC to refer to the class of latent growth-curve models.

Prototypic Data Structures

The most basic data structure for which the methods to be described here are appropriate is a simple design where multiple individuals are measured on a single dependent variable at multiple time points. For example, positive affect might be measured in a group of 40 individuals at 3-month intervals for a year, yielding five scores per individual (at time points we could label as 0,

3, 6, 9, and 12 months). We will see later in the chapter that there are a variety of questions that could be addressed even in this very simple design, but the most typical question would involve whether the data imply a difference in the population mean of positive affect over time. For example, is mean positive affect increasing during this 12-month period? Psychologists trained from an ANOVA tradition should immediately recognize this as a straightforward repeated-measures design, also referred to as a within-subjects design or a subjects-by-time design. From an ANOVA perspective, this can be thought of as a two-factor design, with subjects as a random effect and time as a fixed effect. Standard experimental design texts such as Kirk (1995) and Maxwell and Delaney (2004) explain that the difference between a random effect and a fixed effect pertains to how the levels of the factor are chosen for inclusion in the design. In particular, as the name implies, levels of a random factor are randomly selected from a population of potential levels. For example, each research participant is ideally randomly selected from a population of potential participants, in which case "subjects" is a random factor. In contrast, the levels of the time factor reflect the occasions at which the investigator has chosen to obtain data. It would be unlikely for the specific occasions of measurement to be chosen at random. Instead, the investigator is likely to choose the specific occasions of 0, 3, 6, 9, and 12 months because there are theoretical reasons for believing that intervals of 3 months are appropriate for assessing the dependent measure in question, such as positive affect. From a data analytic perspective, it is important to distinguish random and fixed effects because statistical tests and confidence intervals can be affected by whether factors are fixed or random. When the time factor is fixed but the subjects factor is random, an F test of mean change across time is obtained by dividing the mean square of time by the mean square of the interaction of time by subjects. Intuitively, the numerator represents the magnitude of average change, whereas the denominator represents the extent to which the pattern and magnitude of change differ across individuals. This simple idea provides a foundation for understanding the newer methods to be presented in this chapter.

Limitations of ANOVA

To understand the connection between the simple ANOVA approach and the newer methods, it is helpful to understand the limitations of the ANOVA approach. In particular, the ANOVA approach is well suited and even possesses optimal properties for understanding change in certain situations, but these situations turn out to be extremely limited in practice. Unless all of these restrictive conditions are met, ANOVA loses many of its desirable advantages.

First, ANOVA requires complete data. However, in almost all longitudinal studies, at least some data points will be lost due to attrition of individuals over time as well as other factors beyond the investigator's control. Notice that the planned design of measuring positive affect at five time points for 40 individuals should produce a total of 200 positive affect scores. Except when the investigator is fortunate to have a captive group of research participants, it is highly unlikely to obtain all 200 scores in such a longitudinal design. A number of ad hoc methods have been developed in the ANOVA literature for handling missing data, the most notable being mean substitution and casewise deletion. However, as Schafer and Graham (2002) have shown, both mean substitution and casewise deletion require highly restrictive assumptions in order to handle missing data appropriately. In general, these methods typically introduce bias unless the data are missing completely at random (MCAR), which means that the missingness is unrelated to any variables included in the analysis. Although this is certainly a theoretical possibility, it seems more likely in most psychological studies that the missingness is in fact related to one or more variables measured in the study and included in the data analysis. In this case, statisticians have developed a further distinction between data that are missing at random (MAR) and data that are not missing at random (MNAR). The former means that the missingness is random conditional on certain measured variables, whereas the latter means that it is not. Further details on this distinction are provided in Schafer and Graham (2002). Neither HLM nor LGC requires that the missingness be MCAR. However, both do make the weaker assumption that the missingness is MAR. More generally, HLM and LGC allow the researcher to use all of the data that has been collected, without having to omit subjects and without having to substitute scores for missing data. Indeed, we suspect that in some researchers' minds, this is the reason for the existence of HLM and LGC. Although the ability to proceed with analyses in the face of missing data is a vital advantage of these two methods, we nevertheless feel compelled to emphasize once again that both HLM and LGC still require assumptions about the nature of missing data.

It is also important to note that even if a researcher could succeed in obtaining measures of positive affect at all five time points for all 40 research participants, it is nevertheless unlikely that all measures are obtained literally at the precisely planned times. In other words, the ANOVA design requires that all assessments at the second wave be obtained at the same time for each individual. ANOVA can easily address unequal spacing of time points, so in this respect it is not critical that the second-wave data be collected at exactly the planned moment of 3 months subsequent to baseline. However, it is critical in ANOVA that all Wave 2 measurements be obtained at the same time for each individual. For example, ANOVA could easily handle every person measured 96 days after baseline even though this is clearly later than 3 months. However, ANOVA could not easily handle some individuals measured 88 days after baseline, some other individuals measured at 91 days, and yet others at 96 days. Instead, ANOVA would require that the spacing between time points be identical for each person, regardless of whether the spacing also happens to be equal or unequal. One way of expressing this point is that ANOVA requires balanced data, which means that every person is measured at the exact same occasion and there are no missing data. In contrast, HLM and LGC can handle unbalanced data, where either not everyone is measured at the exact same times, or there are missing data, or both.

Second, the utility of HLM and LGC for handling missing data is so important to longitudinal researchers that it is easy to lose sight of the fact that HLM and LGC provide other equally important advantages over standard ANOVA methods for analyzing longitudinal data. In our judgment, a major limitation of ANOVA is that it focuses narrowly on only one aspect of the data. Specifically, ANOVA addresses a question of mean change. Of course, many fundamental questions in psychological research reduce to questions of mean differences. For this reason, we want to be clear from the outset that HLM and LGC can also answer questions about means. Furthermore, HLM and LGC can sometimes provide better answers to questions about mean change than can ANOVA. One reason that psychological research often focuses on mean change

is that complex questions regarding means can be addressed by incorporating additional factors in the design. For example, in addition to measuring positive affect for 40 individuals at five time points, we might also designate each person as either female or male. The inclusion of a between-subjects factor such as gender opens opportunities for beginning to compare different types of individuals and in particular to examine whether some types display different patterns of change.

Although ANOVA can be expanded in this manner, there are nevertheless many potential questions of interest that ANOVA is not designed to answer. For example, ANOVA does not directly provide information about individual change. Instead, its focus is on mean change. However, psychologists may be more interested in aspects of individual change than in the mean change for a group. New methods of analysis such as HLM and LGC can answer interesting questions about individual change. Furthermore, ANOVA is limited to simple data structures. In reality, however, in addition to measuring positive affect at five time points, we may have also measured negative affect at each of these time points. Although ANOVA could be expanded to MANOVA (multivariate analysis of variance), offering some opportunity to examine correlations as well as means, the model limits the types of questions that could be addressed. HLM and LGC offer many more opportunities in this regard. We may also have measured one or more stable personality traits at baseline. Because such measures are likely to be continuous instead of categorical, they cannot be directly incorporated into ANOVA. Although it would be possible to expand the ANOVA into a general linear model formulation, once again there are additional advantages to an HLM or LGC formulation. Our basic point is that thinking in terms of ANOVA runs a serious risk of greatly restricting researchers' imaginations of the types of research questions they might choose to study. In contrast, HLM and LGC open new vistas for different ways of conceptualizing change, an advantage that stretches far beyond the ability to address problems of missing data.

Third, ANOVA also suffers from a statistical limitation. F tests and confidence intervals require an assumption of sphericity (cf. Maxwell & Delaney, 2004). In practice, this assumption implies that the covariance matrix underlying multiple measures will possess compound symmetry, which in turn implies that any pair of measurements obtained at different time points will have a constant correlation regardless of the spacing between the two time points. For example, according to this assumption, positive affect scores at 3 months and 12 months will correlate the same (in the population) as positive affect scores at 9 months and 12 months. In most situations, correlations actually will be higher for measures spaced more closely in time to one another, in which case the assumption will not hold. One solution to this problem is to use MANOVA instead of ANOVA. Although this successfully circumvents the sphericity assumption, it has its own disadvantages. In particular, MANOVA offers no advantage in this context over ANOVA for handling missing data and also continues to focus primarily on the narrow question of mean change. Once again, HLM and LGC offer alternatives that have the same advantage as MANOVA of not requiring sphericity but offer the additional advantages of handling missing data and addressing a wider range of questions. Furthermore, these alternative methods provide other ways of modeling the covariance structure that represent a compromise between ANOVA and MANOVA. Maxwell and Delaney (2004) provided an introduction to this advantage of these methods, as illustrated most explicitly by SAS PROC MIXED.

Hierarchical Linear Models

Conceptual Rationale for HLM

Analysis of variance is a prototypic method for understanding a phenomenon at a group level. As such, it corresponds to the nomothetic side of psychology, as expressed by Allport (1946). A recurring issue underlying much of the scientific study of human behavior and cognition has been the distinctive advantages of the nomothetic and idiographic approaches to knowledge. Not surprisingly, this issue is also relevant for studying change. Developmental psychologists such as Wohlwill (1973) as well as methodologists such as Nesselroade (1991) and Rogosa (1988) have argued that understanding the true psychological nature of change necessitates understanding change at the individual level, thus requiring an idiographic approach. An essential strength of HLM is that it is ideally suited to understanding change from an idiographic perspective. However, unlike many single-subject designs that suffer from the lack of a clear method for generalizing idiographic results to a broader no-

mothetic perspective, HLM explicitly combines idiographic and nomothetic perspectives. Indeed, the term *multilevel* literally corresponds to one level for each individual and another level for the group.

The essential idea of multilevel modeling in a longitudinal context is to formulate two different models, one that represents individual change and another that represents phenomena across individuals. The essence of multilevel modeling is to formulate these two models in such a way that information about individuals can be passed to the model for phenomena across individuals.

HLM Model Formulation

We will use the data in table 30.1 to illustrate basic principles of multilevel modeling as applied to longitudinal data. We will suppose that an investigator has measured positive affect for 20 adolescents at three time points. The three time points correspond to the beginning of 10th

TABLE 30.1 Hypothetical Positive Affect Scores for 20 Individuals at Three Points in Time

	Grade Level	
10	11	12
Females		
49	37	45
51	56	—
60	57	64
35	36	42
44	49	42
32	28	33
34	30	39
42	55	41
33	42	—
41	49	57
45	56	—
Males		
56	45	37
54	50	52
56	50	—
36	24	34
48	47	—
35	47	39
37	36	—
67	74	65
28	11	24

Note: A missing data point is designated by a dash.

grade, 11th grade, and 12th grade. We will also assume that 11 of the adolescents are females and 9 are males. For the sake of realism, we will also assume that the investigator was not able to obtain measures on everyone at the beginning of 12th grade, resulting in some missing data. (It is important to realize that HLM and LGC approaches can also be used when data are missing at other time points.) We have purposely kept the sample size unrealistically small here in order to make it easy to duplicate our results.

The first step in forming an HLM model for longitudinal data is to develop a model of change for each individual. This model specifies scores on the measure of interest (positive affect in our example) as a function of time. In principle, this function can take on a variety of possible mathematical forms. In practice, most applications of HLM in psychology to date have been based on polynomial models. In other words, the score is expressed in terms of powers (i.e., linear, quadratic, cubic, etc.) of time.

In this context, the individual-level model is known as a Level 1 model. For the data of table 30.1, we will assume that a straight-line growth model is reasonable. In other words, a straight-line growth model presumes that if we could eliminate all sources of error (such as error of measurement) from our data, we would observe each individual's scores changing as a linear function of time. There are a variety of reasons that a straight-line model is frequently the Level 1 model of choice in psychology (Willett, 1989), but all too often a driving force is sheer practicality. The number of powers of time that can be included in the model is limited by the number of time points. With three time points, only one power of time can be specified at the individual level. Although it would be mathematically possible to specify this single power as the square of time (for example), it is not possible with three time points to specify both time itself and the square of time. In most circumstances, it is sensible to include only time itself if forced to choose a single power to include in the model. Even if the real function is not linear, the results can sometimes but not always be interpreted in terms of average rate of change (Willett, 1989). Especially when the true function is anticipated to be nonlinear, the only real solution is to obtain measures at more than three time points.

For our purposes, we will assume that a straight-line model is reasonable for the data of table 30.1. A straight-line growth model for each individual can be written as

$$Y_{it} = \beta_{0i} + \beta_{1i}a_{it} + \varepsilon_{it} \qquad (1)$$

where Y_{it} is the score on the dependent variable for individual i at time t and a_{it} represents a measure of the time at which the Y observation was taken for individual i at time t. At first glance, the i and t subscripts on the a variable might seem superfluous. In reality, however, they play a central role in multilevel modeling. In particular, the i subscript allows different individuals to be measured at different time points. Similarly, the t subscript allows the occasions of measurement to be either equally or unequally spaced. For example, research participant 1 might be measured at the beginning of grades 10, 11, and 12, in which case the a values for this individual would be denoted as $a_{11} = 10$, $a_{12} = 11$, and $a_{13} = 12$. There is no requirement that that the second research participant be measured at these same times. Instead, if this individual were measured at the beginning of the 10th grade, the middle of the 11th grade, and in the middle of the fall semester of 12th grade, the corresponding a values for this individual would be denoted as $a_{21} = 10$, $a_{22} = 11.5$, and $a_{23} = 12.25$. One of the potential advantages of the multilevel modeling approach to longitudinal data is that by allowing each individual to have different values of the a variable, it becomes straightforward to handle situations where different individuals are measured on different occasions. This proves to be especially advantageous in situations where such differences arise because of missing data.

Notice that the model in Equation 1 contains two parameters for each individual, namely an intercept β_{0i} and a slope β_{1i}. The model also allows for error, which reflects all influences that cause observed scores on Y to deviate from a straight line. Especially important is the fact that each individual is allowed to have his or her own value of each parameter, as reflected by the i subscript for these parameters. Thus, while each individual is presumed to follow the same general functional form of change (in this case a straight line), there is no assumption that each individual has the same parameter values, so the specific nature of change is allowed to differ across individuals. As a result, some individuals may have higher intercepts than others, and some individuals may have steeper slopes than others. We will see later that the intercept and the slope may or may not correlate with one another. In other words, the individuals with higher intercepts might also tend to have steeper slopes, or they might tend to have shallower slopes. Alternatively, there might be no relationship whatsoever between intercepts and slopes.

Before proceeding further, it is important to say more about the intercept and slope parameters. In particular, what does it mean that these are literally parameters? The idea here is that each individual has some true but unknown value for both the intercept and the slope of the straight line that is assumed to describe the trajectory of their change over time. There is a very close parallel here with classical test theory, where a person's observed score on some measure is expressed as the sum of their true score and error:

$$X_i = T_i + E_i \qquad (2)$$

Notice that Equation 2 describes how scores will vary from one testing situation to another for a single individual. Examples of situations in this context are a parallel form or a test-restest paradigm. Equation 2 is similar to Equation 1 in that both equations explain why scores within a person may not remain constant. However, Equation 1, unlike Equation 2, describes how scores for this individual will change in some systematic manner as a function of time. The true score T_i in Equation 2 is unknown and in practice unknowable. The best we can hope to do in practice is to estimate any individual's true score. The same is true for the intercept and slope in Equation 1. The parameters β_{0i} and β_{1i} are true scores that cannot be directly observed. Readers who are familiar with structural equation modeling might suspect that this notion of true scores sounds a lot like the idea of latent variables. In fact, there is a definite connection, as expressed, for example, by confirmatory factor analysis. There is a similar connection for longitudinal data. As we will see later in the chapter, we can conceptualize the intercept β_{0i} and the slope β_{1i} as latent variables from the perspective of structural equation modeling, which then leads to latent growth-curve modeling.

The mathematical formulation of the Level 1 model considers only one level of the data, namely data at the level of an individual. We can now augment this idiographic view by developing a nomothetic model across individuals. The fundamental idea here is that the Level 1 model contains information for each individual in the form of the parameters of the model. In the

specific case of a straight-line growth model as in Equation 1, the idiographic information consists of an intercept β_{0i} and a slope β_{1i} for each individual. The nomothetic perspective considers these parameter values across individuals.

Notice that the Level 1 model specifies how scores change across time for a given individual. The nomothetic Level 2 model specifies how change differs across individuals. Specifically, the Level 2 model specifies how Level 1 parameters of change differ across individuals. For this reason, the Level 2 model will consist of as many equations as there are parameters in the Level 1 model. Recall that the Level 1 model for straight-line growth contains two parameters for each individual. Thus, in this case, the Level 2 model will explain individual differences in two parameters. Doing so entails two equations, one for the intercept parameter and another for the slope parameter. A simple example of Level 2 equations for the intercept and slope from the Level 1 model shown in Equation 1 would be

$$\beta_{0i} = \gamma_{00} + U_{0i} \qquad (3)$$

$$\beta_{1i} = \gamma_{10} + U_{1i} \qquad (4)$$

Equation 3 formulates the distribution of intercept parameters across individuals in terms of a grand mean parameter γ_{00} and a unique effect U_{0i}. Notice that there is no i subscript for the grand mean parameter γ_{00} because this parameter, unlike the Level 1 parameters, does not differ from one individual to another. Instead, γ_{00} is the population mean intercept. As a result, U_{0i} is the difference between the population mean intercept and the intercept for individual i. It then follows that every individual will have the same value of U_{0i} only if everyone has the same true intercept. To the extent that different individuals have different intercepts, their values of U_{0i} will differ from one another. In this respect, the variance of U_{0i} reveals the extent to which individuals differ in their intercepts. A similar interpretation holds for the slope parameter, as shown in Equation 4. Specifically, γ_{10} is the population mean slope, and U_{1i} is the difference between the mean slope and the slope for individual i.

As we have just seen, Equations 3 and 4 specify the population mean and population variance of the intercept and slope parameters. The crucial concept here is that in any population of individuals, each person is allowed to have his or her own value of the intercept and slope that describe the presumed straight-line trajectory of change over time. Thus, from the perspective of the population, we can conceptualize both the intercept and the slope as random variables with some type of distribution. The typical assumption is that the intercept and slope parameters have a bivariate normal distribution. This implies that each univariate distribution is normal, so if we could measure each individual's true intercept (or true slope) in an entire population, we would obtain a normal distribution. In this sense, γ_{00} is the mean intercept in this normal distribution of intercepts. Similarly, γ_{10} is the mean slope in a comparable normal distribution of slopes. These two mean parameters, γ_{00} and γ_{10}, are referred to as fixed effects because they do not vary across individuals. The other parameter of any normal distribution besides its mean is its variance (or its standard deviation). Considered simultaneously, the intercept and slope are assumed to have a bivariate normal distribution, which necessitates yet one more parameter, namely the correlation (or the covariance) between the intercept and the slope. Because individual differences in the intercept and the slope are captured by the U_{0i} and U_{1i} parameters, the correlation between the intercept and the slope is identical to the correlation between U_{0i} and U_{1i}. These U variables are referred to as random effects because unlike γ_{00} and γ_{10}, they vary across individuals.

Because the intercept β_{0i} and the slope β_{1i} are true scores (i.e., latent variables), they cannot be directly observed. Despite this limitation, it turns out that it is possible to estimate relevant properties of these variables. In particular, interest will frequently center on estimating the mean intercept and the mean slope. We may also want to know whether one group of individuals has a larger mean than another group. For example, we might want to know whether females have a larger mean intercept than males, or whether a treatment group has a larger mean slope than a control group. The other three parameters of potential interest are (1) the variance of the intercept, (2) the variance of the slope, and (3) the correlation (or covariance) between the intercept and the slope. As is the case with the mean, although we cannot directly observe anyone's true intercept or slope, we can nevertheless estimate all of these parameters of the presumed bivariate normal distribution. Yet another parameter in the model is the variance of the Level 1 error term ε. Although this term plays an important role in the estimation process, it is rarely of direct interest itself.

As a matter of notation, the parameters in the multilevel model depicted by Equations 1, 3, and 4 are:

γ_{00}, the population mean intercept averaging across individuals

γ_{10}, the population mean slope averaging across individuals

$\sigma^2_{U_{0i}}$, the population variance of intercepts

$\sigma^2_{U_{1i}}$, the population variance of slopes

$\rho_{U_{0i}U_{1i}}$, the population correlation of intercepts and slopes

σ^2_{ε}, the population within-person residual variance

It is important to keep in mind that the straight-line growth model shown in Equation 1 is only one of many possible idiographic models that could be stipulated for individual trajectories of change over time. For example, as we mentioned earlier, one option would be to include higher powers of time in the model, such as the square of time or the cube of time. Such terms would allow an examination of the extent to which individual growth trajectories do not follow a straight line. Yet another approach is to use functions that fall outside the polynomial model. Examples of such models are described in such references as Davidian and Giltinan (1995), Pinheiro and Bates (2000), and Vonesh and Chinchilli (1996).

Less obvious is that yet an entirely different type of predictor could also be included as a predictor in the Level 1 model. So far, we have only considered different functional manifestations of time, but the predictor variable itself has always represented some aspect of time per se. However, from a statistical perspective, any variable that changes with time is a potential Level 1 predictor. For example, suppose we are interested in understanding how positive affect changes over time. In other words, the outcome variable Y in the Level 1 model such as that shown in Equation 1 would be a measure of positive affect, which would then be measured repeatedly over time. However, another variable that we would expect to change over time would be negative affect. It would be entirely possible to include a measure of negative affect as another Level 1 predictor variable, resulting in a

Level 1 model of the general form:

$$Y_{it} = \beta_{0i} + \beta_{1i}a_{it} + \beta_{2i}X_{it} + \varepsilon_{it} \qquad (5)$$

where X_{it} represents the negative affect score for individual i at time t. The corresponding regression coefficient β_{2i} then represents the relationship between negative affect and positive affect over time, controlling for the linear effect of time itself. A variable such as X_{it} is referred to as a time-varying covariate because values of this variable change over time and potentially covary with the outcome variable Y. It is especially interesting to notice that adding the time-varying covariate X_{it} to the Level 1 model will alter the value and the meaning of the β_{1i} slope coefficient to the extent that the time-varying covariate changes with time (technically, to the extent that it correlates with the time variable a_{it}). In particular, the β_{1i} slope coefficient in the model that includes negative affect now represents the slope relating positive affect and time at a fixed value of negative affect (i.e., controlling for the linear effect of negative affect). Similarly, the β_{2i} slope coefficient for negative affect reflects the slope relating positive affect to negative affect at a fixed value of time (i.e., controlling for the linear effect of time). It is entirely possible that the researcher might believe that the within-person relationship between positive affect and negative affect becomes either weaker or stronger over time. In such a case, it may be advisable to include the product of time and negative affect as another term in the model (i.e., include a third predictor variable of the form $a_{it} X_{it}$ in Equation 5), just as is sometimes done in multiple regression analysis (see Aiken & West, 1991, for excellent coverage of this topic). The flexibility of the Level 1 model thus opens up a wide range of different types of questions one could ask about the nature of change trajectories in Y over time.

Similarly, other types of models could be specified at Level 2. In particular, it is possible to include additional predictor variables in the Level 2 model. Any variable that differs between individuals is potentially a candidate for inclusion in the Level 2 model. Some examples of such variables would include experimental condition, gender, and Beck Depression Inventory (BDI) score at a fixed point in time. Notice that Level 2 variables do not vary across time. So although the BDI score may certainly change over time, it is included as a Level 2 predictor because it is measured at some fixed point in time, and there is presumably some theoretical

reason to consider its role as measured at this time point vis-à-vis the change parameters of the variable measured at multiple time points. Also, potential Level 2 predictor variables can be either categorical (such as experimental condition and gender) or continuous (such as BDI).

Level 2 models such as Equations 3 and 4 that include only an intercept term (along with a unique effect) as a predictor are referred to as *unconditional models*. In contrast, Level 2 models that include one or more predictors (such as experimental condition, gender, or BDI score) in addition to the intercept (and the unique effect) are referred to as *conditional models*. For example, consider our example where we model change in positive affect in terms of straight-line growth, as reflected by Equation 1. We might now specify that both the intercept and the slope of this trajectory are related to an individual's gender. In this case, we would modify Equations 3 and 4 as follows:

$$\beta_{0i} = \gamma_{00} + \gamma_{01}X_i + U_{0i} \qquad (6)$$

$$\beta_{1i} = \gamma_{10} + \gamma_{11}X_i + U_{1i} \qquad (7)$$

where X_i represents each individual's gender. More generally, X_i could be any variable that varies between individuals.

An earlier statement in the chapter mentioned that multilevel models are sometimes referred to as mixed-effects models, and indeed one of the more popular ways of analyzing data with these models is to use PROC MIXED in SAS. It is straightforward to illustrate the sense in which the HLM models we have presented can also be conceptualized as mixed models. In particular, let's return to Equations 1, 6, and 7. For convenience, Equation 1 is repeated below:

$$Y_{it} = \beta_{0i} + \beta_{1i}a_{it} + \varepsilon_{it} \quad (1, \text{ repeated})$$

Notice that Equation 1 contains β_{0i} and β_{1i} on the right side of the equals sign. However, Equations 6 and 7 provide information about these parameters, making it possible to substitute what we know from Equations 6 and 7 into Equation 1. The resultant equation can be written as

$$Y_{it} = \gamma_{00} + \gamma_{01}X_i + U_{0i} \\ + (\gamma_{10} + \gamma_{11}X_i + U_{1i})a_{it} + \varepsilon_{it} \qquad (8)$$

Rearranging terms yields

$$Y_{it} = \gamma_{00} + \gamma_{01}X_i + \gamma_{10}a_{it} + \gamma_{11}X_i a_{it} \\ + U_{0i} + U_{1i}a_{it} + \varepsilon_{it} \qquad (9)$$

Equation 9 shows that the HLM model can be conceptualized as expressing Y as a combination of fixed effects and random effects. Notice that a portion of the right side of Equation 9 looks like a typical regression equation. Specifically, suppose we had a model of the form

$$Y_{it} = \gamma_{00} + \gamma_{01}X_i + \gamma_{10}a_{it} + \gamma_{11}X_ia_{it} + \varepsilon_{it} \quad (10)$$

This model stipulates that Y is a function of X, a, and the interaction of X with a. Such a model (which consists entirely of fixed effects, except for the error term) could be fit with ordinary least squares (assuming that the usual OLS assumptions were reasonable), and would not require HLM. In reality, however, the longitudinal model of Equation 9 contains two additional terms, namely U_{0i} and U_{1i}. The presence of these random effects in the model provides one way of conceptualizing how HLM differs from ordinary multiple regression analysis. Because the model for Y shown in Equation 9 contains both fixed and random effects, it is referred to as a mixed model. Thus, we have seen how the basic multilevel model can also be thought of as a mixed model.

Numerical Example

Having developed the basic conceptualization of multilevel modeling of longitudinal data, we will now use the data from table 30.1 to illustrate potential practical advantages of this approach. In particular, we will compare ANOVA and HLM analyses of these data. We need to stress that our presentation here is intended simply to highlight benefits of HLM. As such, we do not attempt to provide a thorough analysis of these data, which ideally should consider such issues as distributional assumptions and appropriateness of the model itself. Our goal here is to focus narrowly on gender differences in this example, but it is also important to realize that many other questions of possible interest can be answered with this approach.

ANOVA

From an ANOVA perspective, we can conceptualize these data in terms of a two-factor design, where gender is a between-subjects factor and grade is a within-subjects factor. We will assume that the primary question of interest is whether females and males show different mean changes in positive affect from 10th grade to 12th grade. As such, the effect of greatest interest from an ANOVA perspective is the interaction between gender and grade.

As discussed in many experimental design texts (e.g., Kirk, 1995; Maxwell & Delaney, 2004), there are two basic types of ANOVA tests that can be used to test within-subjects effects, such as the gender by grade interaction of interest here: univariate mixed model or multivariate. In the interest of completeness, we report both types of tests. First, the gender by grade interaction is nonsignificant, $F(2, 24) = 1.299$, $p = .291$, using the univariate mixed-model ANOVA approach. Second, the interaction is also nonsignificant, $F(2, 11) = 1.776$, $p = .215$, using the multivariate approach.

A reasonable argument could be made that we might be especially interested in the linear trend of grade level here. Following this argument, instead of performing an omnibus test of the global grade by gender interaction, we might prefer to test the more focused interaction contrast of the linear trend of grade by gender. Doing so for these data results in a test that just misses being statistically significant at the .05 level, as reflected by $F(1, 12) = 3.873$, $p = .073$.

A major disadvantage of the ANOVA perspective is that all individuals with missing data are eliminated from the analysis. Notice, for example, that the F statistic for the interaction contrast of the linear trend of grade by gender has 12 denominator degrees of freedom. With a total sample size of 20 split into two groups, we would expect this effect to yield 18 denominator degrees of freedom. However, the ANOVA approach excludes the six individuals who are missing a positive affect score in the 12th grade. As a result, the ANOVA results are literally based on only the 14 individuals who provided complete data. Thus, we have effectively discarded 30% of the research participants by analyzing the data this way. One obvious consequence is that power is almost certain to suffer. Less obvious is that unless the missingness mechanism is completely random (i.e., MCAR), the ANOVA approach may also introduce biased parameter estimates. In this particular case, the ANOVA approach estimates the mean difference in slopes between females and males as 3.71. In other words, the single best estimate is that on average, females' positive affect is increasing by 3.71 units per month more than males' positive affect between 10th and 12th grade. A corresponding 95% confidence interval would stretch from -0.40 to 7.81. The fact that this interval contains zero is consistent with the fact that the test itself is nonsignificant at the .05 level.

HLM

The HLM approach also provides a test of whether females and males differ in their mean slopes between 10th grade and 12th grade. Specifically, recall that the γ_{11} parameter in Equation 7 reflects this difference. When the X variable representing gender has been coded in a manner so that the score for one gender differs from the score for the other gender by one unit, the γ_{11} parameter literally equals the mean slope difference. For example, we could code females as 1 and males as 0 on the Level 2 X variable shown in Equation 7. Doing so and analyzing the table 30.1 data with HLM produces a statistically significant effect for the γ_{11} parameter, $t(18) = 2.14$, $p = .046$. Notice that HLM identified a statistically significant gender difference in slopes over time, unlike the ANOVA approaches, which were unable to detect any gender differences in change. We should be cautious not to draw any general conclusions on the basis of a single data set (even though we know that these data were generated by a population model where a gender difference truly exists), but we safely state that the HLM approach will generally provide more power for detecting nonnull effects when some data are missing.

Forming a confidence interval may provide a valuable adjunct to the significant gender difference in slopes. According to the HLM analysis, a 95% confidence interval for the γ_{11} parameter stretches from 0.08 to 8.56. This interval has exactly the same interpretation as the ANOVA-based confidence interval for the gender difference in slopes. However, the HLM interval for these data differs in three important ways.

First, unlike the ANOVA-based interval, the HLM-based interval does not contain zero. Thus, only the HLM interval provides clear evidence that the population parameter is greater than zero. In other words, only the HLM-based interval allows a conclusion that females have steeper slopes than males in the population.

Second, the center of the HLM-based interval is slightly further from zero than is the ANOVA-based interval. If there were no missing data, the intervals would be centered at the same value. However, with missing data, the centers of the intervals will typically differ. In any given data set containing missing data, the intervals might be centered at different values either due to chance or because the ANOVA-based interval requires stronger assumptions about the missing data mechanism and thus can be biased (i.e., the center of the interval is systematically either too high or too low) when the HLM-based interval can be unbiased.

Third, with missing data, the HLM-based interval will tend to be narrower and thus more precise than the ANOVA-based interval. The ANOVA-based interval is based on casewise deletion, and as such ignores any individual with less than complete data. In the numerical example, six individuals are missing a score at 12th grade, so the analysis is based on only the 14 individuals with complete data. Stated differently, ANOVA makes use of a total of 42 positive affect scores, namely three scores for each of 14 individuals. In contrast, HLM uses every observed positive affect score. In the numerical example, HLM makes use of all 54 nonmissing positive affect scores.

HLM is able to use information contained in the data for the six individuals missing scores at 12th grade because of the manner in which the model is formulated. Specifically, HLM can estimate a slope and an intercept for each individual as shown in Equation 1, even though some individuals do not have three waves of data. Conceptually, all 20 slope estimates can be incorporated into Equation 7, and all 20 intercept estimates can be incorporated into Equation 6. Thus, individuals with less than complete data can still contribute to estimates of gender differences. In effect, HLM estimates Level 2 parameters by downweighting those individuals with less than complete data, because their idiographic intercept and slope estimates are less reliable than for those individuals with complete data. However, HLM does not give them a weight of zero, as happens implicitly with ANOVA. As a result, HLM makes better use of the available information, thus relaxing the assumptions under which valid results can be obtained with missing data as well as increasing power and precision. Of course, all this does not take place without some mathematical justification. Parameter estimation in HLM is usually based on maximum likelihood or a variation called *restricted maximum likelihood*. Interested readers are referred to such texts as Raudenbush and Bryk (2001), Verbeke and Molenberghs (2000), and Fitzmaurice, Laird, and Ware (2004) for more details.

Latent Growth-Curve Models

There is a mathematical connection between multilevel models of change and structural equation models of change. In particular, as discussed earlier, Level 1 parameters such as the intercept β_{0i} and the slope β_{1i} can be conceptualized as latent variables. This conceptualization certainly hints at a possible connection, but structural equation modeling is usually thought of in terms of a model whose purpose is to explain observed relationships among manifest variables. As it turns out, this also proves to be a perfectly valid way of thinking about multilevel models, which then leads to an explicit connection to structural equation models.

To understand this connection, we will return to the multilevel model shown in Equations 1, 3, and 4. Although it may not be immediately obvious, this model makes specific predictions about variances and covariances of the outcome variable Y measured at multiple time points. Straightforward application of rules of covariance algebra (such as those presented in Kenny, 1979) shows that according to the model, the population variance of Y at any given time point t will be given by:

$$\text{var}(Y_t) = \sigma_{\beta_0}^2 + a_t^2 \sigma_{\beta_1}^2 + 2a_t \rho_{\beta_0\beta_1} \sigma_{\beta_0} \sigma_{\beta_1} + \sigma_\varepsilon^2$$

$$(11)$$

where $\rho_{\beta_0\beta_1}$ is the population correlation between the intercept and the slope. (Notice that this correlation could also be expressed as $\rho_{U_0 U_1}$, but we have chosen to write it in terms of the Level 1 coefficients to make the meaning clearer.) Similarly, according to the model, the population covariance between scores at two time points t and t' will be given by:

$$\text{cov}(Y_t, Y_{t'}) = \sigma_{\beta_0}^2 + a_t a_{t'} \sigma_{\beta_1}^2 + (a_t + a_{t'}) \rho_{\beta_0\beta_1} \sigma_{\beta_0} \sigma_{\beta_1}$$

$$(12)$$

The important point of Equations 11 and 12 is that the multilevel model formulation implies

that variances and covariances of the outcome variable Y measured at multiple time points will depend on the model parameters and the occasions of measurement.

To demonstrate the implications of Equations 11 and 12, consider the implications of the multilevel model for a design with three equally spaced time points, as in the numerical example of table 30.1. Following typical conventions, suppose time is scaled as 0, 1, and 2, so that the intercept of the Level 1 model corresponds to the value of Y at the beginning of the study. Substituting a values of 0, 1, and 2 into Equations 11 and 12 reveals, according to the multilevel model, the population covariance model for Y measured at these three time points (see Equation 13, bottom of page). All terms are as before except that the subscript for the correlation ρ between the intercept and the slope has been dropped for simplicity.

To gain a better understanding of the covariance matrix shown in Equation 13, it may be helpful to consider a few special cases. First, suppose that individuals do not differ in their true intercepts or slopes. In this case, both $\sigma_{\beta_0}^2$ and $\sigma_{\beta_1}^2$ will equal zero, as will ρ (there can be no correlation when there is no variance). In this case, the covariance matrix shown in Equation 13 simplifies to

$$\begin{bmatrix} \sigma_\varepsilon^2 & 0 & 0 \\ 0 & \sigma_\varepsilon^2 & 0 \\ 0 & 0 & \sigma_\varepsilon^2 \end{bmatrix} \qquad (14)$$

As shown in Equation 14, scores would not correlate across time if individuals did not truly differ in either their intercept or slope (this assumes, as do all the covariance derivations shown here, that errors do not correlate with one another across time, which may or may not be a reasonable assumption in any specific data set). In other words, if there are no true individual differences between trajectories over time, there will be no relationship between scores at any one time and scores at any other time. Of course, such a complete lack of correlation is unlikely in

$$\begin{bmatrix} \sigma_{\beta_0}^2 + \sigma_\varepsilon^2 & \sigma_{\beta_0}^2 + \rho\sigma_{\beta_0}\sigma_{\beta_1} & \sigma_{\beta_0}^2 + 2\rho\sigma_{\beta_0}\sigma_{\beta_1} \\ \sigma_{\beta_0}^2 + \rho\sigma_{\beta_0}\sigma_{\beta_1} & \sigma_{\beta_0}^2 + \sigma_{\beta_1}^2 + 2\rho\sigma_{\beta_0}\sigma_{\beta_1} + \sigma_\varepsilon^2 & \sigma_{\beta_0}^2 + 2\sigma_{\beta_1}^2 + 3\rho\sigma_{\beta_0}\sigma_{\beta_1} \\ \sigma_{\beta_0}^2 + 2\rho\sigma_{\beta_0}\sigma_{\beta_1} & \sigma_{\beta_0}^2 + 2\sigma_{\beta_1}^2 + 3\rho\sigma_{\beta_0}\sigma_{\beta_1} & \sigma_{\beta_0}^2 + 4\sigma_{\beta_1}^2 + 4\rho\sigma_{\beta_0}\sigma_{\beta_1} + \sigma_\varepsilon^2 \end{bmatrix} \qquad (13)$$

psychological data, which is simply another way of saying that in actuality, individuals are likely to differ in their true intercepts or slopes.

Second, suppose individuals differ in true intercepts but do not differ in true slopes. In other words, suppose individuals' trajectories start at different elevations but change at the same true rate. This situation implies that true growth trajectories will be parallel to one another, with any deviations from parallelism being attributable to error. The corresponding covariance matrix can be found from Equation 13 by allowing the variance of intercepts to be nonzero but restricting the variance of slopes to equal zero:

$$\begin{bmatrix} \sigma_{\beta_0}^2 + \sigma_\varepsilon^2 & \sigma_{\beta_0}^2 & \sigma_{\beta_0}^2 \\ \sigma_{\beta_0}^2 & \sigma_{\beta_0}^2 + \sigma_\varepsilon^2 & \sigma_{\beta_0}^2 \\ \sigma_{\beta_0}^2 & \sigma_{\beta_0}^2 & \sigma_{\beta_0}^2 + \sigma_\varepsilon^2 \end{bmatrix} \quad (15)$$

It is apparent that allowing individuals to have different intercepts (but not different slopes) creates a nonzero relationship between scores across time. In particular, the covariance matrix shown in Equation 15 possesses compound symmetry, which is a sufficient condition for the validity of the univariate mixed-model ANOVA for analyzing longitudinal data. In this sense, the model that leads to Equation 15 is still quite restrictive, although it is clearly less restrictive than the model that leads to Equation 14.

More generally, notice that the model that leads to Equation 14 assumes that neither true intercepts nor true slopes differ in the population of individuals. The model that leads to Equation 15 allows true intercepts to differ, but continues to assume that true slopes do not differ. The model that leads to Equation 13 allows both true intercepts and true slopes to differ. The critical point is that these models make different predictions about the covariances to be expected between scores on the outcome variable Y as measured over time. As a consequence, structural equation modeling can be used to assess the extent to which the observed sample covariance matrix for a set of data is consistent with any of the matrix forms implied by a multilevel model, as shown in Equations 13, 14, and 15. It is also important to note that even the most complex model we have considered contains only four covariance parameters, namely a variance for true intercepts, a variance for true slopes, a covariance between true intercepts and

true slopes, and an error variance. However, the 3×3 covariance matrix contains six distinct elements (the matrix must be symmetric, so the six distinct elements are the three variances and the three covariances). Thus, it is possible that even the most complex model we have considered does not provide a good fit to the observed data. While at first glance this might seem to be a problem, in actuality it is an advantage because it provides an opportunity to falsify the model if evidence exists showing that patterns in the data do not conform to the restrictions required by the model.

We have now seen that multilevel models imply certain types of covariance structures. For precisely this reason, structural equation modeling can be used to estimate parameters and test hypotheses in multilevel models. For example, the path diagram shown in figure 30.1 is mathematically equivalent to the multilevel model specified by Equations 1, 3, and 4 for a design with three equally spaced time points and time coded with values of 0, 1, and 2. This equivalence becomes clearer by writing Equation 1 separately for each time point. For example, Equation 1 implies that Y at the first time point can be expressed as

$$Y_{it} = \beta_{0i} + \beta_{1i}(0) + \varepsilon_{it} \quad (16)$$

The connection to the path diagram shown in figure 30.1 becomes even clearer when the implicit multiplier of 1 for β_{0i} is made explicit in the multilevel equation and the multiplier for β_{1i} is moved in front of the coefficient:

$$Y_{it} = (1)\beta_{0i} + (0)\beta_{1i} + \varepsilon_{it} \quad (17)$$

Using this same logic, Equation 1 implies that scores at the second and third time points can be written as

$$Y_{it} = (1)\beta_{0i} + (1)\beta_{1i} + \varepsilon_{it} \quad (18)$$

$$Y_{it} = (1)\beta_{0i} + (2)\beta_{1i} + \varepsilon_{it} \quad (19)$$

respectively. Notice that the multipliers for the intercept and the slope in the multilevel model are exactly the same as those shown in the path diagram as shown in figure 30.1. The diagram is different from many path diagrams in that the paths between manifest variables (i.e., Y at each time point) and the latent variables (i.e., the intercept and the slope) are all fixed. The free parameters of the structural equation model are the same parameters as in the multilevel model.

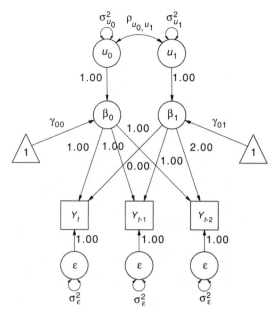

Figure 30.1. Illustrative path model for unconditional straight-line growth.

We have seen that the multilevel model equations imply that the 3×3 covariance matrix for scores measured over time should have the form of Equation 13. Stated differently, the covariance matrix depends on the free parameters shown in figure 30.1. For this reason, standard structural equation programs such as LISREL, AMOS, EQS, MPLUS, and MX can be used to estimate model parameters and test relevant hypotheses.

One further point must be considered in understanding the relationship between multilevel models and structural equation models. In particular, the multilevel model of Equations 1, 3, and 4 not only implies a specific pattern of covariance matrix but also implies a specific pattern of population means for the outcome Y measured over time. Specifically, it follows from these equations that the population mean for Y can be written as

$$E(Y_{it}) = \gamma_{00} + a_t \gamma_{10} \tag{20}$$

Equation 20 shows that if the change trajectory for each individual follows a straight line as specified by Equation 1, then it must be the case that the population means for Y also follow a straight line. The important point here is that the multilevel model not only implies a specific covariance structure but also implies a specific pattern of means. Thus, a corresponding structural equation model must also specify means

as well as covariances. In this respect, the structural equation model formulation is somewhat atypical. Although Sorbom (1978) showed many years ago how structural equation models could incorporate means of latent and manifest variables, most SEM applications have not involved modeling the means. However, the means as well as the covariances must be modeled in latent growth-curve analyses. Willett and Sayer (1994) provide a more detailed but still very accessible explanation of the connection between multilevel models and latent growth-curve models.

Conclusion

This chapter has provided a brief overview of HLM and LGC and the connections between them. Our goal has been to provide a conceptual introduction that will provide a foundation for additional reading on these topics. Not only have we avoided virtually all mathematical details of the methods, but we have been able to illustrate only a small slice of the possible applications of these methods. Ideally, we have succeeded in stimulating readers to pursue additional reading, including additional chapters in this book as well as excellent textbooks on HLM and LGC, such as Singer and Willett (2003), Raudenbush and Bryk (2001), Verbeke and Molenberghs (2000), and Fitzmaurice et al. (2004).

References

Aiken, L. S., & West, S. G. (1991). *Multiple regression: Testing and interpreting interactions.* Thousand Oaks, CA: Sage.

Allport, G. W. (1946). Personalistic psychology as a science: A reply. *Psychological Review, 53,* 132–135.

Cronbach, L. J., & Furby, L. (1970). How we should measure "change"—or should we? *Psychological Bulletin, 74,* 68–80.

Davidian, M., & Giltinan, D. M. (1995). *Nonlinear models for repeated measurement data.* Boca Raton, FL: CRC Press.

Fitzmaurice, G. M., Laird, N. M., & Ware, J. H. (2004). *Applied longitudinal analysis.* New York: Wiley.

Kenny, D. A. (1979). *Correlation and causality.* New York: Wiley.

Kirk, R. E. (1995). *Experimental designs: Procedures for the behavioral sciences* (3rd ed.). Pacific Grove, CA: Brooks/Cole.

Maxwell, S. E., & Delaney, H. D. (2004). *Designing experiments and analyzing data: A model comparison perspective* (2nd ed.). Mahwah, NJ: Erlbaum.

Nesselroade, J. R. (1991). Interindividual differences in intraindividual change. In L. M. Collins & J. L. Horn (Eds.), *Best methods for the analysis of change: Recent advances, unanswered questions, future directions* (pp. 92–105). Washington, DC: American Psychological Association.

Pinheiro, J. C., & Bates, D. M. (2000). *Mixed effects models in S and S-Plus.* New York: Springer.

Raudenbush, S. W., & Bryk, A. S. (2001). *Hierarchical linear models: Applications and data analysis methods* (2nd ed.). Thousand Oaks, CA: Sage.

Rogosa, D. (1988). Myths about longitudinal research. In K. W. Schaie & R. T. Campbell (Eds.), *Methodological issues in aging research* (pp. 171–209). New York: Springer.

Schafer, J. L., & Graham, J. W. (2002). Missing data: Our view of the state of the art. *Psychological Methods, 7,* 147–177.

Singer, J. D., & Willett, J. B. (2003). *Applied longitudinal data analysis: Modeling change and event occurrence.* New York: Oxford University Press.

Sorbom, D. (1978). An alternative to the methodology for analysis of covariance. *Psychometrika, 43,* 381–396.

Verbeke, G., & Molenberghs, G. (2000). *Linear mixed models for longitudinal data.* New York: Springer.

Vonesh, E. F., & Chinchilli, V. M. (1996). *Linear and nonlinear models for the analysis of repeated measurements.* New York: Marcel Dekker.

Willett, J. B. (1989). Some results on reliability for the longitudinal measurement of change: Implications for the design of studies of individual growth. *Educational and Psychological Measurement, 49,* 587–602.

Willett, J. B., & Sayer, A. G. (1994). Using covariance structure analysis to detect correlates and predictors of individual change over time. *Psychological Bulletin, 116,* 363–381.

Wohlwill, J. F. (1973). *The study of behavioral development.* New York: Academic Press.

31

Application of Latent Growth Analyses to Health Outcomes of Adolescent Girls

Paolo Ghisletta and Penelope K. Trickett

This chapter accompanies the reader through three applications of latent growth analysis. The data utilized come from a longitudinal study on the interrelationships between puberty and sexual abuse in a sample of young women. First, we discuss a general modeling strategy when applying latent growth models (LGMs). We posit that the LGMs should not be tested immediately in their most complex specification, but as a series of increasingly complex models. Like any other structural equation model, this strategy allows examining a series of educated research hypotheses. We then proceed to demonstrate the most popular application of LGMs in psychological research: The examination of change in one variable measured directly. Two body appearance scales were analyzed independently to conclude that one was more sensitive to longitudinal change than the other. The second application concerned the simultaneous analyses of change in two variables. The two body appearance scales were this time analyzed simultaneously to conclude that much, but not all, of the information in the scales is shared between them. We further analyzed the two subscales to inquire about differences between the sexually abused and the nonabused subgroup. We

concluded that one scale was more sensitive than the other to group differences in change in body appearance. Finally, we applied a series of increasingly complex LGMs to a latent, as opposed to measured directly, variable, defined by the 11 items of one body appearance scale. This allowed us to examine some psychometric properties of the scale when analyzed longitudinally. We conclude that LGMs are helpful, rigorous, and flexible tools for the analysis of change under certain assumptions.

LGMs are particular specifications of structural equation models (SEMs) and have become a popular choice for the analysis of longitudinal data in many research domains. The close resemblance of LGMs to hierarchical linear models also has furthered the use of LGMs (see chapter 30, this volume). Indeed, the two approaches are conceptually identical under certain conditions (Ghisletta & Lindenberger, 2004; Lindenberger & Ghisletta, 2004; McArdle & Hamagami, 1996; Rovine & Molenaar, 2001) and lead to identical results in empirical applications (Ferrer & McArdle, 2003). In this chapter, we demonstrate the application of LGMs to variables measured directly (i.e., manifest variables) and to variables inferred through indirect measurements (i.e., latent variables). We make use of hierarchical linear model (HLM) software for the former application and of SEM software for the latter application. Finally, we discuss the major issues when fitting LGMs, how to proceed when calculating LGMs, how to interpret LGM results, and how to decide among a series of educated growth hypotheses formalized with LGMs.

Body Image and Competence in Vulnerable Young Women

Thoughts and perceptions about one's body have received much attention in the clinical and pathological literature on adolescence, especially in relation to specific conditions, such as eating disorders. For instance, an essential feature of anorexia nervosa, besides the phobia of gaining weight and the refusal to maintain a minimally normal body weight, is the disturbance in perception of one's body. Body image and its relation to self-esteem has also been considered an important aspect of successful puberty. That is to say, puberty is a developmental period that spans 3 to 4 years of a girl's development in which profound biological changes occur. The rate of physical growth is more rapid than at any other time besides infancy. Studies examining the psychological meaning of these physical changes point to important challenges and necessary tasks of development of the pubertal period (see, e.g., Petersen & Taylor, 1980). One of the important developmental tasks that has been delineated is the need to attain a positive and new sense of self (including two critical components—self-esteem and body image) in the face of these dramatic biological changes and alterations in physical appearance (Simmons, Blyth, & McKinney, 1983).

We posited earlier (Trickett & Putnam, 1993) that sexual abuse experienced by girls prior to puberty was likely to increase the stress and challenges of the pubertal period and place these girls at increased risk of maladaptive developmental outcomes. We also indicated that it was "important to consider the possibility that a child's personal strengths, developed prior to the period in which sexual abuse occurs, will provide defenses against the ravages of abuse, and these strengths may continue to develop at normal or accelerated rates" (p. 84) (Trickett & Putnam, 1993). That is, resilient outcomes for sexually abused females may be enhanced by strengths or

competencies which they are able to maintain through the adolescent period.

A review of research on resilience in abused and neglected children (Trickett, Kurtz, & Pizzigati, 2004) indicated findings supported by research on children's resilience to other adverse conditions (Maton, Schellenbach, Leadbeater, & Solarz, 2004): Intraindividual characteristics such as self-esteem, internal locus of control, intellectual capacity, and good interpersonal resources are predictive of better developmental outcomes for abused and neglected children. So far, only overall self-esteem, not perceived physical competence or body image, has been examined vis-à-vis resilient outcomes in abused or neglected children. In this chapter, we analyze longitudinal measurements of these two aspects of self-esteem: body image, as measured by satisfaction with height, weight, appearance, and other physical changes accompanying puberty; and perceived physical competence, that is, perceptions of competence in sports, games, and other physical activities, in a sample of young women undergoing puberty (Trickett & Putnam, 1993).

Some Basics of Latent Growth Models

An appealing feature of LGMs is that they allow disentangling two mathematically independent but possibly related components: the constant feature (i.e., Level) and the change feature (i.e., Slope or Slopes) of the repeated measurements. Figure 31.1 portrays a SEM representation of an LGM applied to a variable measured directly (i.e., manifest variable). The constant feature of time series is represented within the SEM framework by a factor with equal loadings throughout the time series. In figure 31.1, this is represented by loadings all of 1—all fixed at 1—on the Level factor, symbolized L (any constant value will do, but the value of 1 eases interpretation).

The change feature of the repeated measurements can be represented by a varying number of, and varying values of, loadings. An LGM may contain one Level factor and one or more Slope factors. A variable might be thought to change in time according to a linear pattern only, for instance, in which case the loadings might be simply 1, 2, 3, 4, and so on, for one Slope factor, symbolized S in figure 31.1. But a more complicated, polynomial pattern might be specified for a Slope factor. For example, cyclical changes are not well represented by linear equations; sine and cosine functions will better represent such changes. Also,

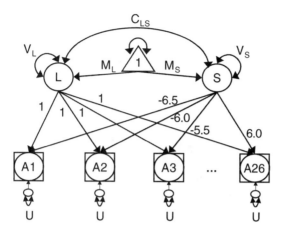

Figure 31.1 Representation of a latent growth model of a manifest variable.

an LGM might have a first Slope factor for linear change and a second Slope factor for quadratic change. The choice of the number and the type of slope to be included in an LGM should be driven by theoretical concerns, although the loadings can be calculated on a purely empirical basis.

The loadings of the Slope factor characterize the change function that is enforced on the time series. If one wishes to estimate parameters relative to linear change, the loadings of the Slope factor will change linearly with respect to the time dimension adopted. If a sine-wave change function is posited in the time series, the loadings of the Slope factor should reflect a sine relationship to the time dimension adopted. In each of these cases, a theory about the nature of the change is invoked (perhaps implicitly). It is possible, also, to estimate the change by fitting a least-squares or maximum-likelihood function to the data (i.e., the manifest variable time interrelationships, with covariances, average cross-products, or even, possibly, correlations). In such an application, a Level factor is specified as per above (to remove the constant longitudinal trend from the time series), and one or more Slope factors is specified in accordance with least-squares or maximum-likelihood criteria. The loadings of the Slope factors are not fixed a priori, but estimated directly from the data (although it is necessary to fix at least one loading per factor for identification purposes and one or more loadings for independence purposes; for more detail, see Ghisletta & McArdle, 2001).

The simplest LGM is a no-change model, meaning that on the average the sample does not exhibit any change. In this case, the function that is said to fit the data is a flat line with zero Slope. In figure 31.1, this is represented by the Level

factor, for which we estimate the mean (M_L) typically scaled to represent the start Level at time one, and then referred to as the intercept on the y-axis of a function of y in terms of x in a Cartesian space. The simplest no-change model does not include individual Level differences; all individuals are posited to start and end at the very same value, the mean (i.e., start value, intercept) which remains invariant over time.

Fit of the LGM also provides an estimation of a variance, namely a portion of total variance that is unrelated to any growth process that is modeled. This variance component is often called uniqueness or residual and is symbolized by the two-headed arrow marked U in figure 31.1. Typically, error of measurement is thought to be a major component of the unique variance. The variation in this no-change model allows for individual differences around the average or intercept. This means that individuals do not change over time but may differ from each other with respect to the average. In figure 31.1, this variability is the variance of the Level factor, portrayed as a two-headed arrow (V_L), which captures individual differences in level. A SEM representation of this no-change, or Level-only, model does not really include a Slope factor.

The purpose of an LGM is to model repeated-measures longitudinal change. A simple change model will include not only a Level factor to model the average starting intercept but also at least one Slope factor to model change. The sample average change may be positive (i.e., growth) or negative (i.e., decline) or may accelerate or decelerate in any of many ways. In figure 31.1, the Slope factor or change is set to be linear. Just as a mean of the means over all occasions, M_L, is calculated for the Level factor, so the mean of the Slopes over all occasions, M_S, is calculated for the Slope factor. And just as there might be individual differences variability around the intercept (V_L), so there might be variability, V_S, around the average change factor. This variation for interindividual differences around the average change can be referred to as interindividual differences in intraindividual change (Baltes & Nesselroade, 1979). In figure 31.1, this is represented by the variance of the Slope factor (the two-headed arrow V_S).

There are several interesting LGMs obtained by specifying M_S and V_S differently. These are, however, often neglected in empirical research. For example, it is possible that on average the sample does not change (hence the average change, M_S, is zero) but that some individuals grow whereas others decline (hence the Slope variance, V_S, is not zero). In this case, the different change effects of different individuals cancel each other in the average, so the mean Slope value is zero (i.e., $M_S = 0$), but a variance in Slope greater than zero (i.e., $V_S > 0$) indicates that individuals are indeed changing, some going up while others are coming down. Of course, this could mean that change was happening by chance and the statistical test of V_S will address this issue (i.e., is V_S really different from zero?).

When the various possible specifications for Level are considered in combination with the various possible Slope factor specifications, many different ideas about change and lack of change can be represented. For instance, it is possible that on average the sample displays interindividual differences in change (i.e., positive variance of the Slope factor) but no interindividual differences in initial level (i.e., zero variance of the Level factor). This situation might depict a learning experiment of totally novel information, in which all participants are uninitiated to the learning material but progressively learn at different rates. Or a sample might be selected with respect to a certain psychological attribute and then asked to undergo a therapeutic treatment, during which some individuals change more quickly, some change more slowly, and some may not change at all. For another example, it is possible that the sample displays interindividual differences in initial level, overall average intraindividual change, but no interindividual differences in intraindividual change (i.e., positive Level variance and nonzero Slope mean but zero Slope variance—or, more realistically, nonsignificant V_S). The different possibilities will increase substantially both as more Slope factors are added to the specification

and as different loadings are considered for the Slope factors (as, e.g., in a change process with an initial Level and linear plus quadratic Slopes). Such different specifications can be tested empirically to describe best the structure of the repeated measurements. In particular, the correlation between the Level and Slope factors can be tested to check to see if Level is indicative of change.

Multivariate extensions of univariate LGM (e.g., MacCallum, Kim, Malarkey, & Kiecolt-Glaser, 1997) open up many other conceptions of change. In a multivariate LGM (MLGM), typically there are several possibilities for considering variable relationships. We can consider whether there is a relation between the Level factor of variable A and the Level factor of variable B, between the Slope factor of variable A and the Slope factor of variable B, and between the Level factor of variable A (or B) and the Slope factor of variable B (or A). We can also consider whether there are nonrandom relations between the portions of the unique factors of the time series of variable A and those of B (given that error by definition does not correlate with anything, we hence prefer to label this portion of variance as unique). Intravariable relations need not be limited to variance and covariances (what are called random effects in HLM). Mean values (or fixed effects in HLM) can also be compared. For example, we could see if the average sample change M_S in variable A is the same as that of variable B.

Figure 31.2 displays a bivariate LGM. Here the two-headed arrows connecting the various Level and Slope factors represent covariances. Likewise, the two-headed arrow between the residuals of variable A and those of B represents a systematic, nonrandom relationship between the change-unrelated portion of the variance of variable A and that of B (this commonly would apply to many or even all measurement points, but is shown here, for simplicity, only for the last occasion). For instance, the test administration medium might affect variables A and B but not affect how the two variables change in time.

When applying MLGMs, it is wise to first fit a univariate LGM on each variable separately. This first step will help to ensure that a series of testable and rejectable change models can be set up for each variable, so that, among the models tested, it is possible to provide a best description of the data of each variable. Then the individual LGMs can be combined, each in its most adequate specification, in an MLGM. By specifying several MLGMs, a series of testable and rejectable hypotheses can then be set up for the

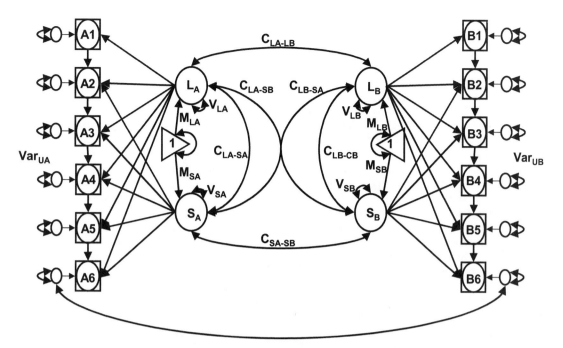

Figure 31.2 Representation of a bivariate latent growth model of two manifest variables. Correlated residuals are only shown for the sixth wave of measurement (but are estimated at all waves).

system of variables as a whole. In contrast, an effort to fit an MLGM directly as a multivariate system may lead to nonsolutions because of variable-specific model misspecifications. Indeed, typically the estimation of variance and covariances (i.e., random effects) is more complex than that of means and intercepts (i.e., fixed effects). A common practice when analyzing the change in two variables consists of skipping the two univariate LGM tests and of specifying from the start a bivariate LGM as that shown in figure 31.2 with variance in Slope for both variables. When either or both of these variances' are nonsignificant, the overall estimation process may become very demanding and lead to nonpermissible solutions (e.g., negative variances).

The residuals deserve a special word. Often it is assumed that the residual variance of a variable's repeated measurements does not change in time. This is a testable hypothesis, although in figures 31.1 and 31.2 it is implied that the residuals do not change: All residuals are represented by the same value, U. This need not be the case. Within the SEM framework, one can easily test several hypotheses concerning the residual structure (although typically this is more difficult within the HLM framework; e.g., Ghisletta & Lindenberger, 2004; Lindenberger & Ghisletta, 2004;

Rovine & Molenaar, 2001). If researchers are particularly interested in questions pertaining to the residual structure, they are advised to use an SEM rather than an HLM framework.

An Example

In the remainder of this chapter, we discuss an application of LGMs to the study of change in body image and physical competence in young women passing through puberty, some of whom have experienced sexual abuse. We briefly describe the study, and then discuss the application of LGM modeling methods.

Study Participants

The variables of interest in these analyses were obtained in a study initiated by Trickett and Putnam (1993) of the psychobiological impact of sexual abuse on female development. Initially, 166 families participated in this research. Approximately half of these families consisted of sexually abused female children and adolescents and their mothers (or other nonabusing caretakers), while the other half were a demographically similar comparison group. Abused females were referred by protective service agencies in the greater Washington, DC, metropolitan area. Eligibility criteria for inclusion in the study were (a) the victim was female, age 6 to 16 years of age; (b) disclosure of referring abuse occurred within 6 months of participation; (c) sexual abuse involved genital contact or penetration; (d) the perpetrator was a family member, including parent, stepparent, or mother's live-in boyfriend, or other relative (e.g., older sibling, uncle, grandparent); and (e) a nonabusing parent or guardian (usually the child's mother) was willing to participate in the project. A group of comparison females recruited via community advertising was similar to the abused subjects in terms of ethnicity, age, socioeconomic status (SES), neighborhood of residence, and family constellation (one- or two-parent families). All families ranged from low to middle SES, with mean Hollingshead (1975) scores of approximately 35 (defined as "blue collar" or working class). Approximately half the families were minorities (primarily African Americans) and half Caucasian.

In repeated measurements at Times 1, 2, and 3, at approximately yearly intervals, there were 166, 139, and 131 participants. A refreshment sample (of nonabused participants) was obtained at Times 4 and 5 (approximately 7 and 9 years after Time 1), so that the sample size for those two waves augmented to 163 and 162 participants respectively. Overall, 105 individuals participated at all five waves of measurement. At the inception of the study, the average age of the sample was 11 years, with a range from 6 to 16 years. More details of the study are provided in Trickett and Putnam (1993), Trickett, Noll, Reiffman, and Putnam (2001), and Nagel, Putnam, Noll, and Trickett (1997).

Variables

Body Image

The Self-Image Questionnaire for Young Adolescents (SIQYA; Petersen, Schulenberg, Abramowitz, Offer, & Jarcho, 1984) is a 98-item self-report questionnaire designed to assess nine aspects of self-concept. In the analyses illustrated here, we limit ourselves to the 11-item body image subscale. These items concern satisfaction with height, weight, appearance, and physical changes accompanying pubertal development. This dimension of self-image has been found to be correlated with the Rosenberg Self-

Image Inventory, self-assessed depressive symptoms, and school problems. The alpha reliability was reported to be 0.77 for girls (Petersen et al., 1984). Longitudinally, the SIQYA has been found to be measurement invariant (i.e., the relations, that is, the factorial loadings between the items and the construct assessed with the items, are the same at different times of measurement; see chapter 11, this volume).

The body image measures were obtained by simply adding the a priori item scores of the 11 five-point Likert-type items. These measures were obtained on 98, 91, 111, 154, and 147 participants at Times 1, 2, 3, 4, and 5, respectively. The Ns are reduced at Times 1, 2, and 3 because this measure was not adequate for participants of ages 6, 7, and 8 years. In our sample, alpha reliability indices were 0.74, 0.79, 0.80, 0.78, and 0.80 at Times 1, 2, 3, 4, and 5, respectively (see figure 31.3).

Physical Competence

The Perceived Competence Scale for Children (Harter, 1982) is a five-factor scale, which weights a child's self-reports of competence in different areas in which a person can cope—social (friendship), physical (athletic), and cognitive (school learning). In this study, only the six-item physical competence subscale is examined. Items on this scale concern perceptions of competence at sports, games, and other physical activities. This was obtained at Times 1, 2, and 3 only on 147, 124, and 119 participants, respectively. A composite score was obtained by adding the six 4-point Likert-type items. In our sample, alpha reliability indices were 0.77, 0.82, and 0.82 at Times 1, 2, and 3, respectively. Figure 31.4 represents the individual longitudinal trajectories of the physical competence composite score plotted by chronological age.

Latent Growth Models of Manifest Variables

In what follows, we demonstrate the application of LGMs to study relationships between body image and perceived physical competence. We first apply a univariate LGM to each variable separately to identify the best-fitting model for each variable. We then combine the two LGMs, in their particular specification form, in a bivariate LGM (BLGM) to ascertain the relationships between the two variables as they change in time, possibly together. We describe the changes

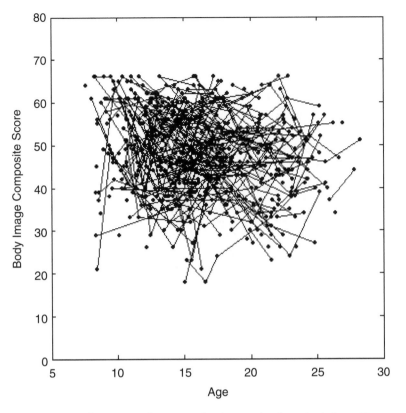

Figure 31.3 Total SIQYA Body Image subscale score by chronological age. Dots represent single measurement points. Lines unify single measurement points of same participant.

occurring over chronological age, so that specific developmental hypotheses regarding young women's acceptance and self-image of their body and physical competence may be tested. We also test for group differences in body image and physical competence, because part of the sample was sexually abused, and this might have affected how they perceive their appearance in general.

As outlined above, body image was assessed on all five time points, but physical competence was measured only on the first three occasions. This difference in number of occasions of measurement does not matter for the separate univariate LGM applications, but it allows us to demonstrate use of incomplete data in the subsequent BLGM. That is, Times 4 and 5 correspond to totally incomplete data on the physical competence subscale. LGMs, however, can accommodate to such data imbalance. It is possible to compute a BLGM with one variable assessed on three occasions and another assessed on five occasions without having to lose the additional

measurements of the variable measured more intensively.

Results of Univariate LGMs

For both the abused and the nonabused subsamples, analyzed first together then separately, table 31.1 displays the parameter estimates and standard errors of the univariate LGMs for the Body Image measures; table 31.2 shows these estimates for the Physical Competence measures. Body Image was best described by an LGM with a linear age Slope. On the average, the overall sample had a score of 47.77 and decreased by 0.47 points per year. However, there were large individual differences in Level and minor individual differences in linear Slope. The variance of the Level factor was 45.78 while that of the linear Slope was 0.58. The covariation between Level and linear Slope was found to be nonsignificant, and the residual variance is 46.46.

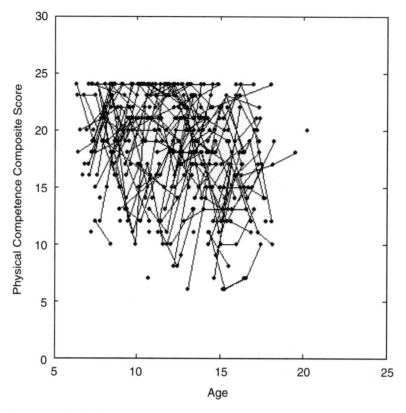

Figure 31.4 Total Physical Competence subscale score by chronological age. Dots represent single measurement points. Lines unify single measurement points of same participant.

No change was detected for the Physical Competence subscale. The average Level for the sample was 18.04. There was wide variability around this average value: The variance of the Level factor was 11.57. The unique variance was 8.49. These analyses suggest that the Body Image and Physical Competence measures tap different constructs of adolescents' perception of their physical selves in this sample: The Body Image scale was sensitive to change, while the Physical Competence scale was not. Hence, it might be important from a theoretical point of view to assess individuals on both instruments.

TABLE 31.1 Parameter Estimates (Standard Errors) of Univariate Latent Growth Models Applied to the SIQYA Body Image for the Total Sample and the Abused and Nonabused Subsamples

	Total Sample	Abused	Nonabused
Mean level	47.77 (0.62)	46.55 (0.84)	48.79 (0.90)
Mean linear age	−0.47 (0.11)	−0.54 (0.14)	−0.38 (0.16)
Variance level	45.78 (7.16)	35.43 (8.81)	52.89(10.87)
Variance linear age	0.58 (0.19)	0.51 (0.25)	0.71 (0.30)
Covariance level-linear age	*ns*	*ns*	*ns*
Unique variance	46.46 (3.88)	48.50 (5.90)	44.20 (5.08)
−2LL	4,041	1,891	2,117

Note: Total Sample means both abused and nonabused together; −2LL is the deviance misfit index.

TABLE 31.2 Parameter Estimates (Standard Errors) of Univariate Latent Growth Models Applied to the Physical Competence Subscale for the Total Sample and the Abused and Nonabused Subsamples

	Total Sample	Abused	Nonabused
Mean level	18.04 (0.32)	16.45 (0.58)	18.75 (0.45)
Mean linear age	*ns*	−0.31 (0.13)	*ns*
Variance level	11.57 (1.83)	9.42 (2.37)	11.60 (2.49)
Variance linear age	*ns*	*ns*	*ns*
Covariance level-linear age	*ns*	*ns*	*ns*
Unique variance	8.49 (0.83)	9.63 (1.39)	7.68 (1.01)
−2LL	1,992	956	1,024

Note: Total Sample means both abused and nonabused together; −2LL is the deviance misfit index.

Results of Bivariate LGMs

Table 31.3 presents the results of the BLGM computed on both subscales simultaneously. In these analyses, the average Level of the Body Image subscale indicated for the total sample was 47.82, while the yearly decrement is estimated at 0.41 points. Individual differences in both Level and linear Slope are still present, and their covariation is again nonsignificant. The average Level for the Physical Competence measures is 17.08 and large individual differences around this mean Level are again indicated. Moreover, now these measures pick up the longitudinal decrease in self-perception and the sample decreases on the average by a rate of 0.29 points per year.

TABLE 31.3 Parameter Estimates (Standard Errors) of Bivariate Latent Growth Models Applied to the SIQYA Body Image and Physical Competence Subscales Simultaneously for the Total Sample and the Abused and Nonabused Subsamples

	Total Sample	Abused	Nonabused
SIQYA Body Image			
Mean level	47.82 (0.60)	46.61 (0.79)	48.98 (0.87)
Mean linear age	−0.41 (0.10)	−0.50 (0.14)	−0.27 (0.12)
Variance level	41.56 (6.62)	30.23 (7.86)	50.66 (10.33)
Variance linear age	0.49 (0.17)	0.58 (0.24)	*ns*
Covariance level-linear age	*ns*	*ns*	*ns*
Unique variance	48.96 (3.93)	49.49 (5.81)	54.84 (5.38)
Physical Competence			
Mean level	17.08 (0.35)	15.93 (0.47)	18.46 (0.44)
Mean linear age	−0.29 (0.07)	−0.46 (0.10)	*ns*
Variance level	9.29 (1.56)	6.39 (1.89)	12.15 (2.51)
Variance linear age	*ns*	*ns*	*ns*
Covariance level-linear age	*ns*	*ns*	*ns*
Unique variance	9.72 (0.91)	11.08 (1.51)	8.29 (1.06)
Intervariable covariances			
Level BI-Level PC	16.57 (2.74)	11.99 (3.22)	21.15(4.42)
Correlation	0.84	0.86	0.85
Uniq. BI-Uniq. PC	11.11 (1.60)	12.57 (2.45)	10.50 (2.10)
Correlation	0.51	0.54	0.49
−2LL	5,879	2,783	1,024

Note: Total Sample means both abused and nonabused together; −2LL is the deviance misfit index; BI = Body Image; PC = Physical Competence.

TABLE 31.4 Likelihood Ratio and Comparative Root Mean Square Error of Approximation Fit Indices for Abused Versus Nonabused Subsamples Comparison

Variable	$\Delta\chi^2$	Δdf	CRMSEA, 95% CI
SIQYA Body Image	6	5	0.03, [0.00–0.13]
Physical Competence	12	4	0.11, [0.02–0.19]
SIQYA BI and Phys. Comp.	10	9	0.03, [0.00–0.10]

Note: $\Delta\chi^2$ = difference in chi square; Δdf = difference in degrees of freedom; CRMSEA = comparative root mean square error of approximation; CI = confidence interval.

The simultaneous modeling of the two composite scores allows estimating the relationships between the two subscales. The Levels of Perceived Physical Competence and of Body Image Self-Concept correlate 0.84, meaning that over 70% of the level variance is shared between the two subscales. At the same time, the unique portions of variance of the two subscales correlate 0.51. This means that the portions of variance unrelated to the change process of the two subscales share about 26% of variance.

Group Differences

Group differences were examined by fitting the separate LGMs and BLGM not only to the overall sample composed of all abused and nonabused girls together, but also to the two subsamples separately. This type of comparison allows us to examine several theoretical questions about group differences, such as whether the shape of change in body image self-concept and perceived physical competence is the same for abused and nonabused girls or whether one subgroup is higher than the other on physical self-perception characteristics or whether one subgroup changes more rapidly than the other on a characteristic examined. A log-likelihood (−2LL) fit index provides a statistical basis for comparing the subgroups to examine whether they are different with respect to the growth model applied. For each model, the −2LL value of the overall sample is compared to the sum of the −2LLs of the two subsamples. The difference between these two amounts is distributed as a chi-square with as many degrees of freedom as the difference in number of parameters estimated under the two conditions. A difference in deviance can be re-expressed as a comparative root mean squared error of approximation (CRMSEA; see Browne & du Toit, 1992) fit index, which takes degrees of freedom, number of

parameters estimated, and total sample size (abused + nonabused) into account in providing a basis for interpretation of the group comparison analyses (for more detail, see Ghisletta & McArdle, 2001).

Tables 31.1–31.3 display the parameter estimates of LGMs fitted separately to the abused and nonabused subsamples. Table 31.4 displays the likelihood ratio tests of the group comparisons, that is, the difference between the overall misfit of both subsamples when examined together and the sum of the misfit indices of both subsamples when examined separately. By rule of thumb, a CRMSEA smaller than 0.05 signifies no reliable group differences, while a value greater than 0.05 suggests that the groups compared are reliably different. Also, if the confidence interval (CI) for the CRMSEA contains 0, we can say that the overall model fits both groups—hence that the two groups are not different.

From the summary of table 31.4, we can see that the abused and nonabused subsamples do not differ on the Body Image subscale, or on the overall description of both subscales when considered together. However, with respect to the Physical Competence subscale only, the abused and the nonabused subsamples are different. For instance, the abused subsample changed by −0.31 each year, where the nonabused subgroup remained stable. Moreover, the average intercept value of the abused subsample is estimated at 16.45, whereas that of the nonabused subsample is higher, at 18.75 (see table 31.2).

This first application of LGM allows us to state that the two subscales tap different yet related areas of children and adolescents' evaluation of their physical self-perception. Much information is shared across the two subscales. In this sample, physical competence and body image are two distinct, but highly related, concepts. Moreover, the two subsamples differ on the Physical Competence subscale only. While the nonabused subsample is stable, the abused subsample decreased in its physical competence score. The two subsamples did not differ on the Body Image scale when considered by itself, or on both subscales when considered together. In other words, both the sexually abused and nonabused females declined in positive body image over time, a finding supported by much other research on American female adolescents (Petersen, 1988). On the other hand, the nonabused females maintained their sense of physical competence over time, whereas the sexually abused females declined in perceived competence over time.

Latent Growth Models of Latent Variables

For over a century now, the use of factor analytical approaches has allowed us to account for unrelated variance, which inevitably contaminates what we are measuring (Spearman, 1904). The use of factor analysis permits us to remove unrelated variance and to ascertain whether we are measuring the same construct across time (e.g., see Meredith, 1964, 1993; Horn & McArdle, 1992; chapter 11, this volume). Indeed, the mere fact that the same instrument was utilized throughout a longitudinal study does not guarantee that the instrument measured the same construct at all time points. Participants could, for instance, react differently to the instrument after repeated exposures (e.g., retest artifacts such as practice, habituation, or fatigue effects).

In this third application of LGMs, we examine in some detail the Body Image Self-Concept subscale of the SIQYA. We initially apply a measurement model on the 11 items of this subscale to define a Body Image factor at each time point. Then we apply an LGM on the five resulting longitudinal factors. This approach was

referred to as an analysis of the "curve of factors" by McArdle (1988). It unites the elegance of the factor analytical approach to the measurement of a construct and the rigor of LGMs for the study of longitudinal change. In this application, for simplicity, change is described over occasions of measurement and not over chronological age.

Results of LGMs of Latent Variables

We first computed separate exploratory factor analyses at each time point, to check the structure of the SIQYA Body Image subscale. That is, at each time point we computed an exploratory factor analysis of the 11 Body Image items. Consistently, at all time points a first strong factor emerged. This motivated us to define a single Body Image factor at each time point. The next step consisted of a detailed study of the longitudinal change in the Body Image factor and its relationships to the 11 items. We defined a series of statistically nested models to test alternative change hypotheses. To reach statistical conclusions about the models fitted, we again relied on the CRMSEA. When comparing two statistically nested models, a CRMSEA greater than 0.05 signifies a reliable difference in fit. In this case, the most parsimonious model describes the data significantly worse than the least parsimonious, so that the latter model is usually retained. However, if the 95% CI includes 0, the two models are said to be close in fit, so that the most parsimonious model may be preferred. Table 31.5 reports the −2LL fit indices of several alternative models and the CRMSEA and 95% CIs for specific model comparisons.

Model 0 is a longitudinal factor model, in which at each time point a single Body Image factor is defined, the five longitudinal Body

TABLE 31.5 Likelihood Ratio and Comparative Root Mean Square Error of Approximation Fit Indices for Longitudinal Factor Models and Curves of Factors Models

Model (−2LL, p)	Comp.	$\Delta\chi^2$	Δdf	CRMSEA, 95% CI
0 Configural invariance (26,410, 235)	0–1	126	40	0.11, [0.08–0.13]
1 Weak factorial invariance (26,536, 195)	—	—	—	—
2 C-o-F, Level only (26,582, 182)	1–2	46	13	0.12, [0.07–0.16]
3 C-o-F, Level and linear Slope (26,573, 185)	1–3	37	10	0.12, [0.07–0.17]
	2–3	9	3	0.10, [0.00–0.20]
4 C-o-F, Level and latent Slope (26,554, 188)	1–4	18	7	0.09, [0.03–0.16]
	3–4	19	3	0.17, [0.09–0.26]

Note: Comp. = models being compared; $\Delta\chi^2$ = difference in chi-square fit statistic; Δdf = difference in degrees of freedom; CRMSEA = comparative root mean square error of approximation; CI = confidence interval; C-o-F = "curve of factors" model.

Image factors are free to covary, and the residual components of longitudinally corresponding items are covarying (e.g., Item 1 at Time 1 correlates with Item 1 at Time 2, but not with Item 2 at Time 1 or 2). However, no constraint is enforced on the longitudinal factor loadings, so that we are in a situation of configural invariance (cf. Widaman & Reise, 1997; chapter 11, this volume). Model 1 is analogous to Model 0, except that now equality constraints are enforced on the longitudinally corresponding factor loadings. Therefore, the same values are estimated for the corresponding factor loadings at all time points. Thus we enforced what some have called weak factorial or metric invariance, a necessary prerequisite to apply the "curve of factors" model. Otherwise, the factors' meaning would be changing in time, so that it would not be sensible to investigate how they progress in time, given their substantial differences. By comparing Models 0 and 1, we see that in our sample, weak configural or metric invariance

does not hold for the Body Image subscale, CRMSEA = 0.11, 95% CI = (0.08 – 0.13). Hence, the application of the "curve of factors" model is not warranted. Nevertheless, for didactical purposes only, we proceeded to fit a series of higher-order LGMs. The remaining models are hence statistically compared to Model 1, as though weak factorial or metric invariance were statistically a feasible description of the longitudinal Body Image subscale.

Model 1 postulates that the structure of the factors' covariances is completely saturated. The higher-order LGM imposed upon the five longitudinal Body Image factors will hence try to explain more parsimoniously the factors' covariances. Model 2 is a Level-only curve of factors. Analogously to the manifest variable LGMs presented previously, this model hypothesizes no change on the (latent) time series. The five longitudinal Body Image factors are assumed to be constant in time with respect to their average mean value and their variance. The

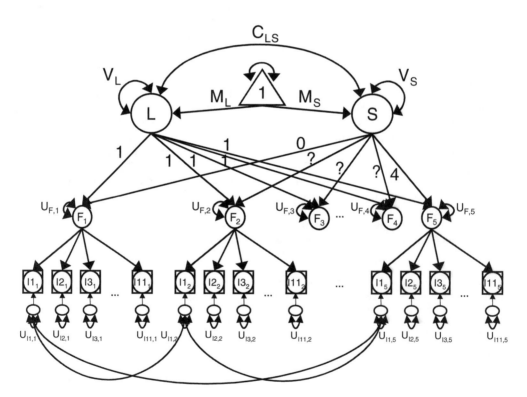

Figure 31.5 A "curve of factors" free Slope latent growth model (McArdle, 1988, #27). For clarity purposes, measurement models are not shown for the third and fourth measurement points (but are estimated at those occasions). Correlated residuals are only shown for the Item 1 (but are estimated for all items). The Slope loadings for the second, third, and fourth measurement points are freely estimated.

comparison of Model 2 to Model 1 leads us to refuse a Level-only representation of the longitudinal Body Image subscale, CRMSEA = 0.12, 95% CI = (0.07 − 0.16). Model 3 adds a higher-order linear Slope to the previous model. This model postulates that the longitudinal Body Image factors change linearly in time. Again, by comparing this to Model 1, we can conclude that the longitudinal factor model better represents the data than the higher-order linear LGM, CRMSEA = 0.12, 95% CI = (0.07 − 0.17). Note that we can also compare Models 2 and 3, to test the gain in fit from adding a linear Slope to the Level-only model. Model 3 better describes the longitudinal structure of the Body Image items, but not convincingly so (despite the CRMSEA of 0.10 greater than 0.05, the 95% CI covers the value 0, indicating a close fit of the two models).

Finally, we fit a "curve of factors" model with a freely estimated Slope. This Model 4 is represented in figure 31.5. Three loadings of the Slope factor are freely estimated from the data as opposed to being fixed at specific values (such as was the case with the linear Slope). We still need to fix two loadings, one for identification of the Slope factor, the other for independence from the Level factor. Hence, the first loading is nonexistent, or fixed at 0, while the last is fixed at 4. This model, although more parsimonious, again loses too much in fit when compared to Model 1, CRMSEA = 0.09, 95% CI = (0.03 − 0.16). We can test the significance of all three freely estimated Slope loadings by comparing Models 3 and 4. The CRMSEA is 0.17 and its 95% CI does not include 0. We can hence conclude that it is more realistic to free the Slope loadings rather forcing them to follow a linear pattern.

This second LGM allowed us to investigate the psychometric properties of the Body Image subscale when examined longitudinally. According to our results, the meaning of the Body Image subscale changes in time, because weak factorial invariance was not obtained (i.e., the longitudinal loadings of the Body Image factor changed in time). This could be due, in part, to the refreshment samples added to the longitudinal design at Times 4 and 5 of the study or to the fact that most participants were in the throes of pubertal development at Times 1, 2, and 3 but were postpubertal by Times 4 and 5. We nevertheless proceeded, for didactical purposes, to examine the shape of the change in the Body Image factor. We concluded that a Level-only

model was not describing the longitudinal evolution of the subscale sufficiently well. A linear change model was better, but the best description of the longitudinal change was obtained when the Slope was freely estimated. However, this more parsimonious model did not describe the covariances among the longitudinal factors sufficiently well.

Conclusion

In this chapter, we have sought to describe three applications of LGMs applied to a typical application in positive psychology. We analyzed data from two subscales measuring aspects of body self-concept and perceived physical competence in young women undergoing puberty, some of whom were sexually abused. The three types of LGMs were (a) univariate LGMs applied to manifest variables, (b) multivariate LGMs applied to manifest variables, and (c) LGMs applied to latent variables. The first two applications allowed us to examine particular change hypotheses about body image and physical competence as well as group differences in these domains between abused and nonabused girls. The third application allowed a more detailed examination of the psychometric properties of the Body Image SIQYA subscale.

Answering the sorts of questions we asked of the data here was difficult previous to LGMs. Particular assumptions, most of which were untenable, had to be accepted. Now we can test specific assumptions about change and address additional substantive questions. Certainly, in years to come other methodological approaches to the analysis of change will be created and available to large audiences through wide software implementation. We are looking forward to more exciting techniques to analyze change.

Acknowledgments   The authors would like to thank John L. Horn for his very thoughtful comments on a previous draft of the chapter.

References

Baltes, P. B., & Nesselroade, J. R. (1979). History and rationale of longitudinal research. In J. R. Nesselroade & P. B. Baltes (Eds.), *Longitudinal research in the study of behavior and development* (pp. 21–27). New York: Academic Press.

Browne, M. W., & du Toit, S. H. C. (1992). Automated fitting of nonstandard models. *Multivariate Behavioral Research, 27,* 269–300.

Ferrer, E., & McArdle, J. J. (2003). Modeling latent growth curves with incomplete data using different types of structural equation modeling and multilevel software. *Structural Equation Modeling, 10,* 493–524.

Ghisletta, P., & Lindenberger, U. (2004). Static and dynamic longitudinal structural analyses of cognitive changes in old age. *Gerontology, 50,* 12–16.

Ghisletta, P., & McArdle, J. J. (2001). Latent growth curve analyses of the development of height. *Structural Equation Modeling, 8,* 531–555.

Harter, S. (1982). The perceived competence scale for children. *Child Development, 53,* 87–97.

Hollingshead, A. (1975). *Four factor index of social status.* Unpublished manuscript, Yale University Department of Sociology.

Horn, J. L., & McArdle, J. J. (1992). A practical and theoretical guide to measurement invariance in aging research. *Experimental Aging Research, 18,* 117–144.

Lindenberger, U., & Ghisletta, P. (2004). Modeling longitudinal changes in old age: From covariance structures to dynamic systems. In R. A. Dixon, L. Bäckman, & L.-G. Nilsson (Eds.), *New frontiers in cognitive aging* (pp. 199–216). Oxford: Oxford University Press.

MacCallum, R. C., Kim, C., Malarkey, W. B., & Kiecolt-Glaser, J. K. (1997). Studying multivariate change using multilevel models and latent curve models. *Multivariate Behavioral Research, 32,* 215–253.

Maton, K. I., Schellenbach, C. J., Leadbeater, B. J., & Solarz, A. L. (Eds.). (2004). *Investing in children, youth, families, and communities: Strengths-based research and policy.* Washington, DC: American Psychological Association.

McArdle, J. J. (1988). Dynamic but structural equation modeling of repeated measures data. In J. R. Nesselroade & R. B. Cattell (Eds.), *Handbook of multivariate experimental psychology* (pp. 561–614). New York: Plenum.

McArdle, J. J., & Hamagami, F. (1996). Multilevel models from a multiple group structural equation perspective. In G. A. Marcoulides & R. E. Schumaker (Eds.), *Advanced structural equation modeling: Issues and techniques* (pp. 89–124). Mahwah, NJ: Erlbaum.

Meredith, W. (1964). Notes on factorial invariance. *Psychometrika, 29,* 177–185.

Meredith, W. (1993). Measurement invariance, factor analysis and factorial invariance. *Psychometrika, 58,* 525–543.

Nagel, D. E., Putnam, F. W., Noll, J. G., & Trickett, P. K. (1997). Disclosure patterns of sexual abuse and psychological functioning at 1-year follow-up. *Child Abuse and Neglect, 21,* 137–147.

Petersen, A. C. (1988). Adolescent development. *Annual Review of Psychology, 39,* 583–272.

Petersen, A. C., Schulenberg, J. E., Abramowitz, R. H., Offer, D., & Jarcho, H. D. (1984). A self-image questionnaire for young adolescents (SIQYA): Reliability and validity studies. *Journal of Youth and Adolescence, 13,* 93–111.

Petersen, A. C., & Taylor, B. (1980). The biological approach to adolescence. In J. Adelson (Ed.), *Handbook of adolescent psychology* (pp. 117–155). New York: Wiley.

Rovine, M. J., & Molenaar, P. C. M. (2001). A structural equations modeling approach to the general linear mixed model. In L. M. Collins & A. G. Sayer (Eds.), *New methods for the analysis of change* (pp. 67–96). Washington, DC: American Psychological Association.

Simmons, R. G., Blyth, D. A., & McKinney, K. L. (1983). The social and psychological effects of puberty on white females. In J. Brooks-Gunn & A. C. Petersen (Eds.), *Girls at puberty: Biological and psychosocial perspectives* (pp. 229–273). New York: Plenum.

Spearman, C. (1904). General intelligence, objectively determined and measured. *American Journal of Psychology, 15,* 201–293.

Trickett, P. K., Kurtz, D. A., & Pizzigati, K. (2004). Resilient outcomes in abused and neglected children: Bases for strengths-based interventions and prevention policies. In K. I. Maton, C. J. Schellenbach, B. J. Leadbeater, & A. L. Solarz (Eds.), *Investing in children, youth, families, and communities: Strengths-based research and policy* (pp. 73–96). Washington, DC: American Psychological Association.

Trickett, P. K., Noll, J. G., Reiffman, A., & Putnam, F. W. (2001). Variants of intrafamilial sexual abuse experience: Implications for long term development. *Journal of Development and Psychopathology, 13,* 1001–1019.

Trickett, P. K., & Putnam, F. W. (1993). Impact of child sexual abuse on females: Toward a developmental, psychobiological integration. *Psychological Science, 4,* 81–87.

Widaman, K. F., & Reise, S. P. (1997). Exploring the measurement invariance of psychological instruments: Applications in the substance use domain. In K. J. Bryant & M. Windle (Eds.), *The science of prevention: Methodological advances from alcohol and substance abuse research* (pp. 281–324). Washington, DC: American Psychological Association.

32

The Use of Growth-Curve Modeling in Estimating Stability and Change in Well-Being Over Time

Daniel K. Mroczek and Paul W. Griffin

One central goal of positive psychology is the understanding of positive psychological growth. Growth implies change. Hence, positive psychology needs tools that can accurately track growth and other types of change over time. This need calls out for longitudinal studies, of course, but also for statistical techniques that can make the most of longitudinal growth data. Growth-curve models are one such technique. Many of the research questions posed by the positive psychology movement are suitable for growth-curve modeling. For example, in what ways do the positively valenced components of well-being change over time? What aspects are stable and which change? More important, who changes and who stays stable? These questions are essential to positive psychology and are amenable to growth-curve models.

This chapter specifically focuses on growth-curve estimation within a mixed modeling framework (Singer & Willett, 2003; Willett & Sayer, 1994), also known as hierarchical linear modeling (HLM; Raudenbush & Bryk, 2002). These mixed modeling techniques for estimating change are best labeled individual growth (or individual trajectory) models. This is because

individual-level growth curves, or trajectories, are estimated, as opposed to modeling data primarily from sample-based variances and covariances, as is done with structural equation modeling (SEM) approaches to growth curves. SEM is the other major technique for estimating growth curves, and when it is used, the term latent growth curve (LGC) models is often employed. The key advantage of LGC models over mixed-model approaches is that the former contains measurement models that allow superior estimation of error. The key advantage of mixed models over LGC is flexibility in handling missing data. As is true in many longitudinal studies, the intervals between measurements are often unequal across participants, creating spacing between measurement occasions that are of varying length. Mixed-model approaches have no problem with this. Researchers should weigh the relative importance of flexibility in handling missing data versus superior estimation of measurement error in making a decision about whether to use mixed-model or SEM-based approaches to growth curves. This chapter focuses on the former. However, the reader may wish to read about the latter (McArdle, 1991).

Applications of Growth-Curve Models to Positive Psychology

Why should researchers study and apply individual growth modeling techniques within the area of positive psychology? Positive psychology is concerned with promoting well-being over time. Ideally, such promotion should be sustained over long periods of time, and not simply comprise flash-in-the-pan bursts of happiness that hold only over the short term. One goal of positive psychology is the identification of mechanisms that increase levels of positive outcomes (positive affect, life satisfaction, flourishing, savoring, etc.) and keep them elevated over time. Sustaining increases in positive outcomes requires upward trajectories. This notion is the hallmark of Sheldon's model of upward spirals of happiness over time (Lyubomirsky, 2001; Sheldon & Houser-Marko, 2001; Sheldon & Kasser, 2001), and is consistent with Fredrickson's broaden-and-build model of positive emotions (Fredrickson, 2003; Fredrickson & Levenson, 1998). If researchers can successfully spark upward trends in positive outcomes, devices will be needed to track these trajectories. If the stimuli used to increase positive variables result in ephemeral changes that are fleeting, we should observe (over the long term) a trend back toward prior levels of the variables. To determine if this happens, methods that track change over time are needed. Individual growth-curve models are well-suited for this purpose.

For example, in the area of affective well-being, few studies have tracked change over time in positive or negative emotion. When such studies have been done, the results are surprising and show systematic changes over time (e.g., Charles, Reynolds, & Gatz, 2001). Other questions remain understudied in the area of affective well-being, such as the extent of individual differences in change (this concept is discussed below) and what variables predict such individual differences in rate of change. Growth models are a valuable tool in answering these questions, both in the area of affective well-being and in the study of change in positive outcomes more generally. Additionally, by conducting longitudinal studies with multiple time points and applying growth models, new questions will inevitably arise. For example, why do some people increase on positive outcomes and others not? By analyzing change in such variables in a sophisticated way, the processes that underlie such changes may become clearer, giving rise to stronger techniques for promoting positive outcomes.

Individual Differences in Intraindividual Change

Investigations of long-term change in positive outcomes require two types of empirical clarity. First, what are the overall, sample-level trends in positive affect, life satisfaction, savoring, and so on over long periods of time? Do sample-level trajectories show increases, decreases, stability, or curvilinearity over time? Second, regardless of the shape and direction of the overall, sample-derived trajectory, are there individual differences in trajectories? Do people vary in rate of change or in the functional form of their trajectory? This latter notion is a central idea in life span developmental theory, which holds that people are characterized by varying developmental trajectories. This is the principle of interindividual differences in intraindividual change (Alwin, 1994; Baltes, Reese, & Nesselroade, 1977; Mroczek & Spiro, 2003a, 2003b; Nesselroade, 1991). The principle holds that people vary in rate of change, in direction of change (if they change at all), and, if curvilinearity characterizes change in a variable, in the amount of curvature that defines people's trajectories. Growth models are well-suited to testing the principle of interindividual differences in intraindividual change because it estimates the latter within persons and the former between persons.

In essence, the concept of interindividual differences in intraindividual change reflects two important types of variability in psychological constructs: within-person and between-person variance (Mroczek & Spiro, 2003b; Mroczek, Spiro, & Almeida, 2003). Long ago, Cattell (1966) realized the importance of this distinction and labeled the two forms of variance ipsative and normative, respectively. Individual trajectories reflect within-person variability, while individual differences across trajectories reflect between-person variability (Nesselroade, 1988, 1991). The distinction between within- and between-person variance is also one of the key differences between the process and structure approaches to personality (Fleeson, 2001; Hooker & McAdams, 2003). For positive psychology, this distinction is also important, because the specific processes that permit growth and flourishing are borne out at the person level (thus creating within-person variance) but very likely manifest themselves differently across people (thus creating between-person variance). Growth-curve models permit the integration of these two forms of variance. Individual growth trajectories are estimated, thus capturing within-person or ipsative variance, but across persons in a sample, estimate between-person or normative variance. This is a useful conceptual and analytic framework for positive psychology and can shed important light on growth processes.

The Data Analytic Framework of Growth Modeling

Let us move to the practicalities of growth modeling. What practical constraints does the researcher face when seeking to estimate change in a variable or process over time?

At Least Three Longitudinal Measurements

First, growth-curve models demand longitudinal data and at least three measurement occasions. In essence, the model is fitting a trajectory or regression line to the longitudinal measurement occasions of an individual. Two measurement occasions can only detect a difference between measurements at two time points. This is suboptimal for assessing rate of change and prohibits the accurate estimation of standard errors for the rate of change, or slope. As others have pointed out, studies composed of only two waves cannot estimate individual trajectories (Rogosa, Brandt, & Zimowski, 1982; Singer, 1998; Singer & Willett, 2003). Hence, to carry out growth modeling adequately, the minimum number of measurement occasions required is three, although for estimation of curvilinear models (e.g., quadratic, cubic), more waves are necessary. The researcher should gauge how many waves of data are required to answer the substantive questions of interest.

Choosing the Time Variable

After obtaining longitudinal data with at least three measurement occasions, the next consideration is how to treat time (Singer & Willett, 2003). Nearly every statistical technique estimates an association between at least two variables. Growth models are no exception. In growth models, the association is between the

variable of interest (e.g., positive emotion) and some variable that represents time (e.g., age). For example, we may hypothesize that wisdom increases as we age. This implies that within a sample of individuals we have followed longitudinally, we should observe a rise in the average wisdom change trajectories. Each individual will have measurements of wisdom at various ages, and the association characterized by the growth model is that between age and wisdom. Imagine two vectors of numbers. One is composed of wisdom measurements and the other is the ages at which the measurements took place. We would expect that, on average, at each age there would be an increase in wisdom from the last age at which the variable was measured. Individual growth models estimate this relationship for each individual, and then put them together to estimate the overall sample trajectory. This hypothetical growth model depicts a longitudinal relationship between a time variable (age) and a substantive variable (wisdom), both at the individual and sample levels.

Thus, as Singer and Willett (2003) argued, the researcher must think hard about what variable should represent time. In many growth-curve models, the metric that represents time is age. However, other ways of clocking time make sense, depending on the study. It can be some calendar metric, such as days, weeks, months, or years. It can be some socially or educationally defined time metric such as grade in school. For example, as mentioned earlier, there is now interest in positive psychology in producing sustainable increases in happiness. Some researchers are investigating possible techniques that spark upward spirals in happiness over time (Lyubomirsky, 2001; Sheldon & Houser-Marko, 2001; Sheldon & Kasser, 2001). If such a technique is applied as an intervention, we can use growth models to track concomitant increases (upward spirals) in the weeks, months, and even years that follow. In this case, rather than using age, it may be more useful and substantively meaningful to use actual elapsed time (e.g., weeks) as the time variable. Regardless of how old someone was at time of intervention, change in happiness is tracked using units of time since the intervention. The first measurement would represent a zero point, and each measurement afterward would record the exact number of days, weeks, months, or years that had elapsed up to that point, from the zero (baseline) occasion. Whether age, weeks, months, calendar year, or some other representative of time is used, researchers using growth models should put serious thought into what time variable best suits the study.

Arranging the Data in Person-Time

Once at least three measurement occasions have been obtained, and the time variable chosen, the data must be arranged in "person-time" (or "person-period"; Singer & Willett, 2003). This requires nesting measurements within persons. Each measurement occasion for a person must be placed on a separate row in the data matrix, with the participant ID serving to unify the multiple rows during the analysis. In essence, each person has his or her own data matrix that is nested within the larger data matrix. An example of this is shown in table 32.1.

The first column in table 32.1 is participant ID, and note that a given participant's measurements are stacked on top of one another in the data matrix. Regardless of the software that is used to estimate the growth model (e.g., HLM, Proc Mixed, MlwiN, xtreg, NLME), data need to be arranged in this stacked fashion. Note also that our fictitious participants are of varying ages, indicating different cohorts as well as differences in interval of measurement. Participant 30 was assessed at regular 3-year intervals (at ages 43, 46, and 49), whereas Participant 32 was assessed at irregular intervals (at ages 17, 19, 23, 25, and 28). Notice that our participants vary not only with respect to length of measurement

interval, but also with regard to number of measurements. This reflects the reality of longitudinal studies, where participants are not available at the desired times of measurement. This kind of variability in spacing of measurements, common in long-term studies, presents no data analytic problem for growth curves estimated in a mixed-modeling framework. However, it violates key assumptions in the repeated-measures ANOVA model and also poses some difficulties for latent growth models estimated via SEM.

Fixed and Random Effects

The mixed-model approach to individual growth models yields two types of effects. These are fixed and random effects. Fixed effects are parameters (coefficients) that define the overall trajectory for the sample. Random effects are parameters that define the variability around the fixed effects. In a simple linear growth-curve model (no quadratic term), there are two fixed effects: an intercept and a slope.

Fixed Effects: Intercept

The intercept is the average amount of outcome (e.g., life satisfaction, positive emotion) where time equals zero. If the time representative is actual time, as in weeks passed since a baseline assessment or intervention, then the intercept defines the leftmost point of the trajectory. It is where the growth curve or trajectory passes through the y-axis. However, if time is clocked by age in a study, then the intercept is the amount of life satisfaction, for example, when age equals zero. This obviously lacks conceptual sense, in that it is impossible to imagine a newborn baby having developed a psychological construct as complex as life satisfaction. Hence it is often desirable to recenter the time variable in order to place the zero point at a more conceptually meaningful spot (Biesanz, Deeb-Sossa, Papadukis, Bollen, & Curran, 2004). This could be the mean entry age of people in your study, the mean overall age across all time points, or even the mean age at study exit. Recentering age around the grand mean has the effect of placing the intercept in the middle of the entire age distribution. As a result, the intercept is the predicted amount of the outcome at a fixed age. This creates ease in interpreting the overall growth curve, yet creates a disadvantage in that

TABLE 32.1 Example of Person Time File in a Growth-Curve Model

ID	Age	Life Satisfaction
30	43	11
30	46	12
30	49	12
30	52	15
31	66	13
31	69	14
31	72	13
31	75	13
32	17	5
32	19	9
32	23	7
32	25	6
32	28	3
33	31	8
33	35	10
33	37	15

some people in the sample may never have been assessed at the age that is the grand mean. For example, say a researcher has followed a group of people for 20 years, and these people represent a wide age range, with a mean age of 50. Some of the younger people in the sample would have been followed from age 20 to 40; some of the older members 60 to 80. None of these people were assessed at age 50, yet the interpretation of the intercept is amount of outcome at age 50 nonetheless. An alternative method of recentering is to person-center. In that technique, the investigator centers each individual around his or her own mean on age. In this case, the interpretation of the intercept is that it is amount of outcome at a given person's age mean. As one can see, it gives rise to less clear language and is a bit harder for readers to understand. Grand-mean and person-mean centering are the most commonly used recentering techniques in growth modeling and, as shown above, each has its advantages and disadvantages. Regardless of the choice a researcher makes, recentering should have the effect of improving interpretation of the intercept in the researcher's own data. The choice should be driven by the substantive concerns of the researcher (Biesanz et al., 2004).

Fixed Effects: Slope

The slope is the amount of change in the variable of interest, per unit of time. If time is clocked in units of weeks, then the slope represents amount of change per week. If it is clocked in units of years, then the slope represents amount of change per year. Fundamentally, the fixed effect for slope quantifies rate of change in the main variable of interest. Together, the intercept and slope define the shape of the overall trajectory, if it is purely linear. The trajectory is no more than a regression line characterized by an intercept and slope. It will tell if the positive outcome of interest increases, decreases, or remains stable over a period of time, but it will also yield the rate of change. Does the variable increase quickly, or decrease slowly? These fixed effects, however, define only the overall, sample-level trajectory. Yet mixed models yield more than this; they also estimate the individual differences around the intercept and slope. These are known as the random effects. It is the estimation of these variances (and covariances) that lead some to label mixed models *random coefficient models*.

Random Effects: Intercept

All random effects estimate individual variability around a growth parameter, be it an intercept, slope, or curvature estimate. The random effect for the intercept is the estimate of variance around the intercept parameter. If statistically significant, it simply tells you if there is a nonzero variance in amount of the outcome at a given point (wherever you have centered the time variable). In the table 32.1 example, there are individual differences in simple level of life satisfaction (ignoring measurement occasion), and these individual differences would show up in a significant intercept variance. This is usually not very interesting to researchers, however, because they usually know if their outcome of interest differs across people or not.

Random Effects: Slope

What is typically much more interesting is the random effect for slope, because it tells us if rate of change varies by person. Imagine change in positive emotion in response to an intervention designed to increase it. Some people will have a strong response and will rise quickly; their trajectories will possess a steep slope. Others will respond in a weaker fashion and display less steep slopes. Others still may have no response and show flat slopes over time. A slope of zero implies stability, or no change over time. Finally, a few people in the study may display declines, or negative slopes, in positive emotion. What this example illustrates is a range of slopes, some large, some small, some zero, some positive, and some negative. Such individual differences in rate of change exemplify the aforementioned life span principle of interindividual differences in intraindividual change (Baltes et al., 1977). It also demonstrates how the fixed effect for slope can be defined by a particular value, but surrounding it there can be considerable individual differences in slope values. The overall sample trajectory may show a rise in positive emotion, but many individuals may nonetheless not conform to the overall pattern.

Modeling Intercept, Linear Growth, and Quadratic Growth Successively

The initial data analytic step in any analysis of change is an unconditional means model (Singer & Willett, 2003), also known as an intercept-only model (Raudenbush & Bryk, 2002). The unconditional means model fits only an overall mean and the variance around that mean across all persons and measurement occasions. The time variable is not even part of the equation at this step (Singer & Willett, 2003). The fixed effect in the unconditional means model is simply the grand mean across all measurements. Sticking with the positive emotion example, this would be the mean amount of positive emotion irrespective of time point. One random effect is estimated as well, the variance around the intercepts. This captures the between-person differences in intercept, or simply the individual differences in level of positive emotion, irrespective of measurement occasion. The remaining variance is the within-person variance in positive emotion, plus error. These estimates of between- and within-person variances are useful. The former tells you how much of the variability is due to between-person differences, or individual differences; the latter represents how much people vary from themselves. The unconditional means model also provides a benchmark of within-person variance that we can use to judge successive models (Raudenbush & Bryk, 2002). The ratio of between- to within-person variance is sometimes called the intraclass correlation, and the rule of thumb is that it should be above .10 to permit moving on to growth-curve models (Raudenbush & Bryk, 2002). Anything less than .10 indicates very little within-person variability.

The next step is to add the time variable into the equation. It may be centered or not, and it can take different forms (age, weeks, grade in school), but the addition of this term to the model allows estimation of fixed and random effects for both intercept and slope. This is the linear growth model. If time is clocked via age, then a formal definition of the model can be expressed as:

$$\text{Positive Outcome} = \pi_{0i} + \pi_{1i}(\text{age}_{ij}) + \varepsilon_{ij} \quad (1)$$

The amount of positive outcome for individual i at measurement occasion j is a function of the person's age at that measurement occasion (age_{ij}). The intercept, π_{0i}, is the predicted amount of positive outcome where age $= 0$ (or if recentered, at some age). The linear coefficient, π_{1i}, is the rate of change (slope); it is the predicted annual amount of change in positive outcome for person i. ε_{ij} represents the errors on each person i at occasion j.

This model is expressed in terms of individuals in that each person's longitudinal trajectory can be described by this equation. The variability in intercepts and slopes across i persons are the random effects. Together, the many intercepts and slopes are used to estimate the overall trajectory intercept and slope, that is, the fixed effects. Standard errors are also estimated for each of the random and fixed effects.

The linear growth model is often adequate for characterizing change in a variable, but sometimes a more complex relationship is necessary. Frequently, curvilinearity best portrays the shape of a growth curve over time. By adding a squared function of our time variable to the linear growth model, we create the quadratic growth model. More formally, the model is expressed as:

$$\text{Positive Outcome} = \pi_{0i} + \pi_{1i}(\text{age}_{ij}) \\ + \pi_{2i}(\text{age}_{ij})^2 + \in_{ij} \quad (2)$$

The quadratic coefficient, π_{2i}, estimates amount of curvature for person i. Note that three parameters are estimated in the quadratic model: intercept, slope, and curvature. Because of the extra estimation, the usual minimum of three measurement occasions is inadequate. At least four occasions are required for the quadratic model. Similarly, if cubic functions of time are estimated, to test for a second bend in the curve, at least five measurement occasions are required. In any case, the usual progression in growth curve modeling is to test simpler models first and then move toward more complex models if conceptual justification is present. An unconditional means model should be estimated first, then a linear growth model, and then, if justified, a quadratic growth model (Singer & Willett, 2003). In the behavioral sciences, complex phenomena such as cubic growth are rare, and it is rarer still to find theory that predicts such phenomena.

Explaining Change: Level 2 Models

All of the growth models described above are Level 1 models (Raudenbush & Bryk, 2002). In multilevel modeling terminology, they reside at the first level, meaning that they describe a within-person association. Even the fixed effects, which reflect sample-level parameters, are nevertheless based on the within-person relationship between time and some outcome. Linear and quadratic growth models are Level 1 models. If the slope or curvature variance (random effects) are significant and large enough at Level 1, the investigator may go on to Level 2 models, which introduce predictors or other explanatory variables to attempt to account for individual differences in the outcome. For example, imagine we estimate longitudinal trajectories of Bryant's (1989, 2003) savoring construct and find that there are statistically significant and considerable individual differences in rate of change. We can then bring in between-person variables in a second level of the model to try to explain some of that variance. Candidates might include a transforming positive experience, such as getting married (or leaving a bad relationship) or some type of spiritual growth. Using a Level 2 that adds one or more of these explanatory variables to the equation permits the researcher to compare slopes of those who had the transforming positive experience versus those who did not. If those who had such an experience displayed slopes that were significantly larger (and positive) compared to those who did not, then we would have identified a between-person variable that accounts for some of the variability in rate of change in savoring life.

In a study that applied individual growth models to personality trait data (Mroczek & Spiro, 2003a), death of spouse was used to predict change in neuroticism over a 12-year period in older adults. The Level 1 model determined that there was statistically significant variability in neuroticism change slopes over 12 years. At Level 2, death of spouse was introduced into the model as a between-person variable. It was a very simple between-person variable in that it was dichotomous. In the sample of older adults, some had experienced the death of their spouse within the 2 years prior to the 12-year longitudinal period, and others had not. This dichotomous variable significantly predicted both intercept and slope of neuroticism. People whose spouses had died started out higher on neuroticism than those who had not endured such a trauma, but then displayed slopes that went down at a faster rate over the next 12 years. In other words, neuroticism was temporarily elevated immediately after the death of one's spouse, but then reverted back in the years following. The between-person variable "death of spouse" accounted for some, but not all, of the individual variability in neuroticism slopes over a 12-year period. This finding is particularly apt

for readers of this volume, because it speaks to the resiliency of humankind in the face of adversity and trauma. It also provides a nice example of how individual growth models can be applied to questions of personality, well-being, or other outcomes relevant to positive psychology.

Future Directions in the Application of Growth Modeling in Positive Psychology

How can growth-curve modeling further our understanding of positive psychological phenomena? We believe that growth modeling is applicable to variety of current issues in positive psychology, and that its use might address some of the current problems in the literature.

Understanding Positive Change

One obvious but powerful way that growth-curve modeling can benefit positive psychology is in furthering our understanding of how different positive characteristics change over time. The longitudinal study of positive states and traits should be a main priority for researchers, especially considering the criticism that most of what we know about positive psychological phenomena is based on cross-sectional studies (Lazarus, 2003). Making the assumption that differences among age cohorts are a reflection of time is a dangerous proposition. For instance, there have been different findings for the association between age and subjective well-being when comparing cross-sectional and longitudinal research (Diener, Suh, Lucas, & Smith, 1999; Mroczek, 2001). What are missing in much of the positive psychology literature are longitudinal trajectories. Growth-curve models allow researchers to estimate trajectories for the variable of interest, be it life satisfaction, gratitude, or hope. In essence, growth models provide a means of understanding the developmental nature of a variety of psychological phenomena, something that has often been lacking in positive psychological research.

Understanding Positive Differences

Another issue related to our lack of understanding of longitudinal change in positive psychological phenomena is the relative inattention given to within-person change (Eid &

Diener, 1999; Lazarus, 2003). While there are a plethora of good studies on between-person differences regarding a number of different constructs in positive psychology, almost no attention has been given to how persons differ from themselves across multiple points in time. Why should positive psychologists care about within-person change? Besides providing a more comprehensive understanding of the variable of interest, studying change within individuals also addresses a fundamental issue in positive psychology, which is whether certain positive characteristics, such as optimism or courage, represent stable dispositions or are more malleable and subject to exogenous influences. We believe that the most comprehensive way of understanding this issue of stability versus change is recognizing that there need not be a mutually exclusive yes-or-no answer (Mroczek & Spiro, 2003a). Some persons change in positive qualities (for better or worse); others do not. As previously discussed, one particular strength of growth models is that by providing estimates of both fixed and random effects, the researcher can attend to group trajectories while also studying how particular individuals deviate from this norm.

Predicting Positive Change

Beyond its descriptive capabilities of estimating both between-persons and within-person differences, an even more attractive quality of growth modeling is that allows the researcher to predict interindividual differences in how persons change over time. Understanding the cause and correlates of positive psychological phenomena is a central aim in positive psychology (Seligman & Csikszentmihalyi, 2000). Up to this point, a preponderance of research has been devoted to predicting between-person differences in levels of positive psychological characteristics (e.g., do levels of neuroticism predict differences in levels of life satisfaction?). Less research, however, has been conducted on what predicts between-persons differences in how individuals change in positive phenomena over time (e.g., do levels of neuroticism predict between-person differences in how persons change in life satisfaction over time?).

Using predictors in growth models not only helps researchers understand how a person comes to change in a particular positive attribute but also enables the investigator to test the influence of some positive psychological

characteristic on the changing nature of some other variable of interest. For example, one researcher might be interested in how the characteristic of hope in patients with cancer changes over the course of their illness. In this case, one can use growth models to test how the variable of spirituality predicts individual differences in how hope changes over the course of these patients' illness. Another researcher might be more concerned with how the characteristic of hope within sickly patients is related to changes in life satisfaction over time. In this case, hope is used as the predictor variable. These two examples illustrate the varied ways that growth modeling can be used to understand the underlying nature and influence of a variety of positive attributes.

Measuring Positive Interventions

This discussion of stability versus change and the prediction of individual differences in intraindividual change brings us to one other prospective use of growth models in positive psychology. As touched upon in our introduction, some researchers in positive psychology are also interested in positive psychological interventions (Seligman, 2000). Are the mechanisms that have been studied in a variety of positive phenomena applicable to real-world treatment? More specifically, can psychologists induce positive change? Answering this question necessitates statistical methodology capable of estimating such change. Growth models provide an advantage over some more traditional methodologies (e.g., repeated measures ANOVA) in that by considering individual differences in intraindividual change they provide a better estimate of not only whether such change occurs, but for whom. Comparing mean scores across time points only tells about the effect of an intervention as it relates to the entire group; it says little about particular individuals. By considering individual change, researchers can better tailor their interventions accordingly. For instance, an intervention that seeks to increase levels of positive affect by having participants engage in more optimistic thinking might lead to significant and sustained differences over time. However, by attending to individual differences in positive affect trajectories, a researcher might observe that these upward trends in positive affect vary according to levels of extraversion. Those high in extraversion show pronounced increases in positive affect, while those low in extraversion show little change at all (a flat trajectory). This valuable information can be used not only in understanding the true nature of the effects of the intervention but also in planning future treatment.

Conclusion

To reiterate what we argued above, the longitudinal study of positive states and traits needs to become a main priority for researchers in positive psychology. As mentioned earlier, the late Richard Lazarus leveled a potent and valid criticism at the positive psychology movement when he stated that most of what we know about positive psychological phenomena is based on cross-sectional studies (Lazarus, 2003). As we have argued throughout this chapter, longitudinal designs coupled with growth-curve models is a powerful corrective to this shortcoming of research in positive psychology. By studying change in positive states and traits, we will gain a deeper and more sophisticated understanding of positive psychological phenomena.

Acknowledgments   The writing of this chapter was supported in part by a grant from the National Institute on Aging (R01-AG18436) to Dan Mroczek.

References

Alwin, D. F. (1994). Aging, personality, and social change: The stability of individual differences over the adult span. In D. L. Featherman, R. M. Lerner, & M. Perlmutter (Eds.), *Life-span development and behavior* (Vol. 12, pp. 135–185). Hillsdale, NJ: Erlbaum.

Baltes, P. B., Reese, H. W., & Nesselroade, J. R. (1977). *Lifespan developmental psychology: Introduction to research methods.* Monterey, CA: Brooks Cole.

Biesanz, J. C., Deeb-Sossa, N., Papadukis, A. A., Bollen, K. A., & Curran, P. J. (2004). The role of coding time in estimating and interpreting growth curve models. *Psychological Methods, 9,* 30–52.

Bryant, F. B. (1989). A four factor model of perceived control: Avoiding, coping, obtaining, savoring. *Journal of Personality 57*(4), 773–797.

Bryant, F. B. (2003). Savoring beliefs inventory (SBI): A scale for measuring beliefs about savoring. *Journal of Mental Health 12*(2), 175–196.

Cattell, R. B. (1966). The data box: Its ordering of total resources in terms of possible relational systems. In R. B. Cattell (Ed.), *Handbook of multivariate experimental psychology* (pp. 97–134). Chicago: Rand-McNally.

Charles, S. T., Reynolds, C. A., & Gatz, M. (2001). Age-related differences and change in positive and negative affect over 23 years. *Journal of Personality and Social Psychology, 80,* 136–151.

Diener, E., Suh, E., Lucas, R. E., & Smith, H. L. (1999). Subjective well-being: Three decades of progress. *Psychological Bulletin, 125,* 276–302.

Eid, M., & Diener, E. (1999). Intraindividual variability in affect: reliability, validity, and personality correlates. *Journal of Personality and Social Psychology, 76,* 662–676.

Fleeson, W. (2001). Toward a structure- and process-integrated view of personality: Traits as density distributions of states. *Journal of Personality and Social Psychology, 80,* 1011–1027.

Fredrickson, B. L. (2003). The value of positive emotions: The emerging science of positive psychology is coming to understand why it's good to feel good. *American Scientist, 91,* 330–335.

Fredrickson, B. L., & Levenson, R. W. (1998). Positive emotions speed recovery from the cardiovascular sequelae of positive emotions. *Cognition and Emotion, 12,* 191–220.

Hooker, K., & McAdams, D. P. (2003). Personality reconsidered: A new agenda for aging research. *Journal of Gerontology: Psychological Sciences, 58,* 296–304.

Lazarus, R. S. (2003). Does the positive psychology movement have legs? *Psychological Inquiry, 14,* 93–109.

Lyubomirsky, S. (2001). Why are some people happier than others? The role of cognitive and motivational processes in well-being. *American Psychologist, 56,* 239–249.

McArdle, J. J. (1991). Structural models of development theory in psychology. *Annals of Theoretical Psychology, 7,* 139–159.

Mroczek, D. K. (2001). Age and emotions in adulthood. *Current Directions in Psychological Science, 10,* 87–90.

Mroczek, D. K., & Spiro, A., III. (2003a). Modeling intraindividual change in personality traits: Findings from the Normative Aging Study. *Journals of Gerontology: Psychological Sciences, 58B,* P153–P165.

Mroczek, D. K., & Spiro, A., III. (2003b). Personality structure and process, variance between and within: Integration by means of developmental framework. *Journal of Gerontology: Psychological Sciences, 58B,* 305–306.

Mroczek, D. K., Spiro, A., & Almeida, D. M. (2003). Between- and within-person variation in affect and personality over days and years: How basic and applied approaches can inform one another. *Ageing International, 28,* 260–278.

Nesselroade, J. R. (1988). Sampling and generalizability: Adult development and aging issues examined within the general methodological framework of selection. In K. W. Schaie, R. T. Campbell, W. M. Meredith, & S. C. Rawlings (Eds.), *Methodological issues in aging research* (pp. 123–141). New York: Springer.

Nesselroade, J. R. (1991). Interindividual differences in intraindividual change. In L. M.Collins & J. L. Horn (Eds.), *Best methods for the analysis of change* (pp. 92–105). Washington, DC: American Psychological Association.

Raudenbush, S. W., & Bryk, A. S. (2002). *Hierarchical linear models: Applications and data analysis methods* (2nd ed.). Thousand Oaks, CA: Sage.

Rogosa, D. R., Brandt, D., & Zimowski, M. (1982). A growth curve approach to the measurement of change. *Psychological Bulletin, 92,* 726–748.

Seligman, M. E. P. (2000). Positive psychology, positive prevention, and positive therapy. In C. R. Snyder & S. J. Lopez (Eds.), *The handbook of positive psychology* (pp. 63–73). Oxford: Oxford University Press

Seligman, M. E. P., & Csikszentmihalyi, M. (2000). Happiness, excellence, and optimal functioning. *American Psychologist, 55,* 5–14.

Sheldon, K. M., & Houser-Marko, A. (2001). Self-concordance, goal-attainment, and the pursuit of happiness: Can there be an upward spiral? *Journal of Personality and Social Psychology, 80,* 152–165.

Sheldon, K. M., & Kasser, T. (2001). Getting older, getting better? Personal strivings and psychological maturity across the life span. *Developmental Psychology, 37,* 491–501.

Singer, J. D. (1998). Using SAS Proc Mixed to fit multilevel models, hierarchical models, and individual growth models. *Journal of Educational and Behavioral Statistics, 23,* 323–355.

Singer, J. D., & Willett, J. B. (2003). *Applied longitudinal analysis: Modeling change and event occurrence.* New York: Oxford University Press.

Willett, J. B., & Sayer, A. G. (1994). Using covariance structure analysis to detect correlates and predictors of individual change over time. *Psychological Bulletin, 116,* 363–381.

33

Understanding Journeys

Growth-Curve Analysis as a Tool for Studying Individual Differences in Change Over Time

Julie K. Norem and Jasmina Burdzovic Andreas

Imagine a race with three runners. Runner A crosses the finish line first, followed fairly closely by Runner B. Runner C finishes last. Studying how the winner of the race trained prior to the race, and the strategies she used while running, may reveal techniques that can improve results for other runners. If one is interested in running a good race, it makes good sense to study winners, and focusing on Runner A would seem the way to go.

Positive psychologists often study winners. There are times, however, when we may learn more about successful life strategies by studying not the absolute winners in a domain, that is, those who report the most satisfaction, the best health, or the best performance; but the also-rans, who may not come in first, but who excel in different ways, overcoming different obstacles and conflicts, and finding ways to adapt to complicated personal life circumstances. There is more than one way to run a good race, and there are many different kinds of races on different kinds of tracks. Sprinters train differently than hurdlers or marathoners, and what works well

for one group may not work for another. If, in our imaginary race, we were to find that Runner A ran in an inside lane with no obstructions, while Runners B and C ran in lanes that included hurdles, our perception of who the winner was might change. When we realize that Runner B almost matched Runner A's time, despite having to jump hurdles along the way, our interest in her training regime and strategies might increase. What allowed Runner B to outpace Runner C, who was running the race most similar to Runner B's?

One of the goals of positive psychology is to further our understanding of how to live the good life. To understand how people can live a good life, we need to pay attention to where people start their life journeys, what they carry with them, what obstacles they do (and do not) encounter along the way, and where they are trying to go. Knowing relative outcomes for different individuals tells us very little: for example, it is doubtful that most people would be able to find their way to the presidency of the United States by following George W. Bush's academic path.

Positive psychologists have tended to use variable-focused methods to study the relations between optimism and outcomes such as health, mood, and life satisfaction. Such an approach, while undeniably important and useful, does have drawbacks, especially to the extent that it becomes an exclusive focus. Specifically, it ignores the fact that personality has structure, and that personality processes arise from, are related to, and influence that structure, such that process and structure must be studied together within individuals. What that abstract statement means more specifically is that optimism is not simply something that exists in a vacuum, or floats around in the ether, ready to attach willy-nilly to different individuals, and thereby independently influence their life outcomes. Rather, optimism is but one aspect of personality, and is, to varying degrees, integrated with other personality characteristics and the particulars of personal history and social context. Its effects, then, will be constrained by or influenced by other aspects of personality and circumstance. Female executives have had to learn that simply adopting the traditionally successful negotiating tactics used by male executives may not lead them to the same success those men have enjoyed because behavior is not simply behavior: It occurs in a social context with gendered expectations, norms, and consequences. In the same way, coping and adaptation do not exist in the abstract: Their consequences and effects vary by culture, gender, race, and personality (Norem & Chang, 2002).

Thus far, there is a relative dearth of research that takes into account the ways in which optimism relates to other aspects of personality and social context: a relative dearth of person-focused research that takes into account not just static levels of optimism, but the challenges, goals, beliefs about the world, and efforts over time of people with different levels and different kinds of optimism. There are specific issues that arise if we ignore the structure or organization of personality and study isolated variables. As a specific example, most research on optimism fails to predict or account for the relative success of those who use defensive pessimism—a markedly nonoptimistic strategy for managing anxiety (Norem, 2001). Indeed, defensive pessimists, cursed with the double whammy of anxiety and pessimism, by most accounts should be failing miserably in their lives, and would at first glance appear to be ideal candidates for a good dose of restorative optimism. As is detailed below, however, there are good reasons to suspect that such a cure would do more harm than good. Without a theoretical perspective that takes into account the ways that this particular kind of pessimism (or lack of optimism) stems from individuals' agentic attempts to respond to their own anxiety in adaptive ways, one arrives at an incomplete and distorted understanding of the varieties of effective human adaptation.

Another hallmark of human adaptation is the ability to learn—especially, to learn from mistakes. To study that human potential effectively, however, requires a longitudinal approach that follows people in real-life circumstances as they work—iteratively—toward their goals over time. This is a rarity both in optimism research and in variable-focused research in general. To address this lack, we need process-focused ways to study individuals over time: methods that take into account differences in where individuals start, differences in paths toward important life outcomes, and the ways in which starting points and pathways influence where individuals finish.

Fortunately, researchers willing to embrace the potential complexity involved in taking seriously individual differences and process in these ways now have available a variety of data collection methods (e.g., experience sampling), advancements in measurement construction (e.g., item-response theory), and tools for data analysis (e.g., hierarchical linear modeling and individual growth-curve analysis) that allow them to identify meaningful coherence within that complexity.

One useful technique among the growing arsenal available to researchers is individual growth modeling (Singer & Willett, 2003). The purpose of this chapter is to provide an example of how this technique can help us to see both changes over time in variables of interest and different kinds of change that may characterize different individuals. Our particular results provide a useful example, because they are somewhat counterintuitive in the context of positive psychology and could be easily obscured without the appropriate analytic techniques. Our purpose is not to provide a detailed technical exposition or how-to manual for these analyses; those are available elsewhere (including other chapters in this volume, and the references listed at the end of this chapter). Rather, our aim is provide a concrete example from ongoing work on human adaptation that may help other researchers see how their theoretical questions can be translated into empirical work that helps do justice to the complexity of human behavior.

Defensive Pessimists and Strategic Optimists: Different Runners, Different Races

Not coincidentally, the particular example we use here is analogous to the imaginary race described initially. Our data come from ongoing research on the construct of *defensive pessimism*. Defensive pessimism is a motivated cognitive strategy that anxious individuals may employ to help them manage or harness their anxiety so that it does not interfere with their performance on a particular task or in a particular situation. From a social cognitive perspective on personality, motivated cognitive strategies describe coherent patterns of appraisal, planning, effort, reaction, and retrospection in the context of personal goals (Cantor & Harlow, 1994; Cantor, Norem, Niedenthal, Langston, & Brower, 1987; Norem, 2001). These strategies describe how people understand the situations that are relevant to their goals, and how they think, feel, and function as those situations unfold. As theoretical units of analysis, these strategies are similar to other affect and self-regulation strategies in the psychological literature (Baumeister, Heatherton, & Tice, 1993; Carver & Scheier, 1990). Here, motivated cognitive strategies are considered person variables because they describe individual differences in characteristic affective responses to and appraisals of similar objective situations.

For people using defensive pessimism, feeling out of control and anxious colors the interpretation of and reaction to particular situations; anxiety is phenomenologically and cognitively inseparable from those situations for these individuals. It is, therefore, part of the problem these individuals need to address if they are to persevere toward their goals, just as Runner B in our example must clear the hurdles in her path. If she simply starts running as if those hurdles are not there, she is certain to fall. If defensive pessimists try simply to ignore their anxiety, they too risk potentially debilitating stumbles. Defensive pessimists need to manage their anxiety so that it does not impair their performance or prevent them from accomplishing their goals. To do so, prior to a task, they set low expectations for how they will do, and mentally rehearse all the negative outcomes they can

imagine occurring. As they think about those negative outcomes in increasingly specific and concrete ways, they switch their focus from their own anxiety about outcome to plans for preventing or coping with potential negative outcomes and bringing about more positive outcomes. This specific and detailed mental rehearsal then generally leads to effective action.

Most previous research has contrasted those who use defensive pessimism with people using a strategy that has been called *strategic optimism*. People who use strategic optimism start out feeling calm, rather than anxious. They set high expectations prior to goal-relevant tasks, performances, or situations, and feel in control. They then actively avoid thinking about possible outcomes, preferring to distract themselves from the impending performance so as to avoid becoming anxious. Like Runner A, their path toward their goal is relatively clear.

Previous research shows that those using defensive pessimism and strategic optimism typically perform equally well when each group uses its characteristic strategy. Experimental manipulations designed to get either group to use the other group's strategy, however, typically result in performance decrements. Thus, increasing positive mood among defensive pessimists leads to poorer performance, as does distracting them, relaxing them, or making them more optimistic; getting strategic optimists to mentally rehearse prior to a performance has similar detrimental effects (Norem & Cantor, 1986; Norem & Illingworth, 1993, 2004; Spencer & Norem, 1996).

We have learned a great deal about these strategies by contrasting them, but sole focus on comparing outcomes for these two groups can also present a somewhat distorted picture, depending on the outcomes one chooses to compare. Specifically, at any given point in time, it is quite likely that defensive pessimists will report more negative affect or less positive affect than strategic optimists. They are also very likely to report lower self-esteem (Norem, 2001; Norem & Illingworth, 2004). If, as is generally the case, their performances are equivalent to the defensive pessimists', but the strategic optimists are happier and feel better about themselves, it is very tempting to conclude that strategic optimists have the better strategy and that they have won the race.

For this interpretation to hold, we would have to be able to argue that strategic optimists showed better adaptation to the same situation as defensive pessimists. This, however, fails to take into account that strategic optimists and defensive pessimists—like Runner A and Runner B—are running different races, starting from different positions, respectively without and with the hurdle of anxiety.

Ideally, to understand fully the adaptive nature and consequences of defensive pessimism, one could hope to do two things: (1) consider defensive pessimists' outcomes—where they end up—in ways that take into account where they began; and (2) compare the pathways and outcomes (e.g., appraisals, performance, progress toward goals) of anxious defensive pessimists over time, not just to those of strategic optimists but also to those of others who are equivalently anxious (i.e., to those who face similar hurdles) but do not use defensive pessimism. Happily, individual growth-curve modeling with longitudinal data allows us to meet both objectives, while avoiding or minimizing some of the problems characteristic of longitudinal studies, analysis of change, and analyses based solely on between-group differences.

An Example: Strategic Optimists, Defensive Pessimists, and Other Anxious Folk

The data for the current example come from a study of women at an elite liberal arts college. An initial sample of 90 women completed a large battery of questionnaires shortly after they arrived on campus for their first semester of college. Subsequently, study participants completed measures at three additional time points: at the end of their first year, the end of their senior year, and the end of their first year out of college. For the purposes of this example, we will only be considering three measures: (1) the measure of defensive pessimism completed at the beginning of the study (Defensive Pessimism Questionnaire, or DPQ; Norem, 2001); (2) the trait measure of anxiety completed at the beginning of the study from the State-Trait Anxiety Inventory (STAI; Spielberger, Gorsuch, Lushene, Vagg, & Jacobs, 1983); and (3) the Rosenberg Self-Esteem Scale completed at each time point (Rosenberg, 1965). Using tripartite splits on the anxiety measure and standard scoring on the DPQ, we identified three groups of participants based on the theoretical distinctions discussed above: low anxious strategic op-

timists (from the upper tertile of the DPQ and the lower tertile of the STAI), highly anxious women who used defensive pessimism (from the upper tertile of both the DPQ and the STAI), and anxious women who did not report using defensive pessimism (from the lower two tertiles of the DPQ and the upper two tertiles of the STAI). (Further details concerning creation of these groups are available from the first author.) The result was a sample of 78 participants ($n = 32$ defensive pessimists, $n = 28$ anxious women, $n = 18$ strategic optimists) for whom we had at least three measures—a recommended minimum for fitting a linear trajectory—of self-esteem over the four testing periods in the study.

Based on previous research, we expected that defensive pessimists would report significantly lower initial self-esteem than the other two groups. Because their strategy allows them to approach their goals in an adaptive way, however, we predicted that they would show significant increases in self-esteem as they progressed through college and began the transition to their lives after college. In contrast, we expected that the anxious women who did not use defensive pessimism would have less success pursuing their goals over time—given their lack of an effective anxiety-management strategy—and thus show decreases in self-esteem over time. We expected little change in self-esteem among the strategic optimists: Their self-esteem is high to begin with, and continued success should only maintain that high level of self-esteem.[1]

We used individual growth modeling (Bryk & Raudenbush, 1992; Singer & Willett, 2003) as the primary analytical and statistical tool in this report (with SAS PROC MIXED procedure; cf. Singer, 1998; Willett, Singer, & Martin, 1998). This method allows for examination of longitudinal data, even if the data are incomplete (i.e., there are missing values at certain assessments), and produces longitudinal growth trajectories as a function of predictor variables. In other words, each student's individual trajectory of self-esteem is defined by its initial estimated status (intercept) and its change over time (slope), which can be modeled independently.

Because students were observed on multiple occasions (a total of four occasions in this specific case), assessment times were nested within students, and a two-level model was used as the most appropriate. In this model, students' self-esteem (SELF-EST) can be expressed as a linear function of time assessments:

$$\text{SELF-EST}_{ti} = \beta_{0i} + \beta_{1i}{}^* \, (\text{Time}) + e_{ti} \quad (1)$$

This equation represents what is also known as the *within-person differences* model (or Level 1 model in hierarchical linear modeling), and it describes the individual growth trajectory of self-esteem for each student i for each time occasion t. Value β_{0i} is the true level of a student's initial self-esteem (i.e., during the year before starting college), while the parameter β_{1i} shows the true rate of change in self-esteem over time. Note that the first assessment time was shortly upon students' college entry, and therefore the estimated intercept value for students' self-esteem when β coefficients are zero would be the year before college entry (rather than the meaningless year 0). Such structuring of the time variable makes interpretation of results both easier and more meaningful (Singer & Willett, 2003).

The next step is to attempt to explain (by adding predictors to the model) the possible variations in students' self-esteem over time. That is the role of a second model (also known as the Level 2 or *between-person differences* model), where substantive predictors are hypothesized to predict both the differences in students' initial levels of self-esteem (β_{0i}) and the changes in self-esteem over time (β_{1i}). In our case, the substantive predictor of interest was students' strategy classification at the beginning of college:[2]

$$\beta_{0i} = \gamma_{00} + \gamma_{01}(\text{DP}) + \gamma_{02}(\text{ANX}) + u_{01}$$
$$\beta_{1i} = \gamma_{10} + \gamma_{11}(\text{DP}) + \gamma_{12}(\text{ANX}) + u_{11} \quad (2)$$

In sum, Equation 2 shows that the individual initial differences in self-esteem and changes in self-esteem over time were hypothesized to be a function of time and student's strategy. Residuals u in the above equations are similar to the residuals in regular regressions and denote the portion of variance unexplained by the substantive predictors. Similarly, the interpretation of γ parameters parallels the interpretation of the regular regression coefficients, with the additional difference that the γ_0 intercept parameters refer to the differences in initial self-esteem (and are similar to main effects in regression), while the γ_1 slope parameters refer to the differences in self-esteem rates of change (and are similar to interaction effects in regression).[3]

We first tested the hypothesized general model without any predictors (also known as the *unconditional growth model*), in which only the effects of time on outcome are examined. It is possible that there is no change in self-esteem over time, or that there are no variations in individual trajectories over time. If that were true, that would mean that there is no change over time to be investigated, and adding predictors to the model would be meaningless. In this case, the examination of variance components revealed that there were significant variations in students' initial levels of self-esteem (estimate = .83, $p < .001$) as well as in rates of change in self-esteem over time (estimate = .0088, $p = .08$). Moreover, the results for the fixed β parameters were also statistically significant: $\beta_0 = 6.73$, $p < .0001$ (indicating that the average true self-esteem in the year before college entry was significantly different than zero for this sample of college students), and $\beta_1 = .074$, $p < .001$ (indicating that the average changes in self-esteem over time were significant for this sample of college students). In short, addition of substantive predictors (i.e., Level 2) would be meaningful in this case and would help explain significant variations in students' self-esteem, both in the initial status (intercept) and in rates of change over time (slope).

The full model (as described in Equation 2) was tested and the estimated parameters are shown in table 33.1:

$$\begin{aligned}
\text{Est. SELF-EST}_{ti} &= [\gamma_{00} + \gamma_{01}(\text{DP})_i + \gamma_{02}(\text{ANX})_i] \\
&\quad + [\gamma_{10} + \gamma_{11}(\text{DP})_i + \gamma_{11}(\text{ANX})_i] \\
&\quad \times [\text{Time}]_{ti}
\end{aligned}$$

The addition of substantive predictors (i.e., students' strategies in this case) significantly reduced the slope variance, which was now reduced to almost zero (estimate = $1.31e^{-20}$). In other words, the significant variance in individual self-esteem trajectories that was observed in the unconditional model (i.e., the time-only model) was fully accounted for by the inclusion of students' strategies in the model. At intercept (i.e., before college entry), the mean self-esteem score was $\gamma_{00} = 7.48$ ($p < .0001$), indicating that most students had self-esteem significantly different from zero. With this particular variable, this test is not meaningful, but with variables that have a meaningful zero point (e.g., amount of drinking), this test could be considerably more informative. Also, the average slope coefficient was $\gamma_{10} = .07$ ($p = .044$), indicating a positive

TABLE 33.1 Growth-Curve Model for Students' Self-Esteem During and After College, as a Function of Student Early Optimistic Orientation

Parameter	Coefficient	SE
Intercept (β_{01})		
Intercept (γ_{00})	7.48***	.23
Defensive pessimist (DP; γ_{01})	−1.17***	.29
Anxious (ANX; γ_{02})	−.72*	.30
Linear Slope (β_{11})		
Intercept (γ_{10})	−.07*	.034
Defensive pessimist (DP; γ_{11})	.11*	.043
Anxious (ANX; γ_{12})	−.129**	.045

Note: For the categorical variable of students' early optimistic orientation, the reference group was Optimists (OPT).

$^{f}p < .10.$ $^{*}p < .05.$ $^{**}p < .01.$ $^{***}p < .001.$

average growth in self-esteem over time for college students in this sample. Finally, additional examination of variance components revealed a negative association between the intercept and slope (estimate = −.0027, $p = .033$), such that students with higher initial self-esteem experienced the least change over time.

As expected, there were significant main effects of students' strategy on intercept (DP $\gamma_{01} = -1.17$, $p < .001$, and ANX $\gamma_{02} = -.72$, $p = .02$), such that defensive pessimists and anxious nonpessimists had lower self-esteem than students who were strategic optimists in the year preceding college entry. More specifically, defensive pessimists had initial self-esteem scores more than one scale point lower than the optimists ($\gamma_{01} = -1.17$), while the anxious students had initial self-esteem scores almost three quarters of a scale point lower than the optimists ($\gamma_{02} = -.72$). Thus, as in previous research, defensive pessimists begin college with lower self-esteem than strategic optimists. The other anxious students, though not as low in self-esteem as the defensive pessimists, are still less positive about themselves than the strategic optimists.

Our primary interest, however, is to go beyond previous work showing mean differences, to look at changes over time as individuals work toward their goals. Our hypothesis was that defensive pessimism would help anxious individuals make progress in their lives, while anxious people without defensive pessimism as a strategy would flounder. In support of this hypothesis, we observed significant effects of students' strategy on the self-esteem slope. In other words, changes in students' self-esteem over time during and in the year after college

were significantly explained by their strategies (or lack thereof; DP $\gamma_{11} = .11$, $p = .01$, and ANX $\gamma_{12} = -.129$, $p = .004$), such that with each additional year, self-esteem increased in defensive pessimists (by approximately one tenth of a point) and decreased in anxious nondefensive pessimists (by approximately one eighth of a point).

Figure 33.1 shows linear growth trajectories for self-esteem for the women in our sample, as predicted by their strategy. We plotted all three groups: strategic optimists (OPT), anxious (ANX), and depressive pessimistic (DP) students. The line for the strategic optimists increases modestly, showing relatively little change in self-esteem over time for this group of women. In contrast, there is significant change from the first year of college to the first year after graduation for the other women, but that change is quite strikingly different for the defensive pessimists than for the other anxious women. The defensive pessimists show significant increases in self-esteem across the 5-year period under study, while the other anxious women—who do not use defensive pessimism—show a significant decline in self-esteem, and end up below where the defensive pessimists were when they began college.

Running the Good Race; Living the Good Life

Considerable research shows that there is a general trend for self-esteem to increase during late adolescence and young adulthood (e.g., Block & Robins, 1993; O'Malley & Backman, 1983). Self-esteem is also consistently positively

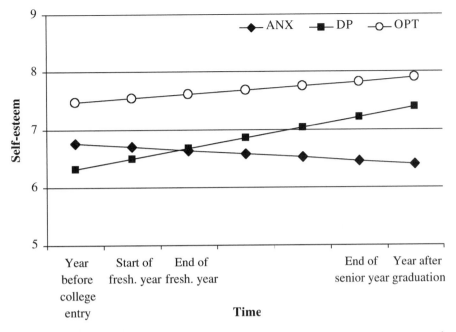

Figure 33.1 Self-esteem trajectories for anxious (ANX, $n = 28$), optimistic (OPT, $n = 18$), and depressive pessimistic ($n = 32$) college students.

correlated with optimism (Scheier, Carver, & Bridges, 1994). Our data illustrate, however, that there is much more going on than either a simple developmental trajectory that is common to everyone, or a between-individuals difference that reflects static levels within individuals over time. Instead, the picture painted with these data is that some people change very little, some change a lot, some go up, and some go down. These changes are not a result of error variance around a mean, but systematic and predictable patterns that make sense in terms of the different situations faced by different individuals, and the different strategies they use to function within those situations.

If we were simply to compare mean levels of self-esteem at different time points for all three groups (e.g., using repeated-measures ANOVA), we would find some of the differences revealed with growth curve analyses: The results would show a main effect for group membership, with strategic optimists having higher self-esteem than the other two groups; a main effect for time showing that self-esteem scores were significantly different at some time periods than others; and an interaction effect showing that the differences across time were different for the different groups. By looking at the group means

for each time period, we could see the relative standings of each group at each time period. It is not appropriate, however, to interpret results from repeated-measures ANOVA as showing the trajectories or rates of change over time for each group, whereas the results from growth-curve analysis do provide that information, both for the entire sample and as a function of predictor variables. Individual growth modeling lets us conclude that the defensive pessimists are indeed increasing in self-esteem over time, while the anxious nondefensive pessimists are decreasing (compared to strategic optimists); in addition, we can see that the anxious nondefensive pessimists decrease at a somewhat faster rate than the defensive pessimists increase. Finally, using an individual growth curve strategy allows us to show that the changes in self-esteem over time are related to where each group begins. More specifically, our results indicated that the greatest changes in self-esteem occurred in students who had the lowest initial self-esteem (i.e., the defensive pessimists), and that the least change occurred in the students who had the highest initial self-esteem (the strategic optimists). Strategic optimists show little positive growth, but given where they start, it seems unrealistic to expect them to do so.

Stability of (or modest increase in) self-esteem itself seems a good outcome for them. In contrast, both the anxious nondefensive pessimists and the defensive pessimists show considerable change or, one could argue, instability—though this change is systematic, which suggests we take care before labeling it instability. For the defensive pessimists, it seems reasonable to interpret that change as positive growth, whereas the downward trend for the other anxious women raises doubts about how well they are doing by the end of the study, and about the meaning and implications of their initially higher self-esteem (Crocker & Park, 2004).

The analysis reported here was conducted in a fairly low-power situation, with relatively few participants and considerable missing data. If we had simply used a repeated-measures ANOVA analysis, we could only have used the subset of participants for whom we had data at all four time points, which means our analysis would have been based on only 44 participants and 176 data points. In this study, as in many situations with repeated testing over time, several participants completed the questionnaires at several but not all of the time points. Adding complexity, different participants missed different testing sessions, so that for some participants there are data from T1, T2, and T4, for others there are data from T1, T3, and T4, and so on.

Individual growth curve modeling handles such cases with ease, as it essentially estimates the regression line for each participant based on the data available for that individual, allowing us to include in the analysis any participant for whom we have at least the three responses recommended for linear regression estimation. The analysis, thus, uses data from 78 participants rather than 44, and 278 data points rather than 176. In other words, individual growth-curve modeling allows us to benefit much more from the imperfect data we have than other traditional analyses do.

The present analysis by no means exhausts the potential individual growth-curve modeling represents for learning from these data. Although it is beyond the scope of this chapter to consider more complex questions and analysis in detail, we can just mention a few possibilities that seem worth pursuing. For example, this study actually includes the defensive pessimism, social satisfaction, and academic performance measures for each of the testing periods throughout the study. That means that in addition to having several self-esteem scores for most participants, we also have multiple measures on other variables that would allow us to use them in further analyses, as either outcome variables of interest (estimating how these three groups differ in terms of initial status and in changes over time in, for example, academic performance) or as predictors of self-esteem (estimating, for example, how academic performance influenced changes in self-esteem during college). Change in self-esteem could then be correlated with change in academic performance to see whether or how they might be related for the different groups. Because individual growth-curve modeling can estimate changes in one outcome (such as self-esteem) as a function not only of time-invariant predictors (as initial cognitive strategy was designated in our example) but of time-variant predictors as well (such as academic performance during each college year), one can theoretically explore a vast range of questions. We could see whether self-esteem change was more strongly related to social outcome predictors or academic outcome predictors—or whether (and if so, how) changes in one variable (such as self-esteem) relate to changes in another domain (such as academic performance). Because, in fact, in this study defensive pessimism was assessed at every time point, one might ask whether the increase in defensive pessimists' self-esteem is related to a decrease in their defensive pessimism, by examining defensive pessimism as a time-varying predictor of self-esteem.

Although the current data lack the power to fully explore hypotheses about nonlinear change, individual growth modeling would certainly allow investigation of quadratic or even more complex relationships (but for such complex equations more than four time points are needed, as there should be at least one time occasion more than the number of parameters in the equation being estimated). This, in turn, opens up the possibility of testing ever more sophisticated hypotheses about who should change on what variables across which contexts over time. One hypothesis of interest in defensive pessimism research, for example, is that the defensive pessimists should show gradual increases in self-confidence as they adapt to particular situations, but subsequent drops in self-esteem upon entering new situations, followed by increases. One or two more data points and a few more participants would allow testing of that hypothesis with individual growth modeling.

Responsibility and Positive Psychology

As work in positive psychology increases in sophistication, exploration of what it means to different individuals to live the good life and how they go about doing just that will need to pay increased attention to border conditions, limitations, costs and benefits, and individual, contextual, and cultural differences that influence when and whether particular processes lead to positive or beneficial outcomes. Theorists have argued, for example, that despite considerable evidence that optimism in various forms is related to positive outcomes, there may be limits to its benefits that are a function of how realistic that optimism is, the context in which it is expressed, or the other personality characteristics with which it is related within an individual (e.g., Norem, 2001; Weinstein & Klein, 1996). Research on defensive pessimism suggests the possibility that the benefits of optimism depend on whether one is anxious or not to begin with, such that changes in optimism that are not accompanied by decreases in anxiety may actually lead to worse outcomes for anxious individuals. Prior to large-scale implementation of efforts to increase optimism as a route to improving the lives of individuals (e.g., Seligman, Reivich, Jaycox, & Gillham, 1995), it would be useful to have further research about the extent to which continued increases in optimism beyond some level continue to be related to positive change. Is more optimism always better for everyone, or does it depend on where one starts? Can one be too optimistic? Does the answer to these questions depend on gender, cultural context, or personality? Exploring such hypotheses requires much more than a cross-sectional or Time 1–Time 2 study design that focuses only on one or two variables such as mood, even if those studies are replicated. Instead, we need a variety of longitudinal studies that allow us to look at short- and long-term effects and relations among sets of variables within different individuals. We also need, of course, the appropriate tools, both theoretical and empirical. Individual growth modeling seems likely to be one of our most useful of those tools. Moreover, by improving our understanding of what analytic methods like individual growth modeling can and cannot tell us about our data, we are likely to improve our theorizing and the design of our studies in corresponding ways.

There may be some disagreement about the extent to which positive psychology as a movement is focused on prescription rather than description, but there can be little doubt that the movement has a prominent public presence: countless newspaper articles, popular books, magazine articles, and radio and television shows have featured members of the movement and their research. It seems somewhat unlikely that the lay public—and the press—will bother with the often fine distinction between reports that describe how individuals do well, and prescriptions for what everyone should do. Members of the movement, thus, have had and are likely to continue to have a unique opportunity to give psychology away to an interested lay audience, who will be looking for prescriptions to follow from research on how to live a good life. Corresponding to this opportunity, therefore, is a unique responsibility to see that our research does justice not just to phenomena we study, but to the individuals whose lives we try to understand.

Notes

1. There are a number of analyses of additional adjustment and performance variables that support the predictions and explanations we offer for the self-esteem patterns growth-curve analysis reveals for these groups, but those analyses are not directly relevant to the demonstration in this chapter. Interested readers should contact the first author for further information about these analyses.

2. Students' strategy was coded as a categorical variable, where DP represented defensive pessimists ($n = 32$) and ANX represented anxious students ($n = 28$), while optimistic students (OPT; $n = 18$) were coded as a reference group through contrast coding similar to dummy coding in the standard multiple regression analyses. The SAS PROC MIXED procedure can distinguish between continuous and categorical variables. In this case, we specified the OPTs as the reference group by giving them the highest code of 3 (SAS uses the highest value as the default reference); the DPs were coded as 1, and the ANX were coded as 2.

3. For example, we can examine the effect of students' anxiety on intercept (or the initial differences in self-esteem before college entry, represented by the coefficient γ_{02}), as well as the effect of anxiety on slope (or on the rates of change in self-esteem, represented by the coefficient γ_{12}). A significant value for γ_{02} would indicate the significant effect of anxiety (i.e., anxious students having significantly different self-esteem than the

optimistic students before entering college), while the significant value for γ_{12} would indicate the significant effect of anxiety in regard to the changes in self-esteem over time (i.e., self-esteem for anxious students is changing at a significantly different rate than is self-esteem for optimistic students). The effects γ_{02} and γ_{12} are independent of each other and are interpreted in relation to the reference group (OPT).

References

Baumeister, R. F., Heatherton, T. F., & Tice, D. M. (1993). When ego threats lead to self-regulation failure: Negative consequences of high self-esteem. *Journal of Personality and Social Psychology, 64,* 141–156.

Block, J., & Robins, R. W. (1993). A longitudinal study of consistency and change in self-esteem from early adolescence to early adulthood. *Child Development, 64,* 909–923.

Bryk, A. S., & Raudenbush, S. W. (1992). *Hierarchical linear models: Applications and data analysis methods.* Newbury Park, CA: Sage.

Cantor, N., & Harlow, R. E. (1994). Personality, strategic behavior, and daily-life problem solving. *Current Directions in Psychological Science, 3*(6), 169–172.

Cantor, N., Norem, J. K., Niedenthal, P. M., Langston, C. A., & Brower, A. (1987). Life tasks, self-concept ideals, and cognitive strategies in a life transition. *Journal of Personality and Social Psychology, 53*(6), 1178–1191.

Carver, C. S., & Scheier, M. (1990). Principles of self-regulation: Action and emotion. In E. T. Higgins (Ed.), *Handbook of motivation and cognition: Foundations of social behavior* (pp. 3–52). New York: Guilford.

Crocker, J., & Park, L. E. (2004). The costly pursuit of self-esteem. *Psychological Bulletin, 130,* 392–414.

Norem, J. K. (2001). Defensive pessimism, optimism, and pessimism. In E. C. Chang (Ed.), *Optimism and pessimism: Implications for theory, research and practice* (pp. 77–100). Washington, DC: American Psychological Association.

Norem, J. K., & Cantor, N. (1986). Defensive pessimism: Harnessing anxiety as motivation. *Journal of Personality and Social Psychology, 51,* 1208–1217.

Norem, J. K., & Chang, E. C. (2002). The positive psychology of negative thinking. *Journal of Clinical Psychology, 58,* 993–1001.

Norem, J. K., & Illingworth, K. S. S. (1993). Strategy-dependent effects of reflecting on self and tasks: Some implications of optimism and defensive pessimism. *Journal of Personality and Social Psychology, 65,* 822–835.

Norem, J. K., & Illingworth, K. S. S. (2004). Mood and performance among defensive pessimists and strategic optimists. *Journal of Research in Personality, 38,* 351–366.

O'Malley, P. M., & Backman, J. G. (1983). Self-esteem: Change and stability between ages 13 and 23. *Developmental Psychology, 19,* 257–268.

Rosenberg, M. (1965). *Society and the adolescent self-image.* Princeton, NJ: Princeton University Press.

Scheier, M. F., Carver, C. S., & Bridges, M. W. (1994). Distinguishing optimism from neuroticism (and trait anxiety, self-mastery, and self-esteem): A reevaluation of the Life Orientation Test. *Journal of Personality and Social Psychology, 67*(6), 1063–1078.

Seligman, M. E. P., Reivich, K., Jaycox, L., & Gillham, J. (1995). *The optimistic child.* Boston: Houghton Mifflin.

Singer, J. D. (1998). Using SAS PROC MIXED to fit multilevel models, hierarchical models, and individual growth models. *Journal of Educational and Behavioral Statistics, 24,* 323–355.

Singer, J. D., & Willett, J. B. (2003). *Applied longitudinal data analysis: Modeling change and event occurrence.* Oxford: Oxford University Press.

Spencer, S. M., & Norem, J. K. (1996). Reflection and distraction: Defensive pessimism, strategic optimism, and performance. *Personality and Social Psychology Bulletin, 22*(4), 354–365.

Spielberger, C., Gorsuch, R., Lushene, R., Vagg, P., & Jacobs, G. (1983). *The manual for the State-Trait Anxiety Inventory.* Palo Alto, CA: Consulting Psychologists Press.

Weinstein, N. D., & Klein, W. M. (1996). Unrealistic optimism: Present and future. *Journal of Social and Clinical Psychology, 15*(1), 1–8.

Willett, J. B., Singer, J. D., & Martin, N. C. (1998). The design and analysis of longitudinal studies of development and psychopathology in context: Statistical models and methodological recommendations. *Development and Psychopathology, 10,* 395–426.

34

Assessing the Ebb and Flow of Daily Life With an Accent on the Positive

Alex J. Zautra, Glenn G. Affleck, Mary C. Davis,
Howard Tennen, and Robert Fasman

In our research, we have embarked on the study of the positive by developing methodologies that we could use to chart stability and change in everyday life experiences. To do so, we needed to build a structure for assessment that could traverse a veritable ocean of experiences, be capable of sailing through both the currents and crosscurrents of social influence, and also stay afloat to record the sometimes violent upheavals in the patterns of engagement that occur on the open sea. The method should be able to record both the ebb and flow of daily life, and at the same time probe the waters for influences on behavior that are both still and deep.

A Brief History of Methods to Study Life as It Is Lived

Two very different traditions in social science provided the initial structure to guide these efforts: the study of quality of life and the study of life stress. The examination of quality of life began in the 1960s with what has been commonly referred to as the social indicators movement (Bauer, 1966). Then social scientists advocated the development of measures that would gauge the progress of our society toward key social goals just as economic indicators were thought to provide evidence of the fiscal strength of the nation. Broad conceptions of what constituted the good life were translated into measurable properties of society like educational attainment, time until reemployment following job loss, and percentage of population with health insurance coverage.

In some countries, most notably the highly managed societies of Eastern Europe, the interest in quality of life translated in part into studies of daily life routines through time-budget methods (Szalai, 1972). A representative sample of people would be asked to record in a notebook what they did each 15 minutes or half hour of a 24-hour day. These data were then aggregated for social groups, communities, even nations, yielding estimates of average time spent in various family, leisure, and compensated work activities. Patterns of engagement in and disengagement from key social roles could be discerned from these data. These first diary methods provided a ledger from which social scientists could judge the quality of living in societies, and record progress toward social goals by repeating the survey in subsequent years. In this country, we have charted progress, or the lack thereof, in improving leisure time with measures such as hours spent by women and men in household chores and average time commuting to work using modified versions of these time budgets.

There were two basic shortcomings of these methods for assessing quality of life. First, there were problems with the assumptions inherent in any behavioral index of quality. How can we be certain that a positive change in the index actually improves the quality of people's lives? To resolve these problems, a number of social indicator researchers proposed methods of assessing affective states and self-reports of satisfaction within life domains that identified levels of quality of life as perceived (Andrews & Withey, 1976; Bradburn, 1969; Campbell, Converse, & Rodgers, 1976). These measures of subjective states paved the way for the application of modern methods of assessment of affective states in studies of the positive in daily life (Zautra & Bachrach, 2000).

The second shortcoming of the time-budget methods of assessing the good life was the problem of discerning patterns of stability and change within the person and distinguishing these patterns from change and stability in the sample as a whole. Usually, time budgets assessed social progress by repeated observations of the same population but not by reinterviewing the same people. This method is appropriate in the study of society but not in the study of persons. Only by studying the same person repeatedly can we hope to estimate stability and change in a person's everyday life.

About the same time that social scientists were developing social indicators of quality of life, public health researchers sought to gain greater specificity in the assessment of social stress through the development of inventories of life stress events (Dohrenwend & Dohrenwend, 1974; Holmes & Rahe, 1967). The early inventories were rudimentary at best, but gave way to more comprehensive methods of identifying and scoring the stressfulness of major life events (Brown & Harris, 1989; Dohrenwend, Krasnoff, Askenasy, & Dohrenwend, 1978; Dohrenwend, Raphael, Schwartz, Stueve, & Skodol, 1993).

The measurement of stressful life events helped resolve one of the difficulties in the assessment of change. In contrast to assessments of time use, events, by definition, signified change. Items on the inventory such as death in the family, divorce, loss of job, retirement, and relocation all pointed to upheavals in everyday life routine. Provided the retrospective accounts of people were accurate, the researchers could estimate degree of change in a person's life through counts of these events, and relate them to other outcomes, most notably changes in health and well-being.

It took approximately a decade or so of this work for researchers to acknowledge that inventories of major life stressors had several shortcomings. Aside from the substantial problems of reliability in retrospective event reporting (Neisser, 1991), there was an increasing awareness that inventories of major life events missed many of the life experiences important to the person. By attending exclusively to major life stressors, these inventories did not account for everyday life stressors (Kanner, Coyne, Shaefer, & Lazarus, 1981), and they failed to account for positive events (Goodhart & Zautra, 1984).

To correct these insufficiencies, one of us (Zautra) along with other researchers developed assessments of everyday life events (Zautra, Guarnaccia, Reich, & Dohrenwend, 1986) and built these measures to assess positive as well as negative events in everyday life. Empirical studies revealed that, by and large, positive event reports were independent of stressful events. Assessments of the positive thus added a new dimension to the study of everyday events. Further, these measures proved strong contributors to the prediction of well-being significantly beyond that provided in the inventories of stressful life events.

Apparent from the outset was the distinctive quality of measures of positive events. In an early review of the relationship between positive events and psychological well-being, we (Zautra & Reich, 1983) found parallel processes at work when examining the effects of events. Although respondents reporting more negative events often reported more distress when compared with those reporting few everyday stressors, those people who reported more positive events did not show lower scores on measures of negative affective states. The occurrence of positive events did show a distinctive relationship to measures of positive emotion, however. People who reported more positive events were significantly happier, reporting more positive emotion on measures of mood and affect than those respondents reporting few positive events. The development of measures of positive affect that were distinct from negative affects only served to strengthen the case for measurement of the positive in everyday events as a dimension of life independent of stress and distress.

The introduction of these parallel assessments of the positive along with the negative provides us with opportunities to understand the dynamics of daily life in ways that would not otherwise be possible. Essential to this exploration, however, are methods that can capture the flow of everyday life events. Indeed, only recently have methods of assessment and data analysis advanced to the point that researchers can assess, score, and analyze data that are collected daily and even within days for many days. Time-series methods developed for the studies of single cases (e.g., Potter & Zautra, 1997) have now given way to methods of analysis that permit us to examine differences both between people and within persons. Of considerable significance is what these new methods provide in the way of information on the patterns of daily life. They can detect the depth of individual differences through estimates of stability in each person's distinctive pattern of daily experience, but also they reveal the extent that unpredictable events arise to influence the quality of our lives.[1]

Within- Versus Across-Person Relations: A Difference That Makes a Difference

To appreciate what a daily process paradigm can contribute to our understanding of emotional processes is to understand first the difference between an across-persons association and a within-person association. We, like many, have been tempted to draw within-person inferences from across-person associations. For example, in early cross-sectional studies of stressful life events, correlations between the number of events and affective disturbance were taken to mean that when a person experiences a stressful event, he or she is more likely to become distressed. But in truth, such correlations only allow us to infer that people who have many stressful events also report more distress. No inference can be made about the potential effects of events directly without observing people when they are under stress and also when they

are not. An across-person correlation, moreover, can depart markedly from a within-person correlation (Snijders & Bosker, 1999). We cannot emphasize this enough. Tennen and Affleck (1996) and Kenny, Kashy, and Bolger (1998) have illustrated that across-persons and within-person correlations can differ not only in magnitude, but also in direction, and that a statistically significant positive across-person association can emerge when not a single individual in the group shows a positive within-person association.

Consider, for example, the findings from a study of rheumatoid arthritis patients, who kept daily diaries of their desirable and undesirable events for 75 consecutive days (Tennen & Affleck, 1996). After aggregating the scores to generate mean levels of both types of events, a moderately high across-person correlation of .50 emerged, as participants who reported more desirable events also reported more undesirable events. The question addressed by this across-person correlation is whether people who experience more undesirable daily events also experience more desirable daily events. Quite a different question is, how are desirable and undesirable events patterned in an individual's life? Is a day with more undesirable events also a day with more desirable events? The across-person analysis cannot answer this question. It requires calculation of a within-person measure of association. Not a single participant exhibited the statistically significant positive association between desirable and undesirable events that was found when the data were analyzed across persons. In fact, the mean within-person correlation was −.25, with a preponderance of significant negative correlations. Even many of those who reported a large number of both desirable and undesirable events showed an inverse relation when these events were examined on a within-person basis.

Other benefits of time-intensive idiographic studies have been advanced by us elsewhere (Affleck, Zautra, Tennen, & Armeli, 1999; Tennen, Suls, & Affleck, 1991) and by others (e.g., Brown & Moskowitz, 1998; Larsen & Kasimatis, 1991). They allow investigators to capture proximal events and behaviors closer to their actual occurrence and to track changes in rapidly fluctuating processes such as emotional reactions closer to their moments of change. These studies also minimize recall error, including systematic error in which individuals who differ on measured or unmeasured variables provide differentially accurate data or use different cognitive heuristics to assist their recall (Neisser, 1991). Because these studies track psychological processes as they unfold, they offer unique opportunities to test the elegant process-oriented models of stress and emotion now in the literature and to narrow the gap between theory and research (Tennen, Affleck, Armeli, & Carney, 2000). Additional benefits of daily process studies include the ability to mitigate some forms of confounding by using informants as their own controls and to establish temporal precedence as a foundation for causal inference (Tennen & Affleck, 1996).

Study Description

We illustrate these methods of assessment and analysis of positive aspects of everyday life with data we are collecting in a diary study of 93 men and women (73% female) with rheumatoid arthritis (RA) verified by medical records. This study was part of an ongoing multiyear project conducted by our research team, assessing a wide range of mental and physical health variables in a community-based sample of RA patients in the Phoenix, Arizona, metropolitan area. Our research team recruited participants through a variety of means, including flyers placed in physicians' offices and other public locations, physicians passing along information to their patients, newspaper ads, senior citizens' groups, arthritis groups, and mass mailings to members of the Arthritis Foundation. We excluded participants involved in health-related litigation, participants with other autoimmune diseases (juvenile rheumatoid arthritis, HIV, AIDS, psoriatic arthritis, and lupus), and participants reporting the current usage of a cyclical hormone replacement therapy. Participants were between the ages of 23 and 86 ($M = 54.3$, $SD = 13.3$). The majority were married (70%) and Caucasian (88%). The average income was roughly $40,000; 98% completed high school and 40% completed 4 years of college; and 43% were employed.

In this study, we made use of data from brief (10–15 minute) questionnaire diaries filled out nightly for 30 days. We required that participants mail in signed consent forms prior to being enrolled in the study and completing diaries. We arranged to compensate participants up to $90 for completing the diary set, depending on their level of compliance. Our diary manager phoned all participants before they began the diary protocol in order to guide them through a sample diary, instruct them to mail their diaries the morning after completing them, and to answer any questions. The diary manager also monitored compliance by checking the postmark date on each envelope, looking through each diary to make sure it was complete, and phoning participants if they were having difficulty following protocol. In total, participants provided 2,713 of 2,790 (93×30) possible person-days of diary data (97% complete).

Measures

Positive Affect

Participants filled out nightly diaries that included the Positive and Negative Affect Schedule (Watson & Clark, 1999). They indicated the extent to which they had experienced each of 10 positive affects (PAs) during that day on a 5-point scale (from 1, *very slightly or not at all*, to 5, *extremely*). The positive affect items were *interested, excited, strong, enthusiastic, proud, alert, inspired, determined, attentive,* and *active*. The mean across the 10 items provided the scores on PA.

In order to examine these scores at the between- and within-person levels independently, we transformed the daily PA scores into mean scores and person-centered daily change scores. First, we computed a mean (between-person) score for each participant by averaging each participant's levels of PA across the 30 days. To obtain person-centered daily change scores (within-person), we then subtracted each participant's mean score from each of the daily observations, resulting in a score representing the participant's daily change in PA compared to his or her own 30-day average. In effect, a positive person-centered score represents a day of above-average PA for that person, and a negative score represents a day of below average PA for that person.

Due to the many observations obtained for each participant, we were able to estimate both within- and between-subject internal consistency reliability. In order to estimate within-person reliability, item values were transformed into z-scores representing deviations from each participant's own mean score (across the 30 days) on each item in the scale. The resulting z-scores (approximately 30 for each participant for each item) were therefore independent of between-person differences in level and variability. The within-subject alpha was .86 for PA. For the estimation of the reliability of the scale across participants, we computed averages of each person's scores (at the item level) across the 30 days, resulting in a mean score for each subject for each item. The between-subject alpha for PA was .95.

Negative Affect

Participants were also queried regarding negative affect (NA) on a nightly basis using the Positive and Negative Affect Schedule (Watson & Clark, 1999). Response format was the same as for PA. The NA items were *distressed, upset, nervous, scared, hostile, irritable, ashamed, jittery, afraid,* and *guilty*. The NA scores were computed in the same manner as described above for PA, yielding satisfactory internal consistency reliabilities. The within-subject alpha was .81 for NA, and the between-subject alpha was .92.

Positive and Negative Social Events

In order to measure daily positive and negative social interactions, we included the Inventory of Small Life Events (ISLE) for older adults (Zautra, Affleck, & Tennen, 1994; Zautra, Guarnaccia, & Dohrenwend, 1986) in our diaries. We asked participants to provide frequency counts of the weekly occurrence of 44 events in all (26 positive, such as "played a sport, game, or cards with friends," and 18 negative, such as "criticized by friend/acquaintance") gathered from the four domains of the ISLE: (1) friends and acquaintances, (2) spouse or live-in partner, (3) family members, and (4) coworkers. Our diaries

also included open-ended questions that queried participants about other life events, both positive and negative, that were not specifically mentioned in the ISLE. We computed total scores for positive and negative events by summing events across the four domains. We also computed both mean and person-centered scores of positive and negative interpersonal events using the same methodology described above for positive and negative affect. Event measures are crafted to sample distinct experiences, ruling out the use of internal consistency methods as a means of estimating the reliability of these indices.

Descriptive Characteristics of Positive and Negative Daily Events and Affects Daily Scores

Table 34.1 provides several statistics that characterize the distributions of the 2,713 person-days of daily positive and negative affect and events. As table 34.1 indicates, PA scores were higher and more variable than NA scores and more closely approximated a normal distribution than did NA scores. The distribution of NA scores was more negatively skewed (i.e., with a preponderance of values toward the low end of the scale) and leptokurtotic (i.e., with greater clustering of values around the peak of the distribution) than was the distribution of PA scores. Table 34.1 tells much the same story about the distributions of daily events: Positive event scores were higher and more variable than negative event scores, and negative event scores were more negatively skewed and leptokurtotic.

The variability in these four series can be decomposed into a between-person source of vari-

TABLE 34.1 Distributional Characteristics of Daily Positive and Negative Affect and Event Scores ($N = 2,713$ Person-Days)

	Affect		Events	
	Positive	Negative	Positive	Negative
Mean	2.792	1.332	4.991	.883
Median	2.800	1.100	5.000	.000
SD	.890	.516	2.963	1.326
Skewness	.122	2.373	.757	2.007
Kurtosis	.094	6.283	.883	4.907
Proportion between-person variance	.68*	.48*	.43*	.32*
Proportion within-person variance	.32*	.52*	.57*	.68*

*p < .05.

ance (i.e., the differences between persons in their mean levels) and a within-person source of variance (i.e., the differences within persons in the dispersion of the scores). Fitting an SAS Proc Mixed model (Singer, 2001), which allowed intercepts (mean levels) to vary randomly, both of these sources of variance were found to be statistically significant for all four daily series (see table 34.1). Notably, a greater proportion of the total variance in PA was due to between-person differences (68%) than was the case for NA (48%). Similarly, but less dramatically, a greater proportion of the total variance in positive event scores was due to differences between persons (43%) than it was for negative event scores (32%). Thus, positive experiences exhibit greater stability day-to-day than negative experiences.

To gain further insight into differences in the patterning of positive and negative daily experiences, additional descriptive analyses were performed at the between-person level using mean daily scores and at the within-person level using person-centered daily scores.

Mean Daily Scores

Table 34.2 presents descriptive statistics for PA and NA and events mean daily scores for the 93 participants. These portrayals echo those of the person-day scores. Mean levels of PA and events were higher and displayed more variation than did NA and negative mean scores, and their distributions were more normal than those of the mean NA and events scores. As was the case with the raw score distributions, mean NA and event scores were more compressed and skewed toward the low end of their respective ranges.

Following conventions introduced by Tukey (1977) for exploratory data analysis, we constructed box-and-whisker plots (not shown) to identify individuals who could be considered outliers in their reports of positive and negative events and affects. It is noteworthy that the distributions of mean PA and mean positive events contained no outlying individuals. However, 5 of the 93 subjects (5.4%) were identified as outliers because of their unusually high levels of NA and seven (7.5%) were identified as outliers because of their unusually high numbers of negative daily events. These scores identify people who have unusually stressful lives, and also when these times of unusually high turbulence occur. Such extremes were not present in the patterns of positive affective experiences for our sample.

Person-Centered Daily Scores

As can be seen in table 34.3, the distributions of the person-centered scores parallel those found with the mean scores. These include greater variability and approximation to normality in both PA and positive events than in NA and negative events. The box-and-whisker plots of PA and NA revealed a substantially higher number of outlying days for NA than for PA. Notably, 9.2% of the days were identified as outliers, because they were characterized by uncommonly high NA (relative to the person's mean level), whereas only 1.5% of the days were outliers because of their uncommonly low level of PA. This was echoed in the outlying days pattern for positive and negative events. Owing to the more compressed range and negative skew of negative daily events, 6.3% of the days were identified as outliers because of the relatively high number of negative events reported on those days, compared with the 0.37% of the days that had relatively low numbers of positive events. Interestingly, more than five times as many days were outliers because the participants reported more positive events than usual than were outliers because participants reported fewer positive events than usual. Of interest for future

TABLE 34.2 Distributional Characteristics of 30-Day Averages for Positive and Negative Affect and Event Scores ($N = 93$ Persons)

	Average Affect		Average Events	
	Positive	Negative	Positive	Negative
Mean	2.786	1.338	5.000	.887
Median	2.765	1.220	4.800	.706
SD	.703	.365	1.984	.783
Skewness	.242	1.961	.143	1.440
Kurtosis	−.206	4.650	−.030	1.678

TABLE 34.3 Distributional Characteristics of Person-Centered Daily Changes in Positive and Negative Affect and Event Scores ($N = 2,713$ Person-Days)

	Change in Affect		Change in Events	
	Positive	Negative	Positive	Negative
Mean	.000	.000	.000	.000
Median	.017	−.040	−.133	−.200
SD	.560	.369	2.216	1.076
Skewness	−.146	1.667	.642	1.363
Kurtosis	.792	6.421	1.571	4.220

research is whether this finding parallels the awareness of positive emotions. Are we more observant of increases in our daily experience of the positive than we are of decreases in positive experience? The data suggest that we are.

Autocorrelation

An autocorrelation pattern in daily reports would indicate that affects, events, or both on one day are able to predict these experiences the next day. To evaluate differences in the extent to which positive and negative experiences are autocorrelated from day to day, we used the SAS Proc Mixed procedure to compare a null model of the person-centered daily report (containing no predictor) with a model in which the lagged (previous day's) value was added as predictor (Littell, Milliken, Stroup, & Wolfinger, 1996). These analyses revealed significant autocorrelation in all four daily series. After comparing each model's residual variance before and after adding the lagged predictor, the effect was similar for PA (reduction in residual variance = 5.8%) and NA (reduction in residual variance = 5.7%). However, autocorrelation was a more prominent feature of negative events (reduction in residual variance = 3.7%) than it was for positive events (reduction in residual variance = 0.4%). Thus, changes in affect and negative events tend to carry over into the next day. Elevations in positive events, however, do not influence the next day's positive events.

Relations Between Positive and Negative Experiences

We next examined the relations between PA and NA, between positive and negative events, and between these affects and events at both the between-person and within-person levels of analysis. We used SAS Proc Mixed procedures because they simultaneously model variances in the intercepts (means) and slopes (within-person relations). For these analyses, we set up the model so that intercepts were allowed to vary randomly, as were all within-person slopes except those that pertained to time-varying covariates. Day-level predictors were person-centered, and the residuals were fit to a first-order autocorrelation pattern. Because we found that outlying persons or days were especially apparent for NA and negative events, we evaluated the effects of including or excluding outlying persons or days for these variables.

Relations Between Positive Affect and Negative Affect

Table 34.4 presents the between-person and within-person relations of NA with PA and relations of negative events with positive events. Although the measures were clearly assessing different emotive states, at both the between- and within-person levels, PA was significantly and inversely correlated with NA, and remained so whether outliers were included or excluded in the analyses. The overlap registered as 7.8% of variance shared between measures of PA and NA between subjects, reflecting a correlation of .28, and 6.4% variance shared within persons in daily fluctuations of PA and NA, reflecting a correlation of .25. The extent of this inverse relationship varied between persons and, as we report later, also varied across days. That some people showed less covariation between PA and NA suggests that there are individual differences in the ability to make fine-grained distinctions between emotions, one component of emotional complexity. This capacity to differentiate affective experiences may be a key to promoting emotion regulation (Feldman Barrett, Gross,

TABLE 34.4 Multilevel Random Coefficient Analyses of Between-Person and Within-Person Relations Between Negative Affect and Positive Affect and Between Negative Events and Positive Events ($N = 2,713$ Person-Days)

	Between-Person		Within-Person	
	b	F	b	F
Negative affect and positive affect	−.569	8.73***	−.417	42.49***
	(−.653)	(5.89)*	(−.415)	(45.20)***
Negative events and positive events	.943	14.51***	−.033	.35
	(−1.163)	(.46)	(−.017)	(.04)

Note: Numbers in parentheses are from analyses that exclude outlying persons for negative affect or events mean scores or outlying days for person-centered negative affect or event scores.

***$p < .001$. *$p < .05$.

Conner, & Benvenuto, 2001) and development of good interpersonal relationships (Kang & Shaver, 2004).

Relations Between Positive Events and Negative Events

Findings presented in table 34.4 reveal a different kind of relation between positive and negative events. At the within-person level—in contrast to the inverse relation between PA and NA—there was no association between positive and negative events. And at the between-person level, there was a positive association between positive and negative events ($r = .37$)—in contrast to the inverse association between PA and NA. However, this association was not statistically significant after individuals with outlying mean negative event scores were omitted from the analyses. Thus, the measurement of positive events introduces an assessment of daily life that is wholly independent of that which is afforded us through the assessment of the daily stress of

negative events. There can hardly be any clearer indication of the need for studies of the positive than findings like this one.

Relations Between Positive Affect/Events and Negative Affect/Events

Two sets of multivariate analyses—one at the between-person level and one at the within-person level—examined how positive and negative events combine to predict PA and NA. Table 34.5 indicates that NA was predicted by negative events, but not independently by positive events. On the other hand, PA was higher among those who had experienced both fewer negative events and more positive events. These findings remained significant even after excluding individuals with outlying mean scores for NA and negative events.

Table 34.6 presents the findings regarding these relations examined at the within-person level. Higher NA scores were reported on days having both a greater number of negative events

TABLE 34.5 Multivariate Multilevel Random Coefficient Analyses of Between-Person Relations of Average Negative and Positive Event Scores With Negative and Positive Affect Scores ($N = 93$ Persons)

	Average Negative Affect[a]		Average Positive Affect[b]	
	b	F	b	F
Average negative events	.097	17.57***	−.307	11.09**
	(.238)	(26.28)***	(−.344)	(13.24)***
Average positive events	−.019	1.04	.140	14.79***
	(−.014)	(2.82)	(.142)	(14.50)***

Note: Numbers in parentheses are from analyses that exclude outlying persons for negative affect or events mean scores.

[a]Adjusting for positive affect.

[b]Adjusting for negative affect.

***$p < .001$ **$p < .01$.

TABLE 34.6 Multivariate Multilevel Random Coefficient Analyses of Within-Person Relations of Change in Negative and Positive Events With Change in Negative and Positive Affect Scores ($N = 2{,}713$ Person-Days)

	Change in Negative Affect[a]		Change in Positive Affect[b]	
	b	F	b	F
Change in negative Events	.094	106.16***	−.001	.02
	(.044)	(139.06)***	(.001)	(.01)
Change in positive events	−.006	3.93*	.065	118.96***
	(−.001)	(.42)	(.057)	(150.55)***

Note: Numbers in parentheses are from analyses that exclude outlying days for person-centered negative affect or events mean scores.

[a]Adjusting for positive affect.

[b]Adjusting for negative affect.

***$p < .001$. *$p < .05$.

and a lower number of positive events, although the latter association did not remain significant after days with outlying negative event occurrences were excluded. PA was higher on days with more positive events but was unaffected by the frequency of that day's negative events, whether or not outlying days were included. This finding stands in contrast to the results of the analysis of the same variables between persons for which negative events had a substantial association with lower PA. These data suggest an important difference in the meaning of assessments of people who have many versus few negative experiences and assessments of times when they have many versus few negative events. People who tend to have more stressful lives also tend to have lower PA, as well as more NA. In contrast, days when many negative experiences occur do not bring lower PA per se. Processes other than the mere accumulation of events must be involved to diminish positive states for people with high levels of chronic stress from negative events. Personality features as well as changes in the structure of the relationship between events and affect over time may underlie these processes.

A Test and Extension of the Dynamic Model of Affect: Effects of Positive and Negative Events on the Link Between Positive and Negative Affect

Within-person assessments allow us to test a process-oriented model that describes conditions that foster greater or lesser differentiation between PA and NA, termed the dynamic model of affect (DMA). It builds on work examining the

contextual determinants of information processing (e.g., Linville, 1985, 1987; Paulhus & Lim, 1994; Ursin & Olff, 1993). Like cognition, the experience of emotion always occurs in an environmental context. In safe and predictable situations, we are able to process information from multiple sources, including emotional inputs to develop an adaptive response. We acquire information arising not only from negatively valenced aspects of a situation, but also from its positively valenced features. Positive and negative affective registers provide little overlapping information here. In times of low stress, then, we would expect PA and NA to be relatively uncorrelated.

During times of stress and uncertainty, the need to process information quickly takes precedence over any advantages that accrue from more differentiated evaluation of stimuli. We can no longer afford to expend our resources on complex, time-consuming processing of information demands. Rather, our attention narrows and our judgments become more simplified and rapid, allowing us to quickly adopt behaviors that are necessary to survive the threatening situation. In such contexts, we preferentially process negative information at the expense of positive. According to the DMA, during times of stress, PA and NA collapse toward a simpler bipolar dimension reflected in a high inverse relationship between the two affect measures.

A multilevel random coefficient model examined the DMA prediction that stressful conditions acted to shrink affective space, resulting in more simplified affective experiencing. NA on a given day j for person i was examined as a function of that day's person-centered PA score

(PA), that day's person-centered negative event score (NEV), and the PA × negative event interaction (PA × NEV). That day's person-centered positive event score (PEV) was entered as a covariate. This produced the following multilevel equation:

$$NA_{ij} = \gamma_{00} + \gamma_{01}(PA) + \gamma_{10}(NEV)$$
$$+ \gamma_{11}(PA \times NEV) + \gamma_{02}(PEV)$$
$$+ u_{0j} + u_{1j} + r_{ij}$$

A significant effect for the interaction term, $b = -.023$, $F(1, 2,591) = 5.78$, $p < .05$, supported the hypothesis. Graphing this interaction revealed that the relation between PA and NA was more strongly negative on days with relatively more negative events.

In contrast to the collapse of affective complexity under stressful conditions, the DMA predicts that the experience of positive events should broaden the capacity for information processing, resulting in greater affective differentiation. A comparable multilevel model examined the effect of that day's positive events on the relation between that day's PA and NA, that is, the significance of the PA × positive event interaction. That day's person-centered negative event score was entered as a covariate. The interaction term was significant, $b = .013$, $F(1, 2,591) = 4.49$, $p < .05$, and consistent with prediction. Graphing this interaction revealed that the relation between PA and NA was closer to zero on days with relatively more positive events. Thus individuals experienced greater affective complexity on days with more positive events, a pattern that highlights the potential of positive affective experiences temporarily to broaden people's emotional, cognitive, and behavioral repertoires (Fredrickson, 1998). Expanding our focus beyond consideration of NA and negative events to include study of the central role of positive engagements thus provides a fuller and more accurate rendering of the experiences of daily life.

Discussion

What do the daily process methods and findings we have described reveal about the nature and value of the positive in daily life? The overarching message is that a focus on both between- and within-person processes permits inclusion of the important and unique information provided by each. The assessment of both positive and negative dimensions of experiencing and the inclusion of not only the affects but also interpersonal events adds to the richness of our understanding of everyday experience.

The intensive within-person assessments shed light on how affects and interpersonal events ebb and flow over time within individuals. Levels of positive affect and events were higher and more variable day-to-day than were those for negative affect and events, suggesting that different factors may hold sway over our experience of the positive compared to the negative. We also examined the extent to which one day's experiences carried over to the next day. Changes in PA and NA on one day tended to be followed by like experiences on the next day to a similar, albeit relatively modest, degree. About 6% of the variance in one day's mood was explained by the previous day's mood for both PA and NA. In contrast, changes in negative but not positive events predicted event experiences the next day, reflecting that social strains tend to perpetuate themselves whereas positive social engagements do not.

The daily process paradigm also allowed us to explore the degree to which fluctuations in PA and NA relate to differences between individuals. More of the variation was attributable to differences between people for the positive than for the negative. Between 40% and 70% of the variance for positive experiences, versus 30% and 50% for negative experiences, was accounted for by between-person factors. Thus, who we are has a more pronounced impact on our experience of joys than on our experience of sorrows. Numerous potential differences between individuals may account for variation in affective experiences, but among likely candidates are those that bear on the capacity to regulate emotion (e.g., Gohm, 2003), including behavioral activation and inhibition (e.g., Gable, Reis, & Elliot, 2000), and neuroticism and extraversion (Watson & Clark, 1992). It is worth noting that despite the substantial between-person effects, much variance within persons remained, suggesting that daily circumstances play an important role in influencing our moods.

The value of focusing on multiple levels of analysis for understanding affective processes is most clear in the pattern of findings relating PA and NA, which demonstrated that the associations between the affects varied both between individuals and within the same individual over time. Initial analyses revealed that PA and NA showed some overlap, such that individuals who reported high levels of NA also reported low levels of PA, and days with high NA were also characterized by low levels of PA. Yet it was only when we considered changes in day-to-day social events that the dynamic nature of the affect associations became apparent. Consistent with predictions derived from the DMA, the inverse relationship between PA and NA became more pronounced on days of high interpersonal stress, and less pronounced on days of high positive social engagement. These and earlier findings suggest shifts in the underlying structure of affective experiences, with a bidimensional structure prevailing during periods of ease and a unidimensional structure dominant during times of stress and uncertainty (e.g., Reich, Zautra, & Davis, 2003; Zautra, Smith, Affleck, & Tennen, 2001).

Several authors (Epstein, 1983; Larsen & Kasimatis, 1991; Tennen & Affleck, 1996) have advocated combining the best of the idiographic and nomothetic traditions in a mixed design that is a hallmark of the daily process paradigm. This permits investigators to determine whether the associations between daily events and emotions relate to differences between individuals. In the data we have presented, for example, the daily process paradigm allows us to ask whether individual difference factors moderate the context-related shifts in affective space. Our previous work suggests that cognitive simplicity and lack of mood clarity may be two factors that increase vulnerability to affective simplification during times of stress (Reich, Zautra, & Potter, 2001; Zautra et al., 2001), but other candidates, particularly those related to emotion regulation skills, are certainly viable.

Here we have focused on assessment of the broad constructs of PA and NA and small events assessed daily at the end of the day. Other strategies that differ in the focus, frequency, and timing of assessments may also be informative. For example, Watson, Wiese, Vaidya, and Tellegen (1999) employed an elegant sampling strategy to assess whether circadian influences differed for the experience of PA and NA by assessing individuals' momentary experience of the affects once per day at different time points throughout the day over 45 days. They found that circadian patterning of PA and NA was quite distinct, such that NA showed little systematic variation and PA varied as a function of time since rising. This example illustrates how the spacing of assessment is dependent on the question being addressed. Multiple within-day

measurements, for instance, may be useful in capturing more transitory processes than are possible with end-of-day daily reports.

In addition to evaluating experiences of general PA and NA and events as we have done, it may be enlightening to evaluate more refined experiences of emotions. For instance, Feldman Barrett and colleagues (2001) employed within-person assessment over time to examine affective differentiation, not between but within PA and NA. They were interested in the extent to which individuals were able to make distinctions within their positive and negative emotional experiences and found that negative but not positive affective differentiation was related to more frequent negative emotion regulation. These findings point to the potential value of including more nuanced assessment of these aspects of affective experiencing.

Being able to muster and maintain positive resources in the face of life's difficulties may be one key to well-being. Our focus here has been on understanding affective experiences in the context of small daily interpersonal events but, of course, monumental events also inevitably occur. A daily process approach may provide a finer understanding of how positive emotions influence recovery from trauma (e.g., Fredrickson, Tugade, Waugh, & Larkin, 2003) and loss (e.g., Tedlie-Moskowitz, Folkman, & Acree, 2003), and offer insights into salient targets in prevention and intervention efforts. Our findings with regard to small daily events, for example, suggest the value of targeting both negative and positive mood, and of scheduling frequent positive events, given that positive mood and events do not carry over from day to day.

Our work also suggests that timing plays a key role in these processes of adaptation. We suspect that the narrowing of attention during acute episodes of stress is highly adaptive. Focused attention allows for a swifter and more uniform response to potential threat. Indeed, the value of positive affective conditions to deter negative states is enhanced during stressful times. However, we also surmise that following the immediate stress response should be a recovery in the depth and scope of attention to affective states, both our own and of those in our social world. Emotional resilience then is manifested as a flexible capacity to shift between focus and extension across a two-dimensional plane. The broader and more complex the possibilities, the more nuanced and rich is the information we have to help us govern our emotional lives. Successful adaptation depends on both awareness of complexity and responsiveness to the changing demands of the daily environment.

Summary

In this chapter, we have shown the development of one approach to the study of the positive. Our methods evolved from earlier approaches concerned with estimating the quality and the stresses of life. Building on both the promise and the shortcomings of those established practices, we were led inexorably to study positive aspects of everyday life. To not do so would have been to ignore essential ingredients of the good life that could not be predicted from extensive knowledge of life's difficulties. Our careful assessment of the positive in events and emotion allowed us to observe just how different our experiences of the positive are from experiences of the negative. The findings from our analyses suggest that two parallel processes infuse our consciousness with emotion and purpose: one that is positive, guiding our approach with promise and hope, and another that is negative, informing us about risk of harm. We can chart their influence on people's lives through careful observations of the ebb and flow of life events and emotion. These processes are embedded within the social fabric as well. Culture and social status, as well as personality, shape our opportunities and also enforce constraints on participation in everyday life. The forces of individual differences in social station and temperament, as powerful as they are, should not overshadow the influence of the dynamic influences of everyday life events. We have shown that it is as important to chart meaningful changes within a person's life as it is to characterize differences between persons and social groups. New methods allow us to look over time within the individual, and they reveal important dynamic relationships between positive and negative affective experiences that would have been neglected without careful attention to the assessment of both positive and negative emotional processes as they unfold over time. More work is needed to be sure in mapping the domains of the positive in everyday life, including greater attention to cognitive processes that influence expectations for and perceptions of benefit or threat from life events. We hope that our attention to detail in the measurement of how events unfold in everyday life will provide some guidance for future endeavors seeking to quantify these aspects of the positive within psychology.

Acknowledgments   This work was supported in part by grants from the National Institute of Arthritis, Musculoskelatal, and Skin Diseases and the Arthritis Foundation.

Note

1. Detailed discussions of the methodological and statistical options now available for such studies have been applied to emotional processes in personality (e.g., Nezlek, 2001), health (e.g., Schwartz & Stone, 1998), clinical (e.g., Affleck et al., 1999), and social phenomena (e.g., Kenny, Kashy, & Bolger, 1997).

References

Affleck, G., Zautra, A., Tennen, H., & Armeli, S. (1999). Multilevel daily process designs for consulting and clinical psychology: A preface for the perplexed. *Journal of Consulting and Clinical Psychology, 67,* 746–754.

Andrews, F. M., & Withey, S. B. (1976). *Social indicators of well-being.* New York: Plenum.

Bauer, R. A. (1966). Detection and anticipation of impact: The nature of the task. In R. A. Bauer (Ed.), *Social indicators* (pp. 1–67). Cambridge, MA: MIT Press.

Bradburn, N. M. (1969). *The structure of psychological well being.* Oxford, UK: Aldine.

Brown, G. W., & Harris, T. O. (1989). *Life events and illness.* New York: Guilford.

Brown, K., & Moskowitz, D. (1998). It's a function of time: A review of the process approach to behavioral medicine research. *Psychosomatic Medicine, 20,* 109–117.

Campbell, A., Converse, P. E., & Rodgers, W. L. (1976). *The quality of American life.* New York: Sage.

Dohrenwend, B. S., & Dohrenwend, B. P. (Eds.). (1974). *Stressful life events: Their nature and effects.* New York: Wiley.

Dohrenwend, B. S., Krasnoff, L., Askenasy, A. R., & Dohrenwend, B. P. (1978). Exemplification of a method for scaling life events: The PERI Life Events Scale. *Journal of Abnormal Psychology, 19,* 205–229.

Dohrenwend, B. P., Raphael, K. G., Schwartz, S., Stueve, A., & Skodol, A. (1993). The structured event probe and narrative rating method for measuring stressful life events. In L. Goldberger & S. Breznitz (Eds.), *Handbook of stress* (2nd ed., pp. 174–199). New York: Free Press.

Epstein, S. (1983). Aggregation and beyond: Some basic issues on the prediction of behavior. *Journal of Personality*, 51(3), 360–392.

Feldman Barrett, L., Gross, J., Conner, T., & Benvenuto, M. (2001). Knowing what you're feeling and knowing what to do about it: Mapping the relation between emotion differentiation and emotion regulation. *Cognition and Emotion, 15*, 713–724.

Fredrickson, B. L. (1998). What good are positive emotions? *Review of General Psychology, 2*, 300–319.

Fredrickson, B. L., Tugade, M. M., Waugh, C. E., & Larkin, G. R. (2003). What good are positive emotions in crisis? A prospective study of resilience and emotions following the terrorist attacks on the United States on September 11th, 2001. *Journal of Personality and Social Psychology, 84*, 365–376.

Gable, S. L., Reis, H. T., & Elliot, A. J. (2000). Behavioral activation and inhibition in everyday life. *Journal of Personality and Social Psychology, 6*, 1135–1149.

Gohm, C. L. (2003). Mood regulation and emotional intelligence: Individual differences. *Journal of Personality and Social Psychology, 84*, 594–607.

Goodhart, D. E., & Zautra, A. (1984). Assessing quality of life in the community: An ecological approach. In W. A. O'Connor & B. Lubin (Eds.), *Ecological approaches to clinical and community psychology* (pp. 251–290). New York: Wiley.

Holmes, T. H., & Rahe, R. H. (1967). The social readjustment scale. *Journal of Psychosomatic Research, 11*, 213–218.

Kang, S.-M., & Shaver, P. R. (2004). Individual differences in emotional complexity: Their psychological implications. *Journal of Personality, 72*, 687–698.

Kanner, A. D., Coyne, J. C., Shaefer, C., & Lazarus, R. S. (1981). Comparison of two modes of stress measurement: Daily hassles and uplifts versus major life events. *Journal of Behavioral Medicine, 4*, 1–39.

Kenny, D., Kashy, D., & Bolger, N. (1998). Data analysis in social psychology. In D. Gilbert, S. Fiske, & G. Linzey (Eds.), *Handbook of social psychology* (4th ed., pp. 233–265). New York: McGraw-Hill.

Larsen, R., & Kasimatis, M. (1991). Day-to day physical symptoms: Individual differences in the occurrence, duration, and emotional concomitants of minor daily illnesses. *Journal of Personality, 59*, 387–424.

Linville, P. W. (1985). Self-complexity and affective extremity: Don't put all your eggs in one basket. *Social Cognition, 3*, 94–120.

Linville, P. W. (1987). Self-complexity as a cognitive buffer against illness and depression. *Journal of Personality and Social Psychology, 62*, 663–676.

Littell, R. C., Milliken, G. A., Stroup, W. W., & Wolfinger, R. D. (1996). *SAS system for linear mixed models*. Cary, NC: SAS Institute.

Neisser, U. (1991). A case of misplaced nostalgia. *American Psychologist, 46*, 34–36.

Nezlek, J. B. (2001). Multilevel random coefficient analyses of event- and interval-contingent data in social and personality psychology research. *Personality and Social Psychology Bulletin, 27*, 771–785.

Paulhus, D. L., & Lim, D. T. K. (1994). Arousal and evaluative extremity in social judgments: A dynamic complexity model. *European Journal of Social Psychology, 24*, 89–99.

Potter, P., & Zautra, A. (1997). Stressful life events' effects on rheumatoid arthritis disease activity. *Journal of Consulting and Clinical Psychology, 65*, 319–323.

Reich, J. W., Zautra, A. J., & Davis, M. C. (2003). Dimensions of affect relationships: Models and their integrative implications. *Review of General Psychology, 7*, 66–83.

Reich, J. W., Zautra, A. J., & Potter, P. T. (2001). Cognitive structure and the independence of positive and negative affect. *Journal of Social and Clinical Psychology, 20*, 99–115.

Schwartz, J., & Stone, A. (1998). Strategies for analyzing ecological momentary assessment data. *Health Psychology, 17*, 6–16.

Singer, J. D. (2001). Fitting individual growth models using SAS PROC MIXED. In D. S. Moskowitz & S. L. Hershberger (Eds.), *Modeling intraindividual variability with repeated measures data: Methods and applications* (pp. 135–170). Mahwah, NJ: Erlbaum.

Snijders, A. B. T., & Bosker, R. J. (1999). *Multilevel analysis: An introduction to basic and advanced multilevel modeling*. London: Sage.

Szalai, A. (Ed.). (1972). *The use of time*. The Hague: Mouton.

Tedlie-Moskowitz, J., Folkman, S., & Acree, M. (2003). Do positive psychological states shed light on recovery from bereavement? Findings from a 3-year longitudinal study. *Death Studies, 27*, 471–500.

Tennen, H., & Affleck, G. (1996). Daily processes in coping with chronic pain: Methods and analytic strategies. In M. Zeidner & N. Endler (Eds.), *Handbook of coping.* (pp. 151–180). New York: Wiley.

Tennen, H., Affleck, G., Armeli, S., & Carney, M. (2000). A daily process approach to coping: Linking theory, research, and practice. *American Psychologist, 55,* 626–636.

Tennen, H., Suls, J., & Affleck, G. (1991). Personality and daily experience: The promise and the challenge. *Journal of Personality, 59,* 313–338.

Tukey, J. (1977). *Exploratory data analysis.* Reading, MA: Addison-Wesley.

Ursin, H., & Olff, M. (1993). The stress response. In S. C. Stanford & P. Solomon (Eds.), *Stress: From synapse to syndrome* (pp. 4–23). New York: Academic Press.

Watson, D., & Clark, L. A. (1992). On traits and temperament: General and specific factors of emotional experience and their relation to the five-factor model. *Journal of Personality, 60,* 441–476.

Watson, D., & Clark, L. A. (1999). *The PANAS-X manual for the positive and negative affect schedule—Expanded form.* Retrieved September 24, 2003, from the University of Iowa Web site: http://www.psychology.uiowa.edu/Faculty/Watson/PANAS-X.pdf

Watson, D., Wiese, D., Vaidya, J., & Tellegen, A. (1999). The two general activation systems of affect: Structural findings, evolutionary considerations, and psychobiological evidence. *Journal of Personality and Social Psychology, 76,* 820–838.

Zautra, A. J., Affleck, G., & Tennen, H. (1994). Assessing life events among older adults. In M. P. Lawton & J. A. Teresi (Eds.), *Annual review of gerontology and geriatrics: Focus on assessment techniques* (Vol. 14, pp. 324–352). New York: Springer.

Zautra, A. J., & Bachrach, K. M. (2000). Psychological dysfunction and well-being. In J. Rappaport & E. Seidman (Eds.), *Handbook of community psychology* (pp. 165–186). New York: Kluwer Academic/Plenum.

Zautra, A. J., Guarnaccia, C. A., & Dohrenwend, B. P. (1986). Measuring small life events. *American Journal of Community Psychology, 14,* 629–655.

Zautra, A. J., Guarnaccia, C. A., Reich, J. W., & Dohrenwend, B. P. (1986). Measuring small events. *American Journal of Community Psychology, 19,* 54–71.

Zautra, A., & Reich, J. W. (1983). Life events and perceptions of life quality: Developments in a two factor approach. *Journal of Community Psychology, 11,* 121–132.

Zautra, A., Smith, B., Affleck, G., & Tennen, H. (2001). Examinations of chronic pain and affect relationships: Applications of a dynamic model of affect. *Journal of Consulting and Clinical Psychology, 69,* 786–795.

35

Using Experience Sampling
and Multilevel Modeling to Study
Person-Situation Interactionist
Approaches to Positive Psychology

William Fleeson

The purpose of this chapter is to describe a method to study interactionism; this method may help rejuvenate interactionist approaches in psychology and may highlight the value of interactionism in positive psychology. Most broadly, interactionism is the view that both environmental and person factors are required for a complete understanding of psychological functioning and that the two factors often interact in producing behavior (Bowers, 1973; Lewin, 1935; Magnusson, 1999; Magnusson & Endler, 1977). Interactionism is valuable to developmental and to social psychology when those fields are interested in how environmental impacts depend on the characteristics and history of the individuals (Magnusson, 1999). Interactionism is valuable to personality psychology as a way to characterize personality in terms of unique responses to situations and as a potential solution to the problems for pure trait or pure situation approaches (Magnusson, 1999). Finally, interactionism is valuable to positive psychology because one of the ways people attain

the good life is through flexibly adapting their behavior in situations to accomplish their goals (Magnusson & Mahoney, 2003; Seligman, 2003).

However, interactionism has not had the empirical success that it should. Although many developmental, social, and personality psychologists agree that behavior is a function of both the situation and the person, few include both factors in their research (Endler & Parker, 1992). A large reason for this is the limited availability of convenient and successful methods for employing the approach. The method described in this study may provide a needed convenient way to study interactionism in a way that solves many of the difficult problems facing previous methods. Specifically, the proposed method uses experience-sampling methodology (ESM; Bolger, Davis, & Rafaeli, 2003; Csikszentmihalyi & Larson, 1992; Hormuth, 1986; Stone, Shiffman, & deVries, 1999) to assess individuals' varying personality states (Fleeson, 2001; Nesselroade, 1988) and the varying psychologically active properties of situations (Funder, 2001; Mischel &

Shoda, 1995), and then employs multilevel modeling (MLM; Nezlek, 2001; Raudenbush & Bryk, 2002, also known as hierarchical linear modeling or multilevel random coefficient modeling) to analyze the associations between situation properties and personality states. None of these components of the method is new to this chapter (although MLM is relatively new to the field) or developed by myself, but in combination they are rare. Because the combination has great potential for many interesting questions, this chapter describes the combined methodology in an attempt to make it less rare.

I illustrate the method with a specific example taken from recent research in my lab, in which I attempt to identify the situation properties that are psychologically active for extraverted behavior. Extraverted individuals are known to experience much more positive affect than do introverted individuals (Eid, Riemann, Angleitner, & Borkenau, 2003), and Fleeson, Malanos, and Achille (2002) showed that each individual also experiences much more positive affect when acting extraverted than when acting introverted. McNiel and Fleeson (in press) employed experimental evidence to add that this relationship is a causal one. Thus, acting extraverted is one opportunity for individuals to increase the positive affect in their lives. The purpose of the illustrative research in this chapter is to determine what kinds of situations induce extraverted behavior, in order to understand the mechanisms underlying extraversion, so that more individuals can take advantage of this opportunity to increase happiness. The prediction is that extraverted behavior is an interactive function both of certain kinds of situations and of the individuals in them.

Goals of Interactionism

Interactionism posits that behavior is a function of the interaction between the person and the situation rather than an additive function of the person's traits and the situation (Bowers, 1973; Lewin, 1935; Magnusson & Endler, 1977). Interactionism assumes that (1) humans are active and flexible, that they adapt their behavior to changing situations; (2) individuals adapt in different unique ways depending on their interpretations of the situation and their desired goals; and (3) therefore, the best prediction of behavior includes situations and individuals as factors, not only additively but also interac-

tively. As a first step, interactionism treats persons and situations as independent variables and attempts to identify situation variables that lead to effective prediction of behavior additively and interactively with persons and person variables.[1] Typically, the situation is operationalized by an interesting experimental manipulation, the person is operationalized by a trait, and a dependent variable is hypothesized to be affected by the manipulation differently for individuals with different traits. For example, a very interesting study showed that knowing the purpose (the situation) of a boring task affected persistence (the dependent variable) more strongly for individuals high in hardiness (the trait) than for individuals low in hardiness. However, the situation did not interact with another trait, conscientiousness, such that highly conscientious individuals persisted regardless of the purpose of the task (Sansone, Weibe, & Morgan, 1999). Thus, to predict behavior at the highest level, it is necessary to know whether and how the effect of the situation differs across individuals. A second step in interactionism assumes that although the situation and the person are independent variables in their production of behavior, they are not independent of each other (Bowers, 1973; Magnusson & Endler, 1977). Rather, person variables affect the situation and situation variables affect the person (Buss, 1987; Ickes, Snyder, & Garcia, 1997; Snyder & Gangestad, 1982). Some of the ways individuals affect situations include choosing which situations to enter, interpreting situations in their own personal ways, and actually changing situations as they interact with them. For example, Sansone et al. (1999) showed that hardy individuals actually changed the task to bolster their own persistence.

There are at least two primary reasons that interactionism became popular throughout psychology. The first is that it provides an integrated, process-based characterization of the individual. Behavior is presumed to be the reaction to the current situation, based on the individual's interpretation of how best to achieve his or her goals in that situation. Thus, interactionism includes cognitive, behavioral, and motivational features working together in everyday life for the developing person (Magnusson, 1999). The second reason is that interactionism promises improvements in the ability to predict behavior. It avoids the attempt to predict behavior from only the situation or from only the personality but rather includes both factors.

Beyond its usefulness to psychology more generally, interactionism is likely to be particularly useful for positive psychology, for at least three reasons. First, one of the goals of positive psychology is to understand how individuals try to improve the quality of their lives; that is, how individuals figure out which goals are afforded by a current situation and then manage their behavior to most effectively pursue those goals. Because interactionism is the approach for studying that process, positive psychologists who are interested in understanding how people use their everyday behavior to try to improve the quality of their lives may find interactionism a promising approach. A second reason that interactionism may be useful for positive psychology is to help steer positive psychology away from a pure situation or a pure personality approach. The quality of life likely is determined not only by the situational conditions of life nor only by the individual living the life. Interactionism encourages focusing on both factors as well as on how the impact of situational conditions depends on the individual.

Finally, interactionism strengthens the link of positive psychology to one of its historical roots—humanism (Seligman & Csikszentmihalyi, 2000). Interactionism takes subjective experience and the uniqueness of individuals seriously in its emphasis on the flexibility of interpretation in the service of personal growth (Cantor & Fleeson, 1994). Furthermore, interactionism does so in a way that adds to the methodological rigor of humanism.

Difficulties for Interactionism

Interactionism has not received sufficient empirical attention. The underlying theory stresses the complexity of human beings and has high standards for the complexity of associated research. Recreating such complexity in actual research can be daunting and seems to require methods that are costly, difficult, or otherwise impractical. Indeed, many attempts to empirically instantiate the approach have met criticism for being too simplistic, specifically, for being arbitrary, atheoretical, and nondynamic. The method described in this chapter is offered as one potential solution that addresses some of the criticisms yet remains relatively convenient and practical as a method.

The first criticism of past attempts to research interactionism, that they have been arbitrary, is directed mainly at some of the laboratory methods (Bowers, 1973; Endler & Parker, 1992). In many studies, situations are manipulated and then variances are decomposed into variance due to the manipulation, variance due to the person, and variance due to the interaction between the manipulation and the person. The problem is that these variance components provide very little information about the relative power of situations, persons, and their interactions in daily life because the selection of situations and the strengths of the manipulations are in the experimenter's hands. It would be trivially easy to select a manipulation and a trait to make it appear as though most behavioral variance is due to situations or as though most behavioral variance is due to persons. In order to determine how much behavioral variance in the course of normal life is due to situations, persons, or their interactions, it is necessary to have situations and persons that are representative of those present in normal life. Even without deliberate effort to preordain the percentages, experimenters have little information about the representativeness of the manipulated situations or of the strengths of the manipulations in their experiments (Bem & Funder, 1978; Bowers, 1973).

The second criticism, that previous attempts to study interactionism have been thin theoretically, rests on two grounds. Often very little general theory of how to characterize situations is offered. Rather, situations are characterized in terms of one variable that is of specific theoretical importance to the researcher. Although this can be valuable, it may not transfer to other research on interactionism. Second, there is often little theory of the process variables, such as cognition and motivation, that predict various patterns of interactions (Mischel & Shoda, 1998; Zuroff, 1986). The interaction is quantified, but the underlying process that produced the interaction may not be addressed (Endler & Parker, 1992).

The final criticism is that most research attempts have not included time as a factor in the research design and so have fewer dynamic elements. Situations are treated as independent entities when it is clear that situations themselves can be influenced by persons (Bowers, 1973; Buss, 1987; Ickes et al., 1997). Also, typical experimental designs measure behavior on one occasion as an output of the experiment rather than tracking changes in behavior as situations change (Larsen, 1989).

The solution described in this chapter has four components: ESM, MLM, psychologically active properties of situations, and personality states. Personality states that change from occasion to occasion are the dynamic dependent variables. Psychologically active properties of situations are identified as the situation variables. ESM allows assessment of behaviors across representative samples of situation properties and situation strengths. MLM allows analyzing both which properties are relevant and how much individuals differ in their reactions to those properties. Finally, combined, the methods are reasonably convenient. Although this solution may not satisfy all criticisms of interactionism, it has promise for understanding what people do in their everyday lives to try to make things better.

Experience-Sampling Methodology

ESM involves obtaining multiple measurements of each individual as he or she lives his or her life. In line with the handbook's nontechnical approach, this chapter covers only enough basics of ESM to enable a researcher to get started on an interactionist approach to positive psychology. For more information, there are many excellent introductions that describe more details, more technical issues, and the multiple variants of ESM (e.g., Bolger et al., 2003; Csikszentmihalyi & Larson, 1992; Hormuth, 1986; Reis & Gable, 2000; Stone et al., 1999).

Personal data assistants (such as Palm Pilots), cell phones, and mobile Web technology have made and continue to make ESM much more handy. Various software for writing questionnaires has been developed, including Experience-Sampling Program, which was developed specifically for psychology uses (Barrett & Barrett, 2001). Participants carry their personal data assistants with them for about 1 to 3 weeks, coming to the lab every couple of days to download their accumulated data.

Several times each day, participants provide a report by answering the programmed questions referring to how they are acting, how they are feeling, what they are thinking, or what the situation is. Reports can refer to the immediate moment or to the previous several hours. A variety of response schedules are possible, depending on the research interests of the investigator. Random schedules are ideal for obtaining a random sample of the individuals' lives. However, random schedules sometimes reduce compliance because participants do not hear the signal when they are not expecting it. Also, random schedules may miss important experiences. Fixed schedules, for example scheduling a report every 3 hours, can aid compliance but sacrifice randomness. If fixed schedules are combined with reports that describe everything that has occurred since the previous report, however, fixed schedules produce representative samples because they produce complete samples. Event-triggered schedules are useful when trying to target responses to specific situations. For example, Wheeler and Reis (1991) described studies in which participants made reports whenever they interacted with others for an extended period of time or whenever certain important relationship events occurred.

ESM provides at least four enhancements to traditional self-report methods. The first enhancement is a reduction in contamination from memory biases or reconstructive processes. Because the reports come close in time to the actual events, emotions, or behaviors, the reports are more likely to be veridical. The second enhancement is the collection of a large amount of information about each individual. Such quantity of information allows more complete person-focused approaches that encompass individuals' ranges and patterns of experiences as well as a characterization of their ecologies. Tracking relationships among the events, situations, behaviors, and emotions can create a dynamic description of the individual's personality.

The third enhancement of ESM, especially useful for interactionism, is that it produces data suited to the investigation of within-person psychological functions rather than only between-person functions. Between-person functions compare people to each other. For example, more extraverted individuals are known to be happier than more introverted individuals (Eid et al., 2003). This is a between-person function because it describes and explains differences between people's happiness levels. A within-person function, in contrast, would be arrived at by comparing the happiness of one individual during the times he or she is extraverted to the same individual's happiness during the times he or she is not extraverted. Such a function, enabled by the centrality of the time dimension in ESM (Larsen, 1989), directly describes the psychological functioning within an individual as he or she moves from one occasion to another.

The fourth enhancement to traditional methods and another one particularly important for interactionist approaches is the opportunity to obtain personalized psychological functions. Different individuals are likely to be characterized by different functions relating variables to each other over time. For example, some individuals are likely to receive more of a mood boost from being extraverted than are other individuals. Similarly, Morf and Rhodewalt (2001) showed that narcissistic individuals' moods are more reactive to praise than are other people's moods. The standard between-person analysis, in contrast, must mathematically assume the same function for all individuals (and relegates any such individual differences to the error term). ESM allows describing both the average function for the typical individual and the unique function for each individual separately.

However, there are at least four potential impediments to obtaining these improvements. Fortunately, safeguards can minimize these impediments. The first impediment is the cost of personal data assistants, which tend to run $100 to $300 per unit. This impediment is mitigated to some extent by the fact that only 30 or so participants are required in many ESM studies. The huge amount of data generated per participant often provides great power for detecting statistical significance, even between subjects, because of the lowered measurement error per participant. To further reduce the cost, researchers can also run only a small number of participants at a time and run the study sequentially, in groups of, for example, 5 or 10 participants (for an initial investment of between $500 and $1,500). Paper recording costs much less but has the disadvantages of not allowing verification of timely completion of reports and requiring many hours of data entry.

A second potential impediment to ESM is the flipside of a strength: overcoming the temptation to collect an unwieldy mass of data. Each participant generates almost as much data as do some experimental studies, meaning that a single ESM study may generate as much data as several experimental studies. When conducting an ESM study, researchers are often tempted to assess as many variables and to test as many hypotheses as possible in one study. Such a temptation is partially based on the belief that ESM is difficult and expensive and partially on the potential to obtain a comprehensive picture of each individual. The resulting data, ironically, are sometimes too overwhelming to get a handle on and too broad to adequately test any particular hypothesis in depth. It is important therefore to focus ESM studies on a small number of hypotheses and

variables in order to make the data and analyses manageable and productive.

A third potential impediment is ensuring adequate compliance on the part of the participants. Typically, participants complete about 70% to 100% of the possible reports, amounting to about 60% to 80% after invalid reports are removed (Fleeson, 2001). Missed reports are primarily due to computer glitches or forgetting rather than due to motivation. Although 60–80% is reasonably good for most sampling procedures, to the extent that the missing reports are not missing randomly, conclusions about within-person functions could be inaccurate.

Finally, a fourth impediment is the cleaning of the data. Data will include at least two types of invalid reports: those due to computer malfunctions and those due to untimely completion. Identifying such reports requires careful review of each report. Even when aided by a statistics package, such review can take several hours.

In sum, these potential impediments can be minimized if identified and addressed. It is my impression that ESM studies are perceived as more daunting than they deserve to be. For example, my lab typically conducts two to five ESM studies per year.

Multilevel Modeling

The statistical component to combine with ESM is MLM. In line with the orientation of this handbook toward nontechnical treatments, this chapter describes only the basics of MLM and the substantive information generated by MLM so that a researcher can start using MLM in an interactionist approach to positive psychology. I present a conceptual interpretation of the results, avoid equations, and focus on MLM as a tool to investigate interactionism. Regarding programs, HLM6 may be the easiest of the programs to use, whereas the SAS and SPSS programs are embedded within complete statistics packages that can do other analyses. For readers desiring more information, there are many excellent introductions to MLM that describe the technical aspects of MLM or the step-by-step instructions (e.g., Kreft & DeLeeuw, 1998; Raudenbush, Bryk, Cheong, & Congdon, 2001; Singer, 1998). Nezlek (2001) is more directly targeted at personality and social psychologists, and Fleeson (in press) is directly targeted at personality psychologists interested in studying processes.

The core of MLM is the psychological function. Just like most statistics models in psychology, the psychological function describes the relationship between an independent variable and a dependent variable. Just as with ordinary regression, the interest is in the direction, magnitude, and significance of the coefficient relating the dependent variable to the independent variable. For example, the question of whether acting extraverted increases positive affect corresponds to the question of what the coefficient is when positive affect is taken as a function of extraversion. The interest is in the direction of the coefficient (whether positive affect increases or decreases with extraversion), the magnitude of the coefficient (how much positive affect changes as extraversion changes), and whether the coefficient is significantly different from zero. Thus, most psychologists are well practiced with the core aspect of MLM. The most conceptually difficult aspect of this function is the fact that it is within-person, that it describes how one individual changes as the moment changes. For example, the above function describes how one individual's positive affect increases and decreases as his or her extraversion increases and decreases from one occasion to another.

In an ESM context, MLM produces four central outputs: (1) a unique function for each individual, (2) the amount that these functions differ across individuals, (3) the weighted average of these functions, and (4) whether a hypothesized characteristic of the individuals predicts their personal functions.

The function for each individual describes how the dependent variable is related to the independent variable for that one individual over time; for example, how that individual's positive affect changes from moment to moment as his or her extraversion changes. The function is unique to that individual and directly describes his or her ongoing psychological functioning. (In most cases, it is best to center the independent variables within person before conducting the analysis in order to focus the function on within-person variation.)

MLM also calculates the amount that the functions of different individuals differ from each other, providing a variance and a standard deviation of the functions. Most important, the output provides a significance test of this variance to determine whether individuals differ from each other systematically in their functions. Systematic individual differences in the function mean that the effect of the situation

property on behavior depends on the individual. That is, it is a significance test on the interaction between person and situation. This is a very different approach to individual differences. Typically, psychologists look for processes common to all people, and consider whether individuals differ in the input or output to the process. In this approach, the process itself differs across individuals. For example, a significant variance for the extraversion function would mean that the rewardingness of acting extraverted differs systematically across individuals; that is, different individuals are characterized by different psychological functions of extraversion. It is important to note that a nonsignificant result does not mean that the function does not differ across subjects—it means only that the function does not differ across subjects more than chance could account for in this particular study with this particular level of power. This is the same as for all null hypothesis testing, but it is important to stress it in the context of MLM.

The output of MLM, however, focuses on a weighted average of these functions. The weighted average is represented by one coefficient, which can be interpreted just like any unstandardized coefficient from a regression. This coefficient is useful in at least two ways. First, the average coefficient describes the function for the typical individual. For example, it describes the typical amount and direction that the typical individual's positive affect changes as his or her extraversion increases. The average coefficient for the extraversion-to-positive-affect function turned out to be .68, meaning that the typical individual's positive affect increased .68 points for every point his or her extraversion increased. Second, it is useful to combine this average coefficient for the typical individual with information about how much individuals differ from each other. The standard deviation of the coefficient across individuals indicates how much individuals' coefficients differ from the typical individual's coefficient. Thus, together, the two pieces of information provide an efficient description of psychological functioning involving those two variables, a description that captures both the commonality and the uniqueness across individuals. The coefficient relating positive affect to extraversion had a standard deviation of .13, $p < .001$, meaning that all individuals became happier when they acted extraverted than when they acted introverted but that individuals differed in how strong the effect was. The significance of the differences also means that those differences are stable differences between individuals.

The final output of MLM is the test of theories to explain the individual differences in such functions. For example, trait extraversion may be associated with the positive affect-extraversion function because it may be that more extraverted individuals are more authentic when acting extraverted than are introverted individuals acting extraverted. The output in this case will be another coefficient, again similar to a beta from a regression. This coefficient describes the direction and magnitude in which the predictor variable is associated with the function, and whether the function is significantly associated with the predictor variable. Fleeson et al. (2002) found that the beta was $-.05$, $p < .05$, meaning that trait extraversion was associated with a weaker function relating positive affect to acting extraverted. That is, extraverts, surprisingly, received smaller boosts from acting extraverted than did introverts.

In sum, MLM provides the statistical analysis to enable ESM's advantages for interactionism and for positive psychology. It allows analyzing and identifying the dynamic within-person psychological functioning in everyday life, as well as each individual's unique functions.

Personality States and the Psychologically Active Properties of Situations

The final components of the method are theoretical: The third is the concept of a personality state (Fleeson, 2004; Nesselroade, 1988; Zuckerman, 1983) and the fourth is the concept of a psychologically active property of a situation (Bowers, 1973; Funder, 2001; Shoda & Lee-Tiernan, 2002). In order to predict behavior from situations, it is necessary to have a way to conceive of and assess both behavior and situation variables. The theoretical propositions are to assess behavior in terms of how much it represents or manifests personality trait contents and to assess situations in terms of properties that vary along continuous dimensions and that have psychological consequences.

Personality States

The central assumption is that, just as people have personality traits, they also have personality states (Fleeson, 2001; Fridhandler, 1986;

Nesselroade, 1988; Zuckerman, 1983). A personality state is the person's personality at a given moment, described in the same terms as are personality traits. For example, how extraverted a person is acting at the moment is his or her extraverted state. States are assessed just like traits, with rating scales, except that the participants are instructed to describe how they are at the moment rather than what they are like in general. For example, a 5 on a 7-point extraversion dimension means that the individual is acting moderately extraverted at the moment. This operationalization of behavior includes all aspects of the trait content, including how the individual is acting, feeling, and thinking at the moment (Pytlik Zillig, Hemenover, & Dienstbier, 2002). It does not assess the concrete, physical actions or movements the person is making, avoiding the problem that superficially similar physical actions can have very different meanings. Admittedly, it may include higher risk of response bias errors.

Although the content of traits can be applied to states, it is not known whether all properties (other than duration) of a given trait are shared by the corresponding state, that is, whether the state is *isomorphic* with the trait. For example, it is unknown whether acting extraverted is the same as being extraverted in all respects other than the duration of time (Fleeson et al., 2002; Zuckerman, 1983). One way to determine what properties of a trait are shared by a state is to test whether the state correlates with other variables similarly to how the trait correlates with them. If the state does correlate similarly to how the trait does, then the state likely shares the properties underlying those correlations; if not, then the state likely lacks the properties underlying those correlations. It is possible that both the state and the trait can be correlated with the same other variable but for two different underlying reasons, but this would be an unparsimonious coincidence.

Cases where the state shares the same underlying property as the trait may even inform about the nature of that property. In general, there are three likely possibilities for reconciling a within-subject correlation involving the state with a between-subject correlation involving the corresponding trait. The unparsimonious possibility is that there are two distinct properties underlying the two correlations. A second possibility is that there is only one property, and it is shared by both the trait and the state. However, there would have to be a stable form of it for the trait and a variable form of it for the state. This possibility requires explaining these two forms without invoking an unparsimonious additional mechanism. The final possibility is that the between-subjects association is present only because the trait increases the likelihood of being in the corresponding state.

For example, using ESM, Fleeson et al. (2002) found that all participants varied in how extraverted they were acting and indeed were happier in those moments when they acted more extraverted than in those moments when they acted less extraverted. Thus, state extraversion was also strongly associated with positive affect, just as trait extraversion is. It would be unparsimonious to assume that extraversion has two completely distinct yet powerful properties that lead to positive affect, whereas no other trait has even one. Rather, it is likely that the same property underlies both trait extraversion's and state extraversion's association with positive affect. Also likely is that extraverts are happier primarily because they are in extraverted states more often.

The within-subject association may inform about the nature of the important property. An individual's complement of dopamine neurons (Depue & Collins, 1999), for example, becomes less likely to be the property responsible for extraverts' increased happiness. When an extravert acts introverted, his or her number of dopamine neurons does not decrease, yet his or her positive affect does decrease. In contrast, amount of dopamine itself could vary with state extraversion and may also be the property underlying the trait-extraversion-to-positive-affect association (Depue & Collins, 1999). Acting extraverted may increase the amount of dopamine at the moment and thereby increase positive affect, and extraverts may have more resting dopamine. However, this possibility is not entirely satisfying because it still requires two distinct mechanisms—one relating state extraversion to positive affect and another mechanism to explain why it is that extraverts would coincidentally have more dopamine in the first place. Susceptibility to positive stimuli (Rusting & Larsen, 1998; chapter 14, this volume) might vary with state extraversion and thereby increase positive affect. That is, when individuals act more extraverted, their susceptibility to positive events may increase. It is also possible that repeated practice at susceptibility may lead more extraverted individuals to more generally have a heightened susceptibility, thus explaining the trait-extraversion-to-positive-affect association as well.

A third possibility is that trait extraversion is associated with positive affect because it increases the likelihood of being in state extraversion. This is an extreme case of isomorphism because it suggests that the properties of extraversion reside first in the state and that the trait's main association to positive affect is through increasing the frequency of the state and its properties. In any event, the within-person correlation suggests that states share at least some of the important properties of traits and that within-subject analysis of states can help determine the nature of traits.

Psychologically Active Properties of Situations

Typically, situations are classified categorically (Shoda, Mischel, & Wright, 1994), such as "social" versus "work." However, the assumption in this approach is that what is powerful about a situation is not its category but rather its properties. For example, what is powerful about social situations is not only that other people are present but the degree to which they are welcoming or hostile. Furthermore, situations differ on continuous dimensions, in the degree to which a property is present, and it is also assumed that multiple important properties are present in each situation, influencing behavior in the same or in different directions. For example, social situations consist of many psychologically active properties that vary from one social situation to the next, such as how friendly others are, how structured the situation is, how interdependent outcomes are, and other properties (Kelley et al., 2003). One job of interactionists is to identify the properties that are psychologically active.

Such knowledge about the properties of situations would be generally useful for psychology for predicting the ebb and flow of behavior (Kelley et al., 2003; Pervin, 1982). More specific theories about specific behaviors and situations will be required to identify the specific properties relevant to those behaviors. For example, interdependence theory provides predictions about the specific properties of social situations relevant to cooperation behaviors (Kelley et al., 2003).

Combining the Four Components: Which Situation Properties Induce Extraversion?

The plan to this method is to use ESM to collect data about the psychologically active properties of situations and individuals' personality states in those situations. Then MLM is used to determine (1) the typical individual's change in personality states as a function of the situation properties, (2) the amount individuals differ from each other in the functions, and (3) whether those differences are significant.

Although this chapter provides the method, the analytic technique, and the abstract theoretical parameters, it does not provide the specific theory for the particular content of an investigation, which will have to be supplied by the researcher. Specifically, it is incumbent upon the researcher to theorize what properties of situations are active for the particular behaviors of interest. For example, researchers could address such questions as: How do people differ in the interpersonal interactions that enhance their relationships? What predicts individual differences in reactions to everyday stressors? Which mood regulation strategies work under which conditions and for whom? What individual differences exist in the conditions that lead to peak performance? What are the mechanisms underlying virtuous behavior? I will illustrate the method for one example question: What situation properties are active in producing extraversion and how much do individuals differ in the power of those properties? Given the strong role of extraversion in positive affect, it is important to identify the mechanisms underlying extraverted behavior to provide one way that individuals might be able to improve their lives. Because of limited space, I only briefly describe the theory and select only a few brief findings to illustrate the method (see Fleeson, 2006, for complete findings).

Fleeson and Jolley (2006) outlined a theory of the processes underlying within-person variability in behavior. One proposed source of variability is that individuals use states (trait content) partially as tools to accomplish their goals; furthermore, individuals are assumed to differ in how they use states to support goals in different situations. This proposal has three basic assumptions: (1) behavior can facilitate or hinder pursuit of personal goals; (2) situations differ in which goals they afford; and (3) one reason individuals behave as they do in a given situation is to facilitate their personal goals that are afforded by that situation. For example, individuals may act extraverted in a situation where other people are being friendly because such a situation affords social goals, and acting in an extraverted manner may facilitate those social goals. The question at issue, then, is what role do extraversion states play in everyday life? Under what conditions do they come into play and when do people enact them? Do different people have different places for extraversion states and use extraversion states in different ways?

The nature of extraversion should provide clues about what kind of tool it is. However, surprisingly little is known about the nature of extraversion (Depue & Collins, 1999; Watson & Clark, 1997). Several theorists have proposed different sets of subtraits of extraversion, ranging from recklessness to leadership; others have proposed different mechanisms underlying extraverted behavior or the development of extraversion. There are some commonalities, and most contemporary theorists include some of the following facets of extraversion: vigorous action (Eysenck & Eysenck, 1975; Hogan, 1983), sensitivity to positive stimuli (Eid et al., 2003; Watson & Clark, 1997), ascendance (Watson & Clark, 1997), and sociability (Hogan, 1983; McCrae & Costa, 2003). Impulsivity has on occasion been included, but a growing consensus is developing that impulsivity belongs more comfortably in other traits (Watson & Clark, 1997). Even less is known about the mechanisms underlying extraversion, that is, why extraverts act extraverted or how extraversion develops in individuals. Extraversion's strong heritable component implicates some genetic source of extraverted behavior, but little is known of the process leading from genes to behavior (Bouchard & Loehlin, 2001).

Thus, current knowledge about the nature or mechanisms of extraversion provides only limited guidance for predicting which situation properties will induce extraverted states. Indeed, identifying those properties may shed light on the nature of extraversion and on the mechanisms underlying individual differences in extraversion—the situation conditions that lead to extraverted states in the moment may be similar to the conditions that lead to the development of extraverted traits in general. For example, if beliefs about other individuals' friendliness are critical in extraverted states, chronic beliefs about the friendliness of others may be critical in stable long-term individual differences in extraverted traits.

A starting point for identifying the types of goals that extraversion facilitates is the facets that most theorists agree are part of extraversion. These facets include vigor, sensitivity to positive stimuli, ascendance, or sociability; thus, individuals may act extraverted when pursuing goals facilitated by these facets. Such goals are afforded by situations that have room for self-initiated, free-form interaction and in which action and sociability are likely to be rewarded (e.g., the goal to make new friends). Such situations were operationalized by the properties of friendliness of others, interestingness, low structure, and low imposition.

I conducted an ESM study to collect data on individuals' variations in these four situation properties and in extraversion. Subjects reported four times per day at fixed times for 2 weeks, describing their behavior and the situation in the half-hour prior to the report. Situation properties were centered within each person.

MLM was then used to analyze the data. For each situation property, a function described state extraversion as a function of the property, just like in a normal regression equation. There were four functions predicting state extraversion, one for each situation property. Table 35.1 shows the results of all functions. The first property was the friendliness of others. MLM revealed a large unstandardized beta for the typical individual, $\beta = .43$, meaning that the typical individual's state extraversion is strongly contingent on the friendliness of others. Additionally, differences between individuals in this function were large and significant, $SD = .30$. Such a result is the key evidence for the interactionist approach, that the association of situations to behavior depended on the individual. The meaning of friendliness for behavior was different for different individuals and reliably so: Friendliness had almost no effect on some individuals' state extraversion, whereas for other individuals, friendliness of others was almost a

prerequisite for acting extraverted. Predicting how extraverted people are acting requires knowledge of which kind of person they are as well as what the situation is. For example, social anxiety may predict the effects of others' friendliness on extraversion, such that more anxious individuals may require more friendliness from others before they will hazard acting extraverted.

The function for interestingness of the situation revealed that for the typical individual, the coefficient relating state extraversion to the interestingness of the situation was .32, meaning that individuals indeed became more extraverted as the situation became more interesting. Importantly, this is a within-person function, describing the ongoing psychological functioning of individuals. Specifically, the comparison is within one person across time—the typical individual was more extraverted on those occasions in which the situation was interesting than on those occasions in which the situation was not so interesting. In this case, the variance between individuals was not significant, $SD = .12$. That is, there was not evidence in the current study that individuals differed from each other in this coefficient more than would be expected from sampling variations.

Both the level of structure and the degree to which the situation was imposed on the individual had small negative associations to extraversion. Thus, they both were indeed psychologically active properties for extraversion, but weak ones and negative ones. The association for structure did not differ significantly across individuals. However, individuals differed reliably in how much an imposed situation was associated with reduced extraversion. Thus, being imposed is a situation property connected to extraversion for some individuals, but not connected to

TABLE 35.1 Psychologically Active Properties of Situations for Extraversion

Property	For the Typical Individual	Individual Differences in the Association
Friendliness	.43***	.30*
Interestingness	.32***	.12
Structure	−.07*	.08
Imposed	−.12**	.11*

Note: Results for the typical individual indicate the average coefficient from MLM analyses and therefore describe the association between the situation property and extraversion state for the typical individual. Individual differences in the association show the standard deviation across individuals in the association and indicate how much individuals differ from each other in the psychological functioning relating a particular situation property to a behavior.

*$p < .05$. **$p < .01$. ***$p < .001$.

extraversion for other individuals. These differences are not just error variance but rather are reliable differences in how individuals react to interest as a feature of their environment.

In sum, these results show that individuals acted more extraverted when the situation was unstructured, freely chosen, full of friendly faces, and interesting, and acted more introverted when the situation became more structured, imposed, unfriendly, and uninteresting. These results may help clarify the mechanisms underlying extraversion, because what produces extraversion in the moment may also produce extraversion in the person. The powerful association of extraversion to others' friendliness suggests that an important mechanism underlying extraversion may be the perception of others' friendliness and the evaluation of extraversion as a tool in promoting social goals (Eaton & Funder, 2003). Such beliefs may provide an opportunity for therapeutic change so that individuals can take advantage of the extraversion-to-positive-affect relationship if they desire to. The weaker associations of structure and imposition to extraversion suggest that such constraints play less of a role in the mechanisms underlying extraversion.

The interactionist approach received strong support in that the association of the situation properties to behavior differed substantially across individuals in half the cases. Predicting behavior will be facilitated by assuming individual differences in the effects of situations. It is important to keep in mind that these significant individual differences are reliable, enduring characteristics of the individuals that operate across situations, that clarify who these people are as individuals, and that may affect how they approach situations and what they try to get out of them.

Conclusion: A Practical Method for Studying Interactionism

This chapter proposes a method to accomplish one underlying goal of interactionism: obtaining a holistic characterization of the individual that is not limited to situation or person effects but rather describes the individual's ongoing psychological functioning in response to changing situations. Furthermore, the method offers interactionism to positive psychologists as a potentially important tool for understanding how individuals go about pursuing what is good in life.

A new method is needed because prior methods have been criticized as not living up to the complexity asserted by the interactionist approach. Specifically, prior methods have been criticized for being arbitrary, atheoretical, and nondynamic. The method described in this chapter reduces arbitrariness because it obtains reasonably representative samples of situations in an individual's everyday life. Thus, variances are less attributable to arbitrary decisions on the part of the researcher and more closely reflect the power of situations as they are encountered in these individuals' daily lives. Such built-in ecological validity means that the description of individuals and their behavioral flexibility will be valid and comprehensive descriptions of how they act in their everyday lives.

Second, this method may reduce the atheoretical criticism. The theory component of the present method is that (1) there are psychologically active properties of situations, (2) such properties vary on continuous dimensions, (3) such properties predict personality states and affective states, and (4) individual differences in such predictions are an important aspect of personality (Shoda & LeeTiernan, 2002). However, this method does not provide the theory describing which situation properties matter, which ones interact with individuals, and which variables predict those interactions. For example, the method does not provide a theory of which properties of situations encourage extraverted states, nor which individuals will find a given property more encouraging. Rather, this method identifies precisely where theoretical work is to be done and what the theory should look like. Specifically, theory is needed on which properties of situations are psychologically active for particular states and which variables predict individual differences in which properties are active. The example for extraversion provided in this chapter was an illustration of one way such theories can be developed.

Third, this method may provide the demanded dynamic descriptions of individuals and their personalities. Magnusson (1999) stated that interactionism views the individual as an "active and purposeful organism, functioning and developing as a total integrated being" (p. 219) and claims that the "task for personality research is to contribute knowledge about how and why individuals think, feel, act, and react in real life situations" (p. 219). This method is dynamic in that it describes the ongoing psychological functioning of individuals in their daily lives by describing how their behavior changes as situations change. Furthermore, this method seamlessly incorporates even more dynamic elements. By incorporating time lags, the reciprocal effects of behavior and situations on each other can be investigated. By adding variables representing expectations and beliefs, cognitive changes in the situation can be addressed. And finally, adding person-level predictors to the model allows prediction of individual differences in situation selection and in the relationships between situations and behaviors.

Solving these problems conveniently is the key to the solution. Conceiving of situations in terms of their psychologically active properties and conceiving of behavior in terms of personality states quantifies them in a way that makes assessing them and calculating variances easy. ESM makes data collection relatively convenient across a wide sample of individuals' lives as they are actually happening. MLM makes the data analyses and interpretations possible and straightforward. A convenient method for obtaining ecologically valid tests of interactionist theories may contribute much to advancing knowledge of how people pursue the good things in life.

Acknowledgments   I would like to thank John Nezlek for comments on an earlier draft. Preparation of this chapter was supported in part by National Institute of Mental Health Grant R01 MH70571.

Note

1. This effort for interactionism has been identified as mechanistic interactionism, whereas the next step has been identified as dynamic interactionism (Endler & Parker, 1992). Because the method I describe in this chapter may aid both types of interactionism in their attempts to describe individuals' flexible actions in everyday situations, I use the more general term *interactionism* to refer to both types. However, I also direct special attention to the criticisms that have been directed at mechanistic interactionism.

References

Barrett, L. F., & Barrett, D. J. (2001). An introduction to computerized experience sampling in psychology. *Social Science Computer Review, 19,* 175–185.

Bem, D. J., & Funder, D. C. (1978). Predicting more of the people more of the time: Assessing the personality of situations. *Psychological Review, 85,* 485–501.

Bolger, N., Davis, A., & Rafaeli, E. (2003). Diary methods: Capturing life as it is lived. *Annual Review of Psychology, 54,* 579–616.

Bouchard, T. J., Jr., & Loehlin, J. C. (2001). Genes, evolution, and personality. *Behavior Genetics, 31,* 243–273.

Bowers, K. S. (1973). Situationism in psychology: An analysis and a critique. *Psychological Review, 80,* 307–336.

Buss, D. M. (1987). Selection, evocation, and manipulation. *Journal of Personality and Social Psychology, 53,* 1214–1221.

Cantor, N., & Fleeson, W. (1994). Social intelligence and intelligent goal pursuit: A cognitive slice of motivation. In R. Dienstbier (Series Ed.) & W. D. Spaulding (Volume Ed.), *Nebraska symposium on motivation: Vol. 41. Integrative views of motivation, cognition, and emotion* (pp. 125–179). Lincoln: University of Nebraska Press.

Csikszentmihalyi, M., & Larson, R. (1992). Validity and reliability of the experience sampling method. In M. W. deVries (Ed.), *The experience of psychopathology: Investigating mental disorders in their natural settings.* New York: Cambridge University Press.

Depue, R. A., & Collins, P. F. (1999). Neurobiology of the structure of personality: Dopamine, facilitation of incentive motivation, and extraversion. *Behavioral and Brain Sciences, 22,* 491–569.

Eaton, L. G., & Funder, D. C. (2003). The creation and consequences of the social world: An interactional analysis of extraversion. *European Journal of Personality, 17,* 375–395.

Eid, M., Riemann, R., Angleitner, A., & Borkenau, P. (2003). Sociability and positive emotionality: Genetic and environmental contributions to the covariation between different facets of extraversion. *Journal of Personality, 71,* 319–346.

Endler, N. S., & Parker, J. D. A. (1992). Interactionism revisited: Reflections on the continuing crisis in the personality area. *European Journal of Personality, 6,* 177–198.

Eysenck, H. J., & Eysenck, S. B. G. (1975). *Manual of the Eysenck Personality Questionnaire.* San Diego, CA: Educational and Industrial Testing Service.

Fleeson, W. (in press). Studying personality processes: Explaining change in between-person longitudinal and within-person multilevel models. In R. W. Robins, R. C. Fraley, & G. R. Krueger (Eds.), *Handbook of research methods in personality psychology.*

Fleeson, W. (2001). Towards a structure- and process-integrated view of personality: Traits as density distributions of states. *Journal of Personality and Social Psychology, 80,* 1011–1027.

Fleeson, W. (2004). Moving personality beyond the person-situation debate: The challenge and the opportunity of within-person variability. *Current Directions, 13,* 83–87.

Fleeson, W. (2006). *Situation-based contingencies underlying trait-content manifestation in behavior.* Manuscript submitted for publication.

Fleeson, W., & Jolley, S. (2006). A proposed theory of the adult development of intraindividual variability in trait-manifesting behavior. In D. Mroczek & T. D. Little (Eds.), *Handbook of personality development* (pp. 41–61). Mahwah, NJ: Erlbaum.

Fleeson, W., Malanos, A., & Achille, N. (2002). An intra-individual process approach to the relationship between extraversion and positive affect: Is acting extraverted as "good" as being extraverted? *Journal of Personality and Social Psychology, 83,* 1409–1422.

Fridhandler, B. M. (1986). Conceptual note on state, trait, and the state-trait distinction. *Journal of Personality and Social Psychology, 50,* 169–174.

Funder, D. C. (2001). Personality. *Annual Review of Psychology, 52,* 197–221.

Hogan, R. T. (1983). A sociaoanalytic theory of personality. In R. Dienstbier (Series Ed.) & M. M. Page (Volume Ed.), *Nebraska symposium on motivation: Vol. 30. Personality—current theory and research* (pp. 125–179). Lincoln: University of Nebraska Press.

Hormuth, S. (1986). The random sampling of experiences in situ. *Journal of Personality, 54,* 262–293.

Ickes, W., Snyder, M., & Garcia, S. (1997). Personality influences on the choice of situations. In R. Hogan, J. Johnson, & S. Briggs (Eds.), *Handbook of personality psychology* (pp. 987). San Diego: Academic Press.

Kelley, H. H., Holmes, J. G., Kerr, N. L., Reis, H. T., Rusbult, C. E., & Van Lange, P. A. M. (2003). *An atlas of interpersonal situations.* Cambridge: Cambridge University Press.

Kreft, I., & De Leeuw, J. (1998). *Introducing multilevel modeling.* Thousand Oaks, CA: Sage.

Larsen, R. J. (1989). A process approach to personality psychology: Utilizing time as a facet of data. In D. M. Buss & N. Cantor (Eds.), *Personality psychology: Recent trends and emerging directions* (pp. 177–193). New York: Springer-Verlag.

Lewin, K. (1935). *A dynamic theory of personality: Selected papers.* New York: McGraw-Hill.

Magnusson, D. (1999). Holistic interactionism: A perspective for research on personality development. In L. A. Pervin & O. P. John (Eds.), *Handbook of personality: Theory and research* (2nd ed., p. 738). New York: Guilford.

Magnusson, D., & Endler, N. S. (1977). *Personality at the crossroads: Current issues in interactional psychology.* Hillsdale, NJ: Erlbaum.

Magnusson, D., & Mahoney, J. L. (2003). A holistic person approach for research on positive development. In L. G. Aspinwall & U. M. Staudinger (Eds.), *A psychology of human strengths: Fundamental questions and future directions for a positive psychology* (pp. 227–243). Washington, DC: American Psychological Association.

McCrae, R. R., & Costa, P. T., Jr. (2003). *Personality in adulthood: A five-factor theory perspective* (2nd ed.). New York: Guilford.

McNiel, J. M., & Fleeson, W. (in press). The causal effects of extraversion on positive affect and neuroticism on negative affect: Manipulating state extraverison and state neuroticism in an experimental approach. *Journal of Research in Personality.*

Mischel, W., & Shoda, Y. (1995). A cognitive-affective system theory of personality: Reconceptualizing situations, dispositions, dynamics, and invariance in personality structure. *Psychological Review, 102,* 246–268.

Mischel, W., & Shoda, Y. (1998). Reconciling processing dynamics and personality dispositions. *Annual Review of Psychology, 49,* 229–258.

Morf, C. C., & Rhodewalt, F. (2001). Unraveling the paradoxes of narcissism: A dynamic self-regulatory processing model. *Psychological Inquiry, 12,* 177–196.

Nesselroade, J. R. (1988). Some implications of the trait-state distinction for the study of development over the life span: The case of personality. In P. B. Baltes, D. L. Featherman, & R. M. Lerner (Eds.), *Life-span development and behavior* (Vol. 8, pp. 163–189). Hillsdale, NJ: Erlbaum.

Nezlek, J. B. (2001). Multilevel random coefficient analyses of event- and interval-contingent data in social and personality psychology research. *Personality and Social Psychology Bulletin, 27,* 771–785.

Pervin, L. A. (1982). The stasis and flow of behavior: Toward a theory of goals. In R. A. Dienstbier (Series Ed.) & M. M. Page (Vol. Ed.), *Nebraska symposium on motivation 1982: Personality—current theory and research* (pp. 1–53). Lincoln, NE: University of Nebraska Press.

Raudenbush, S. W., & Bryk, A. S. (2002). *Hierarchical linear models: Applications and data analysis methods* (2nd ed., Vol. 1). Thousand Oaks, CA: Sage.

Raudenbush, S. W., Bryk, A. S., Cheong, Y. F., & Congdon, R. (2001). *Hierarchical linear and nonlinear modeling* (5th ed.). Lincolnwood, IL: Scientific Software International.

Reis, H. T., & Gable, S. L. (2000). Event-sampling and other methods for studying everyday experiences. In T. H. Reis & M. C. Judd (Eds.), *Handbook of research methods in social and personality psychology* (pp. 190–222). New York: Cambridge University Press.

Rusting, C. L., & Larsen, R. J. (1998). Personality and cognitive processing of affective information. *Personality and Social Psychology Bulletin, 24,* 200–213.

Sansone, C., Weibe, D. J., & Morgan, C. (1999). Self-regulating interest: The moderating role of hardiness and conscientiousness. *Journal of Personality, 67,* 701–733.

Seligman, M. E. P. (2003). Positive psychology: Fundamental assumptions. *Psychologist, 16,* 126–127.

Seligman, M. E. P., & Csikszentmihalyi, M. (2000). Positive psychology: An introduction. *American Psychologist, 55,* 5–14.

Shoda, Y., & LeeTiernan, S. (2002).What remains invariant?: Finding order within a person's thoughts, feelings, and behaviors across situations. In D. Cervone & W. Mischel (Eds.), *Advances in personality science* (pp. 241–270). New York: Guilford.

Shoda, Y., Mischel, W., & Wright, J. C. (1994). Intra-individual stability in the organization of and patterning of behavior: Incorporating psychological situations into the idiographic analysis of personality. *Journal of Personality and Social Psychology, 67,* 674–687.

Singer, J. D. (1998). Using SAS PROC MIXED to fit multilevel models, hierarchical models, and individual growth models. *Journal of Educational and Behavioral Statistics, 24,* 323–355.

Snyder, M., & Gangestad, S. (1982). Choosing social situations: Two investigations of self-monitoring processes. *Journal of Personality and Social Psychology, 43,* 123–135.

Stone, A. A., Shiffman, S. S., & deVries, M. W. (1999). Ecological momentary assessment. In D. Kahneman, E. Diener, & N. Schwarz (Eds.), *Well-being: The foundations of hedonic psychology* (pp. 26–39). New York: Russell Sage.

Watson, D., & Clark, L. A. (1997). Extraversion and its positive emotional core. In R. Hogan, J. Johnson, & S. Briggs (Eds.), *Handbook of personality psychology* (p. 987). San Diego: Academic Press.

Wheeler, L., & Reis, H. T. (1991). Self-recording of everyday life events: Origins, types, and uses. *Journal of Personality, 59,* 339–354.

Zuckerman, M. (1983). The distinction between trait and state scales is not arbitrary: Comment on Allen and Potkay's "On the arbitrary distinction between traits and states." *Journal of Personality and Social Psychology, 44,* 1083–1086.

Zuroff, D. C. (1986). Was Gordon Allport a trait theorist? *Journal of Personality and Social Psychology, 51,* 993–1000.

36

Differentiation of the Distributions of Inspiration and Positive Affect Across Days of the Week

An Application of Logistic Multilevel Modeling

Todd M. Thrash

Positive psychology has been a liberating force in that researchers have more freedom than ever before to investigate what is good and right about human functioning. However, with this increased freedom comes the responsibility to integrate new constructs and theories with, and differentiate them from, those established previously. In our research on inspiration, Andrew Elliot and I (Thrash & Elliot, 2003, 2004) have observed a relatively strong relationship between inspiration and the established construct of activated positive affect (PA; Watson, Wiese, Vaidya, & Tellegen, 1999). Accordingly, we have sought and presented evidence that inspiration is distinct from activated PA. Inspiration has unique correlates (Thrash & Elliot, 2003, 2004), antecedents (Thrash & Elliot, 2004), and consequences (Thrash & Elliot, 2003). The substantive aim of this chapter is to provide additional evidence of the discriminant validity of inspiration and activated PA by documenting different distributions of the two states across days of the week.

The second aim of this chapter is didactic—to illustrate the application of multilevel random coefficient modeling (MRCM) in addressing the above substantive aim. Specifically, I demonstrate how a dummy variable representing assigned condition (inspiration, activated PA) may be modeled as a between-person moderator of the within-person distribution of experiences across days of the week. In doing so, I also illustrate several techniques that may not be familiar to all researchers, such as the prediction of a dichotomous outcome variable using the logit transformation.

Substantive Considerations

Inspiration, Affect, and the Weekly Cycle

The *Oxford English Dictionary* defines *inspiration* as "a breathing in or infusion of some idea, purpose, etc. into the mind; the suggestion,

awakening, or creation of some feeling or impulse, especially of an exalted kind" (Simpson &
Weiner, 1989). A theoretical definition of inspiration, grounded in diverse literatures on inspiration and recent construct validation studies,
includes three core characteristics: transcendence, evocation, and motivation (Thrash & Elliot, 2003, 2004). *Transcendence* refers to the
fact that one becomes oriented toward something that is better or more important than one's
usual concerns; one sees better possibilities.
Evocation refers to the fact that inspiration is
experienced as evoked by a stimulus, and thus
one does not feel directly responsible for becoming inspired. Finally, inspiration involves
motivation to express or make manifest that
which is newly apprehended. Inspiration is
typically operationalized using direct self-report
measures, such as the Inspiration Scale (Thrash
& Elliot, 2003).

Activated PA is an affective state or mood
characterized by positive valence and high activation (Watson et al., 1999). Activated PA
is typically operationalized using the positive
affect scale of the Positive and Negative Affect
Schedule (Watson, Clark, & Tellegen, 1988),
which consists of adjectives such as *interested*,
determined, and *active*. Previous research on
day-of-the-week effects reveals a need to distinguish between activated PA and *pleasant
affect* (Egloff, Tausch, Kohlmann, & Krohne,
1995; Kennedy-Moore, Greenberg, Newman, &
Stone, 1992). Pleasant affect, like activated PA,
has a positive valence, but it does not involve
high activation; it includes moods such as feeling
happy and pleased. A parallel distinction may be
drawn between *activated negative affect* (NA),
which involves feeling tense and anxious, and
unpleasant affect, which involves feeling sad and
unhappy.

Although no research to date has examined
the distribution of inspiration across days of the
week, a number of studies have examined day-
of-the-week effects on mood, as well as participants' beliefs about such effects. Consider, first,
participants' beliefs. In an early study, Farber
(1953) asked participants to rank order the days
of the week in terms of preference, which presumably relates to beliefs about the hedonic tone
of each day. Saturday was most preferred, followed by Friday, Sunday, Thursday, Wednesday, Tuesday, and finally, Monday. Stone,
Hedges, Neale, and Satin (1985) asked participants to judge the day of the week on which their
mood was best or worst; 35% reported having

the best mood on Fridays, followed by 28% on
Sundays and 25% on Saturdays. Further, 65%
of participants reported that they had the worst
mood on Mondays, followed by 9% on Tuesdays
and 5% on Wednesdays. McFarlane, Martin,
and Williams (1988) found that participants recalled experiencing high levels of pleasant affect
on Fridays and Saturdays. Pecjak (1970) reported
that participants associated Saturday with
laughter, love, and passion, Sunday with happiness, and Monday with anger.

These findings indicate, first, that individuals
believe their mood to be better on weekends
than on weekdays. Second, these findings indicate that individuals believe mood to be worse on
Monday than on other weekdays. These two
beliefs are reflected in the expressions "Thank
God it's Friday" and "blue Monday," respectively. These beliefs may or may not correspond
to actual affective experience as measured in
prospective longitudinal research. The following
is a review of the available evidence from diary
studies of affective experience.

Weekend and Blue Monday Effects

In two early studies, Christie and Venables
(1973; Venables & Christie, 1974) examined
Monday–Friday differences in various dimensions of mood. Venables and Christie (1974)
found Friday to be more hedonically positive
than Monday along several affect dimensions
(see also Park, Armeli, & Tennen, 2004, footnote
1), and Christie and Venables (1973) found that
day of the week interacted with personality—for
instance, individuals high in extraversion and
low in neuroticism reported higher arousal and
euphoria on Fridays. However, interpretation of
these findings is complicated by the fact that the
Monday–Friday distinction confounds possible
weekend and blue Monday effects. It is not clear
whether these findings reflect (1) elevated mood
on Friday due to a weekend effect, (2) depressed
mood on Monday due to a blue Monday effect,
or (3) both elevated mood on Friday and depressed mood on Monday.

More recent studies have examined the distribution of affect across all seven days of the
week. Regarding possible weekend effects,
studies have found that pleasant affect (as distinguished from activated PA) peaks on Friday
and Saturday (Csikszentmihalyi & Hunter,
2003; McFarlane et al., 1988; Reis, Sheldon,
Gable, Roscoe, & Ryan, 2000), on Saturday and
Sunday (Egloff et al., 1995; Kennedy-Moore

et al., 1992; Sheldon, Ryan, & Reis, 1996; Stone, Hedges, Neale, & Satin, 1985), or on Friday, Saturday, and Sunday (Rossi & Rossi, 1977). Unpleasant affect (as distinguished from activated NA) has been found to be at a trough on Friday and Saturday (Reis et al., 2000) or on Saturday and Sunday (Kennedy-Moore et al., 1992; Rossi & Rossi, 1977; Stone et al., 1985). Affect balance—that is, pleasant affect minus unpleasant affect—has been found to peak on Friday and Saturday (Larsen & Kasimatis, 1990). Thus, studies have consistently found that weekends involve higher levels of pleasant affect and lower levels of unpleasant affect.

Fewer data are available regarding weekday-weekend differences in activated PA and activated NA. Kennedy-Moore et al. (1992) found that activated PA was lower on Sunday than on other days of the week, but other studies have found activated PA to be invariant across days of the week (Clark & Watson, 1988; Egloff et al., 1995). Activated NA has been found to be lowest on Sunday (Clark & Watson, 1988) or on Saturday and Sunday (Kennedy-Moore et al., 1992). In sum, on weekends, there tends to be an increase in pleasant affect (but not activated PA) and a decrease in unpleasant affect and activated NA.

Although weekend effects have been documented consistently for pleasant affect, unpleasant affect, and activated NA, it is apparent that the timing of the hedonic peak (i.e., Friday, Saturday, or Sunday) has been inconsistent across studies. This inconsistency may be attributable, at least in part, to differences in the populations that have been studied. We might expect Fridays and Saturdays to be the most hedonically positive days for student populations, for whom Friday and Saturday night are often important for socializing, and for whom Sunday often resembles a weekday given the need to study or complete assignments. For nonstudent adult populations, in contrast, Saturday and Sunday may be the most hedonically positive, given that working adults are less likely to actively celebrate on Friday and to have work to complete on Sunday. Indeed, of the studies cited above, those that examined student samples most often documented a hedonic peak on Friday and Saturday (Csikszentmihalyi & Hunter, 2003; Larsen & Kasimatis, 1990; McFarlane et al., 1988; Park et al., 2004; Reis et al., 2000); fewer studies documented a hedonic peak on Saturday and Sunday (Egloff et al., 1995; Sheldon et al., 1996) or on all three days (Rossi & Rossi, 1977). In contrast, both of the

studies that examined nonstudent adult samples documented a hedonic peak on Saturday and Sunday (Kennedy-Moore et al., 1992; Stone et al., 1985). It appears that the timing of the weekend effect varies with the population under investigation.

In contrast to the weekend effect, the blue Monday effect has received little empirical support. A study of mood in work groups failed to uncover a blue Monday effect, despite the fact that employees viewed each other as being in a worse mood on Mondays (Totterdell, Kellett, Teuchmann, & Briner, 1998). Additionally, of all the studies cited above, the only study to report a statistically significant difference between Monday and other weekdays was that by Reis et al. (2000), who found that pleasant affect was lower on Monday than on Tuesday, Wednesday, and Thursday. However, it should be noted that not all of the studies conducted the relevant contrasts, and indeed Monday (or occasionally Sunday) is often the day with the lowest mean in pleasant affect or the highest mean in unpleasant affect. The blue Monday effect may well exist but, if so, appears to be modest in magnitude. Certainly, beliefs about the blue Monday effect, and indeed the weekend effect, overstate reality (McFarlane et al., 1988).

Differential Effects of Weekend on Inspiration and Activated PA

Researchers often attribute weekday-weekend differences in affect to the different types of events and activities that occur on weekdays and weekends. Weekends are known to involve a higher frequency of desirable events and a lower frequency of undesirable events (Kennedy-Moore et al., 1992; Stone, 1987), and much research has linked desirable and undesirable events to mood (e.g., Clark & Watson, 1988; Gable, Reis, & Elliot, 2000; Stone, 1987). However, Kennedy-Moore et al. (1992) found that the weekend effects on pleasant and unpleasant affect remain even after controlling for the frequency of desirable and undesirable events. Perhaps more important is the fact that weekend activities offer greater opportunities for satisfaction of basic psychological needs—relatedness and autonomy in particular (Reis et al., 2000; Sheldon et al., 1996).

Such explanations help explain why, on most measures, weekends are more hedonically positive than weekdays. However, they do not explain the divergence between pleasant affect (which tends to increase on the weekend) and activated PA (which tends not to increase on the weekend). The divergence may reflect the differential involvement of these two types of affect in agentic and communal activities (or *arbeit* and *liebe*, respectively). Brown and Moskowitz (1998) reported that agency is lower, and communion higher, on weekends. Regarding the latter, Reis et al. (2000) found that students reported more hanging out and doing pleasant or fun things with others on the weekend, and doing pleasant or fun things with others was a significant predictor of daily pleasant affect. The well-documented weekend effect for pleasant affect may reflect the fact that weekend social activities are more enjoyable than weekday activities. At the same time, both work and love are evolutionarily significant goals that are likely to activate the underlying approach temperament system, which is posited to be responsible for appetitive affects such as activated PA. In short, individuals may be happier on weekends, yet positively engaged throughout the week—positively engaged with work on weekdays, and positively engaged with relationships on the weekend (cf. Kennedy-Moore et al., 1992).

Whereas weekday and weekend activities both involve forms of positive engagement, several factors suggest that weekday and weekend activities may not be equally conducive to inspiration. First, inspiration is likely to be facilitated by exposure to a cognitively rich and stimulating environment. At least among college students, such exposure is likely to be greater on weekdays than on weekends. Second, inspiration, particularly in the creativity and achievement domains, has long been thought to be facilitated by effort and preparation (Wallas, 1926). Indeed, research has shown that work-mastery motivation predicts increases in inspiration (Thrash & Elliot, 2003). To the extent that weekday activities involve greater effortful task involvement, they are likely to be more conducive to inspiration. Third, the agency-oriented context of the work week may be more compatible with inspired activity, in which one strives to actualize newly recognized possibilities, than with the less explicitly goal-oriented communal context of the weekend. Fourth, to the extent that individuals view the weekend as a time of escape and pleasure seeking, they may be preoccupied with activities (e.g., drinking) that are conducive to pleasant affect but likely inhibitive of inspiration.

In light of these arguments, I hypothesized that activated PA and inspiration would be differentially distributed across days of the week, such that activated PA is approximately equally distributed across weekdays and weekends, and inspiration is more frequent on weekdays than on weekends. No other day-of-the-week effects were expected. These hypotheses were tested using data originally collected for other purposes (Thrash & Elliot, 2004). In one condition, undergraduate participants reported, each night for 2 weeks, whether or not they had experienced inspiration on that day. In the other condition, participants reported whether or not they had experienced activated PA each day.

Statistical Considerations

General Analytic Approach

The present data set consists of nested data—daily assessments (Level 1) are nested within persons (Level 2). The criterion to be predicted is a dichotomous variable representing, for a given day, the presence (1) versus absence (0) of the target experience (i.e., inspiration or activated PA). Day of the week varies at Level 1 and may be represented as a predictor of the presence of the target experience. Condition (inspiration versus activated PA), a Level 2 variable, may be tested as a moderator of the within-person relationship between day of the week and presence of the target experience. Significant moderation would indicate that inspiration and activated PA have different distributions across days of the week.

Several analytic approaches are available for testing whether a between-person variable moderates a within-person relationship. One option is to use a traditional ordinary least squares (OLS) approach such as repeated-measures ANOVA, treating the Level 1 predictor as a repeated measure and the Level 2 predictor as a between-subjects factor, and examining the interaction between them. Although historically ANOVA has been the most widely used approach in studies of day-of-the-week effects, it has several limitations and shortcomings (Kenny, Kashy, & Bolger, 1998; Nezlek, 2001; Reis & Gable, 2000). First, ANOVA is limited to the use of categorical predictors. This is particularly limiting for researchers who wish to use traits or other continuous individual difference variables as moderators of day-of-the-week effects. Second, repeated-measures ANOVA requires complete data for each participant. This limitation is particularly problematic in diary studies, in which a substantial portion of the sample is likely to have missing data on at least one day. A common practice that ameliorates this problem is to compute aggregates (means) for each participant for each day of the week. In a 3-week diary study, for instance, participants would have a complete set of aggregates unless they missed all three Mondays, or all three Tuesdays, or all three of any other day of the week. However, aggregates computed from fewer observations are less reliable than those computed from more observations. Unless a weighting technique is used (e.g., weighted least squares), the aggregation approach may yield imprecise parameter estimates. Third, ANOVA, as typically employed, treats the within-person intercept and slope parameters as fixed effects rather than as random effects; that is, it does not model individuals' intercepts and slopes as arising from populations of possible intercepts and slopes. Because the error structure is misrepresented, misleading parameter estimates and significance tests may result. MRCM, in contrast, can accommodate continuous predictors, unbalanced data, and random intercepts and slopes, using a highly efficient maximum likelihood estimation procedure. This approach is illustrated in the present investigation.

Representation of Day of the Week

A second decision concerns how the day-of-the-week construct is to be represented and modeled. One option is to focus on *weekly cyclicity*, the rhythm that repeats each week. As in spectral analysis, a weekly rhythm may be modeled using a sine or cosine function with a wavelength of 7 days (e.g., Brown & Ryan, 2003). Larsen and Kasimatis (1990) reported that 40% of the variance in daily affect balance, aggregated across individuals, was explained by a sine wave function that peaks around Friday or Saturday and is at a trough around Monday or Tuesday. This approach offers the advantage of statistical parsimony—a single sine or cosine function, or a small number of functions, may be used to characterize the weekly cycle. A second option is to use a coding scheme, such as contrast coding, to represent distinctions among the days of the week. This approach is less parsimonious but permits a fine-tuned analysis of the source of variation across days. Does weekly cyclicity reflect a weekend effect, a blue Monday effect, or both? These are conceptually independent effects for which orthogonal contrast coding is well suited. Accordingly, I use contrast coding in the present investigation.

In the following, I describe the creation of six contrast-coded variables that represent distinctions among the seven days of the week. The values of these six variables were assigned in a two-step process. First, for each contrast variable, the sign of the variable's value for particular days was assigned to reflect the subsets of days to be contrasted by that variable; days assigned a positive code are to be contrasted with days assigned a negative code (see table 36.1).

TABLE 36.1 Signs and Values of Day-of-the-Week Contrast Codes

Day	FS-MTWRU	F-S	U-MTWR	M-TWR	T-WR	W-R
Signs						
Monday (M)	−	0	−	+	0	0
Tuesday (T)	−	0	−	−	+	0
Wednesday (W)	−	0	−	−	−	+
Thursday (R)	−	0	−	−	−	−
Friday (F)	+	+	0	0	0	0
Saturday (S)	+	−	0	0	0	0
Sunday (U)	−	0	+	0	0	0
Values						
Monday (M)	−2/7	0	−1/5	3/4	0	0
Tuesday (T)	−2/7	0	−1/5	−1/4	2/3	0
Wednesday (W)	−2/7	0	−1/5	−1/4	−1/3	1/2
Thursday (R)	−2/7	0	−1/5	−1/4	−1/3	−1/2
Friday (F)	5/7	1/2	0	0	0	0
Saturday (S)	5/7	−1/2	0	0	0	0
Sunday (U)	−2/7	0	4/5	0	0	0

The pattern of contrast codes in table 36.1 is consistent with the requirements of orthogonal contrast coding (see Cohen, Cohen, West, & Aiken, 2003) and was guided by the substantive questions of interest. Given the student sample under investigation, the weekend was operationalized as Friday and Saturday (see Substantive Considerations above). The contrast FS-MTWRU represents the distinction between weekends and weekdays, and the contrast M-TWR represents the distinction between Mondays and other weekdays. The remaining contrast variables are included in order to minimize the effects of having an unequal number of observations across days of the week.

The second step was to assign particular numeric values to each contrast variable for each day of the week (see table 36.1). As recommended by Cohen et al. (2003), values were chosen such that days in the subset having positive signs received the value of $n/(n+p)$, and days in the subset having negative signs received the value of $-p/(n+p)$, where $n =$ the number of days with a negative sign and $p =$ the number of days with a positive sign. Commonly, contrast codes for a particular variable are each multiplied by the value in the denominator $(n+p)$ in order to eliminate fractions. The advantage of using the values of $n/(n+p)$ and $-p/(n+p)$, rather than n and $-p$, is that they differ by exactly 1: $n/(n+p) - [-p/(n+p)] = (n+p)/(n+p) = 1$. For example, in the case of FS-MTWRU, $5/7 - (-2/7) = 1$. Given that an unstandardized regression coefficient indicates the expected change in the dependent variable given a one-unit increase in the independent variable (while holding constant other predictors), this coding scheme will produce unstandardized coefficients that directly indicate the difference in the dependent variable between days having a positive code and those having a negative code (Cohen et al., 2003). If the values of n and $-p$ were used instead, then the unstandardized regression coefficients would indicate $1/(n+p)$ of the difference between the two sets of days, unnecessarily complicating interpretation of regression coefficients.

Logistic Regression/Multilevel Modeling

Dichotomous outcome variables pose a challenge to linear modeling techniques such as regression and MRCM, which require that the criterion be expressed as a linear combination of predictor variables. Consider an example offered by Pampel (2000)—using annual income to predict whether or not an individual owns a home. An increase in income from $0 to $10,000 would be associated with only a modest increase in the probability of owning a home, because a home would not be affordable in either case. An increase in income from $90,000 to $100,000 would also be associated with only a modest increase in the probability of owning a home, because a home would be affordable in both cases. Only at intermediate incomes would a $10,000 increment be associated with a sizable increase in the probability of owning a home. This example illustrates that the relationship between a predictor and the probability of the occurrence of a dichotomous outcome is inherently S-shaped, with the steepest slope at intermediate values of the predictor (see figure 36.1).

One possible response to the problem of nonlinearity would be to ignore it and employ a

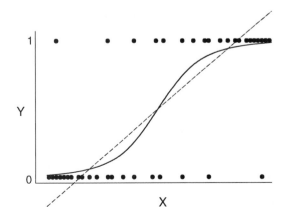

Figure 36.1 The relationship between a continuous predictor variable and a dichotomous outcome variable. Dots indicate observed data points. The solid line indicates the true, nonlinear relationship between the predictor and the probability of the occurrence of the outcome. The dotted line indicates the regression line derived from a traditional regression model that does not take nonlinearity into account.

linear probability model. In this case, a straight line is fitted to the observed data, and predicted values are interpreted as probabilities that the outcome equals 1 rather than 0. This approach is problematic in several respects (Cohen et al., 2003; Pampel, 2000). An interpretation of the resulting predicted values as probabilities is contradicted by the fact that a straight line with a nonzero slope is not constrained to the range of 0–1 (see figure 36.1). Probabilities, by definition, cannot fall outside this range. Even when predicted values are in range, they will tend to be biased, overestimating the slope at extreme values of the predictor and underestimating the slope at intermediate values (see figure 36.1). Furthermore, this approach violates the assumptions of homoscedasticity and normality of residuals, leading to misleading significance tests (see Pampel, 2000).

Logistic regression provides a solution to these problems: proceed with a linear prediction model but interpret the predicted values as representing a nonlinear function of probability, rather than probability per se (Pampel, 2000; Raudenbush & Bryk, 2002). Specifically, the predicted values are interpreted in the logit metric. A logit is defined as follows:

$$\text{logit} = \ln\left(\frac{\varphi}{1-\varphi}\right) \qquad (1)$$

where φ represents the probability of the occurrence of the criterion event—that is, the probability that the criterion variable equals 1 rather than 0. The quantity $\varphi/(1-\varphi)$ is called *odds* and represents the ratio of the probability of occurrence (φ) to the probability of nonoccurrence ($1-\varphi$). The logit is the natural logarithm of the odds. Given its definition, logit units are also called *log-odds*, and I use this more descriptive label hereafter.

Conceiving of predicted values as log-odds rather than probability implies the following regression equation (or Level 1 portion of a multilevel model, if applied separately to each individual):

$$\ln\left(\frac{\varphi}{1-\varphi}\right) = \beta_0 + \beta_1 X \qquad (2)$$

Note that the right side of the equation remains linear in form, and thus X is linearly related to the quantity on the left side of the equation, the predicted log-odds. Nonlinearity is present in the relationship between the predicted log-odds

and their corresponding predicted probability values (φ). As illustrated in the following, a linear increase in log-odds corresponds to a bounded and nonlinear increase in φ that is consistent with the S-shaped curve illustrated in figure 36.1:

log-odds:	-5.00	-4.00	-3.00	-2.00	-1.00	-0.00
φ:	.01	.02	.05	.12	.27	.50
log-odds:	1.00	2.00	3.00	4.00	5.00	
φ:	.73	.88	.95	.98	.99	

In short, in logistic regression, one employs a regression equation that is linear in form but that yields predicted values that are in the log-odds metric and that are nonlinearly related to probability.

Special care must be taken in interpreting predicted values and parameter estimates (i.e., intercepts and slopes) in logistic regression/ multilevel modeling. The log-odds metric, in which predicted values are expressed, has little intuitive meaning. Predicted values may be converted from log-odds to odds using the equation

$$\text{odds} = e^{\text{log-odds}} \qquad (3)$$

and predicted values may be converted from log-odds to probability using the equation

$$\text{probability} = 1/(1+e^{-(\text{log-odds})}) \qquad (4)$$

Given that an intercept represents a predicted value of the dependent variable (specifically, the predicted value when all predictors equal 0), the intercept is also expressed in log-odds units and may be converted into odds or probabilities using Equations 3 or 4.

A slope, or unstandardized regression coefficient, represents the expected change in the log of the odds that the observed criterion equals 1 rather than 0, given a one-unit increase in the independent variable while holding other predictors constant. Conversion into a more interpretable metric is more complex for slopes than for predicted values or intercepts, because neither odds nor probability vary linearly with X, and thus the rate of change cannot be expressed as a constant in these metrics. There is, however, an intuitively meaningful unit that varies linearly with X — the odds ratio, which refers to the multiplicative factor by which the predicted odds change when X is increased by one unit. The odds ratio may be obtained by exponentiating the regression coefficient:

$$\text{odds ratio} = e^{\beta_1}. \tag{5}$$

Equation 5 follows from Equation 2, as derived in the appendix.

Method

Participants

Data collected by Thrash and Elliot (2004, Study 3) were reanalyzed in order to examine the distributions of inspiration and activated PA across days of the week.[1] Participants were 72 undergraduates who participated in return for extra credit in a psychology course. Participants were randomly assigned to a condition. The inspiration condition included 35 individuals (12 male, 23 female), and the activated PA condition included 37 individuals (14 male, 23 female).

Procedure and Measures

Participants completed a short questionnaire via the World Wide Web on 14 consecutive nights, beginning on a Tuesday and ending on a Monday. The Web site permitted participants to complete the nightly diaries no earlier than 5:00 p.m. and no later than 5:00 p.m. the following day. Diaries submitted after 5:00 a.m. were considered late and were excluded from analysis.

Each night, participants in the inspiration condition were asked whether or not they had experienced inspiration in the previous 24 hours. Participants were provided with the *Oxford English Dictionary* definition of inspiration quoted above. Each night, participants in the activated PA condition were asked whether or not they had experienced activated PA in the previous 24 hours. The following definition of activated PA was provided: "being enthusiastic, interested, determined, and excited." These descriptors are the items from the PANAS measure of PA that load more strongly than the item "inspired" (Watson et al., 1999), which also appears on the PANAS. In both conditions, presence of the target experience (i.e., inspiration or activated PA) was coded as present (1) or absent (0), and this variable serves as the criterion in the present investigation.

Results

The Level 1 (day-level) portion of the multilevel model was specified as follows:

$$\begin{aligned} \ln(\varphi_{ij}/1 - \varphi_{ij}) = {} & \beta_{0j} + \beta_{1j}(C_{\text{FS-MTWRU}}) \\ & + \beta_{2j}(C_{\text{F-S}}) + \beta_{3j}(C_{\text{U-MTWR}}) \\ & + \beta_{4j}(C_{\text{M-TWR}}) \\ & + \beta_{5j}(C_{\text{T-WR}}) + \beta_{6j}(C_{\text{W-R}}) \end{aligned} \tag{6}$$

This equation predicts the log-odds of the target experience for person j on day i using six contrast-coded Level 1 variables that represent day of the week. Note that all coefficients in this equation are subscripted j, indicating that each individual j has his or her own regression equation with his or her own intercept (β_{0j}) and slopes ($\beta_{1j} - \beta_{6j}$). The Level 1 intercept, β_{0j}, represents person j's log-odds of the occurrence of the target experience when all predictor variables equal 0. As explained by Cohen et al. (2003), when orthogonal contrast-coded variables all equal 0, the intercept equals the unweighted mean of the dependent variable across contrast units (here, days of the week). Therefore, β_{0j} represents person j's unweighted mean log-odds across the 7 days of the week. Hereafter, references to "average day of the week," "average weekend days," and so on refer to unweighted means.

The remaining six terms in Equation 6 adjust person j's expected log-odds of occurrence upward or downward from his or her average as a function of day of the week. β_{1j}, the slope relating $C_{\text{FS-MTWRU}}$ to the log-odds of occurrence for person j, represents the difference between person j's log-odds on an average weekday and his or her log-odds on an average weekend day. β_{2j}, β_{3j}, β_{4j}, β_{5j}, and β_{6j} may be interpreted in parallel fashion, except that these coefficients represent contrasts within weekends (β_{2j}) or within weekdays ($\beta_{3j} - \beta_{6j}$).

Because each individual j has his or her own regression equation relating day of the week to the presence of the target experience, some degree of variance among individuals in these intercepts (β_{0j}) and slopes ($\beta_{1j} - \beta_{6j}$) is likely. In the Level 2 (person-level) portion of the model, the aim is to account for variance in the Level 1 intercepts and slopes by predicting them from a person-level variable or variables, in this case a dummy-coded variable representing whether the assigned target experience is activated PA

($D_{\text{PA-Insp}} = 0$) or inspiration ($D_{\text{PA-Insp}} = 1$). The Level 2 portion of the model was specified as follows:

$$\beta_{0j} = \gamma_{00} + \gamma_{01}(D_{\text{PA-Insp}}) + u_{0j} \tag{7}$$

$$\beta_{1j} = \gamma_{10} + \gamma_{11}(D_{\text{PA-Insp}}) + u_{1j} \tag{8}$$

$$\beta_{2j} = \gamma_{20} + \gamma_{21}(D_{\text{PA-Insp}}) + u_{2j} \tag{9}$$

$$\beta_{3j} = \gamma_{30} + \gamma_{31}(D_{\text{PA-Insp}}) + u_{3j} \tag{10}$$

$$\beta_{4j} = \gamma_{40} + \gamma_{41}(D_{\text{PA-Insp}}) + u_{4j} \tag{11}$$

$$\beta_{5j} = \gamma_{50} + \gamma_{51}(D_{\text{PA-Insp}}) + u_{5j} \tag{12}$$

$$\beta_{6j} = \gamma_{60} + \gamma_{61}(D_{\text{PA-Insp}}) + u_{6j} \tag{13}$$

Given the present focus on discriminating inspiration and activated PA, the parameters of particular interest are the Level 2 slopes, γ_{k1} ($k = 0, \ldots, 6$), which represent differences between the two conditions in mean Level 1 β_{kj}s. The slope in Equation 7, γ_{01}, indicates the expected change in the Level 1 intercept, β_{0j}, given a one-unit increase in $D_{\text{PA-Insp}}$—that is, given a shift from the activated PA condition ($D_{\text{PA-Insp}} = 0$) to the inspiration condition ($D_{\text{PA-Insp}} = 1$). Thus, γ_{01} indicates the difference between (a) the mean (across individuals) log-odds of occurrence of activated PA on an average day of the week and (b) the mean log-odds of occurrence of inspiration on an average day of the week.

The mean log-odds of occurrence of each state on an average day of the week may be determined by computing the expected value of β_{0j} in Equation 7 under the conditions that $D_{\text{PA-Insp}}$ equals 0 or 1. In the case of activated PA, the mean log-odds of occurrence is $\gamma_{00} + \gamma_{01}(0)$, or γ_{00}. In the case of inspiration, the mean log-odds of occurrence is $\gamma_{00} + \gamma_{01}(1)$, or $\gamma_{00} + \gamma_{01}$.

The slope in Equation 8, γ_{11}, indicates the expected change in β_{1j} given a one-unit increase in $D_{\text{PA-Insp}}$. Thus, γ_{11} indicates the difference between (a) the mean (across individuals) difference in the log-odds of occurrence of activated PA between an average weekday and an average weekend day, and (b) the mean difference in the log-odds of occurrence of inspiration between an average weekday and an average weekend day. More simply, the parameter γ_{11} represents a condition × weekday-weekend contrast interaction.

Simple weekday-weekend slopes for activated PA and inspiration may be estimated by computing the expected value of β_{1j} in Equation 8 under the conditions that $D_{\text{PA-Insp}}$ equals 0 or 1. In the case of activated PA, the mean difference between weekdays and weekends in log-odds of occurrence is $\gamma_{10} + \gamma_{11}(0)$, or γ_{00}. In the case of

inspiration, the mean difference between weekdays and weekends in log-odds of occurrence is $\gamma_{10} + \gamma_{11}(1)$, or $\gamma_{00} + \gamma_{11}$. Equations 9–13, which concern the other day-of-the-week contrasts, may be interpreted in a manner parallel to that of Equation 8.

The program HLM 5.0 (Raudenbush, Bryk, & Congdon, 2000), the multilevel modeling program used for this investigation, provides significance tests for each γ_{k1}, which concern differences between conditions, and for each γ_{k0}, which concern simple effects in the activated PA condition. However, significance tests are not provided for the derived quantities $\gamma_{k0} + \gamma_{k1}$, which concern simple effects in the inspiration condition. The reason is that these derived quantities are not model parameters, because they are completely determined by and redundant with the parameters that constitute them. However, significance tests for simple effects in the inspiration condition may be conducted straightforwardly by reverse recoding the condition variable, such that $D_{\text{PA-Insp}} = 1$ for activated PA and 0 for inspiration. In this case, the parameters γ_{k0} represent simple effects in the inspiration condition and are tested for significance, whereas the quantities $\gamma_{k0} + \gamma_{k1}$ represent simple effects in the activated PA condition and, as derived quantities, are not tested for significance.

The model in Equations 6–13 was analyzed using Laplace estimation with population-average estimates (see Raudenbush & Bryk, 2002, for details). In this analysis, the random effects for the Level 1 slopes (i.e., variances of $u_{1j} - u_{6j}$) were found not to be significant, indicating that they could not be estimated reliably. Therefore, the random error terms in Equations 8–13 were deleted (Kenny et al., 1998), and the model was reanalyzed. Results of this analysis are presented in table 36.2. Although it was not possible to model slopes as varying randomly, it is important to note that there was significant random variance among individuals' intercepts (see table 36.2). Traditional OLS approaches would misrepresent this error structure and could yield misleading parameter estimates and significance levels.

Regarding fixed effects (see table 36.2), the Equation 7 slope was significant, $\gamma_{01} = -1.263$, $p < .001$, indicating that, averaged across days of the week, inspiration and activated PA differed in their likelihood of occurrence. The log-odds of occurrence of activated PA on an average day were $\gamma_{00} = .579$, $p < .001$, corresponding to an odds of $e^{.579} = 1.784$ and a probability of $1/(1 + e^{-(.579)}) = .641$. The log-odds of occurrence

TABLE 36.2 Multilevel Modeling Results

Level 1	Level 2					
	Intercepts		Slopes		Intercepts + Slopes	
Intercept and Slopes	B	SE	B	SE	B	SE
Fixed Effects						
β_{0j}: intercept[a]	$\gamma_{00} = .579^{***}$	.155	$\gamma_{01} = -1.263^{***}$	.237	$\gamma_{00} + \gamma_{01} = -.684^{***}$	.179
β_{1j}: FS vs. MTWRU[b]	$\gamma_{10} = .464$	.293	$\gamma_{11} = -.959^*$	.378	$\gamma_{10} + \gamma_{11} = -.495^*$	.239
β_{2j}: F vs. S[b]	$\gamma_{20} = .425$	.470	$\gamma_{21} = -.728$	.741	$\gamma_{20} + \gamma_{21} = -.303$	.573
β_{3j}: U vs. MTWR[b]	$\gamma_{30} = -.328$	.249	$\gamma_{31} = .228$	.383	$\gamma_{30} + \gamma_{31} = -.100$	.292
β_{4j}: M vs. TWR[b]	$\gamma_{40} = .219$	.323	$\gamma_{41} = -.377$	.401	$\gamma_{40} + \gamma_{41} = -.158$	.238
β_{5j}: T vs. WR[b]	$\gamma_{50} = .607^*$	.282	$\gamma_{51} = -.375$	.388	$\gamma_{50} + \gamma_{51} = .232$	.267
β_{6j}: W vs. R[b]	$\gamma_{60} = -.158$	.367	$\gamma_{61} = -.170$	.521	$\gamma_{60} + \gamma_{61} = -.328$	.370

Variance Component	SD	χ^2	df			
Random Effects						
u_{0j}	.81	171.36^{***}	70			

[a]$df = 70$. [b]$df = 730$.
$^*p < .05.$ $^{***}p < .001.$

of inspiration were $\gamma_{00} + \gamma_{01} = -.684$, $p < .001$, corresponding to an odds of $e^{-.684} = .505$ and a probability of $1/(1 + e^{-(-.684)}) = .335$. Thus, not surprising, activated PA occurred more frequently than inspiration.

The slope in Equation 8, which represents the condition × weekday-weekend contrast interaction, was significant, $\gamma_{11} = -.959$, $p < .05$. In the activated PA condition, the simple slope relating the weekend-weekday contrast to the log-odds of occurrence was not significant, $\gamma_{10} = .464$, *ns*, indicating that activated PA was equally distributed across weekdays and weekends. In the inspiration condition, the simple slope was significant, $\gamma_{10} + \gamma_{11} = -.495$, $p < .05$, corresponding to an odds ratio of $e^{-.495} = .610$; thus, the expected odds of experiencing inspiration decrease by a multiplicative factor of .610 in moving from weekdays to weekend days. These findings support the hypothesis that inspiration, but not activated PA, is less frequent on weekends than on weekdays.

No other condition × day-of-the-week contrasts (i.e., γ_{21}, γ_{31}, γ_{41}, γ_{51}, γ_{61}) were significant, indicating that the distributions of inspiration and activated PA paralleled one another across the weekly cycle, aside from the divergence on weekends. One other significant effect was found, $\gamma_{50} = .607$, $p < .05$, indicating that activated PA was more likely on Tuesdays than on Wednesdays and Thursdays. However, this effect was not predicted and should be considered a tentative finding.

Predicted Values of Inspiration and Activated PA on Each Day of the Week

In order to plot the expected probabilities of the occurrence of inspiration and activated PA for each day of the week, predicted values were derived using the following procedure. First, Equations 7–13 were used to compute predicted values, separately for activated PA and inspiration, of each β_{kj}. Note that these values are already reported in table 36.2 (γ_{k0} represents predicted values in the activated PA condition, and $\gamma_{k0} + \gamma_{k1}$ represents predicted values in the inspiration condition).

Second, Equation 6 was used to compute predicted log-odds separately for each condition on each day of the week. The β_{kj}s in Equation 6 were replaced by the predicted values from table 36.2, and the contrast variables were replaced by the contrast codes in table 36.1. For instance, in the case of activated PA on Monday, the expected log-odds were computed as follows:

$$\ln (\varphi_{ij}/1 - \varphi_{ij})$$
$$= \beta_{0j} + \beta_{1j}(C_{\text{FS-MTWRU}}) + \beta_{2j}(C_{\text{F-S}})$$
$$+ \beta_{3j}(C_{\text{U-MTWR}}) + \beta_{4j}(C_{\text{M-TWR}})$$
$$+ \beta_{5j}(C_{\text{T-WR}}) + \beta_{6j}(C_{\text{W-R}})$$
$$= .579 + (.464)(-2/7) + (.425)(0)$$
$$+ (-.328)(-1/5) + (.219)(3/4)$$
$$+ (.607)(0) + (-.158)(0)$$
$$= .676$$

TABLE 36.3 Predicted Probabilities of the Occurrence of Activated PA and Inspiration by Day of the Week

	Activated PA	Inspiration
Monday	.663	.345
Tuesday	.703	.419
Wednesday	.544	.327
Thursday	.583	.402
Friday	.755	.233
Saturday	.668	.292
Sunday	.546	.349

Finally, these expected log-odds were converted to expected probabilities using Equation 4, which reverses the log-odds function. For instance, the expected probability of activated PA on Monday was computed as follows:

$$\text{probability} = 1/(1 + e^{-(\text{log-odds})})$$
$$= 1/(1 + e^{-(.676)}) = .663$$

The expected probabilities of inspiration and activated PA for each day of the week are reported in table 36.3 and plotted in figure 36.1.

Discussion

The substantive aim of this chapter was to provide evidence of the discriminant validity of inspiration and activated PA by demonstrating that the two states are differentially distributed across days of the week. As expected, the within-person weekday-weekend contrast was found to differ as a function of whether the target experience was activated PA or inspiration. Simple slope analyses demonstrated that the prevalence of activated PA did not differ significantly between weekdays and weekends, whereas inspiration was significantly more prevalent on weekdays than weekends. Neither activated PA nor inspiration demonstrated a blue Monday effect.

Weekend Effects Present and Absent

The lack of a weekend effect for activated PA is consistent with prior research. It may not be surprising that activated PA was quite prevalent on weekends (.76 probability of occurrence on Fridays, and .67 probability of occurrence on Saturdays). Perhaps more surprising is the fact that activated PA is not significantly less prev-

alent on weekdays. This null finding may reflect the fact that activated PA is associated with approach toward a range of evolutionarily significant goals (Watson et al., 1999), some of which (e.g., competence and success) are pursued more on weekdays, and others of which (e.g., intimacy and friendship) are pursued more on weekends. Additional research is needed to examine whether the surface invariance of activated PA is, in fact, undergirded by varying incentives across the week.

The fact that inspiration was more prevalent on weekdays than on weekends is consistent with the theorized causes of inspiration—for instance, inspiration is posited to be facilitated by a cognitively engaging stimulus environment and by effortful involvement, both of which are amply present in the undergraduate work week. It is noteworthy that inspiration was least likely on the day that activated PA was most likely—Friday (see figure 36.2). The dramatic divergence of inspiration and activated PA on Friday may reflect a "TGIF" attitude, a desire to disengage cognitively and reengage with more pleasurable pursuits. Additional research is needed to examine the presumed mediating role, and relative importance, of such factors as cognitive stimulation, effort expenditure, and pleasure seeking.

In addition to mediation, another issue for future research concerns moderation. For instance, for whom is the inspiration weekend effect more or less pronounced? In related research, Larsen and Kasimatis (1990) found that introverts, relative to extraverts, demonstrate a greater entrainment of mood to the weekly cycle. Reis et al. (2000) speculated that individuals high in autonomy may experience as much pleasant affect on weekdays as on weekends; whereas nonautonomous individuals likely drudge through the work week and find joy only once it is over, autonomous individuals are likely to enjoy and value their weekday activities and thus demonstrate a flatter distribution of affect across the week. Perhaps autonomous individuals likewise demonstrate a flatter distribution of inspiration, experiencing inspiration not only during the week but also on weekends. Although communion-oriented weekend activities may be intrinsically less conducive to inspiration even for autonomous individuals, these individuals would be unlikely to hold the TGIF attitude and desire to disengage, which is perhaps the most significant impediment to inspiration on weekends.

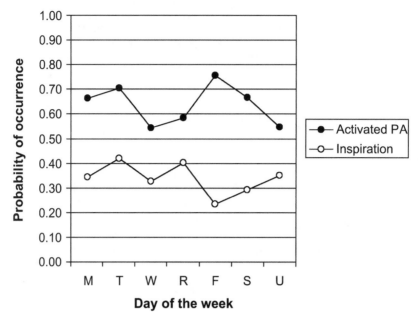

Figure 36.2. Predicted probability of occurrence of inspiration and activated PA by day of the week. M = Monday; T = Tuesday; W = Wednesday; R = Thursday; F = Friday; S = Saturday; U = Sunday.

What Is a Weekend?

Psychologists have given little theoretical attention to what constitutes a weekend. The well-documented weekend effect for certain types of affect has been shown in this chapter to peak at different times in different studies, apparently because the days that are most prototypical of weekends in one population are not necessarily the most prototypical of weekends in another. In the present study, the decrease in inspiration on the weekend occurred on Friday and Saturday; inspiration was as likely on Sunday as on Monday, Tuesday, Wednesday, and Thursday. This finding is consistent with the majority of previous studies on weekend effects with student samples, which tend to find that Friday and Saturday differ affectively from other days of the week. Studies with nonstudent adult samples, in contrast, more often find hedonic peaks on Saturday and Sunday. Accordingly, researchers are encouraged to consider carefully what constitutes a weekend in the population of interest.

Several other factors further complicate an attempt to define *weekend*. First, the subjective transitions between weekdays and weekends may occur midday rather than between days, and they may be continuous rather than dis-

crete. Thus, the Friday-Saturday and Saturday-Sunday definitions of weekend are somewhat crude operationalizations; multiple assessments per day are needed to pinpoint transitions to and from the subjectively defined weekend (e.g., Csikszentmihalyi & Hunter, 2003). Second, given the anticipatory nature of affective experience, the subjective transitions may occur prior to any objective transition markers. Third, a definition of weekend must be culture specific; Sunday is a work day in Israel, for instance (Weinberg, Lubin, Shmushkevich, & Kaplan, 2002). Finally, within a particular population and culture, the timing of the subjectively experienced weekend is likely to vary across individuals as a function of work schedules and activity patterns. Together, these factors suggest that the weekend may be better viewed as a psychological construct than as an objective range of time within the 7-day cycle.

No Blue Monday

To date, there has been only modest evidence for the existence of a blue Monday effect for affect—that is, higher levels of positive affects or lower levels of negative affects on Monday relative to other weekdays. The present data cast further doubt on the existence of a blue Monday effect. Monday did not differ significantly from other weekdays in the probability of experiencing activated PA, nor in the probability of experiencing inspiration. In fact, of the 7 days of the week, Monday was the median day for both activated PA and inspiration. If anything, the present data suggest the possibility of a blue Sunday effect for activated PA (see figure 36.1; see also Kennedy-Moore et al., 1992). A blue Sunday effect would be consistent with a belief in a blue Monday effect—participants may anticipate an unpleasant Monday (which turns out not to be particularly unpleasant). On the other hand, decreased activated PA on Sunday may reflect restfulness more so than feeling blue.

Given the weak evidence for a blue Monday effect, a promising avenue for future research is to identify moderating factors. Perhaps Mondays are blue only for certain individuals (e.g., introverts) or under certain conditions (e.g., being stuck in an undesirable job). This is an important issue, because suicides tend to peak on Mondays (Bradvik & Berglund, 2003; Massing & Angermeyer, 1985; McCleary, Chew, Hellsten, & Flynn-Bransford, 1991), and a blue Monday mood effect, for certain indivividuals or under certain conditions, may be an important contributing factor.

It may also be worthwhile in future studies to assess both affect and attitudes toward the present day of the week. Perhaps there is no contradiction between feeling no worse on Mondays than on other weekdays, yet disliking Monday more than other weekdays because it is so far removed from the weekend.

Methodological and Statistical Issues

A number of methodological and statistical issues have been discussed above, but a few remaining issues should be mentioned briefly. As an alternative to operationalizing the blue Monday effect as a contrast between Monday and other weekdays, researchers may wish to use codes that represent a linear trend across the work week. The present data do not support a trend of this sort, but some previous findings suggest that weekday affect becomes gradually more positive or less negative with increasing proximity to the upcoming weekend (e.g., Larsen & Kasimatis, 1990).

Researchers should bear in mind that day of the week is not a manipulated variable and is therefore susceptible to the various confounds associated with quasi-experimental studies. For instance, geopolitical events, or even a gray sky, may create a history effect that is indistinguishable from the effect of the day of the week on which it occurs. History effects may be minimized by varying the day of the week on which participants begin the study and by collecting data over multiple weeks. Researchers may also wish to assess affect multiple times per day, resulting in a three-level model (assessments nested within days, and days nested within individuals). This approach minimizes biases related to global, end-of-day recollections, and it permits a more fine-grained analysis of transitions between days. Finally, it is often desirable to model lag effects, given that days are sampled serially within persons, rather than independently within persons. Alternatively, a high degree of independence within persons could be achieved by sampling days nonconsecutively, such as every second or third day.

This chapter has illustrated a novel application of multilevel modeling—the differentiation of related constructs by documenting distinct within-person distributions across time. The issue of discriminant validity is most often addressed at the between-person level of analysis. However, a construct's within-person distribution across days (or hours, weeks, etc.) may be viewed profitably as part of its nomological network (see also Watson et al., 1999). In the present case, the wheel of time has provided a natural quasi-experiment that helps illuminate the distinction between the highly correlated constructs of inspiration and activated PA. Equipped with the knowledge that the least inspired day of the week is the beloved and happy Friday, we see that the domain of positive affective-motivational constructs is more differentiated than we might have assumed.

Appendix: Derivation of Equation 5 From Equation 2

Exponentiating both sides of Equation 2 yields the following:

$$\frac{\varphi}{1 - \varphi} = e^{(\beta_0 + \beta_1 X)}, \quad \text{or}$$
$$\text{odds} = e^{(\beta_0 + \beta_1 X)}.$$

An algebraic manipulation yields the following:

$$\text{odds} = e^{\beta_0} e^{\beta_1 X}.$$

Now, consider the effect of increasing X by one unit, from a particular value j to $j+1$. When $X = j$, the predicted odds are as follows:

$$\text{odds}_{X=j} = e^{\beta_0} e^{\beta_1 j}.$$

When $X = j+1$, the predicted odds are as follows:

$$\text{odds}_{X=j+1} = e^{\beta_0} e^{\beta_1 (j+1)}.$$

Algebraic manipulations then yield the following:

$$\text{odds}_{X=j+1} = e^{\beta_0} e^{\beta_1 j} e^{\beta_1}, \text{ or}$$
$$\text{odds}_{X=j+1} = e^{\beta_1} (\text{odds}_{X=j}).$$

Thus, increasing X by one unit increases odds by a multiplicative factor of e^{β_1}. The reason that the quantity e^{β_1} is called the odds ratio is apparent when the above equation is rewritten as follows:

$$e^{\beta_1} = \frac{\text{odds}_{X=j+1}}{\text{odds}_{X=j}}.$$

Acknowledgments   I would like to thank John Nezlek, Harry Reis, and Andrew Elliot for their helpful comments on a previous draft of this chapter.

Note

1. The method section of this chapter only reports information directly relevant to the present investigation. For other details, see Thrash and Elliot (2004).

References

Bradvik, L., & Berglund, M. (2003). A suicide peak after weekends and holidays in patients with alcohol dependence. *Suicide and Life-Threatening Behavior, 33,* 186–191.

Brown, K. W., & Moskowitz, D. S. (1998). Dynamic stability of behavior: The rhythms of our interpersonal lives. *Journal of Personality, 66,* 105–134.

Brown, K. W., & Ryan, R. M. (2003). The benefits of being present: Mindfulness and its role in psychological well-being. *Journal of Personality and Social Psychology, 84,* 822–848.

Christie, M. J., & Venables, P. H. (1973). Mood changes in relation to age, EPI scores, time and day. *British Journal of Social and Clinical Psychology, 12,* 61–72.

Clark, L. A., & Watson, D. (1988). Mood and the mundane: Relations between daily life events and self-reported mood. *Journal of Personality and Social Psychology, 54,* 296–308.

Cohen, J., Cohen, P., West, S. G., & Aiken, L. S. (2003). *Applied multiple regression/correlation analysis for the behavioral sciences* (3rd ed.). Mahwah, NJ: Erlbaum.

Csikszentmihalyi, M., & Hunter, J. (2003). Happiness in everyday life: The uses of experience sampling. *Journal of Happiness Studies, 4,* 185–199.

Egloff, B., Tausch, A., Kohlmann, C.-W., & Krohne, H. W. (1995). Relationships between time of day, day of the week, and positive mood: Exploring the role of the mood measure. *Motivation and Emotion, 19,* 99–110.

Farber, M. L. (1953). Time-perspective and feeling-tone: A study in the perception of the days. *Journal of Psychology, 35,* 253–257.

Gable, S. L., Reis, H. T., & Elliot, A. J. (2000). Behavioral activation and inhibition in everyday life. *Journal of Personality and Social Psychology, 78,* 1135–1149.

Kennedy-Moore, E., Greenberg, M. A., Newman, M. G., & Stone, A. A. (1992). The relationship between daily events and mood: The mood measure may matter. *Motivation and Emotion, 16,* 143–155.

Kenny, D. A., Kashy, D. A., & Bolger, N. (1998). Data analysis in social psychology. In D. T. Gilbert, S. T. Fiske, and G. Lindzey (Eds.), *The handbook of social psychology* (Vol. 1, pp. 233–265). New York: McGraw-Hill.

Larsen, R. J., & Kasimatis, M. (1990). Individual differences in entrainment of mood to the weekly calendar. *Journal of Personality and Social Psychology, 58,* 164–171.

Massing, W., & Angermeyer, M. C. (1985). The monthly and weekly distribution of suicide. *Social Science Medicine, 21,* 433–441.

McCleary, R., Chew, K. S. Y., Hellsten, J. J., & Flynn-Bransford, M. (1991). Age- and sex-specific cycles in United States suicides, 1973–1985. *American Journal of Public Health, 81,* 1494–1497.

McFarlane, J., Martin, C. L., & Williams, T. M. (1988). Mood fluctuations: Women versus men and menstrual versus other cycles. *Psychology of Women Quarterly, 12,* 201–223.

Nezlek, J. B. (2001). Multilevel random coefficient analyses of event- and interval-contingent data in social and personality psychology research. *Personality and Social Psychology Bulletin, 27,* 771–785.

Pampel, F. C. (2000). *Logistic regression: A primer.* Thousand Oaks, CA: Sage.

Park, C. L., Armeli, S., & Tennen, H. (2004). Appraisal-coping goodness of fit: A daily Internet study. *Personality and Social Psychology Bulletin, 30,* 558–569.

Pecjak, V. (1970). Verbal synesthesiae of colors, emotions, and days of the week. *Journal of Verbal Learning and Verbal Behavior, 9,* 623–626.

Raudenbush, S. W., & Bryk, A. S. (2002). *Hierarchical linear models: Applications and data analysis methods* (2nd ed.). Thousand Oaks, CA: Sage.

Raudenbush, S., Bryk, A., & Congdon, R. (2000). *HLM for Windows 5.04.* Computer software. Lincolnwood, IL: Scientific Software International.

Reis, H. T., & Gable, S. L. (2000). Event-sampling and other methods for studying everyday experience. In H. T. Reis & C. M. Judd (Eds.), *Handbook of research methods in social and personality psychology* (pp. 190–222). New York: Cambridge University Press.

Reis, H. T., Sheldon, K. M., Gable, S. L., Roscoe, J., & Ryan, R. M. (2000). Daily well-being: The role of autonomy, competence, and relatedness. *Personality and Social Psychology Bulletin, 26,* 419–435.

Rossi, A. S., & Rossi, P. E. (1977). Body time and social time: Mood patterns by menstrual cycle phase and day of the week. *Social Science Research, 6,* 273–308.

Sheldon, K. M., Ryan, R., & Reis, H. T. (1996). What makes for a good day? Competence and autonomy in the day and in the person. *Personality and Social Psychology Bulletin, 22,* 1270–1279.

Simpson, J. A., & Weiner, S. C. (Eds.). (1989). *Oxford English Dictionary* (2nd ed., Vol. 7). Oxford, UK: Clarendon.

Stone, A. A. (1987). Event content in a daily survey is differentially associated with concurrent mood. *Journal of Personality and Social Psychology, 52,* 56–58.

Stone, A. A., Hedges, S. M., Neale, J. M., & Satin, M. S. (1985). Prospective and cross-sectional mood reports offer no evidence of a "Blue Monday" phenomenon. *Journal of Personality and Social Psychology, 49,* 129–134.

Thrash, T. M., & Elliot, A. J. (2003). Inspiration as a psychological construct. *Journal of Personality and Social Psychology, 84,* 871–889.

Thrash, T. M., & Elliot, A. J. (2004). Inspiration: Core characteristics, component processes, antecedents, and function. *Journal of Personality and Social Psychology, 87,* 957–973.

Totterdell, P., Kellett, S., Teuchmann, K., & Briner, R. B. (1998). Evidence of mood linkage in work groups. *Journal of Personality and Social Psychology, 74,* 1504–1515.

Venables, P. H., & Christie, M. J. (1974). Neuroticism, physiological state and mood: An exploratory study of Friday/Monday changes. *Biological Psychology, 1,* 201–211.

Wallas, G. (1926). *The art of thought.* New York: Harcourt Brace.

Watson, D., Clark, L. A., & Tellegen, A. (1988). Development and validation of brief measures of positive and negative affect: The PANAS scales. *Journal of Personality and Social Psychology, 54,* 1063–1070.

Watson, D., Wiese, D., Vaidya, J., & Tellegen, A. (1999). The two general activation systems of affect: Structural findings, evolutionary considerations, and psychobiological evidence. *Journal of Personality and Social Psychology, 76,* 820–838.

Weinberg, I., Lubin, G., Shmushkevich, M., & Kaplan, Z. (2002). Elevated suicide rates on the first workday: A replication in Israel. *Death Studies, 26,* 681–688.

37

Multilevel Modeling of Motivation

A Self-Determination Theory Analysis of Basic Psychological Needs

Kirk Warren Brown and Richard M. Ryan

Motivation is, by its very nature, a dynamic process. Human motives and desires fluctuate in direction and strength according to inner promptings and environmental contingencies that can facilitate or inhibit the satisfaction of needs, and desires also vary as individuals negotiate their day-to-day lives. This dynamic character of motivation has implications for research designs and analytic approaches used to investigate it. Because traditional one-occasion, experimental, and longitudinal approaches typically provide very limited opportunities to model the dynamic variability of motivation, researchers have begun to pair nontraditional methods such as experience sampling with analytic tools such as multilevel modeling to extend our understanding of motivation as it operates in day-to-day contexts. In this chapter, we discuss recent research using multilevel approaches to modeling the variable nature of motivation and its consequences. Specifically, we focus on recent efforts to understand the expression of three basic psychological needs specified by self-determination theory (SDT; Deci & Ryan, 2000; Ryan, 1995).

Self-Determination Theory and Basic Psychological Needs

Central to SDT is a view of the human organism as active and growth oriented, with a nature endowed with tendencies toward health and well-being (Ryan & Deci, 2000b). SDT proposes that inherent to the adaptive design of the organism is a propensity to exercise one's capacities, to seek connection with others, and to experience behavior as self-organized and congruent. It further suggests that these propensities are innate psychological needs—for competence (Deci, 1975; White, 1959), relatedness (Baumeister & Leary, 1995; Reis & Franks, 1994), and autonomy (deCharms, 1968; Ryan, 1993), respectively—whose fulfillment is essential to ongoing personal well-being, optimal behavioral functioning, and constructive social development (Ryan & Deci, 2000a).

Autonomy concerns volitional, self-endorsed action. When autonomous, individuals perceive that their behavior is willingly undertaken and concordant with the self. The opposite of autonomy is *heteronomy*, or a perception of being controlled by forces felt to be alien to the self. Autonomy is not equivalent to independence or separateness, and in fact dependent acts and connecting behaviors are often highly volitional or autonomous. *Competence* pertains to the experience of mastery, or the effective performance of desired behaviors, which is experienced under conditions that support efficacy and provide optimal challenges. Finally, *relatedness* is the subjective experience of closeness and connection with others. It is maximized within relationships or groups that convey (usually through acts of empathy and caring) the sense that one belongs with and is significant to the other person or group.

Specifying autonomy, competence, and relatedness as basic psychological needs implies that individuals cannot psychologically thrive or function fully without satisfying them, just as they cannot physically thrive without the basic nutriments of food and water. Likewise, just as the physical environment can facilitate or hamper the satisfaction of physical needs, social environments can afford or hinder the fulfillment of autonomy, competence, or relatedness, with consequences for individual functioning and well-being. When a need is thwarted, invariantly there is a deleterious impact on growth and wellness, whether or not that need represents one's values, goals, or desire. Thus a thrust of SDT is to examine variations in need fulfillment across time, contexts, and cultures, as these impact fluctuations in optimal functioning and well-being.

A large literature of empirical research has investigated the social psychology of psychological need support and hindrance (see Deci & Ryan, 2000; Ryan & Deci, 2000b, for reviews). Multilevel modeling approaches have enhanced the sophistication of SDT research by permitting a detailed examination of questions that reflect this person-by-situation character of need fulfillment, and the implications of this dialectic for psychological well-being. Primary questions addressed by this recent research include the following:

- How are basic psychological needs expressed and fulfilled in daily life and other, objective behavioral contexts?
- What consequences does need fulfillment, or lack thereof, have for personal (and collective) well-being across time and contexts?
- What psychological supports exist for need satisfaction?

In this chapter, we discuss research on the basic needs of autonomy, competence, and relatedness within an SDT framework, beginning first with a brief historical overview of research methodology in this area before turning to investigations using multilevel approaches to modeling the dynamic nature of need regulation and the outcomes of such regulation. We also discuss very recent research examining the role of mindfulness (Brown & Ryan, 2003) as a key internal support for healthy behavioral regulation. Finally, we offer suggestions for enhancing the sophistication of research using multilevel approaches as a means to both deepening our understanding of need fulfillment and providing a platform for applied research designed to enhance healthy regulation.

Traditional Approaches to the Study of Motivation: Cross-sectional, Longitudinal, and Experimental Designs

As in many areas of psychology, including positive psychology, a dominant form of measurement in the study of motivation has consisted of scales and questionnaires designed for single-occasion administration. Many such measures of motivation are retrospective in nature, asking individuals to reflect back upon their past psychological experience or behavior. As individual difference measures, they are designed to assess general dispositions or traits and are assumed to reflect stable individual characteristics that have important behavioral consequences. For example, dispositional measures like the General Causality Orientations Scale (Deci & Ryan, 1985), which assesses individual differences in autonomy, have demonstrated criterion validity, assessed both cross-sectionally and predictively over short- and longer-term time intervals.

Despite this, one-occasion assessment relies upon an assumption of temporal stability, regardless of whether the behavior or characteristic measured is theoretically understood to be stable or variable. Yet individuals do not behave according to their trait descriptions in every situation or even across broad classes of situations. Intraindividual variability of this kind has been shown both in research that has tested the situational specificity of motivation and in studies that have repeatedly sampled behavior over time. For example, La Guardia, Ryan, Couchman, and Deci (2000) found significant variations in psychological need fulfillment across different interpersonal relationships. In turn, these within-person differences in need fulfillment from social partner to social partner predicted variability in security of attachment. Although it is often assumed that security of attachment is a stable individual difference variable, contextual variations in support for psychological needs appear to create within-person variations in this presumably stable trait. Other research (e.g., Reis, Sheldon, Gable, Roscoe, & Ryan, 2000) has revealed a marked degree of intraindividual variability in need fulfillment across days of the week. Fluctuations in day-to-day need fulfillment, controlling for individual differences and prior day effects, predicted changes in daily psychological wellness. Such studies showing both contextual and temporal fluctuations thus belie the assumption of stability upon which one-occasion measures are founded.

A reliance upon single-occasion individual difference measures has had a practical basis, as motivational dynamics have, until relatively recently, been difficult to measure and model systematically. Yet the frequent consequence of this dominant approach is that variability in motivation processes has been treated as error, and the assumption of stasis, over situations and over both short and long periods of time, is tacitly relied upon in such research endeavors (Brown & Moskowitz, 1998). A second assumption upon which the reliance on one-occasion, retrospective measures rests is that responses to them will be reasonably accurate. The validity of this assumption can also be questioned, given the inherent limitations to human memory in accurately describing past experience and the variety of sources of error that enter into retrospective reporting, including past event salience, idiosyncratic anchor events, current psychological states, and social desirability.

The incorporation of time into research designs enables the study of whether and how a characteristic will demonstrate stability and change—over time, as in traditional longitudinal designs, or in response to situational factors, as in experimental studies. Both approaches have contributed significantly to our understanding of a variety of motivational issues. Yet the relatively simple way in which these designs are typically employed has imposed limitations on the depth of understanding to be gained about motivational phenomena. Traditional longitudinal designs, which use relatively long inter-measurement intervals, limit investigations to

static or slowly changing phenomena. Researchers using such designs implicitly or explicitly expect that if change occurs, it will be permanent or unidirectional, rather than ongoing or repeated. Change of the latter sort may be embedded in apparently slowly changing or progressive phenomena and the picture provided by measures collected at widely spaced intervals may mask the nonlinear and short-term linear dynamics inherent in behavior. The use of experimental designs reflects a recognition that motivation can vary quickly in response to social and other situational forces, but such designs have typically been used to examine simple pre-post change. In all three traditional research designs discussed here, the lived and often nonlinear nature of motivational processes can easily be missed.

Multilevel Modeling and the Process Approach to Motivation

An important advance in the study of motivational processes came with the introduction of expanded longitudinal studies that measure behavior intensively over time. Following a process approach to research design (Brown & Moskowitz, 1998; Larsen, 1989), this research minimizes the difficulties associated with one-occasion, retrospective measures by collecting data as it occurs in laboratory or natural situations. Also, by expanding the traditional longitudinal design to include many reports or samples of behavior, stability and change can be examined more closely and precisely. Finally, the process approach still permits the study of manipulated effects on behavior but opens the door to examining more complex (but often realistic) responses to experimental inputs as they unfold over time. The process approach provides a frame-by-frame motion picture of behavior (Turk, 1994), rather than snapshots at a single time or at widely spaced time points. A major benefit of this approach is not just that it provides a more detailed and, therefore, accurate look at behavioral processes, but also in uncovering new motivational and other behavioral phenomena, because the focus of research broadens to include both the structure and the dynamics of behavior over time, including behavior that is traditionally viewed as dispositional in nature (Diener, 1996).

The introduction of multilevel modeling (MLM; e.g., Bryk & Raudenbush, 1992; Kreft & deLeeuw,

1998) represents a second important contribution to investigations in motivation, in part because it capitalizes on the process approach to research design. As Maxwell and Tiberio discuss (chapter 30, this volume), it permits the study of inter- and intraindividual variability across situations and across time with a more careful parsing of between- and within-persons variance. It also permits the study of interactions across levels of analysis—between groups and persons, or between persons and occasions—and it allows for the incorporation of time-series variables into analyses, as is discussed below. As this discussion suggests, multilevel modeling capitalizes on the strengths of each of the traditional methodological approaches to motivation discussed above, in its ability to incorporate individual difference effects, experimental group effects, and the study of behavioral variability and change through repeated measurement across situations and time.

Exemplary MLM Research in Motivation

Need Satisfaction and Day-to-Day Personal Well-Being

Several studies have examined two of the primary questions noted earlier, namely, "How are needs expressed and satisfied in daily life and other, objective behavioral contexts?" and "What consequences does need fulfillment, or lack thereof, have for personal well-being?" Sheldon, Ryan, and Reis (1996) examined the role that two of the three basic psychological needs specified by SDT—autonomy and competence—have in creating "good days." In a sample of 60 undergraduates, they collected reports of need satisfaction at both trait and state levels, where the latter was assessed once per day for 14 days. At the close of each day, individuals were asked to rate the degree of autonomy and competence experienced in the three activities in which they had spent the most time. Also measured daily were levels of hedonic well-being (pleasant and unpleasant affect), eudaemonic well-being (subjective vitality), and physical health (common symptoms of illness) experienced over the course of the day.

Using a weighted least squares approach to MLM, with persons treated as a random effect, Sheldon et al. (1996) entered both trait (Level 2) and state (Level 1) autonomy (AUTO) and competence (COMP) need satisfaction terms

into multilevel models predicting each type of daily (Level 1) well-being (WB), as well as a well-being composite. Focusing first on Level 2 effects, the following basic model was tested:

$$WB_{ij} = \beta_{B\text{-}P}AUTO_i + \beta_{B\text{-}P}COMP_i \\ + \beta_{B\text{-}P}SEX_i + \alpha_i + \varepsilon_{ij} \qquad (1)$$

where $i = 1, 2, 3, \ldots I$ and $j = 1, 2, 3, \ldots n_i$.

AUTO and COMP are measured once for each of the I individuals (Level 2), whereas WB is measured n_i times for the ith individual (Level 1). The $\beta_{B\text{-}P}$ terms refer to between-person effects, α_i is the intercept for each person (i.e., each person's well-being on an average day), and ε_{ij} refers to the within-person residuals. Sheldon et al. (1996) found that individuals higher in trait autonomy and competence had better days, on average, than those scoring lower in these dispositions. This result is consistent with a personological approach, which assumes that well-being is determined by stable, enduring qualities of the person. Sheldon et al. (1996) also tested a model including effects of Level 2 traits, gender, and their interaction, and a number of Level 1 predictors, as follows:

$$WB_{ij} = \beta_{B\text{-}P}AUTO_i + \beta_{B\text{-}P}COMP_i \\ + \beta_{B\text{-}P}SEX_i + \beta_{Int}(AUTO_i \times SEX_i) \\ + \beta_{Int}(COMP_i \times SEX_i) \\ + \beta_{W\text{-}P,i}WBLAG_{ij} + \beta_{W\text{-}P,i}IMPORT_{ij} \\ + \beta_{W\text{-}P,i}WE_{ij} + \beta_{W\text{-}P,i}TIME_{ij} \\ + \beta_{W\text{-}P,i}AUTO_{ij} + \beta_{W\text{-}P,i}COMP_{ij} \\ + \alpha_i + \varepsilon_{ij} \qquad (2)$$

In this model, $\beta_{W\text{-}P,i}$ terms refer to within-person effects in which, for example, people report higher well-being at a time when their need for autonomy is more satisfied. Sheldon et al. (1996) found that after factoring in the Level 2 effects of traits and gender, and the effects of several Level 1 variables, including lagged (prior day) well-being (WBLAG), daily activity importance (IMPORT), day of the week (and specifically, a dummy-coded weekend effect, WE), and time of day (TIME), the days on which individuals experienced more autonomy and competence relative to their own baseline were also better days.

In an effort to extend the Sheldon et al. (1996) findings, Reis et al. (2000) employed the same methodological and analytic approach to examine the trait and state effects of all three basic needs—autonomy, competence, and relatedness—upon day-to-day hedonic, eudaemonic, and physical well-being. Insofar as all three represent basic needs, the authors reasoned that each should evidence a unique effect on well-being at both between- and within-person levels of analysis. The Level 2 results of the multilevel analyses showed that trait autonomy and relatedness predicted higher day-to-day positive affect, while autonomy alone predicted higher vitality. Persons higher in dispositional competence showed lower daily negative affect and symptoms. At Level 1, daily autonomy and competence were associated with higher day-to-day levels of all types of well-being examined, while relatedness was most strongly related to higher positive affect and vitality.

As a further extension to Sheldon et al. (1996), Reis et al. (2000) also tested for interaction effects between trait autonomy, competence, and relatedness and their corresponding state expressions in the prediction of daily well-being. Theoretically, this investigation was rooted in the recognition that while the three needs are universal (Deci & Ryan, 2000), some individuals may be more responsive to daily variations in activities or situations that afford or hinder need satisfaction. Reis et al. (2000) tested two competing models that would each indicate that the day-to-day relation between need satisfaction and well-being varied as a function of traits. A deprivation model posited that higher levels of daily need satisfaction would enhance well-being to the extent that individual trait levels were low. That is, when one or more needs was chronically or dispositionally unsatisfied, the opportunity to satisfy those needs would provide a greater well-being benefit than to those higher in dispositional need satisfaction. In contrast, a sensitization model proposed that higher trait need satisfaction reflected a higher value placed on it, and a greater likelihood that such persons would show well-being benefits. This model was tested:

$$
\begin{aligned}
WB_{ij} = {} & \beta_{B\text{-}P}AUTO_i + \beta_{B\text{-}P}COMP_i \\
& + \beta_{B\text{-}P}RELAT_i + \beta_{W\text{-}P,i}WBLAG_{ij} \\
& + \beta_{W\text{-}P,i}AUTO_{ij} + \beta_{W\text{-}P,i}COMP_{ij} \\
& + \beta_{W\text{-}P,i}RELAT_{ij} \\
& + \beta_{Int}(AUTO_i \times AUTO_{ij}) \\
& + \beta_{Int}(COMP_i \times COMP_{ij}) \\
& + \beta_{Int}(RELAT_i \times RELAT_{ij}) \\
& + \alpha_i + \varepsilon_{ij}
\end{aligned}
\tag{3}
$$

The β_{Int} coefficients in this equation estimate the extent to which the day-to-day effects of each type of need satisfaction on well-being (Level 1) vary by trait levels of need satisfaction (Level 2). Each $\beta_{W\text{-}P,i}$ main effect term now represents the effect of day-to-day need satisfaction on well-being for the ith person if trait levels of need satisfaction equaled zero. Together, the $\beta_{W\text{-}P,i}$ assess the individual differences in the effects of day-to-day need satisfaction that cannot be accounted for by trait need satisfaction (cf. Schwartz & Stone, 1998).

The MLM results offered some support for the sensitization model, in that persons higher in each trait variable showed higher daily well-being when daily activities supported the satisfaction of each need. Reis et al. (2000) suggested that higher dispositional need satisfaction might reflect a heightened sensitivity to those needs and therefore a greater responsiveness to environmental events relevant to them. Conversely, lower trait scorers may be comparatively insensitive to such events, which then have less impact on psychological well-being. This person × situation dynamic surrounding the manifestation and consequences of need satisfaction is consistent with both Bem and Funder's (1978) template matching model and Coté and Moskowitz's (1998) behavioral concordance model, which also recognize that responsiveness to situations, and the outcomes of that responsiveness, are guided by dispositional features. However, it is notable that in none of the interactions tested by Reis et al. (2000) was there a negative slope for those low in trait need satisfaction; therefore, while those more highly "traited" in need satisfaction showed higher well-being when their needs were satisfied on a day-to-day basis, those dispositionally low in need satisfaction also generally benefited, but simply not as much, when they had experiences of autonomy, competence, and relatedness. In sum, sensitization effects accounted for some added variance in well-being, atop the main effects expected by a model of basic psychological needs.[1]

Both of the studies reviewed in this section also shed light on the weekly cyclicity of well-being, or the noteworthy tendency for persons to exhibit higher positive affect and lower negative affect on weekends. The two studies' results suggested that weekends were characterized by relative increases in fulfillment of basic psychological needs, and the enhanced satisfaction of these needs explained a significant proportion of this "weekend effect."

A third study examining need satisfaction and its relation to ongoing well-being focused on young athletes in the high-pressure world of competitive sport (Gagné, Ryan, & Bargmann, 2003). While recognizing that psychological and physical benefits can derive from participation in organized athletics, researchers have also documented mood disturbances and damaged self-esteem in children and teenagers experiencing high performance pressure (e.g., Davis, 1997). Of long-standing interest to motivation researchers, as well as parents, teachers, coaches, and other motivators, is how healthy motivation, and, by implication, well-being can be facilitated. Gagné et al. applied multilevel modeling to examine whether need satisfaction derived from athletic involvement was related to well-being outcomes in young female gymnasts. They also examined whether external motivational influences—that is, the motivational climate surrounding athletic participation—affected need satisfaction, motivation, well-being, and the relations between them. Specifically, Gagné et al. conducted a 4-week diary study with 33 female gymnasts aged 7 to 18 years to investigate the predictive relations of perceived parent and coach motivational supports to the athletes' enduring and daily motivation and need satisfaction. They also examined how daily motivation and need satisfaction during practice affected the athletes' well-being.

At the beginning of the study, the athletes completed a measure of self-regulation for gymnastics, which assessed the relative autonomy of their involvement in the sport. They also completed measures of perceived parental and coach autonomy support. At the beginning of each of 15 practices, the gymnasts rated reasons, which varied in degree of autonomy, for attending the practice. At the start and close of each practice, they completed a measure of positive and negative affect, self-esteem, and subjective vitality. A report on need satisfaction during practice was also completed at the end of each practice.

Gagné et al. (2003) first established, using aggregated diary data, that the more autonomy-supportive parents and coaches were perceived to be, the more autonomously motivated was the athletes' sport involvement over time. Perceived autonomy support from coaches also predicted higher levels of need satisfaction over the course of the 15 practice sessions. Gymnasts whose sport involvement was more autonomously regulated showed better well-being over time.

MLM using maximum likelihood estimation found that the relative autonomy of day level (Level 1) incoming, or prepractice, motivation was related to incoming well-being, particularly lower negative affect and both higher vitality and self-esteem. The strongest predictor of Level 1 change in well-being from pre- to postpractice (in which prepractice well-being was included in the equation to control for initial level) was whether each of the needs for autonomy, competence, and relatedness were satisfied during practice. Perceived enduring autonomy support from parents and coaches assessed at the beginning of the study (Level 2) did not moderate these results.

The results of the multilevel investigations reviewed thus far suggest three primary conclusions: First, need satisfaction varies on a day-to-day basis above and below personal baseline levels, and second, these fluctuations have significant consequences for day-to-day well-being. Indeed, Sheldon et al. (1996) and Reis et al. (2000) specifically showed that such variations had influence above and beyond what traits could explain. Finally, the significance of the effects of autonomy, competence, and relatedness at both between- and within-subjects levels of analysis is consistent with SDT's position that each of these three psychological needs has a unique and important impact on well-being, whether examined as a trait characteristic, as intraindividual variation across time, or as interindividual differences in intraindividual experience.

Value Orientation and Collective Well-Being

The interest in active, growth-oriented processes that characterizes SDT has been applied not only to personal well-being but also to social and collective well-being. Sheldon and colleagues have explored the role of individual intrinsic and extrinsic value orientations in the preservation of a natural resource (Sheldon & McGregor, 2000) and in prosocial behavior (Sheldon, Sheldon, & Osbaldiston, 2000). Intrinsic values are theorized to reflect basic psychological needs and include the desire for personal development, affiliation with others, and community involvement (Ryan, Sheldon, Kasser, & Deci, 1996). Extrinsic values include the desire for wealth, attractiveness, and fame, and endorsement of such values is believed to reflect a disconnection from, and lack of fulfillment of, basic psychological needs. Past research has demonstrated that a greater weight given to extrinsic relative to intrinsic values is associated with poorer psychological adjustment, lower subjective well-being, and health risk behavior (e.g., Kasser, 2002; Kasser & Ryan, 1993, 1996).

Sheldon and McGregor (2000) investigated whether these value orientations would have consequences for collective (ecological) well-being as well. Groups of four participants with similar value orientations (all extrinsic and all intrinsic), and groups with mixed orientations (half intrinsic, half extrinsic) were first formed. Each type of group then engaged in a resource dilemma task involving timber harvest in a national forest. This task represented a "tragedy of the commons" paradigm, wherein the procurement of resources in the short term could have long-term effects. It was expected that those with relative intrinsic value orientations would show greater care in preserving the resource, given their stronger sense of community and identification with prosocial norms. Those more extrinsically oriented were expected to deplete the resource more quickly, given their focus on personal material acquisition.

The dependent variable in this study was the total amount of timber that groups, and participants within groups, would harvest over the course of the dilemma task. Each group member submitted a harvest bid each year for 25 years, or until the resource was depleted. MLM using a weighted least squares approach was used to test the hypotheses. Because groups were formed using a median split on individuals' value orientation scale scores, the use of MLM was crucial to separate and thereby "deconfound" the two levels of effect. The following equation was constructed:

$$HARVEST_{ij} = \beta_{B-P}VO_i + \beta_{W-P,i}VO_{ij}$$
$$+ \beta_{Int}(VO_i \times VO_{ij}) + \alpha_i + \varepsilon_{ij} \quad (4)$$

Interestingly, Sheldon and McGregor (2000) hypothesized, and found, contrasting effects of value orientation at the group level (Level 2, represented by $\beta_{B-P}VO_i$) and at the individual, within-group level (Level 1, represented by $\beta_{W-P,i}VO_{ij}$). At Level 1, the study showed that, compared to more intrinsic persons, those more extrinsically oriented made more total profit, because they harvested more timber than their group mates. In contrast, however, Level 2 re-

sults showed that extrinsic groups harvested the least over time, followed by mixed-value groups, and then intrinsic groups, who harvested the most over time because their forest resource was not as quickly depleted by high profit taking. These multilevel results demonstrated that individual self-restraint, rooted in intrinsic values, can benefit a social group, while self-interest can help to maximize personal gain but at the expense of collective well-being.

In a second study, Sheldon et al. (2000) permitted participants to assort themselves into groups, who then participated in an iterated prisoner's dilemma (PD) game, in which they could choose to cooperate or to get ahead over five rounds of play. Results showed, first, that individuals tended to assort themselves into groups of similar value orientation—that is, extrinsics with extrinsics, and likewise for intrinsics. The primary multilevel model was structured identically to Equation 4. The analysis revealed, paralleling the results of the previous study, that individuals scoring higher in extrinsic value orientation made more defection choices during the PD game and thus scored more points than those less extrinsic or those intrinsic in orientation. However, Level 2 results showed that groups with high mean levels of intrinsic values scored more points overall than did groups with lower average levels of intrinsic values. In neither this study nor the Sheldon and McGregor (2000) study did the relation between individual values and outcome vary as a function of the mean level of group value orientation (i.e., there were no Level 1 × Level 2 interaction effects). Thus, the effects of individual-level values and group-level values were independent of each other. These results showed, as before, that selfish gain often came at the expense of collective loss, while altruists accrued both personal and collective benefits, at least when making choices in the company of other prosocial actors.

Theoretically, the multilevel approach taken to these data support hierarchical conceptions of adaptive fitness, in which individuals' fitness level is determined by their behavior within social groups, as well as by the behavior of the aggregate to which those individuals belong (see Sheldon & McGregor, 2000, for review). The results of these studies also support the use of the multilevel approach to explore the long-term social consequences and viability of individual traits, and the behavior that follows from them (Sheldon & McGregor, 2000).

The Role of Mindfulness in Supporting Healthy Motivation

As already noted, there has been long-standing research interest in how social and other contextual supports for autonomy, competence, and relatedness can facilitate self-motivation and well-being (e.g., Gagné et al., 2003). Recent research using MLM has begun to explore the third primary question of interest to SDT researchers noted earlier, namely, "What psychological supports exist for the self-regulation of need satisfaction?" This question is important because even when environments provide an optimal motivational climate, healthy regulation requires a reflective consideration of one's behavior and its fit with personal values, needs, and interests (Ryan & Deci, 2004). Several influential organismic and cybernetic theories of behavioral regulation place central emphasis upon attention and awareness, the capacity to bring consciousness to bear on present events and experience (e.g., Carver & Scheier, 1998; Deci & Ryan, 1985; Varela, Thompson, & Rosch, 1991). Recent research in our laboratory has focused on the concept of *mindfulness*, a quality of consciousness that pertains to an open or receptive attention to and awareness of what is taking place in the present (e.g., Brown & Ryan, 2003).

Several studies have shown that mindfulness conduces to autonomous behavior (see Brown & Ryan, 2004a, for review). For example, Brown and Ryan (2003) asked samples of students and working adults to complete a self-report dispositional measure of mindfulness developed by the authors, called the Mindful Attention Awareness Scale (MAAS). Individuals then recorded the relative autonomy of their behavior at the receipt of a pager signal three times a day over a 2-week (students) or 3-week (adults) period. MLM of unconditional means (see Singer, 1998) first established that there was significant between- and within-subjects variation in day-to-day autonomy. Next, the effects of four important time-series variables, namely, time of day (TIME), day of study (DAY), weekly cyclicity (WKCYCLE), and serial autocorrelation (AUTOCORR), were factored in to produce the following equation:

$$\text{AUTO}_{ij} = \beta_{\text{B-P}}\text{MAAS}_i + \beta_{\text{W-P},i}\text{TIME}_{ij}$$
$$+ \beta_{\text{W-P},i}\text{DAY}_{ij} + \beta_{\text{W-P},i}\text{WKCYCLE}_{ij}$$
$$+ \beta_{\text{W-P},i}\text{AUTOCORR}_{ij}$$
$$+ \alpha_i + \varepsilon_{ij} \qquad (5)$$

The $\beta_{\text{W-P},i}\text{WKCYCLE}_{ij}$ coefficient is represented by a cosine function, which is an alternative way to assess the day-of-week effect to the dummy variable approach used by Sheldon et al. (1996) and Reis et al. (2000). Because Brown and Ryan (2003) were not interested in specific day-of-week (e.g., weekend) effects, the trigonometric approach was used, which allows for fewer terms in model equations. Also in Equation 5, the inclusion of $\beta_{\text{W-P},i}\text{AUTOCORR}_{ij}$ permitted an assessment of first-order lagged effects of within-person autonomy, and is an alternative to the dependent variable lag coefficient used by Sheldon et al. (1996) and Reis et al. (2000; see Equations 2 and 3).[2] In the present study, MLM using restricted maximum likelihood estimation found that more mindful individuals in both samples showed higher levels of autonomous behavior on a day-to-day basis.

This study also included a state measure of mindfulness, such that individuals rated how attentive they were to what was occurring during the activities that they also rated their relative autonomy. Two additional terms were added to Equation 5 to examine the role of state mindfulness on day-to-day autonomy: $\beta_{\text{W-P},i}\text{MAAS}_{ij}$ represented the main effect, and $\beta_{\text{Int}}(\text{MAAS}_i \times \text{MAAS}_{ij})$ represented the trait × state mindfulness interaction. MLM showed that momentary variation in mindfulness was related to fluctuations in autonomy. Specifically, those who were more mindfully attentive to their activities also experienced more autonomous motivation to engage in those activities. The effects of trait (Level 2) and state (Level 1) mindfulness on autonomy were independent in this study, indicating that the regulatory benefits of mindfulness were not limited to those with a mindful disposition. Other research (Brown & Ryan, 2004b) examining day-to-day competence and relatedness has found similar results, providing evidence that trait and state mindfulness offer an important, ongoing internal support for psychological need satisfaction. Moreover, those activities that were associated with greater mindfulness not only fostered autonomy; they also were related to within-person enhancements in well-being.

Future Directions in the Modeling of Motivational Processes

MLM techniques present a number of opportunities and challenges for future research in motivation, several of which we briefly discuss here.

More Intensive Sampling of Day-to-Day Behavior

As is apparent from this review, much of the research modeling motivational processes from within an SDT framework has used diary methods of various kinds. Optimally, these methods have the advantage of capturing psychological and behavioral events and experiences close to the time of their occurrence, and the use of multiple records of experience greatly enhances measurement reliability and statistical power. However, most of the diary research in motivation reviewed here has not taken full advantage of opportunities to model the dynamics of internal experience and behavior, and increasing the sophistication of diary studies would serve important methodological and conceptual purposes. More intensive sampling—multiple times per day rather than just once per day and over longer time intervals than a week or two—would permit the study of diurnal (daily) and septurnal (weekly) dynamic (e.g., cyclic) patterns. For example, there is some evidence for regular daily (Brown & Ryan, 2003) and weekly (Brown & Ryan, 2003; Reis et al., 2000) cyclicity in autonomy and relatedness. Lagged or autocorrelated effects can also be studied in more detail with the collection of measures on a greater than once-per-day basis. Some multilevel modeling software (e.g., SAS PROC MIXED; SAS Institute, 1992, 1997) is well-suited to the incorporation of time series variables like time of day, day of week, day of study, and serial autocorrelation, all characteristics that frequently appear in time-serial data and explain meaningful variance in day-to-day outcomes (West & Hepworth, 1991). Even when interest is not specifically in such variation, time-series variables should be included in multilevel models of day-to-day behavior for control purposes.

More intensive sampling would also permit the study of social and other situational influences on day-to-day motivational processes and behavior. For example, the role of supports for need satisfaction has been understudied in day-to-day contexts. Given evidence that needs are often dependent on social contexts for their expression and fulfillment, and need fulfillment conduces to well-being, it is important to understand how specific kinds of social and other daily activities, and the reasons for engaging in those activities, contribute to dynamic person × situation models of motivation, motivational supports, and the positive well-being consequences that follow from them (Reis et al., 2000).

Effects of Interventions to Enhance Self-Motivation

The majority of research using diary methods in the study of motivation, and a variety of other domains of behavior, has been interested in obtaining detailed pictures of naturally occurring behavior. For reasons already noted, there has been good reason for this. Yet the combination of diary methods and multilevel modeling presents a rich opportunity to examine the real-world effects of clinical, educational, organizational, and other interventions on motivational processes (cf. Deci, Connell, & Ryan, 1989; Williams, Gagné, Ryan, & Deci, 2002). In interrupted time-series designs, for example, a target behavior is recorded repeatedly before (baseline), sometimes during, and following an intervention. Multilevel analysis can then test whether (a) the parameters of the behavior (Level 1) change in response to the Level 2 intervention, as compared to control or other intervention conditions, and (b) whether the effects of the intervention are conditioned by subject and contextual factors. Smyth, Soefer, Hurewitz, and Stone (1999) provided an example of a multilevel analysis of interrupted time-series data in the health domain.

Laboratory-Based Investigations of Motivational Processes

Research in SDT has long been interested in the study of motivation under controlled laboratory conditions (e.g., Deci & Ryan, 1985). Yet little attention has been paid to motivational processes unfolding in real-time laboratory contexts. Sheldon and McGregor's (2000) multilevel analysis of iterated behavioral choices in a resource dilemma task represents an important touchstone for such work, as it models how behavior can change over time in response to both personality and social influences. As alluded to in our discussion of future intervention research, examination of the effects of experimental manipulations on motivational dynamics is well suited to multilevel analysis.

Maximizing the Use of Multilevel Analyses

Beyond the research design possibilities that MLM affords are opportunities to make more complete use of multilevel analyses and statistics. For example, aside from using model parameter estimates, motivation researchers are encouraged to use effect variance estimates, which reflect the estimated variance accounted for by modeled effects within the population. Covariance estimates indicate how much the model intercepts and slopes vary across subjects (or schools, organizations, etc.). Significant covariance in a slope parameter, for example, can point to meaningful individual differences in the covariation between a predictor and outcome (see Singer, 1998). Beyond testing for main effects at each level of a multilevel model, as well as interactions within and across levels, researchers can also use multilevel models to test for mediational effects, using the strategies that are used in ordinary least squares regression (e.g., Baron & Kenny, 1986; MacKinnon, Lockwood, Hoffman, West, & Sheets, 2002), with modifications made to accommodate multilevel testing. Of interest, for example, would be tests of whether need satisfaction mediates the relation between internal or external motivational supports and a variety of motivational outcomes examined over time, including academic or work performance, creative output, social behavior, and well-being.

Conclusion

Because motivation is a dynamic phenomenon that is sensitive to both person and situational changes, it is particularly well suited to multilevel modeling research. In this chapter, we have attempted to show that there is a natural pairing between expanded longitudinal designs, including daily experience and lab-based methods, and multilevel modeling approaches to the study of motivational processes. While this body of work is still small, important findings have been uncovered: The fulfillment of basic psychological needs fluctuates on a day-to-day basis, and subjective well-being is robustly affected by these fluctuations. Other research, discussed only briefly here, indicates that well-being and optimal functioning show intraindividual fluctuations from relationship to relationship and life role to life role. SDT research has shown that this fluctuation in functioning corresponds to changes in supports for psychological needs across these relationships and roles (e.g., La Guardia et al., 2000; Ryan, La Guardia, Solky-Butzel, & Kim, 2005).

Although considerable research has been devoted to the main effects of traits and types of daily events and situations on wellness, multilevel research reviewed herein suggests that day-to-day well-being is contingent on finding personal value or meaning in everyday activities (Reis et al., 2000; see also Sheldon & Kasser, 1995, 1998). Research also suggests that collective or group well-being depends on personal values tied to basic psychological needs. Finally, more recent research indicates that the quality of consciousness known as mindfulness can serve as a dispositional and situational support for basic need fulfillment.

There is still considerable potential to be tapped in the exploration of substantive and analytic questions on motivational processes, and we have outlined several possibilities for future research in multilevel modeling. While beyond the scope of this chapter, it is also worth noting that there are rich research opportunities in joining major analytic forces, such as multilevel modeling with latent variable modeling (e.g., Chou, Bentler, & Pentz, 2000). A defining feature of the recent progress in motivation research, and in the field of psychology as a whole, has been a rapid increase in the sophistication of its research methods and analytic tools. Researchers willing to take a close look at motivational processes through the lens of multilevel and other cutting-edge approaches will do much to expand our basic and applied understanding of this central feature of human behavior.

Notes

1. Reis et al. (2000) also tested gender main effects and interactions with both Level 2 and Level 1 need satisfaction. None of the results qualified the results reported here.

2. First-order autocorrelation is one of the simplest autoregressive error structures and is commonly termed AR(1). When observations on some variable are equally spaced in time, this structure assumes that the residuals for adjacent observations will be most highly correlated, the residuals for observations two intervals apart will be less highly correlated, and so on. There are also continuous-time versions of the usual AR(1) error structure that are capable of assessing first-order autocorrelation when observations are unequally spaced in time (see Schwartz & Stone, 1998).

References

Baron, R. M., & Kenny, D. A. (1986). The moderator-mediator variable distinction in social psychological research: Conceptual, strategic, and statistical considerations. *Journal of Personality and Social Psychology, 51,* 1173–1182.

Baumeister, R. F., & Leary, M. R. (1995). The need to belong: Desire for interpersonal attachments as a fundamental human motivation. *Psychological Bulletin, 117,* 497–529.

Bem, D. J., & Funder, D. C. (1978). Predicting more of the people more of the time: Assessing the personality of situation. *Psychological Review, 85,* 485–501.

Brown, K. W., & Moskowitz, D. S. (1998). It's a function of time: A review of the process approach to behavioral medicine research. *Annals of Behavioral Medicine, 20,* 109–117.

Brown, K. W., & Ryan, R. M. (2003). The benefits of being present: Mindfulness and its role in psychological well-being. *Journal of Personality and Social Psychology, 84,* 822–848.

Brown, K. W., & Ryan, R.M. (2004a). Fostering healthy self-regulation from within and without: A self-determination theory perspective. In P. A. Linley & S. Joseph (Eds.), *Positive psychology in practice* (pp. 105–124). New York: Wiley.

Brown, K. W., & Ryan, R. M. (2004b). *Mindfulness as a facilitator of competence and relatedness.* Unpublished data, University of Rochester.

Bryk, A. S., & Raudenbush, S. W. (1992). *Hierarchical linear models: Applications and data analysis methods.* Newbury Park, CA: Sage.

Carver, C. S., & Scheier, M. F. (1998). *On the self-regulation of behavior.* New York: Cambridge University Press.

Chou, C.-P., Bentler, P. M., & Pentz, M. A. (2000). A two-stage approach to multilevel structural equation models: Application to longitudinal data. In T. D. Little, K. U. Schnabel, & J. Baumert (Eds.), *Modeling longitudinal and multilevel data: Practical issues, applied approaches and specific examples* (pp. 33–49). Mahwah, NJ: Erlbaum.

Coté, S., & Moskowitz, D. S. (1998). On the dynamic covariation between interpersonal behavior and affect: Prediction from neuroticism, extraversion, and agreeableness. *Journal of Personality and Social Psychology, 75,* 1032–1046.

Davis, C. (1997). Body image, exercise, and eating behaviors. In K. R. Fox (Ed.), *The physical self: From motivation to well-being* (pp. 143–174). Champaign, IL: Human Kinetics.

deCharms, R. (1968). *Personal causation: The internal affective determinants of behavior.* New York: Academic Press.

Deci, E. L. (1975). *Intrinsic motivation.* New York: Plenum.

Deci, E. L., Connell, J. P., & Ryan, R. M. (1989). Self-determination in a work organization. *Journal of Applied Psychology, 74,* 580–590.

Deci, E. L., & Ryan, R. M. (1985). *Intrinsic motivation and self-determination in human behavior.* New York: Plenum.

Deci, E. L., & Ryan, R. M. (2000). The "what" and "why" of goal pursuits: Human needs and the self-determination of behavior. *Psychological Inquiry, 11,* 227–268.

Diener, E. (1996). Traits can be powerful, but are not enough: Lessons from subjective well-being. *Journal of Research in Personality, 30,* 389–399.

Gagné, M., Ryan, R. M., & Bargmann, K. (2003). Autonomy support and need satisfaction in the motivation and well-being of gymnasts. *Journal of Applied Sport Psychology, 15,* 372–390.

Kasser, T. (2002). *The high price of materialism.* Cambridge, MA: MIT Press.

Kasser, T., & Ryan, R. M. (1993). A dark side of the American dream: Correlates of financial success as a central life aspiration. *Journal of Personality and Social Psychology, 65,* 410–422.

Kasser, T., & Ryan, R. M. (1996). Further examining the American dream: Differential correlates of intrinsic and extrinsic goals. *Personality and Social Psychology Bulletin, 22,* 80–87.

Kreft, I., & deLeeuw, J. (1998). *Introducing multilevel modeling.* Thousand Oaks, CA: Sage.

La Guardia, J., Ryan, R. M., Couchman, C. E., & Deci, E. L. (2000). Within-person variation in security of attachment: A self-determination theory perspective on attachment, need fulfillment, and well-being. *Journal of Personality and Social Psychology, 79,* 367–384.

Larsen, R. J. (1989). A process approach to personality psychology. Utilizing time as a facet of data. In D. Buss & N. Cantor (Eds.), *Personality psychology: Recent trends and emerging directions* (pp. 177–193). New York: Springer-Verlag.

MacKinnon, D. P., Lockwood, C. M., Hoffman, J. M., West, S. G., & Sheets, V. (2002). A comparison of methods to test mediation and other intervening variable effects. *Psychological Methods, 7,* 83–104.

Reis, H. T., & Franks, P. (1994). The role of intimacy and social support in health outcomes: Two processes or one? *Personal Relationships, 2,* 185–197.

Reis, H. T., Sheldon, K. M., Gable, S. L., Roscoe, J., & Ryan, R. M. (2000). Daily well-being: The role of autonomy, competence, and relatedness. *Personality and Social Psychology Bulletin, 26,* 419–435.

Ryan, R. M. (1993). Agency and organization: Intrinsic motivation, autonomy and the self in psychological development. In J. Jacobs (Ed.), *Nebraska symposium on motivation: Developmental perspectives on motivation* (Vol. 40, pp. 1–56). Lincoln: University of Nebraska Press.

Ryan, R. M. (1995). Psychological needs and the facilitation of integrative processes. *Journal of Personality, 63*, 397–427.

Ryan, R. M., & Deci, E. L. (2004). Autonomy is no illusion: Self-determination theory and the empirical study of authenticity, awareness, and will. In J. Greenberg, S. Koole, & T. Pyszczynski (Eds.), *Handbook of experimental existential psychology* (pp. 449–479). New York: Guilford.

Ryan, R. M., & Deci, E. L. (2000a). Intrinsic and extrinsic motivations: Classic definitions and new directions. *Contemporary Educational Psychology, 25*, 54–67.

Ryan, R. M., & Deci, E. L. (2000b). Self-determination theory and the facilitation of intrinsic motivation, social development, and well-being. *American Psychologist, 55*, 68–78.

Ryan, R. M., La Guardia, J. G., Solky-Butzel, J., & Kim, Y. (2005). On the interpersonal regulation of emotions: Emotional reliance across gender, relationships and cultures. *Personal Relationships, 12*, 145–163.

Ryan, R. M., Sheldon, K. M., Kasser, T., & Deci, E. L. (1996). All goals are not created equal: An organismic perspective on the nature of goals and their regulation. In P. M. Gollwitzer & J. A. Bargh (Eds.), *The psychology of action: Linking cognition and motivation to behavior* (pp. 7–26). New York: Guilford.

SAS Institute. (1992). *SAS technical report P-229, SAS/STAT software: Changes and enhancements.* Cary, NC: Author.

SAS Institute. (1997). *SAS/STAT software: Changes and enhancements through release 6.12.* Cary, NC: Author.

Schwartz, J. E., & Stone, A. A. (1998). Strategies for analyzing ecological momentary assessment data. *Health Psychology, 17*, 6–16.

Sheldon, K. M., & Kasser, T. (1995). Coherence and congruence: Two aspects of personality integration. *Journal of Personality and Social Psychology, 68*, 531–543.

Sheldon, K. M., & Kasser, T. (1998). Pursuing personal goals: Skills enable progress, but not all progress is beneficial. *Personality and Social Psychology Bulletin, 24*, 1319–1331.

Sheldon, K. M., & McGregor, H. A. (2000). Extrinsic value orientation and "The tragedy of the commons." *Journal of Personality, 68*, 383–411.

Sheldon, K. M., Ryan, R. M., & Reis, H. T. (1996). What makes for a good day? Competence and autonomy in the day and in the person. *Personality and Social Psychology Bulletin, 22*, 1270–1279.

Sheldon, K. M., Sheldon, M. S., & Osbaldiston, R. (2000). Prosocial values and group assortation within an N-person prisoner's dilemma game. *Human Nature, 11*, 387–404.

Singer, J. D. (1998). Using SAS PROC MIXED to fit multilevel models, hierarchical models, and individual growth models. *Journal of Educational and Behavioral Statistics, 23*, 323–356.

Smyth, J. M., Soefer, M. H., Hurewitz, A., & Stone, A. A. (1999). The effect of tape-recorded relaxation training on well-being, symptoms, and peak respiratory flow rate in adult asthmatics: A pilot study. *Psychology and Health, 14*, 487–501.

Turk, D. C. (1994). Potentials of process measurement: Motion pictures versus snapshots. *Annals of Behavioral Medicine, 16*, 198.

Varela, F. J., Thompson, E., & Rosch, E. (1991). *The embodied mind: Cognitive science and human experience.* Cambridge, MA: MIT Press.

West, S. G., & Hepworth, J. T. (1991). Statistical issues in the study of temporal data: Daily experiences. *Journal of Personality, 59*, 611–661.

White, R. W. (1959). Motivation reconsidered: The concept of competence. *Psychological Review, 66*, 297–333.

Williams, G. C., Gagné, M., Ryan, R. M., & Deci, E. L. (2002). Facilitating autonomous motivation for smoking cessation. *Health Psychology, 21*, 40–50.

38

Individual and Situational Factors Related to the Experience of Flow in Adolescence

A Multilevel Approach

*Jennifer A. Schmidt, David J. Shernoff,
and Mihaly Csikszentmihalyi*

A fundamental issue pursued by researchers in positive psychology involves defining what constitutes a good life and understanding how individuals can create one. From the perspective of flow theory, "a good life is one that is characterized by complete absorption in what one does" (Nakamura & Csikszentmihalyi, 2002, p. 89). Born out of a desire to understand intrinsically motivated activity, *flow* refers to a state of optimal experience characterized by total absorption in the task at hand: a merging of action and awareness in which the individual loses track of both time and self. The flow state is experientially positive, and out of the flow experience emerges a desire to replicate the experience. Over the past three decades, Csikszentmihalyi and colleagues have developed theoretical constructs and empirical research tools to better understand the nature, origins, and consequences of this state of optimal experience called flow. In this chapter,

we describe the flow model and then present data analyses in which we explore the personal traits and contextual conditions associated with the experience of flow among adolescents in the United States. We demonstrate the utility of hierarchical linear modeling (HLM) for exploring flow using a complex data set characterized by repeated measures.

The Flow Model

In an investigation of the nature of enjoyment, Csikszentmihalyi (1975/2000) interviewed artists, rock climbers, chess players, surgeons, factory workers, and others about their work and leisure activities. The investigation focused on those activities that individuals did for the sheer enjoyment of doing them as opposed to any end product resulting from the activity. Countless interviews with individuals from a variety of backgrounds revealed remarkable similarity in respondents' descriptions of their subjective experience in these activities. These *autotelic* activities (activities for which participation itself is the goal) shared a similar phenomenology in that participants consistently described optimal states of complete absorption, focus, and enjoyment. Further examination also revealed consistency in the conditions under which these optimal states most often occurred. Numerous researchers have confirmed commonalities in optimal experiences and their underlying conditions (Csikszentmihalyi, 1990, 1996; Jackson, 1995, 1996; Massimini & Carli, 1988; Perry, 1999). The optimal state described by individuals is most commonly characterized by: (1) intense concentration on the task at hand; (2) a deep sense of involvement and merging of action and awareness; (3) a sense of control over one's actions in dealing with the task at hand; (4) enjoyment or interest in the activity; and (5) a distorted sense of time (usually that time has passed very quickly). During the process of gathering these descriptions, several interviewees described themselves as "being in flow" or "flowing." Thus, experiences characterized by such descriptions have become known as *flow experiences* or *flow states*.

The specific activities from which individuals derive flow experiences vary widely. Interviews with men and women of different ages, classes, and cultural backgrounds have revealed that the flow state can emerge from involvement in a variety of activities, including athletics, performing surgery, tending cattle, haggling in the marketplace, working on a factory line, reading, and writing. While there is considerable variation in the particular activities that lead people to experience flow, there are a number of phenomenological conditions that are typically present when flow does occur, regardless of the specific activity in which one is engaged. These conditions include: (1) engagement in activity chosen for its own sake—not a necessary, but a facilitative condition; (2) perceived challenges of the task at hand that are relatively high and in balance with one's perceived skills; (3) clear proximal goals that are regarded as important; (4) immediate feedback indicating one's success at meeting these goals; and (5) highly focused, rather than divided or scattered, attention. Of course, some activities by their very nature are structured in such a way that proximal goals and feedback are more salient, challenges can be

manipulated to best match one's skills, and distractions are minimized to focus attention. Indeed, there is some evidence that certain activities (e.g., making music, competitive athletics) are more likely than others to produce flow (Csikszentmihalyi, 1990). Nevertheless, flow refers only to a subjective phenomenology, suggesting that what matters most is that these conditions are salient to the individual, not necessarily inherent to the activity itself. Individuals have the capacity to identify challenges in seemingly unchallenging situations, define proximal goals and rules for engagement, and focus attention in such a way as to create the conditions for flow even when such conditions are absent from the task at hand. What is most essential for the experience of flow appears to be one's subjective perception of challenge, skills, goals, feedback, autonomy, and focused attention. Accordingly, numerous investigations have documented the flow state among individuals while doing daily household chores (Csikszentmihalyi, 1990), working in factory jobs (Le-Fevre, 1988), living in concentration camps (Logan, 1985), and in other situations that might appear on the surface to be counterproductive to the experience of flow (for a review, see Csikszentmihalyi, 1990).

The development and refinement of the flow model has a rich history spanning the past three decades. As a thorough account of the theory's history and development is beyond the scope of this chapter, the reader is referred to Csikszentmihalyi (1990) and Nakamura and Csikszentmihalyi (2002) for a more detailed discussion.

The Systematic Study and Measurement of Flow

The flow model emphasizes the phenomenology of the interaction of the person with one's environment. Like many contemporary theories of human behavior and development (see Magnusson & Stattin, 1998), the flow model acknowledges the dynamic system that is created by the person in context, recognizing that one's experience is a product of interaction with one's environment at that moment (Csikszentmihalyi, 1985; Nakamura & Csikszentmihalyi, 2002). While this interactional viewpoint is fundamental to the theory, capturing the interplay between person and environment can be extremely difficult to accomplish in empirical research studies. The earliest studies of flow relied on qualitative data gathered in open-ended interviews in which participants were asked to describe their subjective experience and antecedent conditions surrounding times of deep enjoyment and absorption (Csikszentmihalyi, 1975/2000). Subsequent research employed paper-and-pencil questionnaires to measure specific dimensions of the flow experience and to compare individuals in the frequency or nature of their flow experiences (Delle Fave & Massimini, 1988; Jackson & Marsh, 1996; Mayers, 1978; Parks, 1996).

Current understanding of flow has been greatly enhanced by the development and use of the experience-sampling method (ESM; Csikszentmihalyi, Larson, & Prescott, 1977). By signaling respondents periodically throughout their waking hours over a period of several days and asking them to report on their immediate experiences, the ESM addresses the problem of recall and estimation errors inherent in surveys and interviews. Respondents carry a paging device (e.g., programmable wristwatch or handheld computer) that signals them at random moments throughout the day. Each time they are signaled, respondents complete a brief questionnaire in which they answer open-ended and scaled questions about the day and time of the signal and their activities and thoughts, as well as the cognitive, affective, and motivational qualities of their experience. The signaling schedule, as well as the particular questions included in the ESM questionnaires, varies depending on the researchers' interests. ESM is the method used to identify and examine flow in this chapter. For a review of the methodological variations employed in ESM research, as well as indications of its reliability and validity, the reader is referred to Hektner, Schmidt, and Csikszentmihalyi (2007), and Csikszentmihalyi and Larson (1987).

The ESM allows researchers to study momentary fluctuations in individuals' cognitive and emotional states in situ and link these fluctuations to particular contextual factors such as one's location, activities, or companions. The ESM is designed to capture both the external and internal dimensions of experience (Csikszentmihalyi & Larson, 1984). External dimensions include the date and time of day, as well as one's physical location, activities, and companions. All of these elements paint the backdrop against which one's daily experience is lived out. Internal dimensions of experience refer to thoughts and feelings as respondents interact with other people and perform the activities that make up their daily life. A given moment can be characterized by both external dimensions (e.g., "It was 10:00 a.m. on Saturday"; "I was with my brother"; "We were playing racquetball"), and internal dimensions (e.g., "That activity was challenging to me"; "I was feeling happy"). While all of the information on the ESM is provided by the respondent and is thus subjective, the external-internal distinction is useful as a means of categorizing the types of experiential information the ESM provides and is the organizing framework for our explorations of the contextual and perceptual factors related to adolescents' experiences of flow.

Challenges and Skills as Primary Conditions for Flow

A substantial body of research has used the ESM to identify moments in individuals' daily lives wherein the conditions for flow are present. The conditions for flow are said to exist when participants report that the challenges of the situation and their skills in the situation are both higher than average. Researchers have examined how often the conditions for flow exist for a given person or group of people, and what types of activities are most likely to produce these conditions (Csikszentmihalyi, 1975/2000; Moneta & Csikszentmihalyi, 1996). Once the moments representing the flow conditions are identified, researchers examine the quality of reported experience to test empirically whether elements of the flow experience are more likely to occur when the flow conditions are present than when they are not. Using this method, researchers have demonstrated that adolescents and adults tend to report greater levels of concentration, enjoyment, involvement, interest, and control when challenges and skills are above average compared to when they are not. These analyses have provided empirical validation for the flow model in that they demonstrate that when the conditions for flow are present, the experience of flow is more likely to occur.

Limitations of Previous Research

As a result of the associations just described, many studies operationalize flow as the combination of simultaneous high challenge and skill (Csikszentmihalyi & Csikszentmihalyi, 1988; Hektner, 1996; Moneta & Csikszentmihalyi, 1996). These studies have contributed greatly to our understanding of flow but are limited in several respects. First, one's perception of high challenges and high skills does not guarantee that the flow state will follow. The conditions of high challenge and high skill are a proxy for flow experiences—telling us only that, statistically speaking, flow may be more likely to occur. To further our understanding of the antecedents of flow, it is necessary to focus on those moments in which participants are actually experiencing flow—that is, when their ratings of concentration, interest, enjoyment, involvement, and control are simultaneously high. Moreover, flow theory identifies conditions for flow other than high challenges and skills—it is important to consider these also.

A second limitation is that most research studies to date examine the associations between challenge-skill and subjective elements of the flow experience independently. For example, in high challenge-high skill situations, average enjoyment has been found to be higher, but participants' levels of concentration, interest, and involvement were not taken into account (Massimini & Carli, 1988; Moneta & Csikszentmihalyi, 1996). To further our understanding of flow, it is necessary to consider multiple elements of the flow experience simultaneously in order to verify that the experiences we examine truly are flow experiences as defined descriptively.

A third limitation of studies on flow to date is that only minimal attention has been paid to person-level variation in the experience of flow among individuals. Several studies have compared the degree to which persons from different age groups, cultural backgrounds, or occupations encounter the flow conditions of high challenges and high skills, but few published studies have used ESM to systematically document person-level variation in the actual experience of flow. Moreover, given the interactional nature of the flow model, it is necessary to use appropriate statistical techniques to simultaneously explore such person-level variation along with variation due to features of momentary experience.

Aims of the Chapter

In this chapter, we begin to address the aforementioned limitations in ESM research on flow. Flow is operationalized in terms of the flow experience rather than the flow conditions. Using an individual's simultaneous ratings of concentration, enjoyment, involvement, interest, and control, each moment is characterized by the degree to which the respondent appears to be in

a flow state. Thus our measurement of flow becomes continuous rather than categorical, and takes into account the full complement of cognitive and affective elements specified by flow theory. We then develop analytical models to identify factors that are predictive of flow experiences. These predictors include the conditions of challenge and skill as they have been measured in previous research but are expanded to examine additional conditions proposed by the theory, including perceived autonomy, the importance of the activity (i.e., the clarity and relevance of goals), the perception of success (as when effective feedback is provided), and focus of attention. We also consider external dimensions of experience such as time of day, activities, location, and companions. Because the structure of ESM data is nested, with repeated observations nested within persons, we use multilevel modeling to more accurately assess the person-level and situational factors associated with flow.

Method

Participants

We employed data from the Sloan Study of Youth and Social Development (SSYSD), a national longitudinal study investigating how students think about their lives in relationship to the future (Csikszentmihalyi & Schneider, 2000). The data were collected in three waves: 1992–1993 (Year 1), 1994–1995 (Year 3), and 1996–1997 (Year 5). Twelve research sites across the United States were selected to represent variation in urbanicity, racial and ethnic composition, labor force composition, and economic stability. Data were collected through elementary, middle, and high schools in each site. While the original study included students who were in 6th, 8th, 10th, and 12th grades, the current analyses included data only from 10th and 12th graders. We focus exclusively on high school students because the daily activities of middle school children and high schoolers are qualitatively different. Because elementary school students frequently stay with the same teacher or classroom for the whole day, salient high school factors such as nonacademic classes or vocational education have little meaning for the elementary school population. There may also be corresponding age-related differences in the experience of engagement or flow. In a review of research on school-age students,

Fredricks, Blumenfeld, and Paris (2004) reported that student engagement is likely to take different forms in elementary and high school. For example, students may not become deeply engaged in learning until they have acquired the intellectual capacity of later ages.

Though the original data were longitudinal, here we use only data collected in a single year for each participant. To maximize the high school sample, we selected 12th grade students ($n = 122$) in Year 1 of the study, 10th graders ($n = 83$) and 12th graders ($n = 87$) in Year 3 of the study, and 10th graders ($n = 80$) in Year 5 of the study. Thus, the sample consisted of 372 adolescents from three separate cohorts in the 1990s. The sample was 60% female and 40% male; 14% of the sample was African American, 6% was Asian American, 10% was Latino, and 70% was European American. Economically, 21% of the sample was drawn from communities that were characterized as lower or working class, while 62% came from middle- or upper-middle-class communities and 17% came from upper-class communities.

Instruments

Experience-Sampling Method

The ESM measures participants' location and activity, as well as affective and cognitive experiences, at random moments. Participants wore wristwatches programmed to emit random signals eight times each day for 7 days, between the hours of 7:30 a.m. and 10:30 p.m. In response to the signal, respondents answered a number of open-ended and scaled questions from an experience-sampling form (ESF; to see a sample self-report form, see Csikszentmihalyi & Schneider, 2000). A week's worth of ESFs was compiled in a logbook that participants carried during the week sampled. Participants selected for this study provided a total of 8,298 ESFs. The data obtained from the ESFs were used to compute measures of flow, as well as indicators of the internal and external dimensions of adolescents' immediate experience.

Surveys

Survey data provided information on participants' demographic characteristics, general self-perceptions, future orientation, and school experiences, as well as their relationships with family members and peers. All person-level variables used in our analyses were derived from these surveys.

Dependent Measure: Flow

A continuous measure of the flow experience (on a 9-point scale) was computed by taking the mean of individuals' momentary rankings of concentration, interest, enjoyment, involvement, and control at the time of the ESM signal. These five variables were chosen because the simultaneous experience of concentration, interest, enjoyment, control, and involvement is definitional to the experience of flow.[1] This construct achieved a moderately high level of reliability ($\alpha = .68$).[2]

Independent Measures

Person-Level Factors

The person-level measures included in our analyses have been suggested by previous research on the autotelic personality and person-level correlates of flow (Adlai-Gail, 1994; Hektner, 1996; Rathunde, 1996). We used measures of students' gender, ethnicity, and socioeconomic status as indicated by the highest level of education attained by either parent. A composite measure of self-esteem was constructed from an abridged version of the Rosenberg (1965) self-esteem scale that contained seven items, each on a 4-point scale. A measure of optimism toward the future was constructed by taking the mean of questionnaire items indicating how powerful and confident respondents felt when thinking about the future on a 5-point scale. Measures of family challenge and family support were constructed using items and procedures developed by Kevin Rathunde (see Csikszentmihalyi, Rathunde, & Whalen, 1993; Rathunde, 1996). Each measure was constructed by summing affirmative answers to 12 statements indicating positive challenge (or support), and then subtracting the sum of four negative challenge (or support) items. Our measure of school support averaged adolescents' responses to five survey items indicating the degree to which they felt cared for and supported by students and teachers at their school, each on a 5-point scale. Peers' value of education was constructed using responses to four questions in which adolescents were asked to indicate the importance of attending classes regularly, studying, getting good grades, and finishing high school to the friends with whom they regularly hang out. A measure of peers' value of cooperative activities was constructed using items in which participants rated the importance of engaging in extracurricular, service, or youth group activities to their friends.

Situational Factors

Situational factors included both external (contextual) and internal (perceptual) dimensions of experience as measured by the ESM. A series of dummy variables was constructed to represent the external dimensions of adolescents' experience. The following variables were created to represent the day and time:[3] weekday, school hours (Monday–Friday, 8 a.m.–3:30 p.m.); weekday, after school (Monday–Friday, 3:30 p.m.–6:30 p.m.); evenings (Monday–Saturday, 6:30 p.m.–10:30 p.m.); Saturday daytime (Saturday, 7:30 a.m.–6:30 p.m.); and Sundays (Sunday, all day and evening). To explore how teens' physical location may impact their experience of flow, all ESM reports of their locations were recoded into five categories: home, academic classes (e.g., math class, English class), nonacademic classes (e.g., art, computer science, etc.), school grounds (other nonclass school locations), and public places. Because one's activities are not always apparent from their physical location, we constructed indicators of adolescents' activities by recoding the hundreds of activities adolescents reported into six general categories: school work, paid work, active leisure, passive leisure, maintenance activities, and other. Active leisure included activities like sports and hobbies, while passive leisure included activities such as watching television. Maintenance referred to chores and errands, as well as personal care and grooming (e.g., brushing one's hair, etc.). These categories are consistent with those used in previous ESM studies of adolescents (e.g., Csikszentmihalyi & Larson, 1984). While there is considerable overlap between the time of day, location, and activity variables, they do represent qualitatively distinct contextual dimensions. For example, there are many times during school hours (even when students are in academic classes) when adolescents report activities other than schoolwork. Likewise, a considerable amount of schoolwork happens after school hours and outside of class.

Each time participants responded to the ESM, they indicated who they were with at the time of the signal. For the purpose of our analyses, these responses were coded into five mutually exclusive categories:[4] alone, with peers only (friends and classmates), with adults only (parents, teachers, coaches), with peers and adults together, and other (other-aged relatives as well as strangers or persons of unspecified relationship to the participant).

We constructed measures of five internal dimensions of experience based on characteristic descriptions of flow experiences. A measure of autonomy was derived from a single item asking participants to choose whether they were engaged in their present activity because they wanted to, they had to, or they had nothing else to do. Anytime participants indicated that they were doing an activity because they wanted to, the autonomy variable was given a value of 1; otherwise, it was given a value of 0. Following procedures used by Hektner (1996), we constructed a measure of the interaction of challenges and skills by taking the geometric mean (the square root of the product) of the challenge and skill items on the ESM. This newly constructed variable also ranged from 0 to 9, as did the challenge and skill items, but was maximized when challenge and skill are both high and in balance. This variable was labeled challenge*skill to symbolize the challenge-skill interaction. The success variable refers to a respondent's answer on a 9-point scale to the question, "Were you succeeding at what you were doing at the time of the signal?" A measure of focus was constructed using adolescents' responses to open-ended questions about what they were doing and what they were thinking about. If responses to these two questions were similar (e.g., the subject was doing math homework and also thinking about math), the focus variable was given a value of 1. If there was a discrepancy between one's actions and thoughts (e.g., doing math homework and thinking about one's girlfriend), the variable was given a value of 0. The importance variable simply represents participants' rating of the importance of the activity on a 9-point scale.

Analytic Approach

Analyses of ESM data can be complex due to the nested levels of data resulting from repeated measures (i.e., beeps) nested within each individual. To analyze the data, we used a series of two-level hierarchical linear models (Raudenbush & Bryk, 2002). HLM is ideal for analyzing repeated measures of participants, solving the unit-of-analysis problem that can occur, estimating appropriate standard errors, and appropriately weighting units by the reliability of the information they provide.

The main objectives of these analyses were to identify individual, perceptual, and contextual factors associated with the experience of flow. The effects of individual factors were modeled as between-persons (or Level 2) effects. The effects of context (external dimensions of experience) and perception (internal dimensions of experience) were modeled as within-participant (or Level 1) effects. In order to demonstrate the utility of multilevel models in analyzing a broad spectrum of possible influences on flow, our analyses were more exploratory and demonstrative than characterized by specific hypothesis testing; such analyses would ordinarily give rise to more specific hypothesis testing in subsequent studies.

When used with ESM data, multilevel modeling techniques allow researchers to examine the interaction between person and context, and capture in a very rudimentary way some of the dynamic quality of human experience. This analytical technique can be used to identify the independent contributions and interactions of situational and personal factors to the experience of flow. Thus we may determine that, in general, certain activities or situations are more likely to produce flow, and that some situations may be more salient for certain types of individuals than others. However, HLM lacks the capacity to capture the truly dynamic nature of ESM data by meaningfully representing a given individual's fluctuations in experience over time. For techniques specifically designed to model such fluctuations and other dynamic systems, see chapters 26 and 29 on dynamic systems-modeling techniques.

Results

Analysis of Variability in Flow

The first analysis was a simple analysis of variance with random effects at Levels 1 and 2, otherwise known as the fully unconditional model. Results show that the maximum likelihood estimate for the grand mean of flow is 6.34 with a standard error of .05. This indicates a 95% confidence interval of $6.34 \pm 1.96(.05) =$ (6.25, 6.43). The variance component at Level 1 (beep level) is 2.71 (77%); and the variance component at Level 2 (person level) is .82 (23%).

This indicates that approximately three quarters of the variation in flow was due to fluctuations experienced by the same person as he or she experienced life throughout the week; approximately a quarter of the variation was attributable to mean differences in flow among participants. The significance test at Level 2 ($\chi^2 = 2,788.81$, $p < 0.001$) indicates that there is statistically significant variation among persons.[5]

Mean Differences in Flow by Person-Level Characteristics

In separate exploratory HLM analyses, person-level means or intercepts in flow were outcomes predicted by a single person-level variable (*means as outcome* models). A wide range of person-level variables were considered as predictors, including background characteristics, psychological factors, family factors, school factors, and peer factors. These independent analyses revealed that individual variation in flow was predicted by a variety of person-level factors, including gender (with girls experiencing greater flow than boys), and race or ethnicity (with African Americans experiencing greater flow than Caucasians). Positive associations with flow were also found for self-esteem, optimism about the future, family challenge, family support, school support, peer valuing of education, and peer valuing of cooperative activities. In these analyses, parental education, grade level of the adolescent (10th vs. 12th), teen's GPA, and educational aspirations did not exert any significant effect on flow.

In order to more fully understand the relationships identified in these independent analyses, an inclusive model was tested to determine which associations would persist while accounting for the effects of the others.[6] Fixed and random effects for this model are presented in table 38.1. Not surprisingly, the magnitude of the fixed effects identified in independent analyses is substantially reduced when multiple person-level factors are taken into account. After controlling on other person-level factors, females still reported significantly higher levels of flow than males. Adolescents with higher levels of self-esteem and greater optimism about the future also experienced more flow in their daily lives. Associations with race or ethnicity and peer values did not remain statistically significant. Though challenge and support in the family are no longer associated with flow once

TABLE 38.1 Fixed and Random Effects of Person Variables on the Mean of Flow as Outcome in a Two-Level HLM Model

Fixed Effect	Coefficient	SE	T-ratio
Flow intercept, γ_{00}	6.16	0.08	78.75***
Female, γ_{01}	0.34	0.10	3.43**
Asian, γ_{02}	−0.31	0.20	−1.51
Latino, γ_{03}	−0.30	0.16	−1.88
Black, γ_{04}	0.16	0.14	1.11
Self-esteem, γ_{05}	0.50	0.11	4.54***
Optimism, γ_{06}	0.14	0.04	3.35**
Family challenge, γ_{07}	0.03	0.02	1.20
Family support, γ_{08}	0.00	0.02	−.02
School support, γ_{09}	0.28	0.11	2.48*
Peers value education, γ_{010}	0.16	0.13	1.21
Peers value cooperative activities, γ_{011}	0.09	0.12	.78

Random Effect	Variance Component	Chi-Square
Flow intercept, u_0	0.61	2157.82***
Level one variance, R	2.71	

*$p < .05$. **$p < .01$. ***$p < .001$.

other factors have been taken into account, the positive effect of school support on flow remains. The Level 2 residual variance component or random effect of the flow intercept for this model was .61, a 26% reduction in variance from the fully unconditional model. This indicates that approximately 26% of the variance in mean flow between participants was accounted for by the variables in the model (as suggested in Raudenbush & Bryk, 2002).[7]

Having identified some relevant person-level characteristics, our remaining models attempt to explain the within-person variation in terms of contextual and perceptual factors, exploring the external and internal dimensions of experience.

External Dimensions of Experience

Time and Day

We next examined whether adolescents felt greater levels of flow at certain times of day or on certain days of the week using the five time blocks described previously. Adolescents reported the highest levels of flow during the evenings ($\gamma = 0.25$, $p < .001$), and during after-school hours on weekdays ($\gamma = 0.15$, $p < .05$). School hours during the week were associated with the lowest levels of flow ($\gamma = -.11$, ns). Participants reported somewhat higher flow on weekends than

during school hours (with slightly higher flow on Saturday than Sunday), but the difference was not statistically significant. Figure 38.1 illustrates the times students were more likely to report relatively high flow versus low flow. The time and day explain little of the within-person variation in flow (2%).[8]

Activities

Analyses of six activity categories revealed that adolescents' experience of flow varied systematically by activity, as illustrated in figure 38.2. Compared to the default category of passive leisure activities, significantly lower levels of flow were reported while engaged in maintenance activities ($\gamma = -0.89$, $p < .001$), schoolwork ($\gamma = -0.37$, $p < .001$), paid work ($\gamma = -0.32$, $p < .05$), and other activity types ($\gamma = -0.86$, $p < .001$). Relative to passive leisure, participants reported significantly higher levels of flow during active leisure activities ($\gamma = 0.65$, $p < .001$). The reduction in the Level 1 variance component of 17% indicates that these activity categories account for some of the within-person variation in flow. Examination of the random effects revealed that, while there was no significant variation among students in their level of flow during schoolwork, there was significant between-persons variation in flow with respect to all other activities.

	Mon	Tues	Wed	Thurs	Fri	Sat	Sun
10:30 p.m.			High	Flow			
6:00 p.m.							
3:30 p.m.							
noon			Low	Flow			
7:30 a.m.							

Figure 38.1 Reported flow by day and time.

Location

When we examined variation in flow by location, we found that adolescents experience lower levels of flow in academic classes relative to all other location categories with the exception of the workplace. The highest levels of flow were reported when adolescents were in public ($\gamma = 0.47$, $p < .001$) and in nonacademic classes ($\gamma = 0.43$, $p < .001$). This latter result suggests that students actually experience their lowest and highest levels of flow while at school, depending on whether the classes are academic or nonacademic. Compared to academic classes, participants also reported greater flow at home ($\gamma = 0.29$, $p < .001$) and while on school grounds but not in classes ($\gamma = 0.23$, $p < .01$). Flow was least likely to occur when teenagers were at work ($\gamma = -0.25$, ns). Modeling location categories produces a 7% reduction in within-person variation in flow, suggesting that simply knowing where a person is physically is not a particularly meaningful predictor of flow experiences.

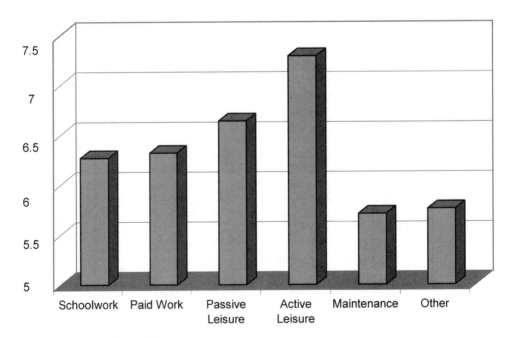

Figure 38.2 Reported level of flow by activity type.

Companionship

Our final analysis of external dimensions of experience examined the relationship between flow and companionship. Adolescents reported the highest levels of flow when with peers only ($\gamma = .11$, *ns*). Relative to the default category *other*, significantly lower levels of flow were reported when adolescents were with adults only ($\gamma = -.22$, $p < .05$), with peers and adults ($\gamma = -.20$, $p < .01$), and when alone ($\gamma = -.14$, $p < .05$). Companionship accounted for approximately 6% of the variance in flow. Random effects showed that the effect of all categories significantly varied among students with the exception of being exclusively with adults.

The external dimensions of experience explain some, though certainly not most, of the variation in an individuals' flow experiences. However, external dimensions represent only a part of subjective experience; one's perceptions of the conditions surrounding an activity or situation may also be quite salient. It is to these internal dimensions of experience that we now turn.

Internal Dimensions of Experience

We next tested the effects on flow of the five conditions for flow specified by flow theory.[9] Fixed and random effects of the internal dimensions of experience are presented in table 38.2. Each of the five factors examined had strong, positive associations with flow even when the effects of other factors were controlled. Autonomy is a strong predictor of flow: When teenagers felt that they were doing a particular activity because they wanted to, they experienced greater levels of flow than when they "had to" or "had nothing else to do." Consistent with flow theory, when challenges and skills were higher and in balance, the experience of flow was more intense. Participants also experienced higher flow when engaged in activities they deemed important. The perception that one was succeeding at the activity at hand was also predictive of greater flow experiences. Finally, situations in which attention was focused by a convergence of thought and action produced greater flow on average than when thoughts and actions diverged. Together, these internal dimensions of experience reduce the within-person residual variation in flow by 45%. The random effects of the coefficients in the model indicated that the average effect of all internal dimensions of experience significantly varied among participants with the exception of focus.

A Comprehensive Model: Multilevel Influences on the Experience of Flow

We conclude our analyses by constructing a comprehensive model combining person-level and contextual variables. Because there is substantial overlap between the external dimensions of experience we have explored, it was not possible to develop a single analytical model to

TABLE 38.2 Fixed and Random Effects of a Two-Level HLM Model: Internal Dimensions of Experience as Predictors of Flow

Fixed Effect	Coefficient	SE	T-ratio
Flow intercept, γ_{00}	6.34	0.05	121.99***
Challenge∗skill slope, γ_{20}	0.17	0.01	15.31***
Success slope, γ_{30}	0.23	0.01	21.47***
Focus slope, γ_{40}	0.31	0.04	8.32***
Autonomy slope, γ_{50}	1.18	0.04	31.29***
Importance slope, γ_{60}	0.18	0.01	17.30***

Random Effect	Variance Component	Chi-Square	
Flow intercept, u_0	0.90	4427.95***	
Challenge∗skill slope, u_1	0.01	450.96***	
Success slope, u_2	0.01	490.09***	
Focus slope, u_3	0.06	348.27	
Autonomy slope, u_4	0.13	416.56***	
Importance slope, u_5	0.02	532.36***	
Level-1 variance, R	1.49		

*$p < .05$. **$p < .01$. ***$p < .001$.

simultaneously estimate the effects of time, day, location, activity, and companionship. We therefore constructed a comprehensive model which appeared to have the greatest predictive power based on the previous analyses, while excluding significant overlap among predictors.

To predict the flow intercept, we included in the model each of the person-level factors significantly predicting mean flow in our means-as-outcomes model (table 38.1). With respect to random coefficients representing external dimensions of experience, we included each of the activity categories and a dummy variable indicating whether participants were alone or with others at the time of the signal. We also included each of the internal dimensions of experience due to their strong predictive power.[10] We also attempted to predict some of the Level 1 co-

efficients that were modeled as random with person-level factors. To simplify, we tested only whether basic demographic factors such as gender, ethnicity, and parental education significantly mediated the random effects included in the model.

Results are presented in table 38.3. Gender, optimism, and self-esteem remain significant predictors of mean differences in flow after accounting for other variables, while school support does not. The effect of activity type on the experience of flow also persists. One unexpected caveat derived from the comprehensive model is that the effect of active leisure activities on flow is further mediated by ethnicity. On average, African American participants reported higher levels of flow during active leisure than those from other races or ethnicities (though all

TABLE 38.3 Fixed and Random Effects of a Comprehensive Two-Level HLM Model

Fixed Effect	Coefficient	SE	T-ratio
Flow intercept, γ_{00}	6.57	0.07	95.99***
Female, γ_{01}	0.26	0.08	3.20**
Optimism, γ_{02}	0.15	0.04	4.04***
Esteem, γ_{03}	0.49	0.09	5.74***
School support, γ_{03}	0.16	0.09	1.78
Autonomy slope, γ_{10}	0.99	0.04	26.00***
Challenge*skill slope, γ_{20}	0.16	0.01	13.79***
Importance slope, γ_{30}	0.20	0.01	20.43***
Success slope, γ_{40}	0.21	0.02	12.68***
Female, γ_{41}	0.05	0.02	2.38*
Focus slope, γ_{50}	0.27	0.03	8.00***
Maintenance activity slope, γ_{60}	−0.73	0.05	−16.01***
Schoolwork slope, γ_{70}	−0.42	0.04	−9.34***
Paid work slope, γ_{80}	−0.54	0.10	−5.39***
Active leisure slope, γ_{90}	0.16	0.06	2.69**
Asian, γ_{91}	−0.14	0.17	−0.86
Latino, γ_{92}	−0.11	0.18	−0.62
African American, γ_{93}	0.36	0.15	2.36*
Other activity slope, γ_{100}	−0.69	0.05	−15.00***
Alone slope, γ_{110}	−0.15	0.04	−4.12***

Random Effect	Variance Component	Chi-Square
Flow intercept, u_0	0.49	454.28***
Autonomy slope, u_1	0.10	107.42*
Challenge*skill slope, u_2	0.01	111.06*
Importance slope, u_3	0.01	127.92**
Succeed slope, u_4	0.01	112.09*
Paid work slope, u_8	0.37	113.77*
Active leisure slope, u_9	0.10	124.09**
Alone slope, u_{11}	0.07	96.06
Level-1 variance, R	1.36	

*$p < .05.$ **$p < .01.$ ***$p < .001.$

participants on average reported greater flow during active leisure than other activities). The negative effect of being alone on flow was also significant in the comprehensive model.

Positive associations persisted between flow and all five internal dimensions of experience in the comprehensive model. The positive effect for success was shown to be greater for females than males, though both genders reported greater flow when perceived success was high. Taken as a whole, all fixed effects tested remained significant even when accounting for the others in the model. The results suggest that both internal and external dimensions of experience exert independent influence on flow.

An examination of the variance components reveals that the model accounted for approximately 40% of the variation in variance in mean flow among persons. Note that this is greater than the amount accounted for in the means-as-outcomes model (table 38.1) alone, in which the same person-level variables accounted for approximately 26% of the Level 2 variance. This is likely due to the additional predictive power of the average effects of the Level 1 coefficients in the model. In other words, the average effect of autonomy, success, and other internal dimensions of experience on flow among participants accounted for additional variation in mean flow. The model accounted for 50% of the Level 1 variation in flow within persons. In addition, significant variation among participants remained in the effects of paid work, active leisure activities, autonomy, the interaction of challenge and skill, importance, and success. Even when variation in such effects was significantly predicted with person-level factors, as with active leisure and success, the residual variation among persons remained significant.

Discussion

The analyses presented in this chapter suggest several things about the nature of flow. We begin with some general trends indicated by the analyses, and then move on to more specific implications for practice, research, and theory. Analyzing the data using a multilevel approach reveals that there is substantial variation in flow experiences both within persons and across persons. These findings support the interactional nature of the flow model, highlighting the importance of considering the interplay between person and environment.

Quantitative research on flow has focused almost exclusively on situational factors, examining the internal and, less commonly, the external dimensions of subjective experience. The use of HLM with ESM data allows researchers to test whether the effects of certain features of one's environment (one's location or activity, for example) have differential effects on the experience of flow for different people (e.g., males vs. females). In this way, the analyses can demonstrate the mediating effect of certain person-level factors on the relationship between environmental factors and flow.

Adolescents' experiences within the contexts of family, peers, and school also influence the degree to which they feel flow. Embedded in these contexts, their perceptions of the nature of activities in which they engage exerts a strong influence on the amount of flow experienced. Our comprehensive model (table 38.3) suggests not only that there are measurable contextual and perceptual factors related to the experience of flow, but also that person-level characteristics may enhance or diminish the effects of these factors. For example, not only is the experience of flow on average greater for females than for males, but the positive impact of perceived success on flow is also greater for females. The factors contributing to the flow experience are complex and are best understood through the use of methods that enable exploration of factors operating and interacting at multiple levels.

Perhaps as notable as the personal factors that were significantly associated with flow were those that were not. We found little evidence that the experience of flow is related to one's socioeconomic status (as indicated by parent education), academic achievement, age, or professional or educational aspirations for the future. This suggests that the capacity to experience flow is not available only to those with affluence, intelligence, and ambition, but rather is accessible to individuals from a variety of backgrounds.

While there is substantial variation in flow at both the person and situational levels, our analyses indicate greater variation within persons than among persons: approximately three quarters of the total variation in flow occurs within persons. Taken as a whole, features of one's situated experience—one's activities, mood, company, and perceptions—may influence one's level of flow to a greater degree than personal characteristics; at the very least, there is more variation to explain at this situational level. But when we attempted to account for this variation ourselves, we found that internal dimensions of experience explain much greater variation in flow than do external dimensions of experience. The experience of flow was not strongly related to the day or time and was only minimally associated with one's physical location or companionship. Among the external dimensions of experience, activity explained the most variance in flow. Leisure activities, and active leisure activities in particular, produced the highest levels of flow. By contrast, the level of flow one experiences seems to depend a great deal on subjective elements of experience such as the perception of autonomy, the match of challenges and skills, success, importance, and focus in relation to daily activities.

Implications for Practice

The results of our investigation have several practical applications for human development and education. Before considering these applications, we must reiterate that the analyses we have presented are exploratory and are intended to demonstrate the use of the ESM and HLM methodologies to deepen our understanding of flow. Before firm recommendations for practice can be made, these findings need to be replicated under conditions in which specific hypotheses are being tested. With this qualification in mind, we offer this tentative discussion of possible suggestions from findings.

Young women appear to experience more flow than young men. We did not anticipate this finding and at present can offer few sound explanations for this result. We only note that it is consistent with a series of studies finding females to be more engaged than males at the elementary and high school levels (e.g., Finn & Cox, 1992; Marks, 2000). An interesting caveat in our study is that the positive effect of success on flow is also greater for females than it is for males. This suggests the possibility that the quality of experience for adolescent girls may be more dependent on feedback and perceptions of competence than it is for boys. Therefore, it might be advisable to provide young females with opportunities to engage activities with clear goals and criteria for success, where they would be most likely to earn positive feedback. Since the perception of success generally enhances the experience of flow for both genders, we wish to make clear that males would benefit from such conditions as well.

Our results suggest an important connection between optimal momentary experience and factors related to mental health and psychological well-being. Both global self-esteem and an optimistic orientation toward the future were associated with momentary levels of flow. Because our analyses are correlational, it is impossible to discern the directionality of this relationship, however. Do adolescents who experience more flow become more optimistic and have more positive self-regard as a result? Do optimism and self-esteem make one more likely to experience flow? Is there a bidirectional relationship? Or are these relationships mediated by some third, confounding factor? Evidence from other studies suggests that the link between flow and mental health may not simply be spurious (Massimini, Csikszentmihalyi, & Carli, 1992). In fact, there is some clinical evidence that enhancing opportunities for flow improves overall mental health (Delle Fave & Massimini, 1992; VanDer Poel & Delespaul, 1992). The clinical and therapeutic implications of flow remain an area ripe for future study.

Findings regarding the external dimensions of experience could have important implications for the promotion of flow among adolescents. Though companionship does not explain a lot of the variation in flow, the results indicate that adolescents experience more flow when with peers than with adults. We believe this result may be confounded with the experience of less flow while in school, and particularly in classrooms, where students are likely to report being in the presence of adults and classmates, but not necessarily peers or chosen friends. By contrast, adolescents are more likely to be with peers during leisure activities, when flow is relatively high. While the effect of being with peers and adults is difficult to separate neatly, it was relatively clear that adolescents report greater flow when in the presence of others than when alone. During adolescence, the presence of others may provide a structure to experience that is necessary for flow. Other researchers (Csikszentmihalyi & Larson, 1984) have similarly found that solitude generally produces negative states like worry and anxiety among adolescents. Providing opportunities for adolescents to interact in productive ways with peers and adults appears to make flow more likely. With the exception of a small percentage of talented youth (e.g., Csikszentmihalyi et al., 1993), only after adolescence may many individuals become increasingly able to structure their attention in order to experience flow while alone.

Adolescents report the greatest level of flow in the pursuit of active leisure. This finding is consistent with previous research (see Nakamura & Csikszentmihalyi, 2002, for a review). It is in these types of activities that the conditions for flow are most salient: Often the task at hand is freely chosen and is well matched to an individual's skill. Furthermore, the goals of the activity tend to be well defined, and feedback in reaching these goals is clear. Thus, to promote flow it is strongly recommended to encourage adolescents to become involved in hobbies, exercise, extracurricular activities, and other active leisure activities rather than spending time in more passive free-time activities like watching television and hanging out. Active leisure activities providing the opportunity for initiative, as opposed to passive leisure, are more likely to occur in the context of organized, voluntary youth programs such as afterschool programs and organized sports (Eccles & Gootman, 2002).

Troubling for the field of education is the finding that students rarely experience flow in school. Adolescents spend considerable amounts of time in school, and school is ideally a place where children and adolescents may identify interests and passions that will lead to meaningful and productive careers. The fact that so little flow occurs in school suggests that this potential is not being harnessed in formal educational settings. Previous ESM studies of high school classrooms have shown that students become particularly disengaged when learning is relatively passive, as during lecture and when watching TV; students become relatively more engaged when involved in individual or group activities (e.g., Shernoff, Csikszentmihalyi, Schneider, & Shernoff, 2003). Consistent with these studies, our results show that when students are in nonacademic classes, such as art, vocational education, and computer science, they experience some of the highest levels of flow. It is interesting to reflect on the fact that one of the most flow-enriched settings—nonacademic classes—exists in the same setting and occurs among the same students as one of the most flow-impoverished settings—academic classes. Nonacademic classes tend to employ more active instructional formats and thereby provide students greater autonomy, interest, and a better match of challenges for their skills. Our findings suggest that one hope for facilitating more flow in schools would be for academic classes to restructure activities in a way that allows more room for autonomy and interest. While such a conversion may sound simple, our study suggests that multiple conditions are operating simultaneously when flow is experienced; no doubt application to the classroom is no exception. To more fully understand flow, researchers and practitioners need to focus on the multiple conditions from which the flow experience may emerge.

Implications for Research Methodology

Several implications for methodology in flow and ESM research emerge from this study. First, it may be useful to distinguish between the experience of flow and conditions for flow when conceptualizing and operationalizing the measure of flow. This distinction, in turn, clarifies the potential relationship between flow as the dependent measure and the influences on flow as independent variables.

Most of the methodological implications stem from the use of multilevel models in the analysis of ESM data, which presents several advantages. Previous analytical approaches chose between analyzing data at either the beep (i.e., response) level or the person level. Studies at the beep level often utilized individually normed z scores, which has the effect of squeezing the individual variation out of the data. Studies at the person level aggregated data across individuals and, in the process, eliminated the rich within-person variation unique to ESM data. By partitioning the variance into within-persons and between-persons components, multilevel models allow researchers to understand effects that occur at both levels simultaneously, rendering both individually normed z scores and cross-subject aggregation unnecessary. Furthermore, multilevel models allow the investigator to examine how within-persons effects may vary randomly across participants, as well as to predict those random effects by individual-level factors.

There are several implications of using multilevel models for future studies of flow. This approach enables researchers to examine measures of the same construct at two levels of analysis. For example, an inventory measuring participants' overall frequency in flow as a Level 2 predictor could complement ESM measures of momentary flow. The inclusion of both momentary and person-level measures of other psychological factors, such as self-esteem, would also be possible in the same study. This would tease out momentary from individual influences on a given outcome. By using HLM in its three-level application, researchers can separate and examine school or community influences using ESM data of individuals who are nested within a number of schools or communities (as demonstrated in Shernoff, 2001). Multilevel models also allow us to examine change over time when using longitudinal data (see Raudenbush & Bryk, 2002), linking momentary experience to long-term developmental outcomes. Despite the variety of potential advantages of multilevel models, we wish to make clear that their use is far from a panacea for understanding many types of research questions. To obtain a deeper understanding of various psychological and social phenomena, or to validate results from multiple sources, mixed methods including qualitative interviews or observations are no less important.

Theoretical Implications

Results of this study have several implications for flow theory. First, flow may be appropriately conceptualized as it is most frequently described: in terms of the subjective experience of deep concentration, enjoyment, interest, involvement, control, and distortion of time.[11] These dimensions may be appropriately separated from the conditions most likely to facilitate flow experiences, which may be further classified into both external and internal dimensions of experience. Our findings with respect to the internal dimensions largely validate flow theory as developed in the past several decades. That is, flow experiences are highly associated with the perception of autonomously chosen activities, high challenges well matched to skills, clear and important goals, feedback with respect to success of achieving goals, and undivided attention. The fact that these factors possess the greatest predictive power of those evaluated in this study lends support to the theory in its current state of development. Our study potentially builds on the theory as well, by suggesting that external dimensions of experience can also be important influences on flow experiences, including time and day, location, companionship, and, most notably, the particular type of activity in which one is engaged. Furthermore, there appear to be significant individual differences in the average experience of flow, as well as in the effects of both perceptual and contextual conditions on momentary experiences of flow.

Limitations

Readers may bear in mind several limitations of the study. First, as in most ESM studies, it relied on self-report data, which is ideal for studying adolescents' subjective experience but vulnerable to problems with memory, hasty completion, exaggeration, and falsification. Second, some of the results may have been influenced by a response bias, particularly if those who responded were somehow different from those who did not. For example, the gender and ethnic differences may have been affected by the underrepresentation of males and Latinos in the sample. Further limitations already discussed relate to the exploratory and correlational nature of the study.

Implications for Positive Psychology

We hope that this study may make a modest theoretical and methodological contribution to the broader field of positive psychology. Flow experiences enhance the quality of life; therefore, understanding the conditions that maximize its likelihood may take us one step closer to understanding the pathways to a good life characterized by psychological well-being. Focusing on the factors that influence the development of the autotelic personality (or persons particularly adept at finding flow) remains an important field for future study, as evidenced by the fact that much of the person-level variation in flow has yet to be explained empirically. Nevertheless, the finding that roughly three quarters of the variation in flow within individuals is due to moving from one situation to another also suggests that considerable attention in the study of flow (and perhaps the study of the good life in general) be spent on understanding situational factors: those features of activities and settings embedded into the structure of experiences composing daily life. Finally, positive psychology has been understandably critiqued for identifying adult constructions of happiness and fulfillment while neglecting the developmental and contextual pathways for achieving them (e.g., Cowen & Kilmer, 2002). Therefore, more studies striving for a full examination of conditions providing opportunities for increasing psychological health in childhood and adolescence are essential to developing a more unified vision of positive psychology.

Acknowledgments The authors wish to thank Dan Bolt for his helpful comments on this manuscript.

Notes

1. Interview studies suggest that perceived alteration of time is also characteristic of flow, but it is difficult to assess this element with ESM.

2. By definition, instances of flow simultaneously pull together frequently uncorrelated aspects of experience (e.g., concentration and enjoyment); therefore, we would not necessarily expect this measure to yield a high level of reliability.

3. These particular day and time distinctions were made because they capture significant shifts in adolescents' physical location and activities and because exploratory analyses indicated corresponding shifts in students' experience of flow.

4. Assessing the effects of companionship is difficult to achieve with a high degree of confidence because very often adolescents are with people who fall into a variety of different categories. For example, adolescents are very often in the same room as parents and friends. Thus, companionship distinctions are somewhat crude.

5. A further implication of this analysis is that it specifies the total amount of variation to be explained at both levels. The variance component in subsequent models with predictors indicates the *residual variance*, or variance left unexplained.

6. Correlations between all independent variables in the model were low enough to suggest that multicolinearity was not a problem. Hence, all variables were included in the model.

7. While Raudenbush and Bryk (2002) demonstrated "variance explained" as the reduction in residual variance after including predictors compared to a fully unconditional model, we wish to acknowledge that several experts have offered alternative formulas to compute variance explained (e.g., Hox, 2002; Snijders & Bosker, 1999).

8. No random effects are significant with the exception of the slope for school hours on weekdays ($u_1 = 0.31$, $p < 0.05$). This indicates that while the effect of flow does not generally vary among participants at particular times of day, there is significant between-person variation during school hours.

9. Correlations between all independent variables in the model were low enough to suggest that colinearity was not a problem. Hence, all variables were included in the model.

10. To avoid overspecification of the model, some coefficients were modeled as fixed (not varying among participants) rather than random.

We fixed variables for which random variation among participants had no meaningful interpretation (e.g., maintenance or other activities), as well those shown not to vary among participants in previous analyses (e.g., schoolwork, focus).

11. We lacked a reliable measure for distortion of time in this study.

References

Adlai-Gail, W. (1994). *Exploring the autotelic personality*. Unpublished doctoral dissertation, University of Chicago.

Cowen, E. L., & Kilmer, R. P. (2002). "Positive psychology": Some plusses and some open issues. *Journal of Community Psychology, 30*, 449–460.

Csikszentmihalyi, M. (1985). Emergent motivation and the evolution of the self. *Advances in Motivation and Achievement, 4*, 93–119.

Csikszentmihalyi, M. (1990). *Flow*. New York: Harper and Row.

Csikszentmihalyi, M. (1996). *Creativity*. New York: HarperCollins.

Csikszentmihalyi, M. (2000). *Beyond boredom and anxiety*. San Francisco: Jossey-Bass. (Original work published 1975)

Csikszentmihalyi, M., & Csikszentmihalyi, I. S. (Eds.). (1988). *Optimal experience*. Cambridge, UK: Cambridge University Press.

Csikszentmihalyi, M., & Larson, R. (1984). *Being adolescent*. New York: Basic Books.

Csikszentmihalyi, M., & Larson, R. (1987). Validity and reliability of the experience-sampling method. *Journal of Nervous and Mental Disease, 175*(9), 525–536.

Csikszentmihalyi, M., Larson, R., & Prescott, S. (1977). The ecology of adolescent activity and experience. *Journal of Youth and Adolescence, 6*, 281–294.

Csikszentmihalyi, M., Rathunde, K., & Whalen, S. (1993). *Talented teenagers*. New York: Cambridge University Press.

Csikszentmihalyi, M., & Schneider, B. (2000). *Becoming adult*. New York: Basic Books.

Delle Fave, A., & Massimini, F. (1988). Modernization and the changing contexts of flow in work and leisure. In M. Csikszentmihalyi & I. S. Csikszentmihalyi (Eds.), *Optimal experience* (pp. 193–213). Cambridge, UK: Cambridge University Press.

Delle Fave, A., & Massimini, F. (1992). The ESM and the measurement of clinical change: A case of anxiety disorder. In M. W. deVries (Ed.), *The experience of psychopathology* (pp. 280–289). Cambridge, UK: Cambridge University Press.

Eccles, J., & Gootman, J. A. (2002). *Community programs to promote youth development.* Washington, DC: National Academy Press.

Finn, J. D., & Cox, D. (1992). Participation and withdrawal among fourth-grade pupils. *American Educational Research Journal, 29,* 141–162.

Fredricks, J. A., Blumenfeld, P. C., & Paris, A. H. (2004). School engagement: Potential of the concept, state of the evidence. *Review of Educational Research, 74,* 59–109.

Hektner, J. (1996). *Exploring optimal personality development: A longitudinal study of adolescents.* Unpublished doctoral dissertation, University of Chicago.

Hektner, J. M., Schmidt, J. A., & Csikszentmihalyi, M. (2007). *Experience sampling method: Measuring the quality of everyday life.* Thousand Oaks, CA: Sage.

Hox, J. (2002). *Multilevel analysis: Techniques and applications.* Mahwah, NJ: Erlbaum.

Jackson, S. (1995). Factors influencing the occurrence of flow state in elite athletes. *Journal of Applied Sport Psychology, 7,* 138–166.

Jackson, S. (1996). Toward a conceptual understanding of the flow experience in elite athletes. *Research Quarterly for Exercise and Sport, 67,* 76–90.

Jackson, S., & Marsh, H. W. (1996). Development and validation of a scale to measure optimal experience: The flow state scale. *Journal of Sport and Exercise Psychology, 18,* 17–35.

LeFevre, J. (1988). Flow and the quality of experience during work and leisure. In M. Csikszentmihalyi & I. S. Csikszentmihalyi (Eds.), *Optimal experience* (pp. 307–326). Cambridge, UK: Cambridge University Press.

Logan, R. (1985). The "flow experience" in solitary ordeals. *Journal of Humanistic Psychology, 25,* 79–89.

Magnusson, D., & Stattin, H. (1998). Person-context interaction theories. In R. M. Lerner (Ed.), *Handbook of child psychology* (Vol. 1, pp. 685–759). New York: Wiley.

Marks, H. M. (2000). Student engagement in instructional activity: Patterns in the elementary, middle and high school years. *American Educational Research Journal, 37,* 153–184.

Massimini, F., & Carli, M. (1988). The systematic assessment of flow in daily experience. In M. Csikszentmihalyi & I. S. Csikszentmihalyi (Eds.), *Optimal experience* (pp. 266–287). Cambridge, UK: Cambridge University Press.

Massimini, F., Csikszentmihalyi, M., & Carli, M. (1992). The monitoring of optimal experience: A tool for psychiatric rehabilitation. In M. W. deVries (Ed.), *The experience of psychopathology* (pp. 270–279). Cambridge, UK: Cambridge University Press.

Mayers, P. (1978). *Flow in adolescence and its relation to school experience.* Unpublished doctoral dissertation, University of Chicago.

Moneta, G., & Csikszentmihalyi, M. (1996). The effect of perceived challenges and skills on the quality of subjective experience. *Journal of Personality, 64,* 275–310.

Nakamura, J., & Csikszentmihalyi, M. (2002). The concept of flow. In C. R. Snyder & S. J. Lopez (Eds.), *Handbook of positive psychology,* pp. 89–105. New York: Oxford.

Parks, B. (1996). *"Flow," boredom, and anxiety in therapeutic work.* Unpublished doctoral dissertation, University of Chicago.

Perry, S. K. (1999). *Writing in flow.* Cincinnati, OH: Writer's Digest Books.

Rathunde, K. (1996). Family context and talented adolescents' optimal experience in school–related activities. *Journal of Research on Adolescence, 6,* 605–628.

Raudenbush, S. W. & Bryk, A.S. (2002). *Hierarchical linear models* (2nd ed.).Thousand Oaks, CA: Sage.

Rosenberg, M. (1965). *Society and the adolescent self-image.* Princeton, NJ: Princeton University Press.

Shernoff, D. J. (2001). *The experience of student engagement in high school classrooms: A phenomenological perspective.* Unpublished doctoral dissertation, University of Chicago.

Shernoff, D. J., Csikszentmihalyi, M., Schneider, B., & Shernoff, E. S. (2003). Student engagement in high school classrooms from the perspective of flow theory. *School Psychology Quarterly, 18*(2), 158–176.

Snijders, T. A. B., & Bosker, R. (1999). *Multilevel analysis: An introduction to basic and advanced multilevel modeling.* Thousand Oaks, CA: Sage.

Van Der Poel, E. G. T., & Delespaul, P. A. E. G. (1992). The applicability of ESM in personalized rehabilitation. In M. W. deVries (Ed.), *The experience of psychopathology* (pp. 290–303). Cambridge, UK: Cambridge University Press.

39

Multilevel Modeling of Social Interactions and Mood in Lonely and Socially Connected Individuals

The MacArthur Social Neuroscience Studies

Louise C. Hawkley, Kristopher J. Preacher,
and John T. Cacioppo

For all the intellectual sophistication and ingenuity of the human species, it is our rudimentary need to belong (Baumeister & Leary, 1995) that motivates much of our behavior and shapes our thoughts and feelings about others. We engage in strategies that facilitate being accepted by others; we cultivate friendships and partnerships; we strive to overcome obstacles that threaten our social bonds; and we suffer when our social relationships are hurting or broken. Ultimately, the success we experience in achieving, negotiating, and maintaining our social relationships helps determine our overall satisfaction with life (Myers, 2000; Myers & Diener, 1995).

Social relationships take shape and substance in social interactions, and the quality of interactions therefore contributes to the impact of social relationships on mood and well-being. In cross-sectional studies, correlations are often observed between mood and interaction type or quality. Moreover, experimental evidence has indicated a bidirectional causal relationship between social interactions and mood. Although experimental manipulations establish the temporal precedence required to infer causality, manipulations of social exchanges or mood are typically low in ecological validity. Experimental constraints on participant choice of interaction partner or setting, for example, are not trivial when we are interested in generalizing reciprocal influences to everyday life. A preferable test of the causal relationship between mood and social exchanges is to examine their reciprocal influence in everyday contexts.

Importantly, permitting individuals to choose when, where, and with whom they interact also allows a realistic evaluation of individual differences in estimates of the relationship between interaction quality and mood. We know that some individuals report dissatisfaction with their social relationships and a feeling of isolation or lack of relational or collective connectedness with friends or groups (Hawkley, Browne, & Cacioppo, 2005). We have begun to learn that potentially adverse health consequences may ensue from these feelings of loneliness and isolation (e.g., Cacioppo et al., 2002; Hawkley, Burleson, Berntson, & Cacioppo, 2003). In marked contrast, very little research has examined how those who are low in feelings of loneliness are protected from these consequences. Studying these socially connected individuals—their cognitions, motives, and interactions—could help us understand what it means to be a successful social being.

In prior research (Hawkley et al., 2003), we found that socially connected individuals reported less negativity and more positivity in feelings about their interaction partners than did their lonely counterparts. Socially connected individuals also reported lower negative affect and higher positive affect over the course of the week than did their less connected counterparts. Several explanations could contribute to these differences in affect and interaction quality. First, the social interactions of socially connected individuals could be objectively different than those of lonely individuals. For example, socially connected individuals may attract or choose the kind of interaction partners that facilitate positive social exchanges, and this could subsequently contribute to higher positive affect and lower negative affect among socially connected than lonely individuals. Second, comparable social interactions may be perceived more positively by socially connected than by lonely individuals. The same perceptual bias may contribute to reported mood differences between socially connected and lonely individuals. Third, socially connected individuals may experience a larger or longer-lasting boost in mood following positive social interactions, or a smaller or shorter-lasting decrement in mood following negative social interactions. This could help to explain why, across a typical week, average positive affect was higher and average negative affect was lower among socially connected than lonely individuals. For each of these explanations, the underlying assumption is that affective aspects of everyday life may contribute to downstream health effects, and more interaction positivity or less negativity could put socially connected individuals at a distinct advantage.

Theoretical Background

Numerous studies have examined the relationship between social interactions and mood, and results suggest a reciprocal causal relationship. For example, in a series of experimental studies, Cunningham (1988a, 1988b) induced mood states and found that a positive mood, relative to a negative mood, stimulated greater interest in social interactions and increased conversation quantity and quality (i.e., self-disclosure). The reverse causal direction has also garnered support, however. In a series of experimental studies, McIntyre and colleagues found that either spontaneous or arranged social interactions increased positive affect relative to affect during a neutral control setting (McIntyre, Watson, Clark, & Cross, 1991; McIntyre, Watson, & Cunningham, 1990). Similarly, when a diary methodology was employed, state positive affect was higher when individuals were socializing (Watson, Clark, McIntyre, & Hamaker, 1992), engaging in physically active social events (Clark & Watson, 1988), interacting with familiar as opposed to relatively unfamiliar partners (Vittengl & Holt, 1998a), and experiencing fun or necessary social interactions (Vittengl & Holt, 1998b). Conversely, negative affect was elevated during arguments and confrontations (Clark & Watson, 1988; Vittengl & Holt, 1998b), interactions marked by the receipt of social support (Vittengl & Holt, 1998b), and interactions with poor communication quality (Vittengl & Holt, 1998a).

Positive and negative affect are largely independent dimensions of mood (Watson, Clark, & Tellegen, 1988) and may be differentially affected by positive and negative qualities of social interactions. In cross-sectional analyses, Rook (2001) found that number of daily positive social exchanges was related to greater daily positive mood but was unrelated to negative mood, whereas number of negative social exchanges was related to dampened positive mood and increased negative mood. Similarly, Finch, Okun, Barrera, Zautra, and Reich (1989) showed that number of positive social ties was associated with well-being, whereas number of negative ties was associated with well-being and psychological distress. More recently, Newsom, Nishishiba, Morgan, and Rook (2003) reported significant correlations between positive and negative social exchanges and both positive and negative affect in both cross-sectional and longitudinal analyses. However, independent of each other, concurrent effects of positive and negative social exchanges were valence-specific. That is, frequency of negative exchanges predicted negative affect and not positive affect when positive exchanges were held constant, and frequency of positive exchanges predicted positive affect and not negative affect when negative exchanges were held constant. On the other hand, longitudinal analyses revealed independent crossover effects: When positive exchanges were held constant, frequency of negative exchanges at baseline predicted both positive and negative affect at follow-up, whereas positive exchanges, independent of negative exchanges, did not predict either positive or negative affect at follow-up.

The foregoing results suggest that inconsistencies in the valence specificity of the effects of social interactions may reflect, at least in part, differing temporal dynamics of positive versus negative exchanges. Vittengl and Holt (1998b) examined these temporal kinetics using time-series analyses of concurrent and time-lagged associations between positive or negative affect and time spent in various types of social interactions. Data consisted of diary reports obtained three times daily for 4 weeks. Positive and negative affect were concurrently associated with qualitatively distinct types of social interactions, but there was no evidence of time-lagged associations within days, possibly because fleeting affective states and infrequent diaries hindered the ability to detect time-lagged associations. On the other hand, the results of longitudinal analyses reported by Newsom et al. (2003) suggest that negative aspects of interactions have an impact on subsequent negative affect, and that these effects may be more long-lasting than the effects of positive aspects of interactions on positive affect.

Our interest is in examining whether degree of loneliness moderates any of these effects linking interaction quality and affect. Prior research indicates that individuals differ in their abilities to benefit from social sources of emotion regulation (reviewed by Mikulincer, Shaver, & Pereg, 2003). Extraverted individuals, for example, are not only more likely to find a willing interaction partner but are also more likely than are shy or introverted individuals to perceive their interactions as positive events (Barrett & Pietromonaco, 1997; Watson et al., 1992). Socially anxious individuals, on the other hand, not only perceive interactions in the natural environment as poorer in quality but also of

greater impact on their mood than do individuals low in social anxiety (Vittengl & Holt, 1998a). Similarly, individuals with less social support show a greater impact of events on next-day mood (Affleck, Tennen, Urrows, & Higgins, 1994).

In our research, we have observed that socially connected individuals perceive their interactions more positively than do less connected individuals (Hawkley et al., 2003). This may dispose them to experience a greater reduction of negative mood or enhancement of positive mood following social interactions than would be true for less connected individuals. Even when interactions have negative aspects, socially connected individuals perceive them less negatively than do less connected individuals (Hawkley et al., 2003), so negative aspects of interactions may have less of an impact on mood in individuals high versus low in social connectedness. In addition, the reciprocal nature of the relationship between affect and interaction quality suggests that the greater positive affect reported by socially connected individuals (Hawkley et al., 2003) may foster better-quality social interactions, thereby perpetuating a cycle of positivity that may be quite resistant to assault in the form of negative interactions. Thus, interaction negativity may have shorter-lasting effects among individuals high versus low in social connectedness.

The Quantitative Approach: Summary of Expectations

A nested repeated-measures design provides a rich source of data permitting the examination of complex questions. We instantiated this design in an experience-sampling study of social isolation and connectedness in young adults (Cacioppo et al., 2000), in which we acquired approximately nine diary entries every day for a week from individuals differing in degree of loneliness. The resulting data structure can be considered hierarchical: Diaries are nested within days, which in turn are nested within individuals. Multilevel modeling (MLM; Goldstein, 1995; Hox, 2002; Kreft & de Leeuw, 1998; Raudenbush & Bryk, 2002; Snijders & Bosker, 1999), also known as hierarchical linear modeling, mixed-effects modeling, and random coefficients modeling, is a technique designed to analyze hierarchically structured data such as these and is the approach we use in this study.

One of the advantages of MLM is that missing data typically do not pose a serious problem; individuals can be measured for different numbers of days, and different days can involve as few or as many measurement occasions as necessary.

In this chapter, we illustrate how MLM has made it possible to examine the following kinds of theoretical questions in incomplete time-series data such as that obtained using an experience-sampling methodology (ESM). For didactic clarity, subsequent MLM analyses will address these questions in the sequence enumerated here.

First, MLM can be used to evaluate the proportion of total variation in a given outcome variable (e.g., affect) that is attributable to variation at a given level of the data hierarchy (e.g., diary, day, or person). Predictors (e.g., loneliness) can then be introduced to explain variation at some of these levels. We expect considerable variability in affect and interaction quality at each level (diary, day, person). Based on our prior work (Hawkley et al., 2003), we hypothesize that loneliness will predict lower levels of positivity and higher levels of negativity in affect and interaction quality.

Second, MLM permits examination of the concurrent relationship between affect and interaction quality in a way that avoids the bias that would result if ordinary linear regression were employed without regard to the hierarchical structure of the data. Based on prior research (Cunningham, 1988a, 1988b; McIntyre et al., 1990, 1991), we expect to find a reciprocal and valence-specific relationship between social interaction quality and affect (i.e., positive interaction quality and positive affect will be mutually predictive, as will negative interaction quality and negative affect). Concurrent interaction quality and affect may also exhibit crossover effects (e.g., Newsom et al., 2003), but prior research has been mixed in this regard.

Third, MLM makes it possible to study intra- and interindividual variability in the concurrent relationship between lower-level variables. Specifically, multilevel modeling permits regression parameters (e.g., slopes) at lower levels to be modeled as dependent variables in regression equations at higher levels. Such effects are termed *cross-level interactions* because they involve variables at higher levels predicting slopes at lower levels. In our case, we study the effects of individual differences in loneliness on the association between interaction quality and affect. We expect that individuals low in loneliness (i.e.,

socially connected individuals) may exhibit more robust positive affect such that negative interaction quality may not have as great an impact on concurrent positive affect as it does among those high in loneliness.

Fourth, MLM can be employed to examine the temporal relationship between variables. Typically, time-series analyses are used to examine time-lagged effects. We introduce a novel alternative means of assessing temporal relationships by testing lagged effects within the context of MLM. Specifically, we use multilevel modeling to examine the lagged effects linking interaction quality and affect. Moreover, by varying the lag between predictor and criterion, we can use the MLM approach to test the duration of the effects of social interaction quality on affect—that is, we can examine the duration as well as the causal direction of effects.

Prior experimental research has shown reciprocal causal effects relating interaction quality and affect (Cunningham, 1988a, 1988b; McIntyre et al., 1990, 1991), and we expect that lagged effects will support this causal structure. Namely, we hypothesize that mood will influence subsequent interaction quality and vice versa. In general, negative exchanges have a greater impact on psychological outcomes than do positive exchanges (a negativity effect; Rook, 1990). The potency of negative exchanges may therefore lengthen the duration of their influence on affect. If this is the case, we expect that negative interaction quality will continue to influence affect when the temporal lag is extended.

Fifth, adding yet another level of complexity, MLM makes it possible to study intra- and interindividual variability in the lagged relationships between lower-level variables. A temporal lag between lower-level variables allows us to ask whether the causal structure linking interpersonal interactions and affect is the same for individuals regardless of degree of loneliness. In addition, we can examine whether loneliness moderates the duration of the effects of interaction quality and affect on each other. If social connectedness facilitates effective emotional regulation, then a given degree of positivity in a social interaction may elicit greater or longer-lasting increases in subsequent positive affect with or without greater or shorter-lasting decreases in subsequent negative affect among individuals low versus high in loneliness. In addition, reciprocal reinforcement between positive interactions and positive affect may lead to more effective buffering of the effects of negative interactions among individuals low as opposed to high in loneliness. Thus, socially connected individuals may recover from negative interactions more quickly than do their lonely counterparts.

Sample and Methods

Over 2,000 students were screened and recruited to represent the lower (total score ≤ 28), middle (total score ≥ 33 and <39), and upper (total score ≥ 46) quintile of scores on the R-UCLA Loneliness Scale (Russell, Peplau, & Cutrona, 1980). The R-UCLA Loneliness Scale consists of 20 items that were originally selected to represent experiences that best distinguished lonely from nonlonely individuals. Examples of these items are "I feel isolated from others"; "I lack companionship"; and "There are people I can turn to." Notably, none of the items refer to the terms *lonely* or *loneliness*. Nevertheless, scores on the R-UCLA Loneliness Scale are highly positively correlated with self-reports of loneliness and inversely correlated with objective measures of social experiences (e.g., amount of time spent alone each day, number of close friends; Russell et al., 1980). Conversely, low scores on the R-UCLA Loneliness Scale represent a high degree of subjective social embeddedness and objective social engagement.

Participants were 135 undergraduate students (83% Caucasian; 7% African American; 7% Asian, Asian American, or Pacific Islander; 3% other or undeclared), equally distributed among the loneliness groups, and males and females were equally represented within each group. Exclusionary criteria have been reported elsewhere (Hawkley et al., 2003). At the time of recruitment, students' mean age was 19.2 ($SD = 1.0$) and they had completed at least one and, on average, 3.2 ($SD = 2.8$) academic quarters; 52% were freshmen, 32% were sophomores, 8% were juniors, and the remaining 8% were seniors or fifth-year students.

We employed ESM (Larson & Csikszentmihalyi, 1983) to collect information about psychosocial and behavioral states. Participants completed diaries for a total of 7 consecutive days. A programmable watch provided to participants was programmed to beep at nine random times between 9:30 a.m. and 12:00 midnight each day, subject to the constraint that the interbeep interval was between 45 and 120 minutes. The 134 participants who completed the 7-day diary study provided 6,772 of a possible 8,442 diaries, representing an 80% return rate. An analysis of covariance revealed that the rate of diary returns did not differ as a function of loneliness, $F(1, 131) = 2.512$, $p = .115$, or gender, $F(1, 131) = 0.539$, $p = .464$.

Diary format consisted primarily of closed-ended questions (multiple options) requiring participants to check the appropriate response. If participants were interacting with someone when they were beeped, they were asked to respond to 16 adjectives, 8 positive and 8 negative (scaled from $1 = not$ at all to $5 = very$), to rate the social interaction. Responses to positive aspects of interactions (i.e., comfortable, intimate, involved, sharing, uninhibited, supported, affectionate, understood) were averaged to create an interaction positivity score (Cronbach's alpha $= 0.867$), and responses to negative aspects of interactions (i.e., cautious, disconnected, conflicted, closed off, distant, phony, dishonest, distrustful) were averaged to create an interaction negativity score (Cronbach's alpha $= 0.886$). Positive and negative affect were calculated by summing responses to the 10 positive and 10 negative items of the Positive and Negative Affect Schedule (PANAS; Watson et al., 1988).

Data Analytic Strategy

In this study, we employed multilevel modeling to capitalize on the hierarchical structure of our repeated measures diary data. As we alluded to earlier, some of the advantages associated with MLM include the fact that lower-level coefficients can be modeled as dependent variables, and missing data typically do not pose a serious problem. In addition, analysis of hierarchical data by MLM avoids problems of (a) severe parameter bias encountered when data are analyzed without regard to nested structure, as with ordinary linear regression; and (b) unclear interpretation and low power attendant upon unnecessarily aggregating Level 1 data to higher levels (Goldstein, 1995). The assumptions necessary for the use of MLM are largely the same as those necessary for ordinary least squares: normality and independence of residuals and random effects, within-unit residual homoscedasticity, and linearity (see Snijders & Bosker, 1999, for a discussion of methods to check these assumptions). Given the nature of the hypotheses and the hierarchical structure of the present data set, MLM was chosen as the most appropriate analytical tool.

Three-Level Models

In MLM, the lowest level of the hierarchy (here the diary level) is commonly denoted Level 1, the next highest as Level 2, and so on. Most applications of MLM involve only two levels, for example, students nested within schools or repeated measures nested within individuals. There is theoretically no limit to the number of levels a multilevel model can contain, but there are often practical and software-related limitations, and few sources discuss MLM with more than two levels. Our data could be organized into the three-level hierarchy depicted in figure 39.1.

The three-level, fully unconditional multilevel model can be represented in terms of Level 1, Level 2, and Level 3 submodels. The Level 1 (diary level) submodel is:

$$Y_{ijk} = \pi_{0jk} + e_{ijk} \qquad e_{ijk} \sim N(0, \sigma^2) \qquad (1)$$

where Y_{ijk} represents the response at diary i on day j for individual k, π_{0jk} represents the mean response on day j for individual k, and e_{ijk} represents the deviation of Y_{ijk} from π_{0jk}.[1] The Level 2 (day-level) model is:

$$\pi_{0jk} = \beta_{00k} + r_{0jk} \qquad r_{0jk} \sim N(0, \tau_\pi) \qquad (2)$$

where β_{00k} represents the mean response for individual k and r_{0jk} represents the deviation of π_{0jk} from β_{00k}, or the random effect for day j. The Level 3 (person-level) model is:

$$\beta_{00k} = \gamma_{000} + u_{00k} \qquad u_{00k} \sim N(0, \tau_\beta) \qquad (3)$$

where γ_{000} represents the grand mean and u_{00k} represents the deviation of β_{00k} from γ_{000}. Combining Equations 1, 2, and 3 yields the following composite model:

$$Y_{ijk} = \gamma_{000} + u_{00k} + r_{0jk} + e_{ijk} \qquad (4)$$

which explicitly models Y_{ijk} as the sum of the grand mean and deviations at Level 3, Level 2, and Level 1, respectively.

Predictor variables may be entered at any level in order to explain variability in random effects at lower levels. For example, if a day-level variable is entered to explain variation in the Level 1 intercept, Equation 2 becomes:

$$\pi_{0jk} = \beta_{00k} + \beta_{01k}(w_{jk}) + r_{0jk} \qquad (5)$$

In this equation, the predictor w is hypothesized to predict intraindividual (intraday or interdiary) variability in the outcome. The slope parameter describing the expected increase in π_{0jk} given a unit change in w is here specified as a *fixed effect*, meaning that it is not permitted to vary across individuals or days. Consequently,

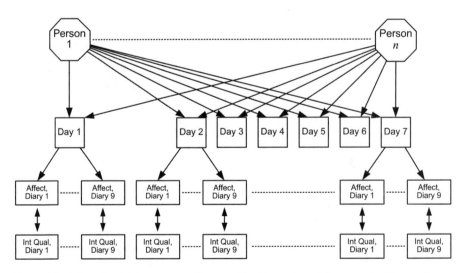

Figure 39.1 Three-level data structure. Data used in this study could be organized into a three-level hierarchy. Level 1 (diary level) consists of repeated measures of affect (positive and negative) and interaction quality (positive and negative) nested within days (Level 2), which in turn are nested within individuals (Level 3).

the equation for β_{01k} may be represented as:

$$\beta_{01k} = \gamma_{010} \qquad (6)$$

The full, conditional, three-level model would now be:

$$Y_{ijk} = \gamma_{000} + \gamma_{010}(w_{jk}) + u_{00k} + r_{0jk} + e_{ijk} \qquad (7)$$

Models such as that in Equation 7 represent only the tip of the iceberg in terms of the potential of MLM to test complex hypotheses about the magnitude and direction of effects in hierarchically structured data sets with more than two levels. Multilevel models may be extended to include nonlinear effects, more than three levels, and multivariate outcomes. Covariates can be entered into the model at any level, and complex error distributions and covariance structures may be specified. In addition, predictors may sometimes be centered (i.e., recast as deviations from their means) in order to improve the stability of estimation and enhance interpretability.[2] For more involved discussions of the possibilities and limitations of MLM, see chapter 30, this volume or any introductory text on the subject (e.g., Hox, 2002; Kreft & de Leeuw, 1998; Raudenbush & Bryk, 2002; Snijders & Bosker, 1999).

Software

Facilities for specifying and estimating multilevel models are included in several statistical software packages, including newer versions of LISREL (8.54) and SPSS (12.0) and dedicated MLM packages such as HLM (Bryk, Raudenbush, Cheong, & Congdon, 2000) and MLwiN (Rasbash et al., 2000). We chose LISREL 8.54 (Jöreskog & Sörbom, 1996) for its speed and ease of use. Complex multilevel models may be easily specified in newer versions of LISREL using PRELIS syntax (du Toit & du Toit,

2001; Jöreskog, Sörbom, du Toit, & du Toit, 1999), examples of which we include in the appendix.

Results and Discussion

Null Models and Other Preliminaries

As a first step, it is often useful to estimate a *null model*. A null model, like Equation 4 above, models the response variable as a function of an intercept and random effects at each level:

$$Y_{ijk} = \gamma_{000} + u_{00k} + r_{0jk} + e_{ijk} \qquad (8)$$

Estimation of a null model allows the partitioning of variance into components at Levels 1, 2, and 3. We estimated a series of null models treating diary-level positive and negative affect (hereafter abbreviated posaff and negaff) and positive and negative interaction quality (hereafter abbreviated posint and negint) as the outcomes of interest. The equation corresponding to the first of these models is:

$$posaff_{ijk} = \gamma_{000} + u_{00k} + r_{0jk} + e_{ijk} \qquad (9)$$

The null model equations for negaff, posint, and negint have identical forms. LISREL provides maximum likelihood point estimates, standard errors, t values, and p values for the random intercept term (γ_{000}) and the Level 1, Level 2, and Level 3 variances (σ^2, τ_π, and τ_β, respectively).[3] Null model results are reported in table 39.1, with LISREL syntax for the posaff model in the appendix. Here and following, values for positive and negative interaction quality were multiplied by 10 to render similar scaling of the affect and interaction quality values. This increased the number of decimal places we could display in parameter estimates involving the

TABLE 39.1 Parameter Estimates for Null Models

	Dependent Variable			
	posaff	negaff	posint*	negint*
$\hat{\gamma}_{000}$	14.284 (0.511)	3.765 (0.307)	30.531 (0.503)	13.821 (0.323)
$\hat{\sigma}^2$	43.829 (0.813)	14.844 (0.276)	54.542 (1.528)	19.225 (0.539)
$\hat{\tau}_\pi$	7.581 (0.705)	3.014 (0.262)	11.486 (1.437)	3.316 (0.465)
$\hat{\tau}_\beta$	32.524 (4.265)	11.729 (1.541)	29.158 (4.147)	12.349 (1.702)

Note: Numbers in parentheses are standard errors.

*Values for positive and negative interaction quality were multiplied by 10, so in original measurement units, the grand mean for posint is 3.053 and the grand mean for negint is 1.382.

interaction quality variables, but does not alter the statistical significance of any reported effects.

In the null model, the point estimate of the intercept is an unconditional estimate of the sample mean, which in all four cases is significantly different from zero ($p < .00001$). The fact that the Level 1, Level 2, and Level 3 variances also are all significantly different from zero implies that there exists variation to be potentially explained in all four outcome variables by adding predictor variables to the model. Variation is additive across levels, such that the variation which exists at a given level in a given outcome variable can be expressed as a proportion of the total variation by the intraclass correlation. For example, the proportions of variability in negaff that exist at the diary, day, and person levels are, respectively:

$$\rho_{diary} = \frac{\sigma^2}{\sigma^2 + \tau_\pi + \tau_\beta}$$
$$= \frac{14.844}{14.844 + 3.014 + 11.729} = 0.502 \quad (10)$$

$$\rho_{day} = \frac{\tau_\pi}{\sigma^2 + \tau_\pi + \tau_\beta}$$
$$= \frac{3.014}{14.844 + 3.014 + 11.729} = 0.102 \quad (11)$$

$$\rho_{person} = \frac{\tau_\beta}{\sigma^2 + \tau_\pi + \tau_\beta}$$
$$= \frac{11.729}{14.844 + 3.014 + 11.729} = 0.396 \quad (12)$$

Most of the explainable variation in all four outcome variables occurs at Level 1, or across diaries (within days and persons).

After specifying null models, the next step in a multilevel analysis is usually to introduce predictor variables. Of primary interest to us was the ability of loneliness to predict variability in affect and interaction quality. Loneliness was measured only once per individual, making it a Level 3 predictor. The success of loneliness in predicting affect and interaction quality can be gauged by noting the magnitude of the regression coefficient associated with loneliness, its significance, and any reduction in Level 1, Level 2, or Level 3 variation when compared to the null model. A typical equation for this type of model is:

$$posaff_{ijk} = \gamma_{000} + \gamma_{001}(loneliness_k)$$
$$+ u_{00k} + r_{0jk} + e_{ijk} \quad (13)$$

Results of fitting this model to data for all four outcome measures are reported in table 39.2. The γ_{001} coefficient in each case represents the slope of the dependent variable regressed on loneliness.

Individual differences in loneliness explain variability in all four outcome variables, but comparison of the variance estimates in tables 39.1 and 39.2 reveals that the explanation occurred mostly at Level 3 (the person level). This means that loneliness does not tend to account for fluctuations in affect or interaction quality observed across diaries or across days within persons. In line with expectations, however, loneliness predicted decreased positivity and increased negativity in affect and interaction quality. Referring to the coefficients in table 39.2, a one-unit increase in loneliness produced an increase in negative affect of 0.120 and a decrease in positive affect of 0.130. Values for posint and negint were multiplied by 10 before analysis, so we can say that a 10-unit increase in loneliness produced a 0.151 increase in interaction negativity and a 0.140 decrease in interaction positivity.

Conversely, in mood and social interactions, experiential domains that arguably are the primary determinants of overall well-being, social connectedness provides a distinct advantage. Specifically, social connectedness predicts higher positive and lower negative affect, and more positive and less negative qualities in social interactions. Not surprisingly, life is

TABLE 39.2 Parameter Estimates for Models With Loneliness as a Predictor

	Dependent Variable			
	posaff	negaff	posint	negint
$\hat{\gamma}_{001}$	−0.130 (0.050)	0.120 (0.029)	−0.140 (0.049)	0.151(0.029)
$\hat{\sigma}^2$	43.828 (0.813)	14.845 (0.276)	54.527 (1.528)	19.219 (0.539)
$\hat{\tau}_\pi$	7.581 (0.705)	3.015 (0.262)	11.515 (1.438)	3.349 (0.467)
$\hat{\tau}_\beta$	30.868 (4.062)	10.272 (1.362)	27.251 (3.913)	9.918 (1.404)

Note: Numbers in parentheses are standard errors.

experienced more positively by socially connected individuals.

Concurrent Effects

As has been noted in prior research (Vittengl & Holt, 1998a, 1998b; Watson et al., 1992), a second key question involves whether affect and interaction quality are concurrently related. In other words, does positive or negative affect predict the positivity or negativity of the current interaction (or vice versa)? To examine this possibility, we specified a series of eight models with posint and negint serving as Level 1 predictors of concurrent affect and posaff and negaff serving as Level 1 predictors of interaction quality. The general form of the equation is:

$$posaff_{ijk} = \pi_{0jk} + \pi_{1jk}(posint_{ijk}) + e_{ijk}$$
$$\pi_{0jk} = \beta_{00k} + r_{0jk}$$
$$\beta_{00k} = \gamma_{000} + u_{00k} \tag{14}$$
$$\pi_{1jk} = \beta_{10k}$$
$$\beta_{10k} = \gamma_{100}$$

The combined equation is thus:

$$posaff_{ijk} = \gamma_{000} + \gamma_{100}(posint_{ijk}) + u_{00k} + r_{0jk} + e_{ijk} \tag{15}$$

Code for this model can be found in the appendix. Results are reported in table 39.3, with point estimates, standard errors, and p values associated with $\hat{\gamma}_{100}$.

In every case, there is a strong concurrent relationship between affect and interaction quality. The direction of these effects was as expected: positive interaction quality predicted higher positive and lower negative affect; negative interaction quality predicted lower positive and higher negative affect. The fact that these concurrent relationships were not valence specific is consistent with valence crossover effects

also reported by Newsom et al. (2003). Moreover, we found reciprocal crossover effects: positive affect predicted higher positive and lower negative interaction quality; negative affect predicted lower positive and higher negative interaction quality.

Intra- and Interindividual Variability in Concurrent Relationships

A complex question that MLM allows us to ask is if the Level 1 slopes relating concurrent affect and interaction quality vary at the day level (within persons) or the person level (across persons). If significant variability is observed at either or both levels, then a case can be made for attempting to predict that variability with Level 2 or Level 3 predictor variables. We adopted the strategy of specifying random effects at both the day and person levels, followed by constraining nonsignificant random effects. The Level 2 variance of the random effect associated with the slope of the predictor will be represented by τ_2 and the Level 3 variance by τ_3. First, we allowed the Level 1 slopes to vary freely across both days and persons. The general form of the equation is:

$$posaff_{ijk} = \pi_{0jk} + \pi_{1jk}(posint_{ijk}) + e_{ijk}$$
$$\pi_{0jk} = \beta_{00k} + r_{0jk}$$
$$\beta_{00k} = \gamma_{000} + u_{00k} \tag{16}$$
$$\pi_{1jk} = \beta_{10k} + r_{1jk}$$
$$\beta_{10k} = \gamma_{100} + u_{10k}$$

The combined equation is:

$$posaff_{ijk} = \gamma_{000} + (\gamma_{100} + r_{1jk} + u_{10k})posint_{ijk} + u_{00k} + r_{0jk} + e_{ijk} \tag{17}$$

Code for this model can be found in the appendix. Results are reported in table 39.4, with point estimates, standard errors, and p values.

TABLE 39.3 Parameter Estimates for Concurrent Fixed-Effects Models

Outcome	Predictor	Effect
posaff	posint	$\hat{\gamma}_{100} = 0.284$ (0.014) $p < .00001$
posaff	negint	$\hat{\gamma}_{100} = -0.134$ (0.025) $p < .00001$
negaff	posint	$\hat{\gamma}_{100} = -0.072$ (0.009) $p < .00001$
negaff	negint	$\hat{\gamma}_{100} = 0.316$ (0.015) $p < .00001$
posint	posaff	$\hat{\gamma}_{100} = 0.391$ (0.019) $p < .00001$
posint	negaff	$\hat{\gamma}_{100} = -0.244$ (0.032) $p < .00001$
negint	posaff	$\hat{\gamma}_{100} = -0.062$ (0.012) $p < .00001$
negint	negaff	$\hat{\gamma}_{100} = 0.375$ (0.018) $p < .00001$

TABLE 39.4 Parameter Estimates for Concurrent Random Effects at the Day and Person Levels

Outcome	Predictor	Effect
posaff	posint	$\hat{\tau}_2 = 0.022$ (0.008) $p = .004$ $\hat{\tau}_3 = 0.022$ (0.007) $p = .001$
posaff	negint	$\hat{\tau}_2 = 0.014$ (0.014) $p = .324$ $\hat{\tau}_3 = 0.041$ (0.016) $p = .010$
negaff	posint	$\hat{\tau}_2 = 0.014$ (0.004) $p < .0001$ $\hat{\tau}_3 = 0.011$ (0.003) $p = .001$
negaff	negint	$\hat{\tau}_2 = 0.062$ (0.013) $p < .00001$ $\hat{\tau}_3 = 0.016$ (0.009) $p = .084$
posint	posaff	$\hat{\tau}_2 = 0.058$ (0.014) $p < .0001$ $\hat{\tau}_3 = 0.011$ (0.009) $p = .221$
posint	negaff	$\hat{\tau}_2 = 0.103$ (0.036) $p = .004$ $\hat{\tau}_3 = 0.175$ (0.048) $p < .001$
negint	posaff	$\hat{\tau}_2 = 0.010$ (0.004) $p = .015$ $\hat{\tau}_3 = 0.007$ (0.003) $p = .040$
negint	negaff	$\hat{\tau}_2 = 0.146$ (0.028) $p < .00001$ $\hat{\tau}_3 = 0.049$ (0.021) $p = .020$

For every pairing of predictor and outcome reported in table 39.4, slopes vary randomly at either the day level or the person level, sometimes both. But do interindividual differences in loneliness explain some of these intra- and interindividual differences in slopes? To address this question, we introduced loneliness as a Level 3 predictor of slopes. Loneliness was not centered because grand-mean centering would not alter the effect of interest, and it is unclear how group-mean centering should be approached or how the results should be interpreted. The full three-level combined equation incorporating a cross-level interaction is (e.g.):

$$posaff_{ijk} = \gamma_{000} + (\gamma_{100} + r_{1jk} + u_{10k})(posint_{ijk})$$
$$+ \gamma_{001}(loneliness_{jk})$$
$$+ \gamma_{101}(loneliness_{jk} \times posint_{ijk})$$
$$+ u_{00k} + r_{0jk} + e_{ijk} \tag{18}$$

Code for this model can be found in the appendix. However, no cross-level interaction effects were found to be significant. That is, the strength of the relationship between affect and concurrent interaction quality did not differ as a function of degree of social connectedness.

Lagged Effects

The results reported thus far do not address the temporal separation (lag) required for establishing causality. Here we depart from assessing purely concurrent effects, and instead focus on examining the relationship between affect and interaction quality when these measures are separated in time. Lagging predictor variables permits us to investigate whether, for example, negative interaction quality at diary $t - 1$ influences affect at time t. Using lagged predictors also allows us to make stronger claims about causality than have heretofore been possible. Granted, the lag intervals are not constant, but diaries tended to be around 92.5 ($SD = 9.5$) minutes apart. The general form of the combined equation is, for example:

$$posaff_{ijk,t} = \gamma_{000} + u_{00k} + r_{0jk}$$
$$+ \gamma_{100}(posint_{ijk,t-1}) + e_{ijk} \tag{19}$$

The LISREL syntax for this model is the same as for the concurrent fixed-effects model; the data are lagged within-day before submitting them to analysis in LISREL. Results are reported in table 39.5, with point estimates, standard errors, and p values associated with $\hat{\gamma}_{100}$.

In virtually every case, there is a strong lagged relationship between affect and interaction quality. These effects were in the expected direction and were not valence-specific. Positive interaction quality at time $t - 1$ positively predicted positive affect and negatively predicted negative affect at the subsequent time point (i.e., about 90 minutes later), and negative interaction quality at time $t - 1$ positively predicted negative affect and negatively predicted positive affect at the subsequent time point. These results suggest that the crossover effects of interaction quality on positive and negative aspects of mood are not limited to concurrent effects, but extend to influence mood as much as 90 minutes later.

The reverse causal direction linking affect and interaction quality was also supported, with only one exception. Negative affect at time $t - 1$ predicted less positivity and more negativity in interactions at the subsequent time point, and positive affect at one time point predicted more positivity (but not less negativity) in interactions at the subsequent time point. Thus, in general, mood had relatively persistent effects on interaction quality.

The strong lagged effects relating interaction quality and affect suggest that their reciprocal influence may last even longer than 90 minutes. We investigated the duration of these effects by lengthening the temporal separation between predictor and outcome. We specified eight

TABLE 39.5 Parameter Estimates for Lag 1 Fixed-Effects Models

Outcome	Predictor	Effect
$posaff_t$	$posint_{t-1}$	$\hat{\gamma}_{100} = 0.079\ (0.017)\ p < .00001$
$posaff_t$	$negint_{t-1}$	$\hat{\gamma}_{100} = -0.058\ (0.028)\ p = .042$
$negaff_t$	$posint_{t-1}$	$\hat{\gamma}_{100} = -0.029\ (0.010)\ p = .003$
$negaff_t$	$negint_{t-1}$	$\hat{\gamma}_{100} = 0.110\ (0.017)\ p < .00001$
$posint_t$	$posaff_{t-1}$	$\hat{\gamma}_{100} = 0.108\ (0.020)\ p < .00001$
$posint_t$	$negaff_{t-1}$	$\hat{\gamma}_{100} = -0.066\ (0.035)\ p = .058$
$negint_t$	$posaff_{t-1}$	$\hat{\gamma}_{100} = 0.002\ (0.012)\ p = .880$
$negint_t$	$negaff_{t-1}$	$\hat{\gamma}_{100} = 0.104\ (0.020)\ p < .00001$

models similar to those above, but employed a lag of two diaries. Results are reported in table 39.6, with point estimates, standard errors, and p values associated with $\hat{\gamma}_{100}$.

These results indicate that some effects are still in evidence even after three diary sessions. For example, negative interaction quality continued to precipitate negative affect even two lags later. Positive interaction quality failed to exhibit effects of comparable duration, in keeping with prior research documenting the greater potency of negative interaction quality in influencing affect (Rook, 1990; see also Newsom et al., 2003). Notably, mood exhibited significant enduring valence-specific effects on interaction quality even two time points later. That is, positive affect enhanced interaction positivity, and negative affect exacerbated interaction negativity during interactions about 3 hours later.

Predicting Intra- and Interindividual Differences in Lagged Effects

Of primary interest to us was the possibility that intra- or interindividual differences in the slopes relating lagged predictors to outcome variables might be functionally related to loneliness. First, we investigated whether the Lag 1 slopes varied

significantly across days or persons. Results are reported in table 39.7.

Note that two of the Level 2 slope variances (for the effects of $negint_{t-1}$ on $posaff_t$ and $posaff_{t-1}$ on $negint_t$) and one Level 3 slope variance (for the effect of $posint_{t-1}$ on $negaff$) were estimated to have negative values. Such solutions are inadmissible and are usually the result of sampling error. In these cases the variances were not significantly different from zero.

The effect of negative interaction quality at time $t-1$ on negative affect at time t varied significantly across days. We investigated the ability of loneliness to predict this random effect. The combined three-level equation is:

$$negaff_{ijk,t}$$
$$= \gamma_{000} + (\gamma_{100} + r_{1jk} + u_{10k})(negint_{ijk,t-1})$$
$$+ \gamma_{001}(loneliness_{jk})$$
$$+ \gamma_{101}(loneliness_k \times negint_{ijk,t-1})$$
$$+ u_{00k} + r_{0jk} + e_{ijk} \tag{20}$$

Intraindividual variability in slopes was not significantly predicted by individual differences in loneliness, $\hat{\gamma}_{101} = -0.001\ (0.004)$, $p = .891$.

TABLE 39.6 Parameter Estimates for Lag 2 Fixed-Effects Models

Outcome	Predictor	Effect
$posaff_t$	$posint_{t-2}$	$\hat{\gamma}_{100} = 0.019\ (0.019)\ p = .321$
$posaff_t$	$negint_{t-2}$	$\hat{\gamma}_{100} = -0.051\ (0.031)\ p = .104$
$negaff_t$	$posint_{t-2}$	$\hat{\gamma}_{100} = 0.001\ (0.011)\ p = .924$
$negaff_t$	$negint_{t-2}$	$\hat{\gamma}_{100} = 0.054\ (0.019)\ p = .004$
$posint_t$	$posaff_{t-2}$	$\hat{\gamma}_{100} = 0.089\ (0.021)\ p < .0001$
$posint_t$	$negaff_{t-2}$	$\hat{\gamma}_{100} = -0.019\ (0.036)\ p = .606$
$negint_t$	$posaff_{t-2}$	$\hat{\gamma}_{100} = -0.008\ (0.013)\ p = .534$
$negint_t$	$negaff_{t-2}$	$\hat{\gamma}_{100} = 0.056\ (0.021)\ p = .008$

TABLE 39.7 Parameter Estimates for Lag 1 Random Effects at the Day and Person Levels

Outcome	Predictor	Effect
posaff	$posint_{t-1}$	$\hat{\tau}_2 = 0.008\ (0.009)\ p = .378$ $\hat{\tau}_3 = 0.004\ (0.005)\ p = .483$
posaff	$negint_{t-1}$	$\hat{\tau}_2 = -0.011\ (0.017)\ p = .509$ $\hat{\tau}_3 = 0.029\ (0.017)\ p = .083$
negaff	$posint_{t-1}$	$\hat{\tau}_2 = 0.005\ (0.003)\ p = .136$ $\hat{\tau}_3 = -0.003\ (0.002)\ p = .154$
negaff	$negint_{t-1}$	$\hat{\tau}_2 = 0.035\ (0.016)\ p = .024$ $\hat{\tau}_3 = 0.001\ (0.015)\ p = .934$
posint	$posaff_{t-1}$	$\hat{\tau}_2 = 0.007\ (0.010)\ p = .466$ $\hat{\tau}_3 = 0.004\ (0.006)\ p = .568$
posint	$negaff_{t-1}$	$\hat{\tau}_2 = 0.010\ (0.024)\ p = .669$ $\hat{\tau}_3 = 0.072\ (0.028)\ p = .011$
negint	$posaff_{t-1}$	$\hat{\tau}_2 = -0.001\ (0.004)\ p = .725$ $\hat{\tau}_3 = 0.002\ (0.003)\ p = .334$
negint	$negaff_{t-1}$	$\hat{\tau}_2 = 0.007\ (0.032)\ p = .817$ $\hat{\tau}_3 = 0.014\ (0.018)\ p = .435$

In addition, the effect of negative affect at time $t-1$ on positive interaction quality at time t varied significantly across people. We investigated the ability of loneliness to predict this random effect. The combined three-level equation is:

$$
\begin{aligned}
posint_{ijk,t} \\
= \gamma_{000} + (\gamma_{100} + r_{1jk} + u_{10k})(negaff_{ijk,t-1}) \\
+ \gamma_{001}(loneliness_{jk}) \\
+ \gamma_{101}(loneliness_k \times negaff_{ijk,t-1}) \\
+ u_{00k} + r_{0jk} + e_{ijk}
\end{aligned}
\qquad (21)
$$

Intraindividual variability in slopes was not significantly predicted by loneliness, $\hat{\gamma}_{101} = 0.0004$ (0.004), $p = .927$.

Given that there was some evidence for Lag 2 effects (see table 39.6), we were curious to discover whether there existed significant intraindividual variability in day-level or person-level slopes for Lag 2 effects and, if so, whether this variability could be predicted by interindividual differences in loneliness. We examined day-level and person-level random effects of Lag 2 predictors. None of these slopes exhibited significant variance at either the day or person level.

Concluding Remarks

In this study, MLM afforded theoretical tests and insights that would not have been visible from other perspectives. Had we taken an ordinary least squares regression approach, for example, we would not have seen that variance in affect and interaction quality was evident not only across diaries, but also across days and across persons. Specifically, variability in mood and interaction quality associated with momentary circumstances exceeded day-to-day and person-to-person variability in mood and interaction quality. Moreover, MLM enabled us to see that loneliness/social connectedness was more powerful in explaining interindividual variance than momentary or daily variance. This finding provides a first clue that loneliness/social connectedness is characterized to a greater extent by a pervasive enduring influence over the affective experience of everyday circumstances (including social interactions) than by a transitory influence on the experience of momentary circumstances.

Second, we saw that concurrent affect and interaction quality were reciprocally related across valence domains, as has been suggested by prior research (Cunningham, 1988a, 1988b; McIntyre et al., 1990, 1991; Newsom et al., 2003). Importantly, lag analyses revealed potentially causal relationships linking interaction quality and affect: These relationships appeared reciprocal, were in the expected directions, and acted across valence domains. In addition, negative aspects of social interactions had a particularly long-lasting influence on negative affect, consistent with the "negativity effect" reported by other researchers (Rook, 1990; see also Newsom et al., 2003).

What distinguishes these findings from prior research is that we acquired online assessments of the co-occurring positive and negative features of social interactions. This is a significant departure from typical, and frequently retrospective, assessments of the number of individuals with whom participants have generally positive or negative exchanges (e.g., Finch et al., 1989; Rook, 2001), or the frequency with which social exchanges are generally positive or negative (Newsom et al., 2003). Our assessments of interaction quality and affect share method variance, and this may have contributed to the associations we observed among the positive and negative aspects of interaction quality and affect. However, this did not prevent us from evaluating possible explanations for social connectedness/loneliness differences in these outcome variables and their interrelationship.

What might account for generally higher positivity and lower negativity in affect and interaction quality among socially connected individuals? Our data support the notion that socially connected individuals differ from lonely individuals in their perceptions of everyday social experiences, with social connectedness characterized by persistently enhanced perceptions of positivity and reduced perceptions of negativity in interaction quality and affect. The results of our lagged analyses indicate that socially connected individuals do not experience longer-lasting effects of positive interactions on mood, or of positive affect on interaction quality, than do lonely individuals, so this explanation does not account for social connectedness/loneliness differences in overall degree of positivity and negativity in these domains. In addition, we know from past research (Hawkley et al., 2003) that these same individuals did not exhibit social connectedness/loneliness differences in time spent with others, ruling out frequency of social opportunities as an explanation for affect differences. On the other hand, we cannot rule out the possibility that socially connected individuals have greater access to better interaction partners, partners that may be similarly inclined toward greater positivity in affect and interaction quality and thereby help foster and maintain positivity in the socially connected individual.

In sum, our data suggest that the combination of greater perceived positivity among socially connected individuals and the tendency for positivity to be self-reinforcing across the domains of affect and interaction quality fosters the re-

current positive interactions and persistently enhanced mood that are characteristic of social connectedness. Unfortunately, the converse is also true: Initially greater negativity and the tendency of negativity to be self-reinforcing fosters greater negativity in interactions and affect among lonely individuals. The advantage of social connectedness may be not only that it triggers upward spirals of positivity (e.g., better coping strategies) that result from the maintenance of positive emotions (Fredrickson & Joiner, 2002), but that it prevents the downward spiraling of negative affect that leads to dysphoria, clinical depression, and anxiety disorders. So what can we learn from socially connected individuals that might help us understand how to be a successful social being? The data presented here suggest that altering perceptions in either domain—interactions or affect—may help to break the cycle of negativity that so profoundly influences well-being and engage the spiral of positivity that moves individuals into the realm of successful social functioning.

Methodological Remarks

In addition to examining the theoretical tests and insights that MLM provides when dealing with complex data sets, we sought to provide a tutorial on some advanced uses of MLM. Tutorials on MLM usually stop at two levels and illustrate how MLM can be used to examine growth or trajectory over time. Our theoretical questions were more complex and required a three-level MLM with tests of lagged effects. Accordingly, the tutorial explained a three-level MLM with instructions. Although rarely used, three-level MLMs can be applied in many settings (e.g., any setting with two levels of nesting plus repeated measures). Our detailed description of how such models can be specified can serve as a useful guide to others who encounter data that are organized according to a hierarchy with at least three levels.

MLM provides an appropriate method for analyzing repeated-measures data that preserves within-person (and in our case within-day) trends that might otherwise become obscured by collapsing across diaries, days, or individuals. Furthermore, whenever researchers encounter data that are organized hierarchically, they run the risk of suffering low power or biased parameter estimates if the nested structure is not modeled. Thus, we structured our model as repeated measures nested within other repeated measures and addressed important theoretical questions that could not otherwise be addressed. For instance, the relationship between variables can be studied within nesting units (e.g., days, people), which allows us to ask questions about both interindividual variability and intraindividual variability.

We further demonstrated that longitudinal designs need not focus on time as a variable or even on trends. The capability of testing lagged effects is very useful, and is an interesting alternative to incorporating time as a predictor (which is how most researchers study trends). We were not interested in trends over time (i.e., growth curves), but rather concurrent and lagged effects of other relevant variables. Our study was characterized by repeated measurements of the same individuals, yet our predictions and hypotheses had little to do with examining growth or trajectory over time.

Finally, in psychological research, there is an unfortunate tendency to address longitudinal hypotheses using cross-sectional data. Temporal separation is a necessary, but not sufficient, condition for causality (Gollob & Reichardt, 1987). To address causality, we used lagged prediction in MLM of longitudinal data. The examination of lagged effects as illustrated in this chapter should be undertaken more often because this modeling strategy recognizes explicitly that independent variables require time to exert effects on dependent variables. Modeling lagged responses in MLM is a novel but powerful statistical approach that overcomes these limitations in traditional longitudinal analyses.

Acknowledgments   This work was supported by Program Project Grant PO1 AG18911 (social isolation, loneliness, health, and the aging process) from the National Institute on Aging and by the Mind-Body Network of the John D. and Catherine T. MacArthur Foundation.

Appendix: Selected LISREL Code

PRELIS Code for Null Model

```
OPTIONS OLS=YES CONVERGE=0.001 MAXITER=100 OUTPUT=STANDARD ;
  ! OLS=YES=Use OLS estimates as start values
  ! CONVERGE=0.001=Convergence criterion=.001
  ! MAXITER=100=Maximum of 100 iterations
TITLE=Null Model; ! Title of analysis
MISSING_DAT =-999.000000; ! Missing data code=-999
SY='C:\data\data1.PSF'; ! Location of data, in PRELIS data format
ID1=BEEPNUM; ! Level-1 unit identifier =diary number
ID2=STUDYDAY; ! Level-2 unit identifier =day of study
ID3=SUBNUM; ! Level-3 unit identifier =subject number
RESPONSE=POSAFF; ! Dependent variable=PANAS positive
FIXED=CONS; ! Requests point estimate of fixed effect
RANDOM1=CONS; ! Diary-level intercept is random
RANDOM2=CONS; ! Day-level intercept is random
RANDOM3=CONS; ! Person-level intercept is random
COV1PAT=DIAG; ! Diary-level covariance matrix is diagonal
COV2PAT=DIAG; ! Day-level covariance matrix is diagonal
COV3PAT=DIAG; ! Person-level covariance matrix is diagonal
```

PRELIS Code for Concurrent Fixed-Effects Model

```
OPTIONS OLS=YES CONVERGE=0.001 MAXITER=100 OUTPUT=STANDARD ;
TITLE=Concurrent Fixed Effects;
MISSING_DAT =-999.000000;
SY='C:\data\data1.PSF';
ID1=BEEPNUM;
ID2=STUDYDAY;
ID3=SUBNUM;
RESPONSE=POSAFF;
FIXED=CONS POSINT; ! Requests point estimates of intercept and slope
```

```
RANDOM1=CONS;
RANDOM2=CONS;
RANDOM3=CONS;
COV1PAT=DIAG;
COV2PAT=DIAG;
COV3PAT=DIAG;
```

PRELIS Code for Concurrent Random-Effects Model

```
OPTIONS OLS=YES CONVERGE=0.001 MAXITER=100 OUTPUT=STANDARD ;
TITLE=Concurrent Random Effects;
MISSING_DAT =-999.000000;
SY='C:\data\data1.PSF';
ID1=BEEPNUM;
ID2=STUDYDAY;
ID3=SUBNUM;
RESPONSE=POSAFF;
FIXED=CONS POSINT;
RANDOM1=CONS;
RANDOM2=CONS POSINT; ! Sets slope of POSINT random at level-2
RANDOM3=CONS POSINT; ! Sets slope of POSINT random at level-3
COV1PAT=DIAG;
COV2PAT=1 ! Requests symmetric covariance matrix at level-2
 2 3;
COV3PAT=1 ! Requests symmetric covariance matrix at level-3
 2 3;
```

PRELIS Code for Predicting Concurrent Random Effects With Loneliness

```
OPTIONS OLS=YES CONVERGE=0.001 MAXITER=100 OUTPUT=STANDARD ;
TITLE=Cross-Level Interaction;
MISSING_DAT =-999.000000;
SY='C:\data\data1.PSF';
ID1=BEEPNUM;
ID2=STUDYDAY;
ID3=SUBNUM;
RESPONSE=POSAFF;
FIXED=CONS POSINT UCPOSINT; ! Fixed effects for POSINT and interac-
  tion term
RANDOM1=CONS;
RANDOM2=CONS POSINT;
RANDOM3=CONS POSINT;
COV1PAT=DIAG;
COV2PAT=1
        2 3;
COV3PAT=1
        2 3;
```

Notes

1. The subscript notation employed for coefficients in MLM can be confusing. The notation convention becomes even more confusing when a third level is added, and is further complicated by the fact that different authors tend to use different subscripting strategies. For purposes of this chapter, we adopt a variation of the notation employed by Raudenbush and Bryk (2002) and Snijders and Bosker (1999), in which i, j, and k denote, respectively, diary, day, and person. When one of these subscripts is replaced by an integer, the integer represents the position of the coefficient in the Level 1, Level 2, and Level 3 equations. In Equation 6, for example, the first 0 in γ_{010} represents the fact

that this Level 3 fixed effect is ultimately related to the intercept in the Level 1 equation; the 1 represents the fact that it is related to the first slope coefficient in the Level 2 equation; and the final 0 represents the fact that γ_{010} is the first (intercept) coefficient in the Level 3 equation.

2. Centering sometimes improves the stability of estimation by reducing collinearity with other predictors, and often renders uninterpretable parameter estimates interpretable. For example, the intercept in traditional regression is interpretable as the value of the dependent variable when all predictors equal zero. If a predictor variable has no meaningful zero point, then mean centering allows the intercept to be interpretable as the predicted value of the dependent variable at the mean of the predictor. In two- and three-level models, centering is more complicated (see Kreft & de Leeuw, 1998; Kreft, de Leeuw, & Aiken, 1995; Raudenbush & Bryk, 2002, for general guidance on centering). In this chapter, we limit analyses to uncentered data because the effects of greatest interest are not altered by the most widely employed kind of centering.

3. For the sake of brevity, only those results directly relevant to the question at hand are reported. More details are available from the authors upon request.

References

Affleck, G., Tennen, H., Urrows, S., & Higgins, P. (1994). Person and contextual features of daily stress reactivity: Individual differences in relations of undesirable daily events with mood disturbance and chronic pain intensity. *Journal of Personality and Social Psychology, 66*, 329–340.

Barrett, L. F., & Pietromonaco, P. R. (1997). Accuracy of the five-factor model in predicting perceptions of daily social interactions. *Personality and Social Psychology Bulletin, 23*, 1173–1187.

Baumeister, R. F., & Leary, M. R. (1995). The need to belong: Desire for interpersonal attachment as a fundamental human motivation. *Psychological Bulletin, 117*, 497–529.

Bryk, A. S., Raudenbush, S. W., Cheong, Y. K., & Congdon, R. (2000). *HLM5: Hierarchical linear and nonlinear modeling.* Chicago: Scientific Software International.

Cacioppo, J. T., Ernst, J. M., Burleson, M. H., McClintock, M. K., Malarkey, W. B., Hawkley, L. C., et al. (2000). Lonely traits and concomitant physiological processes: The MacArthur social neuroscience studies. *International Journal of Psychophysiology, 35*, 143–154.

Cacioppo, J. T., Hawkley, L. C., Crawford, L. E., Ernst, J. M., Burleson, J. M., Kowalewski, R. B.,

et al. (2002). Loneliness and health: Potential mechanisms. *Psychosomatic Medicine, 64*, 407–417.

Clark, L. A., & Watson, D. (1988). Mood and the mundane: Relations between daily life events and self-reported mood. *Journal of Personality and Social Psychology, 54*, 296–308.

Cunningham, M. R. (1988a). Does happiness mean friendliness? Induced mood and heterosexual self-disclosure. *Personality and Social Psychology Bulletin, 14*, 283–297.

Cunningham, M. R. (1988b). What do you do when you're happy or blue? Mood, expectancies, and behavioral interest. *Motivation and Emotion, 12*, 309–331.

du Toit, M., & du Toit, S. (2001). *Interactive LISREL: User's guide.* Lincolnwood, IL: Scientific Software International.

Finch, J. F., Okun, M. A., Barrera, M., Zautra, A. J., & Reich, J. W. (1989). Positive and negative social ties among older adults: Measurement models and the prediction of psychological distress and well-being. *American Journal of Community Psychology, 17*, 585–605.

Fredrickson, B. L., & Joiner, T. (2002). Positive emotions trigger upward spirals toward emotional well-being. *Psychological Science, 13*, 172–175.

Goldstein, H. (1995). *Multilevel statistical models* (2nd ed.). London: Arnold.

Gollob, H. F., & Reichardt, C. S. (1987). Taking account of time lags in causal models. *Child Development, 58*, 80–92.

Hawkley, L. C., Browne, M. W., & Cacioppo, J. T. (2005). How can I connect with thee? Let me count the ways. *Psychological Science, 16*, 798–804.

Hawkley, L. C., Burleson, M. H., Berntson, G. G., & Cacioppo, J. T. (2003). Loneliness in everyday life: Cardiovascular activity, psychosocial context, and health behaviors. *Journal of Personality and Social Psychology, 85*, 105–120.

Hox, J. (2002). *Multilevel analysis: Techniques and applications.* Mahwah, NJ: Erlbaum.

Jöreskog, K. G., & Sörbom, D. (1996). *LISREL 8 user's reference guide.* Chicago: Scientific Software International.

Jöreskog, K. G., Sörbom, D., du Toit, S., & du Toit, M. (1999). *LISREL 8: New statistical features.* Chicago: Scientific Software International.

Kreft, I., & de Leeuw, J. (1998). *Introducing multilevel modeling.* Thousand Oaks, CA: Sage.

Kreft, I. G. G., de Leeuw, J., & Aiken, L. S. (1995). The effect of different forms of centering in hierarchical linear models. *Multivariate Behavioral Research, 30*(1), 1–21.

Larson, R., & Csikszentmihalyi, M. (1983). The experience sampling method. *New Directions for Methodology of Social and Behavioral Science, 15*, 41–56.

McIntyre, C. W., Watson, D., Clark, L. A., & Cross, S. A. (1991). The effect of induced social interaction on positive and negative affect. *Bulletin of the Psychonomic Society, 29*, 67–70.

McIntyre, C. W., Watson, D., & Cunningham, A. C. (1990). The effects of social interaction, exercise, and test stress on positive and negative affect. *Bulletin of the Psychonomic Society, 28*, 141–143.

Mikulincer, M., Shaver, P. R., & Pereg, D. (2003). Attachment theory and affect regulation: The dynamics, development, and cognitive consequences of attachment-related strategies. *Motivation and Emotion, 27*, 77–102.

Myers, D. G. (2000). The funds, friends, and faith of happy people. *American Psychologist, 55*, 56–67.

Myers, D. G., & Diener, E. (1995). Who is happy? *Psychological Science, 6*, 10–19.

Newsom, J. T., Nishishiba, M., Morgan, D. L., & Rook, K. S. (2003). The relative importance of three domains of positive and negative social exchanges: A longitudinal model with comparable measures. *Psychology and Aging, 18*, 746–754.

Rasbash, J., Browne, W., Goldstein, H., Yang, M., Plewis, I., Healy, M., et al. (2000). *A user's guide to MLwiN*. London: Centre for Multilevel Modeling.

Raudenbush, S. W., & Bryk, A. S. (2002). *Hierarchical linear models: Applications and data analysis methods* (2nd ed.). Thousand Oaks, CA: Sage.

Rook, K. S. (1990). Stressful aspects of older adults' social relationships: Current theory and research. In M. A. P. Stephens, J. H. Crowther, S. E. Hobfoll, & D. L. Tennenbaum (Eds.), *Stress and coping in later-life families* (pp. 173–192). Washington, DC: Hemisphere.

Rook, K. S. (2001). Emotional health and positive versus negative social exchanges: A daily diary analysis. *Applied Developmental Science, 5*, 86–97.

Russell, D., Peplau, L. A., & Cutrona, C. (1980). The revised UCLA Loneliness Scale: Concurrent and discriminant validity. *Journal of Personality and Social Psychology, 39*, 472–480.

Snijders, T. A. B., & Bosker, R. J. (1999). *Multilevel analysis: An introduction to basic and advanced multilevel modeling*. Thousand Oaks, CA: Sage.

Vittengl, J. R., & Holt, C. S. (1998a). Positive and negative affect in social interactions as a function of partner familiarity, quality of communication, and social anxiety. *Journal of Social and Clinical Psychology, 17*, 196–208.

Vittengl, J. R., & Holt, C. S. (1998b). A time-series diary study of mood and social interaction. *Motivation and Emotion, 22*, 255–275.

Watson, D., Clark, L. A., McIntyre, C. W., & Hamaker, S. (1992). Affect, personality, and social activity. *Journal of Personality and Social Psychology, 63*, 1011–1025.

Watson, D., Clark, L. A., & Tellegen, A. (1988). Development and validation of brief measures of positive and negative affect: The PANAS scales. *Journal of Personality and Social Psychology, 54*, 1063–1070.

40

Positive Processes in Close Relationships Across Time, Partners, and Context

A Multilevel Approach

Shelly L. Gable and Jennifer G. La Guardia

Clearly, humans operate in a social world. Our close relationships are those in which we derive some of our deepest gratifications as well as our most profound sufferings. It is no wonder that scientists have studied the importance of close relationships to human functioning across the life span (see Reis, Collins, & Berscheid, 2000, for review). Indeed, theoretical and empirical accounts of psychological well-being assert that strong and stable social ties with others are central components of psychological health (e.g., Deci & Ryan, 1985; Ryff, 1995). Further, research has also clearly shown that close relationships are crucial for physical health, so much so that the lack of close bonds is a risk factor for health on par with other risks such as cigarette smoking, high blood pressure, and obesity (House, Landis, & Umberson, 1988).

Historically, although we theoretically model how interpersonal functioning contributes to health, the bulk of research on close relationships focuses on how processes go awry (Spitz-berg & Cupach, 1998) and lead to dysfunction, creating a rather narrow or skewed understanding of relationship functioning. However, a growing emphasis has been on the positive processes in close relationships that lead to greater individual well-being as well as greater growth, commitment, and intimacy within relationships (Gable & Reis, 2001; Reis & Gable, 2003, for reviews). For example, programs of research on empathy (e.g., Ickes & Simpson, 1997), forgiveness (e.g., McCullough, Worthington, & Rachal, 1997), positive emotions (e.g., Gonzaga, Keltner, Londahl, & Smith, 2001), and altruism (e.g., Thompson & DeHarpport, 1998) have begun to shape our understanding of how human flourishing emerges within close relationships.

Regardless of the starting point or framework from which researchers begin, theories of relational processes implicitly, and sometimes explicitly, posit that relationship processes are dynamic. Indeed, processes such as attachment, emotion regulation, and intimacy are viewed as transactional between relationship partners. However, when studying close relationship processes such as these, researchers often employ methods and data analytic strategies focused at the between-person level, thereby essentially ignoring or discounting the important dynamics inherent to these relational processes.

This chapter seeks to challenge the field to conceptualize and design research that simultaneously accounts for important individual differences while attending to within-person variations across partners, contexts, and time. In this chapter, we (1) outline the logic of the within-person approach; (2) highlight the possible advantages and potential pitfalls to studying close relationships across time, contexts, and partners; and (3) discuss data analytic strategies with special attention to techniques of multilevel modeling (MLM). Further, we specifically focus our attention on modeling positive relational processes and discuss new research directions that follow from this exercise.

From a Between-Persons to a Within-Persons Approach

Between-Persons Approach

The hallmark of a between-persons approach is that each person, dyad, or family contributes data at one time point (e.g., "How satisfied are you right now?"), in a particular context (e.g., "How does your partner respond during a conflict?"), or in a particular relationship (e.g., "How much do you and your best friend disclose to each other?"). Typically, from a between-persons approach, people who possess a particular characteristic are compared to those who do not have that characteristic or who have different levels of it. For example, in a study by Fincham, Paleari, and Regalia (2002), people who felt greater empathy for their spouse overall were more likely to forgive their spouse for transgressions than those lower in empathy, with empathy more strongly associated with forgiveness for husbands than for wives. In another typical design, people are placed in a certain situation (e.g., couples asked to discuss a recent positive event) and processes of interest are examined (e.g., eye contact, perceived regard) in the specific interaction or time point. For example, Carstensen, Gottman, and Levenson (1995) assessed emotional behavior in 156 middle and older adult couples in long-term marriages during videotaped interactions of positive and negatively valenced discussions. In terms of positive emotional behaviors, "happy" couples—those who reported being more satisfied with their relationship—showed more positive emotion and were more humorous, affectionate, and validating in interactions than "unhappy" couples.

Although the between-persons approach has certainly yielded valuable information on positive psychological processes in close relationships, the very nature of close relationships prompts us to also take a within-persons perspective (Gable & Reis, 1999). Studies on human behavior that are devoid of the relational context provide us with no better understanding of relational processes because presumably behavior will change as a function of who you are with, when you are with them, and what you are doing. That is, healthy interpersonal functioning is a product of complex interactions within partnerships, as well as across multiple partnerships, over different contexts and time.

Within-Persons Approach

Within close relationships, partners presumably exert mutual influence on each other in meaningful ways (i.e., on nontrivial outcomes), their interactions persist across time with some degree of frequency (although length and frequency vary), and their interactions occur in multiple contexts (Kelley & Thibaut, 1978). As such, each relationship interaction has a rich developmental history to it. How your partner has reacted to you in the past as well as how he or she engages you in the present affects the outcome of any interaction. Further, we can also expect that interactions with one partner may differ significantly from interactions with another partner. Thus, even the same processes (e.g., empathy) may play out very differently with different relationship partners. Therefore, it seems imperative to examine not only the between-person but also the within-person level to adequately understand positive processes in close relationships.

The within-person approach has several specific benefits to methodology and theory. Within-person designs require that each participant rate the variables of interest on multiple occasions, within multiple relationships, or within different contexts. Statistically, multiple data points allow for greater sensitivity in measurement of a given process or phenomenon.

Moreover, multiple data points allow investigators to examine consistency and variation of the sampling units. In addition to statistical considerations, this has important theoretical implications. By considering the within-person perspective, researchers are forced to think dynamically about relationship processes and measure them as such. They must stretch and challenge their theories to address consistency and variation across time, contexts, and partners. Thus, adopting a within-person approach represents an important conceptual decision, not just a methodological convenience or a statistical necessity.

Framing Research Questions and Constructing Theories

When constructing research questions, attention to the between-person and within-person distinctions yields important empirical and theoretical issues. Let's illustrate an example. When we study positive processes in relationships such as passionate love, we might try to understand how the level of couple commitment differs in Couple A (Noah and Beth) and Couple B (Martin and Lisa) as a function of their level of passionate love. However, if our empirical investigation and conceptualization is limited to this between-person strategy, simply understanding the level of commitment or the level of passionate love overlooks the effects of time, context, and partner factors. That is, how each couple arrives at their rated levels of passionate love and commitment is important to understand. More clearly, when we ask Noah, "How passionate is your relationship to Beth?," his answer may be based on comparisons of his relationship to those of other couples (between-persons), how passionate his relationship with Beth is today compared to when they first met (time), how passionate it is today compared to a particularly conflictual period in their relationship (context), or how passionate it is compared to his relationship with his ex-girlfriend (partner). Thus, by ignoring the within-persons perspective we are a priori assuming that there is consistency in the phenomena of interest, or at the very least implying that any inconsistency is meaningless measurement variance.

How, then, do we construct theory and frame research questions to capture the dynamics of time, context, and partner effects? Consider intimacy processes as an example. In the simplest version of Reis and Shaver's intimacy model (Reis & Patrick, 1996; Reis & Shaver, 1988), Partner A (Noah) discloses something to Partner B (Beth), Beth responds to Noah, and to the extent that her reaction conveys that she understands him, validates him, and cares for him, she is deemed responsive. From this model, we would predict that the more responsive Noah perceives Beth to be, the more likely he will be to disclose to Beth, and the more intimate the relationship. This simple formulation, however, does not capture the full picture of intimacy. Indeed, Reis and Shaver incorporated many other facets into this model. First, they suggested that the model must consider the interdependence of the intimacy process—that is, feeling connection or intimacy within the relationship is a product of both partners' contributions of disclosure and responsiveness to the other. So, how Beth engages the relationship will have some effect not only on how intimate she perceives the relationship to be, but also on how intimate Noah perceives the relationship to be, and the same is true for Noah. Further, the model is recursive—that is, the thoughts, feelings, and behaviors that characterize a couple's interaction at any given moment undergo continuous revision. Intimacy is not formed by a single act of disclosure at a single point in time, but instead unfolds over different situations, across time. Finally, Reis and Shaver also suggested that individual differences in needs, goals, and motives influence how each partner engages the other, yielding important couple-level factors that may influence the trajectory of forming intimate bonds. Thus, when we consider the dynamics of intimacy, the theory is multileveled.

In practice, researchers interested in this intimacy process may frame their studies into between-person, within-person, and combined questions. A strictly between-persons question may ask if a particular individual difference factor is associated with perceptions of the partner's level of responsiveness. For example, the researcher can ask whether individual differences in dispositional optimism are associated with differences in perceptions of responsiveness, answering the question, "Do optimists perceive more responsiveness on the part of the partners than pessimists?" Strictly within-persons questions may focus on how disclosure and perceived responsiveness vary across time,

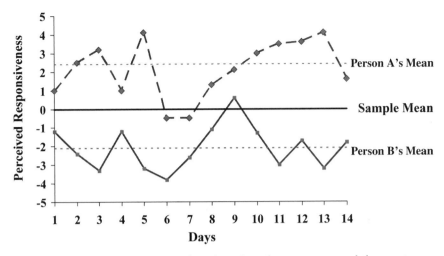

Figure 40.1 Graphic representation of two hypothetical participants in a daily experience study mapping perceptions of spouse's responsiveness over the course of 2 weeks.

partner, and contexts. For example, the researcher can ask if partner responsiveness varies across days (figure 40.1), whether close relationships with more certainty of future stability (e.g., parent-child) are associated with higher responsiveness than relationships with less certainty of future stability (e.g., new dating relationship; figure 40.2), and whether partners are more responsive in the context of activities that require greater shared attention and communi-

cation (e.g., planning a vacation, dining together) than other contexts that demand less (e.g., watching a movie; figure 40.3). Further, we can also examine the covariation of two variables across time, partners, and contexts. For example, we can ask whether people perceive their partners to be more responsive on days that they display more positive emotions; whether more responsiveness is perceived with relationship partners that display more positive emotions;

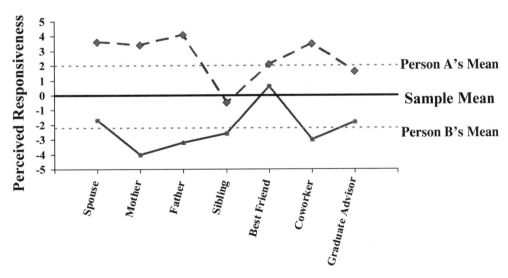

Figure 40.2 Graphic representation of two hypothetical participants in a cross-sectional study of perceptions of responsiveness from different relationship partners.

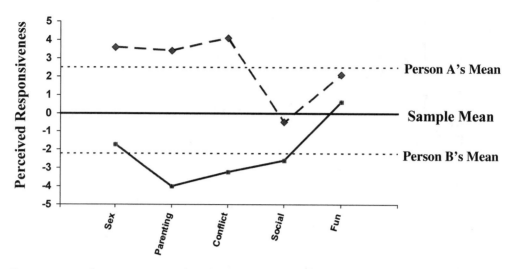

Figure 40.3 Graphic representation of two hypothetical participants in an observational study of perceptions of responsiveness from a dating partner following discussions of desired frequency of sex, preferred parenting styles, an area of relationship conflict, preferred involvement in social activities, and the last fun leisure activity they engaged in.

and whether more positive emotions are perceived in activities that involve greater shared attention and communication. Finally, an interactive question would consider how an individual difference factor moderates how display of positive emotions and perceived responsiveness covary. For example, the researcher can ask whether optimists have a stronger association between displays of positive emotions and perceived responsiveness than do pessimists. In this type of question, a between-persons factor (e.g., dispositional optimism) influences a within-persons association (the covariation between positive emotional displays and perceived responsiveness).

Thus, as illustrated in this example, relational processes when thought of as dynamic entities force us to conceptualize a multifaceted model—attending to between-person, within-person, and interactive effects. By attending to all three levels of analysis, the researcher can address temporal, partner, contextual, and individual difference factors simultaneously, and thereby more fully capture the essence of the relational process.

Methods and Statistical Analysis

Moving away from simply a between-persons approach to a within-persons or mixed design yields significant challenges methodologically

and statistically. Some challenges are practical ones, such as how to most efficiently collect all of the data (e.g., personal handheld devices, internet recordings, multiple taped interviews), while others are theoretical in nature in that they involve choices about how to capture the essence of data in the most sophisticated and precise way possible. Although a thorough description of the varied challenges in design and analysis are beyond the scope of this chapter, we briefly outline some of these issues and provide references for further elaboration of these points.

Practically speaking, within-person approaches require multiple measurement points. The success of the within-person approach relies on the participants' willingness and ability to remain engaged with the increased demands of multiple measurement points. As such, researchers often have to balance capturing a phenomenon thoroughly and accurately while minimizing participant burnout. Thus, designs must favor manageable expectations of the research participants in order to foster adherence to the protocol. Problems such as reactivity in the form of response decay (e.g., response rates declining over time or ratings becoming less thoughtful or accurate) will likely result without this attention (see Reis & Gable, 2000, for further discussion of this issue).

Multiple measurements also pose significant challenges for data analysis. There are several key issues. First, once you introduce multiple data points for any one person, each data point shares some variance in common—they are all nested within the person.[1] Thus, statistical methods must account for this non-independence. Second, the number of data points and the variance of these points for any given person may differ substantially. These differences may be meaningful and important to preserve and assess statistically, as neglect may result in biases of standard error estimates and significance tests. Finally, how we as researchers statistically capture or estimate the dynamics of the data will have implications for the results and interpretation of phenomena. For example, how data are aggregated and the extent to which effects are fixed within models may have a significant impact on results.

Traditionally, within-person designs have been analyzed with repeated-measures ANOVA or multiple linear regression techniques. These methods have several drawbacks that are highlighted when we consider the more recent advances in multilevel modeling (MLM) techniques. We briefly review the mechanisms of each modeling approach, discuss how MLM provides opportunities for improving model estimation over the traditional approaches of ANOVA and multiple linear regression (MLR), and discuss how MLM allows analysis of more complex designs.

Repeated Measures ANOVA and Multiple Linear Regression

Repeated measures ANOVA and MLR are appropriate for designs in which each participant is assessed in all of the same conditions (e.g., same contexts or relationships) or is assessed at the same interval, and the effects are predicted to be fixed. However, within-persons designs often do not adhere to these constraints, both in practice and in theory, and thus problems arise from these approaches. One alternative is to aggregate data across time or conditions and employ an ANOVA or MLR procedure. However, creating an average of data points results in a significant loss of information—precisely the sort of dynamic information that we sought by using a within-persons approach. Moreover, the number of records or data points for each person or the within-person variance may differ substantially from person to person, thereby biasing estimates of standard errors and significance tests or inflating either Type I or Type II errors (see Kashy & Kenny, 2000, for further explanation). To account for this issue, a weighted least squares approach must be employed. Finally, most ANOVA and MLR programs treat predictors as fixed effects as the default, suggesting that they are independent, normally distributed, and have constant variance. As we have already noted, these assumptions are not always met and may lead to biases in results.

Multilevel Modeling

The basic premise behind MLM methods (e.g., hierarchical linear modeling, or HLM, SAS PROC MIXED) is that there exists a hierarchy of observations, in which a lower-level unit is nested within an upper-level unit. These units are non-independent; thus variance in the intercept and slopes of any given effect must be modeled with each level in mind. What does this mean functionally? MLM allows researchers to simultaneously model an upper-level unit (e.g., person) and a lower-level unit that is nested within the upper level (e.g., day), as well as the interaction between these levels. So, in the case of using day and person as units of analysis, the regression line at the lower level estimates the effect on the outcome on a given day as a function of the person's average across all days (all data points), the rating for that day moderated by the regression coefficient (indicating the degree of change in the outcome produced by a one-unit change in the predictor on a given day), and error. The regression line at the upper level models the average intercept and slope for the average person, and further may model whether the lower level is moderated by between-person variables.

Multilevel modeling offers distinct advantages over the traditional ANOVA and MLR approaches (e.g., Nezlek, 2001). First, MLM allows simultaneous estimation of between- and within-person effects and their interactions, thereby addressing the nesting of data. Second, MLM allows researchers to model multiple continuous predictors with an unbalanced number of cases per person, taking advantage of maximum likelihood estimation to weight the effects more heavily for persons who have more data points or greater variance in their predictor variables. Finally, MLM allows the researcher to also treat variables as either random or fixed effects. This innovation allows the intercept and the slope to vary across persons.

These advantages are often difficult to grasp without an example. We present here an illustration of the possibilities afforded by a combined within- and between-persons method using actual data taken from a larger study on marriage, goals, and well-being (Gable, 2000).

A Study of Daily Experiences of Marital Satisfaction

Eighty-nine heterosexual married women from a midsized city in upstate New York were recruited from advertisements in two local newspapers for participation in the study.[2] In the sample, 91% were white; their mean age was 37.1 years ($SD = 9.71$; $Mdn = 37.0$, range 21–69); and they had been married to their current spouse an average of 10.0 years ($SD = 9.39$, $Mdn = 6.5$; range 6 months to 49 years). For 81% of the sample it was their first marriage. Further, 78.4% of them had at least one child, of which 66.3% lived at home.

Participants were scheduled for two appointments, approximately 2 weeks apart. During the first session, participants completed a packet of questionnaires assessing various personality traits and characteristics of their marriage, including perceptions of how responsive their husbands were on average. This was assessed with an 18-item measure of how understood, validated, and cared for they felt by their husbands (Reis, 2000). Participants were then given instructions for the daily experience component. The daily experience records included measures describing their daily interactions with their husbands and their feelings about their marital relationship on each day. Participants were asked to complete one diary record each night before going to bed, and they returned to the laboratory approximately 2 weeks after their initial appointment to hand in their completed diary forms.

There are three variables of interest for the present example. First, daily marital satisfaction was assessed by the item "Overall, today our relationship was...", rated on a 9-point scale ranging from *terrible* (0) to *terrific* (9), with *OK* as its midpoint. Also, participants indicated whether or not they had experienced a conflict with their husbands, as well as whether they had done anything "relaxing" with their spouse each day. Across the sample, the average daily marital satisfaction was 6.65 ($SD = 1.58$). The women reported experiencing a conflict on 20% of the days, and they reported relaxing with their husbands on 26% of the days.

First, we examine marital satisfaction as the dependent variable of interest. In Figure 40.4, marital satisfaction is plotted as a function of time (i.e., days into the study). The figure shows that if we look at the average marital satisfaction score across the 89 women in the sample on any given day, it is very close to the overall average of 6.65. However, the relative stability of the sample across time hides the considerable variability in marital satisfaction reported by

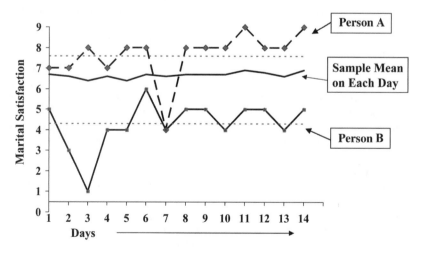

Figure 40.4 Average marital satisfaction on each day in a 14-day study for a sample of 88 wives ($N = 1,144$ days). Individual data from two selected participants from each are also plotted along with their means across the 14 days.

individual participants. To illustrate this point, we randomly chose one participant whose average satisfaction score was above the sample mean (Subject A) and one whose average satisfaction score was below the sample mean (Subject B) and plotted their marital satisfaction scores for each day. As we see from these plots, each woman varies quite substantially across the days, and further, their patterns of variation differ substantially from each other. With this level of analysis, we are able to ask different questions about the nature of marital satisfaction and generate new hypotheses about its variability. For example, on days prior to an increase in marital satisfaction, what happened within the marital relationship? Are there differences in the women's marriages that can explain the differences in their average daily satisfaction? Can these differences explain the fluctuations from day to day?

To address such questions, we analyzed the data using the HLM 5.02 software package (Raudenbush, Bryk, Cheong & Congdon, 1996). At Level 1 (the lower level), each participant contributed up to 14 records, each containing three variables—daily satisfaction level, whether or not there was a disagreement with their husband that day (dummy coded 0 or 1), and whether they did anything relaxing with their husband that day (dummy coded 0 or 1). At Level 2 (the upper level), each participant contributed one record containing one continuous variable—her rating of her husband's typical responsiveness (measured before the daily diary study began and standardized). Thus, we constructed the following equations.

Level 1:

$$Y_{ij} = b_{0j} + b_{1j}(\text{disagree}) + b_{2j}(\text{relax}) + e_{ij} \quad (1)$$

Level 2:

$$b_{0j} = \gamma_{00} + \gamma_{01}(\text{responsiveness}) + u_{0j} \quad (2)$$
$$b_{ij} = \gamma_{00} + \gamma_{11}(\text{responsiveness}) + u_{1j} \quad (3)$$
$$b_{2j} = \gamma_{20} + \gamma_{21}(\text{responsiveness}) + u_{2j} \quad (4)$$

In the Level 1 equation, the two predictor variables (disagree and relax) were not centered, and in the Level 2 equations, responsiveness was grand-mean centered.[3] The equations address the substantive questions of interest and the analyses yield estimated coefficients for each γ in the equations. The intercept ($\gamma_{00} = 6.71$) is the average marital satisfaction on a day where the

other predictors are 0 (i.e., there is neither a fight nor a relaxing activity) for a participant at the mean on responsiveness. The strictly between-persons question, "Does perceived responsiveness of spouse influence average daily marital satisfaction?" is addressed by γ_{01} (.50, $t_{(87)} = 4.89$, $p < .001$). Thus, the average marital satisfaction on a day with no fights or relaxing activities for a woman one unit (standard deviation) above the mean is 7.21 ($6.71 + .50$), and this is a significant difference.[4]

The strictly within-persons question "How are disagreements and relaxing activities related to daily marital satisfaction?" is answered by γ_{10} ($-.84$, $t_{(87)} = -7.51$, $p < .001$) and γ_{20} (.45, $t_{(87)} = -4.67$, $p < .001$). Thus, for the average participant, on days with neither a disagreement nor a relaxing activity with her husband, her satisfaction is 6.71 (i.e., the intercept, γ_{00}). On days she has a disagreement with her spouse, her satisfaction drops by .84, and on days she does something relaxing with him, her satisfaction increases by .45. Further, on days she has both an argument and does something relaxing ($\gamma_{10} + \gamma_{20}$), her satisfaction drops by .39. Figure 40.5 shows the predicted marital satisfaction in each of these contexts.[5] Finally, the interactive question "How does perceived responsiveness moderate the association between disagreements and marital satisfaction?" is answered by γ_{11} (.22, $t_{(87)} = 1.93$. $p = .053$). This marginally significant effect ($\gamma_{11} = .22$) indicates that the difference between a day with no disagreements and a day with a disagreement is $-.62$ for a person who is one standard deviation above the mean on responsiveness (calculated by $\gamma_{10} - \gamma_{11} = -.84 + .22$). Compare this to the difference between a day with no disagreements and a day with a disagreement for someone who is one standard deviation below the mean on responsiveness, -1.06 (calculated by $\gamma_{10} - \gamma_{11} = -.84 - .22$). This effect is plotted in figure 40.6. The second interactive question, "How does perceived responsiveness moderate the association between relaxing activities and marital satisfaction?" is answered by γ_{21} ($-.06$, $t_{(87)} = -0.65$, $p > .50$). This effect was not significant, indicating that responsiveness does not influence the association between relaxing activity and satisfaction (i.e., the benefits of relaxing activities were similar across women).

In summary, women who perceived their husbands to be more responsive before the study began reported higher daily satisfaction with their marital relationships overall. On days

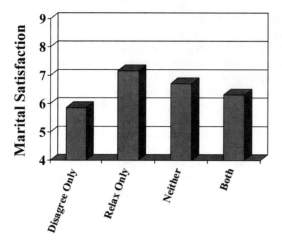

Figure 40.5 Average marital satisfaction on days in which a disagreement occurred, days the couple did something relaxing together, and days when neither or both of those activities were reported.

women had disagreements with their husbands their satisfaction was lower, but the detrimental effects of disagreements were less pronounced for women who perceived their husbands to be more responsive overall. Further, on days women engaged in a relaxing activity with their spouse they reported greater marital satisfaction, and the benefits of the relaxing activity were the same regardless of the level of perceived responsiveness.

Our example can be expanded into a more complex model. For example, although the Level 1 predictors in our example were dichotomous (occurrence of a disagreement or relaxing activity), one could also test the relationships between marital satisfaction and other continuous daily variables such as time spent with spouse or ratings

of social support provided by spouse. Similarly, although our example employed a continuous Level 2 predictor, the effects of dichotomous and categorical variables, such as employment status or attachment style, could also be modeled at Level 2. In multilevel modeling, as in multiple regression, categorical variables are represented with effects coding (see Cohen, Cohen, West, & Aiken, 2003). Finally, the dependent measure itself can be dichotomous or categorical, such as the occurrence of a disagreement (see Cudek & du Toit, 2003; Raudenbush & Bryk, 2002, for analyses on nonlinear models).

The example we have just illustrated looks simply at data from one member of the marriage dyad. What if we wanted to understand a process at the level of the couple, or if we were interested

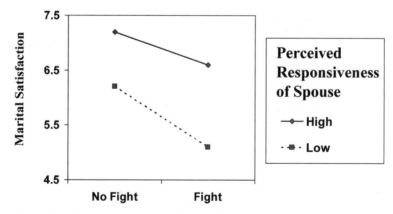

Figure 40.6. Estimated marital satisfaction of women who reported one standard deviation above (High) and one standard deviation below (Low) the mean on perceived responsiveness (feeling understood, validated, and cared for) from their spouse prior to participating in the daily experience study.

in a process at the level of a group? MLM offers opportunities for more complex designs that include modeling of dyadic and group effects, and growth or change across time. Several researchers have blazed the trail for capturing the effects of persons within dyads (Campbell & Kashy, 2002; Griffin & Gonzalez, 1995; Kenny & Cook, 1999; Kenny & La Voie, 1985), within groups (e.g., Kashy & Kenny, 2000; Miller & Kenny, 1986), and change processes across time (Bryk & Raudenbush, 1992; Collins & Sayer, 2000). We recommend reading more detailed accounts of these methods, but we will briefly outline some of the possibilities afforded by these advanced methods below.

In the case of dyads, models share in common the idea that relational outcomes are a function of not only the individuals within a dyad but of the dyad itself. For example, Kenny and Cook (1999) suggested that a person's score on a given dependent variable may be influenced not only by that person's score on an independent variable (actor effect) but also by her partner's score on the independent variable (partner effect). So, returning to our example of intimacy, how Beth engages the relationship will have some effect not only on how intimate she perceives the relationship to be (actor effect), but also on how intimate Noah perceives the relationship to be (partner effect). Of note, practical assistance in analysis is offered by Griffin and Gonzales (1995) for dyads in the exchangeable case and Campbell and Kashy (2002) for estimating dyadic effects using PROC MIXED and HLM programs.

In the case of groups, models can account for individual and group (e.g., family) level effects. For example, a variable may be understood by (1) the tendency of an individual to exhibit a consistent level of that variable across all interaction partners (individual), (2) the tendency for a partner to elicit a consistent level of that variable in his interaction partners (partner), (3) the tendency for individuals with the group to exhibit a similar level of that variable (group), and (4) the unique combination of any two people after removing the other effects (dyad; Kashy & Kenny, 2000). Poignant examples of these group models are found in Miller and Kenny (1986), who examined disclosures among women friends, and Cook (2000), who examined attachment processes within the family unit.

Finally, advances in modeling growth processes over time (e.g., Collins & Sayer, 2000) isolate the nature of individual change (individual growth curves) rather than relying simply on mean growth trajectories. The importance of this approach is that mean growth trajectories may not characterize any given individual change model. Therefore, understanding predictable variations in change patterns is essential to modeling individual change over time.

Multilevel Modeling of Positive Relational Processes

We have said much about the importance of forming dynamic theories of behavior, designing research to capture these ideas, and using advanced statistical tools to adequately represent the data. But just how does this approach manifest in current research on positive relational processes? Although historically much of the field has focused on the between-person perspective, there are clearly some poignant examples of how researchers have adopted a within-person approach to study positive relational phenomena over partners, contexts, and time. We turn now to these examples as illustrations of the power of within-person and multilevel designs.

Positive Processes Across Multiple Close Relationships

The majority of people live in a world in which, on a daily basis, they interact with many others. That is, people are embedded in a social world filled with relationships—from their grocery store clerks to their best friends. Although some of these relationships are peripheral, many are close (albeit not necessarily good or healthy) relationships. Even among people's closest relationships, there are important nuances to how relational processes unfold. For example, how a woman emotionally discloses to her mother (not only level of disclosure but features of that process such as initiation and concurrent emotions) may be very different than how she discloses to her father. Within each relationship, these processes have implications for the quality and dynamics of the particular relationship as well as one's well-being or health. However, what would cause the same person to act differently from one partner to another, and what are the consequences of this variation for the person?

A poignant example of how variability in a process may be shown across different relationships is found in the attachment literature. Attachment is often described as a transactional process with various partners (most typically with mother for children and with romantic partner for adults), but has typically been studied as a between-person or individual difference factor reflecting a general style of engaging relationships (e.g., Hazan & Shaver, 1987). At the between-person level, research attests to the importance of secure attachments for well-being and interpersonal functioning. However, people clearly do not always demonstrate a similar style or model of attachment with each of their varied partners. Simply put, people appear to attach differently to different partners. In the adult literature, people have examined the variation in attachment security across partners and have begun to explain this variability. For example, Baldwin, Keelan, Fehr, Enns, and Koh-Rangarajoo (1996) found that when participants described their 10 most significant relationships, 88% of them endorsed at least two of Hazan and Shaver's adult attachment styles (i.e., secure, avoidant, anxious-ambivalent) and 47% of participants reported all three, suggesting that people do not always enact the same relational style and do not experience the same sense of security with each partner. Further, La Guardia, Ryan, Couchman, and Deci (2000) examined variations in attachment security across people's relationships to their mother, father, romantic partner, best friend, and roommate, and linked variations in security to differences in relational provisions of need support. They found that people varied significantly in their levels of attachment security with important close others, and this variability was systematically linked to variations in need satisfaction, such that greater need satisfaction within relationships predicted greater overall attachment security, as well as more positive views of self and others. Importantly, using this methodology, they were able to further demonstrate that variability in attachment security in itself was not indicative of poorer health, but instead might be quite adaptive—attaching to others who are supportive while withdrawing from others who may not provide for one's needs.

Several important advances are made by this work. First, this research demonstrates the importance of examining relationship-specific dynamics of attachment security, a variable that typically has been viewed as a stable disposition. Second, this work begins to tap into processes (e.g., need fulfillment) that might account for dynamics in attachment behavior across relational partners. Importantly, rather than relying simply on global measures of partner support, this research gets at the heart of the attachment process by using the relationship as the point of analysis. Finally, although prior research (Donahue, Robins, Roberts, & John, 1993) has suggested that such variability might signal fragmentation or ill health, these data importantly suggest that adaptations in accord with need satisfaction may be systematic and instead function to protect overall well-being. Thus, the effects of mean level and variability on health are separable.

Positive Processes in Close Relationships Across Contexts

Context refers to aspects of a situation that modify the individual's experience of that situation and have important psychological consequences. Context may vary as a function of the domain (e.g., work vs. social settings), or it may also vary within relationships (the same behavior is enacted under substantially different circumstances within the partnership). As an example of the former, we could examine how people initiate affiliative behaviors at work versus a social setting (e.g., cocktail party), while as an example of the latter we could examine nonverbal communication used by spouses when discussing child-rearing plans versus financial matters. Again, what this means for research is that we must consider varying contexts to fully understand how relational processes operate. Although there is much research on stressful events across contexts, there remains little research on positive processes across contexts, thus opening up many new opportunities for exploration.

Positive Processes in Close Relationships Over Time

When we take a snapshot of relational behavior at only one point in time, we miss out on the developmental history and future trajectory of the behavior within the relationship. Thus, as we noted previously, relational behavior is not static but instead is characterized by transactions across time.

The component of time has been assessed both by daily experience sampling over relatively short periods of time (e.g., 1 week or 1 month) as well as longer periods of time (e.g., longitudinally over several years or decades). For example, using a daily diary method, Reis, Sheldon, Gable, Roscoe, and Ryan (2000) looked at daily fluctuations in well-being as a function of fluc-tuations in fulfillment of autonomy, compe-tence, and relatedness needs in daily activity. Fulfillment of each of these needs independently predicted variability in daily well-being. Fur-ther, Sheldon, Ryan, and Reis (1996) showed that daily fluctuations of satisfaction of auton-omy and competence needs predicted daily fluctuations in mood, physical symptoms, vital-ity, and self-esteem.

Also, in a study by Bolger, Zuckerman, and Kessler (2000), couples' supportive transactions were recorded over a 35-day period leading up to one of the partners completing the New York State Bar examination. Specifically, examinees' partners rated how much they emotionally supported their partner on a given day, while examinees rated whether or not they received support from their partner on a given day. In-vestigators then related the function of these interactions for the examinees' relief from anx-iety and depression. Results suggested that "invisible support"—situations in which part-ners said they provided emotional support but examinees did not report receiving it—was as-sociated with reductions in depression and dis-couragement over time prior to the bar exam, while little effect was found on reduction of anticipatory anxiety.[6]

Critical examples of longitudinal work on positive relational processes are found in the literature on marriage. For example, in a study of newlywed husbands and wives, Davila, Kar-ney, and Bradbury (1999) found that spouses showed significant increases in their general at-tachment security during the first two years of marriage and that a significant amount of this variance was accounted for by factors in the re-lationship such as the security of their partner's attachment. Also, Huston, Caughlin, Houts, Smith, and George (2001) examined ratings of love (belongingness, closeness, attachment to partner), perceived partner responsiveness, and partner affectionate expression in 156 couples across a 13-year period. For those who remained married and were categorized as happy in year 13, they reported a stronger marital bond, dee-per love for their spouse, and viewed their partner as more responsive when they were newlyweds than couples who remained married but were unhappy or who divorced early. Di-vorced later couples, interestingly, were com-parable to the happily married couples on these positive process dimensions, but they showed more affection than any of the other groups.

In sum, it is clear that many new research questions are afforded by a multilevel concep-tualization of behavior across time, contexts, and relationships. More specifically, research into positive processes will allow a fuller picture of the dynamic landscape of human behavior.

Concluding Comments

Relationships are an integral component of life satisfaction, emotional well-being, and health (Berscheid & Reis, 1998). The critical role that our relationships with close others play spans the life cycle (Reis et al., 2000) and is evident across cultures (Diener & Seligman, 2004). Moreover, the positive processes of interest to psychologists abound in close relationships and therefore it is no surprise that the study of close relationships continues to grow as a field. We have highlighted that many interesting questions in the study of positive processes in close relationships can (and need to) incorporate the effects of context, time, and relationship partner, and we hope that this chapter will encourage theorists and empiricists to integrate the within-person and between-per-son perspectives into the conceptualization of relationship processes and research designs, cre-ating a fuller, more dynamic portrait of rela-tionship functioning.

Notes

1. We use here the example of data points nested within-person. However, the same logic applies to people nested within groups (e.g., families), groups nested within neighborhoods, and so on.

2. Both husbands and wives from 89 couples participated in the study, but only the wives' data are presented here for simplicity. For examples of how to analyze data from both members of couple simultaneously in a multilevel framework, see Barnett, Raudenbush, Brennan, Pleck, and Mar-shall (1995); Gable, Reis, and Downey (2003); Kenny and Cook (1999); Kenny, Kashy, and Bolger (1998).

3. How one chooses to center variables in HLM equations has important implications for the interpretation of coefficients. Coefficients are in-terpreted as the effect of one unit change from 0 of the predictor on the dependent variable. Thus, for uncentered dummy-coded data (0,1), the coefficient is interpreted as the differences between days a person has a 0 and the days the person has a 1 for

that variable. For continuous predictors, one may also choose to center the data around the Level 1 group mean. In the current example, coefficients would be interpreted as changes in the dependent measure associated with a one-unit increase in the predictor variable above the person's own mean on that predictor variable. One may also choose to center the Level 1 predictors around the grand mean, in which case the coefficient is interpreted as changes in the dependent measure associated with a one-unit increase in the predictor variable above the sample mean for that predictor variable. Centering is a difficult but important issue, which is discussed more fully in Raudenbush and Bryk (2002).

4. In our example, a unit increase is a standard deviation increase because responsiveness scores were standardized and thus each person's z score served as her data point. If raw scores are used, a unit increase refers to a unit increase in the scale of the variable. We also grand-mean centered responsiveness scores in the Level 2 equations and therefore, a score of 0 represents a person with average perceived responsiveness.

5. We also created a fight × relaxing activity interaction term by multiplying the fight and relaxing activity dummy codes to test whether the two events interacted; for example, the benefits of engaging in a relaxing activity were more pronounced on days that a fight occurred. This term was tested in a second equation but was not significant, indicating that the benefits of a relaxing activity did not moderate the negative effects of fighting. The inclusion of the interaction term illustrates the possibility of testing within-level interactions, which is conceptually akin to testing interactions in multiple regression.

6. One important note about time effects is that studying processes across time requires the researcher to examine lags in effects. That is, the ripple of a given interaction may exude its effects immediately as well as having prolonged or later emerging effects on outcomes. As such, these types of designs require researchers to statistically model longitudinal change. For example, in the Bolger et al. (2000) study, modeled lag effects assessed whether support provision and receipt of that support on day t affected change in distress levels of the examinee from day t to day $t + 1$. For an in-depth discussion of one approach studying processes over time using time-lagged analysis, see chapter 4, this volume.

References

Baldwin, M. W., Keelan, J. P. R., Fehr, B., Enns, V., & Koh-Rangarajoo, E. (1996). Social-cognitive

conceptualization of attachment working models: Availability and accessibility effects. *Journal of Personality and Social Psychology, 71,* 94–109.

Barnett, R. C., Raudenbush, S. W., Brennan, R. T., Pleck, J. H., & Marshall, N. L. (1995). Change in job and marital experiences and change in psychological distress: A longitudinal study of dual-earner couples. *Journal of Personality and Social Psychology, 69,* 839–850.

Berscheid, E., & Reis, H. T. (1998). Attraction and close relationships. In D. T. Gilbert, S. T. Fiske, & G. Lindzey (Eds.), *The handbook of social psychology* (4th ed.; Vol. 2, pp. 193–281). New York: McGraw-Hill.

Bolger, N., Zuckerman, A., & Kessler, R. C. (2000). Invisible support and adjustment to stress. *Journal of Personality and Social Psychology, 79,* 953–961.

Bryk, A. S., & Raudenbush, S. W. (1992). *Hierarchical linear models.* Newbury Park, CA: Sage.

Campbell, L., & Kashy, D. A. (2002). Estimating actor, partner, and interaction effects for dyadic data using PROC MIXED and HLM: A user-friendly guide. *Personal Relationships, 9,* 327–342.

Carstensen, L. L., Gottman, J. M., & Levenson, R. W. (1995). Emotional behavior in long-term marriage. *Psychology and Aging, 10,* 140–149.

Collins, L. M, & Sayer, A. G. (2000). Modeling growth and change processes: Design, measurement, and analysis for research in social psychology. In H. T. Reis & C. Judd (Eds.), *Handbook of research methods in social and personality psychology (pp. 190–222).* New York: Cambridge University Press.

Cook, W. L. (2000). Understanding attachment security in family context. *Journal of Personality and Social Psychology, 78,* 285–294.

Cudeck, R., & du Toit, S. H. C. (2003). Nonlinear multilevel models for repeated measures data. In N. Duan & S. P. Reise (Eds.), *Multilevel modeling: Methodological advances, issues and applications* (pp. 1–24). Mahwah, NJ: Erlbaum.

Davila, J., Karney, B. R., & Bradbury, T. N. (1999). Attachment change processes in the early years of marriage. *Journal of Personality and Social Psychology, 76,* 783–802.

Deci, E. L., & Ryan, R. M. (1985). *Intrinsic motivation and self-determination in human behavior.* New York: Plenum.

Diener, E., & Seligman, M. E. P. (2004). Beyond money: Toward an economy of well-being. *Psychological Science in the Public Interest, 5,* 1–3.

Donahue, E. M., Robins, R. W., Roberts, B. W., & John, O. P. (1993). The divided self: Concurrent and longitudinal effects of psychological adjustment and social roles on self-concept differentiation. *Journal of Personality and Social Psychology, 64*, 834–846.

Fincham, F. D., Paleari, F. G., & Regalia, C. (2002). Forgiveness in marriage: The role of relationship quality, attributions, and empathy. *Personal Relationships, 9*, 27–37.

Gable, S. L. (2000). *Appetitive and aversive social motivation*. Unpublished doctoral dissertation, University of Rochester.

Gable, S. L., & Reis, H. T. (1999). Now and then, them and us, this and that: Studying relationships across time, partner, context, and person. *Personal Relationships, 6*, 415–432.

Gable, S. L., & Reis, H. T. (2001). Appetitive and aversive social interaction. In J. Harvey & A. Wenzel (Eds.), *Close romantic relationships: Maintenance and enhancement* (pp. 169–194). Mahwah, NJ: Erlbaum.

Gable, S. L., Reis, H. T., & Downey, G. (2003). He said, she said: A quasi-signal detection analysis of spouses' perceptions of everyday interactions. *Psychological Science, 14*, 100–105.

Gonzaga, G. C., Keltner, D., Londahl, E. A., & Smith, M. D. (2001). Love and the commitment problem in romantic relations and friendship. *Journal of Personality and Social Psychology, 81*, 247–262.

Griffin, D., & Gonzalez, R. (1995). Correlational analysis of dyad-level data in the exchangeable case. *Psychological Bulletin, 118*, 430–439.

Hazan, C., & Shaver, P. R. (1987). Romantic love conceptualized as an attachment process. *Journal of Personality and Social Psychology, 52*, 511–524.

House, J. S., Landis, K. R., & Umberson, D. (1988). Social relationships and health. *Science, 241*, 540–545.

Huston, T. L., Caughlin, J. P., Houts, R. M., Smith, S. E., & George, L. E. (2001). The connubial crucible: Newlywed years as a predictor of marital delight, distress, and divorce. *Journal of Personality and Social Psychology, 80*, 237–252.

Ickes, W. J., & Simpson, J. A . (1997). Managing empathic accuracy in close relationships. In W. J. Ickes (Ed.), *Empathic accuracy* (pp. 218–250). New York: Guilford.

Kashy, D. A., & Kenny, D. A. (2000). Social relations and the analysis of nonindependent data. In H. T. Reis & C. M. Judd (Eds.), *Handbook of research methods in social psychology (pp. 451–477)*. New York: Cambridge University Press.

Kelley, H. H., & Thibaut, J. W. (1978). *Interpersonal relations: A theory of interdependence*. New York: Wiley.

Kenny, D. A., & Cook, W. (1999). Partner effects in relationship research: Conceptual issues, analytic difficulties, and illustrations. *Personal Relationships, 6*, 433–438.

Kenny, D. A., Kashy, D. A., & Bolger, N. (1998). Data analysis in social psychology. In D. T. Gilbert, S. T. Fiske, & G. Lindzey (Eds.), *The handbook of social psychology* (4th ed.; *Vol. 1*, pp. 233–265). New York: McGraw-Hill.

Kenny, D. A., & La Voie, L. (1985). Separating individual and group effects. *Journal of Personality and Social Psychology, 48*, 339–348.

La Guardia, J. G., Ryan, R. M., Couchman, C. E., & Deci, E. L. (2000). Within-person variation in security of attachment: A self-determination theory perspective on attachment, need fulfillment, and well-being. *Journal of Personality and Social Psychology, 79*, 367–384.

McCullough, M. E., Worthington, E. L. Jr., & Rachal, K. C. (1997). Interpersonal forgiving in close relationships. *Journal of Personality and Social Psychology, 73*, 321–336.

Miller, L. C., & Kenny, D. A. (1986). Reciprocity of self-disclosure at the individual and dyadic levels: A social relations analysis. *Journal of Personality and Social Psychology, 50*, 713–719.

Nezlek, J. B . (2001). Multilevel random coefficient analyses of event- and interval-contingent data in social and personality psychology research. *Personality and Social Psychology Bulletin, 27*, 771–785

Raudenbush, S. W., & Bryk, A. S. (2002). *Hierarchical linear models: Applications and data analysis methods*. Thousand Oaks, CA: Sage.

Raudenbush, S. W., Bryk, A. S., Cheong, Y. F., & Congdon, R. T. (1996). *HLM 5: Hierarchical linear and nonlinear modeling*. Chicago: Scientific Software International.

Reis, H. T. (2000). *Responsiveness scale*. Unpublished manuscript, University of Rochester.

Reis, H. T., Collins, W. A., & Berscheid, E. (2000). The relationship context of human behavior and development. *Psychological Bulletin, 126*, 844–872.

Reis, H. T., & Gable, S. L. (2000). Event sampling and other methods for studying daily experience. In H. T. Reis & C. M. Judd (Eds.), *Handbook of research methods in social and personality psychology* (pp. 190–222). New York: Cambridge University Press.

Reis, H. T., & Gable, S. L. (2003). Toward a positive psychology of relationships. In C. L. Keyes & J. Haidt (Eds.). *Flourishing: The positive person and the good life* (pp. 129–159). Washington, DC: American Psychological Association.

Reis, H. T., & Patrick, B. C. (1996). Attachment and intimacy: Component processes. In A. Kruglanski & E. T. Higgins (Eds.), *Social psychology: Handbook of basic principles* (pp. 523–563). New York: Guilford.

Reis, H. T., & Shaver, P. (1988). Intimacy as an interpersonal process. In S. Duck (Ed.), *Handbook of personal relationships* (pp. 367–389). Chichester: Wiley.

Reis, H. T., Sheldon, K. M., Gable, S. L., Roscoe, J., & Ryan, R. M. (2000). Daily well-being: The role of autonomy, competence, and relatedness. *Personality and Social Psychology Bulletin, 26,* 419–435.

Ryff, C. D. (1995). Psychological well-being in adult life. *Current Directions in Psychological Science, 4,* 99–104.

Sheldon, K. M., Ryan, R., & Reis, H. T. (1996). What makes for a good day? Competence and autonomy in the day and in the person. *Personality and Social Psychology Bulletin, 22,* 1270–1279.

Spitzberg, B. H., & Cupach, W. R. (Eds.). (1998). *The dark side of close relationships.* Mahwah, NJ: Erlbaum.

Thompson, L., & DeHarpport, T. (1998). Relationships, goal incompatibility, and communal orientation in negotiations. *Basic and Applied Social Psychology, 20,* 33–44.

41

Latent-Class Models for Analyzing Variability and Change

Michael Eid

Variability and change processes in positive psychology, as in most other areas of psychology, have been analyzed predominantly with models for metrical or continuous response variables over a long time. This tendency is well documented in this volume, as the majority of chapters deal with models that assume metrical variables on the observed and the latent level.

The basic measurement process in positive psychology, however, in most cases is not based on metrical response variables but on items that are linked to categorical response scales. There is a tendency to ignore the categorical nature of these response scales by applying statistical methods that have been developed for metrical response variables. Analyzing categorical response scales with models for metrical variables has several shortcomings, and the aim of this chapter is to demonstrate the power and utility of methods for categorical variables to analyze variability and change processes in positive psychology.

Shortcomings of Analyzing Categorical Data With Models for Metrical Variables

The first shortcoming of applying models for metrical variables is that these methods are not able to scrutinize the response process with respect to single response categories. Methods for metrical variables assume that the scores of the scales are equidistant. However, it is widely known in assessment that individuals can have preferences for certain categories and that they avoid others. That means that individuals do not naturally treat the categories as if they were equally spaced on a single continuum. Instead they avoid, for example, middle categories to express their opinion or they choose particularly the middle categories to avoid deciding, and so on. In order to analyze the real response process with respect to the different response categories, it is necessary to have appropriate models that take the categorical nature into account. Moreover, these models are necessary for testing the equivalence of response processes across subgroups. In the cross-cultural context, for example, it is necessary to test the measurement invariance of scales assessing subjective well-being across cultures. The equivalence of measurement and response processes, however, can only be tested on the basis of methodological approaches that are able to model single categories and to compare the responses to single categories across cultures (Eid, Langeheine, & Diener, 2003).

The second shortcoming is that the distributional assumptions of models for metrical variables are often not fulfilled in the area of positive psychology. Life-satisfaction items with two categories, for example, cannot be normally distributed. Moreover, items and scales measuring positive and negative aspects of affective well-being differ in their distribution forms. Scales measuring pleasantness or calmness are often symmetrically distributed, whereas scales measuring unpleasantness and nervousness show skew distributions (Eid, Schneider, & Schwenkmezger, 1999). Consequently, the product-moment correlation coefficient is restricted in its possible range because variables differing in their distributions cannot be maximally correlated. Applying models for metrical variables to non-metrical scales can produce methodological artifacts. For example, applying factor analytic models for metrical response variables to items measuring different poles of a mood continuum can cause an artificial multidimensional solution (difficulty factors) just because of the differences in distributions between the positive and negative items (Eid, Mayer, Steyer, Notz, & Schwenkmezger, 1993; Olsson, 1979).

Aggregating items facilitates applying methods for metrical variables, but in this case the response process itself cannot sufficiently be scrutinized. Choosing many response categories seems to make the scales more metrical but can also cause interindividual differences that question the metrical character of the scales. It is not unlikely that scales with larger numbers of response categories cause interindividual differences in response styles. Eid and Rauber (2000), for example, found in the assessment of satisfaction with leadership behavior that the participants did not use the response scale in the same way. Instead there were two groups differing in their response styles. One group used the scale in the intended way, whereas the other group was overwhelmed by the fineness of a 6-point response scale. They had the tendency to use the scale in the sense of a binary yes-no scale. That means they preferred the extreme categories and avoided the middle ones. The more categories a scale has, the more likely it is that there are individuals who are overwhelmed by the fine grading of the scales and use the scale in quite different ways. Consequently, the responses of individuals cannot easily be compared and one has to take the qualitative differences in response styles into account. Hence, the aim of creating a quasi-metrical scale by increasing the number of categories can have the opposite effect in causing qualitative differences in response styles that hinder the comparison of the individuals with respect to one continuum. Consequently, it is sometimes preferable to use scales with a smaller number of categories to avoid response styles and to analyze these scales with models for categorical variables.

Models for Categorical Variables

The analysis of categorical variables has a long tradition in the social sciences. Psychometric research has focused on models for categorical variables that correct for measurement errors (latent-variable models). With respect to latent-variable models, two groups of models for categorical response variables can be considered. The first group assumes that the observed categorical variables measure latent variables that are metrical in nature. Models of item response theory (e.g., Linden & Hambleton, 1997) and factor analytic models for categorical variables (Muthén, 1983; Takane & de Leeuw, 1987) belong to this category. The second group of models assumes that the latent variables are categorical in nature. These models belong to the family of latent-class models (Clogg, 1995). Latent-class models are appropriate for research questions in positive psychology in which one is not (only) interested in quantitative differences but (also) in qualitative differences between individuals. This refers, for example, to cases in which different items cannot be ordered along a single continuum. Consider, for example, the measurement of different domains of life satisfaction (Eid et al., 2003). For such different life domains as romance, work, friends, and freedom, it might not be reasonable to order the domains on one continuum that is obligatory for all individuals. Instead it makes more sense to assume that there are different types of individuals, which means different profiles of satisfaction with life domains. There might be individuals who are satisfied with their work and their friends, but not with their romance and their freedom. There might also be individuals who are satisfied with their work, but with nothing else, and so forth. The consideration of different types means that there is a hidden categorical variable (types) that explains the observed judgments. Hence, a model measuring latent categorical variables should be used to analyze this data structure.

This chapter gives an overview of latent class models for measuring variability and change. It is structured as follows. First, some basic ideas of analyzing variability and change with categorical variables are discussed by referring to the Markov model, one of the simplest models for analyzing change. Then the basic concepts of latent-class analysis are introduced and latent-class models for measuring variability and change are presented. In particular, the latent Markov model, the latent state-trait model, and the latent state-trait Markov model are described. Next, it is shown how these models can be extended to mixture models that are able to classify individuals according to their change process. This chapter aims at giving a theoretical introduction into the models by avoiding defining the models in a more technical way. Moreover, the examples of applications are theoretically constructed to make them as simple as possible in order to make their understanding as easy as possible. Applications of some of these models to real-life data are presented in chapter 42. For didactic reasons, only the simplest case with dichotomous response variables is presented. The extension to these models to more than two categories is straightforward.

Analyzing Change With Categorical Response Variables

Markov Model

The simplest model for analyzing change with a dichotomous response variable is the Markov model that is depicted in figure 41.1 for a dichotomous response variable measuring a posi-

tive and a negative mood state on four occasions of measurement. In the Markov model, stability and change are represented by transition probabilities (Langeheine, 1988). The transition probabilities describe the probabilities to stay in the same category over time or to change the response category. Figure 41.1 describes an example with a time-homogeneous change process. That means that the probabilities of staying or moving do not depend on the pair of occasions considered but are time-invariant. In the (constructed) example in figure 41.1, the probability of staying in the same category is .80 when a person is in a positive mood and it is .40 when a person is in a negative mood. The probability of moving from a positive to a negative mood state is .20, while the probability of moving from a negative to a positive mood state is .60. According to this model, the probability of maintaining a positive mood is higher than the probability of maintaining a negative mood, and the probability that a negative mood can be repaired is rather high (.60). This simple model shows that change processes can be quite different for the categories of one item.

According to the Markov model, the probability of predicting the category membership later in time, given the category membership at a given moment in time, becomes more uncertain with an increasing time lag. For an individual in a positive mood on the first occasion of measurement in figure 41.1, for example, the probability of belonging to this category on Occasion 2 is .80. The probability that this individual is in the first category on Occasion 3 is .76, because this probability is the sum of the probability of staying in the happy state on all three occasions of measurement ($.80 \times .80 = .64$)

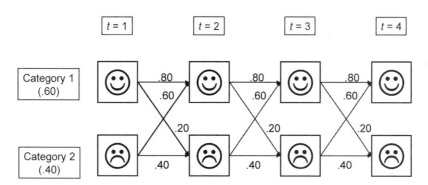

Figure 41.1 Markov model for a dichotomous response variable with two categories (☺, ☹) and four occasions of measurement ($t = 1, \ldots, 4$). Presented are the transition probabilities as well as the (relative) category sizes (in brackets) on the first occasion of measurement.

and the probability of moving from the happy state ($t = 1$) to the unhappy state ($t = 2$) and moving back to the happy state ($t = 3$) ($.20 \times .60 = .12$). The probability of being in the happy state on the fourth occasion of measurement is .66 for an individual who is in a happy state on the first occasion of measurement ($.80 \times .80 \times .80 + .20 \times .60 \times .80 + .20 \times .40 \times .60 = .66$). The probability for the unhappy state can be calculated in the same manner. The Markov model implies a loss of prediction certainty over time. Hence, this model is a typical model for analyzing change processes. It has implications similar to those of the autoregressive model that has been developed for analyzing change with metrical response variables.

Simple Latent-Class Model

This implication of the Markov model might not be appropriate for all kinds of change that can occur in positive psychology. For example, affective well-being is traditionally considered a momentary state that fluctuates around a habitual level of well-being (well-being trait, set point, mood level). According to a state-trait conceptualization of well-being, momentary changes of well-being states are deviations from a well-being trait that are due to situations and the interaction of individuals and situations (Eid & Diener, 2004). These fluctuations are an example of a type of change that Nesselroade (1991) called *variability*. Variability is characterized by short-time fluctuations that are reversible, while *change* in a narrow sense refers to more enduring changes that are often irreversible (such as developmental processes). Whereas the Markov model seems to be appropriate for changes in the narrow sense, it might not be appropriate for measuring short-time fluctuations.

To measure variability, it might be more appropriate to consider models that do not imply a loss of prediction certainty over time but are more in line with the idea of states that fluctuate around a stable trait (set point). One simple model characterizing this type of change for the same data structure is given in figure 41.2. According to this model, there is a latent (hidden) variable with two categories (classes) to which an individual can belong over time. This model is therefore a simple latent-class model. It is assumed that a person can (and must) belong only to one of the two latent classes. The membership of the person is not known beforehand but must

be estimated on the basis of the data. The first class, to which 60% of all individuals belong, characterizes people being happy over time, whereas the second class, to which 40% belong, characterizes people being unhappy over time. The interpretation of the two latent classes as two types of people being happy versus unhappy is inferred from the response probabilities for the observed categories given the latent classes. The class that is interpreted as happy has high conditional response probabilities (.80) for the observed category happy and, consequently, low response probabilities for the observed category unhappy (.20). The two conditional response probabilities must add up to 1 because the individuals have to choose one category. On the other hand, individuals belonging to the second latent class that is interpreted as a class of unhappy people have a probability of .60 to be in an observed unhappy state and a probability of .40 to be in an observed happy state. Moreover, it is assumed that the observed states are independent given the latent-class variables. That means that the latent-class variable explains all associations between the observed variables. All dependencies between the observed states (their stability) can be explained by the fact that there is one latent-class variable representing systematic differences between individuals over time (the two scores of the latent-class variable): There are individuals who are generally happier over time and individuals who are generally less happy over time. The implication of this model for the associations of the observed variables over time is quite different from the implications of the Markov model. For example, for people belonging to the class of happy people, the probability of being in an observed happy state on the first occasion of measurement and the second occasion of measurement is .64. This is calculated by multiplying the two conditional response probabilities ($.80 \times .80$). Moreover, the probability of being in an observed happy state on the first occasion of measurement and the fourth occasion of measurement is also .64 for these individuals. Hence, there is no decline in the associations of the observed variables over time. This model implies a stability of autoassociations over time, whereas the Markov models imply a decline. Hence the two models have different implications and are, therefore, appropriate for measuring different types of change.

Both models are rather simple, but they are restricted in specific ways. The first restriction is due to the fact that the models do not separate

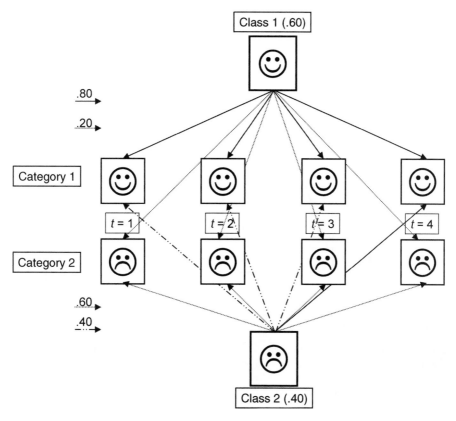

Figure 41.2 A simple latent-class model for one dichotomous response variable with two categories (☺, ☹) and four occasions of measurement ($t = 1, \ldots, 4$). The (relative) class sizes are given in brackets. The arrows indicate the conditional response probabilities.

measurement error from the instability that is due to systematic time-specific influences. Hence, the degree of true variability and change will be overestimated and stability will be underestimated. The second restriction of these models is that they assume that the parameters characterizing the variability and change process are the same for all individuals. For example, in the Markov model, each individual in a positive state has the same probability of .80 of staying in that state and the same probability of .20 of moving to a negative state. In the same vein, in the model with a time-stable latent class, all individuals in the positive latent class have the same probability of .80 of being in a positive observed state on each occasion of measurement. This assumption is rather strong, as it is very likely that individuals differ in their change process.

In order to separate measurement error from true variability and change, it is necessary to assess a construct with multiple indicators and

to choose a measurement model that is able to separate measurement error from systematic occasion-specific influences. Moreover, it is necessary to detect subgroups that differ in their change process.

Models With Multiple Indicators

Latent Markov Model

In multiple-indicator extensions of these models, it is assumed that there are multiple indicators on each occasion of measurement that are fallible indicators of a "true" latent-state variable. In figure 41.3, a multiple-indicator extension of the Markov model with two dichotomous indicators is presented. In this model, called a *latent Markov model* (Wiggins, 1973), it is assumed that there are two different latent-state classes on each occasion of measurement that characterize the state of an individual. In

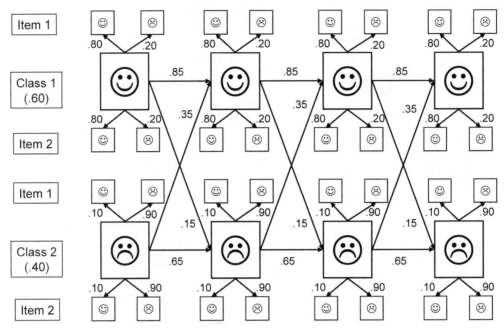

Figure 41.3 A latent Markov model for two dichotomous items with two categories (small ☺, ☹) that are indicators of a dichotomous latent-class variable with two latent classes (large ☺, ☹) on each occasion of measurement ($t = 1, \ldots, 4$). The (relative) class sizes are given in brackets. The arrows indicate the conditional response probabilities and the latent transition probabilities.

this model, it is assumed that there are only two states, a happy state (☺) and an unhappy state (☹) on each occasion of measurement. These different latent-state classes are linked to observable responses by class-specific response probabilities. Because of measurement error, not all individuals in a happy state answer an item in the corresponding positive category and not all individuals in an unhappy state give an answer in the corresponding negative category. But if the item is reliable, there should be a high correspondence between the latent and the observed scores. In the example in figure 41.3, the conditional response probabilities for the observed positive states are rather high for all individuals belonging to the happy latent class (.80) and are rather low for individuals belonging to the unhappy latent class (.10). On the other hand, the conditional probabilities of being in a negative observed state are rather high for all individuals belonging to the unhappy state class (.90) and rather low for all individuals belonging to the positive state class (.20). This shows that the observed variables are reliable indicators of the latent variables.

The process of change is considered by the transition probabilities on the level of the latent-state classes. The change process is characterized in the same way as in the simple Markov model. In the constructed example, there is also a higher probability for maintaining a positive state (.85) than a negative one (.65) and a higher degree of change is provoked by a negative state (.35) than by a positive one (.15). Because measurement error is ubiquitous in psychological and sociological measurements and can cause many artifacts in longitudinal research (Rogosa, 1988), the latent Markov model is a very reasonable extension of the Markov model. Langeheine (1994) presented an application of latent Markov models. Van de Pol and Mannan (2002) gave answers to questions that beginners working with latent Markov models often have.

Latent State-Trait Model

The *latent state-trait model* (Eid & Langeheine, 1999) is based on the same idea as the model in figure 41.2. Like this model, it considers change

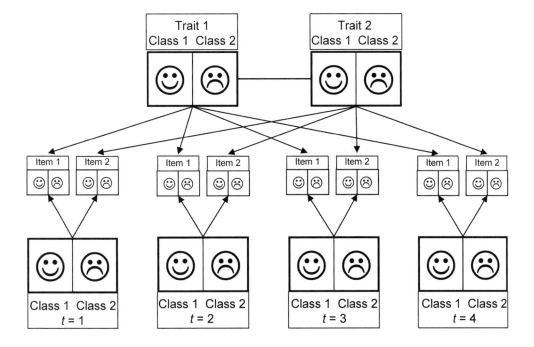

Occasion-specific classes

Figure 41.4 A latent state-trait model for two dichotomous items with two categories (small ☺, ☹) that are indicators of two dichotomous latent-trait variables with two latent classes (large ☺, ☹) and a latent occasion-specific latent-class variable (large ☺, ☹) on each occasion of measurement ($t = 1, \ldots, 4$). The arrows indicate that the response probabilities depend on the trait and occasion-specific class. For each item category on each occasion of measurement, there are four conditional response probabilities for each combination of trait and occasion-specifc class. For reasons of simplicity, these response probabilities are reported in the text.

as situational fluctuations of variable states around stable traits. However, it extends the model in figure 41.2 by considering multiple indicators for one state. It is a latent-class representation of basic measurement ideas that have been developed in latent state-trait theory for metrical (Steyer, Ferring, & Schmitt, 1992; Steyer, Schmitt, & Eid, 1999) and ordinal response variables (Eid & Hoffmann, 1998). This model is depicted in figure 41.4 in a slightly different presentation form in order to avoid too many arrows. In this model, the response probability of an item category depends on two different sources: (1) the membership of an individual in a latent-trait class that characterizes stability over time and represents the idea that there are individuals who are generally more and less happy; and (2) the membership in an occasion-specific class that represents differences

between individuals on the same occasion of measurement.

According to the lower part of the model in figure 41.4, individuals can on each occasion of measurement be in a condition that ameliorates their well-being (latent occasion-specific class ☺) and they can be in conditions that have a negative effect on their well-being (latent occasion-specific class ☹). It is important to note that the individuals do not have to be in the same situation that might be defined by objective characteristics. The occasion-specific classes represent deviations from the values expected by the trait membership that are systematic and might be due to the fact that individuals are in different "outer" and "inner" situations and interact in a different way with the situations in which they are. Situational influences cannot be separated from influences due to an interaction between situations and individuals and are both covered by the occasion-specific variables (see Steyer et al., 1992, for a deeper discussion).

In the model presented in figure 41.4, there is a latent-trait variable (with two latent classes) for each item. The two latent variables can be related. The existence of two latent variables represents the fact that there might be a degree of item specificity. Item specificity means that the two items do not measure a common latent variable. Instead there are stable item-specific influences that one item does not share with the other item. According to this model, there is item homogeneity on the level of the occasion-specific effects as there is only one occasion-specific variable. That means that situations and person-situation interactions have a homogeneous effect on the item responses. However, there are occasion-independent differences between the items. If the two items are perfectly associated on the level of the latent trait variables, the two items are also homogeneous in an occasion-independent way.

The Response Probabilities

In this model, there is for each occasion of measurement a 2×2 table of response probabilities that contains the response probabilities for each combination of trait and occasion-specific classes. This fact is depicted in figure 41.4 by two arrows that link the two categories of an observed variable to the two classes of a latent-trait variable and the two classes of an occasion-specific variable. These probabilities are given in table 41.1 for an observed response to a positive item category (☺) and one occasion of measurement. The conditional probability for a negative response category (☹) is given by 1 minus the conditional response probability of the positive category and is, therefore, not depicted in table 41.1. According to table 41.1, 60 percent of all individuals belong to a positive trait class whereas 40% are in an unhappy trait class. The occasion-specific classes are distributed equally with 50% of individuals in each class. The conditional response probabilities show that the probability of a positive response (☺) is very high (.90) when a happy person (trait class ☺) is in an occasion-specific condition that ameliorates his or her well-being (occasion-specific class ☺); 30% of all individuals belong to this combination of a trait and an occasion-specific class. In an analogous manner, the con-

TABLE 41.1 Conditional Response Probabilities for an Observed Happy Response (☺) Given the Latent Trait and the Latent Occasion-Specific Classes on an Occasion of Measurement

		Trait Classes	
		(.60) ☺	(.40) ☹
Occasion-specific classes	(.50) ☺	(.30) .90	(.20) .60
	(.50) ☹	(.30) .40	(.20) .10

Note: The relative sizes of the classes and the combination of the classes are given in brackets.

ditional response probability of a positive response (☺) is very low (.10) when an unhappy person (trait class ☹) is in a condition that has detrimental influence on her or his well-being (occasion-specific class ☹); 20% of all individuals belong to this combination. There is more response uncertainty in combinations of trait and occasion-specific classes that differ in their valence. Happy individuals in negative occasion-specific conditions characterized by negative effects have a conditional response probability of .40 for a positive category (☺) (30% belong to this combination), whereas unhappy individuals (☹) in conditions that have a positive influence (☺) have a conditional response probability of .60 to the positive category (☺) (20% of all individuals belong to this combination).

The conditional response probabilities that belong to the combinations with different valences of trait and occasion-specific classes are most relevant for comparing the influences of traits and situational or interactional conditions. If the conditional response probabilities are more in line with the trait category, meaning that people in a positive trait class always have high conditional response probabilities for the positive category that are almost independent from the occasion-specific condition to which they belong, then trait influences are more important than occasion-specific influences and there would be low variability in the data. On the other hand, if the response probabilities are more in line with the valence of the occasion-specific classes, meaning that the response probability to a positive category is generally high in positive conditions and generally low in a negative condition and almost independent from the trait class to which an individual belongs, then there is high variability in the data.

The Logit Parameterization

Eid and Langeheine (1999) have shown how a logit parameterization can be used to estimate the degree of association between the observed variable and the latent trait and occasion-specific variables. In fact, the part of the model for one occasion of measurement can be formulated as a log-linear model or a logit model that is, in our example, based on a 2 (observed responses) × 2 (latent-trait classes) × 2 (latent occasion-specific classes) table. For example, the probabilities of this 2 × 2 × 2 table that are calculated on the basis of the conditional response probabilities and class sizes presented in table 41.1 are given in table 41.2. The cells in this table contain the relative sizes of the combinations. The value of .27 in the first cell, for example, means that 27% of all individuals belong to a positive trait class (☺) and a positive occasion-specific class (☺) and give a response to the positive category (☺). The association between two categorical variables can be calculated by the odds ratio. The odds ratio between the occasion-specific classes and the observed responses can be calculated for each trait class separately. To calculate this odds ratio for the positive trait class (☺), the probabilities (cell sizes) of the combinations of the observed response categories and the latent occasion-specific classes that have the same valence ($☺_C☺_S$) and ($☹_C☹_S$) have to be multiplied, whereas the index C indicates the response category and the index S indicates the occasion-specific class. This product has to be divided by the product of the probabilities of the com-

binations differing in their valence, that is, the combinations ($☺_C☹_S$) and ($☹_C☺_S$). That means that the odds ratio (OR) describing the association between the observed responses (C) and the latent occasion-specific classes (S) for the first category of the trait $☺_T$ (index T: trait) is calculated by:

$$OR(C,S) = \frac{Prob(☺_C☺_S)}{Prob(☺_C☹_S)} \frac{Prob(☹_C☹_S)}{Prob(☹_C☺_S)}$$
$$= \frac{.27 \times .18}{.12 \times .03} = 13.5,$$

where *Prob* denotes the probability of a combination, that is, the theoretical relative size given in table 41.2. The odds ratio for the second trait class can be calculated in the same way using the subtable that refers to the second trait category (☹). The odds ratio in the second trait class has the same value as in the first trait class because the model assumes that there is no interaction between trait and occasion-specific classes. The odds ratio of 13.5 indicates that there is a strong relation between the occasion-specific influences and the observed responses. The odds ratio is not limited in its upper value. A value of 1 indicates that two variables are unrelated. A value that is larger than 1 indicates a positive association, whereas a value that is smaller than 1 indicates a negative relation (Hagenaars 1990; Kennedy 1992).

To calculate the odds ratios for the observed responses and the latent-trait classes, the table can be restructured by nesting the trait classes within the occasion-specific classes (see table 41.3). The odds ratio $OR(C,T)$ between the observed response and the trait classes do not depend on the occasion-specific class because it is assumed that there is no interaction between the

TABLE 41.2 Relative Sizes of the Cells of a 2 × 2 × 2 Table Describing the Relations Between the Observed Responses, the Latent Trait Classes, and the Latent Occasion-Specific Classes of a Latent State-Trait Model

| | | Trait Classes | | | |
| | | ☺ Occasion-Specific Class | | ☹ Occasion-Specific Class | |
		☺	☹	☺	☹
Observed	☺	.27	.12	.12	.02
responses	☹	.03	.18	.08	.18
		Odds ratio = 13.5		Odds ratio = 13.5	

TABLE 41.3 Restructured for Analyzing the Odds Ratio Between the Trait Classes and the Observed Responses

		Occasion-Specific Classes			
		☺ Trait Class		☹ Trait Class	
		☺	☹	☺	☹
Observed	☺	.27	.12	.12	.02
responses	☹	.03	.08	.18	.18
		Odds ratio = 6		Odds ratio = 6	

trait and the occasion-specific classes. Hence, the odds ratios are:

$$OR(R,T) = \frac{Prob(☺_C☺_T)}{Prob(☺_C☹_T)} \frac{Prob(☹_C☹_T)}{Prob(☹_C☺_T)}$$
$$= \frac{.27 \times .08}{.12 \times .03} = \frac{.12 \times .18}{.02 \times .18} = 6.$$

The odds ratios are larger than 1, indicating that there is a positive relation between the trait variable and the observed responses. That means that happy individuals more often choose the positive response category. The odds ratio is larger for the occasion-specific classes than for the trait classes, indicating that the influences of situations or interactions are stronger than the influences of trait differences.

In order to obtain the logit parameter for the occasion-specific variable, the odds ratios of the occasion-specific classes that have been calculated for each trait class (see table 41.2) have to be multiplied. Then the eighth root of this product has to be taken (because there are eight cells of the table), and the logarithm of this value has to be calculated. The obtained value must be multiplied by 2. This is the typically calculation rule for logit models that are described in textbooks on categorical data analysis (e.g., Hagenaars, 1990). That means that the logit parameter for the occasion-specific variables is $w_{C,S} = 2 \times \ln(13.5^2)^{1/8} = 1.301$, and the logit parameter for the trait variable is $w_{C,T} = 2 \times \ln(6^2)^{1/8} = 0.896$. A logit model additionally contains a parameter that represents general differences in the distribution of the observed response categories. In our example, this parameter can be calculated by multiplying all probabilities in table 41.2 belonging to the positive response category (☺) and dividing this product by the product of all probabilities belonging to the negative response category (☹). After taking the eighth root of this ratio and

then calculating the logarithm and multiplying the new value by 2, one gets the logit parameter $w_C = 2 \times \ln [(.27 \times .12 \times .12 \times .02)/(.03 \times .18 \times .08 \times .18)]^{1/8} = 0$. This parameter shows that across the different combinations of trait and occasion-specific class, there is no preference in choosing a response category. In our example, the logit model can be formulated as

$$\ln\left(\frac{\Pi_{☺_C|☺_T☺_C}}{\Pi_{☹_C|☺_T☺_S}}\right) = w_C + w_{C,O} + w_{C,T}$$
$$= 0 + 1.301 + 0.896,$$

whereas $\pi_{☺_C|☺_T☺_S}$ is the conditional response probability for the positive category given the positive trait class and the positive occasion-specific class, whereas $\pi_{☺_C|☺_T☺_S}$ is the corresponding conditional response probability for the negative response category. The logarithm of the ratio of the two response probabilities is called *logit*. The logit is decomposed into three components from which the logit parameters for the occasion-specific classes and the trait classes are most interesting. These coefficients only depend on the odds ratios that characterize the associations between the observed and the latent variables. Further coefficients that are of interest for this model are described by Eid and Langeheine (1999).

Latent State-Trait Markov Model

Eid and Langeheine (1999) have also shown how the ideas of the latent Markov model and the latent state-trait model can be integrated into one general model. The basic idea of this model is to start with the structure of a latent state-trait model and to add a Markov structure on the level of the latent occasion-specific variables. That means that the occasion-specific latent classes are not independent as in the model in figure 41.4 but associated. The association structure of the occasion-specific classes in this extended model looks like the structure of the latent variables in figure 41.3. From the scope of the latent state-trait model, the Markov structure on the level of the occasion-specific variables indicates that the occasion-specific influences are not totally independent but there is a kind of inertia, which means that individuals have a tendency to stay in situations and do not change them randomly. As a consequence of this model the autoassociations are not perfectly stable, but there is a decline in stability that is, however, less pronounced as in the latent Markov model.

From the point of view of the latent Markov model, the trait structure in this extended model can be interpreted in such a way that there is a personality bound for the change process. Because of the existence of the latent-trait classes, there is more stability in the data as would be explained by a pure Markov model. Moreover, the item-specific latent-trait variables are able to take item-specific effects into account. Item-specific effects are often present in longitudinal studies and are often discussed under the topic of autocorrelated errors or local dependencies (Hagenaars, 1990). Whereas the latent Markov model is not able to account for these influences, the latent state-trait Markov model is an appropriate way to take item-specific effects into account and might, therefore, be preferable to the latent Markov model whenever the items are not perfectly homogeneous.

Mixture Distribution Models

The latent Markov model and the latent state-trait models allow separating measurement error from true (systematic) variability and change. They are, however, also restricted as they assume that the individuals belonging to the same latent classes do not differ in their change process. For example, in the latent Markov model in figure 41.3, the probability of staying in the first category is .85 for all individuals belonging to the happy latent class on the first occasion of measurement. However, the probabilities for staying and moving might be quite different for different individuals. There might be individuals who stay for the whole period of time in the happy latent state ("true stayers") and whose variability in observed item scores might only be due to measurement error. There might also

be individuals that are unpredictable, which means that their probabilities of staying and of moving are .50. There might even be individuals with an extreme variability indicated by a very high probability of changing. In order to represent interindividual differences in the change process appropriately, latent Markov models and latent state-trait Markov models have been extended to mixture-distribution models that allow a grouping of individuals according to their change process.

Mixed Markov Latent-Class Models

In contrast to the latent Markov model, the *mixed Markov latent-class model* allows interindividual differences in change processes. In this class of models, it is assumed that the population consists of different subpopulations ("chains") that differ in their change processes. These subpopuations are unknown, but the number of relevant subpopulations and their sizes can be estimated. In fact, each subpopulation is characterized by a latent Markov model as depicted in figure 41.3, but the parameters of the model (conditional response probabilities, transition probabilities, class sizes) can differ between latent chains. This class of models is extensively discussed by Langeheine and van de Pol (1990, 1994).

Mixed Latent State-Trait Models

Eid and Langeheine (2003) have shown how the latent state-trait model and the latent state-trait Markov model can be extended to a mixture-distribution model. Like the mixed Markov model, this model consists of different latent chains that differ in their change model. In particular, Eid and Langeheine (2003) discussed four types of models that can explain stability and change in different latent chains: (1) A latent state-trait model, (2) a latent state-trait Markov model, (3) a latent trait model in which perfect latent stability is assumed and all variability in observed responses is due to measurement error, and (4) a latent Markov model with transition probabilities of .5, that is, a model of instability with perfect unpredictability. In this model, there is no association between the occasion-specific classes on different occasions of measurement. They found that a mixed latent state-trait model with two chains consisting of a (1) latent state-trait model with Markov structure and (2) a latent-trait model with perfect latent stability could explain stability and change in negative mood states very well. Moreover, they could show that the mixed latent state-trait model is a special variant of the mixed Markov latent-class model, proving that the mixed Markov latent-class model is a very general modeling approach for analyzing variability and change.

Synopsis of the Models

A synopsis of the models discussed so far is given in figure 41.5. The most general model presented is the mixed Markov latent-class model, which considers latent subgroups (chains) differing in their change process. This model can be used either to test a priori hypotheses in a confirmatory way or to find latent subgroups (chains) differing in their change process in an exploratory way. This model is not generally identified, particularly if there are less than six occasions of measurement (van de Pol, Langeheine, & de Jong, 1996), and many parameters have to be estimated. Therefore, it is recommended to restrict the parameters of this model in order to obtain identified and simpler models. The mixed latent state-trait model is a specific type of a mixed Markov latent-class model that is defined by several restrictions. This model assumes that models belonging to the family of latent state-trait models can characterize the change process

in the latent chains. For example, it might be assumed that there is one chain of traited individuals and one chain of individuals for whom a latent state-trait Markov model holds (Eid & Langeheine, 2003). If there are no latent subgroups differing in their change process, the mixed latent state-trait model reduces to the latent state-trait Markov model, which assumes that the response probabilities on an occasion of measurement depend on latent-trait as well as latent occasion-specific variables. Stability is explained by the existence of latent-trait variables as well as the inertia of the change process represented by latent transition probabilities on the level of the latent occasion-specific variables that are explained by a Markov structure.

If the change process follows totally a latent Markov structure, no latent-trait variables are needed, and the model reduces to a latent Markov model. If there is only one observed variable on an occasion of measurement, instability caused by measurement error cannot be separated from instability caused by occasion-specific influences. Consequently, only a Markov model can be applied to analyze this type of change.

If there is no Markov process on the level of the occasion-specific latent variables, the latent state-trait Markov model reduces to the latent state-trait model, in which the stability is totally explained by the latent trait variables. If there is only one indicator on each occasion of

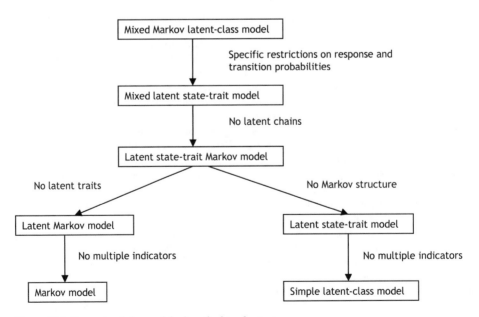

Figure 41.5 Synopsis of the models described in the text.

measurement, situational influences cannot be separated from measurement error, and it is only possible to consider this type of change in a simple latent-class model in which one latent class variable explains the stability.

In order to separate true variability and change from unsystematic error influences, it is recommended to consider at least two indicator variables for each construct considered. In the next step, it would be advisable to analyze a latent state-trait Markov model as a general single-chain model. The fit of this model can be compared to mixed latent state-trait models. If the latent state-trait Markov model fits the data well and a mixture variant of the model does not fit better, one could compare the fit of the latent state-trait Markov model with the two more restricted variants (latent Markov model, latent state-trait model) in order to find out whether or not stability and change could be explained by a simpler model. If the latent state-trait Markov model and its extensions to mixed latent state-trait models do not fit the data, it is recommended to investigate whether the general mixed Markov latent-class model without the specific restrictions of the mixed latent state-trait model could explain the change process sufficiently.

Log-Linear Models with Latent Variables

All models discussed so far are special variants of a very general family of models that is called log-linear models with latent variables (Hagenaars, 1993). Log-linear models with latent variables are multidimensional latent-class models that are restricted according to the principles of log-linear models. This approach is very similar to linear structural equation models, which are often called LISREL models because LISREL was the first computer program for applying this type of model (Jöreskog & Sörbom, 1996). Therefore, Hagenaars (1988) has called this approach a modified LISREL approach. It differs from the structural equation modeling approach at least in two important way: First, the observed and the latent variables are categorical and, second, not only the bivariate relations but also all higher-order associations between the variables can be easily analyzed. The associations between the latent categorical variables (latent classes) as well as the associations between the observed variables and the associations between the observed

and latent variables can be analyzed in quite complex ways. This very flexible structure enables researchers to define complex models for analyzing variability and change that correspond to their theoretical assumptions. An introduction to log-linear models with latent variables is given by Hagenaars (1990, 1993).

All these models are based on the basic ideas of latent class analysis that goes back to the early work of Lazarsfeld (1950) and Lazarsfeld and Henry (1968). Because appropriate estimation procedures and easy-to-handle computer programs were not available in the early years of latent-class analysis, the majority of applications of latent-class analysis have been found in the last 20 years. Introductions to latent-class analysis are given by McCutcheon (1987), Clogg (1995), Rost and Langeheine (1997), and Eid, Langeheine, and Diener (2003).

The latent-class framework, particularly the log-linear models with latent variables, have many advantages for analyzing variability and change in positive psychology. They consider measurement error influences that are not avoidable in psychological research. They do not assume that all items have to be ordered on a latent continuum that is obligatory for all individuals. Instead, there can be typological (qualitative) differences between individuals. These qualitative differences are represented by the different latent classes (types). These latent classes can be ordered on a latent continuum as a result of the analysis, but they must not be ordered and can follow other structures. In the latent class framework, it is comparably easy to formulate models with population heterogeneity that take unobserved structural differences in a population into account. Given the results of a latent-class analysis, each individual can be assigned to a latent class for which his or her assignment probability is maximum. The major disadvantage of latent-class analysis is the requirement regarding the size of a sample, and we will discuss this topic in the framework of estimating and testing a latent-class model.

Estimating and Testing Latent-Class Models

Computer programs for estimating the parameters of a latent-class model use an expectation-maximization (EM) algorithm for obtaining maximum likelihood estimates. This algorithm cannot be described in detail here, but it is explained in books on latent-class analysis (e.g., Hagenaars, 1990). Statistical tests for evaluating the fit of a latent-class model compare the observed frequencies of the different response patterns and the frequencies of the response patterns expected on the basis of a latent-class model. A latent-class model fits the data well when the observed frequencies are close to the expected frequencies. There are several goodness-of-fit criteria for testing the hypothesis that the expected and observed frequencies are equal in the population. The most frequently used statistics are the Pearson χ^2 statistic, the likelihood-ratio test, and the Cressie-Read statistic. All three test statistics are approximately χ^2-distributed with df degrees of freedom, whereas the degrees of freedom are calculated by $df = $ (number of response patterns -1) $-$ (number of estimated parameters). *Approximately* means that this distribution assumption holds when the sample size goes to "infinity." When the samples are small, the condition under which this distributional approximation holds is less clear (see Read & Cressie, 1988, for a deeper discussion of this aspect). There are some rules of thumb such as the recommendation that the expected frequency of each response pattern should be at least 1 or even 5. If the sample size is small compared to the number of possible response patterns, this causes the problem of sparse tables. Sparse tables are contingency tables with many small and zero observed frequencies, which are associated with very small expected frequencies. In the case of sparse tables, the p values of the test statistics, which are calculated on the basis of the χ^2 statistic, might not be valid, and the test statistics cannot be trusted in general. This sample size restriction is the major limitation of latent-class analysis.

There are several ways to deal with the problem of sparse tables. One way is to collapse the categories of an item to get a smaller number of possible response patterns. Collapsing categories, however, is not always possible and meaningful, and the practice of dichotomizing variables has been strongly criticized by MacCallum, Zhang, Preacher, and Rucker (2002). Collapsing categories would be justified if the frequency of one category is very low, so that this category does not contain much information that could be used for estimating the parameters.

If one does not want to collapse categories, a rule of thumb can be used to check whether the test statistics are approximately χ^2-distributed. When all three test statistics differ largely in their values, this indicates that these test statistics are not approximately χ^2-distributed. If the values of the test statistics are very similar, this indicates that the distributional assumption might hold. Another, more promising way to handle the problem of sparse tables is bootstrapping analysis, which is generally recommended by Langeheine, Pannekoek, and van de Pol (1996) in the case of sparse tables. The basic idea of bootstrapping is to estimate the distribution of the test statistics using resampling methods. Based on the estimated distribution, a p value is obtained for the model of interest that is more valid. According to Langeheine et al. (1996), it is sufficient to have 300 bootstrap samples to get appropriate estimates of the distribution. Von Davier (1997) found that in the context of latent-class analysis, bootstrap methods work well with the Pearson χ^2 statistic and the Cressie-Read statistic, but not with the likelihood-ratio test. Consequently, the Pearson χ^2 statistic and the Cressie-Read statistic should be used for testing a latent class model by bootstrap analyses.

The test statistics described so far can be used to test a latent-class model. That means that these test statistics can be used to test a model in a confirmatory way. Applications of latent-class models for analyzing variability and change, however, often have an exploratory component. For example, before applying a model for analyzing variability and change, one might conduct a latent-class analysis only on the first occasion of measurement to find out how many classes are needed to represent interindividual differences sufficiently in the observed variables. One might also not be sure about the number of latent chains needed in a mixture distribution model. Latent models differing in the number of classes or chains cannot be statistically compared by the three test statistics described so far. In these cases, however, the fit of different latent-class models can be compared by information criteria such as Akaikes information criterion (AIC) and the Bayesian information criterion (BIC; for an overview, see Read & Cressie, 1988). These criteria offset the fit of the model with the number of parameters estimated. A model with more parameters is a less restrictive model, and it is therefore likely that this model will fit the data better than a more restrictive model. The information criteria compare the fit of the model in terms of the closeness of observed and expected frequency with the number of parameters needed to obtain this fit. Information criteria are looking for good-fitting models that are rather simple. All latent-class models analyzed can be ranked with respect to their AIC and BIC coefficients, and the model with the smallest values can be chosen as the best-fitting model. According to Lin and Dayton (1997), the AIC seems to be more appropriate for evaluating relatively complex models, whereas the BIC seems to be more appropriate in the case of relatively simple models. However, there is no general rule for preferring one of these coefficients to the other. Generally, the AIC favors models having a larger number of classes than BIC does.

Software

The computer program LEM (Vermunt, 1993) is a general program for analyzing log-linear models with latent variables and can be used to analyze all models presented in this chapter. The program PANMARK (van de Pol et al., 1996) has been developed for analyzing Markov models and its extensions to latent Markov models and mixed Markov models. It is easier to handle than LEM because it is menu-driven but is restricted to all models that can be nested under the general mixed Markov latent-class model. Latent-class models can also be analyzed with the computer program Mplus (Muthén & Muthén, 2002).

Guide to References of Other and Related Approaches

The aim of this chapter is to give a comprehensive introduction to latent-class models for analyzing variability and change. Not all approaches modeling variability and change with latent-class models and not all applications of these models could be considered. Therefore, some hints of other and related approaches are given here. An approach that is closely related to latent Markov models is latent transition analysis, which has been developed for analyzing change with respect to different stages (Collins, Hyatt, & Graham, 2000). This approach is particularly useful for analyzing change in developmental psychology. Langeheine (1994) shows how stage-specific developments can also be analyzed in the context of latent Markov models by constraining latent transition probabilities. The book edited by von Eye and Clogg (1994) contains many chapters about latent-class analysis approaches for analyzing change in developmental psychology. Humphreys and Janson

(2000) extended latent transition models by including covariates. Vermunt, Langeheine, and Böckenholt (1999) showed how time-constant and time-varying covariates can be integrated into latent Markov models.

The models described in this chapter deal with categorical observed variables. Muthén and Muthén (2000) as well as Muthén (2001) combined longitudinal models for metrical response variables such as growth-curve models with latent-class analysis to obtain growth-mixture models. Moreover, the approaches treated in this chapter have focused on models for relatively large samples of individuals. For analyzing change in single case studies, a related approach has been developed that is called hidden Markov models. Hidden Markov models are latent Markov models for single-case applications. Visser, Raijmakers, and Molenaar (2002) discuss advantages and problems of fitting hidden Markov models to psychological data.

References

Clogg, C. C. (1995). Latent class models. In M. E. Sobel (Ed.), *Handbook of statistical modeling for the social and behavioral sciences* (pp. 311–359). New York, Plenum.

Collins, L. M., Hyatt, S. L., & Graham, J. W. (2000). Latent transition analysis as a way of testing models of stage-sequential change in longitudinal data. In T. D. Little, K. U. Schnabel, & J. Baumert (Eds.), *Modeling longitudinal and multilevel data: Practical issues, applied approaches, and specific examples* (pp. 147–161). Mahwah, NJ: Erlbaum.

Eid, M., & Diener, E. (2004). Global judgments of well-being: Situational variability and long-term stability. *Social Indicators Research, 65*, 245–277.

Eid, M., & Hoffmann, L. (1998). Measuring variability and change with an item response model for polytomous variables. *Journal of Educational and Behavioral Statistics, 23*, 193–215.

Eid, M., & Langeheine, R. (1999). The measurement of consistency and occasion specificity with latent class models: A new model and its application to the measurement of affect. *Psychological Methods, 4*, 100–116.

Eid, M., & Langeheine, R. (2003). Separating stable from variable individuals in longitudinal studies by mixture distribution models. *Measurement: Interdisciplinary Research and Perspective*, 179–206.

Eid, M., Langeheine, R., & Diener, E. (2003). Comparing typological structures across cultures by multigroup latent class analysis: A primer. *Journal of Cross Cultural Psychology, 34,* 195–210.

Eid, M., Mayer, A.-K., Steyer, R., Notz, P., & Schwenkmezger, P. (1993). Monopolar mood factors—a methodological artifact? First results of a simulations study with LISCOMP. In R. Steyer, K. F. Wender, & K. Widaman (Eds.), *Proceedings of the 7th European Meeting of the Psychometric Society* (pp. 129–134). Stuttgart: Fischer.

Eid, M., & Rauber, M. (2000). Detecting measurement invariance in organizational surveys. *European Journal of Psychological Assessment, 16,* 20–30.

Eid, M., Schneider, C., & Schwenkmezger, P. (1999). Do you feel better or worse? The validity of perceived deviations of mood states from mood traits. *European Journal of Personality, 13,* 283–306.

Hagenaars, J. A. (1988). LCAG—Loglinear modelling with latent variables: A modified LISREL approach. In W. E. Saris & I. N. Gallhofer (Eds.), *Sociometric research: Vol. 2. Data analysis* (pp. 111–130). London: Macmillan.

Hagenaars, J. A. (1990). *Categorical longitudinal data: Log-linear panel, trend, and cohort analysis.* Newbury Park, CA: Sage.

Hagenaars, J. A. (1993). *Loglinear models with latent variables.* Newbury Park, CA: Sage.

Humphreys, K., & Janson, H. (2000). Latent transition analysis with covariates, nonresponse, summary statistics and diagnostics. *Multivariate Behavioral Research, 35,* 89–118.

Jöreskog, K. G., & Sörbom, D. (1996). *LISREL 8 user's reference guide.* Chicago: Scientific Software International.

Kennedy, J. J. (1992). *Analyzing qualitative data: Log-linear analysis for behavioral research.* New York: Praeger.

Langeheine, R. (1988). Manifest and latent Markov chain models for categorical panel data. *Journal of Educational Statistics, 13,* 299–312.

Langeheine, R. (1994). Latent variables Markov models. In A. von Eye & C. C. Clogg (Eds.), *Latent variable analysis: Applications for developmental research* (pp. 373–395). Thousand Oaks, CA: Sage.

Langeheine, R., Pannekoek, J., & van de Pol, F. (1996). Bootstrapping goodness-of-fit measures in categorical data analysis. *Sociological Methods and Research, 24,* 492–516.

Langeheine, R., & van de Pol, F. (1990). A unifying framework for Markov modeling in discrete space and discrete time. *Sociological Methods and Research, 18,* 416–441.

Langeheine, R., & van de Pol, F. (1994). Discrete-time mixed Markov latent class models. In

A. Dale & R. B. Davies (Eds.), *Analyzing social and political change* (pp. 167–197). London: Sage.

Lazarsfeld, P. F. (1950). Logical and mathematical foundation of latent structure analysis. In S. A. Stouffer, L. Guttman, E. A. Suchman, P. Lazarsfeld, S. A. Star, & J. Clausen (Eds.), *Studies in social psychology in World War II: Vol. IV. Measurement and prediction.* (S.362–412). Princeton, NJ: Princeton University Press.

Lazarsfeld, P. F., & Henry, N. W. (1968). *Latent structure analysis.* Boston: Houghton Mifflin.

Lin, T. H., & Dayton, C. M. (1997). Model selection information criteria for non-nested latent class models. *Journal of Educational and Behavioral Statistics, 22,* 249–264.

Linden, W. J. v. d., & Hambleton, R. K. (1997). *Handbook of modern item response theory.* New York: Springer.

Mac Callum, R. C., Zhang, S., Preacher, K. J., & Rucker, D. D. (2002). On the practice of dichotomization of quantitative variables. *Psychological Methods, 7,* 19–40.

McCutcheon, A. L. (1987). *Latent class analysis.* Newbury Park, CA: Sage.

Muthén, B. (1983). Latent variable structural equation modeling with categorical variables. *Journal of Econometrics, 49,* 22–45.

Muthén, B. (2001). Second-generation structural equation modeling with a combination of categorical and continuous latent variables: New opportunities for latent class/latent growth modeling. In D. M. Collins & A. G. Sayer (Eds.), *New methods for the analysis of change* (pp. 291–322). Washington, DC: American Psychological Association.

Muthén, B., & Muthén, L. K. (2000). Integrating person-centered and variable-centered analyses: Growth mixture modeling with latent trajectory classes. *Alcoholism: Clinical and Experimental Research, 24,* 882–891.

Muthén, B., & Muthén, L. K. (2002). *Mplus users guide.* Los Angeles: Muthén and Muthén.

Nesselroade, J. (1991). Interindividual differences in intraindividual change. In D. M. Collins & J. C. Horn (Eds.), *Best methods for the analysis of change: Recent advances, unanswered questions, future directions* (pp. 92–105). Washington, DC: American Psychological Association.

Olsson, U. (1979). On the robustness of factor analysis against crude classification of the observations. *Multivariate Behavioral Research, 14,* 485–500.

Read, T. R. C., & Cressie, N. A. C. (1988). *Goodness-of-fit statistics for discrete multivariate data.* New York: Springer.

Rogosa, D. R. (1988). Myths about longitudinal research. In K. W. Schaie, R. T. Campbell, W. M. Meredith, & S. C. Rawlings (Eds.),

Methodological issues in aging research (pp. 171–209). New York: Springer.

Rost, J., & Langeheine, R. (1997). *Applications of latent trait and latent class models in the social sciences*. Münster: Waxmann.

Steyer, R., Ferring, D., & Schmitt, M. J. (1992). States and traits in psychological assessment. *European Journal of Psychological Assessment, 8,* 79–98.

Steyer, R., Schmitt, M., & Eid, M. (1999). Latent state-trait theory and research in personality and individual differences. *European Journal of Personality, 13,* 389–408.

Takane, Y., & de Leeuw, J. (1987). On the relationship between item response theory and factor analysis of discretized variables. *Psychometrika, 52,* 393–408.

van de Pol, F., Langeheine, R., & de Jong, W. (1996). *PANMARK 3: User's manual. Panel analysis using Markov chains—A latent class analysis program*. Voorburg, Netherlands: Statistics Netherlands.

van de Pol, F., & Mannan, H. (2002). Questions of a novice in latent Markov modelling. *Methods of Psychological Research, 7,* 1–18.

Vermunt, J. K. (1993). *Lem: Log-linear and event history analysis with missing data using the EM algorithm*. Tilburg: Tilburg University.

Vermunt, J. K., Langeheine, R., & Böckenholt, U. (1999). Discrete-time discrete-state latent Markov models with time-constant and time-varying covariates. *Journal of Educational and Behavioral Statistics, 24,* 179–207.

Von Davier, M. (1997). Bootstrapping goodness-of-fit statistics for sparse categorical data; Results of a Monte Carlo study. *Methods of Psychological Research, 2*(2). Retrieved from http://www.mpr-online.de

Visser, I., Raijmakers, M. E. J., & Molenaar, P. C. M. (2000). Confidence intervals for hidden Markov model parameters. *British Journal of Mathematical and Statistical Psychology, 53*(2), 317–327.

von Eye, A., & Clogg, C. C. (1994). *Latent variable analysis. Applications for developmental research*. Thousand Oaks, CA: Sage.

Wiggins, L. M. (1973). *Panel analysis*. Amsterdam: Elsevier.

42

Detecting Population Heterogeneity in Stability and Change in Subjective Well-Being by Mixture Distribution Models

Michael Eid and Rolf Langeheine

The state-trait distinction has a long tradition in psychology. Particularly in emotion psychology, it is common to distinguish between an emotional state that characterizes the emotion felt at any given moment in time and an emotional trait that describes the disposition of an individual to the repeated experience of a specific emotional state (e.g., Lazarus, 1991; Spielberger, 1977). In positive psychology, it is also common to distinguish, for example, between the momentary well-being of an individual and a general well-being set point that characterizes an individual across situations and time (e.g., Csikszentmihalyi & Wong, 1991; Eid & Diener, 2004). The state-trait distinction enables positive psychologists to simultaneously analyze the effect of stable personality traits as well as fluctuating situational influences on the experience of subjective well-being.

In order to separate stable traits from variable situational influences, psychometric models are needed that allow the decomposition of a momentary state into (1) a component that characterizes an individual over situations and time and (2) a component that indicates effects due to situational influences on an occasion of measurement as well as the interaction between the situation and an individual. Moreover, psychometric models must deal with the influences of measurement error as well, because measurement error usually cannot be avoided in psychological studies.

During the past few years, several approaches have been developed that fulfill these requirements, such as the models of latent state-trait (LST) theory (e.g., Eid & Diener, 2004; Steyer, Ferring, & Schmitt, 1992; Steyer, Schmitt, & Eid, 1999), the state-trait error model (Kenny & Zautra, 1995), and the models of longitudinal factor analysis (Marsh & Grayson, 1994). These approaches are appropriate for measuring latent metrical states and traits by metrical response variables. Based on LST theory, Eid (1996, 1997) has developed a model for measuring metrical latent states and traits by observed ordinal variables (see also Steyer & Partchev, 2001, for

a similar approach). Moreover, Eid and Langeheine (1999) have shown how state-trait models
can be defined in the framework of log-linear
models with latent variables in order to measure
latent categorical state and trait variables on
the basis of categorical observed variables (see
chapter 41, this volume).

Research on positive and negative emotional
states has revealed that there are strong interindividual differences in intraindividual consistency and variability (Eid & Diener, 1999).
What this simply means is that individuals differ
in the degree of their emotional fluctuations.
There are individuals who are rather stable across
situations and time, whereas other individuals
change their emotional states rapidly (e.g., Depue
et al., 1981; Eid & Diener, 1999; Hepburn & Eysenck, 1989; Larsen, 1987; McConville & Cooper,
1992; Penner, Shiffman, Paty, & Fritzsche, 1994).
These results fit into the larger framework of
research on intraindividual consistency (Bem &
Allen, 1974; Schmitt & Borkenau, 1992; Tellegen,
1988) and the metatrait approach (Baumeister,
1991; Baumeister & Tice, 1988; Britt, 1993;
Hershberger, Plomin, & Pedersen, 1995), all of
which represent a theoretical framework for
analyzing individual differences in situation-
specific fluctuations. Baumeister and Tice (1988)
defined a metatrait as "the trait of having versus
not having a particular trait" (p. 573), and they
classified individuals according to their metatrait
into a group of "traited" or a group of "untraited"
individuals. Untraited individuals are more prone
to situational influences than traited individuals,
who should be rather consistent across situations.

As an implication of the metatrait approach,
individuals can differ in their variability across
time. Consequently, psychometric models for
analyzing individuals across time and situations
must consider interindividual differences in intraindividual consistency and variability. Eid and
Langeheine (2003) extended latent state-trait
models for categorical variables to mixture distribution state-trait models. In their extension,
different latent subgroups (classes) are separated
with respect to their intraindividual variability.
In fact, they have distinguished several types
of models in which a latent subgroup of stable
individuals is compared to a subgroup of variable individuals, although the degree of variability can be quite different (perfect variability,
state-traited individuals, Markov state-traited
individuals). Eid and Langeheine (2003) illustrated their approach with binary response
items. Moreover, the model was described more

conceptually than formally. The aim of the
present chapter is to show how this approach can
be extended to variables with more than two
response categories. Furthermore, we describe
how mixture distribution state-trait models can
be formally defined. The model is illustrated by
an application to the measurement of positive
mood, and some practical problems that are related to applying mixture distribution state-trait
models are discussed.

Eid and Langeheine (2003) have shown that the
most fruitful extension of the state-trait model is
a mixture distribution model with one chain of
individuals who are traited (stable over time) and
one chain of individuals for whom a Markov
state-trait model holds; therefore, in this chapter
major emphasis is given to this model. To facilitate the understanding of the model, we introduce it using an empirical example that is first
described in brief.

Observed Variables and Research Plan

The model can be applied to categorical observed
variables that have been repeatedly assessed over
time. The application presented here refers to
two items measuring the momentary positive
mood of an individual. The first item is the
German adjective *heiter*, which can best be
translated into English as *cheerful*. The second
item is the German adjective *vergnügt*, which
can be translated as *happy*. The two items were
assessed using a 5-point response scale. The first
category of the response scale was denoted *not at
all*, the fifth category was labeled *very much*.
The three categories in between were not labeled. The response scale was recoded into three
categories by merging the two extreme categories into one category each. This was done for
two reasons. The first reason is that it reduces
the complexity of the model. The second reason
is that categorical response variables with many
categories can cause problems due to sparse tables (discussed below). The sample consisted of
502 individuals who assessed their current mood
four times with a time lag of 3 weeks between
two measurements.

Hence, the data set consists of eight observed
variables (two items on four occasions of measurement). Each observed variable has three
categories of the intensity of mood: The first category indicates a low mood, the second category
represents a middle mood, and the third category
stands for a high mood. There are $3^8 = 6{,}561$

possible response patterns, of which 374 are considered in this analysis.

The Latent State-Trait Model with Markov Structure

The mixture distribution model is an extension of the latent state-trait model with Markov structure (see chapter 41, this volume). The model of our example, consisting of two items and four occasions of measurement, is depicted in figure 42.1. This figure shows that an observed response variable O_{ik} representing an item i on an occasion k depends on a latent trait variable T_i that is item specific and an occasion-specific variable S_k measuring the influences due to the situations and interactions on an occasion of measurement. This variable S_k represents all occasion-specific influences that cannot be explained by the trait alone. Hence, it is not necessary to actually know the situations in which individuals are. Although measured on the same occasion of measurement, individuals will be in different "inner" situations, and this variability in inner situations across time

causes the variability of states. Moreover, a process might be found at the level of the occasion-specific variables indicating a possible trend in the data, because individuals can become more or less happy over time. This trend is represented by the arrows between the two variables S_k and $S_{(k+1)}$ in figure 42.1. Formally, this model is defined by the following equation (Eid & Langeheine, 1999):

$$\pi_{t_1 t_2 s_1 o_{11} o_{21} s_2 o_{12} o_{22} s_3 o_{13} o_{23} s_4 o_{14} o_{24}}$$

$$= \pi_{t_1 t_2} \pi_{s_1} \pi_{o_{11}|t_1 s_1} \pi_{o_{21}|t_2 s_1} \pi_{s_2|s_1}$$

$$\pi_{o_{12}|t_1 s_2} \pi_{o_{22}|t_2 s_2} \pi_{s_3|s_2} \pi_{o_{13}|t_1 s_3} \pi_{o_{23}|t_2 s_3}$$

$$\pi_{s_4|s_3} \pi_{o_{14}|t_1 s_4} \pi_{o_{24}|t_2 s_4} \tag{1}$$

where $\pi_{t_1 t_2 s_1 o_{11} o_{21} s_2 o_{12} o_{22} s_3 o_{13} o_{23} s_4 o_{14} o_{24}}$ denotes the probability of belonging to cell $(t_1 t_2 s_1 o_{11} o_{21} s_2 o_{12} o_{22} s_3 o_{13} o_{23} s_4 o_{14} o_{24})$ of the joint distribution of the manifest and latent variables. This is the probability that an individual belongs to a latent trait class t_1, a latent trait class t_2, and a latent occasion-specific class s_k on each occasion of measurement, and that he or she answers the first item in a specific category o_{1k} and the second item in a category o_{2k} on each occasion of measurement k. This probability depends on

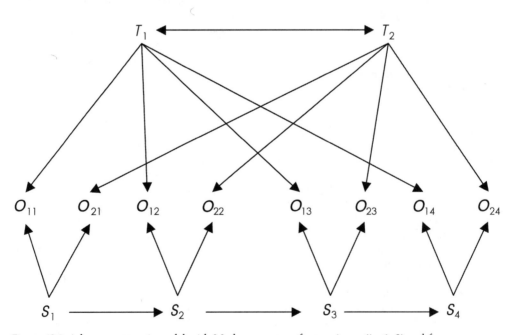

Figure 42.1 A latent state-trait model with Markov structure for two items ($i = 1, 2$) and four occasions of measurement ($k = 1, \ldots, 4$). O_{ik} = observed variables; T_i = item-specific latent-trait variables; S_k = common occasion-specific latent variables. The arrows between the variables S_k indicate carryover effects between occasions of measurement.

(1) the joint distribution of the latent trait variables (π_{t_1,t_2}), (2) the probabilities (sizes) of the occasion-specific latent classes on the first occasion of measurement (π_{s_1}), (3) the conditional response probabilities of the observed item scores given the latent trait and the occasion-specific latent variables ($\pi_{o_{ik}|t,s_k}$), and (4) the transition probabilities of the occasion-specific latent classes ($\pi_{s_{(k+1)}|s_k}$). In this model, all components are multiplicatively combined. The model implies two independence assumptions: (1) the latent-trait variables are independent from the occasion-specific latent variables, and (2) the observed variables are conditionally in-dependent given the latent-trait variables and the occasion-specific variables. The second independence assumption (local independence) means that the latent variables account for all associations among the observed variables.

If the items are measuring not only the same occasion-specific influences but also the same latent trait variable (see lower part of figure 42.2), the model reduces to

$$\pi_{t s_1 o_{11} o_{21} s_2 o_{12} o_{22} s_3 o_{13} o_{23} s_4 o_{14} o_{24}}$$
$$= \pi_t \pi_{s_1} \pi_{o_{11}|ts_1} \pi_{o_{21}|ts_1} \pi_{s_2|s_1} \pi_{o_{12}|ts_2} \pi_{o_{22}|ts_2}$$
$$\pi_{s_3|s_2} \pi_{o_{13}|ts_3} \pi_{o_{23}|ts_3} \pi_{s_4|s_3} \pi_{o_{14}|ts_4} \pi_{o_{24}|ts_4} \quad (2)$$

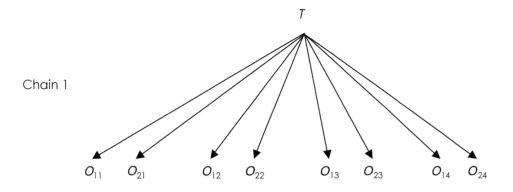

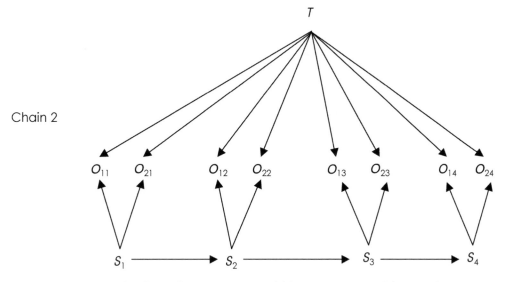

Figure 42.2. A mixture distribution latent state-trait model for separating traited from Markov state-traited individuals for two items ($i = 1, 2$) and four occasions of measurement ($k = 1, \ldots, 4$). O_{ik} = observed variables; T = latent-trait variable; S_k = common occasion-specific latent variables. The arrows between the variables S_k indicate carryover effects between occasions of measurement.

If there is no trend on the level of the latent occasion-specific variables, the transition probabilities are totally random and there is no stability in the occasion-specific part of the model. This model is a pure variability model because the fluctuations on one occasion of measurement are independent from the fluctuations on another occasion of measurement. This type of short-term variability is quite different from changes that are more long-lasting and enduring and are considered, for example, in developmental psychology (e.g., maturation) and in evaluation research (e.g., trait change caused by treatments). Consequently, the model can be simplified by eliminating the transition probabilities. For example, for the case of one latent trait variable this model is defined by:

$$\pi_{ts_1 o_{11} o_{21} s_2 o_{12} o_{22} s_3 o_{13} o_{23} s_4 o_{14} o_{24}}$$

$$= \pi_t \pi_{s_1} \pi_{o_{11}|ts_1} \pi_{o_{21}|ts_1} \pi_{s_2} \pi_{o_{12}|ts_2} \pi_{o_{22}|ts_2}$$

$$\pi_{s_3} \pi_{o_{13}|ts_3} \pi_{o_{23}|ts_3} \pi_{s_4} \pi_{o_{14}|ts_4} \pi_{o_{24}|ts_4} \quad (3)$$

All three models have been applied to our illustrative empirical data set using the computer program LEM (Vermunt, 1997), which can be downloaded from the Internet (http://www.uvt.nl/faculteiten/fsw/organisatie/departementen/mto/software2.html). In all applications, it was assumed that the latent trait and occasion-specific variables have three categories and was based on the idea that each observed category has a latent (error-free) correspondent. Moreover, measurement invariance over time was assumed in all applications. This means that the conditional response probabilities do not differ between occasions of measurement. In addition, the transition probabilities were also assumed to be constant over time. In the model without transition probabilities, the occasion-specific classes are not restricted. The fit coefficients are presented in table 42.1. The implications of these fit coefficients are explained in chapter 41, this volume. The Pearson χ^2 test, the likelihood ratio test, and the Cressie-Read test are all statistical tests for examining the fit of a model by comparing the observed frequencies of the response patterns with the expected frequencies of the response patterns. Moreover, the Akaike information criteria (AIC) and the Bayesian information criteria (BIC) can be used to find the best-fitting model with the minimal number of parameters; in other words, a parsimonious model that represents the data well. Of all

models considered, the best-fitting model is the one with the smallest AIC or BIC value. According to the information criteria in our example, the LST model with one trait and a Markov structure fit the data best. However, the values of the Pearson χ^2 test, the likelihood ratio test, and the Cressie-Read test are quite different, showing that the three test statistics do not follow a χ^2 distribution. If the assumptions on which these fit statistics are based were fulfilled, they all should have shown similar values. However, these large discrepancies indicate that the assumptions are not fulfilled and that the values of these statistics and the related p values should not be used to evaluate the model. We will show how this problem can be solved after first reporting the fit of the mixture distribution models.

Mixture Distribution State-Trait Models

Eid and Langeheine (2003) have shown how Markov state-trait models can be extended to mixture distribution models. In general, mixture distribution extensions are based on introducing a further latent-class variable C. To make the distinction between the latent classes of the trait and occasion-specific variables more clear, the classes c of the variable C are called *latent chains*. This distinction, however, is only a conceptual one, as the latent chains are categories of a latent-class variable indicating the latent chains. The applications in table 42.1 show that the indicators seem to be homogeneous on the trait level. Hence, only extensions of the models with one trait are discussed and analyzed in more detail here. The extensions of models with more than one latent trait variable are straightforward. In its most general form, the mixture distribution LST model with Markov structure is defined by the equation

$$\pi_{cts_1 o_{11} o_{21} s_2 o_{12} o_{22} s_3 o_{13} o_{23} s_4 o_{14} o_{24}}$$

$$= \pi_c \pi_{t|c} \pi_{s_1|c} \pi_{o_{11}|ts_1 c} \pi_{o_{21}|ts_1 c} \pi_{s_2|s_1 c} \pi_{o_{12}|ts_2 c} \pi_{o_{22}|ts_2 c}$$

$$\pi_{s_3|s_2 c} \pi_{o_{13}|ts_3 c} \pi_{o_{23}|ts_3 c} \pi_{s_4|s_3 c} \pi_{o_{14}|ts_4 c} \pi_{o_{24}|ts_4 c} \quad (4)$$

According to this equation, the distribution of the latent trait variable and the occasion-specific variables can be different for different latent chains. Moreover, the conditional probability given the latent trait and occasion-specific classes can be different for different latent chains. The

TABLE 42.1 Goodness-of-Fit Statistics for Different Models

Model	Pearson's χ^2			Likelihood Ratio			Cressie-Read			AIC	BIC
	df	Value	p	df	Value	p	df	Value	p		
One-Chain Models											
I LST model with two traits and Markov structure*	6,524	8,039.22	<.01	6,524	1,477.97	1.00	6,524	3,076.10	1.00	7,333.80	7,485.67
II LST model with one trait and Markov structure	6,530	7,873.18	<.01	6,530	1480.67	1.00	6,530	3,062.54	1.00	7,324.50	7,451.06
III LST model with one trait and without Markov structure	6,530	7,753.40	<.01	6,530	1,489.99	1.00	6,536	3,095.50	1.00	7,330.82	7,457.38
Two-Chain Models											
IV Two-chain LST model with one trait and Markov structure*	6,499	5,459.96	1.00	6,499	1,417.01	1.00	6,499	2,626.64	1.00	7,322.84	7,580.18
V Traited versus Markov state-traited	6,527	6,506.82	.06	6,527	1,464.07	1.00	6,527	2,886.84	1.00	7,313.90	7,453.12
bootstrap p values			.24			.28			.20		
VI Traited versus state-traited	6,527	6,907.25	<.01	6,527	1,468.12	1.00	6,527	2,952.45	1.00	7,317.95	7,457.17

*Eigenvalues of the information matrix ≤ 0 (boundary values).

degree of stability and occasion-specificity can thus differ between chains. Finally, the transition probabilities can differ between chains, indicating differences between latent chains in the trend. To be in line with the LST model, it is assumed that the trait and occasion-specific latent classes are independent of each other, and that the observed responses are locally independent given the latent classes. This is a very general model. However, in its general form, many parameters must be estimated, and this can cause several problems. This general model was applied to the data by assuming that there are two latent chains. In the application of this general model, the program LEM (Vermunt, 1997), the most appropriate computer program for estimating this type of model, provides the warning "9 (nearly) boundary or nonidentified parameters" (see Model IV in table 42.1). Boundary values are estimates of probability parameters that are 0 or 1. Boundary values can have several consequences on model estimation (Hagenaars, 1990; van de Pol, Langeheine, & de Jong, 2000; Vermunt, 1997). If boundary values have been reached during the iterative estimation process, these values will not be changed any more, although they might not provide the optimal solution. Hence, the estimation process might only find a local optimal solution without converging to the general optimal solution (maximum likelihood estimates). Consequently, multiple starting values are necessary to make sure that the algorithm converges to the maximum-likelihood solution. But even with multiple starting values, boundary values can occur. These are only maximum likelihood estimates if the population parameters are also 0 or 1. If the maximum-likelihood solution would be located outside the (0, 1) parameter range, the test statistics would not be asymptotically χ^2 distributed, and bootstrapping analysis should be used (see below). When boundary values occur, the information matrix will contain negative eigenvalues and the standard errors of the boundary values cannot be estimated. Negative eigenvalues of the information matrix can also indicate nonidentified parameters, and it is very important to carefully check whether all parameters are identified.

Consequently, it is generally preferable to avoid boundary values. In many cases, boundary values indicate that the model has too many parameters and is unnecessarily complex. For example, in the Markov LST model with two

latent-trait variables (Model I) in table 42.1, boundary values occurred as well. These boundary values could be found in the bivariate table of the two latent-trait variables, indicating that some combinations (high values of the one trait and low values of the other trait) did not occur because of the homogeneity of the items on the trait level. Hence, a model with two trait variables is unnecessarily too complex, and a model with one trait variable is sufficient, as has been confirmed by a review of the fit statistics. Therefore, in the case of boundary values it would be advisable to look for a simpler, yet still appropriate, model.

Given the distinction between stable (traited) and variable (less traited) individuals, a simpler mixture distribution model with two latent chains was specified (Model V in table 42.1). In one latent chain, an LST model with Markov structure is assumed whereas in the other chain, a simple latent-trait model is assumed, which simply means that the model has no latent occasion-specific classes but only latent trait classes (see figure 42.2). Moreover, other assumptions included measurement invariance over time with respect to the conditional response probabilities, constancy of transition probabilities across time, and finally, measurement invariance with respect to the latent-trait variables between the two latent chains. The latter was done by setting the log-linear parameters of the subtable concerning the trait and the observed variables equal to each other (see below). This model has the best AIC and second best BIC coefficient of the models considered so far and it also has better information criteria values than the mixed model without a Markov process (see table 42.1). In the model without a Markov structure (Model VI in table 42.1), the occasion-specific variables are independent of each other, and the distribution of the occasion-specific variables is not restricted. Therefore, the degrees of freedom are the same for this model and for the model with time-homogeneous transition probabilities. Because the AIC coefficient seems to be more appropriate than the BIC coefficient for complex models (Lin & Dayton, 1997), we selected the mixed Markov latent-state model (Model V) with one chain of traited individuals as the best-fitting model.

The values of the Pearson χ^2 test, the likelihood ratio test, and the Cressie-Read test coefficients are very different for the best-fitting mixture distribution model (Model V), indicating that they are not asymptotically χ^2 distributed. Hence, the fit of the model was tested by bootstrap analysis. Because bootstrap analysis is very time-consuming, only the fit of this best-fitting model was tested using this approach. In the bootstrap analysis, the estimated parameters of the model were taken as population values from which random data sets were drawn. For each of these data sets the model was fitted, resulting in a simulated distribution of each of the three χ^2 statistics for the specific situation given (data, model). The fit of the original model is then compared with the simulated distributions. If the fit statistics of the original application are not extremely bad, meaning that they do not fall in the range of the fit coefficients of the 5% worst-fitting bootstrap samples, the model will not be rejected. Researchers have suggested that in order to estimate the distribution of the fit coefficients, 300 bootstrap samples seem to be sufficient (Langeheine, Pannekoek, & van de Pol, 1996) whereas a smaller number of bootstrap samples is sufficient for simply determining whether the model fits or not. For this purpose, von Davier (1997), for example, considers 40 bootstrap samples appropriate. Moreover, von Davier could show that testing the fit of LCA models by bootstrap analysis works well with the Pearson χ^2 test and the Cressie-Read test, but not with the likelihood ratio test. Because the analysis of mixture distribution LST models is very time consuming, 50 bootstrap samples were analyzed. The bootstrap p values depicted in table 42.1 show that the three test statistics have very similar values and that the model fits the data well. Therefore, the parameters of this model will be explained in detail. The model is a restricted variant of the general mixture distribution LST model defined by Equation 4. In particular, it is assumed that in the first chain of the model (the traited chain), the occasion-specific variables do not influence the response probabilities. In other words, the response probabilities in this chain depend only on the latent trait classes. A detailed listing of the input and output of this model can be found in the appendix.

The results revealed that the first chain of traited individuals comprised 14% of the total sample, and the remaining 86% belong to the second chain of Markov state-traited individuals. The conditional response probabilities and the class sizes for the first chain are presented in table 42.2. The designation of the latent-trait classes arises from the conditional response probabilities. The first trait class is denoted *low* because the probability for the first category is very high for both observed variables. People in this class chose the first category of the item *heiter* (cheerful), with a probability of .82, and the first category of the item *vergnügt* (happy), with a probability of .79. Because the responses in this chain do not depend on systematic occasion-specific influences, individuals in this class show low positive affect on each occasion of measurement. What this finding means is that 4% (chain size × class size: .14 × .28) of all individuals considered in this study belong to the group of stable unpleasant individuals.

The second trait class shows a very low probability for selecting the first category of the two items. This finding means that these individuals do not feel unpleasant affect, and they do not feel this in a stable way. The probabilities for selecting the second and third category of the observed variables are about the same, which means that members of this class fluctuate in feeling their positive affect between medium and

TABLE 42.2 Conditional Response Probabilities and Class Sizes (π_i) in the First Chain (Traited Individuals)

Item Category	Item 1 *Heiter* (Cheerful) Trait Class			Item 2 *Vergnügt* (Happy) Trait Class		
	Low $\pi_1 = .28$	Middle $\pi_2 = .40$	High $\pi_3 = .32$	Low $\pi_1 = .28$	Middle $\pi_2 = .40$	High $\pi_3 = .32$
Low	.82	.00	.01	.79	.01	.02
Middle	.17	.49	.23	.19	.52	.10
High	.01	.51	.76	.02	.47	.88

strong intensity. In other words, members of this group will choose either the middle category or the high one, but it is unpredictable which one will be chosen. Hence, for members of this group it is almost perfectly predictable that they will not feel unpleasant affect, but it is unpredictable whether their positive mood is of medium or strong intensity. Since there are no systematic effects of occasion-specific influences, this might be an indication that these individuals are traited, but that their trait scores are somewhere between the second and the third category, a situation which might cause uncertainty in their responses. In this sample, 5.6% of all individuals ($.14 \times .40$) belong to this class. The third trait class is a class of individuals showing a high probability for the third category. Accordingly, this trait category is denoted *high*, because it comprises individuals in a stable positive mood. This response pattern is shown by 4.5% ($.14 \times .32$) of all individuals.

The conditional response probabilities and the class sizes for the second chain of Markov state-traited individuals are given in table 42.3. Table 42.4 contains the distributions of the occasion-specific classes and the transition probabilities. The conditional response patterns clearly reveal the influence of occasional conditions. In the low occasion-specific class, the conditional response probabilities for the lowest observed categories of the two items (all numbers are rounded in table 42.3) are very high for all trait classes. Hence, this class represents the situational influences that have a negative influence on one's mood.

TABLE 42.4 Probability Distribution of the Latent Occasion-Specific Variables and Transition Probabilities in the Second Chain

Category	Class Sizes $k = 1$	Transition Probabilities Occasion-Specific Classes		
		Low $(k+1)$	Middle $(k+1)$	High $(k+1)$
Low	0.40	.30	.36	.34
Middle	0.35	.36	.38	.26
High	0.25	.28	.32	.40

Note: $k =$ Occasion of measurement.

The middle class of the occasion-specific variable is linked to high probabilities for the middle category of the observed variables, at least for the first two trait classes. The highest occasion-specific class refers to very high probabilities for the highest observed categories, indicating positive occasion-specific influences.

Table 42.3 also shows some interesting differences between the trait classes. The observed response is highly predictable for all observed response categories in the low trait class. It is almost perfectly predictable for members of the middle trait class if they are also in a middle or high occasion-specific class. And it is highly predictable for members of the high trait class if they are in a low or a high occasion-specific class.

The distributions of the occasion-specific classes in table 42.4 reveal that the low and middle classes have almost identical class sizes,

TABLE 42.3 Conditional Response Probabilities and Class Sizes in the Second Chain (Markov State-Traited Individuals)

Occasion-Specific Class	Item Category	Item 1 *Heiter* (Cheerful) Trait Class			Item 2 *Vergnügt* (Happy) Trait Class		
		Low $\pi_1 = .24$	Middle $\pi_2 = .65$	High $\pi_3 = .11$	Low $\pi_1 = .24$	Middle $\pi_2 = .65$	High $\pi_3 = .11$
Low	Low	1.00	0.51	0.95	1.00	0.60	0.92
	Middle	0.00	0.41	0.01	0.00	0.32	0.02
	High	0.00	0.08	.04	0.00	0.08	0.06
Middle	Low	0.00	0.00	0.00	0.50	0.00	0.01
	Middle	0.99	0.91	0.35	0.49	0.78	0.27
	High	.01	0.09	0.65	0.01	0.22	0.72
High	Low	0.01	0.00	0.00	0.04	0.00	0.00
	Middle	0.23	0.02	0.00	0.47	0.08	0.01
	High	0.76	0.98	1.00	0.49	0.92	0.99

whereas the size of the high category is a bit smaller. The transition probabilities belonging to the low occasion-specific class show that there is a slight trend toward improvement: Individuals belonging to this class on the first occasion of measurement will be in a better class on the next occasion of measurement. People in the middle occasion-specific class have a slightly higher probability of staying in or moving to a lower class than of moving to the higher class. For individuals belonging to the high occasion-specific class, there is a relatively high tendency to stay in this class. In general, however, the transition probabilities do not differ much, indicating that there is no strong trend in the data.

Mixture Distribution Latent State-Trait Models as Log-Linear Models With Latent Variables

The way in which the mixed Markov LST model is restricted can best be understood by referring to the log-linear version of this model, because the model has to be formulated and restricted in this way when using the computer program LEM (Vermunt, 1997) for estimating the parameters and testing the fit of the model. In fact, the models considered in table 42.1 are special variants of log-linear models with latent variables (Hagenaars, 1990, 1993). In this formulation of latent-class models, the associations between the categorical variables are specified by log-linear parameters. Log-linear models have been developed to analyze the association structures in multidimensional contingency tables (e.g., Goodman, 1978; Kennedy, 1992). In log-linear models, the expected frequency of a cell of a multidimensional contingency table is decomposed into several parameters, indicating different sources of variations. The mixed Markov LST model will be described referring to the formulation of the log-linear model in terms of effect parameters, because this is the more usual way of formulating log-linear models. Other formulations, such as in terms of dummy-coded variables, are possible as well. In particular, we will show how the parameters of the models need to be restricted to obtain the model discussed above. The parameters we discuss while explaining the model do not refer to parameters explaining the frequencies but rather to the relative frequencies (estimated probabilities).

In the application presented above, we consider eight observed variables with three re- sponse categories (two items on each occasion of measurement). The association between these observed variables is explained by six latent variables: one latent chain variable for separating stable from unstable individuals, one latent trait variable, and four occasion-specific variables. The model was specified as a log-linear model with latent variables in the following way.

1. It is first assumed that there exists a latent variable C with two categories (the two latent chains). The probabilities (relative sizes) of the two categories are not restricted and are freely estimated by the program. The probabilities are .142 for the first and .858 for the second category. The differences in the sizes of the two categories can be represented by log-linear parameters (Hagenaars, 1990). For one variable with two categories, there is one log-linear parameter for each category that indicates the deviation of one class size from the average class size, whereas the average class size is estimated by the geometric mean of the two class sizes. In general, the geometric mean of different cells in the log-linear model is computed by the nth root of the product of the cell probabilities where n denotes the number of cells considered. Concerning the latent-chain variable, we have two categories (cells) with probabilities of .142 and .858, and the geometric mean is $\eta^C = \sqrt[2]{.142 \times .858} = .349$. The deviation of the first category from this mean is calculated by dividing the size of the first category by the geometric mean: $\tau_1^C = .142/.349 = .407$. In an equivalent way, the parameter of the second category is estimated as $\tau_2^C = .858/.349 = 2.458$. These are the parameters of the multiplicative model, and their product equals 1. Taking the logarithm of both parameters gives the parameters of the additive log-linear model: $\lambda_1^C = \ln(\tau_1^C) = \ln(.407) = -.899$ and $\lambda_2^C = \ln(\tau_2^C) = \ln(2.458) = .899$, which add up to 0, the general log-linear parameter of the additive model is $\theta^C = \ln(\eta^C) = \ln(.349) = -1.053$. The parameters indicate that the second chain is larger than the first chain, and this difference in class sizes is significant because the multiplicative parameters differ significantly from 1 and the additive log-linear parameters differ significantly from 0. These tests are based on dividing the estimated parameters by their standard errors that result in an approximately standard normally distributed test statistic (see Hagenaars, 1990). This basic idea of the log-linear model is also applied to the other subtables that consider the associations between the latent and observed variables.

2. In the next step, it is assumed that the distribution of the latent-trait classes depend on the latent chains. What this means is that we allow that the sizes of the latent-trait classes can be different for the different chains. This difference is represented by the conditional probabilities $\pi_{t|c}$. This conditional probability refers to a latent logit model (Vermunt, 1997). In contrast to the log-linear model, in which the associations between categorical variables are considered, in the logit model a difference between dependent and independent variables is made. Therefore, conditional probabilities and conditional probability ratios are considered in the logit model, whereas the log-linear model refers to unconditional probabilities and probability ratios. In fact, the logit model is a regression-type model with a categorical dependent and one or more categorical independent variables. In our case, the latent-trait variable (with three categories) is the dependent variable and the latent-chain variable (with two categories) is the latent independent variable. The logit model is based on the (3×2) table containing the probabilities of each combination of trait class and latent chains, and its parameters can be calculated on the basis of the log-linear parameters of the log-linear model (3×2). For our example, the estimates are given in table 42.5. In the log-linear model of table 42.5, the probability of a cell is decomposed into four parameters. First, it is decomposed into a parameter η, which equals the geometric mean of all cell probabilities:

$$\eta = \sqrt[6]{.040 \times .202 \times .056 \times .561 \times .045 \times .095}$$
$$= .101$$

Second, a parameter τ_i^T is revealed that indicates the deviation of the geometric mean of the categories belonging to one trait category from the general mean η. For example, the parameter τ_i^T represents the deviation of the geometric mean

TABLE 42.5 Probabilities of Each Combination of Trait Classes and Latent Chains

Trait T	Chain c		
	Traited	Markov State-Traited	Sum (Rows)
Low	.040	.202	.242
Middle	.056	.561	.617
High	.045	.095	.140
Sum (columns)	.141	.858	

of the size of the first trait class (low) in the two chains from the general mean:

$$\tau_1^T = \frac{\sqrt[2]{.040 \times .202}}{\eta} = .890$$

Third, and in an analogous way, the parameter τ_{i*}^C indicates the deviation of the average size of one chain category from the general mean. This parameter differs from the parameter τ_i^C discussed above, because the latter refers to the marginal table, that is, the distribution of the chain variable without considering all other variables, whereas the former refers to the bivariate table, and therefore the mean cell sizes across the categories of the trait classes. In order to make this difference clear, the parameter indicating the deviation of the (geometric) mean size is denoted by an index with *. The parameter τ_{i*}^C is calculated by

$$\tau_{1*}^C = \frac{\sqrt[3]{.040 \times .056 \times .045}}{\eta} = .461$$

Finally, the association between the latent trait variable and the latent chain variable is represented by the deviations of the size of a cell from the size expected given the general effect η and the category effects τ_{i*}^C and τ_i^T. For example, for the cell characterizing the size of the first trait category (low) in the first chain (traited) the parameter is

$$\tau_{11}^{CT} = \frac{.040}{\eta \tau_{1*}^C \tau_1^T} = \frac{.040}{.101 \times .461 \times .890} = .965$$

This value shows that the expected relative cell size is only slightly different from the expected value. Therefore, this trait class has almost the same size in the two latent chains. For all other cells of the table, the parameters can be estimated in the same way. Therefore, the log-linear model for this subtable is defined in the multiplicative form by

$$\pi_{ij}^{CT} = \eta \tau_{i*}^C \tau_j^T \tau_{ij}^{CT}$$

and in the additive form by

$$\ln(\pi_{ij}^{CT}) = \theta + \lambda_{i*}^C + \lambda_j^T + \lambda_{ij}^{CT}$$

with

$$\theta = \ln(\eta),$$
$$\lambda_{i*}^C = \ln(\tau_{i*}^C),$$
$$\lambda_j^T = \ln(\tau_j^T),$$
$$\lambda_{ij}^{CT} = \ln(\tau_{ij}^{CT})$$

Based on the parameter of this log-linear model, the parameter of the logit model can be calculated. In the example considered here, the dependent variable is the trait variable and the independent variable is the chain variable. The logit model compares the relative sizes (probabilities) of two categories of the dependent variable with respect to each category of the independent variable. Taking the multiplicative form of this model, the logit model for one category of the independent variable is defined by

$$\Omega_{i1/2}^{C\bar{T}} = \frac{\pi_{i1}}{\pi_{i2}} = \frac{\eta \tau_{i*}^{C} \tau_{1}^{T} \tau_{i1}^{CT}}{\eta \tau_{i*}^{C} \tau_{2}^{T} \tau_{i2}^{CT}} = \frac{\tau_{1}^{T} \tau_{i1}^{CT}}{\tau_{2}^{T} \tau_{i2}^{CT}} = \gamma_{1/2}^{\bar{T}} \gamma_{i1/2}^{C\bar{T}}$$

with

$$\gamma_{1/2}^{\bar{T}} = \frac{\tau_{1}^{T}}{\tau_{2}^{T}} \quad \text{and} \quad \gamma_{i1/2}^{C\bar{T}} = \frac{\tau_{i1}^{CT}}{\tau_{i2}^{CT}}$$

This formulation shows that the logit model depends only on those parameters in which the dependent variable is involved. Therefore, only these log-linear parameters are reported by LEM. The additive form of the logit model is defined by:

$$\Phi_{i1/2}^{C\bar{T}} = \ln\left(\Omega_{i1/2}^{C\bar{T}}\right) = \ln\left(\gamma_{1/2}^{\bar{T}} \gamma_{i1/2}^{C\bar{T}}\right) = \ln\left(\gamma_{1/2}^{\bar{T}}\right)$$
$$+ \ln\left(\gamma_{i1/2}^{C\bar{T}}\right) = \beta_{1/2}^{\bar{T}} + \beta_{i1/2}^{C\bar{T}}$$

The log-linear model for the trait-chain subtable follows the general log-linear model with effect coding, meaning that the parameters indicate deviations from the expected mean cell sizes (Hagenaars, 1990). This model can also be formulated as a design matrix of effect coding variables, a method that makes the whole approach more flexible, particularly if one wants to restrict parameters. The design matrix consists of variables that are used to specify the effect of certain parameters on specific cells. The design matrix follows the effect coding scheme that is also well-known from other statistical approaches such as multiple regression (e.g., Hays, 1994). Using design matrices and the additive parameterization, the log-linear model for the trait-chain subtable can be defined by

$$\begin{pmatrix} \pi_{11}^{CT} \\ \pi_{12}^{CT} \\ \pi_{13}^{CT} \\ \pi_{21}^{CT} \\ \pi_{22}^{CT} \\ \pi_{23}^{CT} \end{pmatrix} = \begin{pmatrix} 1 & 1 & 1 & 0 & 1 & 0 \\ 1 & 1 & 0 & 1 & 0 & 1 \\ 1 & 1 & -1 & -1 & -1 & -1 \\ 1 & -1 & 1 & 0 & -1 & 0 \\ 1 & -1 & 0 & 1 & 0 & -1 \\ 1 & -1 & -1 & -1 & 1 & 1 \end{pmatrix} \begin{pmatrix} \theta \\ \lambda_{1*}^{C} \\ \lambda_{1}^{T} \\ \lambda_{2}^{T} \\ \lambda_{11}^{CT} \\ \lambda_{12}^{CT} \end{pmatrix}$$

The parameter vector does not contain parameters for the second chain and the third trait class. These parameters would be redundant. If the mean cell size of the first chain is known, then the mean chain size of the second chain is also known because the log-linear parameters of the additive model add up to 1. This is also true for the trait classes. If the mean sizes of two trait classes are known, then the mean size of the third class is also known. In general, one needs only $(k-1)$ parameters for indicating the main effect of a categorical variable with k categories. For representing the associations in a bivariate table, the number of parameters necessary can be counted by multiplying the number of parameters needed for the main effects of each variable. In our case we need (1×2) parameters representing the associations between the trait and chain variable (see Hagenaars, 1990, for a deeper discussion). The fifth and sixth columns of the design matrix refer to the parameters indicating the associations. The fifth column of the design matrix is obtained by multiplying the second and third columns, and the sixth column is obtained by multiplying the second and fourth columns.

In the logit model of this subtable, only the parameters involving the trait variable are relevant. Consequently, the design matrix has a reduced form. To analyze a logit structure with the computer program LEM (Vermunt, 1997), it is necessary to refer to the parameter of the log-linear model but to restrict the design matrix in such a way that only the log-linear parameters necessary for calculating the logit parameters are presented. Hence, the design matrix, in combination with the log-linear parameters, does not represent the cell frequencies totally. As a consequence, the way of presenting the design matrix is slightly changed (compared to the design matrix presented above):

Cell CT	Design matrix				Parameter vector
11	1	0	1	0	
12	0	1	0	1	λ_{1}^{T}
13	-1	-1	-1	-1	λ_{2}^{T}
21	1	0	-1	0	λ_{11}^{CT}
22	0	1	0	-1	λ_{12}^{CT}
23	-1	-1	1	1	

For our empirical example, it is not necessary to specify the design matrix in this way because there are no restrictions on the parameters and, therefore, the standard log-linear model can be applied to this subtable. However, formulating a log-linear model on the basis of design matrices is necessary for understanding the other subtables that are restricted in a specific way.

3. The next step of formulating the model concerns the distribution of the first occasion-specific variable. It is assumed that this occasion-specific variable is independent from the trait variable, but that its distribution depends on the latent chain. Therefore, the conditional probability $\pi_{s_1|c}$ is considered. It is assumed that in the chain of traited individuals, the three categories of this variable have the same probability, whereas they can vary freely in the chain of the Markov state-traited individuals. The assumption that the occasion-specific variable has a rectangular distribution in the first chain of traited individuals is equivalent to the assumption that this variable has no main effect in the first chain, which means that the probabilities of the observed responses in the first chain do not depend on a parameter $\lambda_i^{s_1}$ characterizing the main effect of this variable. Consequently, this subtable has to be restricted by a design matrix. In our example, the subtable was restricted in such a way that the occasion-specific variable has an effect only in the second chain of Markov state-traited individuals. In this chain, two parameters are needed to represent a main effect of the occasion-specific variable. These parameters should not have any influence in the first chain of traited individuals. Hence, the design matrix corresponding to these parameters has the following form:

Cell CS_1	Design matrix		Parameter vector
11	0	0	
12	0	0	
13	0	0	$\lambda_{11}^{CS_1}$
21	1	0	
22	0	1	$\lambda_{12}^{CS_1}$
23	−1	−1	

The design matrix contains zeros for all cells belonging to the first chain of traited individuals, indicating that the parameters have no effect in the first chain. In the second chain, the first parameter contrasts the first category with the last category, whereas the second parameter contrasts the second category with the last one. Hence, in the second chain the two parameters

have the usual meaning of log-linear parameters following an effect-coding scheme.

4. The next component of the model equation concerns the transition probabilities, that is, the probabilities of moving from one category of the occasion-specific variable on one occasion of measurement to a category of an occasion-specific variable on another occasion of measurement. These conditional probabilities also depend on the latent chains because it is assumed that there should not be an effect concerning this subtable in the first chain of traited individuals. Hence, it would be necessary to restrict the influence of the parameter of this subtable in such a way that they only influence the second chain of Markov state-traited individuals. Consequently, the design matrix in our example was patterned based on the following considerations. In the chain of Markov state-traited individuals, the conditional transition probabilities could be specified by a logit parametrization. Because the dependent variable (occasion-specific variable on occasion $k + 1$ of measurement) as well as the independent variable (occasion-specific variable on occasion k of measurement) has three categories, two parameters are necessary for representing general differences in the mean category sizes of the dependent variable as well as four parameters are necessary to represent the associations between the two variables. Thus, in general, six parameters are needed to obtain a nonrestricted logit model for this subtable. Because these parameters should not have an effect in the first chain of traited individuals, the cells of the design matrix that correspond to the first chain should contain only zeros. Following an effect-coding scheme in the second chain of Markov state-traited individuals, the design matrix for considering the transition probabilities from the first to second occasion of measurement has been patterned as shown on next page.

The first column and, consequently, the first column contrast the first and the third category of the occasion-specific latent variable on the second occasion of measurement (the dependent variable). The second column contrasts the second and the third categories of the occasion-specific variable on the second occasion of measurement. The third to sixth columns (and parameters) represent the associations. One obtains the values in columns three to six by defining two vectors (not presented here) for the first occasion-specific variable, contrasting the first and last category (first vector) and the

Cell CS_1S_2	Design matrix						Parameter vector
111	0	0	0	0	0	0	
112	0	0	0	0	0	0	
113	0	0	0	0	0	0	
121	0	0	0	0	0	0	
122	0	0	0	0	0	0	
123	0	0	0	0	0	0	$\lambda_{21}^{CS_2}$
131	0	0	0	0	0	0	$\lambda_{22}^{CS_2}$
132	0	0	0	0	0	0	$\lambda_{211}^{CS_1S_2}$
133	0	0	0	0	0	0	$\lambda_{212}^{CS_1S_2}$
211	1	0	1	0	0	0	$\lambda_{221}^{CS_1S_2}$
212	0	1	0	1	0	0	$\lambda_{222}^{CS_1S_2}$
213	−1	−1	−1	−1	0	0	
221	1	0	0	0	1	0	
222	0	1	0	0	0	1	
223	−1	−1	0	0	−1	−1	
231	1	0	−1	0	−1	0	
232	0	1	0	−1	0	−1	
233	−1	−1	1	1	1	1	

second and last category (second vector) of this variable, and by multiplying these two vectors with the two vectors of the second occasion-specific variable. However, as the main effect parameters of the independent variable (the first occasion-specific variable) are irrelevant for the logit model, these parameters and their design vectors are not presented in this chapter. The same design matrix and parameters are assumed for all other transitions probabilities as well. Furthermore, it is assumed that the transition probabilities are time-homogeneous, that is, equivalent for all adjacent pairs of occasions of measurements.

5. Finally, the response probabilities when given the latent trait and latent occasion-specific classes have to be considered. In the chain of Markov state-traited individuals, the response probabilities depend on the trait variable as well as on the occasion-specific variables, whereas in the first chain of traited individuals, the response probabilities must be independent from occasion-specific influences. Consequently, the conditional response probabilities have to be restricted. Based on the logit parametrization of the model, this can be done in the following way.

Given that the dependent variable (the item) has three categories, two parameters are needed to represent mean differences in category sizes. Moreover, it is assumed that also the latent-trait variable has three categories that represent the stable differences between the individuals. To represent the associations between the latent-trait variable and an observed variable, four parameters are needed. In the model considered here, it is assumed that these six parameters do not differ between chains. Therefore, these parameters do not have to be restricted by a design matrix and can be freely estimated. This assumption was made for two reasons. First, it simplifies the model. Second, it implies measurement invariance with respect to the logit parameters across chains. From this point of view, the latent-trait variables have the same significance in the two latent chains, and the two latent chains differ only in their occasion-specific structure, as was intended.

Consequently, the design matrix will restrict only the subtable linking the occasion-specific classes to the observed variables and, therefore, a design matrix restricting only this subtable considering the latent chain variable, an occasion-specific variable, and an observed variable are considered in the following. Because the observed as well as the occasion-specific variables have three categories, four parameters are needed to represent the associations between the two variables. In order to allow occasion-specific influences in the chain of Markov state-traited individuals, these parameters should be freely estimated in the second chain, though they should not have any influence in the first chain. Hence a design matrix has to be chosen that fulfills these needs. The design matrix will be presented for the first item on the first occasion of measurement, but it has the same form for the second item and the other occasions of measurement as well. Moreover, measurement invariance over time was assumed, implying that the parameters should have the same values on all occasions of measurement. An appropriate design matrix based on an effect coding has the following form:

Cell	Design matrix				Parameter
CS_1O_{11}					vector
111	0	0	0	0	
112	0	0	0	0	
113	0	0	0	0	
121	0	0	0	0	
122	0	0	0	0	
123	0	0	0	0	
131	0	0	0	0	
132	0	0	0	0	$\lambda_{211}^{CS_1O_{11}}$
133	0	0	0	0	$\lambda_{212}^{CS_1O_{11}}$
211	1	0	0	0	$\lambda_{221}^{CS_1O_{11}}$
212	0	1	0	0	$\lambda_{222}^{CS_1O_{11}}$
213	−1	−1	0	0	
221	0	0	1	0	
222	0	0	0	1	
223	0	0	−1	−1	
231	−1	0	−1	0	
232	0	−1	0	−1	
233	1	1	1	1	

This design matrix has the same pattern as the third to sixth columns in the design matrix restricting the transition probabilities. Based on this design matrix, the log-linear parameters

can be estimated. When given the estimates of these log-linear parameters, all other log-linear parameters for this table can be estimated given the restriction that the sum of the log-linear parameters belonging to each variable add up to 0 (Hagenaars, 1990).

The log-linear parameters that have been estimated by the computer program LEM (Vermunt, 1997) for the subtables considering the latent-trait variables and the observed variables as well as the subtables considering the latent occasion-specific variable and the observed variables are provided in table 42.6. In the chain of traited individuals, only the trait parameters have an effect and the values are the same as those in the second chain of the Markov state-traited individuals. Therefore, they are not separately depicted here. The parameters of the occasion-specific variables do not have an effect in the first chain of traited individuals, because the design matrix was patterned in such a way that these parameters do not have an influence in the first chain. Hence, the part of table 42.6 that concerns the trait applies to the two latent chains, whereas the part considering the occasion-specific classes is relevant only for the second chain. The log-linear parameters in table 42.6 reflect the results that have been discussed with respect to the conditional response probabilities. The category *low* of both observed variables is positively linked to the category *low* of the latent-trait variable as well as the latent occasion-specific variable and negatively linked to the other categories of the latent variables. This demonstrates that individuals in the low trait and occasion-specific classes have a comparatively high probability to answer in this category. An analogous pattern has been found for the middle categories of the latent and the observed variables. Also, the highest categories of the observed variables have their highest positive parameter values for the highest categories of the latent variables. That shows that each observed category has a latent correspondent.

For each of the two items, the log-linear parameters of the occasion-specific classes are higher than the log-linear parameters of the trait classes, indicating that occasion-specific influences are stronger than trait-specific influences. Moreover, the log-linear parameters are higher for the first item (*heiter*, cheerful) than for the second item (*vergnügt*, happy), indicating that the first item is more closely linked to the latent variables.

TABLE 42.6 Log-Linear Parameters for the Subtables Linking the Observed Variables With the Latent-Trait Variables and the Latent Occasion-Specific Variables

| Observed Variable | Category | Trait | | | Occasion-Specific Variable | | |
		Heiter (Cheerful)	Vergnügt (Happy)	Category	Heiter (Cheerful)	Vergnügt (Happy)
Low	Low	5.92	2.82	Low	8.53	3.97
	Middle	−3.89	−2.05	Middle	−3.85	−0.54
	High	−2.02	−0.77	High	−4.68	−3.43
Middle	Low	−1.55	−0.23	Low	−3.45	−1.32
	Middle	1.97	1.01	Middle	3.09	0.87
	High	−0.43	−0.77	High	0.36	0.45
High	Low	−4.37	−2.58	Low	−5.08	−5.29
	Middle	1.92	1.04	Middle	0.76	0.33
	High	2.45	1.55	High	4.32	2.98

Conclusion

The empirical example presented in this chapter demonstrates the usefulness of the mixed Markov state-trait model for separating traited from untraited individuals. Moreover, it shows that log-linear models with latent variables are an important methodological tool for defining models in a very sophisticated way. This modeling approach, however, also has its limits, as the tables become very large with increasing items under consideration. In this case, the researcher must ensure that the models are identified and that the maximum likelihood solution (global maximum) has been found. Moreover, bootstrap analysis must be applied to test the fit of the model. If there are many items measuring the same construct, it would be easier to define scales and to use methodologies for metrical observed variables. Hence, the modeling approach we have presented is most interesting for situations in which one is interested in the determinants of the responses to few categories of an item.

Appendix: LEM output

In the following, some selected parts of the LEM output are presented and commented upon. Comments are in italics. The first class of a latent occasion-specific variable is interpreted as a "middle" class in the text, the second class is interpreted as a "high," and the third class is interpreted as a "low" class. The first class of a latent trait class is interpreted as "low," the second class as "middle," and the third class as "high."

LEM: log-linear and event history analysis with missing data.
Developed by Jeroen Vermunt (c), Tilburg University, The Netherlands.
Version 1.0 (September 18, 1997).

The first part of the output presents the input. This input can be used for rerunning the analysis.

```
*** INPUT ***

  *Input file for the mixed Markov state-trait model -- Model V
  *number of latent variables
     lat  6
  *number of manifest (observed) variables)
     man  8
  *number of categories of the latent and the observed variables
```

```
*latent variables have to come first
   dim 2 3 3 3 3 3 3 3 3 3 3 3 3 3
*labels of the latent and observed variables
*labels are explained in the text
   lab C T S1 S2 S3 S4 O11 O21 O12 O22 O13 O23 O14 O24
*definition of the model
   mod C
   T|C {TT.C}
   S1|C {cov(C.S1,2)}
   S2|S1.C {cov(C.S1.S2,6)}
   S3|S2.C eq1 S2|S1.C
   S4|S3.C eq1 S2|S1.C
   O11|S1.T.C {O11 T.O11,cov(C.S1.O11,4)}
   O21|S1.T.C {O21 T.O21,cov(C.S1.O21,4)}
   O12|S2.T.C eq1 O11|S1.T.C
   O22|S2.T.C eq1 O21|S1.T.C
   O13|S3.T.C eq1 O11|S1.T.C
   O23|S3.T.C eq1 O21|S1.T.C
   O14|S4.T.C eq1 O11|S1.T.C
   O24|S4.T.C eq1 O21|S1.T.C
 *sample size
   rec 502
 *start values - in this example just needed to make sure that
 *the latent classes have the same meaning as in the text
 *this is also the way how to define the model for bootstrapping
 *the bootstrapping inputs are not provided but available on request
   sta C [0.4065 2.4599]
   sta T [0.8941 1.7324 0.6456]
   sta C.T [0.9700 0.6882 1.4981 1.0309 1.4531 0.6675]
   sta cov(C.S1) [1.0797 0.7579]
   sta cov(C.S1.S2) [1.0006 1.0665 1.0804 0.7877 0.9177
1.2289]
   sta O11 [0.0392 4.8299 5.2848]
   sta T.O11 [173.6975 0.3081 0.0187 0.0293 6.0280 5.6536
0.1962 0.5384 9.4662]
   sta cov(C.S1.O11) [0.0368 16.8495 0.0159 1.0953]
   sta O21 [0.3549 1.7887 1.5754]
   sta T.O21 [16.691 0.7924 0.0756 0.1296 2.7319 2.8254
0.4623 0.4620 4.6823]
   sta cov(C.S1.O21) [0.5729 2.3883 0.0330 1.5566]
 *design matrix
   des [ 0 0 0 1 0 -1
         0 0 0 0 1 -1
         0 0 0 0 0 0 0 0 0 1 -1 0 1 -1 0 1 -1
         0 0 0 0 0 0 0 0 0 1 0 -1 1 0 -1 1 0 -1
         0 0 0 0 0 0 0 0 0 1 0 -1 0 0 0 -1 0 1
         0 0 0 0 0 0 0 0 0 1 -1 0 0 0 0 -1 1
         0 0 0 0 0 0 0 0 0 0 0 1 0 -1 -1 0 1
         0 0 0 0 0 0 0 0 0 0 0 0 1 -1 0 -1 1
         0 0 0 0 0 0 0 0 0 1 0 -1 0 0 0 -1 0 1
         0 0 0 0 0 0 0 0 0 1 -1 0 0 0 0 -1 1
         0 0 0 0 0 0 0 0 0 0 0 1 0 -1 -1 0 1
         0 0 0 0 0 0 0 0 0 0 0 1 -1 0 -1 1
         0 0 0 0 0 0 0 0 1 0 -1 0 0 0 -1 0 1
         0 0 0 0 0 0 0 0 1 -1 0 0 0 0 -1 1
         0 0 0 0 0 0 0 0 0 0 1 0 -1 -1 0 1
         0 0 0 0 0 0 0 0 0 0 1 -1 0 -1 1]
 *data set
   dat heiver3.dat
```

The following part presents the fit statistics and the eigenvalues of the information matrix. Because all eigenvalues are positive, the model is identified and there are no boundary values.

*** STATISTICS ***

```
Number of iterations = 5000
Converge criterion   = 0.0000143905
Seed random values   = 3821

X-squared            = 6506.8172  (0.5679)
L-squared            = 1464.0705  (1.0000)
Cressie-Read         = 2886.8392  (1.0000)
Dissimilarity index  = 0.6282
Degrees of freedom   = 6527
Log-likelihood       = -3623.95115
Number of parameters = 33  (+1)
Sample size          = 502.0
BIC(L-squared)       = -39124.7325
AIC(L-squared)       = -11589.9295
BIC(log-likelihood)  = 7453.1161
AIC(log-likelihood)  = 7313.9023
```

```
Eigenvalues information matrix
  1354.3095   838.0580   635.0247   576.9416   543.0021   371.0856
   297.7193   250.9631   208.4648   184.2312   176.1971   164.4260
   154.6673   133.6904   102.3104    92.4810    83.9994    64.4595
    49.5498    43.0368    40.9250    26.9302    18.6281    13.9174
    12.0927     7.7381     7.0609     5.8888     3.7145     2.8288
     1.1973     0.1323     0.0425
```

The following part presents the observed frequencies of a response pattern, the estimated expected frequencies based on the model, and standardized residuals that are not discussed in the text. Only three response patterns are selected: 1 indicates the first, and 2 the second category.

*** FREQUENCIES ***

```
O11 O21 O12 O22 O13 O23 O14 O24 observed estimated std. res.
 1   1   1   1   1   1   1   1    6.000     5.043     0.426
 1   1   1   1   1   1   1   2    1.000     0.893     0.113
 1   1   1   1   1   1   2   1    1.000     1.443    -0.369
 ...
```

Next, some measures for the explained variance are presented that are not discussed in the text but are explained in the LEM manual.

*** PSEUDO R-SQUARED MEASURES ***

```
 * P(T|C) *
                         baseline   fitted   R-squared
   entropy               0.9174    0.8947    0.0247
   qualitative variance  0.2704    0.2636    0.0253
   classification error  0.3830    0.3830   -0.0000
   -2/N*log-likelihood   1.8347    1.7895    0.0247/0.0433
   likelihood^(-2/N)     6.2635    5.9862    0.0443/0.0527

 * P(S1|C) *
```

	baseline	fitted	R-squared
entropy	1.0845	1.0821	0.0022
qualitative variance	0.3288	0.3280	0.0023
classification error	0.6079	0.6079	-0.0000
-2/N*log-likelihood	2.1690	2.1642	0.0022/0.0048
likelihood^(-2/N)	8.7498	8.7073	0.0049/0.0055

* P(S2|C.S1) *

	baseline	fitted	R-squared
entropy	1.0978	1.0906	0.0066
qualitative variance	0.3331	0.3307	0.0071
classification error	0.6498	0.6287	0.0324
-2/N*log-likelihood	2.1957	2.1812	0.0066/0.0142
likelihood^(-2/N)	8.9860	8.8573	0.0143/0.0161

* P(O11|C.T.S1) *

	baseline	fitted	R-squared
entropy	1.0721	0.3870	0.6390
qualitative variance	0.3250	0.1163	0.6420
classification error	0.6061	0.1798	0.7034
-2/N*log-likelihood	2.1442	0.7732	0.6394/0.5782
likelihood^(-2/N)	8.5350	2.1667	0.7461/0.8452

* P(O21|C.T.S1) *

	baseline	fitted	R-squared
entropy	1.0923	0.5410	0.5047
qualitative variance	0.3313	0.1671	0.4955
classification error	0.6280	0.2534	0.5965
-2/N*log-likelihood	2.1846	1.0820	0.5047/0.5244
likelihood^(-2/N)	8.8873	2.9507	0.6680/0.7527

The following part contains the log-linear parameters and some statistics concerning the significance of the parameters. The log-linear parameters are explained in the text. The log-linear parameters that are calculated in the text differ slightly because of rounding errors. Beta indicates the parameter of the additive model, and exp(beta) the parameters of the multiplicative model (the test statistics are not discussed in the text but explained in the manual). The parameter η is not reported by LEM.

*** LOG-LINEAR PARAMETERS ***

* TABLE C [or P(C)] *

effect	beta	std err	z-value	exp(beta)	Wald	df	prob
C							
1	-0.8993	0.1194	-7.530	0.4069			
2	0.8993			2.4578	56.70	1	0.000

* TABLE C.T [or P(T|C)] *

effect	beta	std err	z-value	exp(beta)	Wald	df	prob
T							
1	-0.1198	0.1937	-0.618	0.8871			
2	0.5564	0.1789	3.109	1.7444			
3	-0.4366			0.6462	10.58	2	0.005
C.T							
1 1	-0.0292	0.1966	-0.149	0.9712			
1 2	-0.3747	0.1821	-2.058	0.6875			
1 3	0.4040			1.4977			
2 1	0.0292			1.0297			
2 2	0.3747			1.4546			
2 3	-0.4040			0.6677	5.87	2	0.053

* TABLE C.S1 [or P(S1|C)] *

effect	beta	std err	z-value	exp(beta)	Wald	df	prob
cov(C.S1)							
1	0.0716	0.1440	0.497	1.0742			
2	−0.2785	0.1474	−1.890	0.7569	5.96	2	0.051

TABLE C.S1.S2 [or P(S2|C.S1)]

effect	beta	std err	z-value	exp(beta)	Wald	df	prob
cov(C.S1.S2)							
1	−0.0012	0.0870	−0.014	0.9988			
2	0.0603	0.1032	0.584	1.0621			
3	0.0735	0.1028	0.715	1.0762			
4	−0.2377	0.0957	−2.484	0.7884			
5	−0.0843	0.0953	−0.884	0.9192			
6	0.2072	0.0929	2.229	1.2302	8.76	6	0.187

* TABLE C.T.S1.O11 [or P(O11|C.T.S1)] *

effect	beta	std err	z-value	exp(beta)	Wald	df	prob
O11							
1	−3.9585	2.3278	−1.701	0.0191			
2	1.9410	1.1760	1.651	6.9657			
3	2.0175			7.5193	2.94	2	0.230
T.O11							
1 1	5.9157	2.3797	2.486	370.7976			
1 2	−1.5459	1.2336	−1.253	0.2131			
1 3	−4.3697	0.0127					
2 1	−3.8948	1.2216	−3.188	0.0203			
2 2	1.9732	0.6329	3.118	7.1935			
2 3	1.9216			6.8318			
3 1	−2.0209			0.1325			
3 2	−0.4272			0.6523			
3 3	2.4481			11.5668	31.30	4	0.000
cov(C.S1.O11)							
1	−3.8525	2.8303	−1.361	0.0212			
2	3.0940	1.4184	2.181	22.0659			
3	−4.6782	2.1652	−2.161	0.0093			
4	0.3637	1.1455	0.317	1.4386	39.09	4	0.000

*TABLE C.T.S1.O21 [or P(O21|C.T.S1)] *

effect	beta	std err	z-value	exp(beta)	Wald	df	prob
O21							
1	−1.0392	0.3624	−2.867	0.3537			
2	0.5821	0.2111	2.758	1.7898			
3	0.4571			1.5795	8.70	2	0.013
T.O21							
1 1	2.8166	0.4764	5.912	16.7199			
1 2	−0.2327	0.2900	−0.802	0.7924			
1 3	−2.5839	0.0755					
2 1	−2.0457	0.3833	−5.337	0.1293			
2 2	1.0072	0.2337	4.309	2.7379			
2 3	1.0385	2.8251					
3 1	−0.7709	0.4626					
3 2	−0.7745	0.4609					
3 3	1.5453			4.6896	76.89	4	0.000
cov(C.S1.O21)							
1	−0.5435	0.3168	−1.716	0.5807			
2	0.8679	0.1627	5.334	2.3818			
3	−3.4250	0.5721	−5.987	0.0325			
4	0.4513	0.3126	1.444	1.5704	78.98	4	0.000

The following part presents the (conditional) probabilities. Because these probabilities do not differ between the occasions of measurement, only the results for the first occasion of measurement and the transition probabilities for the first and second occasions of measurement are given. The rest of the ouput was omitted.

*** (CONDITIONAL) PROBABILITIES ***

Sizes of the chains

* P(C) *

1	0.1420	(0.0291)
2	0.8580	(0.0291)

Sizes of the trait classes in the different chains (see tables 42.2 and 42.3)

* P(T|C) *

1 | 1	0.2845	(0.0932)
2 | 1	0.3960	(0.1097)
3 | 1	0.3196	(0.0937)
1 | 2	0.2353	(0.0625)
2 | 2	0.6536	(0.0660)
3 | 2	0.1111	(0.0374)

Sizes of the occasion-specific classes in the different chains (see tables 42.2 and 42.3)

* P(S1|C) *

1 | 1	0.3333	(0.0000)
2 | 1	0.3333	(0.0000)
3 | 1	0.3333	(0.0000)
1 | 2	0.3509	(0.0472)
2 | 2	0.2473	(0.0407)
3 | 2	0.4018	(0.0353)

Transition probabilities in the different chains (see table 42.4)

* P(S2|C.S1) *

1 | 1	1	0.3333	(0.0000)
2 | 1	1	0.3333	(0.0000)
3 | 1	1	0.3333	(0.0000)
1 | 1	2	0.3333	(0.0000)
2 | 1	2	0.3333	(0.0000)
3 | 1	2	0.3333	(0.0000)
1 | 1	3	0.3333	(0.0000)
2 | 1	3	0.3333	(0.0000)
3 | 1	3	0.3333	(0.0000)
1 | 2	1	0.3758	(0.0454)
2 | 2	1	0.2589	(0.0375)
3 | 2	1	0.3652	(0.0428)
1 | 2	2	0.3213	(0.0503)
2 | 2	2	0.4044	(0.0428)
3 | 2	2	0.2743	(0.0409)
1 | 2	3	0.3569	(0.0473)
2 | 2	3	0.3423	(0.0458)
3 | 2	3	0.3007	(0.0342)

Conditional response probabilities for the observed categories of the first item given the trait and occasion-specific classes (see tables 42.2 and 42.3)

* P(O11|C.T.S1) *

```
1 | 1   1   1    0.8176   (0.0825)
2 | 1   1   1    0.1714   (0.0780)
3 | 1   1   1    0.0110   (0.0110)
1 | 1   1   2    0.8176   (0.0825)
2 | 1   1   2    0.1714   (0.0780)
3 | 1   1   2    0.0110   (0.0110)
1 | 1   1   3    0.8176   (0.0825)
2 | 1   1   3    0.1714   (0.0780)
3 | 1   1   3    0.0110   (0.0110)
1 | 1   2   1    0.0000   (0.0000)
2 | 1   2   1    0.4938   (0.0797)
3 | 1   2   1    0.5062   (0.0797)
1 | 1   2   2    0.0000   (0.0000)
2 | 1   2   2    0.4938   (0.0797)
3 | 1   2   2    0.5062   (0.0797)
1 | 1   2   3    0.0000   (0.0000)
2 | 1   2   3    0.4938   (0.0797)
3 | 1   2   3    0.5062   (0.0797)
1 | 1   3   1    0.0000   (0.0001)
2 | 1   3   1    0.0496   (0.0305)
3 | 1   3   1    0.9503   (0.0305)
1 | 1   3   2    0.0000   (0.0001)
2 | 1   3   2    0.0496   (0.0305)
3 | 1   3   2    0.9503   (0.0305)
1 | 1   3   3    0.0000   (0.0001)
2 | 1   3   3    0.0496   (0.0305)
3 | 1   3   3    0.9503   (0.0305)
1 | 2   1   1    0.0045   (0.0191)
2 | 2   1   1    0.9893   (0.0201)
3 | 2   1   1    0.0061   (0.0083)
1 | 2   1   2    0.0071   (0.0223)
2 | 2   1   2    0.2292   (0.1547)
3 | 2   1   2    0.7637   (0.1552)
1 | 2   1   3    1.0000   (0.0000)
2 | 2   1   3    0.0000   (0.0000)
3 | 2   1   3    0.0000   (0.0000)
1 | 2   2   1    0.0000   (0.0000)
2 | 2   2   1    0.9098   (0.0588)
3 | 2   2   1    0.0902   (0.0588)
1 | 2   2   2    0.0000   (0.0000)
2 | 2   2   2    0.0184   (0.0164)
3 | 2   2   2    0.9816   (0.0164)
1 | 2   2   3    0.5089   (0.0525)
2 | 2   2   3    0.4080   (0.0471)
3 | 2   2   3    0.0832   (0.0248)
1 | 2   3   1    0.0000   (0.0000)
2 | 2   3   1    0.3506   (0.1246)
3 | 2   3   1    0.6494   (0.1246)
1 | 2   3   2    0.0000   (0.0000)
2 | 2   3   2    0.0010   (0.0012)
3 | 2   3   2    0.9990   (0.0012)
1 | 2   3   3    0.9491   (0.0704)
2 | 2   3   3    0.0106   (0.0172)
3 | 2   3   3    0.0403   (0.0550)
```

Conditional response probabilities for the observed categories of the second item given the trait and occasion-specific classes (see tables 42.2 and 42.3)

* P(O21|C.T.S1) *

```
1 | 1   1   1    0.7937   (0.0590)
2 | 1   1   1    0.1903   (0.0548)
3 | 1   1   1    0.0160   (0.0100)
1 | 1   1   2    0.7937   (0.0590)
2 | 1   1   2    0.1903   (0.0548)
3 | 1   1   2    0.0160   (0.0100)
1 | 1   1   3    0.7937   (0.0590)
2 | 1   1   3    0.1903   (0.0548)
3 | 1   1   3    0.0160   (0.0100)
1 | 1   2   1    0.0049   (0.0045)
2 | 1   2   1    0.5209   (0.0524)
3 | 1   2   1    0.4743   (0.0530)
1 | 1   2   2    0.0049   (0.0045)
2 | 1   2   2    0.5209   (0.0524)
3 | 1   2   2    0.4743   (0.0530)
1 | 1   2   3    0.0049   (0.0045)
2 | 1   2   3    0.5209   (0.0524)
3 | 1   2   3    0.4743   (0.0530)
1 | 1   3   1    0.0195   (0.0187)
2 | 1   3   1    0.0983   (0.0397)
3 | 1   3   1    0.8822   (0.0423)
1 | 1   3   2    0.0195   (0.0187)
2 | 1   3   2    0.0983   (0.0397)
3 | 1   3   2    0.8822   (0.0423)
1 | 1   3   3    0.0195   (0.0187)
2 | 1   3   3    0.0983   (0.0397)
3 | 1   3   3    0.8822   (0.0423)
1 | 2   1   1    0.4979   (0.0747)
2 | 2   1   1    0.4896   (0.0711)
3 | 2   1   1    0.0125   (0.0098)
1 | 2   1   2    0.0405   (0.0339)
2 | 2   1   2    0.4687   (0.1087)
3 | 2   1   2    0.4908   (0.1123)
1 | 2   1   3    0.9988   (0.0014)
2 | 2   1   3    0.0012   (0.0014)
3 | 2   1   3    0.0000   (0.0000)
1 | 2   2   1    0.0018   (0.0021)
2 | 2   2   1    0.7821   (0.0368)
3 | 2   2   1    0.2162   (0.0369)
1 | 2   2   2    0.0000   (0.0000)
2 | 2   2   2    0.0810   (0.0424)
3 | 2   2   2    0.9190   (0.0424)
1 | 2   2   3    0.5981   (0.0550)
2 | 2   2   3    0.3239   (0.0496)
3 | 2   2   3    0.0780   (0.0210)
1 | 2   3   1    0.0128   (0.0154)
2 | 2   3   1    0.2650   (0.0893)
3 | 2   3   1    0.7222   (0.0905)
1 | 2   3   2    0.0000   (0.0001)
2 | 2   3   2    0.0089   (0.0057)
3 | 2   3   2    0.9911   (0.0057)
1 | 2   3   3    0.9208   (0.0598)
2 | 2   3   3    0.0235   (0.0225)
3 | 2   3   3    0.0557   (0.0398)
```

References

Baumeister, R. E. (1991). On the stability of variability: Retest reliability of metatraits. *Personality and Social Psychology Bulletin, 17,* 633–639.

Baumeister, R. E., & Tice, D. M. (1988). Metatraits. *Journal of Personality, 56,* 571–598.

Bem, D. J., & Allen, A. (1974). On predicting some of the people some of the time: The search for cross-situational consistency in behavior. *Psychological Review, 81,* 506–520.

Britt, T. W. (1993). Metatraits: Evidence relevant to the validity of the construct and its implications. *Journal of Personality and Social Psychology, 65,* 554–562.

Csikszentmihalyi, M., & Wong, M. M.-H. (1991). The situational and personal correlates of happiness: A cross-national comparison. In F. Strack, M. Argyle, & N. Schwarz (Eds.), *Subjective well-being: An interdisciplinary perspective* (pp. 193–212). Oxford, UK: Pergamon.

Depue, R. A., Slater, J. F., Wolfstetter-Kausch, H., Klein, D., Goplerud, E., & Farr, D. (1981). A behavioral paradigm for identifying persons at risk for bipolar depressive disorder: A conceptual framework and five validation studies. *Journal of Abnormal Psychology Monograph, 90,* 381–437.

Eid, M. (1996). Longitudinal confirmatory factor analysis for polytomous item responses: Model definition and model selection on the basis of stochastic measurement theory. *Methods of Psychological Research, 1,* 65–85. Available at http://www.hsp.de/MPR/

Eid, M. (1997). Happiness and satisfaction: An application of a latent state-trait model for ordinal variables. In J. Rost & R. Langeheine (Eds.), *Applications of latent trait and latent class models in the social sciences* (pp. 145–151). Münster: Waxmann.

Eid, M., & Diener, E. (1999). Intraindividual variability in affect: Reliability, validity, and personality correlates. *Journal of Personality and Social Psychology, 76,* 662–676.

Eid, M., & Diener, E. (2004). Global judgments of well-being: Situational variability and long-term stability. *Social Indicators Research, 65,* 245–277.

Eid, M., & Langeheine, R. (1999). The measurement of consistency and occasion specificity with latent class models: A new model and its application to the measurement of affect. *Psychological Methods, 4,* 100–116.

Eid, M., & Langeheine, R. (2003). Separating stable from variable individuals in longitudinal studies by mixture distribution models. *Measurement, 1,* 179–206.

Goodman, L. A. (1978). *Analyzing qualitative/categorical data.* Lanham, MD: University Press of America.

Hagenaars, J. A. (1990). *Categorical longitudinal data: Log-linear panel, trend, and cohort analysis.* Newbury Park, CA: Sage.

Hagenaars, J. A. (1993). *Loglinear models with latent variables.* Newbury Park, CA: Sage.

Hays, W. L. (1994). *Statistics.* Belmont, CA: Wadsworth.

Hepburn, L., & Eysenck, M. W. (1989). Personality, average mood, and mood variability. *Personality and Individual Differences, 10,* 975–983.

Hershberger, S. L., Plomin, R., & Pedersen, N. L. (1995). Trait and metatraits: Their reliability, stability, and shared genetic influence. *Journal of Personality and Social Psychology, 69,* 673–685.

Kennedy, J. J. (1992). *Analyzing qualitative data: Log-linear analysis for behavioral research* (2nd ed.). New York: Praeger.

Kenny, D. A., & Zautra, A. (1995). The state-trait error model for multiwave data. *Journal of Consulting and Clinical Psychology, 63,* 52–59.

Langeheine, R., Pannekoek, J., & van de Pol, F. (1996). Bootstrapping goodness-of-fit measures in categorical data analysis. *Sociological Methods and Research, 24,* 492–516.

Larsen, R. J. (1987). The stability of mood variability: A spectral analytic approach to daily mood assessment. *Journal of Personality and Social Psychology, 52,* 1195–1204.

Lazarus, R. S. (1991). *Emotion and adaptation.* New York: Oxford University Press.

Lin, T. H., & Dayton, C. M. (1997). Model selection information criteria for non-nested latent class models. *Journal of Educational and Behavioral Statistics, 22,* 249–264.

Marsh, H. W., & Grayson, D. (1994). Longitudinal factor analyses: Common, time-specific, item-specific, and residual-error components of variance. *Structural Equation Modeling, 1,* 116–145.

McConville, C., & Cooper, C. (1992). Mood variability and personality. *Personality and Individual Differences, 13,* 1213–1221.

Penner, L. A., Shiffman, S., Paty, J. A., & Fritzsche, B. A. (1994). Individual differences in intraperson variability in mood. *Journal of Personality and Social Psychology, 66,* 712–721.

Schmitt, M., & Borkenau, P. (1992). The consistency of personality. In G.-V. Caprara & G. L. van Heck (Eds.), *Modern personality psychology: Critical reviews and new directions* (pp. 29–55). New York: Harvester.

Spielberger, C. D. (1977). State-trait anxiety and interactional psychology. In D. Magnusson & N. S. Endler (Eds.), *Personality at the crossroads:*

Current issues in interactional psychology (pp. 173–183). Hillsdale, NJ: Erlbaum.

Steyer, R., Ferring, D., & Schmitt, M. (1992). States and traits in psychological assessment. *European Journal of Psychological Assessment, 2,* 79–98.

Steyer, R., & Partchev, I. (2001). Latent state-trait modeling with logistic item response models. In R. Cudeck, S. Du Toit, & D. Sörbom (Eds.), *Structural equation modeling: Present and future* (pp. 481–520). Chicago: Scientific Software International.

Steyer, R., Schmitt, M., & Eid, M. (1999). Latent state-trait theory and research in personality and individual differences. *European Journal of Personality, 13,* 389–408.

Tellegen, A. (1988). The analysis of consistency in personality assessment. *Journal of Personality, 56,* 621–663.

van de Pol, F., Langeheine, R., & de Jong, W. (2000). *PANMARK 3: User's manual. Panel analysis using Markov chains—A latent class analysis program.* St. Paul, MN: Assessment Systems Corporation.

Vermunt, J. K. (1997). *Lem: A general program for the analysis of categorical data.* Tilburg: Tilburg University.

von Davier, M. (1997). Bootstrapping goodness-of-fit statistics for sparse categorical data—Results of a Monte Carlo study. *Methods of Psychological Research Online, 2,* 29–48. Available at www.mpr-online.de

Index

DATE DUE

JE 19 '08		
DEC 2 4 2010		
DE 25 '08		
DEC 2 4 2010		

DEMCO 38-296